W9-ARY-664

ECONOMICS

CANADA IN THE GLOBAL ENVIRONMENT

FIFTH EDITION

MICHAEL PARKIN
University of Western Ontario

ROBIN BADE

Toronto

Vice President, Editorial Director: Michael J. Young
Acquisitions Editor: Gary Bennett
Marketing Manager: Deborah Meredith
Senior Developmental Editor: Suzanne Schaan
Senior Production Editor: Marisa D'Andrea
Copy Editor: Laurel Sparrow
Production Coordinator: Deborah Starks
Permissions and Photo Research: Lisa Brant
Page Layout: Bill Renaud
Illustrator: Richard Parkin
Art Director: Mary Opper
Interior and Cover Design: Anthony Leung
Cover Image (background): Gary Holscher/Gettyimages
Cover Image (spot image): Michael Pohuski/Gettyimages

National Library of Canada Cataloguing in Publication

Parkin, Michael, 1939–
Economics : Canada in the global environment / Michael Parkin, Robin Bade — 5th ed.

Includes index.
ISBN 0-321-15411-8

1. Economics. 2. Canada—Economic conditions—1991–
I. Bade, Robin II. Title.

HB171.5.P26 2003 330 C2002-902845-0

0-321-15411-8

3 4 5 07 06 05

Printed and bound in the United States of America.

Statistics Canada information is used with the permission of the Minister of Industry, as Minister responsible for Statistics Canada. Information on the availability of the wide range of data from Statistics Canada can be obtained from Statistics Canada's Regional Offices, its World Wide Web site at http://www.statcan.ca, and its toll-free access number 1-800-263-1136.

Photo and figure credits appear on page C-1, which constitutes a continuation of the copyright page.

The cover depicts a common Canadian scene—a wheat field and an ear of wheat—viewed through the lens of the Parkin–Bade icon. You can look at this cover in many different ways. Here is what we see. ◆ First, we see a metaphor for what our text, Web site, and other supplements and the extraordinary publishing effort that created them seek to be—a window that gives students a sharply focused view of the world based on a clear and compelling account of timeless principles. ◆ Second, we see a symbol of what economics (and all scientific endeavour) is about. The Parkin–Bade icon is like an economic model. We use models to understand reality. The model is abstract, like the diamond shape and its hole or aperture. The model distorts our view of the world by omitting some details. But it permits us to see the focus of our interest in the brightest and clearest possible light.

TO OUR STUDENTS

MICHAEL PARKIN received his training as an economist at the Universities of Leicester and Essex in England. Currently in the Department of Economics at the University of Western Ontario, Canada, Professor Parkin has held faculty appointments at Brown University, the University of Manchester, the University of Essex, and Bond University. He is a past president of the Canadian Economics Association and has served on the editorial boards of the *American Economic Review* and the *Journal of Monetary Economics* and as managing editor of the *Canadian Journal of Economics.* Professor Parkin's research on macroeconomics, monetary economics, and international economics has resulted in over 160 publications in journals and edited volumes, including the *American Economic Review*, the *Journal of Political Economy*, the *Review of Economic Studies*, the *Journal of Monetary Economics*, and the *Journal of Money, Credit and Banking.* He became most visible to the public with his work on inflation that discredited the use of wage and price controls. Michael Parkin also spearheaded the movement toward European monetary union.

ROBIN BADE earned degrees in mathematics and economics at the University of Queensland and her Ph.D. at the Australian National University. She has held faculty appointments in the business schools at the University of Edinburgh and Bond University and in the economics departments at the University of Manitoba, the University of Toronto, and the University of Western Ontario. Her research on international capital flows appears in the *International Economic Review* and the *Economic Record.*

Professor Parkin and Dr. Bade are the joint authors of *Modern Macroeconomics* (Pearson Education Canada), an intermediate text, and *Foundations of Economics* (Pearson Education Canada), and have collaborated on many research and textbook writing projects. They are both experienced and dedicated teachers of introductory economics.

PREFACE

This book presents economics as a serious, lively, and evolving science. Its goal is to open students' eyes to the "economic way of thinking" and to help them gain insights into how the economy works and how it might be made to work better. ◆ We provide a thorough and complete coverage of the subject, using a straightforward, precise, and clear writing style. ◆ We are conscious that many students find economics hard, so we place the student at centre stage and write for the student. We use language that doesn't intimidate and that allows the student to concentrate on the substance. ◆ We open each chapter with a clear statement of learning objectives, a real-world student-friendly vignette to grab attention, and a brief preview. We illustrate principles with examples that are selected to hold the student's interest and to make the subject lively. And we put principles to work by using them to illuminate current real-world problems and issues. ◆ We present some new ideas, such as dynamic comparative advantage, game theory, the modern theory of the firm, public choice theory, rational expectations, new growth theory, and real business cycle theory. But we explain these topics with familiar core ideas and tools. ◆ Today's course springs from today's issues—the information revolution, the impending global slowdown of 2003, the Kyoto debate, and the expansion of international trade and investment. But the principles that we use to understand these issues remain the core principles of our science. ◆ Governments and international agencies place renewed emphasis on long-term fundamentals as they seek to sustain economic growth. This book reflects this emphasis. ◆ To help promote a rich, active learning experience, we have developed a comprehensive online learning environment featuring diagnostic quizzes, a dynamic eText, eStudy Guide, interactive tutorials, practice exams, frequent news updates, and more.

The Fifth Edition Revision

ECONOMICS: CANADA IN THE GLOBAL ENVIRONMENT, Fifth Edition, retains all of the improvements achieved in its predecessor with its thorough and detailed presentation of modern economics, emphasis on real-world examples and critical thinking skills, diagrams renowned for pedagogy and precision, and path-breaking technology.

New to this edition are

- New introductory chapter
- All new chapter on global stock markets
- Revised and updated microeconomics content
- Revised and updated macroeconomics content
- Vastly expanded Web site

New Introductory Chapter

Chapter 1 has been completely rewritten to emphasize the central role of tradeoffs in economics, setting the tone for the rest of the book.

All-New Chapter 35 on Global Stock Markets

This exciting addition provides a valuable framework for addressing students' questions about how the stock market works. *What is a stock? What determines stock prices? Why are stock prices volatile? Why is it rational to diversify? How does the stock market influence the economy, and vice versa?*

Revised and Updated Microeconomics Content

The four major revisions in the microeconomics chapters are

1. The Economic Problem (Chapter 2): A revised and more carefully paced explanation of the gains from specialization and exchange.
2. Monopolistic Competition and Oligopoly (Chapter 13): An expanded explanation of repeated games and sequential games. These traditionally advanced topics are explained with examples and illustrations that bring the ideas within the grasp of beginning students.
3. Economic Inequality (Chapter 15): Two chapters from the Fourth Edition have been combined, streamlined, and given a new focus to explain the sources of the trend in the distribution of income—the widening gap between the highest- and lowest-income households.
4. Externalities (Chapter 18): Reorganized to explain the full range of positive and negative production and consumption externalities.

Revised and Updated Macroeconomics Content

The five major revisions in the macroeconomics chapters are

1. Measuring GDP and Economic Growth (Chapter 20): A reorganized and more focused explanation of GDP and its measurement, along with a new and simplified explanation of the chain-weighted method of calculating real GDP.
2. Monitoring Cycles, Jobs, and the Price Level (Chapter 21): A much reorganized chapter that describes how we identify a recession and how Statistics Canada measures the labour market and the CPI. The chapter also explains the significance and interpretation of data on the labour market and price level.
3. Economic Growth (Chapter 30): A simplified and mainstreamed explanation and illustration of the classical, neoclassical, and new theories of economic growth.
4. Macroeconomic Policy Challenges (Chapter 32): Explanation of the Taylor rule and comparison of Bank of Canada interest rate decisions with such a rule.
5. Thorough and extensive updating to reflect the Canadian economy and the global economy of 2001 and 2002 and prospects for 2003 and beyond, as well as the response to the heightened security situation following the September 11 attacks on the United States.

Vastly Expanded Web Site

Our new Web site is the centrepiece of this Fifth Edition revision. The site is organized around "8 steps to success in economics." The 8 steps are

1. Diagnostic quizzes that provide feedback with hyperlinks to all the Web-based learning tools.
2. Online glossary with definitions, examples, and links to related terms.
3. Online eText—the entire textbook in electronic form with hyperlinks to all other components of the Web site and with Flash animations of every figure in the textbook.
4. Online eStudy Guide—the entire study guide in electronic form.

5. *Economics in Action*—our market-leading interactive tutorial software program now accessed on the Web. This Java-based learning tool has been expanded to cover each and every chapter in the textbook. Students manipulate figures from the textbook by changing the conditions that lie behind them and observing how the economy responds to events.
6. PowerPoint lecture notes for students to review.
7. Web-based exercises with links to data and other online sources.
8. Practice exams—students can select from five question types (fill-in-the-blank, true-or-false, multiple-choice, complete-the-graph, and numeric) to be worked with or without detailed feedback.

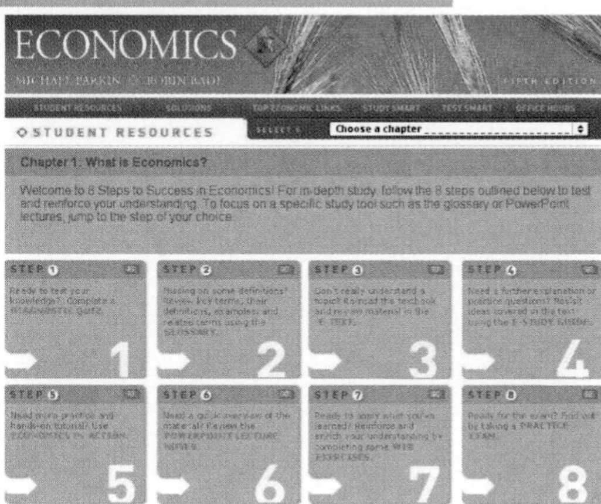

Features to Enhance Teaching and Learning

HERE, WE DESCRIBE THE CHAPTER FEATURES that are designed to enhance the learning process. Each chapter contains the following learning aids.

Chapter Opener

Each chapter opens with a one-page student-friendly, attention-grabbing vignette. The vignette raises questions that both motivate the student and focus the chapter. The Fifth Edition now carries this story into the main body of the chapter, and relates it to the chapter-ending *Reading Between the Lines* feature.

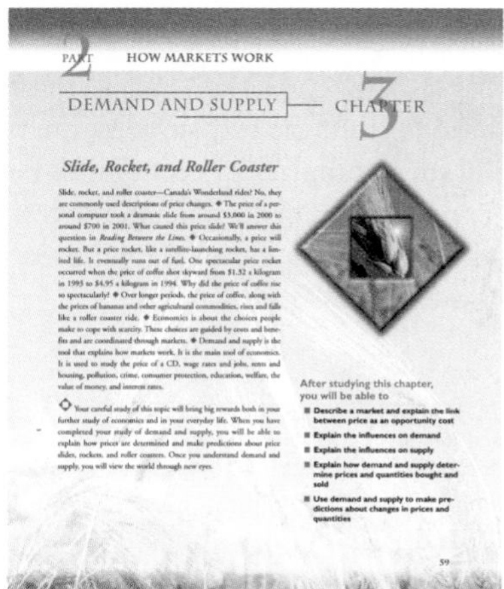

Chapter Objectives

A list of learning objectives enables students to see exactly where the chapter is going and to set their goals before they begin the chapter. We link these goals directly to the chapter's major headings.

After studying this chapter, you will be able to

- **Describe a market and explain the link between price as an opportunity cost**
- **Explain the influences on demand**
- **Explain the influences on supply**
- **Explain how demand and supply determine prices and quantities bought and sold**
- **Use demand and supply to make predictions about changes in prices and quantities**

In-Text Review Quizzes

A review quiz at the end of most major sections enables students to determine whether a topic needs further study before moving on.

REVIEW QUIZ

1. What is scarcity?
2. Give some examples of scarcity in today's world.
3. Define economics.
4. Use the headlines in today's news to illustrate the distinction between microeconomics and macroeconomics.

Key Terms

Highlighted terms within the text simplify the student's task of learning the vocabulary of economics. Each highlighted term appears in an end-of-chapter list with page numbers, in an end-of-book glossary, boldfaced in the index, and on the Parkin–Bade Web site.

KEY TERMS

Absolute advantage, 45
Allocative efficiency, 39
Capital accumulation, 40
Comparative advantage, 42
Dynamic comparative advantage, 45
Economic growth, 40

Above full-employment equilibrium A macroeconomic equilibrium in which real GDP exceeds potential GDP. (p. 510)

Topic: Capital

Factor markets
Factors of production
Human capital
Interest

Diagrams That Show the Action

This book has set new standards of clarity in its diagrams. Our goal has always been to show "where the economic action is." The diagrams in this book continue to generate an enormously positive response, which confirms our view that graphical analysis is the most powerful tool available for teaching and learning economics. But many students find graphs hard to work with. For this reason, we have developed the entire art program with the study and review needs of the student in mind. The diagrams feature

- Shifted curves, equilibrium points, and other important features highlighted in red
- Colour-blended arrows to suggest movement
- Graphs paired with data tables
- Diagrams labelled with boxed notes
- Extended captions that make each diagram and its caption a self-contained object for study and review

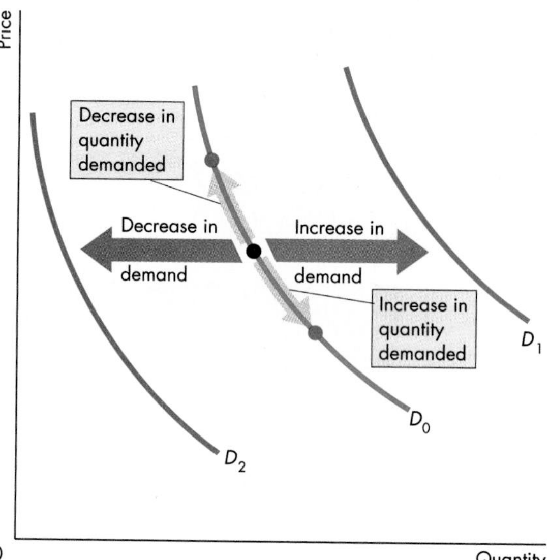

Reading Between the Lines

Each chapter ends with an economic analysis of a significant news article from the popular press together with a thorough economic analysis of the issues raised in the article. The Fifth Edition features all new *Reading Between the Lines* articles. We have chosen each article so that it sheds additional light on the questions first raised in the chapter opener.

Special "You're the Voter" sections in selected chapters invite students to analyze typical campaign topics and to probe their own stances on key public policy issues. Critical thinking questions about the article appear with the end-of-chapter questions and problems.

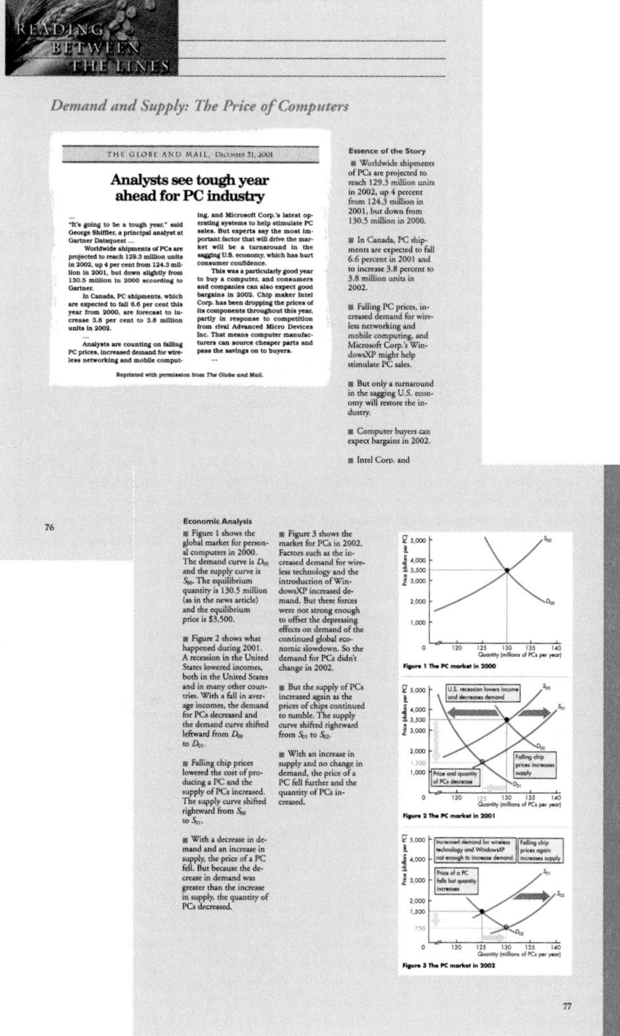

READING BETWEEN THE LINES

Demand and Supply: The Price of Computers

THE GLOBE AND MAIL, DECEMBER 31, 2001

Analysts see tough year ahead for PC industry

...

"It's going to be a tough year," said George Shiffler, a principal analyst at Gartner Dataquest ...

Worldwide shipments of PCs are projected to reach 129.3 million units in 2002, up 4 per cent from 124.3 million in 2001, but down slightly from 130.5 million in 2000 according to Gartner.

In Canada, PC shipments, which are expected to fall 6.6 per cent this year from 2000, are forecast to increase 3.8 per cent to 3.8 million units in 2002.

...

Analysts are counting on falling PC prices, increased demand for wireless networking and mobile computing, and Microsoft Corp.'s latest operating systems to help stimulate PC sales. But experts say the most important factor that will drive the market will be a turnaround in the sagging U.S. economy, which has hurt consumer confidence.

This was a particularly good year to buy a computer, and consumers and companies can also expect good bargains in 2002. Chip maker Intel Corp. has been dropping the prices of its components throughout this year, partly in response to competition from rival Advanced Micro Devices Inc. That means computer manufacturers can source cheaper parts and pass the savings on to buyers.

...

Reprinted with permission from *The Globe and Mail.*

Essence of the Story

- Worldwide shipments of PCs are projected to reach 129.3 million units in 2002, up 4 percent from 124.3 million in 2001, but down from 130.5 million in 2000.
- In Canada, PC shipments are expected to fall 6.6 percent in 2001 and to increase 3.8 percent to 3.8 million units in 2002.
- Falling PC prices, increased demand for wireless networking and mobile computing, and Microsoft Corp.'s WindowsXP might help stimulate PC sales.
- But only a turnaround in the sagging U.S. economy will restore the industry.
- Computer buyers can expect bargains in 2002.
- Intel Corp. and

76

Economic Analysis

- Figure 1 shows the global market for personal computers in 2000. The demand curve is D_{00} and the supply curve is S_{00}. The equilibrium quantity is 130.5 million (as in the news article) and the equilibrium price is $3,500.
- Figure 2 shows what happened during 2001. A recession in the United States lowered incomes, both in the United States and in many other countries. With a fall in average incomes, the demand for PCs decreased and the demand curve shifted leftward from D_{00} to D_{01}.
- Falling chip prices lowered the cost of producing a PC and the supply of PCs increased. The supply curve shifted rightward from S_{00} to S_{01}.
- With a decrease in demand and an increase in supply, the price of a PC fell. But because the decrease in demand was greater than the increase in supply, the quantity of PCs decreased.
- Figure 3 shows the market for PCs in 2002. Factors such as the increased demand for wireless technology and the introduction of WindowsXP increased demand. But these forces were not strong enough to offset the depressing effects on demand of the continued global economic slowdown. So the demand for PCs didn't change in 2002.
- But the supply of PCs increased again as the prices of chips continued to tumble. The supply curve shifted rightward from S_{01} to S_{02}.
- With an increase in supply and no change in demand, the price of a PC fell further and the quantity of PCs increased.

77

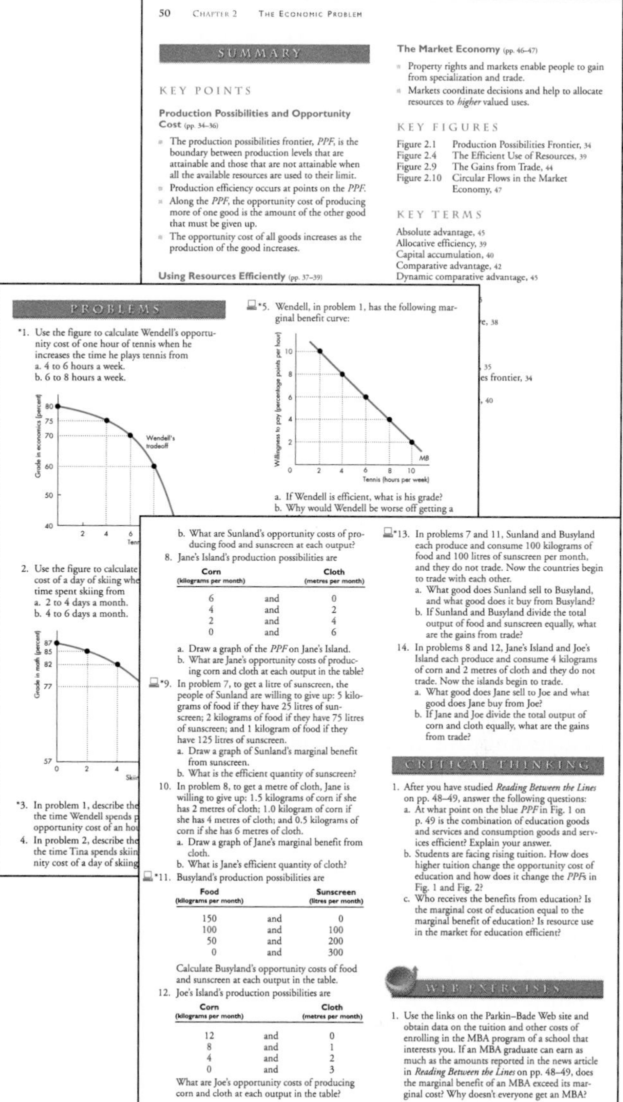

50 CHAPTER 2 THE ECONOMIC PROBLEM

SUMMARY

KEY POINTS

Production Possibilities and Opportunity Cost (pp. 34–36)

- The production possibilities frontier, *PPF*, is the boundary between production levels that are attainable and those that are not attainable when all the available resources are used to their limit.
- Production efficiency occurs at points on the *PPF*.
- Along the *PPF*, the opportunity cost of producing more of one good is the amount of the other good that must be given up.
- The opportunity cost of all goods increases as the production of the good increases.

Using Resources Efficiently (pp. 37–39)

The Market Economy (pp. 46–47)

- Property rights and markets enable people to gain from specialization and trade.
- Markets coordinate decisions and help to allocate resources to *higher* valued uses.

KEY FIGURES

Figure 2.1 Production Possibilities Frontier, 34
Figure 2.4 The Efficient Use of Resources, 39
Figure 2.9 The Gains from Trade, 44
Figure 2.10 Circular Flows in the Market Economy, 47

KEY TERMS

Absolute advantage, 45
Allocative efficiency, 39
Capital accumulation, 40
Comparative advantage, 42
Dynamic comparative advantage, 45

PROBLEMS

*1. Use the figure to calculate Wendell's opportunity cost of one hour of tennis when he increases the time he plays tennis from
a. 4 to 6 hours a week.
b. 6 to 8 hours a week.

*5. Wendell, in problem 1, has the following marginal benefit curve:

a. If Wendell is efficient, what is his grade?
b. Why would Wendell be worse off getting a

b. What are Sunland's opportunity costs of producing food and sunscreen at each output?

8. Jane's Island's production possibilities are

Corn (kilograms per month)		Cloth (metres per month)
6	and	0
4	and	2
2	and	4
0	and	6

a. Draw a graph of the *PPF* on Jane's Island.
b. What are Jane's opportunity costs of producing corn and cloth at each output in the table?

*9. In problem 7, to get a litre of sunscreen, the people of Sunland are willing to give up: 5 kilograms of food if they have 25 litres of sunscreen; 2 kilograms of food if they have 75 litres of sunscreen; and 1 kilogram of food if they have 125 litres of sunscreen.
a. Draw a graph of Sunland's marginal benefit from sunscreen.
b. What is the efficient quantity of sunscreen?

10. In problem 8, to get a metre of cloth, Jane is willing to give up: 1.5 kilograms of corn if she has 2 metres of cloth; 1.0 kilogram of corn if she has 4 metres of cloth; and 0.5 kilograms of corn if she has 6 metres of cloth.
a. Draw a graph of Jane's marginal benefit from cloth.
b. What is Jane's efficient quantity of cloth?

*11. Busyland's production possibilities are

Food (kilograms per month)		Sunscreen (litres per month)
150	and	0
100	and	100
50	and	200
0	and	300

Calculate Busyland's opportunity costs of food and sunscreen at each output in the table.

12. Joe's Island's production possibilities are

Corn (kilograms per month)		Cloth (metres per month)
12	and	0
8	and	1
4	and	2
0	and	3

What are Joe's opportunity costs of producing corn and cloth at each output in the table?

*13. In problems 7 and 11, Sunland and Busyland each produce and consume 100 kilograms of food and 100 litres of sunscreen per month, and they do not trade. Now the countries begin to trade with each other.
a. What good does Sunland sell to Busyland, and what good does it buy from Busyland?
b. If Sunland and Busyland divide the total output of food and sunscreen equally, what are the gains from trade?

14. In problems 8 and 12, Jane's Island and Joe's Island each produce and consume 4 kilograms of corn and 2 metres of cloth and they do not trade. Now the islands begin to trade.
a. What good does Jane sell to Joe and what good does Jane buy from Joe?
b. If Jane and Joe divide the total output of corn and cloth equally, what are the gains from trade?

CRITICAL THINKING

1. After you have studied *Reading Between the Lines* on pp. 48–49, answer the following questions:
a. At what point on the blue *PPF* in Fig. 1 on p. 49 is the combination of education goods and services and consumption goods and services efficient? Explain your answer.
b. Students are facing rising tuition. How does higher tuition change the opportunity cost of education and how does it change the *PPF*s in Fig. 1 and Fig. 2?
c. Who receives the benefits from education? Is the marginal cost of education equal to the marginal benefit of education? Is resource use in the market for education efficient?

WEB EXERCISES

1. Use the links on the Parkin–Bade Web site and obtain data on the tuition and other costs of enrolling in the MBA program of a school that interests you. If an MBA graduate can earn as much as the amounts reported in the news article in *Reading Between the Lines* on pp. 48–49, does the marginal benefit of an MBA exceed its marginal cost? Why doesn't everyone get an MBA?

End-of-Chapter Study Material

Each chapter closes with a concise summary organized by major topics, lists of key terms (all with page references), problems, critical thinking questions, and Web exercises. The problems are arranged in parallel pairs with solutions to the odd-numbered problems provided on the Web site. Most of the even-numbered problems and the Web exercises are new for the Fifth Edition. We provide the links needed for the Web exercises on our Web site.

For the Instructor

THIS BOOK ENABLES YOU TO ACHIEVE THREE objectives in your principles course:

- Focus on the economic way of thinking
- Explain the issues and problems of our time
- Choose your own course structure

Focus on the Economic Way of Thinking

You know how hard it is to encourage a student to think like an economist. But that is your goal. Consistent with this goal, the text focuses on and repeatedly uses the central ideas: choice; tradeoff; opportunity cost; the margin; incentives; the gains from voluntary exchange; the forces of demand, supply, and equilibrium; the pursuit of economic rent; and the effects of government actions on the economy.

Explain the Issues and Problems of Our Time

Students must use the central ideas and tools if they are to begin to understand them. There is no better way to motivate students than by using the tools of economics to explain the issues that confront students in today's world. These issues include the anticipated 2003 global slowdown, environment, widening income gaps, energy deregulation, budget deficits or surpluses, restraining inflation, understanding the stock market, avoiding protectionism, and the long-term growth of output and incomes.

Choose Your Own Course Structure

You want to teach your own course. We have organized this book to enable you to do so. We demonstrate the book's flexibility in the flexibility chart and alternative sequences table that appear on pp. xviii–xxi. You can use this book to teach a traditional course that blends theory and policy or a current policy issues course. Your micro course can emphasize theory or policy. You can structure your macro course to emphasize long-term growth and supply-side fundamentals. Or you can follow a traditional macro sequence and emphasize short-term fluctuations. The choices are yours.

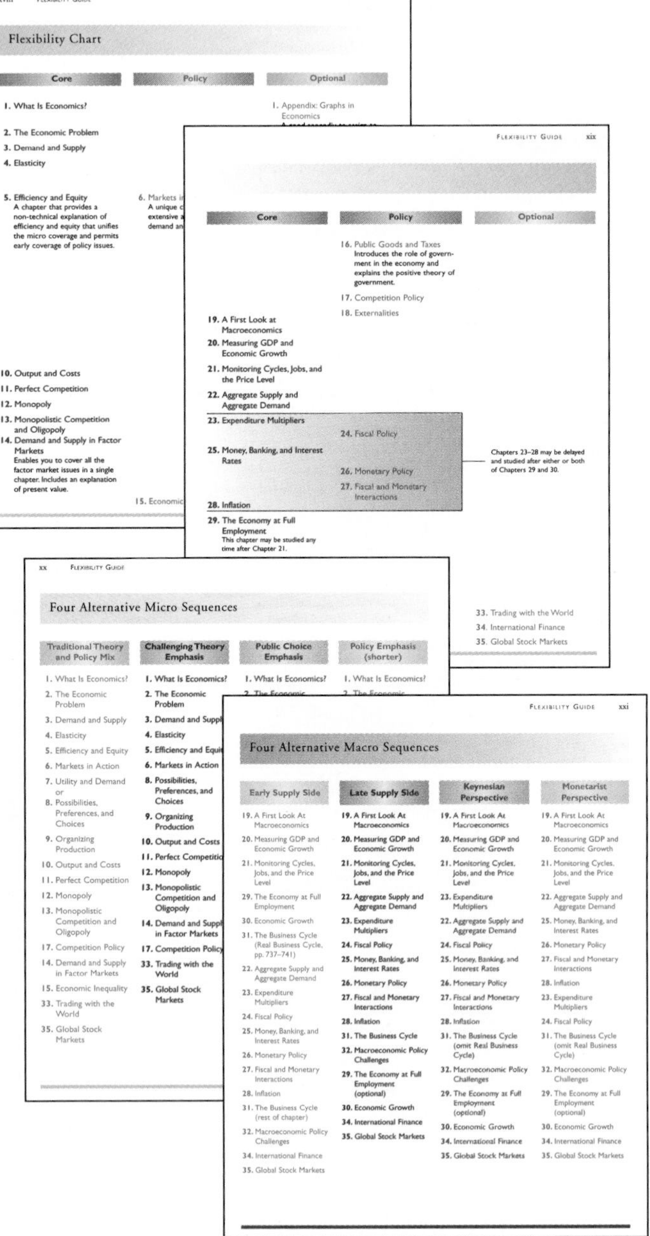

xviii FLEXIBILITY GUIDE

Flexibility Chart

Core | Policy | Optional

1. What Is Economics?
1. Appendix: Graphs in Economics
2. The Economic Problem
3. Demand and Supply
4. Elasticity
5. Efficiency and Equity — A chapter that provides a non-technical explanation of efficiency and equity that unifies the micro coverage and permits early coverage of policy issues.
10. Output and Costs
11. Perfect Competition
12. Monopoly
13. Monopolistic Competition and Oligopoly
14. Demand and Supply in Factor Markets — Enables you to cover all the factor market issues in a single chapter. Includes an explanation of present value.

FLEXIBILITY GUIDE xix

Core | Policy | Optional

16. Public Goods and Taxes — Introduces the role of government in the economy and explains the positive theory of government.
17. Competition Policy
18. Externalities
19. A First Look at Macroeconomics
20. Measuring GDP and Economic Growth
21. Monitoring Cycles, Jobs, and the Price Level
22. Aggregate Supply and Aggregate Demand
23. Expenditure Multipliers
24. Fiscal Policy
25. Money, Banking, and Interest Rates
26. Monetary Policy
27. Fiscal and Monetary Interactions
Chapters 23–28 may be delayed and studied after either or both of Chapters 29 and 30.
28. Inflation
29. The Economy at Full Employment — This chapter may be studied any time after Chapter 21.
33. Trading with the World
34. International Finance
35. Global Stock Markets

xx FLEXIBILITY GUIDE

Four Alternative Micro Sequences

Traditional Theory and Policy Mix	Challenging Theory Emphasis	Public Choice Emphasis	Policy Emphasis (shorter)
1. What Is Economics?	1. What Is Economics?	1. What Is Economics?	1. What Is Economics?
2. The Economic Problem	2. The Economic Problem		
3. Demand and Supply	3. Demand and Supply		
4. Elasticity	4. Elasticity		
5. Efficiency and Equity	5. Efficiency and Equity		
6. Markets in Action	6. Markets in Action		
7. Utility and Demand or 8. Possibilities, Preferences, and Choices	8. Possibilities, Preferences, and Choices		
9. Organizing Production	9. Organizing Production		
10. Output and Costs	10. Output and Costs		
11. Perfect Competition	11. Perfect Competition		
12. Monopoly	12. Monopoly		
13. Monopolistic Competition and Oligopoly	13. Monopolistic Competition and Oligopoly		
17. Competition Policy	14. Demand and Supply in Factor Markets		
14. Demand and Supply in Factor Markets	17. Competition Policy		
15. Economic Inequality	33. Trading with the World		
33. Trading with the World	35. Global Stock Markets		
35. Global Stock Markets			

FLEXIBILITY GUIDE xxi

Four Alternative Macro Sequences

Early Supply Side	Late Supply Side	Keynesian Perspective	Monetarist Perspective
19. A First Look At Macroeconomics	19. A First Look At Macroeconomics	19. A First Look At Macroeconomics	19. A First Look At Macroeconomics
20. Measuring GDP and Economic Growth	20. Measuring GDP and Economic Growth	20. Measuring GDP and Economic Growth	20. Measuring GDP and Economic Growth
21. Monitoring Cycles, Jobs, and the Price Level	21. Monitoring Cycles, Jobs, and the Price Level	21. Monitoring Cycles, Jobs, and the Price Level	21. Monitoring Cycles, Jobs, and the Price Level
29. The Economy at Full Employment	22. Aggregate Supply and Aggregate Demand	23. Expenditure Multipliers	22. Aggregate Supply and Aggregate Demand
30. Economic Growth	23. Expenditure Multipliers	22. Aggregate Supply and Aggregate Demand	25. Money, Banking, and Interest Rates
31. The Business Cycle (Real Business Cycle, pp. 737–741)	24. Fiscal Policy	24. Fiscal Policy	26. Monetary Policy
22. Aggregate Supply and Aggregate Demand	25. Money, Banking, and Interest Rates	25. Money, Banking, and Interest Rates	27. Fiscal and Monetary Interactions
23. Expenditure Multipliers	26. Monetary Policy	26. Monetary Policy	28. Inflation
24. Fiscal Policy	27. Fiscal and Monetary Interactions	27. Fiscal and Monetary Interactions	23. Expenditure Multipliers
25. Money, Banking, and Interest Rates	28. Inflation	28. Inflation	24. Fiscal Policy
26. Monetary Policy	31. The Business Cycle	31. The Business Cycle (omit Real Business Cycle)	31. The Business Cycle (omit Real Business Cycle)
27. Fiscal and Monetary Interactions	32. Macroeconomic Policy Challenges	32. Macroeconomic Policy Challenges	32. Macroeconomic Policy Challenges
28. Inflation	29. The Economy at Full Employment (optional)	29. The Economy at Full Employment (optional)	29. The Economy at Full Employment (optional)
31. The Business Cycle (rest of chapter)	30. Economic Growth	30. Economic Growth	30. Economic Growth
32. Macroeconomic Policy Challenges	34. International Finance	34. International Finance	34. International Finance
34. International Finance	35. Global Stock Markets	35. Global Stock Markets	35. Global Stock Markets
35. Global Stock Markets			

Instructor's Manual

The Instructor's Manual, written by Torben Drewes of Trent University, integrates the teaching and learning package and is a guide to all the supplements. Each chapter contains a chapter outline, what's new in the Fifth Edition, teaching suggestions, a look at where we have been and where we are going, lists of available overhead transparencies, descriptions of the electronic supplements, additional discussion questions, answers to the Review Quizzes, solutions to end-of-chapter problems, additional problems, and solutions to the additional problems. The chapter outline and teaching suggestions sections are keyed to the PowerPoint lecture notes.

Two Test Banks

To provide even greater choice when preparing tests and exams, we now offer two Test Banks with a total of more than 9,000 questions. Test Bank 1, prepared by Jane Waples and Saeed Moshiri of Memorial University, contains over 4,500 multiple-choice questions and is a thoroughly revised, upgraded, and improved version of our previous Test Bank. Test Bank 2, prepared by Glen Stirling of the University of Western Ontario and Ather Akbari of Saint Mary's University, contains about 4,300 *all new* multiple-choice, true-false, and short-answer questions.

PowerPoint Resources

We have developed a full-colour Microsoft PowerPoint Lecture Presentation for each chapter that includes all the figures from the text, animated graphs, and speaking notes. The slide outlines are based on the chapter outlines in the Instructor's Manual, and the speaking notes are based on the Instructor's Manual teaching suggestions. The presentations can be used electronically in the classroom or can be printed to create hard-copy transparency masters, and they can be accessed using Windows or Macintosh.

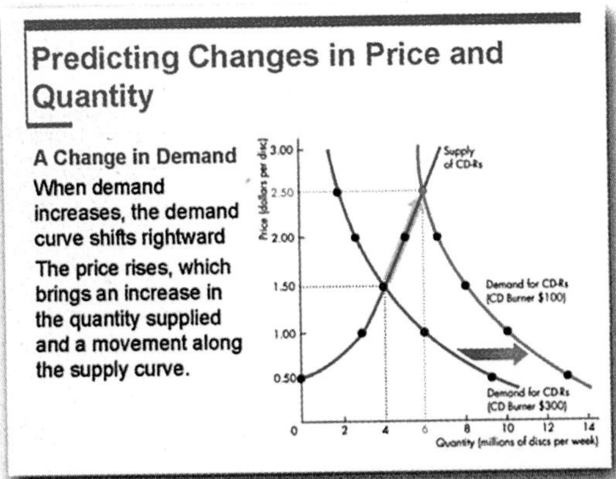

Overhead Transparencies

Full-colour transparencies of key figures from the text will improve the clarity of your lectures. They are available to qualified adopters of the text (contact your Pearson Education Canada sales representative).

Instructor's Resource CD with Computerized Test Banks

This CD contains Computerized Test Bank files, Instructor's Manual files in Microsoft Word, and PowerPoint files. Both test banks are available in Test Generator Software (TestGen-EQ with QuizMaster-EQ). Fully networkable, it is available for Windows and Macintosh. TestGen-EQ's new graphical interface enables instructors to view, edit, and add questions; transfer questions to tests; and print different forms of tests. Tests can be formatted with varying fonts and styles, margins, and headers and footers, as in any word-processing document. Search and sort features let the instructor quickly locate questions and arrange them in a preferred order. QuizMaster-EQ, working with your school's computer network, automatically grades the exams, stores the results on disk, and allows the instructor to view or print a variety of reports.

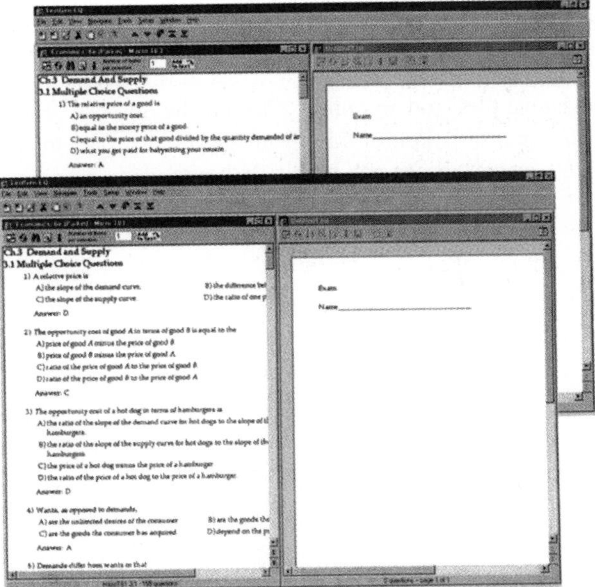

Course Management Systems

We offer three alternative course management systems—CourseCompass, Blackboard, and WebCT. Each system provides a dynamic, interactive, content-rich, and flexible online course management tool that enables instructors to easily and effectively customize online course materials to suit their needs. Instructors can track and analyze student performance on an array of Internet activities. Please contact your Pearson Education Canada representative for more details.

Economics in Action Software

Instructors can use *Economics in Action* interactive software in the classroom. Its many analytical graphs can be used as "electronic transparencies" for live graph manipulation in lectures. Its real-world data sets and graphing utility bring animated time-series graphs and scatter diagrams to the classroom.

The Parkin–Bade Web Site

The Fifth Edition of the textbook continues the tradition of path-breaking technology with *Parkin Online* at www.pearsoned.ca/parkin. The instructor side of *Parkin Online* includes all of the same resources as the student's side, but with the addition of speaking notes in the PowerPoint lecture notes, easy access to Instructor's Manual files, and an online "Consult the Authors" feature: Ask your questions or make your suggestions via e-mail, and we will answer you within 24 hours.

For the Student

Study Guide

The Fifth Edition Study Guide by Avi Cohen of York University and Harvey King of the University of Regina is carefully coordinated with the main text. For the first time, the Study Guide is available online. Print copies are also available.

Each chapter of the Study Guide contains

- Key concepts
- Helpful hints
- True/false questions that ask students to explain their answers
- Multiple-choice questions
- Short-answer questions

Each part allows students to test their cumulative understanding with questions that go across chapters and work a sample midterm examination.

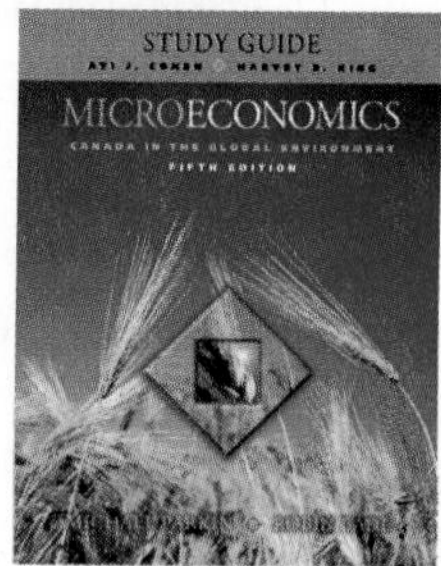

Economics in Action Interactive Software

With *Economics in Action* now available on the Web, students will have fun working the tutorials, answering questions that give instant explanations, and testing themselves ahead of their midterm tests. One of our students told us that using *Economics in Action* is like having a private professor in your dorm room! New modules now cover each and every chapter in the text.

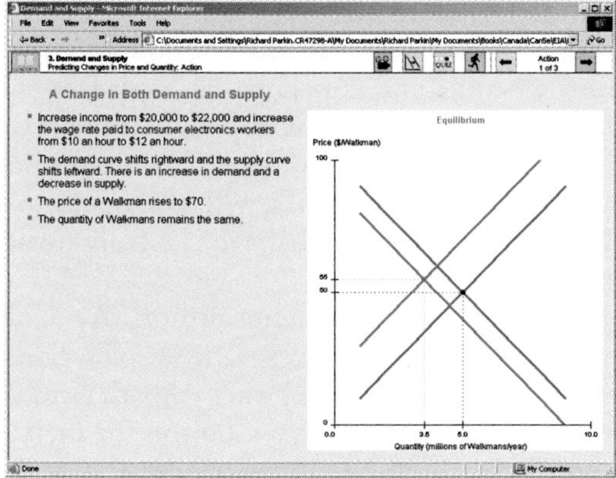

The Parkin–Bade Web Site

Parkin Online is the market-leading Web site for the principles of economics course. No other Web site comes close to matching the material offered on this site, on which students will find

- Diagnostic quizzes with feedback hyperlinked to all the Web-based learning tools
- The textbook—the *entire textbook in PDF format* with hyperlinks and Flash animated figures
- *Economics in Action*—tutorials, quizzes, and graphing tools that make curves shift and graphs come to life with a click of the mouse
- Study Guide—*the entire Study Guide, online*—with online quizzes
- PowerPoint lecture notes
- "Economics in the News" updated several times a week during the school year
- Online "Office Hours": Ask your question via e-mail, and we will answer within 24 hours!
- Economic links—links to Web sites that keep you up to date with what's going on in the economy and that enable you to work end-of-chapter Web exercises
- Solutions to odd-numbered end-of-chapter problems

The power of *Parkin Online* lies not only in the breadth and depth of the learning tools available, but also in the way that we have linked the tools together and provided a mind map to show you these links. When a student submits a diagnostic quiz, he or she receives a report card with an explanation of why answers are correct or incorrect *and hyperlinks* to the part of the eText that the student needs to read to better understand the concept, to the tutorial in *Economics in Action* that the student needs to work, and to related questions in the eStudy Guide and *Economics in Action.* The student is thus able to navigate easily through the site and to maximize the payoff from her or his study efforts.

Acknowledgments

WE THANK OUR CURRENT AND FORMER colleagues and friends at the University of Western Ontario who have taught us so much. They are Jim Davies, Jeremy Greenwood, Ig Horstmann, Peter Howitt, Greg Huffman, David Laidler, Phil Reny, Chris Robinson, John Whalley, and Ron Wonnacott. We also thank Doug McTaggart and Christopher Findlay, co-authors of the Australian edition, and Melanie Powell and Kent Matthews, co-authors of the European edition. Suggestions arising from their adaptations of earlier editions have been helpful to us in preparing this edition.

We thank the several thousand students whom we have been privileged to teach. The instant response that comes from the look of puzzlement or enlightenment has taught us how to teach economics.

It is an especial joy to thank the many outstanding managers, editors, and others at Pearson Education Canada who have contributed to the concerted publishing effort that brought this edition to completion. Tony Vander Woude, Chairman, and Allan Reynolds, President and CEO, have once again provided outstanding corporate direction. They have worked hard to ensure that Pearson evolves a culture that builds on the best of Addison Wesley and Prentice Hall, from which the new company has grown. Michael Young, Vice President and Editorial Director for Higher Education, has been a devoted contributor through his appointment and management of the outstanding editors with whom we've worked. When we began the revision, Dave Ward was our Acquisitions Editor. Dave has moved on to a new range of duties, but we want to place on the record the valuable contribution that he made to this revision in its early stages. Dave was succeeded by Gary Bennett as Acquisitions Editor. Gary played a major role in bringing this revision to completion and in finding and managing a team of outstanding supplements authors. Suzanne Schaan brought her experience and dedicated professionalism to the development effort. Toni Chahley, New Media Developmental Editor, provided direction and leadership in designing our new *Parkin Online* Web site. Deborah Meredith, Marketing Manager, provided inspired marketing direction. Her brochures and, more important, her timely questions and prodding for material had a significant impact on the shape of the text. Anthony Leung, Designer, designed the cover, text, and package and surpassed the challenge of ensuring that we meet the highest design standards. Marisa D'Andrea, our Production Editor, worked miracles on a tight production schedule and coped calmly with late-changing content. Laurel Sparrow copyedited the text manuscript. We thank all of these wonderful people. It has been inspiring to work with them and to share in creating what we believe is a truly outstanding educational tool.

We thank our supplements authors, Avi Cohen, Harvey King, Torben Drewes, Jane Waples, Saeed Moshiri, Glen Stirling, and Ather Akbari. And we thank Kit Pasula and Rosilyn Coulson for their extraordinarily careful accuracy review of near-final pages.

We thank the people who work directly with us. Jeannie Gillmore provided outstanding research assistance on many topics, including all the *Reading Between the Lines* news articles. Jane McAndrew provided excellent library help. Richard Parkin created the electronic art files and offered many ideas that improved the figures in this book. And Laurel Davies managed an ever-growing and more complex *Economics in Action* database.

As with the previous editions, this one owes an enormous debt to our students. We dedicate this book to them and again thank them for their careful reading and critical comments on the previous edition. We especially thank Chang Song and Johnathan Raiken, students at the University of Western Ontario in 2002, for finding errors and less-than-clear passages in the Fourth Edition.

Classroom experience will continue to test the value of this book. We would appreciate hearing from instructors and students about how we can continue to improve it in future editions.

Michael Parkin
Robin Bade
London, Ontario, Canada
michael.parkin@uwo.ca
robin@econ100.com

Reviewers

Ather H. Akbari, Saint Mary's University
Aurelia Best, Centennial College
Caroline Boivin, Université de Sherbrooke
Beverly Cameron, University of Manitoba
Scott Cawfield, Centennial College
Brian Coulter, University College of the Fraser Valley
Torben Drewes, Trent University
C.M. Fellows, Mount Royal College
Brian Ferguson, University of Guelph
Oliver Franke, Athabasca University
David Gray, University of Ottawa
Eric Kam, University of Western Ontario
Gordon Lee, University of Alberta
David Murrell, University of New Brunswick
Steve Rakoczy, Humber College
Kenneth Rea, University of Toronto
Jim Sentance, University of Prince Edward Island
Lance Shandler, Kwantlen University College
Lewis Soroka, Brock University
Glen Stirling, University of Western Ontario
Brian VanBlarcom, Acadia University
Joe Vieira, Confederation College
Graham Voss, University of Victoria
Baotai Wang, University of Northern British Columbia
Richard Watuwa, Saint Mary's University
Christopher Worswick, Carleton University
Emmanuel Yiridoe, Nova Scotia Agricultural College
Ayoub Yousefi, University of Western Ontario

Flexibility Chart

Core

1. What Is Economics?

2. The Economic Problem

3. Demand and Supply

4. Elasticity

5. Efficiency and Equity
A chapter that provides a non-technical explanation of efficiency and equity that unifies the micro coverage and permits early coverage of policy issues.

10. Output and Costs

11. Perfect Competition

12. Monopoly

13. Monopolistic Competition and Oligopoly

14. Demand and Supply in Factor Markets
Enables you to cover all the factor market issues in a single chapter. Includes an explanation of present value.

Policy

6. Markets in Action
A unique chapter that gives extensive applications of demand and supply.

15. Economic Inequality

Optional

1. Appendix: Graphs in Economics
A good appendix to assign to the student with a fear of graphs.

7. Utility and Demand
Although this chapter is optional, it may be covered if desired *before* demand in Chapter 3.

8. Possibilities, Preferences, and Choices
A full chapter on this strictly optional topic to ensure that it is covered clearly with intuitive explanations and illustrations. The standard short appendix treatment of this topic makes it indigestible.

9. Organizing Production
This chapter may be skipped or assigned as a reading.

14. Appendix: Labour Unions

Core	Policy	Optional
	16. Public Goods and Taxes Introduces the role of government in the economy and explains the positive theory of government.	
	17. Competition Policy	
	18. Externalities	
19. A First Look At Macroeconomics		
20. Measuring GDP and Economic Growth		
21. Monitoring Cycles, Jobs, and the Price Level		
22. Aggregate Supply and Aggregate Demand		
23. Expenditure Multipliers		Chapters 23–28 may be delayed and studied after either or both of Chapters 29 and 30.
	24. Fiscal Policy	
25. Money, Banking, and Interest Rates		
	26. Monetary Policy	
	27. Fiscal and Monetary Interactions	
28. Inflation		
29. The Economy At Full Employment This chapter may be studied any time after Chapter 21.		
30. Economic Growth The section on growth theory is optional.		
31. The Business Cycle	**32.** Macroeconomic Policy Challenges	**33.** Trading with the World
		34. International Finance
		35. Global Stock Markets

Four Alternative Micro Sequences

Traditional Theory and Policy Mix

1. What Is Economics?
2. The Economic Problem
3. Demand and Supply
4. Elasticity
5. Efficiency and Equity
6. Markets in Action
7. Utility and Demand
or
8. Possibilities, Preferences, and Choices
9. Organizing Production
10. Output and Costs
11. Perfect Competition
12. Monopoly
13. Monopolistic Competition and Oligopoly
17. Competition Policy
14. Demand and Supply in Factor Markets
15. Economic Inequality
33. Trading with the World
35. Global Stock Markets

Challenging Theory Emphasis

1. What Is Economics?
2. The Economic Problem
3. Demand and Supply
4. Elasticity
5. Efficiency and Equity
6. Markets in Action
8. Possibilities, Preferences, and Choices
9. Organizing Production
10. Output and Costs
11. Perfect Competition
12. Monopoly
13. Monopolistic Competition and Oligopoly
14. Demand and Supply in Factor Markets
17. Competition Policy
33. Trading with the World
35. Global Stock Markets

Public Choice Emphasis

1. What Is Economics?
2. The Economic Problem
3. Demand and Supply
4. Elasticity
5. Efficiency and Equity
6. Markets in Action
7. Utility and Demand
9. Organizing Production
10. Output and Costs
11. Perfect Competition
12. Monopoly
13. Monopolistic Competition and Oligopoly
16. Public Goods and Taxes
17. Competition Policy
18. Externalities

Policy Emphasis (shorter)

1. What Is Economics?
2. The Economic Problem
3. Demand and Supply
4. Elasticity
5. Efficiency and Equity
6. Markets in Action
14. Demand and Supply in Factor Markets
15. Economic Inequality
16. Public Goods and Taxes
18. Externalities
33. Trading with the World

Four Alternative Macro Sequences

Early Supply Side	Late Supply Side	Keynesian Perspective	Monetarist Perspective
19. A First Look At Macroeconomics	**19.** A First Look At Macroeconomics	**19.** A First Look At Macroeconomics	**19.** A First Look At Macroeconomics
20. Measuring GDP and Economic Growth	**20.** Measuring GDP and Economic Growth	**20.** Measuring GDP and Economic Growth	**20.** Measuring GDP and Economic Growth
21. Monitoring Cycles, Jobs, and the Price Level	**21.** Monitoring Cycles, Jobs, and the Price Level	**21.** Monitoring Cycles, Jobs, and the Price Level	**21.** Monitoring Cycles, Jobs, and the Price Level
29. The Economy At Full Employment	**22.** Aggregate Supply and Aggregate Demand	**23.** Expenditure Multipliers	**22.** Aggregate Supply and Aggregate Demand
30. Economic Growth	**23.** Expenditure Multipliers	**22.** Aggregate Supply and Aggregate Demand	**25.** Money, Banking, and Interest Rates
31. The Business Cycle (Real Business Cycle, pp. 737–741)	**24.** Fiscal Policy	**24.** Fiscal Policy	**26.** Monetary Policy
22. Aggregate Supply and Aggregate Demand	**25.** Money, Banking, and Interest Rates	**25.** Money, Banking, and Interest Rates	**27.** Fiscal and Monetary Interactions
23. Expenditure Multipliers	**26.** Monetary Policy	**26.** Monetary Policy	**28.** Inflation
24. Fiscal Policy	**27.** Fiscal and Monetary Interactions	**27.** Fiscal and Monetary Interactions	**23.** Expenditure Multipliers
25. Money, Banking, and Interest Rates	**28.** Inflation	**28.** Inflation	**24.** Fiscal Policy
26. Monetary Policy	**31.** The Business Cycle	**31.** The Business Cycle (omit Real Business Cycle)	**31.** The Business Cycle (omit Real Business Cycle)
27. Fiscal and Monetary Interactions	**32.** Macroeconomic Policy Challenges	**32.** Macroeconomic Policy Challenges	**32.** Macroeconomic Policy Challenges
28. Inflation	**29.** The Economy At Full Employment (optional)	**29.** The Economy At Full Employment (optional)	**29.** The Economy At Full Employment (optional)
31. The Business Cycle (rest of chapter)	**30.** Economic Growth	**30.** Economic Growth	**30.** Economic Growth
32. Macroeconomic Policy Challenges	**34.** International Finance	**34.** International Finance	**34.** International Finance
34. International Finance	**35.** Global Stock Markets	**35.** Global Stock Markets	**35.** Global Stock Markets
35. Global Stock Markets			

BRIEF CONTENTS

PART 1 INTRODUCTION

Chapter 1 What Is Economics?

Chapter 2 The Economic Problem

PART 2 HOW MARKETS WORK

Chapter 3 Demand and Supply

Chapter 4 Elasticity

Chapter 5 Efficiency and Equity

Chapter 6 Markets in Action

PART 3 HOUSEHOLDS' CHOICES

Chapter 7 Utility and Demand

Chapter 8 Possibilities, Preferences, and Choices

PART 4 FIRMS AND MARKETS

Chapter 9 Organizing Production

Chapter 10 Output and Costs

Chapter 11 Perfect Competition

Chapter 12 Monopoly

Chapter 13 Monopolistic Competition and Oligopoly

PART 5 FACTOR MARKETS

Chapter 14 Demand and Supply in Factor Markets

Chapter 15 Economic Inequality

PART 6 MARKET FAILURE AND GOVERNMENT

Chapter 16 Public Goods and Taxes

Chapter 17 Competition Policy

Chapter 18 Externalities

PART 7 ISSUES IN MACROECONOMICS

Chapter 19 A First Look At Macroeconomics

Chapter 20 Measuring GDP and Economic Growth

Chapter 21 Monitoring Cycles, Jobs, and the Price Level

Chapter 22 Aggregate Supply and Aggregate Demand

PART 8 AGGREGATE DEMAND AND INFLATION

Chapter 23 Expenditure Multipliers

Chapter 24 Fiscal Policy

Chapter 25 Money, Banking, and Interest Rates

Chapter 26 Monetary Policy

Chapter 27 Fiscal and Monetary Interactions

Chapter 28 Inflation

PART 9 AGGREGATE SUPPLY AND ECONOMIC GROWTH

Chapter 29 The Economy At Full Employment

Chapter 30 Economic Growth

Chapter 31 The Business Cycle

Chapter 32 Macroeconomic Policy Challenges

PART 10 THE GLOBAL ECONOMY

Chapter 33 Trading with the World

Chapter 34 International Finance

Chapter 35 Global Stock Markets

CONTENTS

PART 1 INTRODUCTION

Chapter 1 What Is Economics? 1

Choice, Change, Challenge, and Opportunity **1**

Definition of Economics **2**
- Scarcity **2**
- Microeconomics **2**
- Macroeconomics **2**

Three Big Microeconomic Questions **3**
- What Goods and Services Are Produced? **3**
- How Are Goods and Services Produced? **4**
- For Whom Are Goods and Services Produced? **5**

Three Big Macroeconomic Questions **6**
- What Determines the Standard of Living? **6**
- What Determines the Cost of Living? **7**
- Why Does Our Economy Fluctuate? **8**

The Economic Way of Thinking **9**
- Choices and Tradeoffs **9**
- Microeconomic Tradeoffs **9**
- Macroeconomic Tradeoffs **10**
- Opportunity Cost **11**
- Margins and Incentives **11**

Economics: A Social Science **12**
- Observation and Measurement **12**
- Model Building **12**
- Testing Models **12**
- Obstacles and Pitfalls in Economics **13**
- Agreement and Disagreement **14**

Chapter 1 Appendix Graphs in Economics 17

Graphing Data 17
- Time-Series Graphs 18
- Cross-Section Graphs 18
- Scatter Diagrams 19

Graphs Used in Economic Models 20
- Variables That Move in the Same Direction 20
- Variables That Move in Opposite Directions 21
- Variables That Have a Maximum or a Minimum 22
- Variables That Are Unrelated 23

The Slope of a Relationship 24
- The Slope of a Straight Line 24
- The Slope of a Curved Line 25

Graphing Relationships Among More Than Two Variables 26

MATHEMATICAL NOTE
Equations to Straight Lines 28

Summary (Key Points, Key Figures and Tables, and Key Terms), Problems, Critical Thinking, and Web Exercises appear at the end of each chapter.

Chapter 2 The Economic Problem 33

Good, Better, Best! 33

Production Possibilities and Opportunity Cost 34
- Production Possibilities Frontier 34
- Production Efficiency 35
- Tradeoff Along the *PPF* 35
- Opportunity Cost 35

Using Resources Efficiently 37
- The *PPF* and Marginal Cost 37
- Preferences and Marginal Benefit 38
- Efficient Use of Resources 39

Economic Growth 40
- The Cost of Economic Growth 40
- Economic Growth in Canada and Hong Kong 41

Gains from Trade 42
- Comparative Advantage 42
- Achieving the Gains from Trade 43
- Absolute Advantage 45
- Dynamic Comparative Advantage 45

The Market Economy 46
- Property Rights 46
- Markets 46
- Circular Flows in the Market Economy 46
- Coordinating Decisions 47

READING BETWEEN THE LINES
POLICY WATCH
The Cost and Benefit of Education 48

PART 1 WRAP UP
Understanding the Scope of Economics 53
- Probing the Ideas: The Sources of Economic Wealth 54
- Talking with Lawrence H. Summers 56

PART 2 HOW MARKETS WORK

Chapter 3 Demand and Supply 59

Slide, Rocket, and Roller Coaster 59

Markets and Prices **60**

Demand **61**
- What Determines Buying Plans? **61**
- The Law of Demand **61**
- Demand Curve and Demand Schedule **62**
- A Change in Demand **63**
- A Change in the Quantity Demanded Versus a Change in Demand **64**

Supply **66**
- What Determines Selling Plans? **66**
- The Law of Supply **66**
- Supply Curve and Supply Schedule **66**
- A Change in Supply **67**
- A Change in the Quantity Supplied Versus a Change in Supply **68**

Market Equilibrium **70**
- Price as a Regulator **70**
- Price Adjustments **71**

Predicting Changes in Price and Quantity **72**
- A Change in Demand **72**
- A Change in Supply **73**
- A Change in Both Demand and Supply **74**

READING BETWEEN THE LINES
Demand and Supply: The Price of Computers **76**

MATHEMATICAL NOTE
Demand, Supply, and Equilibrium **78**

Chapter 4 Elasticity 83

Predicting Prices 83

Price Elasticity of Demand **84**
- Calculating Elasticity **85**
- Inelastic and Elastic Demand **86**
- Elasticity Along a Straight-Line Demand Curve **87**
- Total Revenue and Elasticity **88**
- Your Expenditure and Your Elasticity **89**
- The Factors That Influence the Elasticity of Demand **89**

More Elasticities of Demand **91**
- Cross Elasticity of Demand **91**
- Income Elasticity of Demand **92**
- Real-World Income Elasticities of Demand **93**

Elasticity of Supply **94**
- Calculating the Elasticity of Supply **94**
- The Factors That Influence the Elasticity of Supply **95**

READING BETWEEN THE LINES
Elasticities of Demand and Supply in the Global Oil Market **98**

Chapter 5 Efficiency and Equity 103

More for Less 103

Efficiency: A Refresher **104**
- Marginal Benefit **104**
- Marginal Cost **104**
- Efficiency and Inefficiency **105**

Value, Price, and Consumer Surplus **106**
- Value, Willingness to Pay, and Demand **106**
- Consumer Surplus **107**

Cost, Price, and Producer Surplus **108**
- Cost, Minimum Supply-Price, and Supply **108**
- Producer Surplus **109**

Is the Competitive Market Efficient? **110**
- Efficiency of Competitive Equilibrium **110**
- The Invisible Hand **111**
- The Invisible Hand at Work Today **111**
- Obstacles to Efficiency **111**
- Underproduction **112**
- Overproduction **113**

Is the Competitive Market Fair? **114**
- It's Not Fair If the *Result* Isn't Fair **114**
- It's Not Fair If the *Rules* Aren't Fair **116**

READING BETWEEN THE LINES
POLICY WATCH
Efficiency and Equity in the Market for Drugs **118**

Chapter 6 Markets in Action 123

Turbulent Times 123

Housing Markets and Rent Ceilings **124**
- The Market Response to a Decrease in Supply **124**
- Long-Run Adjustments **125**
- A Regulated Housing Market **125**
- Search Activity **126**
- Black Markets **126**
- Inefficiency of Rent Ceilings **127**

The Labour Market and the Minimum Wage **128**
- The Minimum Wage **129**
- The Minimum Wage in Practice **130**
- Inefficiency of the Minimum Wage **130**

Taxes **131**
- Who Pays a Sales Tax? **131**
- Tax Division and Elasticity of Demand **132**
- Tax Division and Elasticity of Supply **133**
- Sales Taxes in Practice **134**
- Taxes and Efficiency **134**

Markets for Illegal Goods **135**
- A Free Market for Drugs **135**
- A Market for Illegal Drugs **135**
- Legalizing and Taxing Drugs **136**

Stabilizing Farm Revenues **137**
- An Unregulated Agricultural Market **137**
- Speculative Markets in Inventories **138**
- Farm Marketing Boards **139**
- Efficiency and Equity in Farm Markets **141**

READING BETWEEN THE LINES
POLICY WATCH
Who Pays the Airport Security Tax? **142**

PART 2 **WRAP UP**
Understanding How Markets Work 147
- Probing the Ideas: Discovering the Laws of Demand and Supply **148**
- Talking with John McMillan **150**

PART 3 HOUSEHOLDS' CHOICES

Chapter 7 Utility and Demand 153

Water, Water, Everywhere 153

Household Consumption Choices 154
- Consumption Possibilities 154
- Preferences 154
- Total Utility 154
- Marginal Utility 155
- Temperature: An Analogy 155

Maximizing Utility 157
- The Utility-Maximizing Choice 157
- Equalizing Marginal Utility per Dollar Spent 157

Predictions of Marginal Utility Theory 159
- A Fall in the Price of a Movie 159
- A Rise in the Price of Pop 160
- A Rise in Income 162
- Individual Demand and Market Demand 163
- Marginal Utility and Elasticity 164

Efficiency, Price, and Value 164
- Consumer Efficiency and Consumer Surplus 164
- The Paradox of Value 164

READING BETWEEN THE LINES
What's the Marginal Utility of a Boat Ride? 166

Chapter 8 Possibilities, Preferences, and Choices 171

Subterranean Movements 171

Consumption Possibilities 172
- The Budget Equation 173

Preferences and Indifference Curves 175
- Marginal Rate of Substitution 176
- Degree of Substitutability 177

Predicting Consumer Behaviour 178
- A Change in Price 179
- A Change in Income 180
- Substitution Effect and Income Effect 181
- Back to the Facts 182

Work–Leisure Choices 182
- Labour Supply 182
- The Labour Supply Curve 183

READING BETWEEN THE LINES
Regular Books versus Print-on-Demand Books 184

PART 3 WRAP UP
Understanding Households' Choices 189
- Probing the Ideas: People as Rational Decision Makers 190
- Talking with Gary S. Becker 192

PART 4 FIRMS AND MARKETS

Chapter 9 Organizing Production 195

Spinning a Web **195**

The Firm and Its Economic Problem **196**
- The Firm's Goal **196**
- Measuring a Firm's Profit **196**
- Opportunity Cost **196**
- Economic Profit **197**
- Economic Accounting: A Summary **197**
- The Firm's Constraints **198**

Technological and Economic Efficiency **199**
- Technological Efficiency **199**
- Economic Efficiency **199**

Information and Organization **201**
- Command Systems **201**
- Incentive Systems **201**
- Mixing the Systems **201**
- The Principal–Agent Problem **202**
- Coping with the Principal–Agent Problem **202**
- Types of Business Organization **202**
- Pros and Cons of Different Types of Firms **203**
- The Relative Importance of Different Types of Firms **204**

Markets and the Competitive Environment **205**
- Measures of Concentration **206**
- Concentration Measures for the Canadian Economy **207**
- Limitations of Concentration Measures **207**
- Market Structures in the North American Economy **209**

Markets and Firms **210**
- Market Coordination **210**
- Why Firms? **210**

READING BETWEEN THE LINES
Nortel's Problem **212**

Chapter 10 Output and Costs 217

What Does a Doughnut Cost? **217**

Decision Time Frames **218**
- The Short Run **218**
- The Long Run **218**

Short-Run Technology Constraint **219**
- Product Schedules **219**
- Product Curves **219**
- Total Product Curve **220**
- Marginal Product Curve **220**
- Average Product Curve **222**
- Marginal Grade and Grade Point Average **222**

Short-Run Cost **223**
- Total Cost **223**
- Marginal Cost **224**
- Average Cost **224**
- Why the Average Total Cost Curve Is U-Shaped **224**
- Cost Curves and Product Curves **226**
- Shifts in the Cost Curves **226**

Long-Run Cost **228**
- The Production Function **228**
- Short-Run Cost and Long-Run Cost **228**
- The Long-Run Average Cost Curve **230**
- Economies and Diseconomies of Scale **230**

READING BETWEEN THE LINES
The Cost of a Doughnut **232**

Chapter 11 **Perfect Competition 237**

Sweet Competition **237**

Competition **238**
How Perfect Competition Arises **238**
Price Takers **238**
Economic Profit and Revenue **238**

The Firm's Decisions in Perfect Competition **240**
Profit-Maximizing Output **240**
Marginal Analysis **242**
Profits and Losses in the Short Run **243**
The Firm's Short-Run Supply Curve **244**
Short-Run Industry Supply Curve **245**

Output, Price, and Profit in Perfect Competition **246**
Short-Run Equilibrium **246**
A Change in Demand **246**
Long-Run Adjustments **247**
Entry and Exit **247**
Changes in Plant Size **248**
Long-Run Equilibrium **249**

Changing Tastes and Advancing Technology **250**
A Permanent Change in Demand **250**
External Economies and Diseconomies **251**
Technological Change **253**

Competition and Efficiency **254**
Efficient Use of Resources **254**
Choices, Equilibrium, and Efficiency **254**
Efficiency of Perfect Competition **255**

READING BETWEEN THE LINES
Perfect Competition in Maple Syrup **256**

Chapter 12 **Monopoly 261**

The Profits of Generosity **261**

Market Power **262**
How Monopoly Arises **262**
Monopoly Price-Setting Strategies **263**

A Single-Price Monopoly's Output and Price Decision **264**
Price and Marginal Revenue **264**
Marginal Revenue and Elasticity **265**
Output and Price Decision **266**

Single-Price Monopoly and Competition Compared **268**
Comparing Output and Price **268**
Efficiency Comparison **269**
Redistribution of Surpluses **270**
Rent Seeking **270**
Rent-Seeking Equilibrium **270**

Price Discrimination **271**
Price Discrimination and Consumer Surplus **271**
Profiting by Price Discriminating **272**
Perfect Price Discrimination **273**
Efficiency and Rent Seeking with Price Discrimination **274**

Monopoly Policy Issues **275**
Gains from Monopoly **275**
Regulating Natural Monopoly **276**

READING BETWEEN THE LINES
POLICY WATCH
Domestic Airline Monopoly **278**

Chapter 13 Monopolistic Competition and Oligopoly 283

PC War Games **283**

Monopolistic Competition **284**
- Large Number of Firms **284**
- Product Differentiation **284**
- Competing on Quality, Price, and Marketing **284**
- Entry and Exit **285**
- Examples of Monopolistic Competition **285**

Output and Price in Monopolistic Competition **286**
- Short Run: Economic Profit **286**
- Long Run: Zero Economic Profit **287**
- Monopolistic Competition and Efficiency **287**

Product Development and Marketing **288**
- Innovation and Product Development **288**
- Marketing **289**

Oligopoly **291**
- The Kinked Demand Curve Model **291**
- Dominant Firm Oligopoly **292**

Oligopoly Games **293**
- What Is a Game? **293**
- The Prisoners' Dilemma **293**
- An Oligopoly Price-Fixing Game **295**
- Other Oligopoly Games **299**
- An R&D Game **299**

Repeated Games and Sequential Games **301**
- A Repeated Duopoly Game **301**
- A Sequential Entry Game in a Contestable Market **302**

READING BETWEEN THE LINES
POLICY WATCH
Oligopoly in Action: A Book Seller's War **304**

PART 4 **WRAP UP**
Understanding Firms and Markets 309
- Probing the Ideas: Market Power **310**
- Talking with Bengt Holmstrom **312**

PART 5 FACTOR MARKETS

Chapter 14 Demand and Supply in Factor Markets 315

Many Happy Returns **315**

Prices and Incomes in Competitive Factor Markets **316**

Labour Markets **317**
- The Demand for Labour **317**
- Marginal Revenue Product **318**
- The Labour Demand Curve **319**
- Equivalence of Two Conditions for Profit Maximization **320**
- Changes in the Demand for Labour **321**
- Market Demand **322**
- Elasticity of Demand for Labour **322**
- The Supply of Labour **322**
- Labour Market Equilibrium **324**

Capital Markets **325**
- The Demand for Capital **325**
- Discounting and Present Value **326**
- The Present Value of a Computer **327**
- Demand Curve for Capital **329**
- The Supply of Capital **329**
- Supply Curve of Capital **330**
- The Interest Rate **330**

Natural Resource Markets **331**
- The Supply of a Renewable Natural Resource **331**
- The Supply of a Nonrenewable Natural Resource **332**
- Price and the Hotelling Principle **332**

Income, Economic Rent, and Opportunity Cost **334**
- Large and Small Incomes **334**
- Economic Rent and Opportunity Cost **334**

READING BETWEEN THE LINES
Rents and Opportunity Costs on the Ice **336**

Parkin Online
www.pearsoned.ca/parkin

As a student purchasing a new copy of Parkin and Bade's ***Economics: Canada in the Global Environment,* Fifth Edition**, you are entitled to a prepaid subscription to premium services on our Web-based interactive learning environment. You will have unlimited online access to the ***eText***, ***eStudy Guide***, ***Economics in Action*** interactive software tutorial, ***Diagnostic Quizzes*** that link directly to the eText and eStudy Guide, ***Office Hours***, and many other Web resources.

In addition to these resources, you will also have access to **EconomicsCentral**, Pearson Education Canada's online resource for economics students! You'll want to bookmark this site because of its useful features: ***concept tutorials*** for difficult topics, an ***online tutor*** to help you with those tough questions, ***Weblinks***, and much more.

What do you do with this access code?

What do you do with this access code?

1. **Locate the site:**
   Launch your Web browser and type **www.pearsoned.ca/parkin** into the location area.

2. **Use your Pearson Education Canada access code:**
   The first time you access the site, you will be required to register using this access code. Type in the access code on this page (one word per box) and follow the steps indicated. During registration, you will choose a personal User ID and Password for logging onto the site. Your access code can be used only once to establish your subscription, which is non-transferable. Once your registration has been confirmed, you need to enter only your personal User ID and Password each time you enter the site.

   This code is valid for 8 months of access to the Parkin Web site and EconomicsCentral.

   Warning: Once you enter your access code, registration processing may take up to 3 minutes to complete. If you do not wait for confirmation before proceeding, the access code will become invalid.

3. **Log onto the site:**
   Once your registration is confirmed, follow the link to the Web site to log on with your newly established User ID and Password.

CSPECO-FRILL-HAPPY-ARMED-LAPIS-PSHAW

This pincode is only valid with the purchase of a new book.
For help using this access code, please e-mail us at

online.support@pearsoned.com

Chapter 14 Appendix Labour Unions 341

Market Power in the Labour Market **341**
- Union Objectives and Constraints **341**
- A Union in a Competitive Labour Market **342**
- How Unions Try to Change the Demand for Labour **343**
- The Scale of Union–Nonunion Wage Differentials **343**

Monopsony **344**
- Monopsony Tendencies **345**
- Monopsony and a Union **345**
- Monopsony and the Minimum Wage **345**

Chapter 15 Economic Inequality 347

Rags and Riches **347**

Measuring Economic Inequality **348**
- The Distribution of After-Tax Income **348**
- The Income Lorenz Curve **349**
- The Distribution of Wealth **350**
- Wealth Versus Income **350**
- Annual or Lifetime Income and Wealth? **351**
- Trends in Inequality **351**
- Poverty **352**
- Who Are the Rich and the Poor? **352**

The Sources of Economic Inequality **354**
- Human Capital **354**
- Discrimination **357**
- Unequal Ownership of Capital **358**

Income Redistribution **359**
- Income Taxes **359**
- Income Maintenance Programs **359**
- Subsidized Services **359**
- The Scale of Income Redistribution **360**
- The Big Tradeoff **361**

READING BETWEEN THE LINES
Trends in Inequality **362**

PART 5 **WRAP UP**
Understanding Factor Markets 367
- Probing the Ideas: Running Out of Resources **368**
- Talking with Janet Currie **370**

PART 6 MARKET FAILURE AND GOVERNMENT

Chapter 16 Public Goods and Taxes 373

Government: The Solution or the Problem? 373

The Economic Theory of Government 374
- Public Goods 374
- Taxes and Redistribution 374
- Monopoly 374
- Externalities 374
- Public Choice and the Political Marketplace 375
- Political Equilibrium 375

Public Goods and the Free-Rider Problem 376
- Public Goods 376
- The Free-Rider Problem 376
- The Benefit of a Public Good 377
- The Efficient Quantity of a Public Good 378
- Private Provision 378
- Public Provision 378
- The Role of Bureaucrats 380
- Rational Ignorance 380
- Two Types of Political Equilibrium 381
- Why Government Is Large and Grows 381
- Voters Strike Back 381

Taxes 382
- Income Taxes 382
- Employment, Health, and Social Insurance Taxes 384
- Provincial Sales Taxes and the GST 385
- Property Taxes 385
- Excise Taxes 386

READING BETWEEN THE LINES
POLICY WATCH
An Increase in Demand for a Public Good 388

Chapter 17 Competition Policy 393

Public Interest or Special Interests? 393

Market Intervention 394
- Regulation 394
- Public Ownership 394
- Anti-Combine Law 394

Economic Theory of Regulation 394
- Demand for Regulation 394
- Supply of Regulation 395
- Political Equilibrium 395

Regulation and Deregulation 396
- The Scope of Regulation 396
- The Regulatory Process 396
- Natural Monopoly 397
- Public Interest or Capture? 400
- Cartel Regulation 401
- Making Predictions 402

Public Ownership 403
- Efficient Crown Corporation 403
- A Bureaucracy Model of Public Enterprise 404
- Crown Corporations in Reality 405
- Privatization 405

Anti-Combine Law 406
- Canada's Anti-Combine Law 406
- Some Recent Anti-Combine Cases 406
- Public or Special Interest? 407

READING BETWEEN THE LINES
Fixing Vitamin Prices 408

Chapter 18 Externalities 413

Greener and Smarter 413

Externalities in Our Lives **414**
- Negative Production Externalities **414**
- Positive Production Externalities **414**
- Negative Consumption Externalities **414**
- Positive Consumption Externalities **414**

Negative Externalities: Pollution **415**
- The Demand for a Pollution-Free Environment **415**
- The Sources of Pollution **415**
- Private Costs and Social Costs **417**
- Production and Pollution: How Much? **418**
- Property Rights **418**
- The Coase Theorem **419**
- Government Actions in the Face of External Costs **420**

Positive Externalities: Knowledge **421**
- Private Benefits and Social Benefits **421**
- Government Actions in the Face of External Benefits **423**

READING BETWEEN THE LINES
The Air Pollution Debate **426**

PART 6 **WRAP UP**
Understanding Market Failure and Government 431
- Probing the Ideas: Externalities and Property Rights **432**
- Talking with John McCallum **434**

PART 7 ISSUES IN MACROECONOMICS

Chapter 19 A First Look At Macroeconomics 437

What Will Your World Be Like? 437

Origins and Issues of Macroeconomics **438**
- Short-Term Versus Long-Term Goals **438**
- The Road Ahead **438**

Economic Growth **439**
- Economic Growth in Canada **439**
- Economic Growth Around the World **441**
- Benefits and Costs of Economic Growth **443**

Jobs and Unemployment **444**
- Jobs **444**
- Unemployment **444**
- Unemployment in Canada **445**
- Unemployment Around the World **446**
- Why Unemployment Is a Problem **446**

Inflation **447**
- Inflation in Canada **447**
- Inflation Around the World **448**
- Is Inflation a Problem? **448**

Surpluses and Deficits **449**
- Government Budget Surplus and Deficit **449**
- International Surplus and Deficit **449**
- Do Surpluses and Deficits Matter? **450**

Macroeconomic Policy Challenges and Tools **451**
- Policy Challenges and Tools **451**

READING BETWEEN THE LINES
Inflation, Deflation, and Economic Growth **452**

Chapter 20 Measuring GDP and Economic Growth 457

An Economic Barometer **457**

Gross Domestic Product **458**
- GDP Defined **458**
- GDP and the Circular Flow of Expenditure and Income **459**
- Financial Flows **460**
- How Investment Is Financed **460**
- Gross and Net Domestic Product **461**

Measuring Canada's GDP **463**
- The Expenditure Approach **463**
- The Income Approach **463**

Real GDP and the Price Level **465**
- Calculating Real GDP **465**
- Calculating the Price Level **466**
- Deflating the GDP Balloon **467**

Measuring Economic Growth **468**
- Economic Welfare Comparisons **468**
- International Comparisons **470**
- Business Cycle Forecasts **471**

READING BETWEEN THE LINES
The Quarterly GDP Report **472**

Chapter 21 Monitoring Cycles, Jobs, and the Price Level 477

Vital Signs **477**

The Business Cycle **478**
- Business Cycle Dates **478**
- Growth Rate Cycles **478**

Jobs and Wages **480**
- Labour Force **480**
- Four Labour Market Indicators **480**
- Aggregate Hours **483**
- Real Wage Rate **484**

Unemployment and Full Employment **485**
- The Anatomy of Unemployment **485**
- Types of Unemployment **487**
- Full Employment **488**
- Real GDP and Unemployment Over the Cycle **489**

The Consumer Price Index **490**
- Reading the CPI Numbers **490**
- Constructing the CPI **490**
- Measuring Inflation **492**
- The Biased CPI **493**
- The Magnitude of the Bias **493**
- Some Consequences of the Bias **493**

READING BETWEEN THE LINES
The Monthly CPI Report **494**

Chapter 22 Aggregate Supply and Aggregate Demand 499

Production and Prices **499**

Aggregate Supply **500**
- Aggregate Supply Fundamentals **500**
- Long-Run Aggregate Supply **500**
- Short-Run Aggregate Supply **501**
- Movements Along the *LAS* and *SAS* Curves **502**
- Changes in Aggregate Supply **503**

Aggregate Demand **505**
- The Aggregate Demand Curve **505**
- Changes in Aggregate Demand **506**

Macroeconomic Equilibrium **508**
- Short-Run Macroeconomic Equilibrium **508**
- Long-Run Macroeconomic Equilibrium **509**
- Economic Growth and Inflation **510**
- The Business Cycle **510**
- Fluctuations in Aggregate Demand **512**
- Fluctuations in Aggregate Supply **513**

Canadian Economic Growth, Inflation, and Cycles **514**
- Economic Growth **514**
- Inflation **515**
- Business Cycles **515**
- The Evolving Economy: 1961–2001 **515**

READING BETWEEN THE LINES
POLICY WATCH
Kyoto in the *AS–AD* Model **516**

PART 7 WRAP UP

Understanding the Themes of Macroeconomics 521
- Probing the Ideas: Macroeconomic Revolutions **522**
- Talking with Robert J. Barro **524**

PART 8 AGGREGATE DEMAND AND INFLATION

Chapter 23 Expenditure Multipliers 527

Economic Amplifier or Shock Absorber? **527**

Expenditure Plans and GDP **528**
- Consumption and Saving Plans **528**
- Marginal Propensity to Consume **530**
- Marginal Propensity to Save **530**
- Other Influences on Consumption Expenditure and Saving **531**
- The Canadian Consumption Function **532**
- Consumption as a Function of Real GDP **532**
- Import Function **533**

Equilibrium Expenditure at a Fixed Price Level **533**
- The Aggregate Implications of Fixed Prices **533**
- The Aggregate Expenditure Model **534**
- Aggregate Planned Expenditure and Real GDP **535**
- Actual Expenditure, Planned Expenditure, and Real GDP **535**
- Equilibrium Expenditure **536**
- Convergence to Equilibrium **537**

The Multiplier **538**
- The Basic Idea of the Multiplier **538**
- The Multiplier Effect **538**
- Why Is the Multiplier Greater Than 1? **539**
- The Size of the Multiplier **539**
- The Multiplier and the Slope of the *AE* Curve **540**
- Imports and Income Taxes **540**
- Business Cycle Turning Points **541**

The Multiplier and the Price Level **543**
- Aggregate Expenditure and Aggregate Demand **543**
- Aggregate Expenditure and the Price Level **543**
- Equilibrium GDP and the Price Level **545**

READING BETWEEN THE LINES
The Aggregate Expenditure Multiplier in Action **548**

MATHEMATICAL NOTE
The Algebra of the Multiplier **550**

Chapter 24 Fiscal Policy 555

Balancing Acts on Parliament Hill 555

Government Budgets 556
- Budget Making 556
- Highlights of the 2002 Budget 556
- The Budget in Historical Perspective 557
- Provincial and Local Government Budgets 560
- The Canadian Government Budget in Global Perspective 561

Fiscal Policy Multipliers 562
- Government Expenditures Multiplier 562
- Autonomous Tax Multiplier 564
- Induced Taxes and Transfer Payments 565
- International Trade and Fiscal Policy Multipliers 566
- Automatic Stabilizers 566

Fiscal Policy Multipliers and the Price Level 568
- Fiscal Policy and Aggregate Demand 568
- Fiscal Expansion at Potential GDP 570
- Limitations of Fiscal Policy 571

Supply-Side Effects of Fiscal Policy 571
- Fiscal Policy and Potential GDP 571
- Supply Effects and Demand Effects 572

READING BETWEEN THE LINES
POLICY WATCH
Fiscal Policy Projections 574

MATHEMATICAL NOTE
The Algebra of the Fiscal Policy Multipliers 576

Chapter 25 Money, Banking, and Interest Rates 581

Money Makes the World Go Around 581

What Is Money? 582
- Medium of Exchange 582
- Unit of Account 582
- Store of Value 583
- Money in Canada Today 583

Depository Institutions 585
- Chartered Banks 585
- Credit Unions and Caisses Populaires 586
- Trust and Mortgage Loan Companies 586
- Financial Legislation 586
- The Economic Functions of Depository Institutions 586

How Banks Create Money 587
- Reserves: Actual and Desired 587
- Creating Deposits by Making Loans in a One-Bank Economy 587
- The Deposit Multiplier 588
- Creating Deposits by Making Loans with Many Banks 589

The Demand for Money 591
- The Influences on Money Holding 591
- The Demand for Money Curve 592
- Shifts in the Demand for Money Curve 592
- The Demand for Money in Canada 593

Interest Rate Determination 594
- Money Market Equilibrium 595
- Influencing the Interest Rate 595
- Influencing the Exchange Rate 596

The Interest Rate and Expenditure Plans 597
- Nominal Interest and Real Interest 597
- Interest Rate and Opportunity Cost 597
- Consumption Expenditure 597
- Investment 598
- Net Exports and the Interest Rate 598
- Interest-Sensitive Expenditure Curve 598

READING BETWEEN THE LINES
Canada's Changing Demand for Money 600

Chapter 26 Monetary Policy 605

Fiddling with the Knobs 605

The Bank of Canada 606
- The Bank of Canada's Balance Sheet 607
- Making Monetary Policy 607
- Monetary Policy Objectives 607
- Monetary Policy Indicators 608
- Monetary Policy Tools 608

Controlling the Quantity of Money 611
- How an Open Market Operation Works 611
- Monetary Base and Bank Reserves 612
- The Money Multiplier 613
- The Canadian Money Multiplier 615

Ripple Effects of Monetary Policy 615
- Monetary Policy to Lower Unemployment 615
- Monetary Policy to Lower Inflation 616
- Time Lags in the Adjustment Process 617
- Interest Rate Fluctuations 617
- Money Target Versus Interest Rate Target 618
- The Exchange Rate 619
- Interest Rates, Aggregate Demand, and Real GDP Fluctuations 620

The Bank of Canada in Action 621
- Gerald Bouey's Fight Against Inflation 621
- John Crow's Push for Price Stability 621
- Gordon Thiessen's and David Dodge's Balancing Acts 621

READING BETWEEN THE LINES
POLICY WATCH
Monetary Policy in Action 622

Chapter 27 Fiscal and Monetary Interactions 627

Sparks Fly in Ottawa 627

Macroeconomic Equilibrium 628
- The Basic Idea 628
- *AS–AD* Equilibrium 628
- Money Market Equilibrium and Interest-Sensitive Expenditure 628
- Check the Equilibrium 628

Fiscal Policy in the Short Run 630
- First Round Effects of Fiscal Policy 630
- Second Round Effects of Fiscal Policy 630
- Other Fiscal Policies 633
- Crowding Out and Crowding In 633
- The Exchange Rate and International Crowding Out 633

Monetary Policy in the Short Run 634
- Second Round Effects 635
- Money and the Exchange Rate 637

Relative Effectiveness of Policies 637
- Effectiveness of Fiscal Policy 637
- Effectiveness of Monetary Policy 638
- Keynesian–Monetarist Controversy 638
- Sorting Out the Competing Claims 639
- Interest Rate and Exchange Rate Effectiveness 639

Policy Actions at Full Employment 640
- Expansionary Fiscal Policy at Full Employment 640
- Crowding Out at Full Employment 640
- Expansionary Monetary Policy at Full Employment 641
- Long-Run Neutrality 641

Policy Coordination and Conflict 642
- Policy Coordination 642
- Policy Conflict 642

READING BETWEEN THE LINES
POLICY WATCH
Monetary and Fiscal Tensions 644

Chapter 28 Inflation 649

From Rome to Rio de Janeiro 649

Inflation and the Price Level 650

Demand-Pull Inflation 651
- Initial Effect of an Increase in Aggregate Demand 651
- Money Wage Rate Response 651
- A Demand-Pull Inflation Process 652

Cost-Push Inflation 653
- Initial Effect of a Decrease in Aggregate Supply 653
- Aggregate Demand Response 654
- A Cost-Push Inflation Process 654

The Quantity Theory of Money 656
- Evidence on the Quantity Theory 656

Effects of Inflation 658
- Unanticipated Inflation in the Labour Market 658
- Unanticipated Inflation in the Market for Financial Capital 658
- Forecasting Inflation 659
- Anticipated Inflation 659
- Unanticipated Inflation 660
- The Costs of Anticipated Inflation 660

Inflation and Unemployment: The Phillips Curve 662
- The Short-Run Phillips Curve 662
- The Long-Run Phillips Curve 664
- Changes in the Natural Rate of Unemployment 664
- The Canadian Phillips Curve 665

Interest Rates and Inflation 666
- How Interest Rates Are Determined 667
- Why Inflation Influences the Nominal Interest Rate 667

READING BETWEEN THE LINES
Inflation–Unemployment Tradeoff 668

PART 8 WRAP UP
Understanding Aggregate Demand and Inflation 673
- Probing the Ideas: Understanding Inflation 674
- Talking with Michael Woodford 676

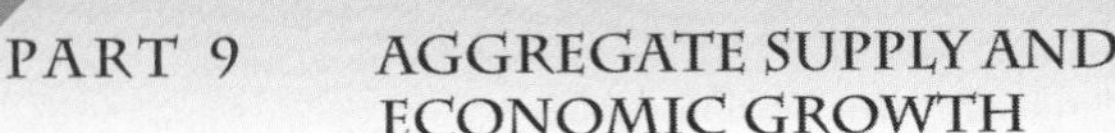

PART 9 AGGREGATE SUPPLY AND ECONOMIC GROWTH

Chapter 29 The Economy At Full Employment 679

Production and Jobs 679

Real GDP and Employment 680
- Production Possibilities 680
- The Production Function 680
- Changes in Productivity 681
- Shifts in the Production Function 682

The Labour Market and Aggregate Supply 683
- The Demand for Labour 683
- The Supply of Labour 685
- Labour Market Equilibrium and Potential GDP 686
- Aggregate Supply 687

Changes in Potential GDP 688
- An Increase in Population 688
- An Increase in Labour Productivity 689
- Population and Productivity in Canada 691

Unemployment at Full Employment 693
- Job Search 693
- Job Rationing 694

READING BETWEEN THE LINES
POLICY WATCH
Canada–U.S. Productivity Gap 696

Chapter 29 Appendix Deriving the Aggregate Supply Curves 698

Deriving the Long-Run Aggregate Supply Curve **698**
- Changes in Long-Run Aggregate Supply **700**

Short-Run Aggregate Supply **700**
- Short-Run Equilibrium in the Labour Market **700**
- Deriving the Short-Run Aggregate Supply Curve **701**
- Changes in Short-Run Aggregate Supply **703**
- Short-Run Changes in the Quantity of Real GDP Supplied **703**
- The Shape of the Short-Run Aggregate Supply Curve **703**

Chapter 30 Economic Growth 707

Transforming People's Lives **707**

Long-Term Growth Trends **708**
- Growth in the Canadian Economy **708**
- Real GDP Growth in the World Economy **709**

The Causes of Economic Growth: A First Look **711**
- Preconditions for Economic Growth **711**
- Saving and Investment in New Capital **711**
- Investment in Human Capital **712**
- Discovery of New Technologies **712**

Growth Accounting **713**
- Labour Productivity **713**
- The Productivity Curve **713**
- Accounting for the Productivity Growth Slowdown and Speedup **715**
- Technological Change During the Productivity Growth Slowdown **716**
- Achieving Faster Growth **716**

Growth Theories **717**
- Classical Growth Theory **717**
- Neoclassical Growth Theory **719**
- New Growth Theory **721**
- Sorting Out the Theories **723**

READING BETWEEN THE LINES
Forecasting Economic Growth **724**

Chapter 31 The Business Cycle 729

Must What Goes Up Always Come Down? 729

Cycle Patterns, Impulses, and Mechanisms **730**
The Role of Investment and Capital **730**
The *AS–AD* Model **730**

Aggregate Demand Theories of the Business Cycle **731**
Keynesian Theory **731**
Monetarist Theory **732**
Rational Expectations Theories **734**
AS–AD General Theory **736**

Real Business Cycle Theory **737**
The RBC Impulse **737**
The RBC Mechanism **738**
Criticisms of Real Business Cycle Theory **740**
Defence of Real Business Cycle Theory **740**

Recessions During the 1990s **741**
The Recession of 1990–1991 **741**
Japanese Stagnation **744**

The Great Depression **746**
Why the Great Depression Happened **747**
Can It Happen Again? **748**

READING BETWEEN THE LINES
Fighting a North American Recession **750**

Chapter 32 Macroeconomic Policy Challenges 755

What Can Policy Do? 755

Policy Goals **756**
Potential GDP Growth **756**
The Business Cycle **756**
Unemployment **756**
Inflation **757**
The Two Core Policy Indicators: Real GDP Growth and Inflation **757**

Policy Tools and Performance **758**
Fiscal Policy Since 1971 **758**
Monetary Policy Since 1971 **759**

Long-Term Growth Policy **760**
National Saving **760**
Investment in Human Capital **762**
Investment in New Technologies **762**

Business Cycle and Unemployment Policy **763**
Fixed-Rule Policies **763**
Feedback-Rule Policies **763**
Discretionary Policies **763**
Stabilizing Aggregate Demand Shocks **763**
Stabilizing Aggregate Supply Shocks **767**
Natural Rate Policies **768**

Anti-Inflation Policy **769**
Avoiding Cost-Push Inflation **769**
Slowing Inflation **771**
Inflation Reduction in Practice **772**
Balancing the Inflation and Real GDP Objective: The Taylor Rule **773**

READING BETWEEN THE LINES
The Stabilization Policy Balancing Act **774**

PART 9 **WRAP UP**
Understanding Aggregate Supply and Economic Growth 779
Probing the Ideas: Incentives to Innovate **780**
Talking with Paul Romer **782**

PART 10 THE GLOBAL ECONOMY

Chapter 33 Trading with the World 785

Silk Routes and Sucking Sounds **785**

Patterns and Trends in International Trade **786**
- Trade in Goods **786**
- Trade in Services **786**
- Geographical Patterns of International Trade **786**
- Trends in the Volume of Trade **786**
- Net Exports and International Borrowing **786**

The Gains from International Trade **787**
- Opportunity Cost in Farmland **787**
- Opportunity Cost in Mobilia **788**
- Comparative Advantage **788**
- The Gains from Trade: Cheaper to Buy Than to Produce **788**
- The Terms of Trade **788**
- Balanced Trade **789**
- Changes in Production and Consumption **789**
- Calculating the Gains from Trade **791**
- Gains for All **791**
- Gains from Trade in Reality **791**

International Trade Restrictions **793**
- The History of Tariffs **793**
- How Tariffs Work **794**
- Nontariff Barriers **796**
- How Quotas and VERs Work **796**

The Case Against Protection **797**
- The Employment Argument **797**
- The Infant-Industry Argument **797**
- The Dumping Argument **798**
- Maintains National Security **798**
- Allows Us to Compete with Cheap Foreign Labour **798**
- Brings Diversity and Stability **799**
- Penalizes Lax Environmental Standards **799**
- Protects National Culture **799**
- Prevents Rich Countries from Exploiting Developing Countries **800**

Why Is International Trade Restricted? **800**
- Tariff Revenue **800**
- Rent Seeking **800**
- Compensating Losers **801**
- Compensating Losers from Protection **801**

The North American Free Trade Agreement **802**
- The Terms of the Canada–United States Agreement **802**
- The Extension of the Agreement: NAFTA **803**
- Effects of the Free Trade Agreement **803**

READING BETWEEN THE LINES
Tariffs in Action: Lumber **804**

Chapter 34 **International Finance 809**

¥€$! **809**

Financing International Trade **810**
- Balance of Payments Accounts **810**
- Borrowers and Lenders, Debtors and Creditors **812**
- Has Canada Borrowed for Consumption or Investment? **812**
- Current Account Balance **813**
- Net Exports **813**
- The Twin Deficits **814**

The Exchange Rate **815**
- Demand in the Foreign Exchange Market **816**
- The Law of Demand for Foreign Exchange **816**
- Changes in the Demand for Dollars **816**
- Supply in the Foreign Exchange Market **818**
- The Law of Supply of Foreign Exchange **818**
- Changes in the Supply of Dollars **819**
- Market Equilibrium **820**
- Changes in the Exchange Rate **820**
- Exchange Rate Expectations **821**
- The Bank of Canada in the Foreign Exchange Market **822**

READING BETWEEN THE LINES
Exchange Rate Projections **824**

Chapter 35 **Global Stock Markets 829**

Irrational Exuberance? **829**

Stock Market Basics **830**
- What Is Stock? **830**
- What Is a Stock Exchange? **830**
- Stock Prices and Returns **831**
- Earnings and the Price-Earnings Ratio **831**
- Reading the Stock Market Report **832**
- Stock Price Indexes **832**
- Stock Price Performance **834**
- Stock Prices **834**
- Earnings Per Share **835**

How Are Stock Prices Determined? **836**
- Market Fundamentals **836**
- Speculative Bubbles **838**
- The Booming Nineties: A Bubble? **839**

Risk and Return **840**
- Risk Premium **840**
- Portfolio Diversification **840**

The Stock Market and the Economy **841**
- Trends and Cycles in Earnings Growth **841**
- Central Bank Monetary Policy **842**
- Taxes **843**
- Wealth, Consumption Expenditure, and Saving **843**
- The Distribution of Wealth **845**

READING BETWEEN THE LINES
Stock Price Uncertainties **846**

PART 10 **WRAP UP**
Understanding the Global Economy 851
- Probing the Ideas: Gains from International Trade **852**
- Talking with Jagdish Bhagwati **854**

Canadian Economy Database **857**

Glossary **G-1**

Index **I-1**

Credits **C-1**

PART 1 INTRODUCTION

WHAT IS ECONOMICS?

CHAPTER 1

Choice, Change, Challenge, and Opportunity

You are studying economics, the science of choice, at a time of enormous change, challenge, and opportunity. Economics studies the choices that we make as we cope with the hard fact of life: we can't have everything we want. ◆ The engine of change is information technology, which has created the Internet and transformed our lives at both work and play. This transformation will continue, but in 2001 it was challenged by a U.S. recession and by the terrorist attacks of September 11. The events of September 11 have brought long-lasting changes to the political and security landscape and to the economic landscape. People now face choices not previously imagined. Some people are avoiding air travel, a choice that is sending shock waves through travel agencies, airports, airlines, airplane builders, and hotels and restaurants. Security at the Canada–U.S. border and at our airports and seaports is stepped up. Governments, airlines, and airport operators are buying more video and electronic surveillance equipment, which is creating new business and job opportunities. ◆ As 2003 began, people were wondering whether economic recovery and renewed expansion was just around the corner or whether there would be a second U.S. recession—a "double dip"—and worrying about how such a development might influence the Canadian economy.

You've just glimpsed some of the economic issues in today's world. Your course in economics will help you to understand the powerful forces that are shaping this world. This chapter takes the first step. It describes the questions that economists try to answer, the way they think about choices, and the methods they use. An appendix provides a guide to the graphical methods that are widely used in economics.

After studying this chapter, you will be able to

- **Define economics and distinguish between microeconomics and macroeconomics**
- **Explain the three big questions of microeconomics**
- **Explain the three big questions of macroeconomics**
- **Explain the ideas that define the economic way of thinking**
- **Explain how economists go about their work as social scientists**

Definition of Economics

ALL ECONOMIC QUESTIONS ARISE BECAUSE WE want more than we can get. We want a peaceful and secure world. We want clean air, lakes, and rivers. We want long and healthy lives. We want good schools, colleges, and universities. We want spacious and comfortable homes. We want an enormous range of sports and recreational gear, from running shoes to jet skis. We want the time to enjoy sports, games, novels, movies, music, travel, and hanging out with our friends.

Scarcity

What each one of us can get is limited by time, by the income we earn, and by the prices we must pay. Everyone ends up with some unsatisfied wants. What we can get as a society is limited by our productive resources. These resources include the gifts of nature, human labour and ingenuity, and tools and equipment that we have produced.

Our inability to satisfy all our wants is called **scarcity.** The poor and the rich alike face scarcity. A child wants a $1.00 can of pop and two 50¢ packs of gum but has only $1.00 in his pocket. He faces scarcity. A millionaire wants to spend the weekend playing golf *and* spend the same weekend at the office attending a business strategy meeting. She faces scarcity. A society wants to provide improved health care, install a computer in every classroom, explore space, clean polluted lakes and rivers, and so on. Even parrots face scarcity!

Not only do I want a cracker—we all want a cracker!

Faced with scarcity, we must make choices. We must *choose* among the available alternatives. The child must *choose* the pop *or* the gum. The millionaire must *choose* the golf game *or* the meeting. As a society, we must *choose* among health care, highways, peacekeeping, the environment, and so on.

Economics is the social science that studies the choices that we make as we cope with scarcity and the institutions that have evolved to influence and reconcile our choices. The subject divides into

- Microeconomics
- Macroeconomics

Microeconomics

Microeconomics is the study of the choices that individuals and businesses make, the way these choices interact, and the influence that governments exert on them. Some examples of microeconomic questions are: Why are more people buying SUVs and fewer people buying minivans? How will a decline in air travel affect the producers of airplanes? How would a tax on e-commerce affect the growth of the Internet? Who benefits from minimum wage laws?

Macroeconomics

Macroeconomics is the study of the effects on the national economy and the global economy of the choices that individuals, businesses, and governments make. Some examples of macroeconomic questions are: Why did production and jobs shrink in 2001? Why has Japan been in a long period of economic stagnation? Can the government bring prosperity by cutting interest rates? Will a tax cut increase the number of jobs and total production?

REVIEW QUIZ

1. What is scarcity?
2. Give some examples of scarcity in today's world.
3. Define economics.
4. Use the headlines in today's news to illustrate the distinction between microeconomics and macroeconomics.

Three Big Microeconomic Questions

LOOK AT THE WORLD AROUND YOU. YOU SEE AN enormous range of things that you might buy and jobs that you might do. You also see a huge range of incomes and wealth. Microeconomics explains much of what you see by addressing three big questions:

- What goods and services are produced?
- How are goods and services produced?
- For whom are goods and services produced?

What Goods and Services Are Produced?

The objects that people value and produce to satisfy wants are called **goods and services.** Goods are physical objects such as golf balls. Services are tasks performed for people such as haircuts.

FIGURE 1.1 What We Produce

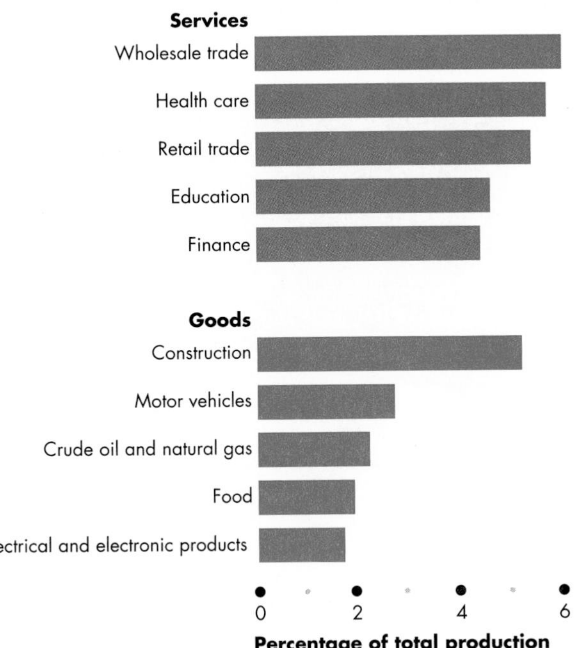

The production of wholesale trade and retail trade greatly exceeds the production of goods such as motor vehicles.

Source: Statistics Canada.

What *are* the goods and services that we produce in Canada today? Figure 1.1 shows the surprising answer. Canada is a service economy. Wholesale trade and retail trade are two of the three largest services. Between them, they represent nearly 12 percent of the value of total production. Health care, education, and financial services, such as banking and stock brokering, complete the five largest services. Among goods, only construction matches the size of the larger service items. Each of the other largest categories of goods—motor vehicles, crude oil and natural gas, food, and electrical and electronic products—accounts for less than 3 percent of the value of total production.

Figure 1.2 shows the trends in what we produce. Fifty years ago, almost 20 percent of Canadians worked on farms, 60 percent in mining, construction, and manufacturing, and 20 percent produced services. Today, more than 70 percent of working Canadians have service jobs. Mining, construction, and manufacturing jobs have shrunk to 25 percent, and farm jobs have almost disappeared.

You've reviewed some of the facts about *what* we produce. These facts raise the deeper question: What determines the quantities of retail services, new homes, DVD players, and wheat that we produce? Microeconomics provides some answers to these questions.

FIGURE 1.2 Trends in What We Produce

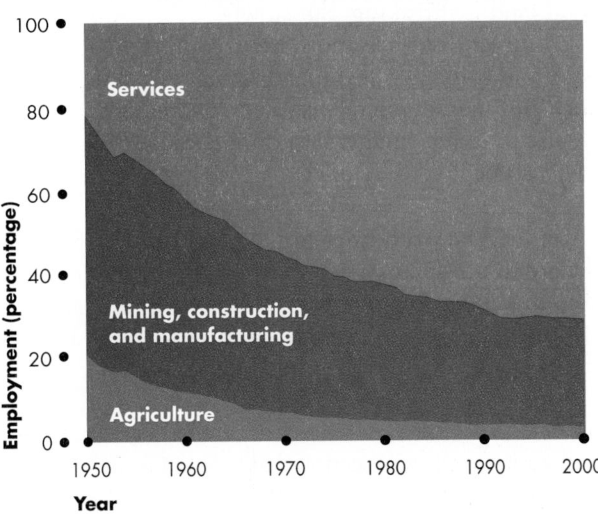

Services have expanded, and agriculture, mining, construction, and manufacturing have shrunk.

Source: Statistics Canada.

How Are Goods and Services Produced?

The range of jobs that you might do keeps changing. When Henry Ford built the world's first auto assembly line, he destroyed the jobs of the skilled craft workers who built cars using hand tools and created jobs for a new type of auto assembly worker. Every year, as businesses adopt new production technologies, similar changes occur. Today, it is information technology businesses that are producing new products, creating new jobs, and destroying old ones.

We call the resources that businesses use to produce goods and services **factors of production**. Factors of production are grouped into four categories:

- Land
- Labour
- Capital
- Entrepreneurship

Land The "gifts of nature" that we use to produce goods and services are called **land.** In economics, land is what in everyday language we call natural resources. It includes land in the everyday sense, minerals, energy, water, and air.

Canada covers 9.9 billion square kilometres and we live on about 3.5 percent of this land. Almost 10 percent of Canada's land surface is water, about 30 percent is forest land, 50 percent is wild land, and 6.5 percent is farmland. Urban land is expanding and rural land is shrinking, but slowly.

Our land surface and water resources are renewable, and some of our mineral resources can be recycled. But many mineral resources, and all those that we use to create energy, are nonrenewable resources—they can be used only once.

Labour The work time and work effort that people devote to producing goods and services is called **labour.** Labour includes the physical and mental efforts of all the people who work on farms and construction sites and in factories, shops, and offices.

In Canada in 2002, 16 million people had jobs or were available for work. An increasing population and an increasing percentage of women with jobs have increased the quantity of labour available.

The *quality* of labour depends on **human capital,** which is the knowledge and skill that people obtain from education, on-the-job training, and work experience. You are building your own human capital right now as you work on your economics course, and your human capital will continue to grow as you become better at your job. Today, more than 80 percent of the Canadian population has completed high school and more than 40 percent has post-secondary certificates, diplomas, or university degrees. Figure 1.3 shows a measure of the growth of human capital in Canada over the past few decades.

Capital The tools, instruments, machines, buildings, and other constructions that businesses now use to produce goods and services are called **capital.** The quantity of capital grows steadily over time.

Entrepreneurship The human resource that organizes labour, land, and capital is called **entrepreneurship.** Entrepreneurs come up with new ideas about what and how to produce, make business decisions, and bear the risks that arise from these decisions.

You've reviewed some of the facts about *how* we produce in Canada. These facts raise deeper questions such as: What determines the quantities of labour and capital that get used? Microeconomics provides some answers to these questions.

FIGURE 1.3 A Measure of Human Capital

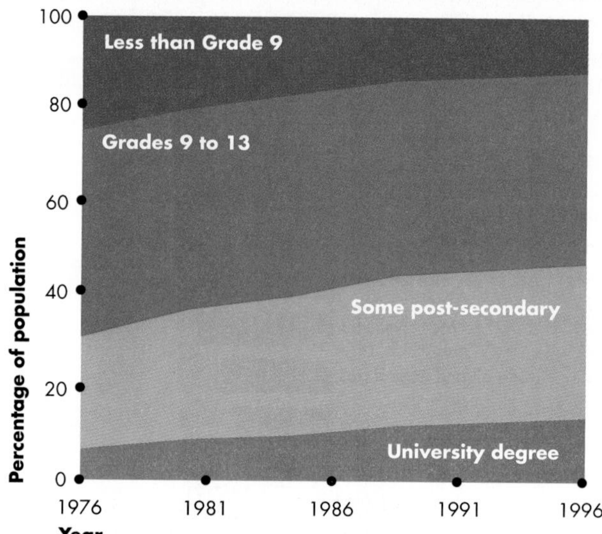

Today, more than 40 percent of the Canadian population has post-secondary certificates, diplomas, or university degrees. A further 41 percent has completed high school.

Source: Statistics Canada.

For Whom Are Goods and Services Produced?

Who gets the goods and services that are produced depends on the incomes that people earn. The movie star who earns a few million dollars a year buys a large quantity of goods and services. A homeless unemployed person has few options and a small quantity of goods and services.

To earn an income, people sell the services of the factors of production they own:

- Land earns **rent.**
- Labour earns **wages.**
- Capital earns **interest.**
- Entrepreneurship earns **profit.**

Which factor of production earns the most income? The answer is labour. Total wages (including fringe benefits) were 69 percent of total income in 2000. Land, capital, and entrepreneurship share the remaining 31 percent. And over time, these percentages have been remarkably constant.

Knowing how income is shared among the factors of production doesn't tell us how it is shared among individuals. You know of lots of people who earn very large incomes. The average NHL player's salary in 2000 was about $3 million, and some stars, such as Mats Sundin of the Toronto Maple Leafs, earn almost $12 million a year. You know of even more people who earn very small incomes. Servers at McDonald's average around $7 an hour; checkout clerks, gas station attendants, and textile and leather workers earn less than $10 an hour.

You probably know about other persistent differences in incomes. Men, on the average, earn more than women. University and college graduates, on the average, earn more than high-school graduates. Canadians and Americans, on the average, earn more than Europeans, who in turn earn more, on the average, than Asians and Africans.

Figure 1.4 shows the incomes for five groups, each of which represents 20 percent of the population. If incomes were equal, each 20 percent group would earn 20 percent of total income. You know that incomes are unequal, and the figure provides a measure of just how unequal they are.

The 20 percent of individuals with the lowest incomes earn only 4 percent of total income. The 20 percent with the second lowest incomes earn 10 percent of total income. The next 20 percent—the middle 20 percent—earn 16 percent of total income.

FIGURE 1.4 The Distribution of Income in Canada

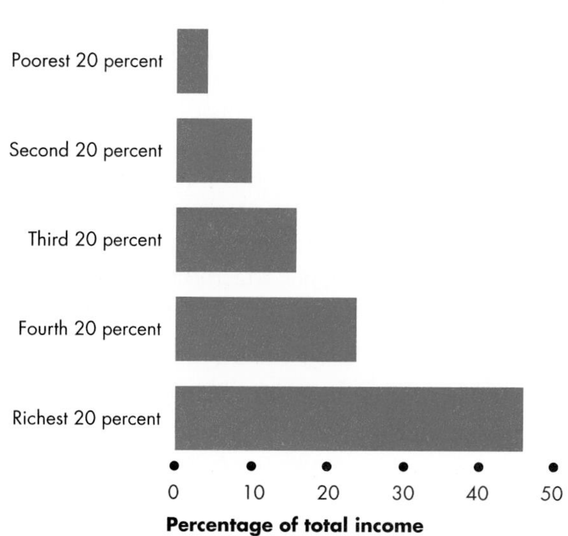

The richest 20 percent of the population earn 46 percent of total income. The poorest 20 percent earn only 4 percent of total income. (The data are for 1998.)

Source: Statistics Canada.

The 20 percent with the second highest incomes earn 24 percent of total income. And the 20 percent of individuals with the highest incomes earn 46 percent of total income.

You've reviewed some of the facts about *for whom* we produce in Canada. These facts raise deeper questions such as: Why do women earn less than men?

The three big microeconomic questions give you a sense of the *scope of microeconomics.* Next, we'll look at the big questions of macroeconomics.

REVIEW QUIZ

1. Does Canada produce more goods than services? What item accounts for the largest percent of the value of what we produce?
2. What are the trends in what we produce?
3. What are the factors of production and what are some of the changes in the way we produce goods and services?
4. Describe the distribution of income that shows for whom goods and services are produced.

Three Big Macroeconomic Questions

YOU'VE LIVED THROUGH A PERIOD OF DRAMATIC change in the way we work and play. The information age has created what has been called a "new economy" with rising living standards and new job opportunities. At the same time, prices have been remarkably stable. But you've also seen that our economy does not always expand. In 2001, economic slowdown brought job losses for millions of people. Macroeconomics explains these events by focusing on three big questions:

- What determines the standard of living?
- What determines the cost of living?
- Why does our economy fluctuate?

What Determines the Standard of Living?

What is the standard of living? How do we measure it? How do we compare the standard of living in Africa with that in Canada and the United States?

The **standard of living** is the level of consumption that people enjoy, on the average, and is measured by average income per person. The greater the income per person, the higher is the standard of living, other things remaining the same.

Figure 1.5 shows the number of Canadian dollars per day earned on the average in different places. You can see that in the United States, the average is $148 a day. This number tells you that an average person in the United States can buy goods and services that cost $148—about five times the world average. Living standards fall off as we move down the figure, with average incomes in India and Africa of only $8 a day.

Most people live in the countries that have incomes below the world average. You can see this fact by looking at the population numbers shown in the figure. The poorest five countries or regions—China, Central Asia, Other Asia, India, and Africa—have a total population of 4 billion, which is two-thirds of the world's population.

What makes the standard of living rise? What can Indians and Africans do to increase their standard of living? Your study of macroeconomics will help you to understand some answers to questions like these.

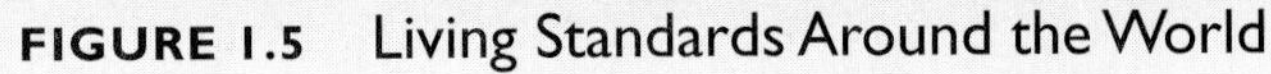

FIGURE 1.5 Living Standards Around the World

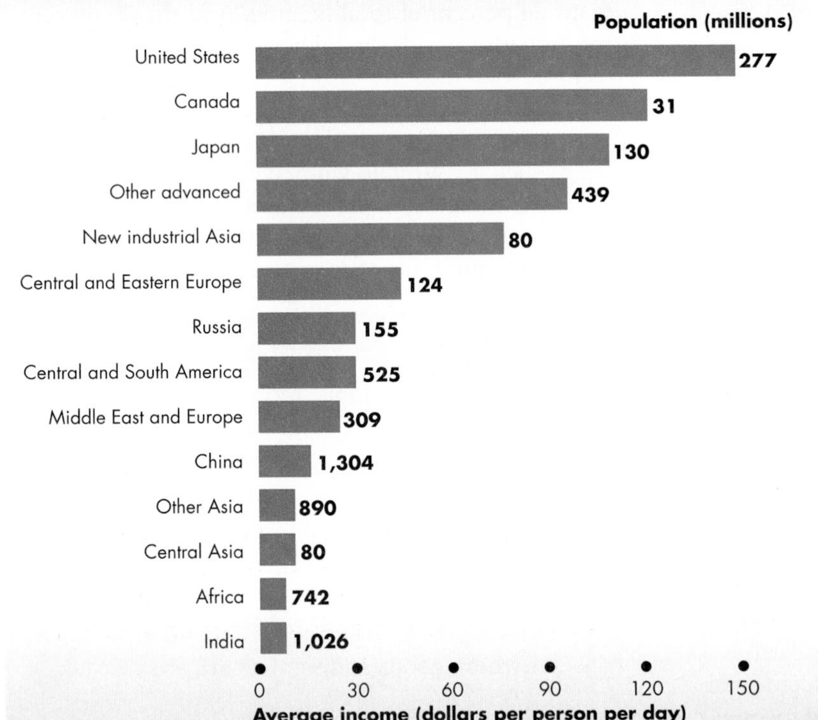

In 2000, average income per person ranged from $148 a day in the United States to $8 a day in Africa. The world average was $30 a day. Russia and Central and South America were close to the average.

Source: International Monetary Fund, *World Economic Outlook*, Washington, D.C., October 2001.

What Determines the Cost of Living?

In your great-grandparents' youth, when the electric light bulb was the latest big thing, the average Canadian earned $1 a day. But your great-grandparents' five cents would buy what you need a dollar to buy. The dollar of 2003 is worth only one-twentieth of the dollar of 1903. If the dollar continues to shrink in value at its average rate of loss, by the time you retire (sure, that's a long time in the future), you'll need almost $5 to buy what $1 buys today. The cost of living is rising.

The **cost of living** is the amount of money it takes to buy the goods and services that the average family consumes. In Canada, we measure money in dollars. So the cost of living in Canada is the number of dollars it takes to buy the goods and services that the average family buys. In the United Kingdom, it is the number of pounds; in Japan, it is the number of yen; and in Russia, it is the number of rubles.

Prices in Different Currencies To make this idea concrete, think about what a Big Mac costs. Table 1.1 shows some prices in 10 countries. The average price of a Big Mac in Canada is $3.00. In the United Kingdom, it is £2.00, and in Japan, it is ¥294. So in the United Kingdom, it costs a smaller number of money units to buy a Big Mac than it does in Canada, and in Japan, it costs a larger number of money units. But a Big Mac costs more in the United Kingdom than in either Canada or Japan. The reason is that a pound is worth 2.40 Canadian dollars, so £2.00 is equivalent to $4.80. And a pound is worth 182 yen, so £2.00 is equivalent to ¥364.

The number of money units that something costs is not so important. But the rate at which the number is changing is very important. A rising cost of living is called **inflation** and a falling cost of living is called **deflation.** Inflation brings a shrinking value of the dollar and deflation brings a rising value of the dollar.

TABLE 1.1 The Cost of a Big Mac in 10 Countries

Country	Name of currency	Price of a Big Mac
United Kingdom	Pound	2.00
United States	U.S. Dollar	2.50
Canada	Canadian Dollar	3.00
Brazil	Real	3.60
South Africa	Rand	9.70
Israel	Shekel	13.90
Russia	Ruble	35.00
Japan	Yen	294
South Korea	Won	3,000
Indonesia	Rupiah	14,700

Source: Economist.com

Inflation and Deflation Have we experienced inflation and a rising cost of living or deflation and a falling cost of living? If we look back over the past 100 years, we see that the cost of living has increased and the value of the dollar has shrunk.

In Canada, on the average between 1902 and 2002, the cost of living increased by 3 percent a year. Most people do not regard inflation at this rate as a big problem. But to place this inflation in perspective, it means that the dollar of 1902 was worth just 5 cents in 2002. At this inflation rate, a dollar earned in 2002 will be worth about 25 cents in 2052, a year in which you will probably be living on your pension!

Most of the advanced economies have low inflation. But the developing economies have higher inflation rates, some of them spectacularly so. In Central and South America, the average inflation rate during the 1980s and 1990s was 107 percent a year. A 100 percent change means a doubling. At this inflation rate, prices are rising by 6 percent a *month*. Inflation this rapid poses huge problems as people struggle to cope with an ever-falling value of money.

During the past few years, the cost of living has increased slowly. Can we count on it rising slowly in the future? What will the dollar buy next year? What will it buy in 10 years when you are paying off your student loan? And what will it buy in 50 years when you are spending your life's savings in retirement?

You've seen that over the years, our standard of living has increased. Why doesn't a rising *cost* of living mean that people must constantly cut back on their spending and endure a falling *standard* of living? Although the cost of living has increased steadily, incomes have increased more quickly. And because incomes have increased faster than the cost of living, the standard of living has increased.

What causes inflation? What can we do to avoid it? Your study of macroeconomics will help you to understand some answers to these questions.

FIGURE 1.6 Business Cycle Phases and Turning Points

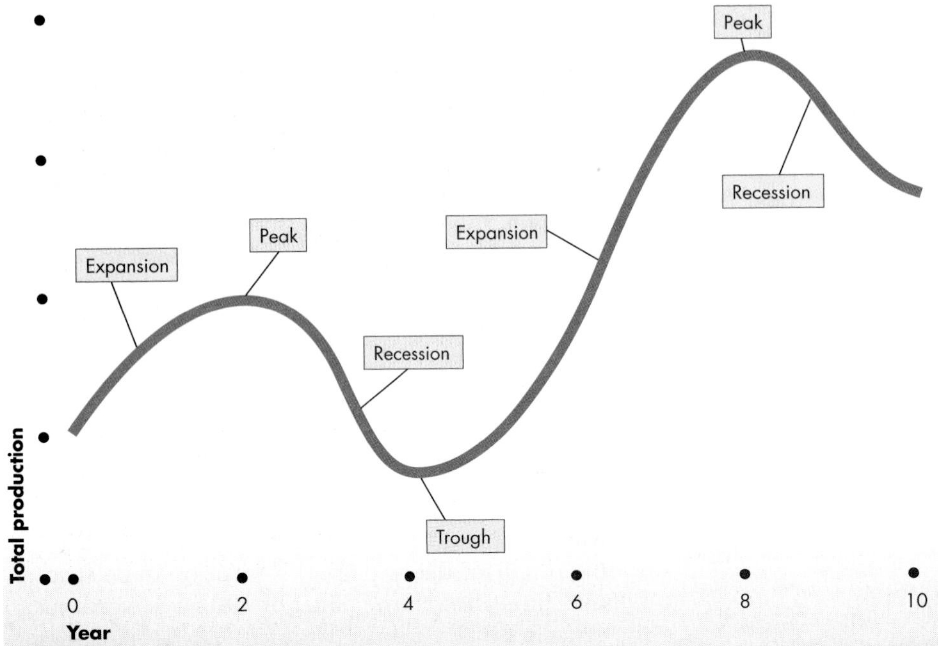

In a business cycle expansion, production and jobs increase more rapidly than normal. In a recession, production and jobs shrink. An expansion ends at a peak, and a recession ends at a trough.

Why Does Our Economy Fluctuate?

Over long periods, both the standard of living and the cost of living increase. But these increases are not smooth and continuous. During 2001, the number of Canadians who wanted a job increased by 330,000. But the Canadian economy created only 103,000 additional jobs. Our economy slowed. We call the periodic but irregular up-and-down movement in production and jobs the **business cycle.**

When production and jobs are increasing more rapidly than normal, the economy is in a business cycle expansion. When production and jobs are shrinking, the economy is in a recession.

Figure 1.6 illustrates the phases and turning points of a business cycle. A *recession* runs from year 2 to year 4, followed by an *expansion* from year 4 through year 8. Another recession runs from year 8 through year 10. A recession ends at a *trough*, and an expansion ends at a *peak.*

The most recent expansion in Canada began in 1991. The deepest recession of the 1990s was in Russia, where production fell by almost 30 percent between 1990 and 1994. The most persistent recession of recent years has been in Japan. The worst recession ever experienced occurred during the 1930s in an episode called the Great Depression. During this period, production in Canada shrank by 28 percent.

When a recession occurs, unemployment increases. During the Great Depression, almost 20 percent of the labour force in Canada was unable to find jobs. During the recession of the early 1990s, the unemployment rate climbed to 12 percent of the labour force.

What causes the business cycle? What can we do to smooth out the business cycle? Economists remain unsure about the answers to these questions. But in your study of macroeconomics, you will learn what economists have discovered about economic fluctuations.

REVIEW QUIZ

1 What are the three big issues that macroeconomics addresses?
2 What do we mean by the standard of living and what is its range from the richest to the poorest countries?
3 What do we mean by the cost of living? If the cost of living keeps rising, does the standard of living keep falling?
4 What are the phases of the business cycle?

The Economic Way of Thinking

THE DEFINITION OF ECONOMICS AND THE questions of microeconomics and macroeconomics tell you about the *scope of economics.* But they don't tell you how economists *think* about these questions and go about seeking answers to them.

You're now going to begin to see how economists approach economic questions. First, in this section, we'll look at the ideas that define the *economic way of thinking.* This way of thinking needs practice, but it is a powerful way of thinking and as you become more familiar with it, you'll begin to see the world around you with a new and sharp focus.

Choices and Tradeoffs

Because we face scarcity, we must make choices. And when we make a choice, we select from the available alternatives. For example, you can spend the weekend studying for your next economics test and having fun with your friends, but you can't do both of these activities at the same time. You must choose how much time to devote to each. Whatever choice you make, you could have chosen something else instead.

You can think about your choice as a tradeoff. A **tradeoff** is an exchange—giving up one thing to get something else. When you choose how to spend your weekend, you trade off between studying and hanging out with your friends.

Guns Versus Butter The classic tradeoff is guns versus butter. "Guns" and "butter" stand for any pair of goods and services. They might actually be guns and butter. Or they might be broader categories such as peacekeeping and food. Or they might be any pair of specific goods or services such as cola and bottled water, baseball bats and tennis racquets, colleges and hospitals, realty services and career counselling.

Regardless of the specific objects that guns and butter represent, the guns-versus-butter tradeoff captures a hard fact of life: If we want more of one thing, we must trade something else in exchange for it.

The idea of a tradeoff is central to the whole of economics. We can pose all the questions of microeconomics and macroeconomics in terms of tradeoffs. Let's return to these questions and view them in terms of tradeoffs.

Microeconomic Tradeoffs

The questions of what, how, and for whom goods and services are produced all involve tradeoffs that are similar to that of guns versus butter.

"What" Tradeoffs What goods and services get produced depends on choices made by each one of us, by our government, and by the businesses that produce the things we buy. Each of these choices involves a tradeoff.

Each one of us faces a tradeoff when we choose how to spend our income. You go to the movies this week, but you forgo a few cups of coffee to buy the ticket—you trade off coffee for a movie.

The federal government faces a tradeoff when it chooses how to spend our tax dollars. Parliament votes for more hospitals but cuts back on educational programs—Parliament trades off education for hospitals.

Businesses face a tradeoff when they decide what to produce. Nike hires Tiger Woods and allocates resources to designing and marketing a new golf ball but cuts back on its development of a new running shoe—Nike trades off running shoes for golf balls.

"How" Tradeoffs How goods and services get produced depends on choices made by the businesses that produce the things we buy. These choices involve a tradeoff. For example, Tim Hortons opens a new doughnut store with an automated production line and closes an older store with a traditional kitchen. Tim Hortons trades off labour for capital.

"For Whom" Tradeoffs For whom goods and services are produced depends on the distribution of buying power. Buying power can be redistributed—transferred from one person to another—in three ways: by voluntary payments, by theft, or through taxes and benefits organized by government. Redistribution brings tradeoffs.

Each of us faces a tradeoff when, for example, we choose how much to contribute to the United Nations famine relief fund. You donate $50 and cut your spending on other items by that amount. You trade off your own level of spending for a small increase in economic equality.

We make choices that influence redistribution by theft when we vote to make theft illegal and to devote resources to law enforcement. We trade off goods and services for an increase in the security of our property.

We also vote for taxes and social programs that redistribute buying power from the rich to the poor. Government redistribution confronts society with what has been called the **big tradeoff**—the tradeoff between equality and efficiency. Taxing the rich and making transfers to the poor bring greater economic equality. But taxing productive activities such as running a business, working hard, saving, and investing in capital discourages these activities. So taxing productive activities means producing less—it creates inefficiency.

You can think of the big tradeoff as being the problem of how to share a pie that everyone contributes to baking. If each person receives a share of the pie that reflects the size of her or his effort, everyone will work hard and the pie will be as large as possible. But if the pie is shared equally, regardless of contribution, some talented bakers will slacken off and the pie will shrink. The big tradeoff is one between the size of the pie and how equally it is shared. We trade off some efficiency for increased equality.

We've reviewed some microeconomic tradeoffs. Let's now look at some macroeconomic tradeoffs.

Macroeconomic Tradeoffs

The three macroeconomic questions about the standard of living, the cost of living, and the business cycle involve tradeoffs that are similar to that of guns versus butter.

Standard of Living Tradeoffs The standard of living is higher in Canada than in Africa. And the standard of living improves over time, so today it is higher than it was a generation ago. Our standard of living and its rate of improvement depend on the many choices made by each one of us, by governments, and by businesses. And these choices involve tradeoffs.

One choice is that of how much of our income to consume and how much to save. Our saving can be channelled through the financial system to finance businesses and to pay for new capital that increases productivity. The more we save and invest, the faster our productivity and our standard of living increase. When you decide to save an extra $1,000 and forgo a vacation, you trade off the vacation for a higher future income. If everyone saves an extra $1,000 and businesses invest in more equipment that increases productivity, the average income per person rises and the standard of living improves. As a society, we trade off current consumption for increased productivity and a higher future standard of living.

A second choice is how much effort to devote to education and training. By becoming better educated and more highly skilled, we become more productive and our standard of living rises. When you decide to remain in school for another two years to complete a professional degree and forgo a huge chunk of leisure time, you trade off leisure for a higher future income. If everyone becomes better educated, productivity increases, income per person rises, and the standard of living improves. As a society, we trade off current consumption and leisure time for increased productivity and a higher future standard of living.

A third choice, usually made by businesses, is how much effort to devote to research and the development of new products and production methods. Ford Motor Company can hire engineers to do research on a new robot assembly line or to operate the existing plant and produce cars. More research brings greater productivity in the future but means smaller current production—a tradeoff of current production for greater future production.

Output-Inflation Tradeoff When policy actions lower the interest rate and speed the pace at which money is created, spending, output, and employment increase. Higher spending brings rising inflation—the cost of living rises more rapidly. Eventually, output returns to its previous level. But the higher inflation rate has been accompanied by a temporary increase in output.

Similarly, when policy actions raise the interest rate and slow the pace at which money is created, spending, output, and employment decrease. Lower spending brings falling inflation—the cost of living rises more slowly. Again, output eventually returns to its previous level and the lower inflation rate has been accompanied by a temporary decrease in output.

When the inflation rate is too high, policy makers would like to lower inflation without lowering output. But they face an **output-inflation tradeoff** because the policy action that lowers inflation also lowers output and a policy action that boosts output increases inflation.

Seeing choices as tradeoffs emphasizes the idea that to get something, we must give up something. What we give up is the *cost* of what we get. Economists call this cost the *opportunity cost*.

Opportunity Cost

The highest-valued alternative that we give up to get something is the **opportunity cost** of the activity chosen. "There's no such thing as a free lunch" is not just a clever throwaway line. It expresses the central idea of economics: that every choice involves a cost.

You can quit school right now, or you can remain in school. If you quit school and take a job at Tim Hortons, you might earn enough to buy some CDs, go to the movies, and spend lots of free time with your friends. If you remain in school, you can't afford these things. You will be able to buy these things later, and that is one of the payoffs from being in school. But for now, when you've bought your books, you might have nothing left for CDs and movies. And doing assignments means that you've got less time for hanging around with your friends. The opportunity cost of being in school is the highest-valued alternative that you would have chosen if you had quit school.

All of the tradeoffs that we've just considered involve opportunity cost. The opportunity cost of some guns is the butter forgone; the opportunity cost of a movie ticket is the number of cups of coffee forgone; the opportunity cost of lower inflation is the output temporarily forgone.

Margins and Incentives

You can allocate the next hour between studying and e-mailing your friends. But the choice is not all or nothing. You must decide how many minutes to allocate to each activity. To make this decision, you compare the benefit of a little bit more study time with its cost—you make your choice at the **margin.**

The benefit that arises from an increase in an activity is called **marginal benefit.** For example, suppose that you're working four nights a week at your courses and your grade point average is 3.0. You decide that you want a higher grade and decide to study an extra night each week. Your grade now rises to 3.5. The marginal benefit from studying for one additional night a week is the 0.5 increase in your grade. It is *not* the 3.5 grade. The reason is that you already have the benefit from studying for four nights a week, so we don't count this benefit as resulting from the decision you are now making.

The cost of an increase in an activity is called **marginal cost.** For you, the marginal cost of increasing your study time by one night a week is the cost of the additional night not spent with your friends (if that is your best alternative use of the time). It does not include the cost of the four nights you are already studying.

To make your decision, you compare the marginal benefit from an extra night of study with its marginal cost. If the marginal benefit exceeds the marginal cost, you study the extra night. If the marginal cost exceeds the marginal benefit, you do not study the extra night.

By evaluating marginal benefits and marginal costs and choosing only those actions that bring greater benefit than cost, we use our scarce resources in the way that makes us as well off as possible.

Our choices respond to incentives. An **incentive** is an inducement to take a particular action. The inducement can be a benefit—a carrot—or a cost—a stick. A change in marginal cost and a change in marginal benefit change the incentives that we face and lead us to change our choices.

For example, suppose your economics instructor gives you some problem sets and tells you that all the problems will be on the next test. The marginal benefit from working these problems is large, so you diligently work them all. Suppose, in contrast, that your math instructor gives you some problem sets and tells you that none of the problems will be on the next test. The marginal benefit from working these problems is lower, so you skip most of them.

The central idea of economics is that we can predict the way choices will change by looking at changes in incentives. More of an activity is undertaken when its marginal cost falls or its marginal benefit rises; less of an activity is undertaken when its marginal cost rises or its marginal benefit falls.

REVIEW QUIZ

1 What is a tradeoff?
2 Provide three examples of microeconomic tradeoffs.
3 What is the big tradeoff and how does it arise?
4 Provide two examples of macroeconomic tradeoffs.
5 What is the short-run tradeoff of macroeconomics?
6 What is opportunity cost?
7 How do economists predict changes in choices?

Economics: A Social Science

ECONOMICS IS A SOCIAL SCIENCE (ALONG WITH political science, psychology, and sociology). Economists try to discover how the economic world works, and in pursuit of this goal (like all scientists), they distinguish between two types of statements:

- What *is*
- What *ought to be*

Statements about what *is* are called *positive* statements and they might be right or wrong. We can test a positive statement by checking it against the facts. When a chemist does an experiment in a laboratory, she is attempting to check a positive statement against the facts.

Statements about what *ought to be* are called *normative* statements. These statements depend on values and cannot be tested. When Parliament debates a motion, it is ultimately trying to decide what ought to be. It is making a normative statement.

To see the distinction between positive and normative statements, consider the controversy over global warming. Some scientists believe that centuries of the burning of coal and oil are increasing the carbon dioxide content of the earth's atmosphere and leading to higher temperatures that eventually will have devastating consequences for life on this planet. "Our planet is warming because of an increased carbon dioxide buildup in the atmosphere" is a positive statement. It can (in principle and with sufficient data) be tested. "We ought to cut back on our use of carbon-based fuels such as coal and oil" is a normative statement. You can agree or disagree with this statement, but you can't test it. It is based on values. Health-care reform provides an economic example of the distinction. "Universal health care cuts the amount of work time lost to illness" is a positive statement. "All Canadians should have equal access to health care" is a normative statement.

The task of economic science is to discover positive statements that are consistent with what we observe and that help us to understand the economic world. This task can be broken into three steps:

- Observation and measurement
- Model building
- Testing models

Observation and Measurement

Economists observe and measure data on such things as natural and human resources, wages and work hours, the prices and quantities of the different goods and services produced, taxes and government spending, and the quantities of goods and services bought from and sold to other countries.

Model Building

The second step towards understanding how the economic world works is to build a model. An **economic model** is a description of some aspect of the economic world that includes only those features of the world that are needed for the purpose at hand. A model is simpler than the reality it describes. What a model includes and what it leaves out result from assumptions about what is essential and what are inessential details.

You can see how ignoring details is useful—even essential—to our understanding by thinking about a model that you see every day: the TV weather map. The weather map is a model that helps to predict the temperature, wind speed and direction, and precipitation over a future period. The weather map shows lines called isobars—lines of equal barometric pressure. It doesn't show the highways. The reason is that our theory of the weather tells us that the pattern of air pressure, not the location of the highways, determines the weather.

An economic model is similar to a weather map. It tells us how a number of variables are determined by a number of other variables. For example, an economic model of Vancouver's bid for the 2010 Winter Olympic Games might tell us the effects of the games on the number of houses and apartments, rents and prices, jobs, transportation facilities, and the outputs and profits of the businesses in the region.

Testing Models

The third step is testing the model. A model's predictions might correspond to the facts or be in conflict with them. By comparing the model's predictions with the facts, we can test a model and develop an economic theory. An **economic theory** is a generalization that summarizes what we think we understand about the economic choices that people make and the performance of industries and entire economies. It is a bridge between an economic model and the real economy.

The process of building and testing models creates theories. For example, meteorologists have a theory that if the isobars form a particular pattern at a particular time of the year (a model), then it will snow (reality). They have developed this theory by repeated observation and by carefully recording the weather that follows specific pressure patterns.

Economics is a young science. It was born in 1776 with the publication of Adam Smith's *Wealth of Nations* (see p. 54). Over the years since then, economists have discovered many useful theories. But in many areas, economists are still looking for answers. The gradual accumulation of economic knowledge gives most economists some faith that their methods will, eventually, provide usable answers to the big economic questions.

But progress in economics comes slowly. Let's look at some of the obstacles to progress in economics.

Obstacles and Pitfalls in Economics

We cannot easily do economic experiments. And most economic behaviour has many simultaneous causes. For these two reasons, it is difficult in economics to unscramble cause and effect.

Unscrambling Cause and Effect By changing one factor at a time and holding all the other relevant factors constant, we isolate the factor of interest and are able to investigate its effects in the clearest possible way. This logical device, which all scientists use to identify cause and effect, is called *ceteris paribus.* ***Ceteris paribus*** is a Latin term that means "other things being equal" or "if all other relevant things remain the same." Ensuring that other things are equal is crucial in many activities, and all successful attempts to make scientific progress use this device.

Economic models (like the models in all other sciences) enable the influence of one factor at a time to be isolated in the imaginary world of the model. When we use a model, we are able to imagine what would happen if only one factor changed. But *ceteris paribus* can be a problem in economics when we try to test a model.

Laboratory scientists, such as chemists and physicists, perform experiments by actually holding all the relevant factors constant except for the one under investigation. In non-experimental sciences such as economics (and astronomy), we usually observe the outcomes of the simultaneous operation of many factors. Consequently, it is hard to sort out the effects of each individual factor and to compare them with what a model predicts. To cope with this problem, economists take three complementary approaches.

First, they look for pairs of events in which other things were equal (or similar). An example might be to study the effects of unemployment benefits on the unemployment rate by comparing the United States with Canada on the presumption that the people in the two economies are sufficiently similar. Second, economists use statistical tools—called econometrics. Third, when they can, they perform experiments. This relatively new approach puts real subjects (usually students) in a decision-making situation and varies their incentives in some way to discover how they respond to a change in one factor at a time.

Economists try to avoid fallacies—errors of reasoning that lead to a wrong conclusion. But two fallacies are common, and you need to be on your guard to avoid them. They are the

- Fallacy of composition
- *Post hoc* fallacy

Fallacy of Composition The fallacy of composition is the (false) statement that what is true of the parts is true of the whole or that what is true of the whole is true of the parts. Think of the true statement "Speed kills" and its implication: Going more slowly saves lives. If an entire highway moves at a lower speed, everyone on the highway has a safer ride.

But suppose that only one driver slows down and all the other drivers try to maintain their original speed. In this situation, there will probably be more accidents because more cars will change lanes to overtake the slower vehicle. So in this example, what is true for the whole is not true for a part.

The fallacy of composition arises mainly in macroeconomics, and it stems from the fact that the parts interact with each other to produce an outcome for the whole that might differ from the intent of the parts. For example, a firm lays off some workers to cut costs and improve its profits. If all firms take similar actions, income falls and so does spending. The firm sells less, and its profits don't improve.

***Post Hoc* Fallacy** Another Latin phrase—*post hoc, ergo propter hoc*—means "after this, therefore because of this." The *post hoc* fallacy is the error of reasoning that a first event *causes* a second event because the first occurred before the second. Suppose you are a visitor from a far-off world. You observe lots of people shopping in early December, and then you see them opening gifts and partying in the holiday season. You wonder, "Does the shopping cause the holiday season?" After a deeper study, you discover that the holiday season causes the shopping. A later event causes an earlier event.

Unravelling cause and effect is difficult in economics. And just looking at the timing of events often doesn't help. For example, the stock market booms, and some months later the economy expands—jobs and incomes grow. Did the stock market boom cause the economy to expand? Possibly, but perhaps businesses started to plan the expansion of production because a new technology that lowered costs had become available. As knowledge of the plans spread, the stock market reacted to *anticipate* the economic expansion. To disentangle cause and effect, economists use economic models and data and, to the extent that they can, perform experiments.

Economics is a challenging science. Does the difficulty of getting answers in economics mean that anything goes and that economists disagree on most questions? Perhaps you've heard the joke "If you laid all the economists in the world end to end, they still wouldn't reach agreement." Surprisingly, perhaps, the joke does not describe reality.

Agreement and Disagreement

Economists agree on a remarkably wide range of questions. And often the agreed-upon view of economists disagrees with the popular and sometimes politically correct view. When Bank of Canada Governor David Dodge testifies before Parliament, his words are rarely controversial among economists, even when they generate endless debate in the press and Parliament.

Here are 12 propositions with which at least 7 out of every 10 economists broadly agree:

- Tariffs and import restrictions make most people worse off.
- A large budget deficit has an adverse effect on the economy.
- A minimum wage increases unemployment among young workers and low-skilled workers.
- Cash payments to welfare recipients make them better off than do transfers-in-kind of equal cash value.
- A tax cut can help to lower unemployment when the unemployment rate is high.
- The distribution of income should be more equal.
- Inflation is primarily caused by a rapid rate of money creation.
- The government should restructure welfare along the lines of a "negative income tax."
- Rent ceilings cut the availability of housing.
- Pollution taxes are more effective than pollution limits.
- The redistribution of income is a legitimate role for the government.
- The federal budget should be balanced on the average over the business cycle but not every year.

Which of these propositions are positive and which are normative? Notice that economists are willing to offer their opinions on normative issues as well as their professional views on positive questions. Be on the lookout for normative propositions dressed up as positive propositions.

REVIEW QUIZ

1. What is the distinction between a positive statement and a normative statement? Provide an example (different from those in the chapter) of each type of statement.
2. What is a model? Can you think of a model that you might use (probably without thinking of it as a model) in your everyday life?
3. What is a theory? Why is the statement "It might work in theory, but it doesn't work in practice" a silly statement?
4. What is the *ceteris paribus* assumption and how is it used?
5. Try to think of some everyday examples of the fallacy of composition and the *post hoc* fallacy.

SUMMARY

KEY POINTS

Definition of Economics (p. 2)

- All economic questions arise from scarcity—from the fact that wants exceed the resources available to satisfy them.
- Economics is the social science that studies the choices that people make as they cope with scarcity.
- The subject divides into microeconomics and macroeconomics.

Three Big Microeconomic Questions (pp. 3–5)

- Three big questions that summarize the scope of microeconomics are
  1. What goods and services are produced?
  2. How are goods and services produced?
  3. For whom are goods and services produced?

Three Big Macroeconomic Questions (pp. 6–8)

- Three big questions that summarize the scope of macroeconomics are
  1. What determines the standard of living?
  2. What determines the cost of living?
  3. Why does our economy fluctuate?

The Economic Way of Thinking (pp. 9–11)

- Every choice is a tradeoff—exchanging more of something for less of something else.
- The classic guns-versus-butter tradeoff represents all tradeoffs.
- All economic questions involve tradeoffs.
- The big social tradeoff is that between equality and efficiency.
- A macroeconomic tradeoff is the short-run tradeoff between output and inflation.
- The highest-valued alternative forgone is the opportunity cost of what is chosen.
- Choices are made at the margin and respond to incentives.

Economics: A Social Science (pp. 12–14)

- Economists distinguish between positive statements—what *is*—and normative statements—what *ought* to be.
- To explain the economic world, economists develop theories by building and testing economic models.
- Economists use the *ceteris paribus* assumption to try to disentangle cause and effect and are careful to avoid the fallacy of composition and the *post hoc* fallacy.
- Economists agree on a wide range of questions about how the economy works.

KEY TERMS

Big tradeoff, 10
Business cycle, 8
Capital, 4
Ceteris paribus, 13
Cost of living, 7
Deflation, 7
Economic model, 12
Economics, 2
Economic theory, 12
Entrepreneurship, 4
Factors of production, 4
Goods and services, 3
Human capital, 4
Incentive, 11
Inflation, 7
Interest, 5
Labour, 4
Land, 4
Macroeconomics, 2
Margin, 11
Marginal benefit, 11
Marginal cost, 11
Microeconomics,2
Opportunity cost, 11
Output-inflation tradeoff, 10
Profit, 5
Rent, 5
Scarcity, 2
Standard of living, 6
Tradeoff, 9
Wages, 5

PROBLEMS

*1. Your friends go the movies one evening and you decide to stay home and do your economics assignment and practice test. You get 80 percent on your next economics exam compared with the 70 percent that you normally score. What is the opportunity cost of your extra points?

2. You go to the movies one evening instead of doing your economics assignment and practice test. You get 50 percent on your next economics exam compared with the 70 percent that you normally score. What is the opportunity cost of going to the movies?

*3. You plan to go to school this summer. If you do, you won't be able to take your usual job that pays $6,000 for the summer, and you won't be able to live at home for free. The cost of tuition is $2,000 and the cost of textbooks is $200, and living expenses are $1,400. What is the opportunity cost of going to summer school?

4. You plan to go skiing next weekend. If you do, you'll have to miss doing your usual weekend job that pays $100, you won't be able to study for 8 hours, and you won't be able to use your prepaid college meal plan. The cost of travel and accommodation will be $350, the cost of renting skis is $60, and your food will cost $40. What is the opportunity cost of the weekend ski trip?

*5. The local mall has free parking, but the mall is always very busy, and it usually takes 30 minutes to find a parking space. Today when you found a vacant spot, Harry also wanted it. Is parking really free at this mall? If not, what did it cost you to park today? When you parked your car today, did you impose any costs on Harry? Explain your answers.

6. The university has built a new movie theatre. Admission for students is free and there are always plenty of empty seats. But when the theatre screened *The Lord of the Rings*, the lines were long. So the theatre decided to charge $4 per student. Cadbury Schweppes offered students a free soft drink. Compare a student's opportunity cost of seeing the movie *The Lord of the Rings* with that of any other movie screened this year. Which is less costly and by how much?

*You can obtain the solutions to the odd-numbered problems on the Parkin–Bade Web site.

CRITICAL THINKING

1. Use the three big questions of microeconomics, the three big questions of macroeconomics, and the economic way of thinking to organize a short essay about the economic life of a homeless man. Does he face scarcity? Does he make choices? Can you interpret his choices as being in his own best interest? Can either his own choices or the choices of others make him better off? If so, how?

WEB EXERCISES

1. Use the link on the Parkin–Bade Web site to visit the CBC.
   a. What is the top economic news story today?
   b. With which of the big questions does it deal? (It must deal with at least one of them and might deal with more than one.)
   c. What tradeoffs does the news item discuss?
   d. Write a brief summary of the news item in a few bulleted points using as much as possible of the economic vocabulary that you have learned in this chapter and that is in the key terms list on p. 15.
2. Use the link on the Parkin–Bade Web site to visit *Resources For Economists on the Internet.* This site is a good place from which to search for economic information on the Internet.
   a. Scroll down the page and click on General Interest.
   b. Visit the "general interest" sites and become familiar with the types of information they contain.
3. Use the link on the Parkin–Bade Web site to visit Statistics Canada.
   a. What is the number of people employed (non-farm employment) in your area?
   b. Has employment increased or decreased?
   c. What is income per person (per capita income) in your area?

APPENDIX

Graphs in Economics

After studying this appendix, you will be able to

- **Make and interpret a time-series graph, a cross-section graph, and a scatter diagram**
- **Distinguish between linear and nonlinear relationships and between relationships that have a maximum and a minimum**
- **Define and calculate the slope of a line**
- **Graph relationships among more than two variables**

Graphing Data

A GRAPH REPRESENTS A QUANTITY AS A DISTANCE on a line. Figure A1.1 shows two examples. Here, a distance on the horizontal line represents temperature, measured in degrees Celsius. A movement from left to right shows an increase in temperature. The point marked 0 represents zero degrees Celsius. To the right of 0, the temperature is positive. To the left of 0 (as indicated by the minus sign), the temperature is negative. A distance on the vertical line represents altitude or height, measured in thousands of metres above sea level. The point marked 0 represents sea level. Points above 0 represent metres above sea level. Points below 0 (indicated by a minus sign) represent metres below sea level.

By setting two scales perpendicular to each other, as in Fig. A1.1, we can visualize the relationship between two variables. The scale lines are called *axes.* The vertical line is the *y-axis,* and the horizontal line is the *x-axis.* Each axis has a zero point, which is shared by the two axes. This zero point, common to both axes, is called the *origin.*

To show something in a two-variable graph, we need two pieces of information: the value of the *x*-variable and the value of the *y*-variable. For example, off the coast of British Columbia on a winter's day, the temperature is 10 degrees—the value of *x*. A fishing boat is located at 0 metres above sea level—the value of *y*. These two bits of information appear as point *A* in Fig. A1.1. A climber at the top of Mt. McKinley on a cold day is 6,194 metres above sea level in a zero-degree gale. These two pieces of information appear as point *B*. The position of the climber on a warmer day might be at the point marked *C*. This point represents the peak of Mt. McKinley at a temperature of 10 degrees.

FIGURE A1.1 Making a Graph

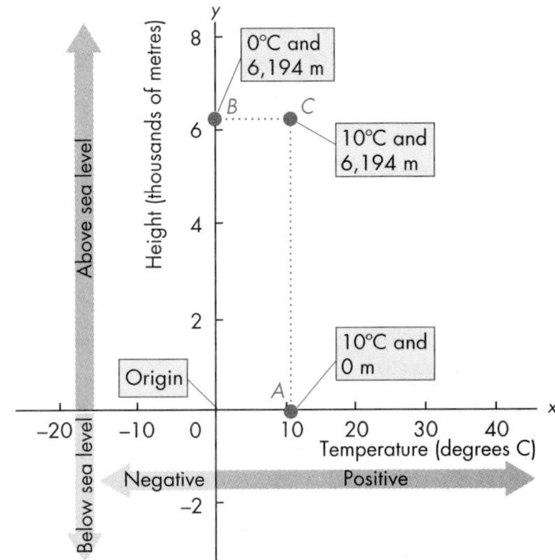

Graphs have axes that measure quantities as distances. Here, the horizontal axis (*x*-axis) measures temperature, and the vertical axis (*y*-axis) measures height. Point *A* represents a fishing boat at sea level (0 on the *y*-axis) on a day when the temperature is 10°C. Point *B* represents a climber on Mt. McKinley, 6,194 metres above sea level, at a temperature of 0°C. Point *C* represents a climber on Mt. McKinley, 6,194 metres above sea level, at a temperature of 10°C.

We can draw two lines, called *coordinates,* from point *C*. One, called the *y*-coordinate, runs from *C* to the horizontal axis. Its length is the same as the value marked off on the *y*-axis. The other, called the *x*-coordinate, runs from *C* to the vertical axis. Its length is the same as the value marked off on the *x-axis.* We describe a point in a graph by the values of its *x*-coordinate and its *y*-coordinate.

Graphs like that in Fig. A1.1 can show any type of quantitative data on two variables. Economists use three types of graphs based on the principles in Fig. A1.1 to reveal and describe the relationships among variables. They are

- Time-series graphs
- Cross-section graphs
- Scatter diagrams

Time-Series Graphs

A **time-series graph** measures time (for example, months or years) on the *x*-axis and the variable or variables in which we are interested on the *y*-axis. Figures 1.2 and 1.3 on pp. 3 and 4 are examples of time-series graphs. So is Fig. A1.2, which provides some information about the price of coffee.

In Fig. A1.2, we measure time in years running from 1971 to 2001. We measure the price of coffee (the variable that we are interested in) on the *y*-axis.

The point of a time-series graph is to enable us to visualize how a variable has changed over time and how its value in one period relates to its value in another period.

A time-series graph conveys an enormous amount of information quickly and easily, as this example illustrates. It shows

- The *level* of the price of coffee—when it is *high* and *low.* When the line is a long way from the *x*-axis, the price is high. When the line is close to the *x*-axis, the price is low.
- How the price *changes*—whether it *rises* or *falls.* When the line slopes upward, as in 1976, the price is rising. When the line slopes downward, as in 1978, the price is falling.
- The *speed* with which the price changes—whether it rises or falls *quickly* or *slowly.* If the line is very steep, then the price rises or falls quickly. If the line is not steep, the price rises or falls slowly. For example, the price rose quickly in 1976 and 1977 and slowly in 1983. The price fell quickly in 1978 and slowly in 1984.

A time-series graph also reveals whether there is a trend. A **trend** is a general tendency for a variable to move in one direction. A trend might be upward or downward. In Fig. A1.2, you can see that the price of coffee had a general tendency to fall from the late 1970s to the early 1990s. That is, although the price rose and fell, the general tendency was for it to fall—the price had a downward trend.

A time-series graph also helps us detect cycles in variables. You can see some peaks and troughs in the price of coffee in Fig. A1.2. Figure 1.6 on p. 8 illustrates the business cycle. We rarely see a cycle as clear as the one shown in that figure.

Finally, a time-series graph also lets us compare the variable in different periods quickly. Figure A1.2 shows that the 1980s were different from the 1970s. The price of coffee fluctuated more violently in the 1970s than it did in the 1980s.

FIGURE A1.2 A Time-Series Graph

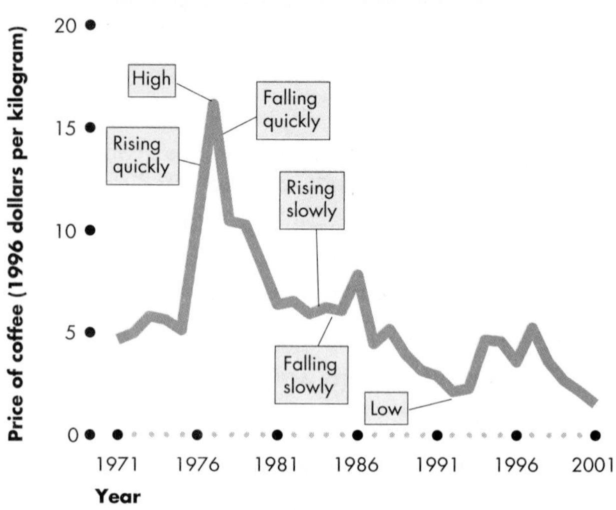

A time-series graph plots the level of a variable on the *y*-axis against time (day, week, month, or year) on the *x*-axis. This graph shows the price of coffee (in 1996 dollars per kilogram) each year from 1971 to 2001. It shows us when the price of coffee was *high* and when it was *low*, when the price *increased* and when it *decreased*, and when it changed *quickly* and when it changed *slowly*.

You can see that a time-series graph conveys a wealth of information. And it does so in much less space than we have used to describe only some of its features. But you do have to "read" the graph to obtain all this information.

Cross-Section Graphs

A **cross-section graph** shows the values of an economic variable for different groups in a population at a point in time. Figure 1.4 on p. 5, called a *bar chart*, is an example of a cross-section graph. Figure A1.3 shows another example.

The bar chart in Fig. A1.3 shows the number of visitors to each province in 1999. The length of each bar indicates the number of visitors. This figure enables you to compare the number of visitors across the provinces. And you can do so much more quickly and clearly than you could by looking at a list of numbers.

FIGURE A1.3 A Cross-Section Graph

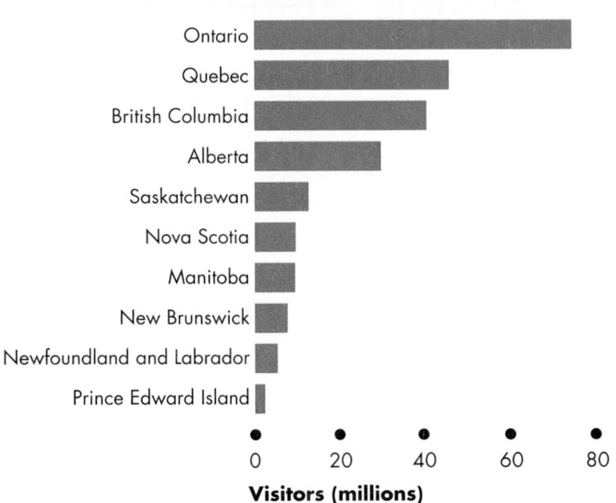

A cross-section graph shows the level of a variable across the members of a population. This bar chart shows the number of visitors to each province in 1999.

Scatter Diagrams

A **scatter diagram** plots the value of one variable against the value of another variable. Such a graph reveals whether a relationship exists between two variables and describes their relationship. Figure A1.4(a) shows the relationship between expenditure and income. Each point shows expenditure per person and income per person in a given year from 1984 to 2001. The points are "scattered" within the graph. The point labelled *A* tells us that in 1996, income per person was $18,095 and expenditure per person was $16,450. The dots in this graph form a pattern, which reveals that as income increases, expenditure increases.

Figure A1.4(b) shows the relationship between the number of international phone calls and the price of a call. This graph show that as the price per minute falls, the number of calls increases.

Figure A1.4(c) shows a scatter diagram of inflation and unemployment in Canada. Here, the dots show no clear relationship between these two variables. The dots in this graph reveal that there is no simple relationship between these variables.

FIGURE A1.4 Scatter Diagrams

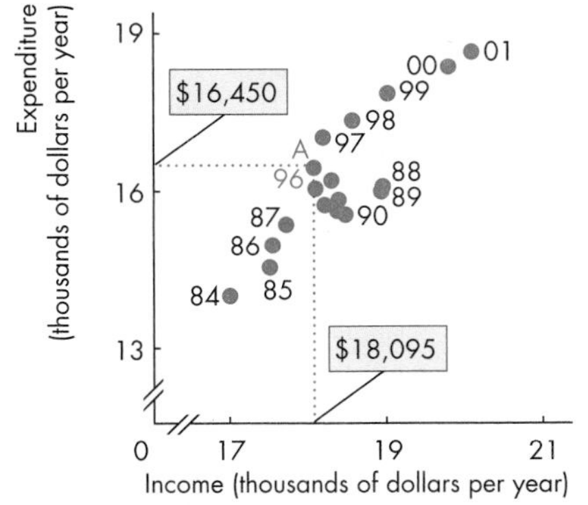

(a) Expenditure and income

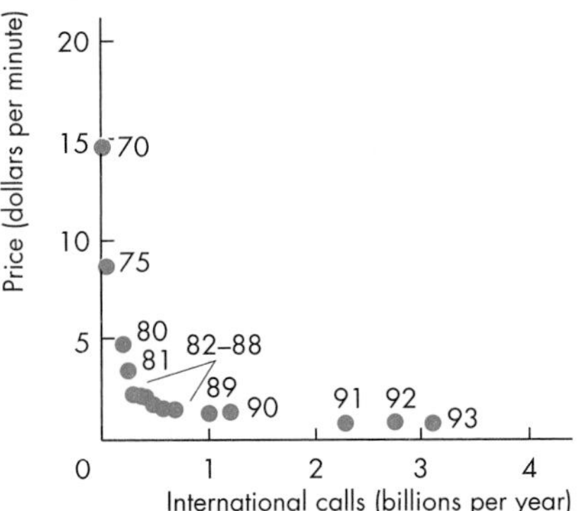

(b) International phone calls and prices

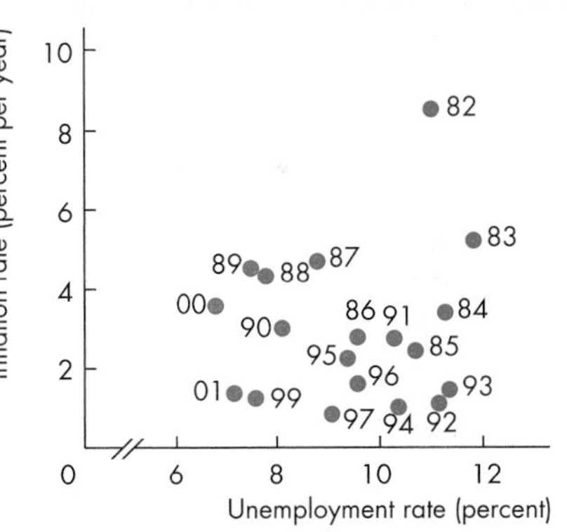

(c) Unemployment and inflation

A scatter diagram reveals the relationship between two variables. Part (a) shows the relationship between expenditure and income. Each point shows the values of the two variables in a specific year. For example, point *A* shows that in 1996, average income was $18,095 and average expenditure was $16,450. The pattern formed by the points shows that as income increases, expenditure increases.

Part (b) shows the relationship between the price of an international phone call and the number of calls made. This graph shows that as the price of a phone call falls, the number of calls made increases. Part (c) shows a scatter diagram of the inflation rate and unemployment rate in Canada. This graph shows that the inflation rate and the unemployment rate are not closely related.

Breaks in the Axes Two of the graphs you've just looked at, Fig. A1.4(a) and Fig. A1.4(c), have breaks in their axes, as shown by the small gaps. The breaks indicate that there are jumps from the origin, 0, to the first values recorded.

In Fig. A1.4(a), the breaks are used because the lowest value of expenditure exceeds $13,000 and the lowest value of income exceeds $17,000. With no breaks in the axes of this graph, there would be a lot of empty space, all the points would be crowded into the top right corner, and we would not be able to see whether a relationship exists between these two variables. By breaking the axes, we are able to bring the relationship into view.

Putting a break in the axes is like using a zoom lens to bring the relationship into the centre of the graph and magnify it so that it fills the graph.

Misleading Graphs Breaks can be used to highlight a relationship. But they can also be used to mislead—to make a graph that lies. The most common way of making a graph lie is to use axis breaks and either to stretch or to compress a scale. For example, suppose that in Fig. A1.4(a), the y-axis ran from zero to $45,000 while the x-axis was the same as the one shown. The graph would now create the impression that despite a huge increase in income, expenditure had barely changed.

To avoid being misled, it is a good idea to get into the habit of always looking closely at the values and the labels on the axes of a graph before you start to interpret it.

Correlation and Causation A scatter diagram that shows a clear relationship between two variables, such as Fig. A1.4(a) or Fig. A1.4(b), tells us that the two variables have a high correlation. When a high correlation is present, we can predict the value of one variable from the value of the other variable. But correlation does not imply causation.

Sometimes a high correlation is a coincidence, but sometimes it does arise from a causal relationship. It is likely, for example, that rising income causes rising expenditure (Fig. A1.4a) and that the falling price of a phone call causes more calls to be made (Fig. A1.4b).

You've now seen how we can use graphs in economics to show economic data and to reveal relationships between variables. Next, we'll learn how economists use graphs to construct and display economic models.

Graphs Used in Economic Models

THE GRAPHS USED IN ECONOMICS ARE NOT always designed to show real-world data. Often they are used to show general relationships among the variables in an economic model.

An *economic model* is a stripped down, simplified description of an economy or of a component of an economy, such as a business or a household. It consists of statements about economic behaviour that can be expressed as equations or as curves in a graph. Economists use models to explore the effects of different policies or other influences on the economy in ways that are similar to the use of model airplanes in wind tunnels and models of the climate.

You will encounter many different kinds of graphs in economic models, but there are some repeating patterns. Once you've learned to recognize these patterns, you will instantly understand the meaning of a graph. Here, we'll look at the different types of curves that are used in economic models, and we'll see some everyday examples of each type of curve. The patterns to look for in graphs are the four cases:

- Variables that move in the same direction
- Variables that move in opposite directions
- Variables that have a maximum or a minimum
- Variables that are unrelated

Let's look at these four cases.

Variables That Move in the Same Direction

Figure A1.5 shows graphs of the relationships between two variables that move up and down together. A relationship between two variables that move in the same direction is called a **positive relationship** or a **direct relationship.** A line that slopes upward shows such a relationship.

Figure A1.5 shows three types of relationships: one that has a straight line and two that have curved lines. But all the lines in these three graphs are called curves. Any line on a graph—no matter whether it is straight or curved—is called a *curve.*

A relationship shown by a straight line is called a **linear relationship**. Figure A1.5(a) shows a linear rela-

FIGURE A1.5 Positive (Direct) Relationships

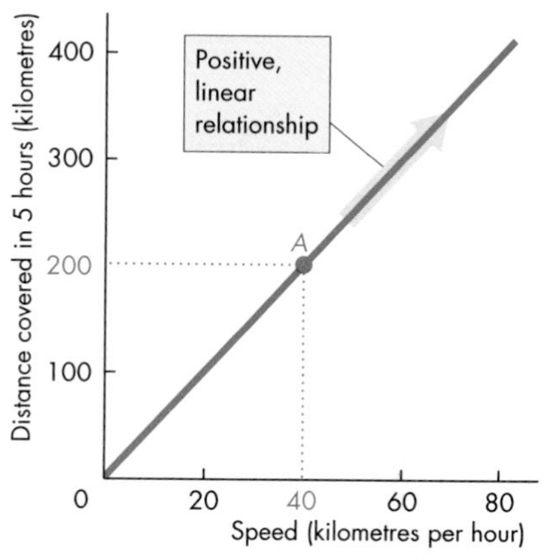

(a) Positive, linear relationship

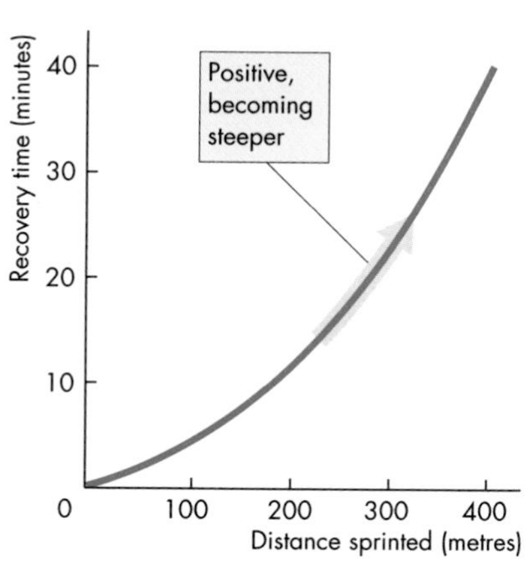

(b) Positive, becoming steeper

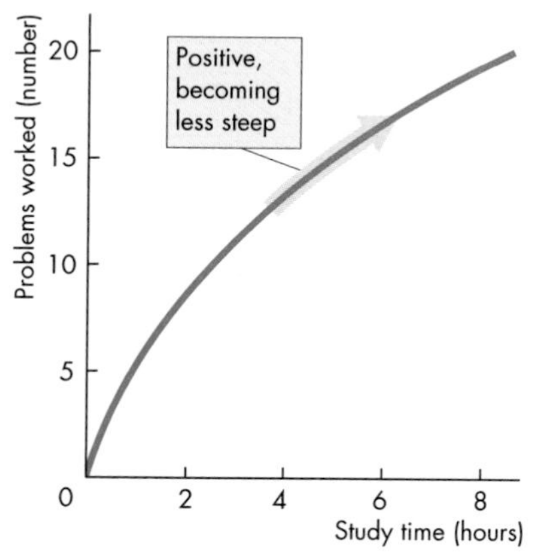

(c) Positive, becoming less steep

Each part of this figure shows a positive (direct) relationship between two variables. That is, as the value of the variable measured on the *x*-axis increases, so does the value of the variable measured on the *y*-axis. Part (a) shows a linear relationship—as the two variables increase together, we move along a straight line. Part (b) shows a positive relationship such that as the two variables increase together, we move along a curve that becomes steeper. Part (c) shows a positive relationship such that as the two variables increase together, we move along a curve that becomes less steep.

tionship between the number of kilometres travelled in 5 hours and speed. For example, point *A* shows that we will travel 200 kilometres in 5 hours if our speed is 40 kilometres an hour. If we double our speed to 80 kilometres an hour, we will travel 400 kilometres in 5 hours.

Figure A1.5(b) shows the relationship between distance sprinted and recovery time (the time it takes the heart rate to return to its normal resting value). This relationship is an upward-sloping one that starts out quite flat but then becomes steeper as we move along the curve away from the origin. The reason this curve slopes upward and becomes steeper is because the additional recovery time needed from sprinting an additional 100 metres increases. It takes less than 5 minutes to recover from the first 100 metres, but it takes more than 10 minutes to recover from the second 100 metres.

Figure A1.5(c) shows the relationship between the number of problems worked by a student and the amount of study time. This relationship is an upward-sloping one that starts out quite steep and becomes flatter as we move away from the origin. Study time becomes less productive as the student spends more hours studying and become more tired.

Variables That Move in Opposite Directions

Figure A1.6 shows relationships between things that move in opposite directions. A relationship between variables that move in opposite directions is called a **negative relationship** or an **inverse relationship.**

Figure A1.6(a) shows the relationship between the number of hours available for playing squash and the number of hours for playing tennis when the total is 5 hours. One extra hour spent playing tennis means one hour less playing squash and vice versa. This relationship is negative and linear.

Figure A1.6(b) shows the relationship between the cost per kilometre travelled and the length of a journey. The longer the journey, the lower is the cost per kilometre. But as the journey length increases, the cost per kilometre decreases, and the fall in the cost is smaller, the longer the journey. This feature of the relationship is shown by the fact that the curve slopes downward, starting out steep at a short journey length and then becoming flatter as the journey length increases. This relationship arises because some of the costs are fixed (such as auto insurance), and the fixed cost is spread over a longer journey.

FIGURE A1.6 Negative (Inverse) Relationships

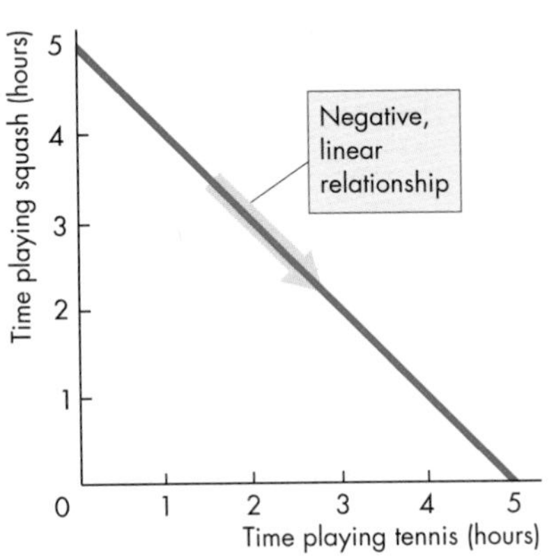

(a) Negative, linear relationship

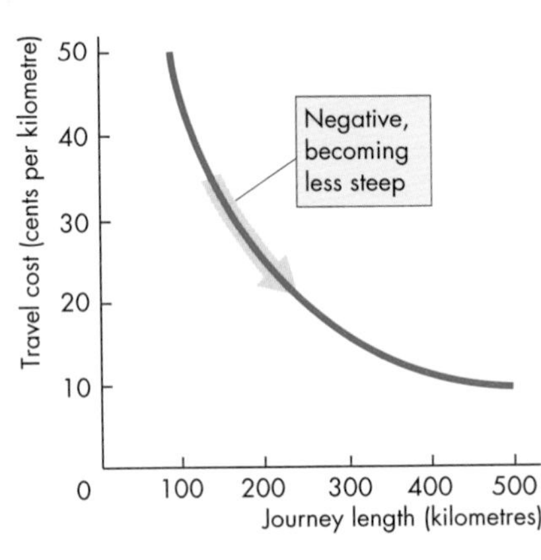

(b) Negative, becoming less steep

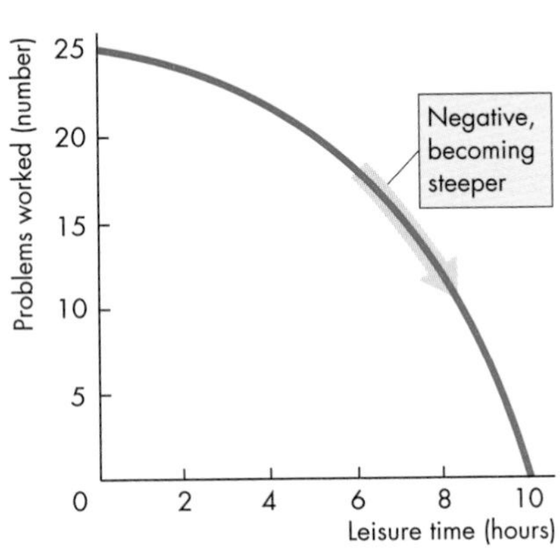

(c) Negative, becoming steeper

Each part of this figure shows a negative (inverse) relationship between two variables. That is, as the value of the variable measured on the *x*-axis increases, the value of the variable measured on the *y*-axis decreases. Part (a) shows a linear relationship. The total time spent playing tennis and squash is 5 hours. As the time spent playing tennis increases, the time spent playing squash decreases, and we move along a straight line. Part (b) shows a negative relationship such that as the journey length increases, the curve becomes less steep. Part (c) shows a negative relationship such that as leisure time increases, the curve becomes steeper.

Figure A1.6(c) shows the relationship between the amount of leisure time and the number of problems worked by a student. Increasing leisure time produces an increasingly large reduction in the number of problems worked. This relationship is a negative one that starts out with a gentle slope at a small number of leisure hours and becomes steeper as the number of leisure hours increases. This relationship is a different view of the idea shown in Fig. A1.5(c).

Variables That Have a Maximum or a Minimum

Many relationships in economic models have a maximum or a minimum. For example, firms try to make the maximum possible profit and to produce at the lowest possible cost. Figure A1.7 shows relationships that have a maximum or a minimum.

Figure A1.7(a) shows the relationship between rainfall and wheat yield. When there is no rainfall, wheat will not grow, so the yield is zero. As the rainfall increases up to 10 days a month, the wheat yield increases. With 10 rainy days each month, the wheat yield reaches its maximum at 2 tonnes per hectare (point *A*). Rain in excess of 10 days a month starts to lower the yield of wheat. If every day is rainy, the wheat suffers from a lack of sunshine and the yield decreases to zero. This relationship is one that starts out sloping upward, reaches a maximum, and then slopes downward.

Figure A1.7(b) shows the reverse case—a relationship that begins sloping downward, falls to a minimum, and then slopes upward. Most economic costs are like this relationship. An example is the relationship between the cost per kilometre and speed for a car trip. At low speeds, the car is creeping in a traffic jam. The number of kilometres per litre is low, so the cost per kilometre is high. At high speeds, the car is travelling faster than its efficient speed, using a large quantity of gasoline, and again the number of kilometres per litre is low and the cost per kilometre is high. At a speed of 100 kilometres an hour, the cost per kilometre is at its minimum (point *B*). This relationship is one that starts out sloping downward, reaches a minimum, and then slopes upward.

FIGURE A1.7 Maximum and Minimum Points

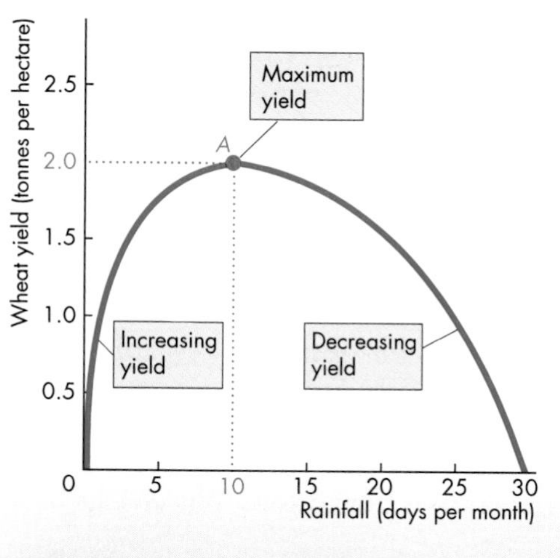

(a) Relationship with a maximum

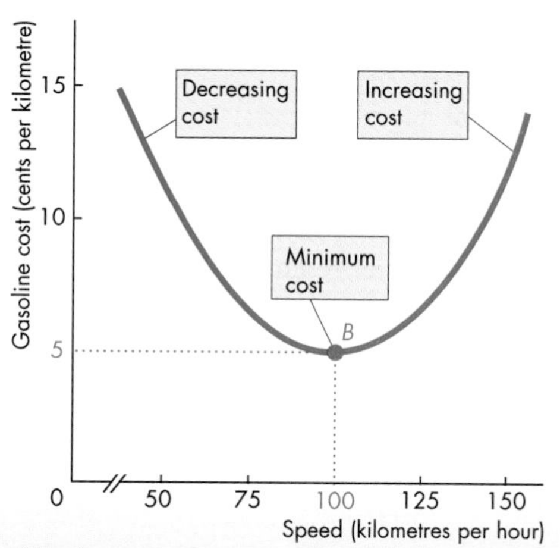

(b) Relationship with a minimum

Part (a) shows a relationship that has a maximum point, *A*. The curve slopes upward as it rises to its maximum point, is flat at its maximum, and then slopes downward.

Part (b) shows a relationship with a minimum point, *B*. The curve slopes downward as it falls to its minimum, is flat at its minimum, and then slopes upward.

Variables That Are Unrelated

There are many situations in which no matter what happens to the value of one variable, the other variable remains constant. Sometimes we want to show the independence between two variables in a graph, and Fig. A1.8 shows two ways of achieving this.

In describing the graphs in Fig. A1.5 through A1.7, we have talked about curves that slope upward and downward, and curves that become less steep or steeper. Let's spend a little time discussing exactly what we mean by slope and how we measure the slope of a curve.

FIGURE A1.8 Variables That Are Unrelated

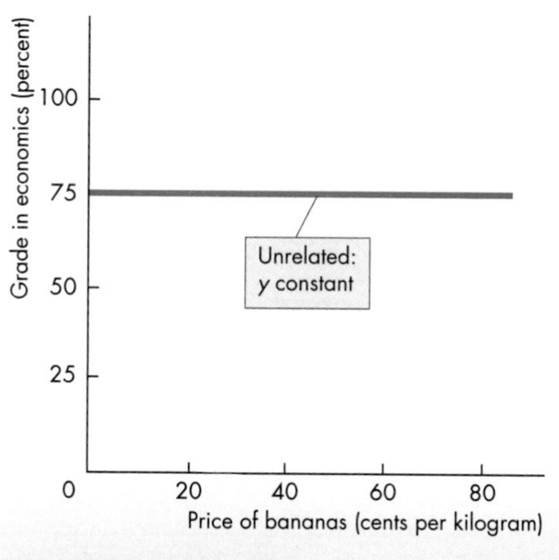

(a) Unrelated: *y* constant

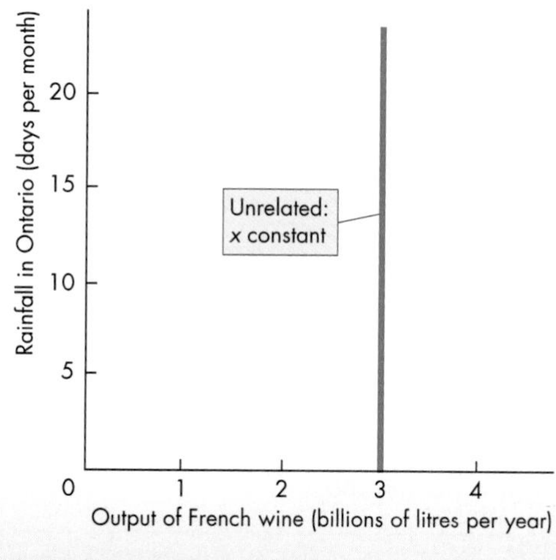

(b) Unrelated: *x* constant

This figure shows how we can graph two variables that are unrelated. In part (a), a student's grade in economics is plotted at 75 percent on the *y*-axis regardless of the price of bananas on the *x*-axis. The curve is horizontal.

In part (b), the output of the vineyards of France on the *x*-axis does not vary with the rainfall in Ontario on the *y*-axis. The curve is vertical.

The Slope of a Relationship

WE CAN MEASURE THE INFLUENCE OF ONE variable on another by the slope of the relationship. The **slope** of a relationship is the change in the value of the variable measured on the *y*-axis divided by the change in the value of the variable measured on the *x*-axis. We use the Greek letter Δ (*delta*) to represent "change in." Thus Δy means the change in the value of the variable measured on the *y*-axis, and Δx means the change in the value of the variable measured on the *x*-axis. Therefore the slope of the relationship is

$$\Delta y/\Delta x$$

If a large change in the variable measured on the *y*-axis (Δy) is associated with a small change in the variable measured on the *x*-axis (Δx), the slope is large and the curve is steep. If a small change in the variable measured on the *y*-axis (Δy) is associated with a large change in the variable measured on the *x*-axis (Δx), the slope is small and the curve is flat.

We can make the idea of slope sharper by doing some calculations.

The Slope of a Straight Line

The slope of a straight line is the same regardless of where on the line you calculate it. The slope of a straight line is constant. Let's calculate the slopes of the lines in Fig. A1.9. In part (a), when x increases from 2 to 6, y increases from 3 to 6. The change in x

FIGURE A1.9 The Slope of a Straight Line

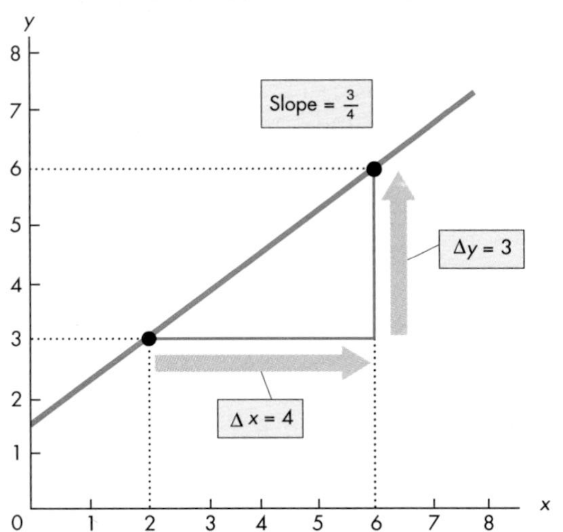

(a) Positive slope

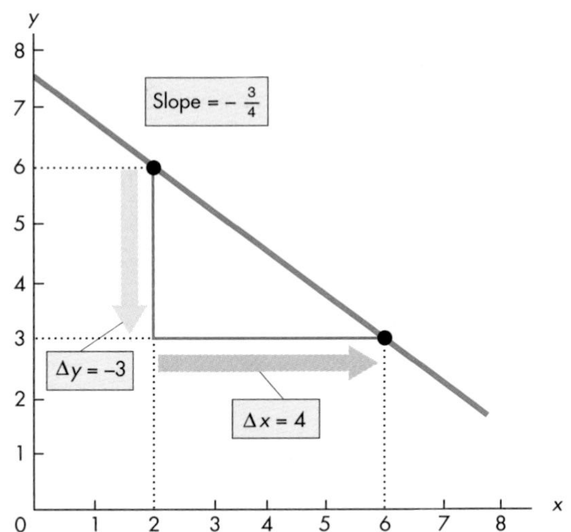

(b) Negative slope

To calculate the slope of a straight line, we divide the change in the value of the variable measured on the *y*-axis (Δy) by the change in the value of the variable measured on the *x*-axis (Δx), as we move along the curve. Part (a) shows the calculation of a positive slope. When *x* increases from 2 to 6, Δx equals 4. That change in *x* brings about an increase in *y* from 3 to 6, so Δy equals 3. The slope ($\Delta y/\Delta x$) equals 3/4. Part (b) shows the calculation of a negative slope. When *x* increases from 2 to 6, Δx equals 4. That increase in *x* brings about a decrease in *y* from 6 to 3, so Δy equals –3. The slope ($\Delta y/\Delta x$) equals –3/4.

is +4—that is, Δx is 4. The change in y is +3—that is, Δy is 3. The slope of that line is

$$\frac{\Delta y}{\Delta x} = \frac{3}{4}.$$

In part (b), when x increases from 2 to 6, y decreases from 6 to 3. The change in y is *minus* 3—that is, Δy is –3. The change in x is *plus* 4—that is, Δx is 4. The slope of the curve is

$$\frac{\Delta y}{\Delta x} = \frac{-3}{4}.$$

Notice that the two slopes have the same magnitude (3/4) but the slope of the line in part (a) is positive (+3/+4 = 3/4), while that in part (b) is negative (–3/+4 = –3/4). The slope of a positive relationship is positive; the slope of a negative relationship is negative.

The Slope of a Curved Line

The slope of a curved line is trickier. The slope of a curved line is not constant. Its slope depends on where on the line we calculate it. There are two ways to calculate the slope of a curved line: You can calculate the slope at a point, or you can calculate the slope across an arc of the curve. Let's look at the two alternatives.

Slope at a Point To calculate the slope at a point on a curve, you need to construct a straight line that has the same slope as the curve at the point in question. Figure A1.10 shows how this is done. Suppose you want to calculate the slope of the curve at point *A*. Place a ruler on the graph so that it touches point *A* and no other point on the curve, then draw a straight line along the edge of the ruler. The straight red line is this line, and it is the tangent to the curve at point *A*. If the ruler touches the curve only at point *A*, then the slope of the curve at point *A* must be the same as the slope of the edge of the ruler. If the curve and the ruler do not have the same slope, the line along the edge of the ruler will cut the curve instead of just touching it.

Now that you have found a straight line with the same slope as the curve at point *A*, you can calculate the slope of the curve at point *A* by calculating the slope of the straight line. Along the straight line, as x increases from 0 to 4 ($\Delta x = 4$) y increases from 2 to 5 ($\Delta y = 3$). Therefore the slope of the line is

$$\frac{\Delta y}{\Delta x} = \frac{3}{4}.$$

Thus the slope of the curve at point A is 3/4.

FIGURE A1.10 Slope at a Point

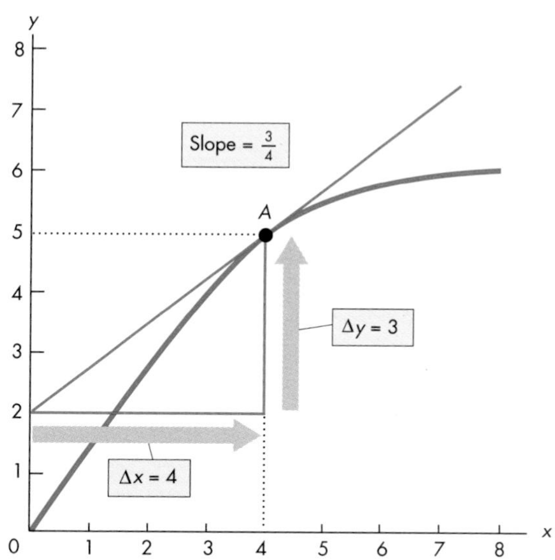

To calculate the slope of the curve at point *A*, draw the red line that just touches the curve at *A*—the tangent. The slope of this straight line is calculated by dividing the change in *y* by the change in *x* along the red line. When *x* increases from 0 to 4, Δx equals 4. That change in *x* is associated with an increase in *y* from 2 to 5, so Δy equals 3. The slope of the red line is 3/4. So the slope of the curve at point *A* is 3/4.

Slope Across an Arc An arc of a curve is a piece of a curve. In Fig. A1.11, you are looking at the same curve as in Fig. A1.10. But instead of calculating the slope at point *A*, we are going to calculate the slope across the arc from *B* to *C*. You can see that the slope at *B* is greater than at *C*. When we calculate the slope across an arc, we are calculating the average slope between two points. As we move along the arc from *B* to *C*, x increases from 3 to 5 and y increases from 4 to 5.5. The change in x is 2 ($\Delta x = 2$), and the change

FIGURE A1.11 Slope Across an Arc

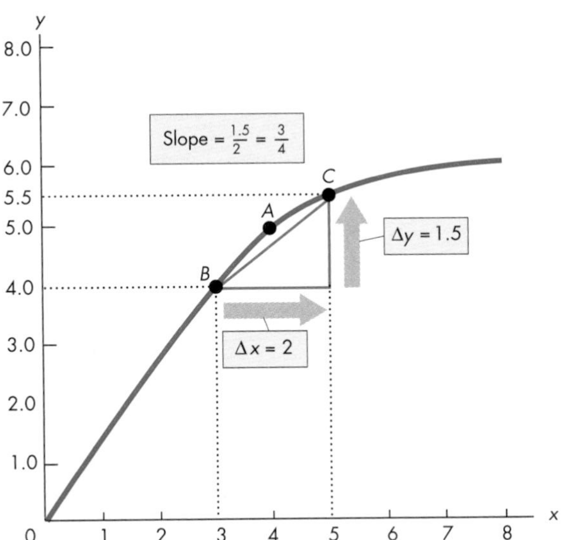

To calculate the average slope of the curve along the arc *BC*, draw a straight line from *B* to *C*. The slope of the line *BC* is calculated by dividing the change in *y* by the change in *x*. In moving from *B* to *C*, Δx equals 2 and Δy equals 1.5. The slope of the line *BC* is 1.5 divided by 2, or 3/4. So the slope of the curve across the arc *BC* is 3/4.

in *y* is 1.5 ($\Delta y = 1.5$). Therefore the slope of the line is

$$\frac{\Delta y}{\Delta x} = \frac{1.5}{2} = \frac{3}{4}.$$

Thus the slope of the curve across the arc *BC* is 3/4.

This calculation gives us the slope of the curve between points *B* and *C*. The actual slope calculated is the slope of the straight line from *B* to *C*. This slope approximates the average slope of the curve along the arc *BC*. In this particular example, the slope across the arc *BC* is identical to the slope of the curve at point *A*. But the calculation of the slope of a curve does not always work out so neatly. You might have some fun constructing some more examples and some counterexamples.

You now know how to make and interpret a graph. But so far, we've limited our attention to graphs of two variables. We're now going to learn how to graph more than two variables.

Graphing Relationships Among More Than Two Variables

WE HAVE SEEN THAT WE CAN GRAPH THE relationship between two variables as a point formed by the *x*- and *y*-coordinates in a two-dimensional graph. You may be thinking that although a two-dimensional graph is informative, most of the things in which you are likely to be interested involve relationships among many variables, not just two. For example, the amount of ice cream consumed depends on the price of ice cream and the temperature. If ice cream is expensive and the temperature is low, people eat much less ice cream than when ice cream is inexpensive and the temperature is high. For any given price of ice cream, the quantity consumed varies with the temperature; and for any given temperature, the quantity of ice cream consumed varies with its price.

Figure A1.12 shows a relationship among three variables. The table shows the number of litres of ice cream consumed each day at various temperatures and ice cream prices. How can we graph these numbers?

To graph a relationship that involves more than two variables, we use the *ceteris paribus* assumption.

Ceteris Paribus We noted in the chapter (see p. 13) that every laboratory experiment is an attempt to create *ceteris paribus* and isolate the relationship of interest. We use the same method to make a graph when more than two variables are involved.

Figure A1.12(a) shows an example. There, you can see what happens to the quantity of ice cream consumed when the price of ice cream varies and the temperature is held constant. The line labelled 21°C shows the relationship between ice cream consumption and the price of ice cream if the temperature remains at 21°C. The numbers used to plot that line are those in the third column of the table in Fig. A1.12. For example, if the temperature is 21°C, 10 litres are consumed when the price is 60¢ a scoop and 18 litres are consumed when the price is 30¢ a scoop. The curve labelled 32°C shows consumption as the price varies if the temperature remains 32°C.

We can also show the relationship between ice cream consumption and temperature when the price of ice cream remains constant, as shown in

FIGURE A1.12 Graphing a Relationship Among Three Variables

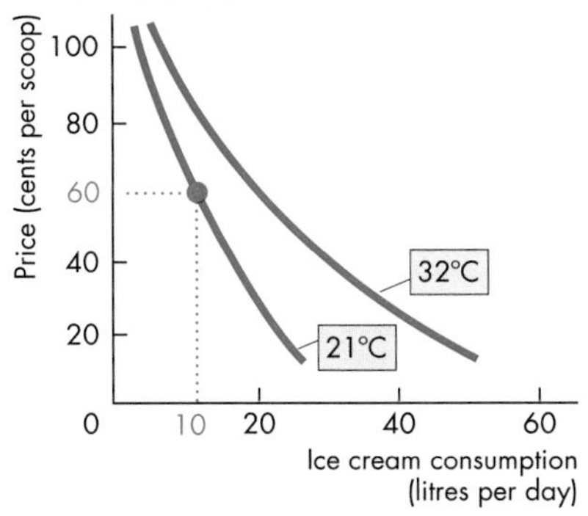

(a) Price and consumption at a given temperature

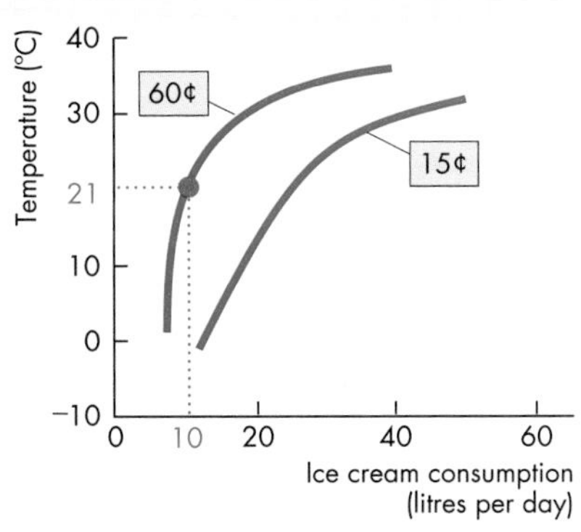

(b) Temperature and consumption at a given price

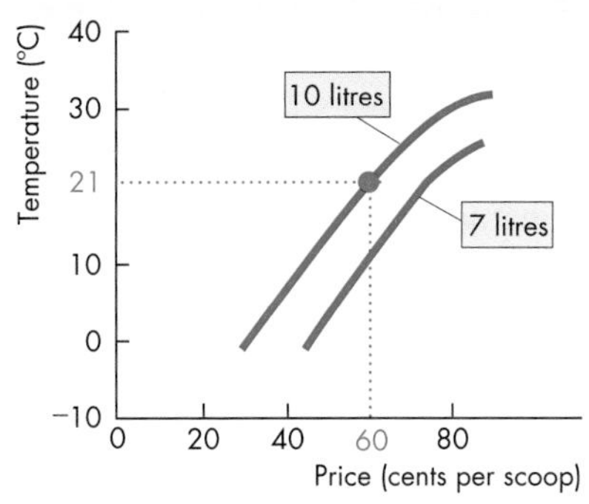

(c) Temperature and price at a given consumption

Price (cents per scoop)	Ice cream consumption (litres per day) −10°C	10°C	21°C	32°C
15	12	18	25	50
30	10	12	18	37
45	7	10	13	27
60	5	7	10	20
75	3	5	7	14
90	2	3	5	10
105	1	2	3	6

The quantity of ice cream consumed depends on its price and the temperature. The table gives some hypothetical numbers that tell us how many litres of ice cream are consumed each day at different prices and different temperatures. For example, if the price is 60¢ a scoop and the temperature is 21°C, 10 litres of ice cream are consumed. This set of values is highlighted in the table and each part of the figure.

To graph a relationship among three variables, the value of one variable is held constant. Part (a) shows the relationship between price and consumption when temperature is held constant. One curve holds temperature at 32°C and the other at 21°C. Part (b) shows the relationship between temperature and consumption when price is held constant. One curve holds the price at 60¢ a scoop and the other at 15¢ a scoop. Part (c) shows the relationship between temperature and price when consumption is held constant. One curve holds consumption at 10 litres and the other at 7 litres.

Fig. A1.12(b). The curve labelled 60¢ shows how the consumption of ice cream varies with the temperature when ice cream costs 60¢ a scoop, and a second curve shows the relationship when ice cream costs 15¢ a scoop. For example, at 60¢ a scoop, 10 litres are consumed when the temperature is 21°C and 20 litres when the temperature is 32°C.

Figure A1.12(c) shows the combinations of temperature and price that result in a constant consumption of ice cream. One curve shows the combination that results in 10 litres a day being consumed, and the other shows the combination that results in 7 litres a day being consumed. A high price and a high temperature lead to the same consumption as a lower price and a lower temperature. For example, 10 litres of ice cream are consumed at 21°C and 60¢ a scoop, 32°C and 90¢ a scoop, and at 10°C and 45¢ a scoop.

◆ With what you have learned about graphs, you can move forward with your study of economics. There are no graphs in this book that are more complicated than those that have been explained in this appendix.

Mathematical Note:
Equations To Straight Lines

IF A STRAIGHT LINE IN A GRAPH DESCRIBES THE relationship between two variables, we call it a **linear relationship**. Figure 1 shows the linear relationship between a person's expenditure and income. This person spends $100 a week (by borrowing or spending previous savings) when income is zero. And out of each dollar earned, this person spends 50 cents (and saves 50 cents).

All linear relationships are described by the same general equation. We call the quantity that is measured on the horizontal (or *x*-axis) *x* and we call the quantity that is measured on the vertical (or *y*-axis) *y*. In the case of Fig. 1, *x* is income and *y* is expenditure.

A Linear Equation

The equation that describes a straight-line relationship between *x* and *y* is

$$y = a + bx.$$

In this equation, *a* and *b* are fixed numbers and they are called constants. The values of *x* and *y* vary so these numbers are called variables. Because the equation describes a straight line, it is called a **linear equation.**

The equation tells us that when the value of *x* is zero, the value of *y* is *a*. We call the constant *a* the *y*-axis intercept. The reason is that on the graph the straight line hits the *y*-axis at a value equal to *a*. Figure 1 illustrates the *y*-axis intercept.

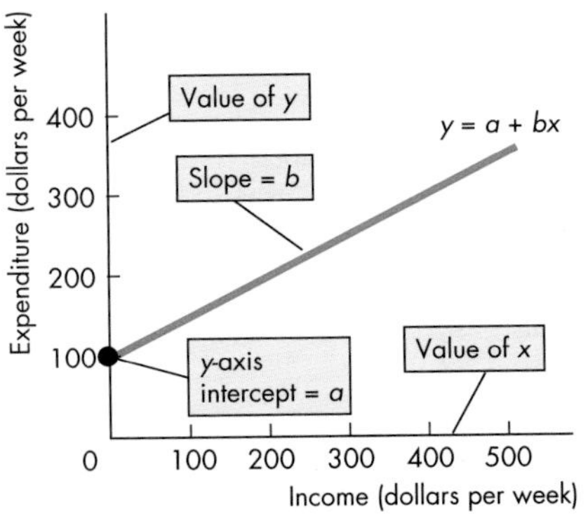

Figure 1 Linear relationship

For positive values of *x*, the value of *y* exceeds *a*. The constant *b* tells us by how much *y* increases above *a* as *x* increases. The constant *b* is the slope of the line.

Slope of Line

As we explain in the chapter, the **slope** of a relationship is the change in the value of *y* divided by the change in the value of *x*. We use the Greek letter Δ (delta) to represent "change in." Thus Δy means the change in the value of the variable measured on the *y*-axis, and Δx means the change in the value of the variable measured on the *x*-axis. Therefore the slope of the relationship is

$$\Delta y / \Delta x.$$

To see why the slope is *b*, suppose that initially the value of *x* is x_1, or $200 in Fig. 2. The corresponding value of *y* is y_1, also $200 in Fig. 2. The equation to the line tells us that

$$y_1 = a + bx_1. \tag{1}$$

Now the value of *x* increases by Δx to $x_1 + \Delta x$ (or $400 in Fig. 2). And the value of *y* increases by Δy to $y_1 + \Delta y$ (or $300 in Fig. 2).

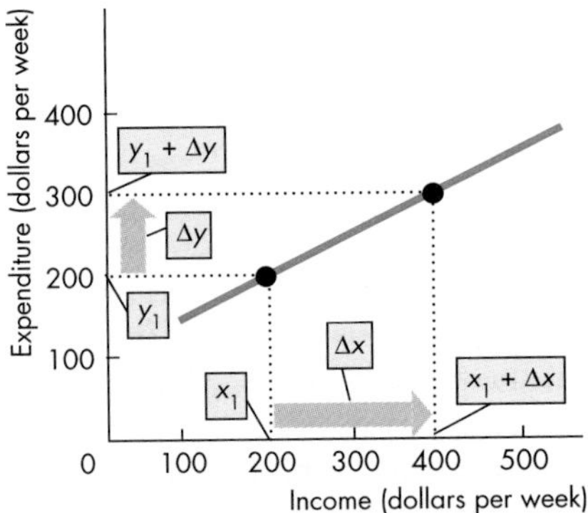

Figure 2 Calculating slope

The equation to the line now tells us that

$$y_1 + \Delta y = a + b(x_1 + \Delta x) \qquad (2)$$

To calculate the slope of the line, subtract equation (1) from equation (2) to obtain

$$\Delta y = b\Delta x \qquad (3)$$

and now divide equation (3) by Δx to obtain

$$\frac{\Delta y}{\Delta x} = b.$$

So, the slope of the line is b.

Position of Line

The y-axis intercept determines the position of the line on the graph. Figure 3 illustrates the relationship between the y-axis intercept and the position of the line on the graph. The y-axis measures saving and the x-axis measures income. When the y-axis intercept, a, is positive, the line hits the y-axis at a positive value of y—as the blue line does. When the y-axis intercept, a, is zero, the line hits the y-axis at the origin—as the purple line does. When the y-axis intercept, a, is negative, the line hits the y-axis at a negative value of y—as the red line does. As the equations to the three lines show, the value of the y-axis intercept does not influence the slope of the line.

Positive Relationships

Figure 1 shows a positive relationship—the two variables x and y move in the same direction. All positive relationships have a slope that is positive. In the equation to the line, the constant b is positive. In this example, the y-axis intercept, a, is 100. The slope b equals $\Delta y/\Delta x$, which is 100/200 or 0.5. The equation to the line is

$$y = 100 + 0.5x.$$

Negative Relationships

Figure 4 shows a negative relationship—the two variables x and y move in the opposite direction. All negative relationships have a slope that is negative. In the equation to the line, the constant b is negative. In the example in Fig. 4, the y-axis intercept, a, is 30. The slope, b, equals $\Delta y/\Delta x$, which is –20/2 or –10. The equation to the line is

$$y = 30 + (-10)x$$

or,

$$y = 30 - 10x.$$

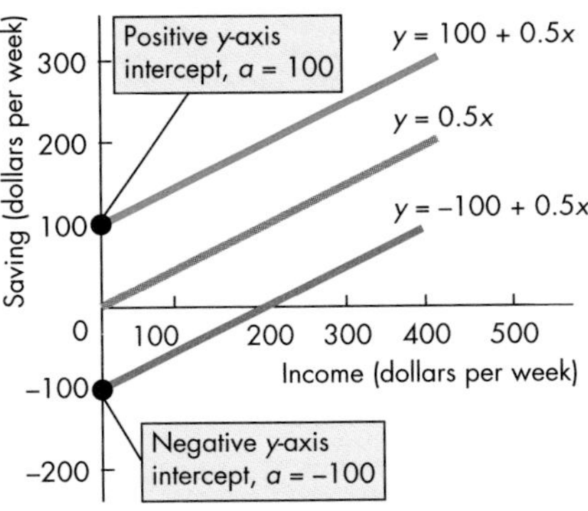

Figure 3 The y-axis intercept

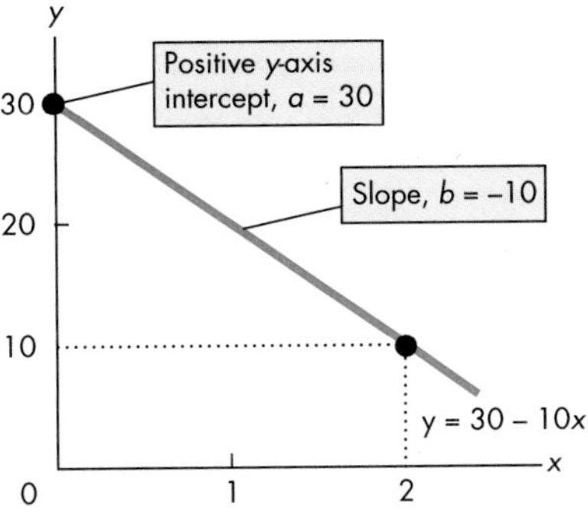

Figure 4 Negative relationship

SUMMARY

KEY POINTS

Graphing Data (pp. 17–20)

- A time-series graph shows the trend and fluctuations in a variable over time.
- A cross-section graph shows how variables change across the members of a population.
- A scatter diagram shows the relationship between two variables. It shows whether two variables are positively related, negatively related, or unrelated.

Graphs Used in Economic Models (pp. 20–23)

- Graphs are used to show relationships among variables in economic models.
- Relationships can be positive (an upward-sloping curve), negative (a downward-sloping curve), positive and then negative (have a maximum point), negative and then positive (have a minimum point), or unrelated (a horizontal or vertical curve).

The Slope of a Relationship (pp. 24–26)

- The slope of a relationship is calculated as the change in the value of the variable measured on the *y*-axis divided by the change in the value of the variable measured on the *x*-axis—that is, $\Delta y/\Delta x$.
- A straight line has a constant slope.
- A curved line has a varying slope. To calculate the slope of a curved line, we calculate the slope at a point or across an arc.

Graphing Relationships Among More Than Two Variables (pp. 26–27)

- To graph a relationship among more than two variables, we hold constant the values of all the variables except two.
- We then plot the value of one of the variables against the value of another.

KEY FIGURES

Figure A1.1 Making a Graph, 17
Figure A1.5 Positive (Direct) Relationships, 21
Figure A1.6 Negative (Inverse) Relationships, 22
Figure A1.7 Maximum and Minimum Points, 23
Figure A1.9 The Slope of a Straight Line, 24
Figure A1.10 Slope at a Point, 25
Figure A1.11 Slope Across an Arc, 26

KEY TERMS

Cross-section graph, 18
Direct relationship, 20
Inverse relationship, 21
Linear relationship, 20
Negative relationship, 21
Positive relationship, 20
Scatter diagram, 19
Slope, 24
Time-series graph, 18
Trend, 18

REVIEW QUIZ

1. What are the three types of graphs used to show economic data?
2. Give an example of a time-series graph.
3. List three things that a time-series graph shows quickly and easily.
4. Give three examples, different from those in the chapter, of scatter diagrams that show a positive relationship, a negative relationship, and no relationship.
5. Draw some graphs to show the relationships between two variables that
   a. Move in the same direction.
   b. Move in opposite directions.
   c. Have a maximum.
   d. Have a minimum.
6. Which of the relationships in question 5 is a positive relationship and which is a negative relationship?
7. What are the two ways of calculating the slope of a curved line?
8. How do we graph a relationship among more than two variables?

PROBLEMS

The spreadsheet provides data on the Canadian economy: Column A is the year, column B is the inflation rate, column C is the interest rate, column D is the growth rate, and column E is the unemployment rate. Use this spreadsheet to answer problems 1, 2, 3, and 4.

	A	B	C	D	E
1	1991	2.8	9.8	–2.1	10.3
2	1992	1.2	8.8	0.9	11.2
3	1993	1.5	7.8	2.3	11.4
4	1994	1.1	8.6	4.8	10.4
5	1995	2.3	8.3	2.8	9.4
6	1996	1.7	7.5	1.6	9.6
7	1997	0.9	6.4	4.2	9.1
8	1998	–0.5	5.5	4.1	8.3
9	1999	1.3	5.7	5.4	7.6
10	2000	3.6	5.9	4.5	6.8
11	2001	1.4	5.8	1.5	7.2

*1. a. Draw a time-series graph of the inflation rate.
b. In which year(s) (i) was inflation highest, (ii) was inflation lowest, (iii) did it increase, (iv) did it decrease, (v) did it increase most, and (vi) did it decrease most?
c. What was the main trend in inflation?

2. a. Draw a time-series graph of the interest rate.
b. In which year(s) was the interest rate highest, (ii) was the interest rate lowest, (iii) did it increase, (iv) did it decrease, (v) did it increase most, and (vi) did it decrease most?
c. What was the main trend in the interest rate?

*3. Draw a scatter diagram to show the relationship between the inflation rate and the interest rate. Describe the relationship.

4. Draw a scatter diagram to show the relationship between the growth rate and the unemployment rate. Describe the relationship.

*5. Draw a graph to show the relationship between the two variables x and y:

x	0	1	2	3	4	5	6	7	8
y	0	1	4	9	16	25	36	49	64

a. Is the relationship positive or negative?
b. Does the slope of the relationship increase or decrease as the value of x increases?
c. Think of some economic relationships that might be similar to this one.

6. Draw a graph that shows the relationship between the two variables x and y:

x	0	1	2	3	4	5
y	25	24	22	16	8	0

a. Is the relationship positive or negative?
b. Does the slope of the relationship increase or decrease as the value of x increases?
c. Think of some economic relationships that might be similar to this one.

*7. In problem 5, calculate the slope of the relationship between x and y when x equals 4.

8. In problem 6, calculate the slope of the relationship between x and y when x equals 3.

*9. In problem 5, calculate the slope of the relationship across the arc when x increases from 3 to 4.

10. In problem 6, calculate the slope of the relationship across the arc when x increases from 4 to 5.

*11. Calculate the slope of the relationship shown at point A in the following figure.

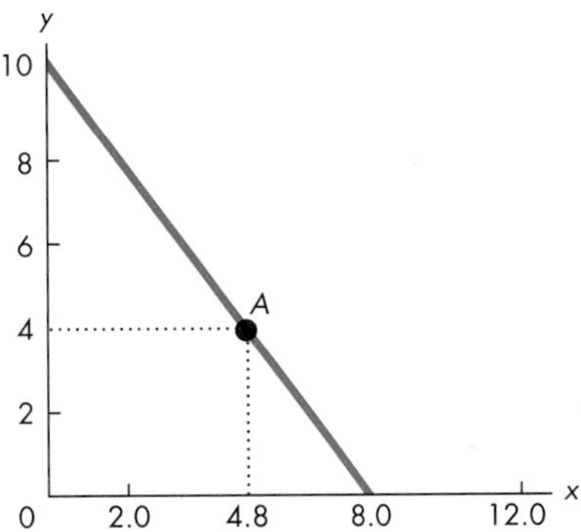

12. Calculate the slope of the relationship shown at point A in the following figure.

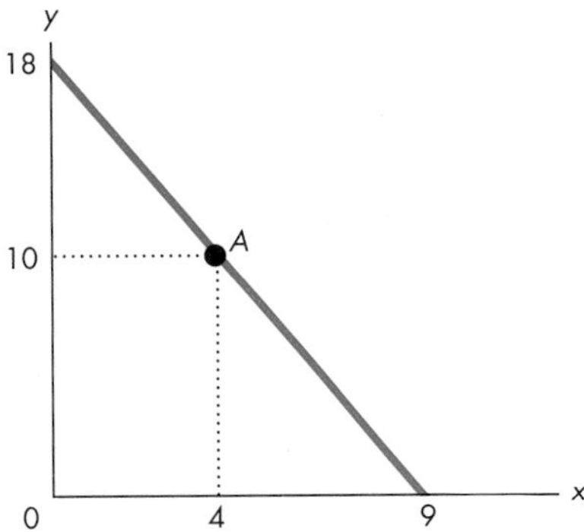

*You can obtain the solutions to the odd-numbered problems at *Parkin Online* (www.pearsoned.ca/parkin).

*13. Use the following figure to calculate the slope of the relationship:

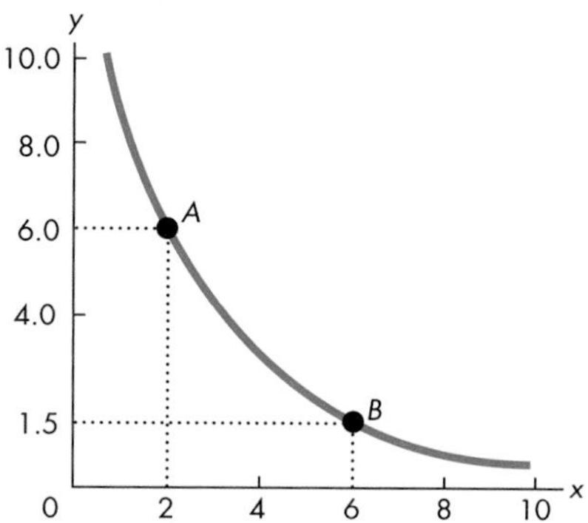

a. At points *A* and *B*.
b. Across the arc *AB*.

14. Use the following figure to calculate the slope of the relationship:

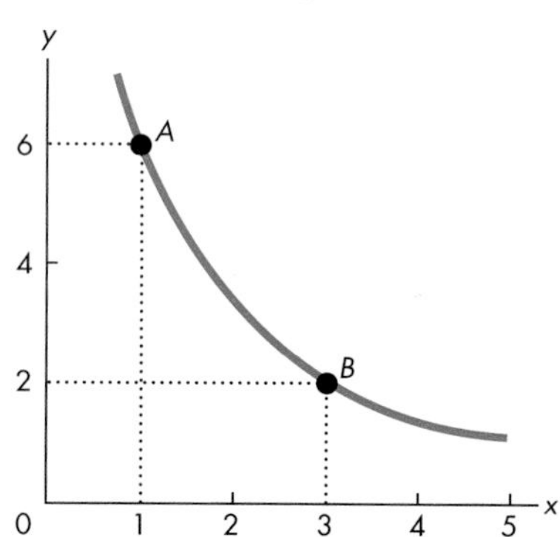

a. At points *A* and *B*.
b. Across the arc *AB*.

*15. The table gives the price of a balloon ride, the temperature, and the number of rides a day.

Price (dollars per ride)	Balloon rides (number per day) 10°C	20°C	30°C
5.00	32	40	50
10.00	27	32	40
15.00	18	27	32
20.00	10	18	27

Draw graphs to show the relationship between
a. The price and the number of rides, holding the temperature constant.
b. The number of rides and temperature, holding the price constant.
c. The temperature and price, holding the number of rides constant.

16. The table gives the price of an umbrella, the amount of rainfall, and the number of umbrellas purchased.

Price (dollars per umbrella)	Umbrellas (number per day) 0	2 (mm of rainfall)	10
10	7	8	12
20	4	7	8
30	2	4	7
40	1	2	4

Draw graphs to show the relationship between
a. The price and the number of umbrellas purchased, holding the amount of rainfall constant.
b. The number of umbrellas purchased and the amount of rainfall, holding the price constant.
c. The amount of rainfall and the price, holding the number of umbrellas purchased constant.

WEB EXERCISES

1. Use the link on the Parkin–Bade Web site and find the Consumer Price Index (CPI) for the latest 12 months. Make a graph of the CPI. During the most recent month, was the CPI rising or falling? Was the rate of rise or fall increasing or decreasing?
2. Use the link on the Parkin–Bade Web site and find the unemployment rate for the latest 12 months. Graph the unemployment rate. During the most recent month, was it rising or falling? Was the rate of rise or fall increasing or decreasing?
3. Use the data that you obtained in Web Exercises 1 and 2. Make a graph to show whether the CPI and the unemployment rate are related to each other.
4. Use the data that you obtained in Web Exercises 1 and 2. Calculate the percentage change in the CPI each month. Make a graph to show whether the percentage change in the CPI and the unemployment rate are related to each other.

THE ECONOMIC PROBLEM

CHAPTER 2

Good, Better, Best!

We live in a style that surprises our grandparents and would have astonished our great-grandparents. MP3s, video games, cell phones, gene splicing, and personal computers, which didn't exist even 25 years ago, have transformed our daily lives. For most of us, life is good, and getting better. But we still make choices and face costs. We still choose what we think is best for us. ◆ Perhaps the biggest choice that you will make is when to quit school and begin full-time work. When you've completed your current program, will you remain in school and work towards a postgraduate degree or a professional degree? What are the costs and consequences of this choice? We'll return to this question in *Reading Between the Lines* at the end of this chapter. ◆ We see an incredible amount of specialization and trade in the world. Each one of us specializes in a particular job—as a lawyer, a journalist, a homemaker. Why? How do we benefit from specialization and trade? ◆ Over many centuries, social institutions have evolved that we take for granted. One of them is property rights and a political and legal system that protects them. Another is markets. Why have these institutions evolved?

These are the questions that we study in this chapter. We begin with the core economic problem—scarcity and choice—and the concept of the production possibilities frontier. We then learn about the central idea of economics: efficiency. We also discover how we can expand production by accumulating capital and by specializing and trading with each other. What you will learn in this chapter is the foundation on which all economics is built.

After studying this chapter, you will be able to

- **Define the production possibilities frontier and calculate opportunity cost**
- **Distinguish between production possibilities and preferences and describe an efficient allocation of resources**
- **Explain how current production choices expand future production possibilities**
- **Explain how specialization and trade expand our production possibilities**
- **Explain why property rights and markets have evolved**

Production Possibilities and Opportunity Cost

EVERY WORKING DAY, IN MINES, FACTORIES, shops, and offices and on farms and construction sites across Canada, 27 million people produce a vast variety of goods and services valued at more than $3 billion. But the quantities of goods and services that we can produce are limited by our available resources and by technology. And if we want to increase our production of one good, we must decrease our production of something else—we face tradeoffs. You are going to learn about the production possibilities frontier, which describes the limit to what we can produce and provides a neat way of thinking about and illustrating the idea of a tradeoff.

The **production possibilities frontier** (*PPF*) is the boundary between those combinations of goods and services that can be produced and those that cannot. To illustrate the *PPF*, we focus on two goods at a time and hold constant the quantities produced of all the other goods and services. That is, we look at a *model* economy in which everything remains the same (*ceteris paribus*) except for the production of the two goods we are considering.

Let's look at the production possibilities frontier for the classic general example of "guns" and "butter," which stand for *any* pair of goods or services.

Production Possibilities Frontier

The *production possibilities frontier* for guns and butter shows the limits to the production of these two goods, given the total resources available to produce them. Figure 2.1 shows this production possibilities frontier. The table lists some combinations of the quantities of butter and guns that can be produced in a month given the resources available. The figure graphs these combinations. The x-axis shows the quantity of butter produced, and the y-axis shows the quantity of guns produced.

Because the *PPF* shows the *limits* to production, we cannot attain the points outside the frontier. They are points that describe wants that can't be satisfied. We can produce at all the points *inside* the *PPF* and *on* the *PPF*. They are attainable points. Suppose that in a typical month, we produce 4 tonnes of butter and 5 guns. Figure 2.1 shows this combination as point *E* and as possibility *E* in the table. The figure also shows

FIGURE 2.1 Production Possibilities Frontier

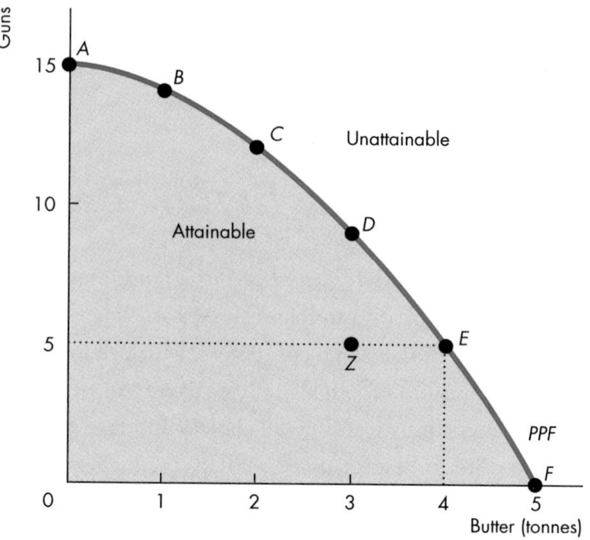

Possibility	Butter (tonnes)		Guns (units)
A	0	and	15
B	1	and	14
C	2	and	12
D	3	and	9
E	4	and	5
F	5	and	0

The table lists six points on the production possibilities frontier for guns and butter. Row *A* tells us that if we produce no butter, the maximum quantity of guns we can produce is 15. Points *A*, *B*, *C*, *D*, *E*, and *F* in the figure represent the rows of the table. The line passing through these points is the production possibilities frontier (*PPF*). It separates the attainable from the unattainable. Production is possible at any point inside the orange area or on the frontier. Points outside the frontier are unattainable. Points inside the frontier, such as point *Z*, are inefficient because resources are wasted or misallocated. At such points, it is possible to use the available resources to produce more of either or both goods.

other production possibilities. For example, we might stop producing butter and move all the people who produce it into producing guns. Point *A* in the figure and possibility *A* in the table show this case. The quantity of guns produced increases to 15, and butter production dries up. Alternatively, we might close the gun factories and switch all the resources into producing butter. In this situation, we produce 5 tonnes of butter. Point *F* in the figure and possibility *F* in the table show this case.

Production Efficiency

We achieve **production efficiency** if we cannot produce more of one good without producing less of some other good. When production is efficient, we are at a point *on* the *PPF.* If we are at a point *inside* the *PPF,* such as point *Z,* production is *inefficient* because we have some *unused* resources or we have some *misallocated* resources or both.

Resources are unused when they are idle but could be working. For example, we might leave some of the gun factories idle or some workers unemployed.

Resources are *misallocated* when they are assigned to tasks for which they are not the best match. For example, we might assign skilled butter-making machine operators to work in a gun factory and skilled gun makers to work in a dairy. We could get more butter *and* more guns from these same workers if we reassigned them to the tasks that more closely match their skills.

If we produce at a point inside the *PPF* such as *Z,* we can use our resources more efficiently to produce more butter, more guns, or more of *both* butter and guns. But if we produce at a point *on* the *PPF,* we are using our resources efficiently and we can produce more of one good only if we produce less of the other. That is, along the *PPF,* we face a *tradeoff.*

Tradeoff Along the *PPF*

Every choice *along* the *PPF* involves a *tradeoff*—we must give up something to get something else. On the *PPF* in Fig. 2.1, we must give up some guns to get more butter or give up some butter to get more guns.

Tradeoffs arise in every imaginable real-world situation, and you reviewed several of them in Chapter 1. At any given point in time, we have a fixed amount of labour, land, capital, and entrepreneurship. By using our available technologies, we can employ these resources to produce goods and services. But we are limited in what we can produce. This limit defines a boundary between what we can attain and what we cannot attain. This boundary is the real world's production possibilities frontier, and it defines the tradeoffs that we must make. On our real-world *PPF,* we can produce more of any one good or service only if we produce less of some other goods or services.

When doctors say that we must spend more on AIDS and cancer research, they are suggesting a tradeoff: more medical research for less of some other things. When the prime minister says that he wants to spend more on education and health care, he is suggesting a tradeoff: more education and health care for less peacekeeping and national security or less private spending (because of higher taxes). When an environmental group argues for less logging, it is suggesting a tradeoff: greater conservation of endangered wildlife for less paper. When your parents say that you should study more, they are suggesting a tradeoff: more study time for less leisure or sleep.

All tradeoffs involve a cost—an opportunity cost.

Opportunity Cost

The *opportunity cost* of an action is the highest-valued alternative forgone. The *PPF* helps us to make the concept of opportunity cost precise and enables us to calculate it. Along the *PPF,* there are only two goods, so there is only one alternative forgone: some quantity of the other good. Given our current resources and technology, we can produce more butter only if we produce fewer guns. The opportunity cost of producing an additional tonne of butter is the number of guns we must forgo. Similarly, the opportunity cost of producing an additional gun is the quantity of butter we must forgo.

For example, at point *C* in Fig. 2.1, we produce less butter and more guns than at point *D.* If we choose point *D* over point *C,* the additional tonne of butter *costs* 3 guns. One tonne of butter costs 3 guns.

We can also work out the opportunity cost of choosing point *C* over point *D* in Fig. 2.1. If we move from point *D* to point *C,* the quantity of guns produced increases by 3 and the quantity of butter produced decreases by 1 tonne. So if we choose point *C* over point *D,* the additional 3 guns *cost* 1 tonne of butter. One gun costs 1/3 of a tonne of butter.

Opportunity Cost Is a Ratio Opportunity cost is a ratio. It is the decrease in the quantity produced of one good divided by the increase in the quantity produced of another good as we move along the production possibilities frontier.

Because opportunity cost is a ratio, the opportunity cost of producing an additional gun is equal to the *inverse* of the opportunity cost of producing an additional tonne of butter. Check this proposition by returning to the calculations we've just worked through. When we move along the *PPF* from *C* to *D*, the opportunity cost of a tonne of butter is 3 guns. The inverse of 3 is 1/3, so if we decrease the production of butter and increase the production of guns by moving from *D* to *C*, the opportunity cost of a gun must be 1/3 of a tonne of butter. You can check that this number is correct. If we move from *D* to *C*, we produce 3 more guns and 1 tonne less of butter. Because 3 guns cost 1 tonne of butter, the opportunity cost of 1 gun is 1/3 of a tonne of butter.

Increasing Opportunity Cost The opportunity cost of a tonne of butter increases as the quantity of butter produced increases. Also, the opportunity cost of a gun increases as the quantity of guns produced increases. This phenomenon of increasing opportunity cost is reflected in the shape of the *PPF*—it is bowed outward.

When a large quantity of guns and a small quantity of butter are produced—between points *A* and *B* in Fig. 2.1—the frontier has a gentle slope. A given increase in the quantity of butter *costs* a small decrease in the quantity of guns, so the opportunity cost of a tonne of butter is a small quantity of guns.

When a large quantity of butter and a small quantity of guns are produced—between points *E* and *F* in Fig. 2.1—the frontier is steep. A given increase in the quantity of butter *costs* a large decrease in the quantity of guns, so the opportunity cost of a tonne of butter is a large quantity of guns.

The *PPF* is bowed outward because resources are not all equally productive in all activities. People with many years of experience working for Smith & Wesson are very good at producing guns but not very good at making butter. So if we move some of these people from Smith & Wesson to Sealtest Dairies, we get a small increase in the quantity of butter but a large decrease in the quantity of guns.

Similarly, people who have spent years working at Sealtest Dairies are good at producing butter but not so good at producing guns. So if we move some of these people from Sealtest Dairies to Smith & Wesson, we get a small increase in the quantity of guns but a large decrease in the quantity of butter. The more we try to produce of either good, the less productive are the additional resources we use to produce that good and the larger is the opportunity cost of a unit of that good.

Increasing Opportunity Costs Are Everywhere Just about every activity that you can think of is one with an increasing opportunity cost. The most skilful farmers use the most fertile land to produce food. The best doctors use the least fertile land to produce health-care services. If hospitals buy fertile land, convert tractors into ambulances, and hire farmers as hospital porters, food production drops drastically and the production of health-care services increases by a tiny amount. The opportunity cost of a unit of health-care services rises. Similarly, if a farmer buys a hospital, converts it to a hydroponic tomato factory, and hires people who were previously doctors and nurses as farm workers, the decrease in the production of health-care services is large, but the increase in food production is small. The opportunity cost of a unit of food rises.

This example is extreme and unlikely, but these same considerations apply to any pair of goods that you can imagine.

REVIEW QUIZ

1. How does the production possibilities frontier illustrate scarcity?
2. How does the production possibilities frontier illustrate production efficiency?
3. How does the production possibilities frontier show that every choice involves a tradeoff?
4. How does the production possibilities frontier illustrate opportunity cost?
5. Why is opportunity cost a ratio?
6. Why does the *PPF* for most goods bow outward so that opportunity cost increases as the quantity produced of a good increases?

We've seen that what we can produce is limited by the production possibilities frontier. We've also seen that production on the *PPF* is efficient. But we can produce many different quantities on the *PPF*. How do we choose among them? How do we know which point on the *PPF* is the best one?

Using Resources Efficiently

YOU'VE SEEN THAT POINTS INSIDE THE *PPF* waste resources or leave them unused and are inefficient. You've also seen that points *on* the *PPF* are efficient—we can't produce more of one good unless we forgo some units of another good. But there are many such points on the *PPF*. Each point on the *PPF* achieves production efficiency. Which point is the best? How can we choose among them? What are the efficient quantities of butter and guns to produce?

These questions are examples of real-world questions of enormous consequence such as: How much should we spend on treating AIDS and how much on cancer research? Should we expand education and health-care programs or cut taxes? Should we spend more on the environment and the conservation of endangered wildlife?

To determine the efficient quantities to produce, we must compare costs and benefits.

The *PPF* and Marginal Cost

The limits to production, which are summarized by the *PPF*, determine the marginal cost of each good or service. **Marginal cost** is the opportunity cost of producing *one more unit*. We can calculate marginal cost in a way that is similar to the way we calculate opportunity cost. *Marginal cost* is the opportunity cost of *one* additional tonne of butter—the quantity of guns that must be given up to get one more tonne of butter—as we move along the *PPF*.

Figure 2.2 illustrates the marginal cost of butter. If butter production increases from zero to 1 tonne—a move from *A* to *B*—the quantity of guns decreases from 15 to 14. So the opportunity cost of the first tonne of butter is 1 gun. If butter production increases from 1 tonne to 2 tonnes—a move from *B* to *C*—the quantity of guns decreases by 2. So the second tonne of butter costs 2 guns.

You can repeat this calculation for an increase in butter production from 2 to 3 tonnes, from 3 to 4 tonnes, and from 4 to 5 tonnes. Figure 2.2 shows the opportunity costs as a series of steps. Each extra tonne of butter costs more guns than the preceding tonne.

We've just calculated the opportunity cost of a tonne of butter and generated the steps in Fig. 2.2(a). The opportunity cost of a tonne of butter is also the *marginal cost* of producing a tonne of butter. In Fig. 2.2(b), the line labelled *MC* shows the marginal cost.

FIGURE 2.2 The *PPF* and Marginal Cost

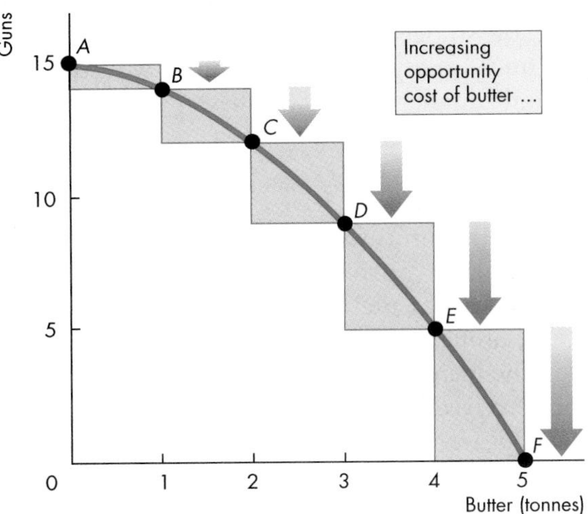

(a) *PPF* and opportunity cost

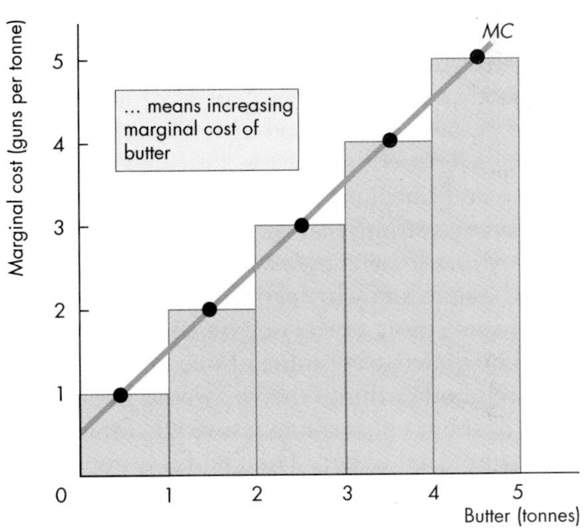

(b) Marginal cost

Opportunity cost is measured along the *PPF* in part (a). If the production of butter increases from zero to 1 tonne, the opportunity cost of a tonne of butter is 1 gun. If the production of butter increases from 1 to 2 tonnes, the opportunity cost of a tonne of butter is 2 guns. The opportunity cost of butter increases as the production of butter increases. Part (b) shows the marginal cost of a tonne of butter as the *MC* curve.

Preferences and Marginal Benefit

Look around your classroom and notice the wide variety of shirts, caps, pants, and shoes that you and your fellow students are wearing today. Why is there such a huge variety? Why don't you all wear the same styles and colours? The answer lies in what economists call preferences. **Preferences** are a description of a person's likes and dislikes.

You've seen that we have a concrete way of describing the limits to production: the *PPF*. We need a similarly concrete way of describing preferences. To describe preferences, economists use the concepts of marginal benefit and the marginal benefit curve. The **marginal benefit** of a good or service is the benefit received from consuming one more unit of it.

We measure the marginal benefit of a good or service by what a person is *willing to pay* for an additional unit of it. The idea is that you are willing to pay what the good is worth to you. It is worth its marginal benefit, and you're willing to pay an amount up to the marginal benefit. So willingness to pay measures marginal benefit.

The **marginal benefit curve** shows the relationship between marginal benefit of a good and the quantity of that good consumed. It is a general principle that the more we have of any good or service, the smaller is its marginal benefit and the less we are willing to pay for an additional unit of it. This tendency is so widespread and strong that we call it a principle—the *principle of decreasing marginal benefit.*

The basic reason why marginal benefit decreases as we consume more of any one item is that we like variety. The more we consume of one item, the more we can see of other things that we would like better.

Think about your willingness to pay for a coffee. You buy a bottomless cup. The first fill is important to you. You'd pay a lot more for it than what it costs. You can refill your cup as often as you wish. But you go back for only one more fill. You enjoy your second cup, but not as much as the first one. And you don't want a third cup, even though it is free.

In everyday life, we think of what we pay for something as the money that we give up—dollars. But you've learned to think about cost as opportunity cost, which is a cost in terms of other goods or services forgone, not a dollar cost. You can think about willingness to pay in the same terms. The price you are willing to pay for something is the quantity of other goods and services that you are willing to forgo. Let's illustrate preferences this way.

FIGURE 2.3 Preferences and the Marginal Benefit Curve

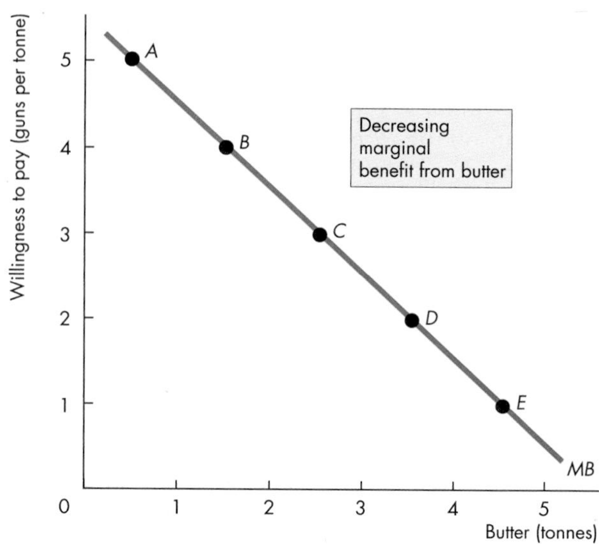

Possibility	Butter (tonnes)	Willingness to pay (guns per tonne)
A	0.5	5
B	1.5	4
C	2.5	3
D	3.5	2
E	4.5	1

The smaller the quantity of butter produced, the more guns people are willing to give up for an additional tonne of butter. If butter production is 0.5 tonnes, people are willing to pay 5 guns per tonne. But if butter production is 4.5 tonnes, people are willing to pay only 1 gun per tonne. Willingness to pay measures marginal benefit. And decreasing marginal benefit is a universal feature of people's preferences.

Figure 2.3 illustrates preferences in this way. In row *A*, butter production is 0.5 tonnes, and at that quantity, people are willing to pay 5 guns per tonne. As the quantity of butter produced increases, the amount that people are willing to pay for it falls. When butter production is 4.5 tonnes, people are willing to pay only 1 gun per tonne.

Let's now use the concepts of marginal cost and marginal benefit to describe the efficient quantity of butter to produce.

Efficient Use of Resources

When we cannot produce more of any one good without giving up some other good, we have achieved *production efficiency*, and we're producing at a point on the *PPF*. When we cannot produce more of any good without giving up some other good that we *value more highly*, we have achieved **allocative efficiency**, and we are producing at the point on the *PPF* that we prefer above all other points.

Suppose in Fig. 2.4, we produce 1.5 tonnes of butter. The marginal cost of butter is 2 guns per tonne, but the marginal benefit from butter is 4 guns per tonne. Because someone values an additional tonne of butter more highly than it costs to produce, resources get used more efficiently if butter production increases and gun production decreases.

Now suppose we produce 3.5 tonnes of butter. The marginal cost of butter is now 4 guns per tonne, but the marginal benefit from butter is only 2 guns per tonne. Because the additional butter costs more to produce than anyone thinks it is worth, we can get more value from our resources by moving some of them away from producing butter and into producing guns.

But suppose we produce 2.5 tonnes of butter. Marginal cost and marginal benefit are now equal at 3 guns per tonne. This allocation of resources between butter and guns is efficient. If more butter is produced, the forgone guns are worth more than the additional butter. If less butter is produced, the forgone butter is worth more than the additional guns.

REVIEW QUIZ

1. What is marginal cost and how is it measured?
2. What is marginal benefit and how is it measured?
3. How does the marginal benefit from a good change as the quantity produced of that good increases?
4. What is production efficiency and how does it relate to the production possibilities frontier?
5. What conditions must be satisfied if resources are used efficiently?

You now understand the limits to production and the conditions under which resources are used efficiently. Your next task is to study the expansion of production possibilities.

FIGURE 2.4 The Efficient Use of Resources

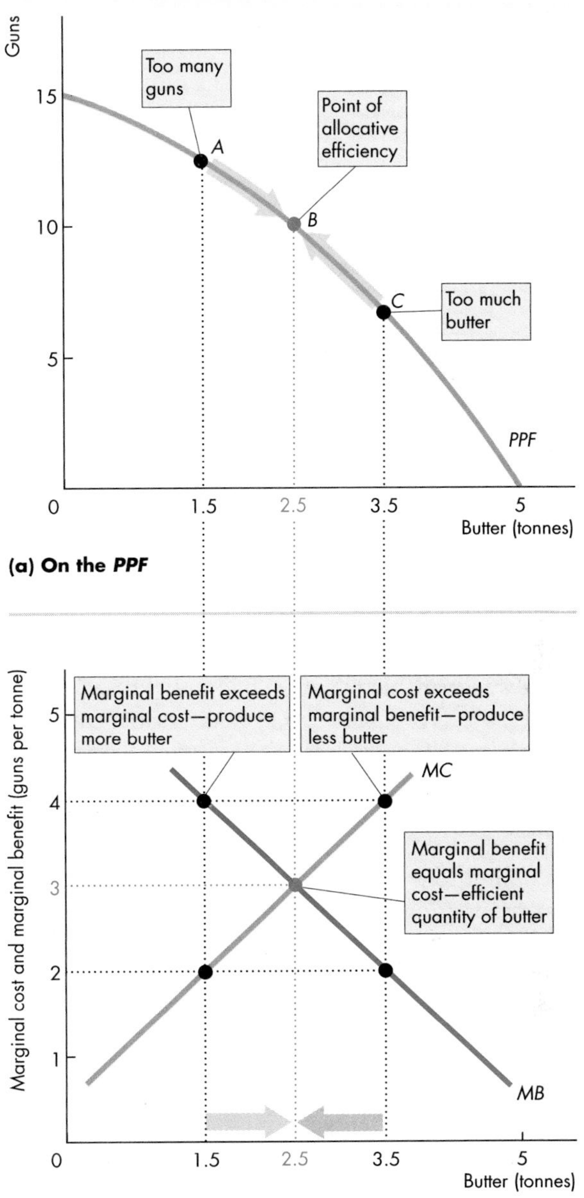

The greater the quantity of butter produced, the smaller is the marginal benefit (*MB*) from it—the fewer guns people are willing to give up to get an additional tonne of butter. But the greater the quantity of butter produced, the greater is the marginal cost (*MC*) of butter—the more guns people must give up to get an additional tonne of butter. When marginal benefit equals marginal cost, resources are being used efficiently.

Economic Growth

DURING THE PAST 30 YEARS, PRODUCTION PER person in Canada has doubled. Such an expansion of production is called **economic growth**. Economic growth increases our standard of living, but it doesn't overcome scarcity and avoid opportunity cost. To make our economy grow, we face a tradeoff—the standard of living tradeoff (p. 10)—and the faster we make production grow, the greater is the opportunity cost of economic growth.

The Cost of Economic Growth

Two key factors influence economic growth: technological change and capital accumulation. **Technological change** is the development of new goods and of better ways of producing goods and services. **Capital accumulation** is the growth of capital resources, which include *human capital*.

As a consequence of technological change and capital accumulation, we have an enormous quantity of cars that enable us to produce more transportation than was available when we had only horses and carriages; we have satellites that make global communications possible on a scale that is much larger than that produced by the earlier cable technology. But new technologies and new capital have an opportunity cost. To use resources in research and development and to produce new capital, we must decrease our production of consumption goods and services. Let's look at this opportunity cost.

Instead of studying the *PPF* of butter and guns, we'll hold the quantity of guns produced constant and examine the *PPF* for butter and butter-making machines. Figure 2.5 shows this *PPF* as the blue curve *ABC*. If we devote no resources to producing butter-making machines, we produce at point *A*. If we produce 3 tonnes of butter, we can produce 6 butter-making machines at point *B*. If we produce no butter, we can produce 10 machines at point *C*.

The amount by which our production possibilities expand depends on the resources we devote to technological change and capital accumulation. If we devote no resources to this activity (point *A*), our *PPF* remains at *ABC*—the blue curve in Fig. 2.5. If we cut the current production of butter and produce 6 machines (point *B*), then in the future, we'll have more capital and our *PPF* will rotate outward to the position shown by the red curve. The fewer resources we devote to producing butter and the more resources we devote to producing machines, the greater is the expansion of our production possibilities.

FIGURE 2.5 Economic Growth

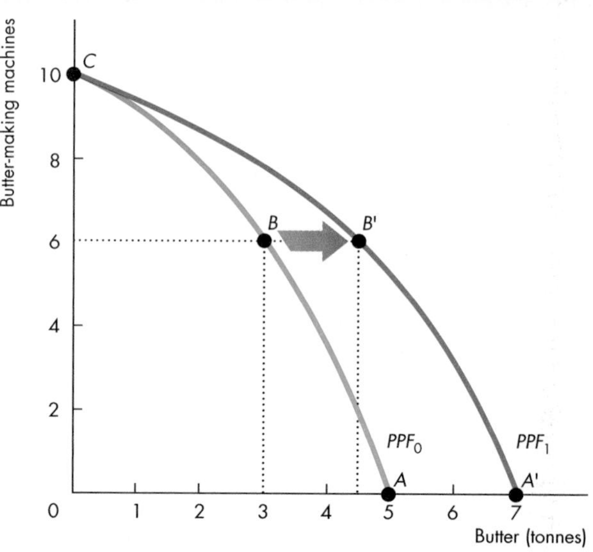

PPF$_0$ shows the limits to the production of butter and butter-making machines, with the production of all other goods and services remaining the same. If we devote no resources to producing butter-making machines and produce 5 tonnes of butter, we remain at point *A*. But if we decrease butter production to 3 tonnes and produce 6 machines, at point *B*, our production possibilities expand. After one period, the *PPF* rotates outward to *PPF*$_1$ and we can produce at point *B'*, a point outside the original *PPF*. We can rotate the *PPF* outward, but we cannot avoid opportunity cost. The opportunity cost of producing more butter in the future is less butter today.

Economic growth is not free. To make it happen, we devote resources to producing new machines and less to producing butter. In Fig. 2.5, we move from *A* to *B*. There is no free lunch. The opportunity cost of more butter in the future is less butter today. Also, economic growth is no magic formula for abolishing scarcity. On the new production possibilities frontier, we continue to face a tradeoff and opportunity cost.

The ideas about economic growth that we have explored in the setting of the dairy industry also apply to nations. Let's look at two examples.

Economic Growth in Canada and Hong Kong

If as a nation we devote all our resources to producing consumer goods and none to research and capital accumulation, production possibilities per person will be the same in the future as they are today. To expand our production possibilities in the future, we must devote fewer resources to producing consumption goods and some resources to accumulating capital and developing technologies so that we can produce more consumption goods in the future. The decrease in today's consumption is the opportunity cost of an increase in future consumption.

The experiences of Canada and Hong Kong make a striking example of the effects of our choices on the rate of economic growth. In 1960, the production possibilities per person in Canada were three times those in Hong Kong (see Fig. 2.6). Canada devoted one-fifth of its resources to accumulating capital and the other four-fifths to consumption. In 1960, Canada was at point *A* on its *PPF*. Hong Kong devoted one-third of its resources to accumulating capital and two-thirds to consumption. In 1960, Hong Kong was at point *A* on its *PPF*.

Since 1960, both countries have experienced economic growth, but growth in Hong Kong has been more rapid than that in Canada. Because Hong Kong devoted a bigger fraction of its resources to accumulating capital, its production possibilities have expanded more quickly.

By 2000, the production possibilities per person in Hong Kong and Canada were similar. If Hong Kong continues to devote more resources to accumulating capital than we do (at point *B* on its 2000 *PPF*), it will continue to grow more rapidly than Canada. But if Hong Kong increases consumption and decreases capital accumulation (moving to point *D* on its 2000 *PPF*), then its rate of economic growth will slow.

Canada is typical of the rich industrial countries, which include the United States, Western Europe, and Japan. Hong Kong is typical of the fast-growing Asian economies, which include Taiwan, Thailand, South Korea, and China. Growth in these countries slowed during the Asia Crisis of 1998 but quickly rebounded. Production possibilities expand in these countries by between 5 percent a year and almost 10 percent a year. If these high growth rates are maintained, these other Asian countries will eventually close the gap on Canada as Hong Kong has done.

FIGURE 2.6 Economic Growth in Canada and Hong Kong

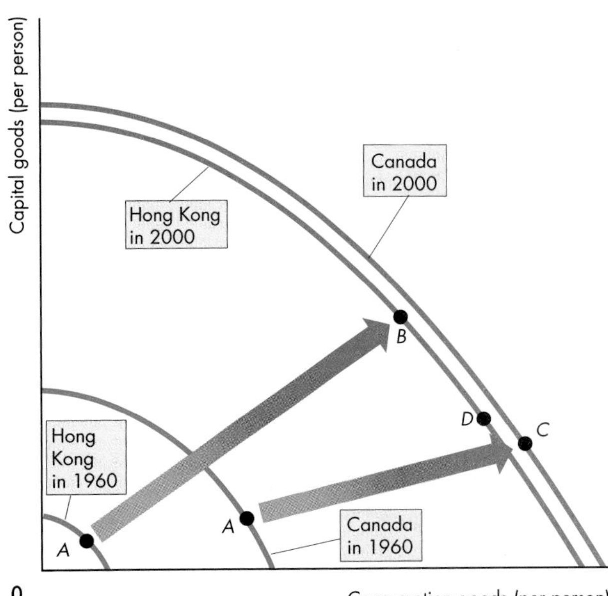

In 1960, the production possibilities per person in Canada were much larger than those in Hong Kong. But Hong Kong devoted more of its resources to accumulating capital than did Canada, so its production possibilities frontier has shifted outward more quickly than has that of Canada. In 2000, Hong Kong's production possibilities per person were similar to those in Canada.

REVIEW QUIZ

1. What are the two key factors that generate economic growth?
2. How does economic growth influence the production possibilities frontier?
3. What is the opportunity cost of economic growth?
4. Why has Hong Kong experienced faster economic growth than Canada has?

Next, we're going to study another way in which we expand our production possibilities—the amazing fact that *both* buyers and sellers gain from specialization and trade.

Gains from Trade

PEOPLE CAN PRODUCE FOR THEMSELVES ALL THE goods that they consume, or they can concentrate on producing one good (or perhaps a few goods) and then trade with others—exchange some of their own goods for those of others. Concentrating on the production of only one good or a few goods is called *specialization.* We are going to discover how people gain by specializing in the production of the good in which they have a *comparative advantage* and trading with each other.

Comparative Advantage

A person has a **comparative advantage** in an activity if that person can perform the activity at a lower opportunity cost than anyone else. Differences in opportunity costs arise from differences in individual abilities and from differences in the characteristics of other resources.

No one excels at everything. One person is an outstanding pitcher but a poor catcher; another person is a brilliant lawyer but a poor teacher. In almost all human endeavours, what one person does easily, someone else finds difficult. The same applies to land and capital. One plot of land is fertile but has no mineral deposits; another plot of land has outstanding views but is infertile. One machine has great precision but is difficult to operate; another is fast but often breaks down.

Although no one excels at everything, some people excel and can outperform others in many activities. But such a person does not have a *comparative* advantage in each of those activities. For example, Robertson Davies was a better actor than most people. But he was an even better writer. So his *comparative* advantage was in writing.

Because people's abilities and the quality of their resources differ, they have different opportunity costs of producing various goods. Such differences give rise to comparative advantage. Let's explore the idea of comparative advantage by looking at two CD factories: one operated by Tom and the other operated by Nancy.

Tom's Factory To simplify the story quite a lot, suppose that CDs have just two components: a disc and a plastic case. Tom has two production lines: one for discs and one for cases. Figure 2.7 shows Tom's production possibilities frontier for discs and cases. It tells us that if Tom uses all his resources to make discs, he can produce 4,000 discs an hour. The *PPF* in Fig. 2.7 also tells us that if Tom uses all his resources to make cases, he can produce 1,333 cases an hour. But to produce cases, Tom must decrease his production of discs. For each case produced, he must decrease his production of discs by 3. So

Tom's opportunity cost of producing 1 case is 3 discs.

Similarly, if Tom wants to increase his production of discs, he must decrease his production of cases. And for each 1,000 discs produced, he must decrease his production of cases by 333. So

Tom's opportunity cost of producing 1 disc is 0.333 of a case.

Tom's *PPF* is linear because his workers have similar skills so if he reallocates them from one activity to another, he faces a constant opportunity cost.

FIGURE 2.7 Production Possibilities in Tom's Factory

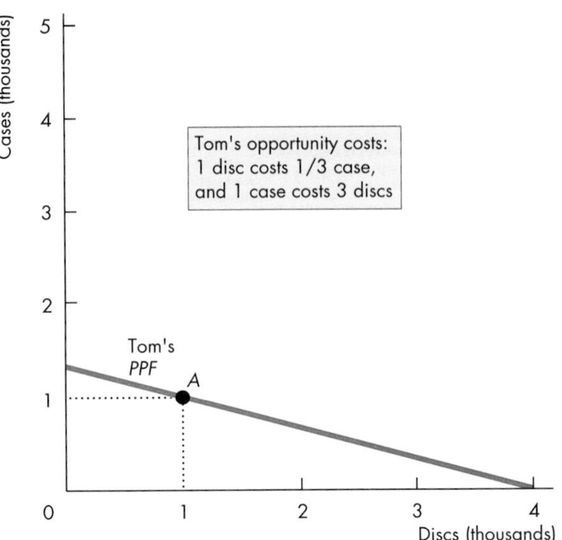

Tom can produce discs and cases along the production possibilities frontier *PPF*. For Tom, the opportunity cost of 1 disc is 1/3 of a case and the opportunity cost of 1 case is 3 discs. If Tom produces at point *A*, he can produce 1,000 cases and 1,000 discs an hour.

Nancy's Factory The other factory, operated by Nancy, also produces cases and discs. But Nancy's factory has machines that are custom made for case production, so they are more suitable for producing cases than discs. Also, Nancy's work force is more skilled in making cases.

These differences between the two factories mean that Nancy's production possibilities frontier—shown along with Tom's *PPF* in Fig. 2.8—is different from Tom's. If Nancy uses all her resources to make discs, she can produce 1,333 an hour. If she uses all her resources to make cases, she can produce 4,000 an hour. To produce discs, Nancy must decrease her production of cases. For each 1,000 additional discs produced, she must decrease her production of cases by 3,000. So

Nancy's opportunity cost of producing 1 disc is 3 cases.

Similarly, if Nancy wants to increase her production of cases, she must decrease her production of discs. For each 1,000 additional cases produced, she must decrease her production of discs by 333. So

Nancy's opportunity cost of producing 1 case is 0.333 of a disc.

Suppose that Tom and Nancy produce both discs and cases and that each produces 1,000 discs and 1,000 cases—1,000 CDs—an hour. That is, each produces at point *A* on his or her *PPF*. Total production is 2,000 CDs an hour.

In which of the two goods does Nancy have a comparative advantage? Recall that comparative advantage is a situation in which one person's opportunity cost of producing a good is lower than another person's opportunity cost of producing that same good. Nancy has a comparative advantage in producing cases. Nancy's opportunity cost of producing a case is 0.333 of a disc, whereas Tom's is 3 discs.

You can see Nancy's comparative advantage by looking at the production possibilities frontiers for Nancy and Tom in Fig. 2.8. Nancy's production possibilities frontier is steeper than Tom's. To produce one more case, Nancy must give up fewer discs than Tom has to. Hence Nancy's opportunity cost of producing a case is less than Tom's. Nancy has a comparative advantage in producing cases.

Tom's comparative advantage is in producing discs. His production possibilities frontier is less steep than Nancy's. This means that to produce one more disc, Tom must give up fewer cases than Nancy has to.

FIGURE 2.8 Comparative Advantage

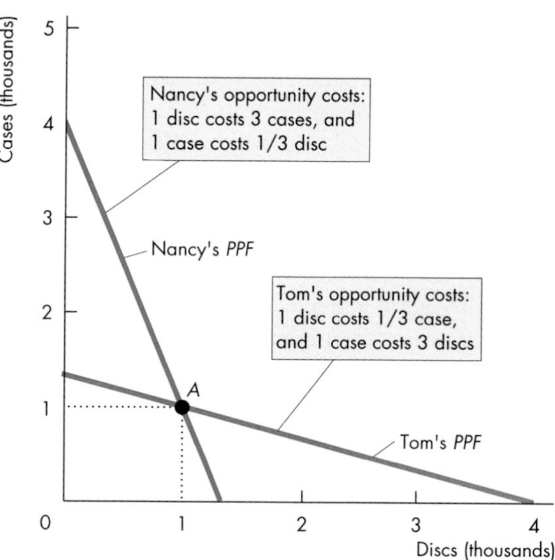

Along Tom's *PPF*, the opportunity cost of 1 disc is 1/3 of a case and the opportunity cost of 1 case is 3 discs. Along Nancy's *PPF*, the opportunity cost of 1 disc is 3 cases and the opportunity cost of 1 case is 1/3 of a disc. Like Tom, Nancy produces 1,000 cases and 1,000 discs an hour at point *A*. Nancy's opportunity cost of a case is less than Tom's, so Nancy has a comparative advantage in cases. Tom's opportunity cost of a disc is less than Nancy's, so Tom has a comparative advantage in discs.

Tom's opportunity cost of producing a disc is 0.333 of a case, which is less than Nancy's 3 cases per disc. So Tom has a comparative advantage in producing discs.

Because Nancy has a comparative advantage in producing cases and Tom has a comparative advantage in producing discs, they can both gain from specialization and exchange.

Achieving the Gains from Trade

If Tom, who has a comparative advantage in producing discs, puts all his resources into that activity, he can produce 4,000 discs an hour—point *B* on his *PPF*. If Nancy, who has a comparative advantage in producing cases, puts all her resources into that activity, she can produce 4,000 cases an hour—point *B'* on her *PPF*. By specializing, Tom and Nancy together can produce 4,000 cases and 4,000 discs an hour, double the total production they can achieve without specialization.

By specialization and exchange, Tom and Nancy can get *outside* their individual production possibilities frontiers. To achieve the gains from specialization, Tom and Nancy must trade with each other.

Figure 2.9 shows how Tom and Nancy gain from trade. They make the following deal: Tom agrees to increase his production of discs from 1,000 an hour to 4,000 an hour—a move along his *PPF* from point *A* to point *B* in Fig. 2.9(a). Nancy agrees to increase her production of cases from 1,000 an hour to 4,000 an hour—a move along her *PPF* from point *A* to point *B*' in Fig. 2.9(b).

They also agree to exchange cases and discs at a "price" of one case for one disc. So Tom sells discs to Nancy for one case per disc, and Nancy sells cases to Tom for one disc per case.

With this deal in place, Tom and Nancy exchange along the red "Trade line." They exchange 2,000 cases and 2,000 discs, and each moves to point *C* (in both parts of the figure). At point *C*, each has 2,000 discs and 2,000 cases, or 2,000 CDs. So each now produces 2,000 CDs an hour—double the previous output. This increase in production of 2,000 CDs an hour is the gain from specialization and trade.

Both parties to the trade share the gains. Nancy, who can produce discs at an opportunity cost of 3 cases per disc, can buy discs from Tom at a cost of 1 case per disc. Tom, who can produce cases at an opportunity cost of 3 discs per case, can buy cases from Nancy at a cost of 1 disc per case.

For Nancy, the cost of a disc falls from 3 cases to 1 case. So she gets her discs more cheaply than she can produce them herself. For Tom, the cost of a case falls from 3 discs to 1 disc. So he gets his cases more cheaply than he can produce them himself.

Because both Tom and Nancy obtain the items they buy from the other at a lower cost than that at which they can produce the items themselves, they both gain from specialization and trade.

The gains that Canada achieves from international trade are similar to those achieved by Tom and Nancy in this example. When Canadians buy T-shirts

FIGURE 2.9 The Gains from Trade

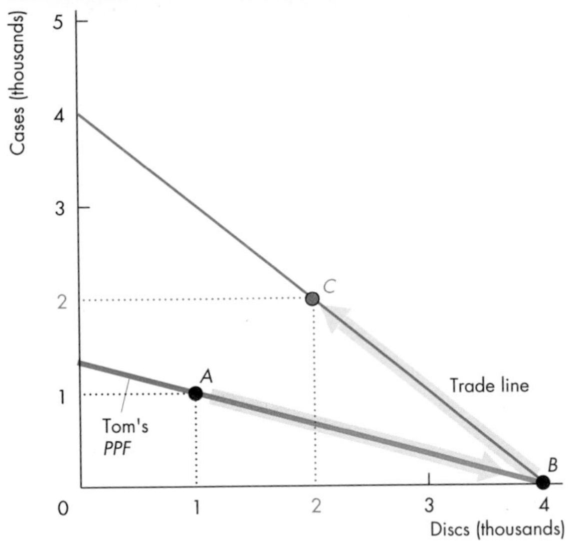

(a) Tom

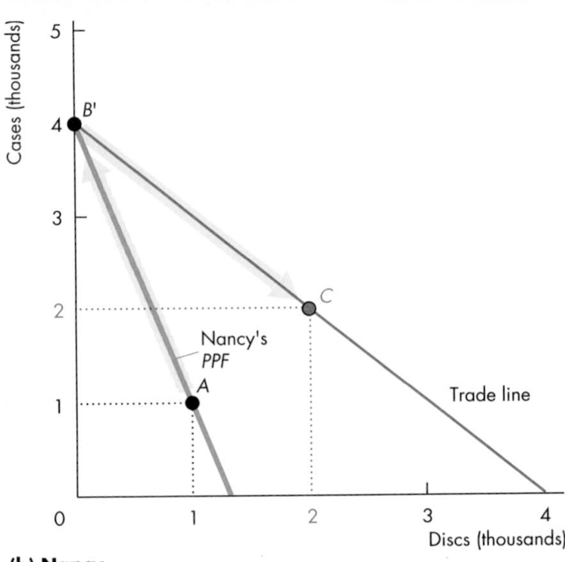

(b) Nancy

Tom and Nancy initially produce at point *A* on their respective *PPFs*. Tom has a comparative advantage in discs, and Nancy has a comparative advantage in cases. If Tom specializes in discs, he produces at point *B* on his *PPF*. If Nancy specializes in cases, she produces at point *B*' on her *PPF*. They exchange cases for discs along the red "Trade line." Nancy buys discs from Tom for less than her opportunity cost of producing them, and Tom buys cases from Nancy for less than his opportunity cost of producing them. Each goes to point *C*—a point outside his or her *PPF*—where each produces 2,000 CDs an hour. Tom and Nancy increase production with no change in resources.

from China and when China buys regional jets from Canada, both countries gain. We get our shirts at a lower cost than that at which we can produce them, and China gets its regional jets at a lower cost than that at which it can produce them.

Tom and Nancy are equally productive. Tom can produce the same quantities of discs as Nancy can produce cases. But this equal productivity is not the source of the gains from specialization and trade. The gains arise from comparative advantage and would be available even if one of the trading partners was much more productive than the other. To see that comparative advantage is the source of the gains, let's look at Tom and Nancy when Nancy is much more productive than Tom.

Absolute Advantage

A person has an **absolute advantage** if that person can produce more goods with a given amount of resources than another person can. Absolute advantage arises from differences in productivity. A person who has a better technology or more capital or is more skilled than another person has an absolute advantage. (Absolute advantage also applies to nations.)

The gains from trade arise from *comparative* advantage, so people can gain from trade in the presence of *absolute* advantage. To see how, suppose that Nancy invents and patents a new production process that makes her *four* times as productive as she was before in the production of both cases and discs. With her new technology, Nancy can produce 16,000 cases an hour (4 times the original 4,000) if she puts all her resources into making cases. Alternatively, she can produce 5,332 discs (4 times the original 1,333) if she puts all her resources into making discs. Nancy now has an absolute advantage.

But Nancy's *opportunity cost* of 1 disc is still 3 cases. And this opportunity cost is higher than Tom's. So Nancy can still get discs at a lower cost by exchanging cases for discs with Tom.

In this example, Nancy will no longer produce only cases. With no trade, she would produce 4,000 discs and 4,000 cases. With trade, she will increase her production of cases to 7,000 and decrease her production of discs to 3,000. Tom will produce 4,000 discs and no cases. Tom will provide Nancy with 2,000 discs in exchange for 2,000 cases. So Tom's CD production will increase from 1,000 to 2,000 as before. Nancy's CD production will increase from 4,000 to 5,000.

Both Tom and Nancy have gained 1,000 CDs by taking advantage of comparative advantage, the same gains as before.

The key point to recognize is that even though someone (or some nation) has an absolute advantage, this fact does not destroy comparative advantage.

Dynamic Comparative Advantage

At any given point in time, the resources and technologies available determine the comparative advantages that individuals and nations have. But just by repeatedly producing a particular good or service, people become more productive in that activity, a phenomenon called **learning-by-doing.** Learning-by-doing is the basis of *dynamic* comparative advantage. **Dynamic comparative advantage** is a comparative advantage that a person (or country) possesses as a result of having specialized in a particular activity and, as a result of learning-by-doing, having become the producer with the lowest opportunity cost.

Hong Kong and Singapore are examples of countries that have pursued dynamic comparative advantage vigorously. They have developed industries in which initially they did not have a comparative advantage but, through learning-by-doing, became low opportunity cost producers in those industries. A specific example is the decision to develop a genetic engineering industry in Singapore. Singapore probably did not have a comparative advantage in genetic engineering initially. But it might develop one as its scientists and production workers become more skilled in this activity.

REVIEW QUIZ

1. What gives a person a comparative advantage?
2. Is production still efficient when people specialize?
3. Why do people specialize and trade?
4. What are the gains from specialization and trade?
5. What is the source of the gains from trade?
6. Distinguish between comparative advantage and absolute advantage.
7. How does dynamic comparative advantage arise?

The Market Economy

INDIVIDUALS AND COUNTRIES GAIN BY specializing in the production of those goods and services in which they have a comparative advantage and then trading with each other. Adam Smith identified this source of economic wealth in his *Wealth of Nations,* published in 1776—see p. 54.

To enable billions of people who specialize in producing millions of different goods and services to reap these gains, trade must be organized. But trade need not be *planned* or *managed* by a central authority. In fact, when such an arrangement has been tried, as it was for 60 years in Russia, the result has been less than dazzling.

Trade is organized by using social institutions. Two key social institutions are

- Property rights
- Markets

Property Rights

Property rights are social arrangements that govern the ownership, use, and disposal of resources, goods, and services. *Real property* includes land and buildings—the things we call property in ordinary speech—and durable goods such as factories and equipment. *Financial property* includes stocks and bonds and money in the bank. *Intellectual property* is the intangible product of creative effort. This type of property includes books, music, computer programs, and inventions of all kinds and is protected by copyrights and patents.

If property rights are not enforced, the incentive to specialize and produce the goods in which each person has a comparative advantage is weakened, and some of the potential gains from specialization and trade are lost. If people can easily steal the production of others, then time, energy, and resources are devoted not to production but to protecting possessions.

Property rights evolved because they enable societies to reap the gains from trade. If we had not developed property rights, we would still be hunting and gathering like our Stone Age ancestors.

Even in countries where property rights are well established, such as Canada, protecting intellectual property is proving to be a challenge in the face of modern technologies that make it relatively easy to copy audio and video material, computer programs, and books.

Markets

In ordinary speech, the word *market* means a place where people buy and sell goods such as fish, meat, fruits, and vegetables. In economics, a *market* has a more general meaning. A **market** is any arrangement that enables buyers and sellers to get information and to do business with each other. An example is the market in which oil is bought and sold—the world oil market. The world oil market is not a place. It is the network of oil producers, users, wholesalers, and brokers who buy and sell oil. In the world oil market, decision makers do not meet physically. They make deals throughout the world by telephone, fax, and direct computer link.

Nancy and Tom can get together and do a deal without markets. But for billions of individuals to specialize and trade millions of goods and services, markets are essential. Like property rights, markets have evolved because they facilitate trade. Without organized markets, we would miss out on a substantial part of the potential gains from trade. Enterprising individuals, each one pursuing his or her own goals, have profited from making markets, standing ready to buy or sell the items in which they specialize.

Circular Flows in the Market Economy

Figure 2.10 identifies two types of markets: goods markets and factor markets. *Goods markets* are those in which goods and services are bought and sold. *Factor markets* are those in which factors of production are bought and sold.

Households decide how much of their labour, land, capital, and entrepreneurship to sell or rent in factor markets. Households receive incomes in the form of wages, rent, interest, and profit. Households also decide how to spend their incomes on goods and services produced by firms. Firms decide the quantities of factors of production to hire, how to use them to produce goods and services, what goods and services to produce, and in what quantities to produce them.

Figure 2.10 shows the flows that result from these decisions by households and firms. The red flows are the factors that go from households through factor markets to firms and the goods and services that go from firms through goods markets to households. The green flows in the opposite direction are the payments made in exchange for these items.

How do markets coordinate all these decisions?

FIGURE 2.10 Circular Flows in the Market Economy

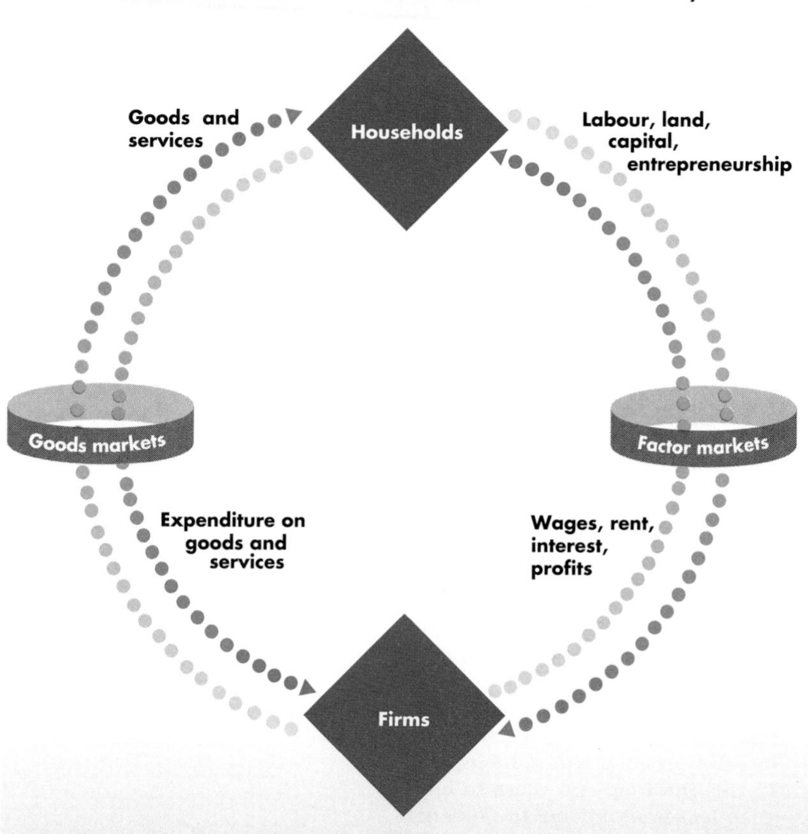

Households and firms make economic choices. Households choose the quantities of labour, land, capital, and entrepreneurship to sell or rent to firms in exchange for wages, rent, interest, and profit. Households also choose how to spend their incomes on the various types of goods and services available. Firms choose the quantities of factors of production to hire and the quantities of the various goods and services to produce. Goods markets and factor markets coordinate these choices of households and firms. Factors of production and goods flow clockwise (red), and money payments flow counterclockwise (green).

Coordinating Decisions

Markets coordinate individual decisions through price adjustments. To see how, think about your local market for hamburgers. Suppose that some people who want to buy hamburgers are not able to do so. To make the choices of buyers and sellers compatible, buyers must scale down their appetites or more hamburgers must be offered for sale (or both must happen). A rise in the price of a hamburger produces this outcome. A higher price encourages producers to offer more hamburgers for sale. It also encourages some people to change their lunch plans. Fewer people buy hamburgers, and more buy hot dogs. More hamburgers (and more hot dogs) are offered for sale.

Alternatively, suppose that more hamburgers are available than people want to buy. In this case, to make the choices of buyers and sellers compatible, more hamburgers must be bought or fewer hamburgers must be offered for sale (or both). A fall in the price of a hamburger achieves this outcome. A lower price encourages firms to produce a smaller quantity of hamburgers. It also encourages people to buy more hamburgers.

REVIEW QUIZ

1. Why are social arrangements such as markets and property rights necessary?
2. What are the main functions of markets?

You have now begun to see how economists approach economic questions. Scarcity, choice, and divergent opportunity costs explain why we specialize and trade and why property rights and markets have developed. You can see all around you the lessons you've learned in this chapter. *Reading Between the Lines* on pp. 48–49 gives an example. It explores the *PPF* of a student like you and the choices that students must make that influence their own economic growth—the growth of their incomes.

The Cost and Benefit of Education

THE GLOBE AND MAIL, AUGUST 28, 2002

Academics leap to defence of the MBA

They don't come with a guarantee, but business degrees offer students well-paying jobs with reputable companies, say many of Canada's top business schools, throwing cold water on a new study questioning the value of an MBA. ...

After surveying decades of research, Jeffrey Pfeffer and Christina Fong of Stanford's graduate school of business have concluded that, with the possible exception of the most elite programs, master's degrees in business administration teach little that would be of real use in the business world. ...

The salaries for these graduates are a telling story. At Queen's University's School of Business, for example, the average starting salary is $95,000. Before joining the program, the average salary of students is $59,750. And at the Rotman School of Management at the University of Toronto, students entering the two-year program have salaries in the $50,000 on average. But the average starting salary for this year's graduate was $89,000. ...

Brian Bemmels, associate dean for academic programs at the University of British Columbia's faculty of commerce, said the research article forces schools to evaluate their programs. He added that the article is based on a lot of opinion.

UBC's business school made a major change in 1995, restructuring its MBA program and reducing it to 15 months from two years to minimize losses of income to students. The average age of students in the program is 31.

Mr. Bemmels said the demand for an MBA degree speaks for itself. UBC had well over 700 applicants for 100 seats this year. Only 17 per cent of the incoming class has a business degree, he said. The rest are graduates of medicine, engineering and general arts.

"All these people wouldn't be doing it if they didn't think it was valuable," Mr. Bemmels said.

"I don't believe the notion that they have been fooled and tricked into something that's no good to them," he added.

Essence of the Story

- Jeffrey Pfeffer and Christina Fong of the Stanford Graduate School of Business say that MBA programs teach little of use in the business world.
- The salaries earned by MBA graduates tell a different story.
- The average starting salary for an MBA is $95,000, up from $59,750 before the MBA.
- At the Rotman School of Management at the University of Toronto, students entering the two-year program have an average salary of $50,000 and an average starting salary of $89,000 after graduation.
- Brian Bemmels said the UBC business school had over 700 applicants for 100 places and most were graduates of medicine, engineering, and general arts.

Economic Analysis

- Education increases human capital and expands production possibilities.

- The opportunity cost of a degree is forgone consumption. The payoff is an increase in lifetime production possibilities.

- Figure 1 shows the choices facing a high school graduate who can consume education goods and services and consumption goods and services on the blue *PPF*.

- Working full time, this person can consume at point *A* on the blue *PPF* in Fig. 1.

- By attending university, the student moves from point *A* to point *B* along her *PPF*, forgoes current consumption (the opportunity cost of education), and increases the use of educational goods and services.

- On graduating from university, earnings jump so production possibilities expand to the red *PPF* in Fig. 1.

- Figure 2 shows a university graduate's choices. The blue curve is the same *PPF* as the red *PPF* in Fig. 1.

- Working full time, this person earns enough to consume at point *C* on the blue *PPF* in Fig. 2.

- By pursuing an MBA, the student moves from point *C* to point *D* along her *PPF*, forgoes current consumption (the opportunity cost of an MBA), and increases the use of educational goods and services.

- With an MBA, a person's earnings jump again, so production possibilities expand to the red *PPF* in Fig. 2.

- For people who have the required ability, the benefits of post-secondary and post-graduate education exceed the costs.

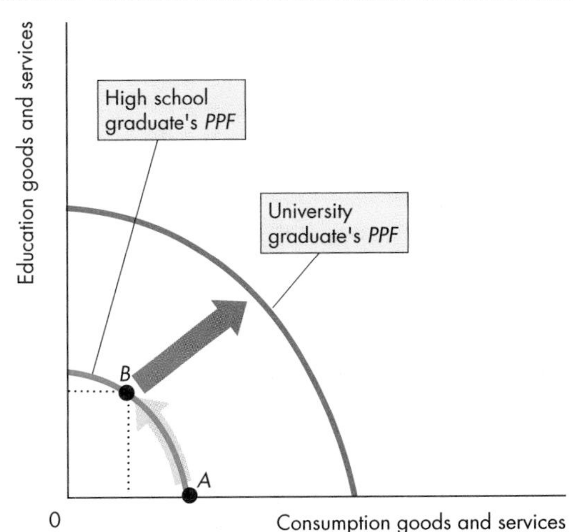

Figure 1 High school graduate's choices

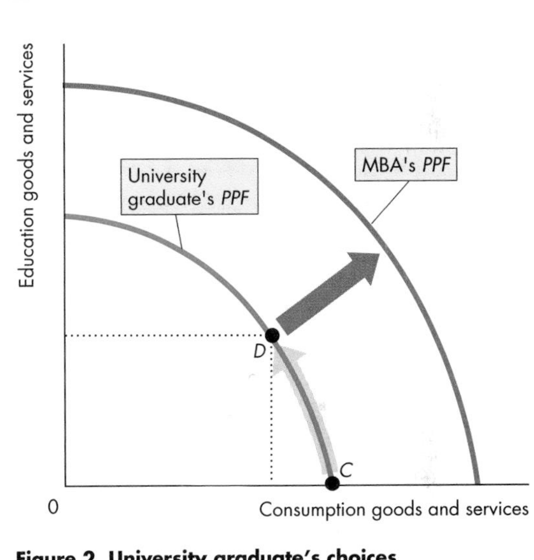

Figure 2 University graduate's choices

You're The Voter

- The Canada Millennium Scholarship Foundation, funded by the federal government, provides $4,000 a year to 900 young Canadians.

- Do you think the Canada Millennium Scholarship Foundation should be expanded so that more students can benefit from it?

- With the huge return from post-secondary and post-graduate education, why don't more people remain in school for longer?

- Would you vote for or against a tax increase to provide greater funding for the Canada Millennium Scholarship Foundation? Why?

SUMMARY

KEY POINTS

Production Possibilities and Opportunity Cost (pp. 34–36)

- The production possibilities frontier, *PPF*, is the boundary between production levels that are attainable and those that are not attainable when all the available resources are used to their limit.
- Production efficiency occurs at points on the *PPF*.
- Along the *PPF*, the opportunity cost of producing more of one good is the amount of the other good that must be given up.
- The opportunity cost of all goods increases as the production of the good increases.

Using Resources Efficiently (pp. 37–39)

- The marginal cost of a good is the opportunity cost of producing one more unit.
- The marginal benefit from a good is the maximum amount of another good that a person is willing to forgo to obtain more of the first good.
- The marginal benefit of a good decreases as the amount available increases.
- Resources are used efficiently when the marginal cost of each good is equal to its marginal benefit.

Economic Growth (pp. 40–41)

- Economic growth, which is the expansion of production possibilities, results from capital accumulation and technological change.
- The opportunity cost of economic growth is forgone current consumption.

Gains from Trade (pp. 42–45)

- A person has a comparative advantage in producing a good if that person can produce the good at a lower opportunity cost than everyone else.
- People gain by specializing in the activity in which they have a comparative advantage and trading with others.
- Dynamic comparative advantage arises from learning-by-doing.

The Market Economy (pp. 46–47)

- Property rights and markets enable people to gain from specialization and trade.
- Markets coordinate decisions and help to allocate resources to *higher* valued uses.

KEY FIGURES

Figure 2.1 Production Possibilities Frontier, 34
Figure 2.4 The Efficient Use of Resources, 39
Figure 2.9 The Gains from Trade, 44
Figure 2.10 Circular Flows in the Market Economy, 47

KEY TERMS

Absolute advantage, 45
Allocative efficiency, 39
Capital accumulation, 40
Comparative advantage, 42
Dynamic comparative advantage, 45
Economic growth, 40
Learning-by-doing, 45
Marginal benefit, 38
Marginal benefit curve, 38
Marginal cost, 37
Market, 46
Preferences, 38
Production efficiency, 35
Production possibilities frontier, 34
Property rights, 46
Technological change, 40

PROBLEMS

*1. Use the figure to calculate Wendell's opportunity cost of one hour of tennis when he increases the time he plays tennis from
a. 4 to 6 hours a week.
b. 6 to 8 hours a week.

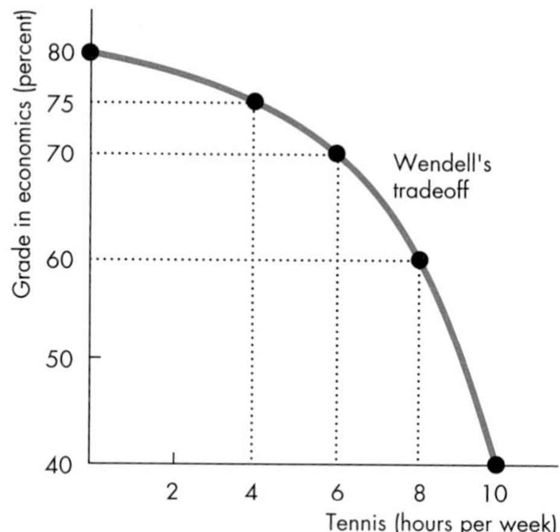

2. Use the figure to calculate Tina's opportunity cost of a day of skiing when she increases her time spent skiing from
a. 2 to 4 days a month.
b. 4 to 6 days a month.

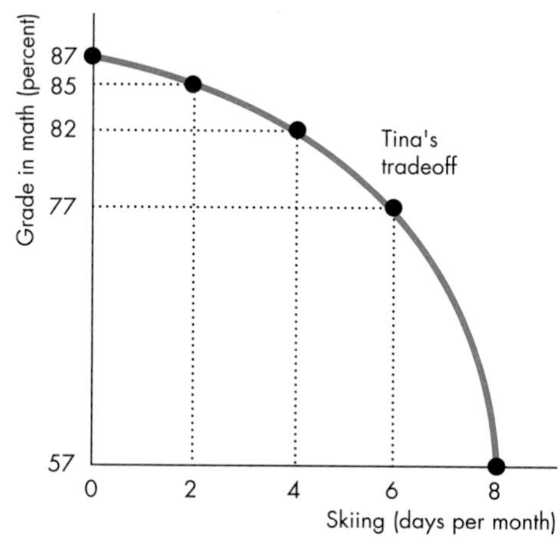

*3. In problem 1, describe the relationship between the time Wendell spends playing tennis and the opportunity cost of an hour of tennis.

4. In problem 2, describe the relationship between the time Tina spends skiing and the opportunity cost of a day of skiing.

*5. Wendell, in problem 1, has the following marginal benefit curve:

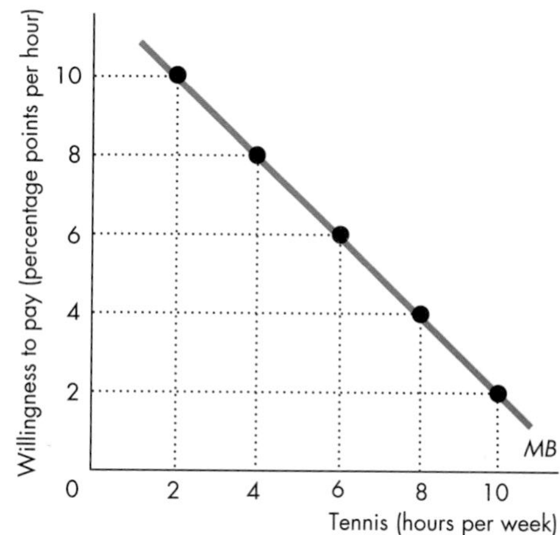

a. If Wendell is efficient, what is his grade?
b. Why would Wendell be worse off getting a higher grade?

6. Tina, in problem 2, has the following marginal benefit curve:

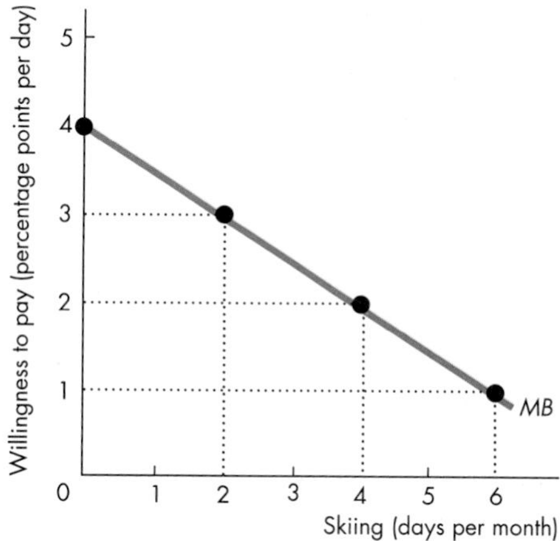

a. If Tina is efficient, how much does she ski?
b. Why would Tina be worse off spending more days a month skiing?

*7. Sunland's production possibilities are

Food (kilograms per month)		Sunscreen (litres per month)
300	and	0
200	and	50
100	and	100
0	and	150

a. Draw a graph of Sunland's production possibilities frontier.

b. What are Sunland's opportunity costs of producing food and sunscreen at each output?

8. Jane's Island's production possibilities are

Corn (kilograms per month)		Cloth (metres per month)
6	and	0
4	and	2
2	and	4
0	and	6

a. Draw a graph of the *PPF* on Jane's Island.
b. What are Jane's opportunity costs of producing corn and cloth at each output in the table?

*9. In problem 7, to get a litre of sunscreen, the people of Sunland are willing to give up: 5 kilograms of food if they have 25 litres of sunscreen; 2 kilograms of food if they have 75 litres of sunscreen; and 1 kilogram of food if they have 125 litres of sunscreen.
a. Draw a graph of Sunland's marginal benefit from sunscreen.
b. What is the efficient quantity of sunscreen?

10. In problem 8, to get a metre of cloth, Jane is willing to give up: 1.5 kilograms of corn if she has 2 metres of cloth; 1.0 kilogram of corn if she has 4 metres of cloth; and 0.5 kilograms of corn if she has 6 metres of cloth.
a. Draw a graph of Jane's marginal benefit from cloth.
b. What is Jane's efficient quantity of cloth?

*11. Busyland's production possibilities are

Food (kilograms per month)		Sunscreen (litres per month)
150	and	0
100	and	100
50	and	200
0	and	300

Calculate Busyland's opportunity costs of food and sunscreen at each output in the table.

12. Joe's Island's production possibilities are

Corn (kilograms per month)		Cloth (metres per month)
12	and	0
8	and	1
4	and	2
0	and	3

What are Joe's opportunity costs of producing corn and cloth at each output in the table?

*13. In problems 7 and 11, Sunland and Busyland each produce and consume 100 kilograms of food and 100 litres of sunscreen per month, and they do not trade. Now the countries begin to trade with each other.
a. What good does Sunland sell to Busyland, and what good does it buy from Busyland?
b. If Sunland and Busyland divide the total output of food and sunscreen equally, what are the gains from trade?

14. In problems 8 and 12, Jane's Island and Joe's Island each produce and consume 4 kilograms of corn and 2 metres of cloth and they do not trade. Now the islands begin to trade.
a. What good does Jane sell to Joe and what good does Jane buy from Joe?
b. If Jane and Joe divide the total output of corn and cloth equally, what are the gains from trade?

CRITICAL THINKING

1. After you have studied *Reading Between the Lines* on pp. 48–49, answer the following questions:
a. At what point on the blue *PPF* in Fig. 1 on p. 49 is the combination of education goods and services and consumption goods and services efficient? Explain your answer.
b. Students are facing rising tuition. How does higher tuition change the opportunity cost of education and how does it change the *PPFs* in Fig. 1 and Fig. 2?
c. Who receives the benefits from education? Is the marginal cost of education equal to the marginal benefit of education? Is resource use in the market for education efficient?

WEB EXERCISES

1. Use the links on the Parkin–Bade Web site and obtain data on the tuition and other costs of enrolling in the MBA program of a school that interests you. If an MBA graduate can earn as much as the amounts reported in the news article in *Reading Between the Lines* on pp. 48–49, does the marginal benefit of an MBA exceed its marginal cost? Why doesn't everyone get an MBA?

UNDERSTANDING THE SCOPE OF ECONOMICS

PART 1

Your Economic Revolution

You are making progress in your study of economics. You've already encountered the big questions and big ideas of economics. And you've learned about the key insight of Adam Smith, the founder of economics: specialization and exchange create economic wealth. ◆ You are studying economics at a time that future historians will call the *Information Revolution.* We reserve the word "Revolution" for big events that influence all future generations. ◆ During the *Agricultural Revolution,* which occurred 10,000 years ago, people learned to domesticate animals and plant crops. They stopped roaming in search of food and settled in villages and eventually towns and cities, where they developed markets in which to exchange their products. ◆ During the *Industrial Revolution,* which began 240 years ago, people used science to create new technologies. This revolution brought extraordinary wealth for some but created conditions in which others were left behind. It brought social and political tensions that we still face today. ◆ During today's *Information Revolution,* people who embraced the new technologies prospered on an unimagined scale. But the incomes and living standards of the less educated are falling behind, and social and political tensions are increasing. Today's revolution has a global dimension. Some of the winners live in previously poor countries in Asia, and some of the losers live here in North America. ◆ So you are studying economics at an interesting time. Whatever *your* motivation is for studying economics, *our* objective is to help you do well in your course, to enjoy it, and to develop a deeper understanding of the economic world around you. ◆ There are three reasons why we hope that we both succeed: First, a decent understanding of economics will help you to become a full participant in the Information Revolution. Second, an understanding of economics will help you play a more effective role as a citizen and voter and enable you to add your voice to those who are looking for solutions to our social and political problems. Third, you will enjoy the sheer fun of *understanding* the forces at play and how they are shaping our world. ◆ If you are finding economics interesting, think seriously about majoring in the subject. A degree in economics gives the best training available in problem solving, offers lots of opportunities to develop conceptual skills, and opens doors to a wide range of graduate courses, including the MBA, and to a wide range of jobs. You can read more about the benefits of an economics degree in the essay by Robert Whaples and Harvey King in the *Study Guide.* ◆ Economics was born during the Industrial Revolution. We'll look at its birth and meet its founder, Adam Smith. Then we'll talk about the progress that economists have made and some of the outstanding policy problems of today with one of today's most distinguished economists, Lawrence H. Summers, President of Harvard University.

PROBING THE IDEAS

The Sources of Economic Wealth

THE FATHER OF ECONOMICS

"It is not from the benevolence of the butcher, the brewer, or the baker that we expect our dinner, but from their regard to their own interests."

ADAM SMITH
The Wealth of Nations

ADAM SMITH *was a giant of a scholar who contributed to ethics and jurisprudence as well as economics. Born in 1723 in Kirkcaldy, a small fishing town near Edinburgh, Scotland, Smith was the only child of the town's customs officer (who died before Adam was born).*

His first academic appointment, at age 28, was as Professor of Logic at the University of Glasgow. He subsequently became tutor to a wealthy Scottish duke, whom he accompanied on a two-year grand European tour, following which he received a pension of £300 a year—ten times the average income at that time.

With the financial security of his pension, Smith devoted ten years to writing An Inquiry into the Nature and Causes of The Wealth of Nations, *which was published in 1776. Many people had written on economic issues before Adam Smith, but he made economics a science. Smith's account was so broad and authoritative that no subsequent writer on economics could advance ideas without tracing their connections to those of Adam Smith.*

THE ISSUES

Why are some nations wealthy while others are poor? This question lies at the heart of economics. And it leads directly to a second question: What can poor nations do to become wealthy?

Adam Smith, who is regarded by many scholars as the founder of economics, attempted to answer these questions in his book *The Wealth of Nations*, published in 1776. Smith was pondering these questions at the height of the Industrial Revolution. During these years, new technologies were invented and applied to the manufacture of cotton and wool cloth, iron, transportation, and agriculture.

Smith wanted to understand the sources of economic wealth, and he brought his acute powers of observation and abstraction to bear on the question. His answer:

- The division of labour
- Free markets

The division of labour—breaking tasks down into simple tasks and becoming skilled in those tasks—is the source of "the greatest improvement in the productive powers of labour," said Smith. The division of labour became even more productive when it was applied to creating new technologies. Scientists and engineers, trained in extremely narrow fields, became specialists at inventing. Their powerful skills accelerated the advance of technology, so by the 1820s, machines could make consumer goods faster and more accurately than any craftsman could. And by the 1850s, machines could make other machines that labour alone could never have made.

But, said Smith, the fruits of the division of labour are limited by the extent of the market. To make the market as large as possible, there must be no impediments to free trade both within a country and among countries. Smith argued that when each person makes the best possible economic choice, that choice leads as if by "an invisible hand" to the best outcome for society as a whole. The butcher, the brewer, and the baker each pursue their own interests but, in doing so, also serve the interests of everyone else.

Then

Adam Smith speculated that one person, working hard, using the hand tools available in the 1770s, might possibly make 20 pins a day. Yet, he observed, by using those same hand tools but breaking the process into a number of individually small operations in which people specialize—by the **division of labour**—ten people could make a staggering 48,000 pins a day. One draws out the wire, another straightens it, a third cuts it, a fourth points it, a fifth grinds it. Three specialists make the head, and a fourth attaches it. Finally, the pin is polished and packaged. But a large market is needed to support the division of labour: One factory employing ten workers would need to sell more that 15 million pins a year to stay in business.

Now

If Adam Smith were here today, the computer chip would fascinate him. He would see it as an extraordinary example of the productivity of the division of labour and of the use of machines to make machines that make other machines. From a design of a chip's intricate circuits, cameras transfer an image to glass plates that work like stencils. Workers prepare silicon wafers on which the circuits are printed. Some slice the wafers, others polish them, others bake them, and yet others coat them with a light-sensitive chemical. Machines transfer a copy of the circuit onto the wafer. Chemicals then etch the design onto the wafer. Further processes deposit atom-sized transistors and aluminum connectors. Finally, a laser separates the hundreds of chips on the wafers. Every stage in the process of creating a computer chip uses other computer chips. And like the pin of the 1770s, the computer chip of today benefits from the large market—a global market—to buy chips in the huge quantities in which they are produced efficiently.

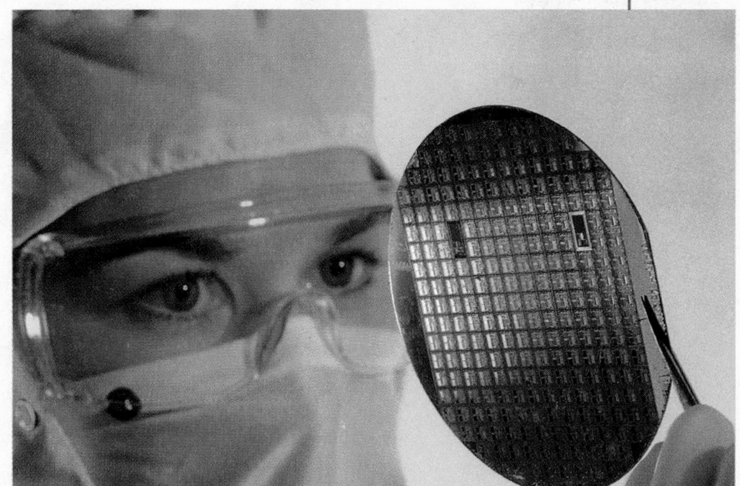

Many economists have worked on the big themes that Adam Smith began. One of these is Lawrence H. Summers, President of Harvard University and distinguished economist.

TALKING WITH

LAWRENCE H. SUMMERS

is President of Harvard University. Born in 1954 in New Haven, Connecticut, into a family of distinguished economists, he was an undergraduate at the Massachusetts Institute of Technology and a graduate student at Harvard University. While still in his 20s, he became one of the youngest tenured economics professors at Harvard University. In Washington, he has held a succession of public service jobs at the World Bank and in the U.S. government, culminating in 1999 with his appointment as Secretary of the Treasury—the chief financial officer of the United States and the president's highest-ranking adviser.

Dr. Summers's research has covered an enormous range of macroeconomic and public policy issues that include capital taxation, unemployment, global financial crises, the transition to a market economy in Eastern Europe, and the problem of speeding progress in the developing countries.

Michael Parkin and Robin Bade talked with Lawrence Summers about his career and the progress that economists have made since the pioneering days of Adam Smith.

Lawrence H. Summers

How does Adam Smith's assessment of the "nature and causes of the wealth of nations" look today in light of the lessons that economists have learned over the past two centuries?

Adam Smith is looking very good today. I think one of the most important insights of the social sciences of the last several centuries is Smith's idea that good things can come from the invisible hand—from decentralization rather than from central planning and direction. But Smith is also prescient in recognizing the various qualifications to the argument for the invisible hand, whether involving fairness, externalities, or monopoly.

What do we know today that Adam Smith didn't know?

We know today much more than Smith did about economic fluctuations and about the role of money—about what we today call macroeconomics. We know more today about economic situations that involve bargaining, whether between two individuals or between small numbers of firms in an industry, or between a buyer and a seller. We know much more today about markets without perfect information. I know how good my used car is when I sell it—you don't when you buy it. I know whether I'm sick when I buy medical insurance, but you the insurance company have to try to figure it out. The role of information in markets, which turns out to be quite profound, is something we understand much better today. And we also understand much better today the role of politics and governments in shaping the economy, which is far larger than it was in Smith's day.

Coincidentally, a few weeks before we're holding this conversation, a new nation was born—East Timor. What advice can economists offer a new and extremely poor nation as it takes its first steps?

Much of economic success involves strong rights to property. Has anyone ever washed a rented car or taken as good care of their hotel room as their home? When people own their farmlands, they're much more likely to farm them sustainably. When businesses own their machinery, they're much more likely to take care of it. When individuals own what they produce, they're much more likely to work hard.

Strong property rights and the framework of laws that support them are profoundly important to the market-based exchanges that are essential to economic success. So also is stable money that can be a basis for exchange. So also is an educated and capable population. But if there is a single lesson that is important for a starting economy, it is that strong property rights can motivate individuals.

One lesson that we've learned from your work at the World Bank is that the return to educating girls in developing countries is very high. What did you discover in that work?

Primary education, and especially for girls, may be the highest return investment available in the developing world. Those who read produce more and therefore earn more. Girls who are educated grow up to be better mothers who have smaller, happier, healthier families. Women who are educated are empowered with greater career options. They are less likely to fall into prostitution, and that reduces the spread of AIDS. Women who are educated are much more likely to take care of the environment. So it is in many respects that primary education, and especially that of girls, generates very large returns.

Are there any other activities that yield comparable returns for developing countries?

Maybe some investments in health care that generate very large returns—it's a difficult evaluation to make. The really crucial lesson is that a country's most precious assets are its people, and investments in people are likely to be the most important investments of all.

> ***"The really crucial lesson is that a country's most precious assets are its people, and investments in people are likely to be the most important investments of all."***

Some of your earliest research was on taxing the income from capital. Why isn't the income from capital just like the income from labour?

Think about it this way: two individuals both earn a hundred dollars. One spends it all this year; the other saves half of it and earns 10 percent interest next year. Who should pay more total taxes? Plausibly, for fairness, both should pay the same tax. A tax on income will lead to the same taxes in the first year for the two individuals; and higher taxes in the second year for the individual who saved.

In effect, taxes on capital income are taxes on future consumption, and it is far from clear why a society should want to tax future consumption more highly than present consumption.

On the other hand, very large fortunes often show up as capital income, and so designing a workable and fair tax system that doesn't tax investment income is something that is very difficult to do.

Would you say that we have not yet managed to figure this one out?

We'll all be working on finding the best tax systems for a long time to come. And it may mean that the income tax is, as Churchill said of democracy, terrible but the best alternative.

The United States has a large and persistent current account deficit, a low personal saving rate, and a projected deficit in the Social Security and Medicare trust funds. Are you concerned about these problems?

Herb Stein, who was a leading American policy economist, once said that the unsustainable cannot be sustained and must surely end!

This is a concern, given that U.S. national debt to foreigners is rising faster than U.S. income. And it's a concern in terms of the financing of Social Security and Medicare as our population ages. In a way, the solution to both these problems is more American saving, because that will put us in a stronger position as our population ages, and will allow us to have investments in the United States without incurring debts to foreigners.

Probably the most potent way of increasing a country's national savings is to improve the position of its budget. Whether to increase taxes or cut expenditures is a judgment for the congress to debate. My guess is that some combination would be appropriate. There are aspects of expenditures that are going to be hard to control. On the other hand, there are other aspects in terms of transfer payments and in terms of various subsidies where economies probably are possible. And one virtue of a strong fiscal position is that it reduces interest expense down the road.

Did you always want to be an economist? How did you choose economics?

I thought I would be a mathematician or a physicist, but found myself very interested in questions of public policy. I was very involved in debate when I was in college. So I found myself wanting very much to combine an interest in public policy issues with an analytical approach, and economics gave me a way to do that. I also found that I had some aptitude, relative to my aptitude for pure mathematics or physics, so I gravitated to economics.

What led a brilliant academic economist to Washington? What did you want to achieve?

I hoped to put to use some of what I had learned in my studies in a direct way and to enhance my understanding of the way actual economies work by seeing how the policy process operated. I had a great time in Washington and feel that my economics training made a huge difference in everything I did. Whether it was thinking about how to respond to the Mexican and Asian financial crises or working on financial deregulation. Whether it was choosing optimal investments for the Customs Department in protecting our borders or designing tax incentives to promote saving. Whether it was supporting the protection of the Social Security trust fund or thinking about enforcement policies against corporate tax shelters. Principles of economics—in terms of maximizing benefits relative to costs, in terms of always thinking of the margin, in terms of always recognizing the opportunity cost of choices taken, in terms of always needing to see things add up—was quite valuable.

And what insights does economics bring to the task of running a major university?

I came to Harvard because I thought after my time in government the two most important resources that were going to shape the economies of the future were leaders and new ideas, and those are the two things that a university produces.

Successful leadership in a university is all about what economists think about all the time—incentives—whether it's for professors to do a good job teaching, attracting the best scholars in a particular area, or motivating concern and research about the most important problems.

Leadership and management for the university are very much about economics because they're very much about incentives. Some of them are pecuniary and involve money, but other incentives come from people's feelings of being appreciated; they come from the teams in which people have an opportunity to work; they come from the way in which the university is organized. If working at the treasury was heavily about applied macroeconomics, leadership in the university is heavily about applied microeconomics.

What is your advice to a student who is just setting out to become an economist? What other subjects work well with economics?

The best advice to students is, don't be a commodity that's available in a perfectly competitive market. Stand out by developing your own distinctive expertise in something you care deeply about. It matters much less what it is and much more that it be yours and it not be a hundred other people's.

I think there is enormous potential in almost every area of economics, but I think that the people who will contribute the most to economics over the next quarter century will be those who have some keen understanding of the context in which economics is playing out—the international context, the technological context, and the political context. So my hope would be that those interested in economics would understand that economics is very different from physics in that it is tracking a changing reality and that in order to do the best economics in a given period, you have to be able to track that changing reality, and that means understanding international, technological, and political contexts.

PART 2 HOW MARKETS WORK

DEMAND AND SUPPLY

CHAPTER 3

Slide, Rocket, and Roller Coaster

Slide, rocket, and roller coaster—Canada's Wonderland rides? No, they are commonly used descriptions of price changes. ◆ The price of a personal computer took a dramatic slide from around $3,000 in 2000 to around $700 in 2001. What caused this price slide? We'll answer this question in *Reading Between the Lines*. ◆ Occasionally, a price will rocket. But a price rocket, like a satellite-launching rocket, has a limited life. It eventually runs out of fuel. One spectacular price rocket occurred when the price of coffee shot skyward from $1.32 a kilogram in 1993 to $4.95 a kilogram in 1994. Why did the price of coffee rise so spectacularly? ◆ Over longer periods, the price of coffee, along with the prices of bananas and other agricultural commodities, rises and falls like a roller coaster ride. ◆ Economics is about the choices people make to cope with scarcity. These choices are guided by costs and benefits and are coordinated through markets. ◆ Demand and supply is the tool that explains how markets work. It is the main tool of economics. It is used to study the price of a CD, wage rates and jobs, rents and housing, pollution, crime, consumer protection, education, welfare, the value of money, and interest rates.

Your careful study of this topic will bring big rewards both in your further study of economics and in your everyday life. When you have completed your study of demand and supply, you will be able to explain how prices are determined and make predictions about price slides, rockets, and roller coasters. Once you understand demand and supply, you will view the world through new eyes.

After studying this chapter, you will be able to

- **Describe a market and explain the link between price and opportunity cost**
- **Explain the influences on demand**
- **Explain the influences on supply**
- **Explain how demand and supply determine prices and quantities bought and sold**
- **Use demand and supply to make predictions about changes in prices and quantities**

Markets and Prices

WHEN YOU NEED A NEW PAIR OF RUNNING shoes, want a bagel and a latte, plan to upgrade your stereo system, or fly to Florida for the winter break, you must find someone who is selling these items or offering these services. You will find them in a *market.* You learned in Chapter 2 (p. 46) that a market is any arrangement that enables buyers and sellers to get information and to do business with each other.

A market has two sides: buyers and sellers. There are markets for *goods* such as apples and hiking boots, for *services* such as haircuts and tennis lessons, for *factors of production* such as computer programmers and earthmovers, and for other manufactured *inputs* such as memory chips and auto parts. There are also markets for money such as Japanese yen and for financial securities such as Yahoo! stock. Only our imagination limits what can be traded in markets.

Some markets are physical places where buyers and sellers meet and where an auctioneer or a broker helps to determine the prices. Examples of this type of market are the New York Stock Exchange and the wholesale fish, meat, and produce markets.

Some markets are groups of people spread around the world who never meet and know little about each other but are connected through the Internet or by telephone and fax. Examples of this type of market are the e-commerce markets and currency markets.

But most markets are unorganized collections of buyers and sellers. You do most of your trading in this type of market. An example is the market for running shoes. The buyers in this vast international market are the millions of joggers (or those who want to make a fashion statement) who are looking for a new pair of shoes. The sellers are the tens of thousands of retail sports equipment and footwear stores. Each buyer can visit several different stores, and each seller knows that the buyer has a choice of stores.

Markets vary in the intensity of competition that buyers and sellers face. In this chapter, we're going to study a **competitive market**—a market that has many buyers and many sellers, so that no single buyer or seller can influence the price.

Producers offer items for sale only if the price is high enough to cover their opportunity cost. And consumers respond to changing opportunity cost by seeking cheaper alternatives to expensive items.

We are going to study the way people respond to *prices* and the forces that determine prices. But to pursue these tasks, we need to understand the relationship between a price and an opportunity cost.

In everyday life, the *price* of an object is the number of dollars that must be given up in exchange for it. Economists refer to this price as the *money price.*

The *opportunity cost* of an action is the highest-valued alternative forgone. If, when you buy a coffee, the highest-valued thing you forgo is some gum, then the opportunity cost of the coffee is the *quantity* of gum forgone. We can calculate the quantity of gum forgone from the money prices of coffee and gum.

If the money price of coffee is $1 a cup and the money price of gum is 50¢ a pack, then the opportunity cost of one cup of coffee is two packs of gum. To calculate this opportunity cost, we divide the price of a cup of coffee by the price of a pack of gum and find the *ratio* of one price to the other. The ratio of one price to another is called a **relative price,** and a *relative price is an opportunity cost.*

We can express the relative price of coffee in terms of gum or any other good. The normal way of expressing a relative price is in terms of a "basket" of all goods and services. To calculate this relative price, we divide the money price of a good by the money price of a "basket" of all goods (called a *price index*). The resulting relative price tells us the opportunity cost of an item in terms of how much of the "basket" we must give up to buy it.

The theory of demand and supply that we are about to study determines *relative prices,* and the word "price" means *relative* price. When we predict that a price will fall, we do not mean that its *money* price will fall—although it might. We mean that its *relative* price will fall. That is, its price will fall *relative* to the average price of other goods and services.

REVIEW QUIZ

1. What is the distinction between a money price and a relative price?
2. Why is a relative price an opportunity cost?
3. Can you think of an example of a good whose money price and relative price have risen?
4. Can you think of an example of a good whose money price and relative price have fallen?

Let's begin our study of demand and supply, starting with demand.

Demand

IF YOU DEMAND SOMETHING, THEN YOU

1. Want it,
2. Can afford it, and
3. Have made a definite plan to buy it.

Wants are the unlimited desires or wishes that people have for goods and services. How many times have you thought that you would like something "if only you could afford it" or "if it weren't so expensive"? Scarcity guarantees that many—perhaps most—of our wants will never be satisfied. Demand reflects a decision about which wants to satisfy.

The **quantity demanded** of a good or service is the amount that consumers plan to buy during a given time period at a particular price. The quantity demanded is not necessarily the same as the quantity actually bought. Sometimes the quantity demanded exceeds the amount of goods available, so the quantity bought is less than the quantity demanded.

The quantity demanded is measured as an amount per unit of time. For example, suppose that you buy one cup of coffee a day. The quantity of coffee that you demand can be expressed as 1 cup per day, 7 cups per week, or 365 cups per year. Without a time dimension, we cannot tell whether the quantity demanded is large or small.

What Determines Buying Plans?

The amount of any particular good or service that consumers plan to buy depends on many factors. The main ones are

1. The price of the good
2. The prices of related goods
3. Expected future prices
4. Income
5. Population
6. Preferences

We first look at the relationship between the quantity demanded and the price of a good. To study this relationship, we keep all other influences on consumers' planned purchases the same and ask: How does the quantity demanded of the good vary as its price varies, other things remaining the same?

The Law of Demand

The **law of demand** states

> Other things remaining the same, the higher the price of a good, the smaller is the quantity demanded.

Why does a higher price reduce the quantity demanded? For two reasons:

- Substitution effect
- Income effect

Substitution Effect When the price of a good rises, other things remaining the same, its *relative* price—its opportunity cost—rises. Although each good is unique, it has *substitutes*—other goods that can be used in its place. As the opportunity cost of a good rises, people buy less of that good and more of its substitutes.

Income Effect When a price rises and all other influences on buying plans remain unchanged, the price rises *relative* to people's incomes. So faced with a higher price and an unchanged income, people cannot afford to buy all the things they previously bought. They must decrease the quantities demanded of at least some goods and services, and normally, the good whose price has increased will be one of the goods that people buy less of.

To see the substitution effect and the income effect at work, think about the effects of a change in the price of a recordable compact disc—a CD-R. Several different goods are substitutes for a CD-R. For example, an audiotape and prerecorded CD provide services similar to those of a CD-R.

Suppose that a CD-R initially sells for $3 and then its price falls to $1.50. People now substitute CD-Rs for audiotapes and prerecorded CDs—the substitution effect. And with a budget that now has some slack from the lower price of a CD-R, people buy more CD-Rs—the income effect. The quantity of CD-Rs demanded increases for these two reasons.

Now suppose that a CD-R initially sells for $3 and then the price doubles to $6. People now substitute prerecorded CDs and audiotapes for CD-Rs—the substitution effect. And faced with a tighter budget, people buy fewer CD-Rs—the income effect. The quantity of CD-Rs demanded decreases for these two reasons.

Demand Curve and Demand Schedule

You are now about to study one of the two most used curves in economics: the demand curve. And you are going to encounter one of the most critical distinctions: the distinction between *demand* and *quantity demanded.*

The term **demand** refers to the entire relationship between the price of the good and the quantity demanded of the good. Demand is illustrated by the demand curve and the demand schedule. The term *quantity demanded* refers to a point on a demand curve—the quantity demanded at a particular price.

Figure 3.1 shows the demand curve for CD-Rs. A **demand curve** shows the relationship between the quantity demanded of a good and its price when all other influences on consumers' planned purchases remain the same.

The table in Fig. 3.1 is the demand schedule for CD-Rs. A *demand schedule* lists the quantities demanded at each price when all other influences on consumers' planned purchases—prices of related goods, expected future prices, income, population, and preferences—remain the same. For example, if the price of a CD-R is 50¢, the quantity demanded is 9 million a week. If the price is $2.50, the quantity demanded is 2 million a week. The other rows of the table show the quantities demanded at prices of $1.00, $1.50, and $2.00.

We graph the demand schedule as a demand curve with the quantity demanded of CD-Rs on the *x*-axis and the price of a CD-R on the *y*-axis. The points on the demand curve labelled *A* through *E* represent the rows of the demand schedule. For example, point *A* represents a quantity demanded of 9 million CD-Rs a week at a price of 50¢ a disc.

Willingness and Ability to Pay Another way of looking at the demand curve is as a willingness-and-ability-to-pay curve. And the willingness-and-ability-to-pay is a measure of *marginal benefit.*

If a small quantity is available, the highest price that someone is willing and able to pay for one more unit is high. But as the quantity available increases, the marginal benefit of each additional unit falls and the highest price that someone is willing and able to pay also falls along the demand curve.

In Fig. 3.1, if only 2 million CD-Rs are available each week, the highest price that someone is willing to pay for the 2 millionth CD-R is $2.50. But if 9 million CD-Rs are available each week, someone is willing to pay 50¢ for the last CD-R bought.

FIGURE 3.1 The Demand Curve

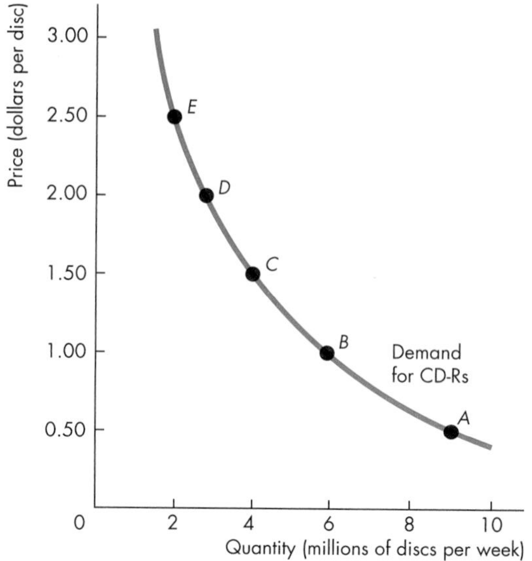

	Price (dollars per disc)	Quantity demanded (millions of discs per week)
A	0.50	9
B	1.00	6
C	1.50	4
D	2.00	3
E	2.50	2

The table shows a demand schedule for CD-Rs. At a price of 50¢ a disc, 9 million a week are demanded; at a price of $1.50 a disc, 4 million a week are demanded. The demand curve shows the relationship between quantity demanded and price, everything else remaining the same. The demand curve slopes downward: As price decreases, the quantity demanded increases.

The demand curve can be read in two ways. For a given price, the demand curve tells us the quantity that people plan to buy. For example, at a price of $1.50 a disc, the quantity demanded is 4 million discs a week. For a given quantity, the demand curve tells us the maximum price that consumers are willing and able to pay for the last disc available. For example, the maximum price that consumers will pay for the 6 millionth disc is $1.00.

A Change in Demand

When any factor that influences buying plans other than the price of the good changes, there is a **change in demand.** Figure 3.2 illustrates an increase in demand. When demand increases, the demand curve shifts rightward and the quantity demanded is greater at each and every price. For example, at $2.50 a disc, the quantity demanded on the original (blue) demand curve is 2 million discs a week. On the new (red) demand curve, the quantity demanded is 6 million discs a week. Look at the numbers in the table and check that the quantity demanded is greater at each price.

Let's look at the factors that bring a change in demand. There are five key factors to consider.

1. Prices of Related Goods The quantity of CD-Rs that consumers plan to buy depends in part on the prices of substitutes for CD-Rs. A **substitute** is a good that can be used in place of another good. For example, a bus ride is a substitute for a train ride; a hamburger is a substitute for a hot dog; and a prerecorded CD is a substitute for a CD-R. If the price of a substitute for a CD-R rises, people buy less of the substitute and more CD-Rs. For example, if the price of a prerecorded CD rises, people buy fewer CDs and more CD-Rs. The demand for CD-Rs increases.

The quantity of CD-Rs that people plan to buy also depends on the prices of complements with CD-Rs. A **complement** is a good that is used in conjunction with another good. Hamburgers and fries are complements. So are spaghetti and meat sauce, and so are CD-Rs and CD burners. If the price of a CD burner falls, people buy more CD burners *and more* CD-Rs. A fall in the price of a CD burner increases the demand for CD-Rs in Fig. 3.2.

2. Expected Future Prices If the price of a good is expected to rise in the future and if the good can be stored, the opportunity cost of obtaining the good for future use is lower today than it will be when the price has increased. So people retime their purchases—they substitute over time. They buy more of the good today before its price is expected to rise (and less after), so the current demand for the good increases.

For example, suppose that Florida is hit by a frost that damages the season's orange crop. You expect the price of orange juice to rise in the future. So you fill your freezer with enough frozen juice to get you through the next six months. Your current demand for frozen orange juice has increased and your future demand has decreased.

FIGURE 3.2 An Increase in Demand

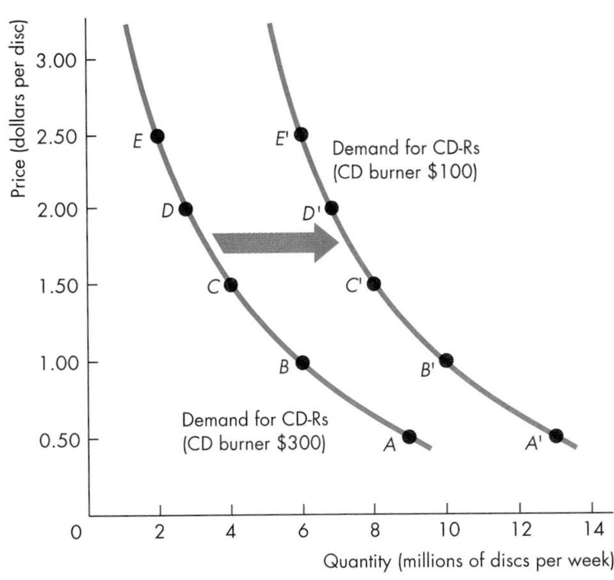

	Original demand schedule CD burner $300			New demand schedule CD burner $100	
	Price (dollars per disc)	**Quantity demanded** (millions of discs per week)		**Price** (dollars per disc)	**Quantity demanded** (millions of discs per week)
A	0.50	9	*A'*	0.50	13
B	1.00	6	*B'*	1.00	10
C	1.50	4	*C'*	1.50	8
D	2.00	3	*D'*	2.00	7
E	2.50	2	*E'*	2.50	6

A change in any influence on buyers' plans other than the price of the good itself results in a new demand schedule and a shift of the demand curve. A change in the price of a CD burner changes the demand for CD-Rs. At a price of $1.50 a disc, 4 million discs a week are demanded when the price of a CD burner is $300 (row *C* of the table) and 8 million CD-Rs a week are demanded when the price of a CD burner is $100. A *fall* in the price of a CD burner *increases* the demand for CD-Rs. The demand curve shifts *rightward*, as shown by the shift arrow and the resulting red curve.

Similarly, if the price of a good is expected to fall in the future, the opportunity cost of buying the good today is high relative to what it is expected to be in the future. So again, people retime their purchases. They buy less of the good now before its price falls, so the demand for the good decreases today and increases in the future.

Computer prices are constantly falling, and this fact poses a dilemma. Will you buy a new computer now, in time for the start of the school year, or will you wait until the price has fallen some more? Because people expect computer prices to keep falling, the current demand for computers is less (the future demand is greater) than it otherwise would be.

3. Income Consumers' income influences demand. When income increases, consumers buy more of most goods, and when income decreases, consumers buy less of most goods. Although an increase in income leads to an increase in the demand for *most* goods, it does not lead to an increase in the demand for *all* goods. A **normal good** is one for which demand increases as income increases. An **inferior good** is one for which demand decreases as income increases. Long-distance transportation has examples of both normal goods and inferior goods. As incomes increase, the demand for air travel (a normal good) increases and the demand for long-distance bus trips (an inferior good) decreases.

4. Population Demand also depends on the size and the age structure of the population. The larger the population, the greater is the demand for all goods and services; the smaller the population, the smaller is the demand for all goods and services.

For example, the demand for parking spaces or movies or CD-Rs or just about anything that you can imagine is much greater in Ottawa than it is in North Bay.

Also, the larger the proportion of the population in a given age group, the greater is the demand for the types of goods and services used by that age group.

For example, in 2001, there were 2.1 million 20-24-year-olds in Canada compared with 2.5 million in 1981. As a result, the demand for college places decreased between 1981 and 2001. During those same years, the number of Canadians aged 85 years and over increased from 195,000 to 430,000. As a result, the demand for nursing home services increased.

TABLE 3.1 The Demand for CD-Rs

The Law of Demand

The quantity of CD-Rs demanded

Decreases if:	*Increases if:*
The price of a CD-R rises	The price of a CD-R falls

Changes in Demand

The demand for CD-Rs

Decreases if:	*Increases if:*
The price of a substitute falls	The price of a substitute rises
The price of a complement rises	The price of a complement falls
The price of a CD-R is expected to fall in the future	The price of a CD-R is expected to rise in the future
Income falls*	Income rises*
The population decreases	The population increases

*A CD-R is a normal good.

5. Preferences Demand depends on preferences. *Preferences* are an individual's attitudes towards goods and services. For example, a rock music fanatic has a much greater preference for CD-Rs than does a tone-deaf technophobe. As a consequence, even if they have the same incomes, their demands for CD-Rs will be very different.

Table 3.1 summarizes the influences on demand and the direction of those influences.

A Change in the Quantity Demanded Versus a Change in Demand

Changes in the factors that influence buyers' plans cause either a change in the quantity demanded or a change in demand. Equivalently, they cause either a movement along the demand curve or a shift of the demand curve.

The distinction between a change in the quantity demanded and a change in demand is the same as that between a movement along the demand curve and a shift of the demand curve.

A point on the demand curve shows the quantity demanded at a given price. So a movement along the demand curve shows a **change in the quantity demanded.** The entire demand curve shows demand. So a shift of the demand curve shows a *change in demand.* Figure 3.3 illustrates and summarizes these distinctions.

Movement Along the Demand Curve If the price of a good changes but everything else remains the same, there is a movement along the demand curve. Because the demand curve slopes downward, a fall in the price of a good or service increases the quantity demanded of it and a rise in the price of the good or service decreases the quantity demanded of it—the law of demand.

In Fig. 3.3, if the price of a good falls when everything else remains the same, the quantity demanded of that good increases and there is a movement down along the demand curve D_0. If the price rises when everything else remains the same, the quantity demanded of that good decreases and there is a movement up along the demand curve D_0.

A Shift of the Demand Curve If the price of a good remains constant but some other influence on buyers' plans changes, there is a change in the demand for that good. We illustrate a change in demand as a shift of the demand curve. For example, if the price of a CD burner falls, consumers buy more CD-Rs regardless of whether the price of a CD-R is high or low. That is what a rightward shift of the demand curve shows—more CD-Rs are bought at each and every price.

In Fig. 3.3, when any influence on buyers' planned purchases changes, other than the price of the good, there is a *change in demand* and the demand curve shifts. Demand *increases* and the demand curve *shifts rightward* (to the red demand curve D_1) if the price of a substitute rises, the price of a complement falls, the expected future price of the good rises, income increases (for a normal good), or the population increases. Demand *decreases* and the demand curve *shifts leftward* (to the red demand curve D_2) if the price of a substitute falls, the price of a complement rises, the expected future price of the good falls, income decreases (for a normal good), or the population decreases.(For an inferior good, the effects of changes in income are in the direction opposite to those described above.)

FIGURE 3.3 A Change in the Quantity Demanded Versus a Change in Demand

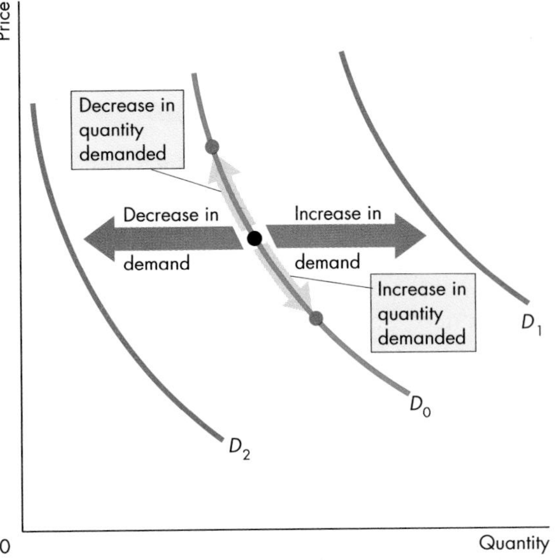

When the price of the good changes, there is a movement along the demand curve and *a change in the quantity demanded,* shown by the blue arrows on demand curve D_0. When any other influence on buyers' plans changes, there is a shift of the demand curve and a *change in demand.* An increase in demand shifts the demand curve rightward (from D_0 to D_1). A decrease in demand shifts the demand curve leftward (from D_0 to D_2).

REVIEW QUIZ

1 Define the quantity demanded of a good or service.
2 What is the law of demand and how do we illustrate it?
3 If a fixed amount of a good is available, what does the demand curve tell us about the price that consumers are willing to pay for that fixed quantity?
4 List all the influences on buying plans that change demand, and for each influence say whether it increases or decreases demand.
5 What happens to the quantity of Palm Pilots demanded and the demand for Palm Pilots if the price of a Palm Pilot falls and all other influences on buying plans remain the same?

Supply

IF A FIRM SUPPLIES A GOOD OR SERVICE, THE FIRM

1. Has the resources and technology to produce it,
2. Can profit from producing it, and
3. Has made a definite plan to produce it and sell it.

A supply is more that just having the *resources* and the *technology* to produce something. *Resources and technology* are the constraints that limit what is possible.

Many useful things can be produced, but they are not produced unless it is profitable to do so. Supply reflects a decision about which technologically feasible items to produce.

The **quantity supplied** of a good or service is the amount that producers plan to sell during a given time period at a particular price. The quantity supplied is not necessarily the same amount as the quantity actually sold. Sometimes the quantity supplied is greater than the quantity demanded, so the quantity bought is less than the quantity supplied.

Like the quantity demanded, the quantity supplied is measured as an amount per unit of time. For example, suppose that GM produces 1,000 cars a day. The quantity of cars supplied by GM can be expressed as 1,000 a day, 7,000 a week, or 365,000 a year. Without the time dimension, we cannot tell whether a particular number is large or small.

What Determines Selling Plans?

The amount of any particular good or service that producers plan to sell depends on many factors. The main ones are

1. The price of the good
2. The prices of resources used to produce the good
3. The prices of related goods produced
4. Expected future prices
5. The number of suppliers
6. Technology

Let's first look at the relationship between the price of a good and the quantity supplied. To study this relationship, we keep all other influences on the quantity supplied the same. We ask: How does the quantity supplied of a good vary as its price varies?

The Law of Supply

The **law of supply** states

> Other things remaining the same, the higher the price of a good, the greater is the quantity supplied.

Why does a higher price increase the quantity supplied? It is because *marginal cost increases.* As the quantity produced of any good increases, the marginal cost of producing the good increases. (You can refresh your memory of increasing marginal cost in Chapter 2, p. 37.)

It is never worth producing a good if the price received for it does not at least cover the marginal cost of producing it. So when the price of a good rises, other things remaining the same, producers are willing to incur the higher marginal cost and increase production. The higher price brings forth an increase in the quantity supplied.

Let's now illustrate the law of supply with a supply curve and a supply schedule.

Supply Curve and Supply Schedule

You are now going to study the second of the two most used curves in economics: the supply curve. And you're going to learn about the critical distinction between *supply* and *quantity supplied.*

The term **supply** refers to the entire relationship between the quantity supplied and the price of a good. Supply is illustrated by the supply curve and the supply schedule. The term *quantity supplied* refers to a point on a supply curve—the quantity supplied at a particular price.

Figure 3.4 shows the supply curve of CD-Rs. A **supply curve** shows the relationship between the quantity supplied of a good and its price when all other influences on producers' planned sales remain the same. The supply curve is a graph of a supply schedule.

The table in Fig. 3.4 sets out the supply schedule for CD-Rs. A *supply schedule* lists the quantities supplied at each price when all the other influences on producers' planned sales remain the same. For example, if the price of a CD-R is 50¢, the quantity supplied is zero—in row *A* of the table. If the price of a CD-R is $1.00, the quantity supplied is 3 million CD-Rs a week—in row *B*. The other rows of the table show the quantities supplied at prices of $1.50, $2.00, and $2.50.

FIGURE 3.4 The Supply Curve

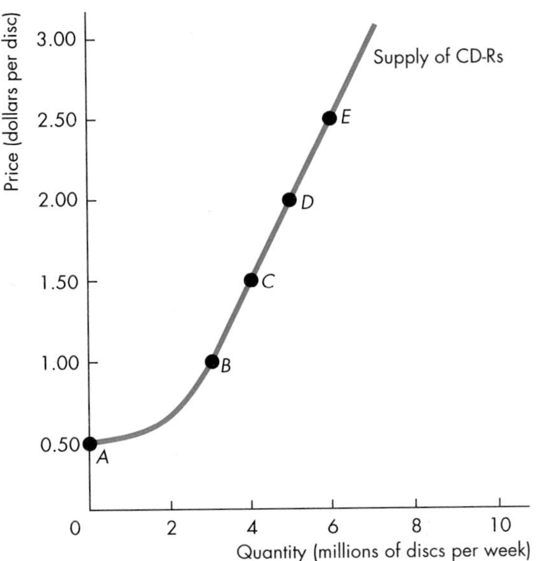

	Price (dollars per disc)	Quantity supplied (millions of discs per week)
A	0.50	0
B	1.00	3
C	1.50	4
D	2.00	5
E	2.50	6

The table shows the supply schedule of CD-Rs. For example, at a price of $1.00, 3 million discs a week are supplied; at a price of $2.50, 6 million discs a week are supplied. The supply curve shows the relationship between the quantity supplied and price, everything else remaining the same. The supply curve usually slopes upward: As the price of a good increases, so does the quantity supplied.

A supply curve can be read in two ways. For a given price, it tells us the quantity that producers plan to sell. And for a given quantity, it tells us the minimum price that producers are willing to accept for that quantity.

To make a supply curve, we graph the quantity supplied on the *x*-axis and the price on the *y*-axis, just as in the case of the demand curve. The points on the supply curve labelled *A* through *E* represent the rows of the supply schedule. For example, point *A* on the graph represents a quantity supplied of zero at a price of 50¢ a CD-R.

Minimum Supply Price Just as the demand curve has two interpretations, so too does the supply curve. The demand curve can be interpreted as a willingness-and-ability-to-pay curve. The supply curve can be interpreted as a minimum-supply-price curve. It tells us the lowest price at which someone is willing to sell another unit.

If a small quantity is produced, the lowest price at which someone is willing to produce one more unit is low. But if a large quantity is produced, the lowest price at which someone is willing to sell one more unit is high.

In Fig. 3.4, if 6 million CD-Rs a week are produced, the lowest price that a producer is willing to accept for the 6 millionth disc is $2.50. But if only 4 million CD-Rs are produced each week, the lowest price that a producer is willing to accept for the 4 millionth disc is $1.50.

A Change in Supply

When any factor that influences selling plans other than the price of the good changes, there is a **change in supply.** Let's look at the five key factors that change supply.

1. Prices of Productive Resources The prices of productive resources influence supply. The easiest way to see this influence is to think about the supply curve as a minimum-supply-price curve. If the price of a productive resource rises, the lowest price a producer is willing to accept rises, so supply decreases. For example, during 2001, the price of jet fuel increased and the supply of air transportation decreased. Similarly, a rise in the minimum wage decreases the supply of hamburgers. If the wages of disc producers rise, the supply of CD-Rs decreases.

2. Prices of Related Goods Produced The prices of related goods and services that firms produce influence supply. For example, if the price of a prerecorded CD rises, the supply of CD-Rs decreases. CD-Rs and prerecorded CDs are *substitutes in production*—goods that can be produced by using the same resources.

If the price of beef rises, the supply of cowhide increases. Beef and cowhide are *complements in production*—goods that must be produced together.

3. Expected Future Prices If the price of a good is expected to rise, the return from selling the good in the future will be higher than it is today. So supply decreases today and increases in the future.

4. The Number of Suppliers The larger the number of firms that produce a good, the greater is the supply of the good. And as firms enter an industry, the supply in that industry increases. As firms leave an industry, the supply in that industry decreases. For example, over the past two years, there has been a huge increase in the number of firms that design and manage Web sites. As a result of this increase, the supply of Internet and World Wide Web services has increased enormously.

5. Technology New technologies create new products and lower the costs of producing existing products. As a result, they change supply. For example, the use of new technologies in the Taiwan factories that make CD-Rs for Imation Enterprises Corporation, a Minnesota based firm, have lowered the cost of producing a CD-R and increased its supply.

Figure 3.5 illustrates an increase in supply. When supply increases, the supply curve shifts rightward and the quantity supplied is larger at each and every price. For example, at a price of $1.00, on the original (blue) supply curve, the quantity supplied is 3 million discs a week. On the new (red) supply curve, the quantity supplied is 6 million discs a week. Look closely at the numbers in the table in Fig. 3.5 and check that the quantity supplied is larger at each price.

Table 3.2 summarizes the influences on supply and the directions of those influences.

A Change in the Quantity Supplied Versus a Change in Supply

Changes in the factors that influence producers' planned sales cause either a change in the quantity supplied or a change in supply. Equivalently, they cause either a movement along the supply curve or a shift of the supply curve.

A point on the supply curve shows the quantity supplied at a given price. A movement along the supply curve shows a **change in the quantity supplied.** The entire supply curve shows supply. A shift of the supply curve shows a *change in supply.*

FIGURE 3.5 An Increase in Supply

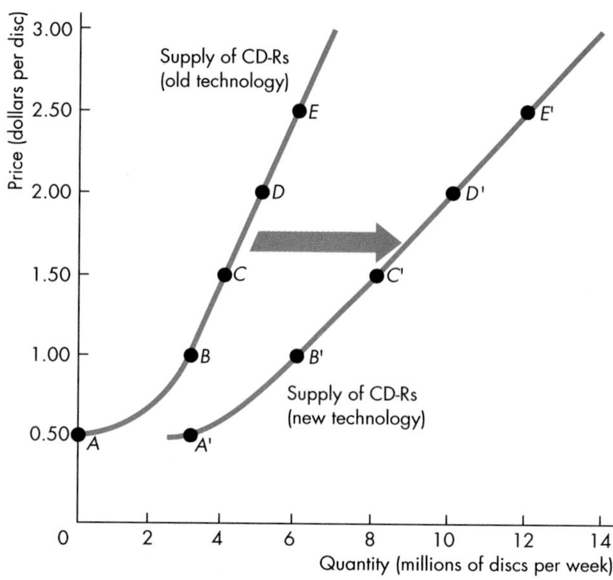

	Original supply schedule Old technology			New supply schedule New technology	
	Price (dollars per disc)	Quantity supplied (millions of discs per week)		Price (dollars per disc)	Quantity supplied (millions of discs per week)
A	0.50	0	A'	0.50	3
B	1.00	3	B'	1.00	6
C	1.50	4	C'	1.50	8
D	2.00	5	D'	2.00	10
E	2.50	6	E'	2.50	12

A change in any influence on sellers' plans other than the price of the good itself results in a new supply schedule and a shift of the supply curve. For example, if Imation invents a new, cost-saving technology for producing CD-Rs, the supply of CD-Rs changes.

At a price of $1.50 a disc, 4 million discs a week are supplied when producers use the old technology (row *C* of the table) and 8 million CD-Rs a week are supplied when producers use the new technology. An advance in technology *increases* the supply of CD-Rs. The supply curve shifts *rightward*, as shown by the shift arrow and the resulting red curve.

Figure 3.6 illustrates and summarizes these distinctions. If the price of a good falls and everything else remains the same, the quantity supplied of that good decreases and there is a movement down along the supply curve S_0. If the price of a good rises and everything else remains the same, the quantity supplied increases and there is a movement up along the supply curve S_0. When any other influence on selling plans changes, the supply curve shifts and there is a *change in supply.* If the supply curve is S_0 and if production costs fall, supply increases and the supply curve shifts to the red supply curve S_1. If production costs rise, supply decreases and the supply curve shifts to the red supply curve S_2.

TABLE 3.2 The Supply of CD-Rs

The Law of Supply

The quantity of CD-Rs supplied

Decreases if:	*Increases if:*
■ The price of a CD-R falls	■ The price of a CD-R rises

Changes in Supply

The supply of CD-Rs

Decreases if:	*Increases if:*
■ The price of a resource used to produce CD-Rs rises	■ The price of a resource used to produce CD-Rs falls
■ The price of a substitute in production rises	■ The price of a substitute in production falls
■ The price of a complement in production falls	■ The price of a complement in production rises
■ The price of a CD-R is expected to rise in the future	■ The price of a CD-R is expected to fall in the future
■ The number of CD-R producers decreases	■ The number of CD-R producers increases
	■ More efficient technologies for producing CD-Rs are discovered

FIGURE 3.6 A Change in the Quantity Supplied Versus a Change in Supply

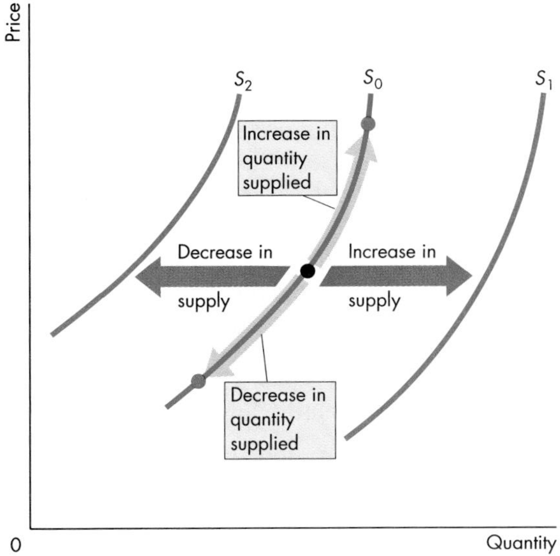

When the price of the good changes, there is a movement along the supply curve and *a change in the quantity supplied,* shown by the blue arrows on supply curve S_0. When any other influence on selling plans changes, there is a shift of the supply curve and a *change in supply.* An increase in supply shifts the supply curve rightward (from S_0 to S_1), and a decrease in supply shifts the supply curve leftward (from S_0 to S_2).

REVIEW QUIZ

1. Define the quantity supplied of a good or service.
2. What is the law of supply and how do we illustrate it?
3. What does the supply curve tell us about the price at which firms will supply a given quantity of a good?
4. List all the influences on selling plans, and for each influence say whether it changes supply.
5. What happens to the quantity of Palm Pilots supplied and the supply of Palm Pilots if the price of a Palm Pilot falls?

Your next task is to use what you've learned about demand and supply and learn how prices and quantities are determined.

Market Equilibrium

WE HAVE SEEN THAT WHEN THE PRICE OF A good rises, the quantity demanded *decreases* and the quantity supplied *increases*. We are now going to see how prices coordinate the plans of buyers and sellers and achieve an equilibrium.

An *equilibrium* is a situation in which opposing forces balance each other. Equilibrium in a market occurs when the price balances the plans of buyers and sellers. The **equilibrium price** is the price at which the quantity demanded equals the quantity supplied. The **equilibrium quantity** is the quantity bought and sold at the equilibrium price. A market moves towards its equilibrium because

- Price regulates buying and selling plans.
- Price adjusts when plans don't match.

Price as a Regulator

The price of a good regulates the quantities demanded and supplied. If the price is too high, the quantity supplied exceeds the quantity demanded. If the price is too low, the quantity demanded exceeds the quantity supplied. There is one price at which the quantity demanded equals the quantity supplied. Let's work out what that price is.

Figure 3.7 shows the market for CD-Rs. The table shows the demand schedule (from Fig. 3.1) and the supply schedule (from Fig. 3.4). If the price of a disc is 50¢, the quantity demanded is 9 million discs a week, but no discs are supplied. There is a shortage of 9 million discs a week. This shortage is shown in the final column of the table. At a price of $1.00 a disc, there is still a shortage, but only of 3 million discs a week. If the price of a disc is $2.50, the quantity supplied is 6 million discs a week, but the quantity demanded is only 2 million. There is a surplus of 4 million discs a week. The one price at which there is neither a shortage nor a surplus is $1.50 a disc. At that price, the quantity demanded is equal to the quantity supplied: 4 million discs a week. The equilibrium price is $1.50 a disc, and the equilibrium quantity is 4 million discs a week.

Figure 3.7 shows that the demand curve and the supply curve intersect at the equilibrium price of $1.50 a disc. At each price *above* $1.50 a disc, there is a surplus of discs. For example, at $2.00 a disc, the

FIGURE 3.7 Equilibrium

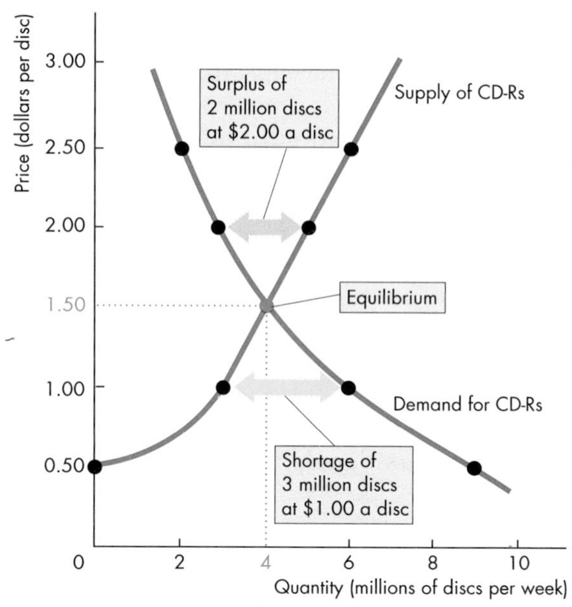

Price (dollars per disc)	Quantity demanded	Quantity supplied	Shortage (–) or surplus (+)
	(millions of discs per week)		
0.50	9	0	–9
1.00	6	3	–3
1.50	4	4	0
2.00	3	5	+2
2.50	2	6	+4

The table lists the quantities demanded and quantities supplied as well as the shortage or surplus of discs at each price. If the price is $1.00 a disc, 6 million discs a week are demanded and 3 million are supplied. There is a shortage of 3 million discs a week, and the price rises. If the price is $2.00 a disc, 3 million discs a week are demanded and 5 million are supplied. There is a surplus of 2 million discs a week, and the price falls. If the price is $1.50 a disc, 4 million discs a week are demanded and 4 million are supplied. There is neither a shortage nor a surplus. Neither buyers nor sellers have any incentive to change the price. The price at which the quantity demanded equals the quantity supplied is the equilibrium price.

surplus is 2 million discs a week, as shown by the blue arrow. At each price *below* $1.50 a disc, there is a shortage of discs. For example, at $1.00 a disc, the shortage is 3 million discs a week, as shown by the red arrow.

Price Adjustments

You've seen that if the price is below equilibrium, there is a shortage, and that if the price is above equilibrium, there is a surplus. But can we count on the price to change and eliminate a shortage or a surplus? We can, because such price changes are beneficial to both buyers and sellers. Let's see why the price changes when there is a shortage or a surplus.

A Shortage Forces the Price Up Suppose the price of a CD-R is $1. Consumers plan to buy 6 million discs a week, and producers plan to sell 3 million discs a week. Consumers can't force producers to sell more than they plan, so the quantity that is actually offered for sale is 3 million discs a week. In this situation, powerful forces operate to increase the price and move it towards the equilibrium price. Some producers, noticing lines of unsatisfied consumers, raise the price. Some producers increase their output. As producers push the price up, the price rises towards its equilibrium. The rising price reduces the shortage because it decreases the quantity demanded and increases the quantity supplied. When the price has increased to the point at which there is no longer a shortage, the forces moving the price stop operating and the price comes to rest at its equilibrium.

A Surplus Forces the Price Down Suppose the price of a CD-R is $2. Producers plan to sell 5 million discs a week, and consumers plan to buy 3 million discs a week. Producers cannot force consumers to buy more than they plan, so the quantity that is actually bought is 3 million discs a week. In this situation, powerful forces operate to lower the price and move it towards the equilibrium price. Some producers, unable to sell the quantities of CD-Rs they planned to sell, cut their prices. In addition, some producers scale back production. As producers cut prices, the price falls towards its equilibrium. The falling price decreases the surplus because it increases the quantity demanded and decreases the quantity supplied. When the price has fallen to the point at which there is no longer a surplus, the forces moving the price stop operating and the price comes to rest at its equilibrium.

The Best Deal Available for Buyers and Sellers When the price is below equilibrium, it is forced up towards the equilibrium. Why don't buyers resist the increase and refuse to buy at the higher price? Because they value the good more highly than the current price and they cannot satisfy all their demands at the current price. In some markets—an example is the market for houses in Canada during 2001 and 2002—the buyers might even be the ones who force the price up by offering higher prices to divert the limited quantities away from other buyers.

When the price is above equilibrium, it is bid down towards the equilibrium. Why don't sellers resist this decrease and refuse to sell at the lower price? Because their minimum supply price is below the current price and they cannot sell all they would like to at the current price. Normally, it is the sellers who force the price down by offering lower prices to gain market share from their competitors.

At the price at which the quantity demanded and the quantity supplied are equal, neither buyers nor sellers can do business at a better price. Buyers pay the highest price they are willing to pay for the last unit bought, and sellers receive the lowest price at which they are willing to supply the last unit sold.

When people freely make offers to buy and sell and when demanders try to buy at the lowest possible price and suppliers try to sell at the highest possible price, the price at which trade takes place is the equilibrium price—the price at which the quantity demanded equals the quantity supplied. The price coordinates the plans of buyers and sellers.

REVIEW QUIZ

1 What is the equilibrium price of a good or service?
2 Over what range of prices does a shortage arise?
3 Over what range of prices does a surplus arise?
4 What happens to the price when there is a shortage?
5 What happens to the price when there is a surplus?
6 Why is the price at which the quantity demanded equals the quantity supplied the equilibrium price?
7 Why is the equilibrium price the best deal available for both buyers and sellers?

Predicting Changes in Price and Quantity

THE DEMAND AND SUPPLY THEORY THAT WE HAVE just studied provides us with a powerful way of analyzing influences on prices and the quantities bought and sold. According to the theory, a change in price stems from a change in demand, a change in supply, or a change in both demand and supply. Let's look first at the effects of a change in demand.

A Change in Demand

What happens to the price and quantity of CD-Rs if the demand for CD-Rs increases? We can answer this question with a specific example. Between 1998 and 2001, the price of a CD burner fell from $300 to $100. Because the CD burner and CD-R discs are complements, the demand for discs increased, as is shown in the table in Fig. 3.8. The original demand schedule and the new one are set out in the first three columns of the table. The table also shows the supply schedule for CD-Rs.

The original equilibrium price is $1.50 a disc. At that price, 4 million discs a week are demanded and supplied. When demand increases, the price that makes the quantity demanded equal the quantity supplied is $2.50 a disc. At this price, 6 million discs are bought and sold each week. When demand increases, both the price and the quantity increase.

Figure 3.8 shows these changes. The figure shows the original demand for and supply of CD-Rs. The original equilibrium price is $1.50 a CD-R, and the quantity is 4 million CD-Rs a week. When demand increases, the demand curve shifts rightward. The equilibrium price rises to $2.50 a CD-R, and the quantity supplied increases to 6 million CD-Rs a week, as highlighted in the figure. There is an *increase in the quantity supplied* but *no change in supply*—a movement along, but no shift of, the supply curve.

We can reverse this change in demand. Start at a price of $2.50 a disc with 6 million CD-Rs a week being bought and sold, and then work out what happens if demand decreases to its original level. Such a decrease in demand might arise from a fall in the price of an MP3 player (a substitute for CD-R technology). The decrease in demand shifts the demand curve leftward. The equilibrium price falls to $1.50 a disc, and the equilibrium quantity decreases to 4 million discs a week.

FIGURE 3.8 The Effects of a Change in Demand

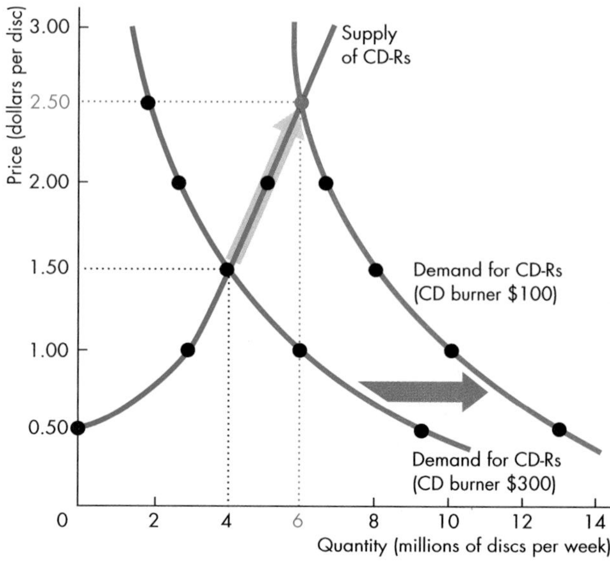

Price (dollars per disc)	Quantity demanded (millions of discs per week)		Quantity supplied (millions of discs per week)
	CD burner $300	CD burner $100	
0.50	9	13	0
1.00	6	10	3
1.50	**4**	8	**4**
2.00	3	7	5
2.50	2	**6**	**6**

With the price of a CD burner at $300, the demand for CD-Rs is shown by the blue demand curve. The equilibrium price is $1.50 a disc, and the equilibrium quantity is 4 million discs a week. When the price of a CD burner falls from $300 to $100, the demand for CD-Rs increases and the demand curve shifts rightward to become the red curve.

At $1.50 a disc, there is now a shortage of 4 million discs a week. The price of a disc rises to a new equilibrium of $2.50. As the price rises to $2.50, the quantity supplied increases—shown by the blue arrow on the supply curve—to the new equilibrium quantity of 6 million discs a week. Following an increase in demand, the quantity supplied increases but supply does not change—the supply curve does not shift.

We can now make our first two predictions:

1. When demand increases, both the price and the quantity increase.
2. When demand decreases, both the price and the quantity decrease.

A Change in Supply

When Imation and other producers introduce new cost-saving technologies in their CD-R production plants, the supply of CD-Rs increases. The new supply schedule (the same one that was shown in Fig. 3.5) is presented in the table in Fig. 3.9. What are the new equilibrium price and quantity? The answer is highlighted in the table: The price falls to $1.00 a disc, and the quantity increases to 6 million a week. You can see why by looking at the quantities demanded and supplied at the old price of $1.50 a disc. The quantity supplied at that price is 8 million discs a week, and there is a surplus of discs. The price falls. Only when the price is $1.00 a disc does the quantity supplied equal the quantity demanded.

Figure 3.9 illustrates the effect of an increase in supply. It shows the demand curve for CD-Rs and the original and new supply curves. The initial equilibrium price is $1.50 a disc, and the quantity is 4 million discs a week. When the supply increases, the supply curve shifts rightward. The equilibrium price falls to $1.00 a disc, and the quantity demanded increases to 6 million discs a week, highlighted in the figure. There is an *increase in the quantity demanded* but *no change in demand*—a movement along, but no shift of, the demand curve.

We can reverse this change in supply. If we start out at a price of $1.00 a disc with 6 million discs a week being bought and sold, we can work out what happens if supply decreases to its original level. Such a decrease in supply might arise from an increase in the cost of labour or raw materials. The decrease in supply shifts the supply curve leftward. The equilibrium price rises to $1.50 a disc, and the equilibrium quantity decreases to 4 million discs a week.

We can now make two more predictions:

1. When supply increases, the quantity increases and the price falls.
2. When supply decreases, the quantity decreases and the price rises.

FIGURE 3.9 The Effects of a Change in Supply

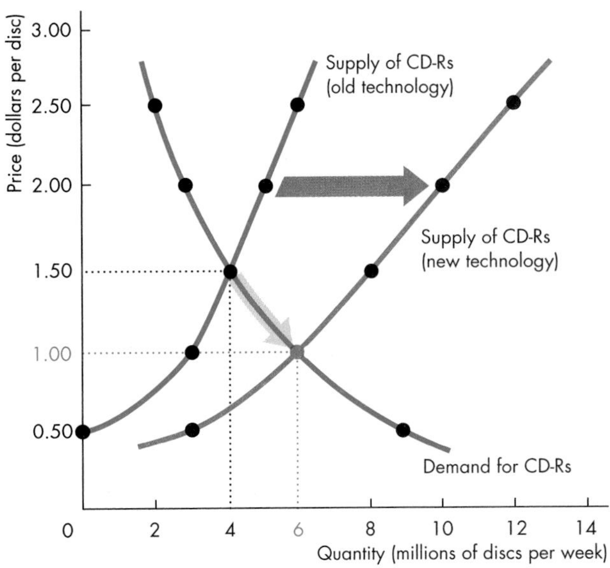

Price (dollars per disc)	Quantity demanded (millions of discs per week)	Quantity supplied (millions of discs per week) Old technology	New technology
0.50	9	0	3
1.00	**6**	3	**6**
1.50	**4**	**4**	8
2.00	3	5	10
2.50	2	6	12

With the old technology, the supply of CD-Rs is shown by the blue supply curve. The equilibrium price is $1.50 a disc, and the equilibrium quantity is 4 million discs a week. When the new technology is adopted, the supply of CD-Rs increases and the supply curve shifts rightward to become the red curve.

At $1.50 a disc, there is now a surplus of 4 million discs a week. The price of a CD-R falls to a new equilibrium of $1.00 a disc. As the price falls to $1.00, the quantity demanded increases—shown by the blue arrow on the demand curve—to the new equilibrium quantity of 6 million discs a week. Following an increase in supply, the quantity demanded increases but demand does not change—the demand curve does not shift.

A Change in Both Demand and Supply

You can now predict the effects of a change in either demand or supply on the price and the quantity. But what happens if *both* demand and supply change together? To answer this question, we look first at the case in which demand and supply move in the same direction—either both increase or both decrease. Then we look at the case in which they move in opposite directions—demand decreases and supply increases or demand increases and supply decreases.

Demand and Supply Change in the Same Direction We've seen that an increase in the demand for CD-Rs raises the price and increases the quantity bought and sold. And we've seen that an increase in the supply of CD-Rs lowers the price and increases the quantity bought and sold. Let's now examine what happens when both of these changes occur together.

The table in Fig. 3.10 brings together the numbers that describe the original quantities demanded and supplied and the new quantities demanded and supplied after the fall in the price of the CD burner and the improved CD-R production technology. These same numbers are illustrated in the graph. The original (blue) demand and supply curves intersect at a price of $1.50 a disc and a quantity of 4 million discs a week. The new (red) supply and demand curves also intersect at a price of $1.50 a disc but at a quantity of 8 million discs a week.

An increase in either demand or supply increases the quantity. So when both demand and supply increase, so does the quantity.

An increase in demand raises the price, and an increase in supply lowers the price, so we can't say whether the price will rise or fall when demand and supply increase together. In this example, the price does not change. But notice that if demand increases by slightly more than the amount shown in the figure, the price will rise. And if supply increases by slightly more than the amount shown in the figure, the price will fall.

We can now make two more predictions:

1. When *both* demand and supply increase, the quantity increases and the price might increase, decrease, or remain the same.
2. When *both* demand and supply decrease, the quantity decreases and the price might increase, decrease, or remain the same.

FIGURE 3.10 The Effects of an Increase in Both Demand and Supply

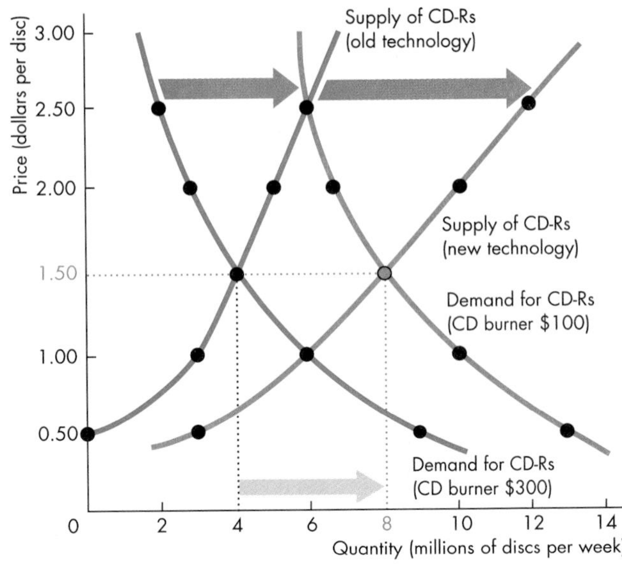

	Original quantities (millions of discs per week)		New quantities (millions of discs per week)	
Price (dollars per disc)	Quantity demanded CD burner $300	Quantity supplied old technology	Quantity demanded CD burner $100	Quantity supplied new technology
0.50	9	0	13	3
1.00	6	3	10	6
1.50	**4**	**4**	**8**	**8**
2.00	3	5	7	10
2.50	2	6	6	12

When a CD burner costs $300 and firms use the old technology to produce discs, the price of a disc is $1.50 and the quantity is 4 million discs a week. A fall in the price of the CD burner increases the demand for CD-Rs, and improved technology increases the supply of CD-Rs. The new supply curve intersects the new demand curve at $1.50 a disc, the same price as before, but the quantity increases to 8 million discs a week. These increases in demand and supply increase the quantity but leave the price unchanged.

Demand and Supply Change in Opposite Directions Let's now see what happens when demand and supply change together in *opposite* directions. A new production technology increases the supply of CD-Rs as before. But now the price of an MP3 download rises. An MP3 download is a *complement* of a CD-R. With more costly MP3 downloads, some people switch from buying CD-Rs to buying prerecorded CDs. The demand for CD-Rs decreases.

Figure 3.11 illustrates the original (blue) and new (red) demand and supply curves. The original equilibrium price is $2.50 a disc, and the quantity is 6 million discs a week. The new supply and demand curves intersect at a price of $1.00 a disc and at the original quantity of 6 million discs a week.

A decrease in demand or an increase in supply lowers the price. So when a decrease in demand and an increase in supply occur together, the price falls.

A decrease in demand decreases the quantity, and an increase in supply increases the quantity, so we can't say for sure which way the quantity will change when demand decreases and supply increases at the same time. In this example, the quantity doesn't change. But notice that if demand had decreased by slightly more than is shown in the figure, the quantity would have decreased. And if supply had increased by slightly more than is shown in the figure, the quantity would have increased.

We can now make two more predictions:

1. When demand decreases and supply increases, the price falls and the quantity might increase, decrease, or remain the same.
2. When demand increases and supply decreases, the price rises and the quantity might increase, decrease, or remain the same.

REVIEW QUIZ

1 What is the effect on the price of a CD-R and the quantity of CD-Rs if (a) the price of a PC falls or (b) the price of an MP3 download rises or (c) more firms produce CD-Rs or (d) CD-R producers' wages rise or (e) any two of these events occur at the same time? (Draw the diagrams!)

To complete your study of demand and supply, take a look at *Reading Between the Lines* on pp. 76–77, which answers the question that we posed at the start of the chapter about falling prices.

FIGURE 3.11 The Effects of a Decrease in Demand and an Increase in Supply

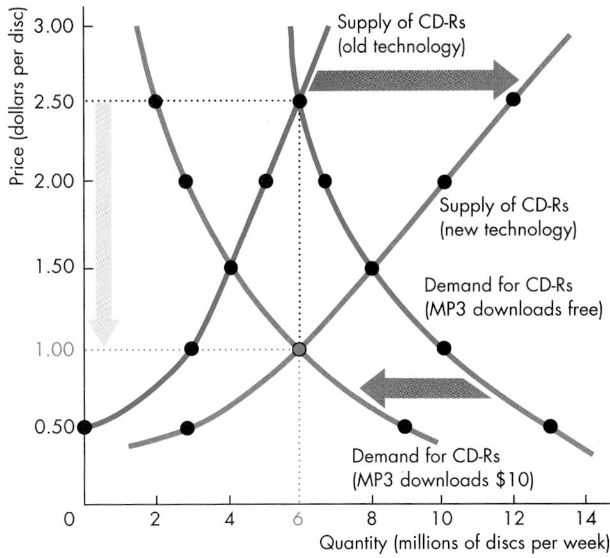

Price (dollars per disc)	Original quantities (millions of discs per week) Quantity demanded MP3 download free	Quantity supplied old technology	New quantities (millions of discs per week) Quantity demanded MP3 download $10	Quantity supplied new technology
0.50	13	0	9	3
1.00	10	3	6	6
1.50	8	4	4	8
2.00	7	5	3	10
2.50	**6**	**6**	2	12

When MP3 downloads are free and firms use the old technology to produce discs, the price of a CD-R is $2.50 and the quantity is 6 million discs a week. A rise in the price of an MP3 download decreases the demand for CD-Rs, and improved technology increases the supply of CD-Rs. The new equilibrium price is $1.00 a disc, a lower price, but in this case the quantity remains constant at 6 million discs a week. This decrease in demand and increase in supply lower the price but leave the quantity unchanged.

READING BETWEEN THE LINES

Demand and Supply: The Price of Computers

THE GLOBE AND MAIL, DECEMBER 31, 2001

Analysts see tough year ahead for PC industry

...

"It's going to be a tough year," said George Shiffler, a principal analyst at Gartner Dataquest ...

Worldwide shipments of PCs are projected to reach 129.3 million units in 2002, up 4 per cent from 124.3 million in 2001, but down slightly from 130.5 million in 2000 according to Gartner.

In Canada, PC shipments, which are expected to fall 6.6 per cent this year from 2000, are forecast to increase 3.8 per cent to 3.8 million units in 2002.

...

Analysts are counting on falling PC prices, increased demand for wireless networking and mobile computing, and Microsoft Corp.'s latest operating systems to help stimulate PC sales. But experts say the most important factor that will drive the market will be a turnaround in the sagging U.S. economy, which has hurt consumer confidence.

This was a particularly good year to buy a computer, and consumers and companies can also expect good bargains in 2002. Chip maker Intel Corp. has been dropping the prices of its components throughout this year, partly in response to competition from rival Advanced Micro Devices Inc. That means computer manufacturers can source cheaper parts and pass the savings on to buyers.

...

Essence of the Story

- Worldwide shipments of PCs are projected to reach 129.3 million units in 2002, up 4 percent from 124.3 million in 2001, but down from 130.5 million in 2000.
- In Canada, PC shipments are expected to fall 6.6 percent in 2001 and to increase 3.8 percent to 3.8 million units in 2002.
- Falling PC prices, increased demand for wireless networking and mobile computing, and Microsoft Corp.'s WindowsXP might help stimulate PC sales.
- But only a turnaround in the sagging U.S. economy will restore the industry.
- Computer buyers can expect bargains in 2002.
- Intel Corp. and Advanced Micro Devices Inc. have cut the prices of chips, which has lowered the costs of PC makers.

Economic Analysis

■ Figure 1 shows the global market for personal computers in 2000. The demand curve is D_{00} and the supply curve is S_{00}. The equilibrium quantity is 130.5 million (as in the news article) and the equilibrium price is $3,500.

■ Figure 2 shows what happened during 2001. A recession in the United States lowered incomes, both in the United States and in many other countries. With a fall in average incomes, the demand for PCs decreased and the demand curve shifted leftward from D_{00} to D_{01}.

■ Falling chip prices lowered the cost of producing a PC and the supply of PCs increased. The supply curve shifted rightward from S_{00} to S_{01}.

■ With a decrease in demand and an increase in supply, the price of a PC fell. But because the decrease in demand was greater than the increase in supply, the quantity of PCs decreased.

■ Figure 3 shows the market for PCs in 2002. Factors such as the increased demand for wireless technology and the introduction of WindowsXP increased demand. But these forces were not strong enough to offset the depressing effects on demand of the continued global economic slowdown. So the demand for PCs didn't change in 2002.

■ But the supply of PCs increased again as the prices of chips continued to tumble. The supply curve shifted rightward from S_{01} to S_{02}.

■ With an increase in supply and no change in demand, the price of a PC fell further and the quantity of PCs increased.

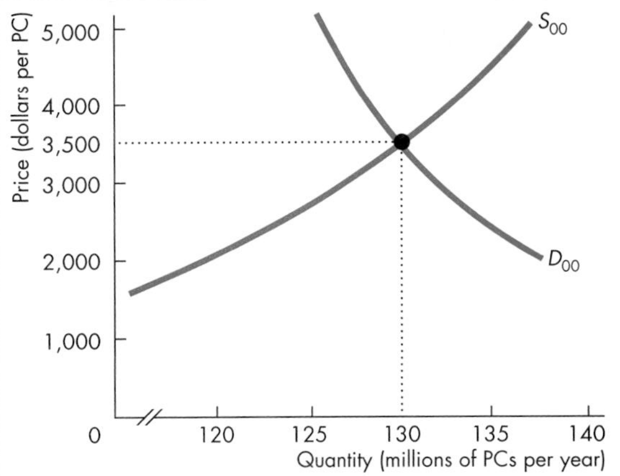

Figure 1 The PC market in 2000

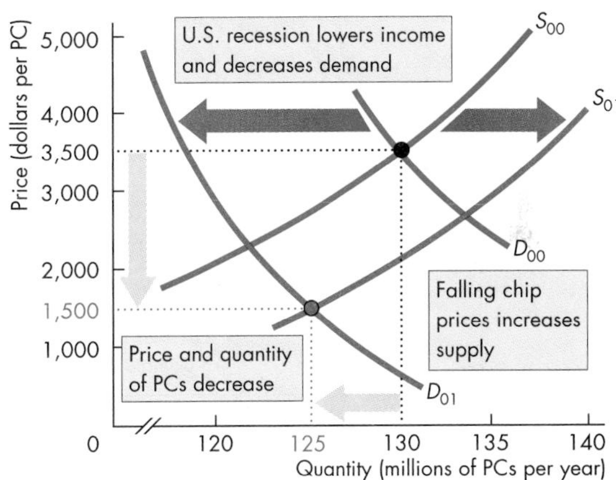

Figure 2 The PC market in 2001

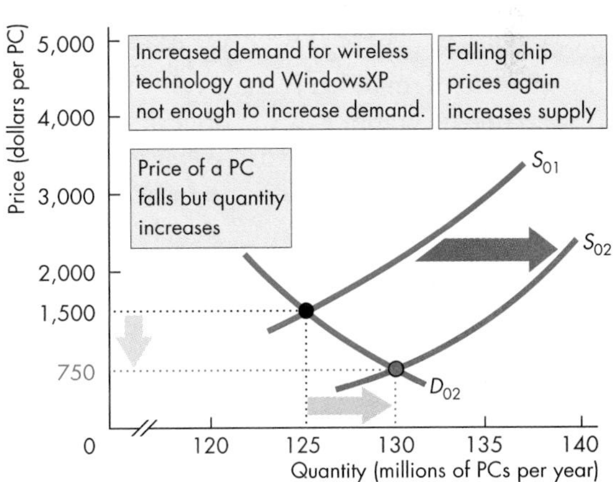

Figure 3 The PC market in 2002

Mathematical Note
Demand, Supply, and Equilibrium

Demand Curve

The law of demand says that as the price of a good or service falls, the quantity demanded of that good or service increases. We illustrate the law of demand by setting out a demand schedule, by drawing a graph of the demand curve, or by writing down an equation. When the demand curve is a straight line, the following linear equation describes it

$$P = a - bQ_D,$$

where P is the price and Q_D is the quantity demanded. The a and b are positive constants.

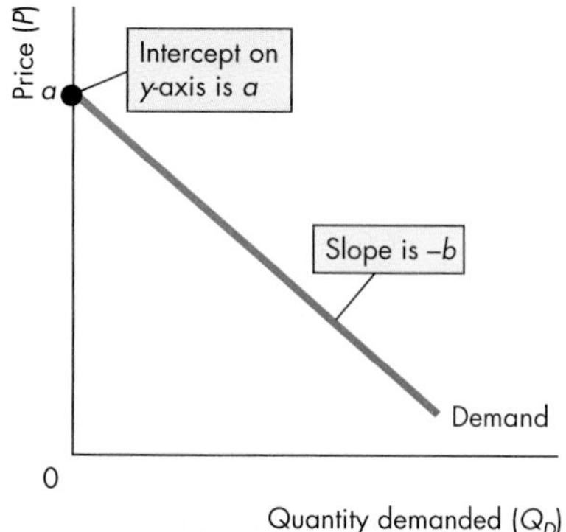

This equation tells us three things:

1. The price at which no one is willing to buy the good (Q_D is zero). That is, if the price is a, then the quantity demanded is zero. You can see the price a on the graph. It is the price at which the demand curve hits the y-axis—what we call the demand curve's "intercept on the y-axis."
2. As the price falls, the quantity demanded increases. If Q_D is a positive number, then the price P must be less than a. And as Q_D gets larger, the price P becomes smaller. That is, as the quantity increases, the maximum price that buyers are willing to pay for the good falls.
3. The constant b tells us how fast the maximum price that someone is willing to pay for the good falls as the quantity increases. That is, the constant b tells us about the steepness of the demand curve. The equation tells us that the slope of the demand curve is $-b$.

Supply Curve

The law of supply says that as the price of a good or service rises, the quantity supplied of that good increases. We illustrate the law of supply by setting out a supply schedule, by drawing a graph of the supply curve, or by writing down an equation. When the supply curve is a straight line, the following linear equation describes it

$$P = c + dQ_S,$$

where P is the price and Q_S is the quantity supplied. The c and d are positive constants.

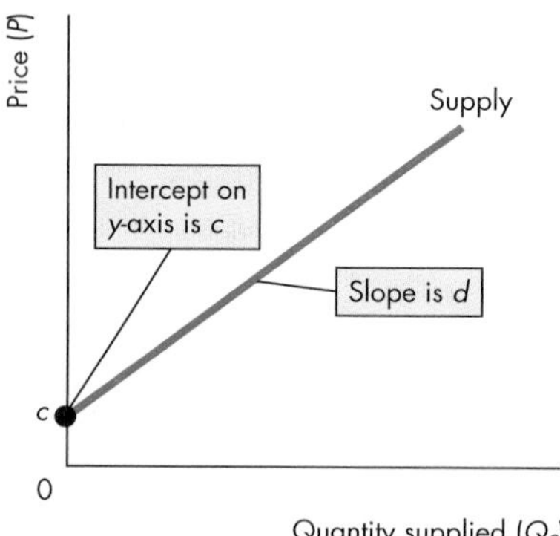

This equation tells us three things:

1. The price at which sellers are not willing to supply the good (Q_S is zero). That is, if the price is c, then no one is willing to sell the good. You can see the price c on the graph. It is the price at which the supply curve hits the y-axis—what we call the supply curve's "intercept on the y-axis."
2. As the price rises, the quantity supplied increases. If Q_S is a positive number, then the price P must be greater than c. And as Q_S increases, the price P gets larger. That is, as the quantity increases, the minimum price that sellers are willing to accept rises.
3. The constant d tells us how fast the minimum price at which someone is willing to sell the good rises as the quantity increases. That is, the constant d tells us about the steepness of the supply curve. The equation tells us that the slope of the supply curve is d.

Market Equilibrium

Demand and supply determine market equilibrium. The figure shows the equilibrium price (P^*) and equilibrium quantity (Q^*) at the intersection of the demand curve and the supply curve.

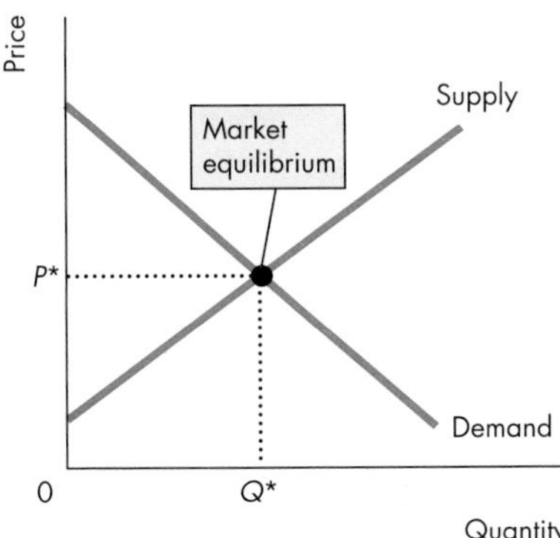

We can use the equations to find the equilibrium price and equilibrium quantity. The price of a good adjusts until the quantity demanded equals the quantity supplied. That is,

$$Q_D = Q_S.$$

So at the equilibrium price (P^*) and equilibrium quantity (Q^*),

$$Q_D = Q_S = Q^*.$$

To find the equilibrium price and equilibrium quantity, substitute Q^* for Q_D in the demand equation and Q^* for Q_S in the supply equation. Then the price is the equilibrium price (P^*), which gives

$$P^* = a - bQ^*$$

$$P^* = c + dQ^*.$$

Notice that

$$a - bQ^* = c + dQ^*.$$

Now solve for Q^*:

$$a - c = bQ^* + dQ^*$$

$$a - c = (b + d)Q^*$$

$$Q^* = \frac{a - c}{b + d}.$$

To find the equilibrium price, (P^*), substitute for Q^* in either the demand equation or the supply equation.

Using the demand equation, we have

$$P^* = a - b\left(\frac{a - c}{b + d}\right)$$

$$P^* = \frac{a(b + d) - b(a - c)}{b + d}$$

$$P^* = \frac{ad + bc}{b + d}.$$

Alternatively, using the supply equation, we have

$$P^* = c + d\left(\frac{a - c}{b + d}\right)$$

$$P^* = \frac{c(b + d) + d(a - c)}{b + d}$$

$$P^* = \frac{ad + bc}{b + d}.$$

An Example

The demand for ice-cream cones is

$$P = 800 - 2Q_D.$$

The supply of ice-cream cones is

$$P = 200 + 1Q_S.$$

The price of a cone is expressed in cents, and the quantities are expressed in cones per day.

To find the equilibrium price (P^*) and equilibrium quantity (Q^*), substitute Q^* for Q_D and Q_S and P^* for P in the demand and supply equations. That is,

$$P^* = 800 - 2Q^*$$

$$P^* = 200 + 1Q^*.$$

Now solve for Q^*:

$$800 - 2Q^* = 200 + 1Q^*$$

$$600 = 3Q^*$$

$$Q^* = 200.$$

And

$$P^* = 800 - 2(200)$$

$$= 400.$$

The equilibrium price is $4 a cone, and the equilibrium quantity is 200 cones per day.

SUMMARY

KEY POINTS

Markets and Prices (p. 60)

- A competitive market is one that has so many buyers and sellers that no one can influence the price.
- Opportunity cost is a relative price.
- Demand and supply determine relative prices.

Demand (pp. 61–65)

- Demand is the relationship between the quantity demanded of a good and its price when all other influences on buying plans remain the same.
- The higher the price of a good, other things remaining the same, the smaller is the quantity demanded—the law of demand.
- Demand depends on the prices of substitutes and complements, expected future prices, income, population, and preferences.

Supply (pp. 66–69)

- Supply is the relationship between the quantity supplied of a good and its price when all other influences on selling plans remain the same.
- The higher the price of a good, other things remaining the same, the greater is the quantity supplied—the law of supply.
- Supply depends on the prices of resources used to produce a good, the prices of related goods produced, expected future prices, the number of suppliers, and technology.

Market Equilibrium (pp. 70–71)

- At the equilibrium price, the quantity demanded equals the quantity supplied.
- At prices above equilibrium, there is a surplus and the price falls.
- At prices below equilibrium, there is a shortage and the price rises.

Predicting Changes in Price and Quantity (pp. 72–75)

- An increase in demand brings a rise in price and an increase in the quantity supplied. (A decrease in demand brings a fall in price and a decrease in the quantity supplied.)
- An increase in supply brings a fall in price and an increase in the quantity demanded. (A decrease in supply brings a rise in price and a decrease in the quantity demanded.)
- An increase in demand and an increase in supply bring an increased quantity, but the price might rise, fall, or remain the same. An increase in demand and a decrease in supply bring a higher price, but the quantity might increase, decrease, or remain the same.

KEY FIGURES

Figure 3.1 The Demand Curve, 62
Figure 3.3 A Change in the Quantity Demanded Versus a Change in Demand, 65
Figure 3.4 The Supply Curve, 67
Figure 3.6 A Change in the Quantity Supplied Versus a Change in Supply, 69
Figure 3.7 Equilibrium, 70
Figure 3.8 The Effects of a Change in Demand, 72
Figure 3.9 The Effects of a Change in Supply, 73

KEY TERMS

Change in demand, 63
Change in supply, 67
Change in the quantity demanded, 65
Change in the quantity supplied, 68
Competitive market, 60
Complement, 63
Demand, 62
Demand curve, 62
Equilibrium price, 70
Equilibrium quantity, 70
Inferior good, 64
Law of demand, 61
Law of supply, 66
Normal good, 64
Quantity demanded, 61
Quantity supplied, 66
Relative price, 60
Substitute, 63
Supply, 66
Supply curve, 66

PROBLEMS

*1. What is the effect on the price of an audiotape and the quantity of audiotapes sold if
 a. The price of a CD rises?
 b. The price of a Walkman rises?
 c. The supply of CD players increases?
 d. Consumers' incomes increase?
 e. Workers who make audiotapes get a pay raise?
 f. The price of a Walkman rises at the same time as the workers who make audiotapes get a pay raise?

2. What is the effect on the price of a DVD player and the quantity of DVD players sold if
 a. The price of a DVD rises?
 b. The price of a DVD falls?
 c. The supply of DVD players increases?
 d. Consumers' incomes decrease?
 e. The wage rate of workers who produce DVD players increases?
 f. The wage rate of workers who produce DVD players rises and at the same time the price of a DVD falls?

*3. Suppose that the following events occur one at a time:
 (i) The price of crude oil rises.
 (ii) The price of a car rises.
 (iii) All speed limits on highways are abolished.
 (iv) Robot technology cuts car production costs.

 Which of these events increases or decreases (state which):
 a. The demand for gasoline?
 b. The supply of gasoline?
 c. The quantity of gasoline demanded?
 d. The quantity of gasoline supplied?

4. Suppose that the following events occur one at a time:
 (i) The price of airfares halves.
 (ii) The price of beef falls.
 (iii) A cheap new strong cloth, a close substitute for leather, is invented.
 (iv) A new high-speed technology for cutting leather is invented.

 Which of these events will increase or decrease (state which):
 a. The demand for leather bags?
 b. The supply of leather bags?
 c. The quantity of leather bags demanded?
 d. The quantity of leather bags supplied?

*5. The figure illustrates the market for pizza.
 a. Label the curves in the figure.
 b. What are the equilibrium price of a pizza and the equilibrium quantity of pizza?

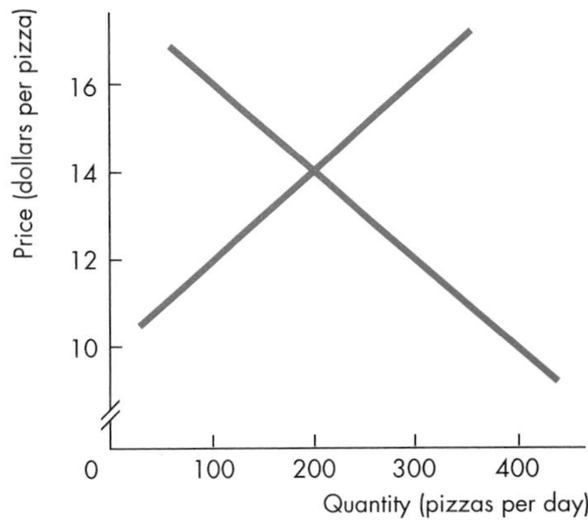

6. The figure illustrates the market for fish.
 a. Label the curves in the figure.
 b. What are the equilibrium price of a fish and the equilibrium quantity of fish?

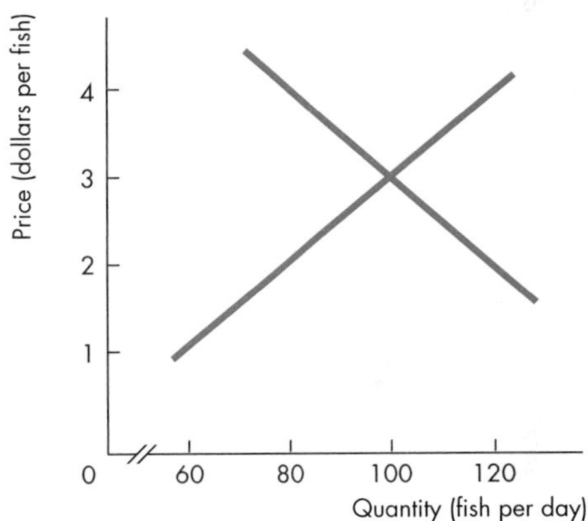

*7. The demand and supply schedules for gum are

Price (cents per pack)	Quantity demanded (millions of packs per week)	Quantity supplied (millions of packs per week)
20	180	60
30	160	80
40	140	100
50	120	120
60	100	140
70	80	160
80	60	180

 a. Draw a graph of the gum market and mark in the equilibrium price and quantity.

b. Suppose that gum is 70 cents a pack. Describe the situation in the gum market and explain how the price of gum adjusts.

8. The demand and supply schedules for potato chips are

Price (cents per bag)	Quantity demanded	Quantity supplied
	(millions of bag per week)	
50	160	130
60	150	140
70	140	150
80	130	160
90	120	170
100	110	180

a. Draw a graph of the potato chip market and mark in the equilibrium price and quantity.
b. Suppose that chips are 60 cents a bag. Describe the situation in the market for chips and explain how the price adjusts.

*9. In problem 7, suppose that a fire destroys some gum-producing factories and the supply of gum decreases by 40 million packs a week.
a. Has there been a shift of or a movement along the supply curve of gum?
b. Has there been a shift of or a movement along the demand curve for gum?
c. What are the new equilibrium price and equilibrium quantity of gum?

10. In problem 8, suppose a new dip comes onto the market and the demand for potato chips increases by 30 million bags per week.
a. Has there been a shift of or a movement along the supply curve of potato chips?
b. Has there been a shift of or a movement along the demand curve for potato chips?
c. What are the new equilibrium price and equilibrium quantity of potato chips?

*11. In problem 9, suppose an increase in the teenage population increases the demand for gum by 40 million packs per week at the same time as the fire occurs. What are the new equilibrium price and quantity of gum?

12. In problem 10, suppose that a virus destroys several potato farms with the result that the supply of potato chips decreases by 40 million bags a week at the same time as the dip comes onto the market. What are the new equilibrium price and quantity of potato chips?

CRITICAL THINKING

1. After you have studied *Reading Between the Lines* on pp. 76–77, answer the following questions:
a. What were the factors that changed the demand for and supply of PCs during 2001 and 2002?
b. How did competition between Intel and AMD influence the market for PCs?
c. How do you think the development of CD-R technology has changed the demand for PCs and the equilibrium price of a PC?

WEB EXERCISES

1. Use the links on the Parkin–Bade Web site and obtain data on the prices and quantities of wheat.
a. Make a figure similar to Fig. 3.7 on p. 70 to illustrate the market for wheat in 1999 and 2000.
b. Show the changes in demand and supply and the changes in the quantity demanded and the quantity supplied that are consistent with the price and quantity data.

2. Use the link on the Parkin–Bade Web site and obtain data on the price of oil.
a. Describe how the price of oil has changed over the past five years.
b. Draw a demand-supply diagram to explain what happens to the price when there is an increase or a decrease in supply and no change in demand.
c. What do you predict would happen to the price of oil if a new drilling technology permitted deeper ocean sources to be used?
d. What do you predict would happen to the price of oil if a clean and safe nuclear technology were developed?
e. What do you predict would happen to the price of oil if automobiles were powered by batteries instead of by internal combustion engines?

ELASTICITY — CHAPTER 4

Predicting Prices

The Organization of Oil Exporting Countries (OPEC) is a big enough player in the global oil market to influence the price of oil. To raise the price, OPEC must cut production. If it does so, by how much will the price rise? Will non-OPEC producers also cut production? Or will they produce more to take advantage of the higher price achieved by OPEC's actions? To answer questions like these, we need to know the quantitative relationship between price and the quantities demanded and supplied. ◆ All firms are interested in the factors that influence prices and in predicting prices. A pizza producer wants to know if the arrival of a new competitor will lower the price of pizza and whether as people's incomes rise they will spend more or less on pizza. A labour union wants to know whether, if it goes for a large wage rise, the number of people employed will fall by a lot or by a little.

◇ In this chapter, you will learn about a tool that helps us to answer questions like the ones we've just considered. You will learn about the elasticity of demand and supply. We'll return to the questions that OPEC needs to answer in *Reading Between the Lines* and see how the concept of elasticity helps us to understand the effects of OPEC's actions on the price of crude oil, a price that has a big impact on the price that you end up paying for gasoline.

After studying this chapter, you will be able to

- **Define, calculate, and explain the factors that influence the price elasticity of demand**
- **Define, calculate, and explain the factors that influence the cross elasticity of demand and the income elasticity of demand**
- **Define, calculate, and explain the factors that influence the elasticity of supply**

Price Elasticity of Demand

YOU KNOW THAT WHEN SUPPLY INCREASES, THE equilibrium price falls and the equilibrium quantity increases. But does the price fall by a large amount and the quantity increase by a little? Or does the price barely fall and the quantity increase by a large amount?

The answer depends on the responsiveness of the quantity demanded to a change in price. You can see why by studying Fig. 4.1, which shows two possible scenarios in a local pizza market. Figure 4.1(a) shows one scenario, and Fig. 4.1(b) shows the other.

In both cases, supply is initially S_0. In part (a), the demand for pizza is shown by the demand curve D_A. In part (b), the demand for pizza is shown by the demand curve D_B. Initially, in both cases, the price is \$20 a pizza and the quantity of pizza produced and consumed is 10 pizzas an hour.

Now a large pizza franchise opens up, and the supply of pizza increases. The supply curve shifts rightward to S_1. In case (a), the price falls by an enormous \$15 to \$5 a pizza, and the quantity increases by only 3 to 13 pizzas an hour. In contrast, in case (b), the price falls by only \$5 to \$15 a pizza and the quantity increases by 7 to 17 pizzas an hour.

The different outcomes arise from differing degrees of responsiveness of the quantity demanded to a change in price. But what do we mean by responsiveness? One possible answer is slope. The slope of demand curve D_A is steeper than the slope of demand curve D_B.

In this example, we can compare the slopes of the two demand curves. But we can't always do so. The reason is that the slope of a demand curve depends on the units in which we measure the price and quantity. And we often must compare the demand curves for different goods and services that are measured in unrelated units. For example, a pizza producer might want to compare the demand for pizza with the demand for soft drinks. Which quantity demanded is more responsive to a price change? This question can't be answered by comparing the slopes of two demand curves. The units of measurement of pizza and soft drinks are unrelated. The question can be answered with a measure of responsiveness that is independent of units of measurement. Elasticity is such a measure.

The **price elasticity of demand** is a units-free measure of the responsiveness of the quantity demanded of a good to a change in its price when all other influences on buyers' plans remain the same.

FIGURE 4.1 How a Change in Supply Changes Price and Quantity

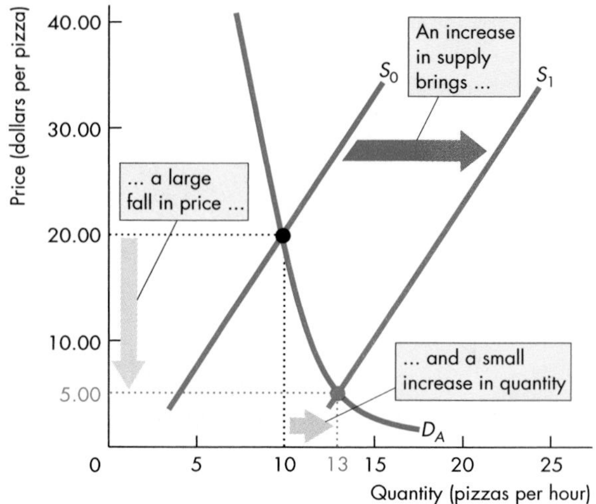

(a) Large price change and small quantity change

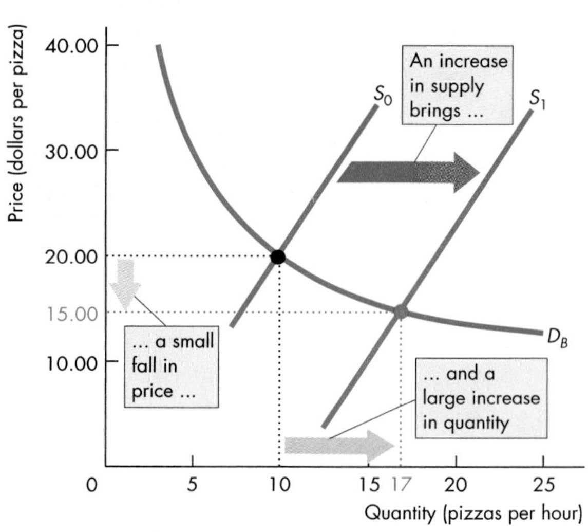

(b) Small price change and large quantity change

Initially the price is \$20 a pizza and the quantity sold is 10 pizzas an hour. Then supply increases from S_0 to S_1. In part (a), the price falls by \$15 to \$5 a pizza, and the quantity increases by only 3, to 13 pizzas an hour. In part (b), the price falls by only \$5 to \$15 a pizza, and the quantity increases by 7, to 17 pizzas an hour. This price change is smaller and the quantity change is larger than in case (a). The quantity demanded is more responsive to price in case (b) than in case (a).

Calculating Elasticity

We calculate the *price elasticity of demand* by using the formula:

$$\text{Price elasticity of demand} = \frac{\text{Percentage change in quantity demanded}}{\text{Percentage change in price}}.$$

To use this formula, we need to know the quantities demanded at different prices when all other influences on buyers' plans remain the same. Suppose we have the data on prices and quantities demanded of pizza and we calculate the price elasticity of demand for pizza.

Figure 4.2 zooms in on the demand curve for pizza and shows how the quantity demanded responds to a small change in price. Initially, the price is \$20.50 a pizza and 9 pizzas an hour are sold—the original point in the figure. The price then falls to \$19.50 a pizza, and the quantity demanded increases to 11 pizzas an hour—the new point in the figure. When the price falls by \$1 a pizza, the quantity demanded increases by 2 pizzas an hour.

To calculate the price elasticity of demand, we express the changes in price and quantity demanded as percentages of the *average price* and the *average quantity*. By using the average price and average quantity, we calculate the elasticity at a point on the demand curve midway between the original point and the new point. The original price is \$20.50 and the new price is \$19.50, so the average price is \$20. The \$1 price decrease is 5 percent of the average price. That is,

$$\Delta P / P_{ave} = (\$1/\$20) \times 100 = 5\%.$$

The original quantity demanded is 9 pizzas and the new quantity demanded is 11 pizzas, so the average quantity demanded is 10 pizzas. The 2 pizza increase in the quantity demanded is 20 percent of the average quantity. That is,

$$\Delta Q / Q_{ave} = (2/10) \times 100 = 20\%.$$

So the price elasticity of demand, which is the percentage change in the quantity demanded (20 percent) divided by the percentage change in price (5 percent) is 4. That is,

$$\text{Price elasticity of demand} = \frac{\%\Delta Q}{\%\Delta P} = \frac{20\%}{5\%} = 4.$$

FIGURE 4.2 Calculating the Elasticity of Demand

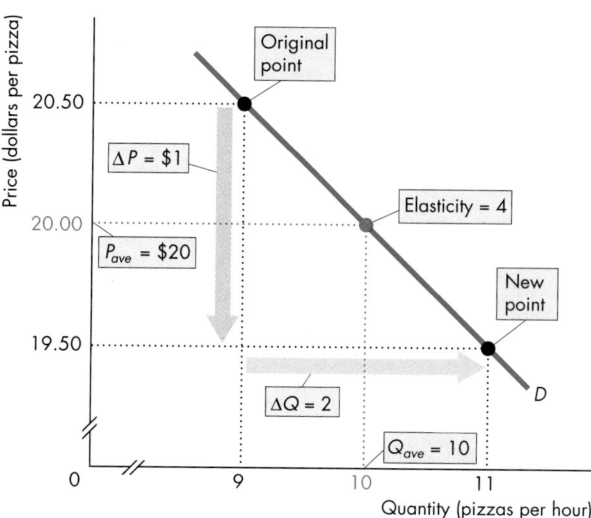

The elasticity of demand is calculated by using the formula:*

$$\text{Price elasticity of demand} = \frac{\text{Percentage change in quantity demanded}}{\text{Percentage change in price}} = \frac{\%\Delta Q}{\%\Delta P} = \frac{\Delta Q / Q_{ave}}{\Delta P / P_{ave}} = \frac{2/10}{1/20} = 4.$$

This calculation measures the elasticity at an average price of \$20 a pizza and an average quantity of 10 pizzas an hour.

*In the formula, the Greek letter delta (Δ) stands for "change in" and $\%\Delta$ stands for "percentage change in."

Average Price and Quantity Notice that we use the *average* price and *average* quantity. We do this because it gives the most precise measurement of elasticity—at the midpoint between the original price and the new price. If the price falls from \$20.50 to \$19.50, the \$1 price change is 4.9 percent of \$20.50. The 2 pizza change in quantity is 22.2 percent of 9, the original quantity. So if we use these numbers, the elasticity of demand is 22.2 divided by 4.9, which equals 4.5. If the price rises from \$19.50 to \$20.50, the \$1 price change is 5.1 percent of $19.50. The 2 pizza change in quantity is 18.2 percent of 11, the original quantity. So if we use these numbers, the elasticity of demand is 18.2 divided by 5.1, which equals 3.6.

By using percentages of the *average* price and *average* quantity, we get the same value for the elasticity regardless of whether the price falls from $20.50 to $19.50 or rises from $19.50 to $20.50.

Percentages and Proportions Elasticity is the ratio of two percentage changes. So when we divide one percentage change by another, the 100s cancel. A percentage change is a *proportionate* change multiplied by 100. The proportionate change in price is $\Delta P / P_{ave}$, and the proportionate change in quantity demanded is $\Delta Q / Q_{ave}$. So if we divide $\Delta Q / Q_{ave}$ by $\Delta P / P_{ave}$ we get the same answer as we get by using percentage changes.

A Units-Free Measure Now that you've calculated a price elasticity of demand, you can see why it is a *units-free measure.* Elasticity is a units-free measure because the percentage change in each variable is independent of the units in which the variable is measured. And the ratio of the two percentages is a number without units.

Minus Sign and Elasticity When the price of a good *rises,* the quantity demanded *decreases* along the demand curve. Because a *positive* change in price brings a *negative* change in the quantity demanded, the price elasticity of demand is a negative number. But it is the magnitude, or absolute value, of the price elasticity of demand that tells us how responsive—how elastic—demand is. To compare elasticities, we use the magnitude of the price elasticity of demand and ignore the minus sign.

Inelastic and Elastic Demand

Figure 4.3 shows three demand curves that cover the entire range of possible elasticities of demand. In Fig. 4.3(a), the quantity demanded is constant regardless of the price. If the quantity demanded remains constant when the price changes, then the price elasticity of demand is zero and the good is said to have **perfectly inelastic demand.** One good that has a very low price elasticity of demand (perhaps zero over some price range) is insulin. Insulin is of such importance to some diabetics that if the price rises or falls, they do not change the quantity they buy.

If the percentage change in the quantity demanded equals the percentage change in price, then the price elasticity equals 1 and the good is said to have **unit elastic demand.** The demand in Fig. 4.3(b) is an example of unit elastic demand.

Between the cases shown in Fig. 4.3(a) and Fig. 4.3(b) is the general case in which the percentage

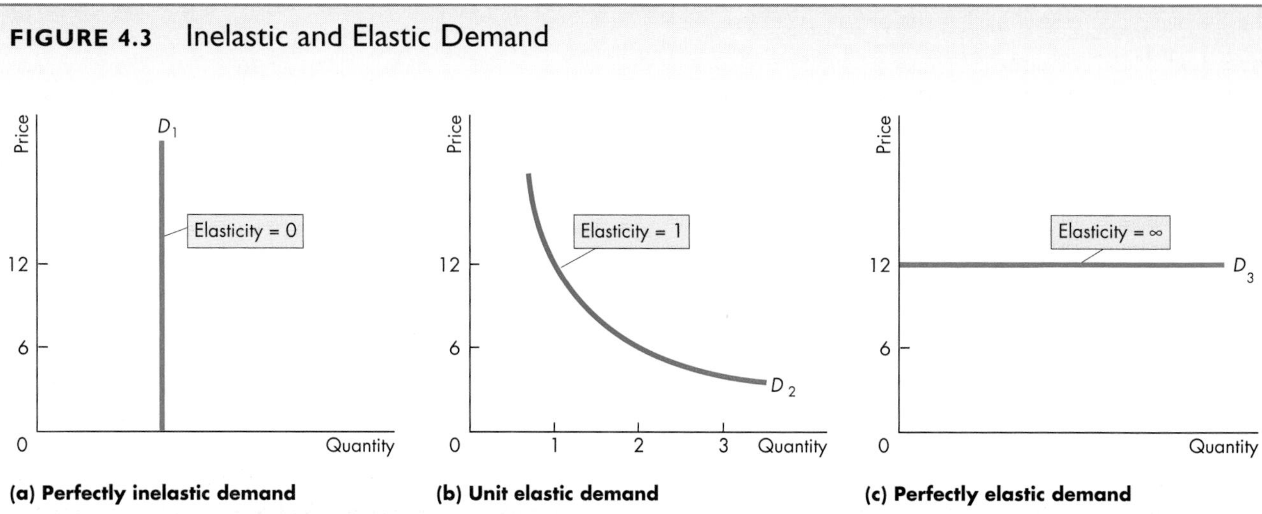

FIGURE 4.3 Inelastic and Elastic Demand

(a) Perfectly inelastic demand **(b) Unit elastic demand** **(c) Perfectly elastic demand**

Each demand illustrated here has a constant elasticity. The demand curve in part (a) illustrates the demand for a good that has a zero elasticity of demand. The demand curve in part (b) illustrates the demand for a good with a unit elasticity of demand. And the demand curve in part (c) illustrates the demand for a good with an infinite elasticity of demand.

change in the quantity demanded is less than the percentage change in price. In this case, the price elasticity of demand is between zero and 1 and the good is said to have **inelastic demand.** Food and housing are examples of goods with inelastic demand.

If the quantity demanded changes by an infinitely large percentage in response to a tiny price change, then the price elasticity of demand is infinity and the good is said to have **perfectly elastic demand.** Figure 4.3(c) shows perfectly elastic demand. An example of a good that has a very high elasticity of demand (almost infinite) is a soft drink from two campus machines located side by side. If the two machines offer the same soft drinks for the same price, some people buy from one machine and some from the other. But if one machine's price is higher than the other's, by even a small amount, no one will buy from the machine with the higher price. Soft drinks from the two machines are perfect substitutes.

Between the cases in Fig. 4.3(b) and Fig. 4.3(c) is the general case in which the percentage change in the quantity demanded exceeds the percentage change in price. In this case, the price elasticity is greater than 1 and the good is said to have **elastic demand.** Automobiles and furniture are examples of goods that have elastic demand.

Elasticity Along a Straight-Line Demand Curve

Along a straight-line demand curve, such as the one in Fig. 4.4, the elasticity varies. At high prices and small quantities, the elasticity is large; at low prices and large quantities, the elasticity is small. To convince yourself of this fact, calculate the elasticity at three average prices.

First, suppose the price falls from \$25 to \$15 a pizza. The quantity demanded increases from zero to 20 pizzas an hour. The average price is \$20, so the percentage change in price is \$10 divided by \$20 multiplied by 100, which equals 50. The average quantity is 10 pizzas, so the percentage change in quantity is 20 pizzas divided by 10 pizzas, multiplied by 100, which equals 200. So dividing the percentage change in the quantity demanded (200) by the percentage change in price (50), you see that the elasticity of demand at an average price of \$20 is 4.

Next, suppose that the price falls from \$15 to \$10 a pizza. The quantity demanded increases from 20 to 30 pizzas an hour. The average price is now \$12.50, so the percentage change in price is \$5 divided by \$12.50 multiplied by 100, which equals 40 percent. The average quantity is 25 pizzas an hour, so the percentage change in the quantity demanded is 10 pizzas divided by 25 pizzas multiplied by 100, which also equals 40 percent. So dividing the percentage change in the quantity demanded (40) by the percentage change in price (40), you see that the elasticity of demand at an average price of \$12.50 is 1. The elasticity of demand is always equal to 1 at the midpoint of a straight-line demand curve.

Finally, suppose that the price falls from \$10 to zero. The quantity demanded increases from 30 to 50 pizzas an hour. The average price is now \$5, so the percentage change in price is \$10 divided by \$5 multiplied by 100, which equals 200 percent. The average quantity is 40 pizzas an hour, so the percentage change in the quantity demanded is 20 pizzas divided by 40 pizzas multiplied by 100, which also equals 50 percent. So dividing the percentage change in the quantity demanded (50) by the percentage change in price (200), you see that the elasticity of demand at an average price of \$5 is 1/4.

FIGURE 4.4 Elasticity Along a Straight-Line Demand Curve

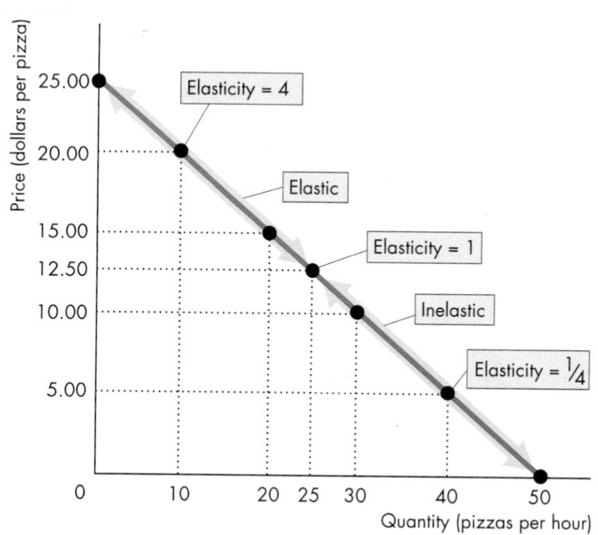

On a straight-line demand curve, elasticity decreases as the price falls and the quantity demanded increases. Demand is unit elastic at the midpoint of the demand curve (elasticity is 1). Above the midpoint, demand is elastic; below the midpoint, demand is inelastic.

Total Revenue and Elasticity

The **total revenue** from the sale of a good equals the price of the good multiplied by the quantity sold. When a price changes, total revenue also changes. But a rise in price does not always increase total revenue. The change in total revenue depends on the elasticity of demand in the following way:

- If demand is elastic, a 1 percent price cut increases the quantity sold by more than 1 percent and total revenue increases.
- If demand is inelastic, a 1 percent price cut increases the quantity sold by less than 1 percent and total revenue decreases.
- If demand is unit elastic, a 1 percent price cut increases the quantity sold by 1 percent and so total revenue does not change.

Figure 4.5 shows how we can use this relationship between elasticity and total revenue to estimate elasticity using the total revenue test. The **total revenue test** is a method of estimating the price elasticity of demand by observing the change in total revenue that results from a change in the price (when all other influences on the quantity sold remain the same).

- If a price cut increases total revenue, demand is elastic.
- If a price cut decreases total revenue, demand is inelastic.
- If a price cut leaves total revenue unchanged, demand is unit elastic.

In Fig. 4.5(a), over the price range from $25 to $12.50, demand is elastic. Over the price range from $12.50 to zero, demand is inelastic. At a price of $12.50, demand is unit elastic.

Figure 4.5(b) shows total revenue. At a price of $25, the quantity sold is zero, so total revenue is also zero. At a price of zero, the quantity demanded is 50 pizzas an hour but total revenue is again zero. A price cut in the elastic range brings an increase in total revenue—the percentage increase in the quantity demanded is greater than the percentage decrease in price. A price cut in the inelastic range brings a decrease in total revenue—the percentage increase in the quantity demanded is less than the percentage decrease in price. At unit elasticity, total revenue is at a maximum.

FIGURE 4.5 Elasticity and Total Revenue

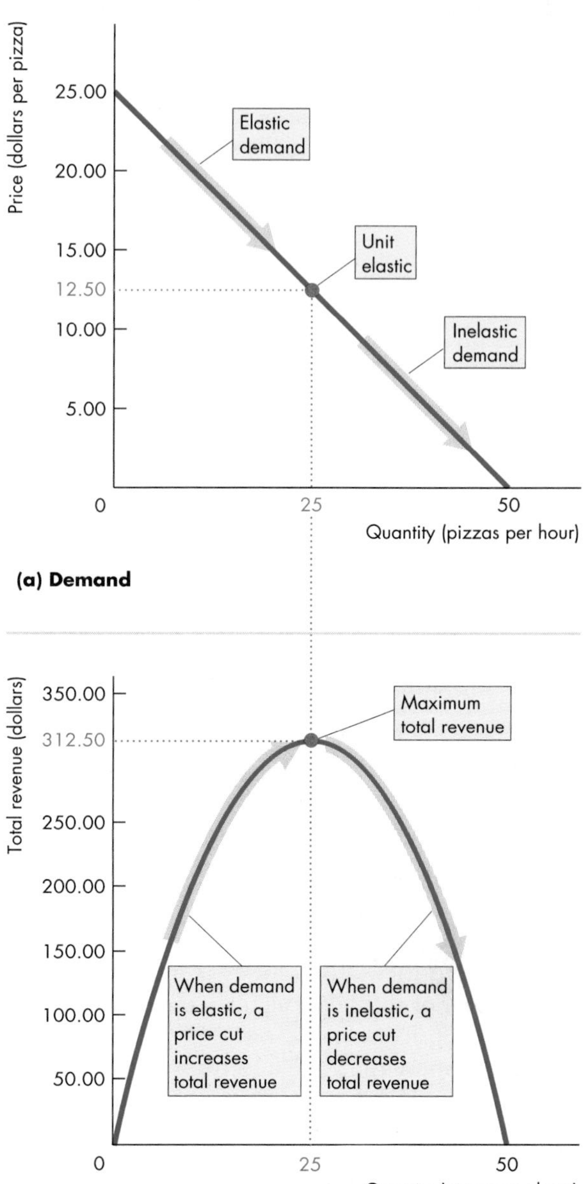

When demand is elastic, in the price range from $25 to $12.50, a decrease in price (part a) brings an increase in total revenue (part b). When demand is inelastic, in the price range from $12.50 to zero, a decrease in price (part a) brings a decrease in total revenue (part b). When demand is unit elastic, at a price of $12.50 (part a), total revenue is at a maximum (part b).

Your Expenditure and Your Elasticity

When a price changes, the change in your expenditure on the good depends on *your* elasticity of demand.

- If your demand is elastic, a 1 percent price cut increases the quantity you buy by more than 1 percent and your expenditure on the item increases.
- If your demand is inelastic, a 1 percent price cut increases the quantity you buy by less than 1 percent and your expenditure on the item decreases.
- If your demand is unit elastic, a 1 percent price cut increases the quantity you buy by 1 percent and your expenditure on the item does not change.

So if when the price of an item falls, you spend more on it, your demand for that item is elastic; if you spend the same amount, your demand is unit elastic; and if you spend less, your demand is inelastic.

The Factors That Influence the Elasticity of Demand

Table 4.1 lists some estimates of actual elasticities in the real world. You can see that these real-world elasticities of demand range from 1.52 for metals, the item with the most elastic demand in the table, to 0.05 for oil, the item with the most inelastic demand in the table. What makes the demand for some goods elastic and the demand for others inelastic?

Elasticity depends on three main factors:

- The closeness of substitutes
- The proportion of income spent on the good
- The time elapsed since the price change

Closeness of Substitutes The closer the substitutes for a good or service, the more elastic is the demand for it. For example, oil from which we make gasoline has substitutes but none that are currently very close (imagine a steam-driven, coal-fueled car). So the demand for oil is inelastic. Plastics are close substitutes for metals, so the demand for metals is elastic.

The degree of substitutability between two goods also depends on how narrowly (or broadly) we define them. For example, the elasticity of demand for meat is low, but the elasticity of demand for beef or pork is high. The elasticity of demand for personal computers is low, but the elasticity of demand for a Compaq, Dell, or IBM is high.

In everyday language we call some goods (such as food and housing) *necessities* and other goods (such as exotic vacations) *luxuries*. A necessity is a good that has poor substitutes and that is crucial for our well-being. So generally, a necessity has an inelastic demand. In Table 4.1, food and oil might be classified as necessities that have inelastic demand.

A luxury is a good that usually has many substitutes, one of which is not buying it. So a luxury generally has an elastic demand. In Table 4.1, furniture and motor vehicles might be classified as luxuries that have elastic demand.

TABLE 4.1 Some Real-World Price Elasticities of Demand

Good or Service	Elasticity
Elastic Demand	
Metals	1.52
Electrical engineering products	1.39
Mechanical engineering products	1.30
Furniture	1.26
Motor vehicles	1.14
Instrument engineering products	1.10
Professional services	1.09
Transportation services	1.03
Inelastic Demand	
Gas, electricity, and water	0.92
Chemicals	0.89
Drinks (all types)	0.78
Clothing	0.64
Tobacco	0.61
Banking and insurance services	0.56
Housing services	0.55
Agricultural and fish products	0.42
Books, magazines, and newspapers	0.34
Food	0.12
Oil	0.05

Sources: Ahsan Mansur and John Whalley, "Numerical Specification of Applied General Equilibrium Models: Estimation, Calibration, and Data," in *Applied General Equilibrium Analysis*, eds. Herbert E. Scarf and John B. Shoven (New York: Cambridge University Press, 1984), 109, and Henri Theil, Ching-Fan Chung, and James L. Seale, Jr., *Advances in Econometrics, Supplement I, 1989, International Evidence on Consumption Patterns* (Greenwich, Conn.: JAI Press Inc., 1989), and Geoffrey Heal, Columbia University, Web site.

Proportion of Income Spent on the Good Other things remaining the same, the greater the proportion of income spent on a good, the more elastic is the demand for it.

Think about your own elasticity of demand for chewing gum and housing. If the price of chewing gum doubles, you consume almost as much gum as before. Your demand for gum is inelastic. If apartment rents double, you shriek and look for more students to share accommodation with you. Your demand for housing is more elastic than your demand for gum. Why the difference? Housing takes a large proportion of your budget, and gum takes only a tiny proportion. You don't like either price increase, but you hardly notice the higher price of gum, while the higher rent puts your budget under severe strain.

Figure 4.6 shows the proportion of income spent on food and the price elasticity of demand for food in 10 countries. This figure confirms the general tendency we have just described. The larger the proportion of income spent on food, the larger is the price elasticity of demand for food. For example, in Tanzania, a nation where 62 percent of income is spent on food, the price elasticity of demand for food is 0.77. In contrast, in Canada, where 14 percent of income is spent on food, the price elasticity of demand for food is 0.13.

Time Elapsed Since the Price Change The longer the time that has elapsed since the price change, the more elastic is demand. When the price of oil increased by 400 percent during the 1970s, people barely changed the quantity of oil and gasoline they consumed. But gradually, as more efficient auto and airplane engines were developed, the quantity consumed decreased. The demand for oil has become more elastic as more time has elapsed since the huge price hike. Similarly, when the price of a PC fell, the quantity of PCs demanded increased only slightly at first. But as more people have become better informed about the variety of ways of using a PC, the quantity of PCs bought has increased sharply. The demand for PCs has become more elastic.

FIGURE 4.6 Price Elasticities in 10 Countries

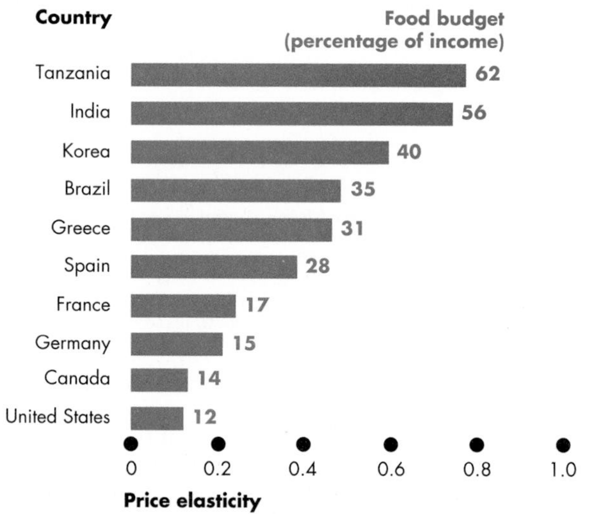

As income increases and the proportion of income spent on food decreases, the demand for food becomes less elastic.

Source: Henri Theil, Ching-Fan Chung, and James L. Seale, Jr., *Advances in Econometrics, Supplement 1, 1989, International Evidence on Consumption Patterns* (Greenwich, Conn.: JAI Press, Inc., 1989).

REVIEW QUIZ

1. Why do we need a units-free measure of the responsiveness of the quantity demanded of a good or service to a change in its price?
2. Can you define and calculate the price elasticity of demand?
3. Why, when we calculate the price elasticity of demand, do we express the change in price as a percentage of the *average* price and the change in quantity as a percentage of the *average* quantity?
4. What is the total revenue test and why does it work?
5. What are the main influences on the elasticity of demand that make the demand for some goods elastic and the demand for other goods inelastic?
6. Why is the demand for a luxury generally more elastic than the demand for a necessity?

You've now completed your study of the *price* elasticity of demand. Two other elasticity concepts tell us about the effects of other influences on demand. Let's look at these other elasticities of demand.

More Elasticities of Demand

BACK AT THE PIZZERIA, YOU ARE TRYING TO WORK out how a price cut by the burger shop next door will affect the demand for your pizza. You know that pizzas and burgers are substitutes. And you know that when the price of a substitute for pizza falls, the demand for pizza decreases. But by how much?

You also know that pizza and soft drinks are complements. And you know that if the price of a complement of pizza falls, the demand for pizza increases. So you wonder whether you might keep your customers by cutting the price you charge for soft drinks. But again by how much? To answer these questions, you need to calculate the cross elasticity of demand. Let's examine this elasticity measure.

Cross Elasticity of Demand

We measure the influence of a change in the price of a substitute or complement by using the concept of the cross elasticity of demand. The **cross elasticity of demand** is a measure of the responsiveness of the demand for a good to a change in the price of a substitute or complement, other things remaining the same. We calculate the *cross elasticity of demand* by using the formula:

$$\text{Cross elasticity of demand} = \frac{\text{Percentage change in quantity demanded}}{\text{Percentage change in price of a substitute or complement}}.$$

The cross elasticity of demand can be positive or negative. It is *positive* for a *substitute* and it is *negative* for a *complement*.

Substitutes Suppose that the price of pizza is constant and 9 pizzas an hour are sold. The price of a burger then rises from \$1.50 to \$2.50. No other influence on buying plans changes, and the quantity of pizzas sold increases to 11 an hour.

The change in the quantity demanded is the new quantity, 11 pizzas, minus the original quantity, 9 pizzas, which is +2 pizzas. The average quantity is 10 pizzas. So the quantity of pizzas demanded increases by 20 percent (+20). That is,

$$\Delta Q / Q_{ave} = (+2/10) \times 100 = +20\%.$$

The change in the price of a burger, a substitute for pizza, is the new price, \$2.50, minus the original price, \$1.50, which is +\$1. The average price is \$2. So the price of a burger rises by 50 percent (+50). That is,

$$\Delta P / P_{ave} = (+1/2) \times 100 = +50\%.$$

So the cross elasticity of demand for pizza with respect to the price of a burger is

$$\frac{+20\%}{+50\%} = 0.4.$$

Figure 4.7 illustrates the cross elasticity of demand. Pizza and burgers are substitutes. Because they are substitutes, when the price of a burger rises, the demand for pizza increases. The demand curve for pizza shifts rightward from D_0 to D_1. Because a *rise* in the price of a burger brings an *increase* in the demand for pizza, the cross elasticity of demand for pizza with respect to the price of a burger is *positive.* Both the price and the quantity change in the same direction.

FIGURE 4.7 Cross Elasticity of Demand

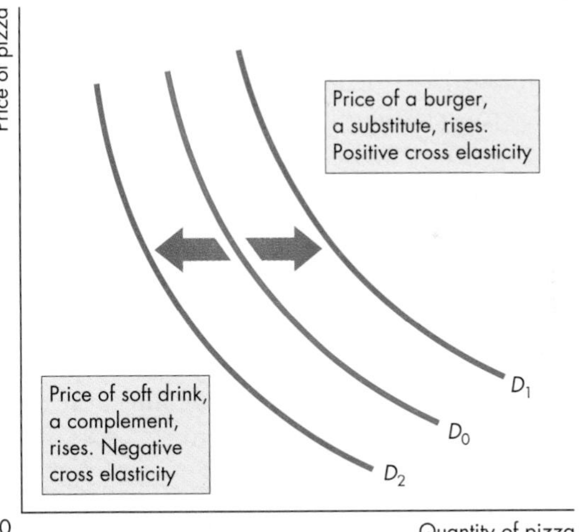

A burger is a *substitute* for pizza. When the price of a burger rises, the demand for pizza increases and the demand curve for pizza shifts rightward from D_0 to D_1. The cross elasticity of the demand for pizza is *positive*.

Soft drinks are a *complement* of pizza. When the price of a soft drink rises, the demand for pizza decreases and the demand curve for pizza shifts leftward from D_0 to D_2. The cross elasticity of the demand for pizza is *negative*.

Complements Now suppose that the price of a pizza is constant and 11 pizzas an hour are sold. The price of a soft drink rises from $1.50 to $2.50. No other influence on buying plans changes, and the quantity of pizzas sold falls to 9 an hour.

The change in the quantity demanded is the opposite of what we've just calculated: The quantity of pizzas demanded decreases by 20 percent (–20).

The change in the price of a soft drink, a complement of pizza, is the same as the percentage change in the price of a burger that we've just calculated: The price rises by 50 percent (+50). So the cross elasticity of demand of pizza with respect to the price of a soft drink is

$$\frac{-20\%}{+50\%} = -0.4.$$

Because pizza and soft drinks are complements, when the price of a soft drink rises, the demand for pizza decreases. In Fig. 4.7, the demand curve for pizza shifts leftward from D_0 to D_2. Because a *rise* in the price of soft drinks brings a *decrease* in the demand for pizza, the cross elasticity of demand for pizza with respect to the price of soft drinks is *negative.* The price and quantity change in *opposite* directions.

The magnitude of the cross elasticity of demand determines how far the demand curve shifts. The larger the cross elasticity (absolute value), the greater is the change in demand and the larger is the shift in the demand curve.

If two items are very close substitutes, such as two brands of spring water, the cross elasticity is large. If two items are close complements, such as movies and popcorn, the cross elasticity is large.

If two items are somewhat unrelated to each other, such as newspapers and orange juice, the cross elasticity is small—perhaps even zero.

Income Elasticity of Demand

Suppose the economy is expanding and people are enjoying rising incomes. This prosperity is bringing an increase in the demand for most types of goods and services. But by how much will the demand for pizza increase? The answer depends on the **income elasticity of demand,** which is a measure of the responsiveness of the demand for a good or service to a change in income, other things remaining the same.

The income elasticity of demand is calculated by using the formula:

$$\text{Income elasticity of demand} = \frac{\text{Percentage change in quantity demanded}}{\text{Percentage change in income}}.$$

Income elasticities of demand can be positive or negative and fall into three interesting ranges:

- Greater than 1 (*normal* good, income elastic)
- Positive and less than 1 (*normal* good, income inelastic)
- Negative (*inferior* good)

Income Elastic Demand Suppose that the price of pizza is constant and 9 pizzas an hour are sold. Then income rises from $975 to $1,025 a week. No other influence on buying plans changes, and the quantity of pizzas sold increases to 11 an hour.

The change in the quantity demanded is +2 pizzas. The average quantity is 10, so the quantity demanded increases by 20 percent. The change in income is +$50 and the average income is $1,000, so the income increases by 5 percent. The income elasticity of demand for pizza is

$$\frac{20\%}{5\%} = 4.$$

As income increases, the quantity of pizza demanded increases faster than does income. The demand for pizza is income elastic. Other goods in this category include ocean cruises, international travel, jewellery, and works of art.

Income Inelastic Demand If the percentage increase in the quantity demanded is less than the percentage increase in income, the income elasticity of demand is positive and less than 1. In this case, the quantity demanded increases as income increases, but income increases faster than does the quantity demanded. The demand for the good is income inelastic. Goods in this category include food, clothing, newspapers, and magazines.

Inferior Goods If when income increases, the quantity demanded of a good decreases, the income elasticity of demand is negative. Goods in this category include small motorcycles, potatoes, and rice. Low-income consumers buy most of these goods.

Real-World Income Elasticities of Demand

Table 4.2 shows estimates of some real-world income elasticities of demand. The demand for a necessity, such as food or gasoline, is income inelastic, while the demand for a luxury, such as transportation, which includes airline and foreign travel, is income elastic.

But what is a necessity and what is a luxury depends on the level of income. For people with a low income, food and clothing can be luxuries. So the *level* of income has a big effect on income elasticities of demand. Figure 4.8 shows this effect on the income elasticity of demand for food in 10 countries. In countries with low incomes, such as Tanzania and India, the income elasticity of demand for food is high. In countries with high incomes, such as Canada, the income elasticity of demand for food is low.

TABLE 4.2 Some Real-World Income Elasticities of Demand

Elastic Demand	
Airline travel	5.82
Movies	3.41
Foreign travel	3.08
Electricity	1.94
Restaurant meals	1.61
Local buses and trains	1.38
Haircuts	1.36
Automobiles	1.07
Inelastic Demand	
Tobacco	0.86
Alcoholic drinks	0.62
Furniture	0.53
Clothing	0.51
Newspapers and magazines	0.38
Telephone	0.32
Food	0.14

Sources: H.S. Houthakker and Lester D. Taylor, *Consumer Demand in the United States* (Cambridge, Mass.: Harvard University Press, 1970), and Henri Theil, Ching-Fan Chung, and James L. Seale, Jr., *Advances in Econometrics, Supplement 1, 1989, International Evidence on Consumption Patterns* (Greenwich, Conn.: JAI Press, Inc., 1989).

FIGURE 4.8 Income Elasticities in 10 Countries

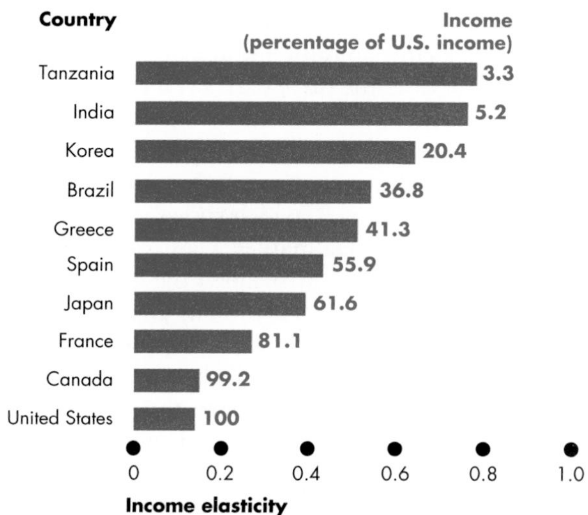

As income increases, the income elasticity of demand for food decreases. The percentage of any increase in income that is spent on food is larger for low-income consumers than for high-income consumers.

Source: Henri Theil, Ching-Fan Chung, and James L. Seale, Jr., *Advances in Econometrics, Supplement 1, 1989, International Evidence on Consumption Patterns* (Greenwich, Conn.: JAI Press, Inc., 1989).

REVIEW QUIZ

1. What does the cross elasticity of demand measure?
2. What does the sign (positive versus negative) of the cross elasticity of demand tell us about the relationship between two goods?
3. What does the income elasticity of demand measure?
4. What does the sign (positive versus negative) of the income elasticity of demand tell us about a good?
5. Why does the level of income influence the magnitude of the income elasticity of demand?

You've now completed your study of the *cross elasticity* of demand and the *income elasticity* of demand. Let's look at the other side of a market and examine the elasticity of supply.

Elasticity of Supply

YOU KNOW THAT WHEN DEMAND INCREASES, THE price rises and the quantity increases. But does the price rise by a large amount and the quantity increase by a little? Or does the price barely rise and the quantity increase by a large amount?

The answer depends on the responsiveness of the quantity supplied to a change in price. You can see why by studying Fig. 4.9, which shows two possible scenarios in a local pizza market. Figure 4.9(a) shows one scenario, and Fig. 4.9(b) shows the other.

In both cases, demand is initially D_0. In part (a), the supply of pizza is shown by the supply curve S_A. In part (b), the supply of pizza is shown by the supply curve S_B. Initially, in both cases, the price is $20 a pizza and the quantity produced and consumed is 10 pizzas an hour.

Now increases in income and population increase the demand for pizza. The demand curve shifts rightward to D_1. In case (a), the price rises by $10 to $30 a pizza, and the quantity increases by only 3 to 13 an hour. In contrast, in case (b), the price rises by only $1 to $21 a pizza, and the quantity increases by 10 to 20 pizzas an hour.

The different outcomes arise from differing degrees of responsiveness of the quantity supplied to a change in price. We measure the degree of responsiveness by using the concept of the elasticity of supply.

Calculating the Elasticity of Supply

The **elasticity of supply** measures the responsiveness of the quantity supplied to a change in the price of a good when all other influences on selling plans remain the same. It is calculated by using the formula:

$$\text{Elasticity of supply} = \frac{\text{Percentage change in quantity supplied}}{\text{Percentage change in price}}.$$

We use the same method that you learned when you studied the elasticity of demand. Let's calculate the elasticity of supply for the supplies illustrated in Fig. 4.9.

In Fig. 4.9(a), when the price rises from $20 to $30, the price rise is $10 and the average price is $25, so the price rises by 40 percent of the average price. The quantity increases from 10 to 13, so the increase

FIGURE 4.9 How a Change in Demand Changes Price and Quantity

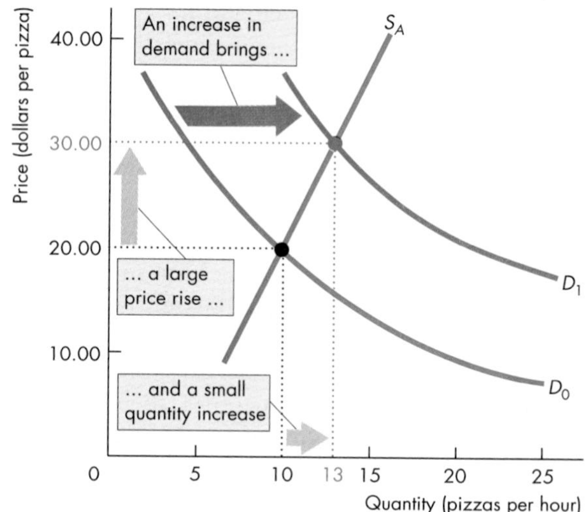

(a) Large price change and small quantity change

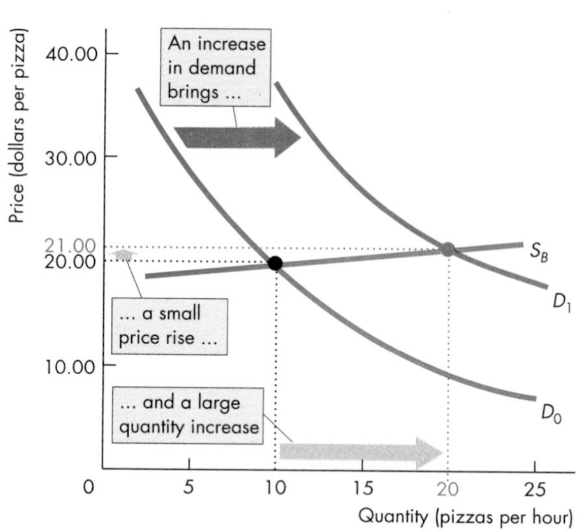

(b) Small price change and large quantity change

Initially, the price is $20 a pizza, and the quantity sold is 10 pizzas an hour. Then increases in income and population increase the demand for pizza. The demand curve shifts rightward to D_1. In part (a) the price rises by $10, to $30 a pizza, and the quantity increases by only 3, to 13 pizzas an hour. In part (b), the price rises by only $1, to $21 a pizza, and the quantity increases by 10, to 20 pizzas an hour. The price change is smaller and the quantity change is larger in case (b) than in case (a). The quantity supplied is more responsive to price in case (b) than in case (a).

is 3, the average quantity is 11.5, and the quantity increases by 26 percent. The elasticity of supply is equal to 26 percent divided by 40 percent, which equals 0.65.

In Fig. 4.9(b), when the price rises from $20 to $21, the price rise is $1 and the average price is $20.50, so the price rises by 4.9 percent of the average price. The quantity increases from 10 to 20, so the increase is 10, the average quantity is 15, and the quantity increases by 67 percent. The elasticity of supply is equal to 67 percent divided by 4.9 percent, which equals 13.67.

Figure 4.10 shows the range of supply elasticities. If the quantity supplied is fixed regardless of the price, the supply curve is vertical and the elasticity of supply is zero. Supply is perfectly inelastic. This case is shown in Fig. 4.10(a). A special intermediate case is when the percentage change in price equals the percentage change in quantity. Supply is then unit elastic. This case is shown in Fig. 4.10(b). No matter how steep the supply curve is, if it is linear and passes through the origin, supply is unit elastic. If there is a price at which sellers are willing to offer any quantity for sale, the supply curve is horizontal and the elasticity of supply is infinite. Supply is perfectly elastic. This case is shown in Fig. 4.10(c).

The Factors That Influence the Elasticity of Supply

The magnitude of the elasticity of supply depends on

- Resource substitution possibilities
- Time frame for the supply decision

Resource Substitution Possibilities Some goods and services can be produced only by using unique or rare productive resources. These items have a low, even perhaps a zero, elasticity of supply. Other goods and services can be produced by using commonly available resources that could be allocated to a wide variety of alternative tasks. Such items have a high elasticity of supply.

A Van Gogh painting is an example of a good with a vertical supply curve and a zero elasticity of supply. At the other extreme, wheat can be grown on land that is almost equally good for growing corn. So it is just as easy to grow wheat as corn, and the opportunity cost of wheat in terms of forgone corn is almost constant. As a result, the supply curve of wheat is almost horizontal and its elasticity of supply is very large. Similarly, when a good is produced in many different countries (for example, sugar and beef), the supply of the good is highly elastic.

FIGURE 4.10 Inelastic and Elastic Supply

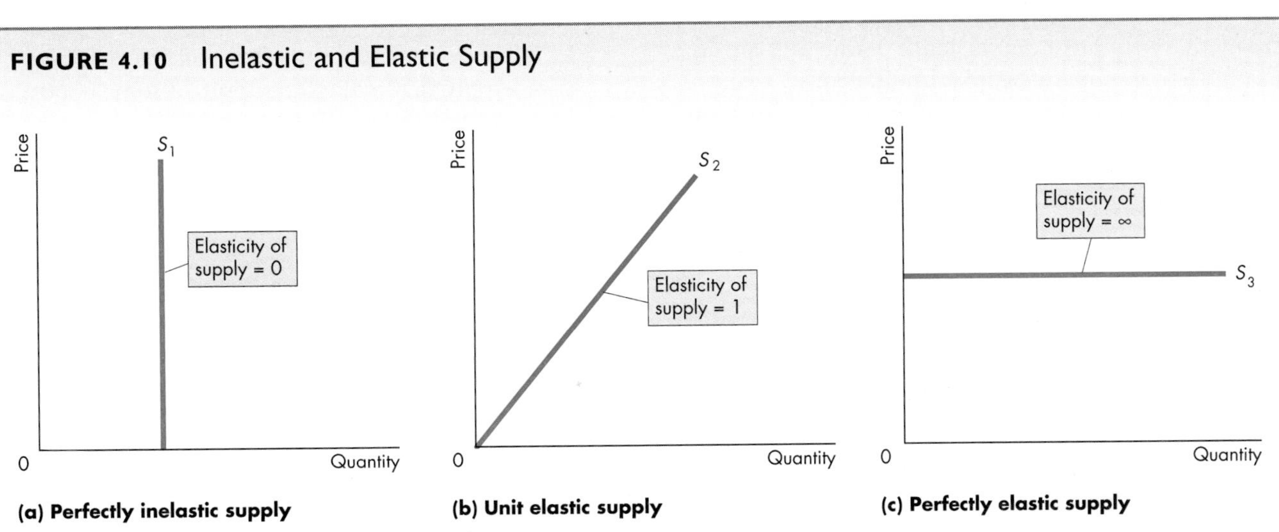

Each supply illustrated here has a constant elasticity. The supply curve in part (a) illustrates the supply of a good that has a zero elasticity of supply. The supply curve in part (b) illustrates the supply for a good with a unit elasticity of supply. All linear supply curves that pass through the origin illustrate supplies that are unit elastic. The supply curve in part (c) illustrates the supply for a good with an infinite elasticity of supply.

The supply of most goods and services lies between the two extremes. The quantity produced can be increased but only by incurring a higher cost. If a higher price is offered, the quantity supplied increases. Such goods and services have an elasticity of supply between zero and infinity.

Time Frame for the Supply Decision To study the influence of the length of time elapsed since a price change, we distinguish three time frames of supply:

1. Momentary supply
2. Long-run supply
3. Short-run supply

When the price of a good rises or falls, the *momentary supply curve* shows the response of the quantity supplied immediately following a price change.

Some goods, such as fruits and vegetables, have a perfectly inelastic momentary supply—a vertical supply curve. The quantities supplied depend on crop-planting decisions made earlier. In the case of oranges, for example, planting decisions have to be made many years in advance of the crop being available. The momentary supply curve is vertical because, on a given day, no matter what the price of oranges, producers cannot change their output. They have picked, packed, and shipped their crop to market, and the quantity available for that day is fixed.

In contrast, some goods have a perfectly elastic momentary supply. Long-distance phone calls are an example. When many people simultaneously make calls, there is a big surge in the demand for telephone cables, computer switching, and satellite time and the quantity bought increases. But the price remains constant. Long-distance carriers monitor fluctuations in demand and reroute calls to ensure that the quantity supplied equals the quantity demanded without changing the price.

The *long-run supply curve* shows the response of the quantity supplied to a change in price after all the technologically possible ways of adjusting supply have been exploited. In the case of oranges, the long run is the time it takes new plantings to grow to full maturity—about 15 years. In some cases, the long-run adjustment occurs only after a completely new production plant has been built and workers have been trained to operate it—typically a process that might take several years.

The *short-run supply curve* shows how the quantity supplied responds to a price change when only *some* of the technologically possible adjustments to production have been made. The short-run response to a price change is a sequence of adjustments. The first adjustment that is usually made is in the amount of labour employed. To increase output in the short run, firms work their labour force overtime and perhaps hire additional workers. To decrease their output in the short run, firms either lay off workers or reduce their hours of work. With the passage of time, firms can make additional adjustments, perhaps training additional workers or buying additional tools and other equipment. The short-run supply curve slopes upward because producers can take action quite quickly to change the quantity supplied in response to a price change. For example, if the price of oranges falls, growers can stop picking and leave oranges to rot on the trees. Or if the price rises, they can use more fertilizer and improved irrigation to increase the yields of their existing trees. In the long run, they can plant more trees and increase the quantity supplied even more in response to a given price rise.

REVIEW QUIZ

1. Why do we need to measure the responsiveness of the quantity supplied of a good or service to a change in its price?
2. Can you define and calculate the elasticity of supply?
3. What are the main influences on the elasticity of supply that make the supply of some goods elastic and the supply of other goods inelastic?
4. Can you provide examples of goods or services whose elasticity of supply are (a) zero, (b) greater than zero but less than infinity, and (c) infinity?
5. How does the time frame over which a supply decision is made influence the elasticity of supply?

You have now studied the theory of demand and supply, and you have learned how to measure the elasticities of demand and supply. All the elasticities that you've met in this chapter are summarized in Table 4.3. In the next chapter, we are going to study the efficiency of competitive markets. But before doing that, take a look at *Reading Between the Lines* on pp. 98–99 to see elasticity in action.

TABLE 4.3 A Compact Glossary of Elasticities

Price Elasticities of Demand

A relationship is described as	When its magnitude is	Which means that
Perfectly elastic or infinitely elastic	Infinity	The smallest possible increase in price causes an infinitely large decrease in the quantity demanded*
Elastic	Less than infinity but greater than 1	The percentage decrease in the quantity demanded exceeds the percentage increase in price
Unit elastic	1	The percentage decrease in the quantity demanded equals the percentage increase in price
Inelastic	Greater than zero but less than 1	The percentage decrease in the quantity demanded is less than the percentage increase in price
Perfectly inelastic or completely inelastic	Zero	The quantity demanded is the same at all prices

Cross Elasticities of Demand

A relationship is described as	When its value is	Which means that
Perfect substitutes	Infinity	The smallest possible increase in the price of one good causes an infinitely large increase in the quantity demanded of the other good
Substitutes	Positive, less than infinity	If the price of one good increases, the quantity demanded of the other good also increases
Independent	Zero	If the price of one good increases, the quantity demanded of the other good remains the same
Complements	Less than zero	If the price of one good increases, the quantity demanded of the other good decreases

Income Elasticities of Demand

A relationship is described as	When its value is	Which means that
Income elastic (normal good)	Greater than 1	The percentage increase in the quantity demanded is greater than the percentage increase in income
Income inelastic (normal good)	Less than 1 but greater than zero	The percentage increase in the quantity demanded is less than the percentage increase in income
Negative income elastic (inferior good)	Less than zero	When income increases, quantity demanded decreases

Elasticities of Supply

A relationship is described as	When its magnitude is	Which means that
Perfectly elastic	Infinity	The smallest possible increase in price causes an infinitely large increase in the quantity supplied
Elastic	Less than infinity but greater than 1	The percentage increase in the quantity supplied exceeds the percentage increase in the price
Inelastic	Greater than zero but less than 1	The percentage increase in the quantity supplied is less than the percentage increase in the price
Perfectly inelastic	Zero	The quantity supplied is the same at all prices

*In each description, the directions of change may be reversed. For example, in this case, the smallest possible *decrease* in price causes an infinitely large *increase* in the quantity demanded.

Elasticities of Demand and Supply in the Global Oil Market

CALGARY HERALD, August 10, 2002

Growth in demand for oil weaker than agency expected

The International Energy Agency, an adviser to 26 nations on oil policy, reduced its forecast for growth in world oil demand this year, citing a "moderate" rate of economic recovery in the U.S. and Europe. ...

The forecast comes six weeks before the Organization of Petroleum Exporting Countries, which has reduced output quotas to the lowest since 1991, meets to discuss whether to raise members' production ceiling. Algeria and Nigeria have asked OPEC for an increase in their quota. ...

The U.S. economy, the world's largest, grew at a 1.1 per cent annual rate in the second quarter after expanding at a five per cent rate in the first quarter. The European Commission trimmed its economic growth forecast after plunging stock prices threatened the region's recovery.

OPEC reduced production quotas three times last year and again on Jan. 1 to support prices as demand declined. The group maintained those quotas in June and will discuss whether to increase supply at a meeting in Osaka, Japan on Sept. 19.

World oil production is rising, in part because OPEC members are pumping more than their official limits, the IEA report shows. In July, supply averaged 76.5 million barrels a day, up 780,000 barrels from June, led by Iran and other members of OPEC.

The 10 OPEC members who agree to limit supply, all except Iraq, produced 23.2 million barrels a day in July, up 360,000 barrels from June and 1.5 million barrels more than their collective target. ...

Calgary Herald, 10 August 2002, page D2.

Essence of the Story

- The U.S. economy grew at a 1.1 percent annual rate in the second quarter and the European Commission trimmed its economic growth forecast.
- The International Energy Agency forecasts that slow economic growth in the United States and Europe will keep the demand for oil low.
- The Organization of Petroleum Exporting Countries (OPEC) cut production quotas three times in 2001 and again on Jan. 1 2002 to the lowest since 1991, but quotas have been exceeded by 1.5 million barrels a day.
- Total oil production in July 2002 was 76.5 million barrels a day.
- OPEC will decide in September 2002 whether to change its production quotas.

Economic Analysis

■ Demand and supply in a global market determine the price of crude oil.

■ OPEC is the largest supplier of oil (with a 36 percent market share), and it tries to limit production to raise the price. But the actions of individual OPEC members and of non-OPEC producers make it impossible for OPEC to control the price of crude oil.

■ Figure 1 shows how the price of crude oil has fluctuated since 1997 (an example of a price roller coaster).

■ Figure 2 shows demand and supply in the market for crude oil in 2000 and 2001.

■ The elasticity of demand is 0.05 and the elasticity of supply is 0.1. These elasticity values are suggested by Geoffrey Heal of Columbia University, a leading natural resource economist.

■ In 2000 and 2001, the supply curve was S_{2001}. In 2001, demand decreased from D_{2000} to D_{2001}. The decrease in demand brought a fall in the price and a decrease in the quantity.

■ Figure 3 shows the market in 2002. OPEC cut its production quotas by 5 million barrels a day. But OPEC members violated the quotas and supply decreased by less than this amount. In 2002, the supply of oil had decreased to S_{2002}.

■ The U.S. and European recessions decreased the demand for oil and, if no other influences had been at work, the demand for oil would have been similar in 2002 to its 2001 level.

■ But another influence was at work. People expected a further decrease in supply to arise from political instability and possibly war in Iraq.

■ Because the demand for oil is inelastic, a small decrease in supply would generate a large rise in the price.

■ With the demand curve D_{2001}, a decrease in supply of just a few million barrels a day would send the price up to $30 a barrel or more.

■ Expecting such a price rise led firms and governments to decide to buy more oil in 2002 and increase their inventories. So the demand for oil increased to D_{2002}.

■ This increase in demand combined with OPEC's cut in its production quotas brought a sharp rise in price.

■ But because the increase in demand exceeded the decrease in supply, the quantity of oil produced actually increased.

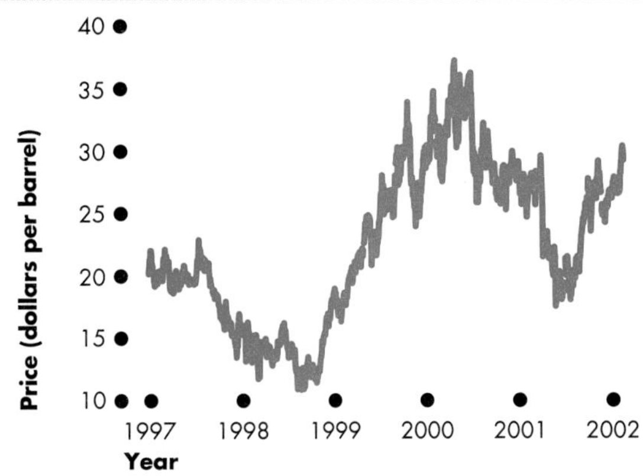

Figure 1 The price of crude oil

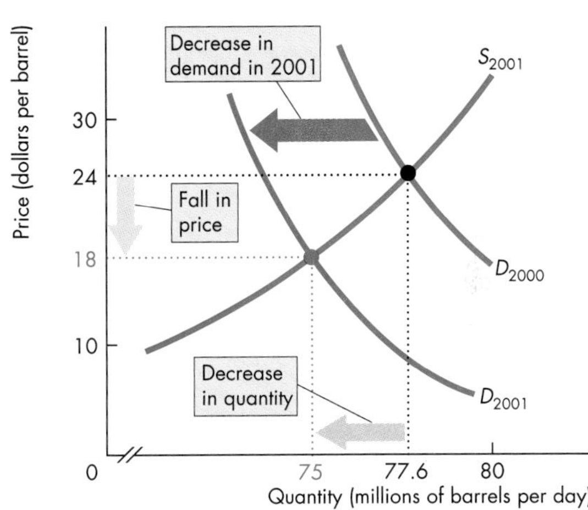

Figure 2 The oil market in 2001

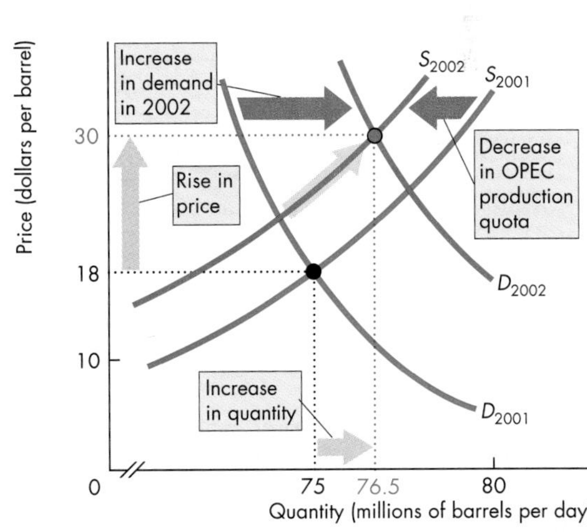

Figure 3 The oil market in 2002

SUMMARY

KEY POINTS

Price Elasticity of Demand (pp. 84–90)

- Elasticity is a measure of the responsiveness of the quantity demanded of a good to a change in its price.
- Price elasticity of demand equals the percentage change in the quantity demanded divided by the percentage change in price.
- The larger the magnitude of the elasticity of demand, the greater is the responsiveness of the quantity demanded to a given change in price.
- Price elasticity of demand depends on how easily one good serves as a substitute for another, the proportion of income spent on the good, and the length of time elapsed since the price change.
- If demand is elastic, a decrease in price leads to an increase in total revenue. If demand is unit elastic, a decrease in price leaves total revenue unchanged. And if demand is inelastic, a decrease in price leads to a decrease in total revenue.

More Elasticities of Demand (pp. 91–93)

- Cross elasticity of demand measures the responsiveness of demand for one good to a change in the price of a substitute or a complement.
- The cross elasticity of demand with respect to the price of a substitute is positive. The cross elasticity of demand with respect to the price of a complement is negative.
- Income elasticity of demand measures the responsiveness of demand to a change in income. For a normal good, the income elasticity of demand is positive. For an inferior good, the income elasticity of demand is negative.
- When the income elasticity is greater than 1, as income increases, the percentage of income spent on the good increases.
- When the income elasticity is less than 1 but greater than zero, as income increases, the percentage of income spent on the good decreases.

Elasticity of Supply (pp. 94–96)

- Elasticity of supply measures the responsiveness of the quantity supplied of a good to a change in its price.
- The elasticity of supply is usually positive and ranges between zero (vertical supply curve) and infinity (horizontal supply curve).
- Supply decisions have three time frames: momentary, long run, and short run.
- Momentary supply refers to the response of sellers to a price change at the instant that the price changes.
- Long-run supply refers to the response of sellers to a price change when all the technologically feasible adjustments in production have been made.
- Short-run supply refers to the response of sellers to a price change after some technologically feasible adjustments in production have been made.

KEY FIGURES AND TABLE

Figure 4.2 Calculating the Elasticity of Demand, 85
Figure 4.3 Inelastic and Elastic Demand, 86
Figure 4.4 Elasticity Along a Straight-Line Demand Curve, 87
Figure 4.5 Elasticity and Total Revenue, 88
Figure 4.7 Cross Elasticity of Demand, 91
Figure 4.10 Inelastic and Elastic Supply, 95
Table 4.3 A Compact Glossary of Elasticities, 97

KEY TERMS

Cross elasticity of demand, 91
Elastic demand, 87
Elasticity of supply, 94
Income elasticity of demand, 92
Inelastic demand, 87
Perfectly elastic demand, 87
Perfectly inelastic demand, 86
Price elasticity of demand, 84
Total revenue, 88
Total revenue test, 88
Unit elastic demand, 86

PROBLEMS

*1. Heavy rain spoils the strawberry crop. As a result, the price of strawberries rises from $4 to $6 a box and the quantity demanded decreases from 1,000 to 600 boxes a week. Over this price range,
a. What is the price elasticity of demand?
b. Describe the demand for strawberries.

2. Good weather brings a bumper tomato crop. The price falls from $7 to $5 a basket, and the quantity demanded increases from 300 to 500 baskets a day. Over this price range,
a. What is the price elasticity of demand?
b. Describe the demand for tomatoes.

*3. The figure shows the demand for videotape rentals.

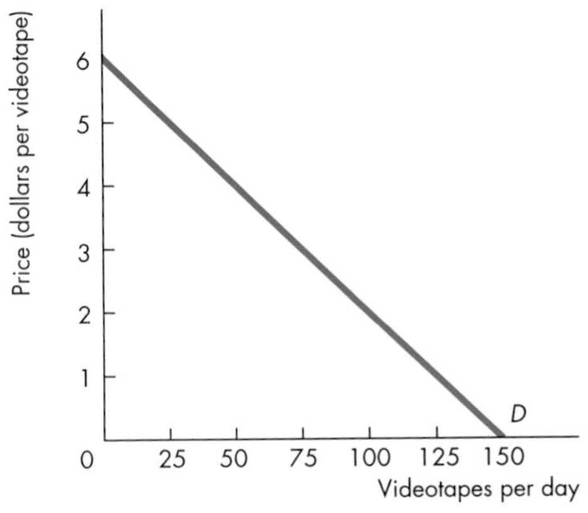

a. Calculate the elasticity of demand for a rise in rental price from $3 to $5.
b. At what price is the elasticity of demand equal to 1?

4. The figure shows the demand for pens.

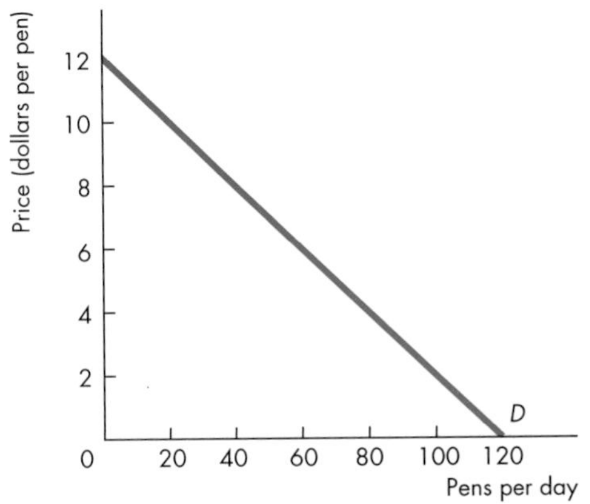

a. Calculate the elasticity of demand for a rise in price from $6 to $10.
b. At what prices is the elasticity of demand equal to 1, greater than 1, and less than 1?

*5. If the quantity of dental services demanded increases by 10 percent when the price of dental services falls by 10 percent, is the demand for dental service inelastic, elastic, or unit elastic?

6. If the quantity of haircuts demanded decreases by 10 percent when the price of a haircut rises by 5 percent, is the demand for haircuts elastic, inelastic, or unit elastic?

*7. The demand schedule for computer chips is

Price (dollars per chip)	Quantity demanded (millions of chips per year)
200	50
250	45
300	40
350	35
400	30

a. What happens to total revenue if the price of a chip falls from $400 to $350?
b. What happens to total revenue if the price of a chip falls from $350 to $300?
c. At what price is total revenue at a maximum? Use the total revenue test to answer this question.
d. At an average price of $350, is the demand for chips elastic or inelastic? Use the total revenue test to answer this question.

8. The demand schedule for sugar is

Price (dollars per kilogram)	Quantity demanded (millions of kilograms per year)
5	25
10	20
15	15
20	10
25	5

a. What happens to total revenue if the price of sugar rises from $5 to $15 per kilogram?
b. What happens to total revenue if the price rises from $15 to $25 per kilogram?
c. At what price is total revenue a maximum? Use the total revenue test to answer this question.
d. At an average price of $20 a kilogram, is the demand for sugar elastic or inelastic? Use the total revenue test to answer this question.

*9. In problem 7, at $250 a chip, is the demand for chips elastic or inelastic? Use the total revenue test to answer this question.

10. In problem 8, at $10 a kilogram, is the demand for sugar elastic or inelastic? Use the total revenue test to answer this question.

*11. If a 12 percent rise in the price of orange juice decreases the quantity of orange juice demanded by 22 percent and increases the quantity of apple juice demanded by 14 percent, calculate the cross elasticity of demand between orange juice and apple juice.

12. If a 5 percent fall in the price of chicken decreases the quantity of beef demanded by 20 percent and increases the quantity of chicken demanded by 15 percent, calculate the cross elasticity of demand between chicken and beef.

*13. Alex's income has increased from $3,000 to $5,000. Alex increased his consumption of bagels from 4 to 8 a month and decreased his consumption of doughnuts from 12 to 6 a month. Calculate Alex's income elasticity of demand for (a) bagels and (b) doughnuts.

14. Judy's income has increased from $13,000 to $17,000. Judy increased her demand for concert tickets by 15 percent and decreased her demand for bus rides by 10 percent. Calculate Judy's income elasticity of demand for (a) concert tickets and (b) bus rides.

*15. The table gives the supply schedule for long-distance phone calls.

Price (cents per minute)	Quantity supplied (millions of minutes per day)
10	200
20	400
30	600
40	800

Calculate the elasticity of supply when
a. The price falls from 40 cents to 30 cents a minute.
b. The price is 20 cents a minute.

16. The table gives the supply schedule for jeans.

Price (dollars per pair)	Quantity supplied (millions of pairs per year)
120	2,400
125	2,800
130	3,200
135	3,600

Calculate the elasticity of supply when
a. The price rises from $125 to $135 a pair.
b. The price is $125 a pair.

CRITICAL THINKING

1. Study *Reading Between the Lines* (pp. 98–99) on the market for crude oil and then answer the following questions:
   a. Why did the price of oil fall during 2001?
   b. What is the elasticity that tells us the effect of a change in supply on the price and quantity of crude oil?
   c. What is the elasticity that tells us the effect of a change in demand on the price and quantity of crude oil?
   d. Why did OPEC want to cut production during 2002?
   e. Calculate the elasticity of supply in Fig. 2 on page 99 when demand decreases and confirm that it is (approximately) 0.1.
   f. If the decrease in supply in Fig. 3 on page 99 was sufficient to increase the price to $30 a barrel along D_{2001}, what would have been the change in the quantity, given the elasticity of demand of 0.05?

WEB EXERCISES

1. Use the link on the Parkin–Bade Web site and
   a. Find the price of gasoline in the summer of 2002.
   b. Use the concepts of demand, supply, and elasticity to explain recent changes in the price of gasoline.
   c. Find the price of crude oil.
   d. Use the concepts of demand, supply, and elasticity to explain recent changes in the price of crude oil.
2. Use the link on the Parkin–Bade Web site and
   a. Find the number of gallons in a barrel and the cost of crude oil in a gallon of gasoline.
   b. What are the other costs that make up the total cost of a gallon of gasoline?
   c. If the price of crude oil falls by 10 percent, by what percentage would you expect the price of gasoline to change, other things remaining the same?
   d. Which demand do you think is more elastic: that for crude oil, or that for gasoline? Why?
3. Use the link on the Parkin–Bade Web site to review and write a brief report on *Geoffrey Heal's* lecture on the oil market during the 1990s.

EFFICIENCY AND EQUITY

CHAPTER 5

More for Less

People constantly strive to get more for less. The government of South Africa was pleased when it found a source of supply of AZT, a drug used to treat AIDS, for $275 per person per year instead of the $23,000 charged by GlaxoSmithKline, the British company that developed the drug. Every time we buy something or decide *not* to buy something, we express our view about how scarce resources should be used. We try to spend our incomes in ways that get the most out of our scarce resources. ◆ Is the allocation of our resources between leisure and education, pizza and sandwiches, inline skates and squash balls, AIDS treatments and other drugs the right one? ◆ Some firms make huge profits year after year. Microsoft, for example, has generated enough profit over the past ten years to rocket Bill Gates, one of its founders, into the position of being one of the richest people in the world. Is that kind of business success a sign of efficiency? ◆ And is it fair that Bill Gates is so incredibly rich while others live in miserable poverty?

These are the issues you'll explore in this chapter. You will discover that competitive markets can be efficient. But you will also discover some sources of inefficiency. You will discover that firms that make huge profits, while efficient in one sense, might be inefficient in a broader sense. And you'll return to the controversial issue of whether South Africa should be able to buy AIDS treatments in a cut-price market in *Reading Between the Lines* at the end of the chapter.

After studying this chapter, you will able to

- **Define efficiency**
- **Distinguish between value and price and define consumer surplus**
- **Distinguish between cost and price and define producer surplus**
- **Explain the conditions under which markets move resources to their highest-valued uses and the sources of inefficiency in our economy**
- **Explain the main ideas about fairness and evaluate claims that markets result in unfair outcomes**

Efficiency: A Refresher

IT IS HARD TO TALK ABOUT EFFICIENCY IN ordinary conversation without generating disagreement. To an engineer, an entrepreneur, a politician, a working mother, or an economist, getting more for less seems like a sensible thing to aim for. But some people think that the pursuit of efficiency conflicts with other, worthier goals. Environmentalists worry about contamination from "efficient" nuclear power plants. And car producers worry about competition from "efficient" foreign producers.

Economists use the idea of efficiency in a special way that avoids these disagreements. An **efficient allocation** of resources occurs when we produce the goods and services that people value most highly (see Chapter 2, pp. 37–39). Equivalently, resource use is efficient when we cannot produce more of a good or service without giving up some other good or service that we value more highly.

If people value a nuclear-free environment more highly than they value cheap electric power, it is efficient to use higher-cost, nonnuclear technologies to produce electricity. Efficiency is not a cold, mechanical concept. It is a concept based on value, and value is based on people's feelings.

Think about the efficient quantity of pizza. To produce more pizza, we must give up some other goods and services. For example, we might give up some sandwiches. So to produce more pizzas, we forgo sandwiches. If we have fewer pizzas, we can have more sandwiches. What is the efficient quantity of pizza to produce? The answer depends on marginal benefit and marginal cost.

Marginal Benefit

If we consume one more pizza, we receive a marginal benefit. **Marginal benefit** is the benefit that a person receives from consuming *one more unit* of a good or service. The marginal benefit from a good or service is measured as the maximum amount that a person is willing to pay for one more unit of it. So the marginal benefit from a pizza is the maximum amount of other goods and services that people are willing to give up to get one more pizza. The marginal benefit from pizza decreases as the quantity of pizza consumed increases —the principle of *decreasing marginal benefit.*

We can express the marginal benefit from a pizza as the number of sandwiches that people are willing to forgo to get one more pizza. But we can also express marginal benefit as the dollar value of other goods and services that people are willing to forgo. Figure 5.1 shows the marginal benefit from pizza expressed in this way. As the quantity of pizza increases, the value of other items that people are willing to forgo to get yet one more pizza decreases.

Marginal Cost

If we produce one more pizza, we incur a marginal cost. **Marginal cost** is the opportunity cost of producing *one more unit* of a good or service. The marginal cost of a good or service is measured as the value of the best alternative forgone. So the marginal cost of a pizza is the value of the best alternative forgone to get one more pizza. The marginal cost of a pizza increases as the quantity of pizza produced increases—the principle of *increasing marginal cost.*

FIGURE 5.1 The Efficient Quantity of Pizza

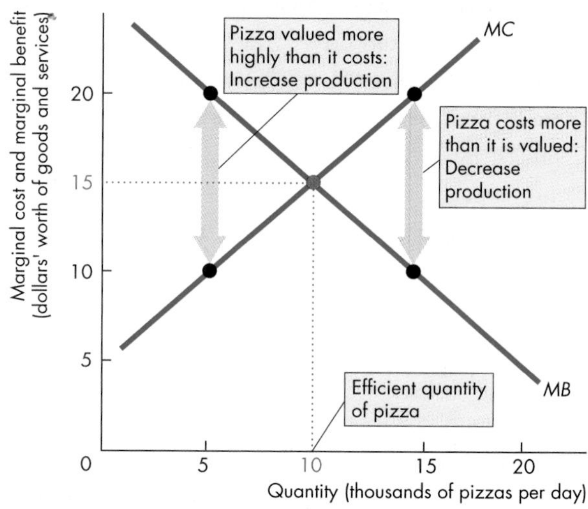

The marginal benefit curve (*MB*) shows what people *are willing to* forgo to get one more pizza. The marginal cost curve (*MC*) shows what people *must* forgo to get one more pizza. If fewer than 10,000 pizzas a day are produced, marginal benefit exceeds marginal cost. Greater value can be obtained by producing more pizzas. If more than 10,000 pizzas a day are produced, marginal cost exceeds marginal benefit. Greater value can be obtained by producing fewer pizzas. If 10,000 pizzas a day are produced, marginal benefit equals marginal cost and the efficient quantity of pizza is available.

We can express marginal cost as the number of sandwiches we must forgo to produce one more pizza. But we can also express marginal cost as the dollar value of other

goods and services we must forgo. Figure 5.1 shows the marginal cost of pizza expressed in this way. As the quantity of pizza produced increases, the value of other items we must forgo to produce yet one more pizza increases.

Efficiency and Inefficiency

To determine the efficient quantity of pizza, we compare the marginal cost of a pizza with the marginal benefit from a pizza. There are three possible cases:

- Marginal benefit exceeds marginal cost.
- Marginal cost exceeds marginal benefit.
- Marginal benefit equals marginal cost.

Marginal Benefit Exceeds Marginal Cost Suppose the quantity of pizza produced is 5,000 a day. Figure 5.1 shows that at this quantity, the marginal benefit of a pizza is $20. That is, when the quantity of pizza available is 5,000 a day, people are willing to pay $20 for the 5,000th pizza. The figure also shows that the marginal cost of the 5,000th pizza is $10. That is, to produce one more pizza, the value of other goods and services that we must forgo is $10.

If pizza production increases from 4,999 to 5,000, the value of the additional pizza is $20 and its marginal cost is $10. If this pizza is produced, the value of the pizza produced exceeds the value of the goods and services we must forgo by $10. Resources will be used more efficiently—they will create more value—if we produce an extra pizza and fewer other goods and services. This same reasoning applies all the way up to the 9,999th pizza. Only when we get to the 10,000th pizza does marginal benefit not exceed marginal cost.

Marginal Cost Exceeds Marginal Benefit Suppose the quantity of pizza produced is 15,000 a day. Figure 5.1 shows that at this quantity, the marginal benefit of a pizza is $10. That is, when the quantity of pizza available is 15,000 a day, people are willing to pay $10 for the 15,000th pizza. The figure also shows that the marginal cost of the 15,000th pizza is $20. That is, to produce one more pizza, the value of the other goods and services that we must forgo is $20.

If pizza production decreases from 15,000 to 14,999, the value of the one pizza forgone is $10 and its marginal cost is $20. So if this pizza is not produced, the value of the other goods and services produced exceeds the value of the pizza forgone by $10. Resources will be used more efficiently—they will create more value—if we produce one fewer pizza and more other goods and services. This same reasoning applies all the way down to the 10,001st pizza. Only when we get to the 10,000th pizza does marginal cost not exceed marginal benefit.

Marginal Benefit Equals Marginal Cost Suppose the quantity of pizza produced is 10,000 a day. Figure 5.1 shows that at this quantity, the marginal benefit of a pizza is $15. That is, when the quantity of pizza available is 10,000 a day, people are willing to pay $15 for the 10,000th pizza. The figure also shows that the marginal cost of the 10,000th pizza is $15. That is, to produce one more pizza, the value of other goods and services that we must forgo is $15.

In this situation, we cannot increase the value of the goods and services produced by either increasing or decreasing the quantity of pizza. If we increase the quantity of pizza, the 10,001st pizza costs more to produce than it is worth. If we decrease the quantity of pizza produced, the 9,999th pizza is worth more than it costs to produce. So when marginal benefit equals marginal cost, resource use is efficient.

REVIEW QUIZ

1. If the marginal benefit of pizza exceeds the marginal cost of pizza, are we producing too much pizza and too little of other goods, or are we producing too little pizza and too much of other goods?
2. If the marginal cost of pizza exceeds the marginal benefit of pizza, are we producing too much pizza and too little of other goods, or are we producing too little pizza and too much of other goods?
3. What is the relationship between the marginal benefit of pizza and the marginal cost of pizza when we are producing the efficient quantity of pizza?

Does a competitive market in pizza produce the efficient quantity of pizza? Let's answer this question.

Value, Price, and Consumer Surplus

TO INVESTIGATE WHETHER A COMPETITIVE market is efficient, we need to learn about the connection between demand and marginal benefit and the connection between supply and marginal cost.

Value, Willingness to Pay, and Demand

In everyday life, we talk about "getting value for money." When we use this expression, we are distinguishing between *value* and *price*. Value is what we get, and the price is what we pay.

The **value** of one more unit of a good or service is its *marginal benefit*. Marginal benefit can be expressed as the maximum price that people are willing to pay for another unit of the good or service. The willingness to pay for a good or service determines the demand for it.

In Fig. 5.2(a) the demand curve *D* shows the quantity demanded at each price. For example, when the price of a pizza is $15, the quantity demanded is 10,000 pizzas a day. In Fig. 5.2(b), the demand curve *D* shows the maximum price that people are willing to pay when there is a given quantity. For example, when 10,000 pizzas a day are available, the most that people are willing to pay for the 10,000th pizza is $15. This second interpretation of the demand curve means that the marginal benefit from the 10,000th pizza is $15. The demand curve is also the marginal benefit curve *MB*.

When we draw a demand curve, we use a *relative price*, not a *money* price. We express the relative price in dollars, but the relative price measures the number of dollars' worth of other goods and services forgone to obtain one more unit of the good in question (see Chapter 3, p. 60). So a demand curve tells us the value of other goods and services that people are willing to forgo to get an additional unit of a good. But this is what a marginal benefit curve tells us too. So

A demand curve is a marginal benefit curve.

We don't always have to pay the maximum price that we are willing to pay. When we buy something, we often get a bargain. Let's see how.

FIGURE 5.2 Demand, Willingness to Pay, and Marginal Benefit

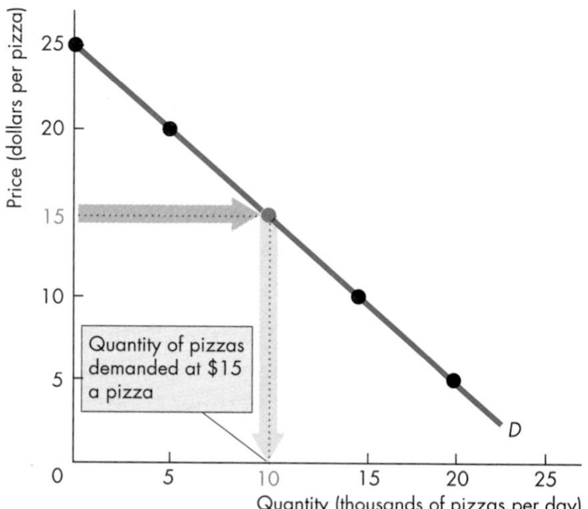

(a) Price determines quantity demanded

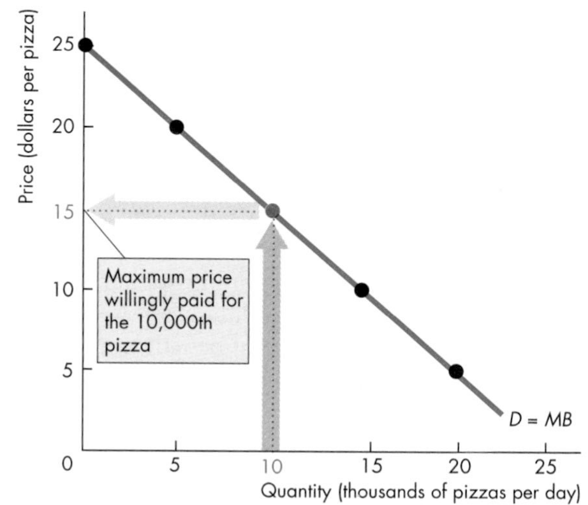

(b) Quantity determines willingness to pay

The demand curve for pizza, *D*, shows the quantity of pizza demanded at each price, other things remaining the same. It also shows the maximum price that consumers are willing to pay if a given quantity of pizza is available. At a price of $15 a pizza, the quantity demanded is 10,000 pizzas a day (part a). If 10,000 pizzas a day are available, the maximum price that consumers are willing to pay for the 10,000th pizza is $15 (part b).

Consumer Surplus

When people buy something for less than it is worth to them, they receive a consumer surplus. A **consumer surplus** is the value of a good minus the price paid for it, summed over the quantity bought.

To understand consumer surplus, let's look at Lisa's demand for pizza in Fig. 5.3. Lisa likes pizza, but the marginal benefit she gets from it decreases quickly as her consumption increases.

To keep things simple, suppose Lisa can buy pizza by the slice and that there are 10 slices in a pizza. If a pizza costs \$2.50 a slice (or \$25 a pizza), Lisa spends her fast-food budget on items that she values more highly than pizza. At \$2 a slice (or \$20 a pizza), she buys 10 slices (1 pizza) a week. At \$1.50 a slice, she buys 20 slices a week; at \$1 a slice, she buys 30 slices a week; and at 50 cents a slice (\$5 a pizza), she eats nothing but pizza and buys 40 slices a week.

Lisa's demand curve for pizza in Fig. 5.3 is also her *willingness-to-pay* or marginal benefit curve. It tells us that if Lisa can have only 10 slices (1 pizza) a week, she is willing to pay \$2 a slice. Her marginal benefit from the 10th slice is \$2. If she can have 20 slices (2 pizzas) a week, she is willing to pay \$1.50 for the 20th slice. Her marginal benefit from the 20th slice is \$1.50.

Figure 5.3 also shows Lisa's consumer surplus from pizza when the price is \$1.50 a slice. At this price, she buys 20 slices a week. The most that Lisa is willing to pay for the 20th slice is \$1.50 a slice, so its marginal benefit equals the price she pays for it.

But Lisa is willing to pay almost \$2.50 for the first slice. So the marginal benefit from this slice is close to \$1 more than she pays for it. So on her first slice of pizza, she receives a *consumer surplus* of almost \$1. At a quantity of 10 slices of pizza a week, Lisa's marginal benefit is \$2 a slice. So on the 10th slice, she receives a consumer surplus of 50 cents.

To calculate Lisa's consumer surplus, we find the consumer surplus on each slice she buys and add them together. This sum is the area of the green triangle—the area below the demand curve and above the market price line. This area is equal to the base of the triangle (20 slices) multiplied by the height of the triangle (\$1) divided by 2, which is \$10.

The area of the blue rectangle in Fig. 5.3 shows what Lisa pays for pizza, which is \$30. This area is equal to 20 slices a week multiplied by \$1.50 a slice.

All goods and services are like the pizza example you've just studied. Because of decreasing marginal benefit, people receive more benefit from their consumption than the amount they pay.

FIGURE 5.3 A Consumer's Demand and Consumer Surplus

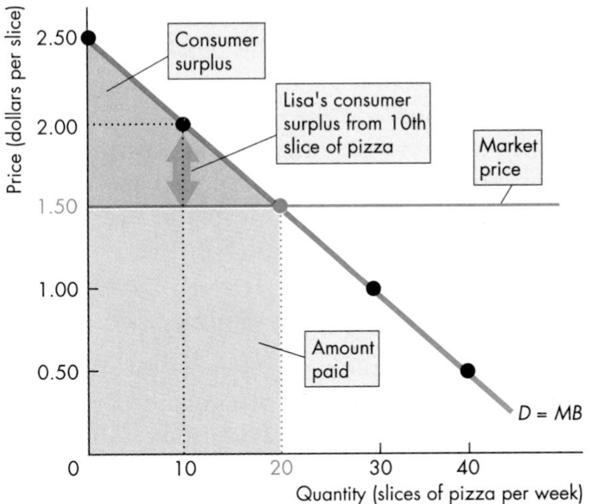

Lisa's demand curve for pizza tells us that at \$2.50 a slice, she does not buy pizza. At \$2 a slice, she buys 10 slices a week; at \$1.50 a slice, she buys 20 slices a week. Lisa's demand curve also tells us that she is willing to pay \$2 for the 10th slice and \$1.50 for the 20th. She actually pays \$1.50 a slice—the market price—and buys 20 slices a week. Her consumer surplus from pizza is \$10—the area of the green triangle.

REVIEW QUIZ

1. How do we measure the value or marginal benefit of a good or service?
2. What is the relationship between marginal benefit and the demand curve?
3. What is consumer surplus? How do we measure it?

You've seen how we distinguish between value—marginal benefit—and price. And you've seen that buyers receive a consumer surplus because marginal benefit exceeds price. Next, we're going to study the connection between supply and marginal cost and learn about producer surplus.

Cost, Price, and Producer Surplus

WHAT YOU ARE NOW GOING TO LEARN ABOUT cost, price, and producer surplus parallels the related ideas about value, price, and consumer surplus that you've just studied.

Firms are in business to make a profit. To do so, they must sell their output for a price that exceeds the cost of production. Let's investigate the relationship between cost and price.

Cost, Minimum Supply-Price, and Supply

Earning a profit means receiving more (or at least receiving no less) for the sale of a good or service than the cost of producing it. Just as consumers distinguish between *value* and *price*, so producers distinguish between *cost* and *price*. Cost is what a producer gives up, and price is what a producer receives.

The cost of producing one more unit of a good or service is its *marginal cost*. And marginal cost is the minimum price that producers must receive to induce them to produce another unit of the good or service. This minimum acceptable price determines supply.

In Fig. 5.4(a), the supply curve *S* shows the quantity supplied at each price. For example, when the price of a pizza is $15, the quantity supplied is 10,000 pizzas a day. In Fig. 5.4(b), the supply curve shows the minimum price that producers must be offered to produce a given quantity of pizza. For example, the minimum price, which producers must be offered to get them to produce 10,000 pizzas a day is $15 a pizza. This second view of the supply curve means that the marginal cost of the 10,000th pizza is $15. The supply curve is also the marginal cost curve *MC*.

Because the price is a relative price, a supply curve tells us the quantity of other goods and services that *sellers must forgo* to produce one more unit of the good. But a marginal cost curve also tells us the quantity of other goods and services that we must

FIGURE 5.4 Supply, Minimum Supply-Price, and Marginal Cost

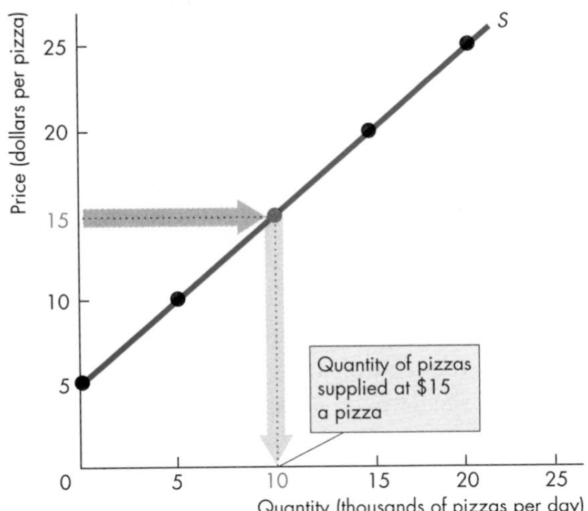

(a) Price determines quantity supplied

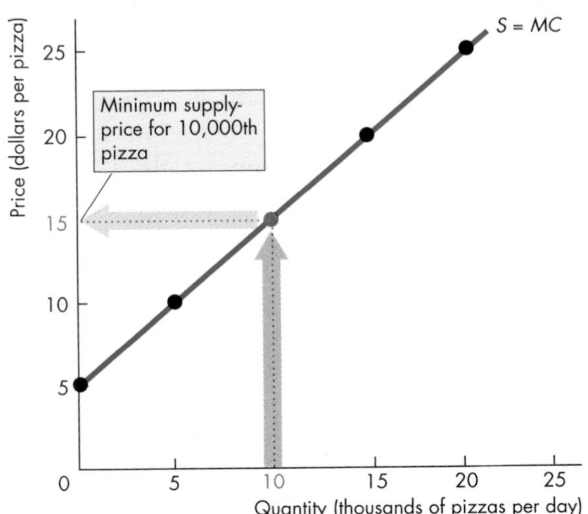

(b) Quantity determines minimum supply-price

The supply curve of pizza, S, shows the quantity of pizza supplied at each price, other things remaining the same. It also shows the minimum price that producers must be offered to get them to produce a given quantity of pizza.

At a price of $15 a pizza, the quantity supplied is 10,000 pizzas a day (part a). To get firms to produce 10,000 pizzas a day, the minimum price they must be offered for the 10,000th pizza is $15 (part b).

forgo to get one more unit of the good. So

A supply curve is a marginal cost curve.

If the price producers receive exceeds the cost they incur, they earn a producer surplus. This producer surplus is analogous to consumer surplus.

Producer Surplus

When price exceeds marginal cost, the firm obtains a producer surplus. A **producer surplus** is the price of a good minus the opportunity cost of producing it, summed over the quantity sold. To understand producer surplus, let's look at Max's supply of pizza in Fig. 5.5.

Max can produce pizza or bake bread that people like a lot. The more pizza he makes, the less bread he can bake. His opportunity cost of a pizza is the value of the bread he must forgo. This opportunity cost increases as Max increases his production of pizza. If a pizza sells for only $5, Max produces no pizza. He uses his kitchen to bake bread. Pizza just isn't worth producing. But at $10 a pizza, Max produces 50 pizzas a day, and at $15 a pizza, he produces 100 a day.

Max's supply curve is also his *minimum supply-price* curve. It tells us that if Max can sell only one pizza a day, the minimum that he must be paid for it is a little more than $5. If he can sell 50 pizzas a day, the minimum that he must be paid for the 50th pizza is $10, and so on.

Figure 5.5 also shows Max's producer surplus. If the price of a pizza is $15, Max plans to sell 100 pizzas a day. The minimum that he must be paid for the 100th pizza is $15. So its opportunity cost is exactly the price he receives for it. But the opportunity cost of the first pizza is just a bit more than $5. So this first pizza costs $10 less to produce than Max receives for it. He receives a *producer surplus* from his first pizza of almost $10. He receives a slightly smaller producer surplus on the second pizza, less on the third, and so on until he receives no producer surplus on the 100th pizza.

Figure 5.5 shows Max's producer surplus as the blue triangle—the area above the supply curve and below the market price line. This area is equal to the base of the triangle (100 pizzas a week) multiplied by the height ($10 a pizza) divided by 2, which equals $500 a day. Figure 5.5 also shows Max's opportunity costs as the red area below the supply curve.

FIGURE 5.5 A Producer's Supply and Producer Surplus

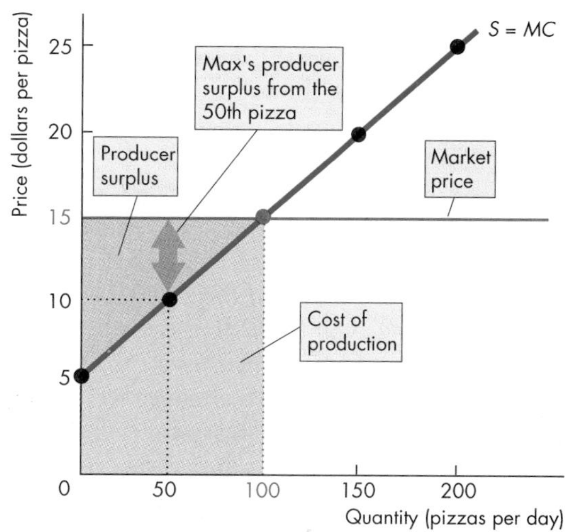

Max's supply curve of pizza tells us that at a price of $5, Max plans to sell no pizza. At a price of $10, he plans to sell 50 pizzas a day; and at a price of $15, he plans to sell 100 pizzas a day. Max's supply curve also tells us that the minimum he must be offered is $10 for the 50th pizza a day and $15 for the 100th pizza a day. If the market price is $15 a pizza, he sells 100 pizzas a day and receives $1,500. The red area shows Max's cost of producing pizza, which is $1,000 a day, and the blue area shows his producer surplus, which is $500 a day.

REVIEW QUIZ

1. What is the relationship between the marginal cost or opportunity cost of producing a good or service and the minimum supply-price—the minimum price that producers must be offered?
2. What is the relationship between marginal cost and the supply curve?
3. What is producer surplus? How do we measure it?

Consumer surplus and producer surplus can be used to measure the efficiency of a market. Let's see how we can use these concepts to study the efficiency of a competitive market.

Is the Competitive Market Efficient?

FIGURE 5.6 SHOWS THE MARKET FOR PIZZA. The demand curve *D* shows the demand for pizza. The supply curve *S* shows the supply of pizza. The equilibrium price is $15 a pizza, and the equilibrium quantity is 10,000 pizzas a day.

The market forces that you studied in Chapter 3 (pp. 70–71) will pull the pizza market to this equilibrium. If the price is greater than $15 a pizza, a surplus will force the price down. If the price is less than $15 a pizza, a shortage will force the price up. Only if the price is $15 a pizza is there neither a surplus nor a shortage and no forces operate to change the price.

So the market price and quantity are pulled towards their equilibrium values. But is this competitive equilibrium efficient? Does a competitive pizza market produce the efficient quantity of pizza?

FIGURE 5.6 An Efficient Market for Pizza

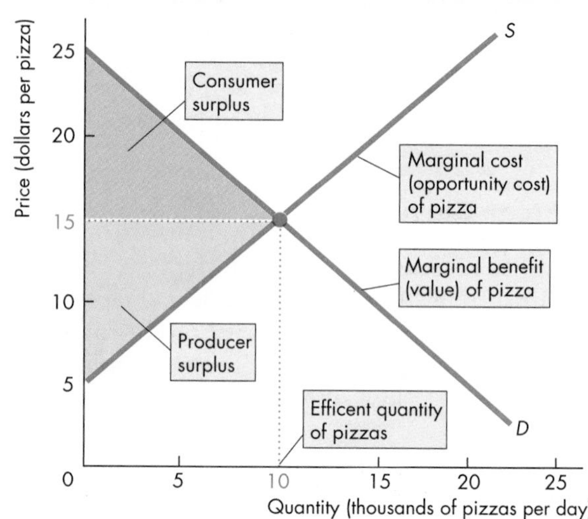

Resources are used efficiently when the sum of consumer surplus and producer surplus is maximized. Consumer surplus is the area below the demand curve and above the market price—the green triangle. Producer surplus is the area below the market price and above the supply curve—the blue triangle. Here, consumer surplus is $50,000, producer surplus is $50,000, and the sum is $100,000. This sum of consumer surplus and producer surplus is maximized when the willingness to pay equals the opportunity cost. The efficient quantity of pizza is 10,000 pizzas per day.

Efficiency of Competitive Equilibrium

The equilibrium in Fig. 5.6 is efficient. Resources are being used to produce the quantity of pizza that people value most highly. It is not possible to produce more pizza without giving up some other good or service that is valued more highly. And if a smaller quantity of pizza is produced, resources are used to produce some other good that is not valued as highly as the pizza forgone.

To see why the equilibrium in Fig. 5.6 is efficient, think about the interpretation of the demand curve as the marginal benefit curve and the supply curve as the marginal cost curve. The demand curve tells us the marginal benefit from pizza. The supply curve tells us the marginal cost of pizza. So where the demand curve and the supply curve intersect, marginal benefit equals marginal cost.

But this condition—marginal benefit equals marginal cost—is the condition that delivers an efficient use of resources. A competitive market puts resources to work in the activities that create the greatest possible value. So a competitive equilibrium is efficient.

If production is less than 10,000 pizzas a day, the marginal pizza is valued more highly than its opportunity cost. If production exceeds 10,000 pizzas a day, the marginal pizza costs more to produce than the value that consumers place on it.

Only when 10,000 pizzas a day are produced is the marginal pizza worth exactly what it costs. The competitive market pushes the quantity of pizza produced to its efficient level of 10,000 a day. If production is less than 10,000 a day, a shortage raises the price, which increases production. If production exceeds 10,000 a day, a surplus lowers the price, which decreases production.

In a competitive equilibrium, resources are used efficiently to produce the goods and services that people value most highly. And when the competitive market uses resources efficiently, the sum of consumer surplus and producer surplus is maximized.

Buyers and sellers each attempt to do the best they can for themselves, and no one plans for an efficient outcome for society as a whole. Buyers seek the lowest possible price, and sellers seek the highest possible price. And the market comes to an equilibrium in which resources are allocated efficiently.

The Invisible Hand

Writing in his *Wealth of Nations* in 1776, Adam Smith was the first to suggest that competitive markets send resources to the uses in which they have the highest value (see pp. 54–55). Smith believed that each participant in a competitive market is "led by an invisible hand to promote an end [the efficient use of resources] which was no part of his intention."

You can see the invisible hand at work in the cartoon. The cold drinks vendor has both cold drinks and shade. He has an opportunity cost of each and a minimum supply-price of each. The park-bench reader has a marginal benefit from a cold drink and from shade. You can see that the marginal benefit from shade exceeds the marginal cost, but the marginal cost of a cold drink exceeds its marginal benefit. The transaction that occurs creates producer surplus and consumer surplus. The vendor obtains a producer surplus from selling the shade for more than its opportunity cost, and the reader obtains a consumer surplus from buying the shade for less than its marginal benefit. In the third frame of the cartoon, both the consumer and the producer are better off than they were in the first frame. The umbrella has moved to its highest-valued use.

The Invisible Hand at Work Today

The market economy relentlessly performs the activity illustrated in the cartoon and in Fig. 5.6 to achieve an efficient allocation of resources. And rarely has the market been working as hard as it is today. Think about a few of the changes taking place in our economy that the market is guiding towards an efficient use of resources.

New technologies have cut the cost of producing computers. As these advances have occurred, supply has increased and the price has fallen. Lower prices have encouraged an increase in the quantity demanded of this now less costly tool. The marginal benefit from computers is brought to equality with their marginal cost.

A Florida frost cuts the supply of oranges. With fewer oranges available, the marginal benefit from oranges increases. A shortage of oranges raises their price, so the market allocates the smaller quantity available to the people who value them most highly.

Market forces persistently bring marginal cost and marginal benefit to equality and maximize the sum of consumer surplus and producer surplus.

Obstacles to Efficiency

Although markets generally do a good job of sending resources to where they are most highly valued, markets do not always get the correct answer. Sometimes they overproduce a good or service, and sometimes they underproduce. The most significant obstacles to achieving an efficient allocation of resources in the market economy are

- Price ceilings and price floors
- Taxes, subsidies, and quotas
- Monopoly
- Public goods
- External costs and external benefits

Price Ceilings and Price Floors A *price ceiling* is a regulation that makes it illegal to charge a price higher than a specified level. An example is a price ceiling on apartment rents, which some cities impose. A *price floor* is a regulation that makes it illegal to pay a lower price than a specified level. An example is the minimum wage. (We study both of these restrictions on buyers and sellers in Chapter 6.)

The presence of a price ceiling or a price floor blocks the forces of demand and supply and might result in a quantity produced that differs from the quantity determined in an unregulated market.

Taxes, Subsidies, and Quotas *Taxes* increase the prices paid by buyers and lower the prices received by sellers. Taxes decrease the quantity produced (for reasons that are explained in Chapter 6, on pp. 131–134). All kinds of goods and services are taxed, but the highest taxes are on gasoline, alcohol, and tobacco.

Subsidies, which are payments by the government to producers, decrease the prices paid by buyers and increase the prices received by sellers. Subsidies increase the quantity produced.

Quotas, which are limits to the quantity that a firm is permitted to produce, restrict output below the quantity that a competitive market produces. Farms are sometimes subject to quotas.

Monopoly A *monopoly* is a firm that has sole control of a market. For example, Microsoft has a near monopoly on operating systems for personal computers. Although a monopoly can earn a large profit, it prevents the market from achieving an efficient use of resources. The goal of a monopoly is to maximize profit. To achieve this goal, it restricts production and raises price. (We study monopoly in Chapter 12.)

Public Goods A *public good* is a good or service that is consumed simultaneously by everyone, even if they don't pay for it. Examples are national security and the enforcement of law and order. Competitive markets would produce too small a quantity of public goods because of a *free-rider problem.* It is not in each person's interest to buy her or his share of a public good. So a competitive market produces less than the efficient quantity. (We study public goods and the free-rider problem in Chapter 16.)

External Costs and External Benefits An *external cost* is a cost that is borne not by the producer but by other people. The cost of pollution is an example of an external cost. When an electric power utility burns coal to generate electricity, it puts sulfur dioxide into the atmosphere. This pollutant falls as acid rain and damages vegetation and crops. The utility does not consider the cost of pollution when it decides the quantity of electric power to supply. Its supply curve is based on its own costs, not on the costs that it inflicts on others. As a result, the utility produces more power than the efficient quantity.

An *external benefit* is a benefit that accrues to people other than the buyer of a good. An example is when someone in a neighbourhood paints her home or landscapes her yard. The homeowner does not consider her neighbour's marginal benefit when she decides whether to do this type of work. So the demand curve for house painting and yard improvement does not include all the benefits that accrue. In this case, the quantity falls short of the efficient quantity. (We study externalities in Chapter 18.)

The impediments to efficiency that we've just reviewed and that you will study in greater detail in later chapters result in two possible outcomes:

- Underproduction
- Overproduction

Underproduction

Suppose that one firm owns all the pizza outlets in a city and that it produces only 5,000 pizzas a day. Figure 5.7(a) shows that at this quantity, consumers are willing to pay $20 for the marginal pizza—marginal benefit is $20. The marginal cost of a pizza is only $10. So there is a gap between what people are willing to pay and what producers must be offered—a gap between marginal benefit and marginal cost.

The sum of consumer surplus and producer surplus is decreased by the amount of the grey triangle in Fig. 5.7(a). This triangle is called deadweight loss. **Deadweight loss** is the decrease in consumer surplus and producer surplus that results from an inefficient level of production.

The 5,000th pizza brings a benefit of $20 and costs only $10 to produce. If we don't produce this pizza, we are wasting $10. Similar reasoning applies all the way up to the 9,999th pizza. By producing more pizza and less of other goods and services, we get more value from our resources.

The deadweight loss is borne by the entire society. It is not a loss for the consumers and a gain for the producer. It is a *social* loss.

FIGURE 5.7 Underproduction and Overproduction

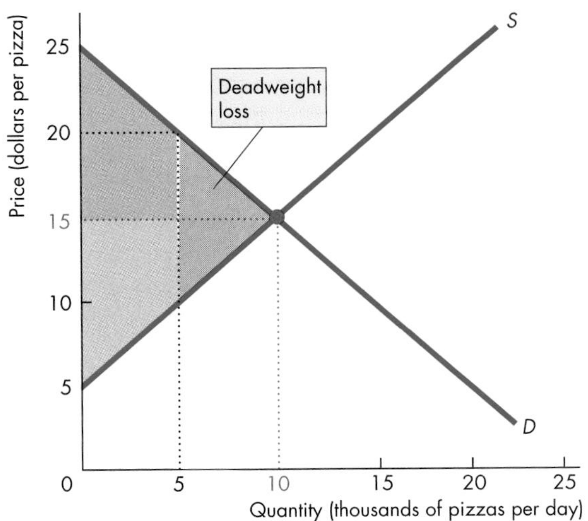

(a) Underproduction

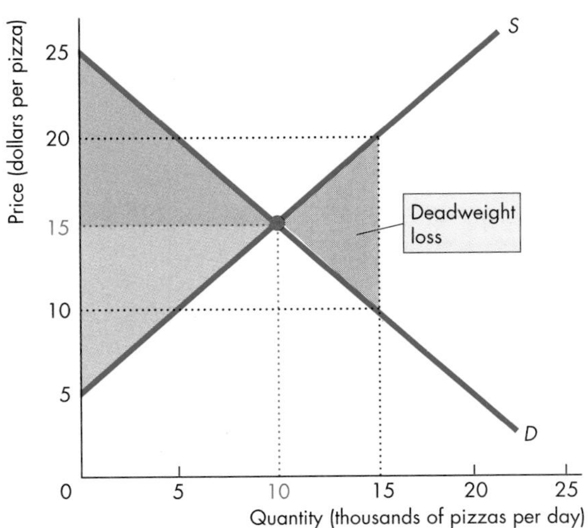

(b) Overproduction

If pizza production is cut to only 5,000 a day, a deadweight loss (the grey triangle) arises (part a). Consumer surplus and producer surplus (the green and blue areas) are reduced. At 5,000 pizzas, the benefit of one more pizza exceeds its cost. The same is true for all levels of production up to 10,000 pizzas a day. If production increases to 15,000, a deadweight loss arises (part b). At 15,000 pizzas a day, the cost of the 15,000th pizza exceeds its benefit. The cost of each pizza above 10,000 exceeds its benefit. Consumer surplus plus producer surplus equals the sum of the green and blue areas minus the grey deadweight loss triangle.

Overproduction

Suppose the pizza lobby gets the government to pay the pizza producers a fat subsidy and that production increases to 15,000 a day. Figure 5.7(b) shows that at this quantity, consumers are willing to pay only $10 for that marginal pizza but the opportunity cost of that pizza is $20. It now costs more to produce the marginal pizza than consumers are willing to pay for it. The gap gets smaller as production approaches 10,000 pizzas a day, but it is present at all quantities greater than 10,000 a day.

Again, deadweight loss is shown by the grey triangle. The sum of consumer surplus and producer surplus is smaller than its maximum by the amount of deadweight loss. The 15,000th pizza brings a benefit of only $10 but costs $20 to produce. If we produce this pizza, we are wasting $10. Similar reasoning applies all the way down to the 10,001st pizza. By producing fewer pizzas and more of other goods and services, we get more value from our resources.

REVIEW QUIZ

1. What is a competitive market? Do competitive markets use resources efficiently? Explain why or why not.
2. Do markets with a price ceiling or price floor, taxes, subsidies, or quotas, monopoly, public goods, or externalities result in the quantity produced being the efficient quantity?
3. What is deadweight loss and under what conditions does it occur?
4. Does a deadweight loss occur in a competitive market when the quantity produced equals the competitive equilibrium quantity and the resource allocation is efficient?

You now know the conditions under which the resource allocation is efficient. You've seen how a competitive market can be efficient, and you've seen some impediments to efficiency.

But is an efficient allocation of resources fair? Does the competitive market provide people with fair incomes for their work? And do people always pay a fair price for the things they buy? Don't we need the government to step into some competitive markets to prevent the price from rising too high or falling too low? Let's now study these questions.

Is the Competitive Market Fair?

WHEN A NATURAL DISASTER STRIKES, SUCH AS A severe winter storm or a hurricane, the prices of many essential items jump. The reason the prices jump is that some people have a greater demand and greater willingness to pay when the items are in limited supply. So the higher prices achieve an efficient allocation of scarce resources. News reports of these price hikes almost never talk about efficiency. Instead, they talk about equity or fairness. The claim often made is that it is unfair for profit-seeking dealers to cheat the victims of natural disaster.

Similarly, when low-skilled people work for a wage that is below what most would regard as a "living wage," the media and politicians talk of employers taking unfair advantage of their workers.

How do we decide whether something is fair or unfair? You know when *you* think something is unfair. But how do you know? What are the *principles* of fairness?

Philosophers have tried for centuries to answer this question. Economists have offered their answers too. But before we look at the proposed answers, you should know that there is no universally agreed-upon answer.

Economists agree about efficiency. That is, they agree that it makes sense to make the economic pie as large as possible and to bake it at the lowest possible cost. But they do not agree about equity. That is, they do not agree about what are fair shares of the economic pie for all the people who make it. The reason is that ideas about fairness are not exclusively economic ideas. They touch on politics, ethics, and religion. Nevertheless, economists have thought about these issues and have a contribution to make. So let's examine the views of economists on this topic.

To think about fairness, think of economic life as a game—a serious game. All ideas about fairness can be divided into two broad groups. They are

- It's not fair if the *result* isn't fair.
- It's not fair if the *rules* aren't fair.

It's Not Fair If the *Result* Isn't Fair

The earliest efforts to establish a principle of fairness were based on the view that the result is what matters. And the general idea was that it is unfair if people's incomes are too unequal. It is unfair that bank presidents earn millions of dollars a year while bank tellers earn only thousands of dollars a year. It is unfair that a store owner enjoys a larger profit and her customers pay higher prices in the aftermath of a winter storm.

There was a lot of excitement during the nineteenth century when economists thought they had made the incredible discovery that efficiency requires equality of incomes. To make the economic pie as large as possible, it must be cut into equal pieces, one for each person. This idea turns out to be wrong, but there is a lesson in the reason that it is wrong. So this nineteenth century idea is worth a closer look.

Utilitarianism The nineteenth century idea that only equality brings efficiency is called *utilitarianism.* **Utilitarianism** is a principle that states that we should strive to achieve "the greatest happiness for the greatest number." The people who developed this idea were known as utilitarians. They included the most eminent thinkers, such as Jeremy Bentham and John Stuart Mill.

Utilitarians argued that to achieve "the greatest happiness for the greatest number," income must be transferred from the rich to the poor up to the point of complete equality—to the point at which there are no rich and no poor.

They reasoned in the following way: First, everyone has the same basic wants and a similar capacity to enjoy life. Second, the greater a person's income, the smaller is the marginal benefit of a dollar. The millionth dollar spent by a rich person brings a smaller marginal benefit to that person than the marginal benefit of the thousandth dollar spent by a poorer person. So by transferring a dollar from the millionaire to the poorer person, more is gained than is lost and the two people added together are better off.

Figure 5.8 illustrates this utilitarian idea. Tom and Jerry have the same marginal benefit curve, *MB.* (Marginal benefit is measured on the same scale of 1 to 3 for both Tom and Jerry.) Tom is at point *A.* He earns $5,000 a year, and his marginal benefit of a dollar of income is 3. Jerry is at point *B.* He earns $45,000 a year, and his marginal benefit of a dollar of income is 1. If a dollar is transferred from Jerry to Tom, Jerry loses 1 unit of marginal benefit and Tom gains 3 units. So together, Tom and Jerry are better off. They are sharing the economic pie more efficiently. If a second dollar is transferred, the same thing happens: Tom gains more than Jerry loses. And the same is true for every dollar transferred until they both reach point *C.* At point *C,* Tom and Jerry have

FIGURE 5.8 Utilitarian Fairness

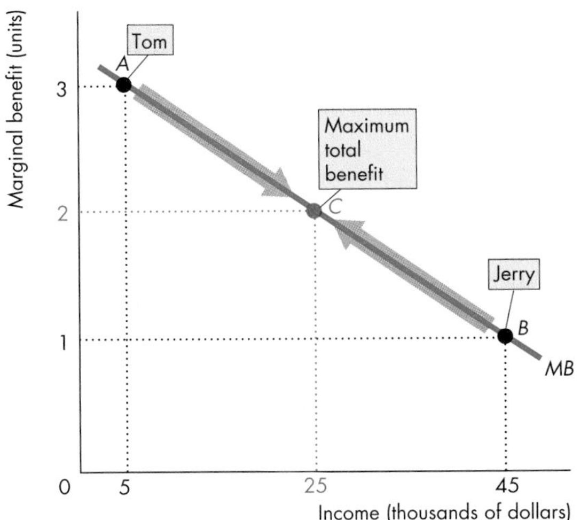

Tom earns $5,000 and has 3 units of marginal benefit at point *A*. Jerry earns $45,000 and has 1 unit of marginal benefit at point *B*. If income is transferred from Jerry to Tom, Jerry's loss is less than Tom's gain. Only when each of them has $25,000 and 2 units of marginal benefit (at point *C*) can the sum of their total benefit increase no further.

$25,000 each, and each has a marginal benefit of 2 units. Now they are sharing the economic pie in the most efficient way. It is bringing the greatest attainable happiness to Tom and Jerry.

The Big Tradeoff One big problem with the utilitarian ideal of complete equality is that it ignores the costs of making income transfers. Recognizing the cost of making income transfers leads to what is called the **big tradeoff,** which is a tradeoff between efficiency and fairness.

The big tradeoff is based on the following facts. Income can be transferred from people with high incomes to people with low incomes only by taxing incomes. Taxing people's income from employment makes them work less. It results in the quantity of labour being less than the efficient quantity. Taxing people's income from capital makes them save less. It results in the quantity of capital being less than the efficient quantity. With smaller quantities of both labour and capital, the quantity of goods and services produced is less than the efficient quantity. The economic pie shrinks.

The tradeoff is between the size of the economic pie and the degree of equality with which it is shared. The greater the amount of income redistribution through income taxes,the greater is the inefficiency—the smaller is the economic pie.

A second source of inefficiency arises because a dollar taken from a rich person does not end up as a dollar in the hands of a poorer person. Some of it is spent on administration of the tax and transfer system. The cost of tax-collecting agencies, such as Canada Customs and Revenue Agency, and welfare-administering agencies, such as Health Canada, must be paid with some of the taxes collected. Also, taxpayers hire accountants, auditors, and lawyers to help them ensure that they pay the correct amount of taxes. These activities use skilled labour and capital resources that could otherwise be used to produce goods and services that people value.

You can see that when all these costs are taken into account, transferring a dollar from a rich person does not give a dollar to a poor person. It is even possible that with high taxes, those with low incomes end up being worse off. Suppose, for example, that highly taxed entrepreneurs decide to work less hard and shut down some of their businesses. Low-income workers get fired and must seek other, perhaps even lower-paid work.

Because of the big tradeoff, those who say that fairness is equality propose a modified version of utilitarianism.

Make the Poorest as Well Off as Possible A Harvard philosopher, John Rawls, proposed a modified version of utilitarianism in a classic book entitled *A Theory of Justice*, published in 1971. Rawls says that, taking all the costs of income transfers into account, the fair distribution of the economic pie is the one that makes the poorest person as well off as possible. The incomes of rich people should be taxed, and after paying the costs of administering the tax and transfer system, what is left should be transferred to the poor. But the taxes must not be so high that they make the economic pie shrink to the point at which the poorest person ends up with a smaller piece. A bigger share of a smaller pie can be less than a smaller share of a bigger pie. The goal is to make the piece enjoyed by the poorest person as big as possible. Most likely, this piece will not be an equal share.

The "fair results" ideas require a change in the results after the game is over. Some economists say that these changes are themselves unfair and propose a different way of thinking about fairness.

It's Not Fair If the *Rules* Aren't Fair

The idea that it's not fair if the rules aren't fair is based on a fundamental principle that seems to be hardwired into the human brain: the symmetry principle. The **symmetry principle** is the requirement that people in similar situations be treated similarly. It is the moral principle that lies at the centre of all the big religions and that says, in some form or other, "behave towards other people in the way you expect them to behave towards you."

In economic life, this principle translates into *equality of opportunity.* But equality of opportunity to do what? This question is answered by the late Harvard philosopher, Robert Nozick, in a book entitled *Anarchy, State, and Utopia,* published in 1974.

Nozick argues that the idea of fairness as an outcome or result cannot work and that fairness must be based on the fairness of the rules. He suggests that fairness obeys two rules:

1. The state must enforce laws that establish and protect private property.
2. Private property may be transferred from one person to another only by voluntary exchange.

The first rule says that everything that is valuable must be owned by individuals and that the state must ensure that theft is prevented. The second rule says that the only legitimate way a person can acquire property is to buy it in exchange for something else that the person owns. If these rules, which are the only fair rules, are followed, then the result is fair. It doesn't matter how unequally the economic pie is shared, provided that it is baked by people each one of whom voluntarily provides services in exchange for the share of the pie offered in compensation.

These rules satisfy the symmetry principle. If these rules are not followed, the symmetry principle is broken. You can see these facts by imagining a world in which the laws are not followed.

First, suppose that some resources or goods are not owned. They are common property. Then everyone is free to participate in a grab to use these resources or goods. The strongest will prevail. But when the strongest prevails, the strongest effectively *owns* the resources or goods in question and prevents others from enjoying them.

Second, suppose that we do not insist on voluntary exchange for transferring ownership of resources from one person to another. The alternative is *involuntary* transfer. In simple language, the alternative is theft.

Both of these situations violate the symmetry principle. Only the strong get to acquire what they want. The weak end up with only the resources and goods that the strong don't want.

In contrast, if the two rules of fairness are followed, everyone, strong and weak, is treated in a similar way. Everyone is free to use their resources and human skills to create things that are valued by themselves and others and to exchange the fruits of their efforts with each other. This is the only set of arrangements that obeys the symmetry principle.

Fairness and Efficiency If private property rights are enforced and if voluntary exchange takes place in a competitive market, resources will be allocated efficiently if there are no

1. Price ceilings and price floors
2. Taxes, subsidies, and quotas
3. Monopolies
4. Public goods
5. External costs and external benefits

And according to the Nozick rules, the resulting distribution of income and wealth will be fair. Let's study a concrete example to examine the claim that if resources are allocated efficiently, they are also allocated fairly.

A Price Hike in a Natural Disaster An earthquake has broken the pipes that deliver drinking water to a city. The price of bottled water jumps from $1 a bottle to $8 a bottle in the 30 or so shops that have water for sale.

First, let's agree that the water is being used *efficiently.* There is a fixed amount of bottled water in the city, and given the quantity available, some people are willing to pay $8 to get a bottle. The water goes to the people who value it most highly. Consumer surplus and producer surplus are maximized.

So the water resources are being used efficiently. But are they being used fairly? Shouldn't people who can't afford to pay $8 a bottle get some of the available water for a lower price that they can afford? Isn't the fair solution for the shops to sell water for a lower price that people can afford? Or perhaps it might be fairer if the government bought the water and then made it available through a government store at a "reasonable" price. Let's think about these alternative solutions to the water problem of this city. Should water somehow be made available at a more reasonable price?

Shop Offers Water for $5 Suppose that Kris, a shop owner, offers water at $5 a bottle. Who will buy it? There are two types of buyers. Chuck is an example of one type. He values water at $8—is willing to pay $8 a bottle. Recall that given the quantity of water available, the equilibrium price is $8 a bottle. If Chuck buys the water, he consumes it. Chuck ends up with a consumer surplus of $3 on the bottle, and Kris receives $3 less of producer surplus.

Mitch is an example of the second type of buyer. Mitch would not pay $8 for a bottle. In fact, he wouldn't even pay $5 to consume a bottle of water. But he buys a bottle for $5. Why? Because he plans to sell the water to someone who is willing to pay $8 to consume it. When Mitch buys the water, Kris again receives a producer surplus of $3 *less* than she would receive if she charged the going market price. Mitch now becomes a water dealer. He sells the water for $8 and earns a producer surplus of $3.

So by being public-spirited and offering water for less than the market price, Kris ends up $3 a bottle worse off and the buyers end up $3 a bottle better off. The same people consume the water in both situations. They are the people who value the water at $8 a bottle. But the distribution of consumer surplus and producer surplus is different in the two cases. When Kris offers the water for $5 a bottle, she ends up with a smaller producer surplus and Chuck and Mitch with a larger consumer surplus and producer surplus.

So which is the fair arrangement? The one that favours Kris or the one that favours Chuck and Mitch? The fair-rules view is that both arrangements are fair. Kris voluntarily sells the water for $5, so in effect, she is helping the community to cope with its water problem. It is fair that she should help, but the choice is hers. She owns the water. It is not fair that she should be compelled to help.

Government Buys Water Now suppose instead that the government buys all the water. The going price is $8 a bottle, so that's what the government pays. Now the government offers the water for sale for $1 a bottle, its "normal" price.

The quantity of water supplied is exactly the same as before. But now, at $1 a bottle, the quantity demanded is much larger than the quantity supplied. There is a shortage of water.

Because there is a large water shortage, the government decides to ration the amount that anyone may buy. Everyone is allocated one bottle. So everyone lines up to collect his or her bottle. Two of these people are Chuck and Mitch. Chuck, you'll recall, is willing to pay $8 a bottle. Mitch is willing to pay less than $5. But they both get a bargain. Chuck drinks his $1 bottle and enjoys a $7 consumer surplus. What does Mitch do? Does he drink his bottle? He does not. He sells it to another person who values the water at $8. And he enjoys a $7 producer surplus from his temporary water-trading business.

So the people who value the water most highly consume it. But the consumer and producer surpluses are distributed in a different way from what the free market would have delivered. Again the question arises, which arrangement is fair?

The main difference between the government scheme and Kris's private charitable contributions lies in the fact that to buy the water for $8 and sell it for $1, the government must tax someone $7 for each bottle sold. So whether this arrangement is fair depends on whether the taxes are fair.

Taxes are an involuntary transfer of private property, so according to the fair-rules view, they are unfair. But most economists, and most people, think that there is such a thing as a fair tax. So it seems that the fair-rules view needs to be weakened a bit. Agreeing that there is such a thing as a fair tax is the easy part. Deciding what is a fair tax brings endless disagreement and debate.

REVIEW QUIZ

1. What are the two big approaches to thinking about fairness?
2. What is the utilitarian idea of fairness and what is wrong with it?
3. Explain the big tradeoff. What idea of fairness has been developed to deal with it?
4. What is the main idea of fairness based on fair rules?

◆ You've now studied the two biggest issues that run right through the whole of economics: efficiency and equity, or fairness. In the next chapter, we study some sources of inefficiency and unfairness. And at many points throughout this book—and in your life—you will return to and use the ideas about efficiency and fairness that you've learned in this chapter. *Reading Between the Lines* on pp. 118–119 looks at an example of an inefficiency and, some would argue, an unfairness in our economy today.

Efficiency and Equity in the Market for Drugs

MONTREAL GAZETTE, February 20, 2001

Drug firms take on South Africa

A critical battle is about to begin in the Pretoria High Court, where 42 pharmaceutical companies, including the British giant GlaxoSmithKline, are attempting to block the South African government from importing the cheap medicines to treat people suffering from such diseases as diarrhea, meningitis, AIDS and tuberculosis. ...

The rest of Africa will be closely watching. So will developing countries on other continents.

With the death toll from infectious diseases inexorably rising, especially in Africa, a tide of outrage is swelling among local activists and international-aid organizations, which see medicines denied to the sick in the name of commerce.

There are more than 32 million men, women and children infected by HIV in developing countries. AZT and 3TC, the basic anti-retroviral drugs in the West, would keep them alive and well, but the price tag is R79,000 (about $15,000 Canadian) to R120,000 (about $23,300 Canadian) per patient per year.

The majority of employed people in South Africa, with families to support, earn less than R20000 ($4,000 Canadian) a year, and by comparison with most of the rest of the continent they are rich.

But there are now alternatives—cheap copies of life-saving medicines called generics, made mainly in Brazil, India and Thailand.

Thailand believes it could reduce the cost to R 1,400 (about $275 Canadian) per patient per year.

It is a price the South African government might be able to pay for the life of its people, but the drug companies, fearing potential worldwide consequences if their prices are undercut, have said no.

Originally appeared as "At the Mercy of the Drug Giants" by Sarah Bosley, February 12, 2001 in *The Guardian*.

Essence of the Story

- Pharmaceutical companies are attempting to block the South African government from importing the cheap medicines to treat diarrhea, meningitis, AIDS, and tuberculosis.
- More than 32 million people are infected by HIV in developing countries.
- The drugs that treat AIDS (such as AZT and 3TC) cost from $15,000 to $23,000 per patient per year.
- The majority of employed people in South Africa earn less than $4,000 a year, and by comparison with the rest of Africa, they are rich.
- Cheap generic copies of AIDS medicines made in Brazil, India, and Thailand cost $275 per patient per year.

Economic Analysis

- The efficient quantity of AZT is that at which its marginal benefit equals its marginal cost.

- We can measure the marginal benefit of AZT by the amount that people are willing to pay for it.

- The marginal benefit to people who buy AZT at its retail price in North America is between $15,000 and $23,000 a year.

- The marginal benefit to the government of South Africa is $275 per person per year.

- We do not know the marginal cost of producing AZT. But we know that producers in Brazil, India, and Thailand are willing to sell AZT for $275 per person per year. So we can be sure that the marginal cost of a year of AZT treatment is not greater than $275 and most likely it is less than this amount.

- Because most AZT sells for a price that exceeds $275, the quantity of AZT produced is less than the efficient quantity.

- Figure 1 illustrates the market for AZT. The demand curve is *D*, and the marginal cost curve is *MC*. (It is an assumption that *MC* is constant at $275 per person per year.)

- The price of a year's treatment per person is $23,000. At this price, the producer earns a large producer surplus shown by the blue rectangle.

- Some consumers would be willing to pay even more than $23,000 for a year's treatment, so there is a consumer surplus shown by the green triangle.

- Because price (marginal benefit) exceeds marginal cost, there is a deadweight loss shown by the grey triangle.

- Figure 2 illustrates the market for AZT if cheap generic versions are available at $275 per person per year.

- The quantity consumed increases, producer surplus and deadweight loss disappear, and consumer surplus expands.

- The market for an existing drug is different from that for a new drug that is still being developed. The development cost of an existing drug is a sunk cost.

- The cost of developing a new drug is part of the opportunity cost that the producer must take into account when deciding whether to continue the development process.

- If a drug developer cannot recover the opportunity cost of development, new drugs might not be developed.

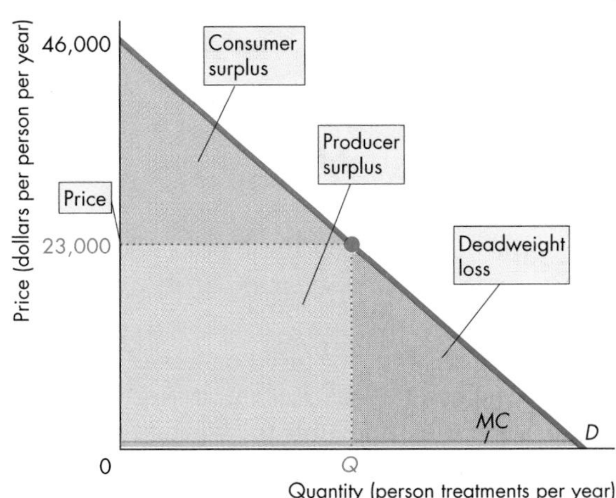

Figure 1 The market without cheap copies

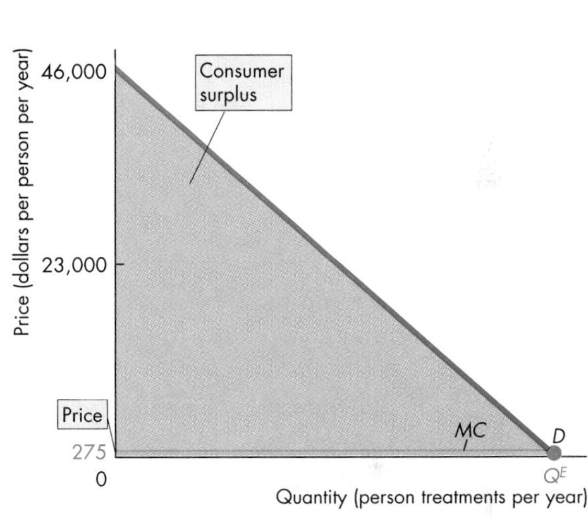

Figure 2 The market with cheap copies

You're The Voter

- Do you support the production of cheap generic drugs to treat AIDS and other diseases that afflict people in poor developing countries? Explain why or why not.

SUMMARY

KEY POINTS

Efficiency: A Refresher (pp. 104–105)

- The marginal benefit received from a good or service—the benefit of consuming one additional unit—is the *value* of the good or service to its consumers.
- The marginal cost of a good or service—the cost of producing one additional unit—is the *opportunity cost* of one more unit to its producers.
- Resource allocation is efficient when marginal benefit equals marginal cost.
- If marginal benefit exceeds marginal cost, an increase in production uses resources more efficiently.
- If marginal cost exceeds marginal benefit, a decrease in production uses resources more efficiently.

Value, Price, and Consumer Surplus (pp. 106–107)

- Marginal benefit is measured by the maximum price that consumers are willing to pay for a good or service.
- Marginal benefit determines demand, and a demand curve is a marginal benefit curve.
- Value is what people are *willing to* pay; price is what people *must* pay.
- Consumer surplus equals value minus price, summed over the quantity consumed.

Cost, Price, and Producer Surplus (pp. 108–109)

- Marginal cost is measured by the minimum price producers must be offered to increase production by one unit.
- Marginal cost determines supply, and a supply curve is a marginal cost curve.
- Opportunity cost is what producers pay; price is what producers receive.
- Producer surplus equals price minus opportunity cost, summed over the quantity produced.

Is the Competitive Market Efficient? (pp. 110–113)

- In a competitive equilibrium, marginal benefit equals marginal cost and resource allocation is efficient.
- Monopoly restricts production and creates deadweight loss.
- A competitive market provides too small a quantity of public goods because of the free-rider problem.
- A competitive market provides too large a quantity of goods and services that have external costs and too small a quantity of goods and services that have external benefits.

Is the Competitive Market Fair? (pp. 114–117)

- Ideas about fairness can be divided into two groups: fair *results* and fair *rules*.
- Fair-results ideas require income transfers from the rich to the poor.
- Fair-rules ideas require property rights and voluntary exchange.

KEY FIGURES

Figure 5.1 The Efficient Quantity of Pizza, 104
Figure 5.3 A Consumer's Demand and Consumer Surplus, 107
Figure 5.5 A Producer's Supply and Producer Surplus, 109
Figure 5.6 An Efficient Market for Pizza, 110
Figure 5.7 Underproduction and Overproduction, 113

KEY TERMS

Big tradeoff, 115
Consumer surplus, 107
Deadweight loss, 112
Efficient allocation, 104
Marginal benefit, 104
Marginal cost, 104
Producer surplus, 109
Symmetry principle, 116
Utilitarianism, 114
Value, 106

PROBLEMS

*1. The figure illustrates the market for floppy discs.

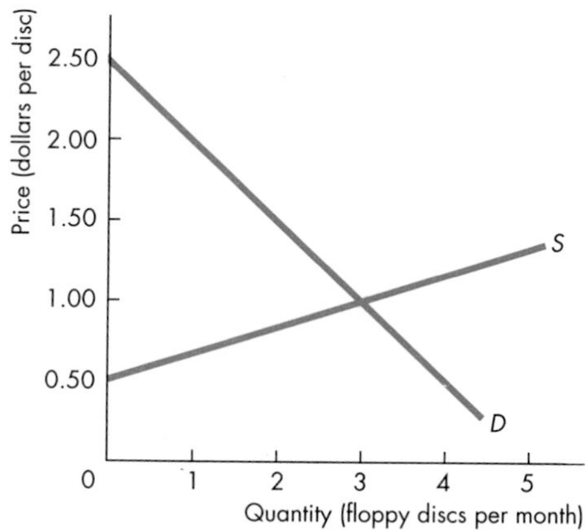

a. What are the equilibrium price and equilibrium quantity of floppy discs?
b. Calculate the amount consumers paid for floppy discs.
c. Calculate the consumer surplus.
d. Calculate the producer surplus.
e. Calculate the cost of producing the floppy discs sold.
f. What is the efficient quantity?

2. The figure illustrates the market for CDs.

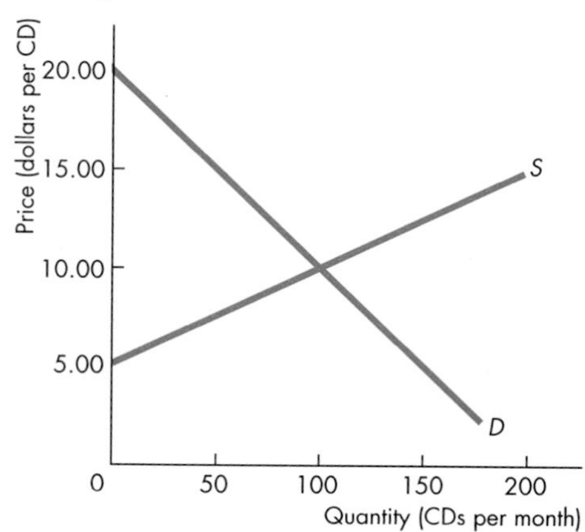

a. What are the equilibrium price and equilibrium quantity of CDs?
b. Calculate the amount consumers paid for CDs.
c. Calculate the consumer surplus.
d. Calculate the producer surplus.
e. Calculate the cost of producing the CDs sold.
f. What is the efficient quantity of CDs?

*3. The table gives the demand and supply schedules for sandwiches.

Price (dollars per sandwich)	Quantity demanded (sandwiches per hour)	Quantity supplied (sandwiches per hour)
0	400	0
1	350	50
2	300	100
3	250	150
4	200	200
5	150	250
6	100	300
7	50	350
8	0	400

a. What is the maximum price that consumers are willing to pay for the 250th sandwich?
b. What is the minimum price that producers are willing to accept for the 250th sandwich?
c. Are 250 sandwiches a day less than or greater than the efficient quantity?
d. If the sandwich market is efficient, what is the consumer surplus? (Draw the graph.)
e. If the sandwich market is efficient, what is the producer surplus? (Draw the graph.)
f. If sandwich makers produce 250 a day, what is the deadweight loss? (Draw the graph.)

4. The table gives the demand and supply schedules for sunscreen.

Price (dollars per bottle)	Quantity demanded (bottles per day)	Quantity supplied (bottles per day)
0	900	0
1	800	100
2	700	200
3	600	300
4	500	400
5	400	500
6	300	600
7	200	700
8	100	800
9	0	900

a. What is the maximum price that consumers are willing to pay for the 300th bottle?
b. What is the minimum price that producers are willing to accept for the 300th bottle?
c. Are 300 bottles a day less than or greater than the efficient quantity? (Draw the graph.)
d. If the market for sunscreen is efficient, what is the consumer surplus? (Draw the graph.)

e. If the market for sunscreen is efficient, what is the producer surplus? (Draw the graph.)
f. If sunscreen bottlers produce 300 bottles a day, what is the deadweight loss?

*5. The table gives the demand schedules for train travel for Ben, Beth, and Bo.

Price (cents per passenger kilometre)	Quantity demanded (passenger kilometres)		
	Ben	Beth	Bo
10	500	300	60
20	450	250	50
30	400	200	40
40	350	150	30
50	300	100	20
60	250	50	10
70	200	0	0

a. If the price of train travel is 40 cents a passenger kilometre, what is the consumer surplus of each traveller?
b. Which traveller has the largest consumer surplus? Explain why.
c. If the price rises to 50 cents a passenger kilometre, what is the change in consumer surplus of each traveller?

6. The table gives the demand schedules for air travel for Ann, Arthur, and Abby.

Price (dollars per passenger kilometre)	Quantity demanded (passenger kilometres)		
	Ann	Arthur	Abby
10.00	500	600	300
12.50	450	500	250
15.00	400	400	200
17.50	350	300	150
20.00	300	200	100
22.50	250	100	50
25.00	200	0	0

a. If the price is $20 a passenger kilometre, what is the consumer surplus of each traveller?
b. Which consumer has the largest consumer surplus? Explain why.
c. If the price falls to $15 a passenger kilometre, what is the change in consumer surplus of each traveller?

CRITICAL THINKING

1. Study *Reading Between the Lines* on pp. 118–119 about AZT and then answer the following questions:
   a. Is the quantity of AZT produced greater than, less than, or equal to the efficient quantity? Explain your answer by using the concepts of marginal benefit, marginal cost, price, consumer surplus, and producer surplus.
   b. If GlaxoSmithKline agreed to sell some AZT for $275 to the government of South Africa, would this deal increase or decrease consumer surplus? Would it increase or decrease GlaxoSmithKline's producer surplus? Would it bring the quantity of AZT closer to the efficient quantity? Explain your answer by using the concepts of marginal benefit, marginal cost, price, consumer surplus, and producer surplus.
   c. Drug producers in Brazil, India, and Thailand make a generic AZT and sell it at a much lower price than GlaxoSmithKline's price. Do generic drugs increase or decrease consumer surplus? Does a generic AZT increase or decrease GlaxoSmithKline's producer surplus? Does it bring the quantity of AZT closer to the efficient quantity? Explain your answer by using the concepts of marginal benefit, marginal cost, price, consumer surplus, and producer surplus.

WEB EXERCISES

1. Use the links on the Parkin-Bade Web site and read the article by Augustine Faucher entitled "Cipro and the Free Riders." Then answer the following questions:
   a. What does the author claim is the problem in the market for antibiotics that can treat anthrax?
   b. What does the author claim is the solution to the problem in this market?
   c. Explain why you agree or disagree with the author.

MARKETS IN ACTION

CHAPTER 6

Turbulent Times

Apartment rents are rising in Toronto, and people are screaming for help. Can the government limit rent increases to help renters live in affordable housing? ◆ Almost every day, a new machine is invented that saves labour and increases productivity. Take a look at the machines in McDonald's that have replaced some low-skilled workers. Can we protect low-skilled workers with minimum wage laws that enable people to earn a living wage? ◆ Almost everything we buy is taxed. And a new tax on air travel has been introduced to pay the cost of increased airport security. How much of the airport security tax gets paid by the traveller and how much by the airlines? We explore this question in *Reading Between the Lines* at the end of the chapter. Do taxes help or hinder the market in its attempt to move resources to where they are valued most highly? ◆ Trade in items such as drugs, automatic firearms, and enriched uranium is illegal. How do laws that make trading in a good or service illegal affect its price and the quantity bought and sold? ◆ In 1996, ideal conditions brought record yields and global grain production increased. But in 2001, yields were low and global grain production decreased. How do farm prices and revenues react to such output fluctuations?

In this chapter, we use the theory of demand and supply (Chapter 3) and the concepts of elasticity (Chapter 4) and efficiency (Chapter 5) to answer questions like those that we've just posed.

After studying this chapter, you will able to

- **Explain how housing markets work and how price ceilings create housing shortages and inefficiency**
- **Explain how labour markets work and how minimum wage laws create unemployment and inefficiency**
- **Explain the effects of the sales tax**
- **Explain how markets for illegal goods work**
- **Explain why farm prices and revenues fluctuate and how speculation and farm marketing boards influence farm prices and farm revenues**

Housing Markets and Rent Ceilings

TO SEE HOW A HOUSING MARKET WORKS, LET'S transport ourselves to San Francisco in April 1906, as the city is suffering from a massive earthquake and fire. You can sense the enormity of San Francisco's problems by reading a headline from the April 19, 1906, *New York Times* about the first days of the crisis:

Over 500 Dead, $200,000,000 Lost in San Francisco Earthquake

Nearly Half the City Is in Ruins and 50,000 Are Homeless

The commander of federal troops in charge of the emergency described the magnitude of the problem:

> Not a hotel of note or importance was left standing. The great apartment houses had vanished ... two hundred-and-twenty-five thousand people were ... homeless.[1]

Almost overnight, more than half the people in a city of 400,000 had lost their homes. Temporary shelters and camps alleviated some of the problem, but it was also necessary to utilize the apartment buildings and houses left standing. As a consequence, they had to accommodate 40 percent more people than they had before the earthquake.

The *San Francisco Chronicle* was not published for more than a month after the earthquake. When the newspaper reappeared on May 24, 1906, the city's housing shortage—what would seem to be a major news item that would still be of grave importance—was not mentioned. Milton Friedman and George Stigler describe the situation:

> *There is not a single mention of a housing shortage!* The classified advertisements listed sixty-four offers of flats and houses for rent, and nineteen of houses for sale, against five advertisements of flats or houses wanted. Then and thereafter a considerable number of all types of accommodation except hotel rooms were offered for rent.[2]

How did San Francisco cope with such a devastating reduction in the supply of housing?

[1] Reported in Milton Friedman and George J. Stigler, "Roofs or Ceilings? The Current Housing Problem," in *Popular Essays on Current Problems*, vol. 1, no. 2 (New York: Foundation for Economic Education, 1946), pp. 3–159.

[2] *Ibid.*, p. 3.

The Market Response to a Decrease in Supply

Figure 6.1 shows the market for housing in San Francisco. The demand curve for housing is *D*. There is a short-run supply curve, labelled *SS*, and a long-run supply curve, labelled *LS*.

The short-run supply curve shows the change in the quantity of housing supplied as the rent changes while the number of houses and apartment buildings remains constant. The short-run supply response arises from changes in the intensity with which existing buildings are used. The quantity of housing supplied increases if families rent out rooms that they previously used themselves, and it decreases if families use rooms that they previously rented out to others.

The long-run supply curve shows how the quantity of housing supplied responds to a change in price after enough time has elapsed for new apartment buildings and houses to be erected or for existing ones to be destroyed. In Fig. 6.1, the long-run supply curve is *perfectly elastic*. We do not actually know that the long-run supply curve is perfectly elastic, but it is a reasonable assumption. It implies that the cost of building an apartment is pretty much the same regardless of whether there are 50,000 or 150,000 apartments in existence.

The equilibrium price (rent) and quantity are determined at the point of intersection of the *short-run* supply curve and the demand curve. Before the earthquake, the equilibrium rent is $16 a month and the quantity is 100,000 units of housing.

Figure 6.1(a) shows the situation immediately after the earthquake. The destruction of buildings decreases the supply of housing and shifts the short-run supply curve *SS* leftward to SS_A. If the rent remains at $16 a month, only 44,000 units of housing are available. But with only 44,000 units of housing available, the maximum rent that someone is willing to pay for the last available apartment is $24 a month. So rents rise. In Fig. 6.1(a), the rent rises to $20 a month.

As the rent rises, the quantity of housing demanded decreases and the quantity supplied increases to 72,000 units. These changes occur because people economize on their use of space and make spare rooms, attics, and basements available to others. The higher rent allocates the scarce housing to the people who value it most highly and are willing to pay the most for it.

But the higher rent has other, long-run effects. Let's look at these long-run effects.

FIGURE 6.1 The San Francisco Housing Market in 1906

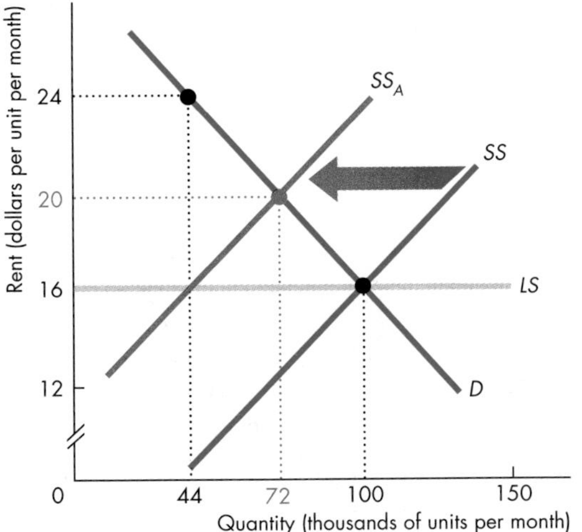

(a) After earthquake

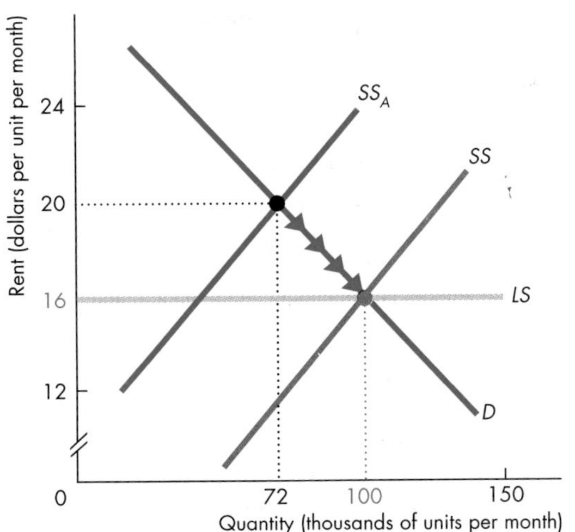

(b) Long-run adjustment

Part (a) shows that before the earthquake, 100,000 housing units were rented at $16 a month. After the earthquake, the short-run supply curve shifts from *SS* to SS_A. The rent rises to $20 a month, and the quantity of housing decreases to 72,000 units.

With rent at $20 a month, there is profit in building new apartments and houses. As the building proceeds, the short-run supply curve shifts rightward (part b). The rent gradually falls to $16 a month, and the quantity of housing increases to 100,000 units—as the arrowed line shows.

Long-Run Adjustments

With sufficient time for new apartments and houses to be constructed, supply increases. The long-run supply curve tells us that in the long run, housing is supplied at a rent of $16 a month. Because the rent of $20 a month exceeds the long-run supply price of $16 a month, there is a building boom. More apartments and houses are built, and the short-run supply curve shifts gradually rightward.

Figure 6.1(b) shows the long-run adjustment. As more housing is built, the short-run supply curve shifts gradually rightward and intersects the demand curve at lower rents and larger quantities. The market equilibrium follows the arrows down the demand curve. The building boom comes to an end when there is no further profit in building new apartments and houses. The process ends when the rent is back at $16 a month, and 100,000 units of housing are available.

We've just seen how a housing market responds to a decrease in supply. And we've seen that a key part of the adjustment process is a rise in the rent. Suppose the government passes a law to stop the rent from rising. What happens then?

A Regulated Housing Market

We're now going to study the effects of a price ceiling in the housing market. A **price ceiling** is a regulation that makes it illegal to charge a price higher than a specified level. When a price ceiling is applied to housing markets, it is called a **rent ceiling.** How does a rent ceiling affect the housing market?

The effect of a price (rent) ceiling depends on whether it is imposed at a level that is above or below the equilibrium price (rent). A price ceiling set *above* the equilibrium price has no effect. The reason is that the price ceiling does not constrain the market forces. The force of the law and the market forces are not in conflict. But a price ceiling *below* the equilibrium price has powerful effects on a market. The reason is that it attempts to prevent the price from regulating the quantities demanded and supplied. The force of the law and the market forces are in conflict, and one (or both) of these forces must yield to some degree. Let's study the effects of a price ceiling that is set below the equilibrium price by returning to San Francisco. What would have happened in San Francisco if a rent ceiling of $16 a month—the rent before the earthquake—had been imposed?

FIGURE 6.2 A Rent Ceiling

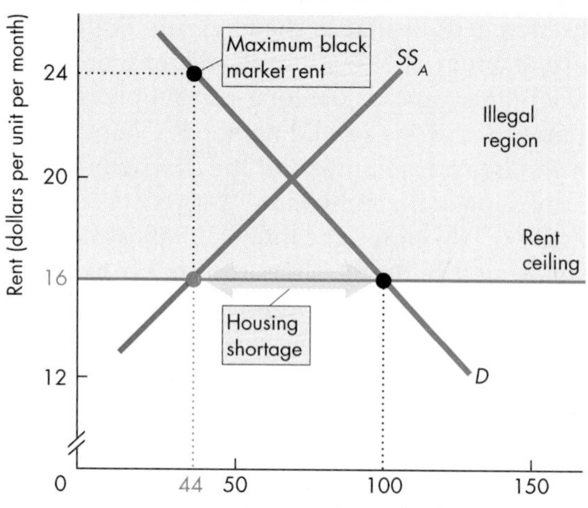

A rent above $16 a month is illegal (in the grey-shaded illegal region). At a rent of $16 a month, the quantity of housing supplied after the earthquake is 44,000 units. Someone is willing to pay $24 a month for the 44,000th unit. Frustrated renters spend time searching for housing and frustrated renters and landlords make deals in a black market.

Figure 6.2 enables us to answer this question. A rent that exceeds $16 a month is in the grey-shaded illegal region in the figure. At a rent of $16 a month, the quantity of housing supplied is 44,000 units and the quantity demanded is 100,000 units. So there is a shortage of 56,000 units of housing.

But the story does not end here. Somehow, the 44,000 units of available housing must be allocated among people who demand 100,000 units. How is this allocation achieved? When a rent ceiling creates a housing shortage, two developments occur. They are

- Search activity
- Black markets

Search Activity

The time spent looking for someone with whom to do business is called **search activity.** We spend some time in search activity almost every time we buy something. You want the latest hot CD, and you know four stores that stock it. But which store has the best deal? You need to spend a few minutes on the telephone finding out. In some markets, we spend a lot of time searching. An example is the used car market. People spend a lot of time checking out alternative dealers and cars.

But when a price is regulated and there is a shortage, search activity increases. In the case of a rent-controlled housing market, frustrated would-be renters scan the newspapers, not only for housing ads but also for death notices! Any information about newly available housing is useful. And they race to be first on the scene when news of a possible supplier breaks.

The *opportunity cost* of a good is equal not only to its price but also to the value of the search time spent finding the good. So the opportunity cost of housing is equal to the rent (a regulated price) plus the time and other resources spent searching for the restricted quantity available. Search activity is costly. It uses time and other resources, such as telephones, cars, and gasoline that could have been used in other productive ways. A rent ceiling controls the rent portion of the cost of housing, but it does not control the opportunity cost, which might even be *higher* than the rent would be if the market were unregulated.

Black Markets

A **black market** is an illegal market in which the price exceeds the legally imposed price ceiling. Black markets occur in rent-controlled housing, and scalpers run black markets in tickets for big sporting events and rock concerts.

When rent ceilings are in force, frustrated renters and landlords constantly seek ways of increasing rents. One common way is for a new tenant to pay a high price for worthless fittings, such as charging $2,000 for threadbare drapes. Another is for the tenant to pay an exorbitant price for new locks and keys—called "key money."

The level of a black market rent depends on how tightly the rent ceiling is enforced. With loose enforcement, the black market rent is close to the unregulated rent. But with strict enforcement, the black market rent is equal to the maximum price that renters are willing to pay.

With strict enforcement of the rent ceiling in the San Francisco example shown in Fig. 6.2, the quantity of housing available remains at 44,000 units. A small number of people offer housing for rent at $24 a month—the highest rent that someone is willing to pay—and the government detects and punishes some of these black market traders.

Inefficiency of Rent Ceilings

In an unregulated market, the market determines the rent at which the quantity demanded equals the quantity supplied. In this situation, scarce housing resources are allocated efficiently. *Marginal benefit* equals *marginal cost* (see Chapter 5, p. 110).

Figure 6.3 shows the inefficiency of a rent ceiling. If the rent is fixed at $16 per month, 44,000 units are supplied. Marginal benefit is $24 a month. The blue triangle above the supply curve and below the rent ceiling line shows producer surplus. Because the quantity of housing is less than the competitive quantity, there is a deadweight loss, shown by the grey triangle. This loss is borne by the consumers who can't find housing and by producers who can't supply housing at the new lower price. Consumers who do find housing at the controlled rent gain. If no one incurs search cost, consumer surplus is shown by the sum of the green triangle and the red rectangle. But search costs might eat up part of the consumer surplus, possibly as much as the entire amount that consumers are willing to pay for the available housing, (the red rectangle).

Equity? So rent ceilings prevent scarce resources from flowing to their highest-valued use. But don't rent ceilings ensure that scarce housing goes to the people whose need is greatest and make the allocation of scarce housing fair?

The complex ideas about fairness are explored in Chapter 5 (pp. 114–117). Blocking rent adjustments that bring the quantity of housing demanded into equality with the quantity supplied doesn't end scarcity. So when the law prevents rents from adjusting and blocks the price mechanism from allocating scarce housing, some other allocation mechanism must be used. One of these factors might be discrimination on the basis of race, ethnicity, or sex. Are these mechanisms fair?

Paris, New York, and Toronto are three cities that have rent ceilings; the best example is New York. One consequence of New York's rent ceilings is that families that have lived in the city for a long time—including some rich and famous ones—enjoy low rents, while newcomers pay high rents for hard-to-find apartments. At the same time, landlords in rent-controlled Harlem abandon entire city blocks to rats and drug dealers. Swedish economist Assar Lindbeck has suggested that rent ceilings are the most effective means yet for destroying cities, even more effective than the hydrogen bomb.

FIGURE 6.3 The Inefficiency of a Rent Ceiling

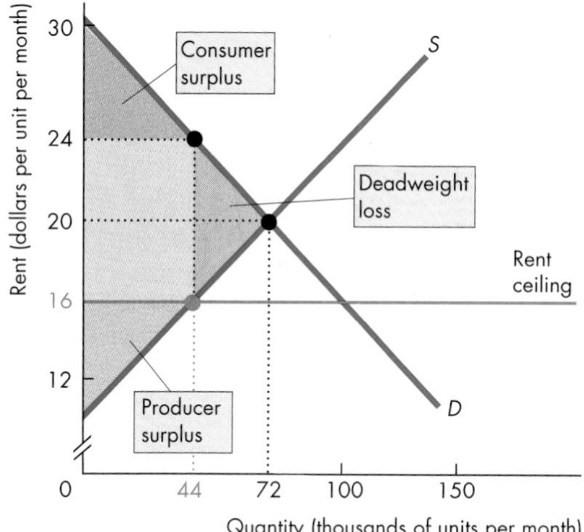

A rent ceiling of $16 a month decreases the quantity of housing supplied to 44,000 units. Producer surplus shrinks, and a deadweight loss arises. If people use no resources in search activity, consumer surplus is the green triangle plus the red rectangle. But if people use resources in search activity equal to the amount they are willing to pay for available housing (the red rectangle), the consumer surplus shrinks to the green triangle.

REVIEW QUIZ

1. How does a decrease in the supply of housing change the equilibrium rent in the short run?
2. What are the effects of a rise in rent? And who gets to consume the scarce housing resources?
3. What are the long-run effects of higher rents following a decrease in the supply of housing?
4. What is a rent ceiling and what are its effects if it is set above the equilibrium rent?
5. What are the effects of a rent ceiling that is set below the equilibrium rent?
6. How do scarce housing resources get allocated when a rent ceiling is in place?

You now know how a price ceiling works. Next, we'll learn about the effects of a price floor by studying minimum wages in the labour market.

The Labour Market and the Minimum Wage

FOR EACH ONE OF US, THE LABOUR MARKET IS the market that influences the jobs we get and the wages we earn. Firms decide how much labour to demand, and the lower the wage rate, the greater is the quantity of labour demanded. Households decide how much labour to supply, and the higher the wage rate, the greater is the quantity of labour supplied. The wage rate adjusts to make the quantity of labour demanded equal to the quantity supplied.

But the labour market is constantly hit by shocks, and wages and employment prospects constantly change. The most pervasive source of these shocks is the advance of technology.

New labour-saving technologies become available every year. As a result, the demand for some types of labour, usually the least-skilled types, decreases. During the 1980s and 1990s, for example, the demand for telephone operators and television repair technicians decreased. Throughout the past 200 years, the demand for low-skilled farm labourers has steadily decreased.

How does the labour market cope with this continuous decrease in the demand for low-skilled labour? Doesn't it mean that the wage rate of low-skilled workers is constantly falling?

To answer these questions, we must study the market for low-skilled labour. And just as we did when we studied the housing market, we must look at both the short run and the long run.

In the short run, there is a given number of people who have a given skill, training, and experience. Short-run supply of labour describes how the number of hours of labour supplied by this given number of workers changes as the wage rate changes. To get workers to work more hours, they must be offered a higher wage rate.

In the long run, people can acquire new skills and find new types of jobs. The number of people in the low-skilled labour market depends on the wage rate in this market compared with other opportunities. If the wage rate of low-skilled labour is high enough, people will enter this market. If the wage rate is too low, people will leave it. Some will seek training to enter higher-skilled labour markets, and others will stop working and stay at home or retire.

The long-run supply of labour is the relationship between the quantity of labour supplied and the wage rate after enough time has passed for people to enter or leave the low-skilled labour market. If people can freely enter and leave the low-skilled labour market, the long-run supply of labour is *perfectly elastic.*

Figure 6.4 shows the market for low-skilled labour. Other things remaining the same, the lower the wage rate, the greater is the quantity of labour demanded by firms. The demand curve for labour, *D* in part (a), shows this relationship between the wage rate and the quantity of labour demanded. Other things remaining the same, the higher the wage rate, the greater is the quantity of labour supplied by households. But the longer the period of adjustment, the greater is the *elasticity of supply* of labour. The short-run supply curve is *SS*, and the long-run supply curve is *LS*. In the figure, long-run supply is assumed to be perfectly elastic (the *LS* curve is horizontal). This market is in equilibrium at a wage rate of $5 an hour and 22 million hours of labour employed.

What happens if a labour-saving invention decreases the demand for low-skilled labour? Figure 6.4(a) shows the short-run effects of such a change. The demand curve before the new technology is introduced is the curve labelled *D*. After the introduction of the new technology, the demand curve shifts leftward to D_A. The wage rate falls to $4 an hour, and the quantity of labour employed decreases to 21 million hours. But this short-run effect on the wage rate and employment is not the end of the story.

People who are now earning only $4 an hour look around for other opportunities. They see many other jobs (in markets for other types of skills) that pay more than $4 an hour. One by one, workers decide to go back to school or take jobs that pay less but offer on-the-job training. As a result, the short-run supply curve begins to shift leftward.

Figure 6.4(b) shows the long-run adjustment. As the short-run supply curve shifts leftward, it intersects the demand curve D_A at higher wage rates and lower levels of employment. The process ends when workers have no incentive to leave the low-skilled labour market and the short-run supply curve has shifted all the way to SS_A. At this point, the wage rate has returned to $5 an hour and employment has decreased to 20 million hours a year.

Sometimes, the adjustment process that we've just described is rapid. At other times, it is slow and the wage rate remains low for a long period. To boost the incomes of the lowest-paid workers, the government intervenes in the labour market and sets the minimum wage that employers are required to pay. Let's look at the effects of the minimum wage.

FIGURE 6.4 A Market for Low-Skilled Labour

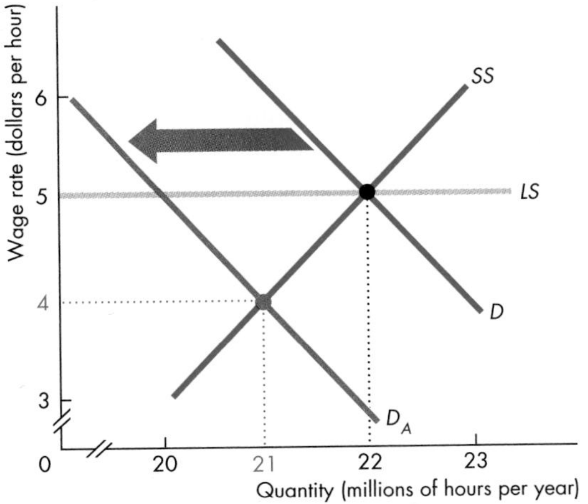

(a) After invention

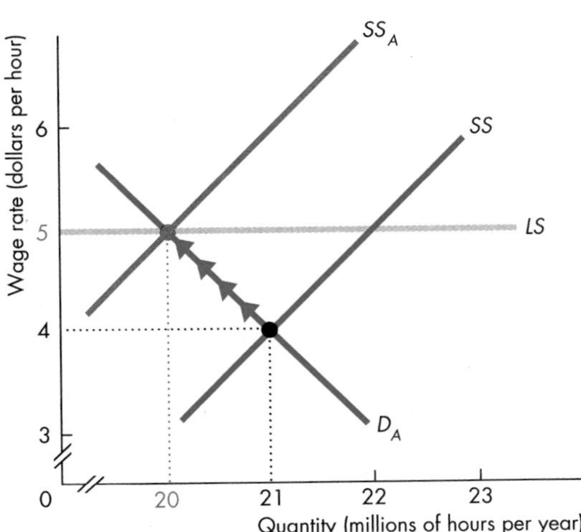

(b) Long-run adjustment

Part (a) shows the immediate effect of a labour-saving invention on the market for low-skilled labour. Initially, the wage rate is $5 an hour and 22 million hours a year are employed. A labour-saving invention shifts the demand curve from D to D_A. The wage rate falls to $4 an hour, and employment decreases to 21 million hours a year. With the lower wage rate, some workers leave this market, and the short-run supply curve starts to shift gradually leftward to SS_A (part b). The wage rate gradually rises, and the employment level decreases. In the long run, the wage rate returns to $5 an hour and employment decreases to 20 million hours a year.

The Minimum Wage

A **price floor** is a regulation that makes it illegal to trade at a price lower than a specified level. When a price floor is applied to labour markets, it is called a **minimum wage.** If the minimum wage is set *below* the equilibrium wage, the minimum wage has no effect. The minimum wage and market forces are not in conflict. If the minimum wage is set *above* the equilibrium wage, the minimum wage is in conflict with market forces and does have some effects on the labour market. Let's study these effects by returning to the market for low-skilled labour.

Suppose that with an equilibrium wage of $4 an hour (Fig. 6.4a), the government sets a minimum wage at $5 an hour. What are the effects of this minimum wage? Figure 6.5 answers this question. It shows the minimum wage as the horizontal red line labelled "Minimum wage." A wage below this level is in the grey-shaded illegal region. At the minimum wage rate, 20 million hours of labour are demanded (point *A*) and 22 million hours are supplied (point *B*), so 2 million hours of available labour are unemployed.

With only 20 million hours demanded, some workers are willing to supply that 20 millionth hour

FIGURE 6.5 Minimum Wage and Unemployment

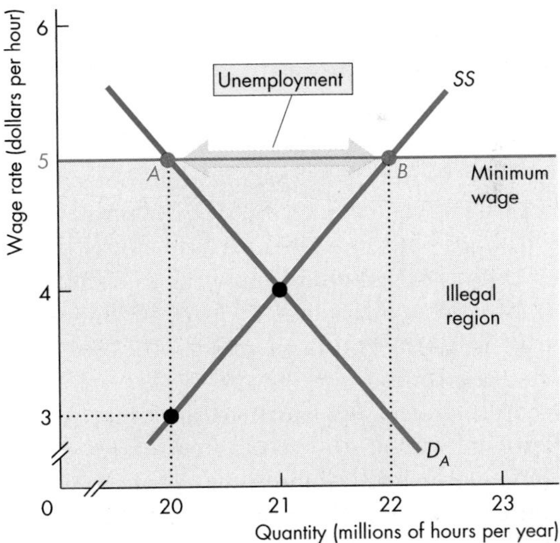

A wage below $5 an hour is illegal, in the grey-shaded illegal region. At the minimum wage of $5 an hour, 20 million hours are hired but 22 million hours are available. Unemployment—*AB*—of 2 million hours a year is created.

for $3. Frustrated unemployed workers spend time and other resources searching for hard-to-find jobs.

The Minimum Wage in Practice

Provincial governments in Canada set minimum wage rates. In 2003, minimum wage rates range from lows of $5.90 an hour in Alberta and $6.00 an hour in Newfoundland and Nova Scotia to highs of $8.00 an hour in British Columbia, $7.30 an hour in Quebec, and $7.20 an hour in the Yukon.

You saw in Fig. 6.5 that the minimum wage brings unemployment. But how much unemployment does it bring? Economists do not agree on the answer to this question. Until recently, most economists believed that the minimum wage was a big contributor to high unemployment among low-skilled young workers. But this view has recently been challenged and the challenge rebutted.

David Card, a Canadian economist who works at the University of California at Berkeley, and Alan Krueger of Princeton University say that increases in the minimum wage have not decreased employment and created unemployment. From their study of minimum wages in California, New Jersey, and Texas, Card and Krueger say that the employment rate of low-income workers increased following an increase in the minimum wage. They suggest three reasons why higher wages might increase employment. First, workers become more conscientious and productive. Second, workers are less likely to quit, so labour turnover, which is costly, is reduced. Third, managers make a firm's operations more efficient.

Most economists are skeptical about Card and Krueger's suggestions. They ask two questions. First, if higher wages make workers more productive and reduce labour turnover, why don't firms freely pay wage rates above the equilibrium wage to encourage more productive work habits? Second, are there other explanations for the employment responses that Card and Krueger have found?

According to Daniel Hamermesh of the University of Texas at Austin, Card and Krueger got the timing wrong and fell into the trap of the *post hoc* fallacy (see pp. 13–14). Hamermesh says that firms cut employment *before* the minimum wage is increased in anticipation of the increase. If he is correct, looking for the effects of an increase *after* it has occurred misses its main effects. Finis Welch of Texas A&M University and Kevin Murphy of the University of Chicago say the employment effects that Card and Krueger found are caused by regional differences in economic growth, not by changes in the minimum wage.

One effect of the minimum wage, according to Fig. 6.5, is an increase in the quantity of labour supplied. If this effect occurs, it might show up as an increase in the number of people who quit school before completing high school to look for work. Some economists say that this response does occur.

Inefficiency of the Minimum Wage

An unregulated labour market allocates scarce labour resources to the jobs in which they are valued most highly. The minimum wage frustrates the market mechanism and results in unemployment—wasted labour resources—and an inefficient amount of job search.

In Fig. 6.5, with firms employing only 20 million hours of labour at the minimum wage, many people who are willing to supply labour are unable to get hired. You can see that the 20 millionth hour of labour is available for $3. That is, the lowest wage at which someone is willing to supply the 20 millionth hour—read off from the supply curve—is $3. Someone who manages to find a job earns $5 an hour—$2 an hour more than the lowest wage rate at which someone is willing to work. So it pays unemployed people to spend time and effort looking for work.

REVIEW QUIZ

1. How does a decrease in the demand for low-skilled labour change the wage rate in the short run?
2. What are the long-run effects of a lower wage rate for low-skilled labour?
3. What is a minimum wage? What are the effects of a minimum wage set below the equilibrium wage?
4. What is the effect of a minimum wage that is set above the equilibrium wage?

Next we're going to study a more widespread government action in markets: taxes, such as the sales taxes that most provinces impose. We'll see how taxes change prices and quantities and discover that usually a sales tax is not paid entirely by the buyer. And we'll see that a tax usually creates a deadweight loss.

Taxes

ALMOST EVERYTHING YOU BUY IS TAXED. BUT who really pays the tax? Because the sales tax is added to the price of a good or service when it is sold, isn't it obvious that the *buyer* pays the tax? Isn't the price higher than it otherwise would be by an amount equal to the tax? It can be, but usually it isn't. And it is even possible that the buyer actually pays none of the tax! Let's see how we can make sense of these apparently absurd statements.

Who Pays a Sales Tax?

Suppose the government puts a $10 sales tax on CD players. What are the effects of the sales tax on the price and quantity of CD players? To answer this question, we need to work out what happens to demand and supply in the market for CD players.

Figure 6.6 shows this market. The demand curve is *D*, and the supply curve is *S*. With no sales tax, the equilibrium price is $100 per CD player and 5,000 CD players are bought and sold each week.

When a good is taxed, it has two prices: a price that excludes the tax and a price that includes the tax. Buyers respond only to the price that includes the tax, because that is the price they pay. Sellers respond only to the price that excludes the tax, because that is the price they receive. The tax is like a wedge between these two prices.

Think of the price on the vertical axis of Fig. 6.6 as the price paid by buyers—the price that *includes* the tax. When a tax is imposed and the price changes, there is a change in the quantity demanded but no change in demand. That is, there is a movement along the demand curve and no shift of the demand curve.

But supply changes, and the supply curve shifts. The sales tax is like an increase in cost, so supply decreases and the supply curve shifts leftward to *S + tax*. To determine the position of this new supply curve, we add the tax to the minimum price that sellers are willing to accept for each quantity sold. For example, with no tax, sellers are willing to offer 5,000 CD players a week for $100 a player. So with a $10 tax, they will supply 5,000 CD players a week for $110—a price that includes the tax. The curve *S + tax* describes the terms under which sellers are willing to offer CD players for sale now that there is a $10 tax.

Equilibrium occurs where the new supply curve intersects the demand curve—at a price of $105 and

FIGURE 6.6 A Sales Tax

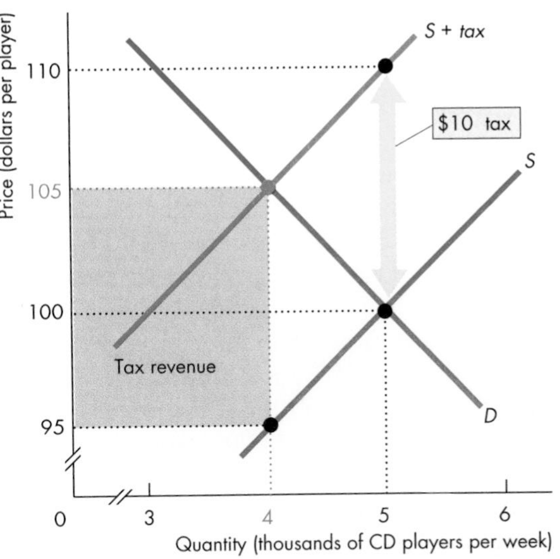

With no sales tax, 5,000 CD players a week are bought and sold at $100 each. A sales tax of $10 a CD player is imposed, and the supply curve shifts leftward to *S + tax*. In the new equilibrium, the price rises to $105 a CD player and the quantity decreases to 4,000 CD players a week. The sales tax raises the price by less than the tax, lowers the price received by the seller, and decreases the quantity. The sales tax brings in revenue to the government equal to the purple rectangle.

a quantity of 4,000 CD players a week. The $10 sales tax increases the price paid by the buyer by $5 a CD player and it decreases the price received by the seller by $5 a CD player. So the buyer and the seller pay the $10 tax equally.

The tax brings in tax revenue to the government equal to the tax per item multiplied by the number of items sold. The purple area in Fig. 6.6 illustrates the tax revenue. The $10 tax on CD players brings in tax revenue of $40,000 a week.

In this example, the buyer and the seller split the tax equally: The buyer pays $5 a CD player, and so does the seller. This equal sharing of the tax is a special case and does not usually occur. But some sharing of the tax between the buyer and seller is usual. And in other special cases, either the buyer or the seller pays the entire tax. The division of the tax between the buyer and the seller depends on the elasticities of demand and supply.

Tax Division and Elasticity of Demand

The division of the tax between the buyer and the seller depends in part on the elasticity of demand. There are two extreme cases:

- Perfectly inelastic demand—buyer pays.
- Perfectly elastic demand—seller pays.

Perfectly Inelastic Demand Figure 6.7(a) shows the market for insulin, a vital daily medication of diabetics. Demand is perfectly inelastic at 100,000 doses a day, regardless of the price, as shown by the vertical curve *D*. That is, a diabetic would sacrifice all other goods and services rather than not consume the insulin dose that provides good health. The supply curve of insulin is *S*. With no tax, the price is $2 a dose and the quantity is 100,000 doses a day.

If insulin is taxed at 20¢ a dose, we must add the tax to the minimum price at which drug companies are willing to sell insulin. The result is the new supply curve *S* + *tax*. The price rises to $2.20 a dose, but the quantity does not change. The buyer pays the entire sales tax of 20¢ a dose.

Perfectly Elastic Demand Figure 6.7(b) shows the market for pink marker pens. Demand is perfectly elastic at $1 a pen, as shown by the horizontal curve *D*. If pink pens are less expensive than the others, everyone uses pink. If pink pens are more expensive than the others, no one uses pink. The supply curve is *S*. With no tax, the price of a pink marker is $1, and the quantity is 4,000 pens a week.

If a sales tax of 10¢ a pen is imposed on pink marker pens but not on other colours, we add the tax to the minimum price at which sellers are willing to offer pink pens for sale, and the new supply curve is *S* + *tax*. The price remains at $1 a pen, and the quantity decreases to 1,000 a week. The 10¢ sales tax leaves the price paid by the buyer unchanged but lowers the amount received by the seller by the full amount of the sales tax. The seller pays the entire tax. As a result, sellers decrease the quantity offered for sale.

We've seen that when demand is perfectly inelastic, the buyer pays the entire tax and when demand is perfectly elastic, the seller pays it. In the usual case, demand is neither perfectly inelastic nor perfectly elastic and the tax is split between the buyer and the seller. But the division depends on the elasticity of demand. The more inelastic the demand, the larger is the amount of the tax paid by the buyer.

FIGURE 6.7 Sales Tax and the Elasticity of Demand

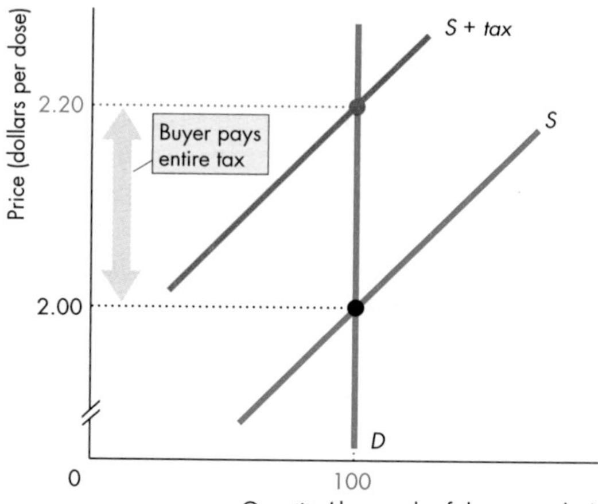

(a) Perfectly inelastic demand

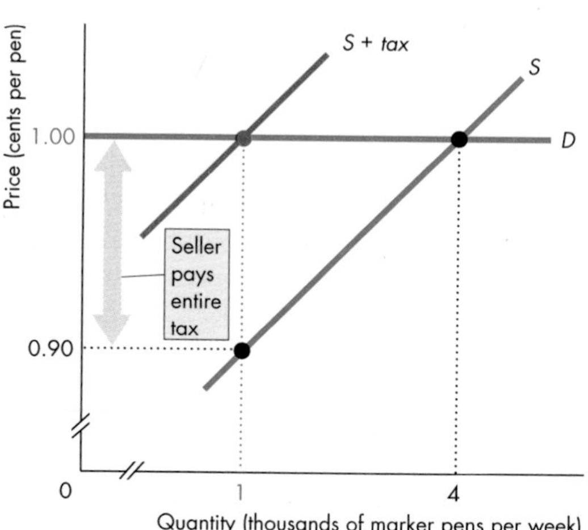

(b) Perfectly elastic demand

Part (a) shows the market for insulin, where demand is perfectly inelastic. With no tax, the price is $2 a dose and the quantity is 100,000 doses a day. A sales tax of 20¢ a dose shifts the supply curve to *S* + *tax*. The price rises to $2.20 a dose, but the quantity bought does not change. The buyer pays the entire tax.

Part (b) shows the market for pink pens. The demand for pink pens is perfectly elastic. With no tax, the price of a pen is $1 and the quantity is 4,000 pens a week. A sales tax of 10¢ a pink pen shifts the supply curve to *S* + *tax*. The price remains at $1 a pen, and the quantity of pink pens sold decreases to 1,000 a week. The seller pays the entire tax.

Tax Division and Elasticity of Supply

The division of the tax between the buyer and the seller also depends, in part, on the elasticity of supply. Again, there are two extreme cases:

- Perfectly inelastic supply—seller pays.
- Perfectly elastic supply—buyer pays.

Perfectly Inelastic Supply Figure 6.8(a) shows the market for water from a mineral spring that flows at a constant rate that can't be controlled. Supply is perfectly inelastic at 100,000 bottles a week, as shown by the supply curve *S*. The demand curve for the water from this spring is *D*. With no tax, the price is 50¢ a bottle and the 100,000 bottles that flow from the spring are bought.

Suppose this spring water is taxed at 5¢ a bottle. The supply curve does not change because the spring owners still produce 100,000 bottles a week even though the price they receive falls. But buyers are willing to buy the 100,000 bottles only if the price is 50¢ a bottle. So the price remains at 50¢ a bottle. The sales tax reduces the price received by sellers to 45¢ a bottle, and the seller pays the entire tax.

Perfectly Elastic Supply Figure 6.8(b) shows the market for sand from which computer-chip makers extract silicon. Supply of this sand is perfectly elastic at a price of 10¢ a kilogram, as shown by the supply curve *S*. The demand curve for sand is *D*. With no tax, the price is 10¢ a kilogram and 5,000 kilograms a week are bought.

If this sand is taxed at 1¢ a kilogram, we must add the tax to the minimum supply-price. Sellers are now willing to offer any quantity at 11¢ a kilogram along the curve *S* + *tax*. A new equilibrium is determined where the new supply curve intersects the demand curve: at a price of 11¢ a kilogram and a quantity of 3,000 kilograms a week. The sales tax has increased the price paid by the buyer by the full amount of the tax—1¢ a kilogram—and has decreased the quantity sold. The buyer pays the entire tax.

We've seen that when supply is perfectly inelastic, the seller pays the entire tax, and when supply is perfectly elastic, the buyer pays it. In the usual case, supply is neither perfectly inelastic nor perfectly elastic and the tax is split between the buyer and the seller. But the division between the buyer and the seller depends on the elasticity of supply. The more elastic the supply, the larger is the amount of the tax paid by the buyer.

FIGURE 6.8 Sales Tax and the Elasticity of Supply

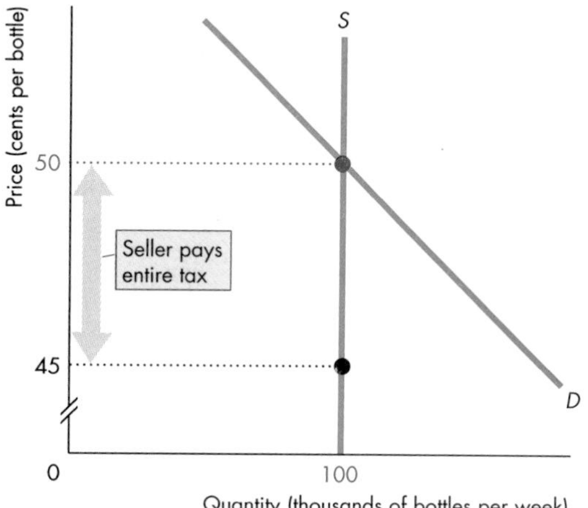

(a) Perfectly inelastic supply

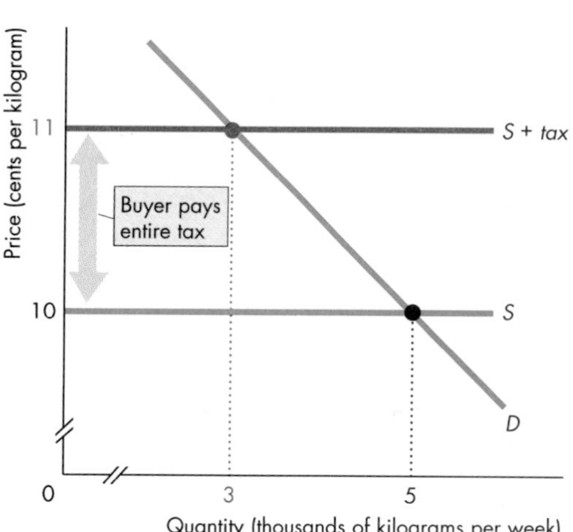

(b) Perfectly elastic supply

Part (a) shows the market for water from a mineral spring. Supply is perfectly inelastic. With no tax, the price is 50¢ a bottle. With a sales tax of 5¢ a bottle, the price remains at 50¢ a bottle. The number of bottles bought remains the same, but the price received by sellers decreases to 45¢ a bottle. The seller pays the entire tax.

Part (b) shows the market for sand. Supply is perfectly elastic. With no tax, the price is 10¢ a kilogram. A sales tax of 1¢ a kilogram increases the minimum supply-price to 11¢ a kilogram. The supply curve shifts to *S* + *tax*. The price increases to 11¢ a kilogram. The buyer pays the entire tax.

Sales Taxes in Practice

We've looked at the range of possible effects of a sales tax by studying the extreme cases. In practice, supply and demand are rarely perfectly elastic or perfectly inelastic. They lie somewhere in between. But some items tend towards one of the extremes. For example, a heavily taxed item such as alcohol, tobacco, or gasoline has a low elasticity of demand. Consequently, the buyer pays most of the tax. Also, because demand is inelastic, the quantity bought does not decrease much and the government collects a large tax revenue.

It is unusual to tax an item heavily if its demand is elastic. Such a good or service has close substitutes. If a tax is levied on such a good or service, people will reduce their purchases of the taxed good and increase their purchases of an untaxed substitute. That is, the quantity of the taxed good bought decreases by a large amount and the government will not collect much tax revenue. This explains why the items that are taxed are those that have inelastic demands and why buyers pay most of the taxes.

Taxes and Efficiency

You've seen that a sales tax places a wedge between the price paid by buyers and the price received by sellers. The price paid by buyers is also the buyers' willingness to pay, which measures marginal benefit. And the price received by sellers is the sellers' minimum supply-price, which equals marginal cost.

So because a tax places a wedge between the buyers' price and the sellers' price, it also puts a wedge between marginal benefit and marginal cost and creates inefficiency. With a higher buying price and a lower selling price, the tax decreases the quantity produced and consumed and a deadweight loss arises. Figure 6.9 shows the inefficiency of a sales tax. With a sales tax, both consumer surplus and producer surplus shrink. Part of each surplus goes to the government in tax revenue—the purple area in the figure. And part of each surplus becomes a deadweight loss—the grey area.

In the extreme cases of perfectly inelastic demand and perfectly inelastic supply, the quantity does not change and there is no deadweight loss. The more inelastic is either demand or supply, the smaller is the decrease in quantity and the smaller is the deadweight loss. When demand or supply is perfectly inelastic, the quantity remains constant and there is no deadweight loss.

FIGURE 6.9 Taxes and Efficiency

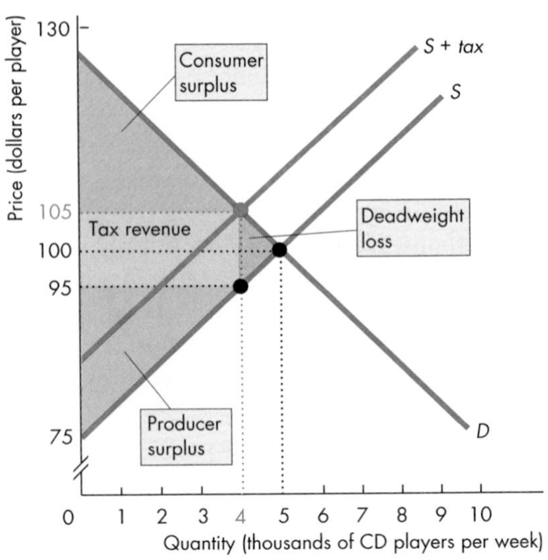

With no sales tax, 5,000 CD players a week are bought and sold at $100 each. With a sales tax of $10 a CD player, the buyer's price rises to $105 a player, the seller's price falls to $95 a player, and the quantity decreases to 4,000 CD players a week. Consumer surplus shrinks to the green area, and the producer surplus shrinks to the blue area. Part of the loss of consumer surplus and producer surplus goes to the government as tax revenue, which is shown as the purple area. A deadweight loss arises, which is shown by the grey area.

REVIEW QUIZ

1. How does the elasticity of demand influence the effect of a sales tax on the price paid by the buyer, the price received by the seller, the quantity, the tax revenue, and the deadweight loss?
2. How does the elasticity of supply influence the effect of a sales tax on the price paid by the buyer, the price received by the seller, the quantity, the tax revenue, and the deadweight loss?
3. Why does a tax create a deadweight loss?

Governments make some types of goods, such as drugs, illegal. Let's see how the market works when trade in an illegal good takes place.

Markets for Illegal Goods

THE MARKETS FOR MANY GOODS AND SERVICES are regulated, and buying and selling some goods is illegal. The best-known examples of such goods are drugs, such as marijuana, cocaine, Ecstasy, and heroin.

Despite the fact that these drugs are illegal, trade in them is a multibillion-dollar business. This trade can be understood by using the same economic model and principles that explain trade in legal goods. To study the market for illegal goods, we're first going to examine the prices and quantities that would prevail if these goods were not illegal. Next, we'll see how prohibition works. Then we'll see how a tax might be used to limit the consumption of these goods.

A Free Market for Drugs

Figure 6.10 shows the market for drugs. The demand curve, *D,* shows that, other things remaining the same, the lower the price of drugs, the larger is the quantity of drugs demanded. The supply curve, *S,* shows that, other things remaining the same, the lower the price of drugs, the smaller is the quantity supplied. If drugs were not illegal, the quantity bought and sold would be Q_C and the price would be P_C.

A Market for Illegal Drugs

When a good is illegal, the cost of trading in the good increases. By how much the cost increases and on whom the cost falls depend on the penalties for violating the law and the effectiveness with which the law is enforced. The larger the penalties and the more effective the policing, the higher are the costs. Penalties might be imposed on sellers, buyers, or both.

Penalties on Sellers Drug dealers in Canada face large penalties if their activities are detected. For example, a marijuana dealer could pay a $200,000 fine and serve a 15-year prison term. A heroin dealer could pay a $500,000 fine and serve a 20-year prison term. These penalties are part of the cost of supplying illegal drugs, and they bring a decrease in supply—a leftward shift in the supply curve. To determine the new supply curve, we add the cost of breaking the law to the minimum price that drug dealers are willing to accept. In Fig. 6.10, the cost of breaking the law by selling drugs (*CBL*) is added to the minimum

FIGURE 6.10 A Market for an Illegal Good

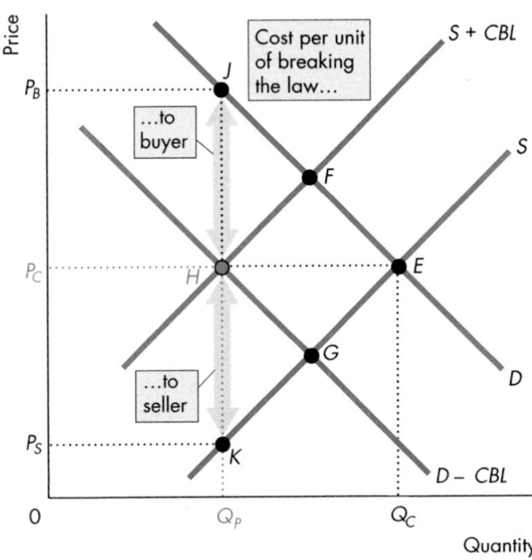

The demand curve for drugs is *D*, and the supply curve is *S*. If drugs are not illegal, the quantity bought and sold is Q_C at a price of P_C—point *E*. If selling drugs is illegal, the cost of breaking the law by selling drugs (*CBL*) is added to the minimum supply-price and supply decreases to *S* + *CBL*. The market moves to point *F*. If buying drugs is illegal, the cost of breaking the law is subtracted from the maximum price that buyers are willing to pay, and demand decreases to *D* – *CBL*. The market moves to point *G*. With both buying and selling illegal, the supply curve and the demand curve shift and the market moves to point *H*. The market price remains at P_C but the market price plus the penalty for buying rises to P_B—point *J*—and the market price minus the penalty for sellers falls to P_S—point *K*.

price that dealers will accept and the supply curve shifts leftward to $S + CBL$. If penalties were imposed only on sellers, the market would move from point *E* to point *F*.

Penalties on Buyers In Canada, it is illegal to *possess* drugs such as marijuana, cocaine, Ecstasy, and heroin. For example, possession of marijuana can bring a prison term of 1 year, and possession of heroin can bring a prison term of 2 years. Penalties fall on buyers, and the cost of breaking the law must be subtracted from the value of the good to determine the maximum price buyers are willing to pay for the drugs. Demand decreases, and the demand curve shifts leftward. In Fig. 6.10, the demand curve shifts to $D - CBL$. If penalties were imposed only on buyers, the market would move from point E to point G.

Penalties on Both Sellers and Buyers Because penalties are imposed on both sellers *and* buyers, supply and demand decrease and the supply curve and the demand curve shift. In Fig. 6.10 the costs of breaking the law are the same for both buyers and sellers, so both curves shift leftward by the same amount. The market moves to point H. The market price remains at the competitive market price P_C, but the quantity bought decreases to Q_P. The buyer pays P_C plus the cost of breaking the law, which is P_B. And the seller receives P_C minus the cost of breaking the law, which is P_S.

The larger the penalties and the greater the degree of law enforcement, the larger is the decrease in demand and/or supply, the smaller is the equilibrium quantity, and the higher is the total price paid by the buyer. That total price is the market price plus the cost of breaking the law imposed on the buyer. But the market price itself might be greater than or less than the free market price P_C. In Canada, the penalties on sellers are much larger than those on buyers, so the quantity of drugs traded decreases and the price increases compared with a free market.

With high enough penalties and effective law enforcement, it is possible to decrease demand and/or supply to the point at which the quantity bought is zero. But in reality, such an outcome is unusual. It does not happen in Canada in the case of illegal drugs. The key reason is the high cost of law enforcement and insufficient resources for the police to achieve effective enforcement. Because of this situation, some people suggest that drugs (and other illegal goods) should be legalized and sold openly but should also be taxed at a high rate in the same way that legal drugs such as alcohol are taxed. How would such an arrangement work?

Legalizing and Taxing Drugs

From your study of the effects of taxes, it is easy to see that the quantity of drugs bought could be decreased if drugs were legalized and taxed. A sufficiently high tax could be imposed to decrease supply, raise the price, and achieve the same decrease in the quantity bought as with a prohibition on drugs. The government would collect a large tax revenue.

Illegal Trading to Evade the Tax It is likely that an extremely high tax rate would be needed to cut the quantity of drugs bought to the level prevailing with a prohibition. It is also likely that many drug dealers and consumers would try to cover up their activities to evade the tax. If they did act in this way, they would face the cost of breaking the law—the tax law. If the penalty for tax law violation is as severe and as effectively policed as drug-dealing laws, the analysis we've already conducted applies also to this case. The quantity of drugs bought would depend on the penalties for law breaking and on the way in which the penalties are assigned to buyers and sellers.

Taxes Versus Prohibition: Some Pros and Cons Which is more effective: prohibition or taxes? In favour of taxes and against prohibition is the fact that the tax revenue can be used to make law enforcement more effective. It can also be used to run a more effective education campaign against illegal drug use. In favour of prohibition and against taxes is the fact that prohibition sends a signal that might influence preferences, decreasing the demand for illegal drugs. Also, some people intensely dislike the idea of the government profiting from trade in harmful substances.

REVIEW QUIZ

1. How does the imposition of a penalty for selling an illegal drug influence demand, supply, price, and the quantity of the drug consumed?
2. How does the imposition of a penalty for possessing an illegal drug influence demand, supply, price, and the quantity of the drug consumed?
3. How does the imposition of a penalty for selling *or* possessing an illegal drug influence demand, supply, price, and the quantity of the drug consumed?
4. Is there any case for legalizing drugs?

You've seen how government action in markets in the form of price ceilings, minimum wages, and taxes limits the quantity and create inefficient resource use. You've also seen how in a market for an illegal good, the quantity can be decreased by imposing penalties on either buyers or sellers or by legalizing and taxing the good. Next, we look at agricultural markets and see how governments try to stabilize farm revenues.

Stabilizing Farm Revenues

EARLY FROST, DROUGHT, HEAVY RAIN, AND flooding all fill the lives of farmers with uncertainty. Fluctuations in the weather bring big fluctuations in farm output. How do changes in farm output affect farm prices and farm revenues? And how might farm revenues be stabilized? Let's begin to answer these questions by looking at an agricultural market.

An Unregulated Agricultural Market

Figure 6.11 shows the market for wheat. In both parts, the demand curve for wheat is *D*. Once farmers have harvested their crop, they have no control over the quantity supplied, and supply is inelastic along a *momentary supply curve*. In normal climate conditions, the momentary supply curve is MS_0 (in both parts of the figure).

The price is determined at the point of intersection of the momentary supply curve and the demand curve. In normal conditions, the price is $200 a tonne. The quantity of wheat produced is 20 million tonnes, and farm revenue is $4 billion. Suppose the opportunity cost to farmers of producing wheat is also $4 billion. Then in normal conditions, farmers just cover their opportunity cost.

Poor Harvest Suppose there is a bad growing season, resulting in a poor harvest. What happens to the price of wheat and the revenue of farmers? These questions are answered in Fig. 6.11(a). The poor harvest decreases supply to 15 million tonnes of wheat, and the momentary supply curve shifts leftward to MS_1. With a decrease in supply, the price rises to $300 a tonne.

What happens to total farm revenue? It *increases* to $4.5 billion. A decrease in supply has brought an increase in price and an increase in farm revenue. It does so because the demand for wheat is *inelastic*. The percentage decrease in the quantity demanded is less than the percentage increase in price. You can verify this fact by noticing in Fig. 6.11(a) that the increase in revenue from the higher price ($1.5 billion—the light blue area) exceeds the decrease in revenue from the smaller quantity ($1.0 billion—the red area). Farmers now make revenue in excess of their opportunity cost.

Although total farm revenue increases when there is a poor harvest, some farmers, whose entire crop is wiped out, suffer a decrease in revenue. Others, whose crop is unaffected, make an enormous gain.

FIGURE 6.11 Harvests, Farm Prices, and Farm Revenue

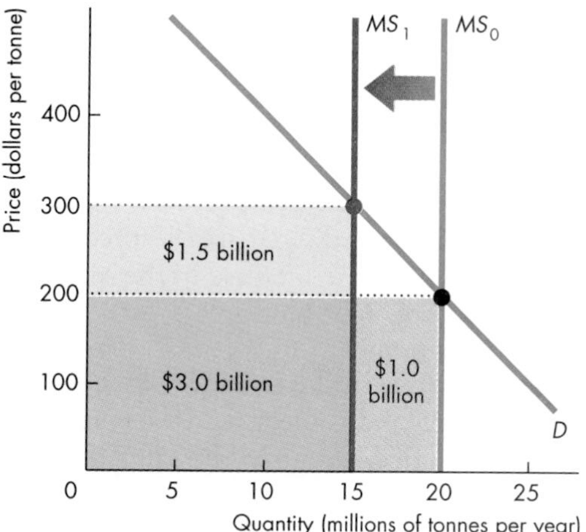

(a) Poor harvest: revenue increases

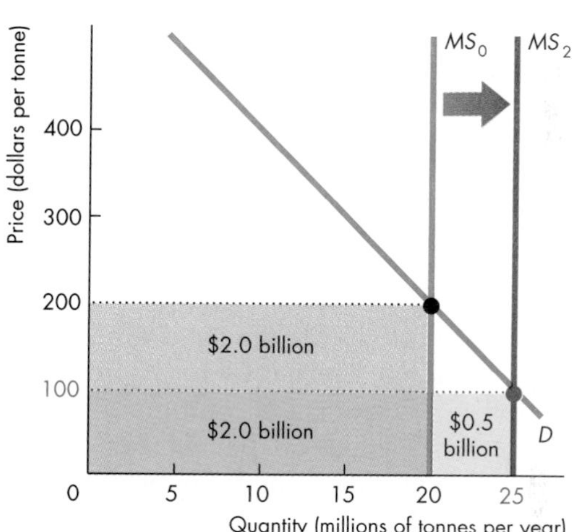

(b) Bumper harvest: revenue decreases

The demand curve for wheat is *D*. In normal times, the supply curve is MS_0 and 20 million tonnes are sold for $200 a tonne. In part (a), a poor harvest decreases supply to MS_1. The price rises to $300 a tonne, and farm revenue increases to $4.5 billion—the $1.5 billion increase from the higher price (light blue area) exceeds the $1.0 billion decrease from the smaller quantity (red area).

In part (b), a bumper harvest increases supply to MS_2. The price falls to $100 a tonne, and farm revenue decreases to $2.5 billion—the $2.0 billion decrease from the lower price (red area) exceeds the $0.5 billion increase from the increase in the quantity sold (light blue area).

Bumper Harvest Figure 6.11(b) shows what happens in the opposite situation, when there is a bumper harvest. Now supply increases to 25 million tonnes, and the momentary supply curve shifts rightward to MS_2. With the increased quantity supplied, the price falls to $100 a tonne. Farm revenue decreases to $2.5 billion. It does so because the demand for wheat is inelastic. To see this fact, notice in Fig. 6.11(b) that the decrease in revenue from the lower price ($2.0 billion—the red area) exceeds the increase in revenue from the increase in the quantity sold ($0.5 billion—the light blue area).

Elasticity of Demand In the example we've just worked through, demand is inelastic. If demand is elastic, the price fluctuations go in the same directions as those we've worked out but revenue fluctuates in the opposite direction. Bumper harvests increase revenue, and poor harvests decrease it. But the demand for most agricultural products is inelastic, and the case we've studied is the relevant one.

Because farm prices fluctuate, institutions have evolved to stabilize them. There are two types of institutions:

- Speculative markets in inventories
- Farm marketing boards

Speculative Markets in Inventories

Many goods, including a wide variety of agricultural products, can be stored. These inventories provide a cushion between production and consumption. If production decreases, goods can be sold from inventory; if production increases, goods can be put into inventory.

In a market that has inventories, we must distinguish production from supply. The quantity produced is *not* the same as the quantity supplied. The quantity supplied exceeds the quantity produced when goods are sold from inventory. And the quantity supplied is less than the quantity produced when goods are put into inventory. Supply therefore depends on the behaviour of inventory holders.

The Behaviour of Inventory Holders Inventory holders speculate. They hope to buy at a low price and sell at a high price. That is, they hope to buy goods and put them into inventory when the price is low and sell them from inventory when the price is high. They make a profit or incur a loss equal to their selling price minus their buying price and minus the cost of storage.

But how do inventory holders know when to buy and when to sell? How do they know whether the price is high or low? To decide whether a price is high or low, inventory holders forecast the future price. If the current price is above the forecasted future price, inventory holders sell goods from inventory. If the current price is below the forecasted future price, inventory holders buy goods to put into inventory. This behaviour by inventory holders makes the supply of the good perfectly elastic at the price forecasted by inventory holders.

Let's work out what happens to price and quantity in a market in which inventories are held when production fluctuates. Let's look again at the wheat market.

Fluctuations in Production In Fig. 6.12, the demand curve for wheat is *D*. Inventory holders expect the future price to be $200 a tonne. The supply curve is *S*—supply is perfectly elastic at the price expected by inventory holders. Production fluctuates between Q_1 and Q_2.

When production fluctuates and there are no inventories, the price and the quantity fluctuate. We saw this result in Fig. 6.11. But if there are inventories, the price does not fluctuate. When production decreases to Q_1, or 15 million tonnes, inventory holders sell 5 million tonnes from inventory and the quantity bought by consumers is 20 million tonnes. The price remains at $200 a tonne. When production increases to Q_2, or 25 million tonnes, inventory holders buy 5 million tonnes and consumers continue to buy 20 million tonnes. Again, the price remains at $200 a tonne. The actions of inventory holders reduce price fluctuations. In Fig. 6.12, the price fluctuations are entirely eliminated. When there are costs of carrying inventories and when inventories become almost depleted, some price fluctuations do occur, but these fluctuations are smaller than those occurring in a market without inventories.

Farm Revenue Even if inventory speculation succeeds in stabilizing the price, it does not stabilize farm revenue. With the price stabilized, farm revenue fluctuates as production fluctuates. But now bumper harvests always bring larger revenues than poor harvests do because the price remains constant and only the quantity fluctuates.

FIGURE 6.12 How Inventories Limit Price Changes

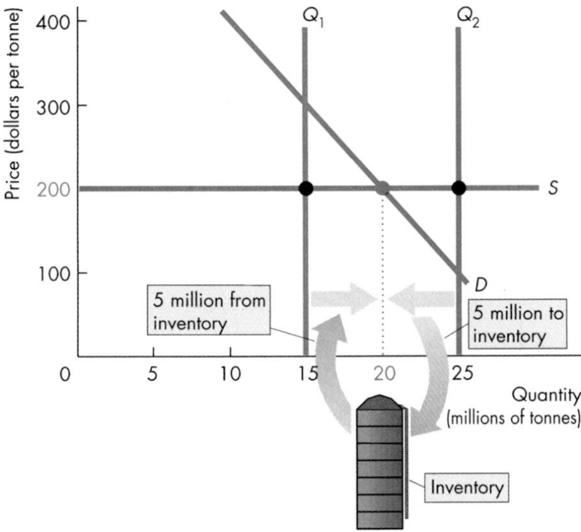

Inventory holders sell wheat from inventory if the price rises above $200 a tonne, and they buy wheat to hold in inventory if the price falls below $200 a tonne, which makes supply (S) perfectly elastic. When production decreases to Q_1, 5 million tonnes are sold from inventory; when production increases to Q_2, 5 million tonnes are added to inventory. The price remains at $200 a tonne.

Farm Marketing Boards

Most governments intervene in agricultural markets. The most extensive such intervention occurs in the European Union and Japan. Farm price intervention is not as extensive in Canada and the United States. But government regulations influence the prices of some agricultural products that include grains, milk, eggs, tobacco, rice, peanuts, cotton, and poultry meats.

In Canada, more than 100 farm marketing boards operate and influence more than one-half of total farm sales. A **farm marketing board** is a regulatory agency that intervenes in an agricultural market to stabilize the price of an agricultural product. Farm marketing boards are often supported by governments. How do agricultural markets work when a stabilization program is in place? The answer depends on which type of intervention takes place. There are three types of intervention:

- Price floor
- Quota
- Subsidy

Price Floor A *price floor* operates in an agricultural market in much the same way that it operates in other markets. Earlier in this chapter, we examined a price floor in the labour market when we studied the effect of minimum wages. The principles are the same in the case of agricultural markets.

Figure 6.13 shows how a price floor works in the market for skim milk powder. The competitive equilibrium price of skim milk powder is $3 a tonne, and 16 million tonnes are produced and bought. If the Canadian Dairy Commission imposes a price floor of $4 a tonne, then the price increases to $4 a tonne and the quantity demanded decreases to 14 million tonnes.

FIGURE 6.13 A Price Floor

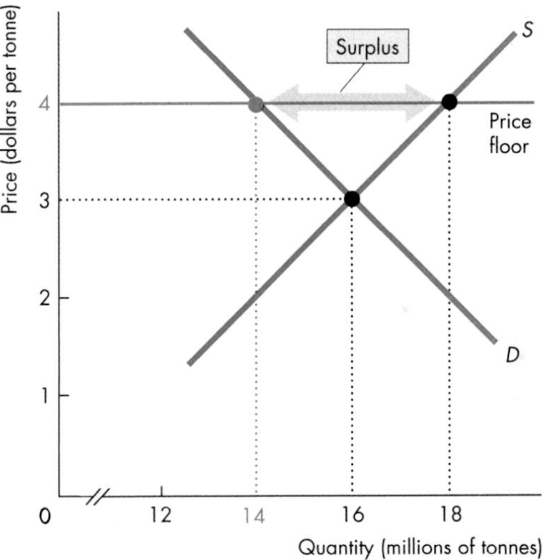

A competitive equilibrium price is $3 tonne and the equivalent quantity produced and bought is 16 million tonnes. A price floor of $4 a tonne increases the price to $4 a tonne, decreases the quantity sold to 14 million tonnes, and increases the quantity produced to 18 million tonnes. The price floor creates a surplus of 4 million tonnes. If the Canadian Dairy Commission does not buy the surplus and allows farmers to find their own market, the price will return to its competitive level of $3 a tonne.

The quantity supplied increases to 18 million tonnes. Farmers produce a surplus of 4 million tonnes.

This method of supporting the price of an agricultural product will fail unless there is some method of taking up the surplus produced. If farmers are left to find a market for their surplus, then the price will fall below the price floor to the competitive price—$3 a tonne. If, on the other hand, the Canadian Dairy Commission purchases the surplus at the price floor, then the price will remain at the price floor. If the marketing board systematically buys more than it sells, then it will end up with a large inventory. Such has been the outcome in the European Union, where stabilization agencies have mountains of butter and lakes of wine! The cost of buying and storing the inventory falls on taxpayers, and the main gainers from a price floor are the large, efficient farms.

Quota A **quota** is a restriction on the quantity of a good that a farm is permitted to produce. If a quota restricts farm production, then the supply curve becomes perfectly inelastic at the quota quantity.

Figure 6.14 illustrates how a quota works in the market for skim milk. The competitive price is $3 a tonne and the competitive quantity is 16 million tonnes. If the Canadian Dairy Commission imposes a quota that restricts total production to 14 million tonnes, the supply curve becomes the vertical line labelled "Quota." With output restricted by the quota, the quantity produced is now 14 million tonnes and the price increases to $4 a tonne.

But this might not be the end of the story. Farmers are willing to produce skim milk at $2 a tonne, so at a market price of $4 a tonne, they will want to increase their output. If the Canadian Dairy Commission does not prevent quotas from being exceeded, a gradual increase in the quantity of skim milk supplied will eventually restore the competitive equilibrium.

Subsidy A **subsidy** is a payment made by the government to the producer. A subsidy is like a tax—a payment made by a producer to the government—but it goes in the reverse direction. Therefore a subsidy works in a similar way to a tax, but instead of adding something to the price paid by the consumer, a subsidy lowers the price to below what it would be in the absence of a subsidy.

FIGURE 6.14 A Quota

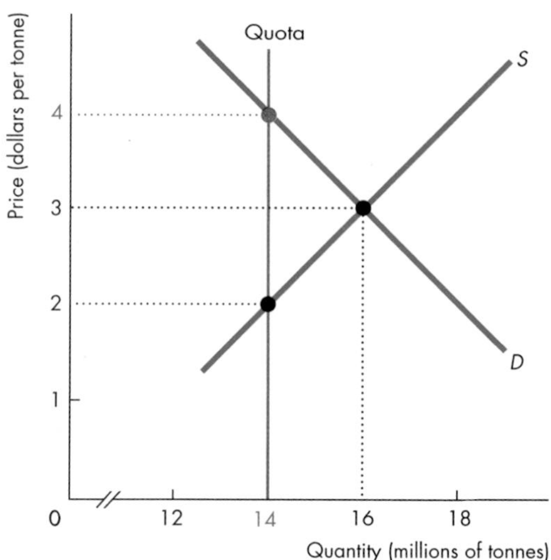

The competitive equilibrium price is $3 a tonne and the equilibrium quantity produced and bought is 16 million tonnes. A quota is set at 14 million tonnes. As a result, the price rises to $4 a tonne and the quantity sold decreases to 14 million tonnes. Producers are willing to supply 14 million tonnes at $2 a tonne, so they will want to increase the quantity that they supply. If the regulatory agency cannot control the quantity produced, then the quantity produced will increase and the price will fall to its competitive level of $3 a tonne.

Figure 6.15 illustrates how a subsidy works in the market for (liquid) milk. The competitive equilibrium is at 30¢ a litre with 16 billion litres produced and bought. The Canadian Dairy Commission then offers a subsidy of 10¢ a litre. The subsidy increases the supply of milk and shifts the supply curve rightward. The magnitude of the shift depends on the size of the subsidy. In this case, farmers are willing to sell each litre for 10¢ less than they would be willing to accept in the absence of a subsidy. The equilibrium price falls to 25¢ a litre, and the quantity produced and bought increases to 17 billion litres. Farmers receive 35¢ a litre, which is the market price of 25¢ a litre plus the subsidy of 10¢ a litre. Thus farmers gain, but taxpayers pay the subsidy. The total subsidy paid is $1.7 billion, which is the 10¢ a litre subsidy

FIGURE 6.15 A Subsidy

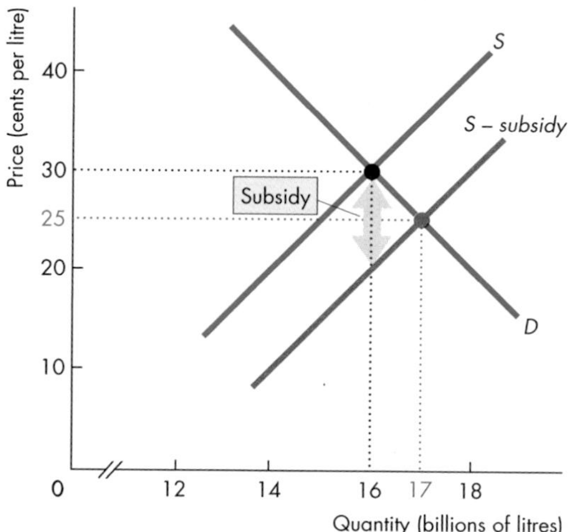

The competitive equilibrium price is 30¢ a litre and the equilibrium quantity produced and bought is 16 billion litres. The Canadian Dairy Commission introduces a subsidy of 10¢ a litre. As a result, producers are now willing to supply each quantity at 10¢ a litre less. The supply curve shifts rightward such that the vertical distance between the supply curve S and the supply curve *S – subsidy* is 10¢ a litre. The price falls to 25¢ a litre, and the quantity produced and sold increases to 17 billion litres. Producers receive 35¢ a litre, which is the market price of 25¢ a litre plus the subsidy of 10¢ a litre. The total subsidy paid is $1.7 billion, which taxpayers will have to pay.

multiplied by the 17 billion litres of milk produced. This method of agricultural support can impose major costs on taxpayers.

Efficiency and Equity in Farm Markets

Are farm marketing boards efficient, and are they fair? It is easy to answer the first question: farm marketing boards are generally inefficient. It is harder to answer the second question, about their fairness.

Inefficiency of Farm Marketing Boards You can see that farm marketing boards are inefficient by looking at what they do to the relationship between marginal cost and marginal benefit. A price floor that exceeds the competitive equilibrium price decreases the quantity demanded and results in a price that equals marginal benefit but exceeds marginal cost. So both consumer surplus and producer surplus shrink and there is a deadweight loss.

A quota restricts output below the quantity that maximizes the sum of consumer surplus and producer surplus. So it, too, creates deadweight loss.

A subsidy increases production above the competitive level. So it results in marginal cost exceeding marginal benefit and creates deadweight loss. All the methods of intervention, then, are inefficient. But are they fair?

Equity of Farm Marketing Boards Farm marketing boards increase the incomes of farmers and decrease the incomes of taxpayers and consumers of farm products compared with what the unregulated market would provide. Because the actions of farm marketing boards create deadweight loss, the gains by farmers are smaller than the losses borne by everyone else.

Whether this redistribution of economic well-being towards farmers is fair is a controversial matter. Most farmers probably think it perfectly fair and most other people probably have their doubts. Whatever the merits of either view, it is a curious and perhaps surprising fact that farmers throughout the world manage to persuade the non-farming majority that redistribution towards the farmers is necessary.

REVIEW QUIZ

1. How do poor harvests and bumper harvests influence farm prices and farm revenues?
2. Explain how inventories and speculation influence farm prices and farm revenues.
3. What are the main actions that farm marketing boards take and how do these actions influence farm prices and farm revenues?

You now know how to use the demand and supply model to predict prices, to study government actions in markets, and to study the sources and costs of inefficiency. Before you leave this topic, take a look at *Reading Between the Lines* on pp. 142–143 and see how the market for air travel has been affected by the new airport security tax.

Who Pays the Airport Security Tax?

THE GLOBE AND MAIL, AUGUST 2, 2002

Impact of air security tax known

The federal government knew its $24 security surcharge could seriously impair passenger traffic before it started collecting the fee on April 1, according to a document obtained by *The Globe and Mail.*

The report, which was prepared for the Department of Finance by investment bank N.M. Rothschild & Sons, reviewed prior studies into price elasticity of air fares and determined there was a potential for a drop in traffic on the short-haul, low-cost market.

"Taken alone, the elasticities imply that a change in the price of air travel of 1 per cent, would result, on average, in an approximately 0.7-per-cent to 2.1-per-cent decline in the demand for air travel services," said the Feb. 19 report, which was released under the Access to Information Act.

However, the report suggests that enhanced security, made possible through the security surcharge, could counteract the drop in traffic by making people feel safer about flying.

Montreal-based Air Canada and Calgary-based WestJet Airlines Ltd. have both complained that the surcharge—$12 on a one-way fare or $24 round-trip—has affected passenger traffic on short-haul routes. ...

WestJet's load factor on Calgary-Edmonton flights fell to 60.5 per cent from 76.2 last year. ... WestJet is selling tickets for fall travel from Calgary to Edmonton for $52.50. Taxes and surcharges bring the total price of the ticket to $89.08. That means the security surcharge, and related GST, raise the total price by 17 per cent.

According to the assumptions in the Rothschild report, that would translate into an anticipated drop in traffic of between 12 per cent and 35 per cent, aside from any increase in traffic as a result of safer skies. ...

Essence of the Story

- Investment bank N.M. Rothschild & Sons has reviewed studies on the price elasticity of demand for air travel for the Department of Finance.
- Estimates of these elasticities range between 0.7 and 2.1.
- The report says that enhanced security made possible through the security surcharge might increase the demand for air travel.
- Airlines complain that the surcharge—$12 on a one-way fare or $24 round-trip—has a big effect on short-haul routes.
- WestJet says that on Calgary–Edmonton flights it is carrying 60.5 percent of its capacity, down from 76.2 percent of capacity the previous year.
- WestJet's base fare for fall travel from Calgary to Edmonton is $52.50, but taxes and surcharges raise the price to $89.08 —17 percent above the base—which means a decrease in traffic between 12 percent and 35 percent, other things remaining the same.

Economic Analysis

- Who pays the airport security tax depends on the elasticities of demand for and supply of air transportation.

- The elasticity of demand for air travel as reported in the news article is estimated to be between 0.7 and 2.1.

- Notice that in reporting the range of elasticity estimates, the news article misuses the term "demand." The elasticity of demand tells us how the *quantity demanded* changes when the price changes for a *given demand.* It does not tell us how demand changes!

- The range of estimates reported in the article is large and implies that demand might be inelastic (0.7) or elastic (2.1).

- The news article does *not* report estimates of the elasticity of supply of air transportation. But the article says that the price will rise by the amount of the tax—the buyer pays the entire tax. So it implicitly assumes that the elasticity of supply is infinite—perfectly elastic.

- Figure 1 shows the possible results of the airport security tax if the elasticity of supply is indeed infinite. The numbers are approximately based on WestJet's Calgary–Edmonton route.

- If the elasticity of demand is 0.7, the demand curve is D_0. If the elasticity of demand is 2.1, the demand curve is D_1. The elasticity of supply is assumed to be infinite, so the supply curve is *S*.

- With no tax, the fare is \$60 a trip and 1,400 passengers a day travel the route.

- The tax shifts the supply curve to *S* + *tax*—a position \$12 above the original supply curve.

- The price rises by the full \$12 of the tax and the quantity decreases to 1,230 if demand is inelastic or to 950 if demand is elastic.

- Figure 2 shows the importance of knowing the elasticity of supply. It shows the outcome if supply is unit elastic.

- Again, with no tax, the fare is \$60 a trip and 1,400 passengers a day travel the route.

- The tax shifts the supply curve to *S* + *tax*—a position \$12 above the original supply curve.

- Now the price rises by between \$4 and \$7 depending on whether demand is elastic or inelastic.

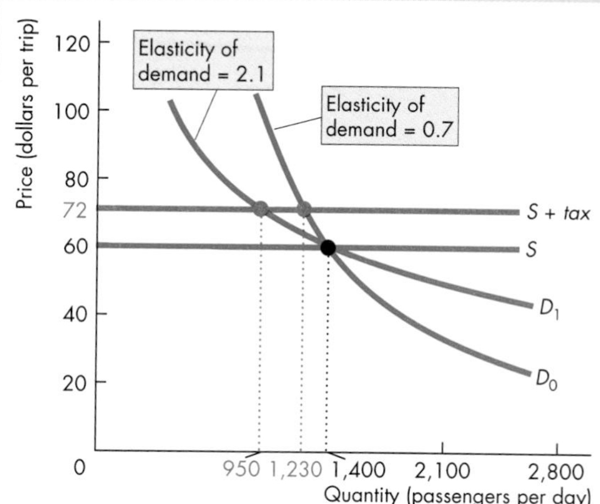

Figure 1 Supply perfectly elastic

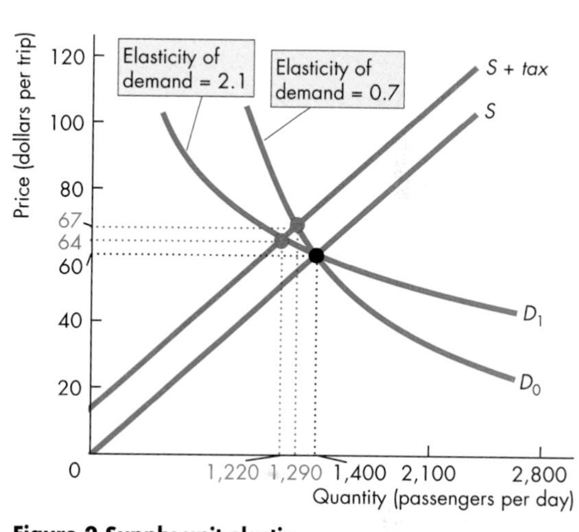

Figure 2 Supply unit elastic

- The effects of the tax on the price and quantity of air travel depend crucially on the elasticity of supply as well as the elasticity of demand.

You're The Voter

- Would you vote for an airport security tax? Why or why not?

- Do you think the airport security tax should be a percentage of the fare rather than a fixed number of dollars? Why or why not?

SUMMARY

KEY POINTS

Housing Markets and Rent Ceilings (pp. 124–127)

- A decrease in the supply of housing raises rents.
- Higher rents stimulate building, and in the long run, the quantity of housing increases and rents fall.
- A rent ceiling that is set below the equilibrium rent creates a housing shortage, wasteful search, and a black market.

The Labour Market and the Minimum Wage (pp. 128–130)

- A decrease in the demand for low-skilled labour lowers the wage rate and reduces employment.
- The lower wage rate encourages low-skilled people to acquire more skills, which decreases the supply of low-skilled labour and, in the long run, raises their wage rate.
- A minimum wage set above the equilibrium wage rate creates unemployment and increases the amount of time people spend searching for a job.
- A minimum wage hits low-skilled young people hardest.

Taxes (pp. 131–134)

- A sales tax raises price but usually by less than the tax.
- The shares of a tax paid by the buyer and by the seller depend on the elasticity of demand and the elasticity of supply.
- The less elastic the demand and the more elastic the supply, the greater is the price increase, the smaller is the quantity decrease, and the larger is the share of the tax paid by the buyer.
- If demand is perfectly elastic or supply is perfectly inelastic, the seller pays the entire tax. And if demand is perfectly inelastic or supply is perfectly elastic, the buyer pays the entire tax.

Markets for Illegal Goods (pp. 135–136)

- Penalties on sellers of an illegal good increase the cost of selling the good and decrease its supply. Penalties on buyers decrease their willingness to pay and decrease the demand for the good.
- The higher the penalties and the more effective the law enforcement, the smaller is the quantity bought.
- A tax that is set at a sufficiently high rate will decrease the quantity of drug consumed, but there will be a tendency for the tax to be evaded.

Stabilizing Farm Revenues (pp. 137–141)

- Farm revenues fluctuate because supply fluctuates.
- The demand for most farm products is inelastic, so a decrease in supply increases the price and increases farm revenues, while an increase in supply decreases price and decreases farm revenues.
- Inventory holders and farm marketing boards act to stabilize farm prices and revenues.

KEY FIGURES

Figure 6.2 A Rent Ceiling, 126
Figure 6.3 The Inefficiency of a Rent Ceiling, 127
Figure 6.5 Minimum Wage and Unemployment, 129
Figure 6.6 A Sales Tax, 131
Figure 6.9 Taxes and Efficiency, 134
Figure 6.10 A Market for an Illegal Good, 135
Figure 6.11 Harvests, Farm Prices, and Farm Revenue, 137

KEY TERMS

Black market, 126
Farm marketing board, 139
Minimum wage, 129
Price ceiling, 125
Price floor, 129
Rent ceiling, 125
Quota, 140
Search activity, 126
Subsidy, 140

PROBLEMS

*1. The figure shows the demand for and supply of rental housing in the Village.

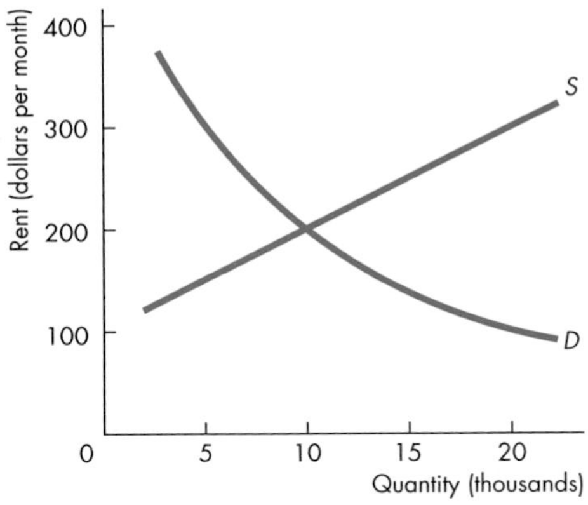

a. What are the equilibrium rent and equilibrium quantity of rental housing?

If a rent ceiling is set at $150 a month, what is

b. The quantity of housing rented?
c. The shortage of housing?
d. The maximum price that someone is willing to pay for the last unit of housing available?

2. The figure shows the demand for and supply of rental housing in Townsville.

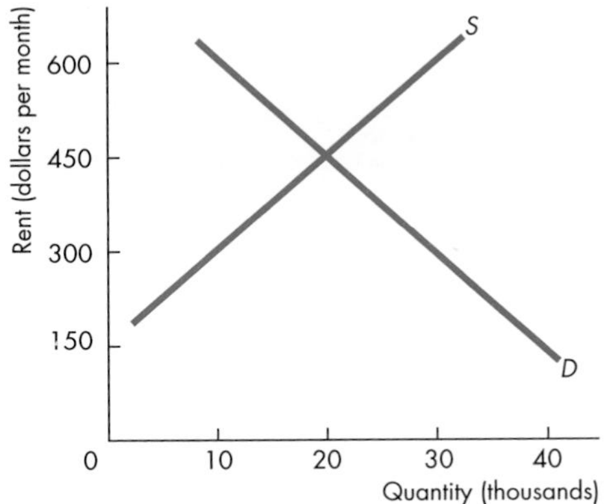

a. What are the equilibrium rent and equilibrium quantity of rental housing?

If a rent ceiling is set at $300 a month, what is

b. The quantity of housing rented?
c. The shortage of housing?
d. The maximum price that someone is willing to pay for the last unit available?

*3. The table gives the demand for and supply of teenage labour.

Wage rate (dollars per hour)	Quantity demanded (hours per month)	Quantity supplied (hours per month)
2	3,000	1,000
3	2,500	1,500
4	2,000	2,000
5	1,500	2,500
6	1,000	3,000

a. What are the equilibrium wage rate and level of employment?
b. What is the quantity of unemployment?
c. If a minimum wage of $3 an hour is set for teenagers, how many hours do they work?
d. With a minimum wage of $3 an hour, how many hours are unemployed?
e. If a minimum wage is set at $5 an hour for teenagers, what are quantities of employment and unemployment?
f. If a minimum wage is set at $5 an hour and demand increases by 500 hours a month, what is the wage rate paid to teenagers and how many hours of their labour are unemployed?

4. The table gives the demand for and supply of labour of high school graduates.

Wage rate (dollars per hour)	Quantity demanded (hours per month)	Quantity supplied (hours per month)
6	10,000	4,000
7	8,000	6,000
8	6,000	8,000
9	4,000	10,000
10	2,000	12,000

a. On a graph, mark in the equilibrium wage rate and level of employment.
b. What is the level of unemployment?
c. If a minimum wage is set at $7 an hour, how many hours do high school graduates work?
d. If a minimum wage is set at $7 an hour, how many hours of labour are unemployed?
e. If a minimum wage is set at $8 an hour, what are employment and unemployment?
f. If the minimum wage is $8 an hour and demand decreases by 2,000 hours a month, what are the wage rate and employment?

*5. The table gives the demand and supply schedules for chocolate brownies.

Price (cents per brownie)	Quantity demanded	Quantity supplied
	(millions per day)	
50	5	3
60	4	4
70	3	5
80	2	6
90	1	7

a. If brownies are not taxed, what is the price of a brownie and how many are consumed?
b. If brownies are taxed at 20¢ each, what is the price and how many brownies are consumed? Who pays the tax?

6. The demand and supply schedules for roses are

Price (dollars per bunch)	Quantity demanded	Quantity supplied
	(bunches per week)	
10	100	40
12	90	60
14	80	80
16	70	100
18	60	120

a. If there is no tax on roses, what is the price and how many bunches are bought?
b. If a tax of $6 a bunch is introduced, what is the price and how many bunches are bought? Who pays the tax?

*7. The demand and supply schedules for rice are

Price (dollars per box)	Quantity demanded	Quantity supplied
	(boxes per week)	
1.20	3,000	500
1.30	2,750	1,500
1.40	2,500	2,500
1.50	2,250	3,500
1.60	2,000	4,500

A storm destroys part of the crop and decreases supply by 500 boxes a week.
a. What do inventory holders do?
b. What is the price and what is farm revenue?

8. In problem 7, instead of a storm, good weather increases supply by 250 boxes a week.
a. What do inventory holders do?
b. What is the price and what is farm revenue?

CRITICAL THINKING

1. Study *Reading Between the Lines* on the airport security tax on pp. 142–143 and answer the following questions:
   a. The airport security tax is a fixed number of dollars per trip. Is this arrangement the best one or would a tax calculated as a percentage of the ticket price work better?
   b. Why do the airlines complain about the airport security tax?
   c. How might the airport security tax increase the demand for air travel?
   d. Do you think the airlines will absorb the tax into their costs and keep ticket prices unchanged? If this outcome did occur, what would it imply about the elasticity of supply of air travel?
   e. Suppose that instead of introducing the airport security tax, the government had put a surcharge on airline fuel to cover the cost of increased security. How would such a tax have affected the price and quantity of air travel? Would it change the distribution of the tax between the traveller and the airlines?

WEB EXERCISES

1. Use the links on the Parkin–Bade Web site to obtain information about cigarette tax rates, tax revenues, purchases, population, and income. Then answer the following questions about the relationship between the number of packs of cigarettes purchased and the price of a pack across Canada.
   a. How would you describe the relationship?
   b. What does the relationship tell you about the demand for cigarettes?
   c. What does the relationship tell you about the amount of cigarette smuggling?
2. Use the links on the Parkin–Bade Web site to obtain information about farm marketing boards in Canada. What are their effects on the quantities of farm products, their prices, and economic efficiency?

UNDERSTANDING HOW MARKETS WORK

PART 2

The Amazing Market

The four chapters that you've just studied explain how markets work. The market is an amazing instrument. It enables people who have never met and who know nothing about each other to interact and do business. It also enables us to allocate our scarce resources to the uses that we value most highly. Markets can be very simple or highly organized. ◆ A simple market is one that the American historian Daniel J. Boorstin describes in *The Discoverers* (p. 161). In the late fourteenth century,

> *The Muslim caravans that went southward from Morocco across the Atlas Mountains arrived after twenty days at the shores of the Senegal River. There the Moroccan traders laid out separate piles of salt, of beads from Ceutan coral, and cheap manufactured goods. Then they retreated out of sight. The local tribesmen, who lived in the strip mines where they dug their gold, came to the shore and put a heap of gold beside each pile of Moroccan goods. Then they, in turn, went out of view, leaving the Moroccan traders either to take the gold offered for a particular pile or to reduce the pile of their merchandise to suit the offered price in gold. Once again the Moroccan traders withdrew, and the process went on. By this system of commercial etiquette, the Moroccans collected their gold.*

An organized market is the Toronto Stock Exchange, which trades many millions of stocks each day. Another is an auction at which a government sells rights to broadcasters and cellular telephone companies for the use of the airwaves. ◆ All of these markets determine the prices at which exchanges take place and enable both buyers and sellers to benefit. ◆ Everything and anything that can be exchanged is traded in markets. There are markets for goods and services; for resources such as labour, capital, and raw materials; for dollars, pounds, and yen; for goods to be delivered now and for goods to be delivered in the future. Only the imagination places limits on what can be traded in markets. ◆ You began your study of markets in Chapter 3 by learning about the laws of demand and supply. There, you discovered the forces that make prices adjust to coordinate buying plans and selling plans. In Chapter 4, you learned how to calculate and use the concept of elasticity to predict the responsiveness of prices and quantities to changes in supply and demand. In Chapter 5, you studied efficiency and discovered the conditions under which a competitive market sends resources to uses in which they are valued most highly. And finally, in Chapter 6, you studied markets in action. There, you learned how markets cope with change and discovered how they operate when governments intervene to fix prices, impose taxes, or make some goods illegal. ◆ The laws of demand and supply that you've learned and used in these four chapters were discovered during the nineteenth century by some remarkable economists. We conclude our study of demand and supply and markets by looking at the lives and times of some of these economists and by talking to one of today's most influential economists who studies and creates sophisticated auction markets.

PROBING THE IDEAS

Discovering the Laws of Demand and Supply

THE ECONOMIST

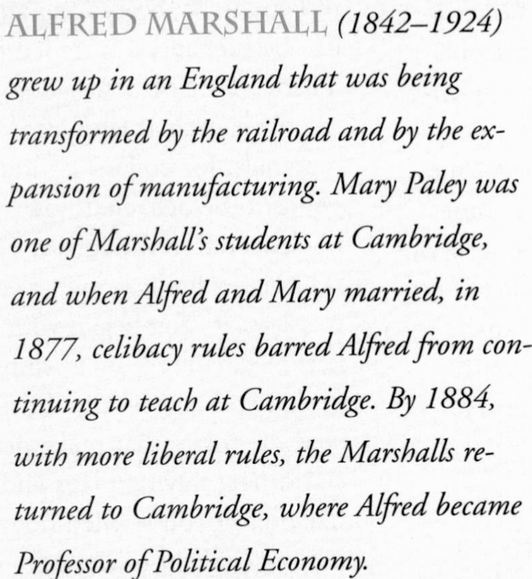

ALFRED MARSHALL *(1842–1924) grew up in an England that was being transformed by the railroad and by the expansion of manufacturing. Mary Paley was one of Marshall's students at Cambridge, and when Alfred and Mary married, in 1877, celibacy rules barred Alfred from continuing to teach at Cambridge. By 1884, with more liberal rules, the Marshalls returned to Cambridge, where Alfred became Professor of Political Economy.*

Many others had a hand in refining the theory of demand and supply, but the first thorough and complete statement of the theory as we know it today was set by Alfred Marshall, with the acknowledged help of Mary Paley Marshall. Published in 1890, this monumental treatise, The Principles of Economics, *became* the *textbook on economics on both sides of the Atlantic for almost half a century. Marshall was an outstanding mathematician, but he kept mathematics and even diagrams in the background. His supply and demand diagram appears only in a footnote.*

"The forces to be dealt with are ... so numerous, that it is best to take a few at a time .... Thus we begin by isolating the primary relations of supply, demand, and price."

ALFRED MARSHALL,
The Principles of Economics

THE ISSUES

The laws of demand and supply that you studied in Chapter 3 were discovered during the 1830s by Antoine-Augustin Cournot (1801–1877), a professor of mathematics at the University of Lyon, France. Although Cournot was the first to use demand and supply, it was the development and expansion of the railroads during the 1850s that gave the newly emerging theory its first practical applications. Railroads then were at the cutting edge of technology just as airlines are today. And as in the airline industry today, competition among the railroads was fierce.

Dionysius Lardner (1793–1859), an Irish professor of philosophy at the University of London, used demand and supply to show railroad companies how they could increase their profits by cutting rates on long-distance business on which competition was fiercest and by raising rates on short-haul business on which they had less to fear from other transportation suppliers. Today, economists use the principles that Lardner worked out during the 1850s to calculate the freight rates and passenger fares that will give airlines the largest possible profit. And the rates calculated have a lot in common with the railroad rates of the nineteenth century. On local routes on which there is little competition, fares per kilometre are highest, and on long-distance routes on which the airlines compete fiercely, fares per kilometre are lowest.

Known satirically among scientists of the day as "Dionysius Diddler," Lardner worked on an amazing range of problems from astronomy to railway engineering to economics. A colourful character, he would have been a regular guest if late-night talk shows had been around in the 1850s. Lardner visited the École des Ponts et Chaussées (School of Bridges and Roads) in Paris and must have learned a great deal from Jules Dupuit.

In France, Jules Dupuit (1804–1866), a French engineer/economist, used demand to calculate the benefits from building a bridge and, once the bridge was built, for calculating the toll to charge for its use. His work was the forerunner of what is today called *cost-benefit analysis.* Working with the principles invented by Dupuit, economists today calculate the costs and benefits of highways and airports, dams, and power stations.

Now

Today, using the same principles that Dupuit devised, economists calculate whether the benefits of expanding airports and air-traffic control facilities are sufficient to cover their costs. Airline companies use the principles developed by Lardner to set their prices and to decide when to offer "seat sales." Like the railroads before them, the airlines charge a high price per kilometre on short flights, for which they face little competition, and a low price per kilometre on long flights, for which competition is fierce.

Then

Dupuit used the law of demand to determine whether a bridge or canal would be valued enough by its users to justify the cost of building it. Lardner first worked out the relationship between the cost of production and supply and used demand and supply theory to explain the costs, prices, and profits of railroad operations. He also used the theory to discover ways of increasing revenue by raising rates on short-haul business and lowering them on long-distance freight.

Markets do an amazing job. And the laws of demand and supply help us to understand how markets work. But in some situations, a market must be designed and institutions must be created to enable the market to operate. In recent years, economists have begun to use their tools to design and create markets. And one of the chief architects of new-style markets is John McMillan, whom you can meet on the following pages.

TALKING WITH

JOHN MCMILLAN *holds the Jonathan B. Lovelace Chair and teaches international management and economics in the Graduate School of Business at Stanford University. Born in Christchurch, New Zealand in 1951, he was an undergraduate at the University of Canterbury, where he studied first mathematics and then economics. For graduate school, he went to the University of New South Wales. John McMillan's research focuses on the way markets work. He wants to dig more deeply than demand and supply and explain how prices get determined, how markets are organized, why some use auctions and some don't, and why different types of auctions get used in different situations. His work has found practical application in the design of mechanisms for selling rights to the electromagnetic spectrum—the air waves that carry your cell-phone messages. His recent book,* Reinventing the Bazaar: A Natural History of Markets *(New York, W.W. Norton, 2002), provides a fascinating account of the rich diversity of market arrangements that have been used through the ages.*

Michael Parkin and Robin Bade talked with John McMillan about his career and the progress that economists have made in understanding markets since the pioneering work of Alfred Marshall.

John McMillan

Professor McMillan, how does Alfred Marshall's assessment of how competitive markets work look today in the light of the progress that economists have made?

Supply and demand is still our basic tool of analysis, but modern microeconomics has dug deeper than Marshall was able to. The supply-demand diagram tells us what prices can do, but it sidesteps the question of where prices come from.

The main insight underlying much of modern microeconomics (and discussed in my book *Reinventing the Bazaar*) is that transaction costs can impede the smooth functioning of markets. Transaction costs include the time and money spent locating trading partners, assessing their reliability, negotiating an agreement, and monitoring performance.

Information is a major source of transaction costs. Often information is unevenly distributed: the seller knows more about the quality of the item for sale than the potential buyer; the buyer knows her willingness to pay but the seller doesn't. Informational asymmetries such as these can mean that transactions that would be mutually beneficial might fail to be realized.

The tools for analyzing the details of deal-making are game theory (as developed by John Nash, the hero of the motion picture *A Beautiful Mind*), and information economics (which was recognized by the Nobel committee in its 2001 economics award to George Akerlof, Michael Spence, and Joseph Stiglitz).

Marshall's economics is like physics without friction. For some questions, the assumption of a frictionless world is a useful short cut: for analyzing, say, the effects of rent controls or minimum-wage laws. For other questions, we need to examine the frictions explicitly. For example, to understand why financial markets are organized as they are we need to bring information asymmetries and transaction costs into the picture.

> ***"The main insight underlying much of modern microeconomics... is that transaction costs can impede the smooth functioning of markets."***

The focus on the costs of transacting has brought a recognition that markets can't operate in thin air. A market is a social construction. To operate well, with transaction costs minimized, any market needs rules and procedures. Some of these rules, perhaps most of them, arise from the bottom up; that is, they evolve through the everyday trial and error of the market participants. Others are set from the top down: government-set laws and regulations can help foster efficient transacting.

Are there any contemporary or recent examples that illustrate the way markets get created, and that perhaps hold some lessons about what works and what doesn't?

Yes. An experiment in the creation of markets is offered to us by the ex-communist countries. In the early 1990s, a common view among those advising Russia, for example, was that the overriding objective was to get the government out. Russia's approach to reform was to abolish all the mechanisms that had run the planned economy and to start with a clean slate. Once the prohibitions on market activity were abolished, the reformers believed, the private sector would quickly take over. Later, in light of Russia's grim performance in the 1990s, this simple view was supplanted by recognition that building a market economy is exceedingly hard. Success requires a complex package of microeconomic reform, macroeconomic stability, and institution-building. Markets don't operate well in an institutional vacuum.

China provides a telling contrast to Russia. China's reforms consisted of leaving the old institutions of the planned economy in place and letting markets grow up around the plan. China boomed during reform; its spectacular economic growth lifted millions out of dire poverty. This growth resulted from the emergence and expansion of the scope of markets and the gradual erosion of the formerly planned economy.

Markets developed in China, paradoxically, in the absence of any laws of contract and of any formal recognition of property rights. In place of the usual market-economy institutions, the pre-existing mechanisms of the planned economy served as a transitional substitute. Highly imperfect as these institutions were, they were enough to support the rapid development of markets. The lesson from the Russia-China comparison is that, for markets to work well, some institutions are better than none.

What is the most remarkable market that you've encountered?

In the Dutch village of Aalsmeer, just outside Amsterdam, operates a flower market of almost unbelievable size and complexity. Its warehouses, full of flowers, cover an area the size of 125 soccer fields. Each morning, 2,000 or so buyers bid around US$5 million for the flowers. The flowers are flown in from far away, from places like Israel, Colombia, and Zimbabwe, and are later dispatched to buyers around the globe.

Sophisticated technology is needed to operate a global market in as perishable an item as cut flowers. The flower auctions are run via a giant clock at the front of the bidding hall, which winds down to successively lower prices. The bidders can stop the clock by pushing a button, meaning they have bought the flowers at the price shown on the clock. Computers then automatically organize the flowers' delivery to the buyer's address.

The auction that you've just described, appropriately called a Dutch auction, starts at a high price and goes down until someone accepts the price. It contrasts with a so-called English

auction, where the price starts low and rises until only one buyer is left. Which works best?

The Dutch auction is used at Aalsmeer because of its speed: a huge volume of flowers must be sold in a few hours. Both buyers and sellers value the speed of the Dutch auction. In other circumstances, the English auction works better from the seller's point of view, but not necessarily from the buyer's point of view.

Consider a situation where there is significant uncertainty about the value of the item for sale. The items has the same value whichever bidder ends up owning it, but at the time of bidding each of the bidders has a different estimate of the value. (This describes, for example, bidding for the right to drill for oil on a tract of land, and each of the bidders has an imperfect estimate of the amount of oil there.) In this situation, there is a risk of what is called the "winner's curse." The bidder who wins is the one with the highest value estimate, which might well be an overestimate. Winning thus conveys bad news: it tells the winner that everyone else believed the item was worth less than the winner believed.

Bidders who understand the winner's curse tend to bid cautiously. But they tend to bid less cautiously—that is, higher—in an English auction than in a Dutch auction. This is because they can see and react to each other's bids. The bids, as they ascend, convey some information about how highly the others value the item, mitigating the winner's curse and thereby usually inducing a higher price. The higher bids induced by the English auction than the other forms of auction are probably the reason that the English auction is the most commonly used auction form around the world.

What is special about selling airwaves that enables expensive economic consultants like you to show governments how to do it?

The spectrum auctions were unusually complex. Thousands of licences were offered. The sale procedure had to recognize complementarities among the licences: that is, the value to a bidder of a licence covering, say, New Jersey, was probably higher if that bidder was going to end up owning a New York licence as well (because the firm could spread its marketing costs across the wider region and in other ways offer more efficient service). None of the tried-and-true auction forms allowed the bidding process to encompass such complementarities. As Vice President Al Gore said at the opening ceremony of one of the auctions, "They couldn't just go look it up in a book."

The auction form that we economists recommend and the government adopted was what came to be known as the "simultaneous ascending auction." Multiple licences were offered for sale at the same time. The ascending bids allowed the bidders to avoid the winner's curse, and the simultaneous bidding on multiple licences allowed the bidders to express their demands for packages of complementary licences. The new auction form has raised many billions of dollars.

What does the Internet mean for markets today? Is it creating gains from trade that were previously unattainable?

It certainly has. By lowering transaction costs—especially the cost of search—to close to zero, it has created global markets in goods that before, because of their lower value, previously had only a local sale. Before the Internet, if you wanted some obscure object, you had to hunt in antique shops, flea markets, and so on. Now you simply use your Internet search engine. Buyers and sellers can quickly and easily contact each other where before it would have been prohibitively expensive. The result is better matches of buyer and seller—and larger gains from trade.

You began your university life studying math. Why did you switch to economics?

I was intrigued that mathematics could be used to help understand how the world works. Of course, as I was to learn, any good piece of economic analysis contains much more than just mathematics, but the mathematics lends the study rigour and precision.

What other subjects work well with economics?

Almost any subject. Mathematics is essential; you can't get to the frontiers of economics research without it. But that's not the only discipline of relevance. Economics uses ideas from fields like biology (for example, natural selection), history (the origins of institutions), sociology (networks and social capital), and philosophy (what is meant by fairness).

PART 3 HOUSEHOLDS' CHOICES

UTILITY AND DEMAND

CHAPTER 7

Water, Water, Everywhere

We need water to live. We don't need diamonds for much besides decoration. If the benefits of water far outweigh the benefits of diamonds, why does water cost practically nothing while diamonds are expensive? ◆ When a winter storm cuts off the power supply, the prices of alternative sources of heat and light, such as firewood and candles, rise dramatically. But people buy as much firewood and as many candles as they can get their hands on. Our demand for goods that provide heat and light is price inelastic. Why? ◆ When the personal computer (PC) was introduced in 1980, it cost more than $5,000 and consumers didn't buy very many. Since then, the price has tumbled and people are buying PCs in enormous quantities. Our demand for PCs is price elastic. What makes the demand for some things price elastic, while the demand for others is price inelastic? ◆ When you buy a monthly transit pass, each additional ride you take is free. What limits the quantity bought when something is "free"?

In the preceding four chapters, we saw that demand has an important effect on the price of a good. But we did not analyze what exactly shapes a person's demand. This chapter examines household behaviour and its influence on demand. It explains why demand for some goods is elastic and the demand for other goods is inelastic. It also explains why the prices of some things, such as diamonds and water, are so out of proportion to their total benefits. And in *Reading Between the Lines* at the end of the chapter, we look at demand when you can buy a monthly pass so the price of an additional unit is zero.

After studying this chapter, you will be able to

- **Describe preferences using the concept of utility and distinguish between total utility and marginal utility**
- **Explain the marginal utility theory of consumer choice**
- **Use marginal utility theory to predict the effects of changing prices and incomes**
- **Explain the paradox of value**

Household Consumption Choices

A HOUSEHOLD'S CONSUMPTION CHOICES ARE determined by many factors, but we can summarize all of these factors in terms of two concepts:

- Consumption possibilities
- Preferences

Consumption Possibilities

A household's consumption choices are constrained by the household's income and by the prices of the goods and services it buys. The household has a given amount of income to spend and cannot influence the prices of the goods and services it buys.

A household's *budget line* describes the limits to its consumption choices. Let's consider Lisa's household. Lisa has an income of $30 a month, and she plans to buy only two goods: movies and pop. The price of a movie is $6; the price of pop is $3 a six-pack. If Lisa spends all her income, she will reach the limits to her consumption of movies and pop.

Figure 7.1 illustrates Lisa's possible consumption of movies and pop. Rows *A* through *F* in the table show six possible ways of allocating $30 to these two goods. For example, Lisa can see 2 movies for $12 and buy 6 six-packs of pop for $18 (row *C*). Points *A* through *F* in the figure illustrate the possibilities presented in the table. The line passing through these points is Lisa's budget line.

Lisa's budget line is a constraint on her choices. It marks the boundary between what she can afford and what she cannot afford. She can afford all the points on the line and inside it. She cannot afford the points outside the line. Lisa's consumption possibilities depend on the price of a movie, the price of pop, and her income. Her consumption possibilities change when the price of a movie, the price of a six-pack of pop, or her income changes.

FIGURE 7.1 Consumption Possibilities

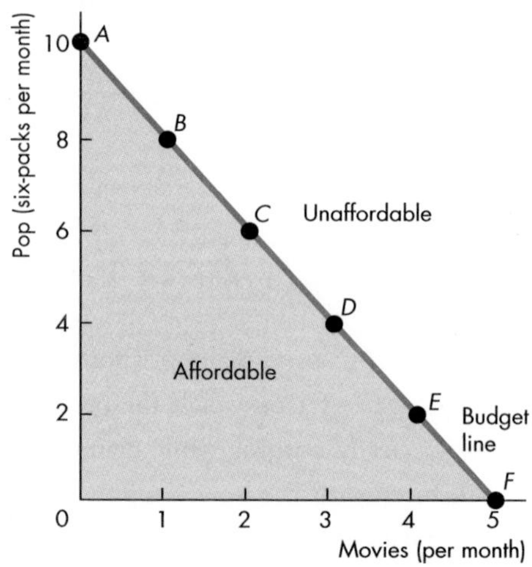

Possibility	Movies Quantity	Movies Expenditure (dollars)	Pop Six-packs	Pop Expenditure (dollars)
A	0	0	10	30
B	1	6	8	24
C	2	12	6	18
D	3	18	4	12
E	4	24	2	6
F	5	30	0	0

Rows *A* through *F* in the table show six possible ways in which Lisa can allocate $30 to movies and pop. For example, Lisa can buy 2 movies and 6 six-packs of pop (row *C*). The combination in each row costs $30. These possibilities are points *A* through *F* in the figure. The line through those points, the budget line, is a boundary between what Lisa can afford and what she cannot afford. Her choices must lie along the line *AF* or inside the orange area.

Preferences

How does Lisa divide her $30 between these two goods? The answer depends on her likes and dislikes—her *preferences*. Economists use the concept of utility to describe preferences. The benefit or satisfaction that a person gets from the consumption of a good or service is called **utility.** Let's now see how we can use the concept of utility to describe preferences.

Total Utility

Total utility is the total benefit that a person gets from the consumption of goods and services. Total utility depends on the level of consumption—more consumption generally gives more total utility. The units of utility are arbitrary. Suppose we tell Lisa that we want to measure her utility. We're going to call the utility from no consumption zero. And we are going

TABLE 7.1 Lisa's Total Utility from Movies and Pop

Movies		Pop	
Quantity per month	Total utility	Six-packs per month	Total utility
0	0	0	0
1	50	1	75
2	88	2	117
3	121	3	153
4	150	4	181
5	175	5	206
6	196	6	225
7	214	7	243
8	229	8	260
9	241	9	276
10	250	10	291
11	256	11	305
12	259	12	318
13	261	13	330
14	262	14	341

to call the utility she gets from 1 movie a month 50 units. We then ask her to tell us, on the same scale, how much she would like 2, 3, and more movies up to 14 a month. We also ask her to tell us, on the same scale, how much she would like 1 six-pack of pop a month, 2 six-packs, and more up to 14 six-packs a month. Table 7.1 shows Lisa's answers.

Marginal Utility

Marginal utility is the change in total utility that results from a one-unit increase in the quantity of a good consumed. When the number of six-packs Lisa buys increases from 4 to 5 a month, her total utility from pop increases from 181 units to 206 units. Thus for Lisa, the marginal utility of consuming a fifth six-pack each month is 25 units. The table in Fig. 7.2 shows Lisa's marginal utility from pop. Notice that marginal utility appears midway between the quantities of pop. It does so because it is the change in consumption from 4 to 5 six-packs that produces the marginal utility of 25 units. The table displays calculations of marginal utility for each number of six-packs that Lisa buys from 1 to 5.

Figure 7.2(a) illustrates the total utility that Lisa gets from pop. The more pop Lisa drinks in a month, the more total utility she gets. Figure 7.2(b) illustrates her marginal utility. This graph tells us that as Lisa drinks more pop, the marginal utility that she gets from pop decreases. For example, her marginal utility decreases from 75 units for the first six-pack to 42 units for the second six-pack and to 36 units for the third. We call this decrease in marginal utility as the quantity of the good consumed increases the principle of **diminishing marginal utility.**

Marginal utility is positive but diminishes as consumption of a good increases. Why does marginal utility have these two features? In Lisa's case, she likes pop, and the more she drinks the better. That's why marginal utility is positive. The benefit that Lisa gets from the last six-pack consumed is its marginal utility. To see why marginal utility diminishes, think about the following two situations: In one, you've just been studying all through the day and evening and you've been too busy finishing an assignment to go shopping. A friend drops by with a six-pack of pop. The utility you get from that pop is the marginal utility from one six-pack. In the second situation, you've been on a pop binge. You've been working on an assignment all day but you've guzzled three six-packs while doing so. You are up to your eyeballs in pop. You are happy enough to have one more can. But the thrill that you get from it is not very large. It is the marginal utility of the nineteenth can in a day.

Temperature: An Analogy

Utility is similar to temperature. Both are abstract concepts, and both have units of measurement that are arbitrary. You know when you feel hot, and you know when you feel cold. But you can't *observe* temperature. You can observe water turning to steam if it is hot enough or turning to ice if it is cold enough. And you can construct an instrument—a thermometer—that can help you to predict when such changes will occur. We call the scale on the thermometer temperature, and we call the units of temperature degrees. But these degree units are arbitrary. For example, we can accurately predict that when a Celsius thermometer shows a temperature of 0, water will turn to ice. This same event occurs when a Fahrenheit thermometer shows a temperature of 32. So the units of measurement of temperature don't matter.

The concept of utility helps us make predictions

FIGURE 7.2 Total Utility and Marginal Utility

Quantity	Total utility	Marginal utility
0	0	
		75
1	75	
		42
2	117	
		36
3	153	
		28
4	181	
		25
5	206	

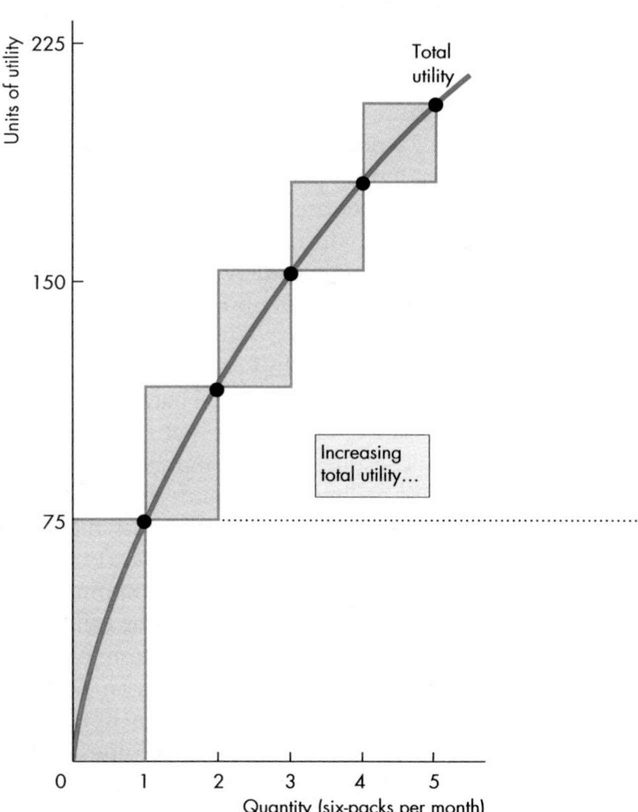

(a) Total utility

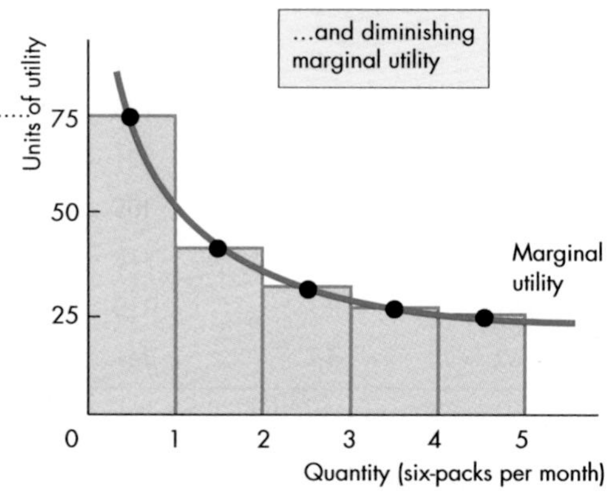

(b) Marginal utility

The table shows that as Lisa drinks more pop, her total utility from pop increases. The table also shows her marginal utility—the change in total utility resulting from the last six-pack she consumes. Marginal utility declines as consumption increases. The figure graphs Lisa's total utility and marginal utility from pop. Part (a) shows her total utility. It also shows as a bar the extra total utility she gains from each additional six-pack—her marginal utility. Part (b) shows how Lisa's marginal utility from pop diminishes by placing the bars shown in part (a) side by side as a series of declining steps.

about consumption choices in much the same way that the concept of temperature helps us make predictions about physical phenomena.

Admittedly, marginal utility theory does not enable us to predict how buying plans change with the same precision that a thermometer enables us to predict when water will turn to ice or steam. But the theory provides important insights into buying plans and has some powerful implications, as you are about to discover. It helps us to understand why people buy more of a good or service when its price falls, why people buy more of most goods when their incomes increase, and it resolves the paradox of value.

REVIEW QUIZ

1 Explain how a consumer's income and the prices of goods limit consumption possibilities.
2 What is utility and how do we use the concept of utility to describe a consumer's preferences?
3 What is the distinction between total utility and marginal utility?
4 What is the key assumption about marginal utility?

Maximizing Utility

A HOUSEHOLD'S INCOME AND THE PRICES THAT the household faces limit its consumption choices, and the household's preferences determine the utility that it can obtain from each consumption possibility. The key assumption of marginal utility theory is that the household chooses the consumption possibility that maximizes its total utility. This assumption of utility maximization is a way of expressing the fundamental economic problem: scarcity. People's wants exceed the resources available to satisfy those wants, so they must make hard choices. In making choices, they try to get the maximum attainable benefit—they try to maximize total utility.

Let's see how Lisa allocates $30 a month between movies and pop to maximize her total utility. We'll continue to assume that the price of a movie is $6 each and the price of pop is $3 a six-pack.

The Utility-Maximizing Choice

The most direct way of calculating how Lisa spends her income to maximize her total utility is by making a table like Table 7.2. The rows of this table show the affordable combinations of movies and pop that lie along Lisa's budget line in Fig. 7.1. The table records three things: first, the number of movies seen and the total utility derived from them (the left side of the table); second, the number of six-packs consumed and the total utility derived from them (the right side of the table); and third, the total utility derived from both movies and pop (the centre column).

The first row of Table 7.2 records the situation when Lisa watches no movies and buys 10 six-packs. In this case, Lisa gets no utility from movies and 291 units of total utility from pop. Her total utility from movies and pop (the centre column) is 291 units. The rest of the table is constructed in the same way.

The consumption of movies and pop that maximizes Lisa's total utility is highlighted in the table. When Lisa sees 2 movies and buys 6 six-packs of pop, she gets 313 units of total utility. This is the best Lisa can do, given that she has only $30 to spend and given the prices of movies and pop. If she buys 8 six-packs of pop, she can see only 1 movie. She gets 310 units of total utility, 3 less than the maximum attainable. If she sees 3 movies, she can drink only 4 six-packs. She gets 302 units of total utility, 11 less than the maximum attainable.

TABLE 7.2 Lisa's Utility-Maximizing Combinations

	Movies		Total utility from movies and pop	Pop	
	Quantity per month	Total utility		Total utility	Six-packs per month
A	0	0	291	291	10
B	1	50	310	260	8
C	2	88	313	225	6
D	3	121	302	181	4
E	4	150	267	117	2
F	5	175	175	0	0

We've just described Lisa's consumer equilibrium. A **consumer equilibrium** is a situation in which a consumer has allocated all his or her available income in the way that, given the prices of goods and services, maximizes his or her total utility. Lisa's consumer equilibrium is 2 movies and 6 six-packs.

In finding Lisa's consumer equilibrium, we measured her *total* utility from movies and pop. But there is a better way of determining a consumer equilibrium, which uses the idea you first met in Chapter 1 that choices are made at the margin. Let's look at this alternative.

Equalizing Marginal Utility per Dollar Spent

A consumer's total utility is maximized by following the rule:

> Spend all the available income and equalize the marginal utility per dollar spent on all goods.

The **marginal utility per dollar spent** is the marginal utility from a good divided by its price. For example, Lisa's marginal utility from seeing 1 movie a month, MU_M, is 50 units of utility. The price of a movie, P_M, is $6, which means that the marginal utility per dollar spent on 1 movie a month, MU_M/P_M, is 50 units divided by $6, or 8.33 units of utility per dollar.

You can see why following this rule maximizes total utility by thinking about a situation in which Lisa has spent all her income but the marginal utilities per dollar spent are not equal. Suppose that Lisa's marginal utility per dollar spent on pop, MU_P/P_P, exceeds that on movies. By spending a dollar more on pop and a dollar less on movies, her total utility from pop rises and her total utility from movies falls. But her utility gain from pop exceeds her utility loss from movies, so her total utility increases. Because she's consuming more pop, her marginal utility from pop has fallen. And because she sees fewer movies, her marginal utility from movies has risen. Lisa keeps increasing her consumption of pop and decreasing her consumption of movies until the two marginal utilities per dollar spent are equal, or when

$$\frac{MU_M}{P_M} = \frac{MU_P}{P_P}.$$

Table 7.3 calculates Lisa's marginal utility per dollar spent on each good. Each row exhausts Lisa's income of \$30. In row *B*, Lisa's marginal utility from movies is 50 units (use Table 7.1 to calculate the marginal utilities). Because the price of a movie is \$6, Lisa's marginal utility per dollar spent on movies is 50 units divided by \$6, which is 8.33. Marginal utility per dollar spent on each good, like marginal utility, decreases as more of the good is consumed.

Lisa maximizes her total utility when the marginal utility per dollar spent on movies is equal to the marginal utility per dollar spent on pop—possibility *C*. Lisa consumes 2 movies and 6 six-packs.

Figure 7.3 shows why the rule "equalize marginal utility per dollar spent on all goods" works. Suppose that instead of consuming 2 movies and 6 six-packs (possibility *C*), Lisa consumes 1 movie and 8 six-packs (possibility *B*). She then gets 8.33 units of utility per dollar spent on movies and 5.67 units per dollar spent on pop. Lisa can increase her total utility by buying less pop and seeing more movies. If she sees one additional movie and spends less on pop, her total utility from movies increases by 8.33 units per dollar and her total utility from pop decreases by 5.67 units per dollar. Her total utility increases by 2.66 units per dollar, as shown by the blue area.

Or suppose that Lisa consumes 3 movies and 4 six-packs (possibility *D*). In this situation, her mar-

TABLE 7.3 Equalizing Marginal Utilities per Dollar Spent

	Movies ($6 each)			Pop ($3 per six-pack)		
	Quantity	Marginal utility	Marginal utility per dollar spent	Six-packs	Marginal utility	Marginal utility per dollar spent
A	0	0		10	15	5.00
B	1	50	8.33	8	17	5.67
C	**2**	**38**	**6.33**	**6**	**19**	**6.33**
D	3	33	5.50	4	28	9.33
E	4	29	4.83	2	42	14.00
F	5	25	4.17	0	0	

FIGURE 7.3 Equalizing Marginal Utilities per Dollar Spent

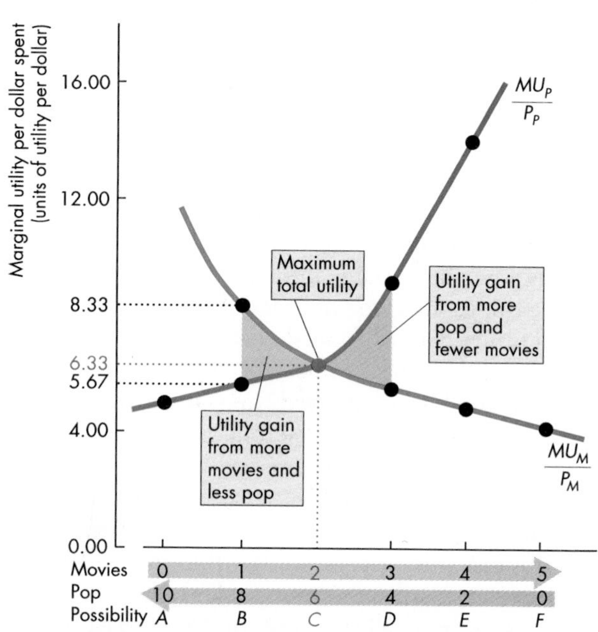

If Lisa consumes 1 movie and 8 six-packs (possibility *B*), she gets 8.33 units of utility from the last dollar spent on movies and 5.67 units of utility from the last dollar spent on pop. She can get more total utility by seeing one more movie and drinking less pop. If she consumes 4 six-packs and sees 3 movies (possibility *D*), she gets 5.50 units of utility from the last dollar spent on movies and 9.33 units of utility from the last dollar spent on pop. She can increase her total utility by seeing one fewer movie and drinking more pop. When Lisa's marginal utilities per dollar spent on both goods are equal, her total utility is maximized.

ginal utility per dollar spent on movies (5.50) is less than her marginal utility per dollar spent on pop (9.33). Lisa can now increase her total utility by seeing one fewer movie and spending more on pop, as the green area shows.

The Power of Marginal Analysis The method we've just used to find Lisa's utility-maximizing choice of movies and pop is an example of the power of marginal analysis. By comparing the marginal gain from having more of one good with the marginal loss from having less of another good, Lisa is able to ensure that she gets the maximum attainable utility.

The rule to follow is simple: If the marginal utility per dollar spent on movies exceeds the marginal utility per dollar spent on pop, see more movies and buy less pop; if the marginal utility per dollar spent on pop exceeds the marginal utility per dollar spent on movies, buy more pop and see fewer movies.

More generally, if the marginal gain from an action exceeds the marginal loss, take the action. You will meet this principle time and again in your study of economics. And you will find yourself using it when you make your own economic choices, especially when you must make a big decision.

Units of Utility In maximizing total utility by making the marginal utilities per dollar spent equal for both goods, the units in which utility is measured do not matter. Any arbitrary units will work. It is in this respect that utility is like temperature. Predictions about the freezing point of water don't depend on the temperature scale; and predictions about a household's consumption choices don't depend on the units of utility.

REVIEW QUIZ

1. What is Lisa's goal when she chooses the quantities of movies and pop to consume?
2. What two conditions are met if a consumer is maximizing utility?
3. Explain why equalizing the marginal utilities of both goods does *not* maximize utility.
4. Explain why equalizing the marginal utilities per dollar spent on both goods *does* maximize utility.

Predictions of Marginal Utility Theory

We're now going to use marginal utility theory to make some predictions. In Chapter 3, we assumed that a fall in the price of a good, other things remaining the same, brings an increase in the quantity demanded of that good—the law of demand. We also assumed that a fall in the price of a substitute decreases demand and a rise in income increases demand for a normal good. We're now going to see that these assumptions are predictions of marginal utility theory.

A Fall in the Price of a Movie

A fall in the price of a movie, other things remaining the same, changes the quantity of movies demanded and brings a movement along the demand curve for movies. We've already found one point on Lisa's demand curve for movies: When the price of a movie is $6, Lisa sees 2 movies a month. Figure 7.4 shows this point on Lisa's demand curve for movies.

To find another point on her demand curve for movies, we need to work out what Lisa buys when the price of a movie changes. Suppose that the price of a movie falls from $6 to $3 and nothing else changes.

To work out the effect of this change in price of a movie on Lisa's buying plans, we must first determine the combinations of movies and pop that she can afford at the new prices. Then we calculate the new marginal utilities per dollar spent. Finally, we determine the combination that makes the marginal utilities per dollar spent on movies and pop equal.

The rows of Table 7.4 show the combinations of movies and pop that exhaust Lisa's $30 of income when the price of a movie is $3 and the price of a six-pack is $3. Lisa's preferences do not change when prices change, so her marginal utility schedule remains the same as that in Table 7.3. Divide her marginal utility from movies by $3 to get the marginal utility per dollar spent on movies.

Lisa now sees 5 movies and drinks 5 six-packs. She *substitutes* movies for pop. Figure 7.4 shows both of these effects. In part (a), we've found another point on Lisa's demand curve for movies. And we've discovered that her demand curve obeys the law of demand. In part (b), we see that a fall in the price of a movie decreases the demand for pop. The demand curve for pop shifts leftward. For Lisa, pop and movies are substitutes.

TABLE 7.4 How a Change in the Price of a Movie Affects Lisa's Choices

Movies ($3 each)		Pop ($3 per six-pack)	
Quantity	Marginal utility per dollar spent	Six-packs	Marginal utility per dollar spent
0		10	5.00
1	16.67	9	5.33
2	**12.67**	8	5.67
3	11.00	7	6.00
4	9.67	**6**	**6.33**
5	8.33	5	8.33
6	7.00	4	9.33
7	6.00	3	12.00
8	5.00	2	14.00
9	4.00	1	25.00
10	3.00	0	

FIGURE 7.4 A Fall in the Price of a Movie

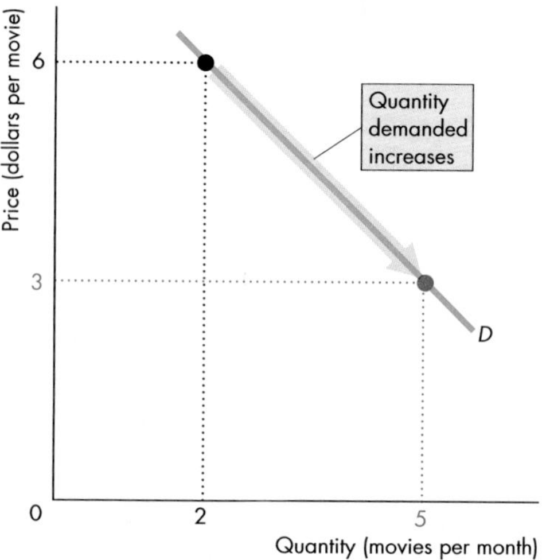

(a) Demand for movies

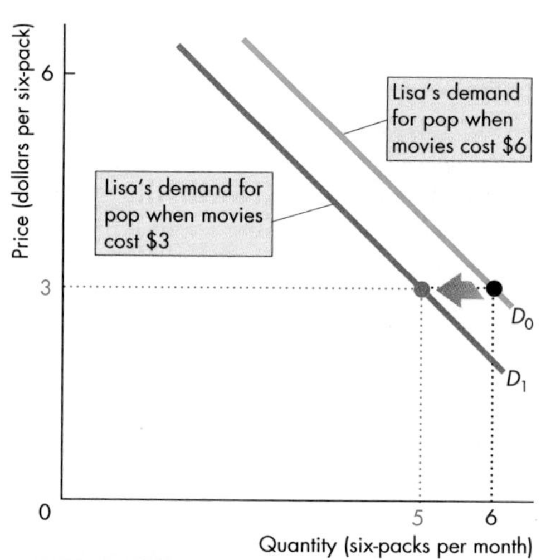

(b) Demand for pop

When the price of a movie falls and the price of pop remains the same, the quantity of movies demanded by Lisa increases, and in part (a), Lisa moves along her demand curve for movies. Also when the price of a movie falls, Lisa's demand for pop decreases, and in part (b), her demand curve for pop shifts leftward.

A Rise in the Price of Pop

In Fig. 7.4(b), we know only one point on Lisa's demand curve for pop when the price of a movie is $3. To find Lisa's demand curve for pop, we must see how Lisa responds to a change in the price of pop. Suppose that the price of pop rises from $3 to $6 a six-pack. The rows of Table 7.5 show the combinations of movies and pop that exhaust Lisa's $30 of income when the price of a movie is $3 and the price of a six-pack is $6. Again, Lisa's preferences don't change when the price changes. Divide Lisa's marginal utility from pop by $6 to get her marginal utility per dollar spent on pop.

Lisa now drinks 2 six-packs a month and sees 6 movies a month. Lisa *substitutes* movies for pop. Figure 7.5 shows both of these effects. In part (a), we've found another point on Lisa's demand curve for pop. And we've confirmed that this demand curve obeys the law of demand. In part (b), we see that Lisa increases the number of movies that she sees when the price of pop rises and the price of a movie remains constant. The demand curve for movies shifts rightward. For Lisa, movies and pop are substitutes.

TABLE 7.5 How a Change in the Price of Pop Affects Lisa's Choices

Movies ($3 each)		Pop ($6 per six-pack)	
Quantity	**Marginal utility per dollar spent**	**Six-packs**	**Marginal utility per dollar spent**
0		5	4.17
2	12.67	4	4.67
4	9.67	3	6.00
6	7.00	2	7.00
8	5.00	1	12.50
10	3.00	0	

Marginal utility theory predicts these two results:

- When the price of a good rises, the quantity demanded of that good decreases.
- If the price of one good rises, the demand for another good that can serve as a substitute increases.

These predictions of marginal utility theory sound familiar because they correspond to the assumptions that we made about demand in Chapter 3. There, we assumed that the demand curve for a good slopes downward and that a rise in the price of a substitute increases demand.

We have now seen that marginal utility theory predicts how the quantities of goods and services that people demand respond to price changes. The theory enables us to derive the consumer's demand curve and predict how the demand curve for one good shifts when the price of another good changes.

Marginal utility theory also helps us to predict how demand changes when income changes. Let's study the effects of a change in income on demand.

FIGURE 7.5 A Rise in the Price of Pop

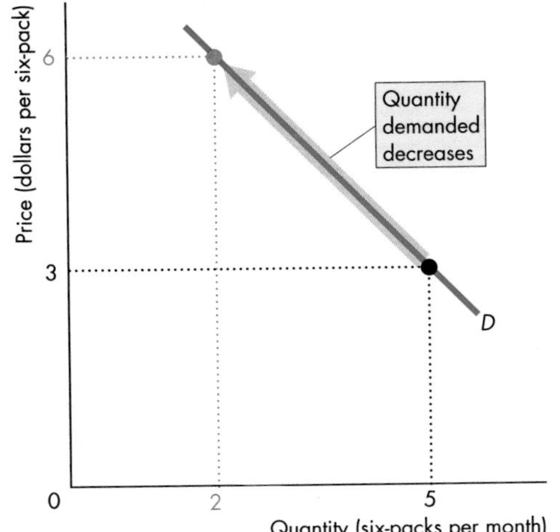

(a) Demand for pop

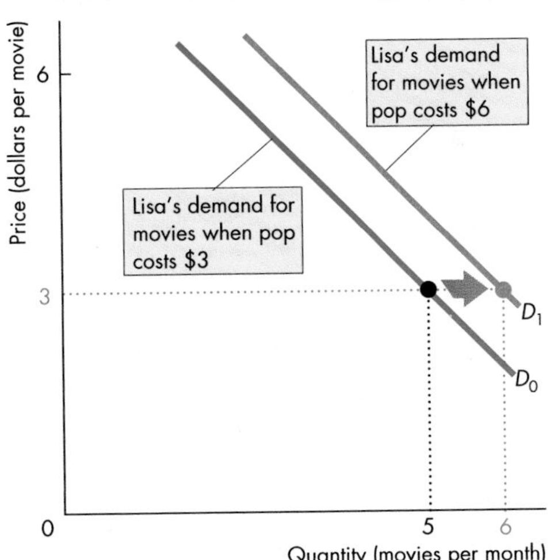

(b) Demand for movies

When the price of pop rises and the price of a movie remains the same, the quantity of pop demanded by Lisa decreases, and in part (a), Lisa moves along her demand curve for pop. Also when the price of pop rises, Lisa's demand for movies increases, and in part (b), her demand curve for movies shifts rightward.

A Rise in Income

Let's suppose that Lisa's income increases to $42 a month, and that the price of a movie is $3 and the price of a six-pack is $3. We saw in Table 7.4 that with these prices and with an income of $30 a month, Lisa sees 5 movies and drinks 5 six-packs a month. We want to compare this choice of movies and pop with Lisa's choice when her income is $42. Table 7.6 shows the calculations needed to make the comparison. With $42, Lisa can see 14 movies a month and buy no pop, or buy 14 six-packs a month and see no movies, or choose any combination of the two goods in the rows of the table. We calculate the marginal utility per dollar spent in exactly the same way as we did before and find the quantities at which the marginal utility per dollar spent on movies and the marginal utility per dollar spent on pop are equal. When Lisa's income is $42, the marginal utilities per dollar spent on both goods are equal when she sees 7 movies and drinks 7 six-packs of pop a month.

By comparing this situation with that in Table 7.4, we see that with an additional $12 a month, Lisa buys 2 more six-packs and sees 2 more movies a month. Lisa's response arises from her preferences, as described by her marginal utilities. Different preferences would produce different quantitative responses. With a larger income, the consumer always buys more of a *normal* good and less of an *inferior* good. For Lisa, pop and movies are normal goods. When her income increases, Lisa buys more of both goods.

You have now completed your study of the marginal utility theory of a household's consumption choices. Table 7.7 summarizes the key assumptions, implications, and predictions of the theory.

TABLE 7.6 Lisa's Choices with an Income of $42 a Month

Movies ($3 each)		Pop ($3 per six-pack)	
Quantity	**Marginal utility per dollar spent**	**Six-packs**	**Marginal utility per dollar spent**
0		14	3.67
1	16.67	13	4.00
2	12.67	12	4.33
3	11.00	11	4.67
4	9.67	10	5.00
5	**8.33**	9	5.33
6	7.00	8	5.67
7	**6.00**	**7**	**6.00**
8	5.00	6	6.33
9	4.00	**5**	**8.33**
10	3.00	4	9.33
11	2.00	3	12.00
12	1.00	2	14.00
13	0.67	1	25.00
14	0.33	0	

TABLE 7.7 Marginal Utility Theory

Assumptions

- A consumer derives utility from the goods consumed.
- Each additional unit of consumption yields additional total utility—marginal utility is positive.
- As the quantity of a good consumed increases, marginal utility decreases.
- A consumer's aim is to maximize total utility.

Implication

- Total utility is maximized when all the available income is spent and when the marginal utility per dollar spent is equal for all goods.

Predictions

- Other things remaining the same, the higher the price of a good, the smaller is the quantity demanded (the law of demand).
- The higher the price of a good, the greater is the quantity bought of substitutes for that good.
- The larger the consumer's income, the greater is the quantity demanded of normal goods.

Individual Demand and Market Demand

Marginal utility theory explains how an individual household spends its income and enables us to derive an individual household's demand curve. In the earlier chapters, we've used *market* demand curves. We can derive a market demand curve from individual demand curves. Let's see how.

The relationship between the total quantity demanded of a good and its price is called **market demand.** The market demand curve is what you studied in Chapter 3. The relationship between the quantity demanded of a good by a single individual and its price is called *individual demand.*

Figure 7.6 illustrates the relationship between individual demand and market demand. In this example, Lisa and Chuck are the only people. The market demand is the total demand of Lisa and Chuck. At $3 a movie, Lisa demands 5 movies a month and Chuck demands 2, so the total quantity demanded by the market is 7 movies a month. Lisa's demand curve for movies in part (a) and Chuck's in part (b) sum *horizontally* to give the market demand curve in part (c).

The market demand curve is the horizontal sum of the individual demand curves and is formed by adding the quantities demanded by each individual at each price.

Because marginal utility theory predicts that individual demand curves slope downward, it also predicts that market demand curves slope downward.

FIGURE 7.6 Individual and Market Demand Curves

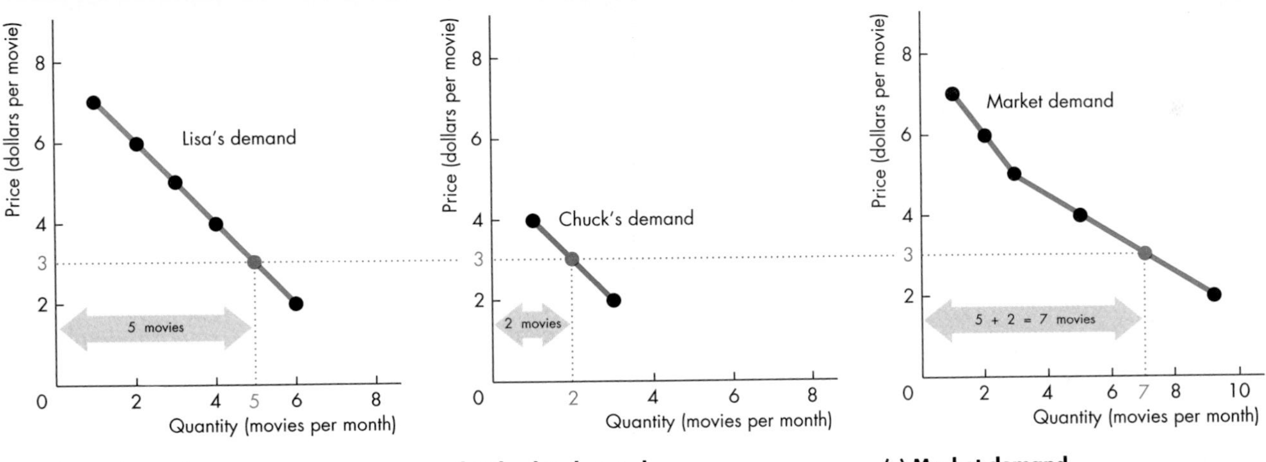

(a) Lisa's demand **(b) Chuck's demand** **(c) Market demand**

Price (dollars per movie)	Quantity of movies demanded		
	Lisa	Chuck	Market
7	1	0	1
6	2	0	2
5	3	0	3
4	4	1	5
3	5	2	7
2	6	3	9

The table and figure illustrate how the quantity of movies demanded varies as the price of a movie varies. In the table, the market demand is the sum of the individual demands. For example, at a price of $3 a movie, Lisa demands 5 movies and Chuck demands 2 movies, so the total quantity demanded in the market is 7 movies. In the figure, the market demand curve is the horizontal sum of the individual demand curves. Thus when the price is $3 a movie, the market demand curve shows that the quantity demanded is 7 movies, the sum of the quantities demanded by Lisa and Chuck.

Marginal Utility and Elasticity

At the beginning of this chapter, we asked why the demand for some things is price elastic while the demand for others is price inelastic. The main answer in Chapter 4 (p. 89) is that a good with close substitutes has an elastic demand and a good with poor substitutes has an inelastic demand. This answer is correct. But you can now provide a deeper answer based on marginal utility theory.

You know that for any pair of goods, X and Y, the consumer maximizes utility when

$$\frac{MU_X}{P_X} = \frac{MU_Y}{P_Y}.$$

If the price of X falls, the consumer will buy more of X to drive the marginal utility of X, MU_X, down. If MU_X diminishes only slightly as the quantity of X consumed increases, then a large increase in the quantity of X restores consumer equilibrium and the demand for X is elastic. If the MU_X diminishes steeply as the quantity of X consumed increases, then a small increase in the quantity of X restores consumer equilibrium and the demand for X is inelastic.

If X has close substitutes, the marginal utility of X diminishes slightly as its quantity consumed increases. If X has poor substitutes, its marginal utility diminishes steeply as its quantity consumed increases.

REVIEW QUIZ

1 When the price of a good falls and the prices of other goods and a consumer's income remain the same, what happens to the consumption of the good whose price has fallen and to the consumption of other goods?
2 Elaborate on your answer to the previous question by using demand curves. For which good does demand change, and for which good does quantity demanded change?
3 If a consumer's income increases and if all goods are normal goods, how does the quantity bought of each good change?

We're going to end this chapter by returning to a recurring theme throughout your study of economics: the concept of efficiency and the distinction between price and value.

Efficiency, Price, and Value

MARGINAL UTILITY THEORY HELPS US TO DEEPEN our understanding of the concept of efficiency and also helps us to see more clearly the distinction between value and price. Let's find out how.

Consumer Efficiency and Consumer Surplus

When Lisa allocates her limited budget to maximize utility, she is using her resources efficiently. Any other allocation of her budget wastes some resources.

But when Lisa has allocated her limited budget to maximize utility, she is *on* her demand curve for each good. A demand curve is a description of the quantity demanded at each price when utility is maximized. When we studied efficiency in Chapter 5, we learned that value equals marginal benefit and that a demand curve is also a willingness-to-pay curve. It tells us a consumer's *marginal benefit*—the benefit from consuming an additional unit of a good. You can now give the idea of marginal benefit a deeper meaning:

Marginal benefit is the maximum price a consumer is willing to pay for an extra unit of a good or service when utility is maximized.

The Paradox of Value

For centuries, philosophers have been puzzled by a paradox that we raised at the start of this chapter. Water, which is essential to life itself, costs little, but diamonds, which are useless in comparison to water, are expensive. Why? Adam Smith tried to solve this paradox. But not until the theory of marginal utility had been developed could anyone give a satisfactory answer.

You can solve this puzzle by distinguishing between *total* utility and *marginal* utility. The total utility that we get from water is enormous. But remember, the more we consume of something, the smaller is its marginal utility. We use so much water that its marginal utility—the benefit we get from one more glass of water—diminishes to a small value. Diamonds, on the other hand, have a small total utility relative to water, but because we buy few diamonds, they have a high marginal utility. When a household has maximized its total utility, it has allocated its budget in the way that makes the marginal

FIGURE 7.7 The Paradox of Value

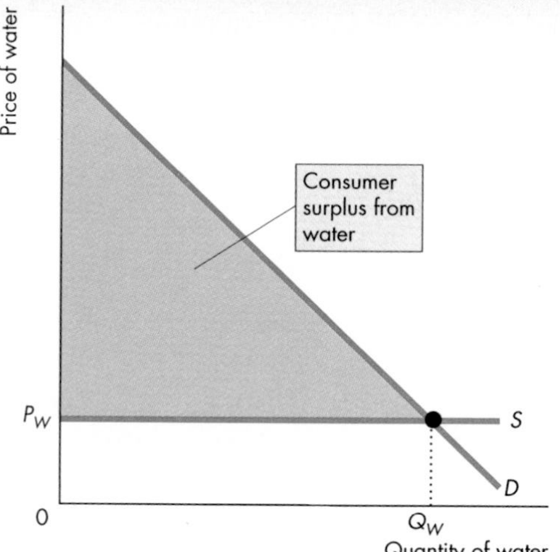

(a) Water

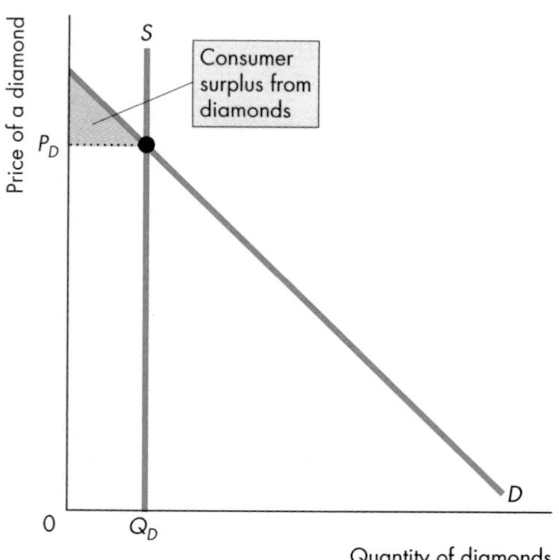

(b) Diamonds

Part (a) shows the demand for water, *D*, and the supply of water, *S*. The supply is assumed to be perfectly elastic at the price P_W. At this price, the quantity of water consumed is Q_W and the consumer surplus from water is the large green triangle. Part (b) shows the demand for diamonds, *D*, and the supply of diamonds, *S*. The supply is assumed to be perfectly inelastic at the quantity Q_D. At this quantity, the price of diamonds is P_D and the consumer surplus from diamonds is the small green triangle. Water is valuable—it has a large consumer surplus—but cheap. Diamonds are less valuable than water—they have a smaller consumer surplus—but are expensive.

utilities per dollar spent equal for all goods. That is, the marginal utility from a good divided by the price of the good is equal for all goods. This equality of marginal utilities per dollar spent holds true for diamonds and water: Diamonds have a high price and a high marginal utility. Water has a low price and a low marginal utility. When the high marginal utility of diamonds is divided by the high price of diamonds, the result is a number that equals the low marginal utility of water divided by the low price of water. The marginal utility per dollar spent is the same for diamonds as for water.

Another way to think about the paradox of value uses *consumer surplus*. Figure 7.7 explains the paradox of value by using this idea. The supply of water (part a) is perfectly elastic at price P_W, so the quantity of water consumed is Q_W and the consumer surplus from water is the large green area. The supply of diamonds (part b) is perfectly inelastic at price Q_D, so the price of diamonds is P_D and the consumer surplus from diamonds is the small green area. Water is cheap but brings a large consumer surplus, while diamonds are expensive but bring a small consumer surplus.

REVIEW QUIZ

1 Can you explain why, along a demand curve, a consumer's choices are efficient?
2 Can you explain the paradox of value?
3 Does water or do diamonds have the greater marginal utility? Does water or do diamonds have the greater total utility? Does water or do diamonds have the greater consumer surplus?

You have now completed your study of the marginal utility theory. And you've seen how the theory can be used to explain our real-world consumption choices. You can see the theory in action once again in *Reading Between the Lines* on pp. 166–167, where it is used to interpret how commuters in Winnipeg will use the new network of water buses along the Assiniboine and Red Rivers.

The next chapter presents an alternative theory of household behaviour. To help you see the connection between the two theories of consumer behaviour, we'll continue with the same example. We'll meet Lisa again and discover another way of understanding how she gets the most out of her $30 a month.

What's the Marginal Utility of a Boat Ride?

WINNIPEG FREE PRESS, JULY 25, 2001

New network of transit boats invite all aboard

With the city skyline behind him, Mayor Glen Murray rode to work yesterday morning, one of the first passengers in the city's new water transit boat.

"This is a fast, hassle-free and affordable way to travel that avoids traffic congestion," Murray said as the system's inaugural ride was filmed and photographed by the media.

The water bus shuttle links six public docks along the Assiniboine and Red Rivers.

Murray boarded the shuttle near his home, a new dock at the foot of Hugo Street, off Wellington Crescent. A 14-minute ride took Murray to the newly constructed dock in Stephen Juba Park at the end of Bannatyne Avenue, where he then walked to city hall.

The new service links the east Exchange area with the Corydon Avenue strip from the Hugo Street dock, with stops in between at The Forks, Tache, the Midtown bridge, and docks at the Legislature and the Osborne Street bridge.

...

For a $2 fee, riders can travel from dock to dock. Passengers are not given life jackets but they will be offered to children. Monthly commuter passes for rush-hour service costs $100. Day passes are $7; $6 for seniors and youths.

The shuttle will operate seven days a week; weekday service has rush-hour departures at eight-minute intervals from 7–9:30 a.m. and 4–6 p.m., with regular 15-minute departures until 11 p.m. On weekends, the service will have departures at 15-minute intervals from 10 a.m.–11 p.m.

The 12-passenger boats travel fully loaded at a maximum speed of about 40 kilometres per hour.

...

Essence of the Story

- A water bus shuttle links six public docks along the Assiniboine and Red Rivers in Winnipeg.
- The price of a one-way trip is $2. The price of a one-day pass is $7 ($6 for seniors and youths). The price of a one-month rush-hour pass is $100.
- The shuttle operates seven days a week. On weekdays boats depart at 15-minute intervals and at eight-minute intervals during rush hours.
- A boat carries 12 passengers at a maximum speed of 40 kilometres per hour.

Economic Analysis

■ The people who live in the region served by the Winnipeg water bus shuttle choose the method of transportation and number of trips that maximize utility.

■ The price of each trip is $2 (no special passes), so each person takes the number of trips that makes the marginal utility per dollar spent on boat trips equal to the marginal utility per dollar spent on other goods.

■ The table illustrates a person's choice if the amount available is $160, the price of a boat ride is $2, and the price of a unit of other goods is $10.

■ The person maximizes utility in this example by taking 20 boat trips and consuming 12 units of other goods.

■ But a Winnipeg commuter must make a more complicated choice because the boat company offers special passes. We'll consider just the $100 monthly pass.

■ Figure 1 shows the consumption possibilities that face the commuter. The commuter can pay $2 a trip or $100 for a month of "free" trips.

■ You can see that the person who takes fewer than 50 trips a month can buy more other goods by paying $2 a trip. The person who takes more than 50 trips a month can buy more other goods by paying $100 for the trips.

■ To decide whether to buy a monthly commuter pass for $100 or pay $2 per trip, the commuter must make two calculations, each similar to the one you've just seen, but with a twist.

■ If the utility-maximizing number of trips at $2 a trip turns out to be greater than 50 a month, the choice is easy: buy a commuter pass and save some money that can be spent on other goods.

■ If the utility-maximizing number of trips at $2 a trip turns out to be less than 50 a month, the commuter needs to reason as follows.

■ If I buy a commuter pass for $100, I can take any number of trips I choose and the cost of one marginal trip is zero. So I will take a trip if its marginal utility is positive.

■ The total utility that I get from these trips is the marginal utility from a commuter pass—it is the change in total utility that results from the decision to buy the pass.

■ So I will buy a commuter pass when the change in total utility that results from the decision to buy the pass divided by $100 is greater than or equal to the marginal utility per dollar spent on other goods.

■ In this case, I will take boat rides until the marginal utility of a ride is zero.

Winnipeg Traveller's Choices at $2 a Trip

	Boat trips ($2 each)			Other goods ($10 each)		
	Quantity	**Marginal utility**	**Marginal utility per dollar spent**	**Quantity**	**Marginal utility**	**Marginal utility per dollar spent**
A	0			16	10	1.00
B	10	10	5.00	14	20	2.00
C	**20**	**8**	**4.00**	**12**	**40**	**4.00**
D	30	6	3.00	10	60	6.00
E	40	4	2.00	8	80	8.00
F	50	3	1.50	6	100	10.00
G	60	2	1.00	4	120	12.00
H	70	1	0.50	2	140	14.00
I	80	0	0	0		

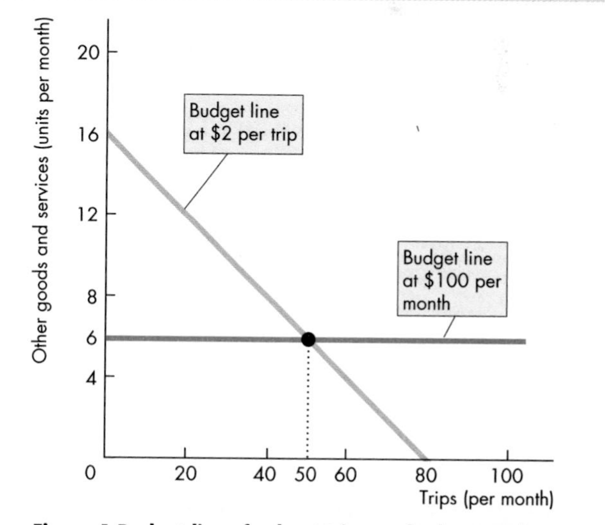

Figure 1 Budget lines for boat trips and other goods

SUMMARY

KEY POINTS

Household Consumption Choices (pp. 154–156)

- A household's choices are determined by its consumption possibilities and preferences.
- A household's consumption possibilities are constrained by its income and by the prices of goods and services. Some combinations of goods and services are affordable, and some are not affordable.
- A household's preferences can be described by marginal utility.
- The key assumption of marginal utility theory is that the marginal utility of a good or service decreases as consumption of the good or service increases.
- Marginal utility theory assumes that people buy the affordable combination of goods and services that maximizes their total utility.

Maximizing Utility (pp. 157–159)

- Total utility is maximized when all the available income is spent and when the marginal utilities per dollar spent on all goods are equal.
- If the marginal utility per dollar spent on good *A* exceeds that on good *B*, total utility increases if the quantity purchased of good *A* increases and the quantity purchased of good *B* decreases.

Predictions of Marginal Utility Theory (pp. 159–164)

- Marginal utility theory predicts the law of demand. That is, other things remaining the same, the higher the price of a good, the smaller is the quantity demanded of that good.
- Marginal utility theory also predicts that, other things remaining the same, the larger the consumer's income, the larger is the quantity demanded of a normal good.
- The market demand curve is found by summing horizontally all the individual demand curves.

Efficiency, Price, and Value (pp. 164–165)

- When a consumer maximizes utility, he or she is using resources efficiently.
- Marginal utility theory resolves the paradox of value.
- When we talk loosely about value, we are thinking of *total* utility or consumer surplus. But price is related to *marginal* utility.
- Water, which we consume in large amounts, has a high total utility and a large consumer surplus, but the price of water is low and the marginal utility from water is low.
- Diamonds, which we consume in small amounts, have a low total utility and a small consumer surplus, but the price of a diamond is high and the marginal utility from diamonds is high.

KEY FIGURES AND TABLE

Figure 7.1 Consumption Possibilities, 154
Figure 7.2 Total Utility and Marginal Utility, 156
Figure 7.3 Equalizing Marginal Utilities per Dollar Spent, 158
Figure 7.4 A Fall in the Price of a Movie, 160
Figure 7.5 A Rise in the Price of Pop, 161
Figure 7.6 Individual and Market Demand Curves, 163
Figure 7.7 The Paradox of Value, 165
Table 7.7 Marginal Utility Theory, 162

KEY TERMS

Consumer equilibrium, 157
Diminishing marginal utility, 155
Marginal utility, 155
Marginal utility per dollar spent, 157
Market demand, 163
Total utility, 154
Utility, 154

PROBLEMS

*1. Jason enjoys rock CDs and spy novels and spends $60 a month on them. The table shows the utility he gets from each good.

Quantity per month	Utility from rock CDs	Utility from spy novels
1	60	20
2	110	38
3	150	53
4	180	64
5	200	70
6	206	75

a. Draw graphs that show Jason's utility from rock CDs and utility from spy novels.
b. Compare the two utility graphs. Can you say anything about Jason's preferences?
c. Draw graphs that show Jason's marginal utility from rock CDs and marginal utility from spy novels.
d. What do the two marginal utility graphs tell you about Jason's preferences?
e. If the price of a rock CD is $10 and the price of a spy novel is $10, how does Jason spend the $60?

2. Martha enjoys classical CDs and travel books and spends $75 a month on them. The table shows the utility she gets from each good.

Quantity per month	Utility from classical CDs	Utility from travel books
1	90	120
2	110	136
3	126	148
4	138	152
5	146	154

a. Draw graphs that show Martha's utility from classical CDs and utility from travel books.
b. Compare the two utility graphs. Can you say anything about Martha's preferences?
c. Draw graphs that show Martha's marginal utility from classical CDs and from travel books.
d. What do the two marginal utility graphs tell you about Martha's preferences?
e. If the price of a classical CD is $15 and the price of a travel book is $15, how does Martha spend the $75 a month?

*3. Max enjoys windsurfing and snorkelling. The table shows the marginal utility he gets from each activity.

Hours per day	Marginal utility from windsurfing	Marginal utility from snorkelling
1	120	40
2	100	36
3	80	30
4	60	22
5	40	12
6	12	10
7	10	8

Max has $35 to spend, and he can spend as much time as he likes on his leisure pursuits. Windsurfing equipment rents for $10 an hour, and snorkelling equipment rents for $5 an hour.

How long does Max spend windsurfing and how long does he spend snorkelling?

4. Pete enjoys rock concerts and the opera. The table shows the marginal utility he gets from each event.

Events per month	Marginal utility from rock concerts	Marginal utility from operas
1	120	200
2	100	160
3	80	120
4	60	80
5	40	40
6	20	0

Pete has $200 a month to spend on these events. The price of a rock concert ticket is $20, and the price of an opera ticket is $40.

How many rock concerts and how many operas does Pete attend?

*5. In problem 3, Max's sister gives him $20 to spend on his leisure pursuits, so he now has a total of $55.
a. Draw a graph that shows Max's consumption possibilities.
b. How many hours does Max choose to windsurf and how many hours does he choose to snorkel now that he has $55 to spend?

6. In problem 4, Pete's uncle gives him $60 to spend on event tickets, so he now has $260.
   a. Draw a graph that shows Pete's budget line.
   b. How many rock concerts and how many operas does Pete now attend?

*7. In problem 5, if the rent on windsurfing equipment decreases to $5 an hour, how many hours does Max now windsurf and how many hours does he snorkel?

8. In Problem 4, if the price of an opera ticket decreases to $20, how many rock concerts and how many operas will Pete attend?

*9. Max, in Problem 3, takes a Club Med vacation, the cost of which includes unlimited sports activities. There is no extra charge for equipment. If Max windsurfs and snorkels for 6 hours a day, how many hours does he windsurf and how many hours does he snorkel?

10. Pete, in Problem 4, wins a prize and has more than enough money to satisfy his desires for rock concerts and operas. He decides to buy a total of 7 tickets each month. How many rock concerts and how many operas does he now attend?

*11. Shirley and Dan are the only two individuals and their demand schedules for popcorn are

Price (cents per carton)	Quantity demanded by Shirley (cartons per week)	Quantity demanded by Dan (cartons per week)
10	12	6
30	9	5
50	6	4
70	3	3
90	1	2

What is the market demand for popcorn?

12. Lee's and Lou's demand schedules for CDs are

Price (dollars per CD)	Quantity demanded by Lee (CDs per year)	Quantity demanded by Lou (CDs per year)
6	12	10
8	9	8
10	6	6
12	3	4
14	0	2

If Lee and Lou are the only two individuals, what is the market demand for CDs?

CRITICAL THINKING

1. Study *Reading Between the Lines* on pp. 166–167 on the Winnipeg water transit boats and then answer the following questions:
   a. If the price of a ride is $2 and the price of a day pass is $6, how does a person decide whether to buy the pass or pay for each ride?
   b. List the components of the opportunity cost of a ride other than the cost of the ticket.
   c. What does marginal utility theory predict will happen to the demand for public transit as incomes rise?

2. Smoking is banned on most airline flights. Use marginal utility theory to explain
   a. The effect of the ban on the utility of smokers.
   b. How the ban influences the decisions of smokers.
   c. The effects of the ban on the utility of non-smokers.
   d. How the ban influences the decisions of non-smokers.

WEB EXERCISES

1. Use the links on the Parkin–Bade Web site and read what Henry Schimberg, former CEO of Coca-Cola, said about the market for bottled water. Use marginal utility theory to explain and interpret his remarks.

2. Use the links on the Parkin–Bade Web site and obtain information about the prices on the Toronto Transit system.
   a. Show the effects of the different ticket options on the consumer's budget line.
   b. How would a person decide whether to pay for each trip, to buy a day pass, or to buy a pass for a longer period? Use marginal utility theory to answer this question.
   c. How do you think the number of riders would change if the price of a single trip fell and the price of a day pass increased?

POSSIBILITIES, PREFERENCES, AND CHOICES

CHAPTER 8

Subterranean Movements

Like the continents floating on the earth's mantle, our spending patterns change steadily over time. On such subterranean movements, business empires rise and fall. One of these movements is occurring with the expansion of Internet access. We now can choose whether to buy a book in the normal way—a regular previously printed and bound book—or to buy a print-on-demand book or an e-book. The price of a print-on-demand book is a bit higher than a regular book, but the buyer can customize the cover and make other custom choices. People are increasingly buying print-on-demand books, but they are still a small part of the overall market for books. Will print-on-demand and other technologies expand and eventually displace the traditional book? ◆ Subterranean movements also govern the way we spend our time. The average workweek has fallen steadily from 70 hours a week in the nineteenth century to 35 hours a week today. While the average workweek is now much shorter than it once was, far more people now have jobs. Why has the average workweek declined?

In this chapter, we're going to study a model of choice that predicts the effects of changes in prices and incomes on what people buy and that explains how much work people do. *Reading Between the Lines* explains why we buy print-on-demand books even though they cost a bit more than regular books.

After studying this chapter, you will be able to

- **Describe a household's budget line and show how it changes when a price or income changes**
- **Make a map of preferences by using indifference curves and explain the principle of diminishing marginal rate of substitution**
- **Predict the effects of changes in prices and income on consumption choices**
- **Predict the effects of changes in wage rates on work–leisure choices**

Consumption Possibilities

CONSUMPTION CHOICES ARE LIMITED BY INCOME and by prices. A household has a given amount of income to spend and cannot influence the prices of the goods and services it buys. A household's **budget line** describes the limits to its consumption choices.

Let's look at Lisa's budget line.[1] Lisa has an income of $30 a month to spend. She buys two goods: movies and pop. The price of a movie is $6, and the price of pop is $3 a six-pack. Figure 8.1 shows alternative affordable ways for Lisa to consume movies and pop. Row *A* says that she can buy 10 six-packs of pop and see no movies, a combination of movies and pop that exhausts her monthly income of $30. Row *F* says that Lisa can watch 5 movies and drink no pop—another combination that exhausts the $30 available. Each of the other rows in the table also exhausts Lisa's income. (Check that each of the other rows costs exactly $30.) The numbers in the table define Lisa's consumption possibilities. We can graph Lisa's consumption possibilities as points *A* through *F* in Fig. 8.1.

Divisible and Indivisible Goods Some goods—called divisible goods—can be bought in any quantity desired. Examples are gasoline and electricity. We can best understand household choice if we suppose that all goods and services are divisible. For example, Lisa can consume a half a movie a month on the average by seeing one movie every two months. When we think of goods as being divisible, the consumption possibilities are not just the points *A* through *F* shown in Fig. 8.1, but those points plus all the intermediate points that form the line running from *A* to *F*. Such a line is a budget line.

Lisa's budget line is a constraint on her choices. It marks the boundary between what is affordable and what is unaffordable. She can afford any point on the line and inside it. She cannot afford any point outside the line. The constraint on her consumption depends on prices and her income, and the constraint changes when prices or her income changes. Let's see how by studying the budget equation.

[1] If you have studied Chapter 7 on marginal utility theory, you have already met Lisa. This tale of her thirst for pop and zeal for movies will sound familiar to you—up to a point. But in this chapter, we're going to use a different method for representing preferences—one that does not require us to resort to the idea of utility.

FIGURE 8.1 The Budget Line

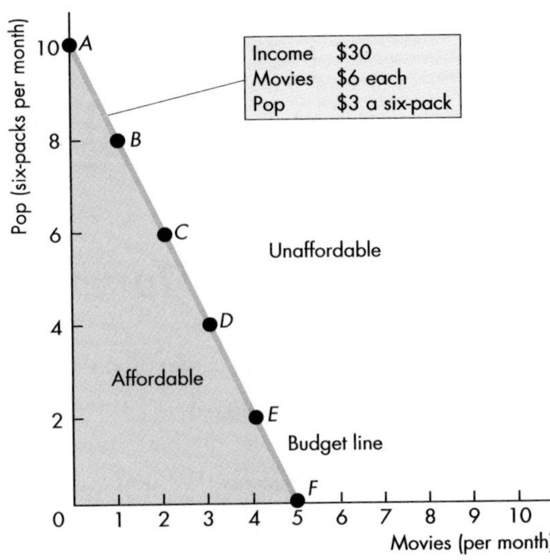

Consumption possibility	Movies (per month)	Pop (six-packs per month)
A	0	10
B	1	8
C	2	6
D	3	4
E	4	2
F	5	0

Lisa's budget line shows the boundary between what she can and cannot afford. The rows of the table list Lisa's affordable combinations of movies and pop when her income is $30, the price of pop is $3 a six-pack, and the price of a movie is $6. For example, row *A* tells us that Lisa exhausts her $30 income when she buys 10 six-packs and sees no movies. The figure graphs Lisa's budget line. Points *A* through *F* on the graph represent the rows of the table. For divisible goods, the budget line is the continuous line *AF*. To calculate the equation for Lisa's budget line, start with expenditure equal to income:

$$\$3Q_P + \$6Q_M = \$30.$$

Divide by $3 to obtain

$$Q_P + 2Q_M = 10.$$

Subtract $2Q_M$ from both sides to obtain

$$Q_P = 10 - 2Q_M.$$

The Budget Equation

We can describe the budget line by using a *budget equation.* The budget equation starts with the fact that

$$\text{Expenditure} = \text{Income.}$$

Expenditure is equal to the sum of the price of each good multiplied by the quantity bought. For Lisa,

$$\text{Expenditure} = (\text{Price of pop} \times \text{Quantity of pop}) + (\text{Price of movie} \times \text{Quantity of movies}).$$

Call the price of pop P_P, the quantity of pop Q_P, the price of a movie P_M, the quantity of movies Q_M, and income Y. We can now write Lisa's budget equation as

$$P_PQ_P + P_MQ_M = Y.$$

Or, using the prices Lisa faces, \$3 for a six-pack and \$6 for a movie, and Lisa's income, \$30, we get

$$\$3Q_P + \$6Q_M = \$30.$$

Lisa can choose any quantities of pop (Q_P) and movies (Q_M) that satisfy this equation. To find the relationship between these quantities, divide both sides of the equation by the price of pop (P_P) to get

$$Q_P + \frac{P_M}{P_P} \times Q_M = \frac{Y}{P_P}.$$

Now subtract the term $P_M/P_P \times Q_M$ from both sides of this equation to get

$$Q_P = \frac{Y}{P_P} - \frac{P_M}{P_P} \times Q_M.$$

For Lisa, income (Y) is \$30, the price of a movie (P_M) is \$6, and the price of pop (P_P) is \$3 a six-pack. So Lisa must choose the quantities of movies and pop to satisfy the equation

$$Q_P = \frac{\$30}{\$3} - \frac{\$6}{\$3} \times Q_M,$$

or

$$Q_P = 10 - 2Q_M.$$

To interpret the equation, look at the budget line in Fig. 8.1 and check that the equation delivers that budget line. First, set Q_M equal to zero. The budget equation tells us that Q_P, the quantity of pop, is Y/P_P, which is 10 six-packs. This combination of Q_M and Q_P is the one shown in row *A* of the table in Fig. 8.1. Next set Q_M equal to 5. Q_P now equals zero (row *F* of the table). Check that you can derive the other rows.

The budget equation contains two variables chosen by the household (Q_M and Q_P) and two variables (Y/P_P and P_M/P_P) that the household takes as given. Let's look more closely at these variables.

Real Income A household's **real income** is the household's income expressed as a quantity of goods the household can afford to buy. Expressed in terms of pop, Lisa's real income is Y/P_P. This quantity is the maximum number of six-packs that she can buy. It is equal to her money income divided by the price of pop. Lisa's income is \$30 and the price of pop is \$3 a six-pack, so her real income in terms of pop is 10 six-packs, which is shown in Fig. 8.1 as the point at which the budget line intersects the *y*-axis.

Relative Price A **relative price** is the price of one good divided by the price of another good. In Lisa's budget equation, the variable P_M/P_P is the relative price of a movie in terms of pop. For Lisa, P_M is \$6 a movie and P_P is \$3 a six-pack, so P_M/P_P is equal to 2 six-packs per movie. That is, to see 1 more movie, Lisa must give up 2 six-packs.

You've just calculated Lisa's opportunity cost of a movie. Recall that the opportunity cost of an action is the best alternative forgone. For Lisa to see 1 more movie a month, she must forgo 2 six-packs. You've also calculated Lisa's opportunity cost of pop. For Lisa to consume 2 more six-packs a month, she must give up seeing 1 movie. So her opportunity cost of 2 six-packs is 1 movie.

The relative price of a movie in terms of pop is the magnitude of the slope of Lisa's budget line. To calculate the slope of the budget line, recall the formula for slope (see the Chapter 1 Appendix): Slope equals the change in the variable measured on the *y*-axis divided by the change in the variable measured on the *x*-axis as we move along the line. In Lisa's case (Fig. 8.1), the variable measured on the *y*-axis is the quantity of pop, and the variable measured on the *x*-axis is the quantity of movies. Along Lisa's budget line, as pop decreases from 10 to 0 six-packs, movies increase from 0 to 5. So the magnitude of the slope of the budget line is 10 six-packs divided by 5 movies, or 2 six-packs per movie. The magnitude of this slope is exactly the same as the relative price we've just calculated. It is also the opportunity cost of a movie.

A Change in Prices When prices change, so does the budget line. The lower the price of the good measured on the horizontal axis, other things remain

FIGURE 8.2 Changes in Prices and Income

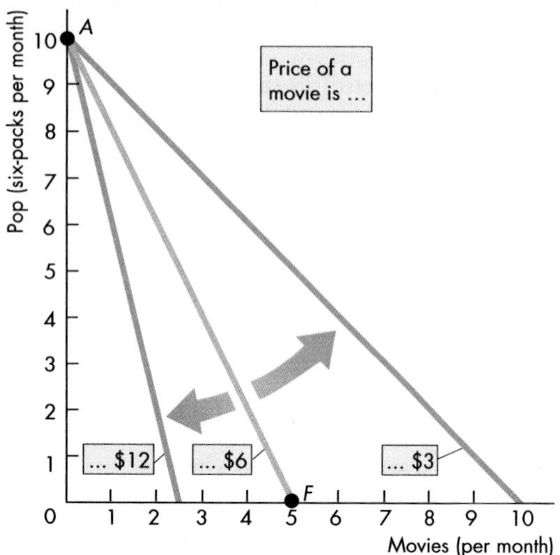

(a) A change in price

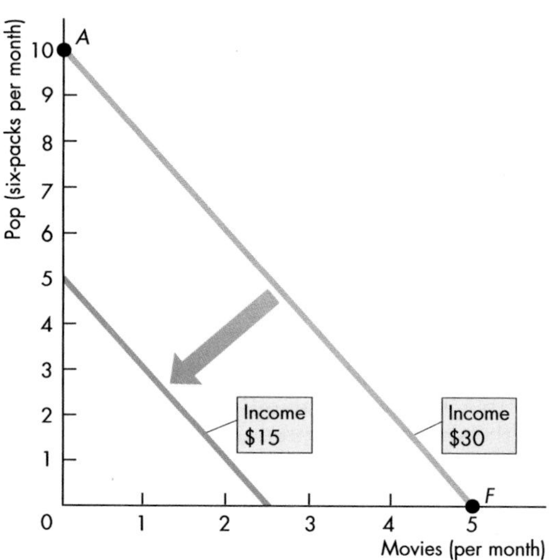

(b) A change in income

In part (a), the price of a movie changes. A fall in the price from \$6 to \$3 a movie rotates the budget line outward and makes it flatter. A rise in the price from \$6 to \$12 a movie rotates the budget line inward and makes it steeper.

In part (b), income falls from \$30 to \$15 while the prices of movies and pop remain constant. The budget line shifts leftward, but its slope does not change.

ing the same, the flatter is the budget line. For example, if the price of a movie falls from \$6 to \$3, real income in terms of pop does not change but the relative price of a movie falls. The budget line rotates outward and becomes flatter, as Fig. 8.2(a) illustrates. The higher the price of the good measured on the horizontal axis, other things remaining the same, the steeper is the budget line. For example, if the price of a movie rises from \$6 to \$12, the relative price of a movie increases. The budget line rotates inward and becomes steeper, as Fig. 8.2(a) illustrates.

A Change in Income A change in money income changes real income but does not change relative prices. The budget line shifts, but its slope does not change. The bigger a household's money income, the bigger is real income and the farther to the right is the budget line. The smaller a household's money income, the smaller is real income and the farther to the left is the budget line. Figure 8.2(b) shows the effect of a change in money income on Lisa's budget line. The initial budget line when Lisa's income is \$30 is the same one that we began with in Fig. 8.1. The new budget line shows how much Lisa can consume if her income falls to \$15 a month. The two budget lines have the same slope because they have the same relative price. The new budget line is closer to the origin than the initial one because Lisa's real income has decreased.

REVIEW QUIZ

1. What does a household's budget line show?
2. How does the relative price and a household's real income influence its budget line?
3. If a household has an income of \$40 and buys only bus rides at \$4 each and magazines at \$2 each, what is the equation of the household's budget line?
4. If the price of one good changes, what happens to the relative price and to the slope of the household's budget line?
5. If a household's money income changes and prices do not change, what happens to the household's real income and budget line?

We've studied the limits to what a household can consume. Let's now learn how we can describe preferences and make a map that contains a lot of information about a household's preferences.

Preferences and Indifference Curves

YOU ARE GOING TO DISCOVER A VERY NEAT IDEA: that of drawing a map of a person's preferences. A preference map is based on the intuitively appealing assumption that people can sort all the possible combinations of goods into three groups: preferred, not preferred, and indifferent. To make this idea more concrete, let's ask Lisa to tell us how she ranks various combinations of movies and pop.

Figure 8.3(a) shows part of Lisa's answer. She tells us that she currently consumes 2 movies and 6 six-packs a month at point *C*. She then lists all the combinations of movies and pop that she says are just as acceptable to her as her current consumption. When we plot these combinations of movies and pop, we get the green curve in Fig. 8.3(a). This curve is the key element in a map of preferences and is called an indifference curve.

An **indifference curve** is a line that shows combinations of goods among which a consumer is *indifferent.* The indifference curve in Fig. 8.3(a) tells us that Lisa is just as happy to consume 2 movies and 6 six-packs a month at point *C* as she is to consume the combination of movies and pop at point *G* or at any other point along the curve.

Lisa also says that she prefers all the combinations of movies and pop above the indifference curve in Fig. 8.3(a)—the yellow area—to those on the indifference curve. And she prefers any combination on the indifference curve to any combination in the grey area below the indifference curve.

The indifference curve in Fig. 8.3(a) is just one of a whole family of such curves. This indifference curve appears again in Fig. 8.3(b) labelled I_1. The curves labelled I_0 and I_2 are two other indifference curves. Lisa prefers any point on indifference curve I_2 to any point on indifference curve I_1, and she prefers any point on I_1 to any point on I_0. We refer to I_2 as being a higher indifference curve than I_1 and I_1 as being higher than I_0.

A preference map is a series of indifference curves that resembles the contour lines on a map. By looking at the shape of the contour lines on a map, we can draw conclusions about the terrain. Similarly, by looking at the shape of indifference curves, we can draw conclusions about a person's preferences.

Let's learn how to "read" a preference map.

FIGURE 8.3 A Preference Map

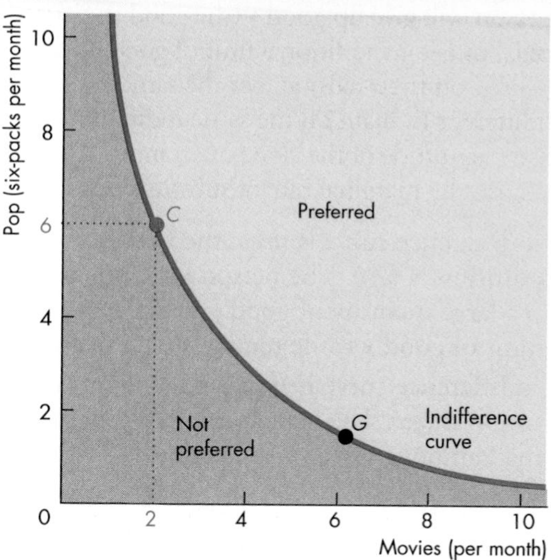

(a) An indifference curve

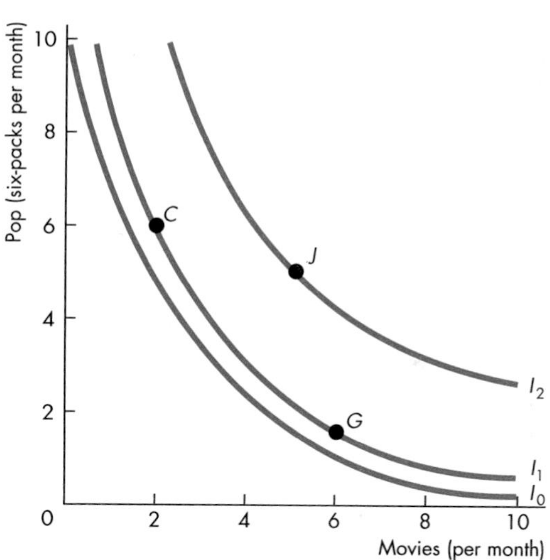

(b) Lisa's preference map

In part (a), Lisa consumes 6 six-packs of pop and 2 movies a month at point *C*. She is indifferent between all the points on the green indifference curve such as *C* and *G*. She prefers any point above the indifference curve (the yellow area) to any point on it, and she prefers any point on the indifference curve to any point below it (the grey area). A preference map is a number of indifference curves. Part (b) shows three indifference curves—I_0, I_1, and I_2—that are part of Lisa's preference map. She prefers point *J* to point *C* or *G*, and so she prefers any point on I_2 to any point on I_1.

Marginal Rate of Substitution

The **marginal rate of substitution** (*MRS*) is the rate at which a person will give up good *y* (the good measured on the *y*-axis) to get an additional unit of good *x* (the good measured on the *x*-axis) and at the same time remain indifferent (remain on the same indifference curve). The magnitude of the slope of an indifference curve measures the marginal rate of substitution.

- If the indifference curve is *steep*, the marginal rate of substitution is *high*. The person is willing to give up a large quantity of good *y* to get an additional unit of good *x* while remaining indifferent.
- If the indifference curve is *flat*, the marginal rate of substitution is *low*. The person is willing to give up a small amount of good *y* to get an additional unit of good *x* while remaining indifferent.

Figure 8.4 shows you how to calculate the marginal rate of substitution. Suppose that Lisa drinks 6 six-packs and sees 2 movies at point *C* on indifference curve I_1. To calculate her marginal rate of substitution, we measure the magnitude of the slope of the indifference curve at point *C*. To measure this magnitude, place a straight line against, or tangent to, the indifference curve at point *C*. Along that line, as the quantity of pop decreases by 10 six-packs, the number of movies increases by 5—an average of 2 six-packs per movie. So at point *C*, Lisa is willing to give up pop for movies at the rate of 2 six-packs per movie—a marginal rate of substitution of 2.

Now suppose that Lisa drinks 1.5 six-packs and sees 6 movies at point *G* in Fig. 8.4. Her marginal rate of substitution is now measured by the slope of the indifference curve at point *G*. That slope is the same as the slope of the tangent to the indifference curve at point *G*. Here, as the quantity of pop decreases by 4.5 six-packs, the number of movies increases by 9—an average of 1/2 six-pack per movie. So at point *G*, Lisa is willing to give up pop for movies at the rate of 1/2 six-pack per movie—a marginal rate of substitution of 1/2.

As Lisa sees more movies and drinks less pop, her marginal rate of substitution diminishes. Diminishing marginal rate of substitution is the key assumption of consumer theory. A **diminishing marginal rate of substitution** is a general tendency for a person to be willing to give up less of good *y* to get one more unit of good *x*, and at the same time remain indifferent, as the quantity of *x* increases. In Lisa's case, she is less willing to give up pop to see one more movie, the more movies she sees.

FIGURE 8.4 The Marginal Rate of Substitution

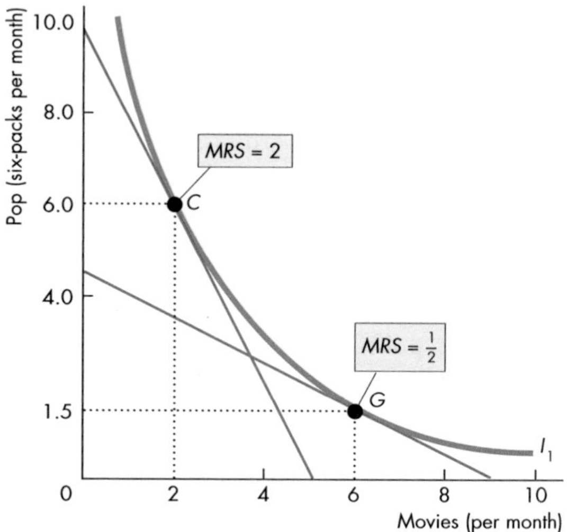

The magnitude of the slope of an indifference curve is called the marginal rate of substitution (*MRS*). The red line at point *C* tells us that Lisa is willing to give up 10 six-packs to see 5 movies. Her marginal rate of substitution at point *C* is 10 divided by 5, which equals 2. The red line at point *G* tells us that Lisa is willing to give up 4.5 six-packs to see 9 movies. Her marginal rate of substitution at point *G* is 4.5 divided by 9, which equals 1/2.

Your Own Diminishing Marginal Rate of Substitution Think about your own diminishing marginal rate of substitution. Imagine that in a week, you drink 10 six-packs of pop and see no movies. Most likely, you are willing to give up a lot of pop so that you can see just 1 movie. But now imagine that in a week, you drink 1 six-pack and see 6 movies. Most likely, you will now not be willing to give up much pop to see a seventh movie. As a general rule, the greater the number of movies you see, the smaller is the quantity of pop you are willing to give up to see one additional movie.

The shape of a person's indifference curves incorporates the principle of the diminishing marginal rate of substitution because the curves are bowed towards the origin. The tightness of the bend of an indifference curve tells us how willing a person is to substitute one good for another while remaining indifferent. Let's look at some examples that make this point clear.

Degree of Substitutability

Most of us would not regard movies and pop as being close substitutes. We probably have some fairly clear ideas about how many movies we want to see each month and how many cans of pop we want to drink. But to some degree, we are willing to substitute between these two goods. No matter how big a pop freak you are, there is surely some increase in the number of movies you can see that will compensate you for being deprived of a can of pop. Similarly, no matter how addicted you are to the movies, surely some number of cans of pop will compensate you for being deprived of seeing one movie. A person's indifference curves for movies and pop might look something like those shown in Fig. 8.5(a).

Close Substitutes Some goods substitute so easily for each other that most of us do not even notice which we are consuming. The different brands of personal computers are an example. As long as it has an "Intel inside" and runs Windows, most of us don't care whether our PC is a Dell, a Compaq, a Sony, or any of a dozen other brands. The same holds true for marker pens. Most of us don't care whether we use a marker pen from the campus bookstore or one from the local supermarket. When two goods are perfect substitutes, their indifference curves are straight lines that slope downward, as Fig. 8.5(b) illustrates. The marginal rate of substitution is constant.

Complements Some goods cannot substitute for each other at all. Instead, they are complements. The complements in Fig. 8.5(c) are left and right running shoes. Indifference curves of perfect complements are L-shaped. One left running shoe and one right running shoe are as good as one left shoe and two right ones. Having two of each is preferred to having one of each, but having two of one and one of the other is no better than having one of each.

The extreme cases of perfect substitutes and perfect complements shown here don't often happen in reality. But they do illustrate that the shape of the indifference curve shows the degree of substitutability between two goods. The more perfectly substitutable the two goods, the more nearly are their indifference curves straight lines and the less quickly does the

FIGURE 8.5 The Degree of Substitutability

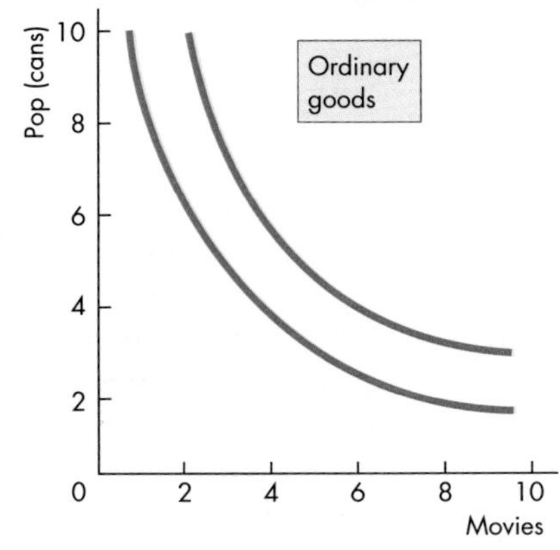

(a) Ordinary goods

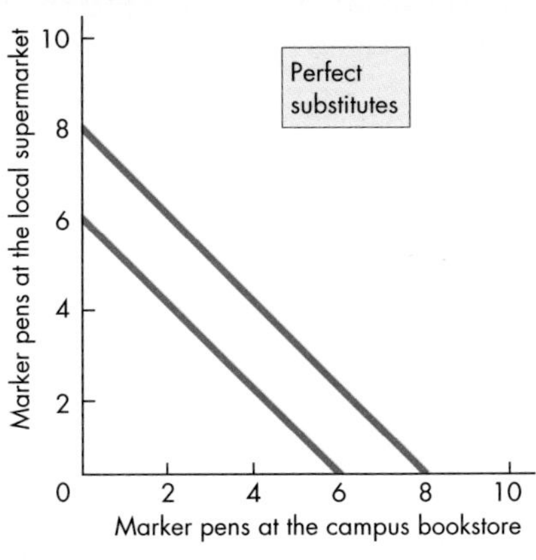

(b) Perfect substitutes

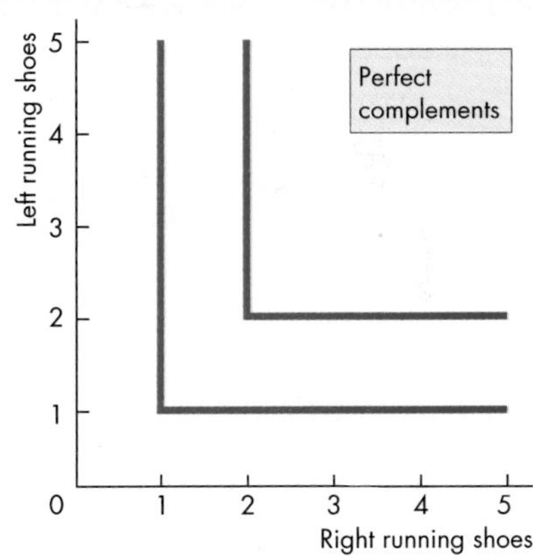

(c) Perfect complements

The shape of the indifference curves reveals the degree of substitutability between two goods. Part (a) shows the indifference curves for two ordinary goods: movies and pop. To drink less pop and remain indifferent, one must see more movies. The number of movies that compensates for a reduction in pop increases as less pop is consumed. Part (b) shows the indifference curves for two perfect substitutes. For the consumer to remain indifferent, one fewer marker pen from the local supermarket must be replaced by one extra marker pen from the campus bookstore. Part (c) shows two perfect complements—goods that cannot be substituted for each other at all. Having two left running shoes with one right running shoe is no better than having one of each. But having two of each is preferred to having one of each.

"With the pork I'd recommend an Alsatian white or a Coke."

marginal rate of substitution diminish. Poor substitutes for each other have tightly curved indifference curves, approaching the shape of those shown in Fig. 8.5(c).

As you can see in the cartoon, according to the waiter's preferences, Coke and Alsatian white wine are perfect substitutes and each is a complement of pork. We hope the customers agree with him.

REVIEW QUIZ

1. What is an indifference curve and how does a preference map show preferences?
2. Why does an indifference curve slope downward and why is it bowed towards the origin?
3. What do we call the magnitude of the slope of an indifference curve?
4. What is the key assumption about a consumer's marginal rate of substitution?

The two components of the model of household choice are now in place: the budget line and the preference map. We will now use these components to work out the household's choice and to predict how choices change when prices and income change.

Predicting Consumer Behaviour

WE ARE NOW GOING TO PREDICT THE QUANTITIES of movies and pop that Lisa chooses to buy. Figure 8.6 shows Lisa's budget line from Fig. 8.1 and her indifference curves from Fig. 8.3(b). We assume that Lisa consumes at her best affordable point, which is 2 movies and 6 six-packs—at point *C*. Here, Lisa

- Is on her budget line.
- Is on her highest attainable indifference curve.
- Has a marginal rate of substitution between movies and pop equal to the relative price.

For every point inside the budget line, such as point *I*, there are points *on* the budget line that Lisa prefers. For example, she prefers all the points on the

FIGURE 8.6 The Best Affordable Point

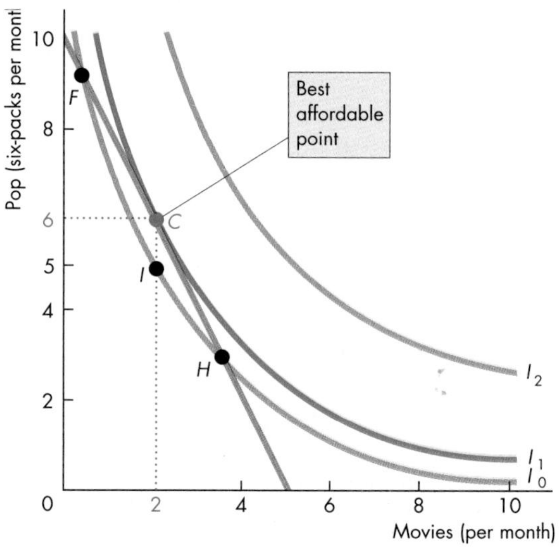

Lisa's best affordable point is *C*. At that point, she is on her budget line and also on the highest attainable indifference curve. At a point such as *H*, Lisa is willing to give up more movies in exchange for pop than she has to. She can move to point *I*, which is just as good as point *H*, and have some unspent income. She can spend that income and move to *C*, a point that she prefers to point *I*.

budget line between F and H to point I. So she chooses a point on the budget line.

Every point on the budget line lies on an indifference curve. For example, point H lies on the indifference curve I_0. At point H, Lisa's marginal rate of substitution is less than the relative price. Lisa is willing to give up more movies in exchange for pop than the budget line says she must. So she moves along her budget line from H towards C. As she does so, she passes through a number of indifference curves (not shown in the figure) located between indifference curves I_0 and I_1. All of these indifference curves are higher than I_0, and therefore Lisa prefers any point on them to point H. But when Lisa gets to point C, she is on the highest attainable indifference curve. If she keeps moving along the budget line, she starts to encounter indifference curves that are lower than I_1. So Lisa chooses point C.

At the chosen point, the marginal rate of substitution (the magnitude of the slope of the indifference curve) equals the relative price (the magnitude of the slope of the budget line).

Let's use this model of household choice to predict the effects on consumption of changes in prices and income. We'll begin by studying the effect of a change in price.

A Change in Price

The effect of a change in the price on the quantity of a good consumed is called the **price effect.** We will use Fig. 8.7(a) to work out the price effect of a fall in the price of a movie. We start with the price of a movie at \$6, the price of pop at \$3 a six-pack, and Lisa's income at \$30 a month. In this situation, she drinks 6 six-packs and sees 2 movies a month at point C.

Now suppose that the price of a movie falls to \$3. With a lower price of a movie, the budget line rotates outward and becomes flatter. (Check back to Fig. 8.2(a) for a refresher on how a price change affects the budget line.) The new budget line is the dark orange one in Fig. 8.7(a).

Lisa's best affordable point is now point J, where she sees 5 movies and drinks 5 six-packs of pop. Lisa drinks less pop and watches more movies now that movies are cheaper. She cuts her pop consumption from 6 to 5 six-packs and increases the number of movies she sees from 2 to 5 a month. Lisa substitutes movies for pop when the price of a movie falls and the price of pop and her income remain constant.

FIGURE 8.7 Price Effect and Demand Curve

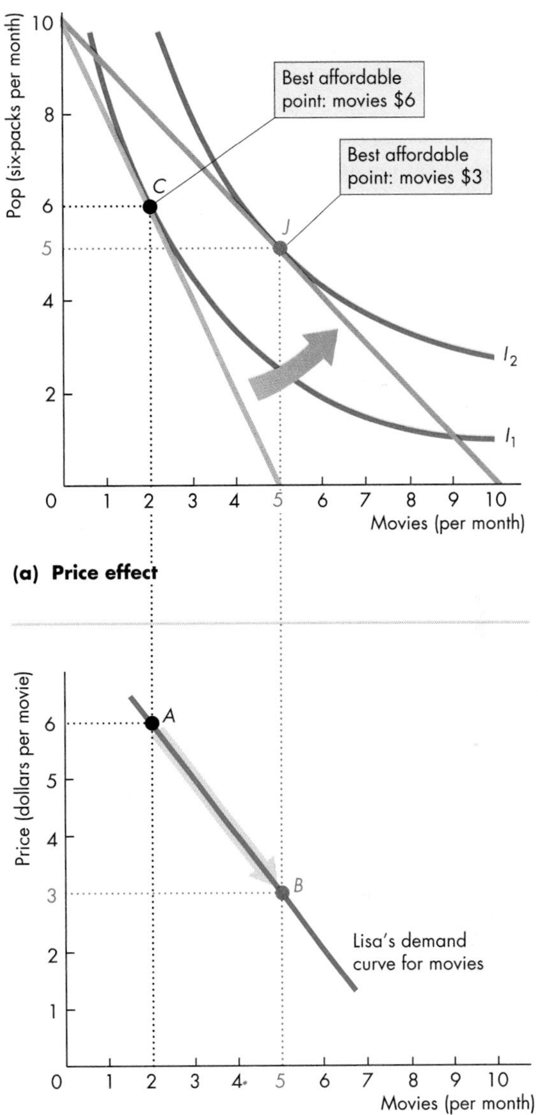

Initially, Lisa consumes at point C (part a). If the price of a movie falls from \$6 to \$3, Lisa consumes at point J. The move from C to J is the price effect.

At a price of \$6 a movie, Lisa sees 2 movies a month—at point A in part (b). At a price of \$3 a movie, she sees 5 movies a month—at point B. Lisa's demand curve traces out her best affordable quantity of movies as the price of a movie varies.

The Demand Curve In Chapter 3, we asserted that the demand curve slopes downward. We can now derive a demand curve from a consumer's budget line and indifference curves. By doing so, we can see that the law of demand and the downward-sloping demand curve are consequences of the consumer's choosing his or her best affordable combination of goods.

To derive Lisa's demand curve for movies, lower the price of a movie and find her best affordable point at different prices. We've just done this for two movie prices in Fig. 8.7(a). Figure 8.7(b) highlights these two prices and two points that lie on Lisa's demand curve for movies. When the price of a movie is \$6, Lisa sees 2 movies a month at point *A*. When the price falls to \$3, she increases the number of movies she sees to 5 a month at point *B*. The demand curve is made up of these two points plus all the other points that tell us Lisa's best affordable consumption of movies at each movie price, given the price of pop and Lisa's income. As you can see, Lisa's demand curve for movies slopes downward—the lower the price of a movie, the more movies she watches each month. This is the law of demand.

Next, let's see how Lisa changes her consumption of movies and pop when her income changes.

A Change in Income

The effect of a change in income on consumption is called the **income effect.** Let's work out the income effect by examining how consumption changes when income changes and prices remain constant. Figure 8.8(a) shows the income effect when Lisa's income falls. With an income of \$30 and with the price of a movie at \$3 and the price of pop at \$3 a six-pack, she consumes at point *J*—she sees 5 movies and drinks 5 six-packs. If her income falls to \$21, she consumes at point *K*—she sees 4 movies and drinks 3 six-packs. When Lisa's income falls, she consumes less of both goods. Movies and pop are normal goods.

The Demand Curve and the Income Effect A change in income leads to a shift in the demand curve, as shown in Fig. 8.8(b). With an income of \$30, Lisa's demand curve for movies is D_0, the same as in Fig. 8.7(b). But when her income falls to \$21, she plans to see fewer movies at each price, so her demand curve for movies shifts leftward to D_1.

FIGURE 8.8 Income Effect and Change in Demand

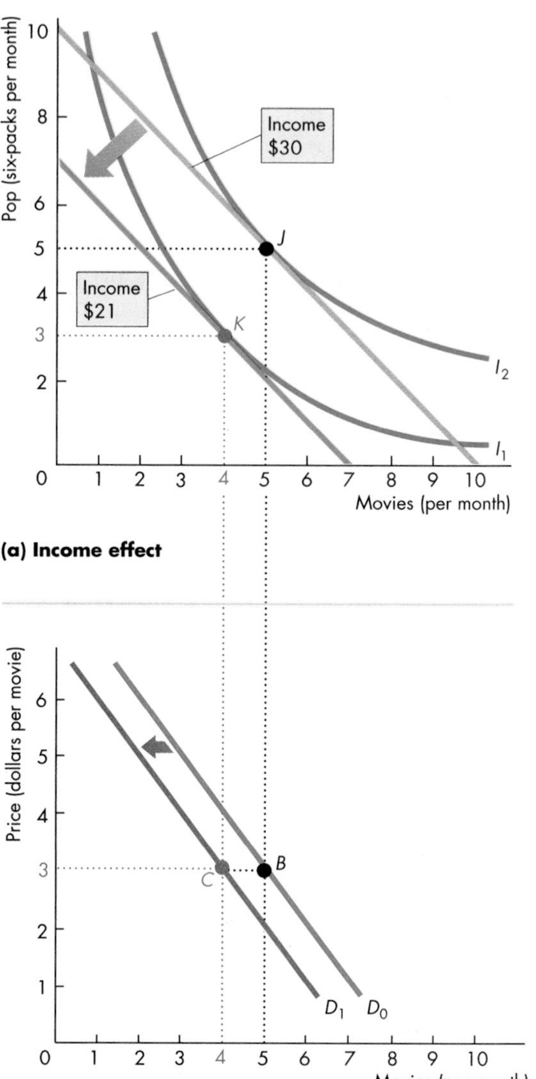

A change in income shifts the budget line and changes the best affordable point and changes consumption. In part (a), when Lisa's income decreases from \$30 to \$21, she consumes less of both movies and pop. In part (b), Lisa's demand curve for movies when her income is \$30 is D_0. When Lisa's income decreases to \$21, her demand curve for movies shifts leftward to D_1. Lisa's demand for movies decreases because she now sees fewer movies at each price.

Substitution Effect and Income Effect

For a normal good, a fall in price *always* increases the quantity bought. We can prove this assertion by dividing the price effect into two parts:

- Substitution effect
- Income effect

Figure 8.9(a) shows the price effect, and Fig. 8.9(b) divides the price effect into its two parts.

Substitution Effect The **substitution effect** is the effect of a change in price on the quantity bought when the consumer (hypothetically) remains indifferent between the original situation and the new one. To work out Lisa's substitution effect, when the price of a movie falls, we cut her income by enough to leave her on the same indifference curve as before.

When the price of a movie falls from \$6 to \$3, suppose (hypothetically) that we cut Lisa's income to \$21. What's special about \$21? It is the income that is just enough, at the new price of a movie, to keep Lisa's best affordable point on the same indifference curve as her original consumption point *C*. Lisa's budget line is now the light orange line in Fig. 8.9(b). With the lower price of a movie and a smaller income, Lisa's best affordable point is *K* on indifference curve I_1. The move from *C* to *K* is the substitution effect of the price change. The substitution effect of the fall in the price of a movie is an increase in the consumption of movies from 2 to 4. The direction of the substitution effect never varies: When the relative price of a good falls, the consumer substitutes more of that good for the other good.

Income Effect To calculate the substitution effect, we gave Lisa a \$9 pay cut. To calculate the income effect, we give Lisa her \$9 back. The \$9 increase in income shifts Lisa's budget line outward, as shown in Fig. 8.9(b). The slope of the budget line does not change because both prices remain constant. This change in Lisa's budget line is similar to the one illustrated in Fig. 8.8. As Lisa's budget line shifts outward, her consumption possibilities expand and her best affordable point becomes *J* on indifference curve I_2. The move from *K* to *J* is the income effect of the price change. In this example, as Lisa's income increases, she increases her consumption of movies. For Lisa, a movie is a normal good. For a normal good, the income effect reinforces the substitution effect.

FIGURE 8.9 Substitution Effect and Income Effect

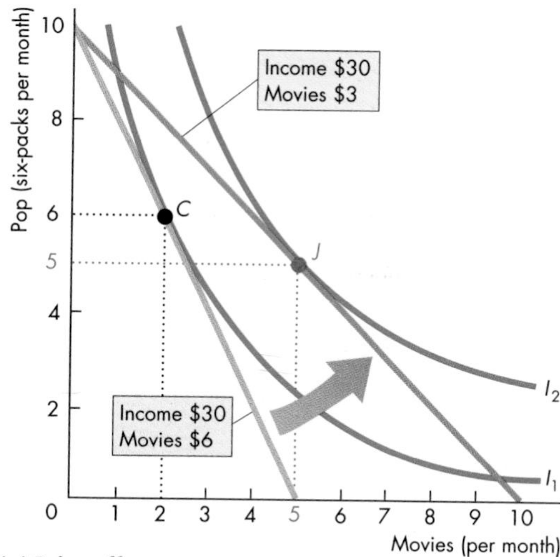

(a) Price effect

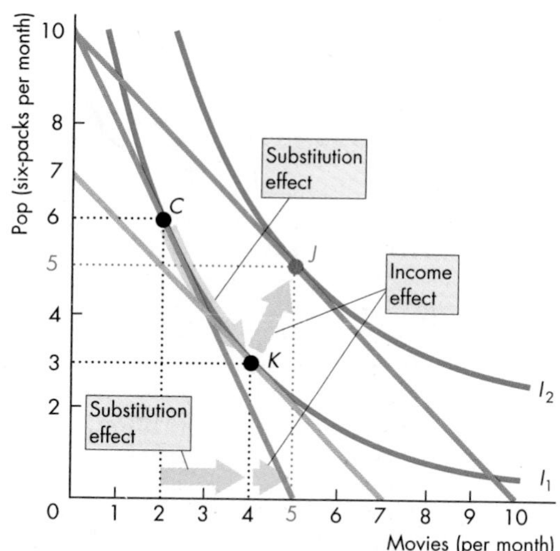

(b) Substitution effect and income effect

The price effect in part (a) can be separated into a substitution effect and an income effect in part (b). To isolate the substitution effect, we confront Lisa with the new price but keep her on her original indifference curve, I_1. The substitution effect is the move from *C* to *K*. To isolate the income effect, we confront Lisa with the new price of a movie but increase her income so that she can move from the original indifference curve, I_1, to the new one, I_2. The income effect is the move from *K* to *J*.

Inferior Goods The example that we have just studied is that of a change in the price of a normal good. The effect of a change in the price of an inferior good is different. Recall that an inferior good is one whose consumption decreases as income increases. For an inferior good, the income effect is negative. Thus for an inferior good, a lower price does not always lead to an increase in the quantity demanded. The lower price has a substitution effect that increases the quantity demanded. But the lower price also has a negative income effect that reduces the demand for the inferior good. Thus the income effect offsets the substitution effect to some degree. If the negative income effect exceeded the positive substitution effect, the demand curve would slope upward. This case does not appear to occur in the real world.

Back to the Facts

We started this chapter by observing how consumer spending has changed over the years. The indifference curve model explains those changes. Spending patterns are determined by best affordable choices. Changes in prices and incomes change the best affordable choice and change consumption patterns.

REVIEW QUIZ

1. When a consumer chooses the combination of goods and services to buy, what is she or he trying to achieve?
2. Can you explain the conditions that are met when a consumer has found the best affordable combination of goods to buy? (Use the terms budget line, marginal rate of substitution, and relative price in your explanation.)
3. If the price of a normal good falls, what happens to the quantity demanded of that good?
4. Into what two effects can we divide the effect of a price change?
5. For a normal good, does the income effect reinforce the substitution effect or does it partly offset the substitution effect?

The model of household choice can explain many other household choices. Let's look at one of them.

Work–Leisure Choices

HOUSEHOLDS MAKE MANY CHOICES OTHER THAN those about how to spend their income on the various goods and services available. We can use the model of household choice to understand many other household choices. Some of these choices are discussed in the part closer on pp. 190–194. Here we'll study a key choice: how much labour to supply.

Labour Supply

Every week, we allocate our 168 hours between working—called *labour*—and all other activities—called *leisure.* How do we decide how to allocate our time between labour and leisure? We can answer this question by using the theory of household choice.

The more hours we spend on *leisure,* the smaller is our income. The relationship between leisure and income is described by an *income–time budget line.* Figure 8.10(a) shows Lisa's income–time budget line. If Lisa devotes the entire week to leisure—168 hours—she has no income and is at point *Z*. By supplying labour in exchange for a wage, she can convert hours into income along the income–time budget line. The slope of that line is determined by the hourly wage rate. If the wage rate is $5 an hour, Lisa faces the flattest budget line. If the wage rate is $10 an hour, she faces the middle budget line. And if the wage rate is $15 an hour, she faces the steepest budget line.

Lisa buys leisure by not supplying labour and by forgoing income. The opportunity cost of an hour of leisure is the hourly wage rate forgone.

Figure 8.10(a) also shows Lisa's indifference curves for income and leisure. Lisa chooses her best attainable point. This choice of income and time allocation is just like her choice of movies and pop. She gets onto the highest possible indifference curve by making her marginal rate of substitution between income and leisure equal to her wage rate. Lisa's choice depends on the wage rate she can earn. At a wage rate of $5 an hour, Lisa chooses point *A* and works 20 hours a week (168 minus 148) for an income of $100 a week. At a wage rate of $10 an hour, she chooses point *B* and works 35 hours a week (168 minus 133) for an income of $350 a week. And at a wage rate of $15 an hour, she chooses point *C* and works 30 hours a week (168 minus 138) for an income of $450 a week.

FIGURE 8.10 The Supply of Labour

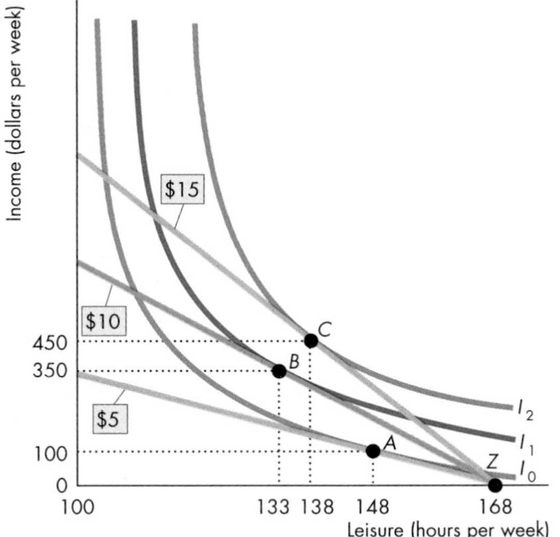

(a) Time allocation decision

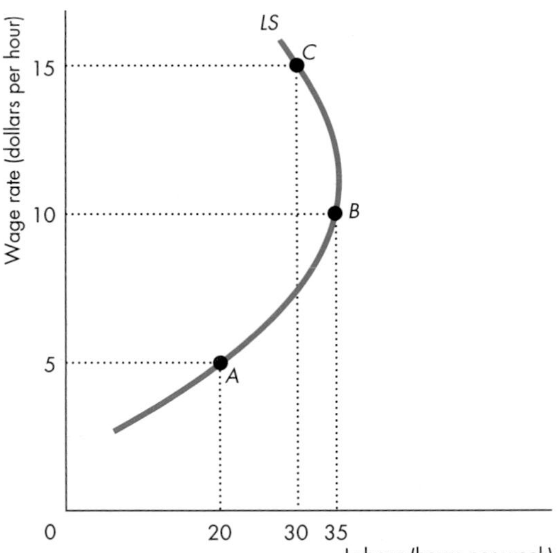

(b) Labour supply curve

In part (a), at a wage rate of $5 an hour, Lisa takes 148 hours of leisure and works 20 hours a week at point *A*. If the wage rate increases from $5 to $10, she decreases her leisure to 133 hours and increases her work to 35 hours a week at point *B*. But if the wage rate increases from $10 to $15, Lisa *increases* her leisure to 138 hours and *decreases* her work to 30 hours a week at point *C*. Part (b) shows Lisa's labour supply curve. Points *A*, *B*, and *C* on the supply curve correspond to Lisa's choices on her income–time budget line in part (a).

The Labour Supply Curve

Figure 8.10(b) shows Lisa's labour supply curve. This curve shows that as the wage rate increases from $5 to $10 an hour, Lisa increases the quantity of labour supplied from 20 hours to 35 hours a week. But when the wage rate increases to $15 an hour, she decreases her quantity of labour supplied to 30 hours a week.

Lisa's supply of labour is similar to that described for the economy as a whole at the beginning of this chapter. As wage rates have increased, work hours have decreased. At first, this pattern seems puzzling. We've seen that the hourly wage rate is the opportunity cost of leisure. So a higher wage rate means a higher opportunity cost of leisure. This fact on its own leads to a decrease in leisure and an increase in work hours. But instead, we've cut our work hours. Why? Because our incomes have increased. As the wage rate increases, incomes increase, so people demand more of all normal goods. Leisure is a normal good, so as incomes increase, people demand more leisure.

The higher wage rate has both a *substitution effect* and an *income effect*. The higher wage rate increases the opportunity cost of leisure and so leads to a substitution effect away from leisure. And the higher wage rate increases income and so leads to an income effect towards more leisure. This outcome of rational household choice explains why the average workweek has fallen steadily as wage rates have increased. With higher wage rates, people have decided to use their higher incomes in part to consume more leisure.

REVIEW QUIZ

1 What is the opportunity cost of leisure?
2 Why might a rise in the wage rate lead to an increase in leisure and a decrease in work hours?

Reading Between the Lines on pp. 184–185 shows you how the theory of household choice explains why people buy print-on-demand books even though they cost more than regular books and what might happen in the market for books as the price of a print-on-demand book gets closer to the price of a regular book.

In the chapters that follow, we study firms' choices. We'll see how, in the pursuit of profit, firms make choices that determine the supply of goods and services and the demand for productive resources.

READING BETWEEN THE LINES

Regular Books versus Print-on-Demand Books

THE GLOBE AND MAIL, April 5, 2002

E-books a new chapter in publishing

Audrey McNeill is an avid reader, so when she heard that her favourite book store in Cambridge, Ont., was selling some tough-to-find classics in a new print-on-demand format, she jumped at the opportunity.

Last week, Ms. McNeill bought three books-on-demand from Books Express as birthday gifts for her daughter: a two-volume set of George Eliot's *Adam Bede* for $20, and Anne Bronte's *Agnes Grey* at $12.50.

It took the retailer five minutes to produce each tome, by downloading the content from a computer, printing the pages, trimming and mechanically binding them together—all at the book seller's new "InstaBook" counter.

A big perk of the InstaBook invention was that it allowed Ms. McNeill to personalize the cover by having her daughter's name printed on it.

"The books weren't available in the store," says the Kitchener resident, who paid slightly more for the books than they would cost in regular paperback. "I wanted to get something personalized. ... My daughter was thrilled."

InstaBook is one of a number of print-on-demand systems slowly coming on stream in North America. Some observers see the technology as an integral step to publishers and book buyers alike becoming more comfortable with electronic books—hyped heavily a couple of years ago but slow to find acceptance.

... Daniel O'Brien, a senior analyst at U.S.-based Forrester Research ... sees potential in print-on-demand books as well as textbooks and technical books in digital form. His research has forecast that print-on-demand will be a $3.9-billion (U.S.) market in the United States by 2005 from a projected $244-million in 2000.

Over all, Forrester expects custom publishing, digital textbooks and consumer e-books to reach $7.8-billion in sales, or 17.5 per cent of the U.S. publishing industry, by 2005.

...

Essence of the Story

- Audrey McNeill bought three books-on-demand from Books Express.
- It took five minutes to produce each book at the book seller's "InstaBook" counter.
- InstaBook allows the consumer to personalize the book's cover.
- The price of an InstaBook is slightly higher than the price of a regular paperback.
- One analyst predicts that print-on-demand will be a $3.9-billion (U.S.) market in the United States by 2005 from a projected $244 million in 2000 and that custom publishing, digital textbooks, and consumer e-books will reach $7.8 billion or 17.5 percent of total revenue in the U.S. publishing industry, by 2005.

Economic Analysis

- Regular books and print-on-demand books are good substitutes, but probably not perfect substitutes for most people.

- When two goods are close substitutes, the marginal rate of substitution doesn't change much as the quantities consumed change, so the indifference curves are relatively straight and a small change in the relative price brings a large change in the quantities bought.

- Figure 1 shows an example of what Audrey McNeill's indifference curves for regular books and print-on-demand books might look like.

- The figure also shows two budget lines, the line *AB* and the line *AC*.

- Along the budget line *AC*, the price of a regular book is the same as the price of a print-on-demand book.

- Along the budget line *AB*, the price of a print-on-demand book is higher than the price of a regular book.

- Suppose that Audrey has a budget for books that enables her to buy 9 regular books a year and no print-on-demand books.

- Because the price of a print-on-demand book is greater than the price of a regular book, she faces the budget line *AB*.

- Audrey's best affordable point, where her budget line just touches her indifference curve I_0, is where she buys 5 regular books and 3 print-on-demand books a year.

- If print-on-demand technology improves and the price of a print-on-demand book falls to that of a regular book, Audrey's budget line rotates outward to become the budget line *AC*.

- With the lower relative price of a print-on-demand book, she substitutes in favour of that type of book.

- Audrey's best affordable point now becomes that at which she buys 6 print-on-demand books and 3 regular books a year.

- If print-on-demand books and regular books are indeed close substitutes, the growth in revenue from print-on-demand and other new technologies predicted in the news article does seem likely.

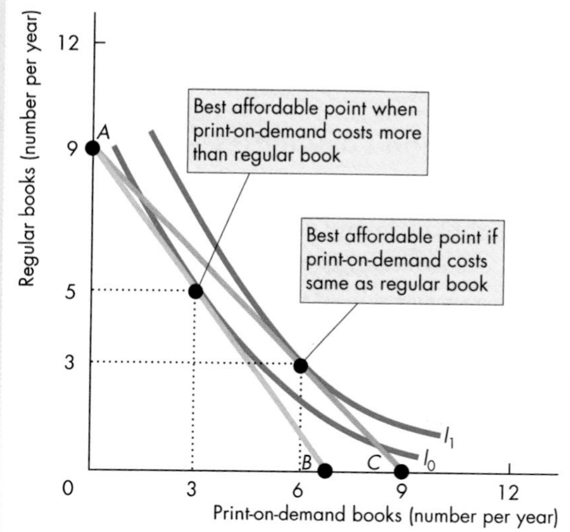

Figure 1 Audrey McNeill's choices

SUMMARY

KEY POINTS

Consumption Possibilities (pp. 172–174)

- The budget line is the boundary between what the household can and cannot afford given its income and the prices of goods.
- The point at which the budget line intersects the *y*-axis is the household's real income in terms of the good measured on that axis.
- The magnitude of the slope of the budget line is the relative price of the good measured on the *x*-axis in terms of the good measured on the *y*-axis.
- A change in price changes the slope of the budget line. A change in income shifts the budget line but does not change its slope.

Preferences and Indifference Curves (pp. 175–178)

- A consumer's preferences can be represented by indifference curves. An indifference curve joins all the combinations of goods among which the consumer is indifferent.
- A consumer prefers any point above an indifference curve to any point on it and any point on an indifference curve to any point below it.
- The magnitude of the slope of an indifference curve is called the marginal rate of substitution.
- The marginal rate of substitution diminishes as consumption of the good measured on the *y*-axis decreases and consumption of the good measured on the *x*-axis increases.

Predicting Consumer Behaviour (pp. 178–182)

- A household consumes at its best affordable point. This point is on the budget line and on the highest attainable indifference curve and has a marginal rate of substitution equal to relative price.
- The effect of a price change (the price effect) can be divided into a substitution effect and an income effect.
- The substitution effect is the effect of a change in price on the quantity bought when the consumer (hypothetically) remains indifferent between the original and the new situation.
- The substitution effect always results in an increase in consumption of the good whose relative price has fallen.
- The income effect is the effect of a change in income on consumption.
- For a normal good, the income effect reinforces the substitution effect. For an inferior good, the income effect works in the opposite direction to the substitution effect.

Work–Leisure Choices (pp. 182–183)

- The indifference curve model of household choice enables us to understand how a household allocates its time between work and leisure.
- Work hours have decreased and leisure hours have increased because the income effect on the demand for leisure has been greater than the substitution effect.

KEY FIGURES

Figure 8.1 The Budget Line, 172
Figure 8.2 Changes in Prices and Income, 174
Figure 8.3 A Preference Map, 175
Figure 8.4 The Marginal Rate of Substitution, 176
Figure 8.6 The Best Affordable Point, 178
Figure 8.7 Price Effect and Demand Curve, 179
Figure 8.8 Income Effect and Change in Demand, 180
Figure 8.9 Substitution Effect and Income Effect, 181

KEY TERMS

Budget line, 172
Diminishing marginal rate of substitution, 176
Income effect, 180
Indifference curve, 175
Marginal rate of substitution, 176
Price effect, 179
Real income, 173
Relative price, 173
Substitution effect, 181

PROBLEMS

*1. Sara's income is $12 a week. The price of popcorn is $3 a bag, and the price of cola is $3 a can.

a. What is Sara's real income in terms of cola?
b. What is her real income in terms of popcorn?
c. What is the relative price of cola in terms of popcorn?
d. What is the opportunity cost of a can of cola?
e. Calculate the equation for Sara's budget line (placing bags of popcorn on the left side of the equation).
f. Draw a graph of Sara's budget line with cola on the *x*-axis.
g. In part (f), what is the slope of Sara's budget line? What determines its value?

2. Rashid's income is $100 per week. The price of a CD is $10, and the price of a book is $20.

a. What is Rashid's real income in terms of CDs?
b. What is his real income in terms of books?
c. What is the relative price of a CD in terms of books?
d. What is the opportunity cost of a book?
e. Calculate the equation for Rashid's budget line (placing books on the left side of the equation).
f. Draw a graph of Rashid's budget line with CDs on the *x*-axis.
g. In part (f), what is the slope of Rashid's budget line? What determines its value?

*3. Sara's income and the prices of popcorn and cola are the same as those in problem 1. The figure illustrates Sara's preferences.

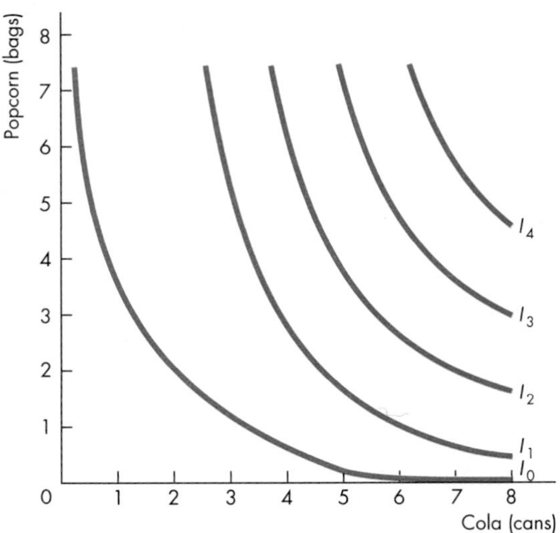

a. What quantities of popcorn and cola does Sara buy?
b. What is Sara's marginal rate of substitution at the point at which she consumes?

4. Rashid's income and the prices of CDs and books are the same as those in problem 2. The figure illustrates his preferences.

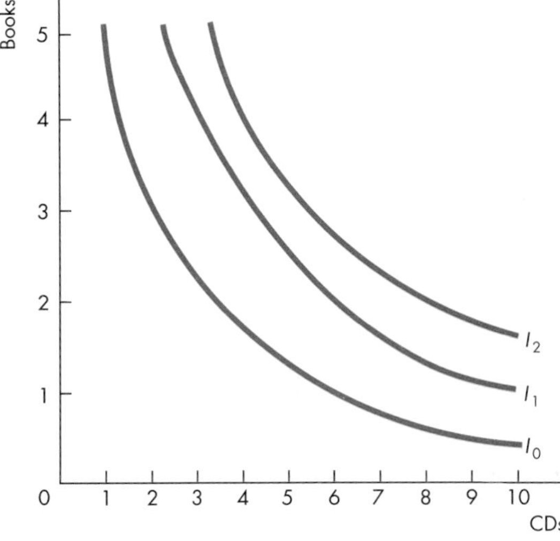

a. What quantities of CDs and books does Rashid buy?
b. What is Rashid's marginal rate of substitution at the point at which he consumes?

*5. Now suppose that in problem 3, the price of cola falls to $1.50 a can and the price of popcorn and Sara's income remain the same.

a. What quantities of cola and popcorn does Sara now buy?
b. Find two points on Sara's demand curve for cola.
c. Find the substitution effect of the price change.
d. Find the income effect of the price change.
e. Is cola a normal good or an inferior good for Sara?

6. Now suppose that in problem 4, the price of a CD rises to $20 and the price of a book and Rashid's income remain the same.

a. What quantities of CDs and books does Rashid now buy?
b. Find two points on Rashid's demand curve for CDs.
c. Find the substitution effect of the price change.
d. Find the income effect of the price change.
e. Is a CD a normal good or an inferior good for Rashid?

*7. Pam buys cookies and comic books. The price of a cookie is $1, and the price of a comic book is $2. Each month, Pam spends all of her income and buys 30 cookies and 5 comic books. Next month, the price of a cookie will fall to 50¢ and the price of a comic book will rise to $5. Assume that Pam's preference map is similar to that in Fig. 8.5(a). Use a graph to answer the following questions.
   a. Will Pam be able to buy 30 cookies and 5 comic books next month?
   b. Will Pam want to buy 30 cookies and 5 comic books?
   c. Which situation does Pam prefer: cookies at $1 and comic books at $2, or cookies at 50¢ and comic books at $3?
   d. If Pam changes the quantities that she buys next month, which good will she buy more of and which will she buy less of?
   e. When the prices change next month, will there be both an income effect and a substitution effect at work or just one of them?

8. Yangjie buys smoothies and sushi. The price of a smoothie is $5, and the price of sushi is $1 a piece. Each month, Yangjie spends all of her income and buys 10 smoothies and 20 pieces of sushi. Next month, the price of a smoothie will fall to $3 and the price of sushi will rise to $2 a piece. Assume that Yangjie's preference map is similar to that in Fig. 8.5(a). Use a graph to answer the following questions.
   a. Will Yangjie be able to buy 10 smoothies and 20 pieces of sushi next month?
   b. Will Yangjie want to buy 10 smoothies and 20 pieces of sushi? Explain why.
   c. Which situation does Yangjie prefer: smoothies at $5 each and sushi at $1 a piece or smoothies at $3 each and sushi at $2 a piece?
   d. If Yangjie changes the quantities that she buys next month, which good will she buy more of and which will she buy less of?
   e. When the prices change next month, will there be both an income effect and a substitution effect at work or just one of them? Explain.

CRITICAL THINKING

1. Study *Reading Between the Lines* about print-on-demand books on pp. 184–185, and then answer the following questions.
   a. How do you buy books?
   b. Sketch your budget constraint for books and other items.
   c. Sketch your indifference curves for books and other goods.
   d. What do you predict would happen to the way that you buy books if the price of a conventional book increased and the price of a print-on-demand book decreased, leaving you able to buy exactly the same quantity of books as you buy now?
2. Some people say that the GST should be scrapped. If the GST, a tax on both goods and services, were replaced by a higher rate of provincial sales tax, a tax on goods but not on services
   a. What would happen to the relative price of CD-Rs and haircuts?
   b. What would happen to the budget line that shows the quantities of CD-Rs and haircuts you can afford to buy?
   c. How would you change your purchases of CD-Rs and haircuts?
   d. Which type of tax is better for the consumer and why?

   Use a graph to illustrate your answers and to show the substitution effect and the income effect of the price change.

WEB EXERCISES

1. Use the links on the Parkin–Bade Web site to obtain information about the prices of cell phone service and first-class mail.
   a. Sketch the budget constraint for a consumer who spent $50 a month on these two goods in 1999 and 2001.
   b. Can you say whether the consumer was better off or worse off in 2001 than in 1999?
   c. Sketch some indifference curves for cell phone calls and first-class letters mailed, and show the income effect and the substitution effect of the changes in prices that occurred between 1999 and 2001.

UNDERSTANDING HOUSEHOLDS' CHOICES

Making the Most of Life

The powerful forces of demand and supply shape the fortunes of families, businesses, nations, and empires in the same unrelenting way that the tides and winds shape rocks and coastlines. You saw in Chapters 3 through 6 how these forces raise and lower prices, increase and decrease quantities bought and sold, cause revenues to fluctuate, and send resources to their most valuable uses. ◆ These powerful forces begin quietly and privately with the choices that each one of us makes. Chapters 7 and 8 probe these individual choices. Chapter 7 explores the marginal utility theory of human decisions. This theory explains people's consumption of leisure time and its flip side, the supply of work time. Marginal utility theory can even be used to explain "non-economic" choices, such as whether to marry and how many children to have. In a sense, there are no non-economic choices. If there is scarcity, there must be choice. And economics studies all such choices. Chapter 8 describes a tool that enables us to make a map of people's likes and dislikes, a tool called an *indifference curve*. Indifference curves are considered an advanced topic, so this chapter is *strictly optional.* But the presentation of indifference curves in Chapter 8 is the clearest and most straightforward available, so if you want to learn about this tool, this chapter is the place to do so. ◆ The earliest economists (Adam Smith and his contemporaries) did not have a very deep understanding of households' choices. It was not until the nineteenth century that progress was made in this area. On the following pages, you can spend some time with Jeremy Bentham, the person who pioneered the use of the concept of utility to the study of human choices, and with Gary Becker of the University of Chicago, who is one of today's most influential students of human behaviour.

PROBING THE IDEAS

People as Rational Decision Makers

The Economist

"... It is the greatest happiness of the greatest number that is the measure of right and wrong."

JEREMY BENTHAM
Fragment on Government

JEREMY BENTHAM *(1748–1832), who lived in London, was the son and grandson of a lawyer and was himself trained as a barrister. But he rejected the opportunity to maintain the family tradition and, instead, spent his life as a writer, activist, and Member of Parliament in the pursuit of rational laws that would bring the greatest happiness to the greatest number of people.*

Bentham, whose embalmed body is preserved to this day in a glass cabinet in the University of London, was the first person to use the concept of utility to explain human choices. But in Bentham's day, the distinction between explaining and prescribing was not a sharp one, and Bentham was ready to use his ideas to tell people how they ought to behave. He was one of the first to propose pensions for the retired, guaranteed employment, minimum wages, and social benefits such as free education and free medical care.

The Issues

The economic analysis of human behaviour in the family, the workplace, the markets for goods and services, the markets for labour services, and financial markets is based on the idea that our behaviour can be understood as a response to scarcity. Everything we do can be understood as a choice that maximizes total benefit subject to the constraints imposed by our limited resources and technology. If people's preferences are stable in the face of changing constraints, then we have a chance of predicting how they will respond to an evolving environment.

The economic approach explains the incredible change that has occurred during the past 100 years in the way women allocate their time as the consequences of changing constraints, not of changing attitudes. Technological advances have equipped the nation's farms and factories with machines that have increased the productivity of both women and men, thereby raising the wages they can earn. The increasingly technological world has increased the return to education for both women and men and has led to a large increase in high school and college graduates of both sexes. And equipped with an ever-widening array of gadgets and appliances that cut the time taken to do household jobs, an increasing proportion of women have joined the labour force.

The economic explanation might not be correct, but it is a powerful one. And if it is correct, the changing attitudes are a consequence, not a cause, of the economic advancement of women.

Then

Economists explain people's actions as the consequences of choices that maximize total utility subject to constraints. In the 1890s, fewer than 20 percent of women chose market employment, and most of those who did had low-paying and unattractive jobs. The other 80 percent of women chose nonmarket work in the home. What constraints led to these choices?

Now

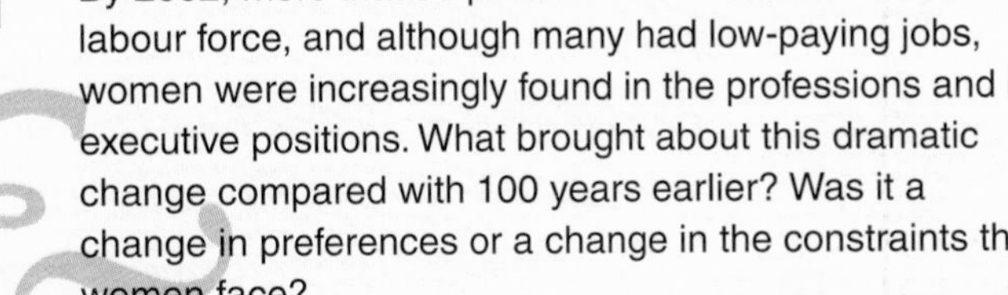

By 2002, more that 60 percent of women were in the labour force, and although many had low-paying jobs, women were increasingly found in the professions and in executive positions. What brought about this dramatic change compared with 100 years earlier? Was it a change in preferences or a change in the constraints that women face?

Today, one economist who stands out above all others and who stands on the shoulders of Jeremy Bentham is Gary Becker of the University of Chicago. Professor Becker has transformed the way we think about human choices. You can meet him on the following pages.

TALKING WITH

GARY S. BECKER *is Professor of Economics and Sociology at the University of Chicago. Born in 1930 in Pottsville, Pennsylvania, he was an undergraduate at Princeton University and a graduate student at the University of Chicago. His graduate supervisor was Milton Friedman, and his Ph.D. thesis became the book* The Economics of Discrimination, *a work that profoundly changed the way we think about discrimination and economic ways of reducing it.*

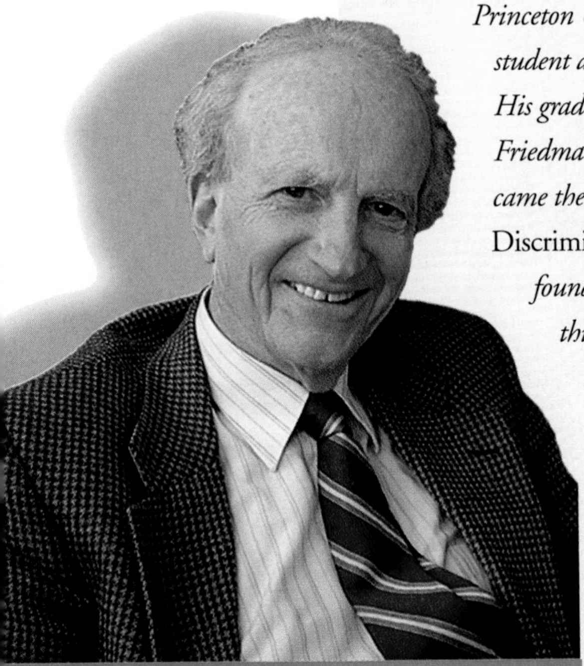

Professor Becker's other major book, Human Capital, *first published in 1964, has become a classic that influenced the thinking of the Clinton Administration on education issues. In 1992, he was awarded the Nobel Prize for Economic Science for his work on human capital.*

Gary S. Becker

Professor Becker has revolutionized the way we think about human decisions in all aspects of life. Michael Parkin and Robin Bade talked with Professor Becker about his work and how it uses and builds on the work of Jeremy Bentham.

Professor Becker, why are you an economist?

When I went to Princeton, I was interested in mathematics, but I wanted to do something for society. I took economics in my freshman year by accident, and it was a lucky accident. I found economics to be tremendously exciting intellectually because it could be used to understand the difference between capitalism and socialism, what determined wages, and how people are taxed. This was so exciting to me that I didn't even worry about job opportunities at the time.

Can we really hope to explain all human choices by using models that were invented initially to explain and predict choices about the allocation of income among alternative consumer goods and services?

I think we can hope to explain all human choices. All choices involve making comparisons and assessing how to allocate our time between work, leisure, and taking care of children. These are choices that are not in principle very different from the type of choices involved in allocating income. Whether economists succeed at the goal of explaining everything, of course, remains to be seen. We certainly haven't done that yet, but I think we've made considerable progress in expanding our horizons with the theory of choice.

You are a professor of both economics and sociology. Do you see these same techniques being used to address questions that are the traditional domain of the sociologist? Or is sociology just a totally different discipline?

Sociology is a discipline with many different approaches. There is a small but growing and vocal group of sociologists who believe in what they call *rational choice theory,* which is the theory economists have used to explain choices in markets. My late colleague, James Coleman, was the leader of that group. One of the issues they deal with is the influence of peers on behaviour. For example, imagine that I am a teenager facing choices of getting involved with drugs or heavy drinking or smoking because of peer pressure. How would rational choice theorists incorporate this peer pressure into an analysis of these choices? The simple approach they take is that my utility, or pleasure, depends not only on what I'm consuming but also on what my peers are doing. If they're doing something very different from what I'm doing, that reduces my utility partly because I receive less respect from them and feel less part of the group.

Therefore when I am trying to get as much utility as possible, I take into account what my peers are doing. But since we're all doing that, this leads to some equilibrium in this peer market. Instead of us all behaving independently, we are all behaving interdependently. I think economists have given social structures such as peer pressure far too little attention. One of the things I learned during my association with Coleman and other sociologists is a better appreciation of the importance of social factors in individual behaviour.

Can you identify the historical figures that have been most influential to your thinking and your career?

Economics is a cumulative field in which we build on the giants who went earlier, and we try to add a little bit. And then other people build on our generation's contributions. The view I take of the broad scope of the economic approach has had a number of major practitioners, including Jeremy Bentham, who stated and applied a very general view of utility-maximizing behaviour to many problems, such as the factors that reduce crime.

Very few people's work, certainly not mine, spring out of nowhere. They have continuity with the past. What we do is try to build on the work of past economists and do a little more and a little better than what they did.

Other nineteenth century people like Wicksteed and Marshall highlighted the rational choice aspect of economics. In the eighteenth century, Adam Smith already applied economic reasoning to political behaviour. My work on human capital was very much influenced by Irving Fisher, Alfred Marshall, Milton Friedman, and Ted Schultz. Very few people's work, certainly not mine, spring out of nowhere. They have continuity with the past. What we do is try to build on the work of past economists and do a little more and a little better than what they did.

How would you characterize the major achievements of the economics of human behaviour? What questions, for example, would have convincing answers?

The area of law and economics has been very successful in analyzing criminal behaviour. Work by many lawyers and economists, particularly Judge Richard Posner and William Landes of the University of Chicago Law School, has produced many successful applications. The question that economics of crime seeks to answer is: What determines the amount of crime that we have and how effective are various actions that governments can take in reducing the amount of crime? This analysis discusses apprehending and punishing criminals, giving better education to people who might commit crimes, reducing unemployment, and so on. They have basically said that fundamentally, the factors determining criminal behaviour are not so different from the factors determining whether people become professors or not. People make choices, and these choices are conditional on their expected benefits and the cost. You can affect the number of people who decide to enter criminal activities by affecting the benefits and costs. To the extent that people make these calculations, they are more likely to enter crime when benefits are high relative to the cost.

One way to affect costs is to make it more likely that if somebody commits a crime they'll be captured, apprehended, convicted, and punished. That raises the cost and reduces crime. I think now that people accept this conclusion for most crimes.

But the economic approach is not simply a law and order approach. It also says that if you can increase the attractiveness to people of working at legal activities rather than illegal or criminal activities, you will also have less crime. One way to increase the attractiveness is to make it easier for people to find jobs and to earn more by improving their skills, their education, and their training and also by improving the functioning of labour markets.

You've made a significant contribution to demographic economics. Nearly 40 years ago, you introduced the idea of children being durable goods. Can you talk about the evolution of this idea?

Demographers initially were extremely hostile to my point of view. However, I recently received the Irene Taeuber Award from the Population Association of America, their most prestigious demographic award. It was given to me in recognition of the value of the economic way of looking at demographic questions, including birth and marriage rates. Over time, the cumulative work of many economists working on population problems around the world made an impact.

The main payoffs from this work have been in our understanding of fertility. The conclusions from the economic approach are that the number of children people have is very much a function of two variables: costs and choices. Costs depend not only on how much food and shelter you give children, but also on the time of parents. In most societies, most of that time is the mother's time, which has a value. As we have become richer, and as women have become better educated and are working outside the home more, the cost to them of spending time on children has risen.

There are about 15 countries of the world that now have birth rates well below replacement levels. If families continue with these rates, the populations will eventually decline—and decline rapidly.

As these costs have risen, families are deterred from having as many children as they had in the past. So one of the factors explaining the big decline in birth rates is the increasing costs of children.

The second variable that economists recognize is that families are making choices about the quality of children's lives in terms of their education, training, and health. In modern economies, this quality component has become very important because the emphasis in modern economies is on knowledge, technology, and skills. But there is a tradeoff. If you spend more on each child's skills, education, and training, you make children more costly and you are likely to have fewer children. Over the past 30 years, birth rates have been decreasing in most countries of the world, including India, China, parts of Asia, Latin America, some parts of Africa, Europe, Canada, and the United States.

How do you respond to people who feel that explaining choices such as how many children to raise is deeply personal and that it is therefore immoral to think of children in these terms?

I think morality is misplaced in this area. We are trying to understand very major changes in the world. There are about 15 countries of the world that now have birth rates well below replacement levels. If families continue with these rates, these populations will eventually decline—and decline rapidly. This includes Germany, Italy, Spain, Portugal, France, and Japan. It is important to understand why birth rates are going down. If this way of looking at it is a powerful tool for understanding why families have made these choices, then it would be immoral, I believe, to neglect this approach. If we are concerned about low birth rates, how can we go about raising them? Or if we want to understand what to expect in other countries that are experiencing significant economic development, we will miss out if we neglect an important set of considerations that help us to understand what's going on.

Is economics a subject that a young person can happily enter today? What are the major incentives for pursuing economics as an undergraduate?

I would certainly encourage a young person to enter economics for several reasons. There are many employment opportunities in economics, and it is also valuable if you decide to go into other areas such as the law, business, or even medicine. Economic issues, including the budget deficit, entitlement programs, minimum wages, and how to subsidize the elderly, are extremely important public policy issues.

I want to stress that economics is a wonderful intellectual activity. To be able to take this very mysterious world we live in and to illuminate parts of it, important parts of it, through the use of economics is enormously intellectually satisfying and challenging for an undergraduate or for anybody else. So I would say it's both practical and satisfying. Who can ask for a better combination?

PART 4 FIRMS AND MARKETS

ORGANIZING PRODUCTION

CHAPTER 9

Spinning a Web

In the fall of 1990, a British scientist named Tim Berners-Lee invented the World Wide Web. This remarkable idea paved the way for the creation and growth of thousands of profitable businesses. One of these businesses is Nortel Networks, founded as Northern Electric and Manufacturing Company Limited at the start of the telephone era more than 100 years ago. ◆ How do Nortel and the other 2 million firms in Canada make their business decisions? How do they operate efficiently? ◆ Businesses range from multinational giants like Nortel to small family restaurants and local Internet service providers. Three-quarters of all firms are operated by their owners. But corporations (such as Nortel) account for 90 percent of all business sales. What are the different forms a firm can take? Why do some firms remain small while others become giants? Why are most firms owner-operated? ◆ Many businesses operate in a highly competitive environment and struggle to make a profit. Others, like Microsoft, seem to have cornered the market for their products and make a large profit. What are the different types of markets in which firms operate? Why is it harder to make a profit in some markets than in others? ◆ GM, Ford, and DaimlerChrysler are household names and we think of them as the makers of our cars. But almost all of the *components* of a car are made by other firms, most of which you've never heard. One firm makes the engine casting, another makes the body panels, and yet another makes the transmission system. Other firms make the windshield, the tires, brakes, and so on. Why doesn't GM make all its own auto components? Why does it leave these activities to other firms and buy from them in markets? How do firms decide what to make themselves and what to buy in the marketplace from other firms?

◇ In this chapter, we are going to learn about firms and the choices they make to cope with scarcity. We begin by studying the economic problems and choices that all firms face.

After studying this chapter, you will be able to

- **Explain what a firm is and describe the economic problems that *all* firms face**
- **Distinguish between technological efficiency and economic efficiency**
- **Define and explain the principal–agent problem and describe how different types of business organizations cope with this problem**
- **Describe and distinguish between different types of markets in which firms operate**
- **Explain why markets coordinate some economic activities and firms coordinate others**

The Firm and Its Economic Problem

THE 2 MILLION FIRMS IN CANADA DIFFER IN SIZE and in the scope of what they do. But they all perform the same basic economic functions. Each **firm** is an institution that hires factors of production and organizes those factors to produce and sell goods and services.

Our goal is to predict firms' behaviour. To do so, we need to know a firm's goals and the constraints it faces. We begin with the goals.

The Firm's Goal

If you asked a group of entrepreneurs what they are trying to achieve, you would get many different answers. Some would talk about making a high-quality product, others about business growth, others about market share, and others about the job satisfaction of their work force. All of these goals might be pursued, but they are not the fundamental goal. They are means to a deeper goal.

A firm's goal is to maximize profit. A firm that does not seek to maximize profit is either eliminated or bought out by firms that do seek to maximize profit.

What exactly is the profit that a firm seeks to maximize? To answer this question, let's look at Sidney's Sweaters.

Measuring a Firm's Profit

Sidney runs a successful business that makes sweaters. Sidney's Sweaters receives $400,000 a year for the sweaters it sells. Its expenses are $80,000 a year for wool, $20,000 for utilities, $120,000 for wages, and $10,000 in interest on a bank loan. With receipts of $400,000 and expenses of $230,000, Sidney's Sweaters' annual surplus is $170,000.

Sidney's accountant lowers this number by $20,000, which he says is the depreciation (fall in value) of the firm's buildings and knitting machines during the year. (Accountants use Canada Customs and Revenue Agency rules based on standards established by the accounting profession to calculate the depreciation.) So the accountant reports that the profit of Sidney's Sweaters is $150,000 a year.

Sidney's accountant measures cost and profit to ensure that the firm pays the correct amount of income tax and to show the bank how its loan has been used. But we want to predict the decisions that a firm makes. These decisions respond to *opportunity cost* and *economic profit.*

Opportunity Cost

The *opportunity cost* of any action is the highest-valued alternative forgone. The action that you choose not to take—the highest-valued alternative forgone—is the cost of the action that you choose to take. For a firm, the opportunity cost of production is the value of the firm's best alternative use of its resources.

Opportunity cost is a real alternative forgone. But so that we can compare the cost of one action with that of another action, we express opportunity cost in money units. A firm's opportunity cost includes both

- Explicit costs
- Implicit costs

Explicit Costs Explicit costs are paid in money. The amount paid for a resource could have been spent on something else, so it is the opportunity cost of using the resource. For Sidney, his expenditures on wool, utilities, wages, and bank interest are explicit costs.

Implicit Costs A firm incurs implicit costs when it forgoes an alternative action but does not make a payment. A firm incurs implicit costs when it

1. Uses its own capital.
2. Uses its owner's time or financial resources.

The cost of using its own capital is an implicit cost—and an opportunity cost—because the firm could rent the capital to another firm. The rental income forgone is the firm's opportunity cost of using its own capital. This opportunity cost is called the **implicit rental rate** of capital.

People rent houses, apartments, cars, and videotapes. And firms rent photocopiers, earth-moving equipment, satellite-launching services, and so on. If a firm rents capital, it incurs an explicit cost. If a firm buys the capital it uses, it incurs an implicit cost. The implicit rental rate of capital is made up of

1. Economic depreciation
2. Interest forgone

Economic depreciation is the change in the *market* value of capital over a given period. It is calculated as the market price of the capital at the beginning of the period minus its market price at the end of the period. For example, suppose that Sidney could have sold his buildings and knitting machines on December 31, 2001, for $400,000. If he can sell the same capital on December 31, 2002, for $375,000, his economic depreciation during 2002 is $25,000—the fall in the market value of the machines. This $25,000 is an implicit cost of using the capital during 2002.

The funds used to buy capital could have been used for some other purpose. And in their next best use, they would have yielded a return—an interest income. This forgone interest is part of the opportunity cost of using the capital. For example, Sidney's Sweaters could have bought government bonds instead of a knitting factory. The interest forgone on the government bonds is an implicit cost of operating the knitting factory.

Cost of Owner's Resources A firm's owner often supplies entrepreneurial ability—the factor of production that organizes the business, makes business decisions, innovates, and bears the risk of running the business. The return to entrepreneurship is profit, and the return that an entrepreneur can expect to receive on the average is called **normal profit.** Normal profit is part of a firm's opportunity cost because it is the cost of a forgone alternative—running another firm. If normal profit in the textile business is $50,000 a year, this amount must be added to Sidney's costs to determine his opportunity cost.

The owner of a firm also can supply labour (in addition to entrepreneurship). The return to labour is a wage. And the opportunity cost of the owner's time spent working for the firm is the wage income forgone by not working in the best alternative job. Suppose that Sidney could take another job that pays $40,000 a year. By working for his knitting business and forgoing this income, Sidney incurs an opportunity cost of $40,000 a year.

Economic Profit

What is the bottom line—the firm's profit or loss? A firm's **economic profit** is equal to its total revenue minus its opportunity cost. The firm's opportunity cost is the sum of its explicit costs and implicit costs. Implicit costs, remember, include *normal profit.* The return to entrepreneurial ability is greater than normal in a firm that makes a positive economic profit. And the return to entrepreneurial ability is less than normal in a firm that makes a negative economic profit—a firm that incurs an economic loss.

Economic Accounting: A Summary

Table 9.1 summarizes the economic accounting concepts that you've just studied. Sidney's Sweaters' total revenue is $400,000. Its opportunity cost (explicit costs plus implicit costs) is $365,000. So its economic profit is $35,000.

To achieve the objective of maximum economic profit a firm must make five basic decisions:

1. What goods and services to produce and in what quantities
2. How to produce—the techniques of production to use
3. How to organize and compensate its managers and workers
4. How to market and price its products
5. What to produce itself and what to buy from other firms

In all these decisions, a firm's actions are limited by the constraints that it faces. Our next task is to learn about these constraints.

TABLE 9.1 Economic Accounting

Item		Amount
Total Revenue		**$400,000**
Opportunity Costs		
Wool	$80,000	
Utilities	20,000	
Wages paid	120,000	
Bank interest paid	10,000	
Total Explicit Costs		$230,000
Sidney's wages forgone	40,000	
Sidney's interest forgone	20,000	
Economic depreciation	25,000	
Normal profit	50,000	
Total Implicit Costs		$135,000
Total Cost		**$365,000**
Economic Profit		**$35,000**

The Firm's Constraints

Three features of its environment limit the maximum profit a firm can make. They are

- Technology constraints
- Information constraints
- Market constraints

Technology Constraints Economists define technology broadly. A **technology** is any method of producing a good or service. Technology includes the detailed designs of machines. It also includes the layout of the workplace. And it includes the organization of the firm. For example, the shopping mall is a technology for producing retail services. It is a different technology from the catalogue store, which in turn is different from the downtown store.

It might seem surprising that a firm's profits are limited by technology, for it seems that technological advances are constantly increasing profit opportunities. Almost every day, we learn about some new technological advance that amazes us. With computers that speak and recognize our own speech and cars that can find the address we need in a city we've never visited before, we are able to accomplish ever more.

Technology advances over time. But at each point in time, to produce more output and gain more revenue, a firm must hire more resources and incur greater costs. The increase in profit that the firm can achieve is limited by the technology available. For example, by using its current plant and work force, Ford can produce some maximum number of cars per day. To produce more cars per day, Ford must hire more resources, which increases Ford's costs and limits the increase in profit that Ford can make by selling the additional cars.

Information Constraints We never possess all the information we would like to have to make decisions. We lack information about both the future and the present. For example, suppose you plan to buy a new computer. When should you buy it? The answer depends on how the price is going to change in the future. Where should you buy it? The answer depends on the prices at hundreds of different computer shops. To get the best deal, you must compare the quality and prices in every shop. But the opportunity cost of this comparison exceeds the cost of the computer!

Similarly, a firm is constrained by limited information about the quality and effort of its work force, the current and future buying plans of its customers, and the plans of its competitors. Workers might slacken off when the manager believes they are working hard. Customers might switch to competing suppliers. Firms must compete against competition from a new firm.

Firms try to create incentive systems for workers to ensure that they work hard even when no one is monitoring their efforts. And firms spend millions of dollars on market research. But none of these efforts and expenditures eliminates the problems of incomplete information and uncertainty. And the cost of coping with limited information itself limits profit.

Market Constraints What each firm can sell and the price it can obtain are constrained by its customers' willingness to pay and by the prices and marketing efforts of other firms. Similarly, the resources that a firm can buy and the prices it must pay for them are limited by the willingness of people to work for and invest in the firm. Firms spend billions of dollars a year marketing and selling their products. Some of the most creative minds strive to find the right message that will produce a knockout television advertisement. Market constraints and the expenditures firms make to overcome them limit the profit a firm can make.

REVIEW QUIZ

1. Why do firms seek to maximize profit? What happens to firms that don't pursue this goal?
2. Why do accountants and economists calculate a firm's cost and profit in different ways?
3. What are the items that make opportunity cost differ from the accountant's cost measure?
4. Why is normal profit an opportunity cost?
5. What are the constraints that firms face? How does each constraint limit the firm's profit?

In the rest of this chapter and in Chapters 10 through 13, we study the decisions that firms make. We're going to learn how we can predict a firm's behaviour as the response to the constraints that it faces and to changes in those constraints. We begin by taking a closer look at the technology constraints, information constraints, and market constraints that firms face.

Technological and Economic Efficiency

MICROSOFT EMPLOYS A LARGE WORK FORCE, AND most Microsoft workers possess a large amount of human capital. But the firm uses a small amount of physical capital. In contrast, a coal-mining company employs a huge amount of mining equipment (physical capital) and almost no labour. Why? The answer lies in the concept of efficiency. There are two concepts of production efficiency: technological efficiency and economic efficiency. **Technological efficiency** occurs when the firm produces a given output by using the least amount of inputs. **Economic efficiency** occurs when the firm produces a given output at the least cost. Let's explore the two concepts of efficiency by studying an example.

Suppose that there are four alternative techniques for making TV sets:

A. *Robot production.* One person monitors the entire computer-driven process.
B. *Production line.* Workers specialize in a small part of the job as the emerging TV set passes them on a production line.
C. *Bench production.* Workers specialize in a small part of the job but walk from bench to bench to perform their tasks.
D. *Hand-tool production.* A single worker uses a few hand tools to make a TV set.

Table 9.2 sets out the amounts of labour and capital required by each of these four methods to make 10 TV sets a day.

Which of these alternative methods are technologically efficient?

Technological Efficiency

Recall that technological efficiency occurs when the firm produces a given output by using the least inputs. Inspect the numbers in the table and notice that method *A* uses the most capital but the least labour. Method *D* uses the most labour but the least capital. Method *B* and method *C* lie between the two extremes. They use less capital but more labour than method *A* and less labour but more capital than method *D*. Compare methods *B* and *C*. Method *C* requires 100 workers and 10 units of capital to produce 10 TV sets. Those same 10 TV sets can be produced by method *B* with 10 workers and the same 10 units of capital. Because method *C* uses the same amount of capital and more labour than method *B*, method *C* is not technologically efficient.

Are any of the other methods not technologically efficient? The answer is no. Each of the other three methods is technologically efficient. Method *A* uses more capital but less labour than method *B*, and method *D* uses more labour but less capital than method *B*.

Which of the methods are economically efficient?

Economic Efficiency

Recall that economic efficiency occurs when the firm produces a given output at the least cost. Suppose that labour costs $75 per person-day and that capital costs $250 per machine-day. Table 9.3(a) calculates the costs of using the different methods. By inspecting the table, you can see that method *B* has the lowest cost. Although method *A* uses less labour, it uses too much expensive capital. And although method *D* uses less capital, it uses too much expensive labour.

Method *C*, which is technologically inefficient, is also economically inefficient. It uses the same amount of capital as method *B* but 10 times as much labour. So it costs more. A technologically inefficient method is never economically efficient.

Although *B* is the economically efficient method in this example, method *A* or *D* could be economically efficient with different input prices.

Suppose that labour costs $150 a person-day and capital costs only $1 a machine-day. Table 9.3(b) now shows the costs of making a TV set. In this case, method *A* is economically efficient. Capital is now so

TABLE 9.2 Four Ways of Making 10 TV Sets a Day

		Quantities of inputs	
	Method	Labour	Capital
A	Robot production	1	1,000
B	Production line	10	10
C	Bench production	100	10
D	Hand-tool production	1,000	1

TABLE 9.3 The Costs of Different Ways of Making 10 TV Sets a Day

(a) Four ways of making TVs

Method	Labour cost ($75 per day)		Capital cost ($250 per day)		Total cost	Cost per TV set
A	$75	+	$250,000	=	$250,075	$25,007.50
B	**750**	+	**2,500**	=	**3,250**	**325.00**
C	7,500	+	2,500	=	10,000	1,000.00
D	75,000	+	250	=	75,250	7,525.00

(b) Three ways of making TVs: High labour costs

Method	Labour cost ($150 per day)		Capital cost ($1 per day)		Total cost	Cost per TV set
A	**$150**	+	**$1,000**	=	**$1,150**	**$115.00**
B	1,500	+	10	=	1,510	151.00
D	150,000	+	1	=	150,001	15,000.10

(c) Three ways of making TVs: High capital costs

Method	Labour cost ($1 per day)		Capital cost ($1,000 per day)		Total cost	Cost per TV set
A	$1	+	$1,000,000	=	$1,000,001	$100,000.10
B	10	+	10,000	=	10,010	1,001.00
D	**1,000**	+	**1,000**	=	**2,000**	**200.00**

cheap relative to labour that the method that uses the most capital is the economically efficient method.

Next, suppose that labour costs only $1 a person-day while capital costs $1,000 a machine-day. Table 9.3(c) shows the costs in this case. Method *D*, which uses a lot of labour and little capital, is now the least-cost method and the economically efficient method.

From these examples, you can see that while technological efficiency depends only on what is feasible, economic efficiency depends on the relative costs of resources. The economically efficient method is the one that uses a smaller amount of a more expensive resource and a larger amount of a less expensive resource.

A firm that is not economically efficient does not maximize profit. Natural selection favours efficient firms and opposes inefficient firms. Inefficient firms go out of business or are taken over by firms with lower costs.

REVIEW QUIZ

1 How do we define technological efficiency? Is a firm technologically efficient if it uses the latest technology? Why or why not?
2 How do we define economic efficiency? Is a firm economically inefficient if it can cut costs by producing less? Why or why not?
3 Explain the key distinction between technological efficiency and economic efficiency.
4 Why do some firms use large amounts of capital and small amounts of labour, while others use small amounts of capital and large amounts of labour?

Next we study information constraints that firms face and the diversity of organization structures they generate.

Information and Organization

EACH FIRM ORGANIZES THE PRODUCTION OF goods and services by combining and coordinating the productive resources it hires. But there is variety across firms in how they organize production. Firms use a mixture of two systems:

- Command systems
- Incentive systems

Command Systems

A **command system** is a method of organizing production that uses a managerial hierarchy. Commands pass downward through the managerial hierarchy, and information passes upward. Managers spend most of their time collecting and processing information about the performance of the people under their control and making decisions about commands to issue and how best to get those commands implemented.

The military uses the purest form of command system. A commander-in-chief makes the big decisions about strategic objectives. Beneath this highest level, generals organize their military resources. Beneath the generals, successively lower ranks organize smaller and smaller units but pay attention to ever-increasing degrees of detail. At the bottom of the managerial hierarchy are the people who operate weapons systems.

Command systems in firms are not as rigid as those in the military, but they share some similar features. A chief executive officer (CEO) sits at the top of a firm's command system. Senior executives who report to and receive commands from the CEO specialize in managing production, marketing, finance, personnel, and perhaps other aspects of the firm's operations. Beneath these senior managers might be several tiers of middle management ranks that stretch downward to the managers who supervise the day-to-day operations of the business. Beneath these managers are the people who operate the firm's machines and who make and sell the firm's goods and services.

Small firms have one or two layers of managers, while large firms have several layers. As production processes have become ever more complex, management ranks have swollen. Today, more people have management jobs than ever before. But the information revolution of the 1990s slowed the growth of management, and in some industries, it reduced the number of layers of managers and brought a shakeout of middle managers.

Managers make enormous efforts to be well informed. And they try hard to make good decisions and issue commands that end up using resources efficiently. But managers always have incomplete information about what is happening in the divisions of the firm for which they are responsible. It is for this reason that firms use incentive systems as well as command systems to organize production.

Incentive Systems

An **incentive system** is a method of organizing production that uses a market-like mechanism inside the firm. Instead of issuing commands, senior managers create compensation schemes that will induce workers to perform in ways that maximize the firm's profit.

Selling organizations use incentive systems most extensively. Sales representatives who spend most of their working time alone and unsupervised are induced to work hard by being paid a small salary and a large performance-related bonus.

But incentive systems operate at all levels in a firm. CEOs' compensation plans include a share in the firm's profit, and factory floor workers sometimes receive compensation based on the quantity they produce.

Mixing the Systems

Firms use a mixture of commands and incentives. And they choose the mixture that maximizes profit. They use commands when it is easy to monitor performance or when a small deviation from an ideal performance is very costly. They use incentives when monitoring performance is either not possible or too costly to be worth doing.

For example, it is easy to monitor the performance of workers on a production line. If one person works too slowly, the entire line slows. So a production line is organized with a command system.

In contrast, it is costly to monitor a CEO. For example, what did John Roth (former CEO of Nortel) contribute to the initial success and subsequent problems of Nortel? This question can't be answered with certainty, yet Nortel's stockholders had to put someone in charge of the business and provide that person with an incentive to maximize their returns. The performance of Nortel illustrates the nature of this problem, known as the principal–agent problem.

The Principal–Agent Problem

The **principal–agent problem** is the problem of devising compensation rules that induce an *agent* to act in the best interest of a *principal.* For example, the stockholders of Nortel are *principals,* and the firm's managers are *agents.* The stockholders (the principals) must induce the managers (agents) to act in the stockholders' best interest. Similarly, Bill Gates (a principal) must induce the programmers who are working on the next generation of Windows (agents) to work efficiently.

Agents, whether they are managers or workers, pursue their own goals and often impose costs on a principal. For example, the goal of stockholders of CIBC (principals) is to maximize the firm's profit. But the firm's profit depends on the actions of its managers (agents) who have their own goals. Perhaps a manager takes a customer to a ball game on the pretense that she is building customer loyalty, when in fact she is simply enjoying on-the-job leisure. This same manager is also a principal, and her tellers are agents. The manager wants the tellers to work hard and attract new customers so that she can meet her operating targets. But the workers enjoy conversations with each other and take on-the-job leisure. Nonetheless, the firm constantly strives to find ways of improving performance and increasing profits.

Coping with the Principal–Agent Problem

Issuing commands does not address the principal–agent problem. In most firms, the shareholders can't monitor the managers and often the managers can't monitor the workers. Each principal must create incentives that induce each agent to work in the interests of the principal. Three ways of attempting to cope with the principal–agent problem are

- Ownership
- Incentive pay
- Long-term contracts

Ownership By assigning to a manager or worker ownership (or part-ownership) of a business, it is sometimes possible to induce a job performance that increases a firm's profits. Part-ownership schemes for senior managers are quite common, but they are less common but not unknown for workers. For example, in 1995 Canadian Pacific Ltd. sold off CP Express and Transport, a coast-to-coast trucking operation, to its 3,500 employees.

Incentive Pay Incentive pay schemes—pay related to performance—are very common. They are based on a variety of performance criteria such as profits, production, or sales targets. Promoting an employee for good performance is another example of an incentive pay scheme.

Long-Term Contracts Long-term contracts tie the long-term fortunes of managers and workers (agents) to the success of the principal(s)—the owner(s) of the firm. For example, a multiyear employment contract for a CEO encourages that person to take a long-term view and devise strategies that achieve maximum profit over a sustained period.

These three ways of coping with the principal–agent problem give rise to different types of business organization. Each type of business organization is a different response to the principal–agent problem. Each type uses ownership, incentives, and long-term contracts in different ways. Let's look at the main types of business organization.

Types of Business Organization

The three main types of business organization are

- Sole proprietorship
- Partnership
- Corporation

Sole Proprietorship A *sole proprietorship* is a firm with a single owner—a proprietor—who has unlimited liability. *Unlimited liability* is the legal responsibility for all the debts of a firm up to an amount equal to the entire wealth of the owner. If a sole proprietorship cannot pay its debts, those to whom the firm owes money can claim the personal property of the owner. Some farmers, computer programmers, and artists are examples of sole proprietorships.

The proprietor makes management decisions, receives the firm's profits, and is responsible for its losses. The profits are taxed at the same rate as other sources of the proprietor's personal income.

Partnership A *partnership* is a firm with two or more owners who have unlimited liability. Partners must agree on an appropriate management structure and on how to divide the firm's profits among themselves. The profits of a partnership are taxed as the personal income of the owners. But each partner is legally liable for all the debts of the partnership (limited only by the wealth of that individual partner). Liability for the full debts of the partnership is called *joint unlimited liability.* Most law firms are partnerships.

Corporation A *corporation* is a firm owned by one or more limited liability stockholders. *Limited liability* means that the owners have legal liability only for the value of their initial investment. This limitation of liability means that if the corporation becomes bankrupt, its owners are not required to use their personal wealth to pay the corporation's debts.

Corporations' profits are taxed independently of stockholders' incomes. The stockholders pay tax on dividends and a capital gains tax on the profit they earn when they sell a stock for a higher price than they paid for it. Corporate stocks generate capital gains when a corporation retains some of its profit and reinvests it in profitable activities.

Pros and Cons of Different Types of Firms

The different types of business organization arise as different ways of trying to cope with the principal–agent problem. Each has advantages in particular situations. And because of its special advantages, each type continues to exist. Each type also has its disadvantages, which explains why it has not driven out the other two.

Table 9.4 summarizes these pros and cons of the different types of firms.

TABLE 9.4 The Pros and Cons of Different Types of Firms

Type of Firm	Pros	Cons
Sole proprietorship	■ Easy to set up ■ Simple decision making ■ Profits taxed only once as owner's income	■ Bad decisions not checked by need for consensus ■ Owner's entire wealth at risk ■ Firm dies with owner ■ Capital is expensive ■ Labour is expensive
Partnership	■ Easy to set up ■ Diversified decision making ■ Can survive withdrawal of partner ■ Profits taxed only once as owners' incomes	■ Achieving consensus may be slow and expensive ■ Owners' entire wealth at risk ■ Withdrawal of partner may create capital shortage ■ Capital is expensive
Corporation	■ Owners have limited liability ■ Large-scale, low-cost capital available ■ Professional management not restricted by ability of owners ■ Perpetual life ■ Long-term labour contracts cut labour costs	■ Complex management structure can make decisions slow and expensive ■ Profits taxed twice as company profit and as stockholders' income

FIGURE 9.1 Relative Importance of the Three Types of Firms

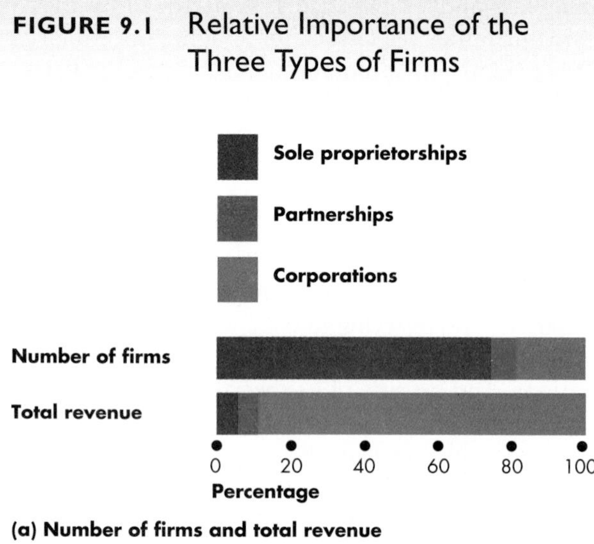

(a) Number of firms and total revenue

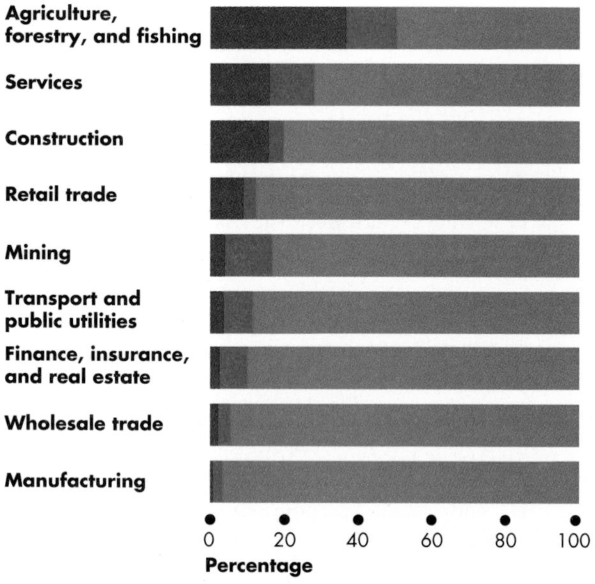

(b) Total revenue in various industries

The data shown are for the United States because we do not have comparable data for Canada. Three-quarters of all U.S. firms are sole proprietorships, almost one-fifth are corporations, and only a twentieth are partnerships. Corporations account for 86 percent of business revenue (part a). But sole proprietorships and partnerships account for a significant percentage of business revenue in some industries (part b).

Source: U.S. Bureau of the Census, *Statistical Abstract of the United States: 2001*.

The Relative Importance of Different Types of Firms

Figure 9.1(a) shows the relative importance of the three main types of firms in the U.S. economy. The figure also shows that the revenue of corporations is much larger than that of the other types of firms. Although only 18 percent of all firms are corporations, they generate 86 percent of revenue.

Figure 9.1(b) shows the percentage of revenue generated by the different types of firms in various industries. Sole proprietorships in agriculture, forestry, and fishing generate about 40 percent of the total revenue in those sectors. Sole proprietorships in the service sector, construction, and retail trades also generate a large percentage of total revenue. Partnerships in agriculture, forestry, and fishing generate about 15 percent of total revenue. Partnerships are more prominent in services; mining; and finance, insurance, and real estate than in other sectors. Corporations are important in all sectors and have the manufacturing field almost to themselves.

Why do corporations dominate the business scene? Why do the other types of business survive? And why are sole proprietorships and partnerships more prominent in some sectors? The answers to these questions lie in the pros and cons of the different types of business organization that are summarized in Table 9.4. Corporations dominate where a large amount of capital is used. But sole proprietorships dominate where flexibility in decision making is critical.

REVIEW QUIZ

1. Explain the distinction between a command system and an incentive system.
2. What is the principal–agent problem? What are the three ways in which firms try to cope with it?
3. What are the three types of firms? Explain the major advantages and disadvantages of each.
4. Why do all three types of firms survive and in which sectors is each type most prominent?

You've now seen how technology constraints influence a firm's use of capital and labour and how information constraints influence a firm's organization. We'll now look at market constraints and see how they influence the environment in which firms compete for business.

Markets and the Competitive Environment

THE MARKETS IN WHICH FIRMS OPERATE VARY A great deal. Some are highly competitive, and profits in these markets are hard to come by. Some appear to be almost free from competition, and firms in these markets earn large profits. Some markets are dominated by fierce advertising campaigns in which each firm seeks to persuade buyers that it has the best products. And some markets display a warlike character.

Economists identify four market types:

1. Perfect competition
2. Monopolistic competition
3. Oligopoly
4. Monopoly

Perfect competition arises when there are many firms, each selling an identical product, many buyers, and no restrictions on the entry of new firms into the industry. The many firms and buyers are all well informed about the prices of the products of each firm in the industry. The worldwide markets for corn, rice, and other grain crops are examples of perfect competition.

Monopolistic competition is a market structure in which a large number of firms compete by making similar but slightly different products. Making a product slightly different from the product of a competing firm is called **product differentiation**. Product differentiation gives the firm in monopolistic competition an element of market power. The firm is the sole producer of the particular version of the good in question. For example, in the market for running shoes, Nike, Reebok, Fila, New Balance, and Asics all make their own version of the perfect shoe. Each of these firms is the sole producer of a particular brand of shoe. Differentiated products are not necessarily different products. What matters is that consumers perceive them to be different. For example, different brands of aspirin are chemically identical (salicylic acid) and differ only in their packaging.

Oligopoly is a market structure in which a small number of firms compete. Computer software, airplane manufacture, and international air transportation are examples of oligopolistic industries. Oligopolies might produce almost identical products, such as the colas produced by Coke and Pepsi. Or they might produce differentiated products such as Chevrolet's Lumina and Ford's Taurus.

Monopoly arises when there is one firm, which produces a good or service that has no close substitutes and in which the firm is protected by a barrier preventing the entry of new firms. In some places, the phone, gas, electricity, and water suppliers are local monopolies—monopolies restricted to a given location. Microsoft Corporation, the software developer that created Windows, the operating system used by PCs, is an example of a global monopoly.

Perfect competition is the most extreme form of competition. Monopoly is the most extreme absence of competition. The other two market types fall between these extremes.

Many factors must be taken into account to determine which market structure describes a particular real-world market. One of these factors is the extent to which the market is dominated by a small number of firms. To measure this feature of markets, economists use indexes called measures of concentration. Let's look at these measures.

Measures of Concentration

Economists use two measures of concentration:

- The four-firm concentration ratio
- The Herfindahl–Hirschman Index

The Four-Firm Concentration Ratio The **four-firm concentration ratio** is the percentage of the value of sales accounted for by the four largest firms in an industry. The range of the concentration ratio is from almost zero for perfect competition to 100 percent for monopoly. This ratio is the main measure used to assess market structure.

Table 9.5 shows two calculations of the four-firm concentration ratio: one for tiremakers and one for printers. In this example, 14 firms produce tires. The largest four have 80 percent of the sales, so the four-firm concentration ratio is 80 percent. In the printing industry, with 1,004 firms, the largest four firms have only 0.5 percent of the sales, so the four-firm concentration ratio is 0.5 percent.

A low concentration ratio indicates a high degree of competition, and a high concentration ratio indicates an absence of competition. A monopoly has a concentration ratio of 100 percent—the largest (and only) firm has 100 percent of the sales. A four-firm concentration ratio that exceeds 40 percent is regarded as an indication of a market that is highly concentrated and dominated by a few firms in an oligopoly. A ratio of less than 40 percent is regarded as an indication of a competitive market.

The Herfindahl–Hirschman Index The **Herfindahl–Hirschman Index**—also called the HHI—is the square of the percentage market share of each firm summed over the largest 50 firms (or summed over all the firms if there are fewer than 50) in a market. For example, if there are four firms in a market and the market shares of the firms are 50 percent, 25 percent, 15 percent, and 10 percent, the Herfindahl–Hirschman Index is

$$\text{HHI} = 50^2 + 25^2 + 15^2 + 10^2 = 3{,}450.$$

TABLE 9.5 Concentration Ratio Calculations

Tiremakers

Firm	Sales (millions of dollars)
Top, Inc.	200
ABC, Inc.	250
Big, Inc.	150
XYZ, Inc.	100
Largest 4 firms	700
Other 10 firms	175
Industry	875

Printers

Firm	Sales (millions of dollars)
Fran's	2.5
Ned's	2.0
Tom's	1.8
Jill's	1.7
Largest 4 firms	8.0
Other 1,000 firms	1,592.0
Industry	**1,600.0**

Four-firm concentration ratios:

Tire makers: $\frac{700}{875} \times 100 = 80\%$

Printers: $\frac{8}{1{,}600} \times 100 = 0.5\%$

In perfect competition, the HHI is small. For example, if each of the largest 50 firms in an industry has a market share of 0.1 percent, then the HHI is $0.1^2 \times 50 = 0.5$. In a monopoly, the HHI is 10,000—the firm has 100 percent of the market: $100^2 = 10{,}000$.

The HHI can be used to classify markets across the spectrum of types. A market in which the HHI is less than 1,000 is regarded as being competitive and the smaller the number, the greater is the degree of competition. A market in which the HHI lies between 1,000 and 1,800 is regarded as being moderately competitive—a form of monopolistic competition. Although the HHI of 10,000 is needed for pure monopoly, a market in which the HHI exceeds 1,800 is regarded as being uncompetitive and a potential matter for concern by competition regulators.

Concentration Measures for the Canadian Economy

Figure 9.2 shows a selection of concentration ratios for Canada that Statistics Canada has calculated.

Industries that produce tobacco products, petroleum and coal products, transport equipment, communications, and beverages have a high degree of concentration and are oligopolies. Services, clothing, furniture, retail trade, and knitting mills have low concentration measures and are highly competitive. Industries that produce food and electrical products are moderately concentrated. These industries are examples of monopolistic competition.

Concentration measures are a useful indicator of the degree of competition in a market. But they must be supplemented by other information to determine a market's structure. Table 9.6 summarizes the range of other information, along with the measures of concentration, that determine which market structure describes a particular real-world market.

Limitations of Concentration Measures

The three main limitations of concentration measures alone as determinants of market structure are their failure to take proper account of

- The geographical scope of the market
- Barriers to entry and firm turnover
- The correspondence between a market and an industry

FIGURE 9.2 Concentration Measures in Canada

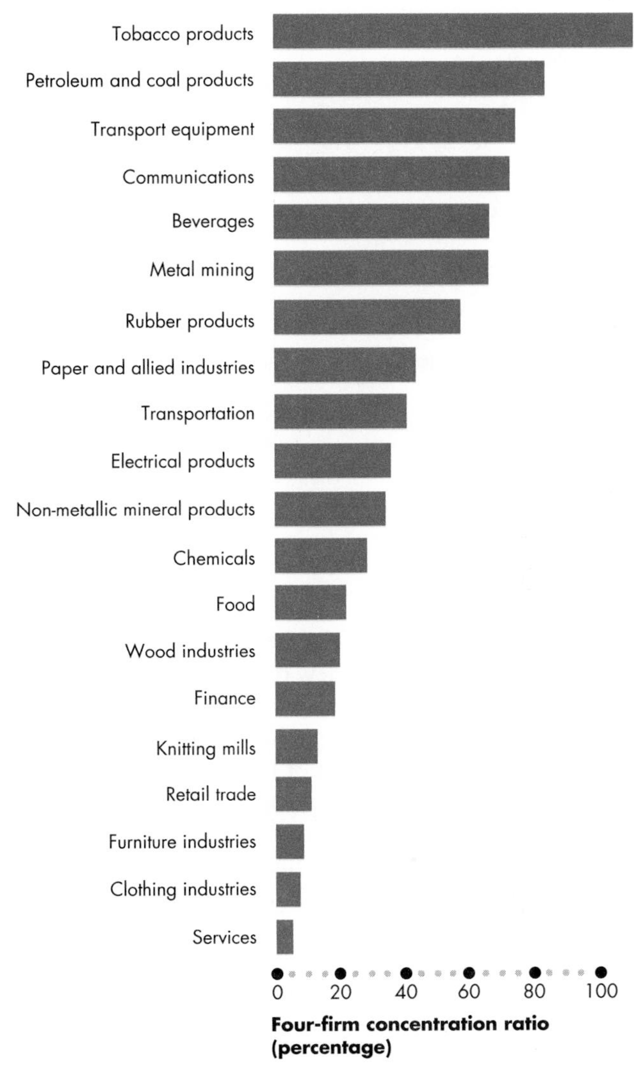

The industries that produce tobacco products, petroleum and coal products, transport equipment, communications, and beverages are highly concentrated, while those that produce services, clothing, furniture, retail trade services, and knitwear are highly competitive. The industries that produce food and electrical products have an intermediate degree of concentration.

Source: Adapted from the Statistics Canada publication *CANSIM DISC*, 10F0007, March 1999.

TABLE 9.6 Market Structure

Characteristics	Perfect competition	Monopolistic competition	Oligopoly	Monopoly
Number of firms in industry	Many	Many	Few	One
Product	Identical	Differentiated	Either identical or differentiated	No close substitutes
Barriers to entry	None	None	Moderate	High
Firm's control over price	None	Some	Considerable	Considerable or regulated
Concentration ratio	0	Low	High	100
HHI (approx. ranges)	Less than 100	101 to 999	More than 1,000	10,000
Examples	Wheat, corn	Food, clothing	Automobiles, cereals	Local water supply

Geographical Scope of Market Concentration measures take a national view of the market. Many goods are sold in a *national* market, but some are sold in a *regional* market and some in a *global* one. The newspaper industry consists of local markets. The concentration measures for newspapers are low, but there is a high degree of concentration in the newspaper industry in most cities. The auto industry has a global market. The three biggest North American car producers don't have much domestic competition, either in Canada or in the United States. But they face tough competition from foreign producers both here and more especially in foreign markets.

Barriers to Entry and Firm Turnover Concentration measures don't measure barriers to entry. Some industries are highly concentrated but have easy entry and an enormous amount of turnover of firms. For example, many small towns have few restaurants, but there are no restrictions on opening a restaurant and many firms attempt to do so.

Also, an industry might be competitive because of *potential entry*—because a few firms in a market face competition from many firms that can easily enter the market and will do so if economic profits are available.

Market and Industry Correspondence To calculate concentration ratios, Statistics Canada classifies each firm as being in a particular industry. But markets do not always correspond closely to industries for three reasons.

First, markets are often narrower than industries. For example, the pharmaceutical industry, which has a low concentration ratio, operates in many separate markets for individual products—for example, measles vaccines and AIDS-fighting drugs. These drugs do not compete with each other, so this industry, which looks competitive, includes firms that are monopolies (or near monopolies) in markets for individual drugs.

Second, most firms make several products. For example, Nortel produces telecommunication equipment and Internet database services, among other things. So this one firm operates in several separate markets. But Statistics Canada classifies Nortel as being in the telecommunication equipment industry. The fact that Nortel competes with other providers of e-commerce database services does not show up in the concentration data for that market.

Third, firms switch from one market to another depending on profit opportunities. For example, Canadian Pacific Ltd., which today produces hotel services, forest products, coal and petroleum products, as well as rail services, has diversified from being just a railroad company. Publishers of newspapers, magazines, and textbooks are today rapidly diversifying into Internet and multimedia products. These switches among industries show that there is much scope for entering and exiting an industry, and so measures of concentration have limited usefulness.

Despite their limitations, concentration measures do provide a basis for determining the degree of competition in an industry when they are combined with information about the geographical scope of the market, barriers to entry, and the extent to which large, multiproduct firms straddle a variety of markets.

FIGURE 9.3 The Market Structure of the North American Economy

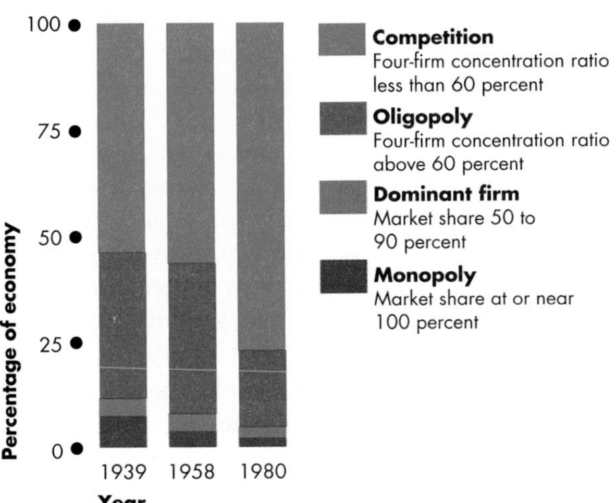

Three-quarters of the North American economy is effectively competitive (perfect competition or monopolistic competition), one-fifth is oligopoly, and the rest is monopoly. The economy became more competitive between 1939 and 1980. (Professor Shepherd, whose 1982 study remains the latest word on this topic, suspects that although some industries have become more concentrated, others have become less concentrated, so the net picture has probably not changed much since 1980.)

Source: William G. Shepherd, "Causes of Increased Competition in the U.S. Economy, 1939–1980," *Review of Economics and Statistics*, November 1982, pp. 613–626.

Market Structures in the North American Economy

How competitive are the markets of North America? Do most firms operate in competitive markets or in non-competitive markets?

Figure 9.3 provides part of the answer to these questions. It shows the market structure of the U.S. economy and the trends in market structure between 1939 and 1980. (Unfortunately, comparable data for Canada alone and data for the 1980s and 1990s are not available.)

In 1980, three-quarters of the value of goods and services bought and sold in the United States were traded in markets that are essentially competitive—markets that have almost perfect competition or monopolistic competition. Monopoly and the dominance of a single firm accounted for about 5 percent of sales. Oligopoly, which is found mainly in manufacturing, accounted for about 18 percent of sales.

Over the period covered by the data in Fig. 9.3, the U.S. economy became increasingly competitive. You can see that the competitive markets have expanded most (the blue areas) and the oligopoly markets have shrunk most (the red areas).

But also during the past decades, the U.S. economy has become much more exposed to competition from the rest of the world. Figure 9.3 does not capture this international competition.

REVIEW QUIZ

1. What are the four market types? Explain the distinguishing characteristics of each.
2. What are the two measures of concentration? Explain how each measure is calculated.
3. Under what conditions do the measures of concentration give a good indication of the degree of competition in a market?
4. Is the North American economy competitive? Is it becoming more competitive or less competitive?

You now know the variety of market types and the way we classify firms and industries into the different market types. Our final question in this chapter is: What determines the things that firms decide to buy from other firms rather than produce for themselves?

Markets and Firms

AT THE BEGINNING OF THIS CHAPTER, WE defined a firm as an institution that hires productive resources and organizes them to produce and sell goods and services. To organize production, firms coordinate the economic decisions and activities of many individuals. But firms are not the only coordinators of economic decisions. You learned in Chapter 3 that markets coordinate decisions. They do so by adjusting prices and making the decisions of buyers and sellers consistent—making the quantity demanded equal to the quantity supplied for each good and service.

Market Coordination

Markets can coordinate production. For example, markets might coordinate the production of a rock concert. A promoter hires a stadium, some stage equipment, audio and video recording engineers and technicians, some rock groups, a superstar, a publicity agent, and a ticket agent—all market transactions—and sells tickets to thousands of rock fans, audio rights to a recording company, and video and broadcasting rights to a television network—another set of market transactions. Alternatively, if rock concerts were produced like cornflakes, the firm producing them would own all the capital used (stadiums, stage, sound and video equipment) and would employ all the labour needed (singers, engineers, salespeople, and so on).

Outsourcing—buying parts or products from other firms—is another example of market coordination. Dell uses outsourcing for all the components of the computers it produces. The major auto makers use outsourcing for windshields and windows, gearboxes, tires, and many other car parts.

What determines whether a firm or a market coordinates a particular set of activities? How does a firm decide whether to buy from another firm or manufacture an item itself? The answer is cost. Taking account of the opportunity cost of time as well as the costs of the other inputs, a firm uses the method that costs least. In other words, it uses the economically efficient method.

Firms coordinate economic activity when they can perform a task more efficiently than markets can. In such a situation, it is profitable to set up a firm. If markets can perform a task more efficiently than a firm can, people will use markets, and any attempt to set up a firm to replace such market coordination will be doomed to failure.

Why Firms?

There are four key reasons why, in many instances, firms are more efficient than markets as coordinators of economic activity. Firms can achieve

- Lower transactions costs
- Economies of scale
- Economies of scope
- Economies of team production

Transactions Costs The idea that firms exist because there are activities in which they are more efficient than markets was first suggested by University of Chicago economist and Nobel Laureate Ronald Coase. Coase focused on the firm's ability to reduce or eliminate transactions costs. **Transactions costs** are the costs that arise from finding someone with whom to do business, of reaching an agreement about the price and other aspects of the exchange, and of ensuring that the terms of the agreement are fulfilled. Market transactions require buyers and sellers to get together and to negotiate the terms and conditions of their trading. Sometimes, lawyers have to be hired to draw up contracts. A broken contract leads to still more expenses. A firm can lower such transactions costs by reducing the number of individual transactions undertaken.

Consider, for example, two ways of getting your creaking car fixed.

1. *Firm coordination*: You take the car to the garage. The garage owner coordinates parts and tools as well as the mechanic's time, and your car gets fixed. You pay one bill for the entire job.
2. *Market coordination*: You hire a mechanic, who diagnoses the problems and makes a list of the parts and tools needed to fix them. You buy the parts from the local wrecker's yard and rent the tools from ABC Rentals. You hire the mechanic again to fix the problems. You return the tools and pay your bills—wages to the mechanic, rental to ABC, and the cost of the parts used to the wrecker.

What determines the method that you use? The answer is cost. Taking account of the opportunity cost of your own time as well as the costs of the other inputs that you would have to buy, you will use the method that costs least. In other words, you will use the economically efficient method.

The first method requires that you undertake only one transaction with one firm. It's true that the firm has to undertake several transactions—hiring the labour and buying the parts and tools required to do the job. But the firm doesn't have to undertake those transactions simply to fix your car. One set of such transactions enables the firm to fix hundreds of cars. Thus there is an enormous reduction in the number of individual transactions that take place if people get their cars fixed at the garage rather than going through an elaborate sequence of market transactions.

Economies of Scale When the cost of producing a unit of a good falls as its output rate increases, **economies of scale** exist. Auto makers, for example, experience economies of scale because as the scale of production increases, the firm can use cost-saving equipment and highly specialized labour. An auto maker that produces only a few cars a year must use hand-tool methods that are costly. Economies of scale arise from specialization and the division of labour that can be reaped more effectively by firm coordination rather than by market coordination.

Economies of Scope A firm experiences **economies of scope** when it uses specialized (and often expensive) resources to produce a *range of goods and services.* For example, Microsoft hires specialist programmers, designers, and marketing experts and uses their skills across a range of software products. As a result, Microsoft coordinates the resources that produce software at a lower cost than can an individual who buys all these services in markets.

Economies of Team Production A production process in which the individuals in a group specialize in mutually supportive tasks is team production. Sport provides the best example of team activity. Some baseball team members specialize in pitching and some in batting, some basketball team members specialize in defence and some in offence. The production of goods and services offers many examples of team activity. For example, production lines in automobile and TV manufacturing plants work most efficiently when individual activity is organized in teams, each specializing in a small task. You can also think of an entire firm as being a team. The team has buyers of raw material and other inputs, production workers, and salespeople. There are even specialists within these various groups. Each individual member of the team specializes, but the value of the output of the team and the profit that it earns depend on the coordinated activities of all the team's members. The idea that firms arise as a consequence of the economies of team production was first suggested by Armen Alchian and Harold Demsetz of the University of California at Los Angeles.

Because firms can economize on transactions costs, reap economies of scale and economies of scope, and organize efficient team production, it is firms rather than markets that coordinate most of our economic activity. But there are limits to the economic efficiency of firms. If a firm becomes too big or too diversified in the things that it seeks to do, the cost of management and monitoring per unit of output begins to rise, and at some point, the market becomes more efficient at coordinating the use of resources. IBM is an example of a firm that became too big to be efficient. In an attempt to restore efficient operations, IBM split up its large organization into a number of "Baby Blues," each of which specializes in a segment of the computer market.

Sometimes firms enter into long-term relationships with each other that effectively cut out ordinary market transactions and make it difficult to see where one firm ends and another begins. For example, GM has long-term relationships with suppliers of windows, tires, and other parts. Wal-Mart has long-term relationships with suppliers of the goods it sells in its stores. Such relationships make transactions costs lower than they would be if GM or Wal-Mart went shopping on the open market each time it wanted new supplies.

REVIEW QUIZ

1. What are the two ways in which economic activity can be coordinated?
2. What determines whether a firm or markets coordinates production?
3. What are the main reasons why firms can often coordinate production at a lower cost than markets can?

Reading Between the Lines on pp. 212–213 explores the economic problem faced by Nortel Networks. We continue to study firms and their decisions in the next four chapters. In Chapter 10, we learn about the relationships between cost and output at different output levels. These cost–output relationships are common to all types of firms in all types of markets. We then turn to problems that are specific to firms in different types of markets.

READING BETWEEN THE LINES

Nortel's Problem

THE CANADIAN PRESS, OCTOBER 3, 2001

Another 20,000 Nortel jobs lost: struggling high-tech giant cuts down to half its size

Nortel Networks is slashing another 20,000 jobs, hiring a new CEO and paring the company to half its size in the wake of another massive quarterly loss and warnings of continued weakness in the telecom industry.

The high-tech giant dropped another bombshell late yesterday, saying it will shrink its workforce by almost 20,000 more jobs to 45,000—less than half the total it started with this year after a spate of acquisitions.

Half of the cuts will be through the sale of assets and non-core businesses and will be completed by the end of this month.

Earlier this year, Nortel cut 30,000 jobs from its peak of 95,000 and reported a loss of $19.4 billion US, one of the biggest in corporate history. The latest cuts mean another 20,000 workers will leave the company, either through layoff or divestment.

Nortel, one of the world's major producers of fibre-optic communications equipment, also announced it will lose about $3.6 billion US in the third quarter, which ended Sunday. Much of that loss came from special charges, but the company also said it will lose $910 million US from operations.

Meanwhile, Nortel appointed its chief financial officer, Frank Dunn, to replace retiring chief executive John Roth, effective Nov. 1. Roth will stay on as vice-chairman until the end of 2002.

The Toronto-area company has been hit hard over the last year by a sharp drop in sales linked to the meltdown of the global technology industry. But stock-swap acquisitions at sky-high prices, overly aggressive expansion and quarterly forecasts it routinely failed to meet have helped batter its share price and produced massive losses.

...

"This has been a challenging period of adjustment," Roth told a telephone news conference, saying the company wants to break even at quarterly revenues of "well below" $4 billion US, down from $5 billion US in earlier estimates. The company is aiming to be at that level in the first quarter of 2002, he said.

...

The Canadian Press.

Essence of the Story

- In 2001, Nortel, one of the world's major producers of fibre-optic communications equipment, announced a loss of $19.4 billion U.S., one of the biggest in corporate history.
- The company cut its work force by 20,000 to 45,000—less than half the total it started the year with and hired a new CEO.
- Half of the job cuts came from the sale of non-core businesses.
- Earlier in 2001, Nortel cut 30,000 jobs from its peak of 95,000.

Economic Analysis

■ Nortel Networks is a very old Canadian corporation that was in business (under a different name) at the birth of the telephone.

■ Nortel produces a wide range of telecommunications equipment and services to customers in more than 150 countries. During the 1990s, Nortel grew to become the world's second largest telecommunications equipment producer (second to Lucent).

■ Nortel's goal is to maximize profit, and the news article illustrates the economic problem that confronted the company during 2001.

■ Nortel's main customers are telecommunications companies such as Bell, AT&T, WorldCom, Global Crossing, and 360network.

■ Fundamentally, Nortel's problems stem from a shrinking market for its products.

■ During 2001, the global market for telecommunications equipment and services collapsed.

■ The collapse came partly from an over expansion as firms scrambled to dominate the $1 trillion global telecommunications market during the 1990s expansion.

■ Faced with a collapse in revenues, Nortel cut back its scale partly by selling assets in businesses outside its core activities and partly by cutting its work force.

■ Nortel also changed its CEO. This move was a change in its entrepreneurial resources.

■ Nortel's goal is to return to profitability but with a much smaller total revenue and total cost.

SUMMARY

KEY POINTS

The Firm and Its Economic Problem
(pp. 196–198)

- Firms hire factors of production and organize them to produce and sell goods and services.
- Firms seek to maximize economic profit, which is total revenue minus opportunity cost.
- Technology, information, and market constraints limit a firm's profit.

Technological and Economic Efficiency
(pp. 199–200)

- A method of production is technologically efficient when the firm produces a given output by using the least amount of inputs.
- A method of production is economically efficient when the cost of producing a given output is as low as possible.

Information and Organization (pp. 201–204)

- Firms use a combination of command systems and incentive systems to organize production.
- Faced with incomplete information and uncertainty, firms induce managers and workers to perform in ways that are consistent with the firm's goals.
- Sole proprietorships, partnerships, and corporations use ownership, incentives, and long-term contracts to cope with the principal–agent problem.

Markets and the Competitive Environment
(pp. 205–209)

- Perfect competition occurs when there are many buyers and sellers of an identical product and when new firms can easily enter a market.
- Monopolistic competition occurs when a large number of firms compete with each other by making slightly different products.
- Oligopoly occurs when a small number of producers compete with each other.
- Monopoly occurs when one firm produces a good or service for which there are no close substitutes and the firm is protected by a barrier that prevents the entry of competitors.

Markets and Firms (pp. 210–211)

- Firms coordinate economic activities when they can perform a task more efficiently—at lower cost—than markets can.
- Firms economize on transactions costs and achieve the benefits of economies of scale, economies of scope, and economies of team production.

KEY FIGURE AND TABLES

Figure 9.1	Relative Importance of the Three Types of Firms, 204
Table 9.4	The Pros and Cons of Different Types of Firms, 203
Table 9.5	Concentration Ratio Calculations, 206
Table 9.6	Market Structure, 208

KEY TERMS

Command system, 201
Economic depreciation, 196
Economic efficiency, 199
Economic profit, 197
Economies of scale, 211
Economies of scope, 211
Firm, 196
Four-firm concentration ratio, 206
Herfindahl–Hirschman Index, 206
Implicit rental rate, 196
Incentive system, 201
Monopolistic competition, 205
Monopoly, 205
Normal profit, 197
Oligopoly, 205
Perfect competition, 205
Principal–agent problem, 202
Product differentiation, 205
Technological efficiency, 199
Technology, 198
Transactions costs, 210

PROBLEMS

*1. One year ago, Jack and Jill set up a vinegar-bottling firm (called JJVB). Use the following information to calculate JJVB's explicit costs and implicit costs during its first year of operation:
   a. Jack and Jill put $50,000 of their own money into the firm.
   b. They bought equipment for $30,000.
   c. They hired one employee to help them for an annual wage of $20,000.
   d. Jack gave up his previous job, at which he earned $30,000, and spent all his time working for JJVB.
   e. Jill kept her old job, which paid $30 an hour, but gave up 10 hours of leisure each week (for 50 weeks) to work for JJVB.
   f. JJVB bought $10,000 of goods and services from other firms.
   g. The market value of the equipment at the end of the year was $28,000.

2. One year ago, Ms. Moffat and Mr. Spieder opened a cheese firm (called MSCF). Use the following information to calculate MSCF's explicit costs and implicit costs during its first year of operation:
   a. Moffat and Spieder put $70,000 of their own money into the firm.
   b. They bought equipment for $40,000.
   c. They hired one employee to help them for an annual wage of $18,000.
   d. Moffat gave up her previous job, at which she earned $22,000, and spent all her time working for MSCF.
   e. Spieder kept his old job, which paid $20 an hour, but gave up 20 hours of leisure each week (for 50 weeks) to work for MSCF.
   f. MSCF bought $5,000 of goods from other firms.
   g. The market value of the equipment at the end of the year was $37,000.

*3. Four methods for doing a tax return are with a personal computer, a pocket calculator, a pocket calculator with pencil and paper, and a pencil and paper. With a PC, the job takes an hour; with a pocket calculator, it takes 12 hours; with a pocket calculator and paper and pencil, it takes 12 hours; and with a pencil and paper, it takes 16 hours. The PC and its software cost $1,000, the pocket calculator costs $10, and the pencil and paper cost $1.
   a. Which, if any, of the methods is technologically efficient?
   b. Which method is economically efficient if the wage rate is
      (i) $5 an hour?
      (ii) $50 an hour?
      (iii) $500 an hour?

4. Shawn is a part-time student and he can do his engineering assignment by using a personal computer, a pocket calculator, a pocket calculator and a pencil and paper, or a pencil and paper. With a PC, Shawn completes the job in 1 hour; with a pocket calculator, it takes15 hours; with a pocket calculator and paper and pencil, it takes 7 hours; and with a pencil and paper, it takes 30 hours. The PC and its software cost $1,000, the pocket calculator costs $20, and the pencil and paper cost $5.
   a. Which, if any, of the methods is technologically efficient?
   b. Which method is economically efficient if Shawn's wage rate is
      (i) $10 an hour?
      (ii) $20 an hour?
      (iii) $250 an hour?

*5. Alternative ways of laundering 100 shirts are

Method	Labour (hours)	Capital (machines)
A	1	10
B	5	8
C	20	4
D	50	1

   a. Which methods are technologically efficient?
   b. Which method is economically efficient if the hourly wage rate and implicit rental rate of capital is
      (i) Wage rate is $1, rental rate is $100?
      (ii) Wage rate is $5, rental rate is $50?
      (iii) Wage rate is $50, rental rate is $5?

6. Four ways of making 10 surfboards a day are

Method	Labour (hours)	Capital (machines)
A	40	10
B	40	20
C	20	30
D	10	40

   a. Which methods are technologically efficient?

b. Which method is economically efficient if the hourly wage rate and implicit rental rate of capital are
(i) Wage rate is $1, rental rate $100?
(ii) Wage rate is $5, rental rate is $50?
(iii) Wage rate is $50, rental rate is $5?

*7. Sales of the firms in the tattoo industry are

Firm	Sales (dollars)
Bright Spots	450
Freckles	325
Love Galore	250
Native Birds	200
Other 15 firms	800

a. Calculate the four-firm concentration ratio.
b. What is the structure of the tattoo industry?

8. Sales of the firms in the dry cleaning industry are

Firm	Sales (thousands of dollars)
SqueakyClean, Inc.	15
Village Cleaners, Inc.	25
Plaza Cleaners, Inc.	30
The Cleanery, Inc.	40
Other 20 firms	300

a. Calculate the four-firm concentration ratio.
b. What is the structure of the industry?

*9. Market shares of chocolate makers are

Firm	Market Share (percent)
Mayfair, Inc.	15
Bond, Inc.	10
Magic, Inc.	20
All Natural, Inc.	15
Truffles, Inc.	25
Gold, Inc.	15

a. Calculate the Herfindahl–Hirschman Index.
b. What is the structure of the industry?

10. Market shares of orange juice suppliers are

Firm	Market Share (percent)
Natural Fresh, Inc.	75
Fresh Squeezed, Inc.	10
Juice-to-Go, Inc.	8
Juiced-Out, Inc.	7

a. Calculate the Herfindahl–Hirschman Index.
b. What is the structure of the industry?

CRITICAL THINKING

1. Study *Reading Between the Lines* about Nortel Network's economic problem on pp. 212–213, and then answer the following questions.
   a. What is the fundamental source of Nortel's economic problem?
   b. What actions did Nortel take in response to its falling revenues in 2001?
   c. How does Nortel seek to return to profitable operations in the face of falling revenues?
   d. Under what circumstances would you expect the firm to increase its work force back to its 2000 level?
2. What is the principal–agent problem? Do you think Nortel has such a problem? Describe the problem and explain how Nortel might cope with it.
3. Do you think that Nortel buys any services from other firms? If so, what types of services do you predict that Nortel buys? Why do you think Nortel doesn't produce these services for itself?

WEB EXERCISES

1. Use the link on your Parkin–Bade Web site and read James D. Miller's views on providing airport security services.
   a. What does Mr. Miller argue concerning the best way to organize airport security?
   b. Explain Mr. Miller's views using the principal–agent analysis. Who is the principal and who is the agent?
   c. What exactly is the principal–agent problem in providing airport security services?
   d. Why might a private provider offer better security than a public provider?
   e. Do you think that a private provider would operate at a lower cost than a public provider? Why or why not?

OUTPUT AND COSTS

What Does a Doughnut Cost?

More doughnuts are sold in Canada (per person) than anywhere else in the world. Tim Hortons, with its more than 2,000 outlets across Canada is the nation's leading producer. But competition has arrived from south of the border. In 2001, a Krispy Kreme outlet opened in Mississauga, Ontario, and more are springing up across the country. At the same time, Country Style is struggling and shrinking. Why? ◆ Firms differ in lots of ways from mom-and-pop convenience stores to multinational giants producing high-tech goods. But regardless of their size or what they produce, all firms must decide how much to produce and how to produce it. How are a firm's costs influenced by these decisions? ◆ Most automakers could produce more cars than they can sell. Why do automakers have expensive equipment lying around that isn't fully used? Electric utilities don't have enough capacity to meet demand on the coldest and hottest days and must buy power from other producers. Why don't these firms install more equipment so that they can supply the market themselves?

We are going to answer these questions in this chapter. To do so, we are going to study the economic decisions of a small, imaginary firm: Cindy's Sweaters, Inc., a producer of knitted sweaters. By studying the economic problems of Cindy's Sweaters we will be able to get a clear view of the problems that face all firms—small ones like Cindy's Sweaters and a mom-and-pop convenience store as well as big firms such as banks, automakers, and electric utilities. We're going to begin by setting the scene and describing the time frames in which Cindy makes her business decisions. At the end of this chapter, in *Reading Between the Lines*, we'll return to Krispy Kreme and Country Style.

After studying this chapter, you will be able to

- **Distinguish between the short run and the long run**
- **Explain the relationship between a firm's output and labour employed in the short run**
- **Explain the relationship between a firm's output and costs in the short run**
- **Derive and explain a firm's short-run cost curves**
- **Explain the relationship between a firm's output and costs in the long run**
- **Derive and explain a firm's long-run average cost curve**

Decision Time Frames

PEOPLE WHO OPERATE FIRMS MAKE MANY decisions. And all of the decisions are aimed at one overriding objective: maximum attainable profit. But the decisions are not all equally critical. Some of the decisions are big ones. Once made, they are costly (or impossible) to reverse. If such a decision turns out to be incorrect, it might lead to the failure of the firm. Some of the decisions are small ones. They are easily changed. If one of these decisions turns out to be incorrect, the firm can change its actions and survive.

The biggest decision that any firm makes is what industry to enter. For most entrepreneurs, their background knowledge and interests drive this decision. But the decision also depends on profit prospects. No one sets up a firm without believing that it will be profitable—that total revenue will exceed opportunity cost (see Chapter 9, pp. 196–197).

The firm that we'll study has already chosen the industry in which to operate. It has also chosen its most effective method of organization, but it has not decided the quantity to produce, the quantities of resources to hire, or the price at which to sell its output.

Decisions about the quantity to produce and the price to charge depend on the type of market in which the firm operates. Perfect competition, monopolistic competition, oligopoly, and monopoly all confront the firm with their own special problems.

But decisions about how to produce a given output do not depend on the type of market in which the firm operates. These decisions are similar for *all* types of firms in *all* types of markets.

The actions that a firm can take to influence the relationship between output and cost depend on how soon the firm wants to act. A firm that plans to change its output rate tomorrow has fewer options than one that plans to change its output rate six months from now.

To study the relationship between a firm's output decision and its costs, we distinguish between two decision time frames:

- The short run
- The long run

The Short Run

The **short run** is a time frame in which the quantities of some resources are fixed. For most firms, the fixed resources are the firm's technology, buildings, and capital. The management organization is also fixed in the short run. We call the collection of fixed resources the firm's *plant*. So in the short run, a firm's plant is fixed.

For Cindy's Sweaters, the fixed plant is its factory building and its knitting machines. For an electric power utility, the fixed plant is its buildings, generators, computers, and control systems. For an airport, the fixed plant is the runways, terminal buildings, and traffic control facilities.

To increase output in the short run, a firm must increase the quantity of variable inputs it uses. Labour is usually the variable input. So to produce more output, Cindy's Sweaters must hire more labour and operate its knitting machines for more hours per day. Similarly, an electric power utility must hire more labour and operate its generators for more hours per day. And an airport must hire more labour and operate its runways, terminals, and traffic control facilities for more hours per day.

Short-run decisions are easily reversed. The firm can increase or decrease its output in the short run by increasing or decreasing the amount of labour it hires.

The Long Run

The **long run** is a time frame in which the quantities of *all* resources can be varied. That is, the long run is a period in which the firm can change its *plant*.

To increase output in the long run, a firm is able to choose whether to change its plant as well as whether to increase the quantity of labour it hires. Cindy's Sweaters can decide whether to install some additional knitting machines, use a new type of machine, reorganize its management, or hire more labour. An electric power utility can decide whether to install more generators. And an airport can decide whether to build more runways, terminals, and traffic control facilities.

Long-run decisions are *not* easily reversed. Once a plant decision is made, the firm usually must live with it for some time. To emphasize this fact, we call the past cost of buying a plant that has no resale value a **sunk cost.** A sunk cost is irrelevant to the firm's decisions. The only costs that influence its decisions are the short-run cost of changing its labour inputs and the long-run cost of changing its plant.

We're going to study costs in the short run and the long run. We begin with the short run and describe the technology constraint the firm faces.

Short-Run Technology Constraint

TO INCREASE OUTPUT IN THE SHORT RUN, A FIRM must increase the quantity of labour employed. We describe the relationship between output and the quantity of labour employed by using three related concepts:

1. Total product
2. Marginal product
3. Average product

These product concepts can be illustrated either by product schedules or by product curves. Let's look first at the product schedules.

TABLE 10.1 Total Product, Marginal Product, and Average Product

	Labour (workers per day)	Total product (sweaters per day)	Marginal product (sweaters per additional worker)	Average product (sweaters per worker)
A	0	0		
			4	
B	1	4		4.00
			6	
C	2	10		5.00
			3	
D	3	13		4.33
			2	
E	4	15		3.75
			1	
F	5	16		3.20

Total product is the total amount produced. Marginal product is the change in total product that results from a one-unit increase in labour. For example, when labour increases from 2 to 3 workers a day (row *C* to row *D*), total product increases from 10 to 13 sweaters. The marginal product of going from 2 to 3 workers is 3 sweaters. Average product is total product divided by the quantity of labour employed. For example, the average product of 3 workers is 4.33 sweaters per worker (13 sweaters a day divided by 3 workers).

Product Schedules

Table 10.1 shows some data that describe Cindy's Sweaters' total product, marginal product, and average product. The numbers tell us how Cindy's Sweaters' production increases as more workers are employed. They also tell us about the productivity of Cindy's Sweaters' workers.

Focus first on the columns headed "Labour" and "Total product." **Total product** is the total output produced. You can see from the numbers in these columns that as Cindy employs more labour, total product increases. For example, when Cindy employs 1 worker, total product is 4 sweaters a day, and when Cindy employs 2 workers, total product is 10 sweaters a day. Each increase in employment brings an increase in total product.

The **marginal product** of labour is the increase in total product that results from a one-unit increase in the quantity of labour employed with all other inputs remaining the same. For example, in Table 10.1, when Cindy increases the number of workers from 2 to 3 and keeps her capital the same, the marginal product of the third worker is 3 sweaters—total product goes from 10 to 13 sweaters.

Average product tells how productive workers are on the average. The **average product** of labour is equal to total product divided by the quantity of labour employed. For example, in Table 10.1, the average product of 3 workers is 4.33 sweaters per worker—13 sweaters a day divided by 3 workers.

If you look closely at the numbers in Table 10.1, you can see some patterns. As the number of workers increases, marginal product at first increases and then begins to decrease. For example, marginal product increases from 4 sweaters a day for the first worker to 6 sweaters a day for the second worker and then decreases to 3 sweaters a day for the third worker. Average product also increases at first and then decreases. You can see the relationships between employment and the three product concepts more clearly by looking at the product curves.

Product Curves

The product curves are graphs of the relationships between employment and the three product concepts you've just studied. They show how total product, marginal product, and average product change as employment changes. They also show the relationships among the three concepts. Let's look at the product curves.

Total Product Curve

Figure 10.1 shows Cindy's Sweaters' total product curve, *TP*. As employment increases, so does the number of sweaters knitted. Points *A* through *F* on the curve correspond to the same rows in Table 10.1.

The total product curve is similar to the *production possibilities frontier* (explained in Chapter 2). It separates the attainable output levels from those that are unattainable. All the points that lie above the curve are unattainable. Points that lie below the curve, in the orange area, are attainable. But they are inefficient—they use more labour than is necessary to produce a given output. Only the points *on* the total product curve are technologically efficient.

Notice especially the shape of the total product curve. As employment increases from zero to 1 to 2 workers per day, the curve becomes steeper. Then, as employment increases to 3, 4, and 5 workers a day, the curve becomes less steep. The steeper the slope of the total product curve, the greater is marginal product, as you are about to see.

FIGURE 10.1 Total Product Curve

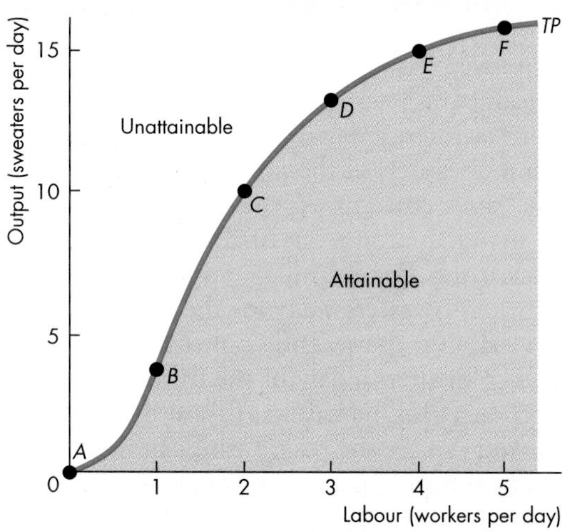

The total product curve, *TP*, is based on the data in Table 10.1. The total product curve shows how the quantity of sweaters changes as the quantity of labour employed changes. For example 2 workers can produce 10 sweaters a day (point *C*). Points *A* through *F* on the curve correspond to the rows of Table 10.1. The total product curve separates attainable outputs from unattainable outputs. Points below the *TP* curve are inefficient.

Marginal Product Curve

Figure 10.2 shows Cindy's Sweaters' marginal product of labour. Part (a) reproduces the total product curve from Fig. 10.1. Part (b) shows the marginal product curve, *MP*.

In part (a), the orange bars illustrate the marginal product of labour. The height of each bar measures marginal product. Marginal product is also measured by the slope of the total product curve. Recall that the slope of a curve is the change in the value of the variable measured on the *y*-axis—output—divided by the change in the variable measured on the *x*-axis—labour input—as we move along the curve. A one-unit increase in labour input, from 2 to 3 workers, increases output from 10 to 13 sweaters, so the slope from point *C* to point *D* is 3, the same as the marginal product that we've just calculated.

We've calculated the marginal product of labour for a series of unit increases in the quantity of labour. But labour is divisible into smaller units than one person. It is divisible into hours and even minutes. By varying the amount of labour in the smallest units imaginable, we can draw the marginal product curve shown in Fig. 10.2(b). The *height* of this curve measures the *slope* of the total product curve at a point. Part (a) shows that an increase in employment from 2 to 3 workers increases output from 10 to 13 sweaters (an increase of 3). The increase in output of 3 sweaters appears on the vertical axis of part (b) as the marginal product of going from 2 to 3 workers. We plot that marginal product at the midpoint between 2 and 3 workers. Notice that marginal product shown in Fig. 10.2(b) reaches a peak at 1.5 workers, and at that point, marginal product is 6. The peak occurs at 1.5 workers because the total product curve is steepest when employment increases from 1 worker to 2 workers.

The total product and marginal product curves are different for different firms and different types of goods. Ford Motor Company's product curves are different from those of Jim's Burger Stand, which in turn are different from those of Cindy's Sweaters. But the shapes of the product curves are similar because almost every production process has two features:

- Increasing marginal returns initially
- Diminishing marginal returns eventually

Increasing Marginal Returns Increasing marginal returns occur when the marginal product of an additional worker exceeds the marginal product of the

FIGURE 10.2 Marginal Product

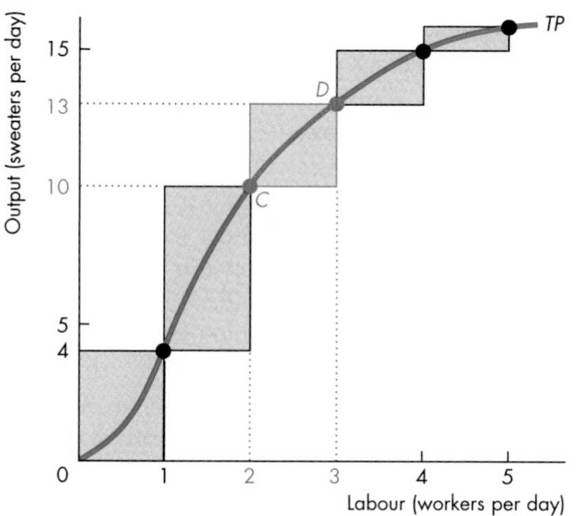

(a) Total product

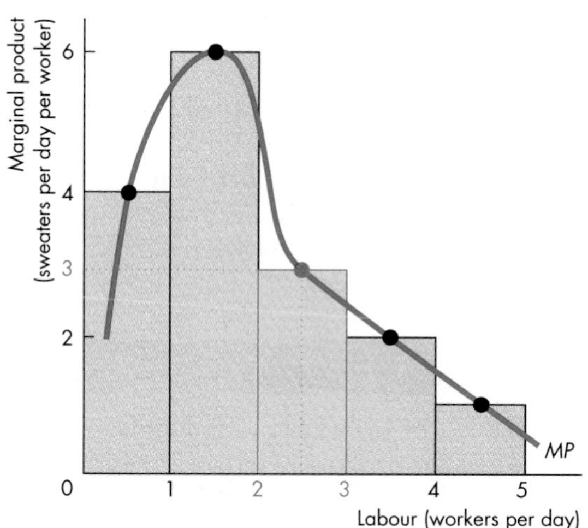

(b) Marginal product

Marginal product is illustrated by the orange bars. For example, when labour increases from 2 to 3, marginal product is the orange bar whose height is 3 sweaters. (Marginal product is shown midway between the labour inputs to emphasize that it is the result of *changing* inputs.) The steeper the slope of the total product curve (*TP*) in part (a), the larger is marginal product (*MP*) in part (b). Marginal product increases to a maximum (in this example when the second worker is employed) and then declines—diminishing marginal product.

previous worker. Increasing marginal returns arise from increased specialization and division of labour in the production process.

For example, if Cindy employs just one worker, that person must learn all the aspects of sweater production: running the knitting machines, fixing breakdowns, packaging and mailing sweaters, buying and checking the type and colour of the wool. All these tasks must be performed by that one person.

If Cindy hires a second person, the two workers can specialize in different parts of the production process. As a result, two workers produce more than twice as much as one. The marginal product of the second worker is greater than the marginal product of the first worker. Marginal returns are increasing.

Diminishing Marginal Returns Most production processes experience increasing marginal returns initially. But all production processes eventually reach a point of *diminishing* marginal returns. **Diminishing marginal returns** occur when the marginal product of an additional worker is less than the marginal product of the previous worker.

Diminishing marginal returns arise from the fact that more and more workers are using the same capital and working in the same space. As more workers are added, there is less and less for the additional workers to do that is productive. For example, if Cindy hires a third worker, output increases but not by as much as it did when she hired the second worker. In this case, after two workers are hired, all the gains from specialization and the division of labour have been exhausted. By hiring a third worker, the factory produces more sweaters, but the equipment is being operated at a rate closer to its limits. There are even times when the third worker has nothing to do because the machines are running without the need for further attention. Hiring more and more workers continues to increase output but by successively smaller amounts. Marginal returns are diminishing. This phenomenon is such a pervasive one that it is called a "law"—the law of diminishing returns. The **law of diminishing returns** states that

> As a firm uses more of a variable input, with a given quantity of fixed inputs, the marginal product of the variable input eventually diminishes.

You are going to return to the law of diminishing returns when we study a firm's costs. But before we do that, let's look at the average product of labour and the average product curve.

Average Product Curve

Figure 10.3 illustrates Cindy's Sweaters' average product of labour, *AP*. It also shows the relationship between average product and marginal product. Points *B* through *F* on the average product curve correspond to those same rows in Table 10.1. Average product increases from 1 to 2 workers (its maximum value at point *C*) but then decreases as yet more workers are employed. Notice also that average product is largest when average product and marginal product are equal. That is, the marginal product curve cuts the average product curve at the point of maximum average product. For the numbers of workers at which marginal product exceeds average product, average product is increasing. For the numbers of workers at which marginal product is less than average product, average product is decreasing.

The relationship between the average and marginal product curves is a general feature of the relationship between the average and marginal values of any variable. Let's look at a familiar example.

FIGURE 10.3 Average Product

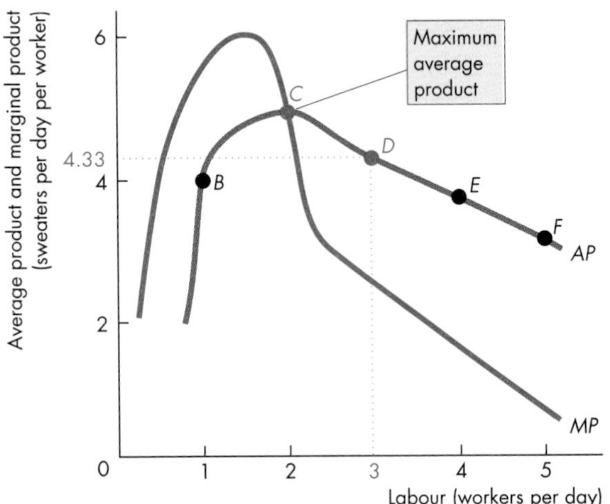

The figure shows the average product of labour and the connection between the average product and marginal product. With 1 worker per day, marginal product exceeds average product, so average product is increasing. With 2 workers per day, marginal product equals average product, so average product is at its maximum. With more than 2 workers per day, marginal product is less than average product, so average product is decreasing.

Marginal Grade and Grade Point Average

To see the relationship between average product and marginal product, think about the similar relationship between Cindy's average grade and marginal grade over five semesters. (Suppose Cindy is a part-time student who takes just one course each semester.) In the first semester, Cindy takes calculus and her grade is a C (2). This grade is her marginal grade. It is also her average grade—her GPA. In the next semester, Cindy takes French and gets a B (3). French is Cindy's marginal course, and her marginal grade is 3. Her GPA rises to 2.5. Because her marginal grade exceeds her average grade, it pulls her average up. In the third semester, Cindy takes economics and gets an A (4)—her new marginal grade. Because her marginal grade exceeds her GPA, it again pulls her average up. Cindy's GPA is now 3, the average of 2, 3, and 4. The fourth semester, she takes history and gets a B (3). Because her marginal grade is equal to her average, her GPA does not change. In the fifth semester, Cindy takes English and gets a D (2). Because her marginal grade, a 2, is below her GPA of 3, her GPA falls.

Cindy's GPA increases when her marginal grade exceeds her GPA. Her GPA falls when her marginal grade is below her GPA. And her GPA is constant when her marginal grade equals her GPA. The relationship between marginal product and average product is exactly the same as that between Cindy's marginal and average grades.

REVIEW QUIZ

1 Explain how the marginal product of labour and the average product of labour change as the quantity of labour employed increases (a) initially and (b) eventually.
2 What is the law of diminishing returns? Why does marginal product eventually diminish?
3 Explain the relationship between marginal product and average product. How does average product change when marginal product exceeds average product? How does average product change when average product exceeds marginal product? Why?

Cindy's Sweaters cares about its product curves because they influence its costs. Let's look at Cindy's Sweaters' costs.

Short-Run Cost

TO PRODUCE MORE OUTPUT IN THE SHORT RUN, a firm must employ more labour, which means that it must increase its costs. We describe the relationship between output and cost by using three cost concepts:

- Total cost
- Marginal cost
- Average cost

Total Cost

A firm's **total cost** (*TC*) is the cost of the productive resources it uses. Total cost includes the cost of land, capital, and labour. It also includes the cost of entrepreneurship, which is *normal profit* (see Chapter 9, p. 197). We divide total cost into total fixed cost and total variable cost.

Total fixed cost (*TFC*) is the cost of the firm's fixed inputs. Because the quantity of a fixed input does not change as output changes, total fixed cost does not change as output changes.

Total variable cost (*TVC*) is the cost of the firm's variable inputs. Because to change its output a firm must change the quantity of variable inputs, total variable cost changes as output changes.

Total cost is the sum of total fixed cost and total variable cost. That is,

$$TC = TFC + TVC.$$

The table in Fig. 10.4 shows Cindy's total costs. With one knitting machine that Cindy rents for \$25 a day, *TFC* is \$25. To produce sweaters, Cindy hires labour, which costs \$25 a day. *TVC* is the number of workers multiplied by \$25. For example, to produce 13 sweaters a day, Cindy hires 3 workers and *TVC* is \$75. *TC* is the sum of *TFC* and *TVC*, so to produce 13 sweaters a day, Cindy's total cost, *TC*, is \$100. Check the calculation in each row of the table.

Figure 10.4 shows Cindy's total cost curves, which graph total cost against total product. The green total fixed cost curve (*TFC*) is horizontal because total fixed cost does not change when output changes. It is a constant at \$25. The purple total variable cost curve (*TVC*) and the blue total cost curve (*TC*) both slope upward because total variable cost increases as output increases. The arrows highlight total fixed cost as the vertical distance between the *TVC* and *TC* curves.

Let's now look at Cindy's marginal cost.

FIGURE 10.4 Total Cost Curves

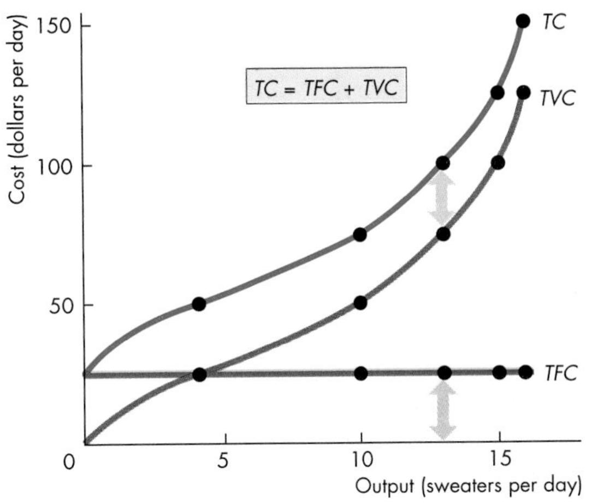

	Labour (workers per day)	Output (sweaters per day)	Total fixed cost (*TFC*)	Total variable cost (*TVC*)	Total cost (*TC*)
			(dollars per day)		
A	0	0	25	0	25
B	1	4	25	25	50
C	2	10	25	50	75
D	3	13	25	75	100
E	4	15	25	100	125
F	5	16	25	125	150

Cindy rents a knitting machine for \$25 a day. This amount is Cindy's total fixed cost. Cindy hires workers at a wage rate of \$25 a day, and this cost is Cindy's total variable cost. For example, if Cindy employs 3 workers, total variable cost is 3 × \$25, which equals \$75. Total cost is the sum of total fixed cost and total variable cost. For example, when Cindy employs 3 workers, total cost is \$100—total fixed cost of \$25 plus total variable cost of \$75. The graph shows Cindy's Sweaters' total cost curves. Total fixed cost (*TFC*) is constant—it graphs as a horizontal line—and total variable cost (*TVC*) increases as output increases. Total cost (*TC*) increases as output increases. The vertical distance between the total cost curve and the total variable cost curve is total fixed cost, as illustrated by the two arrows.

Marginal Cost

In Fig. 10.4, total variable cost and total cost increase at a decreasing rate at small outputs and then begin to increase at an increasing rate as output increases. To understand these patterns in the changes in total cost, we need to use the concept of *marginal cost.*

A firm's **marginal cost** is the increase in total cost that results from a one-unit increase in output. We calculate marginal cost as the increase in total cost divided by the increase in output. The table in Fig. 10.5 shows this calculation. When, for example, output increases from 10 sweaters to 13 sweaters, total cost increases from $75 to $100. The change in output is 3 sweaters, and the change in total cost is $25. The marginal cost of one of those 3 sweaters is ($25 ÷ 3), which equals $8.33.

Figure 10.5 graphs the marginal cost data in the table as the red marginal cost curve, *MC.* This curve is U-shaped because when Cindy hires a second worker, marginal cost decreases, but when she hires a third, a fourth, and a fifth worker, marginal cost successively increases.

Marginal cost decreases at low outputs because of economies from greater specialization. It eventually increases because of *the law of diminishing returns.* The law of diminishing returns means that each additional worker produces a successively smaller addition to output. So to get an additional unit of output, ever more workers are required. Because more workers are required to produce one additional unit of output, the cost of the additional output—marginal cost—must eventually increase.

Marginal cost tells us how total cost changes as output changes. The final cost concept tells us what it costs, on the average, to produce a unit of output. Let's now look at Cindy's Sweaters' average costs.

Average Cost

There are three average costs:

1. Average fixed cost
2. Average variable cost
3. Average total cost

Average fixed cost (*AFC*) is total fixed cost per unit of output. **Average variable cost** (*AVC*) is total variable cost per unit of output. **Average total cost** (*ATC*) is total cost per unit of output. The average cost concepts are calculated from the total cost concepts as follows:

$$TC = TFC + TVC.$$

Divide each total cost term by the quantity produced, *Q*, to get,

$$\frac{TC}{Q} = \frac{TFC}{Q} + \frac{TVC}{Q}$$

or

$$ATC = AFC + AVC.$$

The table in Fig. 10.5 shows the calculation of average total cost. For example, when output is 10 sweaters, average fixed cost is ($25 ÷ 10), which equals $2.50, average variable cost is ($50 ÷ 10), which equals $5.00, and average total cost is ($75 ÷ 10), which equals $7.50. Note that average total cost is equal to average fixed cost ($2.50) plus average variable cost ($5.00).

Figure 10.5 shows the average cost curves. The green average fixed cost curve (*AFC*) slopes downward. As output increases, the same constant fixed cost is spread over a larger output. The blue average total cost curve (*ATC*) and the purple average variable cost curve (*AVC*) are U-shaped. The vertical distance between the average total cost and average variable cost curves is equal to average fixed cost—as indicated by the two arrows. That distance shrinks as output increases because average fixed cost declines with increasing output.

The marginal cost curve (*MC*) intersects the average variable cost curve and the average total cost curve at their minimum points. That is, when marginal cost is less than average cost, average cost is decreasing, and when marginal cost exceeds average cost, average cost is increasing. This relationship holds for both the *ATC* curve and the *AVC* curve and is another example of the relationship you saw in Fig. 10.3 for average product and marginal product and in Cindy's course grades.

Why the Average Total Cost Curve Is U-Shaped

Average total cost, *ATC,* is the sum of average fixed cost, *AFC,* and average variable cost, *AVC.* So the shape of the *ATC* curve combines the shapes of the *AFC* and *AVC* curves. The U shape of the average

FIGURE 10.5 Marginal Cost and Average Costs

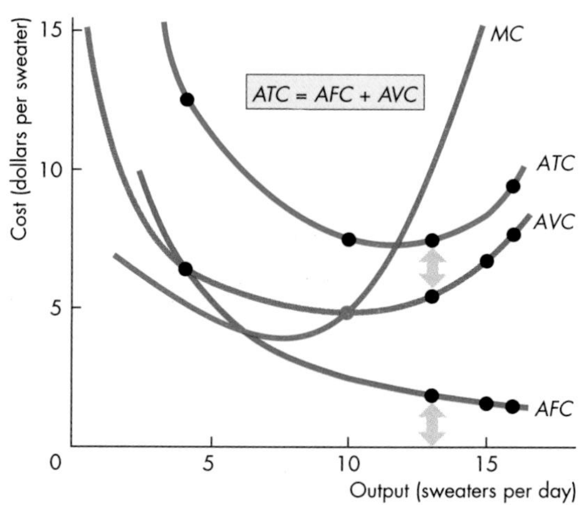

Marginal cost is calculated as the change in total cost divided by the change in output. When output increases from 4 to 10, an increase of 6, total cost increases by $25 and marginal cost is $25 ÷ 6, which equals $4.17. Each average cost concept is calculated by dividing the related total cost by output. When 10 sweaters are produced, *AFC* is $2.50 ($25 ÷ 10), *AVC* is $5 ($50 ÷ 10), and *ATC* is $7.50 ($75 ÷ 10).

The graph shows that the marginal cost curve (*MC*) is U-shaped and intersects the average variable cost curve and the average total cost curve at their minimum points. Average fixed cost (*AFC*) decreases as output increases. The average total cost curve (*ATC*) and average variable cost curve (*AVC*) are U-shaped. The vertical distance between these two curves is equal to average fixed cost, as illustrated by the two arrows.

	Labour (workers per day)	Output (sweaters per day)	Total fixed cost (*TFC*)	Total variable cost (*TVC*)	Total cost (*TC*)	Marginal cost (*MC*) (dollars per additional sweater)	Average fixed cost (*AFC*)	Average variable cost (*AVC*)	Average total cost (*ATC*)
			(dollars per day)				(dollars per sweater)		
A	0	0	25	0	25		—	—	—
						6.25			
B	1	4	25	25	50		6.25	6.25	12.50
						4.17			
C	2	10	25	50	75		2.50	5.00	7.50
						8.33			
D	3	13	25	75	100		1.92	5.77	7.69
						12.50			
E	4	15	25	100	125		1.67	6.67	8.33
						25.00			
F	5	16	25	125	150		1.56	7.81	9.38

total cost curve arises from the influence of two opposing forces:

1. Spreading total fixed cost over a larger output
2. Eventually diminishing returns

When output increases, the firm spreads its total fixed cost over a larger output and so its average fixed cost decreases—its average fixed cost curve slopes downward.

Diminishing returns means that as output increases, ever-larger amounts of labour are needed to produce an additional unit of output. So average variable cost eventually increases, and the *AVC* curve eventually slopes upward.

The shape of the average total cost curve combines these two effects. Initially, as output increases, both average fixed cost and average variable cost decrease, so average total cost decreases and the *ATC* curve slopes downward. But as output increases further and diminishing returns set in, average variable cost begins to increase. Eventually, average variable cost increases more quickly than average fixed cost decreases, so average total cost increases and the *ATC* curve slopes upward.

Cost Curves and Product Curves

The technology that a firm uses determines its costs. Figure 10.6 shows the links between the firm's technology constraint (its product curves) and its cost curves. The upper part of the figure shows the average product curve and the marginal product curve—like those in Fig. 10.3. The lower part of the figure shows the average variable cost curve and the marginal cost curve—like those in Fig. 10.5.

The figure highlights the links between technology and costs. As labour increases initially, marginal product and average product rise and marginal cost and average variable cost fall. Then, at the point of maximum marginal product, marginal cost is a minimum. As labour increases further, marginal product diminishes and marginal cost increases. But average product continues to rise, and average variable cost continues to fall. Then, at the point of maximum average product, average variable cost is a minimum. As labour increases further, average product diminishes and average variable cost increases.

Shifts in the Cost Curves

The position of a firm's short-run cost curves depend on two factors:

- Technology
- Prices of productive resources

Technology A technological change that increases productivity shifts the total product curve upward. It also shifts the marginal product curve and the average product curve upward. With a better technology, the same inputs can produce more output, so technological change lowers costs and shifts the cost curves downward.

For example, advances in robot production techniques have increased productivity in the automobile industry. As a result, the product curves of DaimlerChrysler, Ford, and GM have shifted upward, and their cost curves have shifted downward. But the relationships between their product curves and cost curves have not changed. These curves are still linked in the way shown in Fig. 10.6.

Often, a technological advance results in a firm using more capital (a fixed input) and less labour (a variable input). For example, today the telephone companies use computers to provide directory assistance in place of the human operators they used in

FIGURE 10.6 Product Curves and Cost Curves

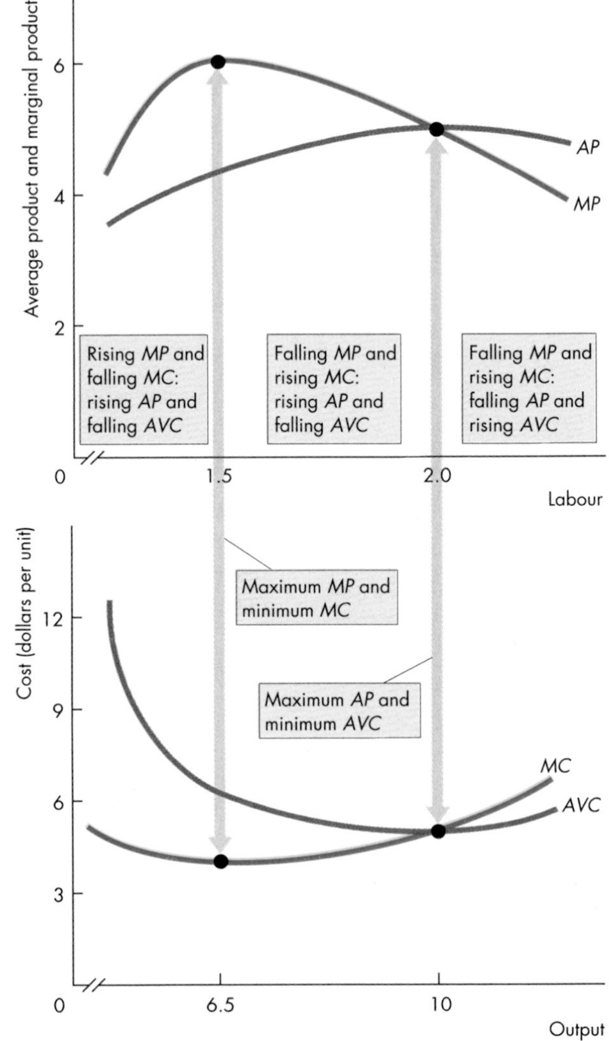

A firm's marginal product curve is linked to its marginal cost curve. If marginal product rises, marginal cost falls. If marginal product is a maximum, marginal cost is a minimum. If marginal product diminishes, marginal cost rises. A firm's average product curve is linked to its average variable cost curve. If average product rises, average variable cost falls. If average product is a maximum, average variable cost is a minimum. If average product diminishes, average variable cost rises.

TABLE 10.2 A Compact Glossary of Costs

Term	Symbol	Definition	Equation
Fixed cost		Cost that is independent of the output level; cost of a fixed input	
Variable cost		Cost that varies with the output level; cost of a variable input	
Total fixed cost	*TFC*	Cost of the fixed inputs	
Total variable cost	*TVC*	Cost of the variable inputs	
Total cost	*TC*	Cost of all inputs	$TC = TFC + TVC$
Output (total product)	*TP*	Total quantity produced (output *Q*)	
Marginal cost	*MC*	Change in total cost resulting from a one-unit increase in total product	$MC = \Delta TC \div \Delta Q$
Average fixed cost	*AFC*	Total fixed cost per unit of output	$AFC = TFC \div Q$
Average variable cost	*AVC*	Total variable cost per unit of output	$AVC = TVC \div Q$
Average total cost	*ATC*	Total cost per unit of output	$ATC = AFC + AVC$

the 1980s. When such a technological change occurs, total cost decreases, but fixed costs increase and variable costs decrease. This change in the mix of fixed cost and variable cost means that at low output levels, average total cost might increase, while at high output levels, average total cost decreases.

Prices of Productive Resources An increase in the price of a productive resource increases costs and shifts the cost curves. But how the curves shift depends on which resource price changes. An increase in rent or some other component of *fixed* cost shifts the fixed cost curves (*TFC* and *AFC*) upward and shifts the total cost curve (*TC*) upward but leaves the variable cost curves (*AVC* and *TVC*) and the marginal cost curve (*MC*) unchanged. An increase in wages or some other component of *variable* cost shifts the variable cost curves (*TVC* and *AVC*) upward and shifts the marginal cost curve (*MC*) upward but leaves the fixed cost curves (*AFC* and *TFC*) unchanged. So, for example, if truck drivers' wages increase, the variable cost and marginal cost of transportation services increase. If the interest expense paid by a trucking company increases, the fixed cost of transportation services increases.

You've now completed your study of short-run costs. All the concepts that you've met are summarized in a compact glossary in Table 10.2.

REVIEW QUIZ

1. What relationships do a firm's short-run cost curves show?
2. How does marginal cost change as output increases (a) initially and (b) eventually?
3. What does the law of diminishing returns imply for the shape of the marginal cost curve?
4. What is the shape of the average fixed cost curve and why?
5. What are the shapes of the average variable cost curve and the average total cost curve and why?

Long-Run Cost

IN THE SHORT RUN, A FIRM CAN VARY THE quantity of labour but the quantity of capital is fixed. So the firm has variable costs of labour and fixed costs of capital. In the long run, a firm can vary both the quantity of labour and the quantity of capital. So in the long run, all the firm's costs are variable. We are now going to study the firm's costs in the long run, when all costs are variable costs and when the quantities of labour and capital vary.

The behaviour of long-run cost depends on the firm's *production function*, which is the relationship between the maximum output attainable and the quantities of both labour and capital.

The Production Function

Table 10.3 shows Cindy's Sweaters' production function. The table lists total product schedules for four different quantities of capital. We identify the quantity of capital by the plant size. The numbers for Plant 1 are for a factory with 1 knitting machine—the case we've just studied. The other three plants have 2, 3, and 4 machines. If Cindy's Sweaters doubles its capital to 2 knitting machines, the various amounts of labour can produce the outputs shown in the second column of the table. The other two columns show the outputs of yet larger quantities of capital. Each column of the table could be graphed as a total product curve for each plant.

Diminishing Returns Diminishing returns occur at all four quantities of capital as the quantity of labour increases. You can check that fact by calculating the marginal product of labour in plants with 2, 3, and 4 machines. At each plant size, as the quantity of labour increases, its marginal product of labour (eventually) diminishes.

Diminishing Marginal Product of Capital Diminishing returns also occur as the quantity of capital increases. You can check that fact by calculating the marginal product of capital at a given quantity of labour. The *marginal product of capital* is the change in total product divided by the change in capital when the quantity of labour is constant—equivalently, the change in output resulting from a one-unit increase in the quantity of capital. For example, if Cindy's has 3 workers and increases its capital from 1 machine to 2 machines, output increases from 13 to 18 sweaters a day. The marginal product of capital is 5 sweaters per day. If Cindy increases the number of machines from 2 to 3, output increases from 18 to 22 sweaters per day. The marginal product of the third machine is 4 sweaters per day, down from 5 sweaters per day for the second machine.

Let's now see what the production function implies for long-run costs.

TABLE 10.3 The Production Function

Labour (workers per day)	Output (sweaters per day)			
	Plant 1	Plant 2	Plant 3	Plant 4
1	4	10	13	15
2	10	15	18	20
3	13	18	22	24
4	15	20	24	26
5	16	21	25	27
Knitting machines (number)	1	2	3	4

The table shows the total product data for four quantities of capital. The greater the plant size, the larger is the total product for any given quantity of labour. But for a given plant size, the marginal product of labour diminishes. And for a given quantity of labour, the marginal product of capital diminishes.

Short-Run Cost and Long-Run Cost

Continue to assume that Cindy can hire a worker for \$25 per day and rent a knitting machine for \$25 per machine per day. Using these input prices and the data in Table 10.3, we can calculate and graph the average total cost curves for factories with 1, 2, 3, and 4 knitting machines. We've already studied the costs of a factory with 1 machine in Figs. 10.4 and 10.5. In Fig. 10.7, the average total cost curve for that case is ATC_1. Figure 10.7 also shows the average total cost curve for a factory with 2 machines, ATC_2, with 3 machines, ATC_3, and with 4 machines, ATC_4.

FIGURE 10.7 Short-Run Costs of Four Different Plants

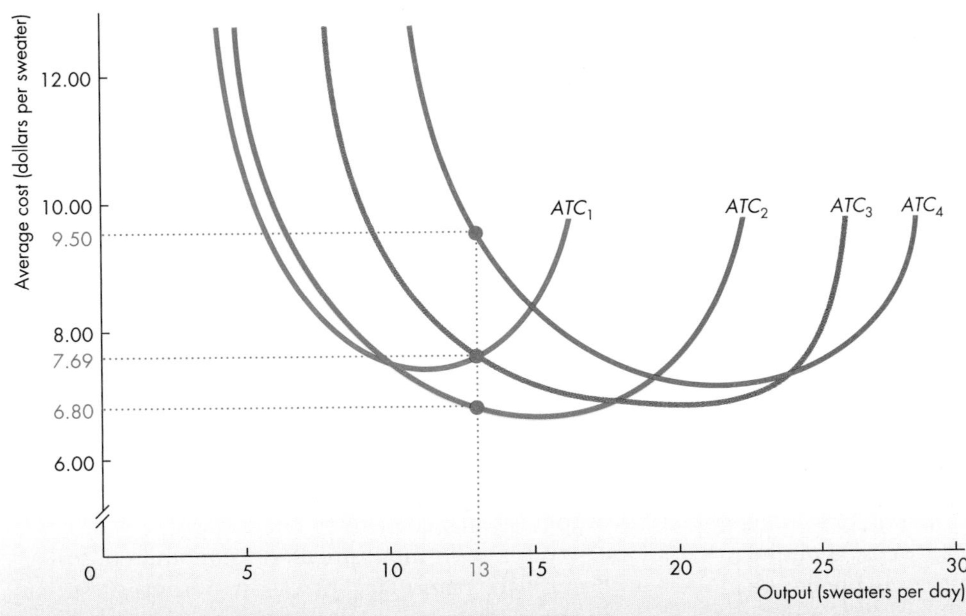

The figure shows short-run average total cost curves for four different quantities of capital. Cindy's can produce 13 sweaters a day with 1 knitting machine on ATC_1 or with 3 knitting machines on ATC_3 for an average cost of $7.69 per sweater. Cindy's can produce the same number of sweaters by using 2 knitting machines on ATC_2 for $6.80 per sweater or by using 4 machines on ATC_4 for $9.50 per sweater. If Cindy's produces 13 sweaters a day, the least-cost method of production—the long-run method—is with 2 machines on ATC_2.

You can see, in Fig. 10.7, that plant size has a big effect on the firm's average total cost. Two things stand out:

1. Each short-run *ATC* curve is U-shaped.
2. For each short-run *ATC* curve, the larger the plant, the greater is the output at which average total cost is a minimum.

Each short-run average total cost curve is U-shaped because, as the quantity of labour increases, its marginal product at first increases and then diminishes. And these patterns in the marginal product of labour, which we examined in some detail for the plant with 1 knitting machine on pp. 220–221, occur at all plant sizes.

The minimum average total cost for a larger plant occurs at a greater output than it does for a smaller plant because the larger plant has a higher total fixed cost and therefore, for any given output level, a higher average fixed cost.

Which short-run average cost curve Cindy's Sweaters operates on depends on its plant size. But in the long run, Cindy chooses the plant size. And which plant size she chooses depends on the output she plans to produce. The reason is that the average total cost of producing a given output depends on the plant size.

To see why, suppose that Cindy plans to produce 13 sweaters a day. With 1 machine, the average total cost curve is ATC_1 (in Fig. 10.7) and the average total cost of 13 sweaters a day is $7.69 per sweater. With 2 machines, on ATC_2, average total cost is $6.80 per sweater. With 3 machines, on ATC_3, average total cost is $7.69 per sweater, the same as with 1 machine. Finally, with 4 machines, on ATC_4, average total cost is $9.50 per sweater.

The economically efficient plant size for producing a given output is the one that has the lowest average total cost. For Cindy's Sweaters, the economically efficient plant to use to produce 13 sweaters a day is the one with 2 machines.

In the long run, Cindy's chooses the plant size that minimizes average total cost. When a firm is producing a given output at the least possible cost, it is operating on its *long-run average cost curve.*

The **long-run average cost curve** is the relationship between the lowest attainable average total cost and output when both the plant size and labour are varied.

The long-run average cost curve is a planning curve. It tells the firm the plant size and the quantity of labour to use at each output to minimize cost. Once the plant size is chosen, the firm operates on the short-run cost curves that apply to that plant size.

The Long-Run Average Cost Curve

Figure 10.8 shows Cindy's Sweaters' long-run average cost curve, *LRAC*. This long-run average cost curve is derived from the short-run average total cost curves in Fig. 10.7. For output rates up to 10 sweaters a day, average total cost is the lowest on ATC_1. For output rates between 10 and 18 sweaters a day, average total cost is the lowest on ATC_2. For output rates between 18 and 24 sweaters a day, average total cost is the lowest on ATC_3. And for output rates in excess of 24 sweaters a day, average total cost is the lowest on ATC_4. The segment of each of the four average total cost curves for which that quantity of capital has the lowest average total cost is highlighted in dark blue in Fig. 10.8. The scallop-shaped curve made up of these four segments is the long-run average cost curve.

Economies and Diseconomies of Scale

Economies of scale are features of a firm's technology that lead to falling long-run average cost as output increases. When economies of scale are present, the *LRAC* curve slopes downward. The *LRAC* curve in Fig. 10.8 shows that Cindy's Sweaters experiences economies of scale for outputs up to 15 sweaters a day.

With given input prices, economies of scale occur if the percentage increase in output exceeds the percentage increase in all inputs. For example, if when a firm increases its labour and capital by 10 percent, output increases by more than 10 percent, its average total cost falls. Economies of scale are present.

The main source of economies of scale is greater specialization of both labour and capital. For example, if GM produces 100 cars a week, each worker must perform many different tasks and the capital must be general-purpose machines and tools. But if GM produces 10,000 cars a week, each worker specializes and becomes highly proficient in a small number of tasks. Also, the capital is specialized and productive.

Diseconomies of scale are features of a firm's technology that lead to rising long-run average cost as output increases. When diseconomies of scale are present, the *LRAC* curve slopes upward. In Fig. 10.8, Cindy's Sweaters experiences diseconomies of scale at outputs greater than 15 sweaters a day.

With given input prices, diseconomies of scale occur if the percentage increase in output is less than the percentage increase in inputs. For example, if when a firm increases its labour and capital by 10 percent, output increases by less than 10 percent,

FIGURE 10.8 Long-Run Average Cost Curve

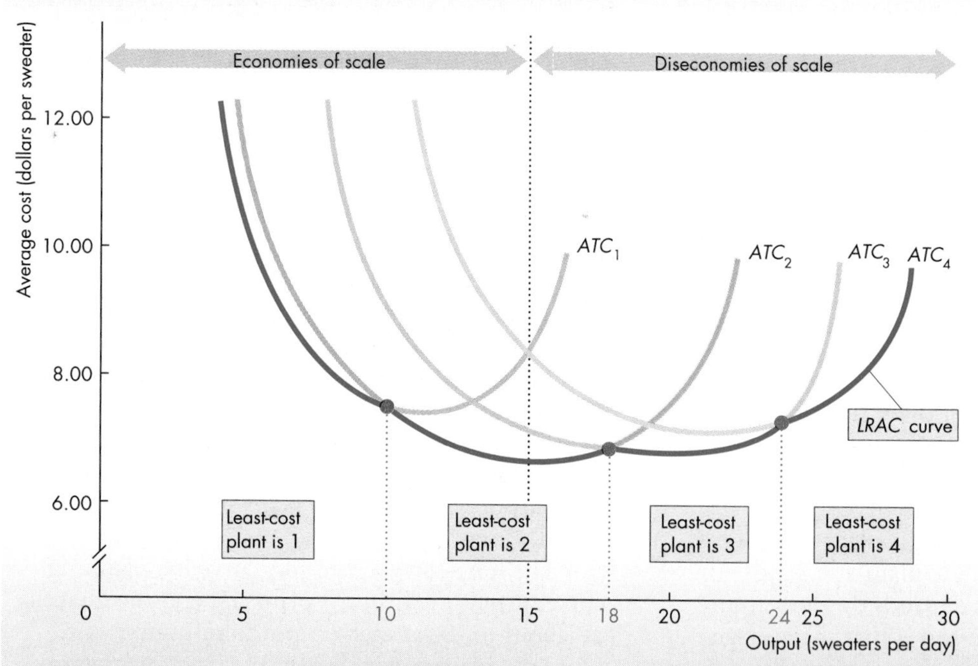

In the long run, Cindy's can vary both capital and labour inputs. The long-run average cost curve traces the lowest attainable average total cost of production. Cindy's produces on its long-run average cost curve if it uses 1 machine to produce up to 10 sweaters a day, 2 machines to produce between 10 and 18 sweaters a day, 3 machines to produce between 18 and 24 sweaters a day, and 4 machines to produce more than 24 sweaters a day. Within these ranges, Cindy's varies its output by varying its labour input.

its average total cost rises. Diseconomies of scale are present.

The main source of diseconomies of scale is the difficulty of managing a very large enterprise. The larger the firm, the greater is the challenge of organizing it and the greater is the cost of communicating both up and down the management hierarchy and among managers. Eventually, management complexity brings rising average cost.

Diseconomies of scale occur in all production processes but perhaps only at a very large output rate.

Constant returns to scale are features of a firm's technology that lead to constant long-run average cost as output increases. When constant returns to scale are present, the *LRAC* curve is horizontal.

Constant returns to scale occur if the percentage increase in output equals the percentage increase in inputs. For example, if when a firm increases its labour and capital by 10 percent, output increases by 10 percent, then constant returns to scale are present.

For example, General Motors can double its production of Cavaliers by doubling its production facility for those cars. It can build an identical production line and hire an identical number of workers. With the two identical production lines, GM produces exactly twice as many cars.

Minimum Efficient Scale A firm experiences economies of scale up to some output level. Beyond that level, it moves into constant returns to scale or diseconomies of scale. A firm's **minimum efficient scale** is the smallest quantity of output at which long-run average cost reaches its lowest level.

The minimum efficient scale plays a role in determining market structure, as you will learn in the next three chapters. The minimum efficient scale also helps to answer some questions about real businesses.

Economies of Scale at Cindy's Sweaters The production technology that Cindy's Sweaters uses, shown in Table 10.3, illustrates economies of scale and diseconomies of scale. If Cindy's Sweaters increases its inputs from 1 machine and 1 worker to 2 of each, a 100 percent increase in all inputs, output increases by more than 100 percent from 4 sweaters to 15 sweaters a day. Cindy's Sweaters experiences economies of scale, and its long-run average cost decreases. But if Cindy's Sweaters increases its inputs to 3 machines and 3 workers, a 50 percent increase, output increases to by less than 50 percent, from 15 sweaters to 22 sweaters a day. Now Cindy's Sweaters experiences diseconomies of scale, and its long-run average cost increases. Its minimum efficient scale is at 15 sweaters a day.

Producing Cars and Generating Electric Power Why do automakers have expensive equipment lying around that isn't fully used? You can now answer this question. An automaker uses the plant that minimizes the average total cost of producing the output that it can sell. But it operates below the efficient minimum scale. Its short-run average total cost curve looks like ATC_1 in Fig. 10.8. If it could sell more cars, it would produce more cars and its average total cost would fall.

Why do many electric utilities have too little production equipment to meet demand on the coldest and hottest days and have to buy power from other producers? You can now see why this happens and why an electric utility doesn't build more generating capacity. A power producer uses the plant size that minimizes the average total cost of producing the output that it can sell on a normal day. But it produces above the minimum efficient scale and experiences diseconomies of scale. Its short-run average total cost curve looks like ATC_3 in Fig. 10.8. With a larger plant size, its average total costs of producing its normal output would be higher.

REVIEW QUIZ

1 What does a firm's production function show and how is it related to a total product curve?
2 Does the law of diminishing returns apply to capital as well as to labour? Explain why or why not.
3 What does a firm's long-run average cost curve show? How is it related to the firm's short-run average cost curves?
4 What are economies of scale and diseconomies of scale? How do they arise? And what do they imply for the shape of the long-run average cost curve?
5 How is a firm's minimum efficient scale determined?

Reading Between the Lines on pp. 232–233 applies what you've learned about a firm's cost curves. It looks at the cost curves of firms like Krispy Kreme and Country Style.

READING BETWEEN THE LINES

The Cost of a Doughnut

THE GLOBE AND MAIL, DECEMBER 12, 2001

Krispy Kreme store mobbed

It was a feeding frenzy yesterday as Krispy Kreme Doughnuts Inc. opened in Canada for the first time. ... And Krispy Kreme sold more than 25,000 doughnuts before 10 a.m., when the store officially opened in Mississauga. ...

That's quite all right with Scott Livengood, chairman, president and chief executive officer, who came up from head office in Winston-Salem, N.C., to oversee the launch. ...

The Krispy Kreme in Mississauga is charging $5.99 for a dozen of its doughnuts — $10.99 for two dozen. That's 35 per cent more than at least one of its competitors charges. ...

"Krispy Kreme is a cultural experience, a multidimensional experience," Mr. Livengood said. "People come for the aroma of coffee, the visual theatre. They come to watch the people.

"They see doughnuts rising through the proof box. It's almost a Circadian rhythm. It's a stimulating visual presentation."...

Mr. Livengood is confident that the formula will work — even in Canada, a country that has more doughnut shops per capita than anywhere in the world.

He has committed to building 31 more outlets over the next six years at a cost of $1.2-million (U.S.) each.

EDMONTON JOURNAL, DECEMBER 15, 2001

Doughnut shop's demise comes as shock to owner

Country Style Food Services Inc. is closing 25 more stores under court-ordered bankruptcy protection so its struggling chain can restructure, the company said Friday.

Fifty stores that were "bleeding" the company's finances will no longer be operating by this weekend, says Country Style, the third largest coffee and doughnut franchiser in Canada.

Dave Mills, the manager of the last Country Style Donut shop in the Edmonton area was shocked to learn Friday that his store was one of the bleeders that would be shut down this morning. ...

Essence of the Stories

- Two news stories separated by only three days report the successful opening of a new doughnut shop and the closing of another.
- Krispy Kreme is expanding its business into Canada and plans to open 31 more outlets over the next six years at a cost of $1.2 million (U.S.) each.
- Country Style Food Services Inc., Canada's third largest coffee and doughnut franchiser, is closing 25 stores.

Economic Analysis

■ Doughnut producers must choose the styles and varieties of doughnuts to produce, the technology for producing them, and the scale of their production plants.

■ Krispy Kreme uses a secret formula to produce doughnuts and makes them in full view of its customers in a doughnut production theatre.

■ The Krispy Kreme technology is capital intensive and has high fixed costs.

■ To produce at a low enough average total cost (*ATC*), Krispy Kreme must produce a large output rate.

■ Figure 1 shows the average cost curves for a production process such as that of Krispy Kreme. (The numbers are assumed.)

■ Average fixed cost (*AFC*) is high and output must exceed 1,500 doughnuts an hour before it falls below 50¢ a doughnut.

■ Average variable cost (*AVC*) is low and is assumed to be constant for output rates up to 2,000 doughnuts an hour.

■ Average total cost (*ATC*) is at its minimum at an output rate of 2,500 doughnuts an hour.

■ Figure 2 shows the average cost curves for a production process such as that of Country Style. (Again, the numbers are assumed.)

■ Average fixed cost (*AFC*) is low and an output of 200 doughnuts an hour keeps it well below the price of a doughnut. But as the output rate falls to around 100 an hour, average costs rise steeply.

■ Average variable cost (*AVC*) is assumed to be constant for output rates up to 200 doughnuts an hour.

■ Average total cost (*ATC*) is at its minimum at an output rate of 300 doughnuts an hour.

■ If the output rate falls below 200 doughnuts an hour, *ATC* rises to exceed the market price of a doughnut and a firm like Country Style has a problem.

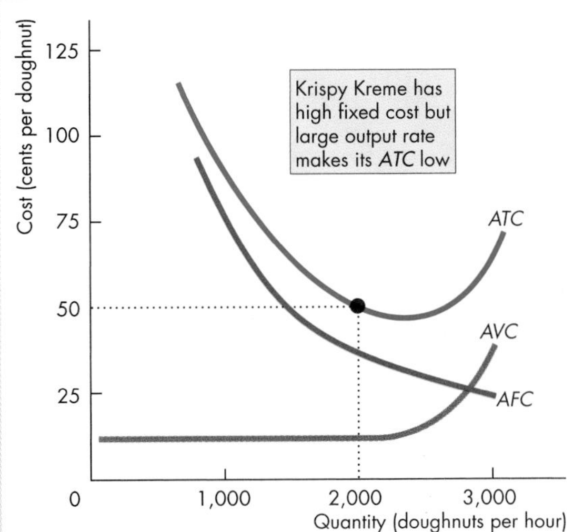

Figure 1 Krispy Kreme cost curves

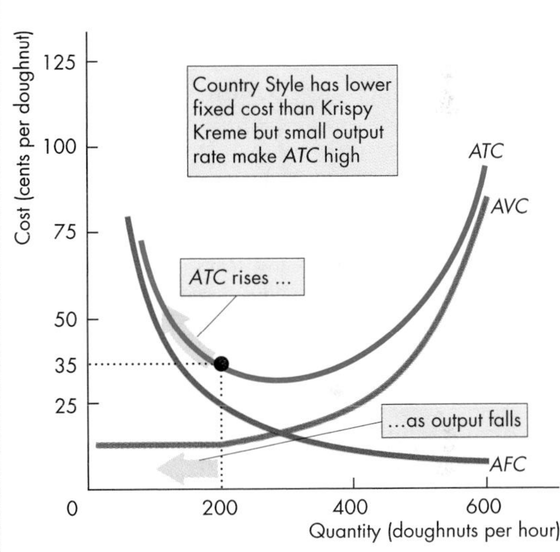

Figure 2 Country Style cost curves

SUMMARY

KEY POINTS

Decision Time Frames (p. 218)

- In the short run, the quantity of some resources are fixed and the quantities of the other resources can be varied.
- In the long run, the quantities of all resources can be varied.

Short-Run Technology Constraint (pp. 219–222)

- A total product curve shows the quantity a firm can produce with a given quantity of capital and different quantities of labour.
- Initially, the marginal product of labour increases as the quantity of labour increases, but eventually, marginal product diminishes—the law of diminishing returns.
- Average product increases initially and eventually diminishes.

Short-Run Cost (pp. 223–227)

- As output increases, total fixed cost is constant, and total variable cost and total cost increase.
- As output increases, average fixed cost decreases and average variable cost, average total cost, and marginal cost decrease at low outputs and increase at high outputs. These cost curves are U-shaped.

Long-Run Cost (pp. 228–231)

- Long-run cost is the cost of production when all inputs—labour and capital—have been adjusted to their economically efficient levels.
- There is a set of short-run cost curves for each different plant size. There is one least-cost plant size for each output. The larger the output, the larger is the plant size that will minimize average total cost.
- The long-run average cost curve traces out the lowest attainable average total cost at each output when both capital and labour inputs can be varied.
- With economies of scale, the long-run average cost curve slopes downward. With diseconomies of scale, the long-run average cost curve slopes upward.

KEY FIGURES AND TABLE

Figure 10.2 Marginal Product, 221
Figure 10.3 Average Product, 222
Figure 10.5 Marginal Cost and Average Costs, 225
Figure 10.6 Product Curves and Cost Curves, 226
Figure 10.7 Short-Run Costs of Four Different Plants, 229
Figure 10.8 Long-Run Average Cost Curve, 230
Table 10.2 A Compact Glossary of Costs, 227

KEY TERMS

Average fixed cost, 224
Average product, 219
Average total cost, 224
Average variable cost, 224
Constant returns to scale, 231
Diminishing marginal returns, 221
Diseconomies of scale, 230
Economies of scale, 230
Law of diminishing returns, 221
Long run, 218
Long-run average cost curve, 229
Marginal cost, 224
Marginal product, 219
Minimum efficient scale, 231
Short run, 218
Sunk cost, 218
Total cost, 223
Total fixed cost, 223
Total product, 219
Total variable cost, 223

PROBLEMS

*1. Rubber Dinghies' total product schedule is

Labour (workers per week)	Output (dinghies per week)
1	1
2	3
3	6
4	10
5	15
6	21
7	26
8	30
9	33
10	35

a. Draw the total product curve.
b. Calculate the average product of labour and draw the average product curve.
c. Calculate the marginal product of labour and draw the marginal product curve.
d. What is the relationship between average product and marginal product when Rubber Dinghies produces (i) fewer than 30 dinghies a week and (ii) more than 30 dinghies a week?

2. Sue's SurfBoards' total product schedule is

Labour (workers per week)	Output (surfboards per week)
1	40
2	100
3	140
4	170
5	190
6	200

a. Draw the total product curve.
b. Calculate the average product of labour and draw the average product curve.
c. Calculate the marginal product of labour and draw the marginal product curve.
d. What is the relationship between the average product and marginal product when Sue's SurfBoards produces (i) less than 100 surfboards a week and (ii) more than 100 surfboards a week?

*3. In problem 1, the price of labour is $400 a week and total fixed cost is $1,000 a week.
a. Calculate total cost, total variable cost, and total fixed cost for each output and draw the short-run total cost curves.
b. Calculate average total cost, average fixed cost, average variable cost, and marginal cost at each output and draw the short-run average and marginal cost curves.

4. In problem 2, the price of labour is $100 per week and total fixed costs are $200 per week.
a. Calculate total cost, total variable cost, and total fixed costs for each level of output and draw the short-run total cost curves.
b. Calculate average total cost, average fixed cost, average variable cost, and marginal cost at each level of output and draw the short-run average and marginal cost curves.

*5. In problem 3, suppose that Rubber Dinghies' total fixed cost increases to $1,100 a week. Explain what changes occur in the short-run average and marginal cost curves.

6. In problem 4, suppose that the price of labour increases to $150 per week. Explain what changes occur in the short-run average and marginal cost curves.

*7. In problem 3, Rubber Dinghies buys a second plant and the total product of each quantity of labour doubles. The total fixed cost of operating each plant is $1,000 a week. The wage rate is $400 a week.
a. Set out the average total cost schedule when Rubber Dinghies operates two plants.
b. Draw the long-run average cost curve.
c. Over what output ranges is it efficient to operate one plant and two plants?

8. In problem 4, Sue's SurfBoards buys a second plant and the total product of each quantity of labour increases by 50 percent. The total fixed cost of operating each plant is $200 a week. The wage rate is $100 a week.
a. Set out the average total cost curve when Sue's SurfBoards operates two plants.
b. Draw the long-run average cost curve.
c. Over what output ranges is it efficient to operate one plant and two plants?

*9. The table shows the production function of Bonnie's Balloon Rides.

Labour (workers per day)	Output (rides per day)			
	Plant 1	Plant 2	Plant 3	Plant 4
1	4	10	13	15
2	10	15	18	20
3	13	18	22	24
4	15	20	24	26
5	16	21	25	27
Balloons (number)	1	2	3	4

Bonnie pays $500 a day for each balloon she rents and $250 a day for each balloon operator she hires.

a. Find and graph the average total cost curve for each plant size.
b. Draw Bonnie's long-run average cost curve.
c. What is Bonnie's minimum efficient scale?
d. Explain how Bonnie uses her long-run average cost curve to decide how many balloons to rent.

10. The table shows the production function of Cathy's Cakes.

Labour (workers per day)	Output (cakes per day)			
	Plant 1	Plant 2	Plant 3	Plant 4
1	20	40	55	65
2	40	60	75	85
3	65	75	90	100
4	65	85	100	110
Ovens (number)	1	2	3	4

Cathy pays $100 a day for each oven she rents and $50 a day for each kitchen worker she hires.

a. Find and graph the average total cost curve for each plant size.
b. Draw Cathy's long-run average cost curve.
c. Over what output range does Cathy experience economies of scale?
d. Explain how Cathy uses her long-run average cost curve to decide how many ovens to rent.

CRITICAL THINKING

1. Study *Reading Between the Lines* on pp. 232–233 and then answer the following questions:
   a. What are the main differences in the cost curves of Krispy Kreme and Country Style?
   b. Why do you think Krispy Kreme is starting to operate in Canada?
   c. Would it ever make sense for Krispy Kreme to make its doughnuts using the same technology as Country Style uses?
   d. Would it ever make sense for Country Style to make its doughnuts using the same technology as Krispy Kreme uses?
   e. Suppose an advance in technology increases the productivity of a Krispy Kreme style doughnut production plant but has no effect on small-scale doughnut production. How would the technological change affect Krispy Kreme's costs and cost curves? Would it change the number of outlets and the number of people it employs? If so, how? Explain.

WEB EXERCISES

1. Use the link on your Parkin–Bade Web site to obtain information about the cost of producing pumpkins.
   a. List all the costs referred to on the Web page.
   b. For each item, say whether it is a fixed cost or a variable cost.
   c. Make some assumptions and sketch the average cost curves and the marginal cost curve for producing pumpkins.
2. Use the link on your Parkin–Bade Web site to obtain information about the cost of producing vegetables. For one of the vegetables (your choice):
   a. List all the costs referred to on the Web page.
   b. For each item, say whether it is a fixed cost or a variable cost.
   c. Sketch the average cost curves and the marginal cost curve for producing the vegetable you've chosen.

PERFECT COMPETITION

CHAPTER 11

Sweet Competition

Maple syrup is sweet, but producing it and selling it is a tough competitive business. Around 12,000 firms in Canada and the United States produce syrup. In 2000 and 2001, bumper crops sent the price of maple syrup tumbling. How did producers react to this drop in price? *Reading Between the Lines* at the end of the chapter answers this question. In recent years, new firms have entered the maple syrup business, while others have been squeezed out. Why do some firms enter an industry and others leave it? What are the effects on profits and prices of new firms entering and old firms leaving an industry? ◆ In September 2002, around 200,000 people were unemployed because they had been laid off by the firms that previously employed them. Why do firms lay off workers? Why do firms temporarily shut down? ◆ Over the past few years, there has been a dramatic fall in the prices of personal computers. For example, a slow computer cost almost $4,000 a few years ago, and a fast one costs only $1,000 today. What goes on in an industry when the price of its output falls sharply? What happens to the profits of the firms producing such goods? Ice cream, computers, and most other goods are produced by more than one firm, and these firms compete with each other for sales.

◆ To study competitive markets, we are going to build a model of a market in which competition is as fierce and extreme as possible—more extreme than in the examples we've just considered. We call this situation "perfect competition."

After studying this chapter, you will be able to

- **Define perfect competition**
- **Explain how price and output are determined in perfect competition**
- **Explain why firms sometimes shut down temporarily and lay off workers**
- **Explain why firms enter and leave the industry**
- **Predict the effects of a change in demand and of a technological advance**
- **Explain why perfect competition is efficient**

Competition

THE FIRMS THAT YOU STUDY IN THIS CHAPTER face the force of raw competition. We call this extreme form of competition perfect competition. **Perfect competition** is an industry in which

- Many firms sell identical products to many buyers.
- There are no restrictions on entry into the industry.
- Established firms have no advantage over new ones.
- Sellers and buyers are well informed about prices.

Farming, fishing, wood pulping and paper milling, the manufacture of paper cups and plastic shopping bags, grocery retailing, photo finishing, lawn service, plumbing, painting, dry cleaning, and the provision of laundry services are all examples of highly competitive industries.

How Perfect Competition Arises

Perfect competition arises if the minimum efficient scale of a single producer is small relative to the demand for the good or service. A firm's *minimum efficient scale* is the smallest quantity of output at which long-run average cost reaches is lowest level. (See Chapter 10, p. 231.) Where the minimum efficient scale of a firm is small relative to demand, there is room for many firms in an industry.

Second, perfect competition arises if each firm is perceived to produce a good or service that has no unique characteristics so that consumers don't care which firm they buy from.

Price Takers

Firms in perfect competition must make many decisions. But one thing they do *not* decide is the price at which to sell their output. Firms in perfect competition are said to be price takers. A **price taker** is a firm that cannot influence the price of a good or service.

The key reason why a perfectly competitive firm is a price taker is that it produces a tiny proportion of the total output of a particular good and buyers are well informed about the prices of other firms.

Imagine that you are a wheat farmer in Saskatchewan. You have 500 hectares under cultivation—which sounds like a lot. But compared to the thousands of hectares across the Canadian prairies and in the Dakotas, Nebraska, Colorado, Oklahoma, and Texas, as well as the thousands more in Argentina, Australia, and Ukraine, your 500 hectares is a drop in the ocean. Nothing makes your wheat any better than any other farmer's, and all the buyers of wheat know the price at which they can do business.

If everybody else sells their wheat for $300 a tonne and you want $310, why would people buy from you? They can go to the next farmer and the next and the one after that and buy all they need for $300 a tonne. This price is determined in the market for wheat, and you are a *price taker.*

A price taker faces a perfectly elastic demand. One farm's wheat is a *perfect substitute* for wheat from the farm next door or from any other farm. Note, though, that the *market* demand for wheat is not perfectly elastic. The market demand curve is downward sloping, and its elasticity depends on the substitutability of wheat for other grains such as barley, rye, corn, and rice.

Economic Profit and Revenue

A firm's goal is to maximize *economic profit,* which is equal to total revenue minus total cost. Total cost is the *opportunity cost* of production, which includes *normal profit,* the return that the entrepreneur can expect to receive on the average in an alternative business. (See Chapter 9, p. 197.)

A firm's **total revenue** equals the price of its output multiplied by the number of units of output sold (price × quantity). **Marginal revenue** is the change in total revenue that results from a one-unit increase in the quantity sold. Marginal revenue is calculated by dividing the change in total revenue by the change in the quantity sold.

Figure 11.1 illustrates these revenue concepts. Cindy's Sweaters is one of a thousand such small firms. Demand and supply in the sweater market determine the price of a sweater. Cindy must take this price. Cindy's Sweaters cannot influence the price by its own actions, so the price remains constant when Cindy changes the quantity of sweaters produced.

The table shows three different quantities of sweaters produced. As the quantity varies, the price remains constant—in this example, at $25 a sweater. Total revenue is equal to the price multiplied by the quantity sold. For example, if Cindy sells 8 sweaters, total revenue is 8 × $25, which equals $200.

Marginal revenue is the change in total revenue resulting from a one-unit change in quantity. For example, when the quantity sold increases from 8 to 9, total revenue increases from $200 to $225, so

FIGURE 11.1 Demand, Price, and Revenue in Perfect Competition

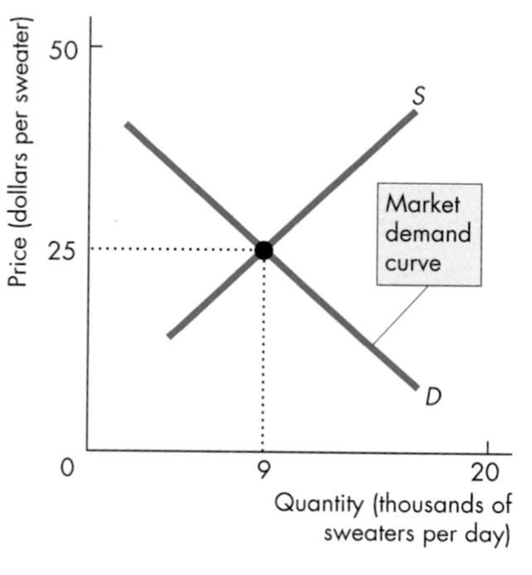

(a) Sweater market

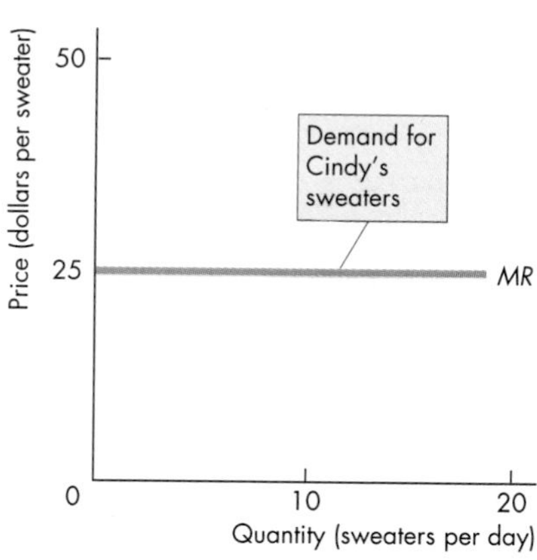

(b) Cindy's marginal revenue

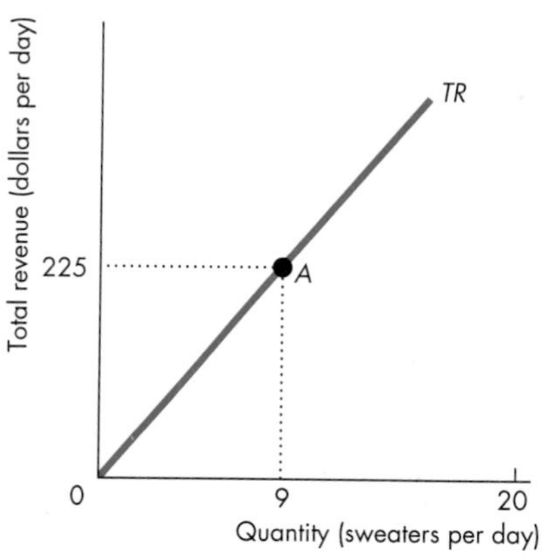

(c) Cindy's total revenue

Quantity sold (*Q*) (sweaters per day)	Price (*P*) (dollars per sweater)	Total revenue (*TR* = *P* × *Q*) (dollars)	Marginal revenue (*MR* = Δ*TR*/Δ*Q*) (dollars per additional sweater)
8	25	200	
			25
9	25	225	
			25
10	25	250	

Market demand and supply determine the market price. In part (a), the market price is \$25 a sweater and 9,000 sweaters are bought and sold. The demand for Cindy's Sweaters is perfectly elastic at the market price of \$25 a sweater. The table calculates total revenue and marginal revenue. Part (b) shows Cindy's Sweaters' marginal revenue curve (*MR*). This curve is also the demand curve for Cindy's sweaters. Part (c) shows Cindy's total revenue curve (*TR*). Point *A* corresponds to the second row of the table.

marginal revenue is \$25 a sweater. (Notice that in the table, marginal revenue appears *between* the lines for the quantities sold to remind you that marginal revenue results from the *change* in the quantity sold.)

Because the price remains constant when the quantity sold changes, the change in total revenue resulting from a one-unit increase in the quantity sold equals price. Therefore in perfect competition, marginal revenue equals price.

Figure 11.1(b) shows Cindy's marginal revenue curve (*MR*). This curve tells us the change in total revenue that results from selling one more sweater. This curve is also the demand curve for Cindy's sweaters. The firm, being a price taker, can sell any quantity it chooses at the market price. The firm faces a perfectly elastic demand for its output.

The total revenue curve (*TR*) in Fig. 11.1(c) shows the total revenue at each quantity sold. For example, if Cindy sells 9 sweaters, total revenue is \$225 (point *A*). Because each additional sweater sold brings in a constant amount—\$25—the total revenue curve is an upward-sloping straight line.

REVIEW QUIZ

1. Why is a firm in perfect competition a price taker?
2. In perfect competition, what is the relationship between the demand for the firm's output and the market demand?
3. In perfect competition, why is a firm's marginal revenue curve also the demand curve for the firm's output?
4. Why is the total revenue curve in perfect competition an upward-sloping straight line?

The Firm's Decisions in Perfect Competition

FIRMS IN A PERFECTLY COMPETITIVE INDUSTRY face a given market price and have the revenue curves that you've studied. These revenue curves summarize the market constraint faced by a perfectly competitive firm.

Firms also face a technology constraint, which is described by the product curves (total product, average product, and marginal product) that you studied in Chapter 10. The technology available to the firm determines its costs, which are described by the cost curves (total cost, average cost, and marginal cost) that you also studied in Chapter 10.

The task of the competitive firm is to make the maximum economic profit possible, given the constraints it faces. To achieve this objective, a firm must make four key decisions: two in the short run and two in the long run.

Short-Run Decisions The *short run* is a time frame in which each firm has a given plant and the number of firms in the industry is fixed. But many things can change in the short run, and the firm must react to these changes. For example, the price for which the firm can sell its output might have a seasonal fluctuation, or it might fluctuate with general business conditions. The firm must react to such short-run price fluctuations and decide

1. Whether to produce or to shut down
2. If the decision is to produce, what quantity to produce

Long-Run Decisions The *long run* is a time frame in which each firm can change the size of its plant and decide whether to leave the industry. Other firms can decide whether to enter the industry. So in the long run, both the plant size of each firm and the number of firms in the industry can change. Also in the long run, the constraints that firms face can change. For example, the demand for the good can permanently fall, or a technological advance can change the industry's costs. The firm must react to such long-run changes and decide

1. Whether to increase or decrease its plant size
2. Whether to stay in an industry or leave it

The Firm and the Industry in the Short Run and the Long Run To study a competitive industry, we begin by looking at an individual firm's short-run decisions. We then see how the short-run decisions of all firms in a competitive industry combine to determine the industry price, output, and economic profit. We then turn to the long run and study the effects of long-run decisions on the industry price, output, and economic profit. All the decisions we study are driven by the pursuit of a single objective: maximization of economic profit.

Profit-Maximizing Output

A perfectly competitive firm maximizes economic profit by choosing its output level. One way of finding the profit-maximizing output is to study a firm's total revenue and total cost curves and find the output level at which total revenue exceeds total cost by the largest amount. Figure 11.2 shows how to do this for Cindy's Sweaters. The table lists Cindy's total revenue and total cost at different outputs, and part (a) of the figure shows Cindy's total revenue and total cost curves. These curves are graphs of the numbers shown in the first three columns of the table. The total revenue curve (*TR*) is the same as that in Fig. 11.1(c). The total cost curve (*TC*) is similar to the one that you met in Chapter 10: As output increases, so does total cost.

Economic profit equals total revenue minus total cost. The fourth column of the table in Fig. 11.2 shows Cindy's economic profit, and part (b) of the figure illustrates these numbers as Cindy's profit curve. This curve shows that Cindy makes an economic profit at outputs between 4 and 12 sweaters a day. At outputs less than 4 sweaters a day, Cindy incurs an economic loss. She also incurs an economic loss if output exceeds 12 sweaters a day. At outputs of 4 sweaters and 12 sweaters a day, total cost equals total revenue and Cindy's economic profit is zero. An output at which total cost equals total revenue is called a *break-even point.* The firm's economic profit at a break-even point is zero. But because normal profit is part of total cost, a firm makes normal profit at a break-even point. That is, at the break-even point, the entrepreneur makes an income equal to the best alternative return forgone.

Notice the relationship between the total revenue, total cost, and profit curves. Economic profit is measured by the vertical distance between the total

FIGURE 11.2 Total Revenue, Total Cost, and Economic Profit

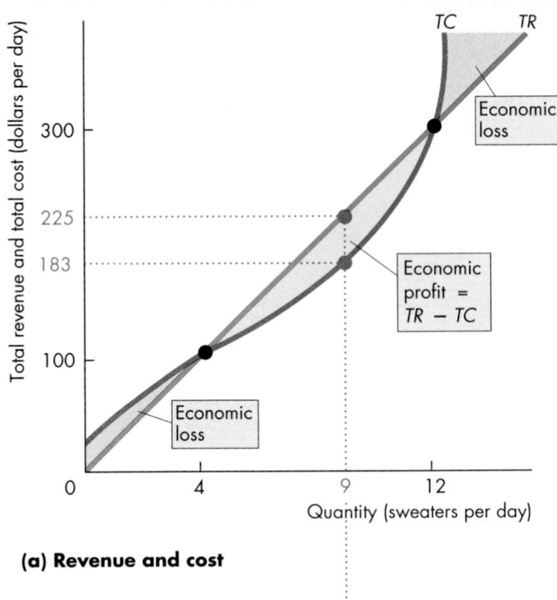

(a) Revenue and cost

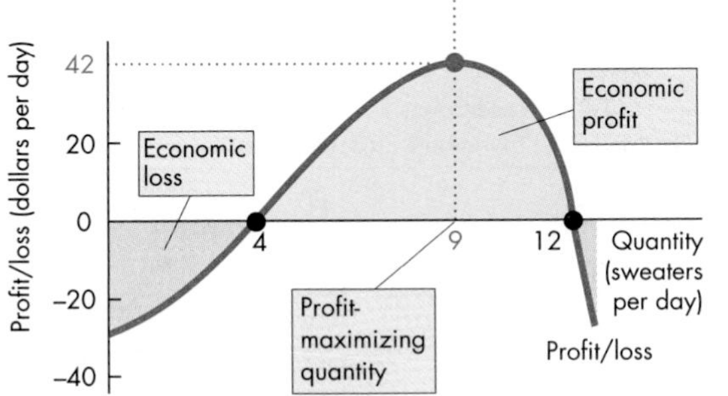

(b) Economic profit and loss

Quantity (Q) (sweaters per day)	Total revenue (TR) (dollars)	Total cost (TC) (dollars)	Economic profit (TR − TC) (dollars)
0	0	22	−22
1	25	45	−20
2	50	66	−16
3	75	85	−10
4	100	100	0
5	125	114	11
6	150	126	24
7	175	141	34
8	200	160	40
9	**225**	**183**	**42**
10	250	210	40
11	275	245	30
12	300	300	0
13	325	360	−35

The table lists Cindy's total revenue, total cost, and economic profit. Part (a) graphs the total revenue and total cost curves. Economic profit, in part (a), is the height of the blue area between the total cost and total revenue curves. Cindy's Sweaters makes maximum economic profit, $42 a day ($225 – $183), when it produces 9 sweaters—the output at which the vertical distance between the total revenue and total cost curves is at its largest. At outputs of 4 sweaters a day and 12 sweaters a day, Cindy makes zero economic profit—these are break-even points. At outputs less than 4 and greater than 12 sweaters a day, Cindy incurs an economic loss. Part (b) of the figure shows Cindy's profit curve. The profit curve is at its highest when economic profit is at a maximum and cuts the horizontal axis at the break-even points.

revenue and total cost curves. When the total revenue curve in part (a) is above the total cost curve, between 4 and 12 sweaters, the firm is making an economic profit and the profit curve in Fig. 11.2(b) is above the horizontal axis. At the break-even points, where the total cost and total revenue curves intersect, the profit curve intersects the horizontal axis. The profit curve is at its highest when the distance between *TR* and *TC* is greatest. In this example, profit maximization occurs at an output of 9 sweaters a day. At this output, Cindy's economic profit is $42 a day.

Marginal Analysis

Another way of finding the profit-maximizing output is to use *marginal analysis* and compare marginal revenue, *MR*, with marginal cost, *MC*. As output increases, marginal revenue remains constant but marginal cost changes. At low output levels, marginal cost decreases, but it eventually increases. So where the marginal cost curve intersects the marginal revenue curve, marginal cost is rising.

If marginal revenue exceeds marginal cost (if $MR > MC$), then the extra revenue from selling one more unit exceeds the extra cost incurred to produce it. The firm makes an economic profit on the marginal unit, so its economic profit increases if output *increases.*

If marginal revenue is less than marginal cost (if $MR < MC$), then the extra revenue from selling one more unit is less than the extra cost incurred to produce it. The firm incurs an economic loss on the marginal unit, so its economic profit decreases if output increases and its economic profit increases if output *decreases.*

If marginal revenue equals marginal cost (if $MR = MC$), economic profit is maximized. The rule $MR = MC$ is an example of marginal analysis. Let's check that this rule works to find the profit-maximizing output by returning to Cindy's Sweaters.

Look at Fig. 11.3. The table records Cindy's marginal revenue and marginal cost. Marginal revenue is a constant $25 a sweater. Over the range of outputs shown in the table, marginal cost increases from $19 a sweater to $35 a sweater.

Focus on the highlighted rows of the table. If Cindy increases output from 8 sweaters to 9 sweaters, marginal revenue is $25 and marginal cost is $23. Because marginal revenue exceeds marginal cost, economic profit increases. The last column of the table shows that economic profit increases from $40 to $42, an increase of $2. This economic profit from the ninth sweater is shown as the blue area in the figure.

If Cindy increases output from 9 sweaters to 10 sweaters, marginal revenue is still $25 but marginal cost is $27. Because marginal revenue is less than marginal cost, economic profit decreases. The last column of the table shows that economic profit decreases from $42 to $40. This loss from the tenth sweater is shown as the red area in the figure.

Cindy maximizes economic profit by producing 9 sweaters a day, the quantity at which marginal revenue equals marginal cost.

FIGURE 11.3 Profit-Maximizing Output

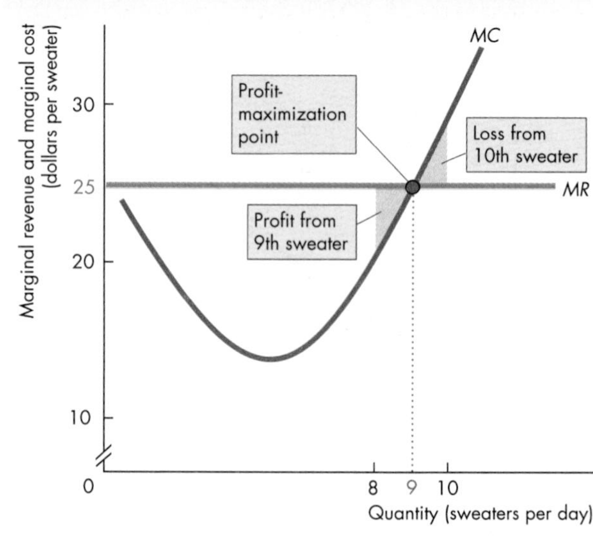

Quantity (Q) (sweaters per day)	Total revenue (TR) (dollars)	Marginal revenue (MR) (dollars per additional sweater)	Total cost (TC) (dollars)	Marginal cost (MC) (dollars per additional sweater)	Economic profit (TR – TC) (dollars)
7	175		141		34
		25		19	
8	200		160		40
		25		**23**	
9	**225**		**183**		**42**
		25		**27**	
10	250		210		40
		25		35	
11	275		245		30

Another way of finding the profit-maximizing output is to determine the output at which marginal revenue equals marginal cost. The table shows that if output increases from 8 to 9 sweaters, marginal cost is $23, which is less than the marginal revenue of $25. If output increases from 9 to 10 sweaters, marginal cost is $27, which exceeds the marginal revenue of $25. The figure shows that marginal cost and marginal revenue are equal when Cindy produces 9 sweaters a day. If marginal revenue exceeds marginal cost, an increase in output increases economic profit. If marginal revenue is less than marginal cost, an increase in output decreases economic profit. If marginal revenue equals marginal cost, economic profit is maximized.

Profits and Losses in the Short Run

In short-run equilibrium, although the firm produces the profit-maximizing output, it does not necessarily end up making an economic profit. It might do so, but it might alternatively break even (earn a normal profit) or incur an economic loss. To determine which of these outcomes occurs, we compare the firm's total revenue and total cost or, equivalently, we compare price with average total cost. If price equals average total cost, a firm breaks even—makes normal profit. If price exceeds average total cost, a firm makes an economic profit. If price is less than average total cost, a firm incurs an economic loss. Figure 11.4 shows these three possible short-run profit outcomes.

Three Possible Profit Outcomes In Fig. 11.4(a), the price of a sweater is $20. Cindy's profit-maximizing output is 8 sweaters a day. Average total cost is $20 a sweater, so Cindy breaks even and makes normal profit (zero economic profit).

In Fig. 11.4(b), the price of a sweater is $25. Profit is maximized when output is 9 sweaters a day. Here, price exceeds average total cost (*ATC*), so Cindy makes an economic profit. This economic profit is $42 a day. It is made up of $4.67 per sweater ($25.00 – $20.33) multiplied by the number of sweaters ($4.67 × 9 = $42). The blue rectangle shows this economic profit. The height of that rectangle is profit per sweater, $4.67, and the length is the quantity of sweaters produced, 9 a day, so the area of the rectangle is Cindy's economic profit of $42 a day.

In Fig. 11.4(c), the price of a sweater is $17. Here, price is less than average total cost and Cindy incurs an economic loss. Price and marginal revenue are $17 a sweater, and the profit-maximizing (in this case, loss-minimizing) output is 7 sweaters a day. Cindy's total revenue is $119 a day (7 × $17). Average total cost is $20.14 a sweater, so the economic loss is $3.14 per sweater ($20.14 – $17.00). This loss per sweater multiplied by the number of sweaters is $22 ($3.14 × 7 = $22). The red rectangle shows this economic loss. The height of that rectangle is economic loss per sweater, $3.14, and the length is the quantity of sweaters produced, 7 a day, so the area of the rectangle is Cindy's economic loss of $22 a day.

FIGURE 11.4 Three Possible Profit Outcomes in the Short Run

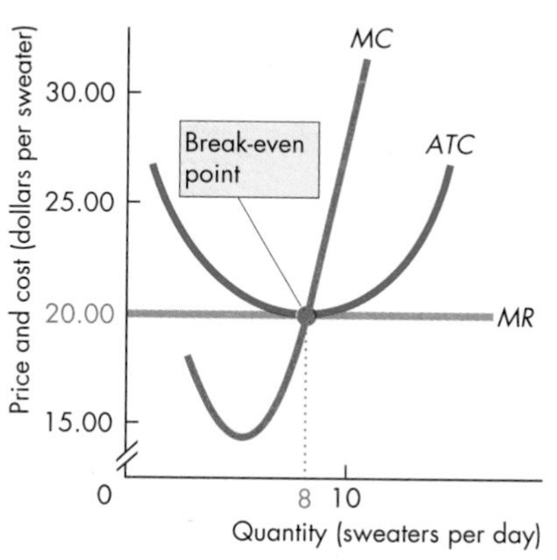

(a) Normal profit

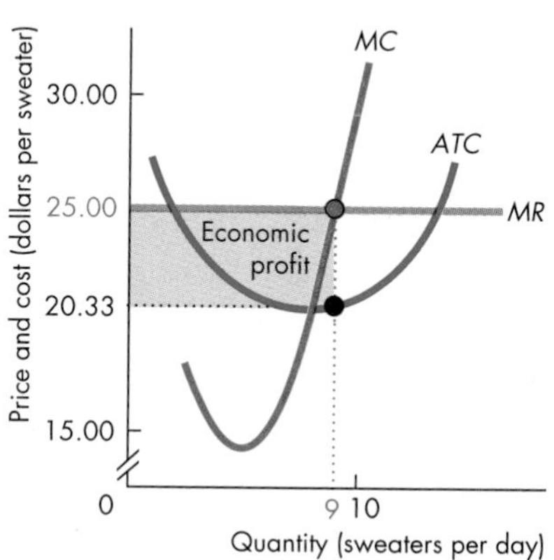

(b) Economic profit

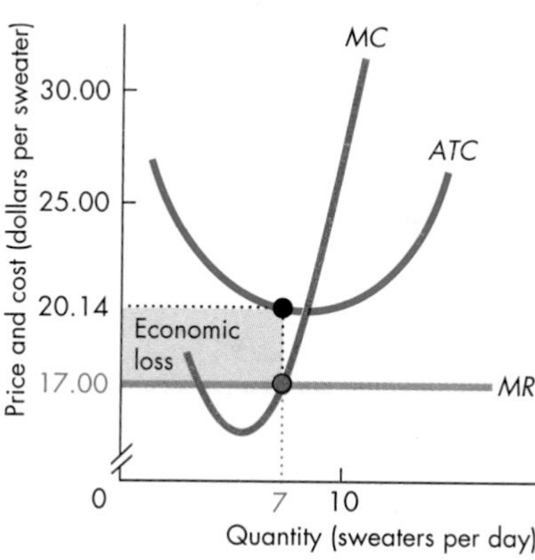

(c) Economic loss

In the short run, the firm might break even (make a normal profit), make an economic profit, or incur an economic loss. If the price equals minimum average total cost, the firm breaks even and makes a normal profit (part a). If the price exceeds the average total cost of producing the profit-maximizing output, the firm makes an economic profit (the blue rectangle in part b). If the price is below minimum average total cost, the firm incurs an economic loss (the red rectangle in part c).

The Firm's Short-Run Supply Curve

A perfectly competitive firm's short-run supply curve shows how the firm's profit-maximizing output varies as the market price varies, other things remaining the same. Figure 11.5 shows how to derive Cindy's supply curve. Part (a) shows Cindy's Sweaters' marginal cost and average variable cost curves, and part (b) shows its supply curve. There is a direct link between the marginal cost and average variable cost curves and the supply curve. Let's see what that link is.

Temporary Plant Shutdown In the short run, a firm cannot avoid incurring its fixed cost. But the firm can avoid variable costs by temporarily laying off its workers and shutting down. If a firm shuts down, it produces no output and it incurs a loss equal to total fixed cost. This loss is the largest that a firm needs to incur. A firm shuts down if the price falls below minimum average variable cost. The **shutdown point** is the output and price at which the firm just covers its total variable cost—point *T* in Fig. 11.5(a). If the price is $17, the marginal revenue curve is MR_0 and the profit-maximizing output is 7 sweaters a day at point *T*. But both price and average variable cost equal $17, so Cindy's total revenue equals total variable cost. Cindy incurs an economic loss equal to total fixed cost. At a price below $17, no matter what quantity Cindy produces, average *variable* cost exceeds price and the firm's loss exceeds total fixed cost. At a price below $17, the firm shuts down temporarily.

The Short-Run Supply Curve If the price is above minimum average variable cost, Cindy maximizes profit by producing the output at which marginal cost equals price. We can determine the quantity produced at each price from the marginal cost curve. At a price of $25, the marginal revenue curve is MR_1 and Cindy maximizes profit by producing 9 sweaters. At a price of $31, the marginal revenue curve is MR_2 and Cindy produces 10 sweaters.

Cindy's short-run supply curve, shown in Fig. 11.5(b), has two separate parts: First, at prices that exceed minimum average variable cost, the supply curve is the same as the marginal cost curve above the shutdown point (*T*). Second, at prices below minimum average variable cost, Cindy shuts down and produces nothing. Its supply curve runs along the vertical axis. At a price of $17, Cindy is indifferent between shutting down and producing 7 sweaters a day. Either way, Cindy incurs a loss of $22 a day.

FIGURE 11.5 A Firm's Supply Curve

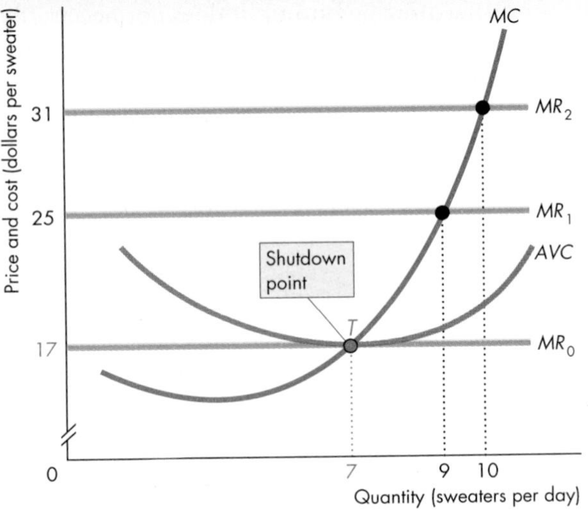

(a) Marginal cost and average variable cost

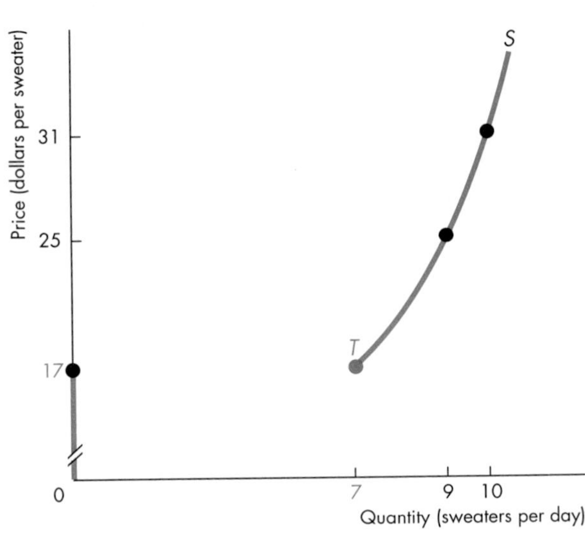

(b) Cindy's short-run supply curve

Part (a) shows Cindy's profit-maximizing output at various market prices. At $25 a sweater, Cindy produces 9 sweaters. At $17 a sweater, Cindy produces 7 sweaters. At any price below $17 a sweater, Cindy produces nothing. Cindy's shutdown point is *T*. Part (b) shows Cindy's supply curve—the number of sweaters Cindy will produce at each price. It is made up of the marginal cost curve (part a) at all points above minimum average variable cost and the vertical axis at all prices below minimum average variable cost.

Short-Run Industry Supply Curve

The **short-run industry supply curve** shows the quantity supplied by the industry at each price when the plant size of each firm and the number of firms remain constant. The quantity supplied by the industry at a given price is the sum of the quantities supplied by all firms in the industry at that price.

Figure 11.6 shows the supply curve for the competitive sweater industry. In this example, the industry consists of 1,000 firms exactly like Cindy's Sweaters. At each price, the quantity supplied by the industry is 1,000 times the quantity supplied by a single firm.

The table in Fig. 11.6 shows the firm's and the industry's supply schedule and how the industry supply curve is constructed. At prices below $17, every firm in the industry shuts down; the quantity supplied by the industry is zero. At a price of $17, each firm is indifferent between shutting down and producing nothing or operating and producing 7 sweaters a day. Some firms will shut down, and others will supply 7 sweaters a day. The quantity supplied by each firm is *either* 0 or 7 sweaters, but the quantity supplied by the industry is *between* 0 (all firms shut down) and 7,000 (all firms produce 7 sweaters a day each).

To construct the industry supply curve, we sum the quantities supplied by the individual firms. Each of the 1,000 firms in the industry has a supply schedule like Cindy's. At prices below $17, the industry supply curve runs along the price axis. At a price of $17, the industry supply curve is horizontal—supply is perfectly elastic. As the price rises above $17, each firm increases its quantity supplied and the quantity supplied by the industry increases by 1,000 times that of each firm.

FIGURE 11.6 Industry Supply Curve

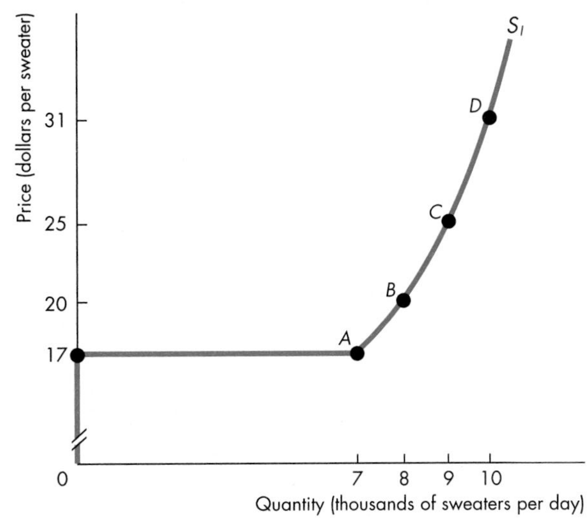

	Price (dollars per sweater)	Quantity supplied by Cindy's Sweaters (sweaters per day)	Quantity supplied by industry (sweaters per day)
A	17	0 or 7	0 to 7,000
B	20	8	8,000
C	25	9	9,000
D	31	10	10,000

The industry supply schedule is the sum of the supply schedules of all individual firms. An industry that consists of 1,000 identical firms has a supply schedule similar to that of the individual firm, but the quantity supplied by the industry is 1,000 times as large as that of the individual firm (see the table). The industry supply curve is S_I. Points *A*, *B*, *C*, and *D* correspond to the rows of the table. At the shutdown price of $17, each firm produces either 0 or 7 sweaters per day. The industry supply is perfectly elastic at the shutdown price.

REVIEW QUIZ

1. Why does a firm in perfect competition produce the quantity at which marginal cost equals price?
2. What is the lowest price at which a firm produces an output? Explain why.
3. What is the relationship between a firm's supply curve, its marginal cost curve, and its average variable cost curve?
4. How do we derive an industry supply curve?

So far, we have studied a single firm in isolation. We have seen that the firm's profit-maximizing actions depend on the market price, which the firm takes as given. But how is the market price determined? Let's find out.

Output, Price, and Profit in Perfect Competition

TO DETERMINE THE MARKET PRICE AND THE quantity bought and sold in a perfectly competitive market, we need to study how market demand and market supply interact. We begin this process by studying a perfectly competitive market in the short run when the number of firms is fixed and each firm has a given plant size.

Short-Run Equilibrium

Industry demand and supply determine the market price and industry output. Figure 11.7(a) shows a short-run equilibrium. The supply curve S is the same as S_I in Fig. 11.6. If demand is shown by the demand curve D_1, the equilibrium price is \$20. Each firm takes this price as given and produces its profit-maximizing output, which is 8 sweaters a day. Because the industry has 1,000 firms, industry output is 8,000 sweaters a day.

A Change in Demand

Changes in demand bring changes to short-run industry equilibrium. Figure 11.7(b) shows these changes.

If demand increases, the demand curve shifts rightward to D_2. The price rises to \$25. At this price, each firm maximizes profit by increasing output. The new output level is 9 sweaters a day for each firm and 9,000 sweaters a day for the industry.

If demand decreases, the demand curve shifts leftward to D_3. The price now falls to \$17. At this price, each firm maximizes profit by decreasing its output. The new output level is 7 sweaters a day for each firm and 7,000 sweaters a day for the industry.

If the demand curve shifts farther leftward than D_3, the price remains constant at \$17 because the industry supply curve is horizontal at that price. Some firms continue to produce 7 sweaters a day, and others temporarily shut down. Firms are indifferent between these two activities, and whichever they choose, they incur an economic loss equal to total fixed cost. The number of firms continuing to produce is just enough to satisfy the market demand at a price of \$17.

FIGURE 11.7 Short-Run Equilibrium

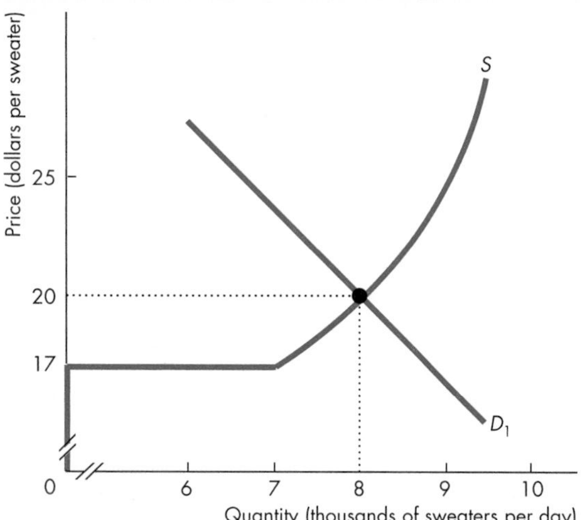

(a) Equilibrium

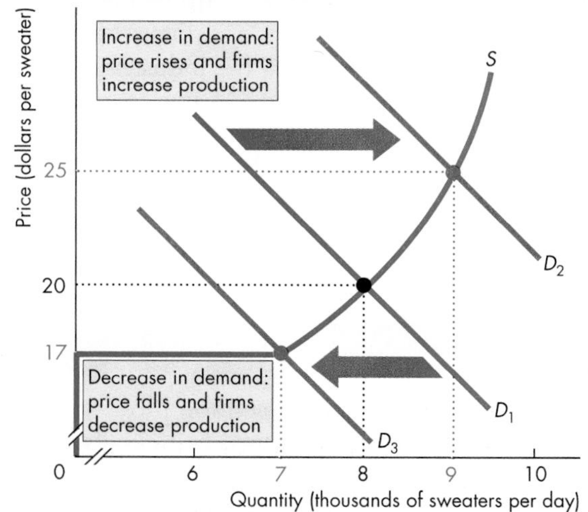

(b) Change in equilibrium

In part (a), the industry supply curve is S. Demand is D_1, and the price is \$20. At this price, each firm produces 8 sweaters a day and the industry produces 8,000 sweaters a day. In part (b), when demand increases to D_2, the price rises to \$25 and each firm increases its output to 9 sweaters a day. Industry output is 9,000 sweaters a day. When demand decreases to D_3, the price falls to \$17 and each firm decreases its output to 7 sweaters a day. Industry output is 7,000 sweaters a day.

Long-Run Adjustments

In short-run equilibrium, a firm might make an economic profit, incur an economic loss, or break even (make normal profit). Although each of these three situations is a short-run equilibrium, only one of them is a long-run equilibrium. To see why, we need to examine the forces at work in a competitive industry in the long run.

In the long run, an industry adjusts in two ways:

- Entry and exit
- Changes in plant size

Let's look first at entry and exit.

Entry and Exit

In the long run, firms respond to economic profit and economic loss by either entering or exiting an industry. Firms enter an industry in which firms are making an economic profit, and firms exit an industry in which firms are incurring an economic loss. Temporary economic profit and temporary economic loss do not trigger entry and exit. But the prospect of persistent economic profit or loss does.

Entry and exit influence price, the quantity produced, and economic profit. The immediate effect of these decisions is to shift the industry supply curve. If more firms enter an industry, supply increases and the industry supply curve shifts rightward. If firms exit an industry, supply decreases and the industry supply curve shifts leftward.

Let's see what happens when new firms enter an industry.

The Effects of Entry Figure 11.8 shows the effects of entry. Suppose that all the firms in this industry have cost curves like those in Fig. 11.4. At any price greater than \$20, firms make an economic profit. At any price less than \$20, firms incur an economic loss. And at a price of \$20, firms make zero economic profit. Also suppose that the demand curve for sweaters is D. If the industry supply curve is S_1, sweaters sell for \$23, and 7,000 sweaters a day are produced. Firms in the industry make an economic profit. This economic profit is a signal for new firms to enter the industry.

As these events unfold, supply increases and the industry supply curve shifts rightward to S_0. With the greater supply and unchanged demand, the market price falls from \$23 to \$20 a sweater and the quantity produced by the industry increases from 7,000 to 8,000 sweaters a day.

Industry output increases, but Cindy's Sweaters, like each other firm in the industry, moves down its supply curve and *decreases* output! Because the price falls, each firm produces less. But because the number of firms in the industry increases, the industry as a whole produces more.

Because price falls, each firm's economic profit decreases. When the price falls to \$20, economic profit disappears and each firm makes a normal profit.

You have just discovered a key proposition:

> As new firms enter an industry, the price falls and the economic profit of each existing firm decreases.

An example of this process occurred during the 1980s in the personal computer industry. When IBM introduced its first PC, there was little competition

FIGURE 11.8 Entry and Exit

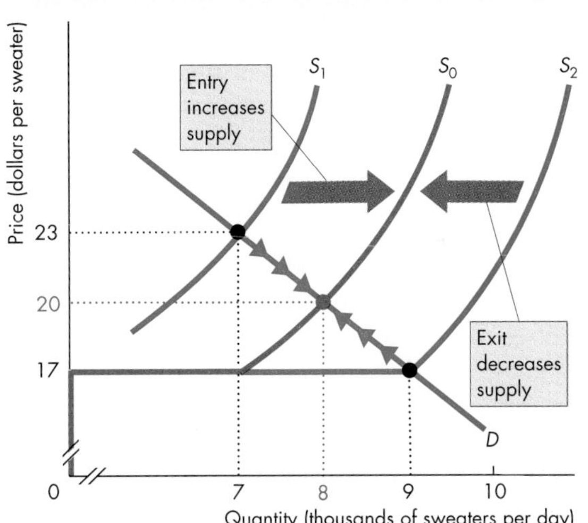

When new firms enter the sweater industry, the industry supply curve shifts rightward, from S_1 to S_0. The equilibrium price falls from \$23 to \$20, and the quantity produced increases from 7,000 to 8,000 sweaters.

When firms exit the sweater industry, the industry supply curve shifts leftward, from S_2 to S_0. The equilibrium price rises from \$17 to \$20, and the quantity produced decreases from 9,000 to 8,000 sweaters.

and the price of a PC gave IBM a big profit. But new firms such as Compaq, NEC, Dell, and a host of others entered the industry with machines that were technologically identical to IBM's. In fact, they were so similar that they came to be called "clones." The massive wave of entry into the personal computer industry shifted the supply curve rightward and lowered the price and the economic profit.

Let's now look at the effects of exit.

The Effects of Exit Figure 11.8 also shows the effects of exit. Suppose that firm's costs and market demand are the same as before. But now suppose the supply curve is S_2. The market price is $17, and 9,000 sweaters a day are produced. Firms in the industry now incur an economic loss. This economic loss is a signal for some firms to exit the industry. As firms exit, the industry supply curve shifts leftward to S_0. With the decrease in supply, industry output decreases from 9,000 to 8,000 sweaters and the price rises from $17 to $20.

As the price rises, Cindy's Sweaters, like each other firm in the industry, moves up along its supply curve and increases output. That is, for each firm that remains in the industry, the profit-maximizing output increases. Because the price rises and each firm sells more, economic loss decreases. When the price rises to $20, each firm makes a normal profit.

You've now discovered a second key proposition:

As firms leave an industry, the price rises and the economic loss of each remaining firm decreases.

The same PC industry that saw a large amount of entry during the 1980s and 1990s is now beginning to see some exit. In 2001, IBM, the firm that first launched the PC, announced that it would no longer produce PCs. The intense competition from Compaq, NEC, Dell, and many others that entered the industry following IBM's lead has lowered the price and eliminated the economic profit on PCs. So IBM will now concentrate on servers and other parts of the computer market.

IBM exited the PC market because it was incurring losses on that line of business. Its exit decreased supply and made it possible for the remaining firms in the industry to earn normal profit.

You've now seen how economic profits induce entry, which in turn lowers profits. And you've seen how economic losses induce exit, which in turn eliminates losses. Let's now look at changes in plant size.

Changes in Plant Size

A firm changes its plant size if, by doing so, it can lower its costs and increase its economic profit. You can probably think of lots of examples of firms that have changed their plant size.

One example that has almost certainly happened near your campus in recent years is a change in the plant size of Kinko's or similar copy shops. Another is the number of FedEx vans that you see on the streets and highways. And another is the number of square feet of retail space devoted to selling computers and video games. These are examples of firms increasing their plant size to seek larger profits.

There are also many examples of firms that have decreased their plant size to avoid economic losses. One of these is Country Style Doughnuts. As competition from other coffee shops became tougher, Country Style Doughnuts closed 45 shops across Canada in late 2002. Many firms have scaled back in a process called *downsizing* in recent years.

Figure 11.9 shows a situation in which Cindy's Sweaters can increase its profit by increasing its plant size. With its current plant, Cindy's marginal cost curve is MC_0, and its short-run average total cost curve is $SRAC_0$. The market price is $25 a sweater, so Cindy's marginal revenue curve is MR_0, and Cindy maximizes profit by producing 6 sweaters a day.

Cindy's Sweaters' long-run average cost curve is *LRAC*. By increasing its plant size—installing more knitting machines—Cindy's Sweaters can move along its long-run average cost curve. As Cindy's Sweaters increases its plant size, its short-run marginal cost curve shifts rightward.

Recall that a firm's short-run supply curve is linked to its marginal cost curve. As Cindy's marginal cost curve shifts rightward, so does its supply curve. If Cindy's Sweaters and the other firms in the industry increase their plants, the short-run industry supply curve shifts rightward. With a given market demand for sweaters, the market price falls. The fall in the market price limits the extent to which Cindy's can profit from increasing its plant size.

Figure 11.9 also shows Cindy's Sweaters in a long-run competitive equilibrium. This situation arises when the market price has fallen to $20 a sweater. Marginal revenue is MR_1, and Cindy maximizes profit by producing 8 sweaters a day. In this situation, Cindy cannot increase her profit by changing the plant size. Cindy is producing at minimum long-run average cost (point *M* on *LRAC*).

FIGURE 11.9 Plant Size and Long-Run Equilibrium

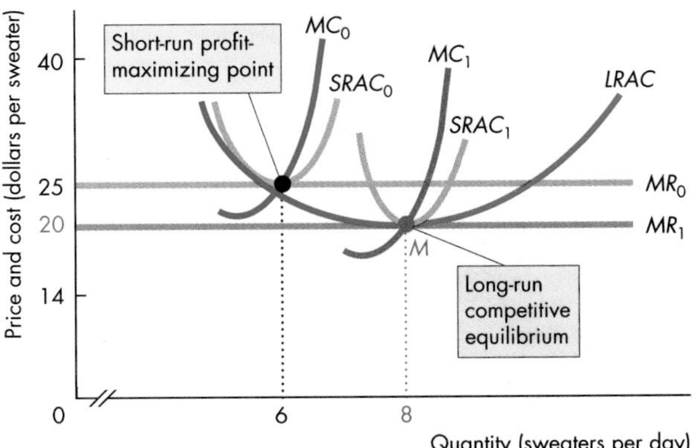

Initially, Cindy's plant has marginal cost curve MC_0 and short-run average total cost curve $SRAC_0$. The market price is \$25 a sweater, and Cindy's marginal revenue is MR_0. The short-run profit-maximizing quantity is 6 sweaters a day. Cindy can increase profit by increasing the plant size.

If all firms in the sweater industry increase their plant sizes, the short-run industry supply increases and the market price falls. In long-run equilibrium, a firm operates with the plant size that minimizes its average cost. Here, Cindy's Sweaters operates the plant with short-run marginal cost MC_1 and short-run average cost $SRAC_1$. Cindy's is also on its long-run average cost curve *LRAC* and produces at point *M*. Its output is 8 sweaters a day, and its average total cost equals the price of a sweater: \$20.

Because Cindy's Sweaters is producing at minimum long-run average cost, it has no incentive to change its plant size. Either a bigger plant or a smaller plant has a higher long-run average cost. If Fig. 11.9 describes the situation of all firms in the sweater industry, the industry is in long-run equilibrium. No firm has an incentive to change its plant size. Also, because each firm is making zero economic profit (normal profit), no firm has an incentive to enter the industry or to leave it.

Long-Run Equilibrium

Long-run equilibrium occurs in a competitive industry when economic profit is zero (when firms earn normal profit). If the firms in a competitive industry are making an economic profit, new firms enter the industry. If firms can lower their costs by increasing their plant size, they expand. Each of these actions increases the industry supply, shifts the industry supply curve rightward, lowers the price, and decreases economic profit.

Firms continue to enter and profit decreases as long as firms in the industry are earning positive economic profits. When economic profit has been eliminated, firms stop entering the industry. And when firms are operating with the least-cost plant size, they stop expanding.

If the firms in a competitive industry are incurring an economic loss, some firms exit the industry. If firms can lower their costs by decreasing their plant size, they downsize. Each of these actions decreases industry supply, shifts the industry supply curve leftward, raises the price, and decreases economic loss.

Firms continue to exit and economic loss continues to decrease as long as firms in the industry are incurring economic losses. When economic loss has been eliminated, firms stop exiting the industry. And when firms are operating with the least-cost plant size, they stop downsizing.

So in long-run equilibrium in a competitive industry, firms neither enter nor exit the industry and old firms neither expand nor downsize. Each firm earns normal profit.

REVIEW QUIZ

1. When the market demand for the good decreases, explain how the price of the good and the output of each firm in perfect competition changes in the short run.
2. If the firms in a competitive industry earn an economic profit, what happens to supply, price, output, and economic profit in the long run?
3. If the firms in a competitive industry incur an economic loss, what happens to supply, price, output, and economic profit?

You've seen how a competitive industry adjusts towards its long-run equilibrium. But a competitive industry is rarely *in* a state of long-run equilibrium. A competitive industry is constantly and restlessly evolving towards such an equilibrium. But the constraints that firms in an industry face are constantly changing. The two most persistent sources of change are in tastes and technology. Let's see how a competitive industry reacts to such changes.

Changing Tastes and Advancing Technology

INCREASED AWARENESS OF THE HEALTH HAZARDS of smoking has caused a decrease in the demand for tobacco and cigarettes. The development of inexpensive car and air transportation has caused a huge decrease in the demand for long-distance trains and buses. Solid-state electronics have caused a large decrease in the demand for TV and radio repair. The development of good-quality inexpensive clothing has decreased the demand for sewing machines. What happens in a competitive industry when there is a permanent decrease in the demand for its products?

The development of the microwave oven has produced an enormous increase in demand for paper, glass, and plastic cooking utensils and for plastic wrap. The widespread use of the personal computer has brought a huge increase in the demand for CD-Rs. What happens in a competitive industry when the demand for its output increases?

Advances in technology are constantly lowering the costs of production. New biotechnologies have dramatically lowered the costs of producing many food and pharmaceutical products. New electronic technologies have lowered the cost of producing just about every good and service. What happens in a competitive industry when technological change lowers its production costs?

Let's use the theory of perfect competition to answer these questions.

A Permanent Change in Demand

Figure 11.10(a) shows a competitive industry that initially is in long-run equilibrium. The demand curve is D_0, the supply curve is S_0, the market price is P_0, and industry output is Q_0. Figure 11.10(b) shows a single firm in this initial long-run equilibrium. The firm produces q_0 and makes a normal profit and zero economic profit.

Now suppose that demand decreases and the demand curve shifts leftward to D_1, as shown in Fig. 11.10(a). The price falls to P_1, and the quantity supplied by the industry decreases from Q_0 to Q_1 as the industry slides down its short-run supply curve S_0. Fig. 11.10(b) shows the situation facing a firm. Price is now below the firm's minimum average total cost, so the firm incurs an economic loss. But to keep its loss to a minimum, the firm adjusts its output to keep marginal cost equal to price. At a price of P_1, each firm produces an output of q_1.

The industry is now in short-run equilibrium but not long-run equilibrium. It is in short-run equilibrium because each firm is maximizing profit. But it is not in long-run equilibrium because each firm is incurring an economic loss—its average total cost exceeds the price.

The economic loss is a signal for some firms to leave the industry. As they do so, short-run industry supply decreases and the supply curve gradually shifts leftward. As industry supply decreases, the price rises. At each higher price, a firm's profit-maximizing output is greater, so the firms remaining in the industry increase their output as the price rises. Each firm slides up its marginal cost or supply curve in Fig. 11.10(b). That is, as firms exit the industry, industry output decreases but the output of the firms that remain in the industry increases. Eventually, enough firms leave the industry for the industry supply curve to have shifted to S_1 in Fig. 11.10(a). At this time, the price has returned to its original level, P_0. At this price, the firms remaining in the industry produce q_0, the same quantity that they produced before the decrease in demand. Because firms are now making normal profit (zero economic profit), no firm wants to enter or exit the industry. The industry supply curve remains at S_1, and industry output is Q_2. The industry is again in long-run equilibrium.

The difference between the initial long-run equilibrium and the final long-run equilibrium is the number of firms in the industry. A permanent decrease in demand has decreased the number of firms. Each remaining firm produces the same output in the new long-run equilibrium as it did initially and earns a normal profit. In the process of moving from the initial equilibrium to the new one, firms incur economic losses.

We've just worked out how a competitive industry responds to a permanent *decrease* in demand. A permanent increase in demand triggers a similar response, except in the opposite direction. The increase in demand brings a higher price, economic profit, and entry. Entry increases industry supply and eventually the price falls to its original level and economic profit returns to normal profit.

The demand for airline travel in the world economy increased permanently during the 1990s and the deregulation of the airlines freed up firms to seek profit opportunities in this industry. The result was a

FIGURE 11.10 A Decrease in Demand

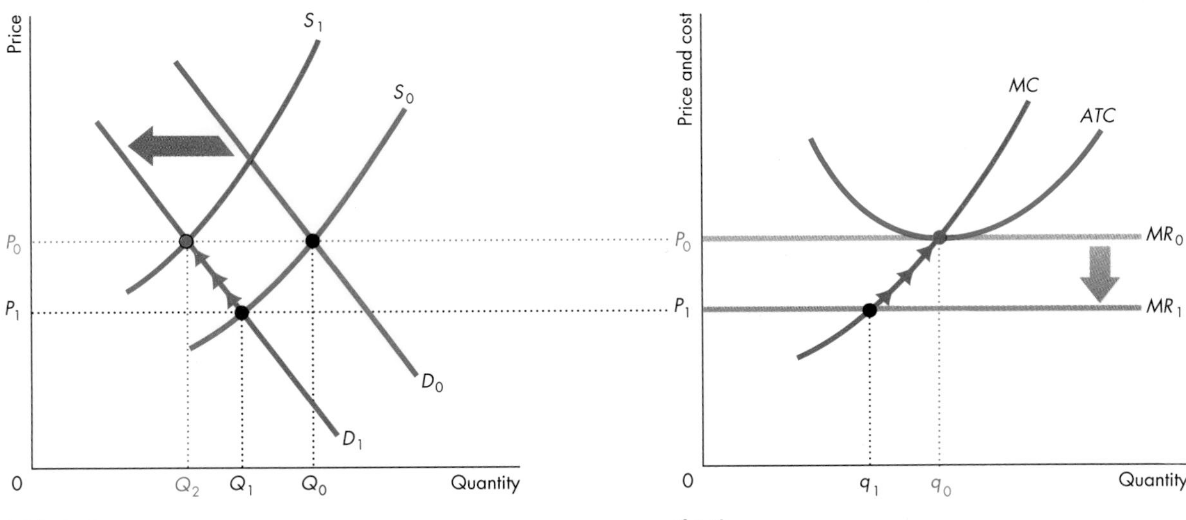

An industry starts out in long-run competitive equilibrium. Part (a) shows the industry demand curve D_0, the industry supply curve S_0, the equilibrium quantity Q_0, and the market price P_0. Each firm sells its output at price P_0, so its marginal revenue curve is MR_0 in part (b). Each firm produces q_0 and makes a normal profit. Demand decreases permanently from D_0 to D_1 (part a). The equilibrium price falls to P_1, each firm decreases its output to q_1 (part b), and industry output decreases to Q_1 (part a).

In this new situation, firms incur economic losses and some firms leave the industry. As they do so, the industry supply curve gradually shifts leftward, from S_0 to S_1. This shift gradually raises the market price from P_1 back to P_0. Once the price has returned to P_0, each firm makes a normal profit. Firms have no further incentive to leave the industry. Each firm produces q_0, and industry output is Q_2.

massive rate of entry of new airlines. The process of competition and change in the airline industry is similar to what we have just studied (but with an increase in demand rather than a decrease in demand).

We've now studied the effects of a permanent change in demand for a good. To study these effects, we began and ended in a long-run equilibrium and examined the process that takes a market from one equilibrium to another. It is this process, not the equilibrium points, that describes the real world.

One feature of the predictions that we have just generated seems odd: In the long run, regardless of whether demand increases or decreases, the price returns to its original level. Is this outcome inevitable? In fact, it is not. It is possible for the long-run equilibrium price to remain the same, rise, or fall.

External Economies and Diseconomies

The change in the long-run equilibrium price depends on external economies and external diseconomies. **External economies** are factors beyond the control of an individual firm that lower the firm's costs as the *industry* output increases. **External diseconomies** are factors outside the control of a firm that raise the firm's costs as industry output increases. With no external economies or external diseconomies, a firm's costs remain constant as the industry output changes.

Figure 11.11 illustrates these three cases and introduces a new supply concept: the long-run industry supply curve.

A **long-run industry supply curve** shows how the quantity supplied by an industry varies as the market price varies after all the possible adjustments have been made, including changes in plant size and the number of firms in the industry.

Figure 11.11(a) shows the case we have just studied—no external economies or diseconomies. The long-run industry supply curve (LS_A) is horizontal. In this case, a permanent increase in demand from D_0 to D_1 has no effect on the price in the long run. The increase in demand brings a temporary increase in price to P_S and a short-run quantity increase from Q_0 to Q_S. Entry increases short-run supply from S_0 to S_1, which lowers the price to its original level, P_0, and increases the quantity to Q_1.

Figure 11.11(b) shows the case of external diseconomies. The long-run supply industry curve (LS_B) slopes upward. A permanent increase in demand from D_0 to D_1 increases the price in both the short run and the long run. As in the previous case, the increase in demand brings a temporary increase in price to P_S and a short-run quantity increase from Q_0 to Q_S. Entry increases short-run supply from S_0 to S_2, which lowers the price to P_2 and increases the quantity to Q_2.

One source of external diseconomies is congestion. The airline industry provides a good example. With bigger airline industry output, there is more congestion of airports and airspace, which results in longer delays and extra waiting time for passengers and airplanes. These external diseconomies mean that as the output of air transportation services increases (in the absence of technological advances), average cost increases. As a result, the long-run supply curve is upward sloping. So a permanent increase in demand brings an increase in quantity and a rise in the price. (Industries with external diseconomies might nonetheless have a falling price because technological advances shift the long-run supply curve downward.)

Figure 11.11(c) shows the case of external economies. In this case, the long-run industry supply curve (LS_C) slopes downward. A permanent increase in demand from D_0 to D_1 increases the price in the short run and lowers it in the long run. Again, the increase in demand brings a temporary increase in price to P_S, and a short-run quantity increase from Q_0 to Q_S. Entry increases short-run supply from S_0 to S_3, which lowers the price to P_3 and increases the quantity to Q_3.

FIGURE 11.11 Long-Run Changes in Price and Quantity

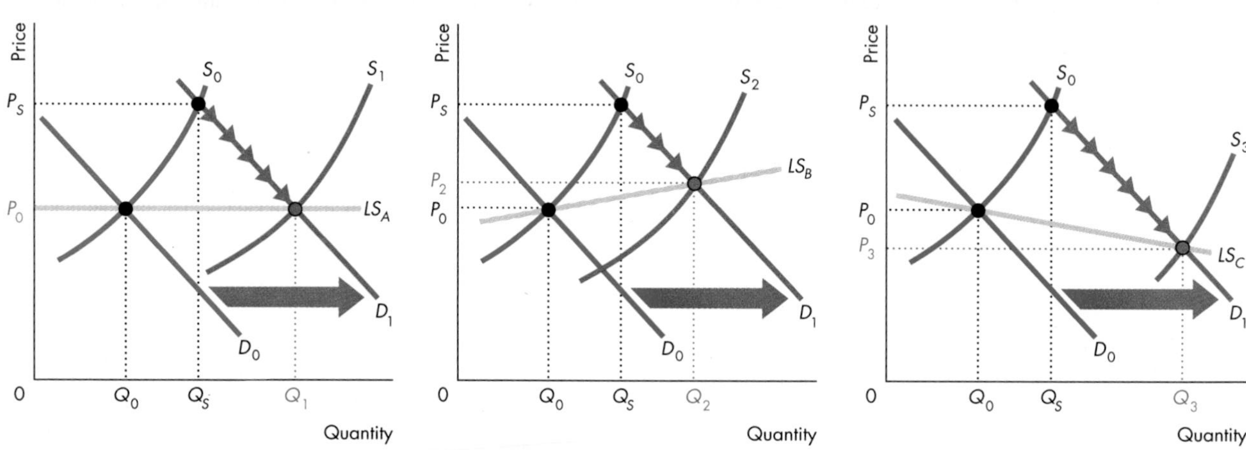

Three possible changes in price and quantity occur in the long run. When demand increases from D_0 to D_1, entry occurs and the industry supply curve gradually shifts rightward from S_0 to S_1.

In part (a), the long-run supply curve, LS_A, is horizontal. The quantity increases from Q_0 to Q_1, and the price remains constant at P_0. In part (b), the long-run supply curve is LS_B; the price rises to P_2, and the quantity increases to Q_2. This case occurs in industries with external diseconomies. In part (c), the long-run supply curve is LS_C; the price falls to P_3, and the quantity increases to Q_3. This case occurs in an industry with external economies.

An example of external economies is the growth of specialist support services for an industry as it expands. As farm output increased in the nineteenth and early twentieth centuries, the services available to farmers expanded. New firms specialized in the development and marketing of farm machinery and fertilizers. As a result, average farm costs decreased. Farms enjoyed the benefits of external economies. As a consequence, as the demand for farm products increased, the output increased but the price fell.

Over the long term, the prices of many goods and services have fallen, not because of external economies but because of technological change. Let's now study this influence on a competitive market.

Technological Change

Industries are constantly discovering lower-cost techniques of production. Most cost-saving production techniques cannot be implemented, however, without investing in new plant and equipment. As a consequence, it takes time for a technological advance to spread through an industry. Some firms whose plants are on the verge of being replaced will be quick to adopt the new technology, while other firms whose plants have recently been replaced will continue to operate with an old technology until they can no longer cover their average variable cost. Once average variable cost cannot be covered, a firm will scrap even a relatively new plant (embodying an old technology) in favour of a plant with a new technology.

New technology allows firms to produce at a lower cost. As a result, as firms adopt a new technology, their cost curves shift downward. With lower costs, firms are willing to supply a given quantity at a lower price or, equivalently, they are willing to supply a larger quantity at a given price. In other words, industry supply increases, and the industry supply curve shifts rightward. With a given demand, the quantity produced increases and the price falls.

Two forces are at work in an industry undergoing technological change. Firms that adopt the new technology make an economic profit. So there is entry by new-technology firms. Firms that stick with the old technology incur economic losses. They either exit the industry or switch to the new technology.

As old-technology firms disappear and new-technology firms enter, the price falls and the quantity produced increases. Eventually, the industry arrives at a long-run equilibrium in which all the firms use the new technology and make a zero economic profit (a normal profit). Because in the long run competition eliminates economic profit, technological change brings only temporary gains to producers. But the lower prices and better products that technological advances bring are permanent gains for consumers.

The process that we've just described is one in which some firms experience economic profits and others experience economic losses. It is a period of dynamic change for an industry. Some firms do well, and others do badly. Often, the process has a geographical dimension—the expanding new-technology firms bring prosperity to what was once the boondocks, and traditional industrial regions decline. Sometimes, the new-technology firms are in a foreign country, while the old-technology firms are in the domestic economy. The information revolution of the 1990s produced many examples of changes like these. The computer programming industry, traditionally concentrated in the United States, now flourishes in Canada, the United Kingdom, and India. Television shows and movies, traditionally made in Los Angeles and New York, are now made in large numbers in Toronto and Vancouver.

Technological advances are not confined to the information and entertainment industries. Even milk production is undergoing a major technological change because of genetic engineering.

REVIEW QUIZ

1. Describe the course of events in a competitive industry following a permanent decrease in demand. What happens to output, price, and economic profit in the short run and in the long run?
2. Describe the course of events in a competitive industry following a permanent increase in demand. What happens to output, price, and economic profit in the short run and in the long run?
3. Describe the course of events in a competitive industry following the adoption of a new technology. What happens to output, price, and economic profit in the short run and in the long run?

Competition and Efficiency

A COMPETITIVE INDUSTRY CAN ACHIEVE AN efficient use of resources. You studied efficiency in Chapter 5 using only the concepts of demand, supply, consumer surplus, and producer surplus. But now that you have learned what lies behind the demand and supply curves of a competitive market, you can gain a deeper understanding of how the competitive market achieves efficiency.

Efficient Use of Resources

Recall that resource use is efficient when we produce the goods and services that people value most highly (see Chapter 5, pp. 104–105). If someone can become better off without anyone else becoming worse off, resources are *not* being used efficiently. For example, suppose we produce a computer that no one wants and that no one will ever use. Suppose also that some people are clamouring for more video games. If we produce one less computer and reallocate the unused resources to produce more video games, some people will become better off and no one will be worse off. So the initial resource allocation was inefficient.

In the more technical language that you have learned, resource use is efficient when marginal benefit equals marginal cost. In the computer and video games example, the marginal benefit of video games exceeds the marginal cost. And the marginal cost of a computer exceeds its marginal benefit. So by producing fewer computers and more video games, we move resources towards a higher-valued use.

Choices, Equilibrium, and Efficiency

We can use what you have learned about the decisions made by consumers and competitive firms and market equilibrium to describe an efficient use of resources.

Choices Consumers allocate their budgets to get the most possible value out of them. And we derive a consumer's demand curve by finding how the best budget allocation changes as the price of a good changes. So consumers get the most value out of their resources at all points along their demand curves, which are also their marginal benefit curves.

Competitive firms produce the quantity that maximizes profit. And we derive the firm's supply curve by finding the profit-maximizing quantities at each price. So firms get the most value out of their resources at all points along their supply curves, which are also their marginal cost curves. (On their supply curves, firms are *technologically efficient*—they get the maximum possible output from given inputs—and *economically efficient*—they combine resources to minimize cost. See Chapter 9, pp. 199–200.)

Equilibrium In competitive equilibrium, the quantity demanded equals the quantity supplied. So the price equals the consumers' marginal benefit and the producers' marginal cost. In this situation, the gains from trade between consumers and producers are maximized. These gains from trade are the consumer surplus plus the producer surplus.

The gains from trade for consumers are measured by *consumer surplus*, which is the area below the demand curve and above the price paid. (See Chapter 5, p. 107.) The gains from trade for producers are measured by *producer surplus*, which is the area above the marginal cost curve and below the price received. (See Chapter 5, p. 109.)The total gains from trade are the sum of consumer surplus and producer surplus.

Efficiency If the people who consume and produce a good or service are the only ones affected by it and if the market for the good or service is in equilibrium, then resources are being used efficiently. They cannot be reallocated to increase their value.

In such a situation, there are no external benefits or external costs. **External benefits** are benefits that accrue to people other than the buyer of a good. For example, you might get a benefit from your neighbour's expenditure on her garden. Your neighbour buys the quantities of garden plants that make *her* as well off as possible, not her *and* you.

In the absence of external benefits, the market demand curve measures marginal *social* benefit—the value that *everyone* places on one more unit of a good or service.

External costs are costs that are borne not by the producer of a good or service but by someone else. For example, a firm might lower its costs by polluting. The cost of pollution is an external cost. Firms produce the output level that maximizes their own profit, and they do not count the cost of pollution as a charge against their profit.

In the absence of external costs, the market supply curve measures marginal *social* cost—the entire marginal cost that *anyone* bears to produce one more unit of a good or service.

An Efficient Allocation Figure 11.12 shows an efficient allocation. Consumers are efficient at all points on the demand curve, *D* (which is also the marginal benefit curve *MB*). Producers are efficient at all points on the supply curve, *S* (which is also the marginal cost curve *MC*). Resources are used efficiently at the quantity Q^* and price P^*. Marginal benefit equals marginal cost, and the sum of producer surplus (blue area) and consumer surplus (green area) is maximized.

If output is Q_0, marginal cost is C_0 and marginal benefit is B_0. Producers can supply more of the good for a cost lower than the price that consumers are willing to pay, and everyone gains by increasing the quantity produced. If output is greater than Q^*, marginal cost exceeds marginal benefit. It costs producers more to supply the good than the price that consumers are willing to pay, and everyone gains by decreasing the quantity produced.

FIGURE 11.12 Efficiency of Competition

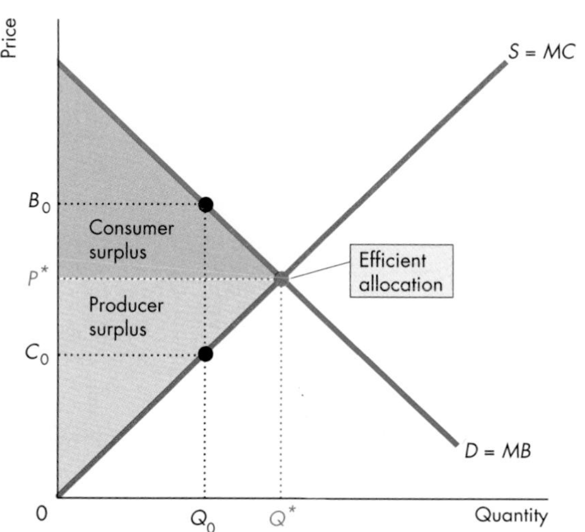

The efficient use of resources requires: consumers to be efficient, which occurs when they are on their demand curves; firms to be efficient, which occurs when they are on their supply curves; and the market to be in equilibrium, with no external benefits or external costs. Resources are used efficiently at the quantity Q^* and the price P^*. With no external benefits or external costs, perfect competition achieves an efficient use of resources. If output is Q_0, the cost of producing one more unit, C_0, is less than its marginal benefit, B_0, and resources are not used efficiently.

Efficiency of Perfect Competition

Perfect competition achieves efficiency if there are no external benefits and external costs. In such a case, the benefits accrue to the buyers of the good and the costs are borne by its producer. In Fig. 11.12, the equilibrium quantity Q^* at the price P^* is efficient.

There are three main obstacles to efficiency:

1. Monopoly
2. Public goods
3. External costs and external benefits

Monopoly Monopoly (Chapter 12) restricts output below its competitive level to raise price and increase profit. Government policies (Chapter 17) arise to limit such use of monopoly power.

Public Goods Goods such as national security, the enforcement of law and order, the provision of clean drinking water, and the disposal of sewage and garbage are examples of public goods. Left to competitive markets, too small a quantity of them would be produced. Government institutions and policies (Chapter 16) help to overcome the problem of providing an efficient quantity of public goods.

External Costs and External Benefits The production of steel and chemicals can generate air and water pollution, and perfect competition might produce too large a quantity of these goods. Government policies (Chapter 18) attempt to cope with external costs and benefits.

You've now completed your study of perfect competition. And *Reading Between the Lines* on pp. 256–257 gives you an opportunity to use what you have learned to understand recent events in the highly competitive maple syrup market.

Although many markets approximate the model of perfect competition, many do not. Your next task is to study markets at the opposite extreme of market power: monopoly. Then, in Chapter 13, we'll study markets that lie between perfect competition and monopoly: monopolistic competition (competition with monopoly elements) and oligopoly (competition among a few producers). When you have completed this study, you'll have a tool kit that will enable you to understand the variety of real-world markets.

Perfect Competition in Maple Syrup

MONTREAL GAZETTE, MARCH 14, 2001

Maple syrup sits unsold in warehouses

A sticky turf war has boiled over in Canada's sugar patch, with farmers and processors feuding over what to do with a glut of maple syrup. ...

... after two bumper crops in a row, producers wonder if it's worth the effort to tap all their trees.

"People naturally aren't encouraged by the prices," said Stanley Holmes, a farmer and maple-syrup producer from Ayer's Cliff who also buys syrup in bulk from neighbouring producers on behalf of Ontario-based processor Delta Foods International.

"Really what they need is less production to get rid of some of this surplus that's hanging over the industry."

Prices alone won't dictate supply, though. Operating conditions, particularly the deep snow still lying in the woods across the province, could also influence the number of trees farmers tap this spring, Holmes said.

"With the snow it's very difficult to get around, and when your prices aren't good, if you have hard conditions like that to overcome, that's another reason not to tackle the job."

Holmes's own sugarbush has a production capacity of 10,000 taps with three-quarters of his trees connected to a pipeline and the rest on buckets. He said he may forego bringing into production those trees that are difficult to reach, especially those not already hooked to a pipeline. ...

The average floor price for syrup has tumbled from a high of around $2.50 per pound in 1997 and 1998 to $1.56 in 2000 and is not expected to be any higher in 2001.

Essence of the Story

- Two back-to-back bumper maple syrup crops have lowered the price of syrup from $2.50 per pound to $1.56.
- At this low price, producers are decreasing the number of trees they tap.
- Supply is influenced by snow, which makes it difficult for producers to tap some of their trees.
- Stanley Holmes has a production capacity of 10,000 taps. 7,500 of these are connected to a pipeline and the rest on buckets.
- At today's low price, Stanley Holmes says he may forego the production on those trees that are difficult to reach and not already hooked to a pipeline.

Economic Analysis

■ Maple syrup—the real kind, not the synthetic syrup such as Aunt Jemima—is produced in Canada and the United States by about 12,000 firms.

■ The market for maple syrup is close to perfectly competitive.

■ Before the bumper crop, the price of maple syrup (in the news article) was $2.50 a pound.

■ After the bumper crop, the price fell to $1.56 a pound.

■ Figure 1 shows why the price fell. The demand curve for maple syrup is *D*, and before the bumper harvest, the supply curve was S_0. The equilibrium price was $2.50 a pound.

■ The bumper harvest shifted the supply curve rightward to S_1. At the price of $2.50 a pound, there was a surplus of syrup, so the price fell. The new equilibrium price is $1.56 a pound.

■ Figure 2 shows the situation facing Stanley Holmes. Stanley is a price taker and maximizes his profit by producing the quantity at which marginal cost (*MC*) equals marginal revenue (*MR*).

■ The figure shows Stanley's cost curves—average total cost curve, *ATC*, average variable cost curve, *AVC*, and marginal cost curve, *MC*.

■ We don't know the exact position of these curves, and those in the figure are assumed. But we do know from Stanley's description of his supply conditions that his marginal cost curve slopes upward.

■ When Stanley says, "With the snow it's very difficult to get around, and when your prices aren't good, if you have hard conditions like that to overcome, that's another reason not to tackle the job," the marginal cost of tapping all his trees is greater than the price he would receive.

■ The figure also shows Stanley's marginal revenue curves before, MR_0, and after, MR_1, the bumper harvest.

■ At $2.50 a pound, Stanley would tap all his trees (10,000 taps according to the news article). At $1.56 a pound, Stanley doesn't bother to tap the distant trees that are not connected to the pipeline.

■ Although the price is low, Stanley says that he will produce from his 7,500 taps that are connected to the pipeline. This fact implies, as the figure shows, that the price of $1.56 exceeds average variable cost. If it didn't, Stanley would temporarily shut down.

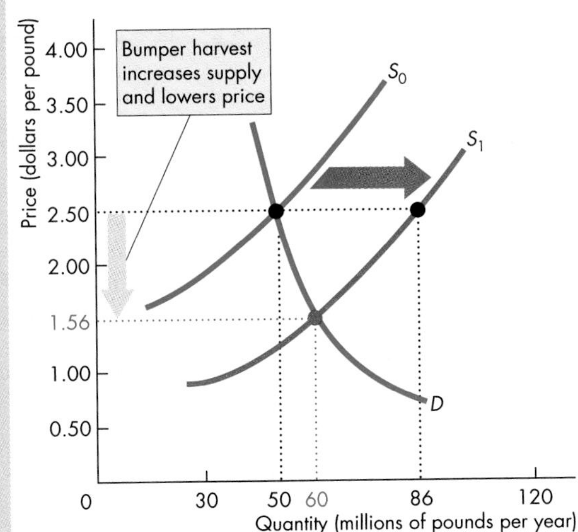

Figure 1 The maple syrup market

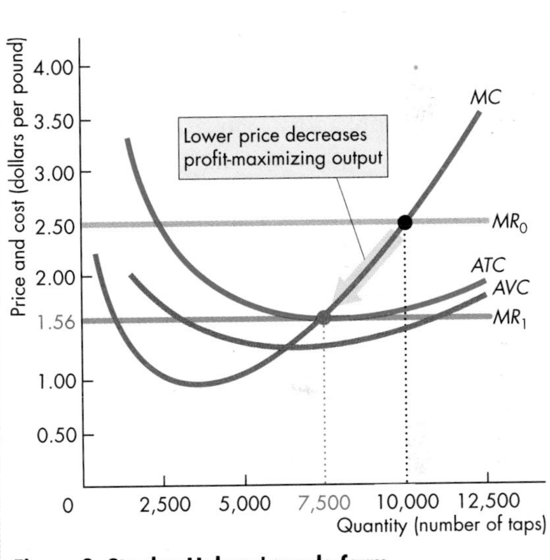

Figure 2 Stanley Holmes' maple farm

SUMMARY

KEY POINTS

Competition (pp. 238–239)

- A perfectly competitive firm is a price taker.

The Firm's Decisions in Perfect Competition (pp. 240–245)

- The firm produces the output at which marginal revenue (price) equals marginal cost.
- In short-run equilibrium, a firm can make an economic profit, incur an economic loss, or make normal profit.
- If price is less than minimum average variable cost, the firm temporarily shuts down.
- A firm's supply curve is the upward-sloping part of its marginal cost curve above minimum average variable cost.
- An industry supply curve shows the sum of the quantities supplied by each firm at each price.

Output, Price, and Profit in Perfect Competition (pp. 246–249)

- Market demand and market supply determine price.
- Persistent economic profit induces entry. Persistent economic loss induces exit.
- Entry and plant expansion increase supply and lower price and profit. Exit and downsizing decrease supply and raise price and profit.
- In long-run equilibrium, economic profit is zero (firms earn normal profit). There is no entry, exit, plant expansion, or downsizing.

Changing Tastes and Advancing Technology (pp. 250–253)

- A permanent decrease in demand leads to a smaller industry output and a smaller number of firms.
- A permanent increase in demand leads to a larger industry output and a larger number of firms.
- The long-run effect of a change in demand on price depends on whether there are external economies (the price falls) or external diseconomies (the price rises) or neither (the price remains constant).
- New technologies increase supply and in the long run lower the price and increase the quantity.

Competition and Efficiency (pp. 254–255)

- Resources are used efficiently when we produce goods and services in the quantities that people value most highly.
- When there are no external benefits and external costs, perfect competition achieves an efficient allocation. Marginal benefit equals marginal cost, and the sum of consumer surplus and producer surplus is maximized.
- The existence of monopoly, public goods, and external costs and external benefits presents obstacles to efficiency.

KEY FIGURES

Figure 11.2 Total Revenue, Total Cost, and Economic Profit, 241
Figure 11.3 Profit-Maximizing Output, 242
Figure 11.4 Three Possible Profit Outcomes in the Short Run, 243
Figure 11.5 A Firm's Supply Curve, 244
Figure 11.7 Short-Run Equilibrium, 246
Figure 11.8 Entry and Exit, 247
Figure 11.12 Efficiency of Competition, 255

KEY TERMS

External benefits, 254
External costs, 254
External diseconomies, 251
External economies, 251
Long-run industry supply curve, 251
Marginal revenue, 238
Perfect competition, 238
Price taker, 238
Short-run industry supply curve, 245
Shutdown point, 244
Total revenue, 238

PROBLEMS

*1. Quick Copy is one of the many copy shops near the campus. The figure shows Quick Copy's cost curves.

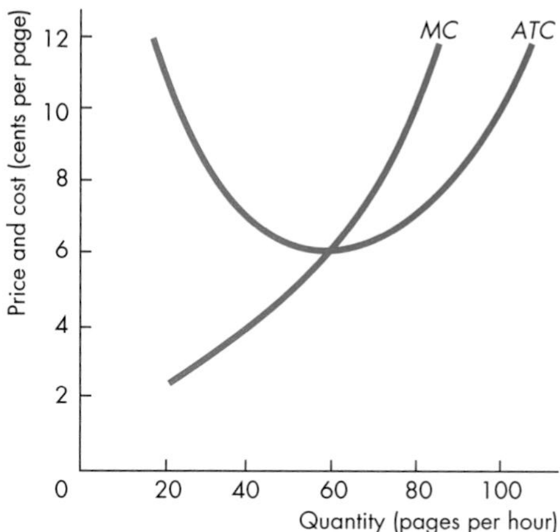

a. If the market price of copying one page is 10 cents, what is Quick Copy's profit-maximizing output?
b. Calculate Quick Copy's profit.
c. With no change in demand or technology, how will the price change in the long run?

2. Jerry's is one of many ice cream stands along the beach. The figure shows Jerry's cost curves.

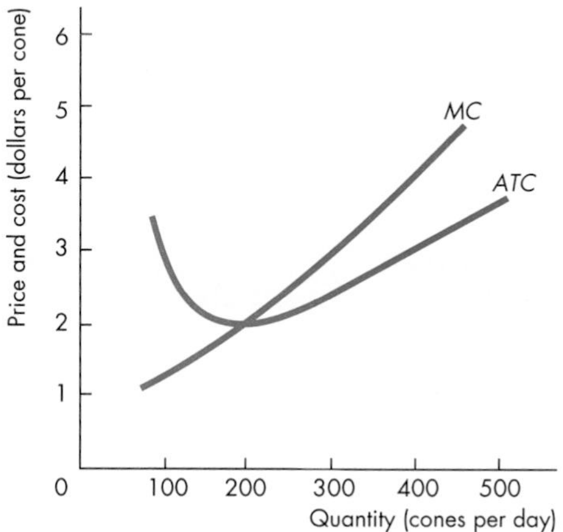

a. If the market price of an ice cream cone is \$3, what is Jerry's profit-maximizing output?
b. Calculate Jerry's profit.
c. With no change in demand or technology, how will the price change in the long run?

*3. Pat's Pizza Kitchen is a price taker. Its costs are

Output (pizzas per hour)	Total cost (dollars per hour)
0	10
1	21
2	30
3	41
4	54
5	69

a. What is Pat's profit-maximizing output and how much economic profit does Pat make if the market price is (i) \$14, (ii) \$12, and (iii) \$10?
b. What is Pat's shutdown point?
c. Derive Pat's supply curve.
d. At what price will Pat exit the pizza industry?

4. Luigi's Lasagna is a price taker. Its costs are

Output (plates per day)	Total cost (dollars per day)
0	14
1	38
2	48
3	62
4	80
5	102
6	128

a. What is Luigi's profit-maximizing output and how much profit does Luigi make if the market price is (i) \$24 a plate, (ii) \$20 a plate, and (iii) \$12 a plate?
b. What is Luigi's shutdown point?
c. What is Luigi's profit at the shutdown point?
d. At what prices will firms with costs the same as Luigi's enter the lasagna market?

*5. The market demand schedule for cassettes is

Price (dollars per cassette)	Quantity demanded (thousands of cassettes per week)
3.65	500
5.20	450
6.80	400
8.40	350
10.00	300
11.60	250
13.20	200
14.80	150

The market is perfectly competitive, and each firm has the following cost structure:

Output (cassettes per week)	Marginal cost (dollars per additional cassette)	Average variable cost (dollars per cassette)	Average total cost
150	6.00	8.80	15.47
200	6.40	7.80	12.80
250	7.00	7.00	11.00
300	7.65	7.10	10.43
350	8.40	7.20	10.06
400	10.00	7.50	10.00
450	12.40	8.00	10.22
500	20.70	9.00	11.00

There are 1,000 firms in the industry.

a. What is the market price?
b. What is the industry's output?
c. What is the output produced by each firm?
d. What is the economic profit made by each firm?
e. Do firms enter or exit the industry?
f. What is the number of firms in the long run?

6. The same demand conditions as those in problem 5 prevail and there are 1,000 firms in the industry, but fixed costs increase by $980. What now are your answers to the questions in problem 5?

*7. In problem 5, the price of compact discs permanently decreases the demand for cassettes and the demand schedule becomes

Price (dollars per cassette)	Quantity demanded (thousands of cassettes per week)
2.95	500
4.13	450
5.30	400
6.48	350
7.65	300
8.83	250
10.00	200
11.18	150

What now are your answers to the questions in problem 5?

8. In problem 6, the price of compact discs permanently decreases the demand for cassettes and the demand schedule becomes that given in the table in problem 7. What now are your answers to the questions in problem 6?

CRITICAL THINKING

1. After you have studied *Reading Between the Lines* on pp. 256–257, answer the following questions.
   a. What are the features of the market for maple syrup that make it an example of perfect competition?
   b. During the 1980s, the technology for extracting sap advanced. What effect do you predict that this development had on the price of syrup and the number of firms that produce it?
   c. Suppose that Aunt Jemima invents a syrup that no one can distinguish (in a blind test) from the real thing and can produce it for half the price of real maple syrup. What effect would you expect this development to have on the market for real maple syrup?
2. Why have the prices of pocket calculators and VCRs fallen? What do you think has happened to the costs and economic profits of the firms that make these products?
3. What has been the effect of an increase in world population on the wheat market and the individual wheat farmer?
4. How has the diaper service industry been affected by the decrease in the Canadian birth rate and the development of disposable diapers?

WEB EXERCISES

1. Use the link on the Parkin–Bade Web site and study the *Web Reading Between the Lines*, "Dumping Steel." Then answer the following questions:
   a. What is the argument in the news article about limiting steel imports?
   b. Do you agree with the argument? Why or why not?
   c. Why do Canada and the United States claim that foreign steel is being dumped in North America? (Use the links in the *Web Reading Between the Lines* to answer this question.)

MONOPOLY

The Profits of Generosity

If you take a trip by air in Canada, it is most likely that you will be flying with Air Canada. Since the disappearance of Canadian Airlines a few years ago, Air Canada has become the only national airline on many major Canadian air routes. Air Canada is obviously not like the firms in perfect competition. It doesn't face a market-determined price. It can choose its own price. How do Air Canada and the firms like it behave? How do these firms choose the quantity to produce and the price at which to sell it? How does their behaviour compare with that of firms in perfectly competitive industries? Do these firms charge prices that are too high and that damage the interests of consumers? Do they bring any benefits? ◆ As a student, you get lots of discounts: when you get your hair cut, go to a museum, or go to a movie. When you take a trip by air, you almost never pay the full fare. Instead, you buy a discounted ticket. Are the people who operate barber shops, museums, movie theatres, and airlines simply generous folks who don't maximize profit? Aren't they throwing profit away by offering discounts?

◇ In this chapter, we study markets in which the firm can influence the price. We also compare the performance of the firm in such a market with that of a competitive market and examine whether monopoly is as efficient as competition. In *Reading Between the Lines* at the end of the chapter, we'll return to Air Canada's monopoly in air travel.

After studying this chapter, you will be able to

- **Explain how monopoly arises and distinguish between single-price monopoly and price-discriminating monopoly**
- **Explain how a single-price monopoly determines its output and price**
- **Compare the performance and efficiency of single-price monopoly and competition**
- **Define rent seeking and explain why it arises**
- **Explain how price discrimination increases profit**
- **Explain how monopoly regulation influences output, price, economic profit, and efficiency**

Market Power

MARKET POWER AND COMPETITION ARE THE TWO forces that operate in most markets. **Market power** is the ability to influence the market, and in particular the market price, by influencing the total quantity offered for sale.

The firms in perfect competition that you studied in Chapter 11 have no market power. They face the force of raw competition and are price takers. The firms that we study in this chapter operate at the opposite extreme. They face no competition and exercise raw market power. We call this extreme monopoly. A **monopoly** is an industry that produces a good or service for which no close substitute exists and in which there is one supplier that is protected from competition by a barrier preventing the entry of new firms.

Examples of monopoly include your local phone, gas, electricity, and water suppliers, as well as De Beers, the South African diamond producer, and Microsoft Corporation, the software developer that created the Windows operating system.

How Monopoly Arises

Monopoly has two key features:

- No close substitutes
- Barriers to entry

No Close Substitutes If a good has a close substitute, even though only one firm produces it, that firm effectively faces competition from the producers of substitutes. Water supplied by a local public utility is an example of a good that does not have close substitutes. While it does have a close substitute for drinking—bottled spring water—it has no effective substitutes for showering or washing a car.

Monopolies are constantly under attack from new products and ideas that substitute for products produced by monopolies. For example, FedEx, Purolator, the fax machine, and e-mail have weakened the monopoly of Canada Post. Similarly, the satellite dish has weakened the monopoly of cable television companies.

But new products also are constantly creating monopolies. An example is Microsoft's monopoly in the DOS operating system during the 1980s and in the Windows operating system today.

Barriers to Entry Legal or natural constraints that protect a firm from potential competitors are called **barriers to entry**. A firm can sometimes create its own barrier to entry by acquiring a significant portion of a key resource. For example, De Beers controls more than 80 percent of the world's supply of natural diamonds. But most monopolies arise from two other types of barriers: legal barriers and natural barriers.

Legal Barriers to Entry Legal barriers to entry create legal monopoly. A **legal monopoly** is a market in which competition and entry are restricted by the granting of a public franchise, government licence, patent, or copyright.

A *public franchise* is an exclusive right granted to a firm to supply a good or service. An example is Canada Post, which has the exclusive right to carry first-class mail. A *government licence* controls entry into particular occupations, professions, and industries. Examples of this type of barrier to entry occur in medicine, law, dentistry, schoolteaching, architecture, and many other professional services. Licensing does not always create monopoly, but it does restrict competition.

A *patent* is an exclusive right granted to the inventor of a product or service. A *copyright* is an exclusive right granted to the author or composer of a literary, musical, dramatic, or artistic work. Patents and copyrights are valid for a limited time period that varies from country to country. In Canada, a patent is valid for 20 years. Patents encourage the *invention* of new products and production methods. They also stimulate *innovation*—the use of new inventions—by encouraging inventors to publicize their discoveries and offer them for use under licence. Patents have stimulated innovations in areas as diverse as soybean seeds, pharmaceuticals, computer memory chips, and video games.

Natural Barriers to Entry Natural barriers to entry create **natural monopoly**, which is an industry in which one firm can supply the entire market at a lower price than two or more firms can.

Figure 12.1 shows a natural monopoly in the distribution of electric power. Here, the market demand curve for electric power is *D*, and the average total cost curve is *ATC*. Because average total cost decreases as output increases, economies of scale prevail over the entire length of the *ATC* curve. One firm can produce 4 million kilowatt-hours at 5 cents a kilowatt-hour. At this price, the quantity demanded is 4 million kilowatt-hours. So if the price were 5 cents, one firm could supply the entire market. If two firms shared the market, it would cost each of them 10 cents a kilowatt-hour to produce a total of 4 million kilowatt-hours. If four firms shared the market, it would cost each of them 15 cents a kilowatt-hour to produce a total of 4 million kilowatt-hours. So in conditions like those shown in Fig. 12.1, one firm can supply the entire market at a lower cost than two or more firms can. The distribution of electric power is an example of natural monopoly. So is the distribution of water and gas.

Most monopolies are regulated in some way by government agencies. We will study such regulation at the end of this chapter. But for two reasons, we'll first study unregulated monopoly. First, we can better understand why governments regulate monopolies and the effects of regulation if we also know how an unregulated monopoly behaves. Second, even in industries with more than one producer, firms often have a degree of monopoly power, and the theory of monopoly sheds light on the behaviour of such firms and industries.

A major difference between monopoly and competition is that a monopoly sets its own price. But in doing so, it faces a market constraint. Let's see how the market limits a monopoly's pricing choices.

FIGURE 12.1 Natural Monopoly

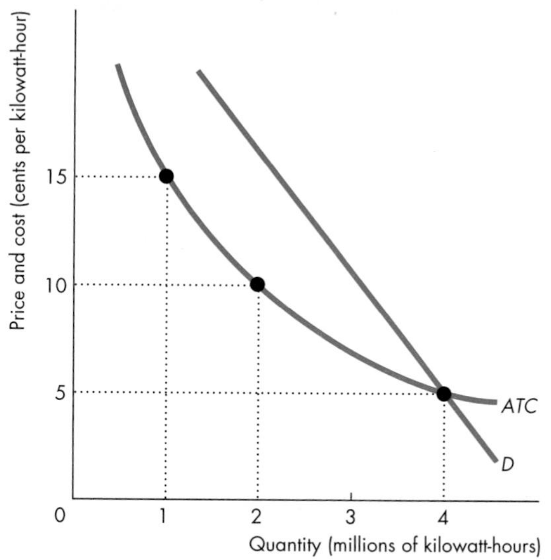

The market demand curve for electric power is *D*, and the average total cost curve is *ATC*. Economies of scale exist over the entire *ATC* curve. One firm can distribute 4 million kilowatt-hours at a cost of 5 cents a kilowatt-hour. This same total output costs 10 cents a kilowatt-hour with two firms and 15 cents a kilowatt-hour with four firms. So one firm can meet the market demand at a lower cost than two or more firms can, and the market is a natural monopoly.

Monopoly Price-Setting Strategies

All monopolies face a tradeoff between price and the quantity sold. To sell a larger quantity, the monopolist must charge a lower price. But there are two broad monopoly situations that create different tradeoffs. They are

- Price discrimination
- Single price

Price Discrimination Many firms price discriminate and most are *not* monopolies. Airlines offer a dizzying array of different prices for the same trip. Pizza producers charge one price for a single pizza and almost give away a second pizza. These are examples of *price discrimination.* **Price discrimination** is the practice of selling different units of a good or service for different prices. Different customers might pay different prices (like airline passengers), or one customer might pay different prices for different quantities bought (like the bargain price for a second pizza).

When a firm price discriminates, it looks as though it is doing its customers a favour. In fact, it is charging the highest possible price for each unit sold and making the largest possible profit.

Not all monopolies can price discriminate. The main obstacle to price discrimination is resale by customers who buy for a low price. Because of resale possibilities, price discrimination is limited to monopolies that sell services that cannot be resold.

Single Price De Beers sells diamonds (of a given size and quality) for the same price to all its customers. If it tried to sell at a low price to some customers and at a higher price to others, only the low-price customers would buy from De Beers. Others would buy from De Beers' low-price customers.

De Beers is a *single-price* monopoly. A **single-price monopoly** is a firm that must sell each unit of its output for the same price to all its customers.

We'll look first at single-price monopoly.

A Single-Price Monopoly's Output and Price Decision

TO UNDERSTAND HOW A SINGLE-PRICE MONOPOLY makes its output and price decision, we must first study the link between price and marginal revenue.

Price and Marginal Revenue

Because in a monopoly there is only one firm, the demand curve facing the firm is the market demand curve. Let's look at Bobbie's Barbershop, the sole supplier of haircuts in Trout River, Newfoundland. The table in Fig. 12.2 shows the market demand schedule. At a price of \$20, Bobbie sells no haircuts. The lower the price, the more haircuts per hour Bobbie can sell. For example, at \$12, consumers demand 4 haircuts per hour (row *E*).

Total revenue (*TR*) is the price (*P*) multiplied by the quantity sold (*Q*). For example, in row *D*, Bobbie sells 3 haircuts at \$14 each, so total revenue is \$42. *Marginal revenue* (*MR*) is the change in total revenue (ΔTR) resulting from a one-unit increase in the quantity sold. For example, if the price falls from \$16 (row *C*) to \$14 (row *D*), the quantity sold increases from 2 to 3 haircuts. Total revenue rises from \$32 to \$42, so the change in total revenue is \$10. Because the quantity sold increases by 1 haircut, marginal revenue equals the change in total revenue and is \$10. Marginal revenue is placed between the two rows to emphasize that marginal revenue relates to the *change* in the quantity sold.

Figure 12.2 shows the market demand curve and marginal revenue curve (*MR*) and also illustrates the calculation we've just made. Notice that at each level of output, marginal revenue is *less* than price—the marginal revenue curve lies below the demand curve. Why is marginal revenue less than price? It is because when the price is lowered to sell one more unit, two opposing forces affect total revenue. The lower price results in a revenue loss, and the increased quantity sold results in a revenue gain. For example, at a price of \$16, Bobbie sells 2 haircuts (point *C*). If she lowers the price to \$14, she sells 3 haircuts and has a revenue gain of \$14 on the third haircut. But she now receives only \$14 on the first two—\$2 less than before. As a result, she loses \$4 of revenue on the first 2 haircuts. To calculate marginal revenue, she must deduct this amount from the revenue gain of \$14. So her marginal revenue is \$10, which is less than the price.

FIGURE 12.2 Demand and Marginal Revenue

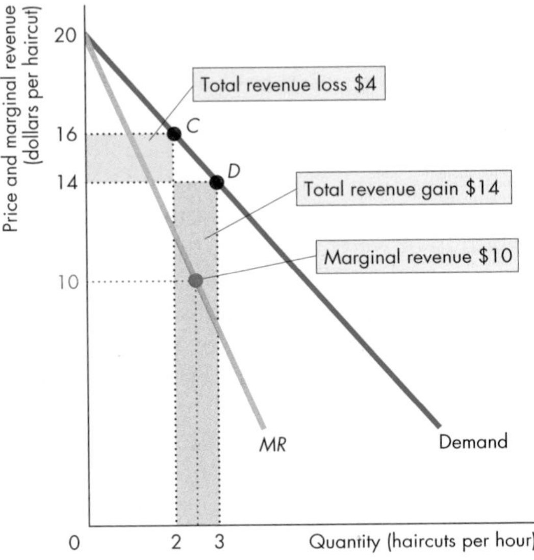

	Price (*P*) (dollars per haircut)	Quantity demanded (*Q*) (haircuts per hour)	Total revenue ($TR = P \times Q$) (dollars)	Marginal revenue ($MR = \Delta TR/\Delta Q$) (dollars per haircut)
A	20	0	0	
				18
B	18	1	18	
				14
C	**16**	**2**	**32**	
				10
D	**14**	**3**	**42**	
				6
E	12	4	48	
				2
F	10	5	50	

The table shows the demand schedule. Total revenue (*TR*) is price multiplied by quantity sold. For example, in row *C*, the price is \$16 a haircut, Bobbie sells 2 haircuts and total revenue is \$32. Marginal revenue (*MR*) is the change in total revenue that results from a one-unit increase in the quantity sold. For example, when the price falls from \$16 to \$14 a haircut, the quantity sold increases by 1 haircut and total revenue increases by \$10. Marginal revenue is \$10. The demand curve and the marginal revenue curve, *MR*, are based on the numbers in the table and illustrate the calculation of marginal revenue when the price of a haircut falls from \$16 to \$14.

Marginal Revenue and Elasticity

A single-price monopoly's marginal revenue is related to the *elasticity of demand* for its good. The demand for a good can be *elastic* (the elasticity of demand is greater than 1), *inelastic* (the elasticity of demand is less than 1), or *unit elastic* (the elasticity of demand is equal to 1). Demand is *elastic* if a 1 percent fall in price brings a greater than 1 percent increase in the quantity demanded. Demand is *inelastic* if a 1 percent fall in price brings a less than 1 percent increase in the quantity demanded. And demand is *unit elastic* if a 1 percent fall in price brings a 1 percent increase in the quantity demanded. (See Chapter 4, pp. 86–87.)

If demand is elastic, a fall in price brings an increase in total revenue—the increase in revenue from the increase in quantity sold outweighs the decrease in revenue from the lower price—and marginal revenue is positive. If demand is inelastic, a fall in price brings a decrease in total revenue—the increase in revenue from the increase in quantity sold is outweighed by the decrease in revenue from the lower price—and marginal revenue is negative. If demand is unit elastic, total revenue does not change—the increase in revenue from the increase in quantity sold offsets the decrease in revenue from the lower price—and marginal revenue is zero. (The relationship between total revenue and elasticity is explained in Chapter 4, on p. 88.)

Figure 12.3 illustrates the relationship between marginal revenue, total revenue, and elasticity. As the price of a haircut gradually falls from $20 to $10, the quantity of haircuts demanded increases from 0 to 5 an hour. Over this output range, marginal revenue is positive (part a), total revenue increases (part b), and the demand for haircuts is elastic. As the price falls from $10 to $0 a haircut, the quantity of haircuts demanded increases from 5 to 10 an hour. Over this output range, marginal revenue is negative (part a), total revenue decreases (part b), and the demand for haircuts is inelastic. When the price is $10 a haircut, marginal revenue is zero, total revenue is a maximum, and the demand for haircuts is unit elastic.

In Monopoly, Demand Is Always Elastic The relationship between marginal revenue and elasticity that you've just discovered implies that a profit-maximizing monopoly never produces an output in the inelastic range of its demand curve. If it did so, it could charge a higher price, produce a smaller quantity, and increase its profit. Let's now look more closely at a monopoly's output and price decision.

FIGURE 12.3 Marginal Revenue and Elasticity

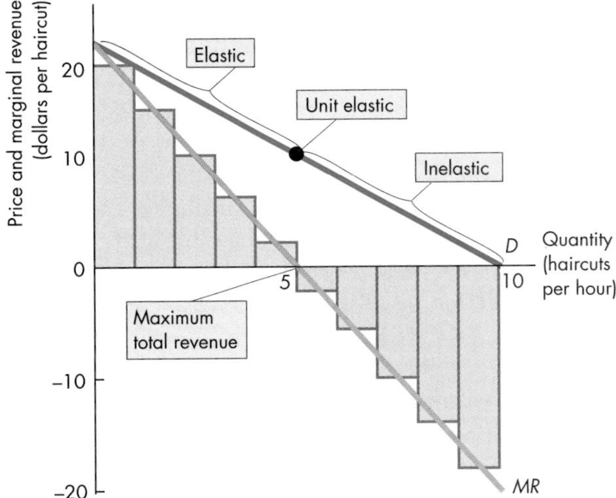

(a) Demand and marginal revenue curves

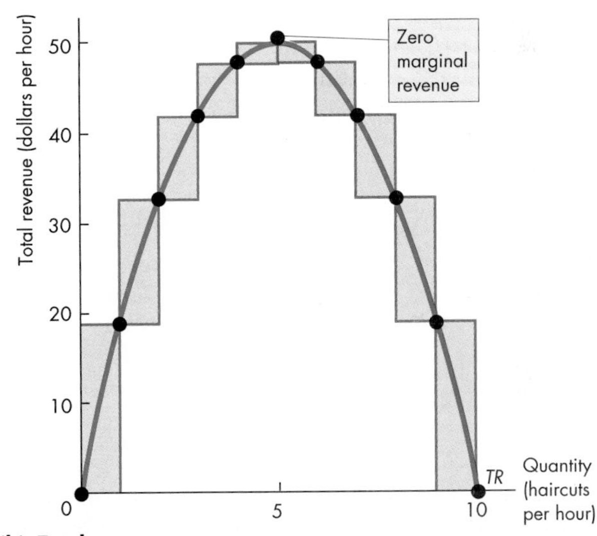

(b) Total revenue curve

In part (a), the demand curve is *D* and the marginal revenue curve is *MR*. In part (b), the total revenue curve is *TR*. Over the range from 0 to 5 haircuts an hour, a price cut increases total revenue, so marginal revenue is positive—as shown by the blue bars. Demand is elastic. Over the range 5 to 10 haircuts an hour, a price cut decreases total revenue, so marginal revenue is negative—as shown by the red bars. Demand is inelastic. At 5 haircuts an hour, total revenue is maximized and marginal revenue is zero. Demand is unit elastic.

Output and Price Decision

To determine the output level and price that maximize a monopoly's profit, we need to study the behaviour of both revenue and costs as output varies. A monopoly faces the same types of technology and cost constraints as a competitive firm. But it faces a different market constraint. The competitive firm is a price taker, whereas the monopoly's output decision influences the price it receives. Let's see how.

Bobbie's revenue, which we studied in Fig. 12.2, is shown again in Table 12.1. The table also contains information on Bobbie's costs and economic profit. Total cost (*TC*) rises as output increases, and so does total revenue (*TR*). Economic profit equals total revenue minus total cost. As you can see in the table, the maximum profit ($12) occurs when Bobbie sells 3 haircuts for $14 each. If she sells 2 haircuts for $16 each or 4 haircuts for $12 each, her economic profit will be only $8.

You can see why 3 haircuts is Bobbie's profit-maximizing output by looking at the marginal revenue and marginal cost columns. When Bobbie increases output from 2 to 3 haircuts, her marginal revenue is $10 and her marginal cost is $6. Profit increases by the difference—$4 an hour. If Bobbie increases output yet further, from 3 to 4 haircuts, her marginal revenue is $6 and her marginal cost is $10. In this case, marginal cost exceeds marginal revenue by $4, so profit decreases by $4 an hour. When marginal revenue exceeds marginal cost, profit increases if output increases. When marginal cost exceeds marginal revenue, profit increases if output decreases. When marginal cost and marginal revenue are equal, profit is maximized.

The information set out in Table 12.1 is shown graphically in Fig. 12.4. Part (a) shows Bobbie's total revenue curve (*TR*) and total cost curve (*TC*). Economic profit is the vertical distance between *TR* and *TC*. Bobbie maximizes her profit at 3 haircuts an hour—economic profit is $42 minus $30, or $12.

A monopoly, like a competitive firm, maximizes profit by producing the output at which marginal cost equals marginal revenue. Figure 12.4(b) shows the market demand curve (*D*), Bobbie's marginal revenue curve (*MR*), and her marginal cost curve (*MC*) and average total cost curve (*ATC*). Bobbie maximizes her profit by doing 3 haircuts an hour. But what price does she charge for a haircut? To set the price, the monopolist uses the demand curve and finds the highest price at which she can sell the profit-maximizing output. In Bobbie's case, the highest price at which she can sell 3 haircuts an hour is $14 per haircut.

TABLE 12.1 A Monopoly's Output and Price Decision

Price (*P*) (dollars per haircut)	Quantity demanded (*Q*) (haircuts per hour)	Total revenue ($TR = P \times Q$) (dollars)	Marginal revenue ($MR = \Delta TR/\Delta Q$) (dollars per haircut)	Total cost (*TC*) (dollars)	Marginal cost ($MC = \Delta TC/\Delta Q$) (dollars per haircut)	Economic profit ($TR - TC$) (dollars)
20	0	0		20		–20
			18		1	
18	1	18		21		–3
			14		3	
16	2	32		24		+8
			10		6	
14	3	42		30		+12
			6		10	
12	4	48		40		+8
			2		15	
10	5	50		55		–5

This table gives the information needed to find the profit-maximizing output and price. Total revenue (*TR*) equals price multiplied by the quantity sold. Profit equals total revenue minus total cost (*TC*). Profit is maximized when 3 haircuts are sold at $14 a haircut. Total revenue is $42, total cost is $30, and economic profit is $12 ($42 – $30).

FIGURE 12.4 A Monopoly's Output and Price

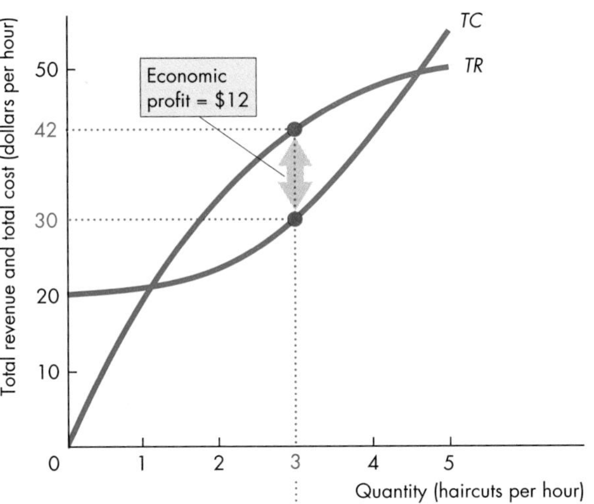

(a) Total revenue and total cost curves

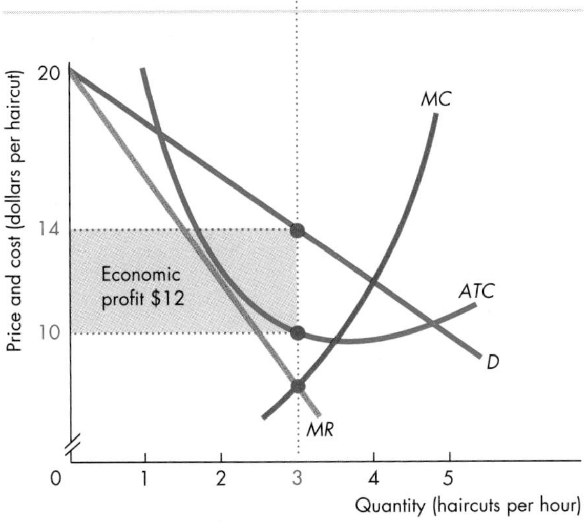

(b) Demand and marginal revenue and cost curves

In part (a), economic profit is the vertical distance equal to total revenue (*TR*) minus total cost (*TC*) and economic profit is maximized at 3 haircuts an hour. In part (b), economic profit is maximized when marginal cost (*MC*) equals marginal revenue (*MR*). The profit-maximizing output is 3 haircuts an hour. The price is determined by the demand curve (*D*) and is $14 a haircut. Her average total cost is $10 a haircut, so economic profit, the blue rectangle, is $12—the profit per haircut ($4) multiplied by 3 haircuts.

All firms maximize profit by producing the output at which marginal revenue equals marginal cost. For a competitive firm, price equals marginal revenue, so price also equals marginal cost. For a monopoly, price exceeds marginal revenue, so price also exceeds marginal cost.

A monopoly charges a price that exceeds marginal cost, but does it always make an economic profit? In Bobbie's case, when she produces 3 haircuts an hour, her average total cost is $10 (read from the *ATC* curve) and her price is $14 (read from the *D* curve). Her profit per haircut is $4 ($14 – $10). Bobbie's economic profit is shown by the blue rectangle, which equals the profit per haircut ($4) multiplied by the number of haircuts (3), for a total of $12.

If firms in a perfectly competitive industry make a positive economic profit, new firms enter. That does not happen in monopoly. Barriers to entry prevent new firms from entering an industry in which there is a monopoly. So a monopoly can make a positive economic profit and continue to do so indefinitely. Sometimes that profit is large, as in the international diamond business.

Bobbie makes a positive economic profit. But suppose that the owner of the shop that Bobbie rents increases Bobbie's rent. If Bobbie pays an additional $12 an hour for rent, her fixed cost increases by $12 an hour. Her marginal cost and marginal revenue don't change, so her profit-maximizing output remains at 3 haircuts an hour. Her profit decreases by $12 an hour to zero. If Bobbie pays more than an additional $12 an hour for her shop rent, she incurs an economic loss. If this situation were permanent, Bobbie would go out of business. But entrepreneurs are a hardy lot, and Bobbie might find another shop where the rent is less.

REVIEW QUIZ

1. What is the relationship between marginal cost and marginal revenue when a single-price monopoly maximizes profit?
2. How does a single-price monopoly determine the price it will charge its customers?
3. What is the relationship between price, marginal revenue, and marginal cost when a single-price monopoly is maximizing profit?
4. Why can a monopoly make a positive economic profit even in the long run?

Single-Price Monopoly and Competition Compared

IMAGINE AN INDUSTRY THAT IS MADE UP OF MANY small firms operating in perfect competition. Then imagine that a single firm buys out all these small firms and creates a monopoly.

What will happen in this industry? Will the price rise or fall? Will the quantity produced increase or decrease? Will economic profit increase or decrease? Will either the original competitive situation or the new monopoly situation be efficient?

These are the questions we're now going to answer. First, we look at the effects of monopoly on the price and quantity produced. Then we turn to the questions about efficiency.

Comparing Output and Price

Figure 12.5 shows the market we'll study. The market demand curve is *D*. The demand curve is the same regardless of how the industry is organized. But the supply side and the equilibrium are different in monopoly and competition. First, let's look at the case of perfect competition.

Perfect Competition Initially, with many small perfectly competitive firms in the market, the market supply curve is ***S***. This supply curve is obtained by summing the supply curves of all the individual firms in the market.

In perfect competition, equilibrium occurs where the supply curve and the demand curve intersect. The quantity produced by the industry is Q_C, and the price is P_C. Each firm takes the price P_C and maximizes its profit by producing the output at which its own marginal cost equals the price. Because each firm is a small part of the total industry, there is no incentive for any firm to try to manipulate the price by varying its output.

Monopoly Now suppose that this industry is taken over by a single firm. Consumers do not change, so the demand curve remains the same as in the case of perfect competition. But now the monopoly recognizes this demand curve as a constraint on its sales. The monopoly's marginal revenue curve is *MR*.

The monopoly maximizes profit by producing the quantity at which marginal revenue equals marginal cost. To find the monopoly's marginal cost curve, first recall that in perfect competition, the industry supply curve is the sum of the supply curves of the firms in the industry. Also recall that each firm's supply curve is its marginal cost curve (see Chapter 11, pp. 244–245). So when the industry is taken over by a single firm, the competitive industry's supply curve becomes the monopoly's marginal cost curve. To remind you of this fact, the supply curve is also labelled *MC*.

The output at which marginal revenue equals marginal cost is Q_M. This output is smaller than the competitive output Q_C. And the monopoly charges the price P_M, which is higher than P_C. We have established that

Compared to a perfectly competitive industry, a single-price monopoly restricts its output and charges a higher price.

We've seen how the output and price of a monopoly compare with those in a competitive industry. Let's now compare the efficiency of the two types of markets.

FIGURE 12.5 Monopoly's Smaller Output and Higher Price

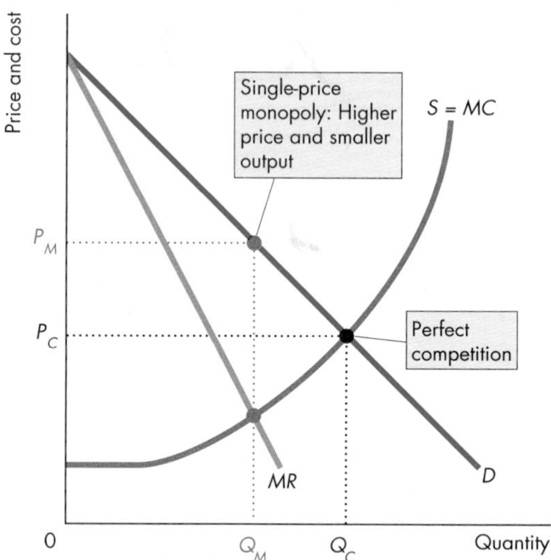

A competitive industry produces the quantity Q_C at price P_C. A single-price monopoly produces the quantity Q_M at which marginal revenue equals marginal cost and sells that quantity for the price P_M. Compared to perfect competition, a single-price monopoly restricts output and raises the price.

Efficiency Comparison

When we studied efficiency in perfect competition, (see Chapter 11, pp. 254–255), we discovered that if there are no external costs and benefits, perfect competition is efficient. Along the demand curve, consumers are efficient. Along the supply curve, producers are efficient. And where the curves intersect—the competitive equilibrium—both consumers and producers are efficient. Price, which measures marginal benefit, equals marginal cost.

Monopoly restricts output below the competitive level and is inefficient. If a monopoly increases its output by one unit, consumers' marginal benefit exceeds the monopoly's marginal cost and resource use will be more efficient.

Figure 12.6 illustrates the inefficiency of monopoly and shows the loss of consumer and producer surpluses in a monopoly. In perfect competition (part a), consumers pay P_C for each unit. The marginal benefit to consumers is shown by the demand curve ($D = MB$). So the price P_C measures the value of the good to the consumer. Value minus the price paid equals *consumer surplus* (see Chapter 5, p. 107). In Fig. 12.6(a), consumer surplus is shown by the green triangle.

The marginal cost of production (opportunity cost) in perfect competition is shown by the supply curve ($S = MC$). The amount received by the producer in excess of this marginal cost is *producer surplus.* In Fig. 12.6(a), the blue area shows producer surplus. At the competitive equilibrium, marginal benefit equals marginal cost and the sum of consumer surplus and producer surplus is maximized. Resource use is efficient.

In Fig. 12.6(b), a monopoly restricts output to Q_M and sells that output for P_M. Consumer surplus decreases to the smaller green triangle. Consumers lose partly by having to pay more for the good and partly by getting less of it. Part of the original producer surplus is also lost. The total loss resulting from the smaller monopoly output (Q_M) is the grey area. The part of the grey area above P_C is the loss of consumer surplus, and the part of the area below P_C is the loss of producer surplus. The entire grey area measures the loss of consumer surplus plus producer surplus. This loss is called the *deadweight loss.* The smaller output and higher price drive a wedge between marginal benefit and marginal cost and eliminate the producer surplus and the consumer surplus on the output that a competitive industry would have produced but the monopoly does not.

FIGURE 12.6 Inefficiency of Monopoly

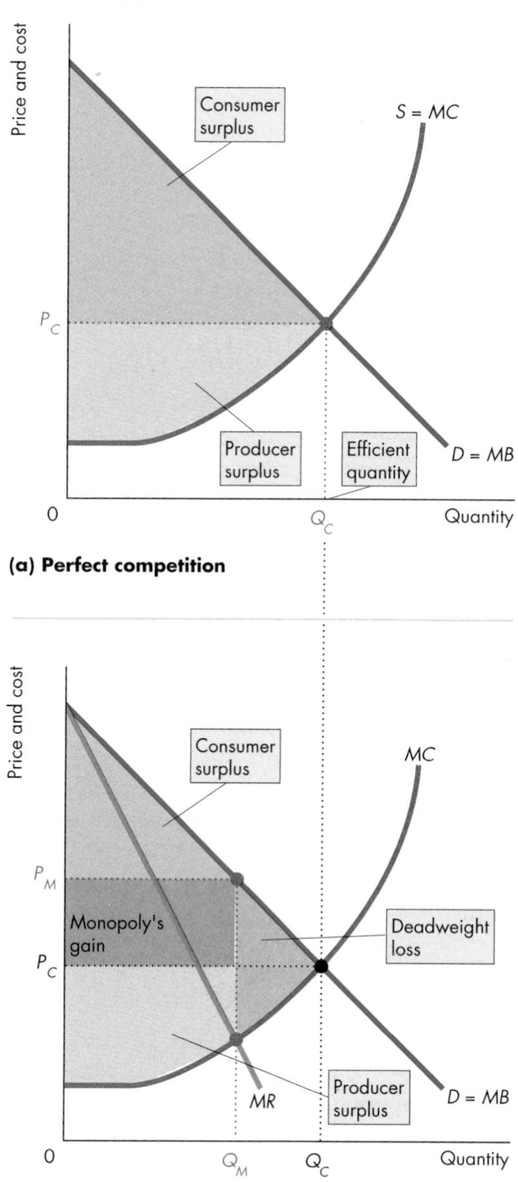

In perfect competition (part a), the quantity Q_C is sold at the price P_C. Consumer surplus is shown by the green triangle. In long-run equilibrium, firms' economic profits are zero and consumer surplus is maximized.

A single-price monopoly (part b) restricts output to Q_M and increases the price to P_M. Consumer surplus is the smaller green triangle. The monopoly takes the darker blue rectangle and creates a deadweight loss (the grey area).

Redistribution of Surpluses

You've seen that monopoly is inefficient because marginal benefit exceeds marginal cost and there is deadweight loss—a social loss. But monopoly also brings a *redistribution* of surpluses.

Some of the lost consumer surplus goes to the monopoly. In Fig. 12.6, the monopoly gets the difference between the higher price, P_M, and the competitive price, P_C, on the quantity sold, Q_M. So the monopoly takes the part of the consumer surplus shown by the darker blue rectangle. This portion of the loss of consumer surplus is not a loss to society. It is redistribution from consumers to the monopoly producer.

Rent Seeking

You've seen that monopoly creates a deadweight loss and so is inefficient. But the social cost of monopoly exceeds the deadweight loss because of an activity called rent seeking. **Rent seeking** is any attempt to capture a consumer surplus, a producer surplus, or an economic profit. The activity is not confined to monopoly. But attempting to capture the economic profit of a monopoly is a major form of rent seeking.

You've seen that a monopoly makes its economic profit by diverting part of consumer surplus to itself. Thus the pursuit of an economic profit by a monopolist is rent seeking. It is the attempt to capture consumer surplus.

Rent seekers pursue their goals in two main ways. They might

- Buy a monopoly
- Create a monopoly

Buy a Monopoly To rent seek by buying a monopoly, a person searches for a monopoly that is for sale at a lower price than the monopoly's economic profit. Trading of taxicab licences is an example of this type of rent seeking. In some cities, taxicabs are regulated. The city restricts both the fares and the number of taxis that can operate so that operating a taxi results in economic profit, or rent. A person who wants to operate a taxi must buy a licence from someone who already has one. People rationally devote their time and effort to seeking out profitable monopoly businesses to buy. In the process, they use scarce resources that could otherwise have been employed to produce goods and services. The value of this lost production is part of the social cost of monopoly. The amount paid for a monopoly is not a social cost because the payment is just a transfer of an existing producer surplus from the buyer to the seller.

Create a Monopoly Rent seeking by creating monopoly is mainly a political activity. It takes the form of lobbying and trying to influence the political process. Such influence might be sought by making campaign contributions in exchange for legislative support or by seeking to influence political outcomes indirectly through publicity in the media or more direct contacts with politicians and bureaucrats. An example of a monopoly right created in this way is the cable television monopoly created and regulated by the Canadian Radio-Television and Telecommunications Commission (CRTC). Another is a regulation that restricts "split-run" magazines. These regulations restrict output and increase price.

This type of rent seeking is a costly activity that uses up scarce resources. Taken together, firms spend billions of dollars lobbying MPs, MPPs, and bureaucrats in the pursuit of licences and laws that create barriers to entry and establish a monopoly right. Everyone has an incentive to rent seek, and because there are no barriers to entry into the rent-seeking activity, there is a great deal of competition for new monopoly rights.

Rent-Seeking Equilibrium

Barriers to entry create monopoly. But there is no barrier to entry into rent seeking. Rent seeking is like perfect competition. If an economic profit is available, a new rent seeker will try to get some of it. And competition among rent seekers pushes up the price that must be paid for a monopoly right to the point at which only a normal profit can be made by operating the monopoly. For example, competition for the right to operate a taxi in Toronto leads to a price of more than $80,000 for a taxi licence, which is sufficiently high to eliminate economic profit for taxi operators and leave them with normal profit.

Figure 12.7 shows a rent-seeking equilibrium. The cost of rent seeking is a fixed cost that must be added to a monopoly's other costs. Rent seeking and rent-seeking costs increase to the point at which no economic profit is made. The average total cost curve, which includes the fixed cost of rent seeking, shifts upward until it just touches the demand curve. Economic profit is zero. It has been lost in rent seeking. Consumer surplus is unaffected. But the

FIGURE 12.7 Rent-Seeking Equilibrium

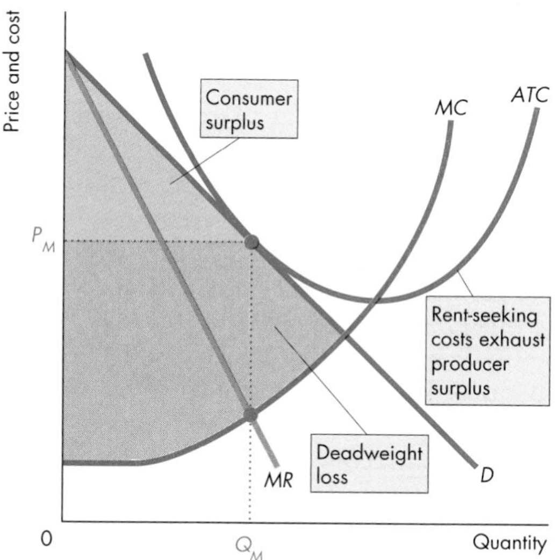

With competitive rent seeking, a monopoly uses all its economic profit to prevent another firm from taking its economic rent. The firm's rent-seeking costs are fixed costs. They add to total fixed cost and to average total cost. The *ATC* curve shifts upward until, at the profit-maximizing price, the firm breaks even.

deadweight loss of monopoly now includes the original deadweight loss triangle plus the lost producer surplus, shown by the enlarged grey area in the figure.

REVIEW QUIZ

1 Why does a single-price monopoly produce a smaller output and charge a higher price than what would prevail if the industry were perfectly competitive?
2 How does a monopoly transfer consumer surplus to itself?
3 Why is a single-price monopoly inefficient?
4 What is rent seeking and how does it influence the inefficiency of monopoly?

So far, we've considered only a single-price monopoly. But many monopolies do not operate with a single price. Instead, they price discriminate. Let's now see how a price-discriminating monopoly works.

Price Discrimination

PRICE DISCRIMINATION—SELLING A GOOD OR service at a number of different prices—is widespread. You encounter it when you travel, go to the movies, get your hair cut, buy pizza, or visit an art museum. Most price discriminators are not monopolies, but monopolies price discriminate when they can do so.

To be able to price discriminate, a monopoly must

1. Identify and separate different buyer types.
2. Sell a product that cannot be resold.

Price discrimination is charging different prices for a single good or service because of differences in buyers' willingness to pay and not because of differences in production costs. So not all price *differences* are price *discrimination.* Some goods that are similar but not identical have different prices because they have different production costs. For example, the cost of producing electricity depends on the time of day. If an electric power company charges a higher price during the peak consumption periods from 7:00 to 9:00 in the morning and from 4:00 to 7:00 in the evening than it does at other times of the day, it is not price discriminating.

At first sight, it appears that price discrimination contradicts the assumption of profit maximization. Why would a movie theatre allow children to see movies at half price? Why would a hairdresser charge students and senior citizens less? Aren't these firms losing profit by being nice to their customers?

Deeper investigation shows that far from losing profit, price discriminators make a bigger profit than they would otherwise. So a monopoly has an incentive to find ways of discriminating and charging each buyer the highest possible price. Some people pay less with price discrimination, but others pay more.

Price Discrimination and Consumer Surplus

The key idea behind price discrimination is to convert consumer surplus into economic profit. Demand curves slope downward because the value that people place on any good decreases as the quantity consumed of that good increases. When all the units consumed are sold for a single price, consumers benefit. The benefit is the value the consumers get from each unit of the good minus the price actually paid for it. This benefit is *consumer surplus.* Price discrimination is an attempt by a monopoly to capture as much of the consumer surplus as possible for itself.

To extract every dollar of consumer surplus from every buyer, the monopoly would have to offer each individual customer a separate price schedule based on that customer's own willingness to pay. Clearly, such price discrimination cannot be carried out in practice because a firm does not have enough information about each consumer's demand curve.

But firms try to extract as much consumer surplus as possible, and to do so, they discriminate in two broad ways:

- Among units of a good
- Among groups of buyers

Discriminating Among Units of a Good One method of price discrimination charges each buyer a different price on each unit of a good bought. A discount for bulk buying is an example of this type of discrimination. The larger the quantity bought, the larger is the discount—and the lower is the price. (Note that some discounts for bulk arise from lower costs of production for greater bulk. In these cases, such discounts are not price discrimination.)

Discriminating Among Groups of Buyers Price discrimination often takes the form of discriminating between different groups of consumers on the basis of age, employment status, or some other easily distinguished characteristic. This type of price discrimination works when each group has a different average willingness to pay for the good or service.

For example, a face-to-face sales meeting with a customer might bring a large and profitable order. For salespeople and other business travellers, the marginal benefit from a trip is large and the price that such a traveller will pay for a trip is high. In contrast, for a vacation traveller, any of several different trips and even no vacation trip are options. So for vacation travellers, the marginal benefit of a trip is small and the price that such a traveller will pay for a trip is low. Because business travellers are willing to pay more than vacation travellers are, it is possible for an airline to profit by price discriminating between these two groups. Similarly, because students have a lower willingness to pay for a haircut than a working person does, it is possible for a hairdresser to profit by price discriminating between these two groups.

Let's see how an airline exploits the differences in demand by business and vacation travellers and increases its profit by price discriminating.

Profiting by Price Discriminating

Global Air has a monopoly on an exotic route. Figure 12.8 shows the demand curve (*D*) and the marginal revenue curve (*MR*) for travel on this route. It also shows Global Air's marginal cost curve (*MC*) and average total cost curve (*ATC*).

Initially, Global is a single-price monopoly and maximizes its profit by producing 8,000 trips a year (the quantity at which *MR* equals *MC*). The price is $1,200 per trip. The average total cost of producing a trip is $600, so economic profit is $600 a trip. On 8,000 trips, Global's economic profit is $4.8 million a year, shown by the blue rectangle. Global's customers enjoy a consumer surplus shown by the green triangle.

FIGURE 12.8 A Single Price of Air Travel

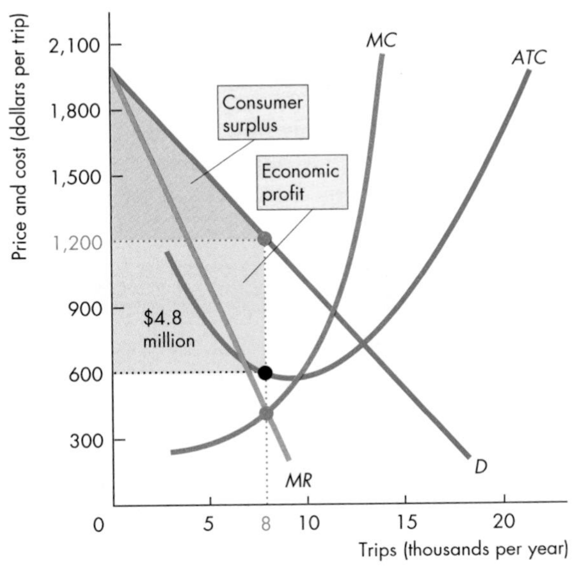

Global Airlines has a monopoly on an air route. The market demand curve is *D*, and marginal revenue curve is *MR*. Global Air's marginal cost curve is *MC*, and its average total cost curve is *ATC*. As a single-price monopoly, Global maximizes profit by selling 8,000 trips a year at $1,200 a trip. Its profit is $4.8 million a year—the blue rectangle. Global's customers enjoy a consumer surplus—the green triangle.

Global is struck by the fact that many of its customers are business travellers, and Global suspects that they are willing to pay more than $1,200 a trip. So Global does some market research, which tells Global that some business travellers are willing to pay as much as $1,800 a trip. Also, these customers frequently change their travel plans at the last moment. Another group of business travellers is willing to pay $1,600. These customers know one week ahead when they will travel, and they never want to stay over a weekend. Yet another group would pay up to $1,400. These travellers know two weeks ahead when they will travel and don't want to stay over a weekend.

So Global announces a new fare schedule: no restrictions, $1,800; 7-day advance purchase, no cancellation, $1,600; 14-day advance purchase, no cancellation, $1,400; 14-day advance purchase, must stay over a weekend, $1,200.

Figure 12.9 shows the outcome with this new fare structure and also shows why Global is pleased with its new fares. It sells 2,000 seats at each of its fare structure and also shows why Global is pleased four prices. Global's economic profit increases by the dark blue steps in Fig. 12.9. Its economic profit is now its original $4.8 million a year plus an additional $2.4 million from its new higher fares. Consumer surplus has shrunk to the smaller green area.

FIGURE 12.9 Price Discrimination

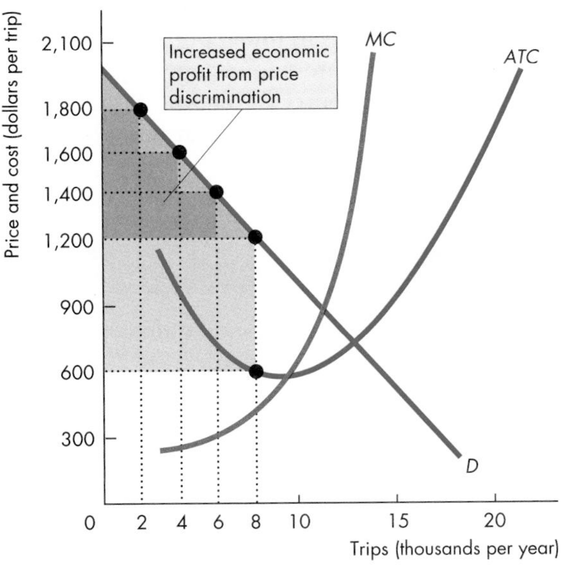

Global revises its fare structure: no restrictions at $1,800, 7-day advance purchase at $1,600, 14-day advance purchase at $1,400, and must stay over a weekend at $1,200. Global sells 2,000 trips at each of its four new fares. Its economic profit increases by $2.4 million a year to $7.2 million a year, which is shown by the original blue rectangle plus the dark blue steps. Global's customers' consumer surplus shrinks.

Perfect Price Discrimination

But Global reckons that it can do even better. It plans to achieve **perfect price discrimination**, which extracts the entire consumer surplus. To do so, Global must get creative and come up with a host of additional fares—ranging between $2,000 and $1,200, each of which appeals to a small segment of the business market—that will extract the entire consumer surplus from the business travellers.

With perfect price discrimination, something special happens to marginal revenue. For the perfect price discriminator, the market demand curve becomes the marginal revenue curve. The reason is that when the price is cut to sell a larger quantity, the firm sells only the marginal unit at the lower price. All the other units continue to be sold for the highest price that each buyer is willing to pay. So for the perfect price discriminator, marginal revenue *equals* price and the demand curve becomes the marginal revenue curve.

With marginal revenue equal to price, Global can obtain yet greater profit by increasing output up to the point at which price (and marginal revenue) is equal to marginal cost.

So Global now seeks additional travellers who will not pay as much as $1,200 a trip but who will pay more than marginal cost. More creative pricing comes up with vacation specials and other fares that have combinations of advance reservation, minimum stay, and other restrictions that make these fares unattractive to its existing customers but attractive to a further group of travellers. With all these fares and specials, Global increases sales, extracts the entire consumer surplus, and maximizes economic profit. Figure 12.10 shows the outcome with perfect price discrimination. The dozens of fares paid by the original travellers who are willing to pay between $1,200 and $2,000 have extracted the entire consumer surplus from this group and converted it into economic profit for Global.

The new fares between $900 and $1,200 have attracted 3,000 additional travellers but taken their entire consumer surplus also. Global is earning an economic profit of more than $9 million.

FIGURE 12.10 Perfect Price Discrimination

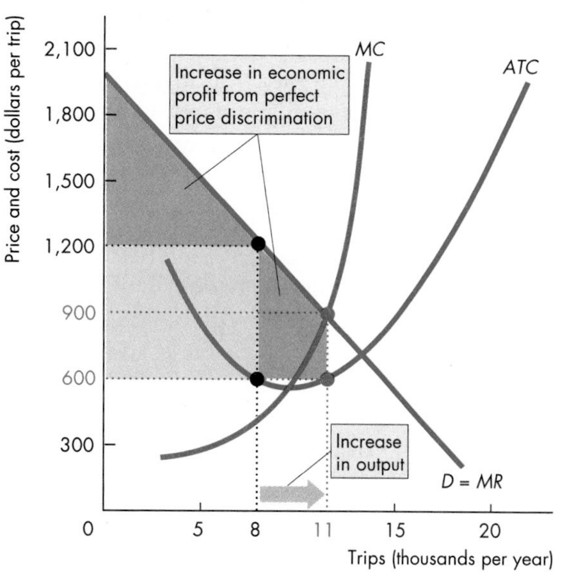

Dozens of fares discriminate among many different types of business travellers, and many new low fares with restrictions appeal to vacation travellers. With perfect price discrimination, Global's demand curve becomes its marginal revenue curve. Economic profit is maximized when the lowest price equals marginal cost. Here, Global sells 11,000 trips and makes an economic profit of $9.35 million a year.

Real-world airlines are just as creative as Global, as you can see in the cartoon!

Would it bother you to hear how little I paid for this flight?

From William Hamilton, "Voodoo Economics," © 1992 by Chronicle Books. Published by Chronicle Books LLC, San Francisco. Used with permission. Visit http://www.chroniclebooks.com.

Efficiency and Rent Seeking with Price Discrimination

With perfect price discrimination, output increases to the point at which price equals marginal cost—where the marginal cost curve intersects the demand curve. This output is identical to that of perfect competition. Perfect price discrimination pushes consumer surplus to zero but increases producer surplus to equal the sum of consumer surplus and producer surplus in perfect competition. Deadweight loss with perfect price discrimination is zero. So perfect price discrimination achieves efficiency.

The more perfectly the monopoly can price discriminate, the closer its output gets to the competitive output and the more efficient is the outcome.

But there are two differences between perfect competition and perfect price discrimination. First, the distribution of the surplus is different. It is shared by consumers and producers in perfect competition, while the producer gets it all with perfect price discrimination. Second, because the producer grabs the surplus, rent seeking becomes profitable.

People use resources in pursuit of rents, and the bigger the rents, the more resources get used in pursuing them. With free entry into rent seeking, the long-run equilibrium outcome is that rent seekers use up the entire producer surplus.

REVIEW QUIZ

1. What is price discrimination and how is it used to increase a monopoly's profit?
2. Explain how consumer surplus changes when a monopoly price discriminates.
3. Explain how consumer surplus, economic profit, and output change when a monopoly perfectly price discriminates.
4. What are some of the ways in which real-world airlines price discriminate?

You've seen that monopoly is profitable for the monopolist but costly for other people. It results in inefficiency. Because of these features of monopoly, it is subject to policy debate and regulation. We'll now study the key monopoly policy issues.

Monopoly Policy Issues

Monopoly looks bad when we compare it with competition. Monopoly is inefficient, and it captures consumer surplus and converts it into producer surplus or pure waste in the form of rent-seeking costs. If monopoly is so bad, why do we put up with it? Why don't we have laws that crack down on monopoly so hard that it never rears its head? We do indeed have laws that limit monopoly power and regulate the prices that monopolies are permitted to charge. But monopoly also brings some benefits. We begin this review of monopoly policy issues by looking at the benefits of monopoly. We then look at monopoly regulation.

Gains from Monopoly

The main reason why monopoly exists is that it has potential advantages over a competitive alternative. These advantages arise from

- Incentives to innovation
- Economies of scale and economies of scope

Incentives to Innovation Invention leads to a wave of innovation as new knowledge is applied to the production process. Innovation may take the form of developing a new product or a lower-cost way of making an existing product. Controversy has raged over whether large firms with market power or small competitive firms lacking such market power are the most innovative. It is clear that some temporary market power arises from innovation. A firm that develops a new product or process and patents it obtains an exclusive right to that product or process for the term of the patent.

But does the granting of a monopoly, even a temporary one, to an innovator increase the pace of innovation? One line of reasoning suggests that it does. Without protection, an innovator is not able to enjoy the profits from innovation for very long. Thus the incentive to innovate is weakened. A contrary argument is that monopolies can afford to be lazy while competitive firms cannot. Competitive firms must strive to innovate and cut costs even though they know that they cannot hang onto the benefits of their innovation for long. But that knowledge spurs them on to greater and faster innovation.

The evidence on whether monopoly leads to greater innovation than competition is mixed. Large firms do more research and development than do small firms. But research and development are inputs into the process of innovation. What matters is not input but output. Two measures of the output of research and development are the number of patents and the rate of productivity growth. On these measures, it is not clear that bigger is better. But as a new process or product spreads through an industry, the large firms adopt the new process or product more quickly than do small firms. So large firms help to speed the process of diffusion of technological change.

Economies of Scale and Economies of Scope Economies of scale and economies of scope can lead to natural monopoly. As you saw at the beginning of this chapter, in a natural monopoly, a single firm can produce at a lower average total cost than can a number of firms.

A firm experiences *economies of scale* when an increase in its output of a good or service brings a decrease in the average total cost of producing it (see Chapter 10, pp. 230–231). A firm experiences *economies of scope* when an increase in the *range of the goods produced* brings a decrease in average total cost (see Chapter 9, p. 211). Economies of scope occur when different goods can share specialized (and usually costly) capital resources. For example, McDonald's can produce both hamburgers and french fries at a lower average total cost than can two separate firms—a burger firm and a french fry firm—because at McDonald's, hamburgers and french fries share the use of specialized food storage and preparation facilities. A firm that produces a wide range of products can hire specialist designers and marketing experts whose skills can be used across the product range, thereby spreading the costs and lowering the average total cost of production of each of the goods.

There are many examples in which combinations of economies of scale and economies of scope arise, but not all of them lead to monopoly. Some examples are the brewing of beer, the manufacture of refrigerators and other household appliances, the manufacture of pharmaceuticals, and the refining of petroleum.

Examples of industries in which economies of scale are so significant that they lead to a natural monopoly are becoming rare. Public utilities such as gas, electric power, local telephone service, and garbage collection once were natural monopolies. But technological advances now enable us to separate the *production* of electric power or natural gas from its *distribution*. The provision of water, though, remains a natural monopoly.

A large-scale firm that has control over supply and can influence price—and therefore behaves like the monopoly firm that you've studied in this chapter—can reap these economies of scale and scope. Small, competitive firms cannot. Consequently, there are situations in which the comparison of monopoly and competition that we made earlier in this chapter is not valid. Recall that we imagined the takeover of a large number of competitive firms by a monopoly firm. But we also assumed that the monopoly would use exactly the same technology as the small firms and have the same costs. If one large firm can reap economies of scale and economies of scope, its marginal cost curve will lie below the supply curve of a competitive industry made up of many small firms. It is possible for such economies of scale and economies of scope to be so large as to result in a larger output and lower price under monopoly than a competitive industry would achieve.

Where significant economies of scale and economies of scope exist, it is usually worth putting up with monopoly and regulating its price.

Regulating Natural Monopoly

Where demand and cost conditions create a natural monopoly, a federal, provincial, or local government agency usually steps in to regulate the prices of the monopoly. By regulating a monopoly, some of the worst aspects of monopoly can be avoided or at least moderated. Let's look at monopoly price regulation.

Figure 12.11 shows the demand curve *D*, the marginal revenue curve *MR*, the long-run average cost curve *ATC*, and the marginal cost curve *MC* for a natural gas distribution company that is a natural monopoly.

The firm's marginal cost is constant at 10 cents per cubic metre. But average total cost decreases as output increases. The reason is that the natural gas company has a large investment in pipelines and so has high fixed costs. These fixed costs are part of the company's average total cost and so appear in the *ATC* curve. The average total cost curve slopes downward because as the number of cubic metres sold increases, the fixed cost is spread over a larger number of units. (If you need to refresh your memory on how the average total cost curve is calculated, look back at Chapter 10, pp. 224–225.)

This one firm can supply the entire market at a lower cost than two firms can because average total cost is falling even when the entire market is supplied. (Refer back to p. 262–263 if you need a quick refresher on natural monopoly.)

Profit Maximization Suppose the natural gas company is not regulated and instead maximizes profit. Figure 12.11 shows the outcome. The company produces 2 million cubic metres a day, the quantity at which marginal cost equals marginal revenue. It prices the gas at 20 cents a cubic metre and makes an economic profit of 2 cents a cubic metre, or $40,000 a day.

This outcome is fine for the gas company, but it is inefficient. The price of gas is 20 cents a cubic metre when its marginal cost is only 10 cents a cubic metre. Also, the gas company is making a big profit. What can regulation do to improve this outcome?

The Efficient Regulation If the monopoly regulator wants to achieve an efficient use of resources, it must require the gas monopoly to produce the quantity of gas that brings marginal benefit into equality with marginal cost. Marginal benefit is what the consumer is willing to pay and is shown by the demand curve. Marginal cost is shown by the firm's marginal cost curve. You can see in Fig. 12.11 that this outcome occurs if the price is regulated at 10 cents per cubic metre and if 4 million cubic metres per day are produced. The regulation that produces this outcome is called a marginal cost pricing rule. A **marginal cost pricing rule** sets price equal to marginal cost. It maximizes total surplus in the regulated industry. In this example, that surplus is all consumer surplus and it equals the area of the triangle beneath the demand curve and above the marginal cost curve.

The marginal cost pricing rule is efficient. But it leaves the natural monopoly incurring an economic loss. Because average total cost is falling as output increases, marginal cost is below average total cost. And because price equals marginal cost, price is below average total cost. Average total cost minus price is the loss per unit produced. It's pretty obvious that a natural gas company that is required to use a marginal cost pricing rule will not stay in business for long. How can a company cover its costs and, at the same time, obey a marginal cost pricing rule?

One possibility is price discrimination in which the firm produces the quantity at which price equals marginal cost but sells some units to some buyers at a higher price (see p. 274).

FIGURE 12.11 Regulating a Natural Monopoly

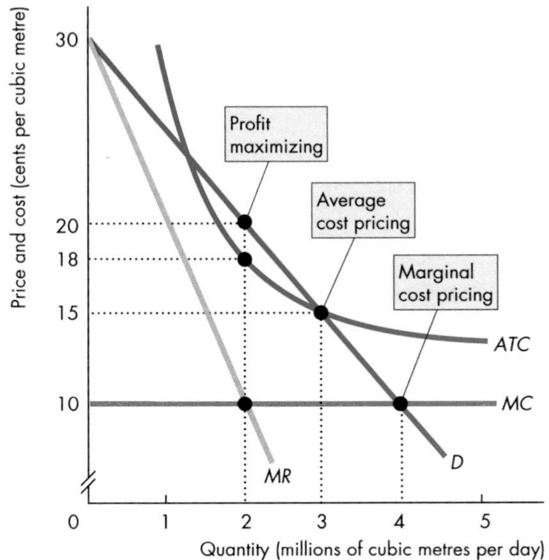

A natural monopoly is an industry in which average total cost is falling even when the entire market demand is satisfied. A natural gas producer faces the demand curve *D*. The firm's marginal cost is constant at 10 cents per cubic metre, as shown by the curve labelled *MC*. Fixed costs are large, and the average total cost curve, which includes average fixed cost, is shown as *ATC*. A marginal cost pricing rule sets the price at 10 cents per cubic metre. The monopoly produces 4 million cubic metres per day and incurs an economic loss. An average cost pricing rule sets the price at 15 cents per cubic metre. The monopoly produces 3 million cubic metres per day and makes normal profit.

Another possibility is to use a two-part price (called a two-part tariff). For example, the gas company might charge a monthly fixed fee that covers its fixed cost and then charge for gas consumed at marginal cost.

But a natural monopoly cannot always cover its costs in these ways. If a natural monopoly cannot cover its total cost from its customers and if the government wants it to follow a marginal cost pricing rule, then the government must give the firm a subsidy. In such a case, the government raises the revenue for the subsidy by taxing some other activity. But as we saw in Chapter 6, taxes themselves generate deadweight loss. Thus the deadweight loss resulting from additional taxes must be subtracted from the efficiency gained by forcing the natural monopoly to adopt a marginal cost pricing rule.

Average Cost Pricing Regulators almost never impose efficient pricing because of its consequences for the firm's profit. Instead, they compromise by permitting the firm to cover its costs and to earn a normal profit. Recall that normal profit is a cost of production and we include it along with the firm's other fixed costs in the average total cost curve. So pricing to cover cost including normal profit means setting price equal to average total cost—called an **average cost pricing rule**.

Figure 12.11 shows the average cost pricing outcome. The natural gas company charges 15 cents a cubic metre and sells 3 million cubic metres per day. This outcome is better for consumers than the unregulated profit-maximizing outcome. The price is 5 cents a cubic metre lower, and the quantity consumed is 1 million cubic metres per day more. And the outcome is better for the producer than the marginal cost pricing rule outcome. The firm earns normal profit. The outcome is inefficient but less so than the unregulated profit-maximizing outcome.

REVIEW QUIZ

1. What are the two main reasons why monopoly is worth tolerating?
2. Can you provide some examples of economies of scale and economies of scope?
3. Why might the incentive to innovate be greater for a monopoly than for a small competitive firm?
4. What is the price that achieves an efficient outcome for a regulated monopoly? And what is the problem with this price?
5. Compare the consumer surplus, producer surplus, and deadweight loss that arise from average cost pricing with those that arise from profit-maximization pricing and marginal cost pricing.

◆ You've now studied perfect competition and monopoly. *Reading Between the Lines* on pp. 278–279 looks at market power in Canadian air travel. In the next chapter, we study markets that lie between the extremes of perfect competition and monopoly and that blend elements of the two.

READING BETWEEN THE LINES

Domestic Airline Monopoly

OTTAWA CITIZEN, AUGUST 13, 2002

Air Canada needs to compete, poll says

A majority of Canadians want to end Air Canada's virtual monopoly, preferring free competition in the country's skies even if it means the end of all major Canadian-owned airlines, a newly released poll indicates.

The survey, conducted for Transport Canada earlier this year, suggests 55 per cent believe that even if opening up the air industry further to U.S.-based airlines means the end of Air Canada and other major Canadian airlines, this is better than having a monopoly.

The comprehensive national poll found great willingness to open up Canadian skies to foreign competitors, with 84 per cent saying they would accept Canadian and American airlines if it meant they could fly all over North America. And a surprising 71 per cent said they would accept U.S.-based airlines in Canada even without equal access for Canadian airlines in the U.S., if it meant lower fares for passengers. This number dropped to 44 per cent, however, if it also meant less service to remote areas in Canada.

The poll indicated that only 15 per cent of Canadians felt the country's airline industry is working well. This is half the number of respondents who said they were satisfied flyers in 1999 when the last survey was performed.

"Overall, Canadians want safety and affordable air fares. They are not happy with the industry as it exists today, and they want to see it fixed," said the poll report. Goldfarb Consultants interviewed 2,083 adult Canadians by telephone between March 5 and 20. It has a margin of error within 2.2 percentage points, 19 times out of 20.

When asked about the problems plaguing the industry, almost two in five respondents mentioned a decline in competition and Air Canada's near monopoly. The report says the second most cited problem—35 per cent mentioned rising airfares and surcharges—may be related to the first.

Laura Cooke, a spokesperson for Air Canada, said she could not offer specific comments about the poll until she had read it, but added that the airline favours free competition with the U.S. airlines in Canada as long as there is a reciprocal deal for Air Canada in the U.S.

"It does not make sense to give up rights or ensure that U.S. carriers have unfettered access to Canada if we were not granted the same consideration in the United States."

Jack Aubrey/*Ottawa Citizen*.

Essence of the Story

- Consultants interviewed 2,083 adult Canadians by telephone in March 2002. The poll has a margin of error within 2.2 percentage points, 19 times out of 20.
- The survey found that 55 percent of Canadians want to end Air Canada's monopoly in domestic air travel.
- The survey found that 84 percent of Canadians are willing to open Canadian skies to foreign competitors.
- The poll found that 71 percent of Canadians say they would accept U.S.-based airlines in Canada even without equal access for Canadian airlines in the United States if it meant lower fares.
- Rising airfares and surcharges give Canadians great concern.
- An Air Canada spokesperson said that the airline favours free competition with U.S. airlines, but only if Air Canada gets the same access to the United States that U.S. carriers get in Canada.

Economic Analysis

- The market for domestic air travel in Canada is effectively a monopoly on many routes.

- The market for international travel is competitive.

- On a day in September 2002, Air Canada quoted the following fares for economy class travel: Toronto–Vancouver round trip, \$3,383.80; Toronto–Los Angeles round trip, \$2,865.27.

- The distances between Toronto and Vancouver and Toronto and Los Angeles are similar and the price difference represents the difference between competition on the international route and monopoly on the domestic route.

- Figure 1 shows the monopoly outcome on a route on which Air Canada has a monopoly. The quantity of trips is that at which marginal cost, *MC*, equals marginal revenue, *MR*, and the price is the highest that the consumer is willing to pay for this quantity—\$1,750 in this example.

- Figure 2 shows the outcome if Air Canada is regulated to price its services at the competitive level. The quantity of trips increases to that at which marginal cost, *MC*, equals price, and the price falls to \$1,250 in this example.

- Figure 3 shows the outcome if other airlines are permitted to compete with Air Canada. With just two airlines similar in size to Air Canada, marginal cost for the route falls from MC_0 to MC_1, and in this example the price falls to \$900 a trip.

- By comparing the outcomes in these three examples, you can see why most Canadians would like to see competition and open skies. You can also see why Air Canada has a different view!

You're The Voter

- Do you think that the federal government should open Canada's skies to competition from foreign-based airlines?

- Do you think the service to remote parts of Canada would suffer if competition replaced monopoly in Canadian air transportation?

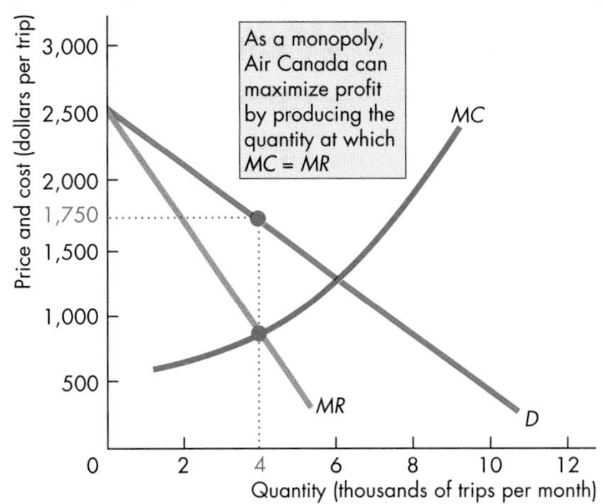

Figure 1 Air Canada operates as a monopoly

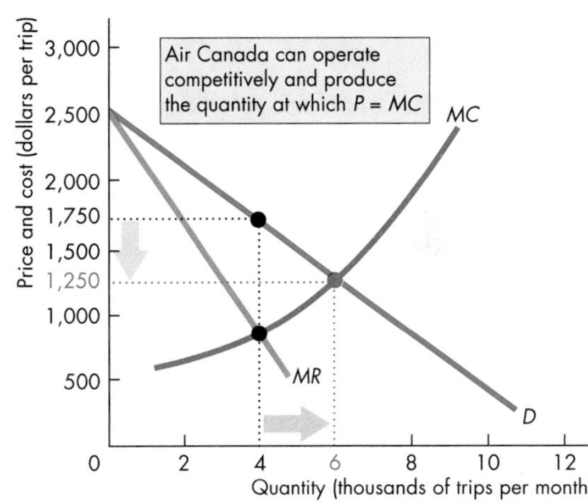

Figure 2 Air Canada operates competitively

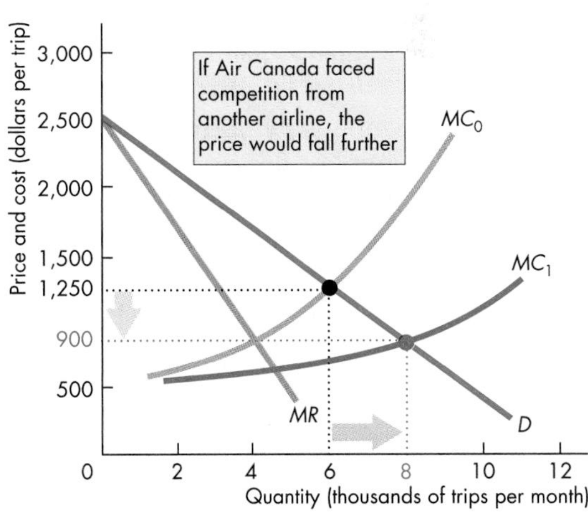

Figure 3 Two airlines the size of Air Canada operate competitively

SUMMARY

KEY POINTS

Market Power (pp. 262–263)

- A monopoly is an industry in which there is a single supplier of a good or service that has no close substitutes and in which barriers to entry prevent competition.
- Barriers to entry may be legal (public franchise, licence, patent, copyright, firm owns control of a resource) or natural (created by economies of scale).
- A monopoly might be able to price discriminate when there is no resale possibility.
- Where resale is possible, a firm charges one price.

A Single-Price Monopoly's Output and Price Decision (pp. 264–267)

- A monopoly's demand curve is the market demand curve, and a single-price monopoly's marginal revenue is less than price.
- A monopoly maximizes profit by producing the output at which marginal revenue equals marginal cost and by charging the maximum price that consumers are willing to pay for that output.

Single-Price Monopoly and Competition Compared (pp. 268–271)

- A single-price monopoly charges a higher price and produces a smaller quantity than a perfectly competitive industry.
- A single-price monopoly restricts output and creates a deadweight loss.
- Monopoly imposes costs that equal its deadweight loss plus the cost of the resources devoted to rent seeking.

Price Discrimination (pp. 271–274)

- Price discrimination is an attempt by the monopoly to convert consumer surplus into economic profit.
- Perfect price discrimination extracts the entire consumer surplus. Such a monopoly charges a different price for each unit sold and obtains the maximum price that each consumer is willing to pay for each unit bought.
- With perfect price discrimination, the monopoly produces the same output as would a perfectly competitive industry.
- Rent seeking with perfect price discrimination might eliminate the entire consumer surplus and producer surplus.

Monopoly Policy Issues (pp. 275–277)

- A monopoly with large economies of scale and economies of scope can produce a larger quantity at a lower price than a competitive industry can achieve, and a monopoly might be more innovative than small competitive firms.
- Efficient regulation requires a monopoly to charge a price equal to marginal cost, but for a natural monopoly, such a price is less than average total cost.
- Average cost pricing is a compromise pricing rule that covers a firm's costs and provides a normal profit but is not efficient. It is more efficient than unregulated profit maximization.

KEY FIGURES AND TABLE

Figure 12.2 Demand and Marginal Revenue, 264
Figure 12.3 Marginal Revenue and Elasticity, 265
Figure 12.4 A Monopoly's Output and Price, 267
Figure 12.5 Monopoly's Smaller Output and Higher Price, 268
Figure 12.6 Inefficiency of Monopoly, 269
Figure 12.9 Price Discrimination, 273
Figure 12.10 Perfect Price Discrimination, 274
Figure 12.11 Regulating a Natural Monopoly, 277
Table 12.1 A Monopoly's Output and Price Decision, 266

KEY TERMS

Average cost pricing rule, 277
Barriers to entry, 262
Legal monopoly, 262
Marginal cost pricing rule, 276
Market power, 262
Monopoly, 262
Natural monopoly, 262
Perfect price discrimination, 273
Price discrimination, 263
Rent seeking, 270
Single-price monopoly, 263

PROBLEMS

*1. Minnie's Mineral Springs, a single-price monopoly, faces the demand schedule.

Price (dollars per bottle)	Quantity demanded (bottles per hour)
10	0
8	1
6	2
4	3
2	4
0	5

a. Calculate Minnie's total revenue schedule.
b. Calculate its marginal revenue schedule.

2. Burma Ruby Mines, a single-price monopoly, faces the demand schedule.

Price (dollars per ruby)	Quantity demanded (rubies per day)
1,100	0
900	1
700	2
500	3
300	4

a. Calculate Burma's total revenue schedule.
b. Calculate its marginal revenue schedule.

*3. Minnie's Mineral Springs in problem 1 has the following total cost:

Quantity produced (bottles per hour)	Total cost (dollars)
0	1
1	3
2	7
3	13
4	21
5	31

a. Calculate the marginal cost of producing each output in the table.
b. Calculate the profit-maximizing output and price.
c. Calculate the economic profit.
d. Does Minnie's use resources efficiently? Explain your answer.

4. Burma Ruby Mines in problem 2 has the following total cost:

Quantity produced (rubies per day)	Total cost (dollars)
1	1,220
2	1,300
3	1,400
4	1,520

a. Calculate the marginal cost of producing each quantity listed in the table.
b. Calculate the profit-maximizing output and price.
c. Calculate the economic profit.
d. Does Burma Ruby Mines use its resources efficiently? Explain your answer.

*5. The figure illustrates the situation facing the publisher of the only newspaper containing local news in an isolated community.

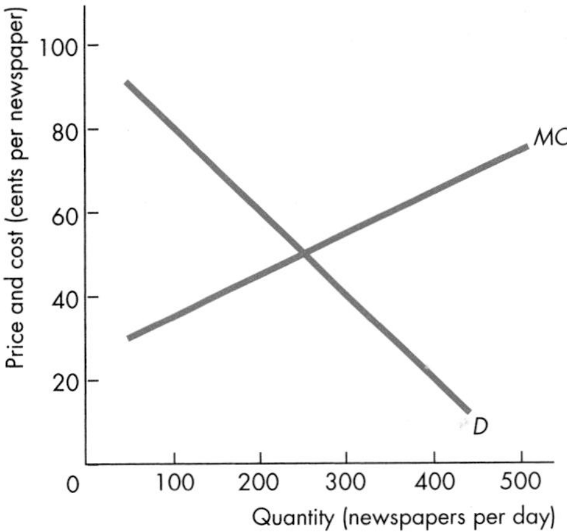

a. On the graph, draw the publisher's marginal revenue curve.
b. What are the profit-maximizing quantity and price?
c. What is the publisher's daily total revenue?
d. At the price charged, is the demand for newspapers elastic or inelastic? Why?
e. On the graph, mark in the consumer surplus and deadweight loss.
f. Might the newspaper try to price discriminate? Explain why or why not.

6. The figure illustrates the situation facing the only coffee shop in an isolated community.

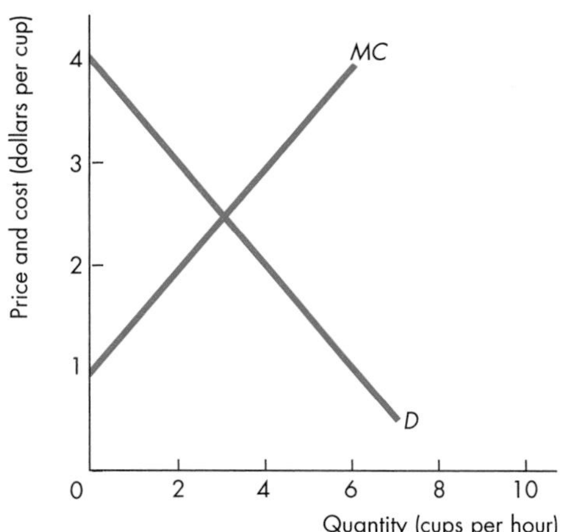

   a. What are the profit-maximizing quantity and price of coffee?
   b. On the graph, mark the coffee shop's profit.
   c. What are consumer surplus and deadweight loss?
   d. What is the efficient quantity? Explain your answer.
   e. Might the coffee shop try to price discriminate? Explain why or why not.

*7. The figure shows the situation facing a natural monopoly that cannot price discriminate.

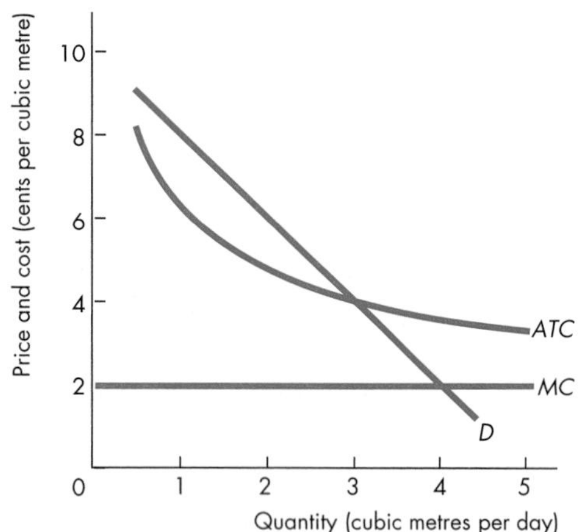

   What quantity will be produced and what will be the deadweight loss if the firm is
   a. An unregulated profit maximizer?
   b. Regulated to earn only normal profit?
   c. Regulated to be efficient?

8. If, in problem 7, marginal cost doubles, what now are your answers?

CRITICAL THINKING

1. Study *Reading Between the Lines* on pp. 278–279 and then answer the following questions.
   a. Is it correct to call Air Canada a monopoly?
   b. How would the arrival of a viable alternative airline affect Air Canada?
   c. How would you regulate the air travel industry to ensure that resources are used efficiently?
   d. "Anyone is free to buy stock in Air Canada, so everyone is free to share in Air Canada's economic profit, and the bigger that economic profit, the better for all." Evaluate this statement.

WEB EXERCISES

1. Use the links on the Parkin–Bade Web site to read the statement by Ralph Nader about Microsoft.
   a. What are Ralph Nader's main claims about Microsoft?
   b. Do you agree with Ralph Nader? Why or why not?
   c. If some other operating systems are better than Windows, why don't they take off?
   d. Does Ralph Nader identify the main costs to the consumer of Microsoft's practices? Explain why or why not.
2. Use the link on the Parkin–Bade Web site to study the market for computer chips.
   a. Is it correct to call Intel a monopoly? Why or why not?
   b. How does Intel try to raise barriers to entry in this market?
3. Use the link on the Parkin–Bade Web site to learn about developments in the Canadian railroad industry of the 1880s.
   a. Was Canadian Pacific a monopoly? Why or why not?
   b. What other elements of market power are discussed on this Web page?
   c. Do you think monopoly was a bigger problem in the 1880s than it is today? Why or why not?

MONOPOLISTIC COMPETITION AND OLIGOPOLY

CHAPTER 13

PC War Games

Since the fall of 2000, our newspapers and magazines have been stuffed with advertising by the big-name PC makers announcing yet lower prices and yet better products and value for money. How do firms like PC makers that are locked in fierce competition with each other set their prices, pick their product lines, and choose the quantities to produce? How are the profits of such firms affected by the actions of other firms? ◆ During the 1990s, a large bookseller, Chapters, began buying up and competing fiercely with smaller independent booksellers. Seeing Chapters' success, another firm with big ideas, Indigo, started to compete with Chapters. Then Indigo bought Chapters! The most recent event in the saga of Canadian book selling was the launch of Amazon.ca, a new online competitor for Indigo, in the summer of 2002. We'll look further at this development in *Reading Between the Lines* at the end of this chapter. How do markets work when only a small number of firms compete for the business?

The theories of monopoly and perfect competition do not predict the kind of behaviour that we've just described. There are no newspaper ads, best brands, or price wars in perfect competition because all firms produce an identical product and each firm is a price taker. And there are none in monopoly because each monopoly firm has the entire market to itself. To understand advertising and price wars, we need the richer models that are explained in this chapter.

After studying this chapter, you will be able to

- **Define and identify monopolistic competition**
- **Explain how output and price are determined in a monopolistically competitive industry**
- **Explain why advertising costs are high in a monopolistically competitive industry**
- **Explain why the price might be sticky in oligopoly**
- **Explain how price and output are determined when there is one dominant firm and several smaller firms in a market**
- **Use game theory to make predictions about price wars and competition among a small number of firms**

Monopolistic Competition

YOU HAVE STUDIED TWO TYPES OF MARKET structure: perfect competition and monopoly. In perfect competition, a large number of firms produce identical goods, there are no barriers to entry, and each firm is a price taker. In the long run, there is no economic profit. In monopoly, a single firm is protected from competition by barriers to entry and can make an economic profit, even in the long run.

Many real-world markets are competitive but not as fiercely so as perfect competition because firms in these markets possess some power to set their prices as monopolies do. We call this type of market *monopolistic competition.*

Monopolistic competition is a market structure in which

- A large number of firms compete.
- Each firm produces a differentiated product.
- Firms compete on product quality, price, and marketing.
- Firms are free to enter and exit.

Large Number of Firms

In monopolistic competition, as in perfect competition, the industry consists of a large number of firms. The presence of a large number of firms has three implications for the firms in the industry.

Small Market Share In monopolistic competition, each firm supplies a small part of the total industry output. Consequently, each firm has only limited power to influence the price of its product. Each firm's price can deviate from the average price of other firms by a relatively small amount.

Ignore Other Firms A firm in monopolistic competition must be sensitive to the average market price of the product. But it does not pay attention to any one individual competitor. Because all the firms are relatively small, no one firm can dictate market conditions, and so no one firm's actions directly affect the actions of the other firms.

Collusion Impossible Firms in monopolistic competition would like to be able to conspire to fix a higher price—called collusion. But because there are many firms, collusion is not possible.

Product Differentiation

A firm practises **product differentiation** if it makes a product that is slightly different from the products of competing firms. A differentiated product is one that is a close substitute but not a perfect substitute for the products of the other firms. Some people will pay more for one variety of the product, so when its price rises, the quantity demanded falls but it does not (necessarily) fall to zero. For example, Adidas, Asics, Diadora, Etonic, Fila, New Balance, Nike, Puma, and Reebok all make differentiated running shoes. Other things remaining the same, if the price of Adidas running shoes rises and the prices of the other shoes remain constant, Adidas sells fewer shoes and the other producers sell more. But sales of Adidas shoes don't disappear unless the price rises by a large enough amount.

Competing on Quality, Price, and Marketing

Product differentiation enables a firm to compete with other firms in three areas: product quality, price, and marketing.

Quality The quality of a product is the physical attributes that make it different from the products of other firms. Quality includes design, reliability, the service provided to the buyer, and the buyer's ease of access to the product. Quality lies on a spectrum that runs from high to low. Some firms—Dell Computers is an example—offer high-quality products. They are well designed and reliable, and the customer receives quick and efficient service. Other firms offer a lower-quality product that is less well designed, that might not work perfectly, and that the buyer must travel some distance to obtain.

Price Because of product differentiation, a firm in monopolistic competition faces a downward-sloping demand curve. So, like a monopoly, the firm can set its price. But there is a tradeoff between the product's quality and price: A firm that makes a high-quality product can charge a higher price than can a firm that makes a low-quality product.

Marketing Because of product differentiation, a firm in monopolistic competition must market its product. Marketing takes two main forms: advertising and packaging. A firm that produces a high-quality product wants to sell it for a suitably high price.

FIGURE 13.1 Examples of Monopolistic Competition

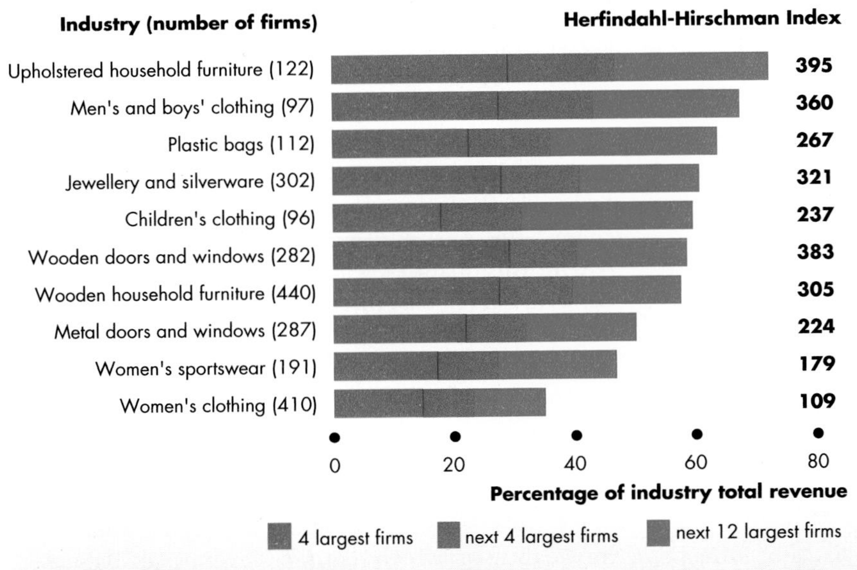

These industries operate in monopolistic competition. The number of firms in the industry is shown in parentheses after the name of the industry. The red bars show the percentage of industry sales by the largest 4 firms. The green bars show the percentage of industry sales by the next 4 largest firms, and the blue bars show the percentage of industry sales by the next 12 largest firms. So the entire length of the red, green, and blue bar combined shows the percentage of industry sales by the largest 20 firms. The Herfindahl–Hirschman Index is shown on the right.

Source: Statistics Canada, *Industrial Organization and Concentration in Manufacturing Industries*, Catalogue No. 31C0024.

To be able to do so, it must advertise and package its product in a way that convinces buyers that they are getting the higher quality for which they are paying a higher price. For example, pharmaceutical companies advertise and package their brand-name drugs to persuade buyers that these items are superior to the lower-priced generic alternatives. Similarly, a low-quality producer uses advertising and packaging to persuade buyers that although the quality is low, the low price more than compensates for this fact.

Entry and Exit

In monopolistic competition, there is free entry and free exit. Consequently, a firm cannot make an economic profit in the long run. When firms make an economic profit, new firms enter the industry. This entry lowers prices and eventually eliminates economic profit. When firms incur economic losses, some firms leave the industry. This exit increases prices and profits and eventually eliminates the economic loss. In long-run equilibrium, firms neither enter nor leave the industry and the firms in the industry make zero economic profit.

Examples of Monopolistic Competition

Figure 13.1 shows 10 industries that are examples of monopolistic competition. These industries have a large number of firms (shown in parentheses after the name of the industry). In the most concentrated of these industries, upholstered household furniture, the largest 4 firms produce 30 percent of the industry's total sales and the largest 20 firms produce 70 percent of total sales. The number on the right is the Herfindahl–Hirschman Index (p. 206–207). Producers of clothing, plastic bags, doors, and windows operate in monopolistic competition.

REVIEW QUIZ

1. What are the distinguishing characteristics of monopolistic competition?
2. How do firms in monopolistic competition compete?
3. In addition to the examples in Fig. 13.1, provide some examples of industries near your university that operate in monopolistic competition.

Output and Price in Monopolistic Competition

WE ARE NOW GOING TO LEARN HOW OUTPUT AND price are determined in monopolistic competition. First, we will suppose that the firm has already decided on the quality of its product and on its marketing program. For a given product and a given amount of marketing activity, the firm faces given costs and market conditions.

Figure 13.2 shows how a firm in monopolistic competition determines its price and output. Part (a) deals with the short run, and part (b) deals with the long run. We'll concentrate first on the short run.

Short Run: Economic Profit

The demand curve *D* shows the demand for the firm's product. It is the demand curve for Nautica jackets, not jackets in general. The curve labelled *MR* is the marginal revenue curve associated with the demand curve. It is derived just like the marginal revenue curve of a single-price monopoly that you studied in Chapter 12. The figure also shows the firm's average total cost (*ATC*) and marginal cost (*MC*). These curves are similar to the cost curves that you first encountered in Chapter 10.

Nautica maximizes profit by producing the output at which marginal revenue equals marginal cost. In Fig. 13.2, this output is 150 jackets a day. Nautica charges the maximum price that buyers are willing to pay for this quantity, which is determined by the demand curve. This price is $190 a jacket. When Nautica produces 150 jackets a day, its average total cost is $140 a jacket, so Nautica makes a short-run economic profit of $7,500 a day ($50 a jacket multiplied by 150 jackets a day). The blue rectangle shows this economic profit.

So far, the firm in monopolistic competition looks just like a single-price monopoly. It produces the quantity at which marginal revenue equals mar-

FIGURE 13.2 Output and Price in Monopolistic Competition

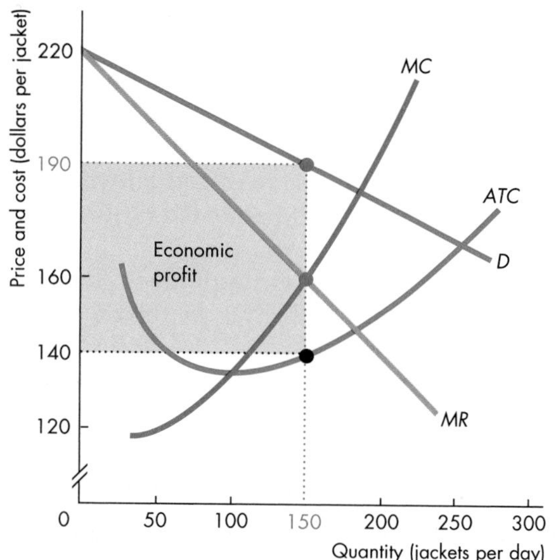

(a) Short run

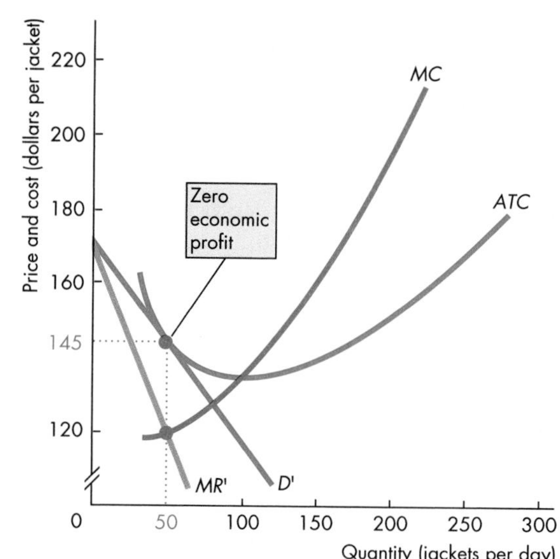

(b) Long run

Part (a) shows the short-run outcome. Profit is maximized by producing 150 jackets per day and selling them for a price of $190 per jacket. Average total cost is $140 per jacket, and the firm makes an economic profit (the blue rectangle) of $7,500 a day ($50 per jacket multiplied by 150 jackets).

Economic profit encourages new entrants in the long run, and part (b) shows the long-run outcome. The entry of new firms decreases the demand for each firm's product and shifts the demand curve and marginal revenue curve leftward. When the demand curve has shifted to *D'*, the marginal revenue curve is *MR'* and the firm is in long-run equilibrium. The output that maximizes profit is 50 jackets a day, and the price is $145 per jacket. Average total cost is also $145 per jacket, so economic profit is zero.

ginal cost and then charges the highest price that buyers are willing to pay for that quantity, determined by the demand curve. The key difference between monopoly and monopolistic competition lies in what happens next.

Long Run: Zero Economic Profit

There is no restriction on entry in monopolistic competition, so economic profit attracts new entrants. As firms enter, each firm has a smaller market share and smaller demand for its product, which means that each firm's demand curve and marginal revenue curve shift leftward. Firms maximize short-run profit by producing the quantity at which marginal revenue equals marginal cost and by charging the highest price that buyers are willing to pay for this quantity. But as the demand for each firm's output decreases, the profit-maximizing quantity and price fall.

Figure 13.2(b) shows the long-run equilibrium. The demand curve for Nautica jackets has shifted leftward to D', and Nautica's marginal revenue curve has shifted leftward to MR'. Nautica produces 50 jackets a day and sells them at a price of \$145 each. At this output level, Nautica's average total cost is also \$145 a jacket. So Nautica is making zero economic profit.

When all the firms are earning zero economic profit, there is no incentive for new firms to enter the industry.

If demand is so low relative to costs that firms are incurring economic losses, exit will occur. As firms leave an industry, the demand for the remaining firms' products increases and their demand curves shift rightward. The exit process ends when all the firms are making zero economic profit.

Monopolistic Competition and Efficiency

When we studied a perfectly competitive industry, we discovered that in some circumstances, such an industry allocates resources efficiently. A key feature of efficiency is that marginal benefit equals marginal cost. Price measures marginal benefit, so efficiency requires price to equal marginal cost. When we studied monopoly, we discovered that such a firm creates an inefficient use of resources because it restricts output to a level at which price exceeds marginal cost. In such a situation, marginal benefit exceeds marginal cost and production is less than its efficient level.

Monopolistic competition shares this feature of monopoly. Even though there is zero economic profit in long-run equilibrium, the monopolistically competitive industry produces an output at which price equals average total cost but exceeds marginal cost. This outcome means that firms in monopolistic competition always have excess capacity in long-run equilibrium.

Excess Capacity A firm's **capacity output** is the output at which average total cost is a minimum—the output at the bottom of the U-shaped *ATC* curve. This output is 100 jackets a day in Fig. 13.3. Firms in monopolistic competition always have *excess capacity* in the long run. In Fig. 13.3, Nautica produces 50 jackets a day and has excess capacity of 50 jackets a day. That is, Nautica produces a smaller output than that which minimizes average total cost.

FIGURE 13.3 Excess Capacity

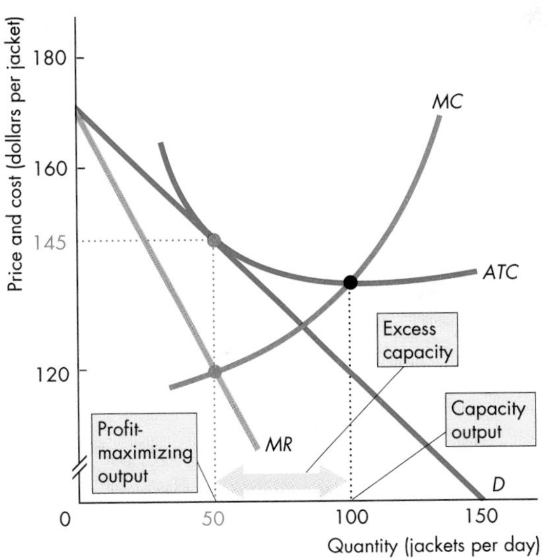

In long-run equilibrium, entry decreases demand to the point at which the firm makes zero economic profit. Nautica produces 50 jackets a day. A firm's capacity output is the output at which average total cost is a minimum. Nautica's capacity output is 100 jackets a day. Because the demand curve in monopolistic competition slopes downward, the profit-maximizing output in the long-run equilibrium is always less than capacity output. In long-run equilibrium, the firm operates with excess capacity.

Consequently, the consumer pays a price that exceeds minimum average total cost. This result arises from the fact that Nautica faces a downward-sloping demand curve. The demand curve slopes downward because of product differentiation, so product differentiation creates excess capacity.

You can see the excess capacity in monopolistic competition all around you. Family restaurants (except for the truly outstanding ones) almost always have some empty tables. You can always get a pizza delivered in less than 30 minutes. It is rare that every pump at a gas station is in use with customers waiting in line. There is always an abundance of realtors ready to help find or sell a home. These industries are examples of monopolistic competition. The firms have excess capacity. They could sell more by cutting their prices, but they would then incur losses.

Because in monopolistic competition price exceeds marginal cost, this market structure, like monopoly, is inefficient. The marginal cost of producing one more unit of output is less than the marginal benefit to the consumer, determined by the price the consumer is willing to pay. But the inefficiency of monopolistic competition arises from product differentiation—from product variety. Consumers value variety, but it is achievable only if firms make differentiated products. So the loss in efficiency that occurs in monopolistic competition must be weighed against the gain of greater product variety.

REVIEW QUIZ

1. How does a firm in monopolistic competition decide how much to produce and at what price to offer its product for sale?
2. Why can a firm in monopolistic competition earn an economic profit only in the short run?
3. Is monopolistic competition efficient?
4. Why do firms in monopolistic competition operate with excess capacity?

You've seen how the firm in monopolistic competition determines its output and price in the short run and the long run when it produces a given product and undertakes a *given* marketing effort. But how does the firm choose its product quality and marketing effort? We'll now study these decisions.

Product Development and Marketing

WHEN WE STUDIED A FIRM'S OUTPUT AND PRICE decision, we supposed that it had already made its product and marketing decisions. We're now going to study these decisions and the impact they have on the firm's output, price, and economic profit.

Innovation and Product Development

To enjoy economic profits, firms in monopolistic competition must be in a state of continuous product development. The reason is that wherever economic profits are earned, imitators emerge and set up business. So to maintain its economic profit, a firm must seek out new products that will provide it with a competitive edge, even if only temporarily. A firm that manages to introduce a new and differentiated variety will temporarily increase the demand for its product and will be able to increase its price temporarily. The firm will make an economic profit. Eventually, new firms that make close substitutes for the new product will enter and compete away the economic profit arising from this initial advantage. So to restore economic profit, the firm must again innovate.

The decision to innovate is based on the same type of profit-maximizing calculation that you've already studied. Innovation and product development are costly activities, but they also bring in additional revenues. The firm must balance the cost and benefit at the margin. At a low level of product development, the marginal revenue from a better product exceeds the marginal cost. When the marginal dollar of product development expenditure brings in a dollar of revenue, the firm is spending the profit-maximizing amount on product development.

For example, when Eidos Interactive released Tomb Raider: Lost Artifact, it was probably not the best game that Eidos could have created. Rather, it was the game that balanced the marginal benefit and willingness of the consumer to pay for further game enhancements against the marginal cost of these enhancements.

Efficiency and Product Innovation Is product innovation an efficient activity? Does it benefit the consumer? There are two views about these questions. One view is that monopolistic competition brings to market many improved products that bring great benefits to the consumer. Clothing, kitchen and other household appliances, computers, computer programs, cars, and many other products keep getting better every year, and the consumer benefits from these improved products.

But many so-called improvements amount to little more than changing the appearance of a product. And sometimes, the improvement is restricted to a different look in the packaging. In these cases, there is little objective benefit to the consumer.

But regardless of whether a product improvement is real or imagined, its value to the consumer is its marginal benefit, which equals the amount the consumer is willing to pay for the improvement. Whether the amount of product improvement is efficient or not depends on the marginal cost of the improvement. Only if the producers' marginal cost of product improvement equals the consumers' marginal benefit do we get the efficient amount of product innovation.

Marketing

Firms can achieve some product differentiation by designing and developing products that are actually different from those of the other firms. But firms also attempt to create a consumer perception of product differentiation even when actual differences are small. Advertising and packaging are the principal means used by firms to achieve this end. An American Express card is a different product from a Visa card. But the actual differences are not the main ones that American Express emphasizes in its marketing. The deeper message is that if you use an American Express card, which Tiger Woods uses, you'll be like Tiger Woods (or some other high-profile successful person).

Marketing Expenditures Firms in monopolistic competition incur huge costs to ensure that buyers appreciate and value the differences between their own products and those of their competitors. So a large proportion of the prices that we pay cover the cost of selling a good. And this proportion is increasing. The cost of advertising in newspapers, in magazines, and on radio and television is the main selling cost. But it is not the only one. Selling costs include the cost of shopping malls that look like movie sets, glossy catalogues and brochures, and the salaries, airfares, and hotel bills of salespeople.

The total scale of selling costs is hard to estimate, but some components can be measured. A survey conducted by a commercial agency suggested that for cleaning supplies and toys, around 15 percent of the price of an item is spent on advertising. Figure 13.4 shows some estimates for other industries.

For the North American economy as a whole, there are some 20,000 advertising agencies, which employ more than 200,000 people and have sales of $45 billion. But these numbers are only part of the total cost of advertising because firms have their own internal advertising departments, the cost of which we can only guess.

Marketing efforts affect a firm's profits in two ways: They increase costs, and if they are effective, they change demand. Let's look at these effects.

Selling Costs and Total Costs Selling costs such as advertising expenditures increase the costs of a monopolistically competitive firm above those of a competitive firm or a monopoly. Advertising costs and other selling costs are fixed costs. They do not vary as total output varies. So, just like fixed production costs, advertising costs per unit decrease as production increases.

FIGURE 13.4 Advertising Expenditures

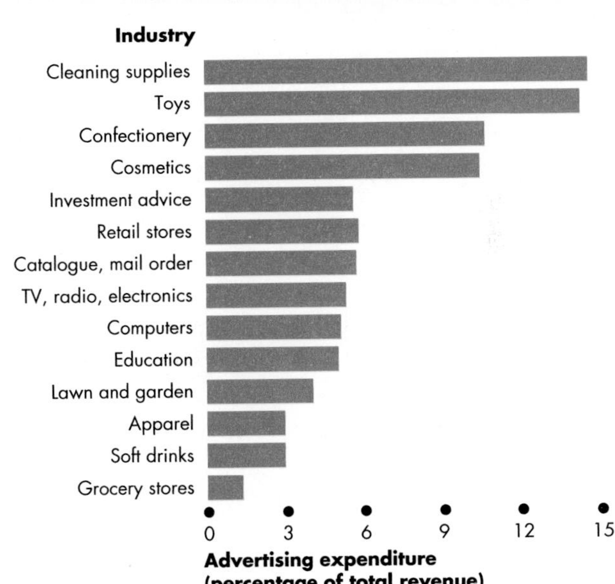

Advertising expenditures are a large part of the total revenue received by producers of cleaning supplies, toys, confectionery, and cosmetics.

Source: Schoenfeld & Associates, Lincolnwood, Illinois, reported at http://www.toolkit.cch.com/text/p03_7006.stm.

Figure 13.5 shows how selling costs and advertising expenditures change a firm's average total cost. The blue curve shows the average total cost of production. The red curve shows the firm's average total cost of production with advertising. The height of the red area between the two curves shows the average fixed cost of advertising. The *total* cost of advertising is fixed. But the *average* cost of advertising decreases as output increases.

The figure shows that if advertising increases the quantity sold by a large enough amount, it can lower average total cost. For example, if the quantity sold increases from 25 jackets a day with no advertising to 130 jackets a day with advertising, average total cost falls from $170 a jacket to $160 a jacket. The reason is that although the *total* fixed cost has increased, the greater fixed cost is spread over a greater output, so average total cost decreases.

Selling Costs and Demand Advertising and other selling efforts change the demand for a firm's product. But does demand increase or decrease? The most natural answer is that advertising increases demand. By informing people about the quality of its products or by persuading people to switch from the products of other firms, a firm that advertises expects to increase the demand for its own products.

But all firms in monopolistic competition advertise. If advertising enables a firm to survive, it might increase the number of firms. To the extent that it increases the number of firms, advertising *decreases* the demand faced by any one firm.

FIGURE 13.5 Selling Costs and Total Cost

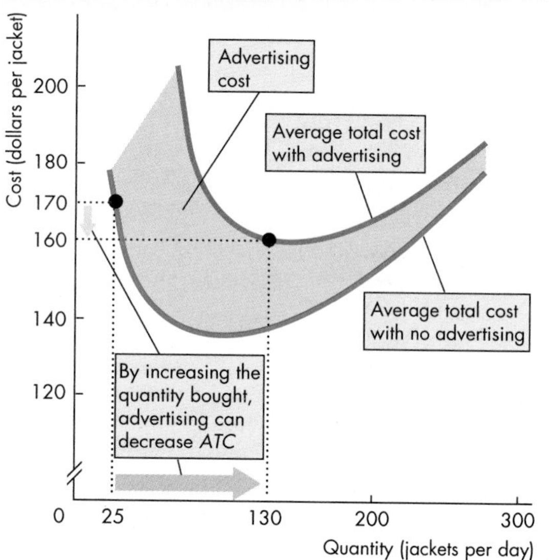

Selling costs such as the cost of advertising are fixed costs, which increase average total cost. Selling costs increase average total cost by a greater amount at small outputs than at large outputs. If advertising enables sales to increase from 25 jackets a day to 130 jackets a day, average total cost *falls* from $170 to $160 a jacket.

Efficiency: The Bottom Line Selling costs that provide consumers with information that they value serve a useful purpose to the consumer and enable a better product choice to be made. But the opportunity cost of the additional services and information must be weighed against the gain to the consumer.

The bottom line on the question of efficiency of monopolistic competition is ambiguous. In some cases, the gains from extra product variety unquestionably offset the selling costs and the extra cost arising from excess capacity. The tremendous varieties of books and magazines, clothing, food, and drinks are examples of such gains. It is less easy to see the gains from being able to buy brand-name drugs that have a chemical composition identical to that of a generic alternative. But some people do willingly pay more for the brand-name alternative.

REVIEW QUIZ

1. What are the two main ways, other than by adjusting price, in which a firm in monopolistic competition competes with other firms?
2. Why might product innovation and development be efficient and why might it be inefficient?
3. How does a firm's advertising expenditure influence its cost curves? Does average total cost increase or decrease?
4. How does a firm's advertising expenditure influence the demand for its product? Does demand increase or decrease?
5. Why is it difficult to determine whether monopolistic competition is efficient or inefficient? What is your opinion about the bottom line and why?

Oligopoly

ANOTHER TYPE OF MARKET THAT LIES between the extremes of perfect competition and monopoly is oligopoly. **Oligopoly** is a market structure in which a small number of firms compete.

In oligopoly, the quantity sold by any one firm depends on that firm's price *and* on the other firms' prices and quantities sold. To see why, suppose you run one of the three gas stations in a small town. If you cut your price and your two competitors don't cut theirs, your sales increase, and the sales of the other two firms decrease. With lower sales, the other firms most likely cut their prices too. If they do cut their prices, your sales and profits take a tumble. So before deciding to cut your price, you must predict how the other firms will react and attempt to calculate the effects of those reactions on your own profit.

Several models have been developed to explain the prices and quantities in oligopoly markets. But no one theory has been found that can explain all the different types of behaviour that we observe in such markets. The models fall into two broad groups: traditional models and game theory models. We'll look at examples of both types, starting with two traditional models.

The Kinked Demand Curve Model

The kinked demand curve model of oligopoly is based on the assumption that each firm believes that

1. If it raises its price, others will not follow.
2. If it cuts its price, so will the other firms.

Figure 13.6 shows the demand curve (D) that a firm believes it faces. The demand curve has a kink at the current price, P, and quantity, Q. At prices above P, a small price rise brings a big decrease in the quantity sold. The other firms hold their current price and the firm has the highest price for the good, so it loses market share. At prices below P, even a large price cut brings only a small increase in the quantity sold. In this case, other firms match the price cut, so the firm gets no price advantage over its competitors.

The kink in the demand curve creates a break in the marginal revenue curve (MR). To maximize profit, the firm produces the quantity at which marginal cost equals marginal revenue. That quantity, Q, is where the marginal cost curve passes through the gap AB in the marginal revenue curve. If marginal cost fluctuates between A and B, as the marginal cost curves MC_0 and MC_1 illustrate, the firm does not change its price or its output. Only if marginal cost fluctuates outside the range AB does the firm change its price and output. So the kinked demand curve model predicts that price and quantity are insensitive to small cost changes.

A problem with the kinked demand curve model is that the firms' beliefs about the demand curve are not always correct and firms can figure out that they are not correct. If marginal cost increases by enough to cause the firm to increase its price and if all firms experience the same increase in marginal cost, they all increase their prices together. The firm's belief that others will not join it in a price rise is incorrect. A firm that bases its actions on beliefs that are wrong does not maximize profit and might even end up incurring an economic loss.

FIGURE 13.6 The Kinked Demand Curve Model

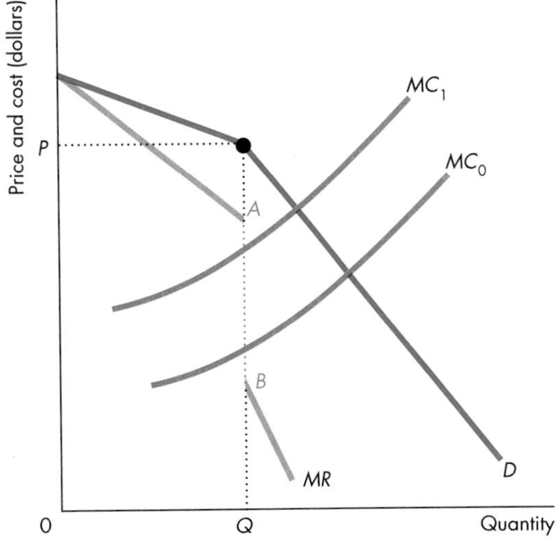

The price in an oligopoly market is P. Each firm believes it faces the demand curve D. At prices above P, a small price rise brings a big decrease in the quantity sold because other firms do not raise their prices. At prices below P, even a big price cut brings only a small increase in the quantity sold because other firms also cut their prices. Because the demand curve is kinked, the marginal revenue curve, MR, has a break, AB. Profit is maximized by producing Q. The marginal cost curve passes through the break in the marginal revenue curve. Marginal cost changes inside the range AB leave the price and quantity unchanged.

Dominant Firm Oligopoly

A second traditional model explains a dominant firm oligopoly, which arises when one firm—the dominant firm—has a big cost advantage over the other firms and produces a large part of the industry output. The dominant firm sets the market price and the other firms are price takers. Examples of dominant firm oligopoly are a large gasoline retailer or a big video rental store that dominates its local market.

To see how a dominant firm oligopoly works, suppose that 11 firms operate gas stations in a city. Big-G is the dominant firm.

Figure 13.7 shows the market for gas in this city. In part (a), the demand curve *D* tells us the total quantity of gas demanded in the city at each price. The supply curve S_{10} is the supply curve of the 10 small suppliers.

Part (b) shows the situation facing Big-G. Its marginal cost curve is *MC*. Big-G faces the demand curve *XD*, and Big-G's marginal revenue curve is *MR*. The demand curve *XD* shows the excess demand not met by the 10 small firms. For example, at a price of $1 a litre, the quantity demanded is 20,000 litres, the quantity supplied by the 10 small firms is 10,000 litres, so the excess quantity demanded is 10,000 litres, which the distance *AB* in both parts of the figure measures.

To maximize profit, Big-G operates like a monopoly. It sells 10,000 litres a week, where marginal revenue equals marginal cost, for a price of $1 a litre. The 10 small firms take the price of $1 a litre. They behave just like firms in perfect competition. The quantity of gas demanded in the entire city at $1 a litre is 20,000 litres, as shown in part (a). Of this amount, Big-G sells 10,000 litres and the 10 small firms each sell 1,000 litres.

The traditional theories of oligopoly do not enable us to understand all oligopoly markets and in recent years, economists have developed new models based on game theory. Let's now learn about game theory.

FIGURE 13.7 A Dominant Firm Oligopoly

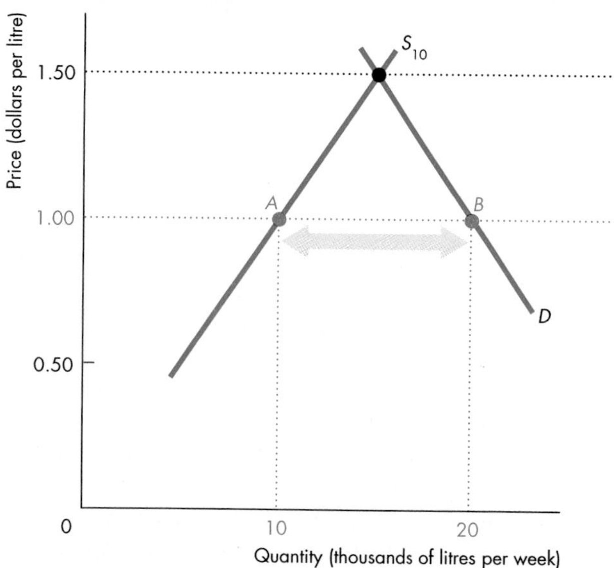

(a) Ten small firms and market demand

The demand curve for gas in a city is *D* in part (a). There are 10 small competitive firms that together have a supply curve of S_{10}. In addition, there is 1 large firm, Big-G, shown in part (b). Big-G faces the demand curve *XD*, determined as the market demand *D* minus the supply of the 10 small firms S_{10}—the demand that is not satisfied by the small firms.

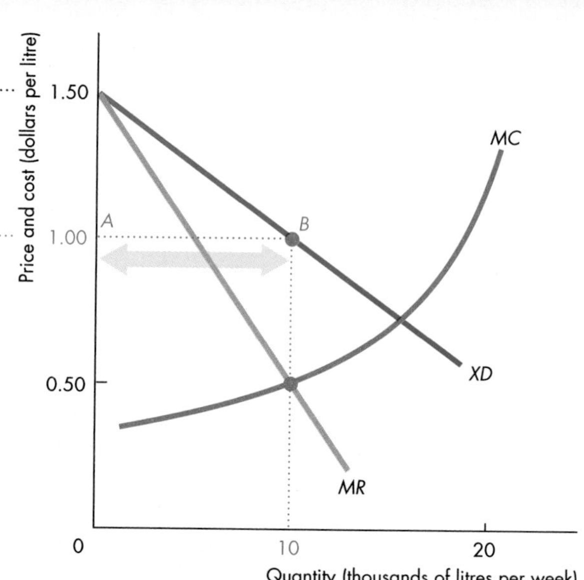

(b) Big-G's price and output decision

Big-G's marginal revenue curve is *MR*, and its marginal cost curve is *MC*. Big-G sets its output to maximize profit by equating marginal cost and marginal revenue. This output is 10,000 litres per week. The price at which Big-G can sell this quantity is $1 a litre. The 10 small firms take this price, and each firm sells 1,000 litres per week, point *A* in part (a).

Oligopoly Games

Economists think about oligopoly as a game, and to study oligopoly markets they use a set of tools called game theory. **Game theory** is a tool for studying *strategic behaviour*—behaviour that takes into account the expected behaviour of others and the recognition of mutual interdependence. Game theory was invented by John von Neumann in 1937 and extended by von Neumann and Oskar Morgenstern in 1944. Today, it is one of the major research fields in economics.

Game theory seeks to understand oligopoly as well as all other forms of economic, political, social, and even biological rivalries by using a method of analysis specifically designed to understand games of all types, including the familiar games of everyday life. We will begin our study of game theory, and its application to the behaviour of firms, by thinking about familiar games.

What Is a Game?

What is a game? At first thought, the question seems silly. After all, there are many different games. There are ball games and parlour games, games of chance and games of skill. But what is it about all these different activities that makes them games? What do all these games have in common? All games share four features:

- Rules
- Strategies
- Payoffs
- Outcome

Let's see how these common features of games apply to a game called "the prisoners' dilemma." This game, it turns out, captures some of the essential features of oligopoly, and it gives a good illustration of how game theory works and how it generates predictions.

The Prisoners' Dilemma

Art and Bob have been caught red-handed, stealing a car. Facing airtight cases, they will receive a sentence of two years each for their crime. During his interviews with the two prisoners, the Crown attorney begins to suspect that he has stumbled on the two people who were responsible for a multimillion-dollar bank robbery some months earlier. But this is just a suspicion. The Crown attorney has no evidence on which he can convict them of the greater crime unless he can get them to confess. The Crown attorney decides to make the prisoners play a game with the following rules.

Rules Each prisoner (player) is placed in a separate room, and cannot communicate with the other player. Each is told that he is suspected of having carried out the bank robbery and that

- If both of them confess to the larger crime, each will receive a sentence of 3 years for both crimes.
- If he alone confesses and his accomplice does not, he will receive an even shorter sentence of 1 year while his accomplice will receive a 10-year sentence.

Strategies In game theory, **strategies** are all the possible actions of each player. Art and Bob each have two possible actions:

1. Confess to the bank robbery.
2. Deny having committed the bank robbery.

Payoffs Because there are two players, each with two strategies, there are four possible outcomes:

1. Both confess.
2. Both deny.
3. Art confesses and Bob denies.
4. Bob confesses and Art denies.

Each prisoner can work out exactly what happens to him—his *payoff*—in each of these four situations. We can tabulate the four possible payoffs for each of the prisoners in what is called a payoff matrix for the game. A **payoff matrix** is a table that shows the payoffs for every possible action by each player for every possible action by each other player.

Table 13.1 shows a payoff matrix for Art and Bob. The squares show the payoffs for each prisoner—the red triangle in each square shows Art's payoff and the blue triangle shows Bob's payoff. If both prisoners confess (top left), each gets a prison term of 3 years. If Bob confesses but Art denies (top right), Art gets a 10-year sentence and Bob gets a 1-year sentence. If Art confesses and Bob denies (bottom left), Art gets a 1-year sentence and Bob gets a 10-year sentence. Finally, if both of them deny (bottom right), neither can be convicted of the bank robbery charge but both are sentenced for the car theft—a 2-year sentence.

Outcome The choices of both players determine the outcome of the game. To predict that outcome, we use an equilibrium idea proposed by John Nash (of Princeton University) who received the Nobel Prize for Economic Science in 1994 and who was the subject of the 2001 movie *A Beautiful Mind.* In **Nash equilibrium**, player *A* takes the best possible action given the action of player *B* and player *B* takes the best possible action given the action of player *A.*

In the case of the prisoners' dilemma, the Nash equilibrium occurs when Art makes his best choice given Bob's choice and when Bob makes his best choice given Art's choice.

To find the Nash equilibrium, we compare all the possible outcomes associated with each choice and eliminate those that are dominated—that are not as good as some other choice. Let's find the Nash equilibrium for the prisoners' dilemma game.

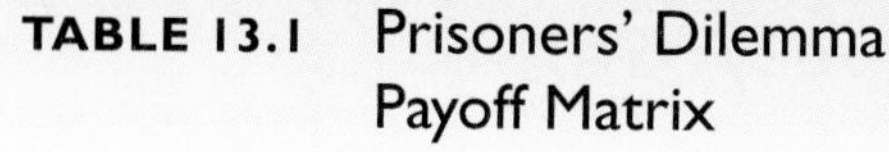
TABLE 13.1 Prisoners' Dilemma Payoff Matrix

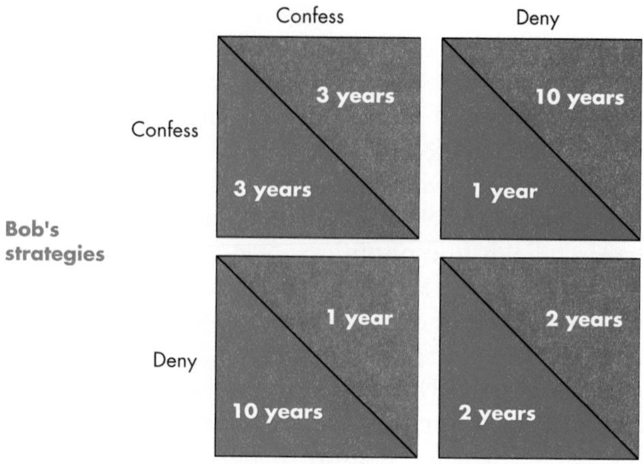

Each square shows the payoffs for the two players, Art and Bob, for each possible pair of actions. In each square, the red triangle shows Art's payoff and the blue triangle shows Bob's. For example, if both confess, the payoffs are in the top left square. The equilibrium of the game is for both players to confess and each gets a 3-year sentence.

Finding the Nash Equilibrium Look at the situation from Art's point of view. If Bob confesses, Art's best action is to confess because in that case, he is sentenced to 3 years rather than 10 years. If Bob does not confess, Art's best action is still to confess because in that case he receives 1 year rather than 2 years. So Art's best action is to confess.

Now look at the situation from Bob's point of view. If Art confesses, Bob's best action is to confess because in that case, he is sentenced to 3 years rather than 10 years. If Art does not confess, Bob's best action is still to confess because in that case, he receives 1 year rather than 2 years. So Bob's best action is to confess.

Because each player's best action is to confess, each does confess, each gets a 3-year prison term, and the Crown attorney has solved the bank robbery. This is the Nash equilibrium of the game.

The Dilemma Now that you have found the solution to the prisoners' dilemma, you can better see the dilemma. The dilemma arises as each prisoner contemplates the consequences of denying. Each prisoner knows that if both of them deny, they will each receive only a 2-year sentence for stealing the car. But neither has any way of knowing that his accomplice will deny. Each poses the following questions: Should I deny and rely on my accomplice to deny so that we will both get only 2 years? Or should I confess in the hope of getting just 1 year (provided that my accomplice denies) knowing that if my accomplice does confess, we will both get 3 years in prison? The dilemma is resolved by finding the equilibrium of the game.

A Bad Outcome For the prisoners, the equilibrium of the game, with each confessing, is not the best outcome. If neither of them confesses, each gets only 2 years for the lesser crime. Isn't there some way in which this better outcome can be achieved? It seems that there is not, because the players cannot communicate with each other. Each player can put himself in the other player's place, and so each player can figure out that there is one best strategy for each of them. The prisoners are indeed in a dilemma. Each knows that he can serve 2 years only if he can trust the other to deny. But each prisoner also knows that it is not in the best interest of the other to deny. So each prisoner knows that he must confess, thereby delivering a bad outcome for both.

The firms in an oligopoly are in a similar situation to Art and Bob in the prisoners' dilemma game. Let's see how we can use this game to understand oligopoly.

An Oligopoly Price-Fixing Game

We can use game theory and a game like the prisoners' dilemma to understand price fixing, price wars, and other aspects of the behaviour of firms in oligopoly. We'll begin with a price-fixing game.

To understand how oligopolies fix prices, we're going to study a special case of oligopoly called duopoly. **Duopoly** is a market structure in which there are only two producers who compete. You can probably find some examples of duopoly near where you live. Many cities have only two suppliers of milk, two local newspapers, two taxi companies, two car rental firms, two copy centres, or two college bookstores. Duopoly captures the essence of all oligopoly situations. Our goal is to predict the prices charged and the quantities produced by the two firms.

Cost and Demand Conditions Two firms, Trick and Gear, produce switchgears. They have identical costs. Figure 13.8(a) shows their average total cost curve (*ATC*) and marginal cost curve (*MC*). Figure 13.8(b) shows the market demand curve for switchgears (*D*). The two firms produce identical switchgears, so one firm's switchgear is a perfect substitute for the other's. So the market prices of both firms' product are identical. The quantity demanded depends on that price—the higher the price, the smaller is the quantity demanded.

This industry is a natural duopoly. Two firms can produce this good at a lower cost than can either one firm or three firms. For each firm, average total cost is at its minimum when production is 3,000 units a week. And when price equals minimum average total cost, the total quantity demanded is 6,000 units a week. So two firms can just produce that quantity.

Collusion We'll suppose that Trick and Gear enter into a collusive agreement. A **collusive agreement** is an agreement between two (or more) producers to restrict output, raise the price, and increase profits. Such an agreement is illegal in Canada and is undertaken in secret. A group of firms that has entered into a collusive agreement to restrict output and increase prices and profits is called a **cartel**. The strategies that firms in a cartel can pursue are to

- Comply
- Cheat

A firm that complies carries out the agreement. A firm that cheats breaks the agreement to its own benefit and to the cost of the other firm.

Because each firm has two strategies, there are four possible combinations of actions for the firms:

1. Both firms comply.
2. Both firms cheat.
3. Trick complies and Gear cheats.
4. Gear complies and Trick cheats.

FIGURE 13.8 Costs and Demand

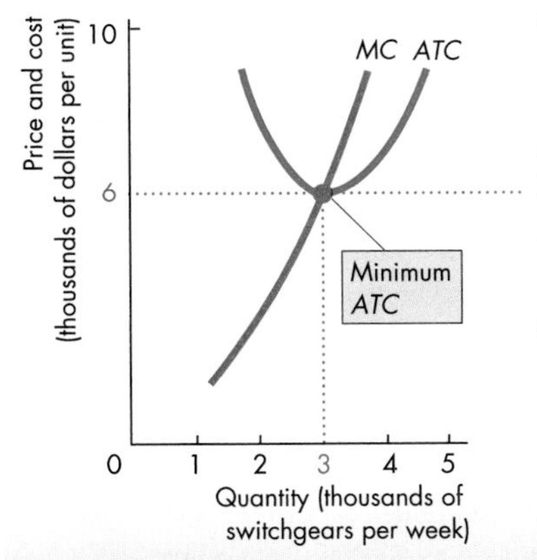

(a) Individual firm

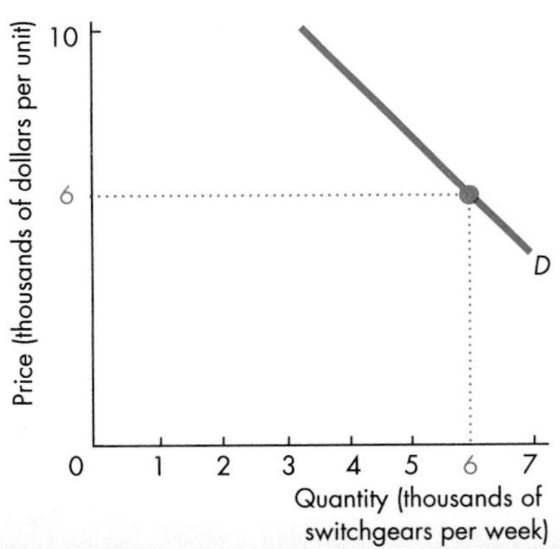

(b) Industry

The average total cost curve for each firm is *ATC*, and the marginal cost curve is *MC* (part a). Minimum average total cost is $6,000 a unit, and it occurs at a production of 3,000 units a week. Part (b) shows the market demand curve. At a price of $6,000, the quantity demanded is 6,000 units per week. The two firms can produce this output at the lowest possible average cost. If the market had one firm, it would be profitable for another to enter. If the market had three firms, one would exit. There is room for only two firms in this industry. It is a natural duopoly.

Colluding to Maximize Profits Let's work out the payoffs to the two firms if they collude to make the maximum profit for the cartel by acting like a monopoly. The calculations that the two firms perform are the same calculations that a monopoly performs. (You can refresh your memory of these calculations by looking at Chapter 12, pp. 266–267.) The only thing that the duopolists must do beyond what a monopolist does is to agree on how much of the total output each of them will produce.

Figure 13.9 shows the price and quantity that maximize industry profit for the duopolists. Part (a) shows the situation for each firm, and part (b) shows the situation for the industry as a whole. The curve labelled *MR* is the industry marginal revenue curve. This marginal revenue curve is like that of a single-price monopoly (see Chapter 12, p. 264). The curve labelled MC_I is the industry marginal cost curve if each firm produces the same level of output. That curve is constructed by adding together the outputs of the two firms at each level of marginal cost. That is, at each level of marginal cost, industry output is twice as much as the output of each individual firm. Thus the curve MC_I in part (b) is twice as far to the right as the curve *MC* in part (a).

To maximize industry profit, the duopolists agree to restrict output to the rate that makes the industry marginal cost and marginal revenue equal. That output rate, as shown in part (b), is 4,000 units a week.

The highest price for which the 4,000 switchgears can be sold is $9,000 each. Trick and Gear agree to charge this price.

To hold the price at $9,000 a unit, production must not exceed 4,000 units a week. So Trick and Gear must agree on the production level for each of them that total 4,000 units a week. Let's suppose that they agree to split the market equally so that each firm produces 2,000 switchgears a week. Because the firms are identical, this division is the most likely.

The average total cost (*ATC*) of producing 2,000 switchgears a week is $8,000, so the profit per unit is $1,000 and economic profit is $2 million (2,000 units × $1,000 per unit). The economic profit of each firm is represented by the blue rectangle in Fig. 13.9(a).

We have just described one possible outcome for a duopoly game: The two firms collude to produce the monopoly profit-maximizing output and divide that output equally between themselves. From the industry point of view, this solution is identical to a monopoly. A duopoly that operates in this way is indistinguishable from a monopoly. The economic profit that is made by a monopoly is the maximum total profit that can be made by colluding duopolists.

But with price greater than marginal cost, either firm might think of trying to increase its profit by cheating on the agreement and producing more than the agreed amount. Let's see what happens if one of the firms does cheat in this way.

FIGURE 13.9 Colluding to Make Monopoly Profits

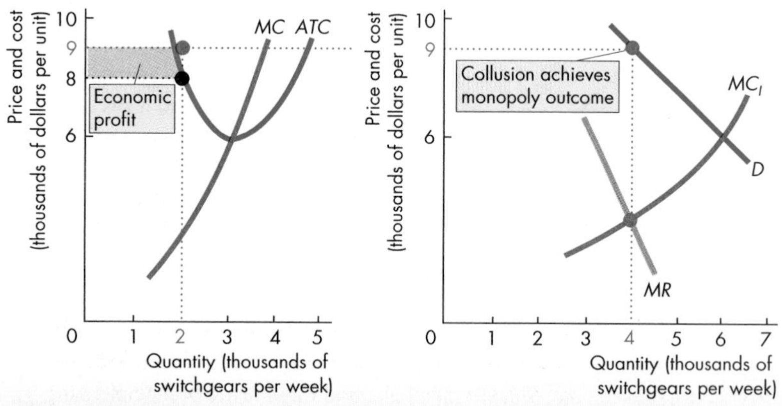

The industry marginal cost curve, MC_I in part (b), is the horizontal sum of the two firms' marginal cost curves, *MC*, in part (a). The industry marginal revenue curve is *MR*. To maximize profit, the firms produce 4,000 units a week (the quantity at which marginal revenue equals marginal cost). They sell that output for $9,000 a unit. Each firm produces 2,000 units a week. Average total cost is $8,000 a unit, so each firm makes an economic profit of $2 million (blue rectangle)—2,000 units multiplied by $1,000 profit a unit.

One Firm Cheats on a Collusive Agreement To set the stage for cheating on their agreement, Trick convinces Gear that demand has decreased and that it cannot sell 2,000 units a week. Trick tells Gear that it plans to cut its price in order to sell the agreed 2,000 units each week. Because the two firms produce an identical product, Gear matches Trick's price cut but still produces only 2,000 units a week.

In fact, there has been no decrease in demand. Trick plans to increase output, which it knows will lower the price, and Trick wants to ensure that Gear's output remains at the agreed level.

Figure 13.10 illustrates the consequences of Trick's cheating. Part (a) shows Gear (the complier); part (b) shows Trick (the cheat); and part (c) shows the industry as a whole. Suppose that Trick increases output to 3,000 units a week. If Gear sticks to the agreement to produce only 2,000 units a week, total output is 5,000 units a week, and given demand in part (c), the price falls to $7,500 a unit.

Gear continues to produce 2,000 units a week at a cost of $8,000 a unit and incurs a loss of $500 a unit, or $1 million a week. This economic loss is represented by the red rectangle in part (a). Trick produces 3,000 units a week at an average total cost of $6,000 each. With a price of $7,500, Trick makes a profit of $1,500 a unit and therefore an economic profit of $4.5 million. This economic profit is the blue rectangle in part (b).

We've now described a second possible outcome for the duopoly game: One of the firms cheats on the collusive agreement. In this case, the industry output is larger than the monopoly output and the industry price is lower than the monopoly price. The total economic profit made by the industry is also smaller than the monopoly's economic profit. Trick (the cheat) makes an economic profit of $4.5 million, and Gear (the complier) incurs an economic loss of $1 million. The industry makes an economic profit of $3.5 million. Thus the industry profit is $0.5 million less than the economic profit a monopoly would make. But the profit is distributed unevenly. Trick makes a bigger economic profit than it would under the collusive agreement, while Gear incurs an economic loss.

A similar outcome would arise if Gear cheated and Trick complied with the agreement. The industry profit and price would be the same, but in this case, Gear (the cheat) would make an economic profit of $4.5 million and Trick (the complier) would incur an economic loss of $1 million.

Let's next see what happens if both firms cheat.

FIGURE 13.10 One Firm Cheats

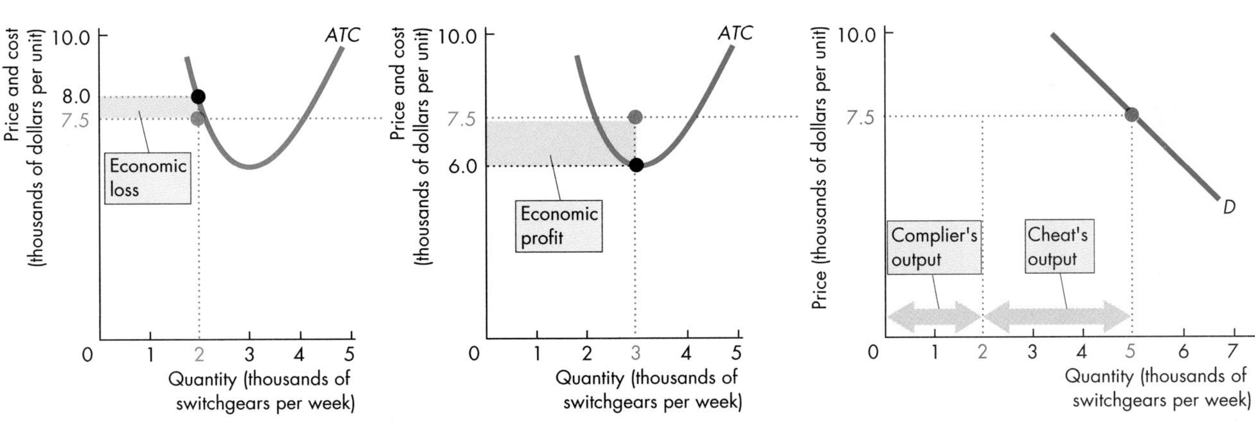

(a) Complier **(b) Cheat** **(c) Industry**

One firm, shown in part (a), complies with the agreement and produces 2,000 units. The other firm, shown in part (b), cheats on the agreement and increases its output to 3,000 units. Given the market demand curve, shown in part (c), and with a total production of 5,000 units a week, the price falls to $7,500. At this price, the complier in part (a) incurs an economic loss of $1 million ($500 per unit × 2,000 units), shown by the red rectangle. In part (b), the cheat makes an economic profit of $4.5 million ($1,500 per unit × 3,000 units), shown by the blue rectangle.

Both Firms Cheat Suppose that both firms cheat and that each behaves in the way that we have just analyzed. Each tells the other that it is unable to sell its output at the going price and that it plans to cut its price. But because both firms cheat, each will propose a successively lower price. As long as price exceeds marginal cost, each firm has an incentive to increase its production—to cheat. Only when price equals marginal cost is there no further incentive to cheat. This situation arises when the price has reached $6,000. At this price, marginal cost equals price. Also, price equals minimum average total cost. At a price less than $6,000, each firm incurs an economic loss. At a price of $6,000, each firm covers all its costs and makes zero economic profit (makes normal profit). Also, at a price of $6,000, each firm wants to produce 3,000 units a week, so the industry output is 6,000 units a week. Given the demand conditions, 6,000 units can be sold at a price of $6,000 each.

Figure 13.11 illustrates the situation just described. Each firm, in part (a), produces 3,000 units a week, and its average total cost is a minimum ($6,000 per unit). The market as a whole, in part (b), operates at the point at which the market demand curve (*D*) intersects the industry marginal cost curve (MC_I). Each firm has lowered its price and increased its output to try to gain an advantage over the other firm. Each has pushed this process as far as it can without incurring an economic loss.

We have now described a third possible outcome of this duopoly game: Both firms cheat. If both firms cheat on the collusive agreement, the output of each firm is 3,000 units a week and the price is $6,000. Each firm makes zero economic profit.

The Payoff Matrix Now that we have described the strategies and payoffs in the duopoly game, we can summarize the strategies and the payoffs in the form of the game's payoff matrix. Then we can find the Nash equilibrium.

Table 13.2 sets out the payoff matrix for this game. It is constructed in the same way as the payoff matrix for the prisoners' dilemma in Table 13.1. The squares show the payoffs for the two firms—Gear and Trick. In this case, the payoffs are profits. (For the prisoners' dilemma, the payoffs were losses.)

The table shows that if both firms cheat (top left), they achieve the perfectly competitive outcome—each firm makes zero economic profit. If both firms comply (bottom right), the industry makes the monopoly profit and each firm earns an economic profit of $2 million. The top right and bottom left squares show what happens if one firm cheats while the other complies. The firm that cheats collects an economic profit of $4.5 million, and the one that complies incurs a loss of $1 million.

Nash Equilibrium in the Duopolists' Dilemma The duopolists have a dilemma like the prisoners' dilemma. Do they comply or cheat? To answer this question, we must find the Nash equilibrium.

FIGURE 13.11 Both Firms Cheat

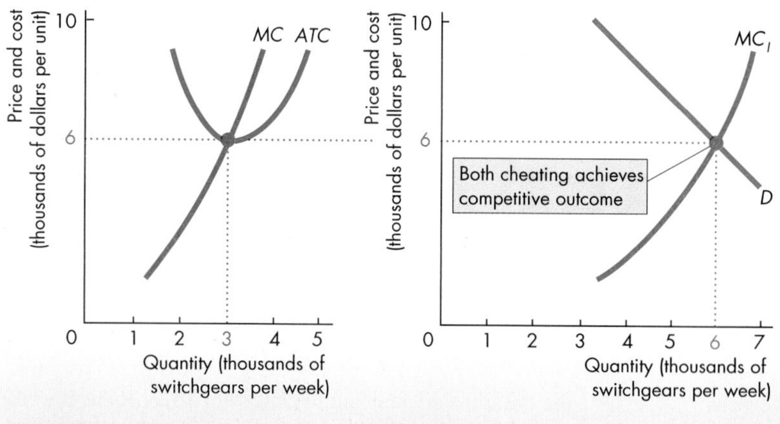

If both firms cheat by increasing production, the collusive agreement collapses. The limit to the collapse is the competitive equilibrium. Neither firm will cut price below $6,000 (minimum average total cost) because to do so will result in losses. In part (a), both firms produce 3,000 units a week at an average total cost of $6,000 a unit. In part (b), with a total production of 6,000 units, the price falls to $6,000. Each firm now makes zero economic profit because price equals average total cost. This output and price are the ones that would prevail in a competitive industry.

TABLE 13.2 Duopoly Payoff Matrix

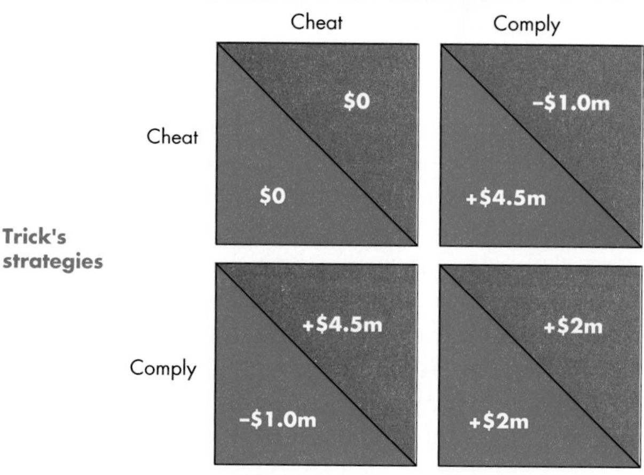

Each square shows the payoffs from a pair of actions. For example, if both firms comply with the collusive agreement, the payoffs are recorded in the bottom right square. The red triangle shows Gear's payoff, and the blue triangle shows Trick's. In Nash equilibrium, both firms cheat.

Look at things from Gear's point of view. Gear reasons as follows: Suppose that Trick cheats. If I comply, I will incur an economic loss of $1 million. If I also cheat, I will make zero economic profit. Zero is better than *minus* $1 million, so I'm better off if I cheat. Now suppose Trick complies. If I cheat, I will make an economic profit of $4.5 million, and if I comply, I will make an economic profit of $2 million. A $4.5 million profit is better than a $2 million profit, so I'm better off if I cheat. So regardless of whether Trick cheats or complies, it pays Gear to cheat. Cheating is Gear's best strategy.

Trick comes to the same conclusion as Gear because the two firms face an identical situation. So both firms cheat. The Nash equilibrium of the duopoly game is that both firms cheat. And although the industry has only two firms, they charge the same price and produce the same quantity as those in a competitive industry. Also, as in perfect competition, each firm makes zero economic profit.

This conclusion is not general and will not always arise. We'll see why not by looking first at some other games that are like the prisoners' dilemma. Then we'll broaden the types of games we consider.

Other Oligopoly Games

Firms in oligopoly must decide whether: to mount expensive advertising campaigns; to modify their product; to make their product more reliable and more durable; to price discriminate and, if so, among which groups of customers and to what degree; to undertake a large research and development (R&D) effort aimed at lowering production costs; and to enter or leave an industry.

All of these choices can be analyzed as games that are similar to the one that we've just studied. Let's look at one example: an R&D game.

An R&D Game

Disposable diapers were first marketed in 1966. The two market leaders from the start of this industry have been Procter & Gamble (the maker of Pampers) and Kimberly-Clark (the maker of Huggies). Procter & Gamble has about 40 percent of the total market, and Kimberly-Clark has about 33 percent. When the disposable diaper was first introduced in 1966, it had to be cost-effective in competition with reusable, laundered diapers. A costly research and development effort resulted in the development of machines that could make disposable diapers at a low enough cost to achieve that initial competitive edge. But new firms tried to get into the business and take market share away from the two industry leaders, and the industry leaders themselves battled each other to maintain or increase their own market share.

During the early 1990s, Kimberly-Clark was the first to introduce Velcro closures. And in 1996, Procter & Gamble was the first to introduce "breathable" diapers into the North American market.

The key to success in this industry (as in any other) is to design a product that people value highly relative to the cost of producing it. The firm that develops the most highly valued product and also develops the least-cost technology for producing it gains a competitive edge, undercutting the rest of the market, increasing its market share, and increasing its profit. But the R&D that must be undertaken to achieve product improvements and cost reductions is costly. So the cost of R&D must be deducted from the profit resulting from the increased market share that lower costs achieve. If no firm does R&D, every firm can be better off, but if one firm initiates the R&D activity, all must follow.

Table 13.3 illustrates the dilemma (with hypothetical numbers) for the R&D game that Kimberly-Clark and Procter & Gamble play. Each firm has two strategies: Spend $25 million a year on R&D or spend nothing on R&D. If neither firm spends on R&D, they make a joint profit of $100 million: $30 million for Kimberly-Clark and $70 million for Procter & Gamble (bottom right of the payoff matrix). If each firm conducts R&D, market shares are maintained but each firm's profit is lower by the amount spent on R&D (top left square of the payoff matrix). If Kimberly-Clark pays for R&D but Procter & Gamble does not, Kimberly-Clark gains a large part of Procter & Gamble's market. Kimberly-Clark profits, and Procter & Gamble loses (top right square of the payoff matrix). Finally, if Procter & Gamble conducts R&D and Kimberly-Clark does not, Procter & Gamble gains market share from Kimberly-Clark, increasing its profit, while Kimberly-Clark incurs a loss (bottom left square).

TABLE 13.3 Pampers versus Huggies: An R&D Game

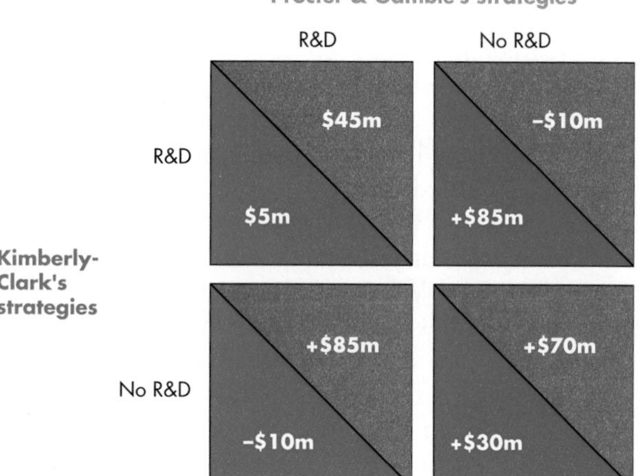

If both firms undertake R&D, their payoffs are those shown in the top left square. If neither firm undertakes R&D, their payoffs are in the bottom right square. When one firm undertakes R&D and the other one does not, their payoffs are in the top right and bottom left squares. The red triangle shows Procter & Gamble's payoff, and the blue triangle shows Kimberly-Clark's. The Nash equilibrium for this game is for both firms to undertake R&D. The structure of this game is the same as that of the prisoners' dilemma.

Confronted with the payoff matrix in Table 13.3, the two firms calculate their best strategies. Kimberly-Clark reasons as follows: If Procter & Gamble does not undertake R&D, we will make $85 million if we do and $30 million if we do not; so it pays us to conduct R&D. If Procter & Gamble conducts R&D, we will lose $10 million if we don't and make $5 million if we do. Again, R&D pays off. Thus conducting R&D is the best strategy for Kimberly-Clark. It pays, regardless of Procter & Gamble's decision.

Procter & Gamble reasons similarly: If Kimberly-Clark does not undertake R&D, we will make $70 million if we follow suit and $85 million if we conduct R&D. It therefore pays to conduct R&D. If Kimberly-Clark does undertake R&D, we will make $45 million by doing the same and lose $10 million by not doing R&D. Again, it pays us to conduct R&D. So for Procter & Gamble, conducting R&D is also the best strategy.

Because conducting R&D is the best strategy for both players, it is the Nash equilibrium. The outcome of this game is that both firms conduct R&D. They make less profit than they would if they could collude to achieve the cooperative outcome of no R&D.

The real-world situation has more players than Kimberly-Clark and Procter & Gamble. A large number of other firms share a small portion of the market, all of them ready to eat into the market share of Procter & Gamble and Kimberly-Clark. So the R&D effort by these two firms not only serves the purpose of maintaining shares in their own battle, but also helps to keep barriers to entry high enough to preserve their joint market share.

REVIEW QUIZ

1. What are the common features of all games?
2. Describe the prisoners' dilemma game and explain why the Nash equilibrium delivers a bad outcome for both players.
3. Why does a collusive agreement to restrict output and raise price create a game like the prisoners' dilemma?
4. What creates an incentive for firms in a collusive agreement to cheat and increase production?
5. What is the equilibrium strategy for each firm in a duopolists' dilemma and why do the firms not succeed in colluding to raise the price and profits?

Repeated Games and Sequential Games

THE GAMES THAT WE'VE STUDIED ARE PLAYED just once. In contrast, many real-world games are played repeatedly. This feature of games turns out to enable real-world duopolists to cooperate, collude, and earn a monopoly profit.

Another feature of the game that we've studied is that the players move simultaneously. But in many real-world situations, one player moves first and then the other moves—the play is sequential rather than simultaneous. This feature of real-world games creates a large number of possible outcomes.

We're now going to examine these two aspects of strategic decision making.

A Repeated Duopoly Game

If two firms play a game repeatedly, one firm has the opportunity to penalize the other for previous "bad" behaviour. If Gear cheats this week, perhaps Trick will cheat next week. Before Gear cheats this week, won't it take into account the possibility that Trick will cheat next week? What is the equilibrium of this game?

Actually, there is more than one possibility. One is the Nash equilibrium that we have just analyzed. Both players cheat, and each makes zero economic profit forever. In such a situation, it will never pay one of the players to start complying unilaterally because to do so would result in a loss for that player and a profit for the other. But a **cooperative equilibrium** in which the players make and share the monopoly profit is possible.

A cooperative equilibrium might occur if cheating is punished. There are two extremes of punishment. The smallest penalty is called "tit for tat." A *tit-for-tat strategy* is one in which a player cooperates in the current period if the other player cooperated in the previous period but cheats in the current period if the other player cheated in the previous period. The most severe form of punishment is called a trigger strategy. A *trigger strategy* is one in which a player cooperates if the other player cooperates but cheats forever thereafter if the other player cheats once.

In the duopoly game between Gear and Trick, a tit-for-tat strategy keeps both players cooperating and earning monopoly profits. Let's see why with an example.

Table 13.4 shows the economic profit that Trick and Gear will make over a number of periods under two alternative sequences of events: colluding and cheating with a tit-for-tat response by the other firm.

If both firms stick to the collusive agreement in period 1, each makes an economic profit of $2 million. Suppose that Trick contemplates cheating in period 1. The cheating produces a quick $4.5 million economic profit and inflicts a $1 million economic loss on Gear. But a cheat in period 1 produces a response from Gear in period 2. If Trick wants to get back into a profit-making situation, it must return to the agreement in period 2 even though it knows that Gear will punish it for cheating in period 1. So in period 2, Gear punishes Trick and Trick cooperates. Gear now makes an economic profit of $4.5 million, and Trick incurs an economic loss of $1 million. Adding up the profits over two periods of play, Trick would have made more profit by cooperating—$4 million compared with $3.5 million.

What is true for Trick is also true for Gear. Because each firm makes a larger profit by sticking with the collusive agreement, both firms do so and the monopoly price, quantity, and profit prevail.

In reality, whether a cartel works like a one-play game or a repeated game depends primarily on the

TABLE 13.4 Cheating with Punishment

	Collude		Cheat with tit-for-tat	
Period of Play	Trick's profit (millions of dollars)	Gear's profit (millions of dollars)	Trick's profit (millions of dollars)	Gear's profit (millions of dollars)
1	2	2	4.5	−1.0
2	2	2	−1.0	4.5
3	2	2	2.0	2.0
4	.	.	.	.

If duopolists repeatedly collude, each makes an economic profit of $2 million per period of play. If one player cheats in period 1, the other player plays a tit-for-tat strategy and cheats in period 2. The profit from cheating can be made for only one period and must be paid for in the next period by incurring a loss. Over two periods of play, the best that a duopolist can achieve by cheating is an economic profit of $3.5 million, compared to an economic profit of $4 million by colluding.

number of players and the ease of detecting and punishing cheating. The larger the number of players, the harder it is to maintain a cartel.

Games and Price Wars A repeated duopoly game can help us understand real-world behaviour and, in particular, price wars. Some price wars can be interpreted as the implementation of a tit-for-tat strategy. But the game is a bit more complicated than the one we've looked at because the players are uncertain about the demand for the product.

Playing a tit-for-tat strategy, firms have an incentive to stick to the monopoly price. But fluctuations in demand lead to fluctuations in the monopoly price, and sometimes, when the price changes, it might seem to one of the firms that the price has fallen because the other has cheated. In this case, a price war will break out. The price war will end only when each firm is satisfied that the other is ready to cooperate again. There will be cycles of price wars and the restoration of collusive agreements. Fluctuations in the world price of oil might be interpreted in this way.

Some price wars arise from the entry of a small number of firms into an industry that had previously been a monopoly. Although the industry has a small number of firms, the firms are in a prisoners' dilemma and they cannot impose effective penalties for price cutting. The behaviour of prices and outputs in the computer chip industry during 1995 and 1996 can be explained in this way. Until 1995, the market for Pentium chips for IBM-compatible computers was dominated by one firm, Intel Corporation, which was able to make maximum economic profit by producing the quantity of chips at which marginal cost equalled marginal revenue. The price of Intel's chips was set to ensure that the quantity demanded equalled the quantity produced. Then in 1995 and 1996, with the entry of a small number of new firms, the industry became an oligopoly. If the firms had maintained Intel's price and shared the market, together they could have made economic profits equal to Intel's profit. But the firms were in a prisoners' dilemma. So prices fell towards the competitive level.

Let's now study a sequential game. There are many such games, and the one we'll examine is among the simplest. But it has an interesting implication and it gives you the flavour of this type of game. The sequential game that we'll study is an entry game in a contestable market.

A Sequential Entry Game in a Contestable Market

If two firms play a game, one firm makes a decision at the first stage of the game and the other makes a decision at the second stage.

We're going to study a sequential game in a **contestable market**—a market in which firms can enter and leave so easily that firms in the market face competition from *potential* entrants. Examples of contestable markets are routes served by airlines and by barge companies that operate on the major waterways. These markets are contestable because firms could enter if an opportunity for economic profit arose and could exit with no penalty if the opportunity for economic profit disappeared.

If the Herfindahl–Hirschman Index (p. 206) is used to determine the degree of competition, a contestable market appears to be uncompetitive. But a contestable market can behave as if it were perfectly competitive. To see why, let's look at an entry game for a contestable air route.

A Contestable Air Route Agile Air is the only firm operating on a particular route. Demand and cost conditions are such that there is room for only one airline to operate. Wanabe, Inc. is another airline that could offer services on the route.

We describe the structure of a sequential game by using a *game tree* like that in Fig. 13.12. At the first stage, Agile Air must set a price. Once the price is set and advertised, Agile can't change it. That is, once set, Agile's price is fixed and Agile can't react to Wanabe's entry decision. Agile can set its price at the monopoly level or at the competitive level.

At the second stage, Wanabe must decide whether to enter or to stay out. Customers have no loyalty (there are no frequent flyer programs) and they buy from the lowest-price airline. So if Wanabe enters, it sets a price just below Agile's and takes all the business.

Figure 13.12 shows the payoffs from the various decisions (Agile's payoffs are in the red triangles and Wanabe's payoffs are in the blue triangles).

To decide on its price, Agile's CEO reasons as follows: Suppose that Agile sets the monopoly price. If Wanabe enters, it earns 90 (think of all payoff numbers as thousands of dollars). If Wanabe stays out it earns nothing. So Wanabe will enter. In this case Agile will lose 50.

FIGURE 13.12 Agile versus Wanabe: A Sequential Entry Game in a Contestable Market

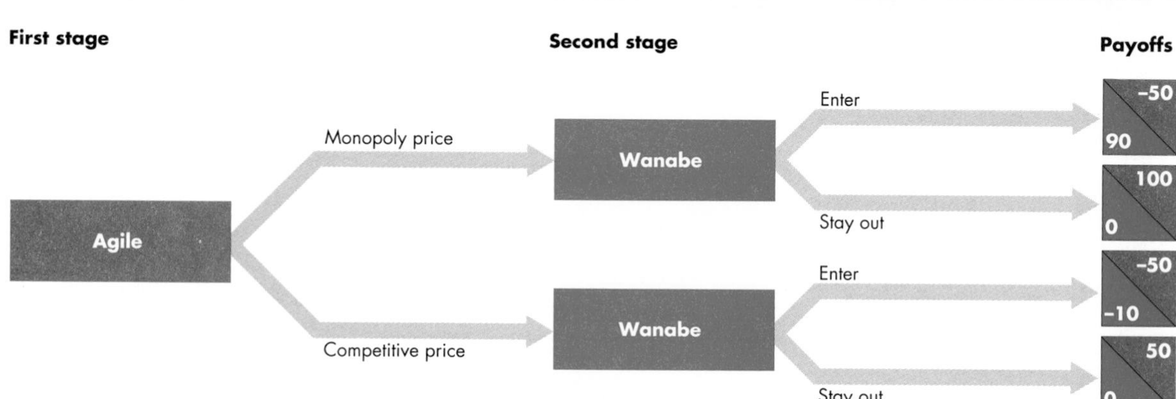

If Agile sets the monopoly price, Wanabe makes 90 (thousand dollars) by entering and earns nothing by staying out. So if Agile sets the monopoly price, Wanabe enters.

If Agile sets the competitive price, Wanabe earns nothing if it stays out and incurs a loss if it enters. So if Agile sets the competitive price, Wanabe stays out.

Now suppose that Agile sets the competitive price. If Wanabe stays out, it earns nothing and if it enters, it loses 10, so Wanabe will stay out. In this case, Agile will earn 50.

Agile's best strategy is to set its price at the competitive level and earn 50 (normal profit). The option of earning 100 by setting the monopoly price with Wanabe staying out is not available to Agile. If Agile sets the monopoly price, Wanabe enters, undercuts Agile, and takes all the business.

In this example, Agile sets its price at the competitive level and earns normal profit. A less costly strategy, called **limit pricing,** sets the price at the highest level that inflicts a loss on the entrant. Any loss is big enough to deter entry, so it is not always necessary to set the price as low as the competitive price. In the example of Agile and Wanabe, at the competitive price, Wanabe incurs a loss of 10 if it enters. A smaller loss would still keep Wanabe out.

This game is interesting because it points to the possibility of a monopoly behaving like a competitive industry and serving the consumer interest without regulation. But the result is not general and depends on one crucial feature of the set up of the game: At the second stage, Agile is locked into the price set at the first stage.

If Agile could change its price in the second stage, it would want to set the monopoly price if Wanabe stayed out—100 with the monopoly price beats 50 with the competitive price. But Wanabe can figure out what Agile would do, so the price set at the first stage has no effect on Wanabe. Agile sets the monopoly price and Wanabe might either stay out or enter.

We've looked at two of the many possible repeated and sequential games, and you've seen how these types of games can provide insights into the complex forces that determine prices and profits.

REVIEW QUIZ

1. If a prisoners' dilemma game is played repeatedly, what punishment strategies might the players employ and how does playing the game repeatedly change the equilibrium?
2. If a market is contestable, how does the equilibrium differ from that of a monopoly?

◆ Monopolistic competition and oligopoly are the most common market structures that you encounter in your daily life. *Reading Between the Lines* on pp. 304–305 shows you oligopoly in action in the Canadian retail book market.

So far, we've been studying the two big questions: What goods and services are produced, and how are they produced? Your next task is to study the forces that determine for whom they are produced.

Oligopoly in Action: A Book Seller's War

THE GLOBE AND MAIL, JUNE 25, 2002

Amazon.ca set to go today

Amazon.com Inc. is set to launch its Canadian on-line site today in a move that is sure to shake up an already shaky publishing industry.

Jeff Bezos, chief executive officer of the world's biggest Internet retailer, will unveil his plans for Canada at a Toronto press conference this morning and later at a cocktail reception for members of the industry.

The long-rumoured arrival of the on-line giant is being applauded by some Canadian publishers who have felt the squeeze of operating in a market dominated by one major player—Indigo Books &Music Inc. ...

Canadian booksellers are less excited about the news.

Earlier this month, the Canadian Booksellers Association called on Ottawa to review Amazon.com's plans, saying the Seattle-based retailer was violating federal foreign investment rules for the industry.

Federal cultural investment regulations require that a majority of any bookseller be Canadian-owned.

A spokeswoman for the association said yesterday that it has received no response from the ministry, other than confirmation that their letter was received. ...

E-commerce consultant and author Rick Broadhead said the arrival of Amazon.ca will likely put instant pressure on the Chapters/Indigo e-commerce site.

"Indigo probably can't afford to compete," he said.

But he said for consumers, the event is good news. "Canadians deserve to have the best retailers to shop at and Amazon is the undisputed king of on-line retailing," he said.

Essence of the Story

- Amazon.com Inc. opened a Canadian on-line site in June 2002.
- Canadian publishers were pleased to see competition for Indigo Books & Music Inc., who they say has squeezed them.
- Canadian booksellers were not pleased about the news.
- The Canadian Booksellers Association claimed that Amazon was violating federal foreign investment rules, which require that a majority of any bookseller be Canadian-owned.
- E-commerce consultant and author Rick Broadhead said the arrival of Amazon.ca will likely put instant pressure on the Chapters/Indigo e-commerce site.

Economic Analysis

■ The retail market for books in Canada is an example of oligopoly.

■ During the 1990s, independent retailers disappeared as Chapters and Indigo expanded.

■ By 2001, these two firms controlled more than 30 percent of the retail book market in Canada and, in some cities, they had a virtual duopoly.

■ Then, in 2001, Indigo Books & Music Inc. bought Chapters.

■ So in 2002, before the arrival of Amazon.ca, Indigo was the major player in the Canadian retail book market and chapters.indigo.ca was the major player in the Canadian e-commerce book market.

■ The table shows the payoff matrix for the game that Indigo and Amazon played in 2002.

■ The numbers in the table are economic profit. (The magnitudes are fictitious, but the relative magnitudes illustrate the nature of the game.)

■ Amazon had two strategies: enter the Canadian market or remain out. Indigo had two strategies: stay in and fight or exit.

■ The payoffs from staying out are zero. If one of the firms had the market to itself, it would earn 100. If both firms shared the market, they would each earn 20.

■ This game is similar to the prisoners' dilemma, but not quite the same because the players can walk away and earn zero.

■ But there is a dilemma. If either firm had the market to itself, it could earn a large profit and sharing the market not only lowers the profit for each but also lowers the total profit that they share. The reason is that basic infrastructure resources are duplicated with two firms.

■ The equilibrium of the assumed game is for Amazon to enter the market and for Indigo to remain.

■ The assumed game might be a poor description of reality. It is possible that there is room for only one firm to earn a positive economic profit. If this turns out to be the case, one of the players will eventually exit and a single dominant firm will win the market.

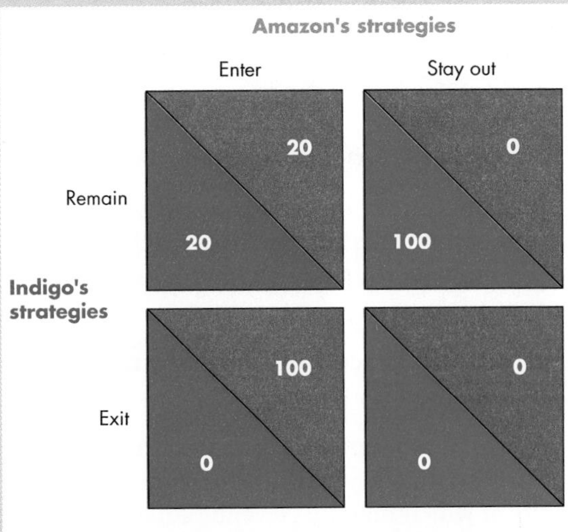

Figure 1 Amazon versus Indigo: An entry game

You're The Voter

■ Do you think the Canadian government should prevent U.S. firms from entering the Canadian book-retailing market?

■ Who would benefit and who would pay for such a ban?

SUMMARY

KEY POINTS

Monopolistic Competition (pp. 284–285)

- Monopolistic competition occurs when a large number of firms compete with each other on product quality, price, and marketing.

Output and Price in Monopolistic Competition (pp. 286–288)

- A firm in monopolistic competition faces downward-sloping demand curve and produces the quantity at which marginal revenue equals marginal cost.
- Entry and exit result in zero economic profit and excess capacity in long-run equilibrium.

Product Development and Marketing (pp. 288–290)

- Firms in monopolistic competition innovate and develop new products in an attempt to maintain economic profit.
- Advertising expenditures increase total cost, but they might lower average total cost if they increase the quantity sold by enough.
- Advertising expenditures might increase demand, but they might also decrease the demand for a firm's product by increasing competition.
- Whether monopolistic competition is inefficient depends on the value we place on product variety.

Oligopoly (pp. 291–292)

- Oligopoly is a market in which a small number of firms compete.
- If rivals match price cuts but do not match price hikes, they face a kinked demand curve and change prices only when large cost changes occur.
- If one firm dominates a market, it acts like a monopoly and the small firms take its price as given and act like perfectly competitive firms.

Oligopoly Games (pp. 293–300)

- Oligopoly is studied by using game theory, which is a method of analyzing strategic behaviour.
- In a prisoners' dilemma game, two prisoners acting in their own interest harm their joint interest.
- An oligopoly (duopoly) price-fixing game is a prisoners' dilemma.
- In Nash equilibrium, both firms cheat and output and price are the same as in perfect competition.
- Firms' decisions about advertising and R&D can be studied by using game theory.

Repeated Games and Sequential Games (pp. 301–303)

- In a repeated game, a punishment strategy can produce a cooperative equilibrium in which price and output are the same as in a monopoly.
- In a sequential contestable market game, a small number of firms can behave like firms in perfect competition.

KEY FIGURES AND TABLES

Figure 13.2	Output and Price in Monopolistic Competition, 286
Figure 13.3	Excess Capacity, 287
Figure 13.5	Selling Costs and Total Cost, 290
Figure 13.8	Costs and Demand, 295
Figure 13.9	Colluding to Make Monopoly Profits, 296
Figure 13.11	Both Firms Cheat, 298
Table 13.1	Prisoners' Dilemma Payoff Matrix, 294
Table 13.2	Duopoly Payoff Matrix, 299

KEY TERMS

Capacity output, 287
Cartel, 295
Collusive agreement, 295
Contestable market, 302
Cooperative equilibrium, 301
Duopoly, 295
Game theory, 293
Limit pricing, 303
Monopolistic competition, 284
Nash equilibrium, 294
Oligopoly, 291
Payoff matrix, 293
Product differentiation, 284
Strategies, 293

PROBLEMS

*1. The figure shows the situation facing Lite and Kool, Inc., a producer of running shoes.

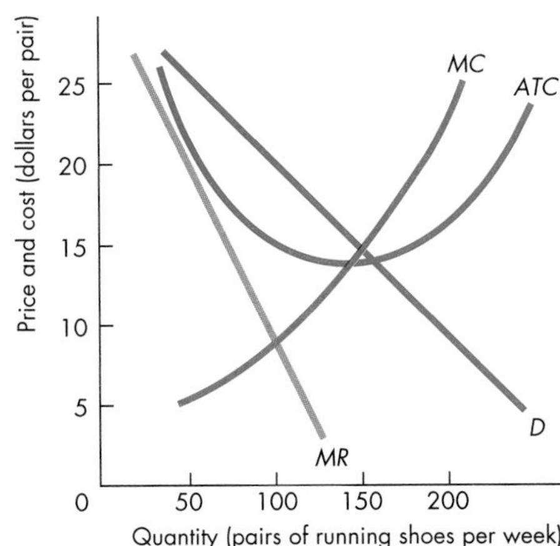

a. What quantity does Lite and Kool produce?
b. What does it charge?
c. How much profit does Lite and Kool make?

2. The figure shows the situation facing The Stiff Shirt, Inc., a producer of shirts.

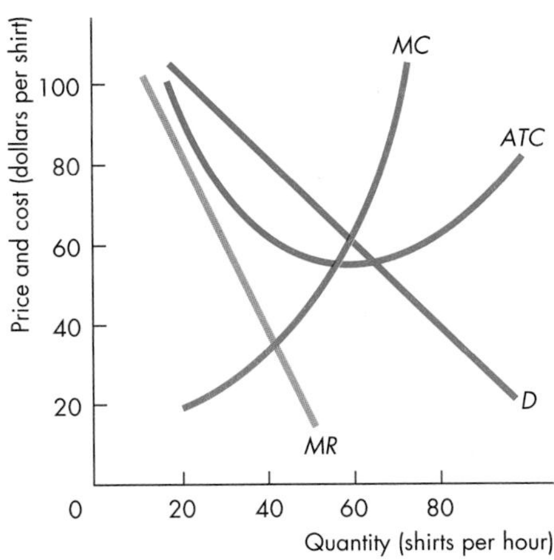

a. What quantity does The Stiff Shirt produce?
b. What does it charge?
c. How much profit does it make?

*3. A firm in monopolistic competition produces running shoes. If it spends nothing on advertising, it can sell no shoes at $100 a pair, and for each $10 cut in price, the quantity of shoes it can sell increases by 25 pairs a day, so at $20 a pair, it can sell 200 pairs a day. The firm's total fixed cost is $4,000 a day. Its average variable cost and marginal cost is a constant $20 per pair. If the firm spends $3,000 a day on advertising, it can double the quantity of shoes sold at each price.
a. If the firm doesn't advertise, what is
(i) The quantity of shoes produced?
(ii) The price per pair?
(iii) The firm's economic profit or loss?
b. If the firm does advertise, what is
(i) The quantity of shoes produced?
(ii) The price per pair?
(iii) The firm's economic profit or loss?
c. Will the firm advertise or not? Why?

4. The firm in problem 3 has the same demand and costs as before if it does not advertise. The firm undertakes some quality improvements in its shoes that raise its marginal and average cost to $40 a pair. If the firm spends $3,000 a day on advertising with an agency, it can double the amount that consumers are willing to pay at each quantity demanded.
a. If the firm hires the agency, what quantity does it produce and what price does it charge?
b. What is the firm's economic profit or loss?
c. What is the firm's profit in the long run?

*5. A firm with a kinked demand curve experiences an increase in fixed costs. Explain how the firm's price, output, and profit change.

6. A firm with a kinked demand curve experiences an increase in variable cost. Explain how the firm's price, output, and profit change.

*7. An industry with one very large firm and 100 very small firms experiences an increase in the demand for its product. Use the dominant firm model to explain the effects on the price, output, and economic profit of
a. The large firm.
b. A typical small firm.

8. An industry with one very large firm and 100 very small firms experiences an increase in total variable cost. Use the dominant firm model to explain the effects on the price, output, and economic profit of
a. The large firm.
b. A typical small firm.

*9. Consider a game with two players in which each player is asked a question. The players can answer the question honestly or lie. If both answer honestly, each receives $100. If one answers honestly and the other lies, the liar receives $500 and the honest player gets nothing. If both lie, then each receives $50.
   a. Describe this game in terms of its players, strategies, and payoffs.
   b. Construct the payoff matrix.
   c. What is the equilibrium for this game?

10. Describe the game known as the prisoners' dilemma. In describing the game,
   a. Make up a story that motivates the game.
   b. Work out a payoff matrix.
   c. Describe how the equilibrium of the game is reached.

*11. Soapy and Suddies, Inc. are the only producers of soap powder. They collude and agree to share the market equally. If neither firm cheats, each makes $1 million profit. If either firm cheats, the cheat makes a profit of $1.5 million, while the complier incurs a loss of $0.5 million. Neither firm can police the other's actions.
   a. If the game is played once,
      (i) What is the profit of each firm if both cheat?
      (ii) Describe the best strategy for each firm.
      (iii) Construct the payoff matrix.
      (iv) What is the equilibrium of the game?
   b. If this duopoly game can be played many times, describe some of the strategies that each firm might adopt.

12. Healthy and Energica are the only producers of a new energy drink. The firms collude and agree to share the market equally. If neither firm cheats, each firm makes $4 million profit. If either firm cheats, the cheat makes $6 million profit, while the complier incurs a loss of $1.5 million. Neither firm can police the other's actions.
   a. If the game is played once,
      (i) What is the payoff matrix?
      (ii) Describe the best strategy for each firm.
      (iii) What is the equilibrium of the game?
   b. If this game can be played many times, what are two strategies that could be adopted?

CRITICAL THINKING

1. Study *Reading Between the Lines* on pp. 304–305 and then answer the following questions.
   a. Why is the Canadian retail book market an example of oligopoly?
   b. How do you think the retail markup on books is determined?
   c. Why did Amazon enter the Canadian market in 2002?
   d. What strategic variables other than price do booksellers use?
   e. Why (aside from the fact that it is illegal) is it impossible for Amazon and Indigo to collude and earn a larger economic profit?
2. Suppose that Netscape and Microsoft develop their own versions of an amazing new Web browser that allows advertisers to target consumers with great precision. Also, the new browser is easier and more fun to use than existing browsers. Each firm is trying to decide whether to sell the browser or to give it away free. What are the likely benefits from each action and which is likely to occur?
3. Why do Coca-Cola Company and PepsiCo spend huge amounts on advertising? Do they benefit? Does the consumer benefit? Explain your answer.

WEB EXERCISES

1. Use the link on the Parkin–Bade Web site to obtain information about the market for vitamins.
   a. In what type of market are vitamins sold?
   b. What illegal act occurred in the vitamin market during the 1990s?
   c. Describe the actions of BASF and Roche as a game and set out a hypothetical payoff matrix for the game.
   d. Is the game played by BASF and Roche played once or is it a repeated game? How do you know which type of game it is?
2. Use the link on the Parkin–Bade Web site to obtain information about the market for art and antiques.
   a. What illegal act occurred in the art and antiques auction market during the 1990s?
   b. Describe the game played by Sotheby's and Christie's and set out a payoff matrix.

UNDERSTANDING FIRMS AND MARKETS

Managing Change

Our economy is constantly changing. Every year, new goods appear and old ones disappear. New firms are born and old ones die. This process of change is initiated and managed by firms operating in markets. When a new product is invented, just one or two firms sell it initially. For example, when the personal computer first became available, there was an Apple or an IBM. The IBM-PC had just one operating system, DOS, made by Microsoft. One firm, Intel, made the chip that ran the IBM-PC. These are examples of industries in which the producer has market power to determine the price of the product and the quantity produced. The extreme case of a single producer that cannot be challenged by new competitors is *monopoly*, which Chapter 12 explained. ◆ But not all industries with just one producer are monopolies. In many cases, the firm that is first to produce a new good faces severe competition from new rivals. One firm facing potential competition is the case of a *contestable market*. If demand increases and makes space for more than one firm, an industry becomes increasingly competitive. Even with just two rivals, the industry changes its face in a dramatic way. *Duopoly*—the case of just two producers—illustrates this dramatic change. The two firms must play close attention to each other's production and prices and must predict the effects of their own actions on the actions of the other firm. We call this situation one of *strategic interdependence*. As the number of rivals grows, the industry becomes an *oligopoly*, in which a small number of firms devise strategies and pay close attention to the strategies of their competitors. ◆ With the continued arrival of new firms in an industry, the market eventually becomes competitive. Competition might be limited because each firm produces its own special version or brand of a good. This case is called *monopolistic competition* because it has elements of both monopoly and competition. Chapter 13 explored the behaviour of firms in all of these types of markets that lie between monopoly at the one extreme and perfect competition at the other. ◆ When competition is extreme—the case that we call *perfect competition*—the market changes again in a dramatic way. Now the firm is unable to influence price. Chapter 11 explained this case. ◆ Often, an industry that is competitive becomes less so as the bigger and more successful firms in the industry begin to swallow up the smaller firms, either by driving them out of business or by acquiring their assets. Through this process, an industry might return to oligopoly or even monopoly. You can see such a movement in the auto and banking industries today. ◆ By studying firms and markets, we gain a deeper understanding of the forces that allocate scarce resources and begin to see the anatomy of the invisible hand. ◆ Many economists have advanced our understanding of these forces and we'll now meet two of them. John von Neumann pioneered the idea of game theory. And Bengt Holmstrom is one of today's leading students of strategic behaviour.

PROBING THE IDEAS

Market Power

The Economist

"Real life consists of bluffing, of little tactics of deception, of asking yourself what is the other man going to think I mean to do."

John von Neumann, ***told to Jacob Bronowski (in a London taxi) and reported in*** **The Ascent of Man**

JOHN VON NEUMANN *was one of the great minds of the twentieth century. Born in Budapest, Hungary, in 1903, Johnny, as he was known, showed early mathematical brilliance. His first mathematical publication was an article that grew out of a lesson with his tutor, which he wrote at the age of 18! But it was at the age of 25, in 1928, that von Neumann published the article that began a flood of research on game theory—a flood that has still not subsided today. In that article, he proved that in a zero-sum game (like sharing a pie), there exists a best strategy for each player.*

Von Neumann invented the computer and built the first modern practical computer, and he worked on the "Manhattan Project," which developed the atomic bomb at Los Alamos, New Mexico, during World War II.

Von Neumann believed that the social sciences would progress only if they used mathematical tools. But he believed that they needed different tools from those developed from the physical sciences.

The Issues

It is not surprising that firms with market power will charge higher prices than those charged by competitive firms. But how much higher?

This question has puzzled generations of economists. Adam Smith said, "The price of a monopoly is upon every occasion the highest which can be got." But he was wrong. Antoine-Augustin Cournot (see p. 148) first worked out the price a monopoly will charge. It is not the "highest which can be got" but the price that maximizes profit. Cournot's work was not appreciated until almost a century later when Joan Robinson explained how a monopoly sets its price.

Questions about monopoly became urgent and practical during the 1870s, a time when rapid technological change and falling transportation costs enabled huge monopolies to emerge in the United States. Monopolies dominated oil, steel, railroads, tobacco, and even sugar. Industrial empires grew ever larger.

The success of the nineteenth century monopolies led to the creation of our anti-combine laws—laws that limit the use of monopoly power. Those laws have been used to prevent monopolies from being set up and to break up existing monopolies. They were used in the United States during the 1960s to end a conspiracy between General Electric, Westinghouse, and other firms when they colluded to fix their prices instead of competing with each other. The laws were used during the 1980s to bring greater competition to long-distance telecommunication. But in spite of anti-combine laws, near monopolies still exist. Among the most prominent today are those in computer chips and operating systems. Like their forerunners, today's near monopolies make huge profits.

But unlike the situation in the nineteenth century, the technological change taking place today is strengthening the forces of competition. Today's information technologies are creating substitutes for services that previously had none. Direct satellite TV is competing with cable, and new phone companies are competing with the traditional phone monopolies.

Then

Ruthless greed, exploitation of both workers and customers—these are the traditional images of monopolies and the effects of their power. These images appeared to be an accurate description during the 1880s, when monopolies stood at their peak of power and influence. One monopolist, John D. Rockefeller, Sr., built his giant Standard Oil Company, which by 1879 was refining 90 percent of the nation's oil and controlling its entire pipeline capacity.

&

Now

Despite anti-combine laws that regulate monopolies, they still exist. One is the monopoly in cable television. In many cities, one firm decides which channels viewers will receive and the price they will pay. During the 1980s, with the advent of satellite technology and specialist cable program producers such as CNN and HBO, the cable companies expanded their offerings. At the same time, they steadily increased prices and their businesses became very profitable. But the very technologies that made cable television profitable are now challenging its market power. Direct satellite TV services are eroding cable's monopoly and bringing greater competition to this market.

Today, many economists who work on microeconomics use the ideas that John von Neumann pioneered. Game theory is the tool of choice. One economist who has made good use of this tool (and many other tools) is Bengt Holmstrom of MIT, whom you can meet on the following pages.

TALKING WITH

BENGT HOLMSTROM *is Paul A. Samuelson Professor of Economics in the department of economics and the Sloan School of Management at the Massachusetts Institute of Technology. Born in 1949 in Helsinki, Finland, he studied mathematics and physics at the University of Helsinki as an undergraduate and then worked as an operations researcher before going to Stanford University as an economics graduate student. Professor Holmstrom's research on the way firms use contracts and incentives is recognized as providing a major advance in our understanding of the mechanisms that operate inside firms. Beyond his academic research, Professor Holmstrom has provided services to a number of major corporations, including Nokia, of which he is currently a director.*

Bengt Holmstrom

Michael Parkin and Robin Bade talked with Bengt Holmstrom about his work and the progress that economists have made in understanding firms and the markets in which they operate since the pioneering ideas about the nature of the firm by Ronald Coase.

Professor Holmstrom, did you study economics as an undergraduate? What drew you to this subject?

No. I was a math and physics major as an undergraduate in Helsinki. I got into economics the way many people do through a side door from mathematics and operations research at Stanford Graduate School of Business.

How did you get interested in the economics of the firm?

I went from my undergraduate degree to work as an operations research analyst at a large conglomerate in Finland. I was hired to implement a company-wide corporate planning model. This was the early 70s, when large optimization models were expected to help firms make better long-term plans and run operations more centrally.

It didn't take me very long to realize that this was a misguided belief. The problem was that the data came from people lower down that had an apparent incentive to misrepresent the numbers. Their minds were focused on outwitting the model. My interest in incentives was entirely driven by this experience.

One of your most profound insights was to view the entire firm as an incentive system. What do you mean when you describe a firm as an incentive system? What implications follow from this view of the firm?

When people talk about incentives, they tend to think about some explicit reward system like a salesperson's commission or a stock option for an executive or something like that.

The key insight has been to understand that incentives are influenced in an enormous number of ways, indirectly and implicitly. For instance, constraints and bureaucratic rules are very important pieces of the overall incentive system. There are many different ways of getting people to do what you think they should be doing.

Sometimes the best incentive is to pay no incentive! Incentives can be terribly damaging if they are poorly designed.

The firm as an incentive system is an expression of the fact that you need to think about *all* the possible ways in which you can influence people's actions and then how you orchestrate the instruments that are available. These instruments include promotion incentives, rewards, or even just praise. The narrow view that it's just a matter of paying a bonus of some sort is very misguided.

Sometimes the best incentive is to pay no incentive! Incentives can be terribly damaging if they are poorly designed.

Can you talk about the role of the economist as economic adviser to a firm? One view is that firms are efficient and the task of the economist is to understand why. Another view is that the economist can help firms to become efficient—for example, by devising better incentive mechanisms. Can the economist help firms to become efficient? And are there other roles for the economist as adviser to a firm?

There's a well-known paradox—and tension—in economics. Positive economics deals with figuring out what is optimal—what is the best that can be done—and then using the description of optimal behaviour as a predictive tool—as a way of explaining why things are the way they are in the world.

And yet at the same time, nothing is presumably perfect so there is room for innovation—organizational innovation and economic innovation—which leads to the economic advice you're asking about.

There are many roles an economist can play as adviser to a firm. If we really understand things better, maybe we can actually make improvements in them. If nothing else, we can understand that if the constraints change, then a system that's designed in a particular way would need to adapt itself to the new circumstances. For example, a firm might have a centralized organization that's good in one set of circumstances and then suddenly the circumstances change and innovation becomes very important, as we seem to think it is right now. Then that situation calls for changes towards organizational structures that are more suited for innovation.

So you can explain the tradeoff between central control and more flexible, innovative structures so that a firm's managers understand these forces. They then might decide to move in the direction that better achieves their objectives. Or they might realize that the reason why other firms change organizational structures may not be relevant in their case.

The economist can help people understand the variety of organizations so that they can pick the right one for the right set of circumstances. There isn't one organization that's good for everything—quite the contrary. Some activities require one kind of organization; some activities require another kind of organization. Charities, for instance, would not be well run by for-profit firms because they would run away with the money. That's an extreme example. So, non-profit organizations play a very important role in running charities.

Joint stock companies have proven to be an extremely flexible and robust form of organization both for small- and large-scale activities. Their scalability is one reason for their enormous success.

Are there any examples of serious progress that we've made in understanding which types of organizations work best in which circumstances?

I think there are lots. There's a big debate right now about airport security that's a wonderful illustration of the insight that the firm is an incentive system and an example of the possibility of having incentives that are too strong in the wrong place. One view is that profit-making companies that run the airport security checking are too oriented towards profit and too little oriented towards quality, because the quality checks come so infrequently. The standard argument is that if they make a mistake they must pay for it, so they have a strong incentive to deliver high-quality work. But if accidents happen infrequently, that sort of feedback mechanism is just too weak. This is a logical reason for moving in the direction of taking away profit-making incentives from airport security checking.

The very existence of the firm comes from the fact that it is there to remove and restructure incorrect incentives—excessively high-powered incentives that come from the market—and to get people to cooperate. In the market, it can be harder to cooperate because everyone is working for his or her own benefit. This works very well if there are a lot of alternatives to choose—if there's competition. But when there is a small number of traders, or where quality is hard to assess, bringing the activity inside the firm is quite natural.

One firm, Enron, was big news during 2002. What do models of incentive systems tell us about what went wrong with Enron?

I think Enron, like most of these disaster cases, teaches that misplaced incentives lead to potentially big mistakes. It's almost tautological to say that if wrongdoing was done, it was done because the incentives weren't aligned correctly. Now, how much of it was a design flaw within Enron and how much was a flaw of the overall system, is harder to judge. There were certainly regulatory problems—energy production regulations had changed; the energy market had been opened up and arbitrage opportunities created. Some of the activities of Enron that sought to profit from this new regulatory environment were entirely legal.

Then there was financial innovation. It's an old, old idea that it would be nice to remove debts from the balance sheet of a firm to make it look better to investors. And apparently new financial instruments had been created to make off-balance sheet operations possible. Some of them were clearly questionable and perhaps some of them illegal.

But the other problem—and this is a system problem, not just an Enron problem—is that when things are going well and everybody believes that the world is moving forward, it's very hard to question something. You go further and further out on a limb, and then the limb breaks and you learn that that was too much.

I don't think that a system that rules out everything that can go wrong is the right system.

I don't see Enron as catastrophically as most people seem to. I think that we would pay a big price if we never let anybody like Enron try. If you regulate things so that nothing like it ever could have happened, it probably would have also thrown out a lot of good innovations with it. It's part of the system to learn by having certain things like this happen.

I'm not defending Enron's actions. But I'm trying to give a different angle to the possible response. System design is different from trying to correct individual cases. I don't think that a system that rules out everything that can go wrong is the right system.

Is it important for an academic economist to have professional interests in the "real world"?

I think everybody's different. For me it has been important because I got interested in incentives through non-academic work. That's where I started, and I was just lucky that incentives happened to be a topical issue when I entered the field.

I don't think one could, in any sense, say that everybody must have real-world experience. You have to find your own sources of stimulation and discover what makes you curious and what makes you interested. For some people, that's just being exceedingly theoretical and not thinking about much else. Some are very talented that way: other people desperately need some connection with the real world. For me, that has been very valuable.

Needless to say, the fact that we are all different is extremely important for overall progress.

What advice do you have for a student who is just starting to study economics? Do you think that economics is a good subject in which to major? What other subjects would you urge students to study alongside economics?

I'm a big believer that people do their best work and have their happiest life when they do the things that they are really interested in. With the wonderful undergraduate system that North America has, I would advise students to sample broadly and go in the direction they get most excited about. But I think there are many reasons to like economics. It spans a fascinating range of questions. At its heart, economics is about understanding social systems, current and past, and how these systems could be improved for the welfare of the human race. I'm confident that economics has contributed a great deal to the current levels of welfare in the West. And I'm optimistic that the developing world will also benefit from our intellectual progress. As an economist, you can have a really big impact, even if the results are less visible than in the natural sciences like physics. For me, it has been incredibly inspiring.

DEMAND AND SUPPLY IN FACTOR MARKETS

CHAPTER 14

Many Happy Returns

It may not be your birthday, and even if it is, chances are you are spending most of it working. But at the end of the week or month (or, if you're devoting all your time to university, when you graduate), you will receive the *returns* from your labour. Those returns vary a lot. Ed Jones, who spends his days in a small container suspended from the top of Toronto's high-rise buildings cleaning windows, makes a happy return of $12 an hour. Antonio Davis, who plays no more than 82 basketball games a year, makes a very happy return of $11 million a year. Some differences in earnings might seem surprising. For example, your university football coach might earn much more than your economics professor. Why aren't *all* jobs well paid? ◆ Most of us have little trouble spending our pay. But most of us do manage to save some of what we earn. What determines the amount of saving that people do and the returns they make on that saving? ◆ Some people earn their income by supplying natural resources such as oil. What determines the price of a natural resource?

In this chapter, we study the markets for factors of production—labour, capital, natural resources—and learn how their prices and people's incomes are determined. And we'll see in *Reading Between the Lines* at the end of the chapter why top-performing hockey players earn such large salaries.

After studying this chapter, you will be able to

- **Explain how firms choose the quantities of labour, capital, and natural resources to employ**
- **Explain how people choose the quantities of labour, capital, and natural resources to supply**
- **Explain how wages, interest, and natural resource prices are determined in competitive factor markets**
- **Explain the concept of economic rent and distinguish between economic rent and opportunity cost**

Prices and Incomes in Competitive Factor Markets

GOODS AND SERVICES ARE PRODUCED BY USING the four resources or *factors of production—labour, capital, land,* and *entrepreneurship* (we defined these factors of production in Chapter 1, p. 4). Incomes are determined by *factor prices*—the *wage* rate for labour, the *interest* rate for capital, the *rental* rate for land, and the rate of *normal profit* for entrepreneurship—and the quantities of the factors used. In addition to the four factor incomes, a residual income, *economic profit* (or *economic loss*), is paid to (or borne by) firms' owners—sometimes the owner is the entrepreneur and sometimes the owners are the stockholders who provide financial capital.

Factors of production, like goods and services, are traded in markets. Some factor markets are competitive and behave like other perfectly competitive markets. Other factors are traded in markets in which there is market power. We focus in this chapter on competitive factor markets to learn how they determine the prices, quantities used, and incomes of factors of production. In an appendix (pp. 341–346), we examine labour markets in which there is market power.

The main tool that we use in this chapter is the demand and supply model. The quantity demanded of a factor of production depends on its price, and the law of demand applies to factors of production just as it does to goods and services. The lower the price of a factor, other things remaining the same, the greater is the quantity demanded. Figure 14.1 shows the demand curve for a factor as the curve labelled *D*.

The quantity supplied of a factor also depends on its price. With a possible exception that we'll identify later in this chapter, the law of supply applies to factors of production. The higher the price of a factor, other things remaining the same, the greater is the quantity supplied of the factor. Figure 14.1 shows the supply curve of a factor as the curve labelled *S*.

The equilibrium factor price is determined at the point of intersection of the demand and supply curves. In Fig. 14.1, the price is *PF* and the quantity used is *QF*.

The income earned by the factor is its price multiplied by the quantity used. In Fig. 14.1, the factor income equals the area of the blue rectangle. This income is the total income received by the factor. Each person who supplies the factor receives the factor price multiplied by the quantity supplied by that person. Changes in demand and supply change the equilibrium price and quantity and change income.

An increase in demand shifts the demand curve rightward and increases price, quantity, and income. An increase in supply shifts the supply curve rightward and decreases price. The quantity used increases, but income might increase, decrease, or remain constant. The change in income that results from a change in supply depends on the elasticity of demand for the factor. If demand is elastic, income rises; if demand is inelastic, income falls; and if demand is unit elastic, income remains constant (see Chapter 4, p. 88).

The rest of this chapter explores the influences on the demand for and supply of factors of production. It also explains the influences on the elasticities of supply and demand for factors of production. These elasticities have major effects on factor prices, quantities used, and incomes.

We begin with the market for labour. But most of what we will learn about the labour market also applies to the other factor markets that we study later in the chapter.

FIGURE 14.1 Demand and Supply in a Factor Market

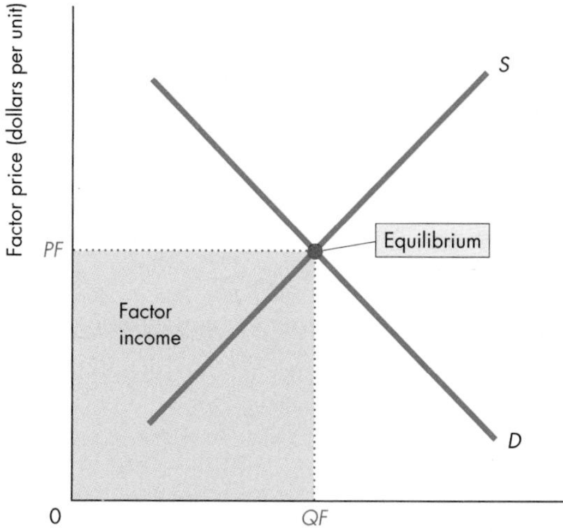

The demand curve for a factor of production (*D*) slopes downward, and the supply curve (*S*) slopes upward. Where the demand and supply curves intersect, the factor price (*PF*) and the quantity of the factor used (*QF*) are determined. The factor income is the factor price multiplied by the quantity of the factor, as represented by the blue rectangle.

Labour Markets

FOR MOST OF US, THE LABOUR MARKET IS OUR only source of income. And in recent years, many people have had a tough time. But over the years, both wages and the quantity of labour have moved steadily upward. Figure 14.2(a) shows the record since 1961. Using 1997 dollars to remove the effects of inflation, total compensation per hour of work increased by about 100 percent, from $9.58 in 1961 to $19.93 in 2001. Over the same period, the quantity of labour employed increased by more than 100 percent, from 12.7 billion hours in 1961 to 27 billion hours in 2001.

Figure 14.2(b) shows why these trends occurred. The demand for labour increased from LD_{61} to LD_{01}, and this increase was much larger than the increase in the supply of labour from LS_{61} to LS_{01}.

A lot of diversity lies behind the average wage rate and the aggregate quantity of labour. During the 1980s and 1990s, some wage rates grew much more rapidly than the average and others fell. To understand the trends in the labour market, we must probe the forces that influence the demand for labour and the supply of labour. This chapter studies these forces. We begin on the demand side of the labour market.

The Demand for Labour

The demand for labour is a derived demand. A **derived demand** is a demand for a factor of production that is *derived* from the demand for the goods and services produced by that factor of production. The derived demand for labour (and for the other factors demanded by firms) is driven by the firm's objective, which is to maximize profit.

You learned in Chapters 11, 12, and 13 that a profit-maximizing firm produces the output at which marginal cost equals marginal revenue. This principle holds true for all firms regardless of whether they operate in perfect competition, monopolistic competition, oligopoly, or monopoly.

A firm that maximizes profit hires the quantity of labour that can produce the profit-maximizing output. What is that quantity of labour? And how does the quantity of labour used change as the wage rate changes? We can answer these questions by comparing the *marginal* revenue earned by hiring one more worker with the *marginal* cost of that worker. Let's look first at the marginal revenue side of this comparison.

FIGURE 14.2 Labour Market Trends in Canada

(a) Labour and wage rate

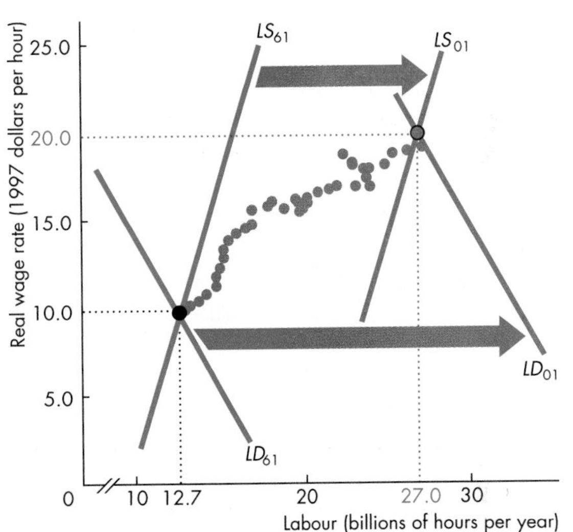

(b) Changes in demand and supply in the labour market

Between 1961 and 2001, the real wage rate doubled and the quantity of labour employed more than doubled. Part (a) shows these increases. Each dot in part (b) shows the real wage rate and the quantity of labour in each year from 1961 to 2001. Part (b) also shows the changes in demand and supply that generated these trends. The demand for labour increased from LD_{61} to LD_{01}, and the supply of labour increased from LS_{61} to LS_{01}. Demand increased by more than supply increased, so both the wage rate and the quantity of labour employed increased.

Source: Statistics Canada, CANSIM tables 282–0002, 282–0022, and 380–0001.

Marginal Revenue Product

The change in total revenue that results from employing one more unit of labour is called the **marginal revenue product** of labour. Table 14.1 shows you how to calculate marginal revenue product for a firm in perfect competition.

The first two columns show the total product schedule for Max's Wash 'n' Wax car wash service. The numbers tell us how the number of car washes per hour varies as the quantity of labour varies. The third column shows the *marginal product of labour*—the change in total product that results from a one-unit increase in the quantity of labour employed. (Look back at p. 219 for a quick refresher on this concept.)

The car wash market in which Max operates is perfectly competitive, and he can sell as many washes as he chooses at $4 a wash, the (assumed) market price. So Max's *marginal revenue* is $4 a wash.

Given this information, we can now calculate *marginal revenue product* (the fourth column). It equals marginal product multiplied by marginal revenue. For example, the marginal product of hiring a second worker is 4 car washes an hour, and because marginal revenue is $4 a wash, the marginal revenue product of the second worker is $16 (4 washes at $4 each).

The last two columns of Table 14.1 show an alternative way to calculate the marginal revenue product of labour. Total revenue is equal to total product multiplied by price. For example, two workers produce 9 washes per hour and generate a total revenue of $36 (9 washes at $4 each). One worker produces 5 washes per hour and generates a total revenue of $20 (5 washes at $4 each). Marginal revenue product, in the sixth column, is the change in total revenue from hiring one more worker. When the second worker is hired, total revenue increases from $20 to $36, an increase of $16. So the marginal revenue product of the second worker is $16, which agrees with our previous calculation.

Diminishing Marginal Revenue Product As the quantity of labour increases, marginal revenue product diminishes. For a firm in perfect competition, marginal revenue product diminishes because marginal product diminishes. In monopoly (or monopolistic competition or oligopoly), marginal revenue product diminishes for a second reason. When more labour is hired and total product increases, the firm must cut its price to sell the extra product. So marginal product and marginal revenue decrease, both of which decrease marginal revenue product.

TABLE 14.1 Marginal Revenue Product at Max's Wash 'n' Wax

	Quantity of labour (L) (workers)	Total product (TP) (car washes per hour)	Marginal product ($MP = \Delta TP/\Delta L$) (washes per worker)	Marginal revenue product ($MRP = MR \times MP$) (dollars per worker)	Total revenue ($TR = P \times TP$) (dollars)	Marginal revenue product ($MRP = \Delta TR/\Delta L$) (dollars per worker)
A	0	0			0	
			5	20		20
B	1	5			20	
			4	16		16
C	2	9			36	
			3	12		12
D	3	12			48	
			2	8		8
E	4	14			56	
			1	4		4
F	5	15			60	

The car wash market is perfectly competitive, and the price is $4 a wash. Marginal revenue is also $4 a wash. Marginal revenue product equals marginal product (column 3) multiplied by marginal revenue. For example, the marginal product of the second worker is 4 washes and marginal revenue is $4 a wash, so the marginal revenue product of the second worker (in column 4) is $16. Alternatively, if Max hires 1 worker (row *B*), total product is 5 washes an hour and total revenue is $20 (column 5). If he hires 2 workers (row *C*), total product is 9 washes an hour and total revenue is $36. By hiring the second worker, total revenue rises by $16—the marginal revenue product of labour is $16.

The Labour Demand Curve

Figure 14.3 shows how the labour demand curve is derived from the marginal revenue product curve. The *marginal revenue product curve* graphs the marginal revenue product of a factor at each quantity of the factor hired. Figure 14.3(a) illustrates the marginal revenue product curve for workers employed by Max. The horizontal axis measures the number of workers that Max hires, and the vertical axis measures the marginal revenue product of labour. The blue bars show the marginal revenue product of labour as Max employs more workers. These bars correspond to the numbers in Table 14.1. The curve labelled *MRP* is Max's marginal revenue product curve.

A firm's marginal revenue product curve is also its demand for labour curve. Figure 14.3(b) shows Max's demand for labour curve (*D*). The horizontal axis measures the number of workers hired—the same as in part (a). The vertical axis measures the wage rate in dollars per hour. In Fig. 14.3(a), when Max increases the quantity of labour employed from 2 workers an hour to 3 workers an hour, his marginal revenue product is \$12 an hour. In Fig. 14.3(b), at a wage rate of \$12 an hour, Max employs 3 workers an hour.

The marginal revenue product curve is also the demand for labour curve because the firm hires the profit-maximizing quantity of labour. If the wage rate is *less* than marginal revenue product, the firm can increase its profit by employing one more worker. Conversely, if the wage rate is *greater* than marginal revenue product, the firm can increase its profit by employing one fewer worker. But if the wage rate *equals* marginal revenue product, then the firm cannot increase its profit by changing the number of workers it employs. The firm is making the maximum possible profit. Thus the quantity of labour demanded by the firm is such that the wage rate equals the marginal revenue product of labour.

Because the marginal revenue product curve is also the demand curve, and because marginal revenue product diminishes as the quantity of labour employed increases, the demand for labour curve slopes downward. The lower the wage rate, other things remaining the same, the more workers a firm hires.

When we studied firms' output decisions, we discovered that a condition for maximum profit is that marginal revenue equals marginal cost. We've now discovered another condition for maximum profit: Marginal revenue product of a factor equals the factor's price. Let's study the connection between these two conditions.

FIGURE 14.3 The Demand for Labour at Max's Wash 'n' Wax

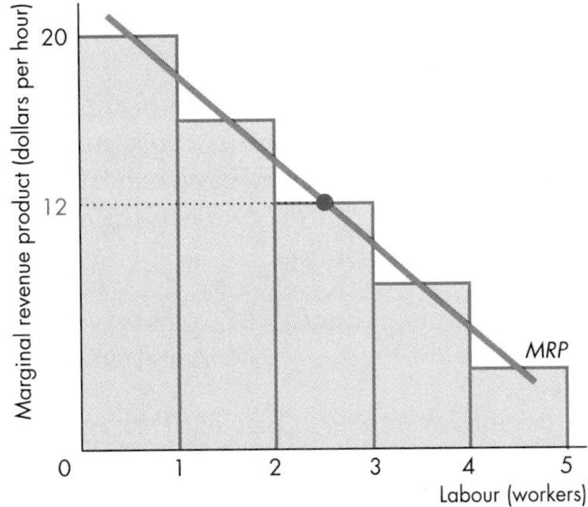

(a) Marginal revenue product

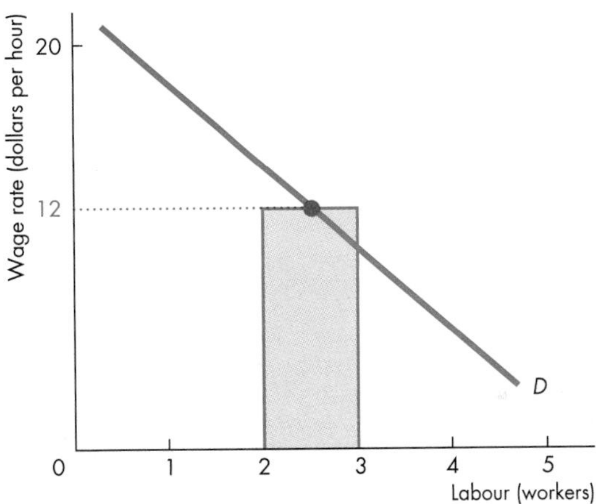

(b) Demand for labour

Max's Wash 'n' Wax operates in a perfectly competitive car wash market and can sell any quantity of washes at \$4 a wash. The blue bars in part (a) represent the firm's marginal revenue product of labour. They are based on the numbers in Table 14.1. The orange line is the firm's marginal revenue product of labour curve. Part (b) shows Max's demand for labour curve. This curve is identical to Max's marginal revenue product curve. Max demands the quantity of labour that makes the wage rate equal to the marginal revenue product of labour. The demand for labour curve slopes downward because marginal revenue product diminishes as the quantity of labour employed increases.

Equivalence of Two Conditions for Profit Maximization

Profit is maximized when, at the quantity of labour hired, *marginal revenue product* equals the wage rate and when, at the quantity produced, *marginal revenue* equals *marginal cost.*

These two conditions for maximum profit are equivalent. The quantity of labour that maximizes profit produces the output that maximizes profit.

To see the equivalence of the two conditions for maximum profit, first recall that

Marginal revenue product = Marginal revenue × Marginal product.

If we call marginal revenue product *MRP*, marginal revenue *MR*, and marginal product *MP*, we have

$$MRP = MR \times MP.$$

If we call the wage rate *W*, the first condition for profit to be maximized is

$$MRP = W.$$

But $MRP = MR \times MP$, so

$$MR \times MP = W.$$

This equation tells us that when profit is maximized, marginal revenue multiplied by marginal product equals the wage rate.

Divide the last equation by marginal product, *MP*, to obtain

$$MR = W \div MP.$$

This equation states that when profit is maximized, marginal revenue equals the wage rate divided by the marginal product of labour.

The wage rate divided by the marginal product of labour equals marginal cost. It costs the firm *W* to hire one more hour of labour. But the labour produces *MP* units of output. So the cost of producing one of those units of output, which is marginal cost, is *W* divided by *MP*.

If we call marginal cost *MC*, then

$$MR = MC,$$

which is the second condition for maximum profit.

Because the first condition for maximum profit implies the second condition, these two conditions are equivalent. Table 14.2 summarizes the calculations you've just done and shows the equivalence of the two conditions for maximum profit.

TABLE 14.2 Two Conditions for Maximum Profit

Symbols

Marginal product	***MP***
Marginal revenue	***MR***
Marginal cost	***MC***
Marginal revenue product	***MRP***
Factor price	***PF***

Two Conditions for Maximum Profit

1. $MR = MC$ 2. $MRP = PF$

Equivalence of Conditions

1. $MRP/MP = MR$ = $MC = PF/MP$

Multiply by *MP* to give *MRP* = *MR* x *MP* Flipping the equation over

Multiply by *MP* to give *MC* x *MP* = *PF* Flipping the equation over

2. $MR \times MP = MRP$ = $PF = MC \times MP$

The two conditions for maximum profit are that marginal revenue (*MR*) equals marginal cost (*MC*) and that marginal revenue product (*MRP*) equals the wage rate (*W*). These two conditions are equivalent because marginal revenue product (*MRP*) equals marginal revenue (*MR*) multiplied by marginal product (*MP*) and the wage rate (*W*) equals marginal cost (*MC*) multiplied by marginal product (*MP*).

Max's Numbers Check the numbers for Max's Wash 'n' Wax and confirm that the conditions you've just examined work. Max's profit-maximizing labour decision is to hire 3 workers if the wage rate is $12 an hour. When Max hires 3 hours of labour, marginal product is 3 washes per hour. Max sells the 3 washes an hour for a marginal revenue of $4 a wash. So marginal revenue product is 3 washes multiplied by $4 a wash, which equals $12 per hour. At a wage rate of $12 an hour, Max is maximizing profit.

Equivalently, Max's marginal cost is $12 an hour divided by 3 washes per hour, which equals $4 per wash. At a marginal revenue of $4 a wash, Max is maximizing profit.

You've discovered that the law of demand applies for labour just as it does for goods and services. Other things remaining the same, the lower the wage rate (the price of labour), the greater is the quantity of labour demanded.

Let's now study the influences that change the demand for labour and shift the demand for labour curve.

Changes in the Demand for Labour

The demand for labour depends on three factors:

1. The price of the firm's output
2. The prices of other factors of production
3. Technology

The higher the price of a firm's output, the greater is its demand for labour. The price of output affects the demand for labour through its influence on marginal revenue product. A higher price for the firm's output increases marginal revenue, which, in turn, increases the marginal revenue product of labour. A change in the price of a firm's output leads to a shift in the firm's demand for labour curve. If the price of the firm's output increases, the demand for labour increases and the demand for labour curve shifts rightward.

The other two influences affect the *long-run demand for labour*, which is the relationship between the wage rate and the quantity of labour demanded when all factors of production can be varied. In contrast, the *short-run demand for labour* is the relationship between the wage rate and the quantity of labour demanded when the quantities of the other factors are fixed and labour is the only variable factor. In the long run, a change in the relative price of factors of production—such as the relative price of labour and capital—leads to a substitution away from the factor whose relative price has increased and towards the factor whose relative price has decreased. So if the price of capital decreases relative to that of using labour, the firm substitutes capital for labour and increases the quantity of capital demanded.

But the demand for labour might increase or decrease. If the lower price of capital increases the scale of production by enough, the demand for labour increases. Otherwise, the demand for labour decreases.

Finally, a new technology that changes the marginal product of labour changes the demand for labour. For example, the electronic telephone exchange has decreased the demand for telephone operators. This same new technology has increased the demand for telephone engineers. Again, these effects are felt in the long run when the firm adjusts all its resources and incorporates new technologies into its production process. Table 14.3 summarizes the influences on a firm's demand for labour.

We saw in Fig. 14.2 that the demand for labour has increased over time and the demand curve has shifted rightward. We can now give some of the reasons for this increase in demand. Advances in technology and investment in new capital increase the marginal product of labour and increase the demand for labour.

TABLE 14.3 A Firm's Demand for Labour

The Law of Demand

(Movements along the demand curve for labour)

The quantity of labour demanded by a firm

Decreases if:	*Increases if:*
■ The wage rate increases	■ The wage rate decreases

Changes in Demand

(Shifts in the demand curve for labour)

A firm's demand for labour

Decreases if:	*Increases if:*
■ The firm's output price decreases	■ The firm's output price increases
■ A new technology decreases the marginal product of labour	■ A new technology increases the marginal product of labour

(Changes in the prices of other factors of production have an ambiguous effect on the demand for labour.)

Market Demand

So far, we've studied the demand for labour by an individual firm. The market demand for labour is the total demand by all firms. The market demand for labour curve is derived (similarly to the market demand curve for any good or service) by adding together the quantities demanded by all firms at each wage rate. Because a firm's demand for labour curve slopes downward, so does the market demand curve.

Elasticity of Demand for Labour

The elasticity of demand for labour measures the responsiveness of the quantity of labour demanded to the wage rate. This elasticity is important because it tells us how labour income changes when the supply of labour changes. An increase in supply (other things remaining the same) brings a lower wage rate. If demand is inelastic, it also brings lower labour income. But if demand is elastic, an increase in supply brings a lower wage rate and an increase in labour income. And if the demand for labour is unit elastic, a change in supply leaves labour income unchanged.

The demand for labour is less elastic in the short run, when only the quantity of labour can be varied, than in the long run, when the quantities of labour and other factors of production can be varied. The elasticity of demand for labour depends on the

- Labour intensity of the production process
- Elasticity of demand for the product
- Substitutability of capital for labour

Labour Intensity of the Production Process A labour-intensive production process is one that uses a lot of labour and little capital. Home building is an example. The greater the degree of labour intensity, the more elastic is the demand for labour. To see why, first suppose that wages are 90 percent of total cost. A 10 percent increase in the wage rate increases total cost by 9 percent. Firms will be sensitive to such a large change in total cost, so if wages increase, firms will decrease the quantity of labour demanded by a relatively large amount. But if wages are 10 percent of total cost, a 10 percent increase in the wage rate increases total cost by only 1 percent. Firms will be less sensitive to this increase in cost, so if wages increase in this case, firms will decrease the quantity of labour demanded by a relatively small amount.

Elasticity of Demand for the Product The greater the elasticity of demand for the good, the larger is the elasticity of demand for the labour used to produce it. An increase in the wage rate increases marginal cost and decreases the supply of the good. The decrease in the supply of the good increases the price of the good and decreases the quantity demanded of the good and the quantities of the factors of production used to produce it. The greater the elasticity of demand for the good, the larger is the decrease in the quantity demanded of the good and so the larger is the decrease in the quantities of the factors of production used to produce it.

Substitutability of Capital for Labour The more easily capital can be used instead of labour in production, the more elastic is the long-run demand for labour. For example, it is easy to use robots rather than assembly-line workers in car factories and grape-picking machines for labour in vineyards. So the demand for these types of labour is elastic. At the other extreme, it is difficult (though possible) to substitute computers for newspaper reporters, bank loan officers, and teachers. So the demand for these types of labour is inelastic.

Let's now turn from the demand side of the labour market to the supply side and examine the decisions that people make about how to allocate their time between working and other activities.

The Supply of Labour

People can allocate their time to two broad activities: labour supply and leisure. (Leisure is a catch-all term. It includes all activities other than supplying labour.) For most people, leisure is more enjoyable than supplying labour. We'll look at the labour supply decision of Jill, who is like most people. She enjoys her leisure time, and she would be pleased if she didn't have to spend her weekends working a supermarket checkout line.

But Jill has chosen to work weekends. The reason is that she is offered a wage rate that exceeds her *reservation wage.* Jill's reservation wage is the lowest wage at which she is willing to supply labour. If the wage rate exceeds her reservation wage, she supplies some labour. But how much labour does she supply? The quantity of labour that Jill supplies depends on the wage rate.

Substitution Effect Other things remaining the same, the higher the wage rate Jill is offered, at least over a range, the greater is the quantity of labour that she supplies. The reason is that Jill's wage rate is her *opportunity cost of leisure.* If she quits work an hour early to catch a movie, the cost of that extra hour of leisure is the wage rate that Jill forgoes. The higher the wage rate, the less willing is Jill to forgo the income and take the extra leisure time. This tendency for a higher wage rate to induce Jill to work longer hours is a *substitution effect.*

But there is also an *income effect* that works in the opposite direction to the substitution effect.

Income Effect The higher Jill's wage rate, the higher is her income. A higher income, other things remaining the same, induces Jill to increase her demand for most goods. Leisure is one of those goods. Because an increase in income creates an increase in the demand for leisure, it also creates a decrease in the quantity of labour supplied.

Backward-Bending Supply of Labour Curve As the wage rate rises, the substitution effect brings an increase in the quantity of labour supplied while the income effect brings a decrease in the quantity of labour supplied. At low wage rates, the substitution effect is larger than the income effect, so as the wage rate rises, people supply more labour. But as the wage rate continues to rise, the income effect eventually becomes larger than the substitution effect and the quantity of labour supplied decreases. The labour supply curve is *backward bending.*

Figure 14.4(a) shows the labour supply curves for Jill, Jack, and Kelly. Each labour supply curve is backward bending, but the three people have different reservation wage rates.

Market Supply The market supply of labour curve is the sum of the individual supply curves. Figure 14.4(b) shows the market supply curve (S_M) derived from the supply curves of Jill, Jack, and Kelly (S_A, S_B, and S_C, respectively) in Fig. 14.4(a). At wage rates of less than $1 an hour, no one supplies any labour. At wage rates greater than $1 an hour, Jill works but Jack and Kelly don't. As the wage rate increases and reaches $7 an hour, all three of them are working. The market supply curve S_M eventually bends backward, but it has a long upward-sloping section.

Changes in the Supply of Labour The supply of labour changes when influences other than the wage rate change. The key factors that change the supply of labour and that over the years have increased it are

FIGURE 14.4 The Supply of Labour

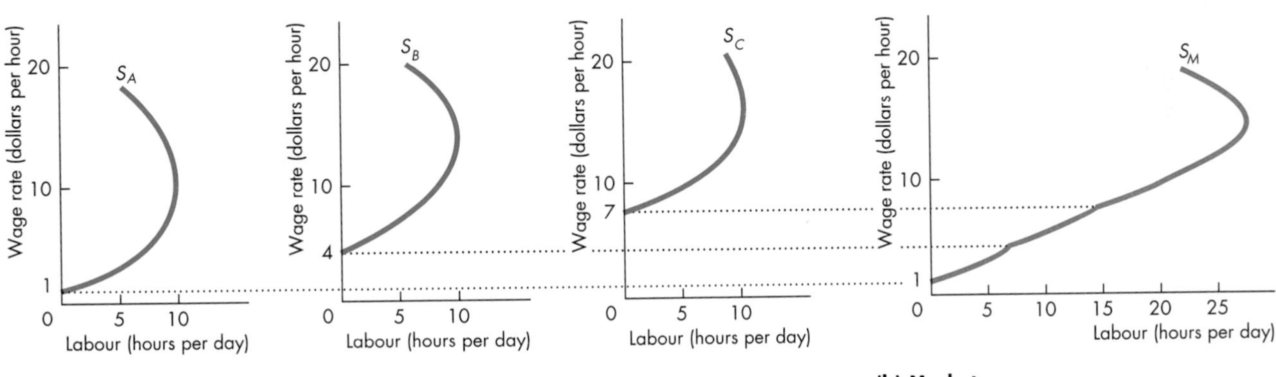

(a) Jill, Jack, and Kelly

(b) Market

Part (a) shows the labour supply curves of Jill (S_A), Jack (S_B), and Kelly (S_C). Each person has a reservation wage below which she or he will supply no labour. As the wage rises, the quantity of labour supplied increases to a maximum. If the wage continues to rise, the quantity of labour supplied begins to decrease. Each person's supply curve eventually bends backward.

Part (b) shows how, by adding the quantities of labour supplied by each person at each wage rate, we derive the market supply curve (S_M). The market supply curve has a long upward-sloping region before it bends backward.

1. Adult population
2. Technological change and capital accumulation

An increase in the adult population increases the supply of labour. So does a technological change or increase in capital in home production (of meals, laundry services, and cleaning services). These factors that increase the supply of labour shift the labour supply curve rightward.

Let's now build on what we've learned about the demand for labour and the supply of labour and study labour market equilibrium and the trends in wage rates and employment.

Labour Market Equilibrium

Wages and employment are determined by equilibrium in the labour market. You saw, in Fig. 14.2, that the wage rate and employment have both increased over the years. You can now explain why.

Trends in the Demand for Labour The demand for labour has *increased* because of technological change and capital accumulation, and the demand for labour curve has shifted steadily rightward.

Many people are surprised that technological change and capital accumulation *increase* the demand for labour. They see new technologies *destroying jobs,* not creating them. Downsizing has become a catchword as the computer and information age has eliminated millions of "good" jobs, even those of managers. So how can it be that technological change *creates* jobs and increases the demand for labour?

Technological change destroys some jobs and creates others. But it creates more jobs than it destroys, and *on the average,* the new jobs pay more than the old ones did. But to benefit from the advances in technology, people must acquire new skills and change their jobs. For example, during the past 20 years, the demand for typists has fallen almost to zero. But the demand for people who can type (on a computer rather than a typewriter) and do other things as well has increased. And the output of these people is worth more than that of a typist. So the demand for people with typing (and other) skills has increased.

Trends in the Supply of Labour The supply of labour has increased because of population growth and technological change and capital accumulation in the home. The mechanization of home production of fast-food preparation services (the freezer and the microwave oven) and laundry services (the automatic washer and dryer and wrinkle-free fabrics) has decreased the time spent on activities that once were full-time jobs and has led to a large increase in the supply of labour. As a result, the labour supply curve has shifted steadily rightward, but more slowly than the labour demand curve has shifted.

Trends in Equilibrium Because technological advances and capital accumulation have increased demand by more than population growth and technological change in home production have increased supply, both wages and employment have increased. But not everyone has shared in the increased prosperity that comes from higher wage rates. Some groups have been left behind, and some have even seen their wage rates fall. Why?

Two key reasons can be identified. First, technological change affects the marginal productivity of different groups in different ways. High-skilled computer-literate workers have benefited from the information revolution while low-skilled workers have suffered. The demand for the services of the first group has increased, and the demand for the services of the second group has decreased. (Draw a supply and demand figure, and you will see that these changes widen the wage difference between the two groups.) Second, international competition has lowered the marginal revenue product of low-skilled workers and so has decreased the demand for their labour. We look further at skill differences and at trends in the distribution of income in Chapter 15.

REVIEW QUIZ

1. Why do we call the demand for labour a *derived demand*? From what is it derived?
2. What is the distinction between marginal revenue product and marginal revenue? Provide an example that illustrates the distinction.
3. When a firm's marginal revenue product equals the wage rate, marginal revenue also equals marginal cost. Why? Provide a numerical example different from that in the text.
4. What determines the amount of labour that households plan to supply?
5. Describe and explain the trends in wage rates and employment.

Capital Markets

CAPITAL MARKETS ARE THE CHANNELS THROUGH which firms obtain *financial* resources to buy *physical* capital resources. These financial resources come from saving. The "price of capital," which adjusts to make the quantity of capital supplied equal to the quantity demanded, is the interest rate.

For most of us, capital markets are where we make our biggest-ticket transactions. We borrow in a capital market to buy a home. And we lend in capital markets to build up a fund on which to live when we retire. Do the rates of return in capital markets increase as wage rates do?

Figure 14.5(a) answers this question by showing the record since 1965. Measuring interest rates as *real* interest rates, which means that we subtract the loss in the value of money from inflation, returns have fluctuated. They ranged 2 to 3 percent a year in the 1960s, became negative in the mid-1970s, bounced back and climbed to 9 percent by the mid-1980s, were steady at about 7 percent in the late 1980s and early 1990s, and fell to about 4 percent in the late 1990s and early 2000s. Over the same period, the quantity of capital employed increased steadily. In 2001, it stood at $2.6 trillion, almost four times its 1965 level.

Figure 14.5(b) shows why these trends occurred. Demand increased from KD_{65} to KD_{01}, and this increase was similar to the increase in supply from KS_{65} to KS_{01}. To understand the trends in the capital market, we must again probe the forces of demand and supply. Many of the ideas you've already met in your study of the labour market apply to the capital market as well. But there are some special features of capital. Its main special feature is that in the capital market, people must compare *present* costs with *future* benefits. Let's discover how people make these comparisons by studying the demand for capital.

The Demand for Capital

A firm's demand for *financial* capital stems from its demand for *physical* capital, and the amount that a firm plans to borrow in a given time period is determined by its planned investment—purchases of new capital. This decision is driven by its attempt to maximize profit. As a firm increases the quantity of capital employed, other things remaining the same, the marginal revenue product of capital eventually

FIGURE 14.5 Capital Market Trends in Canada

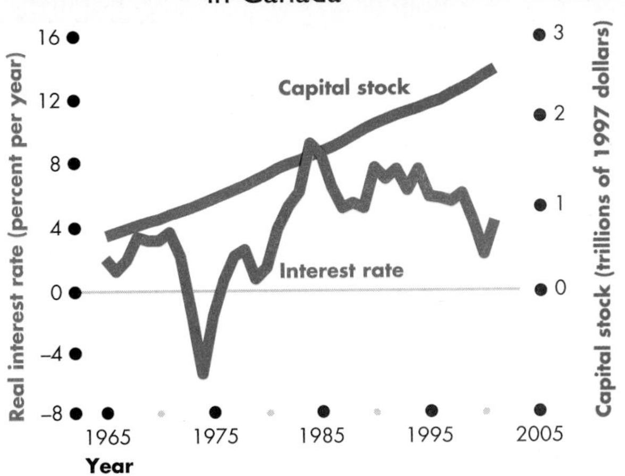

(a) Capital stock and interest rate

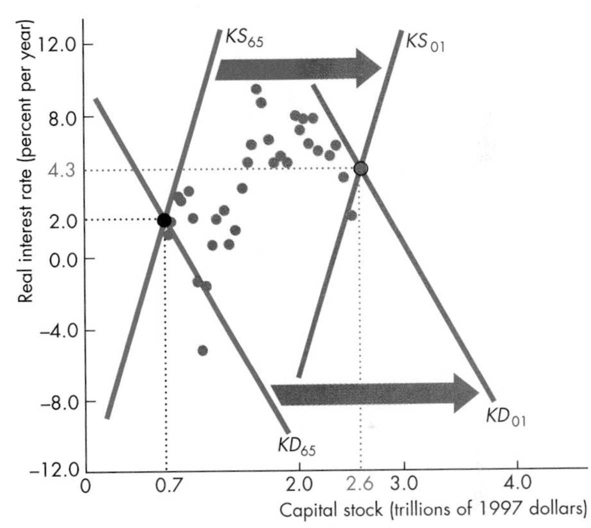

(b) Changes in demand and supply in the capital market

The real interest rate (the interest rate adjusted for inflation) fluctuated between a negative return in 1973 through 1975 and a high of 9 percent in 1984. It fluctuated between 2 and 3 percent during the 1960s and was at about 5 percent during the 1990s and 2000s. During the same period, the quantity of capital increased. By 2001, it was almost four times its 1965 level. Part (a) shows these trends. Part (b) shows the changes in demand and supply of capital that have generated the trends. The demand for capital increased from KD_{65} to KD_{01}, and the supply of capital increased from KS_{65} to KS_{01}.

Sources: Statistics Canada, CANSIM tables 378–0004 and 176–0043.

diminishes. To maximize profit, a firm increases its plant size and uses more capital if the marginal revenue product of capital exceeds the price of capital. But the marginal revenue product comes in the future, and capital must be paid for in the present. So the firm must convert *future* marginal revenue products into a *present value* so that this value can be compared with the price of the new equipment. To make this conversion, we use the technique of discounting.

Discounting and Present Value

Discounting is converting a future amount of money to a present value. And the **present value** of a future amount of money is the amount that, if invested today, will grow to be as large as that future amount when the interest that it will earn is taken into account.

The easiest way to understand discounting and present value is to begin with the relationship among an amount invested today, the interest that it earns, and the amount to which it will grow in the future. The future amount is equal to the present amount (present value) plus the interest it will accumulate in the future. That is,

$$\text{Future amount} = \text{Present value} + \text{Interest income.}$$

The interest income is equal to the present value multiplied by the interest rate, r, so

$$\text{Future amount} = \text{Present value} + (r \times \text{Present value})$$

or

$$\text{Future amount} = \text{Present value} \times (1 + r).$$

If you have \$100 today and the interest rate is 10 percent a year ($r = 0.1$), one year from today you will have \$110—the original \$100 plus \$10 interest. Check that the above formula delivers that answer: $\$100 \times 1.1 = \$110$.

The formula that we have just used calculates a future amount one year from today from the present value and an interest rate. To calculate the present value, we just work backwards. Instead of multiplying the present value by $(1 + r)$, we divide the future amount by $(1 + r)$. That is,

$$\text{Present value} = \frac{\text{Future value}}{(1 + r)}.$$

You can use this formula to calculate present value. This calculation of present value is called discounting. Let's check that we can use the present value formula by calculating the present value of \$110 one year from now when the interest rate is 10 percent a year. You'll be able to guess that the answer is \$100 because we just calculated that \$100 invested today at 10 percent a year becomes \$110 in one year. Thus it follows immediately that the present value of \$110 in one year's time is \$100. But let's use the formula. Putting the numbers into the above formula, we have

$$\text{Present value} = \frac{\$110}{(1 + 0.1)}$$

$$= \frac{\$110}{1.1} = \$100.$$

Calculating the present value of an amount of money one year from now is the easiest case. But we can also calculate the present value of an amount any number of years in the future. As an example, let's see how we calculate the present value of an amount of money that will be available two years from now.

Suppose that you invest \$100 today for two years at an interest rate of 10 percent a year. The money will earn \$10 in the first year, which means that by the end of the first year, you will have \$110. If the interest of \$10 is invested, then the interest earned in the second year will be a further \$10 on the original \$100 plus \$1 on the \$10 interest. Thus the total interest earned in the second year will be \$11. The total interest earned overall will be \$21 (\$10 in the first year and \$11 in the second year). After two years, you will have \$121. From the definition of present value, you can see that the present value of \$121 two years hence is \$100. That is, \$100 is the present amount that, if invested at an interest rate of 10 percent a year, will grow to \$121 two years from now.

To calculate the present value of an amount of money two years in the future, we use the formula:

$$\text{Present value} = \frac{\text{Amount of money two years in future}}{(1 + r)^2}.$$

Use this formula to calculate the present value of \$121 two years from now at an interest rate of 10 percent a year. With these numbers, the formula gives

$$\text{Present value} = \frac{\$121}{(1 + 0.1)^2}$$

$$= \frac{\$121}{(1.1)^2}$$

$$= \frac{\$121}{1.21}$$

$$= \$100.$$

We can calculate the present value of an amount of money n years in the future by using a formula similar to the one we've already used. The general formula is

$$\text{Present value} = \frac{\text{Amount of money } n \text{ years in future}}{(1 + r)^n}.$$

For example, if the interest rate is 10 percent a year, \$100 to be received 10 years from now has a present value of \$38.55. That is, if \$38.55 is invested today at 10 percent a year, the amount will grow to \$100 in 10 years.

You've seen how to calculate the present value of an amount of money one year in the future, two years in the future, and n years in the future. Most practical applications of present value calculate the present value of a sequence of future amounts of money that spread over several years. To calculate the present value of a sequence of amounts over several years, we use the formula you have learned and apply it to each year. We then sum the present values for each year to find the present value of the sequence of amounts.

For example, suppose that a firm expects to receive \$100 a year for each of the next five years. And suppose that the interest rate is 10 percent per year (0.1 per year). The present value of these five payments of \$100 each is calculated by using the following formula:

$$PV = \frac{\$100}{1.1} + \frac{\$100}{1.1^2} + \frac{\$100}{1.1^3} + \frac{\$100}{1.1^4} + \frac{\$100}{1.1^5},$$

which equals

$$PV = \$90.91 + \$82.64 + \$75.13 + \$68.30 + \$62.09$$

$$= \$379.07.$$

You can see that the firm receives \$500 over five years. But because the money arrives in the future, it is not worth \$500 today. Its present value is only \$379.07. And the farther in the future it arrives, the smaller is its present value. The \$100 received one year in the future is worth \$90.91 today. And the \$100 received five years in the future is worth only \$62.09 today.

Let's now see how a firm uses the concept of present value to achieve an efficient use of capital.

The Present Value of a Computer

We'll see how a firm decides how much capital to buy by calculating the present value of a new computer. Tina runs Taxfile, Inc., a firm that sells advice to taxpayers. Tina is considering buying a new computer that costs \$10,000. The computer has a life of two years, after which it will be worthless. If Tina buys the computer, she will pay \$10,000 now and she expects to generate business that will bring in an additional \$5,900 at the end of each of the next two years.

To calculate the present value, PV, of the marginal revenue product of a new computer, Tina calculates

$$PV = \frac{MRP_1}{(1 + r)} + \frac{MRP_2}{(1 + r)^2}.$$

Here, MRP_1 is the marginal revenue product received by Tina at the end of the first year. It is converted to a present value by dividing it by $(1 + r)$, where r is the interest rate (expressed as a proportion). The term MRP_2 is the marginal revenue product received at the end of the second year. It is converted to a present value by dividing it by $(1 + r)^2$.

If Tina can borrow or lend at an interest rate of 4 percent a year, the present value of her marginal revenue product is given by

$$PV = \frac{\$5{,}900}{(1 + 0.04)} + \frac{\$5{,}900}{(1 + 0.04)^2}$$

$$PV = \$5{,}673 + \$5{,}455$$

$$PV = \$11{,}128.$$

The present value (PV) of \$5,900 one year in the future is \$5,900 divided by 1.04 (4 percent as a proportion is 0.04). The present value of \$5,900 two years in the future is \$5,900 divided by $(1.04)^2$. Tina works out those two present values and then adds them to get the present value of the future flow of marginal revenue product, which is \$11,128.

Parts (a) and (b) of Table 14.4 summarize the data and the calculations we've just made. Review these calculations and make sure you understand them.

TABLE 14.4 Net Present Value of an Investment—Taxfile, Inc.

(a) Data

Price of computer	$10,000
Life of computer	2 years
Marginal revenue product	$5,900 at end of each year
Interest rate	4% a year

(b) Present value of the flow of marginal revenue product

$$PV = \frac{MRP_1}{(1 + r)} + \frac{MRP_2}{(1 + r)^2}$$

$$= \frac{\$5,900}{1.04} + \frac{\$5,900}{(1.04)^2}$$

$$= \$5,673 + \$5,455$$

$$= \$11,128.$$

(c) Net present value of investment

$NPV = PV$ of marginal revenue product − Price of computer
= $11,128 − $10,000
= $1,128

Tina's Decision to Buy Tina decides whether to buy the computer by comparing the present value of its future flow of marginal revenue product with its purchase price. She makes this comparison by calculating the net present value (*NPV*) of the computer. **Net present value** is the present value of the future flow of marginal revenue product generated by the capital minus the price of the capital. If the net present value is positive, the firm buys additional capital. If the net present value is negative, the firm does not buy additional capital. Table 14.4(c) shows the calculation of Tina's net present value of a computer. The net present value is $1,128—greater than zero—so Tina buys the computer.

Tina can buy any number of computers that cost $10,000 and have a life of two years. But like all other factors of production, capital is subject to diminishing marginal returns. The greater the amount of capital employed, the smaller is its marginal revenue product. So if Tina buys a second computer or a third one, she gets successively smaller marginal revenue products from the additional machines.

Table 14.5(a) sets out Tina's marginal revenue products for one, two, and three computers. The marginal revenue product of one computer (the case just reviewed) is $5,900 a year. The marginal revenue product of a second computer is $5,600 a year, and the marginal revenue product of a third computer is $5,300 a year. Table 14.5(b) shows the calculations of the present values of the marginal revenue products of the first, second, and third computers.

You've seen that with an interest rate of 4 percent a year, the net present value of one computer is positive. At an interest rate of 4 percent a year, the present value of the marginal revenue product of a second computer is $10,562, which exceeds its price by $562. So Tina buys a second computer. But at an interest rate of 4 percent a year, the present value of the marginal revenue product of a third computer is $9,996, which is $4 less than the price of the computer. So Tina does not buy a third computer.

A Change in the Interest Rate We've seen that at an interest rate of 4 percent a year, Tina buys two computers but not three. Suppose that the interest rate is 8 percent a year. In this case, the present value of the first computer is $10,521 (see Table 14.5b), so Tina still buys one machine because it has a positive net present value. At an interest rate of 8 percent a year, the net present value of the second computer is $9,986, which is less than $10,000, the price of the computer. So at an interest rate of 8 percent a year, Tina buys only one computer.

Suppose that the interest rate is even higher, 12 percent a year. In this case, the present value of the marginal revenue product of one computer is $9,971 (see Table 14.5b). At this interest rate, Tina buys no computers.

These calculations trace Taxfile's demand schedule for capital, which shows the value of computers demanded by Taxfile at each interest rate. Other things remaining the same, as the interest rate rises, the quantity of capital demanded decreases. The higher the interest rate, the smaller is the quantity of *physical* capital demanded. But to finance the purchase of *physical* capital, firms demand *financial* capital. So the higher the interest rate, the smaller is the quantity of *financial* capital demanded.

TABLE 14.5 Taxfile's Investment Decision

(a) Data

Price of computer	\$10,000
Life of computer	2 years
Marginal revenue product:	
Using 1 computer	\$5,900 a year
Using 2 computers	\$5,600 a year
Using 3 computers	\$5,300 a year

(b) Present value of the flow of marginal revenue product

If $r = 0.04$ (4% a year):

Using 1 computer $PV = \frac{\$5{,}900}{1.04} + \frac{\$5{,}900}{(1.04)^2} = \$11{,}128$

Using 2 computers $PV = \frac{\$5{,}600}{1.04} + \frac{\$5{,}600}{(1.04)^2} = \$10{,}562$

Using 3 computers $PV = \frac{\$5{,}300}{1.04} + \frac{\$5{,}300}{(1.04)^2} = \$9{,}996$

If $r = 0.08$ (8% a year):

Using 1 computer $PV = \frac{\$5{,}900}{1.08} + \frac{\$5{,}900}{(1.08)^2} = \$10{,}521$

Using 2 computers $PV = \frac{\$5{,}600}{1.08} + \frac{\$5{,}600}{(1.08)^2} = \$9{,}986$

If $r = 0.12$ (12% a year):

Using 1 computer $PV = \frac{\$5{,}900}{1.12} + \frac{\$5{,}900}{(1.12)^2} = \$9{,}971$

Demand Curve for Capital

The quantity of capital demanded by a firm depends on the marginal revenue product of capital and the interest rate. A firm's demand curve for capital shows the relationship between the quantity of capital demanded by the firm and the interest rate, other things remaining the same. The market demand curve (as in Fig. 14.5b) shows the relationship between the total quantity of capital demanded and the interest rate, other things remaining the same.

Changes in the Demand for Capital Figure 14.5(b) shows that the demand for capital has increased steadily over the years. The demand for capital changes when expectations about the future marginal revenue product of capital change. An increase in the expected marginal revenue product of capital increases the demand of capital. Two main factors that change the marginal revenue product of capital and bring changes in the demand for capital are

1. Population growth
2. Technological change

An increase in the population increases the demand for all goods and services and so increases the demand for the capital that produces them. Advances in technology increase the demand for some types of capital and decrease the demand for other types. For example, the development of diesel engines for railroad transportation decreased the demand for steam engines and increased the demand for diesel engines. In this case, the railroad industry's overall demand for capital did not change much. In contrast, the development of desktop computers increased the demand for office computing equipment, decreased the demand for electric typewriters, and increased the overall demand for capital in the office.

Let's now turn to the supply side of the capital market.

The Supply of Capital

The quantity of capital supplied results from people's saving decisions. The main factors that determine saving are

- Income
- Expected future income
- Interest rate

To see how these factors influence saving, let's see how Aaron makes his saving decisions.

Income Saving is the act of converting *current* income into *future* consumption. When Aaron's income increases, he plans to consume more both in the present and in the future. But to increase *future* consumption, Aaron must save. So, other things remaining the same, the higher Aaron's income, the more he saves. The relationship between saving and income is remarkably stable. People tend to save a constant proportion of their income.

Expected Future Income Because a major reason for saving is to increase future consumption, the amount that Aaron saves depends not only on his current income but also on his *expected future income.* If Aaron's current income is high and his expected future income is low, he will have a high level of saving. But if Aaron's current income is low and his expected future income is high, he will have a low (perhaps even negative) level of saving.

Young people (especially students) usually have low current incomes compared with their expected future incomes. To smooth out their lifetime consumption, they consume more than they earn and incur debts. Such people have a negative amount of saving. In middle age, most people's incomes reach their peak. At this stage in life, saving is at its maximum. After retirement, people spend part of the wealth they have accumulated during their working lives.

Interest Rate A dollar saved today grows into a dollar plus interest tomorrow. The higher the interest rate, the greater is the amount that a dollar saved today becomes in the future. Thus the higher the interest rate, the greater is the opportunity cost of current consumption. With a higher opportunity cost of current consumption, Aaron cuts his consumption and increases his saving.

Supply Curve of Capital

The supply curve of capital (like that in Fig. 14.5b) shows the relationship between the quantity of capital supplied and the interest rate, other things remaining the same. An increase in the interest rate brings an increase in the quantity of capital supplied and a movement along the supply curve. The supply of capital is inelastic in the short run but is probably quite elastic in the long run. The reason is that in any given year, the total amount of saving is small relative to the stock of capital in existence. So even a large change in the saving rate brings only a small change in the quantity of capital supplied.

Changes in the Supply of Capital The main influences on the supply of capital are the size and age distribution of the population and the level of income.

Other things remaining the same, an increase in the population or an increase in income brings an increase in the supply of capital. Also, other things remaining the same, the larger the proportion of middle-aged people, the higher is the saving rate. The reason is that middle-aged people do most of the saving as they build up a pension fund to provide a retirement income. Any one of the factors that increases the supply of capital shifts the supply curve of capital rightward.

Let's now use what we've learned about the demand for and supply of capital and see how the interest rate is determined.

The Interest Rate

Saving plans and investment plans are coordinated through capital markets, and the real interest rate adjusts to make these plans compatible.

Figure 14.6 shows the capital market. Initially, the demand for capital is KD_0, and the supply of capital is KS_0. The equilibrium real interest rate is 6 percent a year, and the quantity of capital is $2 trillion. If the interest rate exceeds 6 percent a year, the quantity of capital supplied exceeds the quantity of capital demanded and the interest rate falls. And if the interest rate is less than 6 percent a year, the quantity of

FIGURE 14.6 Capital Market Equilibrium

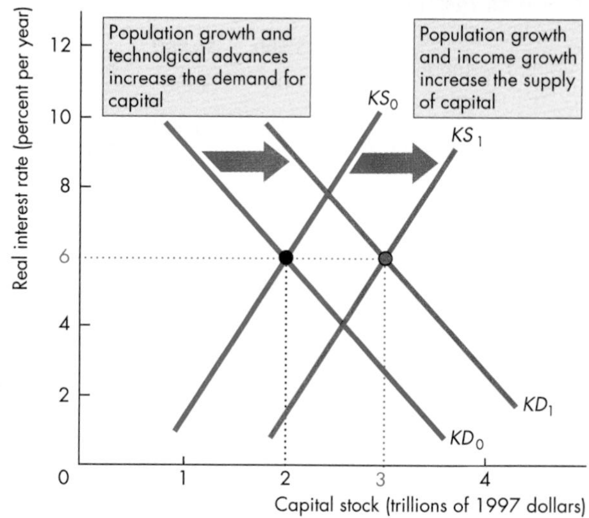

Initially, the demand for capital is KD_0 and the supply of capital is KS_0. The equilibrium interest rate is 6 percent a year, and the capital stock is $2 trillion. Over time, both demand and supply increase to KD_1 and KS_1. The capital stock increases, but the real interest rate is constant. Demand and supply increase because they are influenced by common factors.

capital demanded exceeds the quantity of capital supplied and the interest rate rises

Over time, both the demand for capital and the supply of capital increase. The demand curve shifts rightward to KD_1, and the supply curve also shifts rightward, to KS_1. Both curves shift because the same forces influence both. Population growth increases both demand and supply. Technological advances increase demand and bring higher incomes, which in turn increase supply. Because both demand and supply increase over time, the quantity of capital has an upward trend and the real interest rate has no trend.

Although the real interest rate does not follow a rising or falling trend, it does fluctuate, as you can see in Fig. 14.5. The reason is that the demand for capital and the supply of capital do not change in lockstep. Sometimes rapid technological change brings an increase in the demand for capital *before* it brings rising incomes that increase the supply of capital. When this sequence of events occurs, the real interest rate rises. The first half of the 1980s was such a time, as you can see in Fig. 14.5(a).

At other times, the demand for capital grows slowly or even decreases temporarily. In this situation, supply outgrows demand and the real interest rate falls. Figure 14.5 shows that the mid-1970s, 1984–1991, and the late-1990s were three such periods.

REVIEW QUIZ

1. What is discounting and how is it used to calculate a present value? When might you want to calculate a present value to make a decision?
2. How does a firm compare the future marginal revenue product of capital with the current cost of capital?
3. What are the main influences on a firm's demand for capital?
4. What are the main influences on the supply of capital?
5. What have been the main trends in the quantity of capital and real interest rates, and how can we explain the trends by using the demand for capital and the supply of capital?

The lessons that we've just learned about capital markets can be used to understand the prices of nonrenewable natural resource prices.

Natural Resource Markets

Natural resources, or what economists call *land*, fall into two categories:

- Renewable
- Nonrenewable

Renewable natural resources are natural resources that can be used repeatedly. Examples are land (in its everyday sense), rivers, lakes, rain, and sunshine.

Nonrenewable natural resources are natural resources that can be used only once and that cannot be replaced once they have been used. Examples are coal, natural gas, and oil—the so-called hydrocarbon fuels.

The demand for a natural resource as an input into production is based on the same principle of marginal revenue product as the demand for labour (and the demand for capital). But the supply of a natural resource is special. Let's look first at the supply of renewable natural resources.

The Supply of a Renewable Natural Resource

The quantity of land and other renewable natural resources available is fixed. The quantity supplied cannot be changed by individual decisions. People can vary the amount of land they own. But when one person buys some land, another person sells it. The aggregate quantity of land supplied of any particular type and in any particular location is fixed, regardless of the decisions of any individual. This fact means that the supply of each particular piece of land is perfectly inelastic. Figure 14.7 illustrates such a supply. Regardless of the rent available, the quantity of land supplied in Toronto's Yorkville is a fixed number of square metres.

Because the supply of land is fixed regardless of its price, the price of land is determined by demand. The greater the demand for a specific piece of land, the higher is its price.

Expensive land can be, and is, used more intensively than inexpensive land. For example, high-rise buildings enable land to be used more intensively. However, to use land more intensively, it has to be combined with another factor of production: capital. An increase in the amount of capital per block of land does not change the supply of land itself.

FIGURE 14.7 The Supply of Land

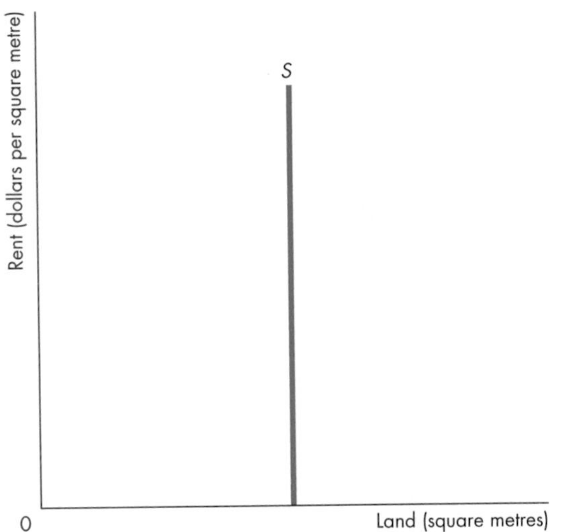

The supply of a given piece of land is perfectly inelastic. No matter what the rent, no more land than the quantity that exists can be supplied.

Although the supply of each type of land is fixed and its supply is perfectly inelastic, each individual firm operating in competitive land markets faces an elastic supply of land. For example, Bloor Street in Toronto has a fixed amount of land, but Chapters, the bookstore, could rent some space from The Bay, the department store. Each firm can rent the quantity of land that it demands at the going rent, as determined in the marketplace. Thus, provided that land markets are competitive, firms are price takers in these markets, just as they are in the markets for other productive resources.

The Supply of a Nonrenewable Natural Resource

The *stock* of a natural resource is the quantity in existence at a given time. This quantity is fixed and is independent of the price of the resource. The *known* stock of a natural resource is the quantity that has been discovered. This quantity increases over time because advances in technology enable ever less accessible sources to be discovered. Both of these *stock* concepts influence the price of a natural resource. But the influence is indirect. The direct influence on price is the rate at which the resource is supplied for use in production—called the *flow* supply.

The flow supply of a nonrenewable natural resource is *perfectly elastic* at a price that equals the present value of the expected price next period.

To see why, think about the economic choices of Saudi Arabia, a country that possesses a large inventory of oil. Saudi Arabia can sell an additional billion barrels of oil right now and use the income it receives to buy U.S. bonds. Or it can keep the billion barrels in the ground and sell them next year. If it sells the oil and buys U.S. bonds, it earns the interest rate on the bonds. If it keeps the oil and sells it next year, it earns the amount of the price increase or loses the amount of the price decrease between now and next year.

If Saudi Arabia expects the price of oil to rise next year by a percentage that equals the current interest rate, the price that it expects next year equals $(1 + r)$ multiplied by this year's price. For example, if this year's price is \$12 a barrel and the interest rate is 5 percent ($r = 0.5$), then next year's expected price is $1.05 \times \$12$, which equals \$12.60 a barrel.

With the price expected to rise to \$12.60 next year, Saudi Arabia is indifferent between selling now for \$12 and not selling now but waiting until next year and selling for \$12.60. It expects to make the same return either way. So at \$12 a barrel, Saudi Arabia will sell whatever quantity is demanded.

But if Saudi Arabia expects the price to rise next year by a percentage that exceeds the current interest rate, it expects to make a bigger return by hanging onto the oil than it can make from selling the oil and buying bonds. So it keeps the oil and sells none. And if it expects the price to rise next year by a percentage that is less than the current interest rate, the bond gives a bigger return than the oil, so Saudi Arabia sells as much oil as it can.

Recall the idea of discounting and present value. The minimum price at which Saudi Arabia is willing to sell oil is the present value of the expected future price. At this price, it will sell as much oil as buyers demand. So its supply is perfectly elastic.

Price and the Hotelling Principle

Figure 14.8 shows the equilibrium in a natural resource market. Because supply is perfectly elastic at the present value of next period's expected price, the actual price of the natural resource equals the present value of next period's expected price. Also, because

FIGURE 14.8 A Nonrenewable Natural Resource Market

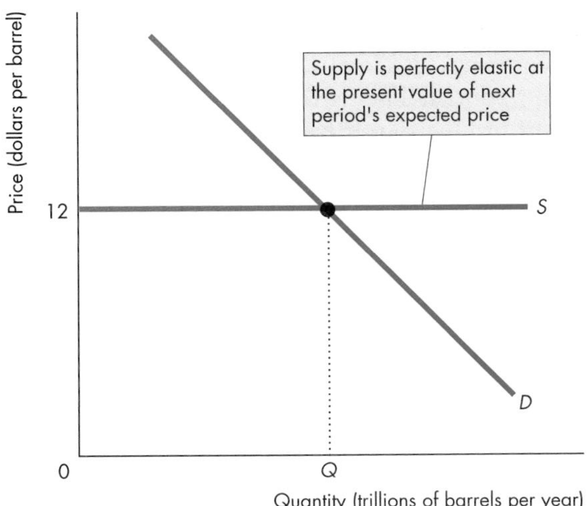

The supply of a nonrenewable natural resource is perfectly elastic at the *present value* of next period's expected price. The demand for a nonrenewable natural resource is determined by its marginal revenue product. The price is determined by supply and equals the *present value* of next period's expected price.

FIGURE 14.9 Falling Resource Prices

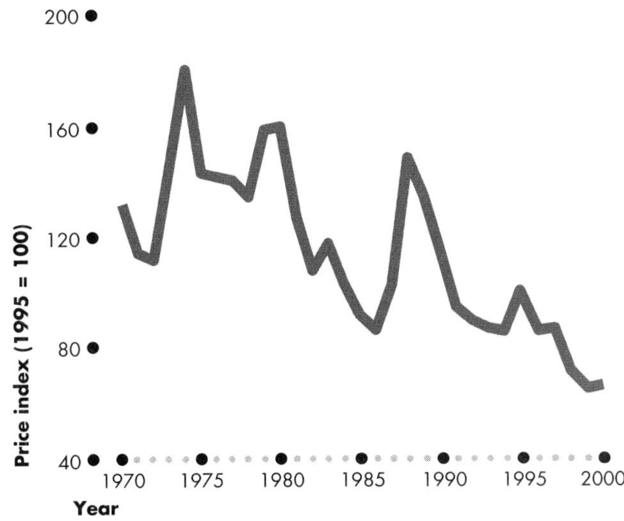

The prices of metals (here an average of the prices of aluminium, copper, iron ore, lead, manganese, nickel, silver, tin, and zinc) have tended to fall over time, not to rise as predicted by the Hotelling Principle. The reason is that unanticipated advances in technology have decreased the cost of extracting resources and greatly increased the exploitable known reserves.

Source: International Financial Statistics (various issues), Washington, DC: International Monetary Fund.

the current price is the present value of the expected future price, the price of the resource is expected to rise at a rate equal to the interest rate.

The proposition that the price of a resource is expected to rise at a rate equal to the interest rate is called the *Hotelling Principle.* It was first realized by Harold Hotelling, a mathematician and economist at Columbia University. But as Fig. 14.9 shows, *actual* prices do not follow the path *predicted* by the Hotelling Principle. Why do natural resource prices sometimes fall rather than follow their expected path and increase over time?

The key reason is that the future is unpredictable. Expected technological change is reflected in the price of a natural resource. But a previously unexpected new technology that leads to the discovery or the more efficient use of a nonrenewable natural resource causes its price to fall. Over the years, as technology has advanced, we have become more efficient in our use of nonrenewable resources. And we haven't just become more efficient. We've become more efficient than we expected to.

REVIEW QUIZ

1. Why is the price of a *renewable* natural resource such as land perfectly inelastic?
2. At what price is the flow supply of a nonrenewable natural resource perfectly elastic and why?
3. Why is the price of a nonrenewable natural resource expected to rise at a rate equal to the interest rate?
4. Why do the prices of nonrenewable resources not follow the path predicted by the Hotelling Principle?

People supply resources to earn an income. But some people earn enormous incomes. Are such incomes necessary to induce people to work and supply other resources? Let's now answer this question.

Income, Economic Rent, and Opportunity Cost

YOU'VE NOW SEEN HOW FACTOR PRICES ARE determined by the interaction of demand and supply. You've also seen that demand is determined by marginal productivity and that supply is determined by the factors of production available and by people's choices about their use. The interaction of demand and supply in factor markets determines who receives a large income and who receives a small income.

Large and Small Incomes

An NBA player earns $11 million a year because he has a high marginal revenue product—reflected in the demand for his services—and the supply of people with the combination of talents needed for this kind of job is small—reflected in the supply. Equilibrium occurs at a high wage rate and a small quantity employed.

People who work at fast-food restaurants earn a low wage rate because they have a low marginal revenue product—reflected in the demand—and many people are able and willing to supply their labour for these jobs. Equilibrium occurs at a low wage rate and a large quantity employed.

If the demand for basketball players increases, their incomes increase by a large amount and the number of players barely changes. If the demand for fast-food workers increases, the number of people doing these jobs increases by a large amount and the wage rate barely changes.

Another difference between a basketball player and a fast-food worker is that if the basketball player were hit with a pay cut, he would probably still supply his services, but if a fast-food worker were hit with a pay cut, he would probably quit. This difference arises from the interesting distinction between economic rent and opportunity cost.

Economic Rent and Opportunity Cost

The total income of a factor of production is made up of its economic rent and its opportunity cost. **Economic rent** is the income received by the owner of a factor of production over and above the amount required to induce that owner to offer the factor for use. Any factor of production can receive an economic rent. The income required to induce the supply of a factor of production is the opportunity cost of using the factor—the value of the factor in its next best use.

Figure 14.10(a) illustrates the way in which a factor income has an economic rent and an opportunity cost component. The figure shows the market for a factor of production. It could be *any* factor of production—labour, capital, or land—but we'll suppose that it is labour. The demand curve is *D*, and the supply curve is *S*. The wage rate is *W*, and the quantity employed is *C*. The income earned is the sum of the yellow and green areas. The yellow area below the supply curve measures opportunity cost, and the green area above the supply curve but below the factor price measures economic rent.

To see why the area below the supply curve measures opportunity cost, recall that a supply curve can be interpreted in two different ways. It shows the quantity supplied at a given price, and it shows the minimum price at which a given quantity is willingly supplied. If suppliers receive only the minimum amount required to induce them to supply each unit of the factor, they will be paid a different price for each unit. The prices will trace the supply curve, and the income received will be entirely opportunity cost—the yellow area in Fig. 14.10(a).

The concept of economic rent is similar to the concept of producer surplus that you met in Chapter 5. Economic rent is the price a person receives for the use of a factor minus the minimum price at which a given quantity of the factor is willingly supplied.

Economic rent is not the same thing as the "rent" that a farmer pays for the use of some land or the "rent" that you pay for your apartment. Everyday "rent" is a price paid for the services of land or a building. *Economic rent* is a component of the income received by any factor of production.

The portion of the income of a factor of production that consists of economic rent depends on the elasticity of the supply of the factor. When the supply of a factor of production is perfectly inelastic, its entire income is economic rent. Most of the income received by Garth Brooks and Pearl Jam is economic rent. Also, a large part of the income of a major-league baseball player is economic rent. When the supply of a factor of production is perfectly elastic, none of its income is economic rent. Most of the

FIGURE 14.10 Economic Rent and Opportunity Cost

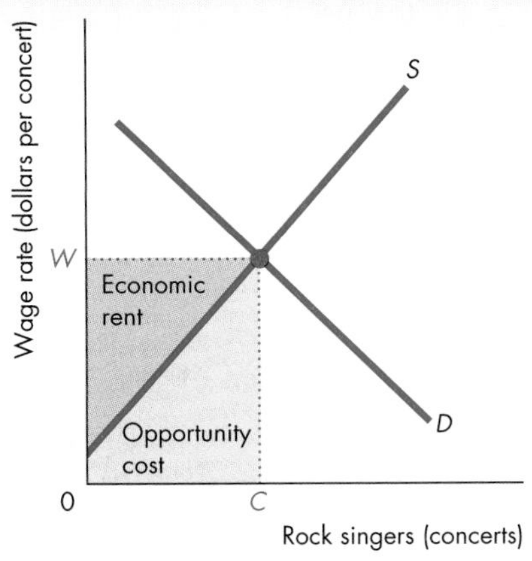

(a) General case

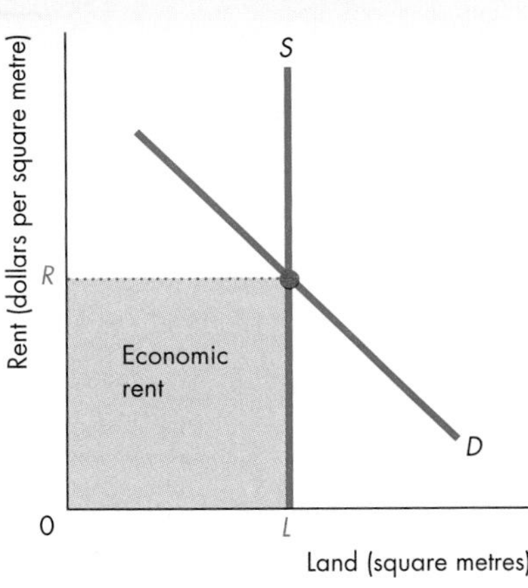

(b) All economic rent

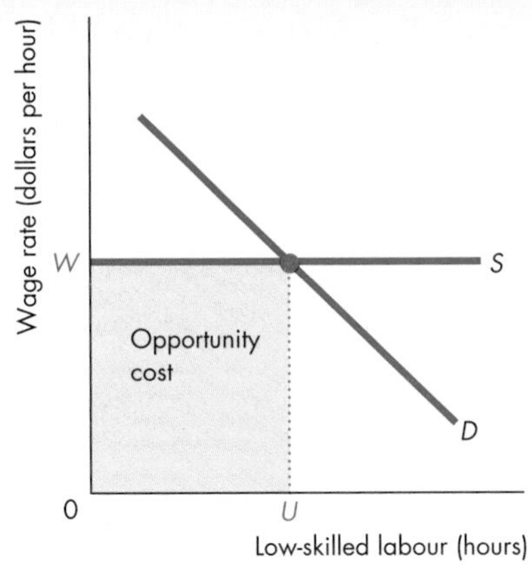

(c) All opportunity cost

When the supply curve of a factor slopes upward—the general case—as in part (a), part of the factor income is economic rent (the green area) and part is opportunity cost (the yellow area). When the supply of a factor is perfectly inelastic (the supply curve is vertical), as in part (b), the entire factor income is economic rent. When the supply of a factor is perfectly elastic, as in part (c), the factor's entire income is opportunity cost.

income of a babysitter is opportunity cost. In general, when supply is neither perfectly elastic nor perfectly inelastic, as Fig. 14.10(a) illustrates, some of the factor income is economic rent and some is opportunity cost.

Figures 14.10(b) and 14.10(c) show the other two possibilities. Part (b) shows the market for a particular parcel of land in Vancouver. The quantity of land is fixed in size at L square metres. So the supply curve of the land is vertical—perfectly inelastic. No matter what the rent on the land is, there is no way of increasing the quantity that can be supplied. Suppose that the demand curve in Fig. 14.10(b) shows the marginal revenue product of this block of land. Then it commands a rent of R. The entire income accruing to the owner of the land is the green area in the figure. This income is *economic rent.*

Figure 14.10(c) shows the market for a factor of production that is in perfectly elastic supply. An example of such a market might be that for low-skilled labour in a poor country such as India or China. In those countries, large numbers of people seeking labour flock to the cities and are available for work at the going wage rate (in this case, W). Thus in these situations, the supply of labour is almost perfectly elastic. The entire income earned by these workers is opportunity cost. They receive no economic rent.

REVIEW QUIZ

1. Why does an NBA player earn a larger income than does a babysitter?
2. What is the distinction between an economic rent and an opportunity cost?
3. Is the income that the Toronto Raptors pays to Antonio Davis an economic rent or compensation for his opportunity cost?
4. Is a Big Mac more expensive in Vancouver than in Brandon, Manitoba because rents are higher in Vancouver, or are rents higher in Vancouver because people in Vancouver are willing to pay more for a Big Mac?

Reading Between the Lines on pp. 336–337 looks at the market for hockey players.

The next chapter looks at how the market economy distributes income and explains the trends in the distribution of income. The chapter also looks at the efforts by governments to redistribute income and modify the market outcome.

READING BETWEEN THE LINES

Rents and Opportunity Costs on the Ice

THE GLOBE AND MAIL, AUGUST 1, 2002

Kariya stays put for $10-million

Anaheim star Paul Kariya agreed to a one-year deal with the Mighty Ducks yesterday after accepting the team's one-year $10 million (U.S.) qualifying offer.

"Having our captain and team leader signed prior to training camp is very important for our club," Anaheim general manager Bryan Murray said in a statement. "Paul's dedication and work ethic continue to make him one of the game's best players."

Kariya, 27, is Anaheim's all-time leader in games (524), goals (275), assists (313) and game-winning goals (42). The 5-foot-10, 173-pound native of North Vancouver, B.C., led the Ducks in goals (32) and points (57) but both totals were his lowest since he had 17 goals and 31 points in 22 games in 1997-98.

"One year at a time at this point is something I feel comfortable with," Kariya said during a conference call. "What it does is put pressure on both myself and the team to continue going in the right direction and for myself to get back playing at the top of my game."

Anaheim (29-42-8-3, 69 points) finished last in the Western Conference's Pacific Division last season. But the Ducks have been busy in the off-season, hiring new coach Mike Babcock and adding defenceman Fredrik Olausson, a free agent from Detroit, and forwards Adam Oates, a free agent from Philadelphia, and Petr Sykora, in a trade with New Jersey.

Kariya is particularly excited about the acquisition of Olausson, Oates and Sykora because he says the three will improve a Ducks' power player that was the NHL's worst last season.

"Our power play really killed us last year," said Kariya, who helped Canada win the men's Olympic hockey gold in Salt Lake City in February. "Getting Adam Oates, who I think is the best power-play guy in the league, and also signing Fredrik Olausson, who is a terrific quarterback out there, is going to help us out a lot.

"I think that will go from being the weakest part of our game to being one of our strongest parts." ...

The Canadian Press.

Essence of the Story

- Paul Kariya signed a one-year deal for $10 million with the Mighty Ducks.
- Kariya says he likes contracting for one year at a time because it puts pressure on both him and the team to perform at the top of their games.
- The Mighty Ducks' general manager says that Paul's dedication and work ethic make him one of the game's best players and having him sign early helps the club.
- Anaheim hired a new defenceman and two forwards that Kariya says will improve the Ducks' power play, which was weak last season.

Economic Analysis

■ This news article illustrates four central economic ideas:

1. Marginal revenue product
2. Economic rent and opportunity cost
3. Incentives
4. Complements

■ The marginal revenue product of Paul Kariya is $10 million a year. Other top hockey players also have a very large marginal revenue product.

■ Having Kariya on the team increases the revenue that the Mighty Ducks generates by $10 million.

■ The supply of top-performing hockey players of Kariya's quality is limited. At a wage rate below the minimum industrial wage, no one would be willing to work and train to perform at the standard of these players. The quantity supplied would be zero.

■ At a wage rate similar to the average industrial wage, a large number of people are willing to work and train to play competition-quality hockey. But few have the talent to perform at the level of Kariya.

■ No matter by how much the wage rate rises above the average industrial wage, the quantity of top-performing hockey players does not increase. The supply is inelastic.

■ The figure shows the market for top-performing hockey players.

■ The demand for top-performing players is determined by their marginal revenue product and is the curve *D*.

■ The supply curve, *S*, shows the willingness of talented people to offer their services as hockey players. The average industrial wage rate is *a*. As the wage rate for hockey players increases above this wage rate, the quantity of star players supplied increases, but up to a maximum of Q_0. This quantity is limited by the available talent pool.

■ Equilibrium in the market for top-performing hockey players occurs at an average wage rate of $1.6 million (U.S.) a year.

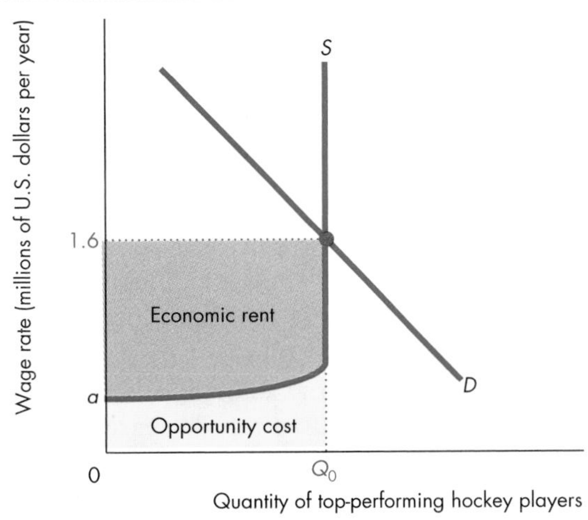

Figure 1 The market for hockey players

■ Most of their income is *economic rent*, which is shown as the green area. The rest, shown by the yellow area, is *opportunity cost*.

■ Paul Kariya and many other players work on a one-year contract. Such a contract provides a stronger *incentive* for the player to perform well so that he can get a new contract the next year. It also provides a strong incentive for the club to hire well and have good coaching and management to make itself attractive to the top players.

■ Hockey players are *complementary* factors of production. Even a great player like Kariya would not perform well without great support from other players.

■ When the Mighty Ducks hired Olausson, Oates, and Sykora, they increased the marginal revenue product of Kariya. And by signing Kariya, they increased the marginal revenue product of the other three players.

SUMMARY

KEY POINTS

Prices and Incomes in Competitive Factor Markets (p. 316)

- An increase in the demand for a factor of production increases the factor's price and total income; a decrease in the demand for a factor of production decreases its price and total income.
- An increase in the supply of a factor of production increases the quantity used but decreases its price and might increase or decrease its total income depending on whether demand is elastic or inelastic.

Labour Markets (pp. 317–324)

- The demand for labour is determined by the marginal revenue product of labour.
- The demand for labour increases if the price of the firm's output rises or if technological change and capital accumulation increase marginal product.
- The elasticity of demand for labour depends on the labour intensity of production, the elasticity of demand for the product, and the ease with which labour can be substituted for capital.
- The quantity of labour supplied increases as the real wage rate increases, but at high wage rates, the supply curve eventually bends backwards.
- The supply of labour increases as the population increases and with technological change and capital accumulation.
- Wage rates and employment increase because demand increases by more than supply.

Capital Markets (pp. 325–331)

- To make an investment decision, a firm compares the *present value* of the marginal revenue product of capital with the price of capital.
- Population growth and technological change increase the demand for capital.
- The higher the interest rate, the greater is the amount of saving and quantity of capital supplied.
- The supply of capital increases as incomes increase.
- Capital market equilibrium determines the real interest rate.

Natural Resource Markets (pp. 331–333)

- The demand for natural resources is determined by marginal revenue product.
- The supply of land is inelastic.
- The supply of nonrenewable natural resources is perfectly elastic at a price equal to the present value of the expected future price.
- The price of a nonrenewable natural resource is expected to rise at a rate equal to the interest rate but fluctuates and sometimes falls.

Income, Economic Rent, and Opportunity Cost (pp. 334–335)

- Economic rent is the income received by the owner of a factor of production over and above the amount needed to induce the owner to supply the factor for use.
- The rest of a factor's income is an opportunity cost.
- When the supply of a factor is perfectly inelastic, its entire income is made up of economic rent; and when supply of a factor is perfectly elastic, its entire income is made up of opportunity cost.

KEY FIGURES AND TABLES

Figure 14.1 Demand and Supply in a Factor Market, 316
Figure 14.3 The Demand for Labour at Max's Wash 'n' Wax, 319
Figure 14.10 Economic Rent and Opportunity Cost, 335
Table 14.2 Two Conditions for Maximum Profit, 320
Table 14.3 A Firm's Demand for Labour, 321

KEY TERMS

Derived demand, 317
Discounting, 326
Economic rent, 334
Marginal revenue product, 318
Net present value, 328
Nonrenewable natural resources, 331
Present value, 326
Renewable natural resources, 331

PROBLEMS

*1. The figure illustrates the market for blueberry pickers.

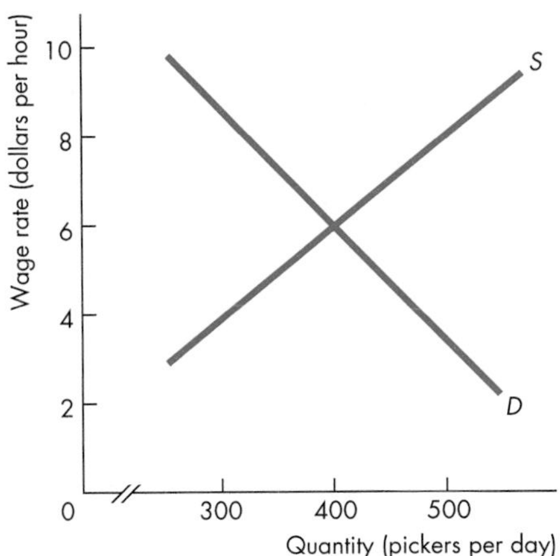

a. What is the wage rate paid to blueberry pickers?
b. How many blueberry pickers get hired?
c. What is the income received by blueberry pickers?

2. In problem 1, if the demand for blueberry pickers decreases by 100 a day:
a. What is the new wage rate paid to the pickers?
b. How many pickers get laid off?
c. What is the total income paid to pickers?

*3. Wanda owns a fish shop. She employs students to sort and pack the fish. Students can pack the following amounts of fish in an hour:

Number of students	Quantity of fish (kilograms)
1	20
2	50
3	90
4	120
5	145
6	165
7	180
8	190

Wanda can sell her fish for 50¢ a kilogram, and the wage rate of packers is $7.50 an hour.
a. Calculate the marginal product of the students and draw the marginal product curve.
b. Calculate the marginal revenue product of the students and draw the marginal revenue product curve.
c. Find Wanda's demand for labour curve.
d. How many students does Wanda employ?

4. Larry makes gourmet ice cream in small batches. He employs workers who can produce the following quantities in a day:

Number of workers	Quantity of ice cream (batches)
1	4
2	10
3	18
4	24
5	29
6	33
7	36
8	38

Larry can sell ice cream for $25 a batch, and the wage rate of his workers is $100 a day.
a. Calculate the marginal product of the workers and draw the marginal product curve.
b. Calculate the marginal revenue product of the workers and draw the marginal revenue product curve.
c. Find Larry's demand for labour curve.
d. How much ice cream does Larry sell?

*5. Back at Wanda's fish shop described in problem 3, the price of fish falls to 33.33¢ a kilogram but fish packers' wages remain at $7.50 an hour.
a. What happens to the students' marginal product?
b. What happens to Wanda's marginal revenue product?
c. What happens to her demand for labour curve?
d. What happens to the number of students that she employs?

6. Back at Larry's ice cream plant described in problem 4, the price of ice cream falls to $20 a batch but the wage rate remains at $100 a day.
a. What happens to the workers' marginal product?
b. What happens to Larry's marginal revenue product?
c. What happens to his demand for labour curve?
d. What happens to the number of workers that he employs?

*7. Back at Wanda's fish shop described in problem 3, packers' wages increase to $10 an hour but the price of fish remains at 50¢ a kilogram.
   a. What happens to marginal revenue product?
   b. What happens to Wanda's demand for labour curve?
   c. How many students does Wanda employ?
8. Back at Larry's ice cream plant described in problem 4, the wage rate rises to $125 a day but the price of ice cream remains at $25 a batch.
   a. What happens to marginal revenue product?
   b. What happens to Larry's demand for labour curve?
   c. How many workers does Larry employ?
*9. Using the information provided in problem 3, calculate Wanda's marginal revenue, marginal cost, and marginal revenue product. Show that when Wanda is making maximum profit, marginal cost equals marginal revenue and marginal revenue product equals the wage rate.
10. Using the information provided in problem 4, calculate Larry's marginal revenue, marginal cost, and marginal revenue product. Show that when Larry is making maximum profit, marginal cost equals marginal revenue and marginal revenue product equals the wage rate.
*11. Greg has found an oil well in his backyard. A geologist estimates that a total of 10 million barrels can be pumped for a pumping cost of a dollar a barrel. The price of oil is $20 a barrel. How much oil does Greg sell each year? If you can't predict how much he will sell, what extra information would you need to be able to do so?
12. Orley has a wine cellar in which he keeps choice wines from around the world. What does Orley expect to happen to the prices of the wines he keeps in his cellar? Explain your answer. How does Orley decide which wine to drink and when to drink it?
*13. Use the figure in problem 1 and show on the figure the blueberry pickers'
   a. Economic rent.
   b. Opportunity cost.
14. Use the figure in problem 1 and the information in problem 2 and show on the figure the blueberry pickers'
   a. Economic rent.
   b. Opportunity cost.

CRITICAL THINKING

1. Study *Reading Between the Lines* on pp. 336–337 and answer the following questions:
   a. What determines the demand for hockey players?
   b. What determines the supply of hockey players?
   c. What do you think Paul Kariya, Fredrik Olausson, Adam Oates, and Petr Sykora would do if they didn't play hockey?
   d. What does your answer to (c) tell you about the opportunity cost of these players?
   e. What does your answer to (c) tell you about the economic rent received by these players?
   f. What are the advantages for the player and the club of a one-year contract over a multi-year contract?
   g. Why do good players like to have other good players on their team?
2. "We are running out of natural resources and must take urgent action to conserve our precious reserves." "There is no shortage of resources that the market cannot cope with." Debate these two views. List the pros and cons for each.
3. Why do we keep finding new reserves of oil? Why don't we do a once-and-for-all big survey that catalogues the earth's entire inventory of natural resources?

WEB EXERCISES

1. Use the link on the Parkin–Bade Web site and read the article on "Trends in Hours of Work Since the Mid 1970s."
   a. What are the trends in hours of work since the mid-1970s?
   b. Are the trends for men the same as those for women? What are the similarities and differences?
   c. Do you think the trends arise from changes on the demand side of the labour market or from changes on the supply side?
   d. What additional information would you need to be sure about your answer to part (c)?

APPENDIX

Labour Unions

After studying this appendix you will be able to

- **Explain why union workers earn more than nonunion workers**
- **Explain how a labour market works in a monopsony**
- **Explain the effects of a minimum wage law in a monopsony**

Market Power in the Labour Market

JUST AS A MONOPOLY FIRM CAN RESTRICT OUTPUT and raise price, so a monopoly owner of a resource can restrict supply and raise the price of the resource.

The main source of market power in the labour market is the labour union. A **labour union** is an organized group of workers that aims to increase wages and influence other job conditions.

Traditionally, a union was formed by a group of workers who had similar skills but who worked for firms in different industries and regions—for example, the electrical workers union. The industrial union was created when workers in mass-production industries unionized. These workers had a variety of skills and they worked in the same industry. Today, most unions have members who work in different industries and have a wide range of skills. For example, the members of the United Steelworkers Union work in steel mills, factories, bakeries, and offices.

Most unions are members of the Canadian Labour Congress, which was created in 1956 with the merger of the Labour Council of Canada (founded in 1883) and the Canadian Congress of Labour (founded in 1940).

Unions vary enormously in size. Some unions are small, but industrial unions are large. Union strength peaked in 1976, when 30 percent of the nonagricultural work force belonged to unions. That percentage has fallen slightly since then and is now about 25 percent.

Union organization is based on a subdivision known as the *local.* The local can be organized as a closed shop, a union shop, or an open shop. A *closed shop* is an arrangement in which the firm can hire only union members. Most closed shops are in the construction industry. A *union shop* is an arrangement in which the firm can hire workers who are not union members, but new workers must join the union, usually at the end of their probationary period. Union shops are common in manufacturing industries and the public sector. An *open shop* is an arrangement in which no employee is required to join the union or pay union dues. There is no restriction on who can work in the "shop." A compromise between the union shop and the open shop is the **Rand Formula:** a requirement that all workers represented by a union must pay union dues, whether they join the union or not.

Unions negotiate with employers or their representatives in a process called *collective bargaining.* The main weapons available to the union and the employer in collective bargaining are the strike and the lockout. A *strike* is a group decision by the workers to refuse to work under prevailing conditions. A *lockout* is a firm's refusal to operate its plant and employ its workers. Each party uses the threat of a strike or a lockout to try to get an agreement in its own favour. Sometimes, when the two parties in the collective bargaining process cannot agree on the wage rate or other conditions of employment, they agree to submit their disagreement to binding arbitration. *Binding arbitration* is a process in which a third party—an arbitrator—determines wages and other employment conditions on behalf of the negotiating parties.

Although they are not labour unions in a legal sense, professional associations act in ways similar to labour unions. A *professional association* is an organized group of professional workers such as lawyers or physicians (for example, the Ontario Medical Association). Professional associations control entry into the professions and license practitioners, ensuring the adherence to minimum standards of competence. But they also influence the compensation and other labour market conditions of their members.

Union Objectives and Constraints

A union has three broad objectives that it strives to achieve for its members:

1. To increase compensation
2. To improve working conditions
3. To expand job opportunities

Each of these objectives contains a series of more detailed goals. For example, in seeking to increase members' compensation, a union operates on a variety of fronts: wage rates, fringe benefits, retirement pay, and such things as vacation allowances. In seeking to improve working conditions, a union is concerned with occupational health and safety as well as the environmental quality of the workplace. In seeking to expand job opportunities, a union tries to get greater job security for existing union members and to find ways of creating additional jobs for them.

A union's ability to pursue its objectives is restricted by two sets of constraints—one on the supply side of the labour market and the other on the demand side. On the supply side, the union's activities are limited by how well it can restrict nonunion workers from offering their labour in the same market as union labour. The larger the fraction of the work force controlled by the union, the more effective the union can be in this regard. It is difficult for unions to operate in markets where there is an abundant supply of willing nonunion labour. For example, the market for part-time checkout clerks is very tough for a union to organize because of the enormous rate of turnover of participants in that market. At the other extreme, unions in the construction industry can better pursue their goals because they can influence the number of people who can obtain skills as electricians, plasterers, and carpenters. The professional associations of dentists and physicians are best able to restrict the supply of dentists and physicians. These groups control the number of qualified workers by controlling either the examinations that new entrants must pass or entrance into professional degree programs.

On the demand side of the labour market, the union faces a tradeoff that arises from firms' profit-maximizing decisions. Because labour demand curves slope downward, anything a union does that increases the wage rate or other employment costs decreases the quantity of labour demanded.

Let's see how unions operate in competitive labour markets.

A Union in a Competitive Labour Market

When a union operates in an otherwise competitive labour market, it seeks to increase wages and other compensation and to limit employment reductions by increasing demand for the labour of its members. That is, the union tries to take actions that shift the demand curve for its members' labour rightward.

Figure A14.1 illustrates a competitive labour market that a union enters. The demand curve is D_C, and the supply curve is S_C. Before the union enters the market, the wage rate is $7 an hour and 100 hours of labour are employed.

Now suppose that a union is formed to organize the workers in this market. The union can attempt to increase wages in this market in two ways. It can try to restrict the supply of labour, or it can try to stimulate the demand for labour. First, look at what happens if the union has sufficient control over the supply of labour to be able to restrict that supply artificially below its competitive level—to S_U. If that is all the union is able to do, employment falls to 85 hours of labour and the wage rate rises to $8 an hour.

FIGURE A14.1 Union in a Competitive Labour Market

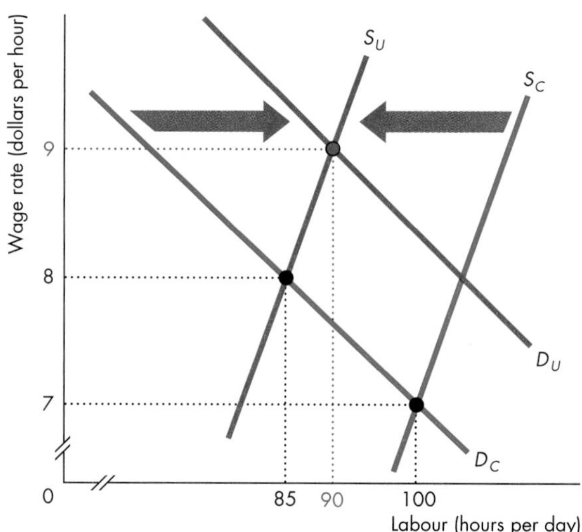

In a competitive labour market, the demand curve is D_C and the supply curve is S_C. Competitive equilibrium occurs at a wage rate of $7 an hour with 100 hours employed. By restricting employment below the competitive level, the union shifts the supply of labour to S_U. If the union can do no more than that, the wage rate will increase to $8 an hour but employment will fall to 85 hours. If the union can increase the demand for labour and shift the demand curve to D_U, then it can increase the wage rate still higher, to $9 an hour, and achieve employment of 90 hours.

The union simply picks its preferred position along the demand curve that defines the tradeoff it faces between employment and the wage rate.

You can see that if the union can only restrict the supply of labour, it raises the wage rate but decreases the number of jobs available. Because of this outcome, unions try to increase the demand for labour and shift the demand curve rightward. Let's see what they might do to achieve this outcome.

How Unions Try to Change the Demand for Labour

Unless a union can take actions that change the demand for the labour that it represents, it has to accept the fact that a higher wage rate can be obtained only at the price of lower employment.

The union tries to operate on the demand for labour in two ways. First, it tries to make the demand for union labour inelastic. Second, it tries to increase the demand for union labour. Making the demand for labour less elastic does not eliminate the tradeoff between employment and the wage rate. But it does make the tradeoff less unfavourable. If a union can make the demand for labour less elastic, it can increase the wage rate at a lower cost in terms of lost employment opportunities. But if the union can increase the demand for labour, it might even be able to increase both the wage rate and the employment opportunities of its members. Some of the methods used by the unions to change the demand for the labour of its members are to

- Increase the marginal product of union members
- Encourage import restrictions
- Support minimum wage laws
- Support immigration restrictions
- Increase demand for the good produced

Unions try to increase the marginal product of their members, which in turn increases the demand for their labour, by organizing and sponsoring training schemes, by encouraging apprenticeship and other on-the-job training activities, and by professional certification.

One of the best examples of import restrictions is the support by the Canadian Auto Workers union (CAW) for import restrictions on foreign cars.

Unions support minimum wage laws to increase the cost of employing low-skilled labour. An increase in the wage rate of low-skilled labour leads to a decrease in the quantity demanded of low-skilled labour and to an increase in demand for high-skilled union labour, a substitute for low-skilled labour.

Restrictive immigration laws decrease the supply of low-skilled workers and increase their wage rate. As a result, the demand for high-skilled union labour increases.

Because the demand for labour is a derived demand, an increase in the demand for the good produced by union labour increases the demand for union labour. The garment workers' union urging us to buy union-made clothes and the CAW asking us to buy only North American cars made by union workers are examples of attempts by unions to increase the demand for union labour.

Figure A14.1 illustrates the effects of an increase in the demand for the labour of a union's members. If the union can increase the demand for labour to D_U, it can achieve an even bigger increase in the wage rate with a smaller fall in employment. By maintaining the restricted labour supply at S_U, the union increases the wage rate to $9 an hour and achieves an employment level of 90 hours of labour.

Because a union restricts the supply of labour in the market in which it operates, its actions increase the supply of labour in nonunion markets. Workers who can't get union jobs must look elsewhere for work. This increase in the supply of labour in nonunion markets lowers the wage rate in those markets and further widens the union–nonunion differential.

The Scale of Union–Nonunion Wage Differentials

We have seen that unions can influence the wage rate by restricting the supply of labour and increasing the demand for labour. How much of a difference to wage rates do unions make in practice?

Union wage rates are, on the average, 30 percent higher than nonunion wage rates. In mining and financial services, union and nonunion wages are similar. In services, manufacturing, and transportation, the differential is between 11 and 19 percent. In wholesale and retail trades, the differential is 28 percent, and in construction, it is 65 percent.

But these union–nonunion wage differentials don't give a true measure of the effects of unions. In some industries, union wages are higher than nonunion wages because union members do jobs that involve greater skill. Even without a union, those workers would receive a higher wage. To calculate the effects of unions, we have to examine the wages of unionized and nonunionized workers who do nearly identical work. The evidence suggests that after allowing for skill differentials, the union–nonunion wage differential lies between 10 percent and 25 percent. For example, airline pilots who belong to the Air Line Pilots' Union earn about 25 percent more than nonunion pilots with the same level of skill.

Let's now look at monopsony.

Monopsony

A MARKET IN WHICH THERE IS A SINGLE BUYER IS called **monopsony.** This market type is unusual, but it does exist. With the growth of large-scale production over the last century, large manufacturing plants such as coal mines, steel and textile mills, and car manufacturers became the major employer in some regions, and in some places a single firm employed almost all the labour. Today, the provincial health insurance plans are the major employers of health-care professionals. These employers have market power.

In monopsony, the employer determines the wage rate and pays the lowest wage at which it can attract the labour it plans to hire. A monopsony makes a bigger profit than a group of firms that compete with each other for their labour. Let's find out how a monopsony achieves this outcome.

Like all firms, a monopsony has a downward-sloping marginal revenue product curve, which is *MRP* in Fig. A14.2. This curve tells us the extra revenue the monopsony receives by selling the output produced by an extra hour of labour. The labour supply curve is *S*. This curve tells us how many hours are supplied at each wage rate. It also tells us the minimum wage for which a given quantity of labour is willing to work.

A monopsony recognizes that to hire more labour, it must pay a higher wage; equivalently, by hiring less labour, it can pay a lower wage. Because a monopsony controls the wage rate, the marginal cost of labour exceeds the wage rate. The marginal cost of labour is shown by the curve *MCL*. The relationship between the marginal cost of labour curve and the supply curve is similar to the relationship between the marginal cost and average cost curves that you studied in Chapter 10. The supply curve is like the average cost of labour curve. In Fig. A14.2, the firm can hire 49 hours of labour for a wage rate of just below \$4.90 an hour. The firm's total labour cost is \$240. But suppose that the firm hires 50 hours of labour. It can hire the 50th hour of labour for \$5 an hour. The total cost of labour is now \$250 an hour. So hiring the 50th hour of labour increases the total cost of labour from \$240 to \$250, which is a \$10 increase. The marginal cost of labour is \$10 an hour. The curve *MCL* shows the \$10 marginal cost of hiring the 50th hour of labour.

To calculate the profit-maximizing quantity of labour to hire, the firm sets the marginal cost of labour equal to the marginal revenue product of labour. That is, the firm wants the cost of the last worker hired to equal the extra total revenue brought in. In Fig. A14.2, this outcome occurs when the monopsony employs 50 hours of labour. What is the wage rate that the monopsony pays? To hire 50 hours of labour, the firm must pay \$5 an hour, as shown by the supply of labour curve. So each worker is paid \$5 an hour. But the marginal revenue product of labour is \$10 an hour, which means that the firm makes an economic profit of \$5 on the last hour of labour that it hires. Compare this outcome with that in a competitive labour market. If the

FIGURE A14.2 A Monopsony Labour Market

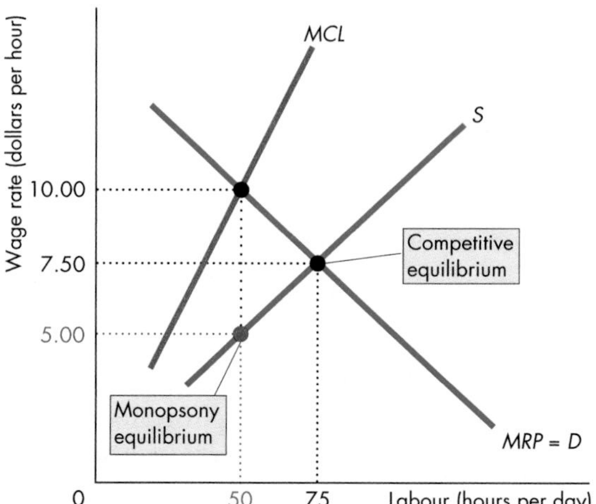

A monopsony is a market structure in which there is a single buyer. A monopsony in the labour market has the marginal revenue product curve *MRP* and faces a labour supply curve *S*. The marginal cost of labour curve is *MCL*. Making the marginal cost of labour equal to the value of marginal product maximizes profit. The monopsony hires 50 hours of labour and pays the lowest wage for which that labour will work, which is \$5 an hour.

labour market shown in Fig. A14.2 were competitive, equilibrium would occur at the point of intersection of the demand curve and the supply curve. The wage rate would be $7.50 an hour, and 75 hours of labour a day would be employed. So compared with a competitive labour market, a monopsony decreases both the wage rate and employment.

The ability of a monopsony to cut the wage and employment to increase its profit depends on the elasticity of labour supply. If the supply of labour is highly elastic, a monopsony has little power to cut the wage and employment to boost its profit.

Monopsony Tendencies

Today, monopsony is rare. Workers can commute long distances to a job, so most people have more than one potential employer. But firms that are dominant employers in isolated communities do face an upward-sloping supply of labour curve and so have a marginal cost of labour that exceeds the wage rate. But in such situations, there is also, usually, a union. Let's see how unions and monopsonies interact.

Monopsony and a Union

In Chapter 12, we discovered that in monopoly, a firm can determine the market price. We've now seen that in monopsony—a market with a single buyer—the buyer can determine the price. Suppose that a union operates in a monopsony labour market. A union is like a monopoly. If the union (monopoly seller) faces a monopsony buyer, the situation is called **bilateral monopoly.** In bilateral monopoly, the wage rate is determined by bargaining.

In Fig. A14.2, if the monopsony is free to determine the wage rate and the level of employment, it hires 50 hours of labour for a wage rate of $5 an hour. But suppose that a union represents the workers. The union agrees to maintain employment at 50 hours but seeks the highest wage rate that the employer can be forced to pay. That wage rate is $10 an hour—the wage rate that equals the marginal revenue product of labour. The union might not be able to get the wage rate up to $10 an hour. But it won't accept $5 an hour. The monopsony firm and the union bargain over the wage rate, and the result is an outcome between $10 an hour and $5 an hour.

The outcome of the bargaining depends on the costs that each party can inflict on the other as a result of a failure to agree on the wage rate. The firm can shut down the plant and lock out its workers, and the workers can shut down the plant by striking. Each party knows the other's strength and knows what it will lose if it does not agree to the other's demands. If the two parties are equally strong and they realize it, they will split the gap between $5 and $10 and agree to a wage rate of $7.50 an hour. If one party is stronger than the other—and both parties know that—the agreed wage will favour the stronger party. Usually, an agreement is reached without a strike or a lockout. The threat is usually enough to bring the bargaining parties to an agreement. When a strike or lockout does occur, it is usually because one party has misjudged the costs each party can inflict on the other.

Minimum wage laws have interesting effects in monopsony labour markets. Let's study these effects.

Monopsony and the Minimum Wage

In a competitive labour market, a minimum wage that exceeds the equilibrium wage decreases employment (see Chapter 6, pp. 129–130). In a monopsony labour market, a minimum wage can *increase* both the wage rate and employment. Let's see how.

Figure A14.3 shows a monopsony labour market in which the wage rate is $5 an hour and 50 hours of labour are employed. A minimum wage law is passed that requires employers to pay at least $7.50 an hour.

FIGURE A14.3 Minimum Wage Law in Monopsony

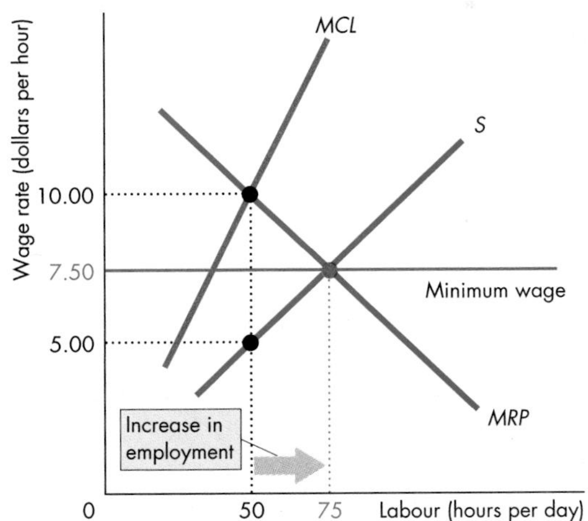

In a monopsony labour market, the wage rate is $5 an hour and 50 hours are hired. If a minimum wage law increases the wage rate to $7.50 an hour, employment increases to 75 hours.

The monopsony in Fig. A14.3 now faces a perfectly elastic supply of labour at $7.50 an hour up to 75 hours. Above 75 hours, a wage above $7.50 an hour must be paid to hire additional hours of labour. Because the wage rate is a fixed $7.50 an hour up to 75 hours, the marginal cost of labour is also constant at $7.50 up to 75 hours. Beyond 75 hours, the marginal cost of labour rises above $7.50 an hour. To maximize profit, the monopsony sets the marginal cost of labour equal to the marginal revenue product of labour. That is, the monopsony hires 75 hours of labour at $7.50 an hour. The minimum wage law has made the supply of labour perfectly elastic and made the marginal cost of labour the same as the wage rate up to 75 hours. The law has not affected the supply of labour curve or the marginal cost of labour at employment levels above 75 hours. The minimum wage law has succeeded in raising the wage rate by $2.50 an hour and increasing the amount of labour employed by 25 hours.

SUMMARY

KEY POINTS

Market Power in the Labour Market
(pp. 341–344)

- In competitive labour markets, unions obtain higher wages only at the expense of lower employment but they try to influence the demand for labour.
- Union workers earn 10 to 25 percent more than comparable nonunion workers.

Monopsony (pp. 344–346)

- A monopsony employs less labour and pays a wage rate below that in a competitive labour market.
- In bilateral monopoly, the wage rate is determined by bargaining.
- In monopsony, a minimum wage law can raise the wage rate and increase employment.

KEY TERMS

Bilateral monopoly, 345
Labour union, 341
Monopsony, 344
Rand Formula, 341

PROBLEMS

*1. A monopsony gold-mining firm operates in an isolated part of the Amazon basin. The table shows the firm's labour supply schedule (columns 1 and 2) and total product schedule (columns 2 and 3). The price of gold is $1.40 a grain.

Wage rate (dollars per day)	Number of workers	Quantity produced (grains per day)
5	0	0
6	1	10
7	2	25
8	3	45
9	4	60
10	5	70
11	6	75

a. What wage rate does the company pay?
b. How many workers does the gold mine hire?
c. What is the value of marginal product at the quantity of labour employed?

2. A monopsony logging firm operates in an isolated part of the Yukon. The table shows the firm's labour supply schedule (columns 1 and 2) and total product schedule (columns 2 and 3). The price of logs is $2 a tonne.

Wage rate (dollars per day)	Number of workers	Quantity produced (tonnes per day)
5	0	0
6	1	9
7	2	17
8	3	24
9	4	30
10	5	35
11	6	39
12	7	42

a. What wage rate does the company pay?
b. How many workers does the company hire?
c. What is the value of marginal product at the quantity of labour employed?

ECONOMIC INEQUALITY

Rags and Riches

Ken Thomson's family fortune, Canada's largest, is estimated at more than $20 billion. The poorest of Canada's richest 100 families is worth a mere $275 million. ◆ In stark contrast to these richest Canadians are the poorest, who can be seen any evening on the park benches of our major cities and in the hostels of the Salvation Army. Here are men and women who have no visible wealth at all other than their clothes and a few meagre possessions. ◆ Most Canadians are not as poor as those who seek help from the Salvation Army, but there is a large amount of relative poverty in our nation. One in 10 families has an income that is so low that it spends close to half its income on rent. ◆ Why are some people exceedingly rich, while others are very poor and own almost nothing?

In this chapter, we study economic inequality—its extent, its sources, and the things governments do to make it less extreme. We begin by looking at some facts about economic inequality in Canada today. We end, in *Reading Between the Lines*, by looking at the widening gap between the rich and the poor in Canada during the past 20 years.

After studying this chapter, you will be able to

- **Describe the inequality in income and wealth and the trends in inequality in Canada**
- **Explain the features of the labour market that contribute to economic inequality**
- **Describe the methods and scale of government income redistribution**

Measuring Economic Inequality

STATISTICS CANADA PROVIDES MEASURES OF economic inequality based on three definitions of income. **Market income** equals the wages, interest, rent, and profit earned in factor markets before paying income taxes. **Total income** equals *market income* plus cash payments to households by governments. **After-tax income** equals *total income* minus tax payments by households to governments.

The Distribution of After-Tax Income

Figure 15.1 shows the distribution of annual after-tax income across all households in Canada in 1998. Note that the *x*-axis measures income and the *y*-axis measures the percentage of households.

The most common household income, called the *mode* income, was received by the 10 percent of the households whose income fell between $10,000 and $14,999.

The income that separated the households into two equal groups, called the *median* income, was $33,227. One-half of Canadian households had an income greater than this amount, and the other half had an income less than this amount. The average household income in 1998, called the *mean* income, was $39,943.

You can see in Fig. 15.1 that the mode income is less than the median income, and the median income is less than the mean income. This feature of the distribution of income tells us that there are more households with low incomes than with high incomes. And some of the high incomes are very high.

The income distribution in Fig. 15.1 is called a *positively skewed* distribution, which means that it has a long tail of high values. This distribution's shape contrasts with a *bell-shaped* distribution like that of people's heights. In a bell-shaped distribution, the mean, median, and mode are all equal.

Another way of looking at the distribution of income is to measure the percentage of after-tax income received by each given percentage of households. Data are reported for five groups—called quintiles or one-fifth shares—each consisting of 20 percent of households.

Figure 15.2 shows the distribution based on

FIGURE 15.1 The Distribution of Income in Canada in 1998

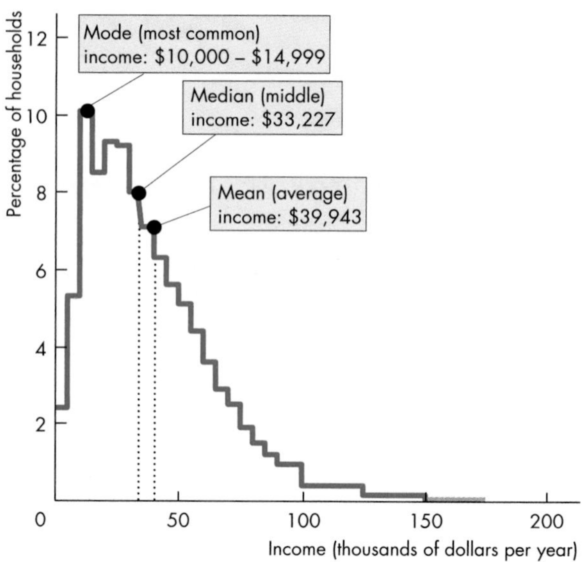

The distribution of income is positively skewed. The mode (most common) income is less than the median (middle) income, which in turn is less than the mean (average) income. A very small percentage of households earn incomes in the range above $150,000 up to several million dollars a year—this part of the distribution is off the scale of this figure.

Source: Statistics Canada, *Income in Canada*, Catalogue 75–202–XIE.

these shares in 1998. The poorest 20 percent of households received 5 percent of after-tax income; the second-poorest 20 percent received 11 percent of after-tax income; the middle 20 percent received 16.7 percent of after-tax income; the second-highest 20 percent received 24.4 percent of after-tax income; and the highest 20 percent received 42.9 percent of after-tax income.

The distribution of after-tax income in Fig. 15.1 and the quintile shares in Fig. 15.2 tell us that income is distributed unequally. But we need a way of comparing the distribution of income in different periods and using different measures. A neat graphical tool called the Lorenz curve enables us to make such comparisons.

FIGURE 15.2 Canadian Quintile Shares in 1998

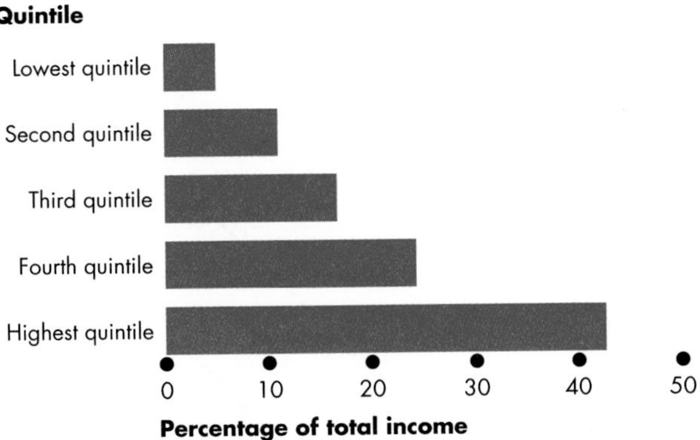

Households (percentage)	Income (percentage of total income)
Lowest 20	5.0
Second-lowest 20	11.0
Middle 20	16.7
Second-highest 20	24.4
Highest 20	42.9

The poorest 20 percent of households received 5 percent of after-tax income; the second-poorest 20 percent received 11 percent; the middle 20 percent received 16.7 percent; the second-highest 20 percent received 24.4 percent; and the highest 20 percent received 42.9 percent.

Source: Statistics Canada, *Income in Canada*, Catalogue 75–202–XIE.

FIGURE 15.3 The Income Lorenz Curve in 1998

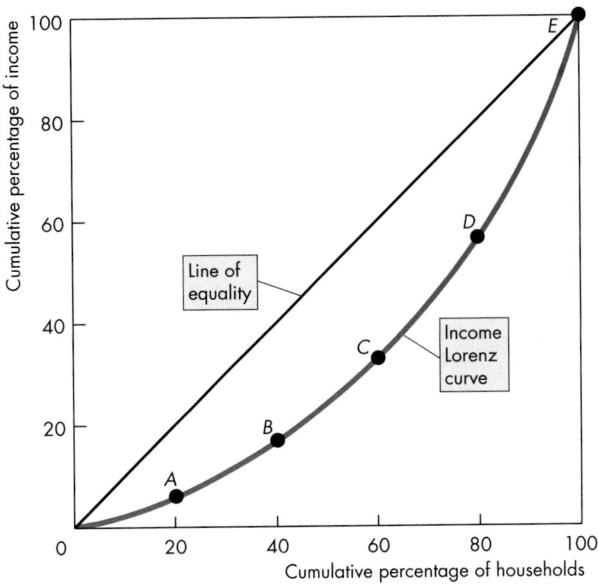

	Households		Income	
	Percentage	Cumulative percentage	Percentage	Cumulative percentage
A	Lowest 20	20	5.0	5.0
B	Second-lowest 20	40	11.0	16.0
C	Middle 20	60	16.7	32.7
D	Second-highest 20	80	24.4	56.1
E	Highest 20	100	42.9	100.0

The cumulative percentage of income is graphed against the cumulative percentage of households. Points *A* through *E* on the Lorenz curve correspond to the rows of the table. If incomes were distributed equally, each 20 percent of households would receive 20 percent of income and the Lorenz curve would fall along the line of equality. The Lorenz curve shows that income is unequally distributed.

Source: Statistics Canada, *Income in Canada*, Catalogue 75–202–XIE.

The Income Lorenz Curve

The income **Lorenz curve** graphs the cumulative percentage of income against the cumulative percentage of households. Figure 15.3 shows the income Lorenz curve using the quintile shares from Fig. 15.2. The table shows the percentage of income in each quintile group. For example, row *A* tells us that the lowest quintile of households receives 5 percent of after-tax income. The table also shows the *cumulative* percentages of households and income. For example, row *B* tells us that the lowest two quintiles (lowest 40 percent) of households receive 16 percent of after-tax income (5 percent for the lowest quintile and 11 percent for the second-lowest). The Lorenz curve graphs the cumulative income shares against the cumulative household percentages.

If income were distributed equally across all the households, each quintile would receive 20 percent of after-tax income and the cumulative percentages of income received by the cumulative percentages of households would fall along the straight line labelled "Line of equality" in Fig. 15.3. The actual distribution of income is shown by the curve labelled "Income Lorenz curve." The closer the Lorenz curve is to the line of equality, the more equal is the distribution.

The Distribution of Wealth

The distribution of wealth provides another way of measuring economic inequality. A household's wealth is the value of the things that it owns at a *point in time.* In contrast, income is the amount that the household receives over a given *period of time.*

Figure 15.4 shows the Lorenz curve for wealth in Canada in 1999. Median household wealth in that year was $64,000. Wealth is extremely unequally distributed, and for this reason, the data are grouped by unequal groups of households. The poorest 40 percent of households owns only 1.1 percent of total wealth (row *A'* in the table). The next poorest 10 percent owns only 2.8 percent of total wealth (row *B'*) and the next poorest 10 percent owns only 4.7 percent of total wealth (row *C'*). So the poorest 60 percent of households owns only 8.6 percent of total wealth. At the other end of the wealth distribution, the wealthiest 10 percent of households owns 55.6 percent of total wealth (row *G'*).

Figure 15.4 shows the income Lorenz curve (from Fig. 15.2) alongside the wealth Lorenz curve. You can see that the Lorenz curve for wealth is much farther away from the line of equality than the Lorenz curve for income is, which means that the distribution of wealth is much more unequal than the distribution of income.

Wealth Versus Income

We've seen that wealth is much more unequally distributed than income. Which distribution provides the better description of the degree of inequality? To answer this question, we need to think about the connection between wealth and income.

Wealth is a stock of assets, and income is the flow of earnings that results from the stock of wealth. Suppose that a person owns assets worth $1 million—has a wealth of $1 million. If the rate of return

FIGURE 15.4 Lorenz Curves for Income and Wealth

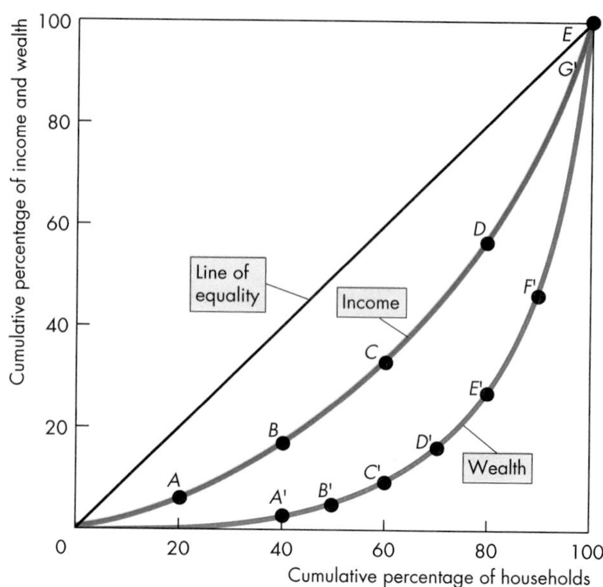

	Households		Wealth	
	Percentage	Cumulative percentage	Percentage	Cumulative percentage
A'	Lowest 40	40	1.1	1.1
B'	Next 10	50	2.8	3.9
C'	Next 10	60	4.7	8.6
D'	Next 10	70	7.4	16.0
E'	Next 10	80	11.0	27.0
F'	Next 10	90	17.4	44.4
G'	Next 10	100	55.6	100.0

The cumulative percentage of wealth is graphed against the cumulative percentage of households. Points *A'* through *G'* on the Lorenz curve for wealth correspond to the rows of the table. By comparing the Lorenz curves for income and wealth, we can see that wealth is distributed much more unequally than income.

Source: Statistics Canada, *Income in Canada*, Catalogue 75–202–XIE.

on assets is 5 percent a year, then this person receives an income of $50,000 a year from those assets. We can describe this person's economic condition by using either the wealth of $1 million or the income of $50,000. When the rate of return is 5 percent a year, $1 million of wealth equals $50,000 of income in perpetuity. Wealth and income are just different ways of looking at the same thing.

But in Fig. 15.4, the distribution of wealth is more unequal than the distribution of income. Why? It is because the wealth data do not include the value of human capital, while the income data measure income from all forms of wealth, including human capital.

Table 15.1 illustrates the consequence of omitting human capital from the wealth data. Lee has twice the wealth and twice the income of Peter. But Lee's human capital is less than Peter's—$200,000 compared with $499,000. And Lee's income from human capital of $10,000 is less than Peter's income from human capital of $24,950. Lee's nonhuman capital is larger than Peter's—$800,000 compared with $1,000. And Lee's income from nonhuman capital of $40,000 is larger than Peter's income from nonhuman capital of $50.

When Lee and Peter are surveyed by Statistics Canada in a national wealth and income survey, their incomes are recorded as $50,000 and $25,000, respectively, which implies that Lee is twice as well off as Peter. And their tangible assets are recorded as $800,000 and $1,000, respectively, which implies that Lee is 800 times as wealthy as Peter.

Because the national survey of wealth excludes human capital, the income distribution is a more accurate measure of economic inequality than the wealth distribution.

Annual or Lifetime Income and Wealth?

A typical household's income changes over time. It starts out low, grows to a peak when the household's workers reach retirement age, and then falls after retirement. Also, a typical household's wealth changes over time. Like income, it starts out low, grows to a peak at the point of retirement, and falls after retirement.

Suppose we look at three households that have identical lifetime incomes. One household is young, one is middle-aged, and one is retired. The middle-aged household has the highest income and wealth, the retired household has the lowest, and the young household falls in the middle. The distributions of annual income and wealth in a given year are unequal, but the distributions of lifetime income and wealth are equal. So some of the inequality in annual income arises because different households are at different stages in the life cycle. But we can see *trends* in the income distribution using annual income data.

TABLE 15.1 Capital, Wealth, and Income

	Lee		Peter	
	Wealth	**Income**	**Wealth**	**Income**
Human capital	200,000	10,000	499,000	24,950
Other capital	800,000	40,000	1,000	50
Total	$1,000,000	$50,000	$500,000	$25,000

When wealth is measured to include the value of human capital as well as other forms of capital, the distribution of income and the distribution of wealth display the same degree of inequality.

Trends in Inequality

Figure 15.5 shows how the distribution of income has changed since 1980. The trends are as follows:

- The share of income received by the richest 20 percent of households has increased from 40.2 percent of total income in 1980 to 42.9 percent in 1998.
- The share of income received by the poorest 20 percent of households has remained constant at 5 percent of total income.
- The shares of income received by the other three groups have decreased, and the share of the third (the middle) 20 percent of households has decreased most from 18.2 percent in 1980 to 16.7 percent in 1998.

No one knows for sure why these trends have occurred, and a large amount of research has been done to try to explain them.

The most likely explanation is one that we'll explore and explain in the next section: Higher-income groups have gained and lower-income groups have lost because the technological change of the past few decades has increased the productivity of higher skilled workers and decreased the productivity of lower-skilled workers. Increased international mobility and competition is another possible explanation.

FIGURE 15.5 Trends in the Distribution of Income: 1980–1998

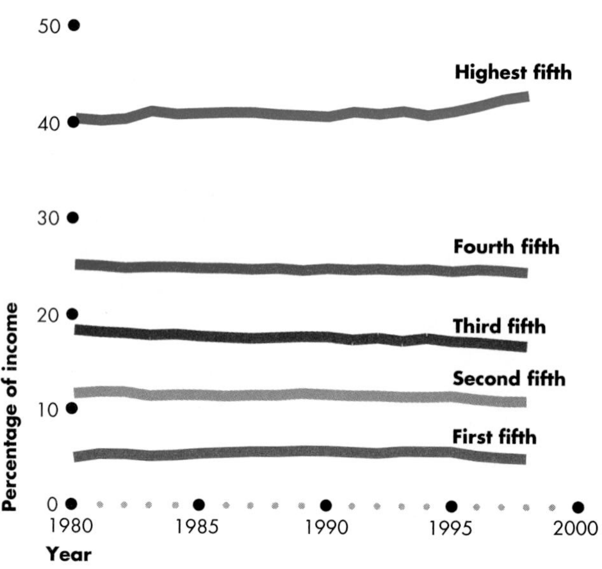

The distribution of income in Canada became more unequal in the 1980s and 1990s. The percentage of income earned by the highest fifth increased the most, and the third (middle) fifth lost the most.

Source: Statistics Canada, *Income Distribution by Size in Canada*, Catalogue 13–207–XPB.

Poverty

Families at the low end of the income distribution are so poor that they are considered to be living in poverty. **Poverty** is a state in which a family's income is too low to be able to buy the quantities of food, shelter, and clothing that are deemed necessary. Poverty is a relative concept. Millions of people living in Africa and Asia survive on incomes of less than $400 a year.

In Canada, poverty is measured in terms of a low-income cutoff. The **low-income cutoff** is the income level, determined separately for different types of families (for example, single persons, couples, one parent), that is selected such that families with incomes below that limit normally spend 54.7 percent or more of their income on food, shelter, and clothing. The low-income cutoffs currently used by Statistics Canada are based on family expenditure data for 1992. Statistics Canada measures the incidence of low income as the percentage of families whose income falls below a low-income cutoff.

Who Are the Rich and the Poor?

The highest incomes in Canada are earned by high-profile sports stars, pop stars, and television personalities and by less well known but very highly paid chief executives of large corporations. The lowest incomes are earned by people who scratch out a living doing seasonal work on farms. Aside from these extremes, what are the characteristics of people who earn high incomes and people who earn low incomes?

Six characteristics stand out:

- Source of income
- Household type
- Age of householder
- Number of children
- Education
- Labour force status

Source of Income In general, a household that earns its income either by working or from investments is more likely to be in the higher income groups. A household that receives its income in the form of a transfer payment from the government is more likely to be poor. Perhaps surprisingly, households that receive a pension income are among those least likely to be poor.

Household Type Statistics Canada classifies households into *family households* and *nonfamily households.* Most nonfamily households are single people who live alone. These households have higher incomes per person than do family households. Family households with two parents present are more likely to have a high income than are single-parent family households. And the most likely to be poor are households with a single female parent. Almost 50 percent of such households are living in poverty.

Age of Householder The youngest and the oldest households have lower incomes than middle-aged households. Income from employment tends to peak in middle age. But income from financial assets increases with age, so older households are less likely to be in poverty than young households.

FIGURE 15.6 The Incidence of Low Income by Family Characteristics

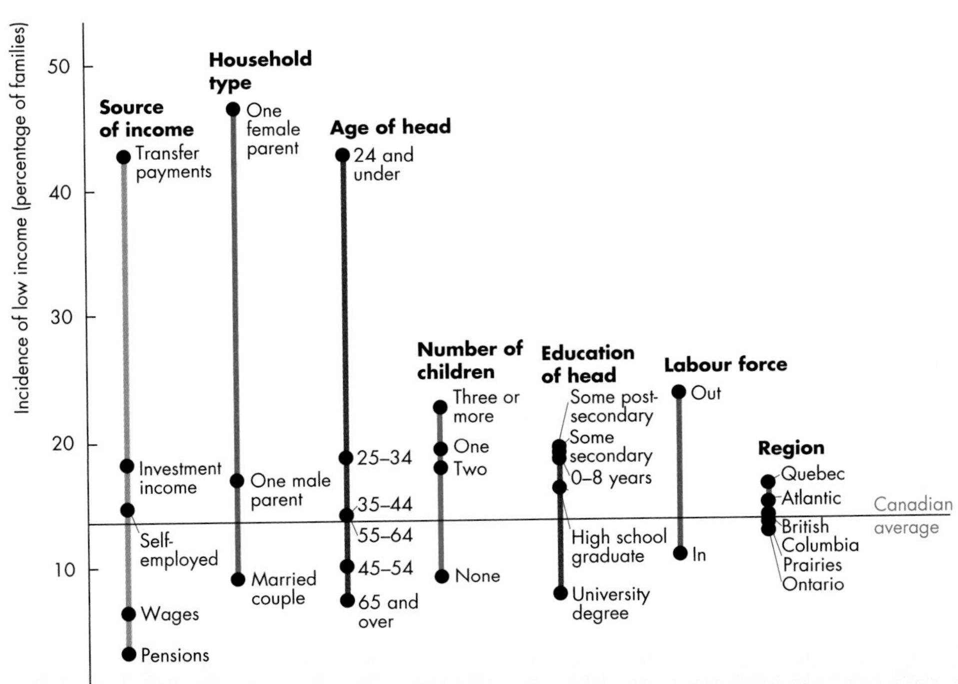

The vertical axis shows the incidence of low income—the percentage of families whose income falls below a low-income cutoff (the income level such that 54.7 percent of income is spent on food, shelter, and clothing). For Canada, on the average, 14 percent of families have incomes below the low-income cutoff. But that percentage varies depending on source of income, family type, sex and age of family head, number of children, education, and region of residence. Source of income, family type, and sex and age of family head are by far the most important factors influencing incidence of low income.

Source: Statistics Canada, *Income in Canada*, Catalogue 75–2002–XIE.

Number of Children On the average, the greater the number of children in a household, the smaller is the income per person. And the greater the number of children, the more likely is the household to be living below the poverty level.

Education Education makes a huge difference to a household's income and to the risk of poverty. A person who has not completed high school earns a fraction of a high school graduate's earnings. And a college or university degree brings a further large gain in income. Post-graduate and professional degrees take earnings even higher.

Labour Force Status Households that are in the labour force, even if unemployed, tend to have higher incomes than those not in the labour force—either because they've retired or because they have become discouraged by a persistent failure to find a suitable job.

Figure 15.6 provides a quick visual summary of the characteristics that we've just described. The figure also shows the small effect that region of residence has on the incidence of low income.

REVIEW QUIZ

1. Which is distributed more unequally: income or wealth? Why? Which is the better measure?
2. Has the distribution of income become more equal or more unequal? The share of which quintile has changed most?
3. What are the main characteristics of people who earn large incomes and small incomes?
4. What is poverty and how does its incidence vary across households?

The Sources of Economic Inequality

WE'VE DESCRIBED ECONOMIC INEQUALITY IN Canada. Our task now is to explain it. We began this task in Chapter 14 by learning about the forces that influence demand and supply in the markets for labour, capital, and land. We're now going to deepen our understanding of these forces.

Inequality arises from unequal labour market outcomes and from unequal ownership of capital. We'll begin by looking at labour markets and two of their features that contribute to differences in incomes:

- Human capital
- Discrimination

Human Capital

A clerk in a law firm earns less than a tenth of the amount earned by the lawyer he assists. An operating room assistant earns less than a tenth of the amount earned by the surgeon with whom she works. A bank teller earns less than a tenth of the amount earned by the bank's CEO. These differences in earnings arise from differences in human capital. We can explain these differences by using a model of competitive labour markets.

We'll study a model economy with two levels of human capital, which we'll call high-skilled labour and low-skilled labour. The low-skilled labour might represent the law clerk, the operating room assistant, or the bank teller, and the high-skilled labour might represent the lawyer, the surgeon, or the bank's CEO. We'll first look at the demand side of the markets for these two types of labour.

The Demand for High-Skilled and Low-Skilled Labour High-skilled workers can perform tasks that low-skilled labour would perform badly or perhaps could not perform at all. Imagine an untrained person doing open-heart surgery. High-skilled labour has a higher marginal revenue product than low-skilled labour. As we learned in Chapter 14, a firm's demand for labour curve is the same as the marginal revenue product of labour curve.

Figure 15.7(a) shows the demand curves for high-skilled and low-skilled labour. The demand curve for high-skilled labour is D_H, and that for low-skilled labour is D_L. At any given level of employment, firms are willing to pay a higher wage rate to a high-skilled worker than to a low-skilled worker. The gap between the two wage rates measures the marginal revenue product of skill. For example, at an employment level of 2,000 hours, firms are willing to pay $12.50 for a high-skilled worker and only $5 for a low-skilled worker, a difference of $7.50 an hour. Thus the marginal revenue product of skill is $7.50 an hour.

The Supply of High-Skilled and Low-Skilled Labour High-skilled labour has more human capital than low-skilled labour, and human capital is costly to acquire. The opportunity cost of acquiring human capital includes actual expenditures on such things as tuition and room and board and also costs in the form of lost or reduced earnings while the skill is being acquired. When a person goes to school full-time, that cost is the total earnings forgone. But some people acquire skills on the job—on-the-job training. Usually, a worker undergoing on-the-job training is paid a lower wage than one doing a comparable job but not undergoing training. In such a case, the cost of acquiring the skill is the difference between the wage paid to a person not being trained and that paid to a person being trained.

The position of the supply curve of high-skilled labour reflects the cost of acquiring human capital. Figure 15.7(b) shows two supply curves: one for high-skilled labour and the other for low-skilled labour. The supply curve for high-skilled labour is S_H, and that for low-skilled labour is S_L.

The high-skilled labour supply curve lies above the low-skilled labour supply curve. The vertical distance between the two supply curves is the compensation that high-skilled labour requires for the cost of acquiring the skill. For example, suppose that the quantity of low-skilled labour supplied is 2,000 hours at a wage rate of $5 an hour. This wage rate compensates the low-skilled workers mainly for their time on the job. Consider next the supply of high-skilled labour. To induce 2,000 hours of high-skilled labour to be supplied, firms must pay a wage rate of $8.50 an hour. This wage rate for high-skilled labour is higher than that for low-skilled labour because high-skilled workers must be compensated not only for the time on the job but also for the time and other costs of acquiring the skill.

Wage Rates of High-Skilled and Low-Skilled Labour To work out the wage rates of high-skilled and low-skilled labour, we have to bring together the effects of skill on the demand for and supply of labour.

FIGURE 15.7 Skill Differentials

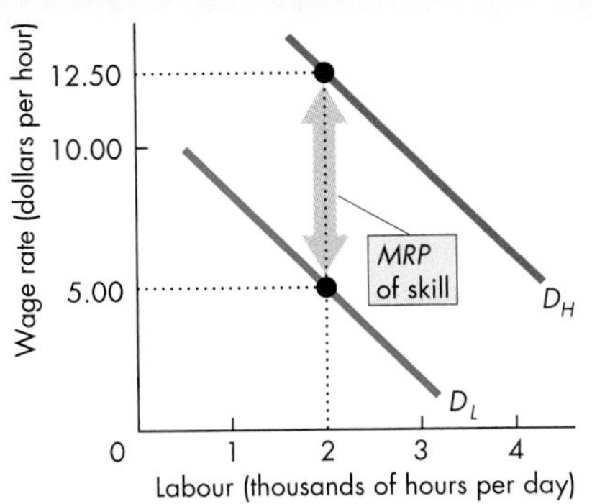

(a) Demand for high-skilled and low-skilled labour

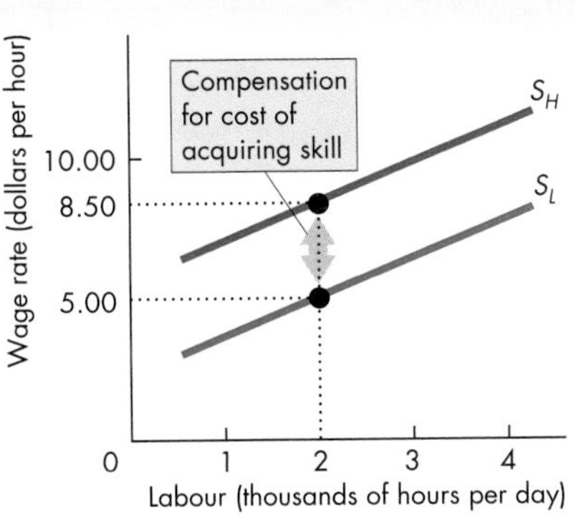

(b) Supply of high-skilled and low-skilled labour

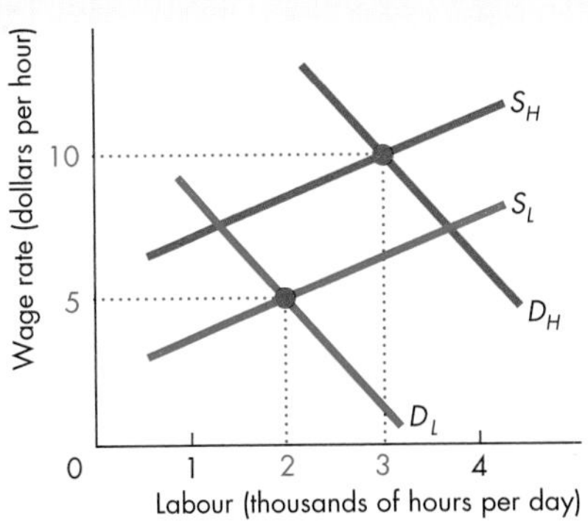

(c) Markets for high-skilled and low-skilled labour

Part (a) illustrates the marginal revenue product of skill. Low-skilled workers have a marginal revenue product that gives rise to the demand curve D_L. High-skilled workers have a higher marginal revenue product than low-skilled labour, so the demand curve for high-skilled labour, D_H, lies to the right of D_L. The vertical distance between these two curves is the marginal revenue product of the skill.

Part (b) shows the effects of the cost of acquiring skills on the supply of labour. The supply curve of low-skilled labour is S_L. The supply curve of high-skilled labour is S_H. The vertical distance between these two curves is the required compensation for the cost of acquiring a skill.

Part (c) shows the equilibrium employment and the wage differential. Low-skilled workers earn $5 an hour, and 2,000 hours of low-skilled labour are employed. High-skilled workers earn $10 an hour, and 3,000 hours of high-skilled labour are employed. The wage rate for high-skilled labour always exceeds that for low-skilled labour.

Figure 15.7(c) shows the demand curves and the supply curves for high-skilled and low-skilled labour. These curves are the same as those plotted in parts (a) and (b). Equilibrium occurs in the market for low-skilled labour where the supply and demand curves for low-skilled labour intersect. The equilibrium wage rate is $5 an hour, and the quantity of low-skilled labour employed is 2,000 hours. Equilibrium in the market for high-skilled labour occurs where the supply and demand curves for high-skilled labour intersect. The equilibrium wage rate is $10 an hour, and the quantity of high-skilled labour employed is 3,000 hours.

As you can see in part (c), the equilibrium wage rate of high-skilled labour is higher than that of low-skilled labour. There are two reasons why this occurs: First, high-skilled labour has a higher marginal revenue product than low-skilled labour, so at a given wage rate, the quantity of high-skilled labour demanded exceeds that of low-skilled labour. Second, skills are costly to acquire, so at a given wage rate, the quantity of high-skilled labour supplied is less than that of low-skilled labour. The wage differential (in this case, $5 an hour) depends on both the marginal revenue product of the skill and the cost of acquiring it. The higher the marginal revenue product of the skill, the larger is the vertical distance between the demand curves. The more costly it is to acquire a skill, the larger is the vertical distance between the supply curves. The higher the marginal revenue product of the skill and the more costly it is to acquire, the larger is the wage differential between high-skilled and low-skilled labour.

Do Education and Training Pay? Rates of return on high school and college education have been estimated to be in the range of 5 to 10 percent a year after allowing for inflation, which suggests that a university or college degree is a better investment than almost any other that a person can undertake.

Inequality Explained by Human Capital Differences Human capital differences help to explain some of the inequality that we've described above. They also help to explain some of the trends in the distribution of income that occurred during the 1990s.

You saw in Fig. 15.6 that better educated, middle-aged, two-parent households are more likely to have a high income than other household types. Human capital differences are correlated with these household characteristics. Education contributes directly to human capital. Age contributes indirectly to human capital because older workers have more experience than younger workers. Human capital differences can also explain a small part of the inequality associated with sex. A larger proportion of men than women have completed a college or university degree. These differences in education levels have disappeared in the current generation and for the population as a whole they are becoming smaller. But they have not yet been eliminated.

Interruptions to a career reduce the effectiveness of job experience in contributing to human capital. Historically, job interruptions have been more common for women than for men because women's careers have been interrupted for bearing and raising children. This factor is a possible source of lower wages, on the average, for women. Although maternity leave and day-care facilities are making career interruptions for women less common, job interruptions remain a problem for many women.

Trends in Inequality Explained by Human Capital Trends You saw in Fig. 15.5 that high-income households have earned an increasing share of after-tax income while low-income households have earned a decreasing share. Human capital differences are a possible explanation for this trend, and Fig. 15.8 illustrates this explanation. The supply of low-skilled labour (part a) and that of high-skilled labour (part b) are *S*, and initially, the demand in each market is D_0. The low-skilled wage rate is \$5 an hour, and the high-skilled wage rate is \$10 an hour.

Information technologies such as computers and laser scanners are *substitutes* for low-skilled labour: they perform tasks that previously were performed by low-skilled labour. The introduction of these technologies has decreased the demand for low-skilled labour (part a), decreased the number of low-skilled jobs, and lowered the wage rate of low-skilled workers.

These same technologies require high-skilled labour to design, program, and run them. High-skilled labour and the information technologies are *complements*. So the introduction of these technologies has increased the demand for high-skilled labour (part b), increased the number of high-skilled jobs, and raised the wage rate of high-skilled workers.

FIGURE 15.8 Explaining the Trend in Income Distribution

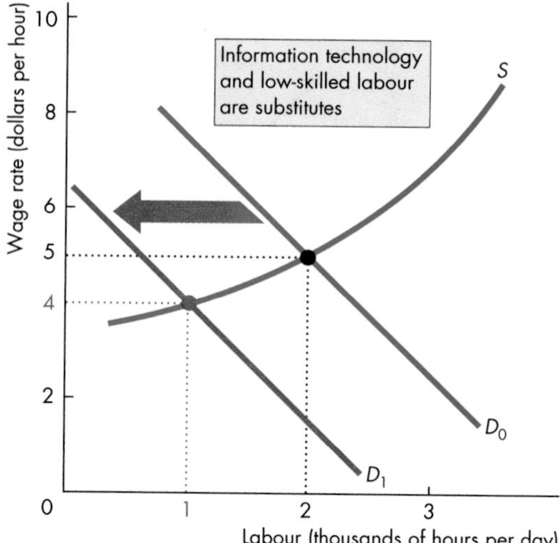

(a) A decrease in demand for low-skilled labour

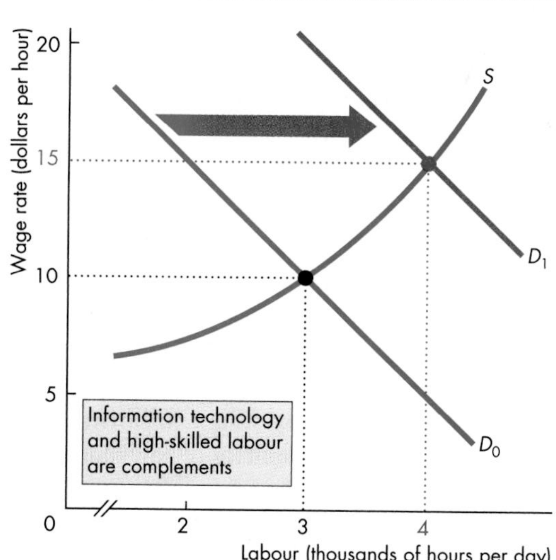

(b) An increase in demand for high-skilled labour

Low-skilled labour in part (a) and information technologies are substitutes. When these technologies were introduced, the demand for low-skilled labour decreased and the quantity of this type of labour and its wage rate decreased. High-skilled labour in part (b) and information technologies are complements. When these technologies were introduced, the demand for high-skilled labour increased and the quantity of this type of labour and its wage rate increased.

Discrimination

Human capital differences can explain some of the economic inequality that we observe. But it can't explain all of it. Discrimination is another possible source of inequality.

Suppose that females and males have identical abilities as investment advisors. Figure 15.9 shows the supply curves of females, S_F (in part a), and of males, S_M (in part b). The marginal revenue product of investment advisors shown by the two curves labelled *MRP* in parts (a) and (b) is the same for both groups.

If everyone is free of sex-based prejudice, the market determines a wage rate of $40,000 a year for investment advisors. But if the customers are prejudiced against women, this prejudice is reflected in the wage rate and employment.

Suppose that the perceived marginal revenue product of the females, when discriminated against, is MRP_{DA}. Suppose that the perceived marginal revenue product for males, the group discriminated in favour of, is MRP_{DF}. With these *MRP* curves, females earn $20,000 a year and only 1,000 females work as investment advisors. Males earn $60,000 a year, and 3,000 of them work as investment advisors.

Counteracting Forces Economists disagree about whether prejudice actually causes wage differentials, and one line of reasoning implies that it does not. In the example you've just studied, customers who buy from men pay a higher service charge for investment advice than do the customers who buy from women. This price difference acts as an incentive to encourage people who are prejudiced to buy from the people against whom they are prejudiced. This force could be strong enough to eliminate the effects of discrimination altogether.

Suppose, as is true in manufacturing, that a firm's customers never meet its workers. If such a firm discriminates against women (or against visible minorities), it can't compete with firms who hire these groups because its costs are higher than those of the unprejudiced firms. Only firms that do not discriminate survive in a competitive industry.

Whether because of discrimination or for some other reason, women on average do earn lower incomes than men. Another possible source of women's lower wage rates arises from differences in the relative degree of specialization of women and men.

FIGURE 15.9 Discrimination

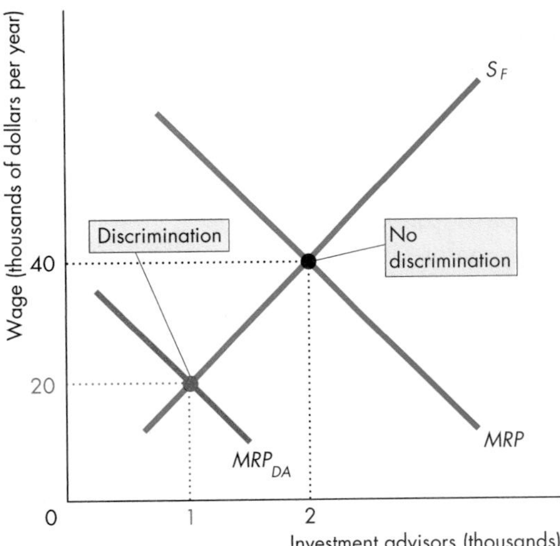

(a) Women

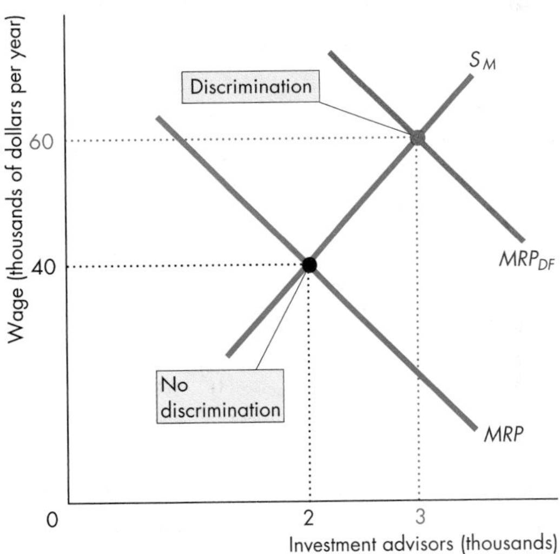

(b) Men

With no discrimination, the wage rate is $40,000 a year and 2,000 of each group are hired. With discrimination against women, the marginal revenue product curve in part (a) is MRP_{DA} and that in part (b) is MRP_{DF}. The wage rate for women falls to $20,000 a year, and only 1,000 are employed. The wage rate for men rises to $60,000 a year, and 3,000 are employed.

Differences in the Degree of Specialization Couples must choose how to allocate their time between working for a wage and doing jobs in the home, such as cooking, cleaning, shopping, organizing vacations, and, most important, bearing and raising children. Let's look at the choices of Bob and Sue.

Bob might specialize in earning an income and Sue in taking care of the home. Or Sue might specialize in earning an income and Bob in taking care of the home. Or both of them might earn an income and share home production jobs.

The allocation they choose depends on their preferences and on the earning potential of each of them. The choice of an increasing number of households is for each person to diversify between earning an income and doing some home chores. But in most households, Bob will specialize in earning an income and Sue will both earn an income and bear a larger share of the task of running the home. With this allocation, Bob will probably earn more than Sue. If Sue devotes time and effort to ensuring Bob's mental and physical well-being, the quality of Bob's market labour will be higher than it would be if he were diversified. If the roles were reversed, Sue would be able to supply market labour that earns more than Bob.

To test whether the degree of specialization accounts for earnings differences between the sexes, economists have compared the incomes of never-married men and women. They have found that, on the average, with equal amounts of human capital, the wages of these two groups are the same.

We've examined some sources of inequality in the labour market. Let's now look at the way inequality arises from unequal ownership of capital.

Unequal Ownership of Capital

You've seen that inequality in wealth (excluding human capital) is much greater than inequality in income. This inequality arises from saving and transfers of wealth from one generation to the next.

The higher a household's income, the more that household tends to save and pass on to the next generation. Saving is not always a source of increased inequality. If a household saves to redistribute an uneven income over its life cycle and enable consumption to fluctuate less than income, saving decreases inequality. If a lucky generation that has a high income saves a large part of that income and leaves capital to a succeeding generation that is unlucky, this act of saving also decreases the degree of inequality. But two features of intergenerational transfers of wealth lead to increased inequality: People can't inherit debt, and marriage tends to concentrate wealth.

Can't Inherit Debt Although a person may die in debt—with negative wealth—a debt can't be forced onto the next generation of a family. So inheritance only adds to a future generation's wealth; inheritance cannot decrease wealth.

Most people inherit nothing or a very small amount. A few people inherit an enormous fortune. As a result, intergenerational transfers make the distribution of income persistently more unequal than the distribution of ability and job skills. A household that is poor in one generation is more likely to be poor in the next. A household that is wealthy in one generation is more likely to be wealthy in the next. And marriage reinforces this tendency.

Marriage and Wealth Concentration People tend to marry within their own socioeconomic class—a phenomenon called *assortative mating*. In everyday language, "like attracts like." Although there is a good deal of folklore that "opposites attract," perhaps such Cinderella tales appeal to us because they are so rare in reality. Wealthy people seek wealthy partners.

Because of assortative mating, wealth becomes more concentrated in a small number of families and the distribution of wealth becomes more unequal.

REVIEW QUIZ

1. What role does human capital play in accounting for income inequality?
2. What role might discrimination play in accounting for income inequality?
3. What are the possible reasons for income inequality by sex and race?
4. What are the possible reasons for income inequality by age group?
5. Does inherited wealth make the distribution of income less equal or more equal?
6. Why does wealth inequality persist across generations?

Next, we're going to see how taxes and government programs redistribute income and decrease the degree of economic inequality.

Income Redistribution

THE THREE MAIN WAYS IN WHICH GOVERNMENTS in Canada redistribute income are

- Income taxes
- Income maintenance programs
- Subsidized services

Income Taxes

Income taxes may be progressive, regressive, or proportional. A **progressive income tax** is one that taxes income at an average rate that increases with the level of income. The **average tax rate** is the percentage of income paid in taxes. A **regressive income tax** is one that taxes income at an average rate that decreases with the level of income. A **proportional income tax** (also called a *flat-rate income tax*) is one that taxes income at a constant rate, regardless of the level of income.

The income tax rates that apply in Canada are composed of two parts: federal and provincial taxes. The highest income tax rates are in Quebec and the lowest are in Alberta. There is variety in the detailed tax arrangements in the individual provinces but the tax system, at both the federal and provincial levels, is progressive.

The poorest Canadians pay no income tax. Even those who earn $30,000 a year, pay a very low rate of income tax. Those whose incomes are $50,000 a year pay about 21 percent of their income in income taxes; those whose incomes are $100,000 a year pay about 28 percent in income tax; and as incomes increase, the average tax rate increases to 45 percent or higher.

Income Maintenance Programs

Three main types of programs redistribute income by making direct payments (in cash, services, or vouchers) to people in the lower part of the income distribution. They are

- Social security programs
- Employment insurance program
- Welfare programs

Social Security Programs Four programs—Old Age Security (OAS), Guaranteed Income Supplement (GIS), the Allowance (for spouses of low-income OAS pensioners), and the Allowance for the Survivor (AS)—ensure a minimum level of income for senior citizens. Monthly cash payments to retired or disabled workers or their surviving spouses are paid for by compulsory payroll taxes on both employers and employees. In December 2002, the maximum OAS was $443.99 a month, the maximum GIS for a single person was $533.99, the maximum Allowance was $797.14, and the maximum AS was $880.06.

Employment Insurance Program To provide an income to unemployed workers, the federal government has established an unemployment compensation program. The Employment Insurance program is funded by employee and employer contributions, and after a qualifying period the worker is entitled to receive a benefit if he or she becomes unemployed. The maximum unemployment benefit is $413 a week or 55 percent of gross weekly earnings over the previous 20 weeks.

Welfare Programs Other welfare programs provide income maintenance for families and persons. They are

1. Canada Assistance Plan, a plan shared equally by the federal and provincial governments that gives financial assistance to families and individuals who are in need, regardless of the cause; the assistance includes food, shelter, fuel, utilities, family supplies, items required to carry on a trade, certain welfare services, and health and social services
2. Family Supplement and Canada Child Tax Benefit programs, designed to help families who have inadequate financial support
3. Canada/Quebec Pension Plans, funded equally by employee and employer contributions, provide retirement benefits, survivor benefits, disability benefits, and death benefits
4. Workers' Compensation, a provincial program funded by employers, designed to provide financial assistance as well as medical care and rehabilitation of workers injured at work

Subsidized Services

A great deal of redistribution takes place in Canada through the provision of subsidized services, which is the provision of goods and services by the government at prices below the cost of production. The taxpayers who consume these goods and services receive a transfer in kind from the taxpayers who do not consume them. The two most important areas in which this form of redistribution takes place are education—both kindergarten through Grade 12 and college and university—and health care.

Canadian students enrolled in the universities in Ontario pay annual tuition fees of around $3,500. The cost of one year's education at one of these universities is about $17,500. Thus families with a member enrolled in these institutions receive a benefit from the government of about $14,000 a year. Those with several college or university students receive proportionately higher benefits.

Government provision of health care to all residents has brought high-quality and high-cost health care to millions of people who earn too little to buy such services themselves. As a result, this program has contributed to reducing inequality.

The Scale of Income Redistribution

To determine the scale of income redistribution, we need to compare the distribution of *market income* with the distribution of *after-tax income.* The data available on benefits exclude the value of subsidized services (such as the value of university education and health care services), so the resulting distribution might understate the total amount of redistribution from the rich to the poor.

Figure 15.10 shows the scale of redistribution based on the calculations just described. In part (a), the blue Lorenz curve describes the market distribution of income and the green Lorenz curve shows the distribution of income after all taxes and benefits. (The Lorenz curve based on *total income*—market income plus transfer payments from governments—lies between these two curves.)

The distribution after taxes and benefits is much less unequal than the market distribution. In 1998, the lowest 20 percent of households received only 0.7 percent of market income but 5 percent of after-tax income. The highest 20 percent of households received 50.8 percent of market income but only 42.9 percent of after-tax income.

Figure 15.10(b) highlights the percentage of total income redistributed among the five groups. The share of total income received by the lowest three quintiles (60 percent) of households increased. The share of total income received by the fourth quintile fell slightly. And the share of total income received by the highest quintile fell by almost 8 percent of total income.

FIGURE 15.10 Income Redistribution

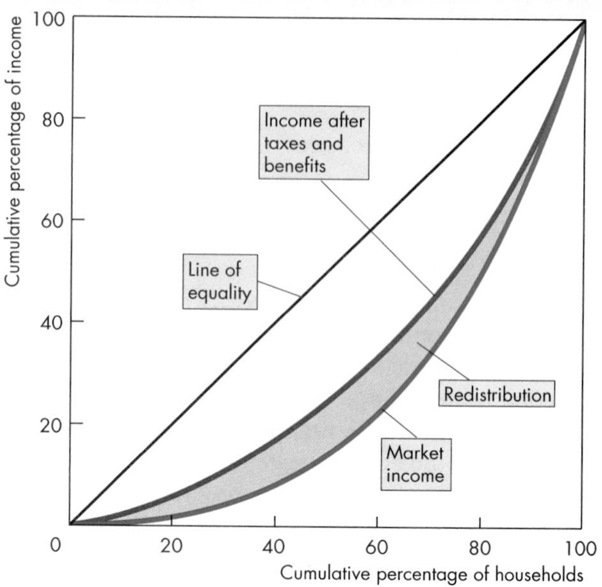

(a) Income distribution before and after redistribution

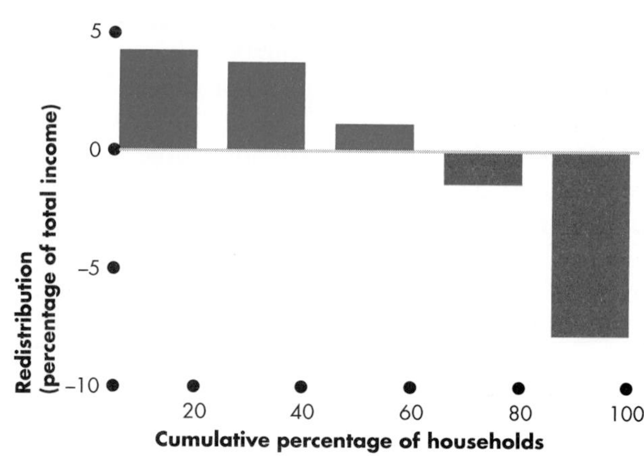

(b) The scale of redistribution

Redistribution reduces the degree of inequality that the market generates. In 1998, the 20 percent of households with the lowest incomes received net benefits that increased their share from 0.7 percent of market income to 5 percent of after-tax income. The 20 percent of households with the highest incomes paid taxes that decreased their share from 50.8 percent of market income to 42.9 percent of income after taxes and redistribution.

Source: Statistics Canada, *Income in Canada*, Catalogue 75–202–XIE.

The Big Tradeoff

The redistribution of income creates what has been called the **big tradeoff**, a tradeoff between equity and efficiency. The big tradeoff arises because redistribution uses scarce resources and weakens incentives.

A dollar collected from a rich person does not translate into a dollar received by a poor person. Some of the dollar collected gets used up in the process of redistribution. Tax-collecting agencies such as the Canada Customs and Revenue Agency and welfare-administering agencies (as well as tax accountants and lawyers) use skilled labour, computers, and other scarce resources to do their work. The bigger the scale of redistribution, the greater is the opportunity cost of administering it.

But the cost of collecting taxes and making welfare payments is a small part of the total cost of redistribution. A bigger cost arises from the inefficiency —deadweight loss—of taxes and benefits. Greater equality can be achieved only by taxing productive activities such as work and saving. Taxing people's income from their work and saving lowers the after-tax income they receive. This lower after-tax income makes them work and save less, which in turn results in smaller output and less consumption not only for the rich who pay the taxes but also for the poor who receive the benefits.

It is not only taxpayers who face weaker incentives to work. Benefit recipients also face weaker incentives. In fact, under the welfare arrangements that prevail in Canada today, the weakest incentives to work are those faced by households that benefit most from welfare. When a welfare recipient gets a job, benefits are withdrawn and eligibility for support is withdrawn. In effect, these households face a marginal tax of more than 100 percent on their earnings. This arrangement locks poor households in a welfare trap.

So the scale and methods of income redistribution must pay close attention to the incentive effects of taxes and benefits.

A Major Welfare Challenge The poorest people in Canada are women who have not completed high school, have a child (or children), and live without a partner. But all single mothers present a major welfare challenge. First, their numbers are large. There are approximately one million single mothers in Canada today. Second, their economic plight and the economic prospects for their children are serious.

Janet Peterson and her four children aged 3 to 13 are one example. Janet has a serious physical disability. She receives a social assistance cheque each month for $1,286, or $15,432 a year. The low-income cutoff for a family of five is $30,910. So Janet and her children live in severe poverty. She spends $625 a month on rent, $400 on food, and the rest on gas, hydro, the phone, and transportation. To provide Janet Peterson (and the other million single mothers) with an income that matches the low-income cutoff would cost more than $10 billion a year.

Janet Peterson has a physical disability that makes it unlikely that she could work. Many other single mothers are in this situation. But this is not the typical case. Most single mothers are physically fit and are capable of working. And some of them are well educated and therefore can earn a high wage rate. Even those single mothers who have not completed high school are capable of either attending school or getting a job.

For physically fit single mothers, the long-term solution to their problem is education and on-the-job training—acquiring human capital. The short-term solution is welfare. But welfare must be designed to minimize the disincentive to pursue the long-term goal. This is the challenge in designing an adequate welfare program.

REVIEW QUIZ

1. How do governments in Canada redistribute income?
2. How large is the scale of redistribution in Canada?
3. What is one of the major welfare challenges today and how is it being tackled in Canada?

We've examined economic inequality in Canada, and we've seen how inequality arises. And we've seen that inequality has increased since 1980. *Reading Between the Lines* on pp. 362–363 looks at the increasing economic inequality in Canada's major cities.

Your task in the following chapters is to look more closely at government actions that modify the outcome of the market economy. We look at sources of market failure and the ways in which government actions aim to overcome it. We also look at what has been called the *political marketplace* and the potential for it to fail too.

READING BETWEEN THE LINES

Trends in Inequality

NATIONAL POST, DECEMBER 14, 2000

Rich and poor growing fastest in Edmonton

The income gap between rich and poor neighbourhoods in Canada's eight largest cities is widening, according to a Statistics Canada report released yesterday.

The 15-year study, based on censuses between 1980 and 1995, indicates the gap has grown the most quickly in Edmonton, by 29.8% — mostly because high-income earners in Alberta's capital tend to cluster in the same areas. Toronto closely follows with a 28.7% increase, mostly because the rich in Canada's largest city are growing richer.

The income gap in Calgary and Winnipeg increased by 20% or more.

Vancouver neighbourhoods showed the smallest increase, at 7.9%. The study said that unlike Edmonton, Calgary, Winnipeg and Quebec City, high-income earners in Vancouver are not concentrated in the same neighbourhoods. But, like Toronto and Montreal, the West Coast city's income gap is still rising.

The report reveals inequality in family incomes between neighbourhoods rose in all cities. Real average earnings fell, sometimes dramatically, in low-income neighbourhoods in virtually all cities while rising moderately in most higher-income neighbourhoods, led by residents living in Toronto, Winnipeg and the Ottawa-Hull region. Only Vancouver marked a decrease in income levels among richer neighbourhoods.

Changes in employment and unemployment patterns were cited as the main reason for the increase, with unemployment the most prevalent in lower-income neighbourhoods.

"The commonly accepted explanation is that it's related to technological change, with increased technology the demand for highly skilled workers rose and the demand for lower skilled workers fell so their wages dropped," said Garnett Picot, director-general of the analytical studies branch at Statistics Canada and an author of the study.

Mr. Picot said the income gap may have improved recently as provincial and local economies flourished. "But I am quite certain it is not reversing the employment issues that we see in the low-income communities."

New census data will not be available until next year. ...

National Post, Financial Post.

Essence of the Story

- A Statistics Canada report published in 2000 says the income gap between rich and poor neighbourhoods in Canada's eight largest cities widened between 1980 and 1995.
- The income gap increased in all cities.
- The gap grew the most in Edmonton, with Toronto close behind.
- The gap grew least in Vancouver.
- Garnett Picot of Statistics Canada said technological change has increased the demand for highly skilled workers and decreased the demand for lower skilled workers.

Economic Analysis

■ In this chapter, we describe the degree of inequality by using quintile income shares and making a Lorenz curve from those numbers.

■ This news article uses the ratio of the average income of the highest 5 percent to the average income of the lowest 5 percent as a measure of inequality.

■ Figure 1 shows this ratio for the eight cities covered by the reported research in 1980 and 1995.

■ The blue bars show the numbers for 1980 and the red bars for 1995.

■ You can see that this measure indicates that the degree of inequality increased in all regions between 1980 and 1995.

■ Figures 2 and 3 illustrate Garnett Picot's explanation for the widening income gap (which is also the explanation provided in this chapter).

■ In Fig. 2, the demand for low-skilled labour in 1980 is D_{80} and the supply of labour is S_{80}. By 1995, demand had increased to D_{95} and supply had increased to S_{95}.

■ Because supply increased by more than demand, the quantity of labour increased but the wage rate fell.

■ In Fig. 3, the demand for high-skilled labour in 1980 is D_{80} and the supply of labour is S_{80}. By 1995, demand had increased to D_{95} and supply had increased to S_{95}, and because demand increased by more than supply, the quantity of labour increased and the wage rate rose.

■ The supply of high-skilled labour increased slowly because the new technologies require a higher level of education to complement them.

■ The demand for high-skilled labour increased by a large amount because the new technologies that have changed the structure of the economy have increased the value of marginal product of highly educated workers.

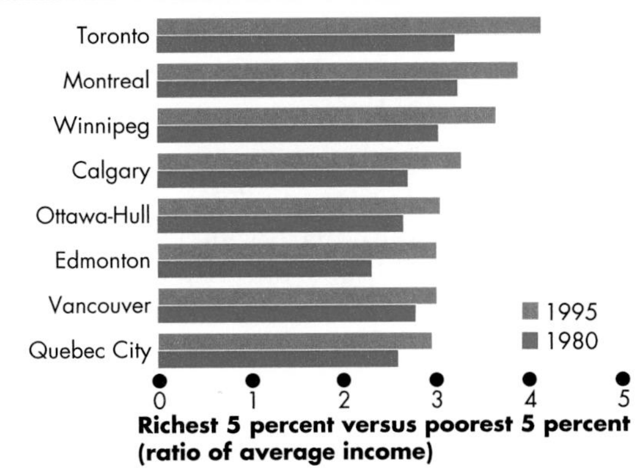

Figure 1 Income gaps in eight cities

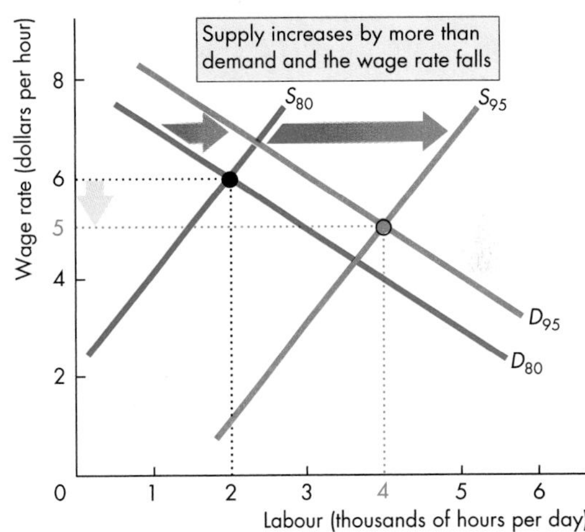

Figure 2 A market for low-skilled labour

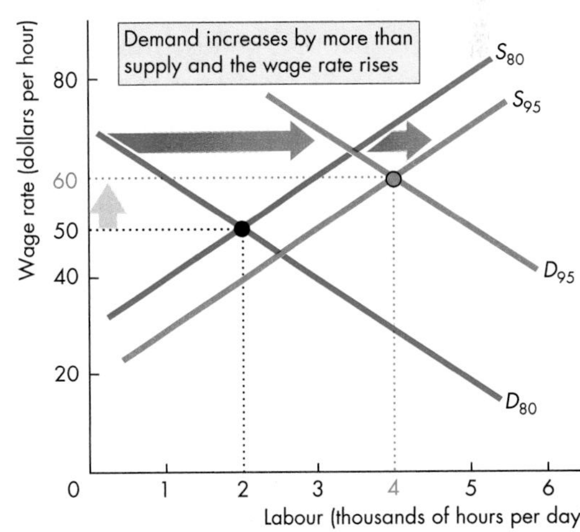

Figure 3 A market for high-skilled labour

SUMMARY

KEY POINTS

Measuring Economic Inequality (pp. 348–353)

- In 1998, the mode after-tax income was in the range between $10,000 and $14,999 a year, the median after-tax income was $33,227, and the mean after-tax income was $39,943.
- The income distribution is positively skewed.
- The poorest 20 percent of households received 5 percent of total income, and the wealthiest 20 percent received 42.9 percent of total income.
- Wealth is distributed more unequally than income because the wealth data exclude the value of human capital.
- Since 1980, the share of income received by the richest 20 percent of households has increased, the share of the poorest 20 percent has remained constant, and the shares of income received by the other three groups of households have decreased.
- Source of income, household type, age of householder, number of children, education, and labour market status all influence household income.

The Sources of Economic Inequality (pp. 354–358)

- Inequality arises from differences in human capital.
- Inequality might arise from discrimination.
- Inequality between men and women might arise from differences in the degree of specialization.
- Intergenerational transfers of wealth lead to increased inequality because people can't inherit debt, and assortative mating tends to concentrate wealth.

Income Redistribution (pp. 359–361)

- Governments redistribute income through progressive income taxes, income maintenance programs, and subsidized services.
- Redistribution increases the share of total income received by the lowest three quintiles (60 percent) of households and decreases the share of total income received by the highest quintile. The share of the fourth quintile falls slightly.
- Because the redistribution of income weakens incentives, it creates a tradeoff between equity and efficiency.
- Effective redistribution seeks to support the long-term solution to low income, which is education and job training—acquiring human capital.

KEY FIGURES

Figure 15.1 The Distribution of Income in Canada in 1998, 348
Figure 15.4 Lorenz Curves for Income and Wealth, 350
Figure 15.5 Trends in the Distribution of Income: 1980–1998, 352
Figure 15.6 The Incidence of Low Income by Family Characteristics, 353
Figure 15.7 Skill Differentials, 355
Figure 15.8 Explaining the Trend in Income Distribution, 356
Figure 15.9 Discrimination, 357
Figure 15.10 Income Redistribution, 360

KEY TERMS

Average tax rate, 359
After-tax income, 348
Big tradeoff, 361
Low-income cutoff, 352
Lorenz curve, 349
Market income, 348
Poverty, 352
Progressive income tax, 359
Proportional income tax, 359
Regressive income tax, 359
Total income, 348

PROBLEMS

*1. The table shows income shares in the United States in 2000.

Households (percentage)	Income (percent of total)
Lowest 20	4.8
Second-lowest 20	10.5
Third-lowest 20	15.8
Fourth-lowest 20	22.8
Highest 20	46.1

a. Draw a Lorenz curve for the United States in 2000 and compare it with that for Canada in 1998 shown in Fig. 15.3.
b. Was Canadian income distributed more equally or less equally than that in the United States?
c. Can you think of some reasons for the differences in the distribution of income in Canada and the United States?

2. The table shows income shares in Sweden in 1992.

Households (percentage)	Income (percent of total)
Lowest 20	6.7
Second-lowest 20	12.2
Third-lowest 20	17.6
Fourth-lowest 20	24.5
Highest 20	39.0

a. Draw the Lorenz curve for income in Sweden in 1992.
b. Was income distributed more equally or less equally in Canada in 1998 than in Sweden in 1992?
c. Use the information provided in problem 1 on the distribution of income in the United States in 2000. Was income distributed more equally or less equally in the United States in 2000 than in Sweden in 1992?
d. Can you think of some reasons for the differences in the distribution of income in Canada and Sweden?

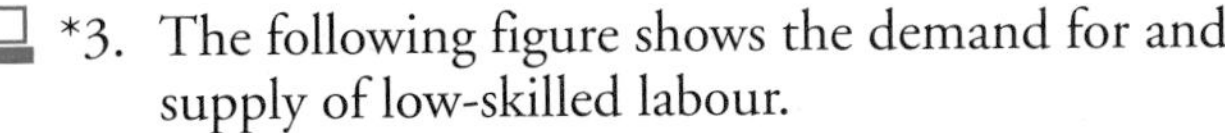

*3. The following figure shows the demand for and supply of low-skilled labour.

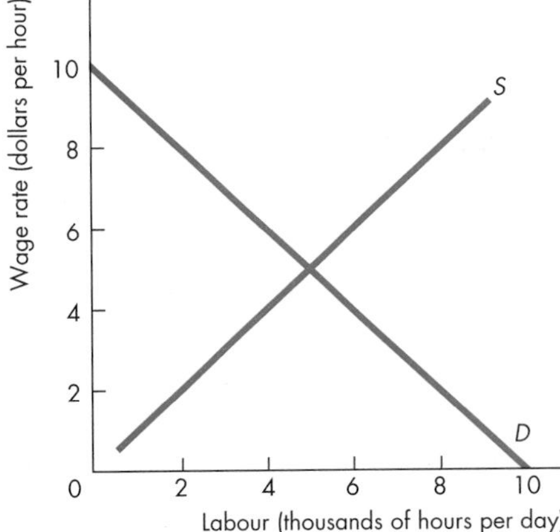

High-skilled workers have twice the marginal product of low-skilled workers. (The marginal product at each employment level is twice the marginal product of a low-skilled worker.) But the cost of acquiring the skill adds $2 an hour to the wage that must be offered to attract high-skilled labour. What is

a. The wage rate of low-skilled labour?
b. The quantity of low-skilled labour employed?
c. The wage rate of high-skilled labour?
d. The quantity of high-skilled labour employed?

4. The following figure shows the demand for and supply of low-skilled labour.

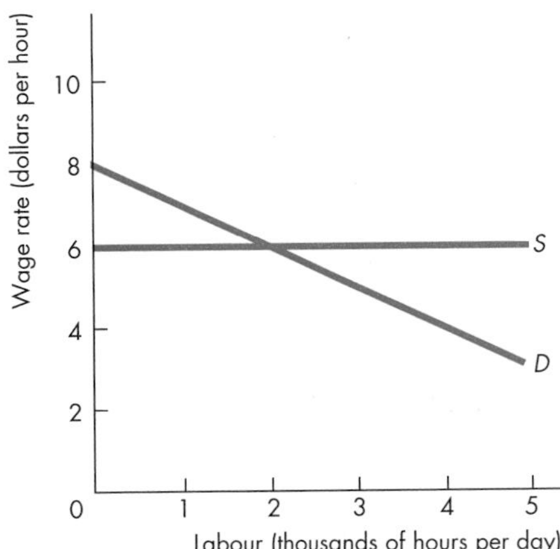

The marginal productivity of a high-skilled worker is $10 an hour greater than that of a low-skilled worker. (The marginal product at each employment level is $10 greater than that of a low-skilled worker.) The cost of acquiring the skill adds $6 an hour to the wage that must be offered to attract high-skilled labour.
a. What is the wage rate of low-skilled labour?
b. What is the quantity of low-skilled labour employed?
c. What is the wage rate of high-skilled labour?
d. What is the quantity of high-skilled labour employed?
e. Why does the wage rate of a high-skilled worker exceed that of a low-skilled worker by exactly the cost of acquiring the skill?

*5. The table shows the distribution of market income in Canada in 1998.

Households (percentage)	**Market income** (percent of total)
Lowest 20	0.7
Second-lowest 20	7.2
Third-lowest 20	15.5
Fourth-lowest 20	25.8
Highest 20	50.8

a. What is market income?
b. Draw the Lorenz curve for the distribution of market income.
c. Compare the distribution of market income with the distribution of after-tax income shown in Fig. 15.3. Which distribution is more unequal and why?

6. Use the information provided in problem 5 and in Fig. 15.3.
a. What is the percentage of market income that is redistributed from the highest income group?
b. What are the percentages of market income that are redistributed to the lower income groups?
c. Describe the effects of increasing the amount of income redistribution in Canada to the point at which the lowest income group receives 15 percent of after-tax income and the highest income group receives 30 percent of after-tax income.

CRITICAL THINKING

1. Study *Reading Between the Lines* on pp. 362–363 and then
a. Describe the main facts about the changes in the distribution of income in Canada reported in the news article.
b. In which cities is the distribution of income more unequal or less unequal?
c. Why, according to the news article, has the gap between the rich and the poor widened?
d. Do you think the explanation for the widening gap between high and low incomes explains the regional differences? Explain why or why not using the ideas that you have learned in this chapter.
e. What policy issues are raised by the news article?
f. How do you think the tax system and the welfare system should be changed to influence the distribution of after-tax income in Canada today?

WEB EXERCISES

1. Use the link on the Parkin–Bade Web site to obtain data on income distribution among major league baseball players. Then
a. Describe the main facts about the income distribution of major league players.
b. Compare the income distribution of these players with the income distribution of Canada.
c. Which is more unequal?
d. What is the problem with inequality?

2. Use the link on the Parkin–Bade Web site to download the World Bank's Deininger and Squire Data Set on income distribution in a large number of countries.
a. Which country in the data set has the most unequal distribution?
b. Which country in the data set has the most equal distribution?
c. Can you think of reasons that might explain the differences in income distribution in the two countries you've identified?

UNDERSTANDING FACTOR MARKETS

For Whom?

During the past 35 years, the rich have been getting richer and the poor poorer. This trend is new. From the end of World War II until 1965, the poor got richer at a faster pace than the rich and the gap between rich and poor narrowed a bit. What are the forces that generate these trends? The answer to this question is the forces of demand and supply in factor markets. These forces determine wages, interest rates, and the prices of land and natural resources. These forces also determine people's incomes. ◆ The three categories of resources are human, capital, and natural. Human resources include labour, human capital, and entrepreneurship. The income of labour and human capital depends on wage rates and employment levels, which are determined in labour markets. The income from capital depends on interest rates and the amount of capital, which are determined in capital markets. The income from natural resources depends on prices and quantities that are determined in natural resource markets. Only the return to entrepreneurship is not determined directly in a market. That return is normal profit plus economic profit, and it depends on how successful each entrepreneur is in the business that he or she runs. ◆ The chapters in this part study the forces at play in factor markets and explain how those forces have led to changes in the distribution of income. ◆ The overview of all the factor markets in Chapter 14 explained how the demand for factors of production results from the profit-maximizing decisions of firms. You studied these decisions from a different angle in Chapters 9–13, where you learned how firms choose their profit-maximizing output and price. Chapter 14 explained how a firm's profit-maximizing decisions determine its demand for factors of production. It also explained how factor supply decisions are made and how equilibrium in factor markets determines factor prices and the incomes of owners of factors of production. ◆ Some of the biggest incomes earned by superstars are a surplus that we call economic rent. ◆ Chapter 14 used labour resources and the labour market as its main example. But it also looked at some special features of capital markets and natural resource markets. ◆ Chapter 15 studied the distribution of income. This chapter took you right back to the fundamentals of economics and answered one of the big economic questions: Who gets to consume the goods and services that are produced? ◆ Many outstanding economists have advanced our understanding of factor markets and the role they play in helping to resolve the conflict between the demands of humans and the resources available. One of them is Thomas Robert Malthus, whom you can meet on the following page. You can also enjoy the insights of Janet Currie, a professor of economics at UCLA and a prominent contemporary Canadian labour economist.

PROBING THE IDEAS

Running Out of Resources

THE ECONOMIST

"The passion between the sexes has appeared in every age to be so nearly the same, that it may always be considered, in algebraic language, as a given quantity."

THOMAS ROBERT MALTHUS
An Essay on the Principle of Population

THOMAS ROBERT MALTHUS *(1766–1834), an English clergyman and economist, was an extremely influential social scientist. In his best-selling* An Essay on the Principle of Population, *published in 1798, he predicted that population growth would outstrip food production and said that wars, famine, and disease were inevitable unless population growth was held in check by what he called "moral restraint." By "moral restraint," he meant marrying at a late age and living a celibate life. He married at the age of 38 a wife of 27, marriage ages that he recommended for others. Malthus's ideas were regarded as too radical in their day. And they led Thomas Carlyle, a contemporary thinker, to dub economics the "dismal science." But the ideas of Malthus had a profound influence on Charles Darwin, who got the key idea that led him to the theory of natural selection from reading* An Essay on the Principle of Population. *And David Ricardo and the classical economists were strongly influenced by Malthus's ideas.*

THE ISSUES

Is there a limit to economic growth, or can we expand production and population without effective limit? Thomas Malthus gave one of the most influential answers to these questions in 1798. He reasoned that population, unchecked, would grow at a geometric rate—1, 2, 4, 8, 16...—while the food supply would grow at an arithmetic rate—1, 2, 3, 4, 5.... To prevent the population from outstripping the available food supply, there would be periodic wars, famines, and plagues. In Malthus's view, only what he called moral restraint could prevent such periodic disasters.

As industrialization proceeded through the nineteenth century, Malthus's idea came to be applied to all natural resources, especially those that are exhaustible.

Modern-day Malthusians believe that his basic idea is correct and that it applies not only to food but also to every natural resource. In time, these prophets of doom believe, we will be reduced to the subsistence level that Malthus predicted. He was a few centuries out in his predictions but not dead wrong.

One modern-day Malthusian is ecologist Paul Ehrlich, who believes that we are sitting on a "population bomb." Governments must, says Ehrlich, limit both population growth and the resources that may be used each year.

In 1931, Harold Hotelling developed a theory of natural resources with different predictions from those of Malthus. The Hotelling Principle is that the relative price of an exhaustible natural resource will steadily rise, bringing a decline in the quantity used and an increase in the use of substitute resources.

Julian Simon (who died in 1998) challenged both the Malthusian gloom and the Hotelling Principle. He believed that people are the "ultimate resource" and predicted that a rising population lessens the pressure on natural resources. A bigger population provides a larger number of resourceful people who can work out more efficient ways of using scarce resources. As these solutions are found, the prices of exhaustible resources actually fall. To demonstrate his point, in 1980, Simon bet Ehrlich that the prices of five metals—copper, chrome, nickel, tin, and tungsten—would fall during the 1980s. Simon won the bet!

Then

No matter whether it is agricultural land, an exhaustible natural resource, or the space in the centre of Winnipeg, and no matter whether it is 1998 or, as shown here, 1913, there is a limit to what is available, and we persistently push against that limit. Economists see urban congestion as a consequence of the value of doing business in the city centre relative to the cost. They see the price mechanism, bringing ever-higher rents and prices of raw materials, as the means of allocating and rationing scarce natural resources. Malthusians, in contrast, explain congestion as the consequence of population pressure, and they see population control as the solution.

Now

In Tokyo, the pressure on space is so great that in some residential neighbourhoods, a parking space costs $1,700 a month. To economize on this expensive space—and to lower the cost of car ownership and hence boost the sale of new cars—Honda, Nissan, and Toyota, three of Japan's big car producers, have developed a parking machine that enables two cars to occupy the space of one. The most basic of these machines costs a mere $10,000—less than 6 months' parking fees.

Malthus developed his ideas about population growth in a world in which women played a limited role in the economy. Malthus did not consider the opportunity cost of women's time a factor to be considered in predicting trends in the birth rate and population growth. But today, the opportunity cost of women's time is a crucial factor because women play an expanded role in the labour force. One woman who has made significant contributions to our knowledge of labour markets is Janet Currie of UCLA. You can meet Professor Currie on the following pages.

TALKING WITH

JANET CURRIE *is a professor of economics at the University of California, Los Angeles. Born in 1960 in Kingston, Ontario, she attended the University of Toronto, where she received her B.A. and M.A. in economics before moving to Princeton University, where she completed her Ph.D. in 1988. Professor Currie's research examines a wide range of public programs—medical, nutritional, educational, and housing—for (mainly) poor families. She has provided valuable assessments of the short-term and long-term effects of the Head Start program (enriched preschool for children in poor households) and Medicaid (government-provided health insurance for poor mothers and their children).*

Janet Currie

Michael Parkin and Robin Bade talked with Janet Currie about her work and the progress that economists have made in understanding how public policies can influence the distribution of income and economic well-being as well as the supply of labour and human capital.

Professor Currie, what attracted you to economics?

I was attracted to economics because it addresses questions of broad human interest (such as poverty and inequality) with intellectual rigour. Some may view the economic paradigm as restrictive (does everyone really maximize utility all the time?), but it provides a set of tools that yield powerful predictions about human behaviour, and it can be tested. For example, the "Law of Demand" (people consume less of a good when the price goes up) can be adopted to think about why many eligible people do not participate in social programs that might benefit them.

Why are there still relatively few women in our field?

Like other scientific careers, that of an economist requires an initial investment in mathematical skills. Mathematics is the language of science, and it is difficult to become a scientist if you don't speak the language. Undergraduate programs in economics may be partially to blame for not preparing students adequately for graduate work in the field. Many programs are aimed more at preparing students for careers in law or business. While this may be what the majority of undergraduate economics students want, we should also serve those who may go on to study economics in graduate school.

Difficulties in combining work and family are also an issue, but economics is not unique in requiring women to devote a lot of time to their careers at precisely the point when traditionally women would spend most time with their families. However, supports such as maternity leave and child care are improving, and making it easier for younger women to "do it all."

Could you briefly describe Head Start and summarize your main conclusions about its effects?

Head Start is a U.S. preschool program for disadvantaged three- to five-year-old children. In a series of studies comparing Head Start children to siblings who did not attend, I find evidence of lasting effects of Head Start in terms of schooling attainment and reductions in criminal activity. These findings are important because, while everyone would like to believe that investments in children pay off, there was little prior evidence of longer-term effects of Head Start.

You asked in a recent paper, "Are public housing projects good for kids?" What's the answer?

The title of this paper is intentionally provocative. Given all the negative publicity about some housing projects, most people assume that public housing must be bad for children. However, the key question is not whether kids in public housing do worse than other kids (they do) but whether they do better than they would have done in the absence of the program. For example, without the program, some children might have become homeless or had to move many times. It turns out that on average, public housing programs do improve the housing available to poor families, and have some positive effects in terms of schooling attainments.

In another paper, published in 1998, you summarized what we know and need to know about the effects of welfare programs on children. What, in a nutshell, do we know? What do we still need to know? And how would we set about finding the needed answers?

One striking conclusion from this review of welfare programs is that the available evidence suggests that in-kind programs are more effective than traditional welfare programs, which give cash to parents. This might account for the growing proportion of aid to poor families that is given in the form of specific in-kind benefits (e.g., Head Start, medical insurance, housing assistance). However, the evidence is far from complete. We need a lot more information about effects of programs on children, since anti-poverty programs are often justified in terms of their possible beneficial effects on children. We also need more information about longer-term effects of programs. For example, does it matter at what age the benefits are received?

In terms of how to find out what we need to know, I am a big supporter of social experiments, since a real random-assignment, treatment-control design provides more convincing answers than most statistical studies. On the other hand, it isn't possible to mount an experiment for every question. Much more could be done with exiting data if more of it was made available to researchers and if governments were more willing to allow linkages of different data sources.

What are some of the social experiments that have provided convincing answers? And how could economists do better work if governments were more willing to allow linkages of different data sources?

The great thing about a well-designed experiment is that anyone can understand the results. For example, in a drug trial, we randomly assign people to a treatment group that gets the drug, and a control group that gets a placebo. Because of the random assignment, the two groups are the same on average, so that any *ex poste* differences in how they do can be attributed to the treatment.

"The great thing about a well-designed experiment is that anyone can understand the results."

Social experiments like the "Moving to Opportunity" project also rely on random assignment. In this experiment, the treatment consisted of giving a voucher to families in public housing projects that allowed the families to move into a low-poverty neighbourhood and gave them some assistance in relocating. The initial results indicate that the experiment had an effect on youth crime, as well as on criminal victimization. So far, there are no positive effects on schooling attainment or parental employment, but it is possible that these will emerge in the followup that is currently being conducted.

Another interesting experiment involves Early Head Start, a U.S. program that extends Head Start benefits to infants and toddlers. This program has demonstrated short-term effects of the program on cognitive test scores. Again, it will be necessary to do some long-term followup in order to see whether these benefits are retained.

The downside of experiments is that they are very expensive, relative to a statistical study, and cannot be used to answer questions other than those they were designed to address. Some of my work on the effects of Medicaid expansions provides an example of what can be done by linking various types of data. The U.S. government collects a good deal of survey data about health insurance and health care utilization. Because my co-author, Jon Gruber, was working in Washington, we were able to get state identifiers so that we could link information about Medicaid income cutoffs in each state to the individual-level records. This enabled us to ask how changing the income cutoffs affected health care utilization. In recent years, the government has been unwilling to release geographic identifiers, so that it is not possible to do a similar study of more recent health insurance expansions.

A few years ago, you stuck out your neck on the never-to-end minimum wage issue. What, according to your work, is the effect of the minimum wage on youth employment?

We found compelling evidence that youths affected by minimum wage legislation were less likely to be employed than those who were not (because they had wages either above or below the affected group). There are some obvious methodological flaws with some of the work arguing that minimum wages actually increase employment (such as failure to properly control for increases in demand, which might be driving increases in employment even at the higher minimum wages). However, much of the work (my own included) ignores an important question, which is whether we actually want to increase employment among youths. If higher minimum wages reduced employment but increased schooling, perhaps this would be a good outcome.

You've studied the effects of restrictions on the use of public funds for abortion. What did you discover?

Many people have argued that restrictions on abortion may cause more unwanted children to be born and hence worsen infant and child outcomes. The basic idea of my paper was that if this were true, then one ought to be able to see the effect in the distribution of birthweights. That is, if children who would have been aborted are more likely to be of low birthweight (because their mothers did not take care of themselves), then one should see more low birthweight infants in areas that adopt abortion restrictions.

> ***"...economics are increasingly contributing to debate (and frequently having the last word) on questions that used to be considered far outside their scope."***

We did not, however, find this effect. In hindsight, it is not obvious that children who are born as a result of abortion restrictions ought to be less healthy than average, since the majority of women seeking abortions are young and non-poor.

What advice do you have for a student who is just starting to study economics? Do you think that economics is a good subject in which to major? What other subjects would you urge students to study alongside economics?

I have never regretted choosing economics as a major. Economics gives one the tools to study a vast array of social issues in a rigorous manner. Not surprisingly, economists are increasingly contributing to debate (and frequently having the last word) on questions that used to be considered far outside their scope. Economics concepts such as "opportunity cost," "selection bias," and "cost-benefit analysis" are central to the discussion of a vast array of policy issues.

Students who want to leave open the option of graduate work in economics should make sure they take enough mathematics courses to get them through a good graduate program.

PUBLIC GOODS AND TAXES

CHAPTER 16

Government: The Solution or the Problem?

Canada's federal, provincial, and municipal governments employ 1.5 million people and spend more than 40 cents of every dollar that we earn. Do we need this much government? Is government too big, as some Progressive Conservatives and Canadian Alliance Party members suggest? Is government "the problem"? Or, despite its enormous size, is government too small to do all the things it must? Is government, as some Liberals and New Democrats suggest, not contributing enough to economic life? ◆ After the terrorist attacks on New York and Washington on September 11, 2001, almost everyone agreed that governments around the world need to step up the scope and quality of domestic and global security. What determines the scale on which the government provides a public service such as domestic security? And why can't the market provide the security that people demand? To pay for the things they provide, governments collect taxes. What determines the types and scale of the taxes that we pay?

We begin our study of government by describing the areas in which the market economy fails to achieve an efficient allocation of resources. We then explain what determines the scale of government provision of public services and the taxes that pay for them. In *Reading Between the Lines* at the end of the chapter, we return to the consequences of September 11 and look at the increased public expenditure on Canada's border security.

After studying this chapter, you will be able to

- **Explain how government arises from market failure and redistribution**
- **Distinguish between public goods and private goods, explain the free-rider problem, and explain how the quantity of public goods is determined**
- **Explain why most of the government's revenue comes from income taxes, why income taxes are progressive, and why some goods are taxed at a much higher rate than others**

The Economic Theory of Government

THE ECONOMIC THEORY OF GOVERNMENT explains the purpose of governments, the economic choices that governments make, and the consequences of those choices.

Governments exist for two major reasons. First, they establish and maintain property rights and set the rules for the redistribution of income and wealth. Property rights are the foundation on which all market activity takes place. They replace stealing with a rule-based and law-enforced system for redistributing income and wealth.

Second, governments provide a nonmarket mechanism for allocating scarce resources when the market economy results in *inefficiency*—a situation called **market failure.** When market failure occurs, too many of some things and too few of other things are produced. By reallocating resources, it is possible to make some people better off while making no one worse off. So people support government activity that modifies the market outcome and corrects market failure.

We're going to study four economic problems that are dealt with by government or public choices:

- Public goods
- Taxes and redistribution
- Monopoly
- Externalities

Public Goods

Some goods and services are consumed either by everyone or by no one. Examples are national defence, law and order, and sewage and waste disposal services. National defence systems cannot isolate individuals and refuse to protect them. Airborne diseases from untreated sewage do not avoid some people and target others. A good or service that is consumed either by everyone or by no one is called a *public good.*

The market economy fails to deliver the efficient quantity of public goods because of a free-rider problem. Everyone tries to free-ride on everyone else because the good is available to all whether they pay for it or not. We'll study public goods and the free-rider problem later in this chapter. We'll study the factors that influence the scale of provision of public goods, and we'll also study the taxes that pay for them.

Taxes and Redistribution

You saw in Chapter 15 that the market economy delivers an unequal distribution of income and wealth and that income support systems and progressive income taxes influence the distribution.

Taxes play a dual role: They pay for public goods, and they redistribute income. In this chapter, we'll look further at taxes and explain why Canada's income tax is progressive and why some goods are taxed at high rates and others at lower rates.

Monopoly

Monopoly and *rent seeking* prevent the allocation of resources from being efficient. Every business tries to maximize profit, and when a monopoly exists, it can increase profit by restricting output and keeping the price high. For example, some years ago, Bell Canada had a monopoly on long-distance telephone services and the quantity of long-distance services was much smaller and the price much higher than they are today. Since the end of Bell Canada's monopoly, the quantity of long-distance calls has exploded.

Some monopolies arise from *legal barriers to entry*—barriers to entry created by governments—but a major activity of government is to regulate monopoly and to enforce laws that prevent cartels and other restrictions on competition. We study these regulations and laws in Chapter 17.

Externalities

When a chemical factory (legally) dumps its waste into a river and kills the fish, it imposes a cost—called an *external cost*—on the members of a fishing club who fish downstream. When a homeowner fills her garden with spring bulbs, she generates an external benefit for all the passersby. External costs and benefits are not usually taken into account by the people whose actions create them. The chemical factory does not take the fishing club's wishes into account when it decides whether to dump waste into the river. The homeowner does not take her neighbours' views into account when she decides to fill her garden with flowers. We study externalities in Chapter 18.

Before we begin to study each of these problems from which government activity arises, let's look at the arena in which governments operate: the "political marketplace."

Public Choice and the Political Marketplace

Government is a complex organization made up of millions of individuals, each with his or her own economic objectives. Government policy is the outcome of the choices made by these individuals. To analyze these choices, economists have developed a public choice model of the political marketplace. The actors in the political marketplace are

- Voters
- Politicians
- Bureaucrats

Figure 16.1 illustrates the choices and interactions of these actors. Let's look at each in turn.

Voters Voters are the consumers in the political marketplace. In markets for goods and services, people express their preferences by their willingness to pay. In the political marketplace, they express their preferences by their votes, campaign contributions, and lobbying activity. Public choice theory assumes that people support the policies they believe will make them better off and oppose the policies they believe will make them worse off. It is voters' *perceptions* rather than reality that guide their choices.

Politicians Politicians are the entrepreneurs of the political marketplace. Public choice theory assumes that the objective of a politician is to get elected and to remain in office. Votes to a politician are like economic profit to a firm. To get enough votes, politicians propose policies that they expect will appeal to a majority of voters.

Bureaucrats Bureaucrats are the hired officials in government departments. They are the producers or firms in the political marketplace. Public choice theory assumes that bureaucrats aim to maximize their own utility and that to achieve this objective, they try to maximize the budget of their department.

The bigger the budget of a department, the greater is the prestige of its chief and the larger is the opportunity for promotion for people farther down the bureaucratic ladder. So all the members of a department have an interest in maximizing the department's budget. To maximize their budgets, bureaucrats devise programs that they expect will appeal to politicians and they help politicians to explain their programs to voters.

FIGURE 16.1 The Political Marketplace

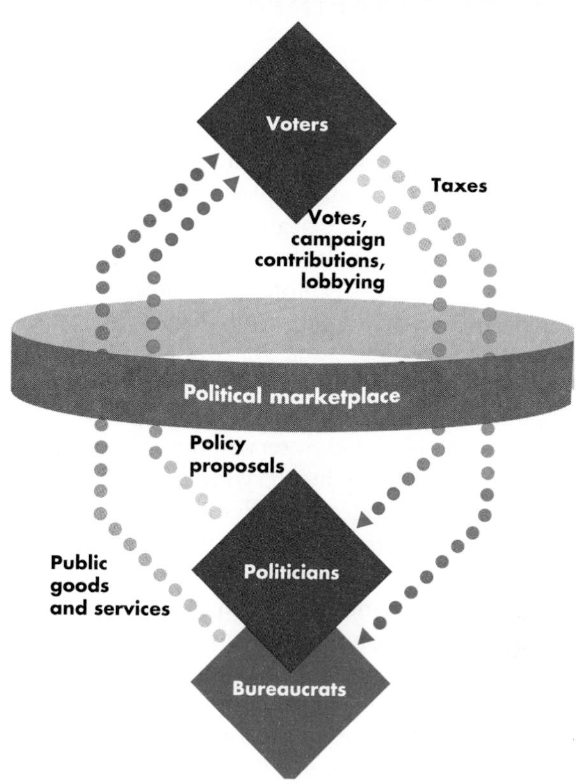

Voters express their demands for policies by voting, making campaign contributions, and lobbying. Politicians propose policies to appeal to a majority of voters. Bureaucrats try to maximize the budgets of their departments. A political equilibrium emerges in which no group can improve its position by making a different choice.

Political Equilibrium

Voters, politicians, and bureaucrats make choices to best further their own objectives. But each group is constrained by the preferences of the other groups and by what is technologically feasible. The outcome that results from the choices of voters, politicians, and bureaucrats is a **political equilibrium**, which is a situation in which all their choices are compatible and in which no group can improve its position by making a different choice. Let's see how voters, politicians, and bureaucrats interact to determine the quantity of public goods.

Public Goods and the Free-Rider Problem

WHY DOES THE GOVERNMENT PROVIDE GOODS and services such as national defence and public health? Why don't we buy environmental protection from Arctic Ozone, Inc., a private firm that competes for our dollars in the marketplace in the same way that Tim Hortons and Coca-Cola do? The answer to these questions lies in the free-rider problem created by public goods. Let's explore this problem. We begin by looking at the nature of a public good.

Public Goods

A **public good** is a good or service that can be consumed simultaneously by everyone and from which no one can be excluded. The first feature of a public good is called nonrivalry. A good is *nonrival* if consumption of it by one person does not decrease consumption of it by another person. An example is watching a television show. The opposite of nonrival is rival. A good is *rival* if consumption of it by one person decreases consumption of it by another person. An example is eating a hot dog.

The second feature of a public good is that it is nonexcludable. A good is *nonexcludable* if it is impossible, or extremely costly, to prevent someone from benefiting from a good. An example is national defence. It would be difficult to exclude someone from being defended. The opposite of nonexcludable is excludable. A good is *excludable* if it is possible to prevent a person from enjoying the benefits of a good. An example is cable television. Cable companies can ensure that only those people who have paid the fee receive programs.

Figure 16.2 classifies goods according to these two criteria and gives examples of goods in each category. National defence is a *pure* public good. One person's consumption of the security provided by our national defence system does not decrease the security of someone else—defence is nonrival. And the military cannot select those whom it will protect and those whom it will leave exposed to threats—defence is nonexcludable.

Many goods have a public element but are not pure public goods. An example is a highway. A highway is nonrival until it becomes congested. One more car on a highway with plenty of space does not reduce anyone else's consumption of transportation services. But once the highway becomes congested, one extra vehicle lowers the quality of the service available to everyone else—it becomes rival like a private good. Also, users can be excluded from a highway by tollgates. Another example is fish in the ocean. Ocean fish are rival because a fish taken by one person is not available for anyone else. Ocean fish are also nonexcludable because it is difficult to prevent people from catching them.

FIGURE 16.2 Public Goods and Private Goods

	Rival	Nonrival
Excludable	**Pure private goods** Food Car House	**Excludable and nonrival** Cable television Bridge Highway
Nonexcludable	**Nonexcludable and rival** Fish in the ocean Air	**Pure public goods** Lighthouse National defence

A pure public good (bottom right) is one for which consumption is nonrival and from which it is impossible to exclude a consumer. Pure public goods pose a free-rider problem. A pure private good (top left) is one for which consumption is rival and from which consumers can be excluded. Some goods are nonexcludable but are rival (bottom left), and some goods are nonrival but are excludable (top right).

Source: Adapted from and inspired by E.S. Savas, *Privatizing the Public Sector* (Chatham, N.J.: Chatham House Publishers, 1982), p. 34.

The Free-Rider Problem

Public goods create a free-rider problem. A **free rider** is a person who consumes a good without paying for it. Public goods create a *free-rider problem* because the quantity of the good that a person is able to consume is not influenced by the amount the person pays for the good. So no one has an incentive to pay for a public good. Let's look more closely at the free-rider problem by studying an example.

The Benefit of a Public Good

Suppose that a device has been invented that makes it possible to eliminate acid rain. Let's call this device an acid-rain check. The benefit provided by an acid-rain check is the *value* of its services. The *value* of a *private* good is the maximum amount that a person is willing to pay for one more unit, which is shown by the person's demand curve. The value of a *public* good is the maximum amount that all the *people* are willing to pay for one more unit of it.

Total benefit is the dollar value that a person places on a given level of provision of a public good. The greater the quantity of a public good, the larger is a person's total benefit. *Marginal benefit* is the increase in total benefit that results from a one-unit increase in the quantity of a public good.

Figure 16.3 shows the marginal benefit that arises from acid-rain checks for a society with just two members, Lisa and Max. Lisa's and Max's marginal benefits are graphed as MB_L and MB_M, in parts (a) and (b). The marginal benefit from a public good is similar to the marginal utility from a private good—it diminishes as the quantity of the good increases. For Lisa, the marginal benefit from the first acid-rain check is \$80 and from the second it is \$60. By the time 5 acid-rain checks are deployed, Lisa's marginal benefit is zero. For Max, the marginal benefit from the first acid-rain check is \$50 and from the second it is \$40. By the time 5 acid-rain checks are installed, Max's marginal benefit is only \$10.

Part (c) shows the economy's marginal benefit curve, *MB*. An individual's marginal benefit curve for a public good is similar to the individual's demand curve for a private good. But the economy's marginal benefit curve for a public good is different from the market demand curve for a private good. To obtain the market demand curve for a *private* good, we sum the quantities demanded by all individuals at each price—we sum the individual demand curves *horizontally* (see Chapter 7, p. 163). But to find the economy's marginal benefit curve of a *public* good, we sum the marginal benefits of all individuals at each quantity—we sum the individual marginal benefit curves *vertically*. The resulting marginal benefit for the economy made up of Lisa and Max is the economy's marginal benefit curve graphed in part (c)—the curve *MB*. Lisa's marginal benefit from the first acid-rain check gets added to Max's marginal benefit from the first acid-rain check because they *both* consume the first acid-rain check.

FIGURE 16.3 Benefits of a Public Good

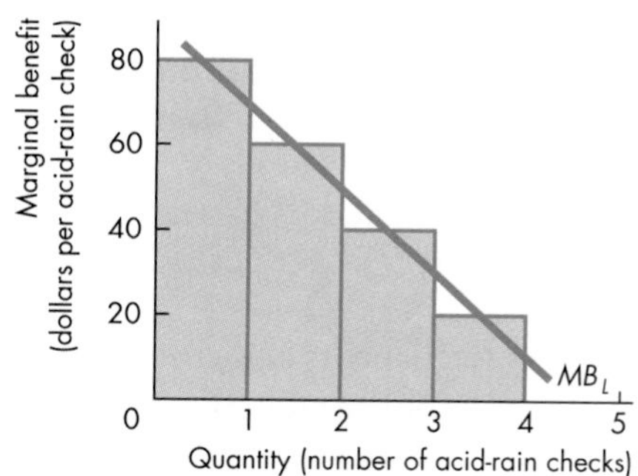

(a) Lisa's marginal benefit

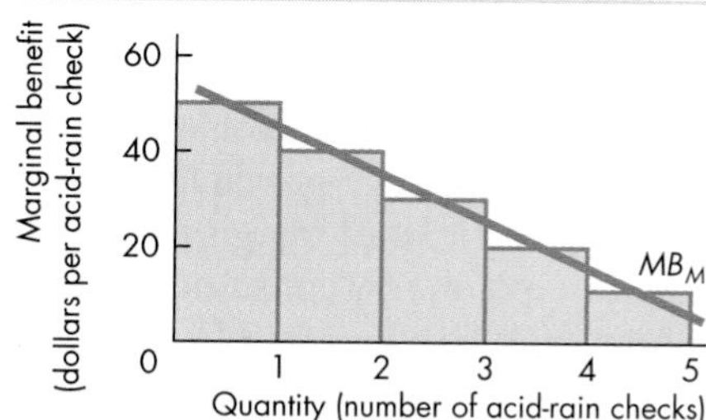

(b) Max's marginal benefit

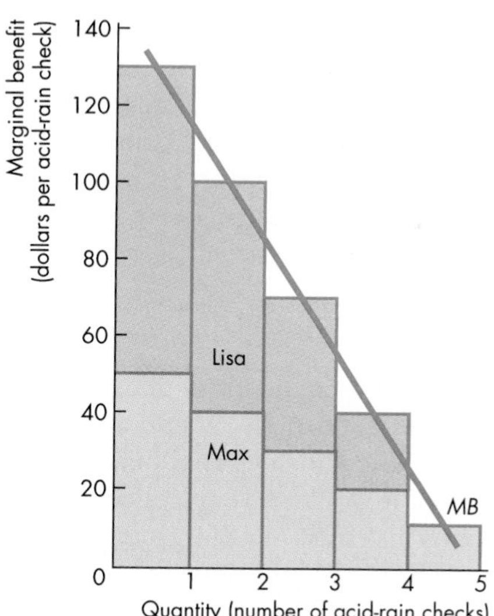

(c) Economy's marginal benefit

The marginal benefit to the economy at each quantity of the public good is the sum of the marginal benefits of all individuals. The marginal benefit curves are MB_L for Lisa, MB_M for Max, and *MB* for the economy.

The Efficient Quantity of a Public Good

An economy with two people would not buy any acid-rain checks—because the total benefit falls far short of the cost. But an economy with 25 million people might. To determine the efficient quantity, we need to take the cost as well as the benefit into account.

The cost of an acid-rain check is based on technology and the prices of the resources used to produce it (see Chapter 10).

Figure 16.4 shows the benefits and costs. The second and third columns of the table show the total and marginal benefits. The next two columns show the total and marginal cost of producing acid-rain checks. The final column shows net benefit. Part (a) graphs total benefit, *TB,* and total cost, *TC.*

The efficient quantity is the one that maximizes *net benefit*—total benefit minus total cost—and occurs when 2 acid-rain checks are provided.

The fundamental principles of marginal analysis that you have used to explain how consumers maximize utility and how firms maximize profit can also be used to calculate the efficient scale of provision of a public good. Figure 16.4(b) shows this alternative approach. The marginal benefit curve is *MB* and the marginal cost curve is *MC.* When marginal benefit exceeds marginal cost, net benefit increases if the quantity produced increases. When marginal cost exceeds marginal benefit, net benefit increases if the quantity produced decreases. Marginal benefit equals marginal cost with 2 acid-rain checks. So making marginal cost equal to marginal benefit maximizes net benefit and uses resources efficiently.

Private Provision

We have now worked out the quantity of acid-rain checks that maximizes net benefit. Would a private firm—Arctic Ozone, Inc.—deliver that quantity? It would not. To do so, it would have to collect $1.5 billion to cover its costs—or $60 from each of the 25 million people in the economy. But no one would have an incentive to buy his or her "share" of the acid-rain check system. Everyone would reason as follows: "The number of acid-rain checks provided by Arctic Ozone, Inc., is not affected by my $60. But my own private consumption is greater if I free-ride and do not pay my share of the cost of the acid-rain check system. If I do not pay, I enjoy the same level of security and I can buy more private goods. Therefore I will spend my $60 on other goods and free-ride on the public good." This is the free-rider problem.

If everyone reasons the same way, Arctic Ozone has zero revenue and so provides no acid-rain checks. Because two acid-rain checks is the efficient level, private provision is inefficient.

Public Provision

Suppose there are two political parties, the Greens and the Smokes, which agree on all issues except for the quantity of acid-rain checks. The Greens would like to provide 4 acid-rain checks at a cost of $5 billion, with benefits of $5 billion and a net benefit of zero, as shown in Fig. 16.4. The Smokes would like to provide 1 acid-rain check at a cost of $0.5 billion, a benefit of $2 billion, and a net benefit of $1.5 billion—see Fig. 16.4.

Before deciding on their policy proposals, the two political parties do a "what-if" analysis. Each party reasons as follows. If each party offers the acid-rain check program it wants—Greens 4 acid-rain checks and Smokes 1 acid-rain check—the voters will see that they will get a net benefit of $1.5 billion from the Smokes and zero net benefit from the Greens, and the Smokes will win the election.

Contemplating this outcome, the Greens realize that they are too "green" to get elected. They figure that they must scale back their proposal to 2 acid-rain checks. At this level of provision, total cost is $1.5 billion, total benefit is $3.5 billion, and net benefit is $2 billion. If the Smokes stick with 1 acid-rain check, the Greens will win the election.

But contemplating this outcome, the Smokes realize that they must match the Greens. They too propose to provide 2 acid-rain checks on exactly the same terms as the Greens. If the parties offer the same number of acid-rain checks, the voters are indifferent between them. Each party receives around 50 percent of the vote.

The result of the politicians' "what-if" analysis is that each party offers 2 acid-rain checks, so regardless of who wins the election, this is the quantity of acid-rain checks installed. And this quantity is efficient. It maximizes the perceived net benefit of the voters. Thus in this example, competition in the political marketplace results in the efficient provision of a public good. But for this outcome to occur, voters must be well informed and evaluate the alternatives. But as you will see below, voters do not always have an incentive to be well informed.

FIGURE 16.4 The Efficient Quantity of a Public Good

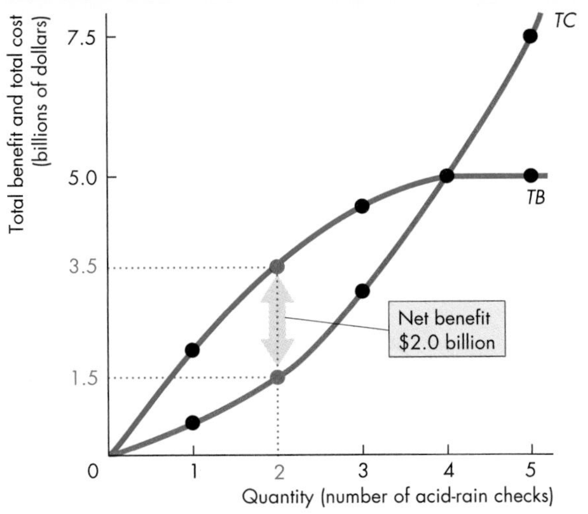

(a) Total benefit and total cost

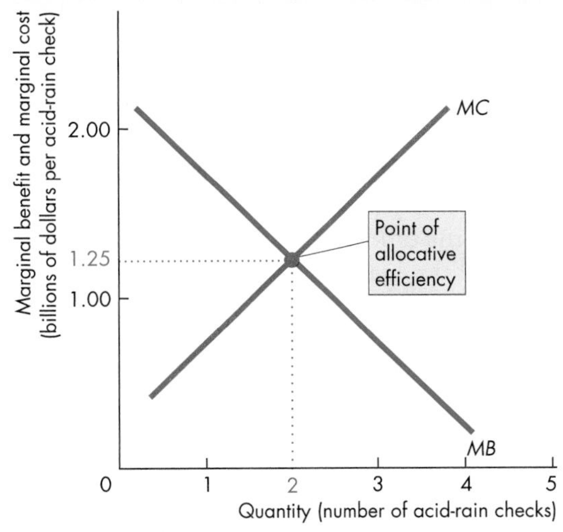

(b) Marginal benefit and marginal cost

Quantity (number of acid-rain checks)	**Total benefit** (billions of dollars)	**Marginal benefit** (billions of dollars per acid-rain check)	**Total cost** (billions of dollars)	**Marginal cost** (billions of dollars per acid-rain check)	**Net benefit** (billions of dollars)
0	0		0		0
		2.0		0.5	
1	2.0		0.5		1.5
		1.5		1.0	
2	**3.5**		**1.5**		**2.0**
		1.0		1.5	
3	4.5		3.0		1.5
		0.5		2.0	
4	5.0		5.0		0
		0		2.5	
5	5.0		7.5		–2.5

Net benefit—the vertical distance between total benefit, *TB*, and total cost, *TC*—is maximized when 2 acid-rain checks are installed (part a) and where marginal benefit, *MB*, equals marginal cost, *MC* (part b). The Smokes would like 1 acid-rain check, and the Greens would like 4. But each party recognizes that its only hope of being elected is to provide 2 acid-rain checks—the quantity that maximizes net benefit and so leaves no room for the other party to improve on.

The Principle of Minimum Differentiation In the example we've just studied, both parties propose identical policies. This tendency towards identical policies is an example of the **principle of minimum differentiation,** which is the tendency for competitors to make themselves identical to appeal to the maximum number of clients or voters. This principle not only describes the behaviour of political parties but also explains why fast-food restaurants cluster in the same block and even why new auto models have similar features. If McDonald's opens a restaurant in a new location, it is likely that Burger King will open next door to McDonald's rather than a kilometre down the road. If Chrysler designs a new van with a sliding door on the driver's side, most likely Ford will too.

The Role of Bureaucrats

We have analyzed the behaviour of politicians but not that of the bureaucrats who translate the choices of the politicians into programs and who control the day-to-day activities that deliver public goods. Let's now see how the economic choices of bureaucrats influence the political equilibrium.

To do so, we'll stick with the previous example. We've seen that competition between two political parties delivers the efficient quantity of acid-rain checks. But will the Department of the Environment (DOE) cooperate and accept this outcome?

Suppose the objective of the DOE is to maximize its budget. With 2 acid-rain checks being provided at minimum cost, the budget is $1.5 billion (see Fig. 16.5). To increase its budget, the DOE might do two things. First, it might try to persuade the politicians that 2 acid-rain checks cost more than $1.5 billion. As Fig. 16.5 shows, if possible, the DOE would like to convince Parliament that 2 acid-rain checks cost $3.5 billion—the entire benefit. Second, and pressing its position even more strongly, the DOE might argue for more acid-rain checks. It might press for 4 acid-rain checks and a budget of $5 billion. In this situation, total benefit and total cost are equal and net benefit is zero.

The DOE wants to maximize its budget, but won't the politicians prevent it from doing so because the DOE's preferred outcome costs votes? The politicians will do this if voters are well informed and know what is best for them. But voters might be rationally ignorant. In this case, well-informed interest groups might enable the DOE to achieve its objective.

FIGURE 16.5 Bureaucratic Overprovision

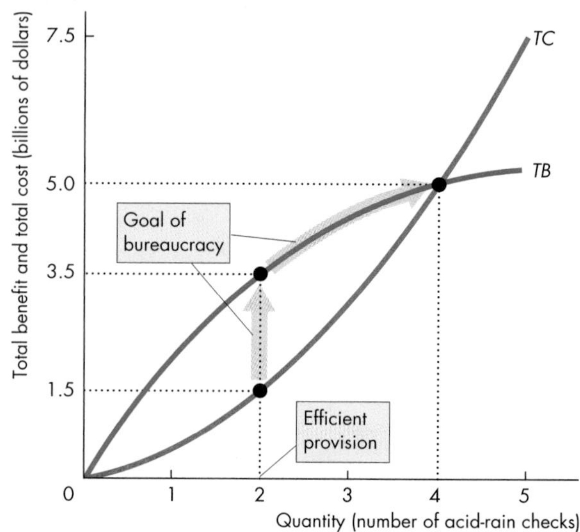

The goal of a bureaucracy is to maximize its budget. A bureaucracy will seek to increase its budget so that its total cost equals total benefit, and then use its budget to expand output and expenditure. Here, the DOE tries to get $3.5 billion to provide 2 acid-rain checks. It would like to increase the quantity to 4 with a budget of $5.0 billion.

Rational Ignorance

A principle of public choice theory is that it is rational for a voter to be ignorant about an issue unless that issue has a perceptible effect on the voter's income. **Rational ignorance** is the decision *not* to acquire information because the cost of doing so exceeds the expected benefit. For example, each voter knows that he or she can make virtually no difference to Canada's environment policy. Each voter also knows that it would take an enormous amount of time and effort to become even moderately well informed about alternative approaches. So voters remain relatively uninformed about the technicalities of issues. (Although we are using environment policy as an example, the same idea applies to all public choices.)

All voters are consumers of clean air. But not all voters are producers of the equipment needed to monitor and maintain good air quality. Only a small number are in this latter category. Voters who own or work for firms that produce acid-rain checks have a direct personal interest in the government's policy because it affects their incomes. These voters have an incentive to become well informed about environmental issues and to operate a political lobby aimed at furthering their own interests. In collaboration with the bureaucracy, these voters exert a larger influence than do the relatively uninformed voters who only consume this public good.

When the rationality of the uninformed voter and special interest groups are taken into account, the political equilibrium provides public goods in excess of the efficient quantity. So in the current example, three or four acid-rain checks might be bought rather than the efficient quantity of two acid-rain checks.

Two Types of Political Equilibrium

We've seen that two types of political equilibrium are possible: efficient and inefficient. These two types of political equilibrium correspond to two theories of government:

- Public interest theory
- Public choice theory

Public Interest Theory Public interest theory predicts that governments make choices that achieve efficiency. This outcome occurs in a perfect political system in which voters are fully informed about the effects of policies and refuse to vote for outcomes that can be improved upon.

Public Choice Theory Public choice theory predicts that governments make choices that result in inefficiency. This outcome occurs in political markets in which voters are rationally ignorant and base their votes only on issues that they know affect their own net benefit. Voters pay more attention to their interests as producers than their interests as consumers, and public officials also act in their own best interest. The result is *government failure* that parallels market failure.

Why Government Is Large and Grows

Now that we know how the quantity of public goods is determined, we can explain part of the reason for the growth of government. Government grows in part because the demand for some public goods increases at a faster rate than the demand for private goods. There are two possible reasons for this growth:

- Voter preferences
- Inefficient overprovision

Voter Preferences The growth of government can be explained by voter preferences in the following way. As voters' incomes increase (as they do in most years), the demand for many public goods increases more quickly than income. (Technically, the *income elasticity of demand* for many public goods is greater than 1—see Chapter 4, pp. 92–93.) These goods include public health, education, national defence, highways, airports, and air-traffic control systems. If politicians did not support increases in expenditures on these items, they would not get elected.

Inefficient Overprovision Inefficient overprovision might explain the *size* of government but not its *growth rate.* It (possibly) explains why government is *larger* than its efficient scale, but it does not explain why governments use an increasing proportion of total resources.

Voters Strike Back

If government grows too large relative to the value that voters place on public goods, there might be a voter backlash against government programs and a large bureaucracy. Electoral success during the 1990s at the provincial and federal levels required politicians of all parties to embrace smaller, leaner, and more efficient government. The September 11 attacks have led to a greater willingness to pay for security, but have probably not lessened the desire for lean government.

Another way in which voters—and politicians—can try to counter the tendency of bureaucrats to expand their budgets is to privatize the production of public goods. Government *provision* of a public good does not automatically imply that a government-operated bureau must *produce* the good. Garbage collection (a public good) is often handled by a private firm, and experiments are being conducted with private fire departments and even private prisons.

REVIEW QUIZ

1. What is the free-rider problem and why does it make the private provision of a public good inefficient?
2. Under what conditions will competition among politicians for votes result in an efficient quantity of a public good?
3. How do rationally ignorant voters and budget-maximizing bureaucrats prevent competition in the political marketplace from producing the efficient quantity of a public good? Do they result in too much or too little public provision of public goods?

We've now seen how voters, politicians, and bureaucrats interact to determine the quantity of a public good. But public goods are paid for with taxes. Taxes also redistribute income. How does the political marketplace determine the taxes we pay?

Taxes

TAXES GENERATE THE FINANCIAL RESOURCES that provide public goods. Taxes also redistribute income. Governments use five major types of taxes:

- Income taxes
- Employment, health, and social insurance taxes
- Provincial sales taxes and the GST
- Property taxes
- Excise taxes

Figure 16.6 shows the relative amounts raised by these five major taxes in 2001. Income taxes raised 52 percent of tax revenue in 2001. Provincial sales taxes and the GST raised 15 percent of total taxes. Property taxes and employment, health, and social insurance taxes each raised 11 percent of total taxes. Finally, excise taxes raised 6 percent of total taxes. Although excise taxes raise a small amount of tax revenue, they nevertheless have a big impact on some markets, as you'll discover later in this chapter. Let's take a closer look at each type of tax.

Income Taxes

Income taxes are paid on personal incomes and corporate profits. In 2001, the personal income tax raised $88 billion for the federal government and another $53 billion for provincial governments. Corporate profits taxes raised $28 billion for the federal government and $14 billion for the provincial governments. We'll look first at the effects of personal income tax and then at corporate profits tax.

FIGURE 16.6 Government Tax Revenues

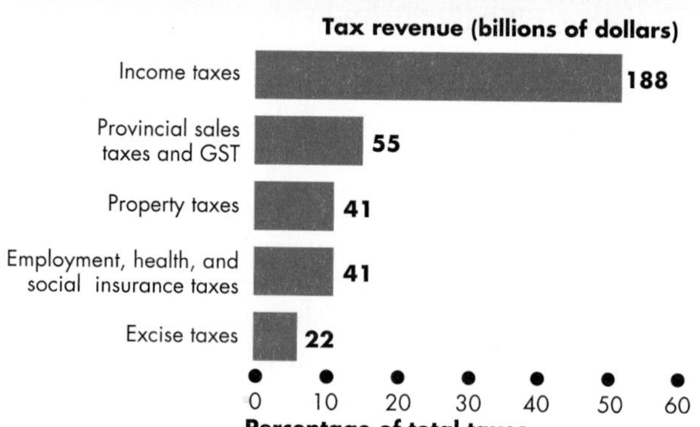

More than half of government tax revenue comes from income taxes. Excise taxes bring in a small amount of revenue, but these taxes have big effects on a small number of markets.

Source: Adapted from the Statistics Canada publication *CANSIM DISC*, 10F0007, March 1999.

Personal Income Tax The amount of income tax that a person pays depends on her or his *taxable income*, which equals total income minus expenses and other allowances. In 2001, the basic personal deduction from total income was $7,634 for a single person and a further $6,482 for a spouse.

The *tax rate* (percent) depends on the taxable income and province of residence. For Ontario, the tax rate increases according to the following scale:

$0 to $31,677	22.05 percent
$31,678 to $63,354	31.15 percent
$63,355 to $63,786	35.15 percent
$63,787 to $103,000	37.16 percent
Over $103,000	40.16 percent

The percentages in this list are marginal tax rates. A **marginal tax rate** is the percentage of an additional dollar of income that is paid in tax. For example, if taxable income increases from $25,000 to $25,001, the additional tax paid is 22.05 cents and the marginal tax rate is 22.05 percent. If taxable income increases from $103,000 to $103,001, the additional tax paid is 40.16 cents and the marginal tax rate is 40.16 percent.

The **average tax rate** is the percentage of income that is paid in tax. Let's calculate the average tax rate for a single person who earns $50,000 in a year. Tax is zero on the first $7,634, plus $6,985 (22.05 percent) on the next $31,677, plus $3,330 on the remaining $10,689. Total tax is $10,315, which is 20.6 percent of $50,000. The average tax rate is 20.6 percent.

If the marginal tax rate exceeds the average tax rate, the average tax rate increases as income increases and the tax is a *progressive tax* (see p. 359). The personal income tax is a progressive tax. To see this feature of the income tax, calculate the average tax rate for someone whose income is $100,000 a year. Tax is zero on the first $7,634, plus $6,985 (22.05 percent) on the next $31,677, plus $9,867 (31.15 percent) on the next $31,677, plus $152 (35.15 percent) on the next $432, plus $10,620 (37.16 percent) on the remaining $28,580. Total tax is $27,624, which is 27.62 percent of $100,000. So the average tax rate is 27.62 percent.

The Effect of Income Taxes Figure 16.7 shows how the income tax affects labour markets. Part (a) shows the market for low-wage workers, and part (b) shows the market for high-wage workers. These labour markets are competitive, and with no income taxes, they work just like all the other competitive markets you have studied. The demand curves are *LD*, and the supply curves are *LS* (in both parts of the figure). Both groups work 40 hours a week. Low-wage workers earn $9.50 an hour, and high-wage workers earn $175 an hour. What happens when an income tax is introduced?

If low-wage workers are willing to supply 40 hours a week for $9.50 an hour when there is no tax, then they are willing to supply that same quantity in the face of a 15 percent tax only if the wage rises by enough to provide an after-tax wage rate of $9.50 an hour. That is, they want to get the $9.50 an hour they received before plus enough to pay 15 percent of their income to the government. So the supply of labour decreases because the amount received from work is lowered by the amount of income tax paid. The acceptable wage rate at each level of employment rises by the amount of the tax that must be paid. For low-wage workers who face a tax rate of 15 percent, the supply curve shifts to *LS* + *tax*. The equilibrium wage rate rises to $10 an hour, but the after-tax wage rate falls to $8.50 an hour. Employment falls to 36 hours a week.

For high-wage workers who face a tax rate of 39.6 percent, the supply curve shifts to *LS* + *tax*. The equilibrium wage rate rises to $200 an hour, and the after-tax wage rate falls to $121 an hour. Employment falls to 32 hours a week. The decrease in employment of high-wage workers is larger than that of low-wage workers because of the differences in the marginal tax rates each type of worker faces.

FIGURE 16.7 The Effects of Income Taxes

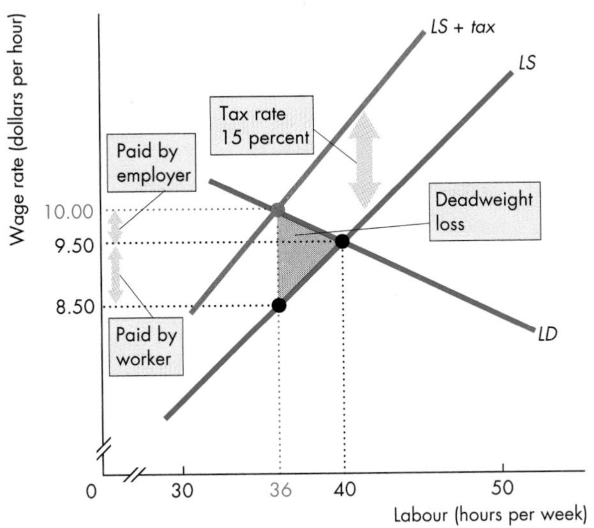

(a) Lowest income tax rate

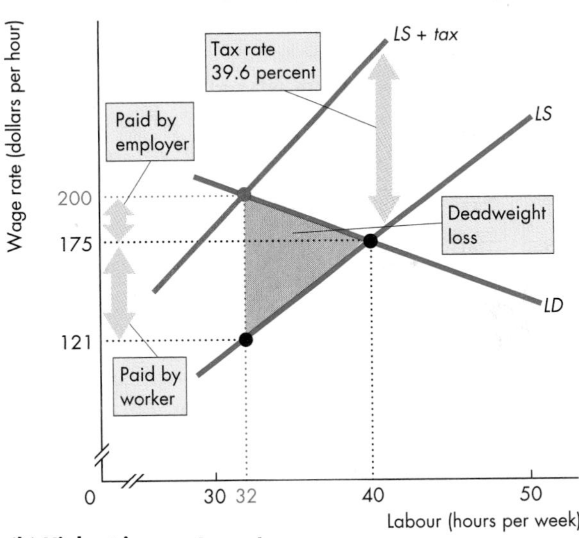

(b) Highest income tax rate

The demand for labour is *LD*, and with no income taxes, the supply of labour is *LS* (both parts). In part (a), low-wage workers earn $9.50 an hour and each works 40 hours a week. In part (b), high-wage workers earn $175 an hour and each works 40 hours a week. An income tax decreases the supply of labour, and the labour supply curve shifts leftward. For low-wage workers in part (a), whose marginal tax rate is 15 percent, supply decreases to *LS* + *tax*. Employment falls to 36 hours a week. For high-wage workers in part (b), whose marginal tax rate is 39.6 percent, supply decreases to *LS* + *tax*. Employment falls to 32 hours a week. The deadweight loss from the high marginal tax rate on high-wage workers is much larger than that from the low marginal tax rate on low-wage workers.

Notice that the income tax is paid by both the employer and the worker. In the case of low-wage workers, the employer pays an extra 50 cents an hour and the worker pays $1 an hour. In the case of high-wage workers, employers pay an extra $25 an hour and workers pay $54 an hour. The exact split depends on the elasticities of demand and supply.

Notice also the difference in the *deadweight loss* for the two groups. The deadweight loss is larger for the high-wage workers than for the low-wage workers.

Why Do We Have a Progressive Income Tax? We have a progressive income tax because it is part of the political equilibrium. A majority of voters support it, so politicians who also support it get elected.

The economic model that predicts progressive income taxes is called the *median voter* model. The core idea of the median voter model is that political parties pursue policies that are most likely to attract the support of the median voter. The median voter is the one in the middle—one-half of the population lies on one side and one-half on the other. Let's see how the median voter model predicts a progressive income tax.

Imagine that government programs benefit everyone equally and are paid for by a proportional income tax. Everyone pays the same percentage of income. In this situation, there is a redistribution from high-income voters to low-income voters. Everyone benefits equally, but because they have higher incomes, the high-income voters pay a larger amount of taxes.

Is this situation the best one possible for the median voter? It is not. Suppose that instead of using a proportional tax, the marginal tax rate is lowered for low-income voters and increased for high-income voters—a progressive tax. Low-income voters are now better off, and high-income voters are worse off. Low-income voters will support this change, and high-income voters will oppose it. But there are many more low-income voters than high-income voters, so the low-income voters win.

The median voter is a low-income voter. In fact, because the distribution of income is skewed, the median voter has a smaller income than the average income (see Fig. 15.1 on p. 348). This fact raises an interesting question: Why doesn't the median voter support taxes that skim off all income above the average and redistribute it to everyone with a below-average income? This tax would be so progressive that it would result in equal incomes after taxes and transfers were paid.

The answer is that high taxes discourage effort and saving and the median voter would be worse off with such radical redistribution than under the arrangements that prevail today.

Let's now look at corporate profits tax.

Corporate Profits Tax In popular discussions of taxes, corporate profits taxes are seen as a free source of revenue for the government. Taxing people is bad, but taxing corporations is just fine.

It turns out that taxing corporations is very inefficient. We use an inefficient tax because it redistributes income in favour of the median voter, just like the income tax. Let's see why taxing corporate profits is inefficient.

The corporate profits tax is misnamed. It is only partly a tax on economic profit. It is mainly a tax on the income from capital. Taxing the income from capital works like taxing the income from labour except for two critical differences: The supply of capital is highly (perhaps perfectly) elastic, and the quantity of capital influences the productivity of labour and wage income. Because the supply of capital is highly elastic, firms pay the entire tax and the quantity of capital decreases. With a smaller capital stock than we would otherwise have, the productivity of labour and incomes are lower than they would otherwise be.

Employment, Health, and Social Insurance Taxes

Social insurance taxes are the contributions paid by employers and employees to provide social security benefits, unemployment compensation, and health benefits.

Unions lobby to get employers to pay a bigger share of these taxes, and employers' organizations lobby to get workers to pay a bigger share. But this lobbying effort is not worth much, for who *really* pays these taxes depends in no way on who writes the cheques. It depends on the elasticities of demand and supply for labour.

Figure 16.8 shows you why. The demand curve, *LD*, and the supply curve, *LS*, are identical in the two parts of the figure. With no social insurance taxes, the quantity of labour employed is *QL** and the wage rate is *W**.

A social insurance tax is now introduced. In part (a), the employee pays the tax, and in part (b), the employer pays. When the employee pays, supply decreases and the supply of labour curve shifts leftward to *LS* + *tax*. The vertical distance between the supply curve *LS* and the new supply curve *LS* + *tax* is the amount of the tax. The wage rate rises to *WC*, the after-tax wage rate falls to *WT*, and employment decreases to QL_0.

When the employer pays, in Fig. 16.8(b), demand decreases and the demand for labour curve shifts leftward to *LD* – *tax*. The vertical distance between the demand curve *LD* and the new demand curve *LD* – *tax* is the amount of the tax. The wage rate falls to *WT*, but the cost of labour rises to *WC* and employment decreases to QL_0.

So regardless of which side of the market is taxed, the outcomes are identical. If the demand for labour is perfectly inelastic or if the supply of labour is perfectly elastic, the employer pays the entire tax. And if the demand for labour is perfectly elastic or if the supply of labour is perfectly inelastic, the employee pays the entire tax. These cases are like those for the sales tax that you studied in Chapter 6 (pp. 131–134).

Provincial Sales Taxes and the GST

Sales taxes are the taxes levied by the provinces on a wide range of goods and services. The GST is the tax levied by the federal government on most goods and services. We studied the effects of these taxes in Chapter 6. There is one feature of these taxes, though, that we need to note: They are *regressive.* The reason they are regressive is that saving increases with income and sales taxes are paid only on the part of income that is spent.

Suppose, for example, that the sales tax rate is 8 percent. A family that earns $20,000 and spends $18,000 on goods and services pays $1,440 in sales tax. Its taxes are 7.2 percent of its income. A family that earns $100,000 and spends $60,000 on goods and services pays $4,800 in sales taxes. So this family's taxes are only 4.8 percent of its income.

If the sales tax is regressive, why does the median voter support it? It is the entire tax code that matters, not an individual tax. So a regressive sales tax is voted for only as part of an overall tax regime that is progressive.

Property Taxes

Property taxes are collected by local governments and are used to provide local public goods. A **local public good** is a public good that is consumed by all the people who live in a particular area. Examples of local public goods are parks, museums, and safe neighbourhoods.

FIGURE 16.8 Social Insurance Taxes

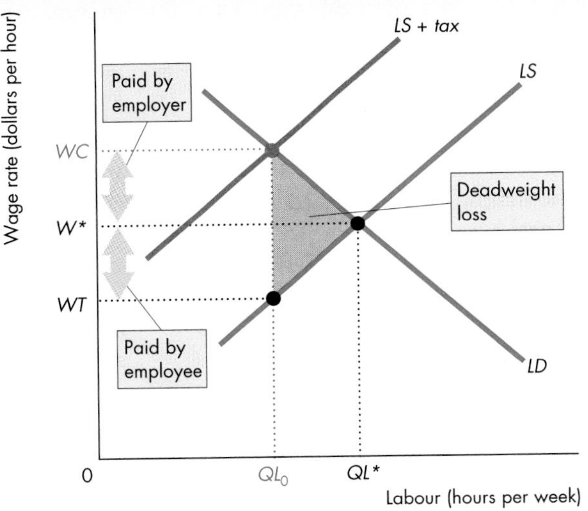

(a) Tax on employees

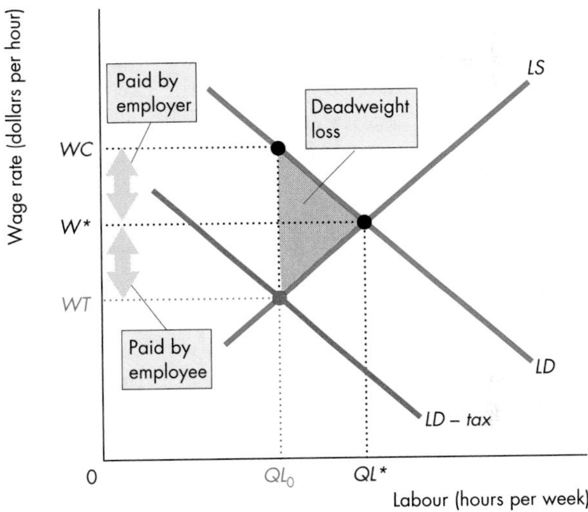

(b) Tax on employers

With no social insurance tax, the quantity of labour employed is QL^* and the wage rate is W^* (in both parts). In part (a), employees pay a social insurance tax. Supply decreases, and the supply of labour curve shifts leftward to *LS + tax*. The wage rate rises to *WC*, the after-tax wage rate falls to *WT*, and employment decreases to QL_0. In part (b), employers pay a social insurance tax. Demand decreases, and the demand for labour curve shifts leftward to *LD – tax*. The wage rate falls to *WT*, but the cost of labour rises to *WC* and employment decreases to QL_0. The outcomes are identical in the two cases.

There is a much closer connection between property taxes paid and benefits received than in the case of federal and provincial taxes. This close connection makes property taxes similar to a price for local services. Because of this connection, property taxes change both the demand for and supply of property in a neighbourhood. A higher tax lowers supply, but improved local public goods increase demand. So some neighbourhoods have high taxes and high-quality local government services, and other neighbourhoods have low taxes and low-quality services. Both can exist in the political equilibrium.

Excise Taxes

An **excise tax** is a tax on the sale of a particular commodity. The total amount raised by these taxes is small, but they have a big impact on some markets. Let's study the effects of an excise tax by considering the tax on gasoline shown in Fig. 16.9. The demand curve is *D*, and the supply curve is *S*. If there is no tax on gasoline, its price is 60¢ a litre and 400 million litres of gasoline a day are bought and sold.

Now suppose that a tax is imposed on gasoline at the rate of 60¢ a litre. As a result of the tax, the supply of gasoline decreases and the supply curve shifts leftward. The magnitude of the shift is such that the vertical distance between the original and the new supply curve is the amount of the tax. The new supply curve is the red curve, *S* + *tax*. The new supply curve intersects the demand curve at 300 million litres a day and $1.10 a litre. Sellers receive 50¢ a litre, the price at which they are willing to supply 300 million litres a day. This situation is the new equilibrium after the imposition of the tax.

The excise tax creates a deadweight loss made up of the loss of consumer surplus and producer surplus. The dollar value of that loss is $30 million a day. Because 300 million litres of gasoline are sold each day and the tax is 60¢ a litre, total revenue from the gasoline tax is $180 million a day (300 million litres multiplied by 60¢ a litre). So to raise tax revenue of $180 million a day by using the gasoline tax, a deadweight loss of $30 million a day—one-sixth of the tax revenue—is incurred.

One of the main influences on the deadweight loss arising from a tax is the elasticity of demand for the product. The demand for gasoline is fairly inelastic. As a consequence, when a tax is imposed, the quantity demanded falls by a smaller percentage than the percentage rise in price.

FIGURE 16.9 An Excise Tax

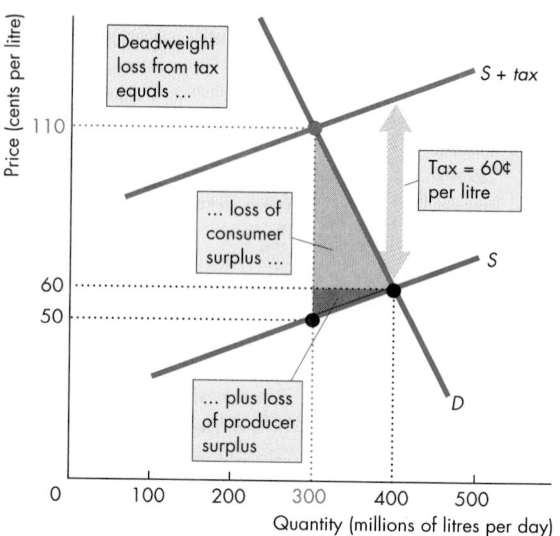

The demand curve for gasoline is *D*, and the supply curve is *S*. In the absence of any taxes, gasoline sells for 60¢ a litre and 400 million litres a day are bought and sold. With a tax of 60¢ a litre, the supply curve shifts leftward to become the curve *S* + *tax*. The new equilibrium price is $1.10 a litre, and 300 million litres a day are bought and sold. The excise tax creates a deadweight loss represented by the grey triangle. The tax revenue collected is 60¢ a litre on 300 million litres, which is $180 million a day. The deadweight loss is $30 million a day. That is, to raise tax revenue of $180 million a day, a deadweight loss of $30 million a day is incurred.

To see the importance of the elasticity of demand, let's consider a different commodity: orange juice. So that we can make a quick and direct comparison, let's assume that the orange juice market is exactly as big as the market for gasoline. Figure 16.10 illustrates this market. The demand curve for orange juice is *D*, and the supply curve is *S*. Orange juice is not taxed, and so the price of orange juice is 60¢ a litre—where the supply curve and the demand curve intersect—and the quantity of orange juice traded is 400 million litres a day.

Now suppose that the government contemplates abolishing the gasoline tax and taxing orange juice instead. The demand for orange juice is more elastic than the demand for gasoline. Orange juice has many good substitutes in the form of other fruit juices. The

FIGURE 16.10 Why We Don't Tax Orange Juice

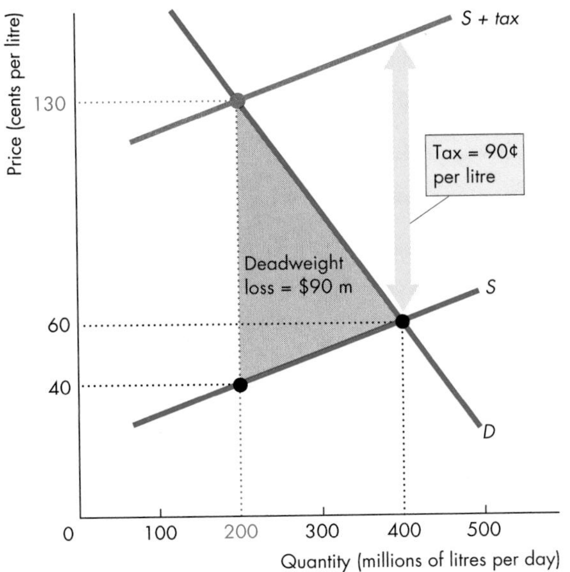

The demand curve for orange juice is *D*, and the supply curve is *S*. The price is 60¢ a litre, and 400 million litres of juice a day are traded. To raise $180 million of tax revenue, a tax of 90¢ a litre is imposed. This tax shifts the supply curve to *S* + *tax*. The price rises to $1.30 a litre, and the quantity falls to 200 million litres a day. The deadweight loss, the grey triangle, equals $90 million a day. The deadweight loss from taxing orange juice is larger than that from taxing gasoline (Fig. 16.9) because the demand for orange juice is more elastic than the demand for gasoline.

government wants to raise $180 million a day so that its total revenue is not affected by this tax change. The government's economists, armed with their statistical estimates of the demand and supply curves for orange juice that appear in Fig. 16.10, work out that a tax of 90¢ a litre will do the job. With such a tax, the supply curve shifts leftward to become the curve labelled *S* + *tax*. This new supply curve intersects the demand curve at a price of $1.30 a litre and at a quantity of 200 million litres a day. The price at which suppliers are willing to produce 200 million litres a day is 40¢ a litre. The government collects a tax of 90¢ a litre on 200 million litres a day, so it collects a total revenue of $180 million a day—exactly the amount that it requires.

But what is the deadweight loss? The answer can be seen by looking at the grey triangle in Fig. 16.10. The deadweight loss is $90 million. Notice how much bigger the deadweight loss is from taxing orange juice than from taxing gasoline. In the case of orange juice, the deadweight loss is one-half the revenue raised, while in the case of gasoline, it is only one-sixth. What accounts for this difference? The supply curves are identical in each case, and the examples were also set up to ensure that the initial no-tax prices and quantities were identical. The difference between the two cases is the elasticity of demand: In the case of gasoline, the quantity demanded falls by only 25 percent when the price almost doubles. In the case of orange juice, the quantity demanded falls by 50 percent when the price only slightly more than doubles.

You can see why taxing orange juice is not on the political agenda of any of the major parties. Vote-seeking politicians seek out taxes that benefit the median voter. Other things being equal, this means that they try to minimize the deadweight loss of raising a given amount of revenue. Equivalently, they tax items with poor substitutes more heavily than items with close substitutes. That is, they tax items with inelastic demands, such as tobacco products and alcohol, more heavily than items with more elastic demands.

REVIEW QUIZ

1. How do income taxes influence employment and efficiency? Why are income taxes progressive?
2. Can parliament make employers pay a larger share of social insurance tax?
3. Why do some neighbourhoods have high taxes and high-quality services, and others have low taxes and low-quality services?
4. Why does the government impose excise taxes at high rates on goods that have a low elasticity of demand?.

Reading Between the Lines on pp. 388–389 looks at the changing scale of provision of border security services brought about by the increased awareness of terrorism. In the next two chapters, we are going to look at government economic actions in the face of monopolies and externalities.

READING BETWEEN THE LINES

An Increase in Demand for a Public Good

OTTAWA CITIZEN, December 11, 2001

Spending reveals urgent need for extra security

Beefing up border security and refugee screening will cost taxpayers an additional $2.2 billion over the next five years as the federal government responds to the Sept. 11 attacks.

The new spending is a loud admission from the Chrétien government that better protection is needed immediately.

The effort is aimed at shoring up Canadian and, perhaps more important, U.S. confidence in the government's ability to ensure terrorists will not enter the U.S. or Canada. ...

Finance Minister Paul Martin's budget spelled out more than $1.2 billion will be dedicated to beefing up the border, including $646 million for new technology, including explosive-detecting equipment. ...

To complement the border developments, an additional $1 billion will be spent screening immigrants, refugees and visitors coming into Canada. ...

Mr. Martin's budget also foreshadowed improvements to Canada's passport system in the new year but the details, including the actual cost, are under wraps. The budget only said: "Further state-of-the-art security features will be incorporated into the passport system."

Overall, the government is budgeting $287 million to make its documents fraud-proof in the next five years.

"We will tighten control in our refugee system so that only those truly in need can enjoy the privilege of our welcome. To that end, we will increase resources so that enhanced security checks can be done on claimants as soon as they arrive," said Mr. Martin.

Officials said the additional $210 million being spent on refugee determination, detention and possible removal in the next five years will not build detention facilities. Individuals will be detained in existing facilities if they do not satisfy immigration officers as to their identities, pose security risks or try to enter the country illegally.

The Immigration Refugee Board will also get more money to shorten the time necessary to validate refugee claims.

The other $395 million will go towards hiring more immigration control officers as part of the effort to improve screening... .

Jack Aubrey/*Ottawa Citizen*

Essence of the Story

- Finance Minister Paul Martin announced an additional $2.2 billion of expenditure on border security over the next five years as the federal government responds to the September 11 attacks.
- More than $1.2 billion will be spent on items that include explosive-detecting equipment to improve border security.
- An additional $1 billion will be spent on items that include a new passport system and more immigration control officers to screen immigrants, refugees, and visitors coming into Canada.

Economic Analysis

■ After the terrorist attacks of September 11, 2001, Canadian citizens and politicians revised their assessment of the benefit of border security.

■ Border security is a public good, and its efficient provision requires that its marginal benefit equal its marginal cost.

■ The total cost and marginal cost curve of border security did not change on September 11, 2001. Figure 1 shows an example of the total cost curve, *TC*, and Fig. 2 shows an example of the marginal cost curve, *MC*.

■ But the terrorist attacks changed the assessment of total benefit and marginal benefit. Before September 11, 2001, the benefit curves were TB_0 in Fig. 1 and MB_0 in Fig. 2.

■ The efficient quantity of border security was 50 units (an index number), and expenditure on this public good was $600 million a year (on the *y*-axis in Fig.1).

■ After the attacks, total benefit and marginal benefit increased to TB_1 in Fig. 1 and MB_1 in Fig. 2.

■ The efficient quantity increased to 75 (an assumed value) in Fig. 2, and expenditure in the 2002 budget increased to $1,000 million (on the *y*-axis in Fig. 1).

■ The increase in expenditure is $400 million in 2002 but will be a little higher over the succeeding years and will total $2.2 billion over five years.

■ We don't know that the efficient quantity of border security was being provided before September 11 and we don't know that the efficient quantity will be provided in the coming years. The figures show the efficient quantities.

■ Possibly, there is and will continue to be an overprovision through the pursuit of budget maximization by the government departments that provide border security.

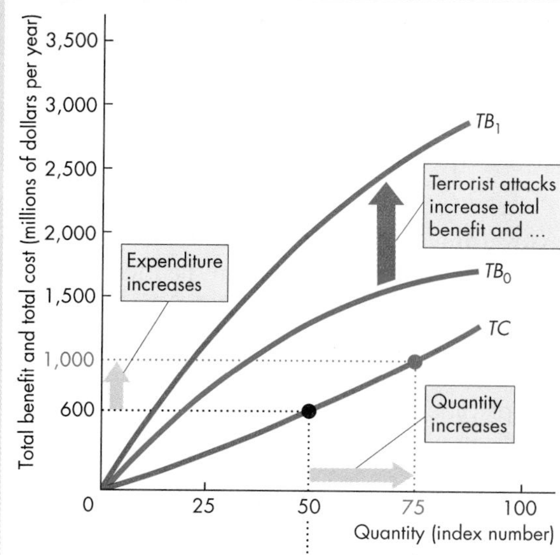

Figure 1 Total benefit and total cost

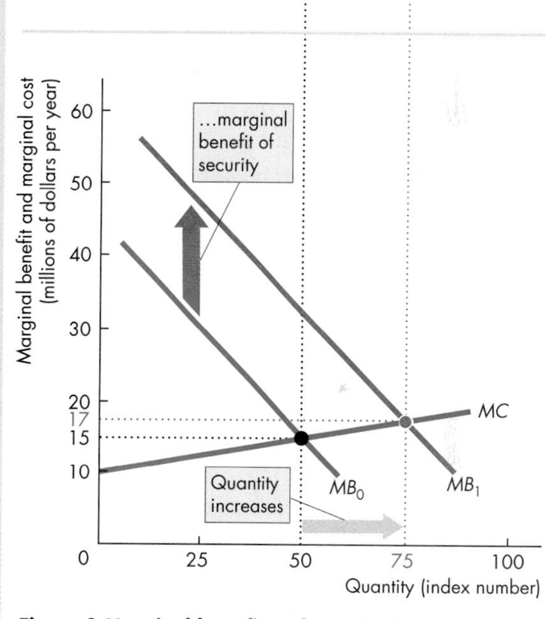

Figure 2 Marginal benefit and marginal cost

You're The Voter

■ Do you think that Canada and the United States should adopt common rules and procedures for North American security and have an open common border?

■ Would you vote for increased expenditure and harmonization for Canada–U.S. security arrangements? Explain why or why not.

SUMMARY

KEY POINTS

The Economic Theory of Government
(pp. 374–375)

- Government exists to provide public goods, regulate monopoly, cope with externalities, and reduce economic inequality.
- Public choice theory explains how voters, politicians, and bureaucrats interact in a political marketplace.

Public Goods and the Free-Rider Problem
(pp. 376–381)

- A public good is a good or service that is consumed by everyone and that is *nonrival* and *nonexcludable.*
- A public good creates a *free-rider* problem: No one has an incentive to pay his or her share of the cost of providing a public good.
- The efficient level of provision of a public good is that at which net benefit is maximized. Equivalently, it is the level at which marginal benefit equals marginal cost.
- Competition between political parties, each of which tries to appeal to the maximum number of voters, can lead to the efficient scale of provision of a public good and to both parties proposing the same policies—the principle of minimum differentiation.
- Bureaucrats try to maximize their budgets and, if voters are rationally ignorant, producer interests may result in voting to support taxes that provide public goods in quantities that exceed those that maximize net benefit.

Taxes (pp. 382–387)

- Government revenue comes from income taxes, social insurance taxes, sales taxes and the GST, property taxes, and excise taxes.
- Income taxes decrease the level of employment and create a deadweight loss.
- Taxes can be progressive (the average tax rate rises with income), proportional (the average tax rate is constant), or regressive (the average tax rate falls with income).
- Income taxes are progressive because this arrangement is in the interests of the median voter.
- Social insurance taxes are paid by the employer and the employee (and sales taxes are paid by the buyer and the seller) in amounts that depend on the elasticities of demand and supply.
- Property taxes change both demand and supply and can result in high-tax/high-quality service areas and low-tax/low-quality service areas.
- Excise taxes at high rates on gasoline, alcoholic beverages, and tobacco products create a smaller deadweight loss than would taxes on items with more elastic demands.

KEY FIGURES

Figure 16.3 Benefits of a Public Good, 377
Figure 16.4 The Efficient Quantity of a Public Good, 379
Figure 16.5 Bureaucratic Overprovision, 380
Figure 16.7 The Effects of Income Taxes, 383
Figure 16.8 Social Insurance Taxes, 385
Figure 16.9 An Excise Tax, 386

KEY TERMS

Average tax rate, 382
Excise tax, 386
Free rider, 376
Local public good, 385
Marginal tax rate, 382
Market failure, 374
Political equilibrium, 375
Principle of minimum differentiation, 379
Public good, 376
Rational ignorance, 380

PROBLEMS

*1. You are provided with the following information about a sewage disposal system that a city of 1 million people is considering installing.

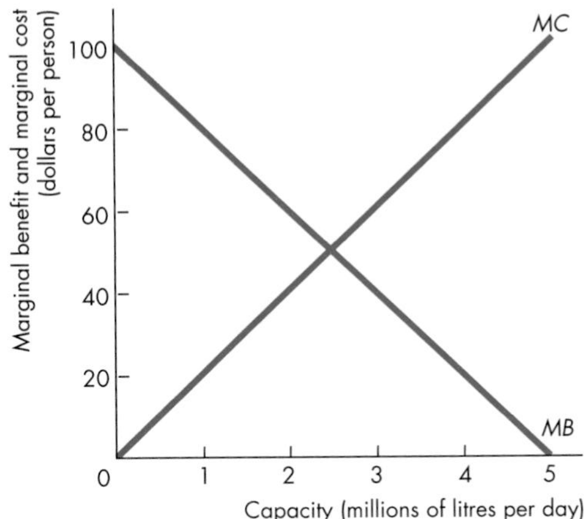

a. What is the capacity that achieves maximum net benefit?
b. How much will each person have to pay in taxes to pay for the efficient capacity level?
c. What is the political equilibrium if voters are well informed?
d. What is the political equilibrium if voters are rationally ignorant and bureaucrats achieve the highest attainable budget?

2. You are provided with the following information about a mosquito control program.

Quantity (square kilometres sprayed per day)	Marginal cost (dollars per day)	Marginal benefit (dollars per day)
0	0	0
1	1,000	5,000
2	2,000	4,000
3	3,000	3,000
4	4,000	2,000
5	5,000	1,000

a. What is the quantity of spraying that achieves maximum net benefit?
b. What is the total tax revenue needed to pay for the efficient quantity of spraying?
c. What is the political equilibrium if voters are well informed?
d. What is the political equilibrium if voters are rationally ignorant and bureaucrats achieve the highest attainable budget?

*3. An economy has two groups of people: A-types and B-types. The population consists of 80 percent A-types and 20 percent B-types. A-types have a perfectly elastic supply of labour at a wage rate of $10 an hour. B-types have a perfectly inelastic supply of labour, and their equilibrium wage rate is $100 an hour.
a. What kinds of tax arrangements do you think this economy will adopt?
b. Analyze the labour market in this economy and explain what will happen to the wage rates and employment levels of the two groups when the taxes you predict in your answer to part (a) are introduced.

4. Suppose that in the economy described in problem 3, the proportion of A-types is 20 percent and the proportion of B-types is 80 percent. Everything else remains the same.
a. Now what kinds of tax arrangements do you think the economy will adopt?
b. Analyze the labour market in this economy and explain what will happen to the wage rates and employment levels of the two groups when the taxes you predict in your answer to part (a) are introduced.
c. Compare the economy in problem 3 with the economy in this problem. Which economy more closely resembles our actual economy?

*5. An economy has a competitive labour market, which is described by the following demand and supply schedule:

Wage rate (dollars per hour)	Quantity demanded (hours per week)	Quantity supplied (hours per week)
20	0	50
16	15	40
12	30	30
8	45	20
4	60	10
0	75	0

a. What are the equilibrium wage rate and hours of work done?
b. If a $4 social insurance tax is imposed on employers
(i) What is the new wage rate?
(ii) What is the new number of hours worked?
(iii) What is the after-tax wage rate?

(iv) What is the tax revenue?
(v) What is the deadweight loss?

6. In the economy described in problem 5, the social insurance tax on employers is eliminated and a new social insurance tax of $4 is imposed on employees.
   a. What is the new wage rate?
   b. What is the new number of hours worked?
   c. What is the after-tax wage rate?
   d. What is the tax revenue?
   e. What is the deadweight loss?
   f. Compare the situation in problem 5 with that in this problem and explain the similarities and differences in the two situations.
*7. A competitive market for cookies has the following demand and supply schedule:

Price (dollars per kilogram)	**Quantity demanded** (kilograms per month)	**Quantity supplied** (kilograms per month)
7	0	8
6	1	7
5	2	6
4	3	5
3	4	4
2	5	3
1	6	2
0	7	1

   a. Find the equilibrium price and quantity.
   b. If cookies are taxed at $2 a kilogram
      (i) What is the new price of cookies?
      (ii) What is the new quantity bought?
      (iii) What is the tax revenue?
      (iv) What is the deadweight loss?
8. In the competitive market for cookies in problem 7, the government wants to change the tax to the rate that brings in the greatest possible amount of revenue.
   a. What is that tax rate?
   b. What is the new price of cookies?
   c. What is the new quantity bought?
   d. What is the tax revenue?
   e. What is the deadweight loss?

CRITICAL THINKING

1. Study *Reading Between the Lines* on pp. 388–389 and then answer the following:
   a. Describe some of the items included in border security and explain whether they are public goods or private goods.
   b. Why might the provision of border security exceed the efficient level?
   c. Can you think of any reasons why the provision of border security might be less than the efficient level?
2. Your city council is contemplating upgrading its system for controlling traffic signals. The council believes that by installing computers, it can improve the speed of the traffic flow. The bigger the computer the council buys, the better the job it can do. The mayor and the other elected officials who are working on the proposal want to determine the scale of the system that will win them the most votes. The city bureaucrats want to maximize the budget. Suppose that you are an economist who is observing this public choice. Your job is to calculate the quantity of this public good that uses resources efficiently.
   a. What data would you need to reach your own conclusions?
   b. What does the public choice theory predict will be the quantity chosen?
   c. How could you, as an informed voter, attempt to influence the choice?

WEB EXERCISES

1. Use the links on the Parkin–Bade Web site and read the article on demand revealing processes.
   a. What is a demand revealing process and what is its purpose?
   b. Why might using a demand revealing process deliver a more efficient level of public goods than our current political system?
   c. Why might our current political system deliver a more efficient level of public goods than would a demand revealing process?

COMPETITION POLICY

CHAPTER 17

Public Interest or Special Interests?

When you consume water, electric power, cable TV, or local telephone service, you buy from a regulated monopoly. Why do we regulate the industries that produce these goods and services? How do we regulate them? Does regulation work in the interests of consumers—the public interest—or does it serve the interests of producers—special interests? ◆ The government used its anti-combine laws to end Northern Telecom's monopoly on phone equipment and Bell Canada's monopoly on long-distance phone calls as well as the installation of phone lines. This action brought competition into all three markets. Now you can choose where to buy your phone equipment, which long-distance telephone service to use, and the company to install your phone line. ◆ You will see, in *Reading Between the Lines* at the end of the chapter, that similar laws in Europe have been used to fine companies for fixing the prices of vitamins. What are the anti-combine laws? How have they evolved over the years? How are they used today? Do they serve the public interest of consumers or the special interests of producers?

◆ This chapter studies these questions.

After studying this chapter, you will be able to

- **Define regulation, public ownership, and anti-combine law**
- **Distinguish between the public interest and capture theories of regulation**
- **Explain how regulation affects prices, outputs, profits, and the distribution of the gains from trade between consumers and producers**
- **Explain how public ownership affects prices, outputs, and allocative efficiency**
- **Explain how anti-combine law is used in Canada today**

Market Intervention

THE GOVERNMENT INTERVENES IN MONOPOLISTIC and oligopolistic markets to influence what, how, and for whom various goods and services are produced in three main ways:

- Regulation
- Public ownership
- Anti-combine law

Regulation

Regulation consists of rules administered by a government agency to influence economic activity by determining prices, product standards and types, and the conditions under which new firms may enter an industry. To implement its regulations, the government establishes agencies to oversee the regulations and ensure their enforcement. The first such economic regulation in Canada was the Railway Act of 1888, which regulated railway rates. Since then and up to the late 1970s, regulation spread to banking and financial services, telecommunications, gas and electric utilities, railways, trucking, airlines and buses, and dozens of agricultural products. Since the early 1980s, there has been a tendency to deregulate the Canadian economy.

Deregulation is the process of removing restrictions on prices, product standards and types, and entry conditions. In recent years, deregulation has occurred in domestic air transportation, telephone service, interprovincial trucking, and banking and financial services.

Public Ownership

In Canada, a publicly owned firm is called a **Crown corporation**. The most important Crown corporations are Canada Post, the CBC, VIA Rail, and Atomic Energy of Canada. There are many provincial Crown corporations, the most important of which are the provincial hydro companies. Just as there has been a tendency to deregulate the Canadian economy in recent years, there has also been a tendency to privatize it. **Privatization** is the process of selling a publicly owned corporation to private shareholders. Petro-Canada was privatized in 1991.

Anti-Combine Law

An **anti-combine law** is a law that regulates and prohibits certain kinds of market behaviour, such as monopoly and monopolistic practices. The main thrust of the anti-combine law is the prohibition of monopoly practices and of restricting output in order to achieve higher prices and profits. Until 1971, these laws were part of the Criminal Code. As a consequence, the test of guilt was much more stringent than under civil law, and Canada's anti-combine laws were used less vigorously than the parallel laws (called "anti-trust laws") in the United States.

To understand why the government intervenes in markets and to work out the effects of interventions, we need to identify the gains and losses that government actions can create. These gains and losses are the consumer surplus and producer surplus associated with different output levels and prices. We first study the economics of regulation.

Economic Theory of Regulation

THE ECONOMIC THEORY OF REGULATION IS PART of the broader theory of public choice that is explained in Chapter 16. We're going to re-examine the main features of public choice theory but with an emphasis on the regulatory aspects of government behaviour. We'll examine the demand for government actions, the supply of those actions, and the political equilibrium that emerges.

Demand for Regulation

The demand for regulation is expressed through political activity—voting, lobbying, and making campaign contributions. But engaging in political activity is costly and people demand political action only if the benefit that they individually receive from such action exceeds their individual costs in obtaining the action. The four main factors that affect the demand for regulation are

1. Consumer surplus per buyer
2. Number of buyers
3. Producer surplus per firm
4. Number of firms

The larger the consumer surplus per buyer resulting from regulation, the greater is the demand for regulation by buyers. Also, as the number of buyers increases, so does the demand for regulation. But numbers alone do not necessarily translate into an effective political force. The larger the number of buyers, the greater is the cost of organizing them, so the demand for regulation does not increase proportionately with the number of buyers.

The larger the producer surplus per firm arising from a particular regulation, the larger is the demand for that regulation by firms. Also, as the number of firms that might benefit from some regulation increases, so does the demand for that regulation. But again, large numbers do not necessarily mean an effective political force. The larger the number of firms, the greater is the cost of organizing them.

For a given surplus, consumer or producer, the smaller the number of households or firms who share that surplus, the larger is the demand for the regulation that creates it.

Supply of Regulation

Politicians and bureaucrats supply regulation. According to public choice theory, politicians choose policies that appeal to a majority of voters, thereby enabling themselves to achieve and maintain office. Bureaucrats support policies that maximize their budgets (see Chapter 16, p. 380). Given these objectives of politicians and bureaucrats, the supply of regulation depends on the following factors:

1. Consumer surplus per buyer
2. Producer surplus per firm
3. The number of voters who benefit

The larger the consumer surplus per buyer or producer surplus per firm generated and the larger the number of voters who benefit by a regulation, the greater is the tendency for politicians to supply that regulation. Politicians are likely to supply regulation that benefits a large number of people by a large amount per person. They are also likely to supply regulation that benefits a small number of people when the benefit per person is large and the cost is spread widely and not easily identified. But they are unlikely to supply regulation that brings a small benefit per person.

Political Equilibrium

In equilibrium, the regulation that exists is such that no interest group finds it worthwhile to use additional resources to press for changes and no group of politicians finds it worthwhile to offer different regulations. Being in a political equilibrium is not the same thing as everyone being in agreement. Lobby groups will devote resources to trying to change regulations that are already in place. And others will devote resources to maintaining the existing regulations. But no one will feel it is worthwhile to *increase* the resources that he or she is devoting to such activities. Also, political parties might not agree with each other. Some support the existing regulations, and others propose different regulations. In equilibrium, no one wants to change the proposals that they are making.

What will a political equilibrium look like? The answer depends on whether the regulation serves the public interest or the interest of the producer. Let's look at these two possibilities.

Public Interest Theory The **public interest theory** is that regulations are supplied to satisfy the demand of consumers and producers to maximize total surplus—that is, to attain allocative efficiency. Public interest theory implies that the political process relentlessly seeks out deadweight loss and introduces regulations that eliminate it. For example, where monopoly practices exist, the political process will introduce price regulations to ensure that outputs increase and prices fall to their competitive levels.

Capture Theory The **capture theory** is that the regulations are supplied to satisfy the demand of producers to maximize producer surplus—that is, to maximize economic profit. The key idea of capture theory is that the cost of regulation is high and only those regulations that increase the surplus of small, easily identified groups and that have low organization costs are supplied by the political process. Consumers bear the cost of such regulation, but the costs are spread thinly and widely so the politicians do not lose votes.

The predictions of the capture theory are less clear-cut than the predictions of the public interest theory. According to the capture theory, regulations benefit cohesive interest groups by large and visible amounts and impose small costs on everyone else. But those costs are so small, in per person terms, that no one feels it is worthwhile to incur the cost of organizing an interest group to avoid them. To make these predictions concrete enough to be useful, the capture theory needs a model of the costs of political organization.

Whichever theory of regulation is correct, according to public choice theory, the political system delivers amounts and types of regulations that best further the electoral success of politicians. Because producer-oriented and consumer-oriented regulations are in conflict with each other, the political process can't satisfy both groups in any particular industry. Only one group can win. This makes the regulatory actions of government a bit like a unique product—for example, a painting by Emily Carr. There is only one original and it will be sold to just one buyer. Normally, a unique commodity is sold through an auction; the highest bidder takes the prize.

Equilibrium in the regulatory process can be thought of in much the same way: The suppliers of regulation will satisfy the demands of the higher bidder. If the producer demand offers a bigger return to the politicians, either directly through votes or indirectly through campaign contributions, then the regulation will serve the producers' interests. If the consumer demand translates into a larger number of votes, then the regulation will serve the consumers' interests.

REVIEW QUIZ

1. How do consumers and producers express their demand for regulation? What are their objectives? What are the costs of expressing a demand for regulation?
2. When politicians and bureaucrats supply regulation, what are they trying to achieve? Do politicians and bureaucrats have the same objectives?
3. What is a political equilibrium? When does the political equilibrium achieve allocative efficiency? When does the political equilibrium serve the interests of producers? When do the bureaucrats win?

We have now completed our study of the *theory* of regulation in the marketplace. Let's turn our attention to the regulations that exist in our economy today. Which theory of regulation best explains these real-world regulations? Which of these regulations are in the public interest and which are in the interest of producers?

Regulation and Deregulation

THE PAST DECADE OR SO HAS SEEN DRAMATIC changes in the way in which the government has regulated the Canadian economy. We're going to examine some of these changes. To begin, we'll look at what the government regulates and also at the scope of regulation. Then we'll turn to the regulatory process itself and examine how regulators control prices and other aspects of market behaviour. Finally, we'll tackle the more difficult and controversial questions: Why does the government regulate some things but not others? Who benefits from the regulation that we have—consumers or producers?

The Scope of Regulation

Regulation in Canada touches a wide range of economic activity. Table 17.1 sets out the major federal regulatory agencies, together with a brief statement of their responsibilities. As you can see by inspecting that table, the predominant sectors subject to regulation are agriculture, energy, transport, and telecommunications.

Provincial and municipal governments also establish regulations covering a wide range of economic activity. Some of these—for example, municipal regulation of the taxicab industry—have important direct effects on the marketplace. Our analysis of the regulatory process and the effects of regulation apply with equal force to price, output, and profit regulation at these other governmental levels.

What exactly do regulatory agencies do? How do they regulate?

The Regulatory Process

Though regulatory agencies vary in size and scope and in the detailed aspects of economic life that they control, there are certain features common to all agencies.

First, the government appoints the senior bureaucrats who are the key decision makers in a regulatory agency. In addition, all agencies have a permanent bureaucracy made up of experts in the industry being regulated and who are often recruited from the regulated firms. Agencies have financial resources, voted by Parliament, to cover the costs of their operations.

TABLE 17.1 Federal Regulatory Agencies

Agency	Responsibility
Atomic Energy Control Board	Administers the Atomic Energy Control Act governing all uses of radioactive material.
Canadian Dairy Commission	Administers national dairy policy, which seeks to give producers an adequate return and keep the price to consumers low.
Canadian Radio-Television and Telecommunications Commission	Regulates all aspects of radio, television, and telecommunications.
Canadian Grain Commission	Regulates grain handling, establishes and maintains quality standards, audits grain stocks, and supervises future trading.
Canadian Wheat Board	Regulates exports of wheat and barley and domestic sales for human consumption.
National Energy Board	Regulates oil, gas, and electrical industries.
National Farm Products Marketing Council	Advises government on the establishment and operation of national agricultural marketing agencies and works with those agencies and provincial governments to promote marketing of farm products. Chicken, egg, and turkey agencies have been established under its aegis.
Canadian Transport Commission	Regulates transports under federal jurisdiction including rail, air, water, and pipeline and some interprovincial commercial motor transport.

Source: Adapted from the Statistics Canada publication *Canada Year Book*, catalogue 11-402, 1992, pp. 543–558.

Second, each agency adopts a set of practices or operating rules for controlling prices and other aspects of economic performance. These rules and practices are based on well-defined physical and financial accounting procedures that are relatively easy to administer and to monitor.

In a regulated industry, individual firms are usually free to determine the technology that they will use in production. But they are not free to determine the prices at which they will sell their output, the quantities that they will sell, or the markets that they will serve. The regulatory agency grants certification to a company to serve a particular market and with a particular line of products. The agency also determines the level and structure of prices that the company can charge. In some cases, the agency also determines the scale of output permitted.

To analyze the way in which regulation works, it is convenient to distinguish between the regulation of a natural monopoly and the regulation of cartels. Let's begin with the regulation of a natural monopoly.

Natural Monopoly

A **natural monopoly** was defined in Chapter 12 (p. 262) as an industry in which one firm can supply the entire market at a lower price than two or more firms can. As a consequence, a natural monopoly experiences economies of scale, no matter how large an output rate it produces. Examples of natural monopolies include local distribution of cable television signals, electricity, and gas, and urban rail services. It is much more expensive to have two or more competing sets of wires, pipes, and train tracks serving every neighbourhood than it is to have a single set. (What is a natural monopoly changes over time as technology changes. With the introduction of fibre optic cables, both telephone companies and cable television companies will be able to compete with each other in both markets, so what is a natural monopoly will become a more competitive industry.)

Let's consider the example of cable TV, which is shown in Fig. 17.1. The demand curve for cable TV is *D*. The cable TV company's marginal cost curve is *MC*. That marginal cost curve is (assumed to be)

FIGURE 17.1 Natural Monopoly: Marginal Cost Pricing

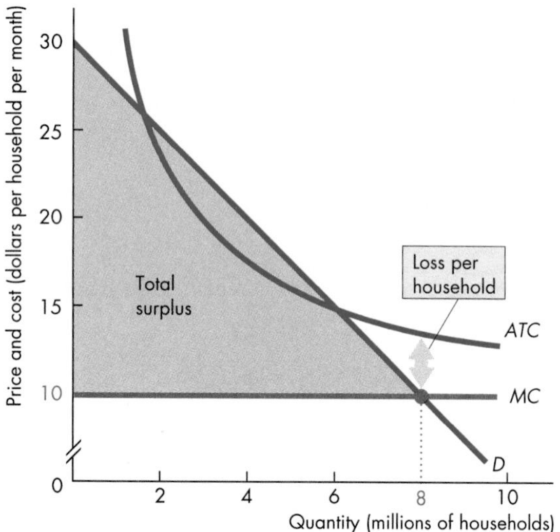

A natural monopoly is an industry in which average total cost is falling even when the entire market demand is satisfied. The demand for cable TV is shown by the curve *D*. The firm's marginal cost is constant at $10 per household per month, as shown by the curve *MC*. Fixed costs are large, and the average total cost curve, which includes average fixed cost, is shown as *ATC*. A marginal cost pricing rule that maximizes total surplus sets the price at $10 a month, with 8 million households being served. The resulting consumer surplus is shown as the green area. The firm incurs a loss on each household, indicated by the red arrow. To remain in business, the firm must price discriminate, use a two-part tariff, or receive a subsidy.

horizontal at $10 per household per month—that is, the cost of providing each additional household with a month of cable programming is $10. The cable company has a heavy investment in satellite receiving dishes, cables, and control equipment and so has high fixed costs. These fixed costs are part of the company's average total cost curve, shown as *ATC*. The average total cost curve slopes downward because as the number of households served increases, the fixed cost is spread over a larger number of households. (If you need to refresh your memory on how the average total cost curve is calculated, take a quick look back at Chapter 10, p. 224.)

Regulation in the Public Interest How will cable TV be regulated according to the public interest theory? It will be regulated to maximize total surplus, which occurs if marginal cost equals price. As you can see in Fig. 17.1, that outcome occurs if the price is regulated at $10 per household per month and if 8 million households are served. Such a regulation is called a marginal cost pricing rule. A **marginal cost pricing rule** sets price equal to marginal cost. It maximizes total surplus in the regulated industry.

A natural monopoly that is regulated to set price equal to marginal cost incurs an economic loss. Because its average total cost curve is downward sloping, marginal cost is below average total cost. Because price equals marginal cost, price is below average total cost. Average total cost minus price is the loss per unit produced. It's pretty obvious that a cable TV company that is required to use a marginal cost pricing rule will not stay in business for long. How can a company cover its costs and, at the same time, obey a marginal cost pricing rule?

One possibility is price discrimination (see Chapter 12, pp. 271–274). Another is to use a two-part price (called a two-part tariff). For example, local telephone companies can charge consumers a monthly fee for being connected to the telephone system and then charge a price equal to marginal cost for each local call. A cable TV operator can charge a one-time connection fee that covers its fixed cost and then charge a monthly fee equal to marginal cost.

But a natural monopoly cannot always cover its costs in these ways. If a natural monopoly cannot cover its total cost from its customers and if the government wants it to follow a marginal cost pricing rule, then the government must give the firm a subsidy. In such a case, the government raises the revenue for the subsidy by taxing some other activity. But as we saw in Chapter 16, taxes themselves generate deadweight loss. Thus the deadweight loss resulting from additional taxes must be subtracted from the efficiency gained by forcing the natural monopoly to adopt a marginal cost pricing rule.

Deadweight loss might be minimized by making the natural monopoly cover its costs rather than by taxing another sector of the economy. When a monopoly covers its costs, it uses an average cost pricing rule. An **average cost pricing rule** sets price equal to average total cost. Figure 17.2 shows the average cost pricing outcome. The cable TV operator charges $15 a month and serves 6 million households. A deadweight loss arises, which is shown by the grey triangle in the figure.

FIGURE 17.2 Natural Monopoly: Average Cost Pricing

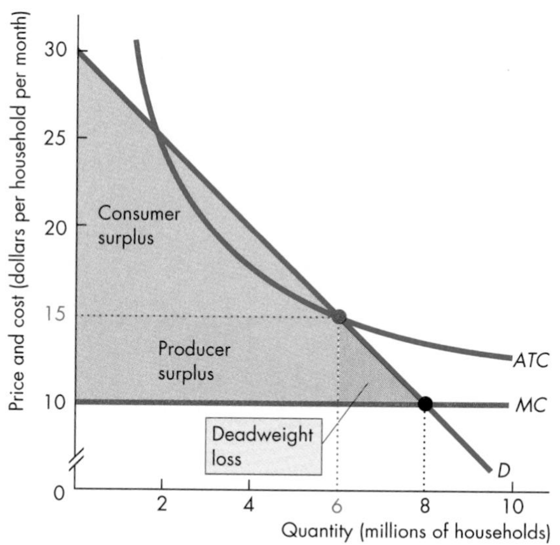

An average cost pricing rule sets the price equal to average total cost. The cable TV operator charges $15 a month and serves 6 million households. In this situation, the firm breaks even—average total cost equals price. Deadweight loss, shown by the grey triangle, is generated. Consumer surplus is reduced to the green area.

FIGURE 17.3 Natural Monopoly: Profit Maximization

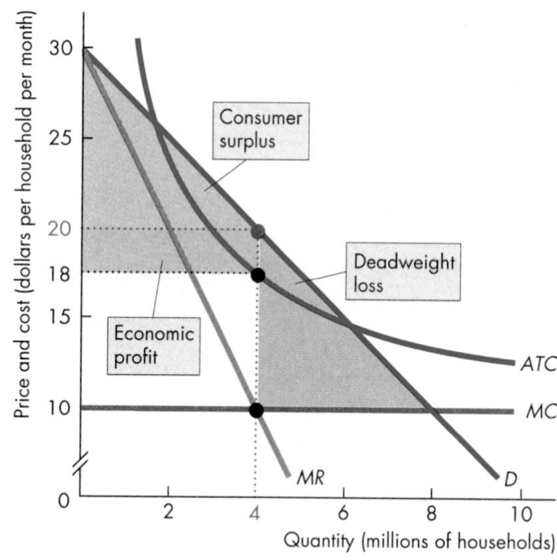

The cable TV operator would like to maximize profit. To do so, marginal revenue (*MR*) is made equal to marginal cost (*MC*). At a price of $20 a month, 4 million households buy cable service. Consumer surplus is reduced to the green triangle. The deadweight loss increases to the grey triangle. The monopoly makes the profit shown by the blue rectangle. If the producer can capture the regulator, the outcome will be the situation shown here.

Capturing the Regulator What does the capture theory predict about the regulation of this industry? According to the capture theory, the producer gets the regulator to set rules that work to serve the interest of the producer. But the producer interest is served by being able to operate at the same output and price as an unregulated monopoly. In Fig. 17.3, the monopoly's marginal revenue curve is the curve labelled *MR*. Marginal revenue equals marginal cost when output is 4 million households and the price is $20 a month. At this output and price, the producer makes the maximum profit. So regulation in the interest of the producer maintains the unregulated monopoly outcome.

But how can a producer go about capturing the regulator and obtaining regulation that results in this monopoly profit-maximizing outcome? To answer this question, we need to look at the way in which agencies determine a regulated price. A key method used is called rate of return regulation.

Rate of Return Regulation **Rate of return regulation** determines a regulated price by setting the price at a level that enables the regulated firm to earn a specified target percent return on its capital. The target rate of return is determined with reference to what is normal in competitive industries. This rate of return is part of the opportunity cost of the natural monopoly and is included in the firm's average total cost. By examining the firm's total cost, including the normal rate of return on capital, the regulator attempts to determine the price at which average total cost is covered. Thus rate of return regulation is equivalent to an average cost pricing rule.

In Fig. 17.2, average cost pricing results in a regulated price of $15 a month with 6 million households being served. Thus rate of return regulation, based on a correct assessment of the producer's average total cost curve, results in a price that favours the consumer and does not enable the producer to maximize monopoly profit. The special interest group will have failed to capture the regulator, and the outcome will be closer to that predicted by the public interest theory of regulation.

But there is a feature of many real-world situations that the above analysis does not take into account: the ability of the monopoly firm to mislead the regulator about its true costs.

Inflating Costs The managers of a firm might be able to inflate the firm's costs by spending part of the firm's revenue on inputs that are not strictly required for the production of the good. By this device, the firm's apparent costs exceed the true costs. On-the-job luxury in the form of sumptuous office suites, limousines, free baseball tickets (disguised as public relations expenses), company jets, lavish international travel, and entertainment are all ways in which managers can inflate costs.

If the cable TV operator makes the regulator believe that its true cost is *ATC (inflated)* in Fig. 17.4, then the regulator will set the price at $20 a month. In this example, the price and quantity will be the same as those under unregulated monopoly. It might be impossible for firms to inflate their costs by as much as the amount shown in the figure. But to the extent that costs can be inflated, the apparent average total cost curve lies somewhere between the true average total cost curve and *ATC (inflated)*. The greater the ability of the firm to inflate its costs in this way, the more closely its profit (measured in economic terms) approaches the maximum possible. The stockholders of this firm don't receive this economic profit because it is used up in baseball tickets, luxury offices, and the other actions taken by the firm's managers to inflate the company's costs.

FIGURE 17.4 Natural Monopoly: Inflating Costs

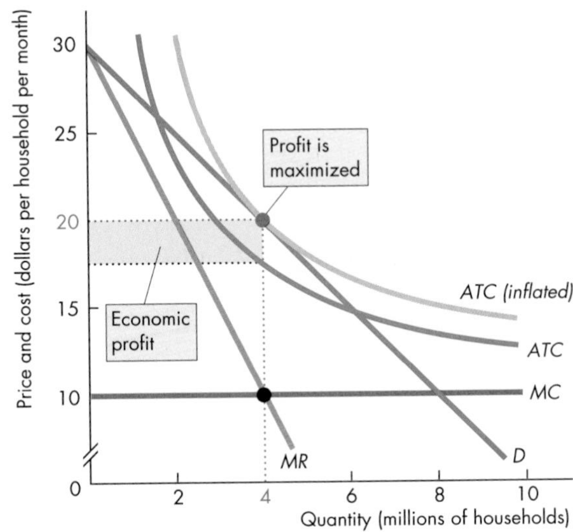

If the cable TV operator is able to inflate its costs to *ATC (inflated)* and persuade the regulator that these are genuine minimum costs of production, rate of return regulation results in a price of $20 a month—the profit-maximizing price. To the extent that the producer can inflate costs above average total cost, the price rises, output decreases, and deadweight loss increases. The managers, not the shareholders (owners) of the firm, capture the profit.

Public Interest or Capture?

It is not clear whether actual regulation produces prices and quantities that more closely correspond with the predictions of capture theory or of public interest theory. One thing is clear, however. Price regulation does not require natural monopolies to use the marginal cost pricing rule. If it did, most natural monopolies would incur losses and receive hefty government subsidies to enable them to remain in business. But there are even exceptions to this conclusion. For example, many local telephone companies do appear to use marginal cost pricing for local telephone calls. These phone companies cover their total cost by charging a flat fee each month for being connected to their telephone system but then permitting each local call to be made at its marginal cost—zero or something very close to it.

We can test whether natural monopoly regulation is in the public interest or producer interest by comparing the rates of return in regulated natural monopolies with average returns. If regulated natural monopolies have rates of return that are significantly higher than those in the rest of the economy, then, to some degree, the regulator may have been captured by the producer. There is plenty of empirical evidence that many natural monopolies in Canada do earn higher rates of return than the economy average.

One recent striking example is cable television service; telephone service is another. The rates of return in these two industries exceed 10 percent a year, approaching double the economy average. Perhaps the most dramatic piece of evidence that regulation benefits the regulated firm is the profits of Bell Canada Enterprises (BCE), prior to deregulation of long-distance phone services. BCE is a conglomerate that produced *regulated* long-distance telephone services and *unregulated* phone equipment (Northern Telecom) and financial services (Montreal Trustco). In 1992, BCE made a total profit of $1.4 billion on total assets of $12.3 billion, a profit rate of 11.4 percent. But this total was made up of a profit of $0.9 billion on assets of $7 billion—a return of 12.9 percent—for the regulated Bell Canada and a profit of $0.5 billion on assets of $5.3 billion—9.4 percent—for all of BCE's *unregulated* operations.

Until the early 1990s, long-distance telephone service was a natural monopoly, but technological advances in telecommunications have changed the situation. Today, the industry is an oligopoly. But oligopoly is also regulated. Let's examine regulation in oligopolistic industries—the regulation of cartels.

Cartel Regulation

A *cartel* is a collusive agreement among a number of firms designed to restrict output and achieve a higher profit for the cartel's members. Cartels are illegal in Canada and in most other countries. But international cartels can sometimes operate legally, as does the international cartel of oil producers known as OPEC (the Organization of the Petroleum Exporting Countries).

Illegal cartels can arise in oligopolistic industries. An oligopoly is a market structure in which a small number of firms compete with each other. We studied oligopoly (and duopoly—two firms competing for a market) in Chapter 13. There we saw that if firms manage to collude and behave like a monopoly, they can set the same price and sell the same total quantity as a monopoly firm would. But we also discovered that in such a situation, each firm will be tempted to cheat, increasing its own output and profit at the expense of the other firms. The result of such cheating on the collusive agreement is the unravelling of the monopoly equilibrium and the emergence of a competitive outcome with zero economic profit for producers. Such an outcome benefits consumers at the expense of producers.

How is oligopoly regulated? Does regulation prevent monopoly practices or does it encourage those practices?

According to the public interest theory, oligopoly is regulated to ensure a competitive outcome. Consider, for example, the market for trucking tomatoes from the fields of southwestern Ontario to a ketchup factory at Leamington, illustrated in Fig. 17.5. The demand curve for trips is *D*. The industry marginal cost curve—and the competitive supply curve—is *MC*. Public interest regulation will regulate the price of a trip at $20 and there will be 300 trips a week.

FIGURE 17.5 Collusive Oligopoly

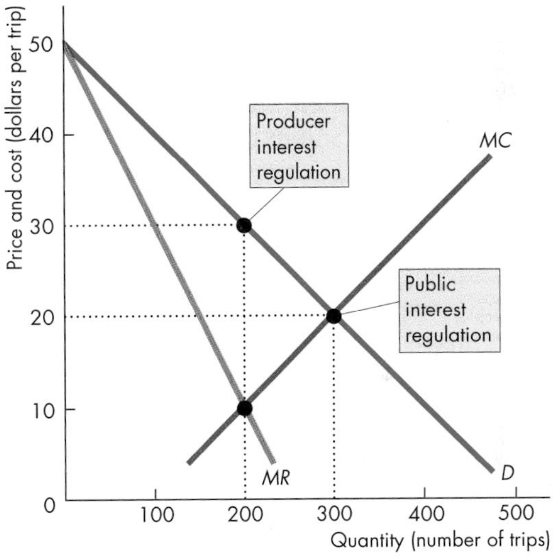

Ten trucking firms transport tomatoes from southwestern Ontario to Leamington. The demand curve is *D*, and the industry marginal cost curve is *MC*. Under competition, the *MC* curve is the industry supply curve. If the industry is competitive, the price of a trip will be $20 and 300 trips will be made each week. Producers will demand regulation that restricts entry and limits output to 200 trips a week where industry marginal revenue (*MR*) is equal to industry marginal cost (*MC*). This regulation raises the price to $30 a trip and results in each producer making maximum profit—as if the 10 firms were a monopoly.

How would this industry be regulated according to the capture theory? Regulation that is in the interest of producers will maximize profit. To find the outcome in this case, we need to determine the price and quantity when marginal cost equals marginal revenue. The marginal revenue curve is *MR*. So marginal revenue equals marginal cost at 200 trips a week. The price of a trip is $30.

One way of achieving this outcome is to place an output limit on each firm in the industry. If there are 10 trucking companies, an output limit of 20 trips per company ensures that the total number of trips in a week is 200. Penalties can be imposed to ensure that no single producer exceeds its output limit.

All the firms in the industry would support this type of regulation because it helps to prevent cheating and to maintain a monopoly outcome. Each firm knows that without effectively enforced production quotas, every firm has an incentive to increase output. (For each firm, price exceeds marginal cost, so a greater output brings a larger profit.) So each firm wants a method of preventing output from rising above the industry's profit-maximizing level, and the quotas enforced by regulation achieve this end. With this type of cartel regulation, the regulator enables a cartel to operate legally and in its own best interest.

What does cartel regulation do in practice? Although there is disagreement about the matter, the consensus view is that regulation tends to favour the producer. Trucking and airlines (when they were regulated by the Canadian Transport Commission) and taxicabs (regulated by cities) are specific examples in which profits of producers increased as a result of regulation. But the most dramatic examples of regulation favouring the producer are in agriculture. An Economic Council of Canada study, based on the situation prevailing in the early 1980s, estimated that regulation of the egg-producing and broiler chicken industries alone transferred more than $100 million a year to just 4,600 individual producers.[1]

Further evidence on cartel and oligopoly regulation can be obtained from the performance of prices and profit following deregulation. If, following deregulation, prices and profit fall, then, to some degree, the regulation must have been serving the interest of the producer. In contrast, if, following deregulation, prices and profits remain constant or increase, then the regulation may be presumed to have been serving the public interest. Because there has been a substantial amount of deregulation in recent years, we may use this test of oligopoly regulation to see which of the two theories better fits the facts. The evidence is mixed, but in the cases of airlines, trucking, and long-distance phone calls, three oligopolies to be deregulated, prices fell and there was a large increase in the volume of business.

Making Predictions

Most industries have a few producers and many consumers. In these cases, public choice theory predicts that regulation will protect producers because a small number of people stand to gain a large amount and so they will be fairly easy to organize as a cohesive lobby. Under such circumstances, politicians will be rewarded with campaign contributions rather than votes. But there are situations in which the consumer interest is sufficiently strong and well organized and thus able to prevail. There are also cases in which the balance switches from producer to consumer, as seen in the deregulation process that began in the late 1970s.

Deregulation raises some hard questions for economists seeking to understand and make predictions about regulation. Why were the transportation and telecommunications sectors deregulated? If producers gained from regulation and if the producer lobby was strong enough to achieve regulation, what happened in the 1970s to change the equilibrium to one in which the consumer interest prevailed? We do not have a complete answer to this question at the present time. But regulation had become so costly to consumers, and the potential benefits to them from deregulation so great, that the cost of organizing the consumer voice became a price worth paying.

One factor that increased the cost of regulation borne by consumers and brought deregulation in the transportation sector was the large increase in energy prices in the 1970s. These price hikes made route regulation by the Canadian Transport Commission extremely costly and changed the balance of the political equilibrium to favour consumers. Technological change was the main factor at work in the telecommunications sector. New satellite-based, computer-controlled long-distance technologies enabled smaller producers to offer low-cost services. These producers wanted a share of Bell Canada's business—and profit. Furthermore, as communica-

[1] J. D. Forbes, R. D. Hughes, and T.K. Warley, *Economic Intervention and Regulation in Canadian Agriculture* (Ottawa: Department of Supply and Services, 1982).

tions technology improved, the cost of communication fell and the cost of organizing larger groups of consumers also fell. If this line of reasoning is correct, we can expect to see more consumer-oriented regulation in the future. In practice, more consumer-oriented regulation often means deregulation —removing the regulations that are already in place to serve the interests of producer groups.

REVIEW QUIZ

1 What are the main regulatory agencies in Canada?
2 Why does natural monopoly need to be regulated?
3 What pricing rule enables a natural monopoly to operate in the public interest?
4 Why is a marginal cost pricing rule difficult to implement?
5 What pricing rule is typically used to regulate a natural monopoly and what problems does it create?
6 Why is it necessary to regulate a cartel?
7 How might cartels be regulated in the public interest?

Let's now turn to the second method of intervention in markets—public ownership.

Public Ownership

CROWN CORPORATIONS HAVE A SIGNIFICANT AND historical presence in Canadian society. Before Confederation, Crown corporations were used for building canals and operating ports and harbours. The establishment of the Canadian nation involved a commitment to build a railway to link New Brunswick and Nova Scotia to central Canada. Over the years, vast distances, a sparse population, the presence of a powerful neighbour, strong and distinct national interests, and the existence of two main cultural and linguistic groups nurtured the establishment of Crown corporations.

A Crown corporation is a corporation in which the government has 100 percent ownership. There are federal and provincial Crown corporations, and they are involved in many sectors of the economy, including transportation; energy and resources; agriculture and fisheries; development and construction; government services; culture; financial intermediaries; telecommunications and broadcasting; provincial lotteries; housing; and alcoholic beverages. Examples of Crown corporations include the Business Development Bank of Canada, the Canadian Museum of Nature, and the Ontario Lottery Corporation.

Public ownership provides another way in which the government can influence the behaviour of a natural monopoly. What are the effects of this method of natural monopoly control? How does a publicly owned corporation operate? Let's explore some alternative patterns of behaviour for such corporations.

Efficient Crown Corporation

One possibility is that a Crown corporation is operated in a manner that results in economic efficiency—maximization of total surplus. Let's consider the example of a railway. Figure 17.6(a) illustrates the demand for freight service and the railway's costs. The demand curve is *D*. The marginal cost curve is *MC*. Notice that the marginal cost curve is horizontal at $2 a tonne. The railway has a heavy investment in track, trains, and control equipment, so it has large fixed costs. These fixed costs feature in the company's average total cost curve *ATC*. The average total cost curve slopes downward because as the number of tonnes of freight carried increases, the fixed costs are spread over a larger number of tonnes. To be efficient, a Crown corporation obeys the rule:

> Produce the output at which price equals marginal cost.

In this example, that output level is 8 billion tonnes a year at a price—and marginal cost—of $2 a tonne. To be able to operate in this manner, a publicly owned railway has to be subsidized; the subsidy on each unit of output must equal the difference between average total cost and marginal cost. And the subsidy has to be collected in a way other than through the price of the good or service produced—in other words, by taxation. If the government taxes each household a fixed amount, the consumer surplus will shrink to the green triangle shown in Fig. 17.6(a), but consumer surplus will be at its maximum.

FIGURE 17.6 Crown Corporation

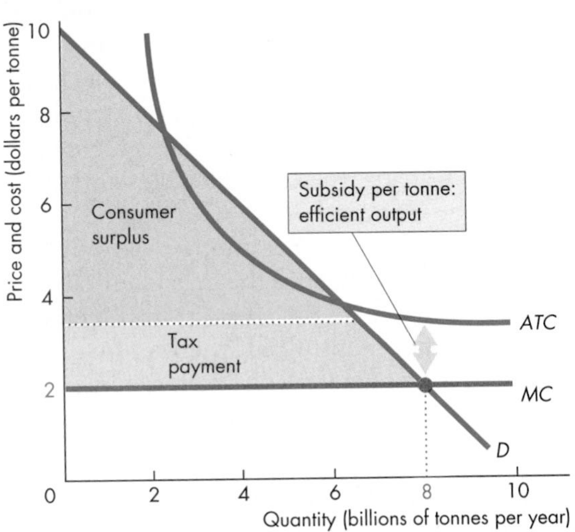

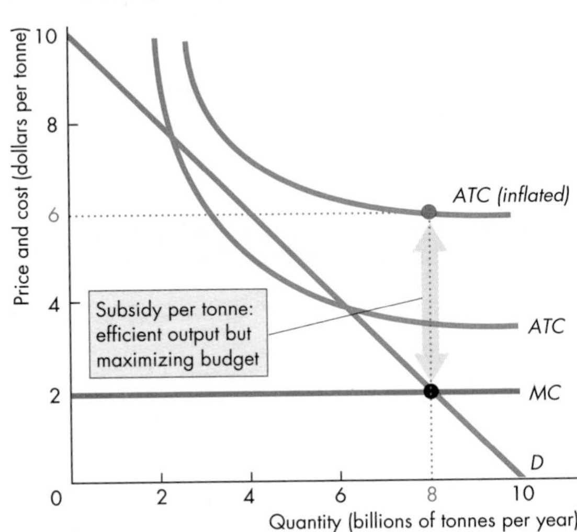

Part (a) shows a railway operated by a Crown corporation that produces the output at which price equals marginal cost. Its output is 8 billion tonnes a year and the price is $2 a tonne. The Crown corporation receives a subsidy that enables it to cover its total cost, and that cost is the minimum possible cost of providing the efficient quantity. Part (b) shows what happens if the managers of the Crown corporation pursue their own interest and maximize their budget by padding costs. Average total cost now increases to *ATC (inflated)*. If the corporation is required to keep price equal to marginal cost, the quantity produced is efficient, but the managers divert the consumer surplus to themselves.

The situation depicted in Fig. 17.6(a) achieves an efficient outcome because consumer surplus is maximized. But it is not an outcome that is necessarily compatible with the interests of the managers of the Crown corporation. One model of the behaviour of managers is that suggested by the economic theory of bureaucracy. What does that alternative model predict about Crown corporation behaviour?

A Bureaucracy Model of Public Enterprise

The basic assumption of the economic theory of bureaucracy is that bureaucrats aim to maximize the budget of their bureau. The equivalent assumption for the managers of a Crown corporation is that they seek to maximize the budget of the Crown corporation. The effect of budget maximization by the managers of a Crown corporation depends on the pricing constraints under which the managers operate. We will consider two alternative cases:

- Budget maximization with marginal cost pricing
- Budget maximization at a zero price

Budget Maximization with Marginal Cost Pricing

If the bureau maximizes its budget but obeys the marginal cost pricing rule, it will produce the efficient outcome. It will produce 8 billion tonnes a year and it will sell its output for $2 a tonne, as Fig. 17.6(b) illustrates. But the corporation will not minimize its production cost. It will inflate its costs and become inefficient. It will hire more workers than the number required to produce 8 billion tonnes a year, and its internal control mechanisms, which would ensure internal efficiency (as in a private profit-maximizing firm), will be weak. As a result, the average total cost of the corporation will rise to *ATC (inflated)*.

What determines the limit on the extent to which the corporation can inflate its costs? The answer is the maximum amount that the users of the output can be made to pay through taxation. That maximum is the total consumer surplus. That maximum consumer surplus is the area beneath the demand curve and above the marginal cost curve. You can work out how big it is by using the usual formula for the area of the triangle. The height of this triangle is $8 and its base is 8 billion tonnes a year, so the consumer surplus is $32 billion. Spread over 8 billion tonnes, $32 billion gives a subsidy of $4 a tonne, the amount shown in the figure. $32 billion will be the upper limit that any government—in a political democracy—can extract from the taxpayer-consumers of the product of this corporation. If the subsidy were higher, people would vote to shut down the Crown corporation because the subsidy would exceed the consumer surplus.

Budget Maximization at Zero Price What happens if a government bureau provides its goods or services free? Of course, it is improbable that a publicly owned railway would be able to persuade politicians and taxpayers that its activities should be expanded to the point of providing its services free. But there are several examples of publicly provided goods that are indeed free. Primary and secondary education and health care are two outstanding examples. For the sake of comparison, we'll continue with our railway, improbable though it is.

If in Fig. 17.6(b) the bureau increases output to the point at which the price that consumers are willing to pay for the last unit produced is zero, output rises to 10 billion tonnes a year. A deadweight loss is created because the marginal cost of production, $2 a tonne, is higher than the marginal benefit or willingness to pay, $0 per tonne. The bureau will be inefficient in its internal operations and inflate its costs. The subsidy will increase to the highest that the public will be willing to pay. The maximum subsidy will equal the consumer surplus.

Compromise Outcome There will be a tendency for the corporation to overproduce and to inflate its budget, but not to the extent shown in Fig. 17.6(b). There will be a tendency for consumer interest to have some influence, but not to the degree shown in Fig. 17.6(a). The basic prediction about the behaviour of a Crown corporation, then, is that it will overproduce and be less efficient than a private firm.

Crown Corporations in Reality

How do actual Crown corporations behave? Several studies have been directed to answering this question. One of the most fruitful ways of approaching the question is to compare public and private enterprises in which, as far as possible, other things are equal. There are two well-known and well-studied cases for which other things seemed to be fairly equal. One such comparison is of Canada's public and private railways—Canadian National (CN) and Canadian Pacific (CP). The other is from Australia, which had two domestic airlines, one private and the other public, that flew almost identical routes at almost identical times every day. Economists studied the costs of these similar enterprises and concluded that each of the publicly owned enterprises operated with a cost structure that was significantly higher than that of the corresponding private firm. In the case of CN and CP, the estimated difference was 14 percent.[2]

Privatization

Largely because of an increasing understanding of how bureaucracies work and of the inefficiency of publicly operated enterprises, there has been a move to sell off publicly owned corporations. Since the mid-1980s, the federal government has sold a dozen companies, including Air Canada and CN.

REVIEW QUIZ

1. How might a Crown corporation operate efficiently?
2. What are the effects of budget maximization by the managers of a Crown corporation?
3. What limits the maximum budget of a Crown corporation?

Let's now turn to anti-combine law.

---

[2] W.S.W. Caves and Lauritis Christensen, "The Relative Efficiency of Public *v.* Private Firms in a Competitive Environment: The Case of Canada's Railroads," *Journal of Political Economy* 88, 5 (September–October 1980), 958–76.

Anti-Combine Law

ANTI-COMBINE LAW GIVES POWERS TO THE courts and to government agencies to influence markets. Like regulation, anti-combine law can work in the public interest to maximize total surplus or in private interests to maximize the surpluses of particular special interest groups such as producers. We'll describe Canada's anti-combine law and then examine some recent cases.

Canada's Anti-Combine Law

Canada's anti-combine law dates from 1889. At that time, monopoly was a major political issue and people were concerned about the absence of competition in industries as diverse as sugar and groceries, biscuits and confectionery, coal, binder twine, agricultural implements, stoves, coffins, eggs, and fire insurance.

Canada's anti-combine law today is defined in the Competition Act of 1986, which is described in Table 17.2. The Act established a Competition Bureau and a Competition Tribunal. The Competition Act distinguishes between practices that are

1. Criminal
2. Noncriminal

Conspiracy to fix prices, bid-rigging, other anti-competitive price-fixing actions, and false advertising are criminal offences. The courts handle alleged offences, and the standard level of proof beyond a reasonable doubt must be established.

Mergers, abuse of a dominant market position, refusal to deal, and other actions designed to limit competition such as exclusive dealing are noncriminal offences. The Director of the Competition Bureau sends alleged violations of a noncriminal nature to the Competition Tribunal for examination.

Some Recent Anti-Combine Cases

Let's see how the Competition Act has been working by looking at some recent cases. The first case we'll examine is important because it confirms the Competition Tribunal's power to enforce its orders.

Chrysler In 1986, Chrysler stopped supplying auto parts to Richard Brunet, a Montreal auto dealer. Chrysler also discouraged other dealers from supplying Brunet. The Competition Tribunal claimed that Chrysler wanted Brunet's business for itself and ordered Chrysler to resume doing business with Brunet. Chrysler did not resume sending supplies and the Tribunal cited Chrysler for contempt. Appeals against this ruling eventually reached the Supreme Court of Canada, which confirmed the Tribunal's power over contempt for its ruling. But the Tribunal subsequently dropped its contempt charge.

The second case we'll look at concerns aspartame, the sweetener in many soft drinks.

NutraSweet NutraSweet, the maker of aspartame, tried to gain a monopoly in aspartame. It did so by licensing the use of its "swirl" only on products for which it had an exclusive deal. The Competition Tribunal ruled that this action unduly limited competition and told NutraSweet that it may not enforce existing contracts, enter into new contracts in which it is the exclusive supplier, or give inducements to encourage the display of its "swirl." The result of this case was an increase in competition and a fall in the price of aspartame in Canada.

The third case we'll examine concerns a publication you use almost every day: the Yellow Pages.

Bell Canada Enterprises Two subsidiaries of Bell Canada Enterprises have a 90 percent share of the market for the publication of telephone directories in their territories. These companies tie the sale of advertising services to the sale of advertising space in the Yellow Pages. If you want to advertise in the Yellow Pages, you must buy the advertising services of one of these two companies. As a result, other advertising agencies cannot effectively compete for business in Yellow Pages advertising. The Director of the Competition Bureau applied for an order prohibiting the tied-sale practice of these two companies.

Other Recent Anti-Competitive Agreements During 1995 and 1996, the Competition Bureau took action against several anti-competitive agreements. Among such cases were driving schools in Sherbrooke, ready-mix concrete in the Saguenay-Lac St-Jean region, real estate dealing in Calgary, the importing of Australian mandarin oranges, wire for baling pulp, and ambulance services in Alberta.

The Competition Bureau is extremely active in

TABLE 17.2 Canada's Anti-Combine Law: The Competition Act, 1986

Abuse of Dominant Position

79 (1) Where on application by the Director, the Tribunal finds that:
- (a) one or more persons substantially or completely control, throughout Canada or any area thereof, a class or species of business,
- (b) that person or those persons have engaged in or are engaging in a practice of anti-competitive acts, and
- (c) the practice has had, is having or is likely to have the effect of preventing or lessening competition substantially in a market, the Tribunal may make an order prohibiting all or any of those persons from engaging in that practice.

Mergers

92 (1) Where on application by the Director, the Tribunal finds that a merger or proposed merger prevents or lessens, or is likely to prevent or lessen, competition substantially . . . the Tribunal may . . . [,] in the case of a completed merger, order any party to the merger
- (i) to dissolve the merger . . .
- (ii) to dispose of assets and shares . . .

[or]
in the case of a proposed merger, make an order directed against any party to the proposed merger
- (i) ordering the person . . . not to proceed with the merger
- (ii) ordering the person not to proceed with part of the merger

reviewing and, in some cases, blocking mergers. The next cases we examine fall into this category.

Canada Packers and Labatt Canada Packers Inc. and John Labatt Ltd. proposed a merger of their flour milling operations that would have made them the biggest miller in Canada and the fifth biggest in North America. The Competition Tribunal stopped this merger, saying that the Canadian flour milling business had been run too much like a cartel and that more, not less, competition was needed.

Banks Some attempts to merge are so politically sensitive that they are decided at the highest political level. One example is the decision of the federal government to block an attempted merger by the Royal Bank and the Bank of Montreal. If Canada's two major banks eventually merge, the sanction of the federal government will be needed.

Public or Special Interest?

The intent of anti-combine law is to protect the public interest and restrain the profit-seeking and anti-competitive actions of producers. On the whole, the overall thrust of the law and its enforcement has been in line with its intent and has served the public interest. Further, if the recent cases we have examined are setting a trend, we can expect a continuation of pro-consumer decisions from the courts and the Competition Tribunal in future cases.

REVIEW QUIZ

1. What is the Act of Parliament that provides our anti-combine law?
2. What actions violate the anti-combine law?
3. Under what circumstances is a merger unlikely to be approved?

In this chapter, we've seen how the government intervenes in markets to affect prices, quantities, consumer surplus, and producer surplus. *Reading Between the Lines* on pp. 408–409 looks at price fixing in global markets for vitamins.

READING BETWEEN THE LINES

Fixing Vitamin Prices

THE WALL STREET JOURNAL, NOVEMBER 22, 2001

EU levies $755.1 million fine in vitamin price-fixing case

The European Commission fined eight companies a record 855.2 million euros ($755.1 million) for allegedly fixing vitamin prices, but let one drug maker almost completely off the hook for turning on its former partners.

The supposed ringleader of the price-fixing cartel, Roche Holding AG of Switzerland, was fined 462 million euros, or 2.6% of world-wide sales in 1999.

Under the commission's rules, fines start at 20 million euros per offense and increase by 10% for each additional year of illegal activity. The figures in that formula are subject to mitigating or aggravating factors.

The commission said although it would have been justified in fining Roche as much as 962 million euros, the sum was reduced because Roche cooperated in the investigation by, among other things, willingly giving the commission documents for which it asked.

Roche was the "prime mover and main beneficiary" of the scheme to fix prices on 12 separate vitamins in the 1990s, the commission said. BASF AG of Germany was another "paramount" player, the commission said, and was fined 296.2 million euros. Fines for the six other companies ranged from 5 million euros to 37.1 million euros.

Mario Monti, the commissioner responsible for antitrust policy, said the eight companies operated the "most damaging series of cartels the commission has ever investigated" in terms of harm to consumers. But the commission didn't impose the maximum penalty possible under the law: 10% of a company's annual sales during the last year in which the cartel operated. Altogether, that could have run into the billions of euros.

Mr. Monti insisted the commission wasn't letting the companies off lightly. But he lamented the fact that under European Union law, there are no criminal sanctions for price-fixing, as there are in the U.S. "We're working to make penalties more and more effective and more and more deterrent," he said.

In the 1999 U.S. case, Roche paid a fine of $500 million, and a former executive went to prison.

Amelia Torres, a spokeswoman for Mr. Monti, said the commission had wide discretion on the final amount of the fine, in part because it wanted to maintain "a certain degree of uncertainty" so companies didn't calculate likely fines into their business plans. However, Roche said it had already figured the fine into its spending plans back in 1999.

Essence of the Story

- Price fixing is illegal in the European Union, but it is not subject to criminal sanctions.
- Under European Commission (EC) rules, fines start at 20 million euros per offence and increase by 10 percent for each additional year of illegal activity.
- In 2001, the EC fined eight companies for allegedly fixing vitamin prices.
- The largest fine imposed was on Roche of Switzerland (462 million euro—2.6 percent of its 1999 worldwide sales).
- The EC could have fined Roche 962 million euros but reduced the fine because Roche cooperated in the investigation.
- Roche said that it had budgeted for the fine in its spending plans.

Economic Analysis

- In Canada, price fixing is a criminal offence that can be punished by a combination of fines and imprisonment.

- In the European Union (EU), price fixing is illegal but subject only to a fine.

- The formula for a fine is a fixed amount per violation per year. For the firm, the fine is a fixed cost.

- Even when the EC uses discretion to keep the firm guessing about the scale of the fine, the firm can figure out the maximum fine and can compare paying the fine with the alternative of not engaging in price fixing.

- If the profit that results from price fixing minus the fine exceeds the profit from not price fixing, it is rational, but illegal, for a firm to price fix.

- Figure 1 shows the situation that Roche of Switzerland faces.

- The demand curve for Roche's products depends on the prices set by its competitors.

- When Roche's competitors engage in price fixing, the demand curve for Roche's products is *D* and its marginal revenue curve is *MR*.

- Roche's average total cost curve is *ATC*, and its marginal cost curve is *MC*.

- Roche maximizes profit by selling 3 billion items a year (where *MC* equals *MR*) at a price of $6 per item.

- Roche's economic profit, shown by the sum of the two blue rectangles, is $6 billion a year. (Roche's actual economic profit in 2000 was about $5 billion.)

- Because Roche pays a price-fixing fine, which is about $0.4 billion, its *ATC* curve shifts upward to *ATC* + *fine*.

- Even if Roche paid a price-fixing fine of $4 billion, ten times as large as the one imposed, its *ATC* curve would shift upward to *ATC* + *fine** and the firm would still make an economic profit.

- Figure 2 illustrates the alternative of competing without price fixing. Competition, from other producers decreases the demand for Roche's products to D_{comp}. The price is driven down to the point at which economic profit is eliminated and the firm earns normal profit (included in *ATC*).

- The Canadian law is more powerful than the EU law and makes it harder for firms to use price fixing as a business strategy.

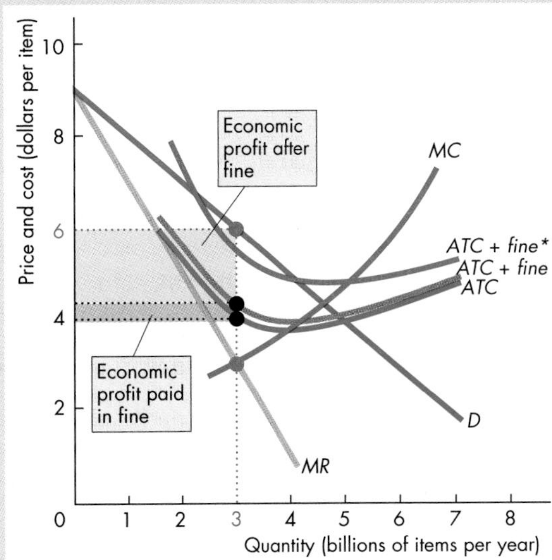

Figure 1 Roche in 2000

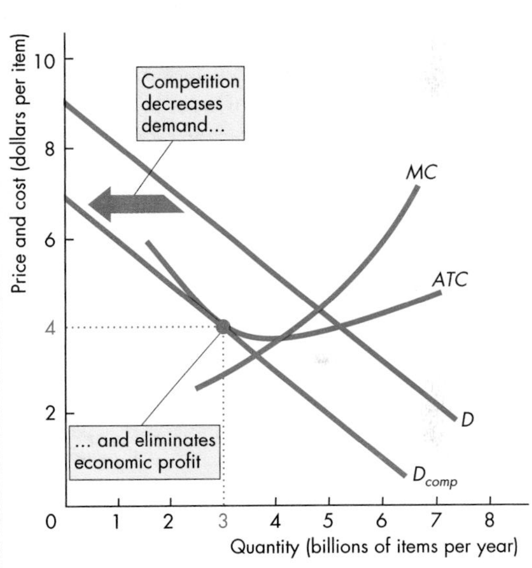

Figure 2 Roche in competition

SUMMARY

KEY POINTS

Market Intervention (p. 394)

- The government intervenes to regulate monopolistic and oligopolistic markets in three ways: regulation, public ownership, and anti-combine law.

Economic Theory of Regulation (pp. 394–396)

- Consumers and producers express their demand for the regulation by voting, lobbying, and making campaign contributions.
- The larger the surplus per person generated by a regulation or the smaller the number of people who share a given surplus, the larger is the demand for the regulation.
- Regulation is supplied by politicians who pursue their own best interest.
- The larger the surplus per person generated and the larger the number of people who benefit from it, the larger is the supply of regulation.
- Public interest theory predicts that regulation will maximize total surplus; capture theory predicts that producer surplus will be maximized.

Regulation and Deregulation (pp. 396–403)

- Natural monopolies and cartels are regulated by agencies controlled by politically appointed bureaucrats and staffed by a permanent bureaucracy of experts.
- Regulated firms must comply with rules about price, product quality, and output levels.
- Regulation has not lowered the profit rates of regulated firms.

Public Ownership (pp. 403–405)

- Crown corporations are 100 percent owned by federal and provincial governments and they produce such items as broadcasting, hydroelectric power, and telecommunications.
- The economic theory of bureaucracy is that managers maximize their budgets subject to political constraints.
- Crown corporations tend to be inefficient: They overproduce and their costs are too high.

Anti-Combine Law (pp. 406–407)

- Anti-combine law provides an alternative way for government to control monopoly and monopolistic practices.
- The Competition Act of 1986 sets out Canada's anti-combine law and places responsibility for enforcement with the Competition Tribunal.

KEY FIGURES AND TABLES

Figure 17.1	Natural Monopoly: Marginal Cost Pricing, 398
Figure 17.2	Natural Monopoly: Average Cost Pricing, 399
Figure 17.3	Natural Monopoly: Profit Maximization, 399
Figure 17.5	Collusive Oligopoly, 401
Figure 17.6	Crown Corporation, 404
Table 17.1	Federal Regulatory Agencies, 397
Table 17.2	Canada's Anti-Combine Law: The Competition Act, 1986, 407

KEY TERMS

Anti-combine law, 394
Average cost pricing rule, 398
Capture theory, 395
Crown corporation, 394
Marginal cost pricing rule, 398
Natural monopoly, 397
Privatization, 394
Public interest theory, 395
Rate of return regulation, 399

PROBLEMS

*1. Elixir Springs, Inc., is an unregulated natural monopoly that bottles Elixir, a unique health product with no substitutes. The total fixed cost incurred by Elixir Springs is $150,000, and its marginal cost is 10 cents a bottle. The figure illustrates the demand for Elixir.

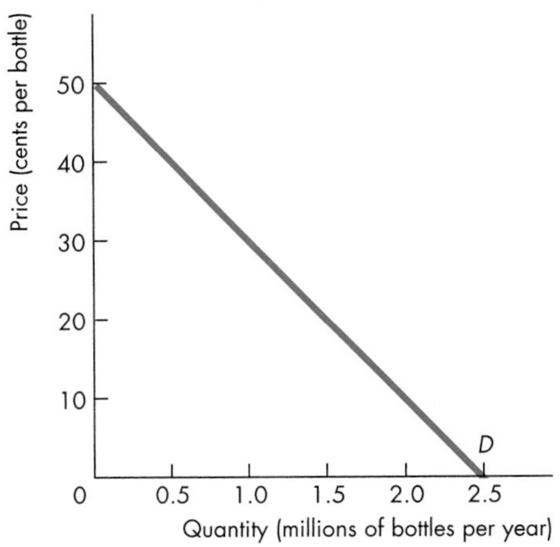

a. What is the price of a bottle of Elixir?
b. How many bottles does Elixir Springs sell?
c. Does Elixir Springs maximize total surplus or producer surplus?

2. Cascade Springs, Inc., is a natural monopoly that bottles water from a spring in the Rocky Mountains. Cascade Springs' total fixed cost is $80,000, and its marginal cost is 5 cents a bottle. The figure illustrates the demand for Cascade Springs bottled water.

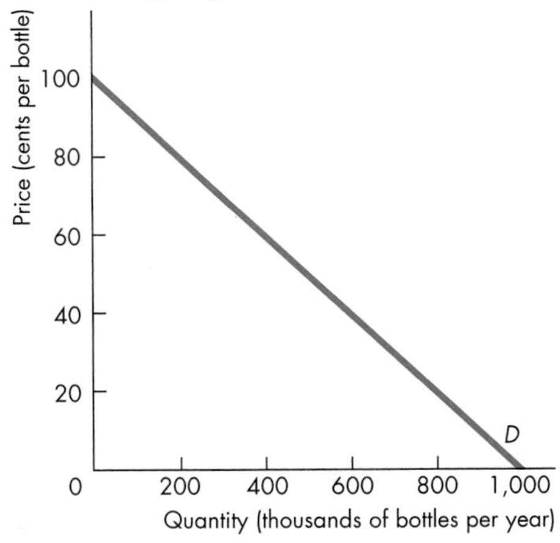

a. What is the price of Cascade Springs water?
b. How many bottles does Cascade Springs sell?
c. Does Cascade Springs maximize total surplus or producer surplus?

*3. The government imposes a marginal cost pricing rule on Elixir Springs in problem 1.
a. What is the price of a bottle of Elixir?
b. How many bottles does Elixir Springs sell?
c. What is Elixir Springs' producer surplus?
d. What is the consumer surplus?
e. Is the regulation in the public interest? Explain.

4. The government imposes a marginal cost pricing rule on Cascade Springs in problem 2.
a. What is the price of Cascade Springs water?
b. How many bottles does Cascade Springs sell?
c. What is the economic profit?
d. What is the consumer surplus?
e. Is the regulation in the public interest? Explain.

*5. The government imposes an average cost pricing rule on Elixir Springs in problem 1.
a. What is the price of a bottle of Elixir?
b. How many bottles does Elixir Springs sell?
c. What is Elixir Springs' producer surplus?
d. What is the consumer surplus?
e. Is the regulation in the public interest? Explain.

6. The government imposes an average cost pricing rule on Cascade Springs in problem 2.
a. What is the price of Cascade Springs water?
b. How many bottles does Cascade Springs sell?
c. What is Cascade Springs' economic profit?
d. What is the consumer surplus?
e. Is the regulation in the public interest or in the private interest?

*7. Two airlines share an international route. The figure shows the demand curve for trips on this route and each firm's marginal cost. This air route is regulated.

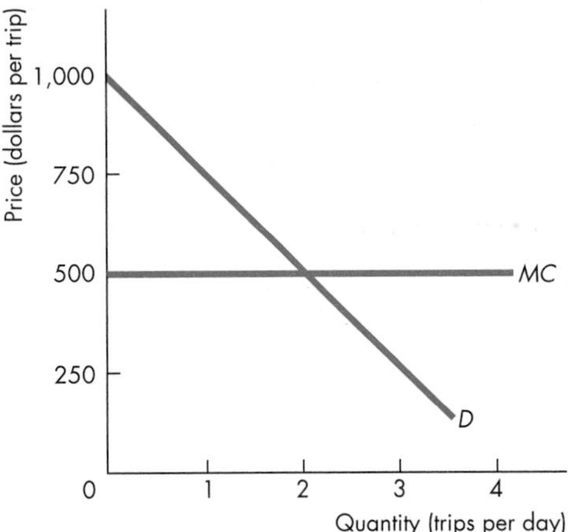

a. What is the price of a trip and what is the number of trips per day if the regulation is in the public interest?
b. What is the price of a trip and what is the number of trips per day if the airlines capture the regulator?
c. What is the deadweight loss in part (b)?
d. What do you need to know to predict whether the regulation is in the public interest or the producer interest?

8. Two telephone companies offer local calls in an area. The figure shows the market demand curve for calls and the marginal cost curves of each firm. These firms are regulated.

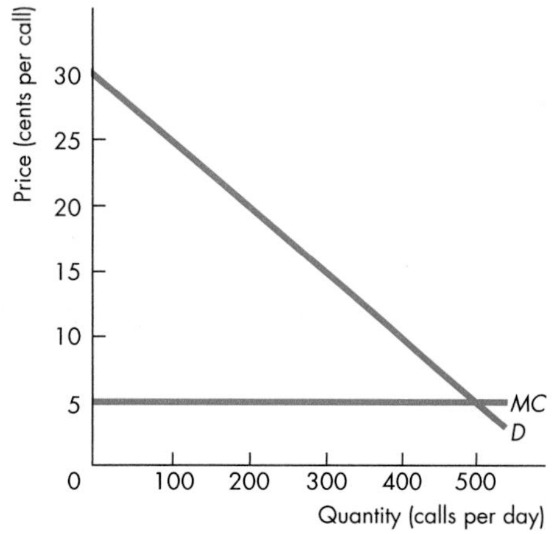

a. What is the price of a call and what is the number of calls per day if the regulation is in the public interest?
b. What is the price of a call and what is the number of calls per day if the telephone companies capture the regulator?
c. What is the deadweight loss in part (b)?
d. What do you need to know to predict whether the regulation will be in the public interest or in the producer interest?

CRITICAL THINKING

1. After you have studied *Reading Between the Lines* on pp. 408–409, answer the following questions.
   a. What did Roche and BASF do that is illegal?
   b. Would their actions have been illegal if they had been carried out in Canada?
   c. How does the European Commission try to discourage price fixing? Do you think this method works?
   d. What changes would you recommend to the EU law and why?
2. The government of Canada regulates the production and sale of many goods and services. For example, it regulates the prices of local phone and cable TV services, the grain prices paid to wheat and cereal farmers and to whom they can sell the grain. The suppliers of local phone and cable TV services are monopolies, but there are many grain farmers. Why are grain farmers regulated? Is the regulation in the interest of grain farmers or consumers?
3. "Now that Canada has free trade with the United States, the government of Canada should not regulate monopolies in Canada because they are in direct competition with U.S. producers." Do you agree with this argument? If so, explain why. If not, explain why the argument is incorrect.

WEB EXERCISES

1. Use the link on the Parkin–Bade Web site to visit Competition Law Review. Look for cases of collusive agreement, abuse of dominant position, and mergers to restrict competition. In each case, describe the means cited as used to lessen competition.

EXTERNALITIES

CHAPTER 18

Greener and Smarter

We burn huge quantities of fossil fuels—coal, natural gas, and oil—that cause acid rain and possibly global warming. We use chlorofluorocarbons (CFCs) that may damage the earth's ozone layer, expose us to additional ultraviolet rays, and increase the risk of skin cancer. We dump toxic waste into rivers, lakes, and oceans. These environmental issues are simultaneously everybody's problem and nobody's problem. How can we take account of the damage that we cause others every time we turn on our heating or air conditioning systems? ◆ Almost every day, we hear about a new discovery—in medicine, engineering, chemistry, physics, or even economics. The advance of knowledge seems boundless. And more and more people are learning more and more of what is already known. The stock of knowledge is increasing, apparently without bound. We are getting smarter. But are we getting smarter fast enough? Are we spending enough on research and education? Do enough people remain in school for long enough? And do we work hard enough at school? Would we be better off if we spent more on research and education?

In this chapter, we study the problems that arise because many of our actions create externalities. They affect other people, for ill or good, in ways that we do not usually take into account when we make our own economic choices. We study two big areas—pollution and knowledge—in which externalities are especially important. Externalities are a major source of *market failure*. When market failure occurs, we must either live with the inefficiency it creates or try to achieve greater efficiency by making some *public choices*. We close the chapter in *Reading Between the Lines* by looking at air pollution in Ontario today.

After studying this chapter, you will be able to

- **Explain how property rights can sometimes be used to overcome externalities**
- **Explain how emission charges, marketable permits, and taxes can be used to achieve efficiency in the face of external costs**
- **Explain how subsidies can be used to achieve efficiency in the face of external benefits**
- **Explain how scholarships, below-cost tuition, and research grants make the quantity of education and invention more efficient**
- **Explain how patents improve economic efficiency**

Externalities in Our Lives

A COST OR A BENEFIT THAT ARISES FROM production and falls on someone other than the producer or a cost or a benefit that arises from consumption and falls on someone other than the consumer is called an **externality**. Let's review the range of externalities, classify them, and look at some everyday examples.

An externality can arise from either *production* or *consumption* and it can be either a **negative externality**, which imposes an external cost, or a **positive externality**, which provides an external benefit. So there are four types of externalities:

- Negative production externalities
- Positive production externalities
- Negative consumption externalities
- Positive consumption externalities

Negative Production Externalities

Every weekday morning and afternoon, Highway 401 that runs across the northern end of Toronto slows to a crawl as trucks and commuters compete for positions on what looks more like an expensive parking lot than an expressway. A similar situation occurs in every major Canadian city from Vancouver to Halifax and in every major city around the world. Each road user imposes a negative production externality on the other road users.

Logging and the clearing of forests are the source of another negative production externality. These activities destroy the habitat of wildlife and influence the amount of carbon dioxide in the atmosphere, which has a long-term effect on temperature. Everyone living and future generations bear these external costs. Pollution, which we examine in the next section, is another example of this type of externality.

Positive Production Externalities

When Labonte Honey Inc. moves its bees into a blueberry orchard in the Lac St-Jean area of northern Quebec, the honeybees collect pollen and nectar from the fruit blossoms to make the honey. At the same time, they pollinate the blueberry flowers, which increases the output of blueberries. Two positive production externalities are present in this example: Labonte Honey gets a positive production externality from the owner of the fruit orchard, and the fruit grower gets a positive production externality from Labonte.

Negative Consumption Externalities

Negative consumption externalities are a source of irritation for most of us. Smoking tobacco in a confined space creates fumes that many people find unpleasant and that pose a health risk. So smoking in restaurants and on airplanes generates a negative externality. To avoid this negative externality, many restaurants and all airlines ban smoking. But while a smoking ban avoids a negative consumption externality for most people, it imposes a negative consumption externality on smokers. The majority imposes a cost on the minority—the smokers who would prefer to enjoy the consumption of tobacco while dining or taking a plane trip.

Noisy parties and outdoor rock concerts are other examples of negative consumption externalities. They are also examples of the fact that a simple ban on an activity is not a solution. Banning noisy parties avoids the external cost on sleep-seeking neighbours, but it results in the sleepers imposing an external cost on the fun-seeking partygoers.

Permitting dandelions to grow in lawns, not picking up leaves in the fall, and allowing a dog to bark loudly or to foul a neighbour's lawn are other sources of negative consumption externalities.

Positive Consumption Externalities

When you get a flu vaccination, you lower your risk of getting infected this winter. And if you avoid the flu, your neighbour who didn't get vaccinated has a better chance of avoiding it too. Flu vaccination generates positive consumption externalities.

When its owner restores a historic building, everyone who sees the building gets pleasure from it. Similarly, when someone erects a spectacular house—such as those built in Montreal's "Golden Square Mile" in the 1800s—or another exciting structure—such as the CN Tower or SkyDome in Toronto—an external consumption benefit flows to everyone who has an opportunity to view it. Education, which we examine in this chapter, is another example of this type of externality.

Negative Externalities: Pollution

POLLUTION IS NEITHER A NEW PROBLEM NOR IS IT only an industrial problem. Pre-industrial Europe had sewage disposal problems that created cholera epidemics and plagues that killed millions. London's air in the Middle Ages was dirtier than that of Los Angeles today. Some of the worst pollution today is in China and Thailand. Nor is the desire to find solutions to pollution new. The developments of fourteenth-century garbage and sewage disposal is an example of early attempts to tackle pollution.

Popular discussions of pollution usually pay little attention to economics. They focus on physical aspects of the problem, not on the costs and the benefits. A common assumption is that *any* action that causes pollution must cease. In contrast, an economic study of pollution emphasizes costs and benefits. An economist talks about the efficient amount of pollution. This emphasis on efficiency does not mean that economists, as citizens, do not share the same goals as others and value a healthy environment. Nor does it mean that economists have the right answers and everyone else has the wrong ones (or vice versa). Economics provides a set of tools and principles that clarify the issues. It does not provide an agreed list of solutions. The starting point for an economic analysis of pollution is the demand for a pollution-free environment.

The Demand for a Pollution-Free Environment

The demand for a pollution-free environment is greater today than it has ever been. We express this demand in several ways. We join organizations that lobby for anti-pollution regulations and policies. We vote for politicians who support the policies that we want to see implemented. We buy "green" products and avoid hazardous products, even if we pay a bit more to do so. And we pay higher housing costs and commuting costs to live in pleasant neighbourhoods.

The demand for a pollution-free environment has grown for two main reasons. First, as our incomes increase, we demand a larger range of goods and services, and one of these "goods" is a pollution-free environment. We value clean air, unspoiled natural scenery, and wildlife, and we are willing and able to pay for them.

Second, as our knowledge of the effects of pollution grows, we are able to take measures that reduce those effects. For example, now that we know how sulfur dioxide causes acid rain and how clearing rain forests destroys natural stores of carbon dioxide, we are able, in principle, to design measures that limit these problems.

Let's look at the range of pollution problems that have been identified and the actions that create those problems.

The Sources of Pollution

Economic activity pollutes air, water, and land, and these individual areas of pollution interact through the *ecosystem.*

Air Pollution Sixty percent of our air pollution comes from road transportation and industrial processes. Only 16 percent arises from electric power generation.

A common belief is that air pollution is getting worse. In many developing countries, air pollution *is* getting worse. But air pollution in North America is getting less severe for most substances. Figure 18.1 shows the trends in the concentrations of six air pollutants. Lead has been almost eliminated from our air. Sulfur dioxide, carbon monoxide, and suspended particulates have been reduced to around one-half of their 1980 levels. And even the more stubborn ozone and nitrogen dioxide are at around 70 percent of their 1980 levels.

These reductions in levels of air pollution are even more impressive when they are compared with the level of economic activity. Between 1970 and 2000, total production in North America increased by 158 percent. During this same period, vehicle kilometres travelled increased by 143 percent, energy consumption increased by 45 percent, and the population increased by 36 percent. While all this economic activity was on the increase, air pollution from all sources *decreased* by 29 percent.

While the facts about the sources and trends in air pollution are not in doubt, there is disagreement about the *effects* of air pollution. The least controversial is *acid rain* caused by sulfur dioxide and nitrogen oxide emissions from coal- and oil-fired generators of electric utilities. Acid rain begins with air pollution, and it leads to water pollution and vegetation damage.

More controversial are airborne substances (suspended particulates) such as lead from leaded gasoline. Some scientists believe that in sufficiently

FIGURE 18.1 Trends in Air Pollution

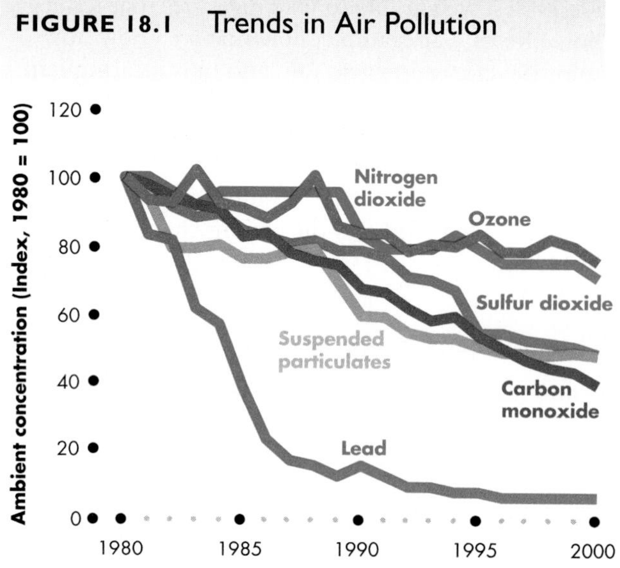

Lead has almost been eliminated from our air; concentrations of carbon monoxide, sulfur dioxide, and suspended particulates have decreased to about one-half of their 1980 levels; and nitrogen dioxide and ozone have fallen to about 70 percent of their 1980 levels.

Source: U.S. Environmental Protection Agency, *National Air Quality and Emissions Trends Report,* 1999 and 2000.

large concentrations, these substances (189 of which have currently been identified) cause cancer and other life-threatening conditions.

Even more controversial is *global warming,* which some scientists believe results from the carbon dioxide emissions. The earth's average temperature has increased over the past 100 years, but most of the increase occurred *before* 1940. Determining what causes changes in the earth's temperature and isolating the effect of carbon dioxide from other factors are proving to be difficult.

Equally controversial is the problem of *ozone layer depletion.* There is no doubt that a hole in the ozone layer exists over Antarctica and that the ozone layer protects us from cancer-causing ultraviolet rays from the sun. But how our industrial activity influences the ozone layer is simply not understood at this time.

One air pollution problem has almost been eliminated: lead from gasoline. In part, this happened because the cost of living without leaded gasoline, it turns out, is not high. But sulfur dioxide and the so-called greenhouse gases are a much tougher problem to tackle. Their alternatives are costly or have pollution problems of their own. The major sources of these pollutants are road vehicles and electric utilities. Road vehicles can be made "greener" in a variety of ways. One is with new fuels, and some alternatives being investigated are alcohol, natural gas, propane and butane, and hydrogen. Another way of making cars and trucks "greener" is to change the chemistry of gasoline. Refiners are working on reformulations of gasoline that reduce tailpipe emissions. Similarly, electric power can be generated in cleaner ways by harnessing solar power, tidal power, or geothermal power. While technically possible, these methods are more costly than conventional carbon-fuelled generators. Another alternative is nuclear power. This method is good for air pollution but creates a potential long-term problem for land and water pollution because there is no known entirely safe method of disposing of spent nuclear fuel.

Water Pollution The largest sources of water pollution are the dumping of industrial waste and treated sewage into lakes and rivers and the runoff from fertilizers. A more dramatic source is the accidental spilling of crude oil into the oceans, such as in the *Prestige* spill off the coast of Spain in 2002.

There are two main alternatives to polluting the waterways and oceans. One is the chemical processing of waste to render it inert or biodegradable. The other, widely used for nuclear waste, is to use land sites for storage in secure containers.

Land Pollution Land pollution arises from dumping toxic waste. Ordinary household garbage does not pose a pollution problem unless contaminants from dumped garbage seep into the water supply. This possibility increases as landfills reach capacity and less suitable landfill sites are used. It is estimated that 80 percent of existing landfills will be full by 2010. Some regions (New York, New Jersey, and other U.S. East Coast states) and some countries (Japan and the Netherlands) are seeking less costly alternatives to landfill, such as recycling and incineration. Recycling is an apparently attractive alternative, but it requires an investment in new technologies to be effective. Incineration is a high-cost alternative to landfill, and it produces air pollution. Furthermore, these alternatives are not free, and they become efficient only when the cost of using landfill is high.

We've seen that the demand for a pollution-free environment has grown, and we've described the range of pollution problems. Let's now look at the economics of these problems. The starting point is the distinction between private costs and social costs.

Private Costs and Social Costs

A *private cost* of production is a cost that is borne by the producer of a good or service. *Marginal cost* is the cost of producing an *additional unit* of a good or service. So **marginal private cost** (MC) is the cost of producing an additional unit of a good or service that is borne by the producer of that good or service.

You've seen that an *external cost* is a cost of producing a good or service that is *not* borne by the producer but borne by other people. A **marginal external cost** is the cost of producing an additional unit of a good or service that falls on people other than the producer.

Marginal social cost (MSC) is the marginal cost incurred by the entire society—by the producer and by everyone else on whom the cost falls—and is the sum of marginal private cost and marginal external cost. That is,

$$MSC = MC + \text{Marginal external cost.}$$

We express costs in dollars. But we must always remember that a cost is an opportunity cost—what we give up to get something. A marginal external cost is what someone other than the producer of a good or service must give up when the producer makes one more unit of the item. Something real, such as a clean river or clean air, is given up.

Valuing an External Cost Economists use market prices to put a dollar value on the cost of pollution. For example, suppose that there are two similar rivers, one polluted and the other clean. Five hundred identical homes are built along each river. The homes on the clean river rent for $2,500 a month, and those on the polluted river rent for $1,500 a month. If the pollution is the only detectable difference between the two rivers and the two locations, the rent decrease of $1,000 per month is the cost of the pollution. For the 500 homes, the external cost is $500,000 a month.

External Cost and Output Figure 18.2 shows an example of the relationship between output and cost in a chemical industry that pollutes. The marginal cost curve, MC, describes the private marginal cost borne by the firms that produce the chemical. Marginal cost increases as the quantity of chemical produced increases. If the firms dump waste into a river, they impose a marginal external cost that increases with the amount of the chemical produced. The marginal social cost curve, MSC, is the sum of marginal private cost and marginal external cost. For example, when output is 4,000 tonnes per month, marginal private cost is $100 a tonne, marginal external cost is $125 a tonne, and marginal social cost is $225 a tonne.

Figure 18.2 shows that when the quantity of chemicals produced increases, the amount of pollution increases and the external cost of pollution increases. But the figure doesn't tell us how much pollution gets created. That quantity depends on how the market for chemicals operates. First, we'll see what happens when the industry is free to pollute.

FIGURE 18.2 An External Cost

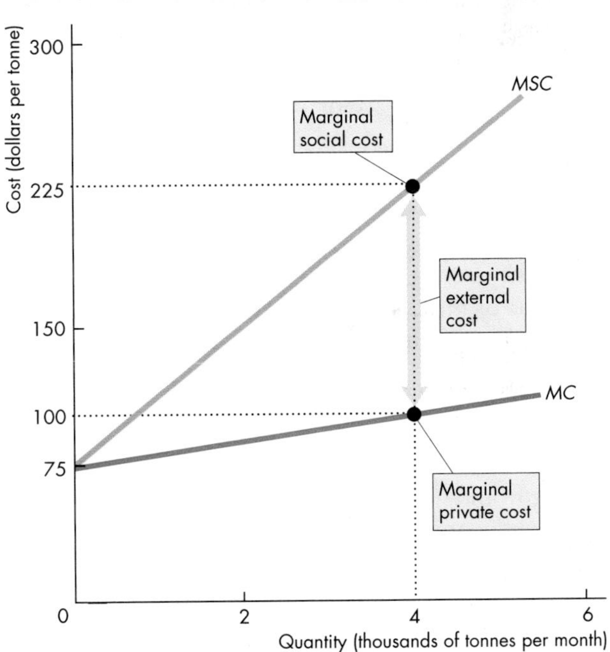

The MC curve shows the private marginal cost borne by the factories that produce a chemical. The MSC curve shows the sum of marginal private cost and marginal external cost. When output is 4,000 tonnes of chemicals per month, marginal private cost is $100 a tonne, marginal external cost is $125 a tonne, and marginal social cost is $225 a tonne.

Production and Pollution: How Much?

When an industry is unregulated, the amount of pollution it creates depends on the market equilibrium price and quantity of the good produced. In Fig. 18.3, the demand curve for a pollution-creating chemical is *D*. This curve also measures the marginal benefit, *MB*, to the buyers of the chemical. The supply curve is *S*. This curve also measures the marginal private cost, *MC*, of the producers. The supply curve is the marginal private cost curve because when firms make their production and supply decisions, they consider only the costs that they will bear. Market equilibrium occurs at a price of $100 a tonne and a quantity of 4,000 tonnes a month.

This equilibrium is inefficient. You learned in Chapter 5 that the allocation of resources is efficient when marginal benefit equals marginal cost. But we must count all the costs—private and external—when we compare marginal benefit and marginal cost. So with an external cost, the allocation is efficient when marginal benefit equals marginal *social* cost. This outcome occurs when the quantity of chemicals produced is 2,000 tonnes a month. The market equilibrium overproduces by 2,000 tonnes a month and creates a deadweight loss, the grey triangle.

How can the people who live beside the polluted river get the chemical factories to decrease their output of chemicals and create less pollution? If some method can be found to achieve this outcome, everyone—the owners of the chemical factories and the residents of the riverside homes—can gain. Let's explore some solutions.

FIGURE 18.3 Inefficiency with an External Cost

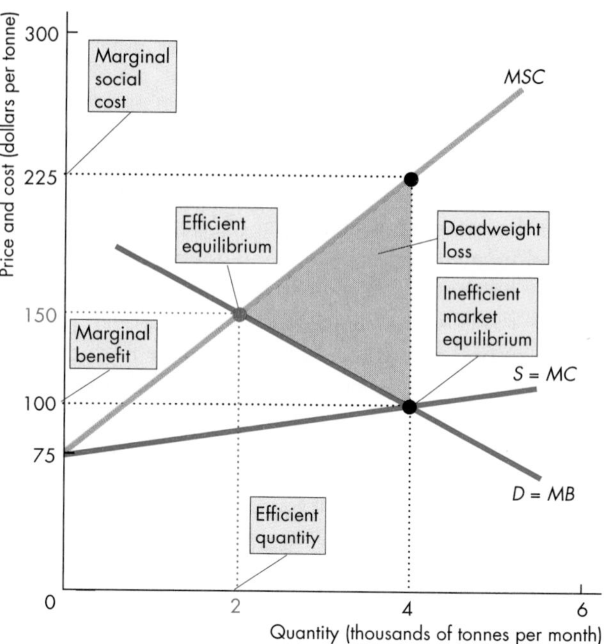

The market supply curve is the marginal private cost curve, *S* = *MC*. The demand curve is the marginal benefit curve, *D* = *MB*. Market equilibrium at a price of $100 a tonne and 4,000 tonnes a month is inefficient because marginal social cost exceeds marginal benefit. The efficient quantity is 2,000 tonnes a month. The grey triangle shows the deadweight loss created by the pollution externality.

Property Rights

Sometimes it is possible to reduce the inefficiency arising from an externality by establishing a property right where one does not currently exist. **Property rights** are legally established titles to the ownership, use, and disposal of factors of production and goods and services that are enforceable in the courts.

Suppose that the chemical factories own the river and the 500 homes alongside it. The rent that people are willing to pay depends on the amount of pollution. Using the earlier example, people are willing to pay $2,500 a month to live alongside a pollution-free river, but only $1,500 a month to live with the pollution created by 4,000 tonnes of chemicals a month. If the factories produce this quantity, they lose $1,000 a month for each home, a total of $500,000 a month.

The chemical factories are now confronted with the cost of their pollution—forgone rent from the people who live beside the river.

Figure 18.4 illustrates the outcome by using the same example as in Fig. 18.3. With property rights in place, the *MC* curve no longer measures all the costs that the factories face in producing the chemical. It excludes the pollution costs that they must now bear. The *MSC* curve now becomes the marginal private cost curve *MC*. All the costs fall on the factories, so the market supply curve is based on all the marginal costs and is the curve labelled $S = MC = MSC$.

Market equilibrium now occurs at a price of $150 a tonne and a quantity of 2,000 tonnes a month. This outcome is efficient. The factories still produce some pollution, but it is the efficient quantity.

FIGURE 18.4 Property Rights Achieve an Efficient Outcome

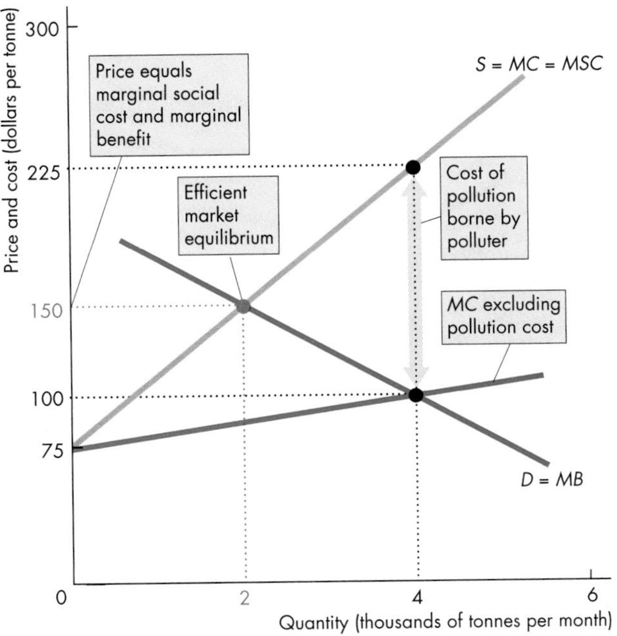

With property rights, the marginal cost curve that excludes pollution costs shows only part of the producers' marginal cost. The marginal private cost curve includes the cost of pollution, and the supply curve is $S = MC = MSC$. Market equilibrium is at a price of $150 a tonne and a quantity of 2,000 tonnes a month and is efficient because marginal social cost equals marginal benefit.

The Coase Theorem

Does it matter how property rights are assigned? Does it matter whether the polluter or the victim of the pollution owns the resource that might be polluted? Until 1960, everyone—including economists who had thought long and hard about the problem—thought that it did matter. But in 1960, Ronald Coase had a remarkable insight, which is now called the Coase theorem.

The **Coase theorem** is the proposition that if property rights exist, if only a small number of parties is involved, and if transactions costs are low, then private transactions are efficient. There are no externalities because the transacting parties take all the costs and benefits into account. Furthermore, it doesn't matter who has the property rights.

Application of the Coase Theorem In the example that we've just studied, the factories own the river and the homes. Suppose that instead, the residents own their homes and the river. Now the factories must pay a fee to the homeowners for the right to dump their waste. The greater the quantity of waste dumped into the river, the more the factories must pay. So again, the factories face the opportunity cost of the pollution they create. The quantity of chemicals produced and the amount of waste dumped are the same whoever owns the homes and the river. If the factories own them, they bear the cost of pollution because they receive a lower income from home rents. And if the residents own the homes and the river, the factories bear the cost of pollution because they must pay a fee to the homeowners. In both cases, the factories bear the cost of their pollution and dump the efficient amount of waste into the river.

The Coase solution works only when transactions costs are low. **Transactions costs** are the opportunity costs of conducting a transaction. For example, when you buy a house, you incur a series of transactions costs. You might pay a realtor to help you find the best place and a lawyer to run checks that assure you that the seller owns the property and that after you've paid for it, the ownership has been properly transferred to you.

In the example of the homes alongside a river, the transactions costs that are incurred by a small number of chemical factories and a few homeowners might be low enough to enable them to negotiate the deals that produce an efficient outcome. But in many situations, transactions costs are so high that it would be inefficient to incur them. In these situations, the Coase solution is not available.

Suppose that everyone owns the airspace above his or her home up to, say, 10 kilometres. If someone pollutes your airspace, you can charge a fee. But to collect the fee, you must identify who is polluting your airspace and persuade them to pay you. Imagine the costs of negotiating and enforcing agreements with the 300 million people who live in Canada and the United States (and perhaps Mexico) and the several thousand factories that emit sulfur dioxide and create acid rain that falls on homeowners' property! In this situation, we use public choices to cope with externalities. But the transactions costs that block a market solution are real costs, so attempts by the government to deal with externalities offer no easy solution. Let's look at some of these attempts.

Government Actions in the Face of External Costs

The three main methods that governments use to cope with externalities are

- Taxes
- Emission charges
- Marketable permits

Taxes The government can use taxes as an incentive for producers to cut back on an activity that creates an external cost. Taxes used in this way are called **Pigovian taxes**, in honour of Arthur Cecil Pigou, the British economist who is credited with first working out this method of dealing with externalities during the 1920s.

By setting the tax rate equal to the marginal external cost, firms can be made to behave in the same way as they would if they bore the cost of the externality directly. To see how government actions can change market outcomes in the face of externalities, let's return to the example of the chemical factories and the river.

Assume that the government has assessed the marginal external cost accurately and imposes a tax on the factories that exactly equals this cost. Figure 18.5 illustrates the effects of this tax.

The demand curve and marginal benefit curve, $D = MB$, and the firms' marginal cost curve, MC, are the same as in Fig. 18.3. The pollution tax equals the marginal external cost of the pollution. We add this tax to marginal cost to find the market supply curve. This curve is the one labelled $S = MC + tax = MSC$. This curve is the market supply curve because it tells us the quantities supplied at each price given the firms' marginal cost and the tax they must pay. This curve is also the marginal social cost curve because the pollution tax has been set equal to the marginal external cost.

Demand and supply now determine the market equilibrium price at $150 a tonne and the equilibrium quantity at 2,000 tonnes a month. At this scale of chemical production, the marginal social cost is $150 and the marginal benefit is $150, so the outcome is efficient. The firms incur a marginal cost of $88 a tonne and pay a tax of $62 a tonne. The government collects tax revenue of $124,000 a month.

FIGURE 18.5 A Pollution Tax

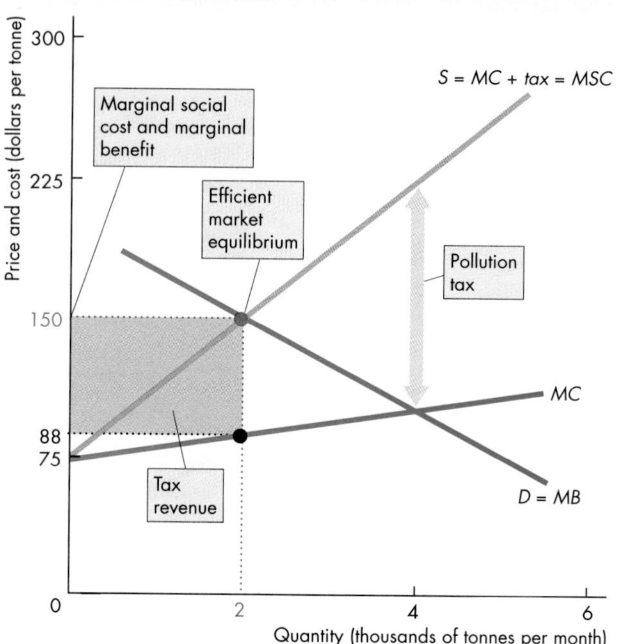

A pollution tax is imposed equal to the marginal external cost of pollution. The supply curve becomes the marginal private cost curve, MC, plus the tax—$S = MC + tax$. Market equilibrium is at a price of $150 a tonne and a quantity of 2,000 tonnes a month and is efficient because marginal social cost equals marginal benefit. The government collects a tax revenue shown by the purple rectangle.

Emission Charges Emission charges are an alternative to a tax for confronting a polluter with the external cost of pollution. The government sets a price per unit of pollution. The more pollution a firm creates, the more it pays in emission charges. This method of dealing with pollution externalities has been used only modestly in North America but is common in Europe where, for example, France, Germany, and the Netherlands make water polluters pay a waste disposal charge.

To work out the emission charge that achieves efficiency, the government needs a lot of information about the polluting industry that, in practice, is rarely available.

Marketable Permits Instead of taxing or imposing emission charges on polluters, each potential polluter might be assigned a permitted pollution limit. Each firm knows its own costs and benefits of pollution, and making pollution limits marketable is a clever way of using this private information that is unknown to the government. The government issues each firm a permit to emit a certain amount of pollution, and firms can buy and sell these permits. Firms that have a low marginal cost of reducing pollution sell their permits, and firms that have a high marginal cost of reducing pollution buy permits. The market in permits determines the price at which firms trade permits. And firms buy or sell permits until their marginal cost of pollution equals the market price.

This method of dealing with pollution provides an even stronger incentive than do emission charges to find technologies that pollute less because the price of a permit to pollute rises as the demand for permits increases.

A Real-World Market for Emission Permits

Environment Canada has not used marketable permits but the Environmental Protection Agency (EPA) in the United States has. The EPA first implemented air quality programs following the passage of the Clean Air Act in 1970.

Trading in lead pollution permits became common during the 1980s, and this marketable permit program has been rated a success. It enabled lead to be virtually eliminated (see Fig. 18.1). But this success might not easily translate to other situations because lead pollution has some special features. First, most lead pollution came from a single source: leaded gasoline. Second, lead in gasoline is easily monitored. Third, the objective of the program was clear: to eliminate lead in gasoline. The EPA is now considering using marketable permits to promote efficiency in the control of chlorofluorocarbons, the gases that are believed to damage the ozone layer.

REVIEW QUIZ

1. What is the distinction between a negative production externality and a negative consumption externality?
2. What is the distinction between private cost and social cost?
3. How does an externality prevent a competitive market from allocating resources efficiently?
4. How can an externality be eliminated by assigning property rights? How does this method of coping with an externality work?
5. How do taxes help us to cope with externalities? At what level must a pollution tax be set if it is to induce firms to produce the efficient quantity of pollution?

Positive Externalities: Knowledge

KNOWLEDGE COMES FROM EDUCATION AND research. To study the economics of knowledge, we must distinguish between private benefits and social benefits.

Private Benefits and Social Benefits

A *private benefit* is a benefit that the consumer of a good or service receives. *Marginal benefit* is the benefit from an *additional unit* of a good or service. So a **marginal private benefit** (*MB*) is the benefit from an additional unit of a good or service that the consumer of that good or service receives.

The *external benefit* from a good or service is the benefit that someone other than the consumer receives. A **marginal external benefit** is the benefit from an additional unit of a good or service that people other than the consumer enjoy.

Marginal social benefit (*MSB*) is the marginal benefit enjoyed by society—by the consumer of a good or service (marginal private benefit) plus the marginal benefit enjoyed by others (the marginal external benefit). That is,

$$MSB = MB + \text{Marginal external benefit.}$$

Figure 18.6 shows an example of the relationship between marginal private benefit, marginal external benefit, and marginal social benefit. The marginal benefit curve, *MB*, describes the marginal private benefit—such as expanded job opportunities and higher incomes—enjoyed by university graduates. Marginal private benefit decreases as the quantity of education increases.

But university graduates generate external benefits. On the average, university graduates communicate more effectively with others and tend to be better citizens. Their crime rates are lower, and they are more tolerant of the views of others. And a society with a large number of university graduates can support high-quality newspapers and television channels, music, theatre, and other organized social activities.

In the example in Fig. 18.6, the marginal external benefit is \$15,000 per student per year when 15 million students enrol in university. The marginal social benefit curve, *MSB*, is the sum of marginal private benefit and marginal external benefit. For example, when 15 million students a year enrol in university, the

FIGURE 18.6 An External Benefit

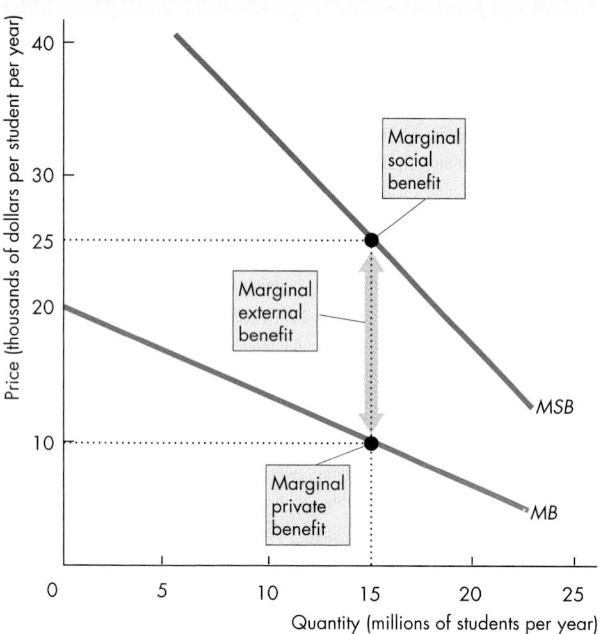

The *MB* curve shows the private marginal benefit enjoyed by the people who receive a university education. The *MSB* curve shows the sum of marginal private benefit and marginal external benefit. When 15 million students attend university, marginal private benefit is $10,000 per student, marginal external benefit is $15,000 per student, and marginal social benefit is $25,000 per student.

FIGURE 18.7 Inefficiency with an External Benefit

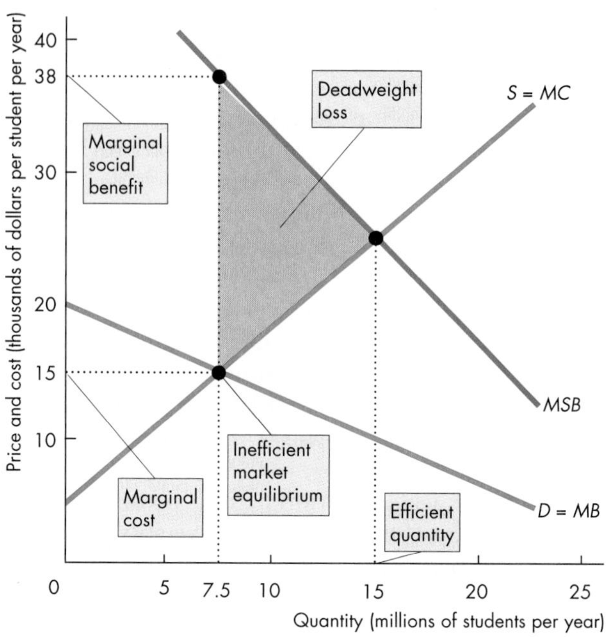

The market demand curve is the marginal private benefit curve, $D = MB$. The supply curve is the marginal cost curve, $S = MC$. Market equilibrium at a tuition of $15,000 a year and 7.5 million students is inefficient because marginal social benefit exceeds marginal cost. The efficient quantity is 15 million students. The grey triangle shows the deadweight loss created because too few students enrol in university.

marginal private benefit is $10,000 per student and the marginal external benefit is $15,000 per student, so the marginal social benefit is $25,000 per student.

When people make schooling decisions, they ignore its external benefits and consider only its private benefits. So if education were provided by private schools that charged full-cost tuition, we would produce too few university graduates.

Figure 18.7 illustrates the underproduction that would result if the government left education to the private market. The supply curve is the marginal cost curve of the private schools, $S = MC$. The demand curve is the marginal private benefit curve, $D = MB$. Market equilibrium occurs at a tuition of $15,000 per student per year and 7.5 million students per year. At this equilibrium, marginal social benefit is $38,000 per student, which exceeds marginal cost by $23,000. There are too few students in university. The efficient number is 15 million, where marginal social benefit equals marginal cost. The grey triangle shows the deadweight loss.

Underproduction similar to that in Fig. 18.7 would occur at primary school and secondary school if an unregulated market produced education. When children learn basic reading, writing, and number skills, they receive the private benefit of increased earning power. But even these basic skills bring the external benefit of developing better citizens.

External benefits also arise from the discovery of new knowledge. When Isaac Newton worked out the formulas for calculating the rate of response of one variable to another—calculus—everyone was free to use his method. When a spreadsheet program called VisiCalc was invented, Lotus Corporation and Microsoft were free to copy the basic idea and create Lotus 1-2-3 and Microsoft Excel. When the first shopping mall was built and found to be a successful way of arranging retailing, everyone was free to copy the idea, and malls spread like mushrooms.

Once someone has discovered how to do something, others can copy the basic idea. They do have to work to copy an idea, so they face an opportunity cost. But they do not usually have to pay the person who made the discovery to use it. When people make decisions, they ignore its external benefits and consider only its private benefits.

When people make decisions about the quantity of education or the amount of research to undertake, they balance the marginal private cost against the marginal private benefit. They ignore the external benefit. As a result, if we left education and research to unregulated market forces, we would get too little of these activities.

To get closer to producing the efficient quantity of a good or service that generates an external benefit, we make public choices, through governments, to modify the market outcome.

Government Actions in the Face of External Benefits

Four devices that governments can use to achieve a more efficient allocation of resources in the presence of external benefits are

- Public provision
- Private subsidies
- Vouchers
- Patents and copyrights

Public Provision Under **public provision**, a public authority that receives its revenue from the government produces the good or service. The education services produced by the public universities, colleges, and schools are examples of public provision.

Figure 18.8(a) shows how public provision might overcome the underproduction that arises in Fig. 18.7. Public provision cannot lower the cost of

FIGURE 18.8 Public Provision or Private Subsidy to Achieve an Efficient Outcome

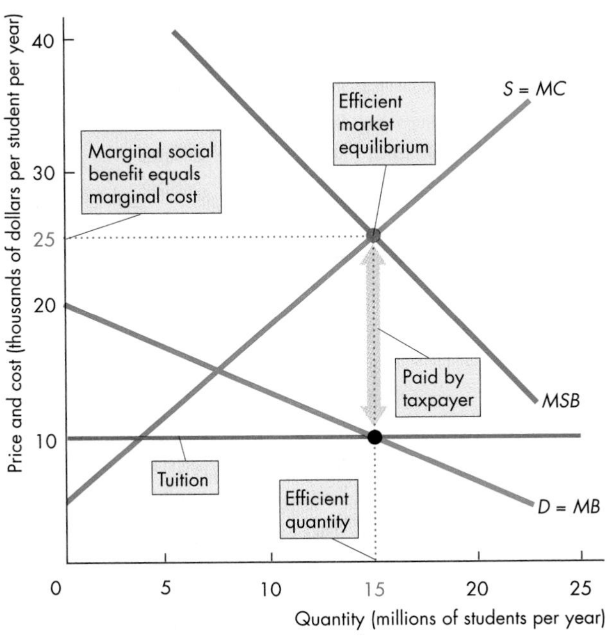

(a) Public provision

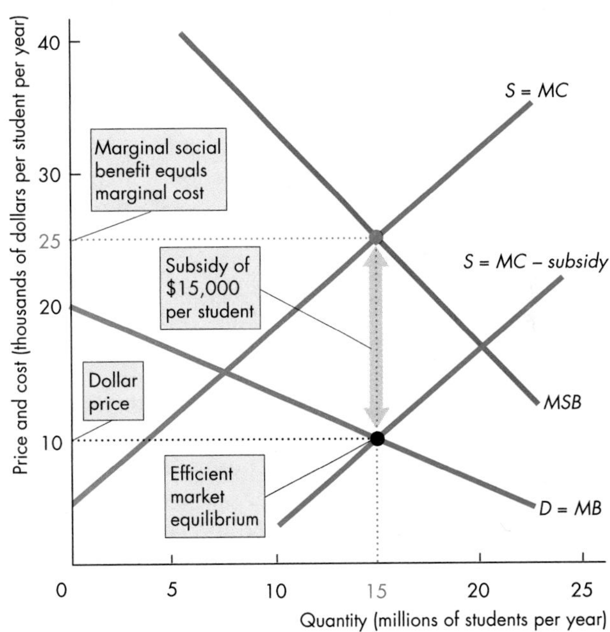

(b) Private subsidy

In part (a), marginal social benefit equals marginal cost with 15 million students enrolled in university, the efficient quantity. Tuition is set at $10,000, and the taxpayers cover the other $15,000 marginal cost per student. In part (b), with a subsidy of $15,000 per student, the supply curve is *S* = *MC* – *subsidy*. The equilibrium price is $10,000, and the market equilibrium is efficient with 15 million students enrolled. Marginal social benefit equals marginal cost.

production, so marginal cost is the same as before. Marginal private benefit and marginal external benefit are also the same as before.

The efficient quantity occurs where marginal social benefit equals marginal cost. In Fig. 18.8(a), this quantity is 15 million students. Tuition is set to ensure that the efficient number of students enrols. That is, tuition is set at the level that equals the marginal private benefit at the efficient quantity. In Fig. 18.8(a), tuition is $10,000 a year. The rest of the cost of the public university is borne by the taxpayers and, in this example, is $15,000 per student per year.

Private Subsidies A **subsidy** is a payment that the government makes to private producers. By making the subsidy depend on the level of output, the government can induce private decision makers to consider external benefits when they make their choices.

Suppose that all schools are private. Figure 18.8(b) shows how a subsidy to private schools would work. In the absence of a subsidy, the marginal cost curve is the market supply curve, $S = MC$. The marginal benefit is the demand curve, $D = MB$. In this example, the government provides a subsidy to schools of $15,000 per student per year. We must subtract the subsidy from the marginal cost of education to find the schools' supply curve. That curve is $S = MC - subsidy$ in the figure. The equilibrium tuition (market price) is $10,000 a year, and the equilibrium quantity is 15 million students. To educate 15 million students, schools incur a marginal cost of $25,000 a year. The marginal social benefit is also $25,000 a year. So with marginal cost equal to marginal social benefit, the subsidy has achieved an efficient outcome. The tuition and the subsidy just cover the schools' marginal cost.

Vouchers A **voucher** is a token that the government provides to households, which they can use to buy specified goods or services. U.S. economist Milton Friedman has long advocated vouchers as a means of providing parents with greater choice and control over the education of their children. Some people advocate them for college and university so that students can both receive financial help and exercise choice. The Canadian Alliance party has advocated the use of vouchers.

A school voucher allows parents to choose the school their children will attend and to use the voucher to pay part of the cost. The school cashes the vouchers to pay its bills. A voucher provided to a university student would work in a similar way. Because vouchers can be spent only on a specified item, they increase the willingness to pay for that item and so increase the demand for it.

FIGURE 18.9 Vouchers Achieve an Efficient Outcome

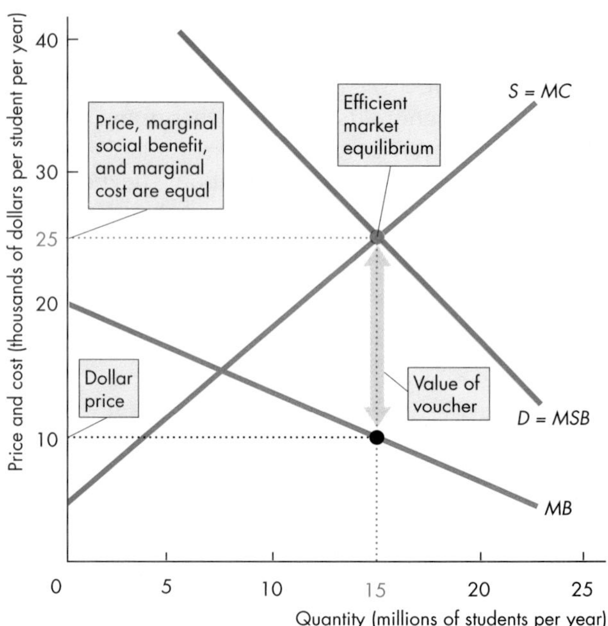

With vouchers, buyers are willing to pay MB plus the value of the voucher, so the demand curve becomes the marginal social benefit curve, $D = MSB$. Market equilibrium is efficient with 15 million students enrolled because price, marginal social benefit, and marginal cost are equal. The tuition consists of the dollar price of $10,000 and the value of the voucher.

Figure 18.9 shows how a voucher system works. The government provides a voucher equal to the marginal external benefit. Students use these vouchers to supplement the dollars they pay for university education. The marginal social benefit curve becomes the demand for university education, $D = MSB$. The market equilibrium occurs at a price of $25,000 per student per year, and 15 million students enrol in universities. Each student pays $10,000 tuition, and universities collect an additional $15,000 per student from the voucher.

If the government estimates the value of the external benefit correctly and makes the value of the voucher equal the marginal external benefit, the outcome from the voucher scheme is efficient. Marginal cost equals marginal social benefit, and the deadweight loss is eliminated.

Vouchers are similar to subsidies, but their advocates say that they are more efficient than subsidies because the consumer can monitor school performance more effectively than the government can.

Patents and Copyrights Knowledge might be an exception to the principle of diminishing marginal benefit. Additional knowledge (about the right things) makes people more productive. And there seems to be no tendency for the additional productivity from additional knowledge to diminish.

For example, in 15 years, advances in knowledge about microprocessors have given us chips that have made our personal computers increasingly powerful. Each advance in knowledge about how to design and manufacture a processor chip has brought apparently ever larger increments in performance and productivity. Similarly, each advance in knowledge about how to design and build an airplane has brought apparently ever larger increments in performance: Orville and Wilbur Wright's 1903 Flyer was a one-seat plane that could hop a farmer's field. The Lockheed Constellation, designed in 1949, was an airplane that could fly 120 passengers from New York to London, but with two refuelling stops in Newfoundland and Ireland. The latest version of the Boeing 747 can carry 400 people nonstop from Los Angeles to Sydney, Australia, or Toronto to Tokyo (flights of 12,000 kilometres that take 13 hours). Similar examples can be found in agriculture, biogenetics, communications, engineering, entertainment, medicine, and publishing.

One reason why knowledge increases without diminishing returns is the sheer number of different things that can be tried. Paul Romer explains this fact with an amazing example. Suppose, says Romer, "that to make a finished good, 20 different parts have to be attached to a frame, one at a time. A worker could proceed in numerical order, attaching part one first, then part two.... Or the worker could proceed in some other order, starting with part 10, then adding part seven.... With 20 parts, ... there are [more] different sequences ... than the total number of seconds that have elapsed since the Big Bang created the universe, so we can be confident that in all activities, only a very small fraction of the possible sequences have ever been tried."*

* Paul Romer, "Ideas and Things," in *The Future Surveyed*, supplement to *The Economist*, September 11, 1993, pp. 71–72.

Think about all the processes, all the products, and all the different bits and pieces that go into each process and product, and you can see that we have only begun to scratch around the edges of what is possible.

Because knowledge is productive and generates external benefits, it is necessary to use public policies to ensure that those who develop new ideas have incentives to encourage an efficient level of effort. The main way of providing the right incentives uses the central idea of the Coase theorem and assigns property rights—called **intellectual property rights**—to creators. The legal device for establishing intellectual property rights is the patent or copyright. A **patent** or **copyright** is a government-sanctioned exclusive right granted to the inventor of a good, service, or productive process to produce, use, and sell the invention for a given number of years. A patent enables the developer of a new idea to prevent others from benefiting freely from an invention for a limited number of years.

Although patents encourage invention and innovation, they do so at an economic cost. While a patent is in place, its holder has a monopoly. And monopoly is another source of inefficiency (which is explained in Chapter 12). But without a patent, the effort to develop new goods, services, or processes is diminished and the flow of new inventions is slowed. So the efficient outcome is a compromise that balances the benefits of more inventions against the cost of temporary monopoly in newly invented activities.

REVIEW QUIZ

1. What is special about knowledge that creates external benefits?
2. How might governments use public provision, private subsidies, and vouchers to achieve an efficient amount of education?
3. How might governments use public provision, private subsidies, vouchers, and patents and copyrights to achieve an efficient amount of research and development?

Reading Between the Lines on pp. 426–427 looks at the pollution created by generating electricity and the debate over whether the regulation of power utilities is too lax or too severe.

READING BETWEEN THE LINES

The Air Pollution Debate

THE GLOBE AND MAIL, APRIL 16, 2002

Three plants spew bulk of pollutants

Three large coal-fired power plants in Southern Ontario produce 83 per cent of all the harmful air pollutants from the province's electric-power sector, according to documents obtained under the Freedom of Information Act.

In the first full look at air emissions from the province's 143 generating facilities, the coal plants—located near Toronto, Simcoe and Sarnia—stand out because they produced 24 million tonnes of contaminants that cause global warming, acid rain, smog, and heavy-metal poisoning in wildlife.

The bulk of the pollutants, tracked over an eight-month period in 2000, are carbon dioxide, sulphur dioxide and nitrogen oxides, but they also include nerve poisons, such as mercury, that are toxic to humans and wildlife even in small concentrations.

The figures also show that the province's publicly owned utility, Ontario Power Generation, is the worst polluter, producing the lion's share of the emissions, with nearly 91 per cent of the total.

The company that was the next-largest emitter, TransAlta Cogen LP, produced only 1.4 per cent.

Ontario Power is such a big polluter partly because it generates the bulk of the province's electricity, and partly because of its use of coal to carry out this task.

Essence of the Story

- Newly available data show that Ontario Power Generation creates 91 percent of total emissions from the electric power producing sector and its three largest power plants account for 83 percent of the province's air pollution.
- These emissions include carbon dioxide, sulfur dioxide, and nitrogen oxides, as well as mercury.

Economic Analysis

- In producing electricity, there is a tradeoff between the private cost and the social cost of production.

- The cheapest fuels and production technologies are extremely dirty.

- None of these technologies are used in Canada today. But they are used in China and Russia (among other countries) where air pollution is a serious problem.

- Canada, in contrast, has achieved a high standard of air quality.

- But is the standard high enough? Or is it too high?

- To answer this question, we need to consider the economics of pollution from producing electricity.

- Figure 1 shows the demand for electricity and its marginal benefit as the curve $D = MB$.

- The curve *MC* shows the marginal cost of producing electricity in dirty plants.

- With an unregulated and competitive market, the quantity produced is 6 megawatt hours.

- Because the plants are dirty, a pollution problem arises. The curve *MSC* shows the marginal social cost of producing electricity.

- The vertical distance between the *MC* curve and the *MSC* curve is the marginal external cost.

- Taking the marginal external cost into account, we can find the efficient quantity of electricity to produce and the efficient amount of pollution.

- In the example in Fig. 1, the efficient quantity is 4 megawatt hours. Notice that at the efficient quantity, we still have pollution, but a smaller amount than with the unregulated outcome.

- Figure 2 shows the same demand and cost curves as Fig. 1 but focuses on the overall cost of pollution—its deadweight loss.

- If production is cut to 4 megawatt hours, the deadweight loss disappears and we have the efficient outcome.

- If power companies are regulated to use a more costly but cleaner technology, the *MC* curve shifts upward, the cost of electricity rises, the quantity produced decreases, and the deadweight loss from pollution shrinks.

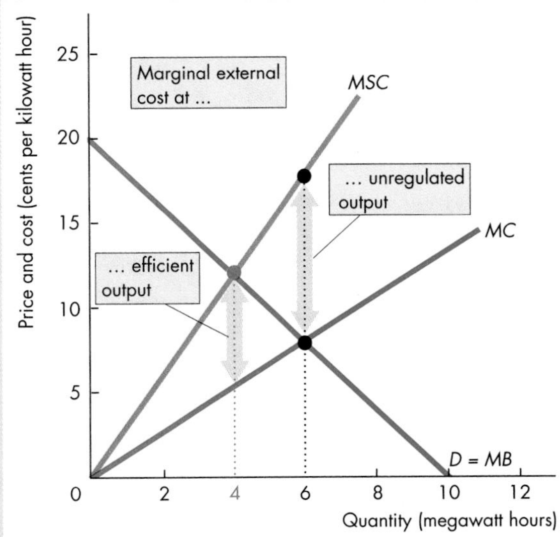

Figure 1 Efficient and unregulated outcomes compared

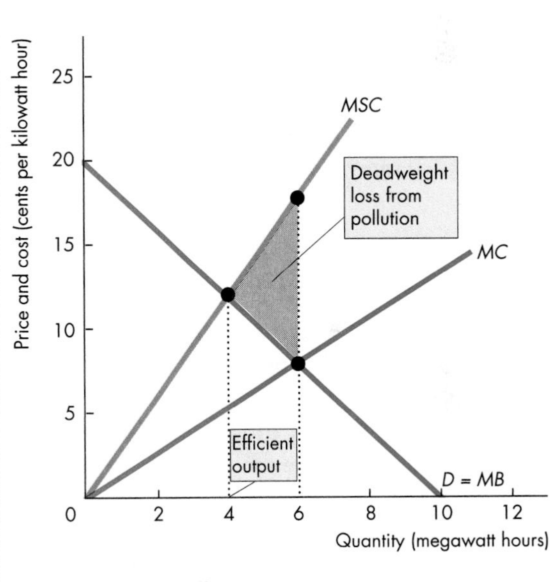

Figure 2 Cost of pollution

- If the additional cost imposed by regulation on the power companies is less than the marginal external cost of pollution, production and pollution move towards but remain above their efficient levels.

- If the additional cost imposed by regulation on the power companies exceeds the marginal external cost of pollution, production and pollution move below their efficient levels.

SUMMARY

KEY POINTS

Externalities in Our Lives (p. 414)

- An externality can arise from either a production activity or a consumption activity.
- A negative externality imposes an external cost.
- A positive externality provides an external benefit.

Negative Externalities: Pollution (pp. 415–421)

- External costs are costs of production that fall on people other than the producer of a good or service. Marginal social cost equals marginal private cost plus marginal external cost.
- Producers take account only of marginal private cost and overproduce when there is a marginal external cost.
- Sometimes it is possible to overcome a negative externality by assigning a property right.
- When property rights cannot be assigned, governments might overcome externalities by using taxes, emission charges, or marketable permits.

Positive Externalities: Knowledge (pp. 421–425)

- External benefits are benefits that are received by people other than the consumer of a good or service. Marginal social benefit equals marginal private benefit plus marginal external benefit.
- External benefits from education arise because better-educated people tend to be better citizens, commit fewer crimes, and support social activities.
- External benefits from research arise because once someone has worked out a basic idea, others can copy it.
- Vouchers or subsidies to schools or the provision of public education below cost can achieve a more efficient provision of education.
- Patents and copyrights create intellectual property rights and an incentive to innovate. But they do so by creating a temporary monopoly, the cost of which must be balanced against the benefit of more inventive activity.

KEY FIGURES

Figure 18.3 Inefficiency with an External Cost, 418
Figure 18.4 Property Rights Achieve an Efficient Outcome, 419
Figure 18.5 A Pollution Tax, 420
Figure 18.7 Inefficiency with an External Benefit, 422
Figure 18.8 Public Provision or Private Subsidy to Achieve an Efficient Outcome, 423
Figure 18.9 Vouchers Achieve an Efficient Outcome, 424

KEY TERMS

Coase theorem, 419
Copyright, 425
Externality, 414
Intellectual property rights, 425
Marginal external benefit, 421
Marginal external cost, 417
Marginal private benefit, 421
Marginal private cost, 417
Marginal social benefit, 421
Marginal social cost, 417
Negative externality, 414
Patent, 425
Pigovian taxes, 420
Positive externality, 414
Property rights, 418
Public provision, 423
Subsidy, 424
Transactions costs, 419
Voucher, 424

PROBLEMS

*1. The table provides information about costs and benefits arising from the production of pesticide that pollutes a lake used by a trout farmer.

Quantity of pesticide (tonnes per week)	Pesticide producer's MC	Trout farmer's MC from pesticide production	Marginal benefit of pesticide
	(dollars per tonne)		
0	0	0	250
1	5	33	205
2	15	67	165
3	30	100	130
4	50	133	100
5	75	167	75
6	105	200	55
7	140	233	40

a. If no one owns the lake and if there is no regulation of pollution, what is the quantity of pesticide produced per week and what is the marginal cost of pollution borne by the trout farmer?
b. If the trout farmer owns the lake, how much pesticide is produced per week and what does the pesticide producer pay the farmer per tonne?
c. If the pesticide producer owns the lake, and if a pollution-free lake rents for $1,000 a week, how much pesticide is produced per week and how much rent per week does the farmer pay the factory for the use of the lake?
d. Compare the quantities of pesticide produced in your answers to parts (b) and (c) and explain the relationship between these quantities.

2. The table at the top of the next column provides information about the costs and benefits of steel smelting that pollutes the air of a city.
a. With no property rights in the city's air and no regulation of pollution, what is the quantity of steel produced per week and what is the marginal cost of pollution borne by the citizens?
b. If the city owns the steel plant, how much steel is produced per week and what does the city charge the steel producer per tonne?

Quantity of steel (tonnes per week)	Steel producer's MC	Marginal external cost	Marginal benefit of steel
	(dollars per tonne)		
0	0	0	1,200
10	100	15	1,100
20	200	25	1,000
30	300	50	900
40	400	100	800
50	500	200	700
60	600	300	600
70	700	400	500
80	800	500	400

c. If the steel firm owns the city, and if the residents of a pollution-free city are willing to pay $15,000 a week in property taxes, how much steel is produced per week and how much are the citizens willing to pay in property taxes to live in the polluted city?
d. Compare the quantities of steel produced in your answers to parts (b) and (c) and explain the relationship between these quantities.

*3. Back at the pesticide plant and trout farm described in problem 1, suppose that no one owns the lake and that the government introduces a pollution tax.
a. What is the tax per tonne of pesticide produced that achieves an efficient outcome?
b. Explain the connection between your answers to problem 3(a) and problem 1.

4. Back at the steel smelter and city in problem 2, suppose that the city introduces a pollution tax.
a. What is the tax per tonne of steel produced that will achieve an efficient outcome?
b. Explain the connection between your answers to problem 4(a) and problem 2.

*5. Using the information provided in problem 1, suppose that no one owns the lake and that the government issues two marketable pollution permits: one to the farmer, and one to the factory. Each may pollute the lake, and the total amount of pollution is the efficient amount.
a. What is the quantity of pesticide produced?
b. What is the market price of a pollution permit? Who buys and who sells a permit?
c. What is the connection between your answers to problems 5(a) and (b) and problems 1 and 3?

6. Using the information given in problem 2, suppose that the city issues two marketable pollution permits: one to the city government, and one to the smelter. Each may pollute the air by the same amount, and the total is the efficient amount.
   a. How much steel is produced?
   b. What is the market price of a permit? Who buys and who sells a permit?
   c. What is the connection between your answers to problems 2 and 4?

*7. The marginal cost of educating a student is $4,000 a year and is constant. The figure shows the marginal private benefit curve.

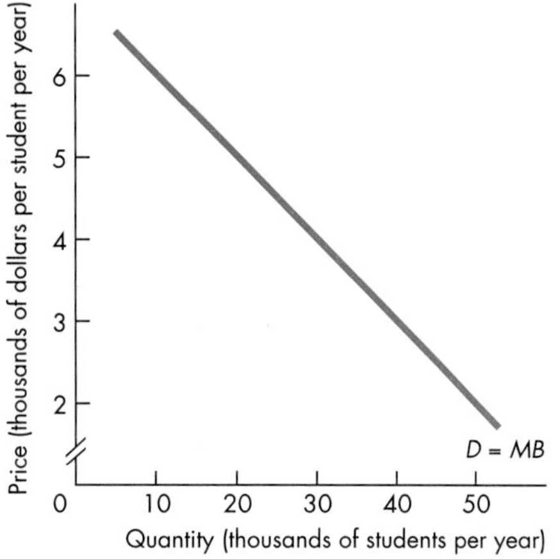

   a. With no government involvement and if the schools are competitive, how many students are enrolled and what is the tuition?
   b. The external benefit from education is $2,000 per student per year and is constant. If the government provides the efficient amount of education, how many school places does it offer and what is the tuition?

8. A technological advance cuts the marginal cost of educating a student to $2,000 a year and is constant. The marginal private benefit is the same as that in problem 7. The external benefit from education increases to $4,000 per student per year and is constant.
   a. With no government involvement and if the schools are competitive, how many students are enrolled and what is the tuition?
   b. If the government provides the efficient amount of education, how many school places does it offer and what is the tuition?
   c. Compare the outcomes in problem 8 with those in problem 7. Explain the differences between the two situations.

CRITICAL THINKING

1. After you have studied *Reading Between the Lines* on pp. 426–427, answer the following questions:
   a. Which electric power companies create most of the air pollution in the electricity industry in Ontario?
   b. What are the pros and cons of stiffening the regulations that power utilities face?
   c. If a technological advance lowers the cost of producing electricity but leaves the marginal external pollution cost unchanged, would the adoption of this technology in an unregulated market increase or decrease pollution? Explain using a figure like those on p. 427.

WEB EXERCISES

1. Use the links on the Parkin–Bade Web site to get two viewpoints on global warming. Then answer these questions:
   a. What are the benefits and costs of greenhouse gas emissions?
   b. Do you think the environmentalists are correct in the view that greenhouse gas emissions must be cut, or do you think the costs of reducing greenhouse gas emissions exceed the benefits?
   c. If greenhouse gas emissions are to be reduced, should reductions be achieved by assigning production limits or marketable permits?
2. To decrease the amount of overfishing of southern bluefin tuna in its territorial waters, the government of Australia introduced private property rights with an allocation of Individual Transferable Quotas (ITQs). To check out the effects of this system, use the link on your Parkin–Bade Web site to read the review by John Coombs of Colby College, Maine. Also look at the Greenpeace view. Then answer the following questions:
   a. Would the introduction of ITQs in North America help to replenish Canadian fish stocks?
   b. Explain why ITQs give an incentive not to overfish.
   c. Why does Greenpeace oppose ITQs?

UNDERSTANDING MARKET FAILURE AND GOVERNMENT

PART 6

Making the Rules

Creating a system of responsible democratic government is a huge enterprise and one that can easily go wrong. Creating a constitution that makes despotic and tyrannical rule impossible is relatively easy. And we have achieved such a constitution in Canada by using some sound economic ideas. We have designed a sophisticated system of incentives—of carrots and sticks—to make the government responsive to public opinion and to limit the ability of individual special interests to gain at the expense of the majority. But we have not managed to create a constitution that effectively blocks the ability of special interest groups to capture the consumer and producer surpluses that result from specialization and exchange. ◆ We have created a system of government to deal with four economic problems. The market economy would produce too small a quantity of those public goods and services that we must consume together, such as national defence and air-traffic control. It enables monopoly to restrict production and charge too high a price. It produces too large a quantity of some goods and services, the production of which creates pollution. And it generates a distribution of income and wealth that most people believe is too unequal. So we need a government to help cope with these economic problems. But as the founding fathers knew would happen, when governments get involved in the economy, people try to steer the government's actions in directions that bring personal gains at the expense of the general interest. ◆ The three chapters in this part explained the problems with which the market has a hard time coping. Chapter 16 overviewed the entire range of problems and studied one of these problems, public goods, more deeply. Chapter 17 studied competition policy and the regulation of natural monopoly. And Chapter 18 dealt with externalities. It examined the external costs imposed by pollution and the external benefits that come from education and research. It described some of the ways in which externalities can be dealt with. And it explained that one way of coping with externalities is to strengthen the market and "internalize" the externalities rather than to intervene in the market. ◆ Many economists have thought long and hard about the problems discussed in this part. But none has had as profound an effect on our ideas in this area as Ronald Coase, whom you can meet on the following page. You can also meet John McCallum, Canada's Minister of National Defence, who wrestles with some of the issues you've studied in this part every day.

PROBING THE IDEAS

Externalities and Property Rights

THE ECONOMIST

"The question to be decided is: is the value of fish lost greater or less than the value of the product which contamination of the stream makes possible?"

RONALD H. COASE
The Problems of Social Cost

RONALD COASE *(1910–), was born in England and educated at the London School of Economics, where he was deeply influenced by his teacher, Arnold Plant, and by the issues of his youth: communist central planning versus free markets. Professor Coase has lived in the United States since 1951. He first visited America as a 20-year-old on a travelling scholarship during the depths of the Great Depression. It was on this visit, and before he had completed his bachelor's degree, that he conceived the ideas that 60 years later were to earn him the 1991 Nobel Prize for Economic Science. He discovered and clarified the significance of transactions costs and property rights for the functioning of the economy. Ronald Coase has revolutionized the way we think about property rights and externalities and has opened up the growing field of law and economics.*

THE ISSUES

As knowledge accumulates, we are becoming more sensitive to environmental externalities. We are also developing more sensitive methods of dealing with them. But all the methods involve a public choice.

Urban smog, which is both unpleasant and dangerous to breathe, forms when sunlight reacts with emissions from the tailpipes of automobiles. Because of this external cost of auto exhaust, we set emission standards and tax gasoline. Emission standards increase the cost of a car, and gasoline taxes increase the cost of the marginal kilometre travelled. The higher costs decrease the quantity demanded of road transportation and so decrease the amount of pollution it creates. Is the value of cleaner urban air worth the higher cost of transportation? The public choices of voters, regulators, and lawmakers answer this question.

Acid rain, which imposes a cost on everyone who lives in its path, falls from sulfur-laden clouds produced by electric utility smokestacks. This external cost is being tackled with a market solution. This solution is marketable permits, the price and allocation of which are determined by the forces of supply and demand. Private choices determine the demand for marketable permits, but a public choice determines the supply.

As cars stream onto an urban highway during the morning rush hour, the highway clogs and becomes an expensive parking lot. Each rush hour traveller imposes external costs on all the others. Today, road users bear private congestion costs but do not face a share of the external congestion costs that they create. But a market solution to this problem is now technologically feasible. It is a solution that charges road users with a fee similar to a toll that varies with time of day and degree of congestion. Confronted with the social marginal cost of their actions, each road user makes a choice and the market for highway space is efficient. Here, a public choice to use a market solution leaves the final decision about the degree of congestion to private choices.

THEN

Chester Jackson, a Lake Erie fisherman, recalls that when he began fishing on the lake, boats didn't carry drinking water. Fishermen drank from the lake. Speaking after World War II, Jackson observed, "Can't do that today. Those chemicals in there would kill you." Farmers used chemicals, such as the insecticide DDT, that got carried into the lake by runoff. Industrial waste and trash were also dumped in the lake in large quantities. As a result, Lake Erie became badly polluted during the 1940s and became incapable of sustaining a viable fish stock.

NOW

Today, Lake Erie supports a fishing industry, just as it did in the 1930s. No longer treated as a garbage dump for chemicals, the lake is regenerating its ecosystem. Fertilizers and insecticides are now recognized as products that have potential externalities, and their external effects are assessed by Environment Canada before new versions are put into widespread use. Dumping industrial waste into rivers and lakes is now subject to much more stringent regulations and penalties. Lake Erie's externalities have been dealt with by one of the methods available: government regulation.

Fundamental to protecting property rights is our national defence. John McCallum, whom you can meet on the following pages, is Canada's Minister of National Defence. But he is also an economist, and one whose career provides an outstanding example of the enormous range of jobs that the economist is equipped to perform.

TALKING WITH

JOHN McCALLUM

is Canada's Minister of National Defence and Member of Parliament for the Ontario constituency of Markham. Born in Montreal in 1950, he was an undergraduate at Cambridge University and a graduate student at Université de Paris and McGill University, where he earned his PhD in 1977. Dr. McCallum's career path has been extraordinarily broad. He has been a professor of economics at the University of Manitoba, Simon Fraser University, Université du Québec à Montréal, and McGill University, Dean of Arts at McGill, and Senior Vice President and Chief Economist at the Royal Bank of Canada. He has become well known for his strongly held and clearly stated views on economic policy and is a prolific contributor to economic policy debates and now to defence policy issues in Canada.

John McCallum

Robin Bade and Michael Parkin talked with John McCallum about his work and his views on the role of economics and the economist in the wide range of jobs that he has held.

How did you become an economist?

By fluke. I went to Cambridge University as an undergraduate, and under the British system one had to choose a single subject. I liked both the humanities and mathematics, and, by a process of elimination, I discovered that economics was about the only subject offering a combination of the two. So, never having heard the name John Maynard Keynes, I went to Cambridge, the home of Keynes and the bastion of Keynesianism. I was much too young to meet the great man himself, but just old enough to be taught by his direct disciples, people like Joan Robinson, Nicholas Kaldor, Richard Kahn, and Luigi Pasinetti. So, naturally, not being a child prodigy equipped to challenge the thinking of my great teachers, I emerged a Keynesian.

Are you still a Keynesian, and does the label matter much today?

I emerged a Keynesian. But given the world in which I live, with the passage of time I gradually lost some of my ardour as a Keynesian. But I'd still say that I'm a modern-day Keynesian, which is a different definition of what a Keynesian was back when I was an undergraduate—much more modest in ambition.

You've been an economics professor and a dean, the chief economist at a major bank, and now a Member of Parliament and Canada's Minister of Defence. Reflecting on this broad career, what are the principles of economics that you find yourself repeatedly coming back to?

The principles of economics that are relevant depend on the job. When I was Chief Economist of the Royal Bank I was concerned with macroeconomics. I was commenting on the macroeconomy and trying to forecast it. I might say that one of the things I miss least about being a bank chief economist is that I don't have to pretend I know what the currency will be in the future! So a bank economist's job is mainly macro and relies on macroeconomic principles.

But any job that involves the management of people or resources, whether as a

Dean of Arts or Minister of Defence, uses microeconomic principles. Although I am trying to get more resources, that's not entirely under my control, and whether I get new resources or not, at the end of the day I'll have a fixed amount of resources. So the challenge is always to get the greatest value—the most bang for the buck—out of a finite amount of resources.

The economics that is valuable in this activity is not complicated mathematical economics (which I never was very good at anyway) but basic principles like opportunity cost and benefits and costs and benefits at the margin. Those are the concepts I find useful today.

Does the Department of National Defence have economists working on defence resource allocation questions?

Economists are not in evidence here in the way they are at the Bank of Canada or in the Department of Finance. But there are some economic studies performed in the Department of National Defence on topics such as the economic benefits that accrue to the various regions of Canada as a result of defence spending.

How does the Minister of National Defence use the concepts of opportunity cost, benefit, and the margin to get the best bang for the buck? Can you provide an example?

Think about strategic air lift—the capacity to carry people and heavy equipment long distances. We don't have that capacity, and neither does any other NATO country except for the UK and the US. Right now we rent airplanes to carry our troops and equipment around the world and that's not necessarily a bad option. But we, along with some other NATO nations, are looking at alternatives.

One option is the status quo. A second option is buying the airplanes ourselves. A third option is a European joint-ownership plan. And a fourth option might be to try to reach a deal with the Americans. Resolving the issue clearly involves trying to get the benefit that we want in the most cost effective way.

The status quo—renting planes when we need them—is a low-cost solution but it has two main problems. First, there might be times when everyone is looking for strategic lift at the same time. Second, it can sometimes take too long to negotiate agreements and get the planes operating.

Buying our own planes would give us the greatest flexibility. But that solution has a high cost and for much of the time the planes would be sitting on the ground.

The European joint-ownership time-sharing proposal might offer an efficient compromise and be the most cost-effective solution. The idea would be to work together with our NATO allies and acquire a share in jointly owned NATO lift capacity.

This arrangement would be similar to sharing a condo. The amount of time you get is proportional to the money you put in. So that's one option, which we're exploring. We would need to make sure that some of these airplanes were in Canada and that we had access when we needed them. We have a special geography compared with everyone of our European NATO partners.

So solving the problem acquiring strategic lift at least cost is a classic economic problem.

What about an area that is less clear cut—where you're trying to figure out something much less well defined? For example, how do we decide how much we should be spending on Canada's national defence?

I come at this issue from the point of view that has grown out of my experience in a number of large organizations (the bank, university, and now defence). I think any large organization has a tendency to have inefficiencies and turf issues. Large organizations don't respond quickly to changing circumstances. For example, in the defence area, the Cold War has been over for more than a decade. Yet many countries, especially in Europe, still have hundreds of tanks hanging around as if the next challenge is a Soviet invasion.

We are also into the post-September 11 world, which has brought a radical change to the kinds of response capability that is required.

Then we have a military technological revolution, which is bringing the high tech sort of warfare like we saw in the Gulf War such as precision bombs and unmanned aerial vehicles.

Put together the totally different world and the radical changes in technology and it's definitely a challenge to adapt.

But large organizations don't just automatically reinvent themselves to deal with the changing world. I'm not sure that an economist in particular has an advantage here.

What I'm trying to do is bring in people from the private sector with expertise in restructuring to try to find ways to improve our administrative efficiency and to have a debate on what military capabilities are very important, not important, or middle important in today's world.

Things in large organizations don't always go fast but in terms of the private sector people I'm hoping to get answers of some savings within six months.

There are more fundamental issues like defence capabilities. We may have a much broader defence review where these will be discussed and we'll get input from stakeholders and ordinary Canadians before making a decision.

Can we talk a bit about the complaint that you sometimes hear from the Americans that we're not spending enough on our national defence? Do you think there's a conflict of interest for the Americans? Are they trying to get us to buy their stuff? Or do you think that indeed we do have an incentive to be a free rider and that we need to guard against that?

I think both are correct. In fact I've commented publicly on this before. When the American ambassador tells us to spend more on defence in part he has in mind buying American-made big airplanes for strategic lift. And that's not a criticism. Any ambassador has the job to sell his country's product. So in part there is a double interest. The Americans would like us to spend more, but they'd also like us to buy their products. So there's a bit of a mix when you get those messages. But at the same time, living next to the world's only superpower, there is a risk of becoming a free rider. Because the Americans have an interest in defending the whole continent by means of defending their own country, there's a possibility that we could become a free rider.

Now I personally am lobbying for more money for defence. It is true that relative to our GDP we're near the bottom in terms of our spending so some may argue that we're free riders to a certain degree. But if you compare our own situation with a country like Holland or France we're not in clear and present danger of being invaded. We've never been invaded in our history or not at least since 1812 unlike the Europeans so I think we feel less vulnerable to terrorist attack rightly or wrongly than Americans do.

So I think in the minds of Canadians there is less urgency or need for defence compared with some other countries with different histories. There has been a significant increase in public support for defence spending over the last few years—certainly since September 11, but starting earlier than that.

So my answer is: I think that Canadians feel less-threatened militarily than do many other countries, so they're not inclined to spend a lot. But I think that's changing as there's more public support now for stronger defence spending.

Do you have any final words for the beginning student?

My own career suggests that economics can lead you into a variety of different areas. I still think it's highly relevant as a way of thinking that will help you, perhaps only subconsciously, in a number of different jobs even if they're not specifically related to economics. There's only a relatively limited number of areas where I think people can work explicitly as economists—you can go into the academic world or you can work for a bank or the government or a lobbyist such as the Chamber of Commerce. But I think the training you get in economics is important even if you don't work in a job as an economist. Maybe some of the examples I've given illustrate that.

Beyond that, I would encourage all students to focus on three points, not necessarily in order of importance: Get good marks; show imagination in combining sound economic principles with real-world issues and problems; and be a good team player.

PART 7 ISSUES IN MACROECONOMICS

A FIRST LOOK AT MACROECONOMICS

CHAPTER 19

What Will Your World Be Like?

During the past 100 years, the quantity of goods and services produced in Canada's farms, factories, shops, and offices has expanded more than twentyfold. As a result, we have a much higher standard of living than our grandparents had. Will production always expand? ◆ For most of us, a high standard of living means finding a good job. What kind of job will you find when you graduate? Will you have lots of choice, or will you face a labour market with a high unemployment rate in which jobs are hard to find? ◆ A high standard of living means being able to afford to buy life's necessities and have some fun. If prices rise too quickly, some people get left behind and must trim what they buy. What will the dollar buy next year; in 10 years when you are paying off your student loan; and in 50 years when you are spending your life's savings in retirement? ◆ Every year between 1971 and 1997, the federal government spent more than it raised in taxes. And most years, we spend more on imports from the rest of the world than we earn on our exports. How will these deficits affect your future? ◆ To keep production expanding and prevent an economic slowdown, the federal government and the Bank of Canada—the nation's financial managers—take policy actions. How do their actions influence production, jobs, prices, and the ability of Canadians to compete in the global marketplace?

These are the questions of macroeconomics that you are about to study. In *Reading Between the Lines* at the end of the chapter, we'll take a quick look at macroeconomic performance—inflation, deflation, and economic growth—around the world in 2002.

After studying this chapter, you will be able to

- **Describe the origins and issues of macroeconomics**
- **Describe the trends and fluctuations in economic growth**
- **Describe the trends and fluctuations in jobs and unemployment**
- **Describe the trends and fluctuations in inflation**
- **Describe the trends and fluctuations in government and international deficits**
- **Identify the macroeconomic policy challenges and describe the tools available for meeting them**

Origins and Issues of Macroeconomics

ECONOMISTS BEGAN TO STUDY ECONOMIC growth, inflation, and international payments as long ago as the 1750s, and this work was the origin of macroeconomics. But modern macroeconomics did not emerge until the **Great Depression,** a decade (1929–1939) of high unemployment and stagnant production throughout the world economy. In the Depression's worst year, 1933, the production of Canada's farms, factories, shops, and offices was only 70 percent of its 1929 level and 20 percent of the labour force was unemployed. These were years of human misery on a scale that is hard to imagine today. They were also years of extreme pessimism about the ability of the market economy to work properly. Many people believed that private ownership, free markets, and democratic political institutions could not survive.

The science of economics had no solutions to the Great Depression. The major alternative system of central planning and socialism seemed increasingly attractive to many people. It was in this climate of economic depression and political and intellectual turmoil that modern macroeconomics emerged with the publication in 1936 of John Maynard Keynes' *The General Theory of Employment, Interest, and Money* (see pp. 522–523).

Short-Term Versus Long-Term Goals

Keynes' theory was that depression and high unemployment result from insufficient private spending and that to cure these problems, the government must increase its spending. Keynes focused primarily on the *short term.* He wanted to cure an immediate problem almost regardless of the *long-term* consequences of the cure. "In the long run," said Keynes, "we're all dead."

But Keynes believed that after his cure for depression had restored the economy to a normal condition, the long-term problems of inflation and slow economic growth would return. And he suspected that his cure for depression, increased government spending, might trigger inflation and might lower the long-term growth rate of production. With a lower long-term growth rate, the economy would create fewer jobs. If this outcome did occur, a policy aimed at lowering unemployment in the short run might end up increasing it in the long run.

By the late 1960s and through the 1970s, Keynes' predictions became a reality. Inflation increased, economic growth slowed, and in some countries unemployment became persistently high. The causes of these developments are complex. But they point to an inescapable conclusion: The long-term problems of inflation, slow growth, and persistent unemployment and the short-term problems of depression and economic fluctuations intertwine and are most usefully studied together. So although macroeconomics was reborn during the Great Depression, it has now returned to its older tradition. Today, macroeconomics is a subject that tries to understand long-term economic growth and inflation as well as short-term business fluctuations and unemployment.

The Road Ahead

There is no unique way to study macroeconomics. Because its rebirth was a product of depression, the common practice for many years was to pay most attention to short-term output fluctuations and unemployment, but never to completely lose sight of the long-term issues. When a rapid inflation emerged during the 1970s, this topic returned to prominence. During the 1980s, when long-term growth slowed in Canada and other rich industrial countries but exploded in East Asia, economists redirected their energy towards economic growth. During the 1990s, as information technologies further shrank the globe, the international dimension of macroeconomics became more prominent. The result of these developments is that modern macroeconomics is a broad subject that studies all the issues we've just identified: economic growth and fluctuations, unemployment, inflation, and government and international deficits.

Over the past 40 years, economists have developed a clearer understanding of the forces that determine macroeconomic performance and have devised policies that they hope will improve this performance. Your main goal is to become familiar with the theories of macroeconomics and the policies that they make possible. To set you on your path towards this goal, we're going to take a first look at economic growth, jobs and unemployment, inflation, and surpluses and deficits, and learn why these macroeconomic phenomena merit our attention.

Economic Growth

YOUR PARENTS ARE RICHER THAN YOUR GRANDparents were when they were young. But are you going to be richer than your parents are? And are your children going to be richer than you? The answers depend on the rate of economic growth.

Economic growth is the expansion of the economy's production possibilities. It can be pictured as an outward shift of the production possibilities frontier (*PPF*)—see Chapter 2, pp. 40–41.

We measure economic growth by the increase in real gross domestic product. **Real gross domestic product** (also called **real GDP**) is the value of the total production of all the nation's farms, factories, shops, and offices measured in the prices of a single year. Real GDP in Canada is currently measured in the prices of 1997 (called 1997 dollars). We use the dollar prices of a single year to eliminate the influence of *inflation*—the increase in the average level of prices—and determine how much production has grown from one year to another. (Real GDP is explained more fully in Chapter 20 on pp. 458–462.)

Real GDP is not a perfect measure of total production because it does not include everything that is produced. It excludes the things we produce for ourselves at home (preparing meals, doing laundry, house painting, gardening, and so on). It also excludes production that people hide to avoid taxes or because the activity is illegal—the underground economy. But despite its shortcomings, real GDP is the best measure of total production available. Let's see what it tells us about economic growth.

Economic Growth in Canada

Figure 19.1 shows real GDP in Canada since 1961 and highlights two features of economic growth:

- The growth of potential GDP
- Fluctuations of real GDP around potential GDP

The Growth of Potential GDP When all the economy's labour, capital, land, and entrepreneurial ability are fully employed, the value of production is called **potential GDP.** Real GDP fluctuates around potential GDP and the rate of long-term economic growth is measured by the growth rate of potential GDP. It is shown by the steepness of the potential GDP line (the black line) in Fig. 19.1.

From 1960 through 1974, potential GDP grew at an unusually rapid rate of 4.9 percent a year. But the growth rate slowed from the mid-1970s to the mid-1990s. The growth rate of output per person sagged during these years in a phenomenon called the **productivity growth slowdown**. The growth rate of potential GDP increased during the late 1990s and 2000s, but it is too soon to tell whether this increase is the beginning of a new phase of more rapid growth.

Why did the productivity growth slowdown occur? This question is controversial. We explore the causes of the productivity growth slowdown in Chapter 30. Whatever its cause, the slowdown means that we all have smaller incomes today than we would have had if the economy had continued to grow at its 1960s rate.

Let's now look at real GDP fluctuations around potential GDP.

FIGURE 19.1 Economic Growth in Canada

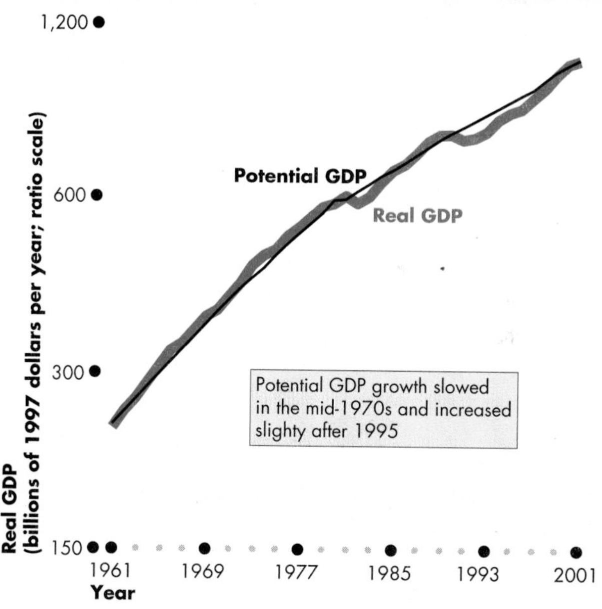

The long-term economic growth rate, measured by the growth of potential GDP, was 4.9 percent a year from 1960 through 1974. Growth slowed from the mid-1970s to the mid-1990s but sped up slightly after 1995. Real GDP fluctuates around potential GDP.

Sources: Statistics Canada, CANSIM series v1992292 and International Monetary Fund, *World Economic Outlook* database, Output gap series.

Fluctuations of Real GDP Around Potential GDP

Real GDP fluctuates around potential GDP in a business cycle. A *business cycle* is the periodic but irregular up-and-down movement in production.

Business cycles are not regular, predictable, or repeating cycles like the phases of the moon. Their timing changes unpredictably. But cycles do have some things in common. Every business cycle has two phases:

1. A recession
2. An expansion

and two turning points:

1. A peak
2. A trough

Figure 19.2 shows these features of the most recent business cycle in Canada. A **recession** is a period during which real GDP decreases—the growth rate of real GDP is negative—for at least two successive quarters. The most recent recession, which is highlighted in the figure, began in the first quarter of 1990 and ended in the first quarter of 1991. This recession lasted for four quarters. An **expansion** is a period during which real GDP increases. The most recent expansion began in the second quarter of 1991. This expansion is the longest expansion on record. An earlier expansion ended in the first quarter of 1990.

When a business cycle expansion ends and a recession begins, the turning point is called a **peak**. The most recent peak occurred in the first quarter of 1990. When a business cycle recession ends and an expansion begins, the turning point is called a **trough**. The most recent trough occurred in the first quarter of 1991.

Sometimes, during a business cycle expansion phase, the growth rate slows down. A slowdown in the growth rate of real GDP but with the growth rate *not* becoming negative for two quarters is called a **growth recession**. Two growth recessions occurred during the long expansion of the 1990s and 2000s. The first of these ran from the beginning of 1995 to the first quarter of 1996 and the second one ran from mid 2000 to mid 2001. During a growth recession, real GDP dips below potential GDP.

FIGURE 19.2 The Most Recent Canadian Business Cycle

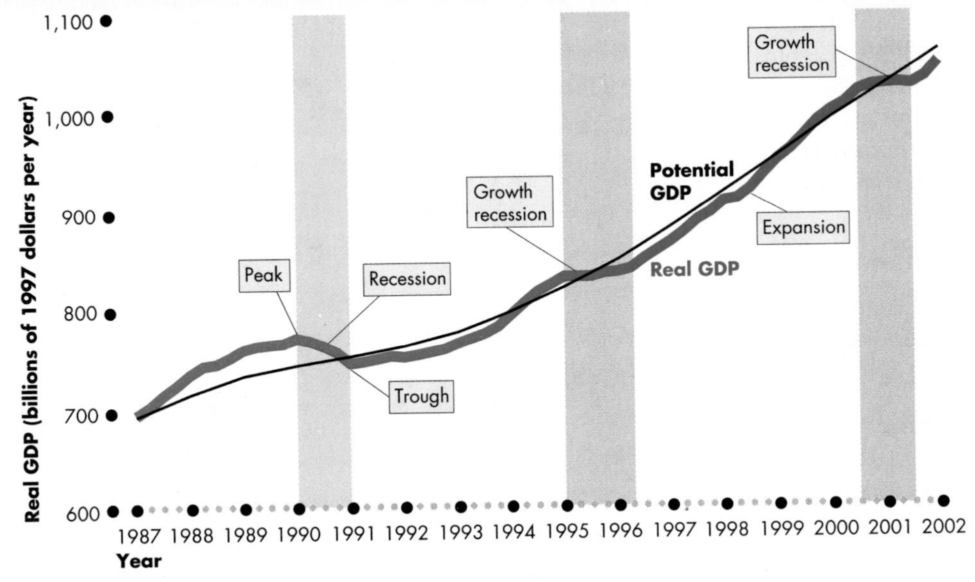

A business cycle has two phases: recession and expansion. The most recent recession (highlighted) ran from the first quarter of 1990 through the first quarter of 1991. Then a new expansion began in the second quarter of 1991. A business cycle has two turning points, a peak and a trough. In the most recent business cycle, the peak occurred in the first quarter of 1990 and the trough occurred in the first quarter of 1991. Growth recessions occurred in 1995–1996 and in 2000–2001.

Sources: Statistics Canada, CANSIM series v1992292 and International Monetary Fund, *World Economic Outlook* database, Output gap series.

The Most Recent Recession in Historical Perspective The recession of 1990–1991 seemed severe while we were passing through it, but compared with earlier recessions, it was mild. You can see how mild it was by looking at Fig. 19.3, which shows a longer history of Canadian economic growth. The biggest decrease in real GDP occurred during the Great Depression of the 1930s. A decrease also occurred in 1946 and 1947, after a huge World War II expansion. A serious recession also occurred during the early 1980s, when the Bank of Canada and the Federal Reserve Board in the United States hiked interest rates to previously unimagined levels.

Each of these economic downturns was more severe than that in 1990–1991. But you can see that the Great Depression was much more severe than anything that followed it. This episode was so extreme that we don't call it a recession. We call it a *depression.*

This last truly great depression occurred before governments started taking policy actions to stabilize the economy. It also occurred before the birth of modern macroeconomics. Is the absence of another great depression a sign that macroeconomics has contributed to economic stability? Some people believe it is. Others doubt it. We'll evaluate these opinions on a number of occasions in this book.

We've looked at real GDP growth and fluctuations in Canada. But is the Canadian experience typical? Do other countries share our experience? Let's see whether they do.

Economic Growth Around the World

A country might have a rapid growth rate of real GDP, but it might also have a rapid population growth rate. To compare growth rates over time and across countries, we use the growth rate of real GDP *per person.* Real GDP per person is real GDP divided by the population. For example, Canadian real GDP in the first quarter of 2002 was $1,048 billion a year. The population of Canada was 31.4 million. So Canadian real GDP per person was $1,048 billion divided by 31.4 million, which equals $33,376.

Figure 19.4 shows real GDP per person between 1960 and 2000 for Canada alongside the world's

FIGURE 19.3 Long-Term Economic Growth in Canada

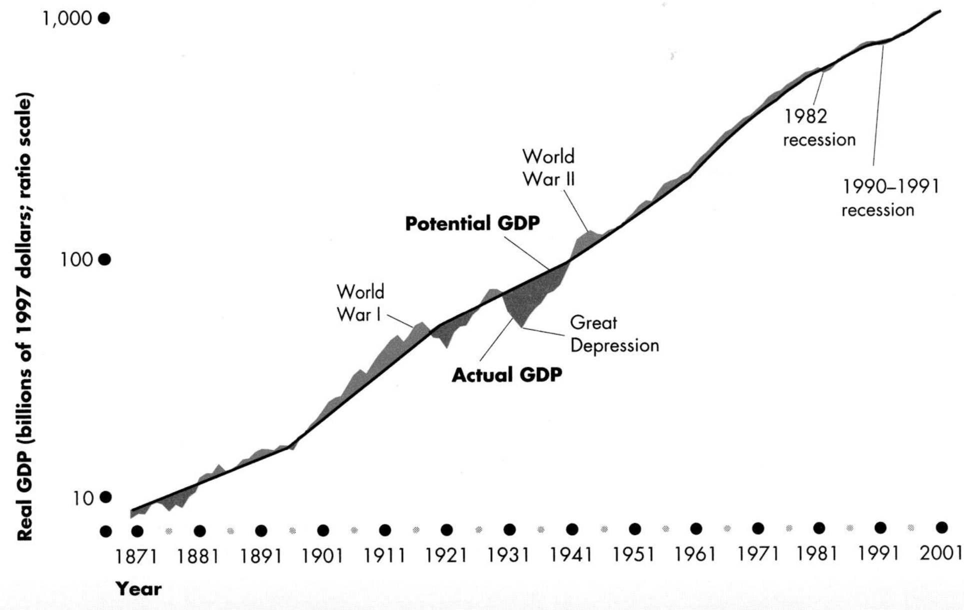

The thin black line shows potential GDP. Along this line, real GDP grew at an average rate of 3.7 percent a year between 1870 and 2001. The blue areas show when real GDP was above potential GDP, and the red areas show when it was below potential GDP. During some periods, such as World War II, real GDP expanded quickly. During other periods, such as the Great Depression and more recently in 1982 (following interest rate hikes) and 1990–1991, real GDP declined.

Sources: 1870–1925, Angus Maddison, *Dynamic Forces in Capitalist Development*, Oxford University Press, New York, 1991. 1926–2001, and Statistics Canada, *Historical Statistics of Canada*, series F 55 and CANSIM series v1992292.

three largest economies: the United States, Japan, and Germany. In these countries, four features of the paths of real GDP per person stand out:

- Similar business cycles before 1990
- Different business cycles in the 1990s
- Similar 1970s growth recessions
- Different long-term growth trends

Similar Business Cycles Before 1990 Each of the three big economies had an expansion running from the early or mid-1960s through 1973, a recession from 1973 to 1975, an expansion through 1979, another recession in the early 1980s, and a long expansion through the rest of the 1980s.

Different Business Cycles in the 1990s The 1990s saw Canada and the United States in a long and strong business cycle expansion. But the decade brought severe recession in Japan and only moderate expansion in Germany. This divergence of business cycles is relatively uncommon.

Similar 1970s Growth Recessions Canadian real GDP per person grew at 3.8 percent a year from 1960 through 1973, but slowed to 2.5 percent between 1974 and 1988 and to only 1.2 percent after 1988. Growth in the United States slowed from 2.9 percent to 1.7 percent and then to 1.8 percent, in Germany from 3.5 percent to 2.0 percent and then to 1.6 percent, and in Japan from 8.5 percent to 3.3 percent and then to 0.8 percent.

Different Long-Term Growth Trends In 1960, real GDP per person in Canada exceeded that in Germany, exceeded that in Japan by a large amount, but was less than that in the United States.

During the 1960s, Japan's real GDP streaked upward like a rocket departing Cape Canaveral. Canada and Germany grew quickly too, and all three countries closed the gap on the United States. Growth slowed in all four countries during the 1970s and Japan's growth rate more than halved. Even so, Japan's growth of real GDP per person equalled the U.S. rate *before* the slowdown. Because it achieved such a high growth rate, Japan narrowed the gap

FIGURE 19.4 Economic Growth in Canada and the Three Largest Economies

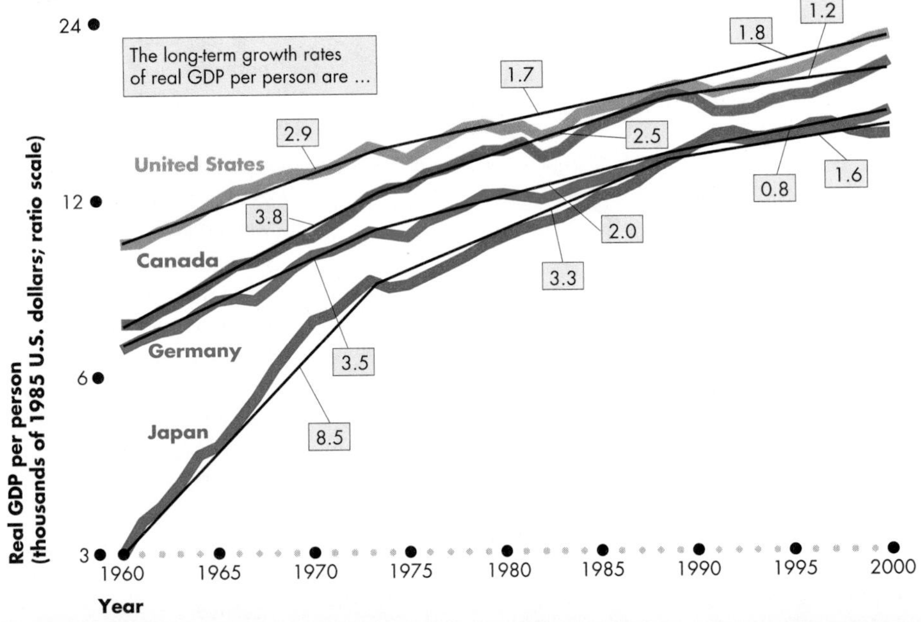

Economic growth in Canada and the three large economies—the United States, Germany, and Japan—was the most rapid during the 1960s. The growth rate in all four countries slowed during the 1970s, and the countries had similar business cycles. The United States has grown slowest and Canada has narrowed the gap on the United States. Japan has grown fastest, and Germany too has grown faster than the United States. But in the mid-1990s, growth in Canada and in Japan had slowed to a crawl.

Sources: The data for 1960 through 1992 are from "The Penn World Table," *Quarterly Journal of Economics*, May 1991, pp. 327–368. New computer disk supplement (Mark 5.6a). The data use comparable international relative prices converted to 1985 U.S. dollars. The data for 1993–2000 are from the International Monetary Fund, *International Financial Statistics*, Washington, D.C., 2002.

between its own level of real GDP per person and those of Canada and the United States and overtook that of Germany.

During the 1990s, Japan's real GDP per person fell below Germany's and because the growth of Canada's real GDP per person slowed to a crawl, the gap between the levels of real GDP per person in Canada and the United States widened.

Figure 19.5 compares the growth of the Canadian economy with that of several other countries and regions since 1980. Among the industrial economies, the European Union has grown the slowest and the other industrial countries, mainly those of newly industrialized Asia, have grown the fastest. Among the developing economies the most rapid growth has occurred in Asia, where the average growth rate has exceeded 7 percent a year. The slowest growing developing countries are in Africa and the Western Hemisphere (Central and South America). The transition economies have grown the slowest. These are countries such as Russia and the other countries of Central Europe that are making a transition from a state-managed economy to a market economy. Production has been shrinking severely in these countries.

World average growth has been just over 3 percent a year. The Canadian growth rate is slightly below the world average and much below the growth rates that the developing economies of Asia have achieved.

FIGURE 19.5 Growth Rates Around the World

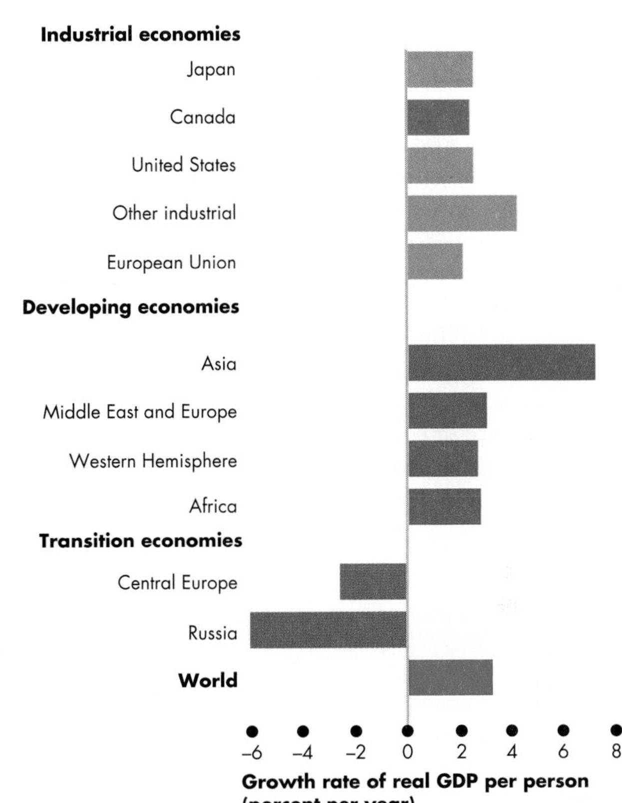

Since 1980, the growth rate of real GDP per person has been lower in Canada than in some other industrial economies. The developing economies of Asia have had the most rapid growth rates and those of Central Europe and Russia have had the slowest growth.

Source: International Monetary Fund, *World Economic Outlook*, Washington D.C., October 1988, p.145.

Benefits and Costs of Economic Growth

What are the benefits and costs of economic growth? Does it matter if the long-term growth rate slows as it did during the 1970s?

The main benefit of long-term economic growth is expanded consumption possibilities, including more health care for the poor and elderly, more cancer and AIDS research, more space research and exploration, better roads, and more and better housing. We can even have cleaner lakes, more trees, and cleaner air by devoting more resources to environmental problems.

When the long-term growth rate slows, some of these benefits are lost, and the loss can be large. For example, if long-term growth had not slowed in Canada during the 1970s, real GDP in 2001 would have been about $1,700 billion, or $54,000 per person. Instead, real GDP was $1,035 billion, or $33,000 per person. So if the long-term trend of the 1960s had persisted, as a nation we would have had $665 billion more to spend. Each person (on the average) would have had $21,000 more each year. If the government had taken one-third of this extra income, it could have provided more health care, more education, more day-care services, and more and better highways. All these items could have been obtained with no cut in the provision of other goods and services. At the same time, you might have had another $14,000 a year to spend on whatever pleased you.

The main cost of economic growth is forgone consumption. To sustain a high growth rate, resources must be devoted to advancing technology and accumulating capital rather than to producing goods and services for current consumption. This cost cannot be avoided. But it brings the benefit of greater consumption in the future.

Two other possible costs of faster growth are a more rapid depletion of exhaustible natural resources such as oil and natural gas and increased pollution of the air, rivers, and oceans. But neither of these two costs is inevitable. The technological advances that bring economic growth help us to economize on natural resources and to clean up the environment. For example, more efficient auto engines cut gasoline use and tailpipe emissions.

A fourth possible cost of faster growth is more frequent job changes and more frequent moves from one region of the country to another. For example, during the 1990s, the economy of central Canada expanded and people migrated there from the Maritimes and the Prairies.

The pace of economic growth is determined by the choices that people make to balance the benefits and costs of economic growth. You'll study these choices and their consequences in Chapter 30.

REVIEW QUIZ

1. What is economic growth and how is the long-term economic growth rate measured?
2. What is the distinction between real GDP and *potential* GDP?
3. What is a business cycle and what are its phases?
4. What is a *recession*?
5. In what phase of the business cycle was the Canadian economy during 2001?
6. What happened to economic growth in Canada and other countries during the 1970s?
7. What are the similarities and differences in growth among the major economies?
8. What are the benefits and the costs of long-term economic growth?

We've seen that real GDP grows and that it fluctuates over the business cycle. The business cycle brings fluctuations in the number of jobs available and in unemployment. Let's now examine these core macroeconomic problems.

Jobs and Unemployment

WHAT KIND OF LABOUR MARKET WILL YOU ENTER when you graduate? Will there be plenty of good jobs to choose from, or will there be so much unemployment that you will be forced to take a low-paying job that doesn't use your education? The answer depends, to a large degree, on the total number of jobs available and on the unemployment rate.

Jobs

Finance Minister Paul Martin introduced the 1995 federal budget with what seemed to be an astonishing fact: "Canada is enjoying a period of strong economic growth and job creation. In the past year, 433,000 jobs have been created."

The Canadian economy is an incredible job-creating machine. In 2001, 15.1 million Canadians had jobs. That number is 2.2 million more than in 1991 and 3.8 million more than in 1981. But a year in which we create 433,000 new jobs is unusual. Every year, on the average, the Canadian economy creates about 200,000 *additional* jobs.

The pace of job creation and destruction fluctuates over the business cycle. More jobs are destroyed than created during a recession, so the number of jobs decreases. But more jobs are created than destroyed during an expansion, so the number of jobs increases. For example, during the recession of 1990–1991, Canadian production shrank and 250,000 jobs disappeared. But through the expansion that followed, the number of jobs created expanded quickly.

Unemployment

Not everyone who wants a job can find one. On any one day in a normal or average year, more than 1 million people are unemployed, and during a recession or depression, unemployment rises above this level. For example, in November 1992, the worst month for unemployment in recent times, 1,740,000 people were looking for jobs.

Unemployment is defined as a state in which a person does not have a job but is available for work, willing to work, and has made some effort to find work within the previous four weeks. The total number of people who are employed and unemployed is called the **labour force.** The **unemployment rate** is the percentage of the people in the labour force who are unemployed. (The concepts of the labour force and unemployment are explained more fully in Chapter 21 on pp. 480–481.)

The unemployment rate is not a perfect measure of the underutilization of labour for two main reasons. First, the unemployment rate excludes discouraged workers. A **discouraged worker** is a person who does not have a job, is available for work, and is willing to work but who has given up the effort to find work. Many people switch between the unemployed and discouraged worker categories in both directions every month. Second, the unemployment rate measures unemployed people rather than unemployed labour hours. As a result, the unemployment rate excludes part-time workers who want full-time jobs.

Despite these two limitations, the unemployment rate is the best available measure of underused labour resources. Let's look at some facts about unemployment.

Unemployment in Canada

Figure 19.6 shows the unemployment rate in Canada from 1926 through 2001. Three features stand out. First, during the Great Depression of the 1930s, the unemployment rate climbed to an all-time high of almost 20 percent during 1933 and remained high throughout the 1930s.

Second, the unemployment rate reached an all-time low of 1.2 percent during World War II.

Third, although in recent years we have not experienced anything as devastating as the Great Depression, we have seen some high unemployment rates during recessions. The figure highlights two of them—the 1982 recession and the 1990–1991 recession.

Fourth, the unemployment rate never falls to zero. In the period since World War II, the average unemployment rate has been 6.7 percent.

How does Canadian unemployment compare with unemployment in other countries?

FIGURE 19.6 Unemployment in Canada

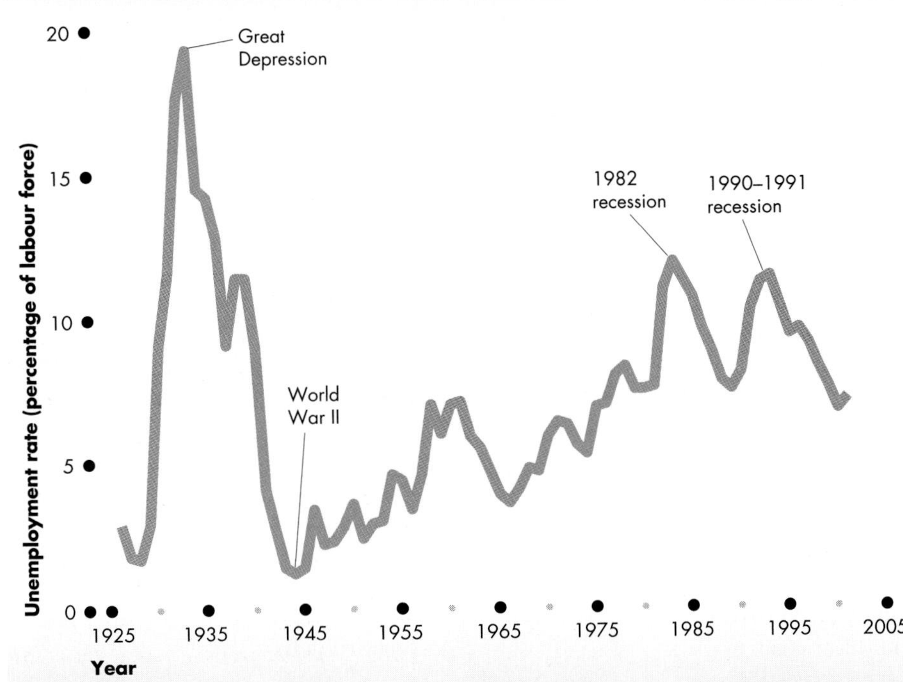

Unemployment is a persistent feature of economic life, but its rate varies. At its worst—during the Great Depression—20 percent of the labour force was unemployed. Even in recent recessions, the unemployment rate climbed towards 12 percent. Between the late 1960s and 1982, there was a general tendency for the unemployment rate to increase. Since 1982, the unemployment rate has remained below its 1982 peak and fell during the 1990s.

Sources: Statistics Canada, *Historical Statistics of Canada*, 2nd edition, 1983 and CANSIM Table 282-0002.

Unemployment Around the World

Figure 19.7 compares the unemployment rate in Canada with those in Western Europe, Japan, and the United States. Over the period shown in this figure, Canadian unemployment averaged 9.3 percent, much higher than Japanese unemployment (which averaged 3.0 percent), and higher than U.S. unemployment (which averaged 6.3 percent) and European unemployment (which averaged 8.6 percent).

Canadian unemployment fluctuates over the business cycle. It increases during a recession and decreases during an expansion. Like Canadian unemployment, U.S. and European unemployment increase during recessions and decrease during expansions. The cycles in Canadian unemployment are similar to those in U.S. unemployment, but the European cycle is out of phase with the North American cycle.

During the past 20 years, U.S. unemployment has been on a falling trend and during the past 10 years, Japanese unemployment has been on a rising trend. There have been no trends in the unemployment rates of Canada and Western Europe.

Let's now look at some of the consequences of unemployment that make it the serious problem that it is.

FIGURE 19.7 Unemployment in Industrial Economies

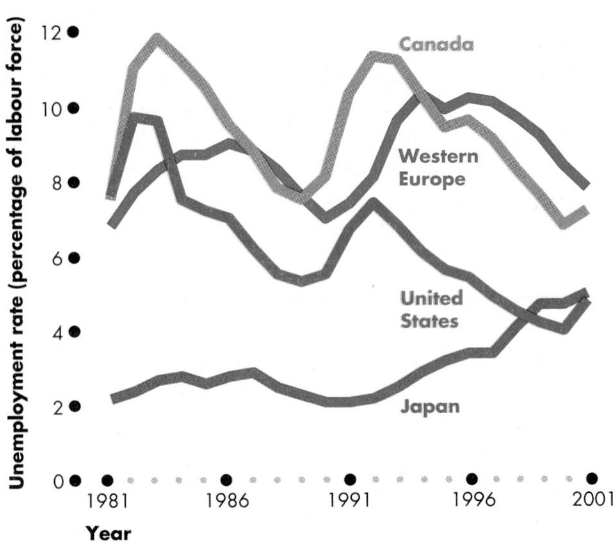

The unemployment rate in Canada has been higher, on the average, than the unemployment rates of the United States, Western Europe, and Japan. The cycles in Canadian unemployment are similar to those in the United States. Western European unemployment has a cycle that is out of phase with the North American unemployment cycle. Unemployment in Japan has drifted upward in recent years.

Source: International Monetary Fund, *World Economic Outlook*, September 2002, Washington, D.C.

Why Unemployment Is a Problem

Unemployment is a serious economic, social, and personal problem for two main reasons:

- Lost production and incomes
- Lost human capital

Lost Production and Incomes The loss of a job brings an immediate loss of income and production. These losses are devastating for the people who bear them and make unemployment a frightening prospect for everyone. Employment insurance creates a safety net, but it does not provide the same living standard that having a job provides.

Lost Human Capital Prolonged unemployment can permanently damage a person's job prospects. For example, a manager loses his job when his employer downsizes. Short of income, he becomes a taxi driver. After a year in this work, he discovers that he can't compete with new MBA graduates. He eventually gets hired as a manager but in a small firm and at a low wage. He has lost some of his human capital.

The costs of unemployment are spread unequally, which makes unemployment a highly charged political problem as well as a serious economic problem.

REVIEW QUIZ

1. What is unemployment?
2. What have been the main trends and cycles in the unemployment rate in Canada since 1926?
3. Compare unemployment in Canada, the United States, Western Europe, and Japan.
4. What are the main costs of unemployment that make it a serious problem?

Let's now turn to the third major macroeconomic issue: inflation.

Inflation

PRICES ON THE AVERAGE CAN BE RISING, FALLING, or stable. **Inflation** is a process of rising prices. We measure the *inflation rate* as the percentage change in the *average* level of prices or the **price level.** A common measure of the price level is the *Consumer Price Index* (CPI). The CPI tells us how the average price of all the goods and services bought by a typical urban household changes from month to month. (The CPI is explained in Chapter 21, p. 490.)

So that you can see how the inflation rate is measured, let's do a calculation. In December 2000, the CPI was 115.1, and in December 2001, it was 115.9, so the inflation rate during 2001 was

$$\text{Inflation rate} = \frac{115.9 - 115.1}{115.1} \times 100$$

$$= 0.7 \text{ percent.}$$

Inflation in Canada

Figure 19.8 shows the Canadian inflation rate from 1961 through 2001. During the early 1960s, the inflation rate was low. It began to increase during the late 1960s at the time of the Vietnam War. But the largest increases occurred in 1974 and 1980, years in which the actions of the Organization of Petroleum Exporting Countries (OPEC) resulted in exceptionally large increases in the price of oil. Inflation was brought under control in the early 1980s when Bank of Canada Governor Gerald Bouey and U.S. Federal Reserve Chairman Paul Volcker pushed interest rates up and people cut back on their spending. Since 1983, inflation has been relatively mild, and during the 1990s its rate continued to fall until 1998 when it began to increase again.

The inflation rate rises and falls over the years, but it rarely becomes negative. If the inflation rate is negative, the price *level* is falling and we have **deflation.** Since the 1930s, the price level has generally increased—the inflation rate has been positive.

FIGURE 19.8 Inflation in Canada

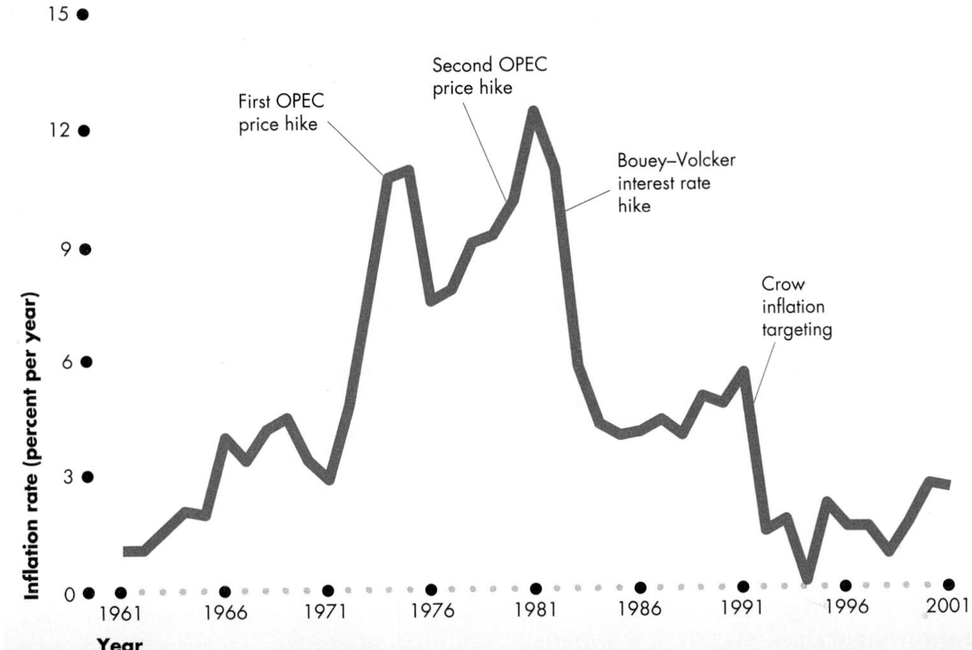

Inflation is a persistent feature of economic life in Canada. The inflation rate was low in the first half of the 1960s, but it increased during the late 1960s at the time of the Vietnam War. The inflation rate increased further with the OPEC oil price hikes but eventually declined in the early 1980s because of policy actions taken by the Bank of Canada. Since 1983, inflation has been mild, and during the 1990s it fell further. In the late 1990s, the inflation rate increased slightly and in 2001 was 2.6 percent.

Source: Statistics Canada CANSIM table 362-0002.

Inflation Around the World

Figure 19.9 shows inflation around the world since 1970. It also shows the Canadian inflation rate in a broader perspective. Part (a) shows that the other industrial countries shared Canada's burst of double-digit inflation during the 1970s and the decline in inflation during the 1980s and 1990s. But Canada has achieved a lower inflation rate than most countries. Part (b) shows that the average inflation rate of industrial countries has been very low compared with that of the developing counties. Among the developing countries, the most extreme inflation in recent times has occurred in the former Yugoslavia, where its rate has exceeded 6,000 percent per year.

FIGURE 19.9 Inflation Around the World

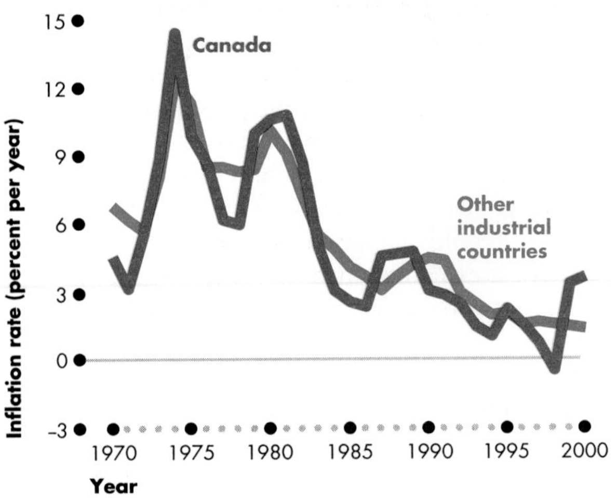

(a) Canada and other industrial countries

(b) Industrial countries and developing countries

Inflation in Canada is similar to that in the other industrial countries. Compared with the developing countries, inflation in Canada and the other industrial countries is low.

Sources: International Monetary Fund, *International Financial Statistics Yearbook*, Washington, D.C., 2001, and *World Economic Outlook*, October 2001.

Is Inflation a Problem?

A very low inflation rate is not much of a problem. But a high inflation rate is a serious problem. It makes inflation hard to predict, and unpredictable inflation makes the economy behave a bit like a casino in which some people gain and some lose and no one can predict where the gains and losses will fall. Gains and losses occur because of unpredictable changes in the value of money. Money is used as a measuring rod of value in the transactions that we undertake. Borrowers and lenders, workers and employers, all make contracts in terms of money. If the value of money varies unpredictably over time, then the amounts *really* paid and received—the quantity of goods that the money will buy—also fluctuate unpredictably. Measuring value with a measuring rod whose units vary is a bit like trying to measure a piece of cloth with an elastic ruler. The size of the cloth depends on how tightly the ruler is stretched.

In a period of rapid, unpredictable inflation, resources get diverted from productive activities to forecasting inflation. It becomes more profitable to forecast the inflation rate correctly than to invent a new product. Doctors, lawyers, accountants, farmers—just about everyone—can make themselves better off, not by specializing in the profession for which they have been trained but by spending more of their time dabbling as amateur economists and inflation forecasters and managing their investment portfolios.

From a social perspective, this diversion of talent resulting from inflation is like throwing scarce resources onto the garbage heap. This waste of resources is a cost of inflation.

The most serious type of inflation is called *hyperinflation*—an inflation rate that exceeds 50 percent a month. At the height of a hyperinflation, workers are often paid twice a day because money loses its value so quickly. As soon as workers are paid, they rush out to spend their wages before they lose too much value.

Hyperinflation is rare but there have been some spectacular examples of it. Several European countries experienced hyperinflation during the 1920s after World War I and again during the 1940s after World War II. But hyperinflation is more than just a historical curiosity. It occurs in today's world. In 1994, the African nation of Zaire had a hyperinflation that peaked at a *monthly* inflation rate of 76 percent, which is 88,000 percent a year! Brazil has also been close to the hyperinflation stratosphere with a monthly inflation rate of 40 percent. A cup of coffee that cost 15 cruzeiros in 1980 cost 22 *billion* cruzeiros in 1994.

Inflation imposes costs, but getting rid of inflation is also costly. Policies that lower the inflation rate increase the unemployment rate. Most economists think the increase in the unemployment rate that accompanies a fall in the inflation rate is temporary. But some economists say that higher unemployment is a permanent cost of low inflation. The cost of lowering inflation must be evaluated when an anti-inflation policy is pursued. You will learn more about inflation and the costs of curing it in Chapter 28.

REVIEW QUIZ

1. What is inflation and how does it influence the value of money?
2. How is inflation measured?
3. What has been Canada's inflation record since 1961?
4. How does inflation in Canada compare with inflation in other industrial countries and in developing countries?
5. What are some of the costs of inflation that make it a serious economic problem?

Now that you've studied economic growth and fluctuations, unemployment, and inflation, let's turn to the fourth macroeconomic issue: surpluses and deficits. What happens when a government spends more than it collects in taxes? And what happens when a nation buys more from other countries than it sells to them? Do governments and nations face the problem that you and I would face if we spent more than we earned? Do they run out of funds? Let's look at these questions.

Surpluses and Deficits

In 1998, for the first time in almost 30 years, the federal government had a budget surplus. For 28 years, it had a deficit. And most years, Canada has an international deficit. What is the government budget surplus and deficit? What is an international deficit?

Government Budget Surplus and Deficit

If a government collects more in taxes than it spends, it has a surplus—a **government budget surplus.** If a government spends more than it collects in taxes, it has a deficit—a **government budget deficit.** The federal government had a surplus in 2001.

Figure 19.10(a) shows the federal government and total government budget surplus and deficit from 1971 to 2001. (Total government is federal, provincial, and local government.) So that we can compare the surplus or deficit in one year with that in another year, we measure the surplus or deficit as a percentage of GDP. (The concept of GDP, which is explained more fully in Chapter 20, pp. 458–462, equals total income in the economy.) You can think of this measure as the number of cents of surplus or deficit per dollar of income earned by an average Canadian.

The total government had a budget deficit every year from 1975 through 1996. The government deficit fluctuated and swelled during recessions. From 1982 through 1996, the deficit was never less than 2 percent of GDP.

Since 1993, the federal government deficit has shrunk, and in 1998, a surplus emerged. Since 1998, the federal budget surplus has become larger. In 2001, the federal government surplus was 1.6 percent of GDP.

International Surplus and Deficit

When we import goods and services from the rest of the world, we make payments to foreigners. When we export goods and services to the rest of the world, we receive payments from foreigners. If our imports exceed our exports, we have an international deficit.

Figure 19.10(b) shows the history of Canada's international balance from 1971 to 2001. The figure shows the balance on the **current account,** which includes our exports minus our imports but also takes into account interest payments paid to and received from the rest of the world. To compare one year with

FIGURE 19.10 Government Budget and International Surpluses and Deficits

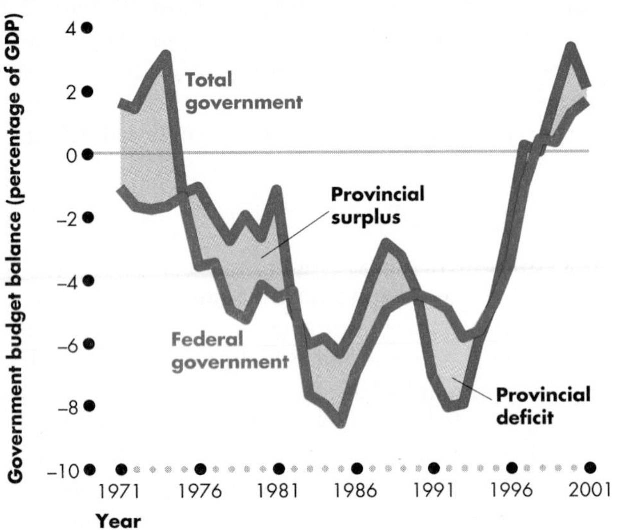

(a) Canadian government budget balance

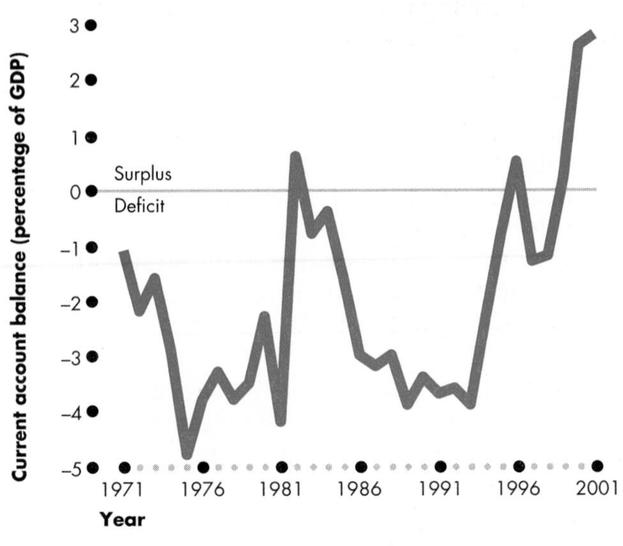

(b) Canadian international deficit

In part (a), the federal government had a large and persistent deficit between 1971 and the late-1990s. The provincial governments had a large deficit during the early 1990s. In part (b), the Canadian current account shows the balance of our exports minus our imports. In most years since 1970, Canada has had an international deficit. The deficit became large during the mid-1970s and early 1980s. It has persisted at around 3 to 4 percent of GDP through the mid-1990s. From 1999 to 2001, Canada had an international surplus.

Sources: Statistics Canada, CANSIM tables 376-0001, 380-0002, and 380-0007.

another, the figure shows the current account as a percentage of GDP. In 2001, Canada had a current account surplus of 2.8 percent of GDP. But in most years, Canada has had a current account deficit and it has fluctuated. From 1986 to 1995, the deficit was persistently around 3 percent to 4 percent of GDP. Our imports have exceeded our exports during these years. In 1996 and between 1999 and 2001, Canada had a current account surplus.

Do Surpluses and Deficits Matter?

Why do deficits cause anxiety? What happens when a government cannot cover its spending with taxes, or when a country buys more from other countries than it sells to them?

If you spend more than you earn, you have a deficit. And to cover your deficit, you go into debt. But when you borrow, you must pay interest on your debt. Just like you, if a government or a nation has a deficit, it must borrow. And like you, the government and the nation must pay interest on their debts.

Whether borrowing and paying out huge amounts of interest is a good idea depends on what the borrowed funds are used for. If you borrow to finance a vacation, you must eventually tighten your belt, cut spending, and repay your debt as well as pay interest on the debt. But if you borrow to invest in a business that earns a large profit, you might be able to repay your debt and pay the interest on it while continuing to increase your spending. It is the same with a government and a nation. A government or a nation that borrows to increase its consumption might be heading for trouble later. But a government or a nation that borrows to buy assets that earn a profit might be making a sound investment.

You will learn more about the government's budget surplus in Chapter 24 and about the international current account in Chapter 34.

REVIEW QUIZ

1. What determines a government's budget deficit or budget surplus?
2. How have the budgets of the federal government and the provincial governments evolved since 1971?
3. What is a country's international deficit?
4. How has the Canadian international deficit changed since 1971?

Macroeconomic Policy Challenges and Tools

FROM THE TIME OF ADAM SMITH'S *Wealth of Nations* in 1776 until the publication of Keynes' *General Theory of Employment, Interest, and Money* in 1936, it was widely believed that the only economic role for government was to enforce property rights. The economy behaved best, it was believed, if the government left people free to pursue their own best interests. The macroeconomics of Keynes challenged this view. Keynes' central point was that the economy will not fix itself and that government actions are needed to achieve and maintain full employment. The Canadian government declared full employment as a policy goal soon after World War II ended.

Policy Challenges and Tools

Today, the five widely agreed challenges for macroeconomic policy are to

1. Reduce unemployment
2. Boost economic growth
3. Stabilize the business cycle
4. Keep inflation low
5. Reduce government and international deficits

But how can we do all these things? What are the tools available to pursue the macroeconomic policy challenges? Macroeconomic policy tools are divided into two broad categories:

- Fiscal policy
- Monetary policy

Fiscal Policy Making changes in tax rates and in government spending programs is called **fiscal policy**. This range of actions is under the control of the federal government. Fiscal policy can be used to try to boost long-term growth by creating incentives that encourage saving, investment, and technological change. Fiscal policy can also be used to try to smooth out the business cycle. When the economy is in a recession, the government might cut taxes or increase its spending. Conversely, when the economy is in a rapid expansion, the government might increase taxes or cut its spending in an attempt to slow real GDP growth and prevent inflation from increasing. Fiscal policy is discussed in Chapter 24.

Monetary Policy Changing interest rates and changing the amount of money in the economy is called **monetary policy**. These actions are under the control of the Bank of Canada. The principal aim of monetary policy is to keep inflation in check. To achieve this objective, the Bank prevents the quantity of money from expanding too rapidly. Monetary policy can also be used to smooth the business cycle. When the economy is in recession, the Bank might lower interest rates and inject money into the economy. And when the economy is in a rapid expansion, the Bank might increase interest rates in an attempt to slow real GDP growth and prevent inflation from increasing. We study monetary policy in Chapters 25 and 26.

REVIEW QUIZ

1. What are the main challenges of macroeconomic policy?
2. What are the main tools of macroeconomic policy?
3. Can you distinguish between fiscal policy and monetary policy?

In your study of macroeconomics, you will learn what is currently known about the causes of unemployment, economic growth, business cycles, inflation, and government and international surpluses and deficits. You will also learn more about the policy choices and challenges that the government and the Bank of Canada face. *Reading Between the Lines* on pp. 452–453 examines inflation, deflation, and economic growth around the world in 2002.

READING BETWEEN THE LINES

Inflation, Deflation, and Economic Growth

NATIONAL POST, NOVEMBER 15, 2002

Buy technology stocks to hedge against deflation

Global economists are becoming worried about the risk of deflation. They are warning us of potential massive unemployment, terrible stock markets, economic collapse and widespread cannibalism. (OK... I made up the bit about cannibalism but economists tend to be a dry lot, and their pronouncements could use a little spicing up.)

Why the concern? Deflation is not a lowering of inflation rates; it is an absolute decline in prices. This creates a vicious cycle. Since goods get cheaper over time, why not wait and defer purchases?

If enough people do this, companies don't make money, nobody has jobs, prices go lower, and then even more people defer spending. Bad stuff. This spiral has crippled Japan for more than a decade. ...

In a recent newsletter, Toron Strategist Arthur Heinmaa talked about the possibility of deflation, the fact that the U.S. Federal Reserve is becoming increasingly aware of the dangers, and which kinds of companies are likely to do best if we do slip into deflation.

Mr. Heinmaa doesn't say that deflation is going to happen for sure, but says it is a big enough risk that as investors, we should at least partially deflation-proof our portfolios.

Investors should look for companies whose products are not commodities, with strong cash flows and minimal fixed debt. ...

Names like Microsoft, Cisco, Amgen and Intel (or Canada's Cognos, QLT or Dalsa) have good balance sheets and strong margins that reflect their considerable intellectual property.

Even after the bubble, Cisco is posting record gross margins (almost 70%), and over US$10-billion in cash. Software and drug makers routinely spend billions on research, but are still over 10 times as profitable as most industries.

Better yet, these companies already operate in a deflationary environment! The technology "industry has lived with deflation its entire existence," says University of British Columbia professor (and *Financial Post* columnist) Paul Kedrosky. ...

Essence of the Story

- Economists are warning about the risk of deflation—an absolute decline in the price level.
- Deflation is said to bring unemployment, a fall in the stock market, and economic collapse.
- Japan's economy is named as an example of the bad effects of deflation.
- Investors can protect themselves against deflation by buying stock in companies such as Microsoft, Cisco, Amgen, Intel, Cognos, QLT, and Dalsa, which have strong cash flows and small fixed debt.
- These companies already operate in a deflationary environment because the prices of their products have fallen every year.

Economic Analysis

■ Some economists fear the possibility of deflation in major economies such as the United States, but the consensus view is that deflation will not occur.

■ Deflation occurs when the quantity of money in the economy decreases. The opposite is happening in the United States and Canada today—we have inflation, not deflation.

■ It is true that Japan has had deflation and a poor economic performance.

■ But there is no simple and strong relationship between inflation and deflation on the one hand, and broader economic performance on the other hand.

■ Some countries have deflation and a strong economy, while others have deflation and a weak economy.

■ Also, some countries have inflation and a strong economy, while others have inflation and a weak economy.

■ Figure 1 shows the inflation and deflation rates in 2002 around the world. They ranged from an inflation rate of almost 140 percent per year in Zimbabwe to a deflation rate of 7 percent a year in Ethiopia.

■ Six countries (or territories) had deflation: Ethiopia, Hong Kong, Uganda, Bahrain, Japan, and China.

■ Compare these inflation and deflation rates with economic growth rates—a measure of the overall strength of the economy—shown in Fig. 2.

■ As the news article notes, Japan has deflation and a negative growth rate (a shrinking economy).

■ Angola, with the fastest growth rate, has a high inflation rate.

■ But high inflation and fast growth do not go together—neither do deflation and negative growth.

■ China, with the second-fastest growth rate, has a small deflation rate. Argentina, with the fastest shrinking rate, has one of the highest inflation rates. The biggest deflation occurred in Ethiopia—a country whose growth rate in 2002 was one of the highest.

■ The news article might be correct about the stocks that give the best protection against deflation. (We are not endorsing those recommendations!)

■ But the news article is incorrect when it says that these technology firms have experienced deflation. They have not—deflation is a falling price *level*, not a falling price of a particular group of goods.

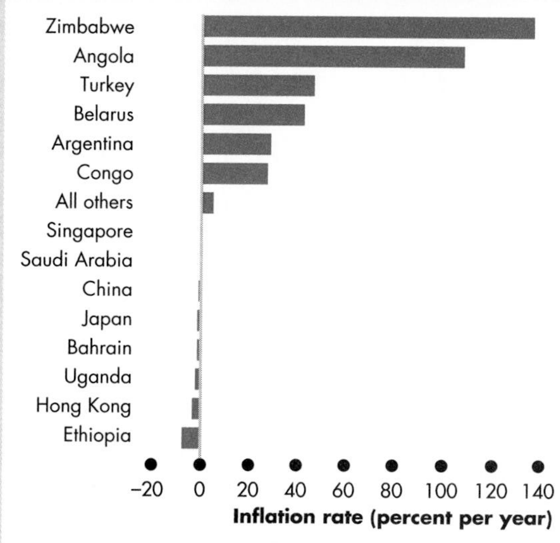

Figure 1 Inflation rates in 2002

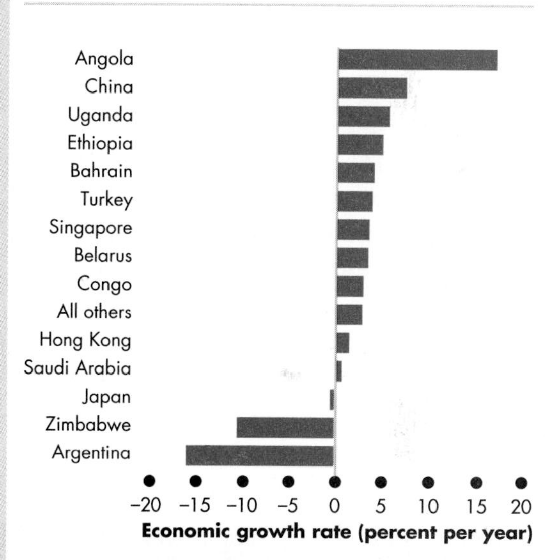

Figure 2 Economic growth rates in 2002

SUMMARY

KEY POINTS

Origins and Issues of Macroeconomics (p. 438)

- Macroeconomics studies economic growth and fluctuations, jobs and unemployment, inflation, and surpluses and deficits.

Economic Growth (pp. 439–444)

- Economic growth is the expansion of potential GDP. Real GDP fluctuates around potential GDP in a business cycle.
- Countries have similar business cycles but different long-term trends in potential GDP.
- The main benefit of long-term economic growth is higher future consumption, and the main cost is lower current consumption.

Jobs and Unemployment (pp. 444–446)

- The Canadian economy creates about 200,000 jobs a year but unemployment persists.
- Canadian unemployment increases during a recession and decreases during an expansion.
- The Canadian unemployment rate is higher than that in the United States and Japan.
- Unemployment can permanently damage a person's job prospects.

Inflation (pp. 447–449)

- Inflation, a process of rising prices, is measured by the percentage change in the CPI.
- Inflation is a problem because it lowers the value of money and makes money less useful as a measuring rod of value.

Surpluses and Deficits (pp. 449–451)

- When the government collects more in taxes than it spends, the government has a budget surplus. When the government spends more than it collects in taxes, the government has a budget deficit.
- When imports exceed exports, a nation has an international deficit.
- Deficits are financed by borrowing.

Macroeconomic Policy Challenges and Tools (p. 451)

- The macroeconomic policy challenge is to use fiscal policy and monetary policy to boost long-term growth, stabilize the business cycle, lower unemployment, tame inflation, and prevent large deficits.

KEY FIGURES

Figure 19.1 Economic Growth in Canada, 439
Figure 19.2 The Most Recent Canadian Business Cycle, 440
Figure 19.3 Long-Term Economic Growth in Canada, 441
Figure 19.6 Unemployment in Canada, 445
Figure 19.8 Inflation in Canada, 447
Figure 19.10 Government Budget and International Surpluses and Deficits, 450

KEY TERMS

Current account, 449
Deflation, 447
Discouraged worker, 445
Economic growth, 439
Expansion, 440
Fiscal policy, 451
Government budget deficit, 449
Government budget surplus, 449
Great Depression, 438
Growth recession, 440
Inflation, 447
Labour force, 444
Monetary policy, 451
Peak, 440
Potential GDP, 439
Price level, 447
Productivity growth slowdown, 439
Real gross domestic product (real GDP), 439
Recession, 440
Trough, 440
Unemployment, 444
Unemployment rate, 444

PROBLEMS

*1. Use Data Graphing in Chapter 19 of *Economics in Action* to answer the following questions. In which country in 1992 was
   a. The growth rate of real GDP highest: Canada, Japan, or the United States?
   b. The unemployment rate highest: Canada, Japan, the United Kingdom, or the United States?
   c. The inflation rate lowest: Canada, Germany, the United Kingdom, or the United States?
   d. The government budget deficit (as a percentage of GDP) largest: Canada, Japan, the United Kingdom, or the United States?

2. Use Data Graphing in Chapter 19 of *Economics in Action* to answer the following questions. In which country in 2000 was
   a. The growth rate of real GDP highest: Canada, Japan, or the United States?
   b. The unemployment rate lowest: Canada, Japan, the United Kingdom, or the United States?
   c. The inflation rate lowest: Canada, the United Kingdom, Japan, or the United States?
   d. The government budget surplus (as a percentage of GDP) smallest: Canada, the United Kingdom, or the United States?
   e. Is it possible to say in which country consumption possibilities are growing fastest? Why or why not?

*3. The figure shows the real GDP growth rates in India and Pakistan from 1989 to 1996.

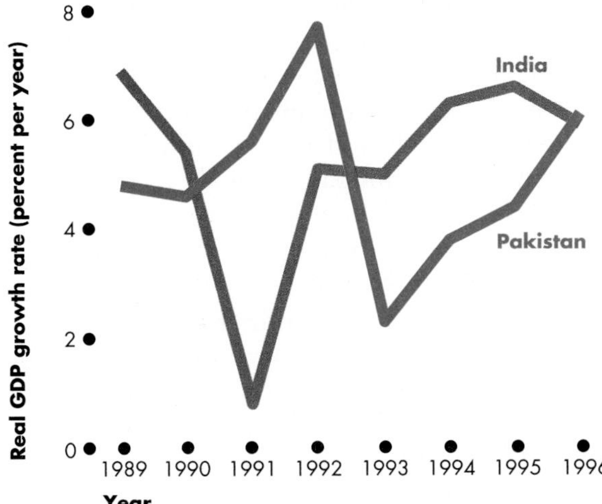

In which years did economic growth in
   a. India increase? And in which year was growth the fastest?
   b. Pakistan decrease? And in which year was growth the slowest?
   c. Compare the paths of economic growth in India and Pakistan during this period.

4. The figure shows real GDP per person in Australia and Japan from 1989 to 1996.

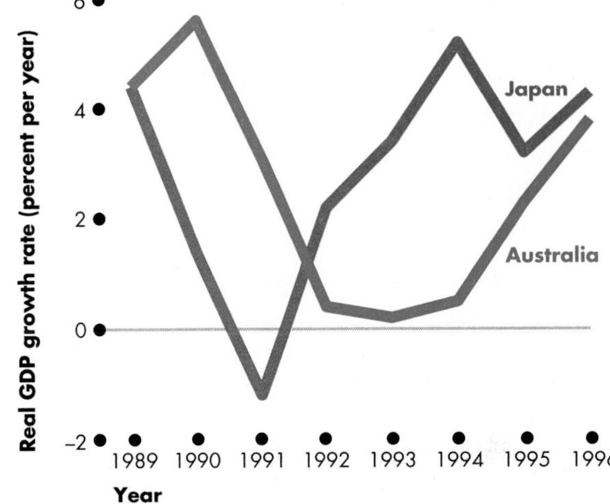

In which years did economic growth in
   a. Australia increase? And in which year was growth the fastest?
   b. Japan decrease? And in which year was growth the slowest?
   c. Compare the paths of economic growth in Australia and Japan during this period.

*5. The figure shows real GDP in Germany from the first quarter of 1991 to the fourth quarter of 1994.

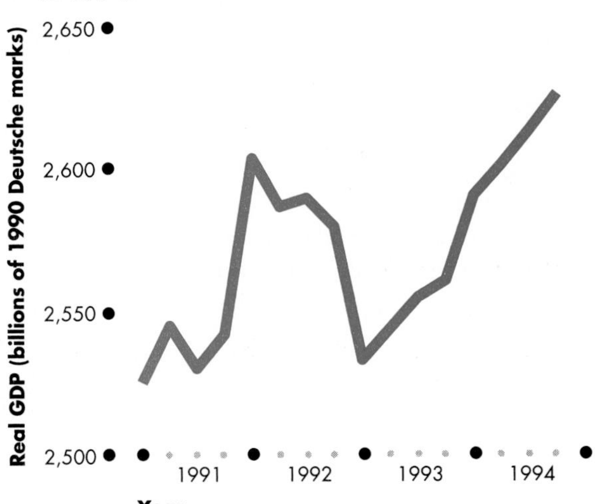

a. How many recessions did Germany experience during this period?
b. In which quarters, if any, did Germany experience a business cycle peak?
c. In which quarters, if any, did Germany experience a business cycle trough?
d. In which quarters, if any, did Germany experience an expansion?

6. The table shows Canada's rate of economic growth during 2001 and the first three quarters of 2002.

	2001	2002
First quarter	0.6	5.8
Second quarter	0.3	4.1
Third quarter	–0.5	3.0
Fourth quarter	2.9	

a. Did Canada experience a recession during this period?
b. Did the economic growth rate speed up or slow down during 2002?
c. Which of the two years had the highest average economic growth rate?

*7. Use Data Graphing in Chapter 19 of *Economics in Action* to answer the following questions. Which country, in 1998, had
a. The largest budget deficit: Canada, Japan, the United Kingdom, or the United States?
b. A current account surplus: Canada, Japan, Germany, or the United States?

8. Use Data Graphing in Chapter 19 of *Economics in Action* to answer the following questions. Which country, in 2002, had
a. The largest budget surplus: Canada, Japan, the United Kingdom, or the United States?
b. The largest current account deficit: Canada, Japan, Germany, or the United States?

*9. Use Data Graphing in Chapter 19 of *Economics in Action* to make a scatter diagram of the inflation rate and the unemployment rate in Canada.
a. Describe the relationship.
b. Do you think that low unemployment brings an increase in the inflation rate?

10. Use Data Graphing in Chapter 19 of *Economics in Action* to make a scatter diagram of the government budget deficit as a percentage of GDP and the unemployment rate in Canada.
a. Describe the relationship.
b Do you think that low unemployment brings a decrease in the budget deficit?

CRITICAL THINKING

1. Study *Reading Between the Lines* on pp. 452–453 and then answer the following questions:
a. Which countries experienced deflation during 2002?
b. Of the countries that experienced deflation, which experienced negative economic growth?
c. Which countries experienced high inflation rates during 2002?
d. Of the countries that experienced high inflation rates, which experienced negative economic growth?
e. What do you think the data presented in the figures on page 453 tell us about the effects of deflation?

WEB EXERCISES

1. Use the links on the Parkin–Bade Web site to obtain the latest data on real GDP, unemployment, and inflation in Canada
a. Update the figures on pages 440, 445, and 447.
b. What dangers does the Canadian economy face today?
c. What actions, if any, do you think might be needed to keep the economy strong?

2. Use the links on the Parkin–Bade Web site to obtain data on unemployment in your home province.
a. Compare unemployment in your home province with that in Canada as a whole.
b. Why do you think your province might have a higher or a lower unemployment rate than the Canadian average?

3. Use the links on the Parkin–Bade Web site to obtain data on the Consumer Price Index for the capital city in your home province.
a. Compare the inflation rate in your home province with that in Canada as a whole.
b. Compare the inflation rate in your home province with that of the capital cities in neighbouring provinces.

4. Use the links on the Parkin–Bade Web site to obtain data on the following variables for Canada for the most recent period. Describe how the following variables have changed over the last year.
a. The unemployment rate
b. The inflation rate
c. The government budget surplus or deficit
d. The international deficit

MEASURING GDP AND ECONOMIC GROWTH

CHAPTER 20

An Economic Barometer

Has our economy avoided the recession that in 2001 and 2002 hit the United States and several other parts of the world? In the fall of 2002, many Canadian and foreign corporations wanted to know the answer to this question. Nortel wanted to know whether to lay off more workers or delay the layoffs for a while in the hope that the economy might expand. Bombardier wanted to know whether to expand its capacity to build railroad engines. To assess the state of the economy and to make big decisions about business contraction and expansion, firms such as Nortel and Bombardier use forecasts of GDP. What exactly *is* GDP and how can we use it to tell us whether we are in a recession or how rapidly our economy is expanding? ◆ To reveal the growth or shrinkage of GDP, we must remove the effects of inflation and assess how *real* GDP is changing. How do we remove the inflation component of GDP to reveal *real* GDP? ◆ Some countries are rich while others are poor. How do we compare economic well-being in one country with that in another? How can we make international comparisons of GDP?

◇ In this chapter, you will find out how economic statisticians measure GDP, real GDP, and the economic growth rate. You will also learn about the limitations of these measures. In *Reading Between the Lines* at the end of the chapter, we'll look at Canadian real GDP during 2002.

After studying this chapter, you will be able to

- **Define GDP and use the circular flow model to explain why GDP equals aggregate expenditure and aggregate income**
- **Explain the two ways of measuring GDP**
- **Explain how we measure *real* GDP and the GDP deflator**
- **Explain how we use real GDP to measure economic growth and describe the limitations of our measure**

Gross Domestic Product

WHAT EXACTLY IS GDP, HOW IS IT CALCULATED, what does it mean, and why do we care about it? You are going to discover the answers to these questions in this chapter. First, what *is* GDP?

GDP Defined

GDP, or **gross domestic product**, is the market value of all the final goods and services produced within a country in a given time period. This definition has four parts:

- Market value
- Final goods and services
- Produced within a country
- In a given time period

We'll examine each in turn.

Market Value To measure total production, we must add together the production of apples and oranges, computers and popcorn. Just counting the items doesn't get us very far. For example, which is the greater total production: 100 apples and 50 oranges, or 50 apples and 100 oranges?

GDP answers this question by valuing items at their *market values*—at the prices at which each item is traded in markets. If the price of an apple is 10 cents, the market value of 50 apples is $5. If the price of an orange is 20 cents, the market value of 100 oranges is $20. By using market prices to value production, we can add the apples and oranges together. The market value of 50 apples and 100 oranges is $5 plus $20, or $25.

Final Goods and Services To calculate GDP, we value the *final goods and services* produced. A **final good** (or service) is an item that is bought by its final user during a specified time period. It contrasts with an **intermediate good** (or service), which is an item that is produced by one firm, bought by another firm, and used as a component of a final good or service.

For example, a Ford SUV is a final good, but a Firestone tire on the SUV is an intermediate good. A Dell computer is a final good, but an Intel Pentium chip inside it is an intermediate good.

If we were to add the value of intermediate goods and services produced to the value of final goods and services, we would count the same thing many times—a problem called *double counting*. The value of an SUV already includes the value of the tires, and the value of a Dell PC already includes the value of the Pentium chip inside it.

Some goods can be an intermediate good in some situations and a final good in other situations. For example, the ice cream that you buy on a hot summer day is a final good, but the ice cream that a café buys and uses to make sundaes is an intermediate good. The sundae is the final good. So whether a good is an intermediate good or a final good depends on what it is used for, not on what it is.

Produced Within a Country Only goods and services that are produced *within a country* count as part of that country's GDP. Bata Limited, a Canadian firm, produces shoes in Thailand, and the market value of those shoes is part of Thailand's GDP, not part of Canada's GDP. Toyota, a Japanese firm, produces automobiles in Cambridge, Ontario, and the value of this production is part of Canada's GDP, not part of Japan's GDP.

In a Given Time Period GDP measures the value of production *in a given time period*—normally either a quarter of a year (called the quarterly GDP data) or a year (called the annual GDP data). Some components of GDP are measured for a period as short as a month, but we have no reliable monthly GDP data.

Businesses such as Bell Canada and the Bank of Montreal and governments use the quarterly GDP data to keep track of the short-term evolution of the economy. They use the annual GDP data to examine long-term trends and changes in production and the standard of living.

GDP measures not only the value of total production but also total income and total expenditure. The equality between the value of total production and total income is important because it shows the direct link between productivity and living standards. Our standard of living rises when our incomes rise and we can afford to buy more goods and services. But we must produce more goods and services if we are to be able to buy more goods and services.

Rising incomes and a rising value of production go together. They are two aspects of the same phenomenon—increasing productivity. To see why, we study the circular flow of expenditure and income.

GDP and the Circular Flow of Expenditure and Income

Figure 20.1 illustrates the circular flow of expenditure and income. The economy consists of households, firms, governments, and the rest of the world (the diamonds), which trade in factor markets, goods (and services) markets, and financial markets. We focus first on households and firms.

Households and Firms Households sell and firms buy the services of labour, capital, and land in factor markets. For these factor services, firms pay income to households: wages for labour services, interest for the use of capital, and rent for the use of land. A fourth factor of production, entrepreneurship, receives profit.

Firms' retained earnings—profits that are not distributed to households—are part of the household sector's income. You can think of retained earnings as being income that households save and lend back to firms. Figure 20.1 shows the total income—*aggregate income*—received by households, including retained earnings, by the blue dots labelled *Y*.

Firms sell and households buy consumer goods and services—such as inline skates and haircuts—in the markets for goods and services. The total payment for these goods and services is **consumption expenditure,** shown by the red dots labelled *C*.

Firms buy and sell new capital equipment—such as computer systems, airplanes, trucks, and assembly line equipment—in the goods market. Some of what firms produce is not sold but is added to inventory. For example, if GM produces 1,000 cars and sells 950 of them, the other 50 cars remain in GM's inventory of unsold cars, which increases by 50 cars. When a firm adds unsold output to inventory, we can think of the firm as buying goods from itself. The

FIGURE 20.1 The Circular Flow of Expenditure and Income

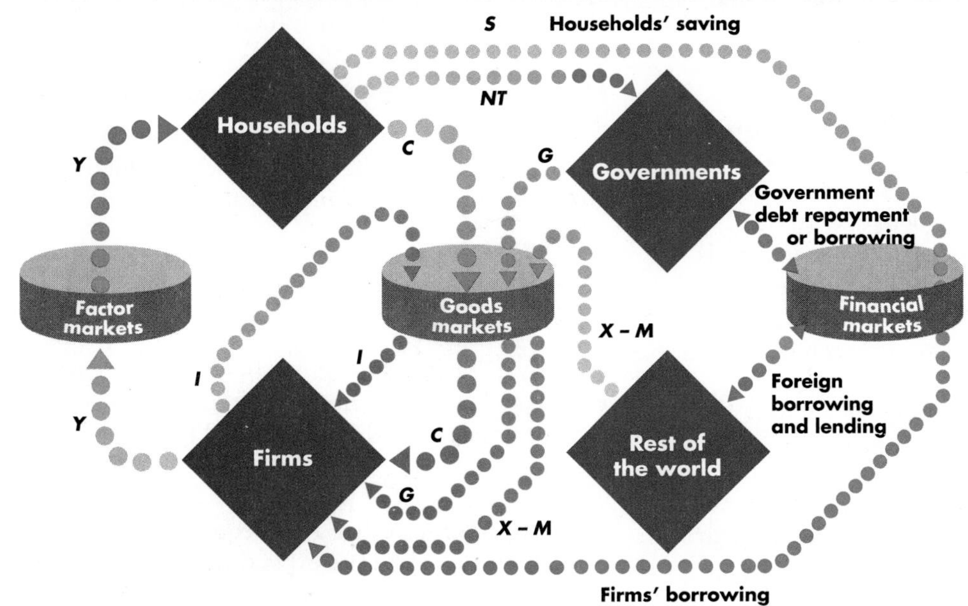

Billions of dollars in 2001		
C	=	621
I	=	184
G	=	231
X – *M*	=	56
Y	=	1,092
C	=	621
S	=	218
NT	=	253
Y	=	1,092

Source: Statistics Canada, CANSIM table 380-0002.

In the circular flow of expenditure and income, households make consumption expenditures (*C*); firms make investment expenditures (*I*); governments purchase goods and services (*G*); and the rest of the world purchases net exports (*X* – *M*)—(red flows). Households receive incomes (*Y*) from firms (blue flow).

Aggregate income (blue flow) equals aggregate expenditure (red flows). Households use their income to consume (*C*), save (*S*), and pay net taxes (*NT*). Firms borrow to finance their investment expenditures, and governments and the rest of the world borrow to finance their deficits or lend their surpluses (green flows).

purchase of new plant, equipment, and buildings and the additions to inventories are **investment,** shown by the red dots labelled I.

Governments Governments buy goods and services, called **government expenditures,** from firms. In Fig. 20.1, government expenditures on goods and services are shown as the red flow G. Governments use taxes to pay for their purchases. Figure 20.1 shows taxes as net taxes by the green dots labelled NT. **Net taxes** are equal to taxes paid to governments minus transfer payments received from governments. *Transfer payments* are cash transfers from governments to households and firms, such as social security benefits, unemployment compensation, and subsidies, and interest payments on the governments' debt.

Rest of the World Firms sell goods and services to the rest of the world, **exports**, and buy goods and services from the rest of the world, **imports**. The value of exports minus the value of imports are called **net exports**, which Fig. 20.1 shows by the red flow $X-M$.

If net exports are positive, there is a net flow from the rest of the world to Canadian firms. If net exports are negative, there is net flow from Canadian firms to the rest of the world.

GDP Equals Expenditure Equals Income Gross domestic product can be determined in two ways: by the total expenditure on goods and services or by the total income earned producing goods and services.

The total expenditure—*aggregate expenditure*—is the sum of the red flows in Fig. 20.1. Aggregate expenditure equals consumption expenditure plus investment plus government expenditures plus net exports.

Aggregate income earned producing goods and services is equal to the total amount paid for the factors used—wages, interest, rent, and profit. This amount is shown by the blue flow in Fig. 20.1. Because firms pay out as incomes (including retained profits) everything they receive from the sale of their output, income (the blue flow) equals expenditure (the sum of the red flows). That is,

$$Y = C + I + G + X - M.$$

The table in Fig. 20.1 shows the numbers for 2001. You can see that the sum of the expenditures is $1,092 billion, which also equals aggregate income.

Because aggregate expenditure equals aggregate income, these two methods of valuing GDP give the same answer. So

GDP equals aggregate expenditure and equals aggregate income.

The circular flow model is the foundation on which the national economic accounts are built.

Financial Flows

The circular flow model also enables us to see the connection between the expenditure and income flows and flows through the financial markets that finance deficits and pay for investment. These flows are shown in green in Fig. 20.1. Household **saving** (S) is the amount that households have left after they have paid their net taxes and bought their consumption goods and services. Government borrowing finances a government budget deficit. (Government lending arises when the government has a budget surplus.) And foreign borrowing pays for a deficit with the rest of the world. These financial flows are the sources of the funds that firms use to pay for their investment in new capital. Let's look a bit more closely at how investment is financed.

How Investment Is Financed

Investment adds to the stock of capital and is one of the determinants of the rate at which production grows. Investment is financed from three sources:

1. Private saving
2. Government budget surplus
3. Borrowing from the rest of the world

Private saving is the green flow labelled S in Fig. 20.1. Notice that households' income is consumed, saved, or paid in net taxes. That is,

$$Y = C + S + NT.$$

But you've seen that Y also equals the sum of the components of aggregate expenditure. That is,

$$Y = C + I + G + X - M.$$

By using these two equations, you can see that

$$I + G + X - M = S + NT$$

Now subtract G and X from both sides of the last equation and add M to both sides to obtain

$$I = S + (NT - G) + (M - X).$$

In this equation, $(NT - G)$ is the government budget surplus and $(M - X)$ is borrowing from the rest of the world.

If net taxes (NT) exceed government expenditures (G), the government has a budget surplus equal to $(NT - G)$, and this surplus contributes towards paying for investment. If net taxes are less than government expenditures, the government has a budget deficit equal to $(NT - G)$, which is now negative. This deficit subtracts from the sources that finance investment.

If we import more than we export, we borrow an amount equal to $(M - X)$ from the rest of the world. So part of the rest of the world's saving finances investment in Canada. If we export more than we import, we lend an amount equal to $(X - M)$ to the rest of the world. So part of Canadian saving is used to finance investment in other countries.

The sum of private saving (S) and government saving $(NT - G)$ is called **national saving.** So investment is financed by national saving and foreign borrowing. In 2002, Canadian investment was \$184 billion. National saving was \$240 billion and $X - M$ was \$56 billion. Canada lent \$56 billion to the rest of the world.

Gross and Net Domestic Product

What does the "gross" in GDP mean? *Gross* means *before* accounting for the depreciation of capital. The opposite of gross is *net*, which means *after* accounting for the depreciation of capital. To understand what the depreciation of capital is and how it affects aggregate expenditure and income, we need to expand the accounting framework that we use and distinguish between flows and stocks.

Flows and Stocks in Macroeconomics A **flow** is a quantity per unit of time. The water that is running from an open faucet into a bathtub is a flow. So is the number of CDs you buy during a month and the amount of income that you earn during a month. GDP is a flow—the value of the goods and services produced in a country *during a given time period.* Saving and investment are also flows.

A **stock** is a quantity that exists at a point in time. The water in a bathtub is a stock. So are the number of CDs that you own and the amount of money in your savings account. The two key stocks in macroeconomics are wealth and capital. And the flows of saving and investment change these stocks.

Wealth and Saving The value of all the things that people own is called **wealth.** What people own (a stock) is related to what they earn (a flow). People earn an income, which is the amount they receive during a given time period from supplying the services of factors of production. Income that is left after paying net taxes is either consumed or saved. *Consumption expenditure* is the amount spent on consumption goods and services. *Saving* is the amount of income remaining after consumption expenditures are met. So saving adds to wealth.

For example, suppose that at the end of the school year, you have \$250 in a savings account and some textbooks that are worth \$300. That's all you own. Your wealth is \$550. Suppose that you take a summer job and earn an income after taxes of \$5,000. You are extremely careful and spend only \$1,000 through the summer on consumption goods and services. At the end of the summer, when school starts again, you have \$4,250 in your savings account. Your wealth is now \$4,550. Your wealth has increased by \$4,000, which equals your saving of \$4,000. Your saving of \$4,000 equals your income of \$5,000 minus your consumption expenditure of \$1,000.

National wealth and national saving work just like this personal example. The wealth of a nation at the start of a year equals its wealth at the start of the previous year plus its saving during the year. Its saving equals its income minus its consumption expenditure.

Capital and Investment *Capital* is the plant, equipment, buildings, and inventories of raw materials and semi-finished goods that are used to produce other goods and services. The amount of capital in the economy exerts a big influence on GDP.

Two flows change the stock of capital: investment and depreciation. *Investment,* the purchase of new capital, increases the stock of capital. (Investment includes additions to inventories.) **Depreciation** is the decrease in the stock of capital that results from wear and tear and obsolescence. Another name for depreciation is **capital consumption.** The total amount spent on purchases of new capital and on replacing depreciated capital is called **gross investment.** The amount by which the stock of capital increases is called **net investment.** Net investment equals gross investment minus depreciation.

Figure 20.2 illustrates these concepts. On January 1, 2003, Tom's Tapes, Inc., had 3 machines.

This quantity was its initial capital. During 2003, Tom's scrapped an older machine. This quantity is its depreciation. After depreciation, Tom's stock of capital was down to 2 machines. But also during 2003, Tom's bought 2 new machines. This amount is its gross investment. By December 31, 2003, Tom's Tapes had 4 machines, so its capital had increased by 1 machine. This amount is Tom's net investment. Tom's net investment equals its gross investment (the purchase of 2 new machines) minus its depreciation (1 machine scrapped).

The example of Tom's Tapes can be applied to the economy as a whole. The nation's capital stock decreases because capital depreciates and increases because of gross investment. The change in the nation's capital stock from one year to the next equals its net investment.

FIGURE 20.2 Capital and Investment

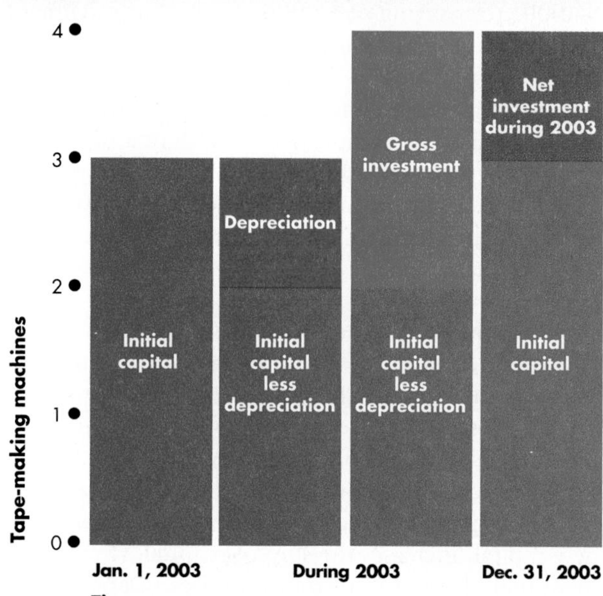

Tom's Tapes has a capital stock at the end of 2003 that equals its capital stock at the beginning of the year plus its net investment. Net investment is equal to gross investment less depreciation. Tom's gross investment is the 2 new machines bought during the year, and its depreciation is the 1 machine that Tom's scrapped during the year. Tom's net investment is 1 machine.

Back to the Gross in GDP We can now see the distinction between gross domestic product and net domestic product. On the income side of the flows that measure GDP, a firm's *gross* profit is its profit *before* subtracting *depreciation.* A firm's gross profit is part of aggregate income, so depreciation is counted as part of gross income and GDP. Similarly, on the expenditure side of the flows that measure GDP, *gross investment* includes depreciation, so depreciation is counted as part of aggregate expenditure, and total expenditure is a gross measure.

Net domestic product excludes depreciation. Like GDP, net domestic product can be viewed as the sum of incomes or expenditures. Net income includes firms' *net* profits—profits *after* subtracting depreciation. And net expenditure includes *net* investment, which also excludes depreciation.

The Short Term Meets the Long Term The flows and stocks that you've just studied influence GDP growth and fluctuations. One of the reasons why GDP grows is that the capital stock grows. Investment adds to capital, so GDP grows because of investment. But investment fluctuates, which brings fluctuations to GDP. So capital and investment along with wealth and saving are part of the key to understanding both the growth and the fluctuations of GDP.

Investment and saving interact with income and consumption expenditure in a circular flow of expenditure and income. In this circular flow, income equals expenditure, which also equals the value of production. This equality is the foundation on which a nation's economic accounts are built and from which its GDP is measured.

REVIEW QUIZ

1. Define GDP and distinguish between a final good and an intermediate good. Provide examples.
2. Why does GDP equal aggregate income and also equal aggregate expenditure?
3. How is Canadian investment financed? What determines national saving?
4. What is the distinction between gross and net?

Let's now see how the ideas that you've just studied are used in practice. We'll see how GDP and its components are measured in Canada today.

Measuring Canada's GDP

STATISTICS CANADA USES THE CONCEPTS THAT you met in the circular flow model to measure GDP and its components in the *National Income and Expenditure Accounts.* Because the value of aggregate output equals aggregate expenditure and aggregate income, there are two approaches available for measuring GDP, and both are used. They are

- The expenditure approach
- The income approach

The Expenditure Approach

The *expenditure approach* measures GDP as the sum of consumption expenditure (*C*), investment (*I*), government expenditures on goods and services (*G*), and net exports of goods and services (*X* – *M*), corresponding to the red flows in the circular flow model in Fig. 20.1. Table 20.1 shows the result of this approach for 2001. The table uses the terms in the *National Income and Expenditure Accounts.*

Personal expenditures on consumer goods and services are the expenditures by households on goods and services produced in Canada and in the rest of the world. They include goods such as CDs and books and services such as banking and legal advice. They do *not* include the purchase of new homes, which is counted as part of investment. But they do include the purchase of consumer durable goods, which technically are capital like homes.

Business investment is expenditure on capital equipment and buildings by firms and expenditure on new homes by households. It also includes the change in business inventories.

Government expenditures on goods and services are the purchases of goods and services by all levels of government. This item includes expenditures on national defence and garbage collection. But it does *not* include *transfer payments* because they are not purchases of goods and services.

Net exports of goods and services are the value of exports minus the value of imports. This item includes telephone equipment that Nortel sells to AT&T in the United States (a Canadian export), and Japanese DVD players that Sears buys from Sony (a Canadian import).

Table 20.1 shows the relative magnitudes of the four items of aggregate expenditure.

TABLE 20.1 GDP: The Expenditure Approach

Item	Symbol	Amount in 2001 (billions of dollars)	Percentage of GDP
Personal expenditures on consumer goods and services	*C*	621	56.9
Business investment	*I*	184	16.8
Government expenditures on goods and services	*G*	231	21.2
Net exports of goods and services	*X* – *M*	56	5.1
Gross domestic product	*Y*	1,092	100.0

The expenditure approach measures GDP as the sum of personal expenditures on consumer goods and services (*C*), business investment (*I*), government expenditures on goods and services (*G*), and net exports (*X* – *M*). In 2001, GDP measured by the expenditure approach was $1,092 billion. Personal expenditures on consumer goods and services is the largest expenditure item.

Source: Statistics Canada, CANSIM table 380-0002.

The Income Approach

The *income approach* measures GDP by summing the incomes that firms pay households for the factors of production they hire—wages for labour, interest for capital, rent for land, and profits for entrepreneurship. Let's see how the income approach works.

The *National Income and Expenditure Accounts* divide incomes into five categories:

1. Wages, salaries, and supplementary labour income
2. Corporate profits
3. Interest and miscellaneous investment income
4. Farmers' income
5. Income from non-farm unincorporated businesses

Wages, salaries, and supplementary labour income is the payment for labour services. It includes net wages and salaries (called "take-home pay") plus taxes withheld plus benefits such as pension contributions.

Corporate profits are the profits of corporations, some of which are paid to households in the form of dividends and some of which are retained by corporations as undistributed profits. They are all income.

Interest and miscellaneous investment income is the interest households receive on loans they make minus the interest households pay on their own borrowing.

Farmers' income and *income from non-farm unincorporated businesses* are a mixture of the previous three items. They include compensation for labour, payment for the use of capital, and profit, lumped together in these two catch-all categories.

Table 20.2 shows these five incomes and their relative magnitudes.

The sum of the incomes is called *net domestic income at factor cost.* The term *factor cost* is used because it is the cost of the *factors of production* used to produce final goods and services. When we sum all the expenditures on final goods and services, we arrive at a total called *domestic product at market prices.* Market prices and factor cost would be the same except for indirect taxes and subsidies.

An *indirect tax* is a tax paid by consumers when they buy goods and services. (In contrast, a *direct tax* is a tax on income.) Provincial sales taxes, GST, and taxes on alcohol, gasoline, and tobacco products are indirect taxes. Because of indirect taxes, consumers pay more for some goods and services than producers receive. Market price exceeds factor cost. For example, if the sales tax is 7 percent, when you buy a $1 chocolate bar you pay $1.07. The factor cost of the chocolate bar including profit is $1. The market price is $1.07.

A *subsidy* is a payment by the government to a producer. Payments made to grain growers and dairy farmers are subsidies. Because of subsidies, consumers pay less for some goods and services than producers receive. Factor cost exceeds market price.

To get from factor cost to market price, we add indirect taxes and subtract subsidies. Making this adjustment brings us one step closer to GDP, but it does not quite get us there.

The final step is to add depreciation (or capital consumption). You can see the reason for this adjustment by recalling the distinction between gross and net profit and between gross and net investment. Total income is a net number because it includes firms' net profits, which exclude depreciation. Total expenditure is a gross number because it includes gross investment. So to get from total income to GDP, we must add depreciation to total income.

TABLE 20.2 GDP: The Income Approach

Item	**Amount in 2001** (billions of dollars)	**Percentage of GDP**
Wages, salaries, and supplementary labour income	569	52.1
Corporate profits	128	11.7
Interest and miscellaneous investment income	53	4.9
Farmers' income	3	0.3
Income from non-farm unincorporated businesses	67	6.1
Indirect taxes *less* subsidies	128	11.7
Capital consumption (depreciation)	144	13.2
Gross domestic product	1,092	100.0

The sum of all incomes equals net domestic income at factor cost. GDP equals net domestic income at factor cost plus indirect taxes less subsidies plus capital consumption (depreciation). In 2001, GDP measured by the income approach was $1,092 billion. Wages, salaries, and supplementary labour income was by far the largest part of aggregate income.

Source: Statistics Canada, CANSIM table 380-0001.

REVIEW QUIZ

1. What is the expenditure approach to measuring GDP?
2. What is the income approach to measuring GDP?
3. What adjustments must be made to total income to make it equal GDP?

You now know how GDP is defined and measured. The dollar value of GDP can change because either prices change or the volume of goods and services produced changes. You are next going to learn how we unscramble these two sources of change in GDP to reveal changes in the volume of goods and services produced—changes in what we call *real* GDP.

Real GDP and the Price Level

YOU'VE SEEN THAT GDP MEASURES TOTAL expenditure on final goods and services in a given period. In 2001, GDP was $1,092 billion. The year before, in 2000, GDP was $1,065 billion. Because GDP in 2001 was greater than in 2000, we know that one or two things must have happened during 2001:

- We produced more goods and services in 2001 than in 2000.
- We paid higher prices for our goods and services in 2001 than we paid in 2000.

Producing more goods and services contributes to an improvement in our standard of living. Paying higher prices means that our cost of living has increased but our standard of living has not. So it matters a great deal why GDP has increased.

You're now going to learn how economists at Statistics Canada split GDP into two parts. One part tells us the change in production, and the other part tells us the change in prices. The method that is used has changed in recent years, and you are going to learn about the new method.

We measure the change in production by using a number that we call real GDP. **Real GDP** is the value of final goods and services produced in a given year when valued at constant prices. By comparing the value of the goods and services produced at constant prices, we can measure the change in the volume of production.

Calculating Real GDP

Table 20.3 shows the quantities produced and the prices in 2002 for an economy that produces only two goods: balls and bats. The first step towards calculating real GDP is to calculate **nominal GDP**, which is the value of the final goods and services produced in a given year valued at the prices that prevailed in that same year. Nominal GDP is just a more precise name for GDP that we use when we want to be emphatic that we are not talking about real GDP.

Nominal GDP Calculation To calculate nominal GDP in 2002, sum the expenditures on balls and bats in 2002 as follows:

Expenditure on balls = 100 balls × $1 = $100.

Expenditure on bats = 20 bats × $5 = $100.

Nominal GDP in 2002 = $100 + $100 = $200.

Table 20.4 shows the quantities produced and the prices in 2003. The quantity of balls produced increased to 160, and the quantity of bats produced increased to 22. The price of a ball fell to 50¢, and the price of a bat increased to $22.50. To calculate nominal GDP in 2003, we sum the expenditures on balls and bats in 2003 as follows:

Expenditure on balls = 160 balls × $0.50 = $80.

Expenditure on bats = 22 bats × $22.50 = $495.

Nominal GDP in 2003 = $80 + $495 = $575.

To calculate real GDP, we choose one year, called the *base year*, against which to compare the other years. In Canada today, the base year is 1997. The choice of the base year is not important. It is just a common reference point. We'll use 2002 as the base year. By definition, real GDP equals nominal GDP in the base year. So real GDP in 2002 is $200.

Base-Year Prices Value of Real GDP The base-year prices method of calculating real GDP, which is the traditional method, values the quantities produced in each year at the prices of the base year. Table 20.5 shows the prices in 2002 and the quantities in 2003 (based on the information in Tables 20.3

TABLE 20.3 GDP Data for 2002

Item	Quantity	Price
Balls	100	$1.00
Bats	20	$5.00

TABLE 20.4 GDP Data for 2003

Item	Quantity	Price
Balls	160	$ 0.50
Bats	22	$22.50

TABLE 20.5 2003 Quantities and 2002 Prices

Item	Quantity	Price
Balls	160	$1.00
Bats	22	$5.00

and 20.4). The value of the 2003 quantities at the 2002 prices is calculated as follows:

Expenditure on balls = 160 balls × $1.00 = $160.

Expenditure on bats = 22 bats × $5.00 = $110.

Value of the 2003 quantities at 2002 prices = $270.

Using the traditional base-year prices method, $270 would be recorded as real GDP in 2003.

Chain-Weighted Output Index Calculation The **chain-weighted output index** method, which is the new method of calculating real GDP, uses the prices of two adjacent years to calculate the real GDP growth rate. So to find the real GDP growth rate in 2003, we compare the quantities produced in 2002 and 2003 by using both the 2002 prices and the 2003 prices. We then average the two sets of numbers in a special way that we'll now describe.

To compare the quantities produced in 2002 and 2003 at 2003 prices, we need to calculate the value of 2002 quantities at 2003 prices. Table 20.6 summarizes these quantities and prices. The value of the 2002 quantities at the 2003 prices is calculated as follows:

Expenditure on balls = 100 balls × $0.50 = $50.

Expenditure on bats = 20 bats × $22.50 = $450.

Value of the 2002 quantities at 2003 prices = $500.

We now have two comparisons between 2002 and 2003. At the 2002 prices, the value of production increased from $200 in 2002 to $270 in 2003.

TABLE 20.6 2002 Quantities and 2003 Prices

Item	Quantity	Price
Balls	100	$ 0.50
Bats	20	$22.50

The increase in value is $70, and the percentage increase is ($70 ÷ $200) × 100, which is 35 percent.

At the 2003 prices, the value of production increased from $500 in 2002 to $575 in 2003. The increase in value is $75, and the percentage increase is ($75 ÷ $500) × 100, which is 15 percent.

The new method of calculating real GDP uses the average of these two percentage increases. The average of 35 percent and 15 percent is (35 + 15) ÷ 2, which equals 25 percent. Real GDP is 25 percent greater in 2003 than in 2002. Real GDP in 2002 is $200, so real GDP in 2003 is $250.

Chain Linking The calculation that we've just described is repeated each year. Each year is compared with its preceding year. So in 2004, the calculations are repeated but using the prices and quantities of 2003 and 2004. Real GDP in 2004 equals real GDP in 2003 increased by the calculated percentage change in real GDP for 2004. For example, suppose that real GDP for 2004 is calculated to be 20 percent greater than that in 2003. You know that real GDP in 2003 is $250. So real GDP in 2004 is 20 percent greater than this value and is $300. In every year, real GDP is valued in base-year (2002) dollars.

By applying the calculated percentage change to the real GDP of the preceding real GDP, each year is linked back to the dollars of the base year like the links in a chain.

Calculating the Price Level

You've seen how real GDP is used to reveal the change in the quantity of goods and services produced. We're now going to see how we can find the change in prices that increases our cost of living.

The average level of prices is called the **price level.** One measure of the price level is the **GDP deflator,** which is an average of current-year prices expressed as a percentage of base-year prices. We calculate the GDP deflator by using nominal GDP and real GDP in the formula:

GDP deflator = (Nominal GDP ÷ Real GDP) × 100.

You can see why the GDP deflator is a measure of the price level. If nominal GDP rises but real GDP remains unchanged, it must be that the price level has risen. The formula gives a higher value for the GDP deflator. The larger the nominal GDP for a given real GDP, the higher is the price level and the larger is the GDP deflator.

TABLE 20.7 Calculating the GDP Deflator

Year	Nominal GDP	Real GDP	GDP deflator
2002	$200	$200	100
2003	$575	$250	230

Table 20.7 shows how the GDP deflator is calculated. In 2002, the deflator is 100. In 2003, it is 230, which equals nominal GDP of $575 divided by real GDP of $250 and then multiplied by 100.

Deflating the GDP Balloon

You can think of GDP as a balloon that is blown up by growing production and rising prices. In Fig. 20.3, the GDP deflator lets the inflation air out of the nominal GDP balloon—the contribution of rising prices—so that we can see what has happened to *real* GDP. The red balloon for 1981 shows real GDP in that year. The green balloon shows *nominal* GDP in 2001. The red balloon for 2001 shows real GDP for that year. To see real GDP in 2001, we *deflate* nominal GDP using the GDP deflator.

REVIEW QUIZ

1. What is the distinction between nominal GDP and real GDP?
2. What is the traditional method of calculating real GDP?
3. What is the new method of calculating real GDP?
4. How is the GDP deflator calculated?

You now know how to calculate real GDP and the GDP deflator. Your next task is to learn how to use real GDP to calculate economic growth and to make economic welfare comparisons. We also look at some limitations of real GDP as a measure of economic welfare and as a tool for comparing living standards across countries.

FIGURE 20.3 The Canadian GDP Balloon

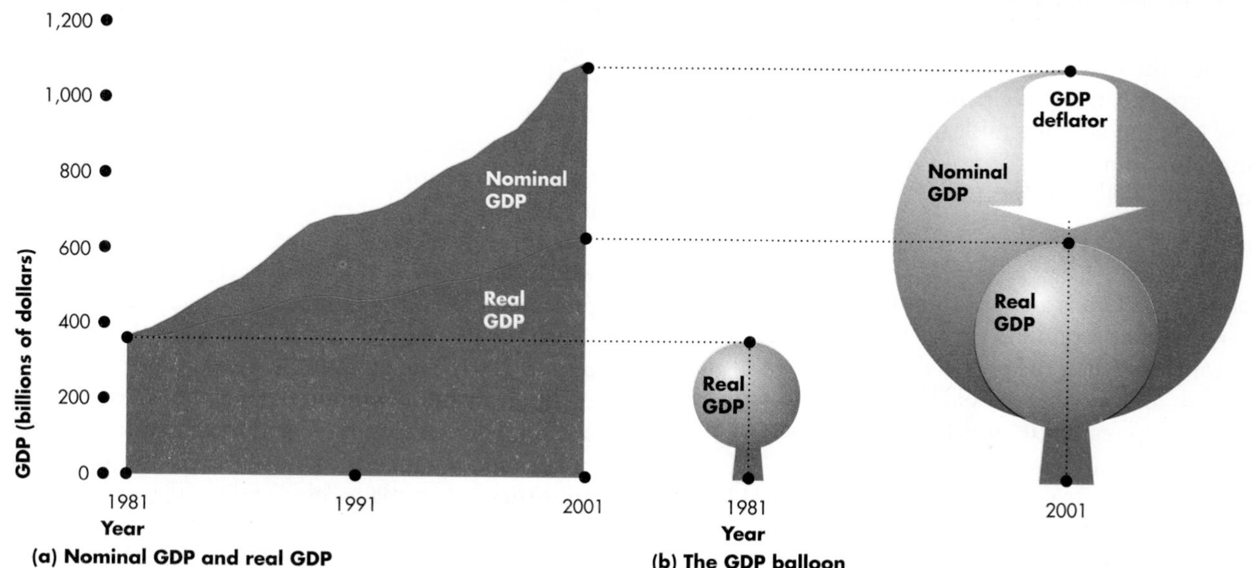

Part of the rise in GDP comes from inflation and part from increased production—an increase in real GDP. The GDP deflator lets some air out of the GDP balloon so that we can see the extent to which production has increased.

Source: Statistics Canada, CANSIM table 380-0003.

Measuring Economic Growth

WE USE ESTIMATES OF REAL GDP TO CALCULATE the economic growth rate. The **economic growth rate** is the percentage change in the quantity of goods and services produced from one year to the next. To calculate the economic growth rate, we use the formula:

$$\text{Economic growth rate} = \frac{\text{Real GDP this year} - \text{Real GDP last year}}{\text{Real GDP last year}} \times 100.$$

For example, real GDP was \$1,028 billion in 2001 and \$1,012 billion in 2000. So the economic growth rate (percent per year) during 2001 was

$$\text{Economic growth rate} = \frac{(\$1{,}028 - \$1{,}012)}{\$1{,}012} \times 100$$
$$= 1.58 \text{ percent.}$$

We want to measure the economic growth rate so that we can make

- Economic welfare comparisons
- International comparisons
- Business cycle forecasts

Although the real GDP growth rate is used for these three purposes, it is not a perfect measure for any of them. Nor is it a totally misleading measure. We'll evaluate the limitations of real GDP and its growth rate in each of the three cases.

Economic Welfare Comparisons

Economic welfare is a comprehensive measure of the general state of economic well-being. Economic welfare improves when the production per person of *all* the goods and services grows. The goods and services that make up real GDP growth are only a part of all the items that influence economic welfare.

Today, because of real GDP growth, real GDP per person in Canada of \$33,000 is 80 percent higher that it was in 1971. But are we 80 percent better off? Does this growth of real GDP provide a full and accurate measure of the change in economic welfare?

It does not. The reason is that economic welfare depends on many factors that are not measured by real GDP or that are not measured accurately by real GDP. Some of these factors are

- Overadjustment for inflation
- Household production
- Underground economic activity
- Health and life expectancy
- Leisure time
- Environment quality
- Political freedom and social justice

Overadjustment for Inflation The price indexes that are used to measure inflation give an upward-biased estimate of true inflation. (You will learn about the sources of this bias on p. 493.) If we overestimate the rise in prices, we underestimate the growth of real GDP. When car prices rise because cars have gotten better (safer, more fuel efficient, more comfortable), the GDP deflator counts the price increase as inflation. So what is really an increase in production is counted as an increase in price rather than an increase in real GDP. It is deflated away by the wrongly measured higher price level. The magnitude of this bias is probably less than 1 percentage point a year, but its exact magnitude is not known.

Household Production An enormous amount of production takes place every day in our homes. Preparing meals, cleaning the kitchen, changing a light bulb, cutting the grass, washing the car, and helping a high school student with homework are all examples of productive activities that do not involve market transactions and are not counted as part of GDP.

If these activities grew at the same rate as real GDP, then not measuring them would not be a problem. But it is likely that market production, which is part of GDP, is increasingly replacing household production, which is not part of GDP. Two trends point in this direction. One is the number of people who have jobs, which has increased from 58 percent in 1970 to 65 percent in 2001. The other is the trend in the purchase of traditionally home-produced goods and services in the market. For example, more and more families now eat in fast-food restaurants—one of the fastest-growing industries in Canada today—and use day-care services. This trend means that an increasing proportion of food preparation and child care that were part of household production are now measured as part of GDP. So real GDP grows more rapidly than does real GDP plus home production.

Underground Economic Activity The *underground economy* is the part of the economy that is purposely hidden from the view of the government to avoid taxes and regulations or because the goods and services being produced are illegal. Because underground economic activity is unreported, it is omitted from GDP.

The underground economy is easy to describe, even if it is hard to measure. It includes the production and distribution of illegal drugs, production that uses illegal labour that is paid less than the minimum wage, and jobs done for cash to avoid paying income taxes. This last category might be quite large and includes tips earned by cab drivers, hairdressers, and hotel and restaurant workers.

Estimates of the scale of the underground economy range between 5 and 15 percent of GDP ($50 billion to $150 billion) in Canada and much more in some countries. It is particularly large in some Eastern European countries that are making a transition from communist economic planning to a market economy.

If the underground economy is a constant proportion of the total economy, the growth rate of real GDP provides a useful estimate of *changes* in economic welfare. But production can shift from the underground economy to the rest of the economy, and can shift the other way. The underground economy expands relative to the rest of the economy if taxes rise sharply or if regulations become especially restrictive. And the underground economy shrinks relative to the rest of the economy if the burdens of taxes and regulations ease.

During the 1980s, when tax rates were cut, there was an increase in the reporting of previously hidden income and tax revenues increased. So some part (but probably a small part) of the expansion of real GDP during the 1980s represented a shift from the underground economy rather than an increase in production.

Health and Life Expectancy Good health and a long life—the hopes of everyone—do not show up in real GDP, at least not directly. A larger real GDP does enable us to spend more on medical research, health care, a good diet, and exercise equipment. And as real GDP has increased, our life expectancy has lengthened—from 70 years at the end of World War II to approaching 80 years today. Infant deaths and death in childbirth, two fearful scourges of the nineteenth century, have almost been eliminated.

But we face new health and life expectancy problems every year. AIDS and drug abuse are taking young lives at a rate that causes serious concern. When we take these negative influences into account, we see that real GDP growth overstates the improvements in economic welfare.

Leisure Time Leisure time is an economic good that adds to our economic welfare. Other things remaining the same, the more leisure we have, the better off we are. Our working time is valued as part of GDP, but our leisure time is not. Yet from the point of view of economic welfare, leisure time must be at least as valuable to us as the wage that we earn for the last hour worked. If it were not, we would work instead of taking the leisure. Over the years, leisure time has steadily increased. The workweek has become shorter, more people take early retirement, and the number of vacation days has increased. These improvements in economic well-being are not reflected in real GDP.

Environmental Quality Economic activity directly influences the quality of the environment. The burning of hydrocarbon fuels is the most visible activity that damages our environment. But it is not the only example. The depletion of exhaustible resources, the mass clearing of forests, and the pollution of lakes and rivers are other major environmental consequences of industrial production.

Resources that are used to protect the environment are valued as part of GDP. For example, the value of catalytic converters that help to protect the atmosphere from automobile emissions are part of GDP. But if we did not use such pieces of equipment and instead polluted the atmosphere, we would not count the deteriorating air that we were breathing as a negative part of GDP.

An industrial society possibly produces more atmospheric pollution than an agricultural society does. But pollution does not always increase as we become wealthier. Wealthy people value a clean environment and are willing to pay for one. Compare the pollution in East Germany in the late 1980s with pollution in Canada. East Germany, a poor country, polluted its rivers, lakes, and atmosphere in a way that is unimaginable in Canada or in wealthy West Germany.

Political Freedom and Social Justice Most people value political freedoms such as those provided by the Charter of Human Rights and the Constitution of Canada. And they value social justice or fairness—equality of opportunity and social security safety nets that protect people from the extremes of misfortune.

A country might have a very large real GDP per person but have limited political freedom and equity. For example, an elite might enjoy political liberty and extreme wealth while the vast majority are effectively enslaved and live in abject poverty. Such an economy would generally be regarded as having less economic welfare than one that had the same amount of real GDP but in which political freedoms were enjoyed by everyone. Today, China has rapid real GDP growth but limited political freedoms, while Russia has slow real GDP growth and an emerging democratic political system. Economists have no easy way to determine which of these countries is better off.

The Bottom Line Do we get the wrong message about the growth in economic welfare by looking at the growth of real GDP? The influences that are omitted from real GDP are probably important and could be large. Developing countries have a larger underground economy and a larger amount of household production than do developed countries. So as an economy develops and grows, part of the apparent growth might reflect a switch from underground to regular production and from home production to market production. This measurement error overstates the rate of economic growth and the improvement in economic welfare.

Other influences on living standards include the amount of leisure time available, the quality of the environment, the security of jobs and homes, and the safety of city streets. It is possible to construct broader measures that combine the many influences that contribute to human happiness. Real GDP will be one element in those broader measures but by no means the whole of them.

International Comparisons

All the problems we've just reviewed affect economic welfare of every country, so to make international comparisons of economic welfare, factors additional to real GDP must be used. But real GDP comparisons are major components of international welfare comparisons, and two special problems arise in making these comparisons. First, the real GDP of one country must be converted into the same currency units as the real GDP of the other country. Second, the same prices must be used to value the goods and services in the countries being compared. Let's look at these two problems by using a striking example, a comparison of Canada and China.

In 1992 (the most recent year for which we can make this comparison), real GDP per person in Canada was $25,453. The official Chinese statistics published by the International Monetary Fund say that real GDP per person in China in 1992 was 2,028 yuan. (The yuan is the currency of China.) On the average, during 1992, a Canadian dollar was worth 4.768 yuan. If we use this exchange rate to convert Chinese yuan into Canadian dollars, we get a value of $425.

The official comparison of China and Canada makes China look extremely poor. In 1992, real GDP per person in Canada was 60 times that in China.

Figure 20.4 shows the official story of real GDP in China from 1980 to 1998. Figure 20.4 also shows another story based on an estimate of real GDP per person that is much larger than the official measure. Let's see how this alternative measurement is made.

GDP in Canada is measured by using prices that prevail in Canada. China's GDP is measured by using prices that prevail in China. But the relative prices in the two countries are very different. Some goods that are expensive in Canada cost very little in China. These items get a small weight in China's real GDP. If, instead of using China's prices, all the goods and services produced in China are valued at the prices prevailing in Canada, then a more valid comparison can be made of GDP in the two countries. Such a comparison uses prices called *purchasing power parity prices.*

Robert Summers and Alan Heston, economists in the Center for International Comparisons at the University of Pennsylvania, have used purchasing power parity prices to construct real GDP data for more than 100 countries. These data, which are published in the Penn World Table (PWT), tell a remarkable story about China. The PWT data use 1985 as the base year, so they are measured in 1985 dollars. According to the PWT, in 1992, real GDP per person in Canada was 11 times that of China, not the 60 times shown in the official data.

Figure 20.4 shows the PWT view of China's real GDP and compares it with the official view. The difference in the two views arises from the prices used. The official statistics use Chinese prices, while the PWT data use purchasing power parity prices.

Another China scholar, Thomas Rawski of the University of Pittsburgh, doubts both sets of data shown in Fig. 20.4. He believes that the growth rate

FIGURE 20.4 Two Views of Real GDP in China

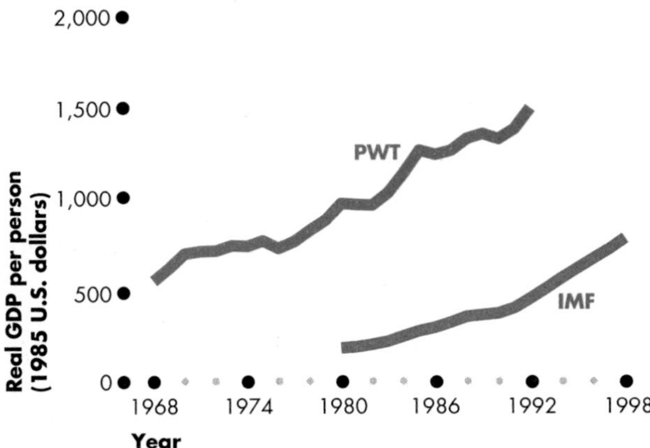

According to the official statistics of the International Monetary Fund (IMF) and the World Bank, China is a poor developing country. But according to an alternative view, Penn World Table (PWT), which is based on purchasing power parity prices, China's real GDP is more than 6 times the official view. Yet other China scholars think that even the official numbers are too big. So there is much uncertainty about China's real GDP.

Sources: International Monetary Fund, *World Economic Outlook 2001* (Washington, DC, 2001) and "The Penn World Table" (Mark 5.6).

of China's real GDP has been exaggerated for some years and that even the official data overstate real GDP in China.

Canada's real GDP is measured pretty reliably. But China's is not. The alternative measures of China's real GDP are unreliable, and the truth about real GDP in China is not known. But China is growing, and many businesses are paying close attention to the prospects of expanding their activities in China and other fast-growing Asian economies.

Business Cycle Forecasts

If policymakers plan to raise interest rates to slow an expansion that they believe is too strong, they look at the latest estimates of real GDP. But suppose that for the reasons that we've just discussed, real GDP is mismeasured. Does this mismeasurement hamper our ability to identify the phases of the business cycle? It does not. The reason is that although the omissions from real GDP do change over time, they probably do not change in a systematic way with the business cycle. So inaccurate measurement of real GDP does not necessarily cause a wrong assessment of the phase of the business cycle.

The fluctuations in economic activity measured by real GDP tell a reasonably accurate story about the phase of the business cycle that the economy is in. When real GDP grows, the economy is in a business cycle expansion; when real GDP shrinks (for two successive quarters), the economy is in a recession. Also, as real GDP fluctuates, so do production and jobs.

But real GDP fluctuations probably exaggerate or overstate the fluctuations in total production and economic welfare. The reason is that when business activity slows in a recession, household production increases and so does leisure time. When business activity speeds up in an expansion, household production and leisure time decrease. Because household production and leisure time increase in a recession and decrease in an expansion, real GDP fluctuations tend to overstate the fluctuations in total production and in economic welfare. But the directions of change of real GDP, total production, and economic welfare are probably the same.

REVIEW QUIZ

1. Does real GDP measure economic welfare? If not, why not?
2. Does real GDP measure total production of goods and services? If not, what are the main omissions?
3. How can we make valid international comparisons of real GDP?
4. Does the growth of real GDP measure the economic growth rate accurately?
5. Do the fluctuations in real GDP measure the business cycle accurately?

You've now studied the methods used to measure GDP, economic growth, and the price level. And you've learned about some of the limitations of these measures. *Reading Between the Lines* on pp. 472–473 looks at Canadian real GDP during 2002.

Your next task is to learn how we measure employment and unemployment and inflation.

READING BETWEEN THE LINES

The Quarterly GDP Report

THE CANADIAN PRESS, AUGUST 30, 2002

Economy slowed in Q2 compared with Q1 but still showed healthy advance

The economy grew by 4.3 per cent on an annualized basis in the second quarter of this year, Statistics Canada said Friday. Second-quarter growth alone came in at 1.1 per cent, driven by domestic demand and a buildup of inventories.

That compared with 1.5 per cent growth in the first quarter and an annualized rate of 6.2 per cent. "GDP lost momentum towards the end of the (second) quarter, edging up in June," the agency said. "Canada's current account surplus with the rest of the world fell slightly, but remained strong at $4.9 billion."

Second-quarter growth in the gross domestic product "matched the average over the previous two quarters and was well above the flat showing of the first three quarters of 2001," Statistics Canada said.

Domestic demand, which gained 0.9 per cent and matched its first-quarter pace, "was boosted by strong consumer spending on services and a pick-up of business investment in machinery and equipment, which more than offset an easing of housing investment."

Manufacturers, wholesalers and retailers began to replenish inventory after drawing them down for three quarters.

"Corporate profits continued to recover from their tumble in 2001 and healthy gains in employment pushed up labour income," the agency said. "Imports were up strongly to satisfy domestic demand and the rebuilding of inventory."

Statistics Canada said that in the second quarter:

—Consumer spending was up a robust 0.7 per cent.
—Housing investment remained at historically high levels.
—Personal disposable income was up a healthy 1.5 per cent.
—Corporate profits advanced 9.8 per cent.
—Business plant and equipment spending recorded its strongest gain since the fourth quarter of 1999, boosted by a 4.8 per cent increase in spending on machinery and equipment.
—Imports jumped 4.0 per cent.
—Exports decelerated to 0.4 per cent from 1.3 per cent in the first quarter.

...

The Canadian Press

Essence of the Story

- Statistics Canada reported that real GDP grew by 1.1 percent (a 4.3 percent annual rate) in the second quarter of 2002.
- Real GDP had grown by 1.5 percent (a 6.2 percent annual rate) in the first quarter of 2002, so the growth rate slowed in the second quarter but was above the growth rate of the first three quarters of 2001.
- The components of aggregate expenditure that grew quickly during the second quarter of 2002 were business inventories, consumer expenditure, and business fixed investment.
- Exports slowed and imports jumped, so these components of aggregate expenditure contributed to the slowdown in the second quarter.
- The components of aggregate income that grew quickly during the second quarter of 2002 were corporate profits and labour income.

Economic Analysis

■ Statistics Canada reports the nation's GDP numbers every three months.

■ To make the quarterly numbers easy to compare with annual numbers, growth rates are reported at annual rates.

■ An annual growth rate is calculated from quarterly data by using the formula:

$$g = [(x_t/x_{t-1})^4 - 1] \times 100,$$

where g is the annualized growth rate, x_t is the value of the variable in the current quarter, and x_{t-1} is the value of the variable in the preceding quarter.

■ The change in real GDP in a quarter is equal to

$$\Delta C + \Delta I + \Delta G + \Delta X - \Delta M$$

■ Figure 1 shows the composition of the change in real GDP in the second quarter of 2002 with the change in inventories, a component of investment, shown separately from the rest of investment.

■ You can see that consumption expenditure and the change in inventories were the items that changed most.

■ Notice that the increase in imports was large.

■ The news article compares the second quarter with the first quarter, and Fig. 2 shows the differences between the two quarters.

■ You can see that real GDP jumped by more in the first quarter of 2002 than it did in the second quarter.

■ In the first quarter, the change in inventories was much smaller than in the second quarter. Exports increased by more and imports by much less than in the second quarter.

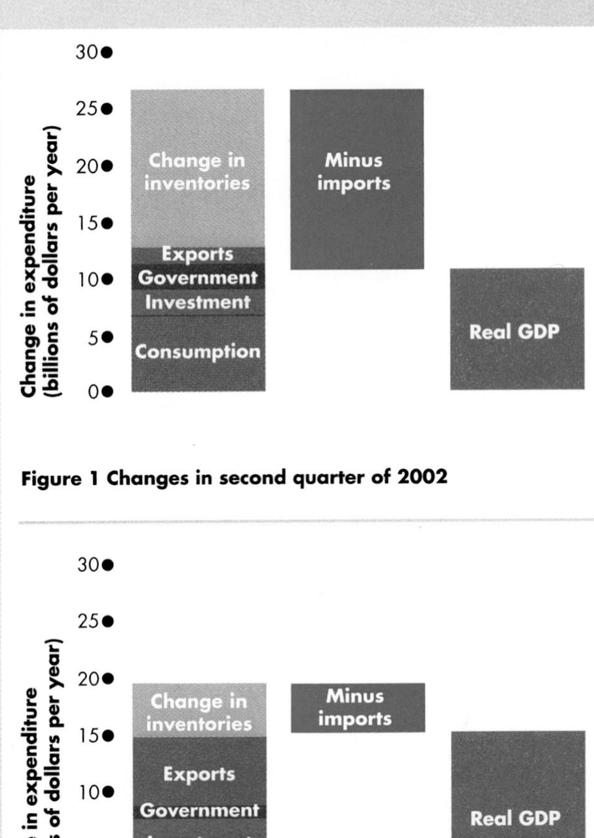

Figure 1 Changes in second quarter of 2002

Figure 2 Changes in first quarter of 2002

SUMMARY

KEY POINTS

Gross Domestic Product (pp. 458–462)

- GDP, or gross domestic product, is the market value of all the final goods and services produced in a country during a given period.
- A final good is an item that is bought by its final user during a specified time period, and contrasts with an intermediate good, which is a component of a final good.
- GDP is calculated by using the expenditure and income totals in the circular flow of expenditure and income.
- Aggregate expenditure on goods and services equals aggregate income and GDP.

Measuring Canada's GDP (pp. 463–464)

- Because aggregate expenditure, aggregate income, and the value of aggregate production are equal, we can measure GDP by using the expenditure approach or the income approach.
- The expenditure approach sums consumption expenditure, investment, government expenditures on goods and services, and net exports.
- The income approach sums wages, interest, rent, and profit (and indirect taxes and depreciation).

Real GDP and the Price Level (pp. 465–467)

- Real GDP is measured by a chain-weighted output index that compares the value of production each year with its value at the previous year's prices.
- The GDP deflator measures the price level based on the prices of the items that make up GDP.

Measuring Economic Growth (pp. 468–471)

- We measure the economic growth rate as the percentage change in real GDP.
- Real GDP growth is not a perfect measure of economic growth because it excludes quality improvements, household production, the underground economy, environmental damage, health and life expectancy, leisure time, political freedom, and social justice.
- The growth rate of real GDP gives a good indication of the phases of the business cycle.

KEY FIGURES AND TABLES

Figure 20.1 The Circular Flow of Expenditure and Income, 459
Figure 20.2 Capital and Investment, 462
Table 20.1 GDP: The Expenditure Approach, 463
Table 20.2 GDP: The Income Approach, 464

KEY TERMS

Capital consumption, 461
Chain-weighted output index, 466
Consumption expenditure, 459
Depreciation, 461
Economic growth rate, 468
Economic welfare, 468
Exports, 460
Final good, 458
Flow, 461
GDP deflator, 466
Government expenditures, 460
Gross domestic product (GDP), 458
Gross investment, 461
Imports, 460
Intermediate good, 458
Investment, 460
National saving, 461
Net exports, 460
Net investment, 461
Net taxes, 460
Nominal GDP, 465
Price level, 466
Real GDP, 465
Saving, 460
Stock, 461
Wealth, 461

PROBLEMS

*1. The figure at the bottom of the page shows the flows of expenditure and income on Lotus Island. During 2002, *A* was \$20 million, *B* was \$60 million, *C* was \$24 million, *D* was \$30 million, and *E* was \$6 million. Calculate
   a. Aggregate expenditure.
   b. Aggregate income.
   c. GDP.
   d. Government budget deficit.
   e. Household saving.
   f. Government saving.
   g. National saving.
   h. Borrowing from the rest of the world.

2. In problem 1, during 2003, *A* was \$25 million, *B* was \$450 million, *C* was \$30 million, *D* was \$30 million, and *E* was –\$10 million. Calculate the quantities in problem 1 during 2003.

*3. Martha owns a copy shop that has 10 copiers. One copier wears out each year and is replaced. In addition, this year Martha will expand her business to 14 copiers. Calculate Martha's initial capital stock, depreciation, gross investment, net investment, and final capital stock.

4. Wendy operates a weaving shop with 20 looms. One loom wears out each year and is replaced. But this year, Wendy will expand her business to 24 looms. Calculate Wendy's initial capital stock, depreciation, gross investment, net investment, and final capital stock.

*5. The transactions in Ecoland last year were

Item	Dollars
Wages paid to labour	800,000
Consumption expenditure	600,000
Taxes	250,000
Transfer payments	50,000
Profits	200,000
Investment	250,000
Government expenditures	200,000
Exports	300,000
Saving	300,000
Imports	250,000

   a. Calculate Ecoland's GDP.
   b. Did you use the expenditure approach or the income approach to make this calculation?
   c. How is investment financed?

6. The transactions in Highland last year were

Item	Dollars
Wages paid to labour	400,000
Consumption expenditure	350,000
Net taxes	125,000
Profits	140,000
Investment	150,000
Government expenditures	130,000
Exports	120,000
Saving	135,000
Imports	140,000

   a. Calculate Highland's GDP.
   b. What extra information do you need to calculate net domestic product at factor cost?
   c. Where does Highland get the funds to finance its investment?

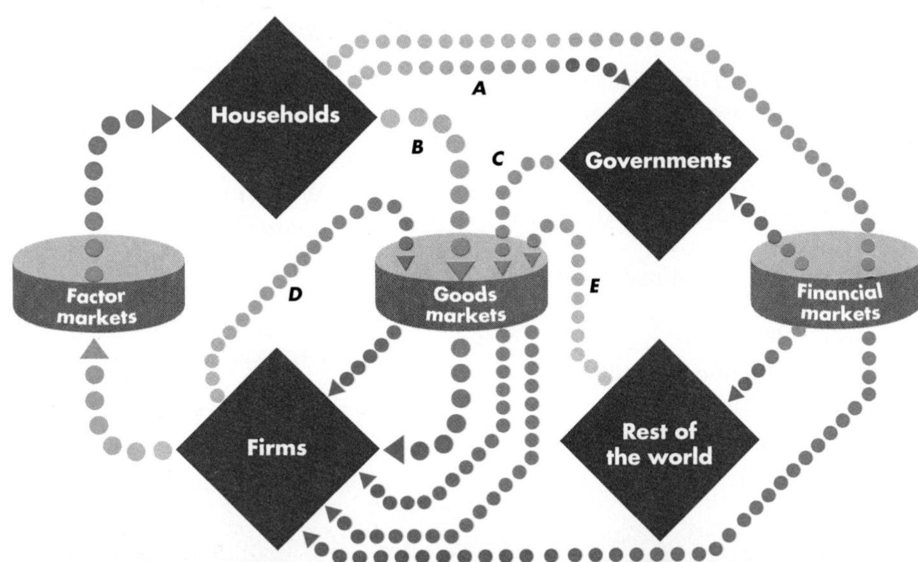

*7. Bananaland produces only bananas and sunscreen. The base year is 2002, and the tables give the quantities produced and prices.

	Quantity	
Good	**2002**	**2003**
Bananas	1,000 bunches	1,100 bunches
Sunscreen	500 bottles	525 bottles

	Price	
Good	**2002**	**2003**
Bananas	$2 a bunch	$3 a bunch
Sunscreen	$10 a bottle	$8 a bottle

a. Calculate nominal GDP in 2002 and 2003.
b. Calculate real GDP in 2003 using the base-year prices method.

8. Sea Island produces only lobsters and crabs. The base year is 2003, and the tables give the quantities produced and the prices.

	Quantity	
Good	**2003**	**2004**
Lobsters	1,000	1,450
Crabs	500	525

	Price	
Good	**2003**	**2004**
Lobsters	$20 each	$25 each
Crabs	$10 each	$12 each

a. Calculate nominal GDP in 2003 and 2004.
b. Calculate real GDP in 2004 using the base-year prices method.

*9. Bananaland (in problem 7) decides to use the chain-weighted output index method to calculate real GDP. Using this method,
a. Calculate the growth rate of real GDP in 2003.
b. Calculate the GDP deflator in 2003.
c. Compare and comment on the differences in real GDP using the base-year prices and chain-weighted output index methods.

10. Sea Island (in problem 8) decides to use the chain-weighted output index method to calculate real GDP. Using this method,
a. Calculate the growth rate of real GDP in 2004.
b. Calculate the GDP deflator in 2004.
c. Compare and comment on the differences in real GDP using the base-year prices and chain-weighted output index methods.

CRITICAL THINKING

1. Study *Reading Between the Lines* on pp. 472–473 and then answer the following questions:
a. In the first and second quarters of 2002, which components of aggregate expenditure increased most?
b. According to the news article, which components of aggregate income increased most during the first and second quarters of 2002?
c. What happened to net exports during the first two quarters of 2002? Did they increase or decrease? Did Canada increase or decrease its net lending to the rest of the world during those two quarters?
d. Was Canada in a recession, growth recession, or expansion during the first half of 2002?
e. What happened to total investment during the first two quarters of 2002?
f. Where, in the circular flow model, do changes in business inventories appear?

WEB EXERCISES

1. Use the link on the Parkin–Bade Web site to visit Statistics Canada. There you can obtain all the available data on GDP and the components of aggregate expenditure and aggregate income. You will find data in current prices (nominal GDP) and constant prices (real GDP).
a. What is the value of nominal GDP in the current quarter?
b. What is the value of real GDP in the current quarter using the chain-weighted index method?
c. What is the GDP deflator in the current quarter?
d. What was the value of real GDP in the same quarter of the previous year?
e. By how much has real GDP changed over the past year? (Express your answer as a percentage.)
f. Did real GDP increase or decrease and what does the change tell you about the state of the economy over the past year?

MONITORING CYCLES, JOBS, AND THE PRICE LEVEL

CHAPTER 21

Vital Signs

When the U.S. economy went into recession during 2001, Canada's economy slowed but avoided recession. What exactly is a recession, who decides when one begins and ends, and what criteria are used to make these decisions? ◆ Each month, we chart the unemployment rate as a measure of Canadian economic health. How do we measure the unemployment rate? What does it tell us? Is it a reliable vital sign for the economy? ◆ Every month, we also chart the number of people working, the number of hours they work, and the wages they receive. Are most new jobs full time or part time? And are they high-wage jobs or low-wage jobs? ◆ As the Canadian economy continued to slow in the first half of 2002, these questions about the health of the labour market became of vital importance to millions of Canadian families. We put the spotlight on the labour market during 2002 in *Reading Between the Lines* at the end of this chapter. ◆ Having a good job that pays a decent wage is only half of the equation that translates into a good standard of living. The other half is the cost of living. We track the cost of the items that we buy with another number that is published every month—the Consumer Price Index, or CPI. What is the CPI? How is it calculated? And does it provide a reliable guide to the changes in our cost of living?

These are the questions we study in this chapter. We begin by looking at the way in which a recession is identified and dated. And we end, in *Reading Between the Lines,* by putting the spotlight on the CPI in 2002.

After studying this chapter, you will be able to

- **Explain how we date business cycles**
- **Define the unemployment rate, the labour force participation rate, the employment-to-population ratio, and aggregate hours**
- **Describe the sources of unemployment, its duration, the groups most affected by it, and how it fluctuates over a business cycle**
- **Explain how we measure the price level and the inflation rate using the CPI**

The Business Cycle

THE BUSINESS CYCLE IS A PERIODIC BUT IRREGULAR up-and-down movement in production and jobs (see p. 440). There is no official, government-sponsored record of the dating of business cycles. Instead, business cycles are identified by two private agencies: the Economic Cycle Research Institute (ECRI) and the National Bureau of Economic Research (NBER). The ECRI identifies and dates the business cycles in Canada and 17 other countries and the NBER dates the U.S. business cycle. The working definition of the business cycle used by the ECRI is as follows:

> ... pronounced, pervasive and persistent advances and declines in aggregate economic activity, which cannot be defined by any single variable, but by the consensus of key measures of output, income, employment and sales.[1]

A business cycle has two phases—expansion and recession—and two turning points—peak and trough. The NBER, whose methods the ECRI uses, defines the phases and turning points of the cycle as follows.

> A *recession* is a significant decline in activity spread across the economy, lasting more than a few months, visible in industrial production, employment, real income, and wholesale-retail trade. A recession begins just after the economy reaches a *peak* of activity and ends as the economy reaches its *trough*. Between trough and peak, the economy is in an *expansion*.[2]

Real GDP is the broadest measure of economic activity, and another popular working definition of a recession is a decrease in real GDP that lasts for at least two quarters. But we don't measure real GDP each month, so the ECRI and NBER do not use the real GDP numbers. Instead, they look at employment, which is the broadest *monthly* indicator of economic activity, along with other monthly measures that include personal income, sales of goods, and industrial production.

[1] You can find this definition and the dates of the business cycles in 18 countries at the ECRI Web site (www.businesscycle.com).

[2] "The NBER's Business-Cycle Dating Procedure," January 10, 2002, NBER Web site (www.nber.org). (Italicizing of key terms added.)

Business Cycle Dates

Figure 21.1(a) provides a quick summary of the Canadian business cycle since 1926. The figure shows the average per-year percentage change in real GDP during successive recessions and expansions.

The Great Depression, which began with a recession that ran from August 1929 to March 1933, was the most severe contraction of economic activity ever experienced. Over a 43-month period, real GDP shrank by 33 percent. Canada has had only four other recessions, at the end of World War II, 1954, 1982, and 1990–1991. The ECRI identified one other recession during 1957, but it was so mild that it doesn't show up in the real GDP data.

Expansion is the normal state of the economy, and the biggest expansion occurred during World War II. But the longest expansion ran from 1954 to 1982 (except for a mild stop in 1957). There is no correlation between the length of an expansion and the length of the preceding recession.

Growth Rate Cycles

Because recessions are rare, just looking at expansions and recessions misses a lot of the volatility in our economy. An alternative and more sensitive approach is to examine growth rate cycle downturns. A **growth rate cycle downturn** is a

> ... pronounced, pervasive and persistent decline in the *growth rate* of aggregate economic activity. The procedures used to identify peaks and troughs in the growth rate cycle are analogous to those used to identify business cycle turning points, except that they are applied to the growth rates of the same time series, rather than their levels.[3]

Figure 21.1(b) shows the growth rate cycles since 1961 (the first year for which we have quarterly real GDP data).

REVIEW QUIZ

1. What are the phases of the business cycle?
2. Have recessions been getting worse?

[3] This definition is from the ECRI Web site (with small changes).

FIGURE 21.1 Two Views of Canadian Business Cycles

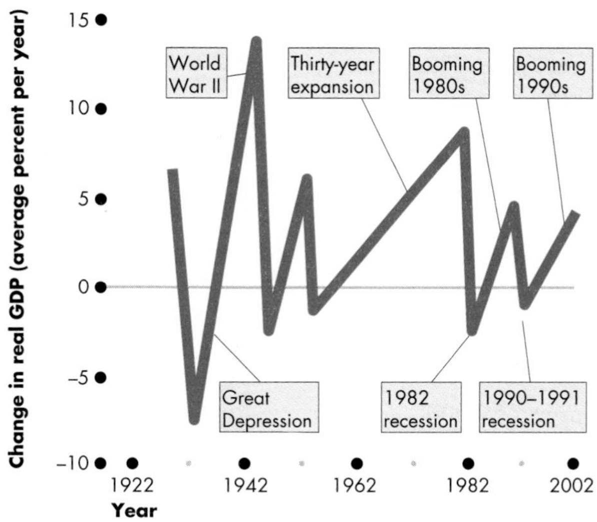

(a) Business cycle patterns

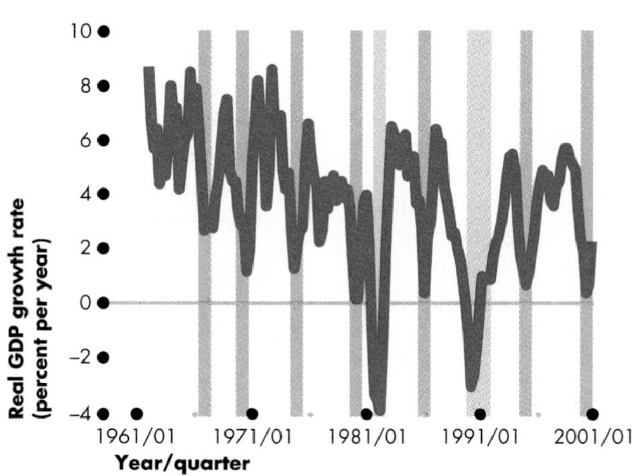

(b) Growth rate cycles

Part (a) shows the patterns of recession and expansion since the mid-1920s using real GDP as the measuring rod. Recessions have lasted from almost four years during the Great Depression, when real GDP fell by 33 percent, to a year in 1953–1954, when real GDP fell by 1.2 percent. Canada has had only four recessions since World War II.

Part (b) shows the higher frequency growth rate cycles since 1961, again using real GDP as the measuring rod of economic activity. The two deepest growth rate recessions occurred during 1982 and 1990–1991, the periods in which real GDP shrank and the economy was in recession in part (a). The other growth rate recessions identified by the shading in the figure were milder and did not take real GDP growth into negative territory.

Sources: Business cycle dates and growth rate cycle dates: the Economic Cycle Research Institute.
Real GDP: Statistics Canada, CANSIM table 1992292.

Jobs and Wages

YOU HAVE SEEN THAT EMPLOYMENT IS ONE OF THE key features of the economy that helps the ECRI and NBER to determine the onset of recession. The state of the labour market has a large impact on our incomes and our lives. We become concerned when jobs are hard to find and more relaxed when they are plentiful. But we want a good job, which means that we want a well-paid and interesting job.

You are now going to learn how economists track the health of the labour market.

Labour Force

Every month, Statistics Canada surveys 59,000 households and asks a series of questions about the age and job market status of their members. This survey is called the Labour Force Survey. Statistics Canada uses the answers to describe the anatomy of the labour force.

Figure 21.2 shows the population categories used by Statistics Canada and the relationships among the categories. It divides the population into two groups: the working-age population and others who are too young to work. The **working-age population** is the total number of people aged 15 years and over. Statistics Canada divides the working-age population into two groups: those in the labour force and those not in the labour force. It also divides the labour force into two groups: the employed and the unemployed. So the **labour force** is the sum of the employed and the unemployed.

To be counted as employed in the Labour Force Survey, a person must have either a full-time job or a part-time job. To be counted as *un*employed, a person must be available for work and must be in one of three categories:

1. Without work but has made specific efforts to find a job within the previous four weeks
2. Waiting to be called back to a job from which he or she has been laid off
3. Waiting to start a new job within four weeks

Anyone surveyed who satisfies one of these three criteria is counted as unemployed. People in the working-age population who are neither employed nor unemployed are classified as not in the labour force.

In 2001, the population of Canada was 31.08 million. There were 6.46 million people under 15 years of age. The working-age population was 24.62 million. Of this number, 8.37 million were not in the labour force. Most of these people were in school full time or had retired from work. The remaining 16.25 million people made up the Canadian labour force. Of these, 15.08 million were employed and 1.17 million were unemployed.

FIGURE 21.2 Population Labour Force Categories

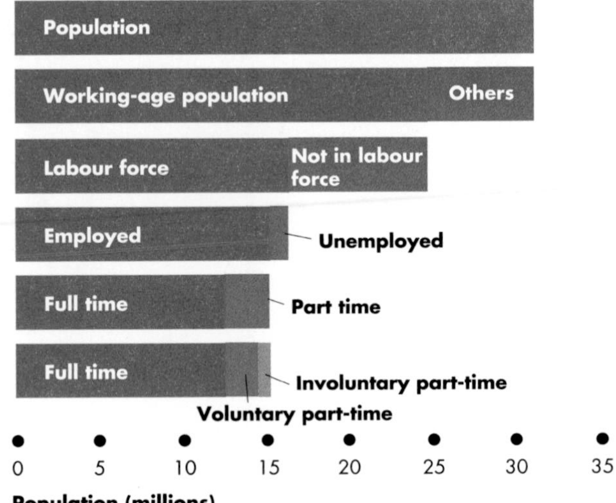

The population is divided into the working-age population and others. The working-age population is divided into those in the labour force and those not in the labour force. The labour force is divided into those employed and those unemployed. The people employed are divided into those with full-time jobs and those with part-time jobs. And part-time workers are divided into those who are voluntary and involuntary part-time workers.

Source: Statistics Canada, *Labour Force Historical Review*, CD-ROM 2001 and CANSIM tables 282-0002 and 051-0001.

Four Labour Market Indicators

Statistics Canada calculates four indicators of the state of the labour market:

- The unemployment rate
- The involuntary part-time rate
- The labour force participation rate
- The employment-to-population ratio

The Unemployment Rate The amount of unemployment is an indicator of the extent to which people who want jobs can't find them. The **unemployment rate** is the percentage of the people in the labour force who are unemployed. That is,

$$\text{Unemployment rate} = \frac{\text{Number of people unemployed}}{\text{Labour force}} \times 100$$

and

$$\text{Labour force} = \begin{array}{l}\text{Number of people employed} + \\ \text{Number of people unemployed.}\end{array}$$

In 2001, the number of people employed was 15.08 million and the number unemployed was 1.17 million. So the labour force was 16.25 million (15.08 million plus 1.17 million) and the unemployment rate was 7.2 percent (1.17 million divided by 16.25 million, multiplied by 100).

Figure 21.3 shows the unemployment rate (the orange line and plotted on the right-hand scale) and three other labour market indicators between 1961 and 2001. The average unemployment rate has been 7.7 percent, and it reached peak values at the ends of the 1982 and 1990–1991 recessions.

The Involuntary Part-Time Rate Part-time workers who want full-time work do not get counted as being unemployed. To measure the extent of this type of underemployment, Statistics Canada counts the number of involuntary part-time workers—part-time workers who want full-time jobs. The involuntary part-time rate is the percentage of the people in the labour force who have part-time jobs and want full-time jobs. That is,

$$\begin{array}{c}\text{Involuntary} \\ \text{part-time rate}\end{array} = \frac{\text{Number of involuntary part-time workers}}{\text{Labour force}} \times 100.$$

In 2001, the number of involuntary part-time workers was 700,000, the labour force was 16.25 million, and the involuntary part-time rate was 4.3 percent.

Figure 21.3 shows the involuntary part-time rate (plotted on the right-hand scale) from 1976 to 1995 and then a new definition after 1997. You can see that an increasing percentage of the labour force wants full-time work but is not able to get full-time work. You can also see that the fluctuations in the involuntary part-time rate are like those in the unemployment rate.

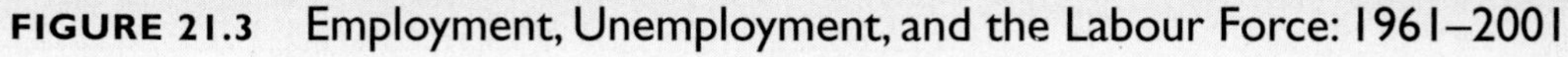

FIGURE 21.3 Employment, Unemployment, and the Labour Force: 1961–2001

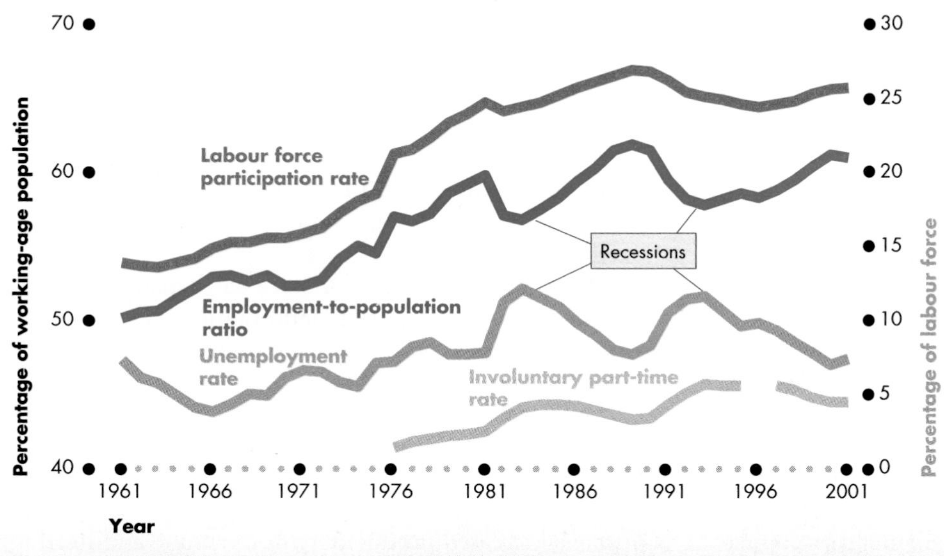

The unemployment rate increases in recessions and decreases in expansions. The labour force participation rate and the employment-to-population ratio have upward trends and fluctuate with the business cycle. The employment-to-population ratio fluctuates more than the labour force participation rate and reflects cyclical fluctuations in the unemployment rate. Fluctuations in the labour force participation rate arise mainly because of discouraged workers.

Source: Statistics Canada, *Labour Force Historical Review*, CD-ROM, 2001 and CANSIM table 282-0002.

The Labour Force Participation Rate The number of people who join the labour force is an indicator of the willingness of people of working age to take jobs. The **labour force participation rate** is the percentage of the working-age population who are members of the labour force. That is,

$$\text{Labour force participation rate} = \frac{\text{Labour force}}{\text{Working-age population}} \times 100.$$

In 2001, the labour force was 16.25 million and the working-age population was 24.62 million. By using the above equation, you can calculate the labour force participation rate. It was 66 percent (16.25 million divided by 24.62 million, multiplied by 100).

Figure 21.3 shows the labour force participation rate (graphed in red and plotted on the left-hand scale). It has followed an upward trend and has increased from 54 percent during the early 1960s to 66 percent in 2001. It has also had some mild fluctuations. They result from unsuccessful job seekers becoming discouraged workers. **Discouraged workers** are people who are available and willing to work but have not made specific efforts to find a job within the previous four weeks. These workers often temporarily leave the labour force during a recession and re-enter during an expansion and become active job seekers.

The Employment-to-Population Ratio The number of people of working age who have jobs is an indicator of both the availability of jobs and the degree of match between people's skills and jobs. The **employment-to-population ratio** is the percentage of people of working age who have jobs. That is,

$$\text{Employment-to-population ratio} = \frac{\text{Number of people employed}}{\text{Working-age population}} \times 100.$$

In 2001, the number of people employed was 15.08 million and the working-age population was 24.62 million. By using the above equation, you can calculate the employment-to-population ratio. It was 61.3 percent (15.08 million divided by 24.62 million, multiplied by 100).

Figure 21.3 shows the employment-to-population ratio (graphed in blue and plotted against the left-hand scale). It increased from 50 percent during the early 1960s to 61 percent in 2001. The increase in the employment-to-population ratio means that the Canadian economy has created jobs at a faster rate than the working-age population has grown. This labour market indicator also fluctuates, and its fluctuations coincide with but are opposite to those in the unemployment rate. The employment-to-population ratio falls during a recession and increases during an expansion.

FIGURE 21.4 The Changing Face of the Labour Market

The upward trends in the labour force participation rate and the employment-to-population ratio are accounted for mainly by the increasing participation of women in the labour market. The male labour force participation rate and employment-to-population ratio have decreased.

Source: Statistics Canada, CANSIM table 282-0002.

Why have the labour force participation rate and the employment-to-population ratio increased? The main reason is an increase in the number of women in the labour force. Figure 21.4 shows this increase. Shorter work hours, higher productivity, and an increased emphasis on white-collar jobs have expanded the job opportunities and wages available to women. At the same time, technological advances have increased productivity in the home and freed up women's time to take jobs outside the home.

Figure 21.4 also shows another remarkable trend in the Canadian labour force: The labour force participation rate and the employment-to-population ratio for men have *decreased.* These indicators decreased because increasing numbers of men were remaining in school longer and because some were retiring earlier.

Aggregate Hours

The four labour market indicators that we've just examined are useful signs of the health of the economy and directly measure what matters to most people: jobs. But these four indicators don't tell us the quantity of labour used to produce real GDP, and we cannot use them to calculate the productivity of labour. The productivity of labour is significant because it influences the wages people earn.

The reason why the number of people employed does not measure the quantity of labour employed is that jobs are not all the same. People in part-time jobs might work just a few hours a week. People in full-time jobs work around 35 to 40 hours a week. And some people regularly work overtime. For example, a 7-11 store might hire six students who work for three hours a day each. Another 7-11 store might hire two full-time workers who work nine hours a day each. The number of people employed in these two stores is eight, but the total hours worked by six of the eight is the same as the total hours worked by the other two. To determine the total amount of labour used to produce real GDP, we measure labour in hours rather than in jobs. **Aggregate hours** are the total number of hours worked by all the people employed, both full time and part time, during a year.

Figure 21.5(a) shows aggregate hours in the Canadian economy from 1961 to 2001. Like the employment-to-population ratio, aggregate hours have an upward trend. But aggregate hours have not grown as quickly as has the number of people employed. Between 1961 and 2001, the number of people employed in the Canadian economy increased by 150 percent. During that same period, aggregate hours increased by a bit more than 110 percent. Why the difference? Because average hours per worker decreased.

Figure 21.5(b) shows average hours per worker. After hovering at a bit more than 40 hours a week during the early 1960s, average hours per worker decreased to about 34 hours a week during the 1990s. This shortening of the average workweek arose partly because of a decrease in the average hours worked by full-time workers, but mainly because the

FIGURE 21.5 Aggregate Hours: 1961–2001

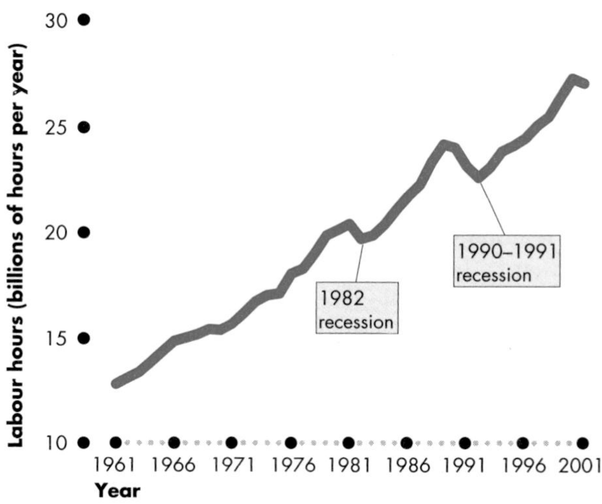

(a) Aggregate hours

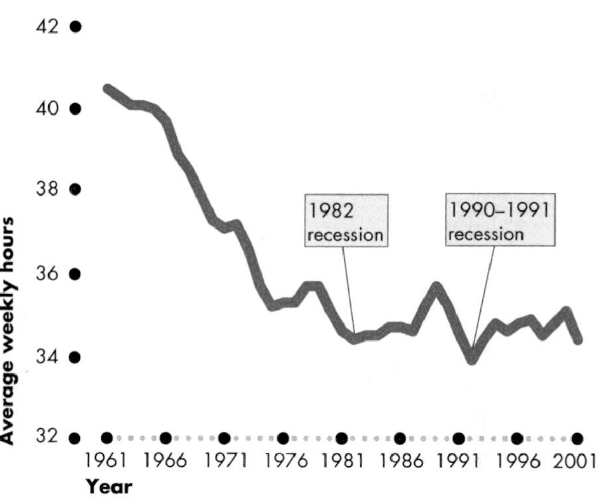

(b) Average weekly hours per person

Aggregate hours (part a) measure the total labour used to produce real GDP more accurately than does the number of people employed because an increasing proportion of jobs are part time. Between 1961 and 2001, aggregate hours increased by an average of 1.9 percent a year. Fluctuations in aggregate hours coincide with the business cycle. Aggregate hours have increased at a slower rate than the number of jobs because the average workweek has shortened (part b).

Source: Statistics Canada, CANSIM tables 282-0002 and 282-0022 and authors' calculations.

number of part-time jobs increased faster than the number of full-time jobs.

Fluctuations in aggregate hours and average hours per worker line up with the business cycle. Figure 21.5 highlights the past two recessions, during which aggregate hours decreased and average hours per worker decreased more quickly than the trend.

Real Wage Rate

The **real wage rate** is the quantity of goods and services that an hour's work can buy. It is equal to the money wage rate (dollars per hour) divided by the price level. If we use the GDP deflator to measure the price level, the real wage rate is expressed in 1997 dollars because the GDP deflator is 100 in 1997. The real wage rate is a significant economic variable because it measures the reward for labour.

FIGURE 21.6 Real Wage Rates: 1961–2001

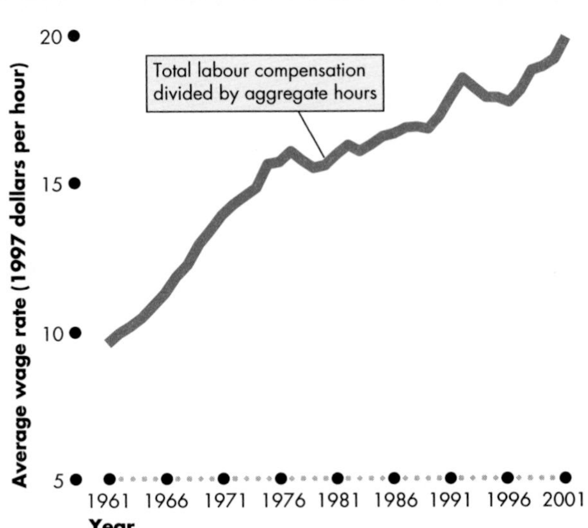

The average hourly real wage rate follows an upward trend. But the trend growth rate of the real wage rate slowed during the 1970s and early 1980s. Occasionally, the real wage rate falls, as it did in the late 1970s and early 1990s.

Sources: Statistics Canada CANSIM tables 282-0002, 282-0022, and 380-0001, and the authors' calculations.

What has happened to the real wage rate in Canada? Figure 21.6 answers this question. Figure 21.6 shows the broadest measure of the average hourly real wage rate in the Canadian economy

The money wage rate is calculated from the national income accounts and aggregate hours. We know from the income side of the national income accounts the total amount of labour income. This total includes wages and salaries and all forms of supplementary labour income such as health and insurance benefits. It includes all labour income, not just that of people who are paid by the hour. If we divide this total by aggregate hours, we arrive at an estimate of the economy-wide average money wage rate. This average includes all types of labour in all parts of the economy.

The real wage rate follows an upward path. But the trend growth rate slowed during the 1970s and early 1980s in the *productivity growth slowdown.* This productivity growth slowdown is the main reason for this behaviour of the average real wage rate.

The average real wage rate usually increases but you can see in Fig. 21.6 that it sometimes decreases. The real wage rate decreased during the late 1970s, and it decreased again during the 1990s.

REVIEW QUIZ

1. What are the trends in the unemployment rate, the labour force participation rate, and the employment-to-population ratio?
2. How do the unemployment rate, the labour force participation rate, and the employment-to-population ratio fluctuate over the business cycle?
3. Has the female labour force participation rate been similar to or different from the male labour force participation rate?
4. How have aggregate hours changed since 1961?
5. How did the average hourly real wage rate change during the 1990s?

You've now seen how we measure employment, unemployment, and the real wage rate. Your next task is to study the anatomy of unemployment and see why it never disappears, even at full employment.

Unemployment and Full Employment

HOW DO PEOPLE BECOME UNEMPLOYED, AND how does a period of unemployment end? How long do people remain unemployed on the average? Who is at greatest risk of becoming unemployed? Let's answer these questions by looking at the anatomy of unemployment.

The Anatomy of Unemployment

People become unemployed if they

1. Lose their jobs and search for another job.
2. Leave their jobs and search for another job.
3. Enter or re-enter the labour force to search for a job.

People end a spell of unemployment if they

1. Are hired or recalled.
2. Withdraw from the labour force.

People who are laid off from their jobs, either permanently or temporarily, are called **job losers.** Some job losers become unemployed, but some immediately withdraw from the labour force. People who voluntarily quit their jobs are called **job leavers.** Like job losers, some job leavers become unemployed and search for a better job, while others withdraw from the labour force temporarily or permanently retire from work. People who enter or re-enter the labour force are called **entrants** and **re-entrants.** Entrants are mainly people who have just left school. Some entrants get a job right away and are never unemployed, but many spend time searching for their first job, and during this period, they are unemployed. Re-entrants are people who have previously withdrawn from the labour force. Most of these people are formerly discouraged workers. Figure 21.7 shows these labour market flows.

FIGURE 21.7 Labour Market Flows

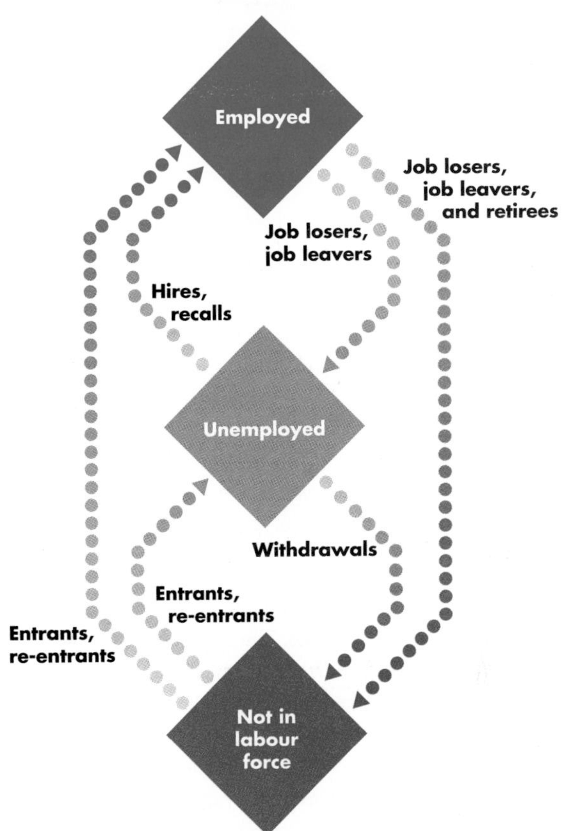

Unemployment results from employed people losing or leaving their jobs (job losers and job leavers) and from people entering the labour force (entrants and re-entrants). Unemployment ends because people get hired or recalled or because they withdraw from the labour force.

The Sources of Unemployment Figure 21.8 shows unemployment by reason for becoming unemployed. Job losers are the biggest source of unemployment. On the average, they account for around half of total unemployment. Also, their number fluctuates a great deal. At the trough of the recession of 1990–1991, on any given day, almost 1 million of the 1.6 million unemployed were job losers. In contrast, at the business cycle peak year of 1989, fewer than 600,000 of the 1 million unemployed were job losers.

Entrants and re-entrants also make up a large component of the unemployed, and their number fluctuates but more mildly than the fluctuations in the number of job losers.

Job leavers are the smallest and most stable source of unemployment. On any given day, less than 200,000 people are unemployed because they are job leavers. The number of job leavers is remarkably

FIGURE 21.8 Unemployment by Reason

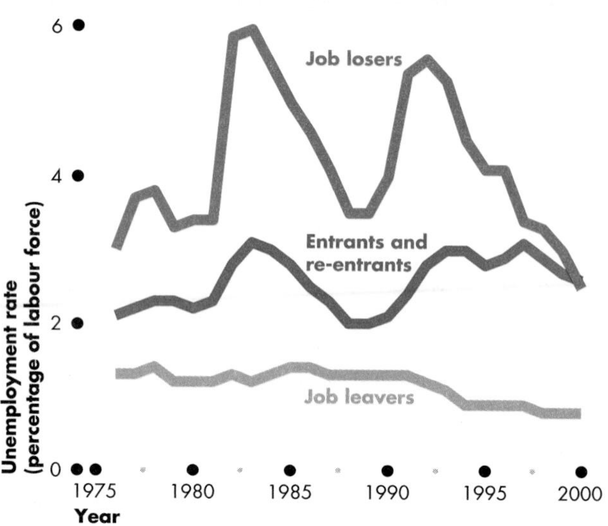

Everyone who is unemployed is a job loser, a job leaver, or an entrant or re-entrant into the labour force. Most unemployment results from job loss. The number of job losers fluctuates more closely with the business cycle than do the numbers of job leavers and entrants and re-entrants. Entrants and re-entrants are the second most common type of unemployed people. Their number fluctuates with the business cycle because of discouraged workers. Job leavers are the least common type of unemployed people.

Source: Statistics Canada, *Labour Force Historical Review* CD-ROM, 2001.

FIGURE 21.9 Unemployment by Duration

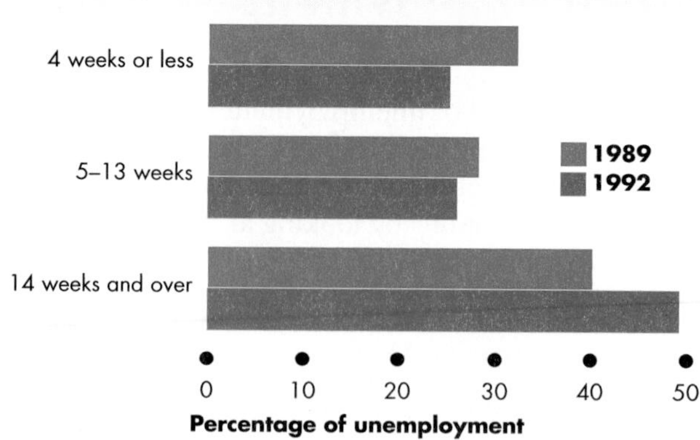

Close to a business cycle peak in 1989, when the unemployment rate was 7.5 percent, 32 percent of unemployment lasted for 4 weeks or less, 28 percent lasted for 5 to 13 weeks, and less than 40 percent lasted for 14 weeks or more. In a business cycle trough in 1992, when the unemployment rate was 11 percent, 25 percent of unemployment lasted for 4 weeks or less, 26 percent lasted for 5 to 13 weeks, and 49 percent lasted for 14 weeks or more.

Source: Statistics Canada, *Labour Force Historical Review* CD-ROM, 2001.

constant, although to the extent that it fluctuates, it does so in line with the business cycle: A slightly larger number of people leave their jobs in good times than in bad times.

The Duration of Unemployment Some people are unemployed for a week or two, and others are unemployed for periods of a year or more. The longer the spell of unemployment, the greater the personal cost to the unemployed. The average duration of unemployment varies over the business cycle.

Figure 21.9 compares the duration of unemployment at a business cycle peak in 1989, when the unemployment rate was low, with that at a business cycle trough in 1992, when the unemployment rate was high. In 1989, when the unemployment rate hit a low of 7.5 percent, 32 percent of the unemployed were in that situation for less than 4 weeks and less than 40 percent of the unemployed were jobless for longer than 13 weeks. In 1992, when the unemployment rate reached a high of 11 percent, only 25 percent of the unemployed found a new job in 4 weeks or less and 49 percent were unemployed for more than 13 weeks. At both low and high unemployment rates, about 27 percent of the unemployed take between 4 weeks and 13 weeks to find a job.

The Demographics of Unemployment Figure 21.10 shows unemployment for different demographic groups. The figure shows that high unemployment rates occur among young workers. In the business cycle trough in 1992, the teenage unemployment rate was 20 percent. Even in 1989, when the national unemployment rate was 7.5 percent, the teenage unemployment rate was 13 percent.

FIGURE 21.10 Unemployment by Demographic Group

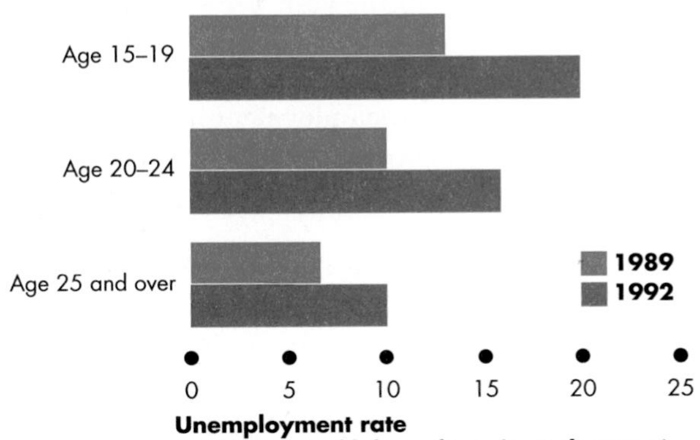

Teenagers experience the highest unemployment rates. In the 1992 business cycle trough (when unemployment was at its highest rate, 11 percent), the teenage unemployment rate was 20 percent. Even at the 1989 business cycle peak (when the unemployment rate was at its lowest, 7.5 percent), the teenage unemployment rate was 13 percent.

Source: Statistics Canada, CANSIM table 282-0002.

Why is the unemployment rate of young people so high? There are three reasons. First, young people are still in the process of discovering what they are good at and trying different lines of work. So they leave their jobs more frequently than do older workers. Second, firms sometimes hire teenagers on a short-term trial basis. So the rate of job loss is higher for teenagers than for other people. Third, most young persons are not in the labour force but are in school. This fact means that the percentage of the young adult population that is unemployed is much lower than the percentage of the young labour force that is unemployed. In 2001, for example, 340,000 15-to-24 year olds were unemployed and 2.3 million were employed. So the 15-to-24 year olds' unemployment rate was 12.9 percent. But 4 million were enrolled in post-secondary education. If we considered being in school as the equivalent of having a job and measured the unemployment rate as the percentage of the labour force plus the school population, we would record a 5.1 percent unemployment rate among 15-to-24 year olds.

Types of Unemployment

Unemployment is classified into four types that are based on its origins. They are

- Frictional
- Structural
- Seasonal
- Cyclical

Frictional Unemployment The unemployment that arises from normal labour turnover—from people entering and leaving the labour force and from the ongoing creation and destruction of jobs—is called **frictional unemployment.** This type of unemployment is a permanent and healthy phenomenon in a dynamic, growing economy.

The unending flow of people into and out of the labour force and the processes of job creation and job destruction create the need for people to search for jobs and for businesses to search for workers. Always, there are businesses with unfilled jobs and people seeking jobs. Look in your local newspaper, and you will see that there are always some jobs being advertised. Businesses don't usually hire the first person who applies for a job, and unemployed people don't usually take the first job that comes their way. Instead, both firms and workers spend time searching out what they believe will be the best match available. By this search process, people can match their own skills and interests with the available jobs and find a satisfying job and income. While these unemployed people are searching, they are frictionally unemployed.

The amount of frictional unemployment depends on the rate at which people enter and re-enter the labour force and on the rate at which jobs are created and destroyed. During the 1970s, the amount of frictional unemployment increased as a consequence of the post-war baby boom that began during the 1940s. By the late 1970s, the baby boom created a bulge in the number of people leaving school. As these people entered the labour force, the amount of frictional unemployment increased.

The amount of frictional unemployment is influenced by unemployment compensation. The greater the number of unemployed people covered by employment insurance and the more generous the unemployment benefits they receive, the longer is the average time taken in job search and the greater is the amount of frictional unemployment. Canadian employment insurance is among the most comprehensive and generous in the world. It is much more comprehensive than that in the United States. This factor is one reason why the Canadian unemployment rate has exceeded the U.S. unemployment rate since the early 1980s. But there are other reasons. Canadian workers, especially young workers who make up the so-called Generation X, have shorter spells of employment and more frequent intervening spells of unemployment, supported by employment insurance, than do young U.S. workers.[4]

Structural Unemployment The unemployment that arises when changes in technology or international competition change the skills needed to perform jobs or change the locations of jobs is called **structural unemployment.** This type of unemployment usually lasts longer than frictional unemployment because workers must retrain and possibly relocate to find a job. For example, when a steel plant in Hamilton, Ontario, is automated, some jobs in that city are destroyed. Meanwhile, in the Ottawa valley and Vancouver, new jobs for security guards, life-insurance salespeople, and retail clerks are created. The unemployed former steelworkers remain unemployed for several months until they move, retrain, and get one of these jobs. Structural unemployment is painful, especially for older workers for whom the best available option might be to retire early but with a lower income than they had expected.

At some times the amount of structural unemployment is modest. At other times it is large, and at such times, structural unemployment can become a serious long-term problem. It was especially large during the late 1970s and early 1980s. During those years, oil price hikes and an increasingly competitive international environment destroyed jobs in traditional Canadian industries, such as auto and steel, and created jobs in new industries, such as electronics and bioengineering, as well as in banking and insurance. Structural unemployment was also present during the early 1990s as many businesses and governments "downsized."

Seasonal Unemployment Many jobs are available only at certain times of the year. **Seasonal unemployment** is the unemployment that arises because the number of jobs available has decreased because of the season. Most seasonal unemployment in Canada occurs in the winter because construction and outdoor farming essentially close down for several months.

Cyclical Unemployment The unemployment that fluctuates over the business cycle is called **cyclical unemployment.** This type of unemployment increases during a recession and decreases during an expansion. An auto worker who is laid off because the economy is in a recession and who gets rehired some months later when the expansion begins has experienced cyclical unemployment.

Full Employment

There is always *some* unemployment. So what do we mean by *full employment*? **Full employment** occurs when there is no cyclical unemployment or, equivalently, when all the unemployment is frictional, structural, and seasonal. The unemployment rate at full employment is called the **natural rate of unemployment**. The divergence of the unemployment rate from the natural rate of unemployment is cyclical unemployment.

There can be a lot of unemployment at full employment, and the term "full employment" is an example of a technical economic term that does not correspond with everyday language. The term "natural rate of unemployment" is another technical economic term whose meaning does not correspond with everyday language. For most people—especially for unemployed workers—there is nothing *natural* about unemployment.

So why do economists call a situation with a lot of unemployment "full employment"? And why is the unemployment at full employment called "natural"?

The reason is that the economy is a complex mechanism that is always changing. Every day, some people retire, new workers enter the labour force, some businesses downsize or fail and others expand or start up. This process of change creates unavoidable frictions and dislocations, which create unemployment. Economists don't agree about the size of the natural rate of unemployment or the extent to which it fluctuates.

[4] These conclusions are based on the work of David Card and Craig W. Riddell, "A Comparative Analysis of Unemployment in Canada and the United States" *Small Differences that Matter: Labour Markets and Income Maintenance in Canada and the United States*, edited by Richard Freeman and David Card, Chicago: University of Chicago Press and NBER, 1993, pp. 149–189, and Audra J. Bowlus, "What Generation X Can Tell Us About the U.S.—Canadian Unemployment Rate Gap" University of Western Ontario, 1996.

FIGURE 21.11 Unemployment and Real GDP

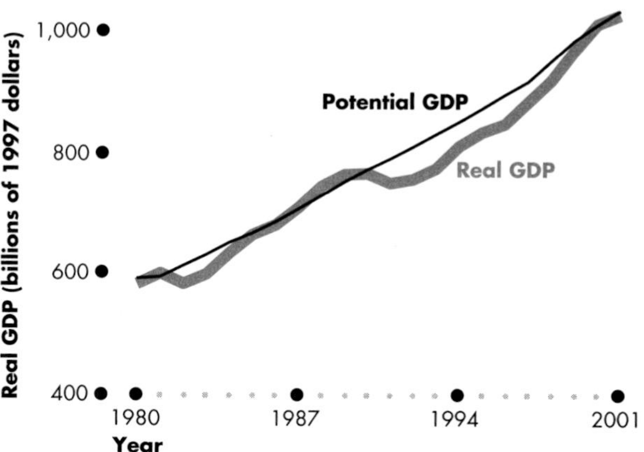

(a) Real GDP

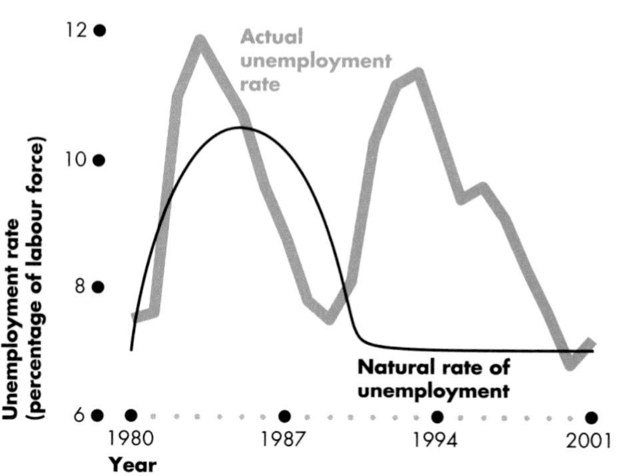

(b) Unemployment rate

As real GDP fluctuates around potential GDP (part a), the unemployment rate fluctuates around the natural rate of unemployment (part b). In the deep recession of 1982, the unemployment rate reached almost 12 percent. In the milder recession of 1990–1991, the unemployment rate peaked at about 11 percent. The natural rate of unemployment increased during the 1980s and decreased during the 1990s.

Sources: Statistics Canada, CANSIM tables 282-0002 and 380-0002, International Monetary Fund, *World Economic Outlook*, Output gap series, and the authors' assumptions.

Real GDP and Unemployment Over the Cycle

The quantity of real GDP at full employment is called **potential GDP.** You will study the forces that determine potential GDP in Chapter 29 (pp. 686–687). Over the business cycle, real GDP fluctuates around potential GDP and the unemployment rate fluctuates around the natural rate of unemployment. Figure 21.11 illustrates these fluctuations in Canada between 1980 and 2001—real GDP in part (a) and the unemployment rate in part (b).

When the economy is at full employment, the unemployment rate equals the natural rate of unemployment and real GDP equals potential GDP. When the unemployment rate is less than the natural rate of unemployment, real GDP is greater than potential GDP. And when the unemployment rate is greater than the natural rate of unemployment, real GDP is less than potential GDP.

Figure 21.11(b) shows one view of the natural rate of unemployment. Keep in mind that economists do not know the magnitude of the natural rate of unemployment and the natural rate shown in the figure is only one estimate. In Fig. 21.11(b), the natural rate of unemployment rose during the 1980s and then fell through the late 1980s and stabilized during the 1990s at around 7 percent. This estimate of the natural rate of unemployment in Canada is one that many, but not all, economists would accept.

REVIEW QUIZ

1 What are the categories of people who become unemployed?
2 Define frictional unemployment, structural unemployment, and cyclical unemployment and provide an example of each type of unemployment.
3 What is the natural rate of unemployment?
4 How might the natural rate of unemployment change and what factors might make it change?
5 How does the unemployment rate fluctuate over the business cycle?

Your final task in this chapter is to learn about another vital sign that gets monitored every month: the Consumer Price Index (CPI). What is the CPI, how do we measure it, and what does it mean?

The Consumer Price Index

STATISTICS CANADA CALCULATES THE CONSUMER Price Index every month. The **Consumer Price Index (CPI)** is a measure of the average of the prices paid by urban consumers for a fixed "basket" of consumer goods and services. What you learn in this section will help you to make sense of the CPI and relate it to your own economic life. The CPI tells you what has happened to the value of the money in your pocket.

Reading the CPI Numbers

The CPI is defined to equal 100 for a period called the **base period.** Currently, the base period is 1992. That is, for the average of the 12 months of 1992, the CPI equals 100.

In May 2002, the CPI was 118.6. This number tells us that the average of the prices paid by urban consumers for a fixed market basket of consumer goods and services was 18.6 percent higher in May 2002 than it was on the average during 1992.

In May 2001, the CPI was 117.4. Comparing the May 2002 CPI with the May 2001 CPI tells us that the index of the prices paid by urban consumers for a fixed basket of consumer goods and services increased during the year ended May 2002 by 1.2—from 117.4 to 118.6.

Constructing the CPI

Constructing the CPI is a huge operation that costs millions of dollars and involves three stages:

- Selecting the CPI basket
- Conducting the monthly price survey
- Calculating the CPI

Selecting the CPI Basket The first stage in constructing the CPI is to select what is called the CPI basket. This "basket" contains the goods and services represented in the index and the relative importance attached to each of them. The idea is to make the relative importance of the items in the CPI basket the same as that in the budget of an average urban household. For example, because people spend more on housing than on bus rides, the CPI places more weight on the price of housing than on the price of bus rides.

Statistics Canada uses several baskets and calculates several alternative CPIs. The goal of the alternatives is to omit items that are highly volatile and that mask the deeper changes in the index. Here, we'll look only at the main "All-Items" index.

To determine the spending patterns of households and to select the CPI basket, Statistics Canada conducts a Consumer Expenditure Survey. This survey is costly and so is undertaken only once every few years. Today's CPI basket is based on data gathered in a Consumer Expenditure Survey of 1996.

Figure 21.12 shows the CPI basket at the end of 2001. The basket contains thousands of individual goods and services arranged in the eight large groups shown in the figure. The most important item in a household's budget is shelter, which accounts for 27 percent of total expenditure. Transportation comes next at 19 percent. Third in relative importance is food at 18 percent. These three groups account for almost two-thirds of the average household budget.

FIGURE 21.12 The CPI Basket

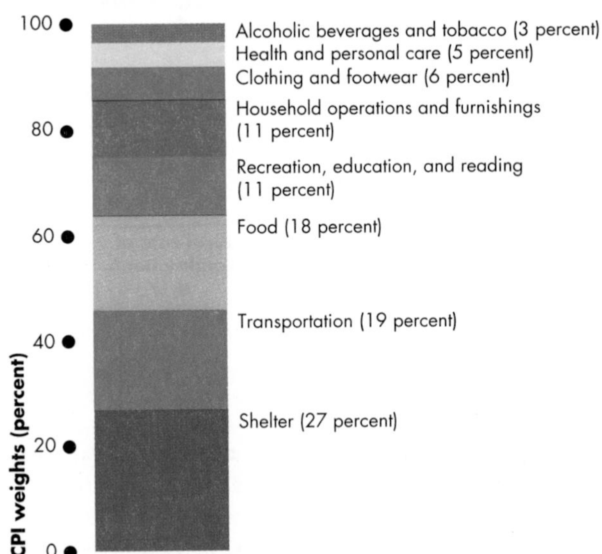

The CPI basket consists of the items that an average urban household buys. It consists mainly of shelter (27 percent), transportation (19 percent), and food (18 percent). All other items add up to 36 percent of the total.

Source: Statistics Canada, Catalogue 62-557-XIB.

Statistics Canada breaks down each of these categories into smaller ones. For example, the recreation, education, and reading category breaks down into textbooks and supplies, tuition, telephone services, and personal computer services.

As you look at the relative importance of the items in the CPI basket, remember that they apply to the *average* household. *Individual* households are spread around the average. Think about your own expenditure and compare the basket of goods and services you buy with the CPI basket.

Conducting the Monthly Price Survey Each month, Statistics Canada employees check the prices of the goods and services in the CPI basket in 64 urban centres. Because the CPI aims to measure price *changes*, it is important that the prices recorded each month refer to exactly the same item. For example, suppose that the price of a box of jellybeans has increased, but a box now contains more beans. Has the price of jellybeans increased? Statistics Canada employees must record the details of changes in quality or packaging so that price changes can be isolated from other changes.

Once the raw price data are in hand, the next task is to calculate the CPI.

Calculating the CPI The CPI calculation has three steps:

1. Find the cost of the CPI basket at base period prices.
2. Find the cost of the CPI basket at current period prices.
3. Calculate the CPI for the base period and the current period.

We'll work through these three steps for a simple example. Suppose the CPI basket contains only two goods and services: oranges and haircuts. We'll construct an annual CPI rather than a monthly CPI with the base period 2002 and the current period 2003.

Table 21.1 shows the quantities in the CPI basket and the prices in the base period and current period.

Part (a) contains the data for the base period. In that period, consumers bought 10 oranges at \$1 each and 5 haircuts at \$8 each. To find the cost of the CPI basket in the base period prices, multiply the quantities in the CPI basket by the base period prices. The cost of oranges is \$10 (10 at \$1 each), and the cost of haircuts is \$40 (5 at \$8 each). So total expenditure in the base period on the CPI basket is \$50 (\$10 + \$40).

Part (b) contains the price data for the current period. The price of an orange increased from \$1 to \$2, which is a 100 percent increase (\$1 ÷ \$1 × 100 = 100). The price of a haircut increased from \$8 to \$10, which is a 25 percent increase (\$2 ÷ \$8 × 100 = 25).

The CPI provides a way of averaging these price increases by comparing the costs of the baskets rather than the prices of the items. To find the cost of the CPI basket in the current period, 2003, multiply the quantities in the basket by their 2003 prices. The cost of oranges is \$20 (10 at \$2 each), and the cost of haircuts is \$50 (5 at \$10 each) So total expenditure on the fixed CPI basket at current period prices is \$70 (\$20 + \$50).

You've now taken the first two steps towards calculating the CPI: calculating the cost of the CPI basket in the base period and the cost in the current period. The third step uses the numbers you've just calculated to find the CPI for 2002 and 2003.

The formula for the CPI is

$$\text{CPI} = \frac{\text{Cost of CPI basket at current period prices}}{\text{Cost of CPI basket at base period prices}} \times 100.$$

TABLE 21.1 The CPI: A Simplified Calculation

(a) The cost of the CPI basket at base period prices: 2002

Item	CPI basket Quantity	Price	Cost of CPI basket
Oranges	10	\$1	\$10
Haircuts	5	\$8	\$40
Cost of CPI basket at base period prices			\$50

(b) The cost of the CPI basket at current period prices: 2003

Item	CPI basket Quantity	Price	Cost of CPI basket
Oranges	10	\$ 2	\$20
Haircuts	5	\$10	\$50
Cost of CPI basket at current period prices			\$70

In Table 21.1, you have established that in 2002, the cost of the CPI basket was \$50 and in 2003, it was \$70. You also know that the base period is 2002. So the cost of the CPI basket at base period prices is \$50. If we use these numbers in the CPI formula, we can find the CPI for 2002 and 2003. For 2002, the CPI is

$$\text{CPI in 2002} = \frac{\$50}{\$50} \times 100 = 100.$$

For 2003, the CPI is

$$\text{CPI in 2003} = \frac{\$70}{\$50} \times 100 = 140.$$

The principles that you've applied in this simplified CPI calculation apply to the calculations performed every month by Statistics Canada.

Measuring Inflation

A major purpose of the CPI is to measure *changes* in the cost of living and in the value of money. To measure these changes, we calculate the **inflation rate,** which is the percentage change in the price level from one year to the next. To calculate the inflation rate, we use the formula:

$$\text{Inflation rate} = \frac{(\text{CPI this year} - \text{CPI last year})}{\text{CPI last year}} \times 100.$$

We can use this formula to calculate the inflation rate. The CPI in May 2002 was 118.6, and the CPI in May 2001 was 117.4. So the inflation rate during the year to May 2002 was

$$\text{Inflation rate} = \frac{(118.6 - 117.4)}{117.4} \times 100 = 1.02.$$

Figure 21.13 shows the CPI and the inflation rate in Canada during the 30 years between 1971 and 2001. The two parts of the figure are related.

Figure 21.13 shows that when the price *level* in part (a) rises rapidly, the inflation rate in part (b) is high, and when the price level in part (a) rises slowly, the inflation rate in part (b) is low. Notice in part (a) that the CPI increased every year during this period.

During the late 1970s and early 1980s, the CPI increased rapidly, but its rate of increase slowed during the 1980s and 1990s.

FIGURE 21.13 The CPI and the Inflation Rate

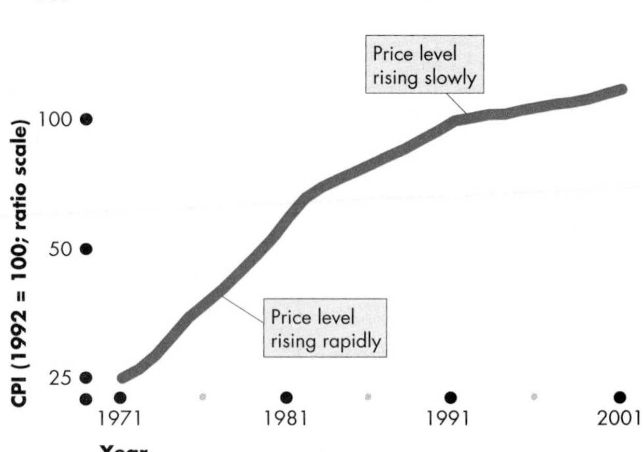

(a) CPI: 1971–2001

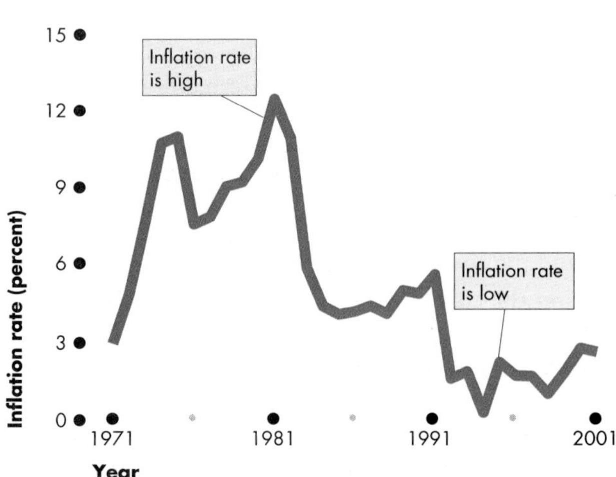

(b) Inflation rate: 1971–2001

In part (a), the CPI (the price level) has increased every year. In part (b), the inflation rate has averaged 5.25 percent a year. During the 1970s and early 1980s, the inflation rate was high and sometimes exceeded 10 percent a year. But after 1985, the inflation rate fell to an average of 3 percent a year.

Source: Statistics Canada, CANSIM table 326-0002.

The CPI is not a perfect measure of the price level, and changes in the CPI probably overstate the inflation rate. Let's look at the sources of bias.

The Biased CPI

The main sources of bias in the CPI are

- New goods bias
- Quality change bias
- Commodity substitution bias
- Outlet substitution bias

New Goods Bias If you want to compare the price level in 2003 with that in 1973, you must somehow compare the price of a computer today with that of a typewriter in 1973. Because a PC is more expensive than a typewriter was, the arrival of the PC puts an upward bias into the CPI and its inflation rate.

Quality Change Bias Cars, CD players, and many other items get better every year. Part of the rise in the prices of these items is a payment for improved quality and is not inflation. But the CPI counts the entire price rise as inflation and so overstates inflation.

Commodity Substitution Bias Changes in relative prices lead consumers to change the items they buy. For example, if the price of beef rises and the price of chicken remains unchanged, people buy more chicken and less beef. Suppose they switch from beef to chicken on a scale that provides the same amount of protein and the same enjoyment as before and their expenditure is the same as before. The price of protein has not changed. But because it ignores the substitution of chicken for beef, the CPI says the price of protein has increased.

Outlet Substitution Bias When confronted with higher prices, people use discount stores more frequently and convenience stores less frequently. This phenomenon is called *outlet substitution.* The CPI surveys do not monitor outlet substitutions.

The Magnitude of the Bias

How big is the bias in the measurement of the CPI? The answer varies from country to country. In the United States, the bias is believed to range between 1 percent and 2 percent a year. But in Canada, it is believed to be at most 1 percent a year and probably less than this amount.

To reduce the bias problems, Statistics Canada revises the basket used for calculating the CPI about every 10 years. Also, Statistics Canada tries to estimate the quantitative effects of the various sources of bias and eliminate them by statistical adjustments. It is these adjustments that make Canada's CPI a more reliable measure of the price level than the CPI in the United States is of the U.S. price level.

Some Consequences of the Bias

The bias in the CPI has three main consequences. It

- Distorts private contracts.
- Increases government outlays.
- Biases estimates of real earnings.

Many private agreements, such as wage contracts, are linked to the CPI. For example, a firm and its workers might agree to a three-year wage deal that increases the wage rate by 2 percent a year *plus* the percentage increase in the CPI. Such a deal ends up giving the workers more *real* income than the firm intended.

Close to a third of federal government outlays are linked directly to the CPI. And while a bias of 1 percent a year seems small, accumulated over a decade, it adds up to billions of dollars of additional expenditures.

Trade unions and businesses bargain over wages based in part on changes in the CPI. If the CPI is biased upwards, businesses might agree to wage increases that are larger than they would accept if the CPI were measured accurately.

REVIEW QUIZ

1. What is the CPI and how is it calculated?
2. How do we calculate the inflation rate and what is the relationship between the CPI and the inflation rate?
3. What are the four main ways in which the CPI is an upward-biased measure of the price level?
4. What problems arise from the CPI bias?

Readings Between the Lines on pp. 494–495 looks at the CPI in 2002. You've now completed your study of the measurement of macroeconomic performance. Your task in the following chapters is to learn what determines that performance and how policy actions might improve it.

READING BETWEEN THE LINES

The Monthly CPI Report

THE GLOBE AND MAIL, SEPTEMBER 21, 2002

Ont. electricity jolts inflation

A huge jump in electricity prices in Ontario triggered by a heat wave that hit shortly after the province moved to open-market pricing drove the Canadian inflation rate in August to 2.6 per cent.

That was up from an annualized 2.1 per cent in July, Statistics Canada said yesterday. Some economists said the rise in the cost of living was steep enough to cause concern. ...

Electricity prices climbed 18.3 per cent in Ontario in August from a month earlier, Statscan said in its monthly inflation report. That followed a 9.2-per-cent increase in July from June. ...

Upward pressure on gasoline prices and car insurance also pushed up the cost of living in August as the cost of filling the gas tank climbed 2.5 per cent, and insurance premiums rose 2.6 per cent.

The core rate of inflation closely monitored by the Bank of Canada climbed 2.5 per cent in August from an annual rate of 2.1 per cent in July, the biggest advance since September of 1995. Without electricity, the core rate was 2.2 per cent in August.

The Bank of Canada's core measure excludes the eight most volatile items, such as food, energy and indirect taxes, but includes electricity prices. ...

The increase in gasoline, electricity and auto insurance premiums accounted for almost the entire upward movement in inflation in August—without those items, the rise was a tepid 0.6 per cent, ...

Some prices fell in August, including fresh vegetables, which dropped 13.8 per cent because of the increased availability as local crops came on the market.

Essence of the Story

- Statistics Canada reported that the inflation rate in August 2002 was 2.6 percent (annual rate) up from 2.1 percent in July 2002.
- Ontario electricity prices increased by 18.3 percent in August and by 9.2 percent in July, and these increases are reported as the source of the jump in the inflation rate.
- Gasoline and car insurance prices also increased at a faster pace in August.
- The core inflation rate, which excludes food, energy, and indirect taxes but includes electricity, increased at an annual rate of 2.5 percent in August, up from 2.1 percent in July.
- This jump in the core inflation rate in August 2002 was the biggest since September 1995.
- Some prices fell in August, including those of fresh vegetables, which dropped 13.8 percent.

Economic Analysis

■ Statistics Canada reports the nation's Consumer Price Index (CPI) numbers every month.

■ The Consumer Price Index is an indicator of the changes in consumer prices experienced by Canadians.

■ The Consumer Price Index is obtained by comparing the price of a fixed basket of commodities purchased by Canadians over different time periods.

■ The fixed basket includes food, shelter, household operations and furnishings, clothing and footwear, transportation, health and personal care, recreation, education and reading, and alcoholic beverages and tobacco products.

■ Figure 1 shows the Consumer Price Index for each month from January 2000 through October 2002.

■ In August 2001, the Consumer Price Index was 116.7 and in August 2002, it was 119.2.

■ The annual inflation rate between August 2001 and August 2002 was 2.1 percent. This inflation rate is calculated as

$$\frac{(119.2 - 116.7)}{116.7} \times 100.$$

■ Figure 2 shows the inflation rate for each month between January 2000 and October 2002. You can see that the inflation rate was on a slightly rising trend through 2000 and the first half of 2001, fell in the second half of 2001, and increased during 2002.

■ In addition to reporting the Consumer Price Index, Statistics Canada also reports a monthly index for each component of the Consumer Price Index basket.

■ Figure 3 shows the percentage changes in each component of the Consumer Price Index basket between July and August 2002.

■ These price changes tell us about *relative prices.* They do not tell us anything about inflation. Nor do they tell us *why* the inflation rate changed.

■ It is a common mistake in the media to say that the inflation rate increased (or decreased) *because* a particular price increased (or decreased).

■ The price of Ontario electricity increased. But this change in relative prices provides no information about why the inflation rate changed. Lots of relative prices changed, as Fig. 3 shows.

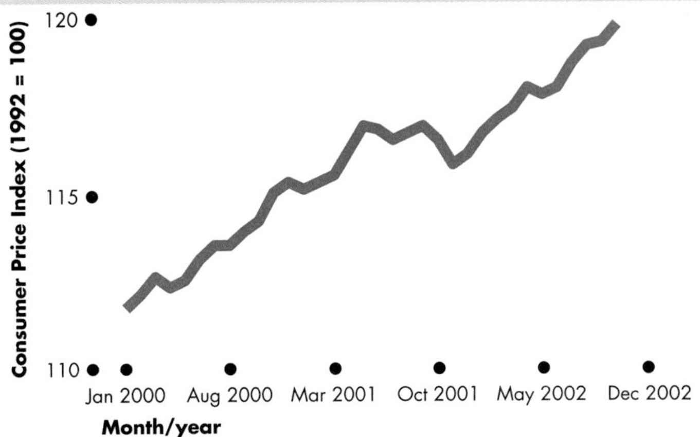

Figure 1 Consumer Price Index

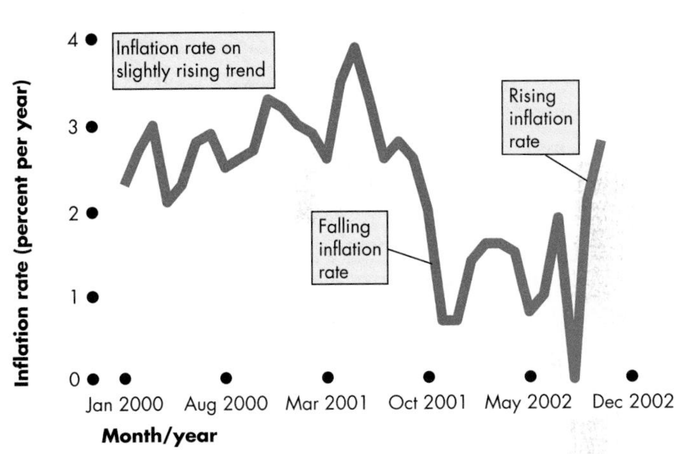

Figure 2 Inflation rate

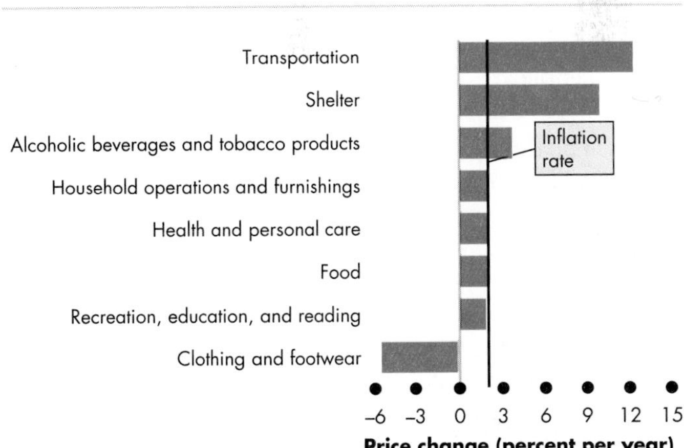

Figure 3 Relative price changes between July and August 2002

SUMMARY

KEY POINTS

The Business Cycle (pp. 478–479)

- A recession is a significant decline in activity spread across the economy and lasting more than a few months.
- Another definition of recession is a decrease in real GDP that lasts for at least two quarters.
- The ECRI has identified only 4 recessions and expansions in Canada since World War II.

Jobs and Wages (pp. 480–484)

- The unemployment rate averaged 7.7 percent between 1961 and 2001. It increases in recessions and decreases in expansions.
- The labour force participation rate and the employment-to-population ratio have an upward trend and fluctuate with the business cycle.
- The labour force participation rate has increased for females and decreased for males.
- Aggregate hours have an upward trend, and they fluctuate with the business cycle.
- Real hourly wage rates grow but their growth rates slowed during the 1970s.

Unemployment and Full Employment (pp. 485–489)

- People are constantly entering and leaving the state of unemployment.
- The duration of unemployment fluctuates over the business cycle. But the demographic patterns of unemployment are constant.
- Unemployment can be frictional, structural, seasonal, and cyclical.
- When all unemployment is frictional, structural, and seasonal, the unemployment rate equals the natural rate of unemployment, the economy is at full employment, and real GDP equals potential GDP.
- Over the business cycle, real GDP fluctuates around potential GDP and the unemployment rate fluctuates around the natural rate of unemployment.

The Consumer Price Index (pp. 490–493)

- The Consumer Price Index (CPI) measures the average of the prices paid by urban consumers for a fixed basket of consumer goods and services.
- The CPI is defined to equal 100 for the base period—currently 1992.
- The inflation rate is the percentage change in the CPI from one year to the next.
- Changes in the CPI probably overstate the inflation rate slightly.
- The bias in the CPI distorts private contracts and increases government outlays.

KEY FIGURES

Figure 21.1 Two Views of Canadian Business Cycles, 479
Figure 21.2 Population Labour Force Categories, 480
Figure 21.7 Labour Market Flows, 485
Figure 21.11 Unemployment and Real GDP, 489
Figure 21.12 The CPI Basket, 490

KEY TERMS

Aggregate hours, 483
Base period, 490
Consumer Price Index (CPI), 490
Cyclical unemployment, 488
Discouraged workers, 482
Employment-to-population ratio, 482
Entrants, 485
Frictional unemployment, 487
Full employment, 488
Growth rate cycle downturn, 478
Inflation rate, 492
Job leavers, 485
Job losers, 485
Labour force, 480
Labour force participation rate, 482
Natural rate of unemployment, 488
Potential GDP, 489
Real wage rate, 484
Re-entrants, 485
Seasonal unemployment, 488
Structural unemployment, 488
Unemployment rate, 481
Working-age population, 480

PROBLEMS

*1. Statistics Canada reported the following data for January 2000: Labour force: 15,537,700 Employment: 14,339,200 Working-age population: 24,137,100. Calculate for that month the
   a. Unemployment rate.
   b. Labour force participation rate.
   c. Employment-to-population ratio.

2. Statistics Canada reported the following data for January 2001: Labour force: 16,219,800 Employment: 14,990,400 Working-age population: 24,764,100. Calculate for that month the
   a. Unemployment rate.
   b. Labour force participation rate.
   c. Employment-to-population ratio.

*3. During 2000, the working-age population in Canada increased by 327,100, employment increased by 280,900, and the labour force increased by 330,400. Use these numbers and the data in problem 1 to calculate the change in unemployment and the change in the number of people not in the labour force during 2000.

4. During 2001, the working-age population in Canada increased by 299,900, employment decreased by 16,600, and the labour force increased by 329,200. Use these numbers and the data in problem 2 to calculate the change in unemployment and the change in the number of people not in the labour force during 2001.

*5. In August 2000, the unemployment rate was 7.2 percent. In August 2001, the unemployment rate was 7.5 percent. Use this information to predict what happened between August 2000 and August 2001 to the numbers of
   a. Job losers and job leavers.
   b. Labour force entrants and re-entrants.

6. In January 2001, the unemployment rate was 7.5 percent. In January 2002, the unemployment rate was 8.6 percent. Use these data to predict what happened between January 2001 and January 2002 to the numbers of
   a. Job losers and job leavers.
   b. Labour force entrants and re-entrants.

*7. In July 2002, on Sandy Island, 10,000 people were employed, 1,000 were unemployed, and 5,000 were not in the labour force. During August 2002, 80 people lost their jobs, 20 quit their jobs, 150 were hired or recalled, 50 withdrew from the labour force, and 40 entered or re-entered the labour force. Calculate for July 2002
   a. The labour force.
   b. The unemployment rate.
   c. The working-age population.
   d. The employment-to-population ratio.

   And calculate for the end of August 2002
   e. The number of people unemployed.
   f. The number of people employed.
   g. The labour force.
   h. The unemployment rate.

8. In July 2003 on Sandy Island, 11,000 people were employed, 900 were unemployed, and 5,000 were not in the labour force. During August 2003, 40 people lost their jobs, 10 quit their jobs, 180 were hired or recalled, 20 withdrew from the labour force, and 60 entered or re-entered the labour force. Calculate for July 2003
   a. The labour force.
   b. The unemployment rate.
   c. The working-age population.
   d. The employment-to-population ratio.

   And calculate for the end of August 2003
   e. The number of people unemployed.
   f. The number of people employed.
   g. The labour force.
   h. The unemployment rate.

9. A typical family on Sandy Island consumes only juice and cloth. Last year, which was the base year, the family spent $40 on juice and $25 on cloth. In the base year, juice was $4 a bottle and cloth was $5 a length. In the current year, juice is $4 a bottle and cloth is $6 a length. Calculate
   a. The basket used in the CPI.
   b. The CPI in the current year.
   c. The inflation rate in the current year.

10. A typical family on Lizard Island consumes only mangoes and nuts. In the base year, the family spent $60 on nuts and $10 on mangoes. In the base year, mangoes were $1 each and nuts were $3 a bag. In the current year, mangoes are $1.50 each and nuts are $4 a bag. Calculate
   a. The basket used in the CPI.
   b. The CPI in the current year.
   c. The inflation rate in the current year.

CRITICAL THINKING

1. Study *Reading Between the Lines* on pp. 494–495 and then answer the following questions:
   a. Describe the changes in the CPI that occurred during 2002.
   b. Explain the difference between a change in a relative price and inflation. Which relative prices increased most in August 2002 and which increased least or fell?
   c. Do you think the news article did a good job reporting the August CPI numbers? Write a brief report that does a better job and explain why it is better.
2. Thinking about the economy of Sandy Island in problems 7 and 8:
   a. In what phase of its business cycle was Sandy Island during 2003?
   b. What do you predict would be happening to real GDP on Sandy Island? Why?
   c. What do you predict would be happening to real GDP per person on Sandy Island? Why?
3. Describe the main features of the labour market at the peak of the business cycle.
4. Describe the main features of the labour market at the trough of the business cycle.
5. You've seen in this chapter that the average workweek has shortened over the years. Do you think that shorter work hours are a problem or a benefit? Do you expect the average workweek to keep getting shorter? Why or why not?
6. An increasing number of jobs are part-time jobs. Can you think of some reasons for this trend? Who benefits from part-time jobs: the employer, the worker, or both? Explain with examples.
7. You've seen that the CPI is biased and overstates the true inflation rate. It would be a simple matter to adjust the CPI for the known average bias. Yet we continue to keep a flawed measure of inflation in place. Why do you think we don't adjust the CPI for the known average bias so that its measure of the inflation rate is more accurate? Explain who gains from the biased measure and who loses from it. Try to think of reasons why those who lose have not persuaded those who win to adopt a more accurate measure.

WEB EXERCISES

1. Use the link on the Parkin–Bade Web site to review the Bank of Canada's latest Monetary Policy Report. In which phase of the business cycle is the economy in your region? How does your region compare to the nation as a whole?
2. Use the link on the Parkin–Bade Web site to visit the Web site of Statistics Canada and find labour market data for your own province.
   a. What have been the trends in employment, unemployment, and labour force participation in your province during the past two years?
   b. On the basis of what you know about your own province, how would you set about explaining these trends?
   c. Try to identify those industries that have expanded most and those that have shrunk.
   d. What are the problems with your own provincial labour market that you think need provincial government action to resolve?
   e. What actions do you think your provincial government must take to resolve these problems? Answer this question by using the demand and supply model of the labour market and predict the effects of the actions you prescribe.
   f. Compare the labour market performance of your own province with that of Canada.
   g. If your province is performing better than the national average, to what do you attribute the success? If your province is performing worse than the national average, to what do you attribute its problems? What federal actions are needed in your provincial labour market?
3. Use the link on the Parkin–Bade Web site to visit the Web site of Statistics Canada and find CPI data for your own province.
   a. What have been the trends in the CPI in your province during the past two years?
   b. Compare the CPI performance of your own province with that of Canada as a whole.
   c. On the basis of what you know about your own province, how would you set about explaining its deviation from the Canadian average?

AGGREGATE SUPPLY AND AGGREGATE DEMAND

CHAPTER 22

Production and Prices

During the 10 years from 1992 to 2002, Canadian real GDP increased by 40 percent. Expanding at this pace, real GDP doubles every 21 years. What forces bring persistent and rapid expansion of real GDP? ◆ Expanding real GDP brings a rising standard of living. Inflation brings a rising cost of living. Because of inflation, you need $2 today to buy what $1 bought in 1980. What causes inflation? ◆ Our economy does not expand at a constant pace. Instead, it ebbs and flows over the business cycle. For example, we had a recession during 1990 and early 1991. For half a year, real GDP decreased. Since that time, our economy has expanded, but at a variable rate. Why do we have a business cycle? ◆ Because our economy fluctuates, the government and the Bank of Canada try to smooth its path. How do the policy actions of the government and the Bank of Canada affect production and prices?

◆ To answer these questions, we need a *model* of real GDP and the price level. Our main task in this chapter is to study such a model: the *aggregate supply–aggregate demand model.* Our second task is to use the aggregate supply–aggregate demand (or *AS–AD*) model to answer the questions we've just posed. You'll discover that this model enables us to understand the forces that make our economy expand, that bring inflation, and that cause business cycle fluctuations. At the end of the chapter, in *Reading Between the Lines,* we'll put the *AS–AD* model to work to understand the macroeconomic effects of implementing the Kyoto agreement on climate control.

After studying this chapter, you will be able to

- **Explain what determines aggregate supply**
- **Explain what determines aggregate demand**
- **Explain macroeconomic equilibrium**
- **Explain the effects of changes in aggregate supply and aggregate demand on economic growth, inflation, and the business cycle**
- **Explain Canadian economic growth, inflation, and the business cycle by using the *AS–AD* model**

Aggregate Supply

THE AGGREGATE SUPPLY–AGGREGATE DEMAND model enables us to understand three features of macroeconomic performance:

- Growth of potential GDP
- Inflation
- Business cycle fluctuations

The model uses the concepts of *aggregate* supply and *aggregate* demand to determine *real GDP* and the *price level* (the GDP deflator). We begin by looking at the limits to production that influence aggregate supply.

Aggregate Supply Fundamentals

The *quantity of real GDP supplied* (*Y*) depends on

1. The quantity of labour (*L*)
2. The quantity of capital (*K*)
3. The state of technology (*T*)

The influence of these three factors on the quantity of real GDP supplied is described by the **aggregate production function,** which is written as the equation:

$$Y = F(L, K, T).$$

In words, the quantity of real GDP supplied is determined by (is a function *F* of) the quantities of labour and capital and the state of technology. The larger is *L*, *K*, or *T*, the greater is *Y*.

At any given time, the quantity of capital and the state of technology are fixed. They depend on decisions that were made in the past. The population is also fixed. But the quantity of labour is not fixed. It depends on decisions made by people and firms about the supply of and demand for labour.

The labour market can be in any one of three states: at full employment, above full employment, or below full employment.

Even at full employment, there are always some people looking for jobs and some firms looking for people to hire. The reason is that there is a constant churning of the labour market. Every day, some jobs are destroyed as businesses reorganize or fail. Some jobs are created as new businesses start up or existing ones expand. Some workers decide, for any of a thousand personal reasons, to quit their jobs. And other people decide to start looking for a job. This constant churning in the labour market prevents unemployment from ever disappearing. The unemployment rate at full employment is called the **natural rate of unemployment.**

Another way to think about full employment is as a state of the labour market in which the quantity of labour demanded equals the quantity supplied. Firms demand labour only if it is profitable to do so. And the lower the wage rate, which is the cost of labour, the greater is the quantity of labour demanded. People supply labour only if doing so is the most valuable use of their time. And the higher the wage rate, which is the return to labour, the greater is the quantity of labour supplied. The wage rate that makes the quantity of labour demanded equal to the quantity of labour supplied is the equilibrium wage rate. At this wage rate, there is full employment. (You can study the labour market at full employment in Chapter 29 on pp. 686–687.)

The quantity of real GDP at full employment is *potential GDP*, which depends on the full-employment quantity of labour, the quantity of capital, and the state of technology. Over the business cycle, employment fluctuates around full employment and real GDP fluctuates around potential GDP.

To study aggregate supply in different states of the labour market, we distinguish two time frames:

- Long-run aggregate supply
- Short-run aggregate supply

Long-Run Aggregate Supply

The economy is constantly bombarded by events that move real GDP away from potential GDP and, equivalently, that move employment away from full employment. Following such an event, forces operate to take real GDP back towards potential GDP and restore full employment. The **macroeconomic long run** is a time frame that is sufficiently long for these forces to have done their work so that real GDP equals potential GDP and full employment prevails.

The **long-run aggregate supply curve** is the relationship between the quantity of real GDP supplied and the price level in the long run when real GDP equals potential GDP. Figure 22.1 shows this relationship as the vertical line labelled *LAS*. Along the long-run aggregate supply curve, as the price level changes, real GDP remains at potential GDP, which in Fig. 22.1 is $1,000 billion. The long-run aggregate supply curve is always vertical and is located at potential GDP.

FIGURE 22.1 Long-Run Aggregate Supply

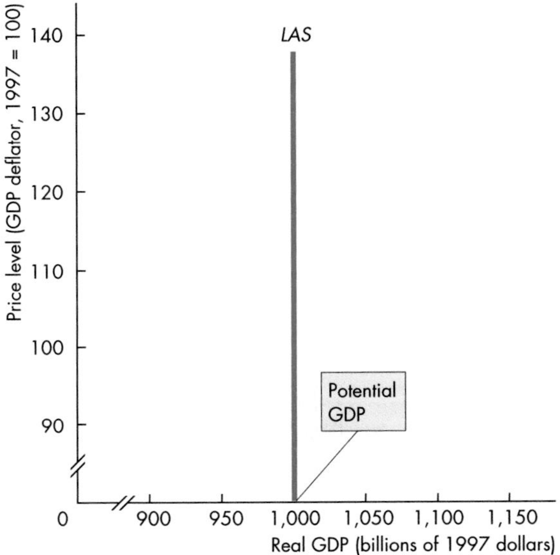

The long-run aggregate supply curve (*LAS*) shows the relationship between potential GDP and the price level. Potential GDP is independent of the price level, so the *LAS* curve is vertical at potential GDP.

The long-run aggregate supply curve is vertical because potential GDP is independent of the price level. The reason for this independence is that a movement along the *LAS* curve is accompanied by a change in *two* sets of prices: the prices of goods and services—the price level—and the prices of productive resources. A 10 percent increase in the prices of goods and services is matched by a 10 percent increase in the money wage rate and other resource prices. That is, the price level, money wage rate, and other resource prices all change by the same percentage, and *relative prices* and the *real wage rate* remain constant. When the price level changes but relative prices and the real wage rate remain constant, real GDP also remains constant.

Production at a Pepsi Plant You can see why real GDP remains constant when all prices change by the same percentage if you think about production decisions at a Pepsi bottling plant. The plant is producing the quantity of Pepsi that maximizes profit. The plant can increase production but only by incurring a higher *marginal cost* (see Chapter 2, p. 37). So the firm has no incentive to change production.

Short-Run Aggregate Supply

The **macroeconomic short run** is a period during which real GDP has fallen below or risen above potential GDP. At the same time, the unemployment rate has risen above or fallen below the natural rate of unemployment.

The **short-run aggregate supply curve** is the relationship between the quantity of real GDP supplied and the price level in the short run when the money wage rate, the prices of other resources, and potential GDP remain constant. Figure 22.2 shows a short-run aggregate supply curve as the upward-sloping curve labelled *SAS*. This curve is based on the short-run aggregate supply schedule, and each point on the aggregate supply curve corresponds to a row of the aggregate supply schedule. For example, point *A* on the short-run aggregate supply curve and row *A* of the schedule tell us that if the price level is 100, the quantity of real GDP supplied is $900 billion.

At point *C*, the price level is 110 and the quantity of real GDP supplied is $1,000 billion, which equals potential GDP. If the price level is higher than 110, real GDP exceeds potential GDP; if the price level is below 110, real GDP is less than potential GDP.

Back at the Pepsi Plant You can see why the short-run aggregate supply curve slopes upward by returning to the Pepsi bottling plant. The plant produces the quantity that maximizes profit. If the price of Pepsi rises and the money wage rate and other costs don't change, the *relative price* of Pepsi rises and the firm has an incentive to increase its production. The higher relative price of Pepsi covers the higher marginal cost of producing more Pepsi, so the firm increases production.

Similarly, if the price of Pepsi falls and the money wage rate and other costs don't change, the lower relative price is not sufficient to cover the marginal cost of Pepsi, so the firm decreases production.

Again, what's true for Pepsi bottlers is true for the producers of all goods and services. So when the price level rises and the money wage rate and other resource prices remain constant, the quantity of real GDP supplied increases.

FIGURE 22.2 Short-Run Aggregate Supply

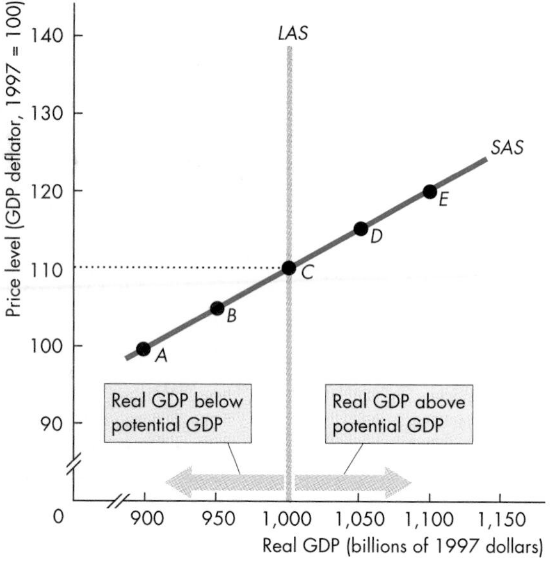

	Price level (GDP deflator)	Real GDP (billions of 1997 dollars)
A	100	900
B	105	950
C	110	1,000
D	115	1,050
E	120	1,100

The short-run aggregate supply curve shows the relationship between the quantity of real GDP supplied and the price level when the money wage rate, other resource prices, and potential GDP remain the same. The short-run aggregate supply curve, *SAS*, is based on the schedule in the table. This curve is upward-sloping because firms' marginal costs increase as output increases, so a higher price is needed, relative to the prices of productive resources, to bring forth an increase in the quantity produced. On the *SAS* curve, when the price level is 110, real GDP equals potential GDP. If the price level is greater than 110, real GDP exceeds potential GDP; if the price level is below 110, real GDP is less than potential GDP.

Movements Along the *LAS* and *SAS* Curves

Figure 21.3 summarizes what you've just learned about the *LAS* and *SAS* curves. When the price level, the money wage rate, and other resource prices rise by the same percentage, relative price remains constant and real GDP remains at potential GDP. There is a *movement along* the *LAS* curve.

When the price level rises but the money wage rate and other resource prices remain the same, the quantity of real GDP supplied increases and there is a *movement along* the *SAS* curve.

Let's next study the influences that bring changes in aggregate supply.

FIGURE 22.3 Movements Along the Aggregate Supply Curves

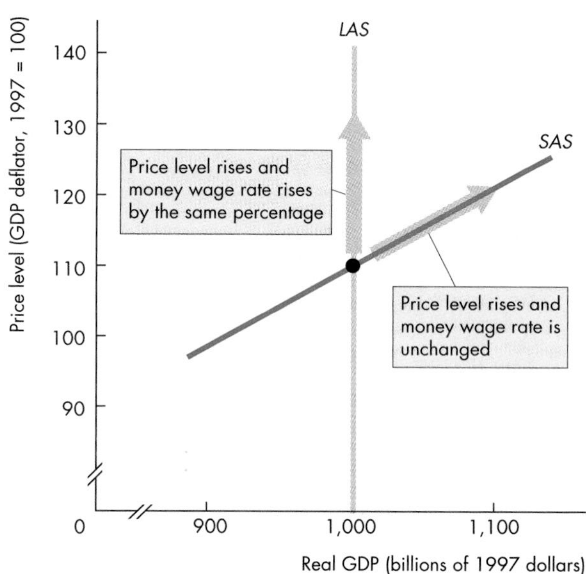

A rise in the price level with no change in the money wage rate and other resource prices brings an increase in the quantity of real GDP supplied and a movement along the short-run aggregate supply curve, *SAS*.

A rise in the price level with equal percentage increases in the money wage rate and other resource prices keeps the quantity of real GDP supplied constant at potential GDP and brings a movement along the long-run aggregate supply curve, *LAS*.

Changes in Aggregate Supply

You've just seen that a change in the price level brings a movement along the aggregate supply curves but does not change aggregate supply. Aggregate supply changes when influences on production plans other than the price level change. Let's begin by looking at factors that change potential GDP.

Changes in Potential GDP When potential GDP changes, both long-run aggregate supply and short-run aggregate supply change. Potential GDP changes for three reasons:

1. A change in the full-employment quantity of labour
2. A change in the quantity of capital
3. An advance in technology

An increase in the full-employment quantity of labour, an increase in the quantity of capital, or an advance in technology increases potential GDP. And an increase in potential GDP changes both the long-run aggregate supply and short-run aggregate supply.

Figure 22.4 shows these effects of a change in potential GDP. Initially, the long-run aggregate supply curve is LAS_0 and the short-run aggregate supply curve is SAS_0. If an increase in the quantity of capital or a technological advance increases potential GDP to $1,100 billion, long-run aggregate supply increases and the long-run aggregate supply curve shifts rightward to LAS_1. Short-run aggregate supply also increases, and the short-run aggregate supply curve shifts rightward to SAS_1.

Let's look more closely at the influences on potential GDP and the aggregate supply curves.

FIGURE 22.4 A Change in Potential GDP

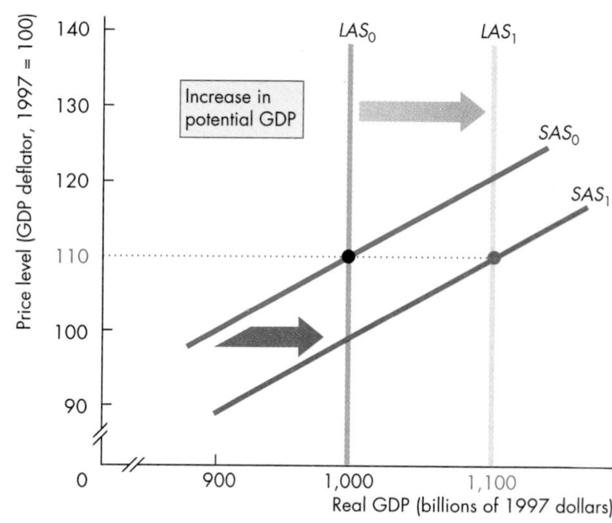

An increase in potential GDP increases both long-run aggregate supply and short-run aggregate supply and shifts both aggregate supply curves rightward, from LAS_0 to LAS_1 and from SAS_0 to SAS_1.

A Change in the Full-Employment Quantity of Labour A Pepsi bottling plant that employs 100 workers bottles more Pepsi than an otherwise identical plant that employs 10 workers. The same is true for the economy as a whole. The larger the quantity of labour employed, the greater is GDP.

Over time, potential GDP increases because the labour force increases. But (with constant capital and technology) *potential* GDP increases only if the full-employment quantity of labour increases. Fluctuations in employment over the business cycle bring fluctuations in real GDP. But these changes in real GDP are fluctuations around potential GDP. They are not changes in potential GDP and long-run aggregate supply.

A Change in the Quantity of Capital A Pepsi bottling plant with two production lines bottles more Pepsi than an otherwise identical plant that has only one production line. For the economy, the larger the quantity of capital, the more productive is the labour force and the greater is its potential GDP. Potential GDP per person in capital-rich Canada is vastly greater than that in capital-poor China and Russia.

Capital includes *human capital*. One Pepsi plant is managed by an economics major with an MBA and has a labour force with an average of 10 years of experience. This plant produces a much larger output than an otherwise identical plant that is managed by someone with no business training or experience and that has a young labour force that is new to bottling. The first plant has a greater amount of human capital than the second. For the economy as a whole, the larger the quantity of *human capital*—the skills that people have acquired in school and through on-the-job training—the greater is potential GDP.

An Advance in Technology A Pepsi plant that has pre-computer age machines produces less than one that uses the latest robot technology. Technological change enables firms to produce more from any given amount of inputs. So even with fixed quantities of labour and capital, improvements in technology increase potential GDP.

Technological advances are by far the most important source of increased production over the past two centuries. Because of technological advances, one farmer in Canada today can feed 100 people and one auto worker can produce almost 14 cars and trucks in a year.

Let's now look at the effects of changes in the money wage rate.

Changes in the Money Wage Rate and Other Resource Prices When the money wage rate or the money prices of other resources (such as the price of oil) change, short-run aggregate supply changes but long-run aggregate supply does not change.

Figure 22.5 shows the effect on aggregate supply of an increase in the money wage rate. Initially, the short-run aggregate supply curve is SAS_0. A rise in the money wage rate *decreases* short-run aggregate supply and shifts the short-run aggregate supply curve leftward to SAS_2.

The money wage rate (and resource prices) affect short-run aggregate supply because they influence firms' costs. The higher the money wage rate, the higher are firms' costs and the smaller is the quantity that firms are willing to supply at each price level. So an increase in the money wage rate decreases short-run aggregate supply.

A change in the money wage rate does not change long-run aggregate supply because on the *LAS* curve, a change in the money wage rate is accompanied by an equal percentage change in the price level. With no change in *relative* prices, firms have no incentive to change production and real GDP remains constant at potential GDP.

In Fig. 22.5, the vertical distance between the original *SAS* curve and the new *SAS* curve is determined by the percentage change in the money wage rate. That is, the percentage increase in the price level between point *A* and point *B* equals the percentage increase in the money wage rate.

Because potential GDP does not change when the money wage rate changes, long-run aggregate supply does not change. The long-run aggregate supply curve remains at *LAS*.

FIGURE 22.5 A Change in the Money Wage Rate

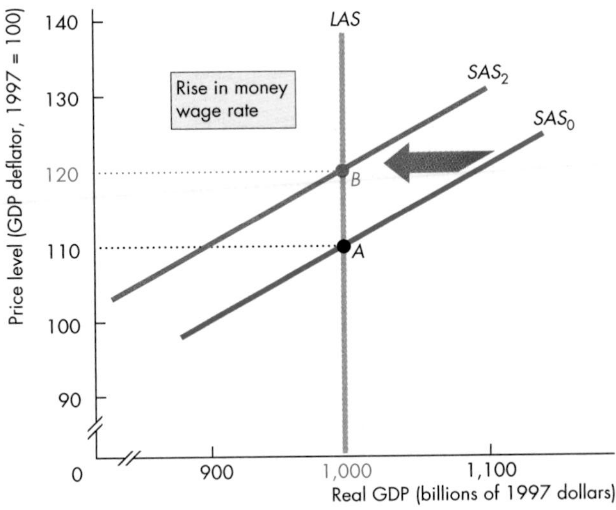

A rise in the money wage rate decreases short-run aggregate supply and shifts the short-run aggregate supply curve leftward from SAS_0 to SAS_2. A rise in the money wage rate does not change potential GDP, so the long-run aggregate supply curve does not shift.

REVIEW QUIZ

1. If the price level rises and if the money wage rate also rises by the same percentage, what happens to the quantity of real GDP supplied? Along which aggregate supply curve does the economy move?
2. If the price level rises and the money wage rate remains constant, what happens to the quantity of real GDP supplied? Along which aggregate supply curve does the economy move?
3. If potential GDP increases, what happens to aggregate supply? Is there a shift of or a movement along the *LAS* curve and the *SAS* curve?
4. If the money wage rate rises and potential GDP remains the same, what happens to aggregate supply? Is there a shift of or a movement along the *LAS* curve and the *SAS* curve?

Aggregate Demand

THE QUANTITY OF REAL GDP DEMANDED IS THE sum of the real consumption expenditure (C), investment (I), government expenditures (G), and exports (X) minus imports (M). That is,

$$Y = C + I + G + X - M.$$

The *quantity of real GDP demanded* is the total amount of final goods and services produced in Canada that people, businesses, governments, and foreigners plan to buy.

These buying plans depend on many factors. Some of the main ones are

- The price level
- Expectations
- Fiscal policy and monetary policy
- The world economy

We first focus on the relationship between the quantity of real GDP demanded and the price level. To study this relationship, we keep all other influences on buying plans the same and ask: How does the quantity of real GDP demanded vary as the price level varies?

The Aggregate Demand Curve

Other things remaining the same, the higher the price level, the smaller is the quantity of real GDP demanded. This relationship between the quantity of real GDP demanded and the price level is called **aggregate demand.** Aggregate demand is described by an aggregate demand schedule and an aggregate demand curve.

Figure 22.6 shows an aggregate demand curve (AD) and an aggregate demand schedule. Each point on the AD curve corresponds to a row of the schedule. For example, point C' on the AD curve and row C' of the schedule tell us that if the price level is 110, the quantity of real GDP demanded is $1,000 billion.

The aggregate demand curve slopes downward for two reasons:

- Wealth effect
- Substitution effects

Wealth Effect When the price level rises but other things remain the same, *real* wealth decreases. Real wealth is the amount of money in the bank, bonds, stocks, and other assets that people own, measured not in dollars but in terms of the goods and services that this money, bonds, and stocks will buy.

FIGURE 22.6 Aggregate Demand

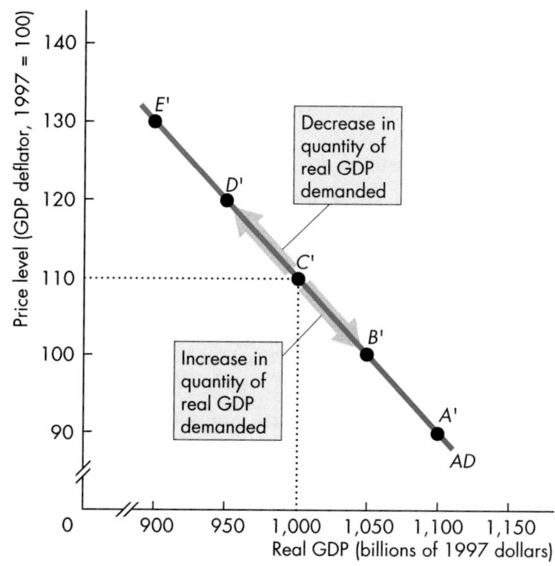

	Price level (GDP deflator)	Real GDP (billions of 1997 dollars)
A'	90	1,100
B'	100	1,050
C'	110	1,000
D'	120	950
E'	130	900

The aggregate demand curve (AD) shows the relationship between the quantity of real GDP demanded and the price level. The aggregate demand curve is based on the aggregate demand schedule in the table. Each point A' through E' on the curve corresponds to the row in the table identified by the same letter. Thus when the price level is 110, the quantity of real GDP demanded is $1,000 billion, shown by point C' in the figure. A change in the price level with all other influences on aggregate buying plans remaining the same brings a change in the quantity of real GDP demanded and a movement along the AD curve.

People save and hold money, bonds, and stocks for many reasons. One reason is to build up funds for education expenses. Another reason is to build up enough funds to meet possible medical or other big bills. But the biggest reason is to build up enough funds to provide a retirement income.

If the price level rises, real wealth decreases. People then try to restore their wealth. To do so, they must increase saving and, equivalently, decrease current consumption. Such a decrease in consumption is a decrease in aggregate demand.

Maria's Wealth Effect You can see how the wealth effect works by thinking about Maria's buying plans. Maria lives in Moscow, Russia. She has worked hard all summer and saved 20,000 rubles (the ruble is the currency of Russia), which she plans to spend attending graduate school when she has finished her economics degree. So Maria's wealth is 20,000 rubles. Maria has a part-time job, and her income from this job pays her current expenses. The price level in Russia rises by 100 percent, and now Maria needs 40,000 rubles to buy what 20,000 once bought. To try to make up some of the fall in value of her savings, Maria saves even more and cuts her current spending to the bare minimum.

Substitution Effects When the price level rises and other things remain the same, interest rates rise. The reason is related to the wealth effect that you've just studied. A rise in the price level decreases the real value of the money in people's pockets and bank accounts. With a smaller amount of real money around, banks and other lenders can get a higher interest rate on loans. But faced with higher interest rates, people and businesses delay plans to buy new capital and consumer durable goods and cut back on spending.

This substitution effect involves substituting goods in the future for goods in the present and is called an *intertemporal* substitution effect—a substitution across time. Saving increases to increase future consumption.

To see this intertemporal substitution effect more clearly, think about your own plan to buy a new computer. At an interest rate of 5 percent a year, you might borrow $2,000 and buy the new machine you've been researching. But at an interest rate of 10 percent a year, you might decide that the payments would be too high. You don't abandon your plan to buy the computer, but you decide to delay your purchase.

A second substitution effect works through international prices. When the Canadian price level rises and other things remain the same, Canadian-made goods and services become more expensive relative to foreign-made goods and services. This change in *relative prices* encourages people to spend less on Canadian-made items and more on foreign-made items. For example, if the Canadian price level rises relative to the U.S. price level, Americans buy fewer Canadian-made cars (Canadian exports decrease) and Canadians buy more U.S.-made cars (Canadian imports increase). Canadian GDP decreases.

Maria's Substitution Effects In Moscow, Russia, Maria makes some substitutions. She was planning to trade in her old motor scooter and get a new one. But with a higher price level and faced with higher interest rates, she decides to make her old scooter last one more year. Also, with the prices of Russian goods sharply increasing, Maria substitutes a low-cost dress made in Malaysia for the Russian-made dress she had originally planned to buy.

Changes in the Quantity of Real GDP Demanded When the price level rises and other things remain the same, the quantity of real GDP demanded decreases—a movement up the *AD* curve as shown by the arrow in Fig. 22.6. When the price level falls and other things remain the same, the quantity of real GDP demanded increases—a movement down the *AD* curve.

We've now seen how the quantity of real GDP demanded changes when the price level changes. How do other influences on buying plans affect aggregate demand?

Changes in Aggregate Demand

A change in any factor that influences buying plans other than the price level brings a change in aggregate demand. The main factors are

- Expectations
- Fiscal policy and monetary policy
- The world economy

Expectations An increase in expected future disposable income increases consumption goods (especially big-ticket items such as cars) that people plan to buy today and increases aggregate demand today.

An increase in the expected future inflation rate

increases aggregate demand today because people decide to buy more goods and services at today's relatively lower prices. An increase in expected future profit increases the investment that firms plan to undertake today and increases aggregate demand today.

Fiscal Policy and Monetary Policy The government's attempt to influence the economy by setting and changing taxes, making transfer payments, and purchasing goods and services is called **fiscal policy.** A tax cut or an increase in transfer payments—for example, unemployment benefits or welfare payments—increases aggregate demand. Both of these influences operate by increasing households' disposable income. **Disposable income** is aggregate income minus taxes plus transfer payments. The greater the disposable income, the greater is the quantity of consumption goods and services that households plan to buy and the greater is aggregate demand.

Government expenditures on goods and services are one component of aggregate demand. So if the government spends more on hospitals, schools, and highways, aggregate demand increases.

Monetary policy consists of changes in interest rates and in the quantity of money in the economy. The quantity of money is determined by the Bank of Canada and the banks (in a process described in Chapters 25 and 26). An increase in the quantity of money in the economy increases aggregate demand. To see why money affects aggregate demand, imagine that the Bank of Canada borrows the army's helicopters, loads them with millions of new $10 bills, and sprinkles these bills like confetti across the nation. People gather the newly available money and plan to spend some of it. So the quantity of goods and services demanded increases. But people don't plan to spend all the new money. They plan to save some of it and lend it to others through the banks. Interest rates fall, and with lower interest rates, people plan to buy more consumer durables and firms plan to increase their investment.

The World Economy Two main influences that the world economy has on aggregate demand are the foreign exchange rate and foreign income. The *foreign exchange rate* is the amount of a foreign currency that you can buy with a Canadian dollar. Other things remaining the same, a rise in the foreign exchange rate decreases aggregate demand. To see how the foreign exchange rate influences aggregate demand, suppose that $1 exchanges for 100 Japanese yen. A Fujitsu phone (made in Japan) costs 12,500 yen, and an equivalent Nortel phone (made in Canada) costs $110. In Canadian dollars, the Fujitsu phone costs $125, so people around the world buy the cheaper

FIGURE 22.7 Changes in Aggregate Demand

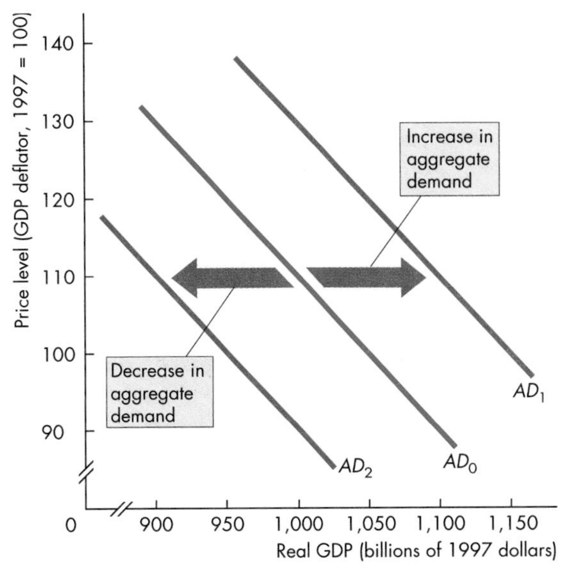

Aggregate demand

Decreases if:	*Increases if:*
■ Expected future disposable income, inflation, or profits decrease	■ Expected future disposable income, inflation, or profits increase
■ Fiscal policy decreases government expenditures, increases taxes, or decreases transfer payments	■ Fiscal policy increases government expenditures, decreases taxes, or increases transfer payments
■ Monetary policy decreases the quantity of money and increases interest rates	■ Monetary policy increases the quantity of money and decreases interest rates
■ The exchange rate increases or foreign income decreases	■ The exchange rate decreases or foreign income increases

Canadian phone. Now suppose the foreign exchange rate rises to 125 yen per dollar. At 125 yen per dollar, the Fujitsu phone costs $100 and is now cheaper than the Nortel phone. People will switch from the Canadian phone to the Japanese phone. Canadian exports will decrease and Canadian imports will increase, so Canadian aggregate demand will decrease.

An increase in foreign income increases Canadian exports and increases Canadian aggregate demand. For example, an increase in income in Japan and Germany increases Japanese and German consumers' and producers' planned expenditures on Canadian-made goods and services.

Shifts of the Aggregate Demand Curve When aggregate demand changes, the aggregate demand curve shifts. Figure 22.7 shows two changes in aggregate demand and summarizes the factors that bring about such changes.

Aggregate demand increases and the aggregate demand curve shifts rightward from AD_0 to AD_1 when expected future income, inflation, or profit increases; government expenditures on goods and services increase; taxes are cut; transfer payments increase; the quantity of money increases and interest rates fall; the foreign exchange rate falls; or foreign income increases.

Aggregate demand decreases and the aggregate demand curve shifts leftward from AD_0 to AD_2 when expected future income, inflation, or profit decreases; government expenditures on goods and services decrease; taxes increase; transfer payments decrease; the quantity of money decreases and interest rates rise; the foreign exchange rate rises; or foreign income decreases.

REVIEW QUIZ

1. What does the aggregate demand curve show? What factors change and what factors remain the same when there is a movement along the aggregate demand curve?
2. Why does the aggregate demand curve slope downward?
3. How do changes in expectations, fiscal policy and monetary policy, and the world economy change aggregate demand and shift the aggregate demand curve?

Macroeconomic Equilibrium

THE PURPOSE OF THE AGGREGATE SUPPLY–aggregate demand model is to explain changes in real GDP and the price level. To achieve this purpose, we combine aggregate supply and aggregate demand and determine macroeconomic equilibrium. There is a macroeconomic equilibrium for each of the time frames for aggregate supply: a long-run equilibrium and a short-run equilibrium. Long-run equilibrium is the state towards which the economy is heading. Short-run equilibrium is the normal state of the economy as it fluctuates around potential GDP.

We'll begin our study of macroeconomic equilibrium by looking first at the short run.

Short-Run Macroeconomic Equilibrium

The aggregate demand curve tells us the quantity of real GDP demanded at each price level, and the short-run aggregate supply curve tells us the quantity of real GDP supplied at each price level. **Short-run macroeconomic equilibrium** occurs when the quantity of real GDP demanded equals the quantity of real GDP supplied. That is, short-run equilibrium occurs at the point of intersection of the *AD* curve and the *SAS* curve. Figure 22.8 shows such an equilibrium at a price level of 110 and real GDP of $1,000 billion (points *C* and *C'*).

To see why this position is the equilibrium, think about what happens if the price level is something other than 110. Suppose, for example, that the price level is 120 and that real GDP is $1,100 billion (at point *E* on the *SAS* curve). The quantity of real GDP demanded is less than $1,100 billion, so firms are unable to sell all their output. Unwanted inventories pile up, and firms cut both production and prices. Production and prices are cut until firms can sell all their output. This situation occurs only when real GDP is $1,000 billion and the price level is 110.

Now suppose the price level is 100 and real GDP is $900 billion (at point *A* on the *SAS* curve). The quantity of real GDP demanded exceeds $900 billion, so firms are unable to meet the demand for their output. Inventories decrease, and customers clamour for goods and services. So firms increase production and raise prices. Production and prices increase until firms can meet demand. This situation

FIGURE 22.8 Short-Run Equilibrium

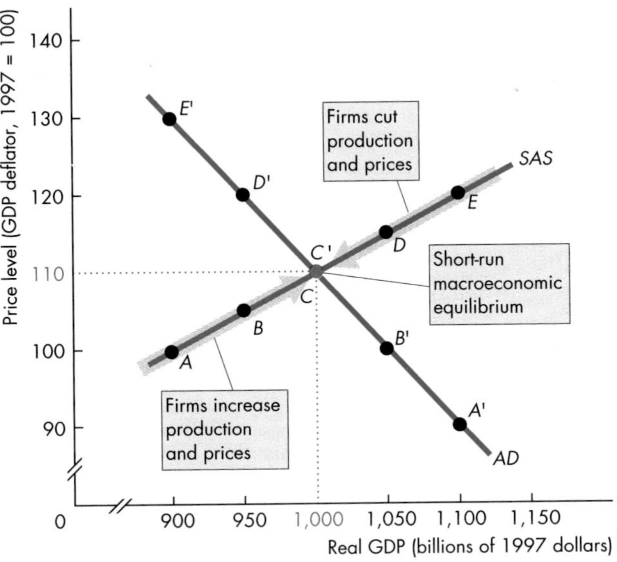

Short-run macroeconomic equilibrium occurs when real GDP demanded equals real GDP supplied—at the intersection of the aggregate demand curve (*AD*) and the short-run aggregate supply curve (*SAS*). Here, such an equilibrium occurs at points *C* and *C'*, where the price level is 110 and real GDP is $1,000 billion. If the price level is 120 and real GDP is $1,100 billion (point *E*), firms will not be able to sell all their output. They will decrease production and cut prices. If the price level is 100 and real GDP is $900 billion (point *A*), people will not be able to buy all the goods and services they demand. Firms will increase production and raise their prices. Only when the price level is 110 and real GDP is $1,000 billion can firms sell all that they produce and can people buy all that they demand. This is the short-run macroeconomic equilibrium.

occurs only when real GDP is $1,000 billion and the price level is 110.

In short-run equilibrium, the money wage rate is fixed. It does not adjust to bring full employment. So in the short run, real GDP can be greater than or less than potential GDP. But in the long run, the money wage rate does adjust and real GDP moves towards potential GDP. We are going to study this adjustment process. But first, let's look at the economy in long-run equilibrium.

Long-Run Macroeconomic Equilibrium

Long-run macroeconomic equilibrium occurs when real GDP equals potential GDP—equivalently, when the economy is on its *long-run* aggregate supply curve. Figure 22.9 shows *long-run* equilibrium, which occurs at the intersection of the aggregate demand curve and the long-run aggregate supply curve (the blue curves). Long-run equilibrium comes about because the money wage rate adjusts. Potential GDP and aggregate demand determine the price level, and the price level influences the money wage rate. In long-run equilibrium, the money wage rate has adjusted to put the (green) short-run aggregate supply curve through the long-run equilibrium point.

We'll look at this money wage adjustment process later in this chapter. But first, let's see how the *AS–AD* model helps us to understand economic growth and inflation.

FIGURE 22.9 Long-Run Equilibrium

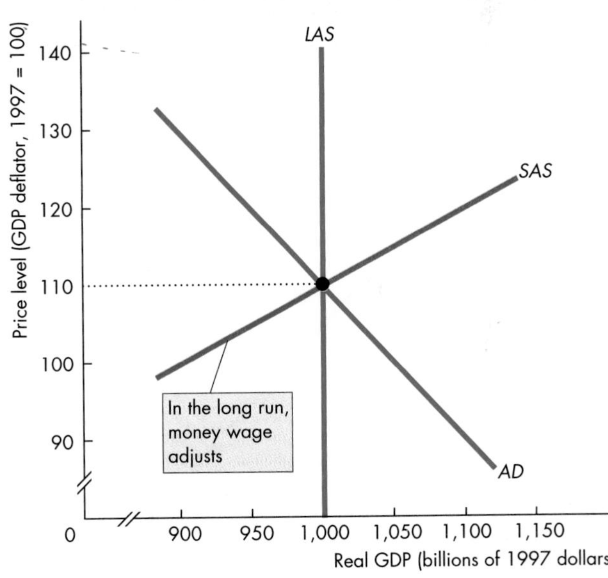

In long-run macroeconomic equilibrium, real GDP equals potential GDP. So long-run equilibrium occurs where the aggregate demand curve intersects the long-run aggregate supply curve. In the long run, aggregate demand determines the price level and has no effect on real GDP. The money wage rate adjusts in the long run, so the *SAS* curve intersects the *LAS* curve at the long-run equilibrium price level.

Economic Growth and Inflation

Economic growth occurs because over time, the quantity of labour grows, capital is accumulated, and technology advances. These changes increase potential GDP and shift the long-run aggregate supply curve rightward. Figure 22.10 shows such a shift. The growth rate of potential GDP is determined by the pace at which labour grows, capital is accumulated, and technology advances.

Inflation occurs when, over time, aggregate demand increases by more than long-run aggregate supply. That is, inflation occurs if the aggregate demand curve shifts rightward by more than the rightward shift in the long-run aggregate supply curve. Figure 22.10 shows such shifts.

If aggregate demand increased at the same pace as long-run aggregate supply, we would experience real GDP growth with no inflation.

In the long run, the main influence on aggregate demand is the growth rate of the quantity of money. At times when the quantity of money increases rapidly, aggregate demand increases quickly and the inflation rate is high. When the growth rate of the quantity of money slows, other things remaining the same, the inflation rate eventually decreases.

Our economy experiences growth and inflation, like that shown in Fig. 22.10. But it does not experience *steady* growth and *steady* inflation. Real GDP fluctuates around potential GDP in a business cycle, and inflation also fluctuates. When we study the business cycle, we ignore economic growth. By doing so, we can see the business cycle more clearly.

FIGURE 22.10 Economic Growth and Inflation

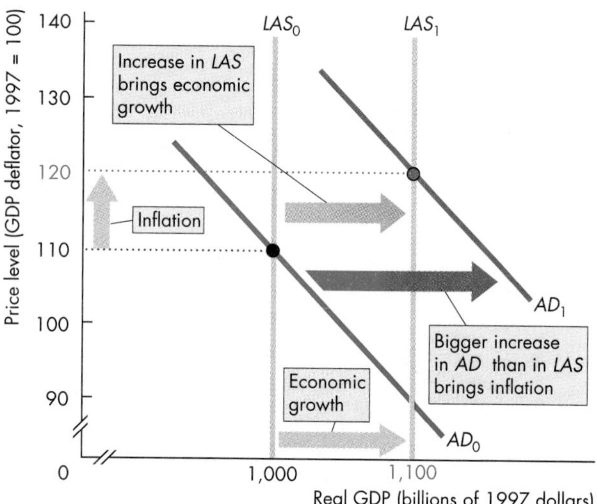

Economic growth is the persistent increase in potential GDP. Economic growth is shown as an ongoing rightward movement in the *LAS* curve. Inflation is the persistent rise in the price level. Inflation occurs when aggregate demand increases by more than the increase in long-run aggregate supply.

The Business Cycle

The business cycle occurs because aggregate demand and short-run aggregate supply fluctuate but the money wage rate does not adjust quickly enough to keep real GDP at potential GDP. Figure 22.11 shows three types of short-run equilibrium.

In part (a), there is a below full-employment equilibrium. A **below full-employment equilibrium** is a macroeconomic equilibrium in which potential GDP exceeds real GDP. The amount by which potential GDP exceeds real GDP is called a **recessionary gap.** This name reminds us that a gap has opened up between potential GDP and real GDP either because the economy has experienced a recession or because real GDP, while growing, has grown more slowly than potential GDP.

The below full-employment equilibrium shown in Fig. 22.11(a) occurs where the aggregate demand curve AD_0 intersects the short-run aggregate supply curve SAS_0 at a real GDP of $980 billion and a price level of 110. The recessionary gap is $20 billion. The Canadian economy was in a situation similar to that shown in Fig. 22.11(a) during the early 1980s, and again during the early 1990s. In those years, real GDP was less than potential GDP.

Figure 22.11(b) is an example of *long-run equilibrium*, in which real GDP equals potential GDP. In this example, the equilibrium occurs where the aggregate demand curve AD_1 intersects the short-run aggregate supply curve SAS_1 at an actual and potential GDP of $1,000 billion. The Canadian economy was in a situation such as that shown in Fig. 22.11(b) in 1999.

Figure 22.11(c) shows an above full-employment equilibrium. An **above full-employment equilibrium** is a macroeconomic equilibrium in which real GDP exceeds potential GDP. The amount by which real GDP exceeds potential GDP is called an **inflationary gap.** This name reminds us that a gap has opened up between real GDP and potential GDP and that this gap creates inflationary pressure.

The above full-employment equilibrium shown in Fig. 22.11(c) occurs where the aggregate demand curve AD_2 intersects the short-run aggregate supply curve SAS_2 at a real GDP of $1,020 billion and a price level of 110. There is an inflationary gap of $20 billion. The Canadian economy was last in a situation similar to that depicted in Fig. 22.11(c) in 2000.

The economy moves from one type of equilibrium to another as a result of fluctuations in aggregate demand and in short-run aggregate supply. These fluctuations produce fluctuations in real GDP and the price level. Figure 22.11(d) shows how real GDP fluctuates around potential GDP.

Let's now look at some of the sources of these fluctuations around potential GDP.

FIGURE 22.11 The Business Cycle

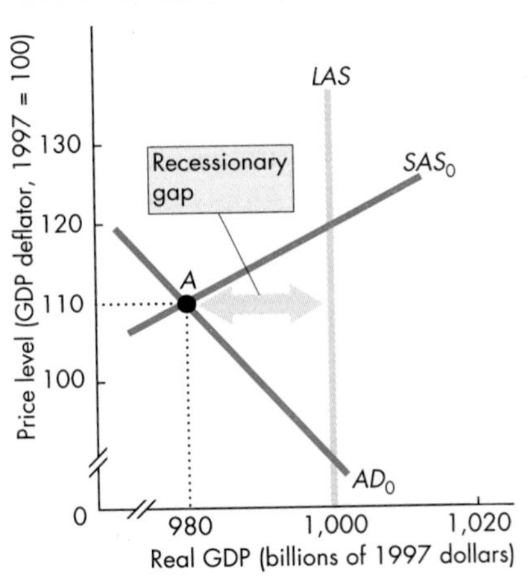

(a) Below full-employment equilibrium

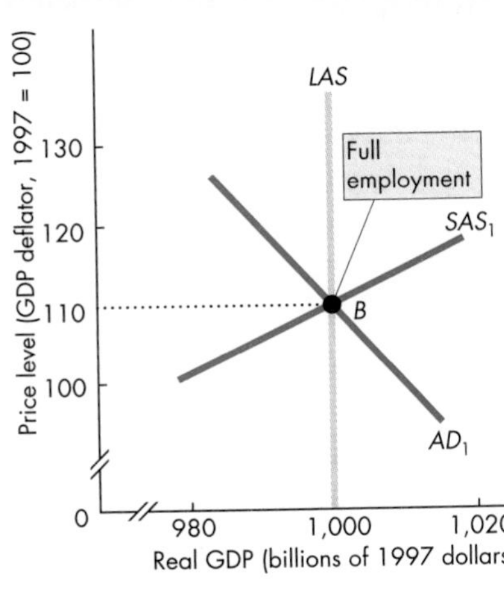

(b) Long-run equilibrium

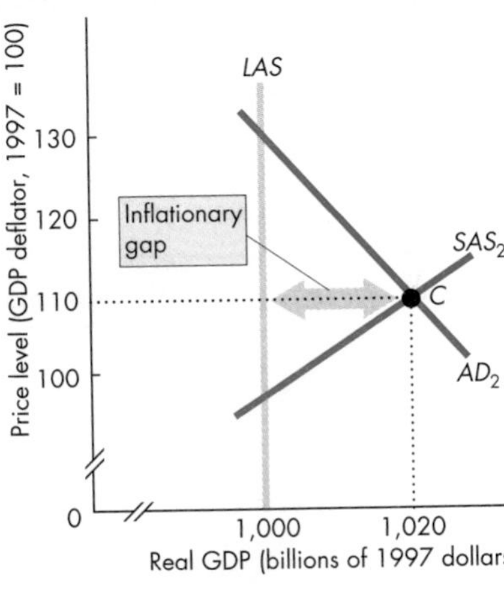

(c) Above full-employment equilibrium

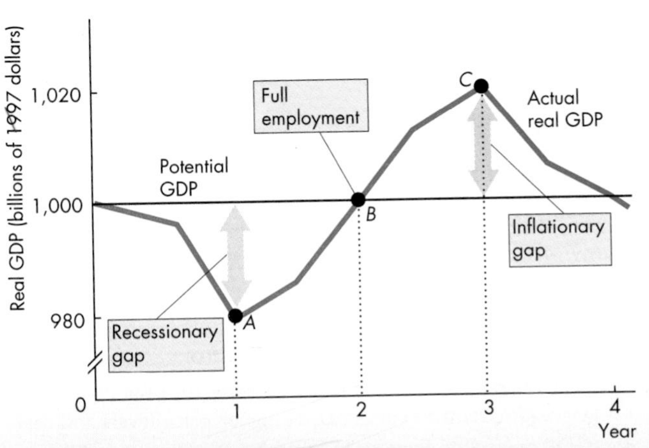

(d) Fluctuations in real GDP

Part (a) shows a below full-employment equilibrium in year 1; part (b) shows a long-run equilibrium in year 2; and part (c) shows an above full-employment equilibrium in year 3. Part (d) shows how real GDP fluctuates around potential GDP in a business cycle.

In year 1, a recessionary gap exists and the economy is at point *A* (in parts a and d). In year 2, the economy is in long-run equilibrium and the economy is at point *B* (in parts b and d). In year 3, an inflationary gap exists and the economy is at point *C* (in parts c and d).

Fluctuations in Aggregate Demand

One reason real GDP fluctuates around potential GDP is that aggregate demand fluctuates. Let's see what happens when aggregate demand increases.

Figure 22.12(a) shows an economy in long-run equilibrium. The aggregate demand curve is AD_0, the short-run aggregate supply curve is SAS_0, and the long-run aggregate supply curve is *LAS*. Real GDP equals potential GDP at $1,000 billion, and the price level is 110.

Now suppose that the world economy expands and that the demand for Canadian-made goods increases in Japan and Europe. The increase in Canadian exports increases aggregate demand, and the aggregate demand curve shifts rightward from AD_0 to AD_1 in Fig. 22.12(a).

Faced with an increase in demand, firms increase production and raise prices. Real GDP increases to $1,050 billion, and the price level rises to 115. The economy is now in an above full-employment equilibrium. Real GDP exceeds potential GDP, and there is an inflationary gap.

The increase in aggregate demand has increased the prices of all goods and services. Faced with higher prices, firms have increased their output rates. At this stage, prices of goods and services have increased but the money wage rate has not changed. (Recall that as we move along a short-run aggregate supply curve, the money wage rate is constant.)

The economy cannot produce in excess of potential GDP forever. Why not? What are the forces at work that bring real GDP back to potential GDP?

Because the price level has increased and the money wage rate is unchanged, workers have experienced a fall in the buying power of their wages and firms' profits have increased. In these circumstances, workers demand higher wages and firms, anxious to maintain their employment and output levels, meet those demands. If firms do not raise the money wage rate, they will either lose workers or have to hire less productive ones.

As the money wage rate rises, the short-run aggregate supply curve begins to shift leftward. In Fig. 22.12(b), the short-run aggregate supply curve moves

FIGURE 22.12 An Increase in Aggregate Demand

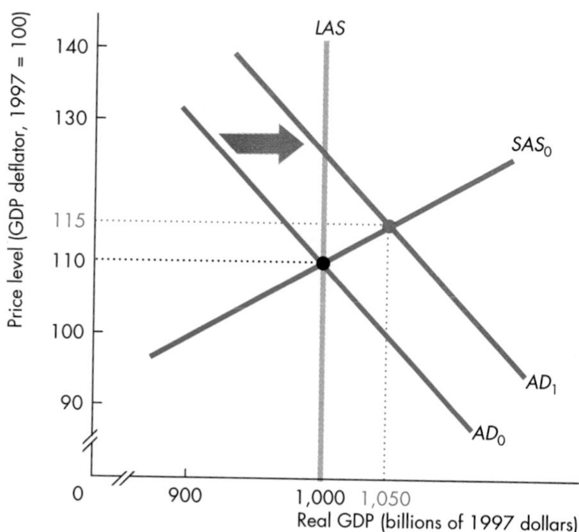

(a) Short-run effect

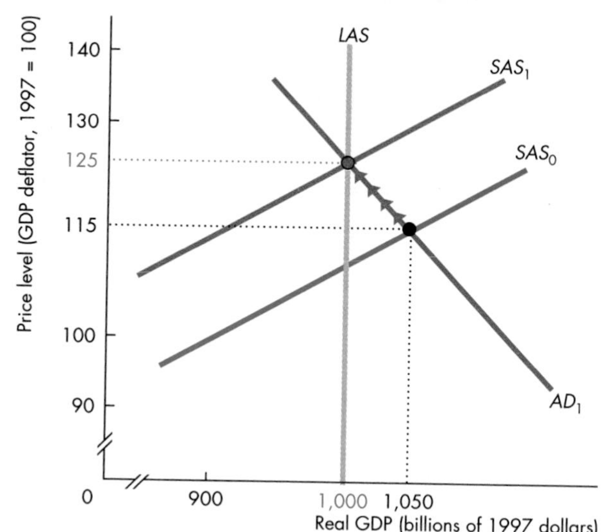

(b) Long-run effect

An increase in aggregate demand shifts the aggregate demand curve from AD_0 to AD_1. In short-run equilibrium, real GDP increases to $1,050 billion and the price level rises to 115. In this situation, an inflationary gap exists. In the long run, the money wage rate rises and the short-run aggregate supply curve shifts leftward from SAS_0 to SAS_1 in part (b). As the *SAS* curve shifts leftward, it intersects the aggregate demand curve AD_1 at higher price levels and real GDP decreases. Eventually, the price level rises to 125 and real GDP decreases to $1,000 billion—potential GDP.

from SAS_0 towards SAS_1. The rise in the money wage rate and the shift in the *SAS* curve produce a sequence of new equilibrium positions. Along the adjustment path, real GDP decreases and the price level rises. The economy moves up along its aggregate demand curve as the arrowheads show.

Eventually, the money wage rate rises by the same percentage as the price level. At this time, the aggregate demand curve AD_1 intersects SAS_1 at a new long-run equilibrium. The price level has risen to 125, and real GDP is back where it started, at potential GDP.

A decrease in aggregate demand has similar but opposite effects to those of an increase in aggregate demand. That is, a decrease in aggregate demand shifts the aggregate demand curve leftward. Real GDP decreases to less than potential GDP, and a recessionary gap emerges. Firms cut prices. The lower price level increases the purchasing power of wages and increases firms' costs relative to their output prices because the money wage rate remains unchanged. Eventually, the money wage rate falls and the short-run aggregate supply curve shifts rightward. But the money wage rate changes slowly, so real GDP slowly returns to potential GDP and the price level falls slowly.

Let's now work out how real GDP and the price level change when aggregate supply changes.

Fluctuations in Aggregate Supply

Fluctuations in short-run aggregate supply can bring fluctuations in real GDP around potential GDP. Suppose that initially real GDP equals potential GDP. Then there is a large but temporary rise in the price of oil. What happens to real GDP and the price level?

Figure 22.13 answers this question. The aggregate demand curve is AD_0, the short-run aggregate supply curve is SAS_0, and the long-run aggregate supply curve is *LAS*. Real GDP is $1,000 billion, which equals potential GDP, and the price level is 110. Then the price of oil rises. Faced with higher energy and transportation costs, firms decrease production. Short-run aggregate supply decreases, and the short-run aggregate supply curve shifts leftward to SAS_1. The price level rises to 120, and real GDP decreases to $950 billion. Because real GDP decreases, the economy experiences recession. Because the price level increases, the economy experiences inflation. A combination of recession and inflation, called *stagflation*, actually occurred in the United States in the mid-1970s. But events like this are not common and Canada escaped the worst of that recession.

FIGURE 22.13 A Decrease in Aggregate Supply

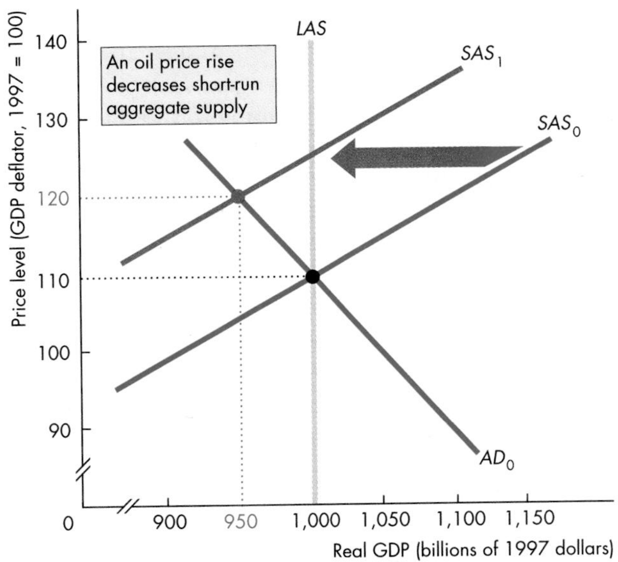

An increase in the price of oil decreases short-run aggregate supply and shifts the short-run aggregate supply curve from SAS_0 to SAS_1. Real GDP decreases from $1,000 billion to $950 billion, and the price level increases from 110 to 120. The economy experiences both recession and inflation—a situation known as stagflation.

REVIEW QUIZ

1. Does economic growth result from increases in aggregate demand, short-run aggregate supply, or long-run aggregate supply?
2. Does inflation result from increases in aggregate demand, short-run aggregate supply, or long-run aggregate supply?
3. Describe three types of short-run macroeconomic equilibrium.
4. How do fluctuations in aggregate demand and short-run aggregate supply bring fluctuations in real GDP around potential GDP?

Let's put our new knowledge of aggregate supply and aggregate demand to work and see how we can explain recent Canadian macroeconomic performance.

Canadian Economic Growth, Inflation, and Cycles

THE ECONOMY IS CONTINUALLY CHANGING. IF you imagine the economy as a video, then an aggregate supply–aggregate demand figure such as Fig. 22.13 is a freeze-frame. We're going to run the video—an instant replay—but keep our finger on the freeze-frame button and look at some important parts of the previous action. Let's run the video from 1961.

Figure 22.14 shows the state of the economy in 1961 at the point of intersection of its aggregate demand curve, AD_{61}, and short-run aggregate supply curve, SAS_{61}. Real GDP was $240 billion, and the GDP deflator was 17 (less than one-fifth of its 2001 level). In 1961, real GDP equalled potential GDP—the economy was on its long-run aggregate supply curve, LAS_{61}.

By 2001, the economy had reached the point marked by the intersection of aggregate demand curve AD_{01} and short-run aggregate supply curve SAS_{01}. Real GDP was $1,027 billion, and the GDP deflator was 106. The *LAS* curve assumes that potential GDP in 2001 was also $1,027 billion.

The path traced by the blue and red dots in Fig. 22.14 shows three key features:

- Economic growth
- Inflation
- Business cycles

Economic Growth

Over the years, real GDP grows—shown in Fig. 22.14 by the rightward movement of the points. The faster real GDP grows, the larger is the horizontal distance between successive dots in the figure. The forces that generate economic growth are those that increase potential GDP. Potential GDP grows because the quantity of labour grows, we accumulate physical capital and human capital, and our technologies advance.

These forces that bring economic growth were strongest during the early 1970s, mid-1980s, and late 1990s.

FIGURE 22.14 Aggregate Supply and Aggregate Demand: 1961–2001

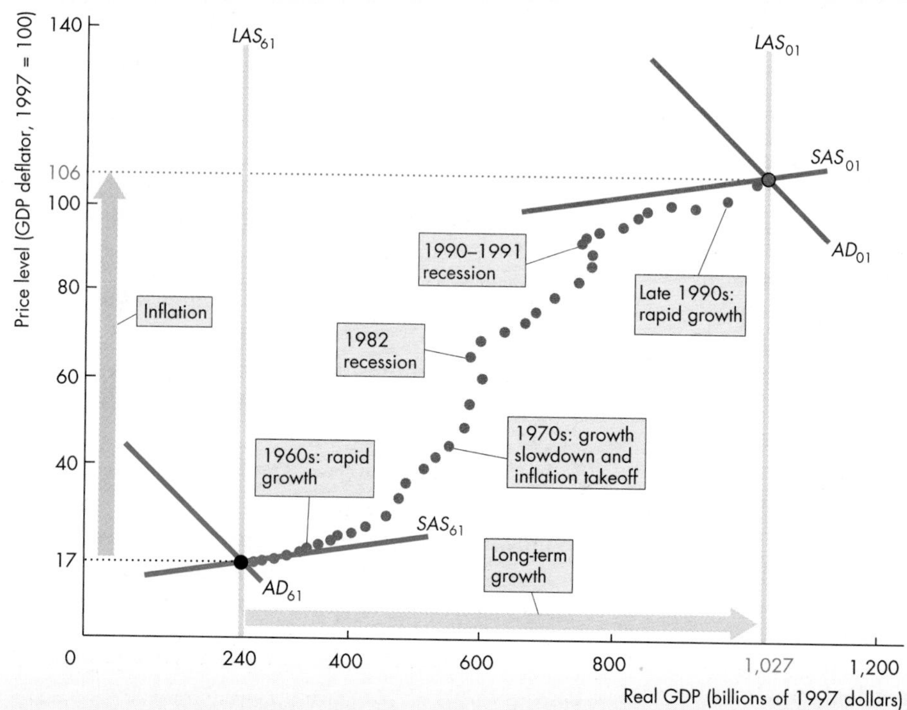

Each point shows the GDP deflator and real GDP in a given year. In 1961, the aggregate demand curve, AD_{61}, and the short-run aggregate supply curve, SAS_{61}, determined these variables. Each point is generated by the gradual shifting of the *AD* and *SAS* curves. By 2001, the curves were AD_{01} and SAS_{01}. Real GDP grew, and the price level increased. Real GDP grew quickly and inflation was moderate during the 1960s; real GDP growth sagged in 1974–1975 and again in 1982. Inflation was rapid during the 1970s but slowed after the 1982 recession. The period from 1982 to 1989 was one of strong, persistent expansion. A recession began in 1990, and a further strong and sustained expansion resumed in the late 1990s and through 2001.

Sources: Statistics Canada, CANSIM tables 326–0002 and 380–0003 and authors' assumptions.

Inflation

The price level rises over the years—shown in Fig. 22.14 by the upward movement of the points. The larger the rise in the price level, the larger is the vertical distance between successive dots in the figure. The main force generating the persistent increase in the price level is a tendency for aggregate demand to increase at a faster pace than the increase in long-run aggregate supply. All of the factors that increase aggregate demand and shift the aggregate demand curve influence the pace of inflation. But one factor—the growth of the quantity of money—is the main source of *persistent* increases in aggregate demand and persistent inflation.

"Please stand by for a series of tones. The first indicates the official end of the recession, the second indicates prosperity, and the third the return of the recession."

Business Cycles

Over the years, the economy grows and shrinks in cycles—shown in Fig. 22.14 by the wavelike pattern made by the points, with the recessions highlighted. The cycles arise because both the expansion of short-run aggregate supply and the growth of aggregate demand do not proceed at a fixed, steady pace. Although the economy has cycles, recessions do not usually follow quickly on the heels of their predecessors; "double-dip" recessions like the one in the cartoon are rare.

The Evolving Economy: 1961–2001

During the 1960s, real GDP growth was rapid and inflation was low. This was a period of rapid increases in aggregate supply and of moderate increases in aggregate demand.

The mid-1970s were years of rapid inflation and slow growth. The major source of these developments was a series of massive oil price increases that slowed the rightward movement of the long-run aggregate supply curve and rapid increases in the quantity of money that speeded the rightward movement of the aggregate demand curve. The short-run aggregate supply curve shifted leftward at a faster pace than the aggregate demand curve shifted rightward.

The rest of the 1970s saw high inflation—the price level increased quickly—and only moderate growth in real GDP. By 1980, inflation was a major problem and the Bank of Canada decided to take strong action against it. It permitted interest rates to rise to previously unknown levels. Consequently, aggregate demand decreased. By 1982, the decrease in aggregate demand put the economy in a deep recession.

During the years 1983–1990, capital accumulation and steady technological advance resulted in a sustained rightward shift of the long-run aggregate supply curve. Wage growth was moderate, and the short-run aggregate supply curve shifted rightward. Aggregate demand growth kept pace with the growth of aggregate supply. Sustained but steady growth in aggregate supply and aggregate demand kept real GDP growing and inflation steady. The economy moved from a recession with real GDP less than potential GDP in 1982 to above full employment in 1990. It was in this condition when a decrease in aggregate demand led to the 1990–1991 recession. The economy stagnated for a year and then began to expand again, expanding rapidly during the late 1990s. Growth slowed again in 2001.

◆ The *AS–AD* model explains economic growth, inflation, and the business cycle. The model is a useful one because it enables us to keep our eye on the big picture. But it lacks detail. It does not tell us as much as we need to know about the deeper forces that lie behind aggregate supply and aggregate demand. The chapters that follow begin to fill in the details on aggregate demand. But before you embark on this next stage, take a look at *Reading Between the Lines* on pp. 516–517, which looks at the effects of implementing the Kyoto agreement on climate control on aggregate supply and aggregate demand in the Canadian economy in 2010.

Kyoto in the AS–AD Model

FINANCIAL POST, OCTOBER 12, 2002

Kyoto could cost 244,000 jobs

The federal government conceded yesterday that implementing the Kyoto Protocol on climate change could cost the Canadian economy as many as a quarter of a million jobs, and $21-billion in output, by the end of the decade.

In a long awaited impact study of Kyoto, federal officials predicted the accord could mean between 61,000 and 244,000 fewer jobs by 2010. They also forecast the accord could mean gross domestic product would be between 0.4% ($5-billion) and 1.6% ($21-billion) lower than expected by the same year.

The federal document argued that the 244,000 job figure and 1.6% drop in GDP growth was a worst-case scenario. Officials said the lower figures were more likely. ...

Private-sector estimates place the cost of implementing Kyoto at 450,000 jobs by 2010, and $4.5-billion annually.

Pierre Alvarez, president of the Canadian Association of Petroleum Producers, called the federal calculations "empty numbers," adding that Ottawa's Kyoto plan remains a mystery.

"This is a model based on hypothetical assumptions, assumptions no one else has ever seen," he said.

"To extrapolate from that, they are simply empty numbers that are of little value to the current debate."

He added: "The assumptions are based on estimates we don't necessarily agree with—we've had inadequate information—they are based on assumptions that we don't understand and have only had one presentation on."

Nancy Hughes Anthony, president of the Canadian Chamber of Commerce, charged yesterday the government's economic model leaves a "false impression" about the impact of the Kyoto Protocol by presenting optimistic projections.

But she said it is even clear from the best and worst-case scenarios in the federal analysis that the prosperity of Canadians will suffer if Jean Chrétien, the Prime Minister, pushes ahead with ratification of Kyoto by the end of the year. ...

Essence of the Story

- The federal government predicts that ratifying the Kyoto accord will lower employment by between 61,000 and 244,000 persons by 2010.
- The government also predicts that ratifying the Kyoto accord will lower real GDP by between 0.4 percent ($5 billion) and 1.6 percent ($21 billion) by 2010.
- The government regards the higher numbers—244,000 jobs and $21 billion real GDP—as the worst-case scenario.
- Private-sector estimates place the cost of implementing Kyoto at 450,000 jobs by 2010.
- Private-sector estimates also place the cost of implementing Kyoto at $4.5 billion annually.

Economic Analysis

- Implementing the Kyoto accord requires Canada to cut its emissions of "greenhouse" gasses, measured as carbon dioxide equivalent, from more than 700 million tonnes a year in 2002 to 540 million tonnes a year by 2010.

- To achieve this large cut in emissions, we must generate electricity more cleanly and use technologies that are more costly and less productive.

- We must also increase the fuel efficiency of automobiles and trucks.

- These activities decrease the productivity of labour, slow the accumulation of productive capital, and slow the pace of productivity-enhancing technological change.

- The overall consequence of this slowdown in productivity growth is a slower growth rate of potential GDP.

- By not implementing the Kyoto accord and maintaining recent trends, real GDP will grow by 3 percent a year.

- Maintaining the recent inflation trends (and the Bank of Canada's target for inflation), the annual inflation rate will be 2 percent a year.

- Figure 1 shows where the economy will be by 2010 if these trends persist—the base line case.

- Real GDP will be $1,240 billion, up by 27 percent from its 2002 level; and the price level will be 125, up by 17 percent from its 2002 level.

- Figure 2 shows the difference that implementing Kyoto will make, using the numbers that the government describes as the worst-case scenario.

- Relative to the base line case, long-run aggregate supply will be lower at LAS_1, and real GDP will be $21 billion less than it otherwise would have been.

- If the Bank of Canada continues to pursue an inflation target of 2 percent a year, aggregate demand growth will slow to match the slower growth of potential GDP. The *AD* curve and *SAS* curve will be at AD_1 and SAS_1, and the price level will be unaffected by Kyoto.

- If aggregate demand growth does not slow to match the slower growth rate of potential GDP, Kyoto will bring a higher price level and increased inflation.

- The decrease in employment that results from Kyoto will either decrease the labour force or increase the natural rate of unemployment. It will not affect cyclical unemployment.

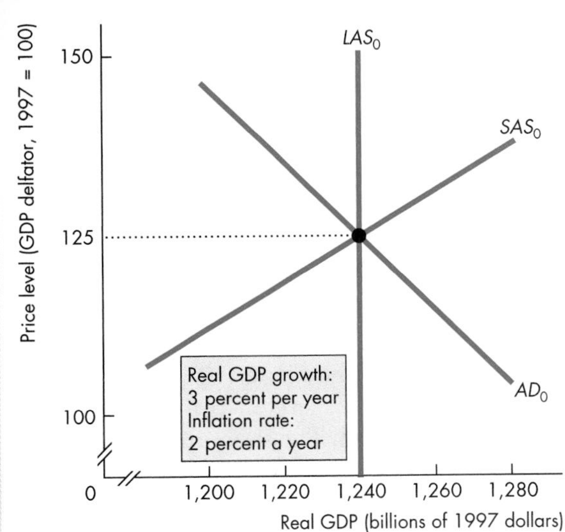

Figure 1 Base line case--no Kyoto

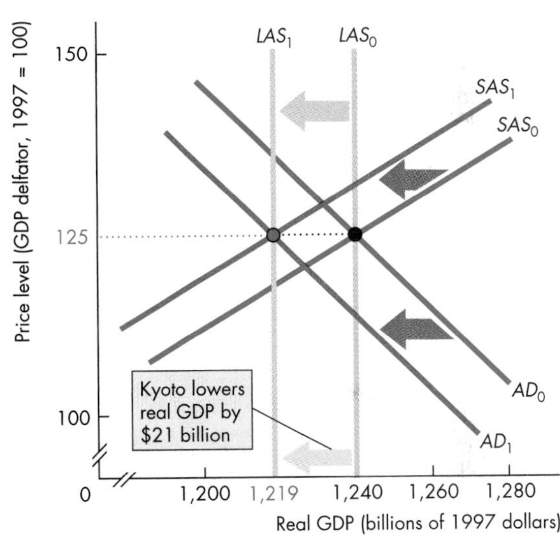

Figure 2 Government's Kyoto worst-case scenario

You're The Voter

- Based just on its macroeconomic consequences, do you think that implementing Kyoto is a big deal?

- What macroeconomic reasons would you give for supporting or opposing the implementation of Kyoto?

SUMMARY

KEY POINTS

Aggregate Supply (pp. 500–504)

- In the long run, the quantity of real GDP supplied is potential GDP, which is independent of the price level. The long-run aggregate supply curve is vertical.
- In the short run, the money wage rate is constant, so a rise in the price level increases the quantity of real GDP supplied. The short-run aggregate supply curve is upward sloping.
- A change in potential GDP changes both long-run and short-run aggregate supply. A change in the money wage rate or other resource prices changes only short-run aggregate supply.

Aggregate Demand (pp. 505–508)

- A rise in the price level decreases the quantity of real GDP demanded, other things remaining the same.
- The reason is that the higher price level decreases the quantity of *real* money, raises the interest rate, and raises the price of domestic goods compared with foreign goods.
- Changes in expected future disposable income, inflation, and profit; changes in fiscal policy and monetary policy; and changes in world real GDP and the foreign exchange rate change aggregate demand.

Macroeconomic Equilibrium (pp. 508–513)

- In the short run, real GDP and the price level are determined by aggregate demand and short-run aggregate supply.
- In the long run, real GDP equals potential GDP and aggregate demand determines the price level and the money wage rate.
- Economic growth occurs because potential GDP increases.
- Inflation occurs because aggregate demand grows more quickly than potential GDP.
- Business cycles occur because aggregate demand and aggregate supply fluctuate.

Canadian Economic Growth, Inflation, and Cycles (pp. 514–515)

- Potential GDP grew fastest during the early 1970s, mid-1980s, and late 1990s and slowest during the late 1970s and early 1990s.
- Inflation persists because aggregate demand grows faster than potential GDP.
- Business cycles occur because aggregate supply and aggregate demand change at an uneven pace.

KEY FIGURES

Figure 22.2 Short-Run Aggregate Supply, 502
Figure 22.3 Movements Along the Aggregate Supply Curves, 502
Figure 22.4 A Change in Potential GDP, 503
Figure 22.5 A Change in the Money Wage Rate, 504
Figure 22.6 Aggregate Demand, 505
Figure 22.7 Changes in Aggregate Demand, 507
Figure 22.8 Short-Run Equilibrium, 509
Figure 22.9 Long-Run Equilibrium, 509
Figure 22.10 Economic Growth and Inflation, 510
Figure 22.11 The Business Cycle, 511
Figure 22.12 An Increase in Aggregate Demand, 512
Figure 22.14 Aggregate Supply and Aggregate Demand: 1961–2001, 514

KEY TERMS

Above full-employment equilibrium, 510
Aggregate demand, 505
Aggregate production function, 500
Below full-employment equilibrium, 510
Disposable income, 507
Fiscal policy, 507
Inflationary gap, 511
Long-run aggregate supply curve, 500
Long-run macroeconomic equilibrium, 509
Macroeconomic long run, 500
Macroeconomic short run, 501
Monetary policy, 507
Natural rate of unemployment, 500
Recessionary gap, 510
Short-run aggregate supply curve, 501
Short-run macroeconomic equilibrium, 508

PROBLEMS

*1. The following events occur that influence the economy of Toughtimes:
- A deep recession hits the world economy.
- Oil prices rise sharply.
- Businesses expect huge losses in the near future.

a. Explain the separate effects of each of these events on real GDP and the price level in Toughtimes, starting from a position of long-run equilibrium.
b. Explain the combined effects of these events on real GDP and the price level in Toughtimes, starting from a position of long-run equilibrium.
c. Explain what the Toughtimes government and the Bank of Toughtimes can do to overcome the problems faced by the economy.

2. The following events occur that influence the economy of Coolland:
- There is a strong expansion in the world economy.
- Businesses expect huge profits in the near future.
- The Coolland government cuts its expenditure.

a. Explain the separate effects of each of these events on real GDP and the price level in Coolland, starting from a position of long-run equilibrium.
b. Explain the combined effects of these events on real GDP and the price level in Coolland, starting from a position of long-run equilibrium.
c. Explain why the Coolland government or the Bank of Coolland might want to take action to influence the Coolland economy.

*3. The economy of Mainland has the following aggregate demand and supply schedules:

Price level	Real GDP demanded	Real GDP supplied in the short run
	(billions of 1997 dollars)	
90	450	350
100	400	400
110	350	450
120	300	500
130	250	550
140	200	600

a. In a figure, plot the aggregate demand curve and the short-run aggregate supply curve.
b. What are the values of real GDP and the price level in Mainland in a short-run macroeconomic equilibrium?
c. Mainland's potential GDP is $500 billion. Plot the long-run aggregate supply curve in the same figure in which you answered part (a).

4. The economy of Miniland has the following aggregate demand and supply schedules:

Price level	Real GDP demanded	Real GDP supplied in the short run
	(billions of 1997 dollars)	
90	600	150
100	500	200
110	400	250
120	300	300
130	200	350
140	100	400

a. In a figure, plot the aggregate demand curve and the short-run aggregate supply curve.
b. What are the values of real GDP and the price level in Miniland in a short-run macroeconomic equilibrium?
c. Miniland's potential GDP is $250 billion. Plot the long-run aggregate supply curve in the same figure in which you answered part (a).

*5. In problem 3, aggregate demand increases by $100 billion. How do real GDP and the price level change in the short run?

6. In problem 4, aggregate demand decreases by $150 billion. How do real GDP and the price level change in the short run?

*7. In problem 3, aggregate supply decreases by $100 billion. What now is the short-run macroeconomic equilibrium?

8. In problem 4, aggregate supply increases by $150 billion. What now is the short-run macroeconomic equilibrium?

*9. In the economy shown in the figure on the next page, initially the short-run aggregate supply is SAS_0 and aggregate demand is AD_0. Then some events change aggregate demand, and the aggregate demand curve shifts rightward to AD_1. Later, some other events change aggregate supply, and the short-run aggregate supply curve shifts leftward to SAS_1.

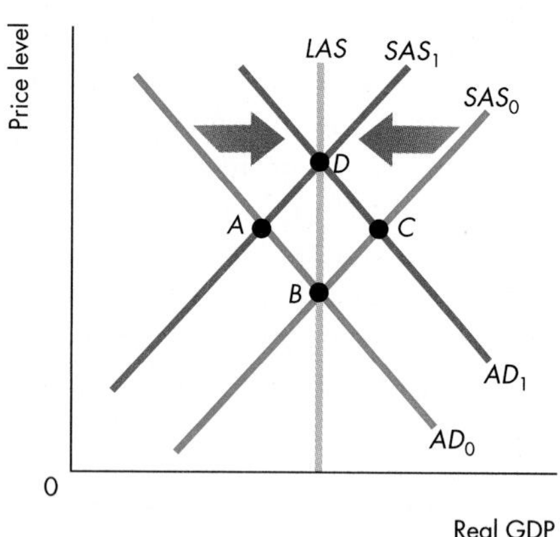

a. What is the short-run equilibrium point after the change in aggregate demand?
b. What is the equilibrium point after the change in aggregate supply?
c. What events could have changed aggregate demand from AD_0 to AD_1?
d. What events could have changed aggregate supply from SAS_0 to SAS_1?

10. In the economy shown in the figure, initially long-run aggregate supply is LAS_0, short-run aggregate supply is SAS_0, and aggregate demand is AD. Then some events change aggregate supply, and the aggregate supply curves shift rightward to LAS_1 and SAS_1.

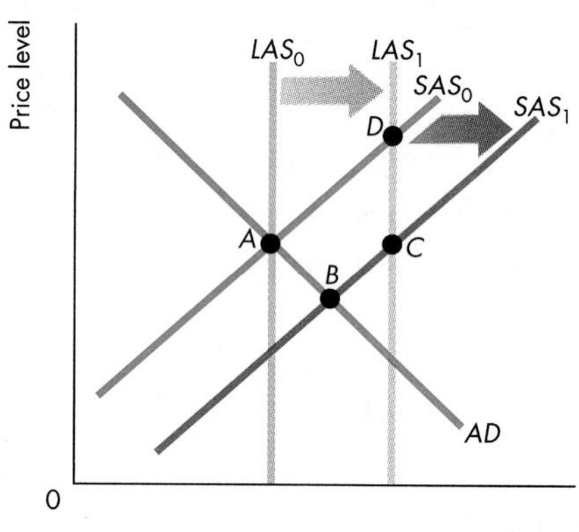

a. What is the short-run equilibrium point after the change in aggregate supply?
b. What events could have changed long-run aggregate supply from LAS_0 to LAS_1?
c. What events could have changed short-run aggregate supply from SAS_0 to SAS_1?
d. After the increase in aggregate supply, is real GDP greater than or less than potential GDP?
e. What change in aggregate demand will make real GDP equal to potential GDP?

CRITICAL THINKING

1. After you have studied the effects of implementing the Kyoto agreement on aggregate supply and aggregate demand in the Canadian economy in *Reading Between the Lines* on pp. 516–517:
   a. List the factors that influence long-run aggregate supply and explain how Kyoto might impact each of these factors.
   b. List the factors that influence short-run aggregate supply and explain how Kyoto might impact each of these factors.
   c. List the factors that influence aggregate demand and explain how Kyoto might impact each of these factors.
   d. Use the *AS–AD* model to illustrate and to explain why Kyoto need not increase the inflation rate, even if it brings a large decrease in potential GDP.

WEB EXERCISES

1. Use the links on the Parkin–Bade Web site to find data on recent changes in and forecasts of real GDP and the price level in Canada.
   a. What is your forecast of next year's real GDP?
   b. What is your forecast of next year's price level?
   c. What is your forecast of the inflation rate?
   d. What is your forecast of the growth rate of real GDP?
   e. Do you think there will be a recessionary gap or an inflationary gap next year?
2. Use the links on the Parkin–Bade Web site to find data on recent changes in and forecasts of real GDP and the price level in Japan.
   a. What is your forecast of next year's real GDP?
   b. What is your forecast of next year's price level?
   c. What is your forecast of the inflation rate?
   d. What is your forecast of the growth rate of real GDP?
   e. Compare and contrast the performance of the Canadian and Japanese economies.

UNDERSTANDING THE THEMES OF MACROECONOMICS

PART 7

The Big Picture

Macroeconomics is a large and controversial subject that is interlaced with political ideological disputes. And it is a field in which charlatans as well as serious thinkers have much to say. This page is a map that looks back at the road you've just travelled and forward at the path you will take from here. ◆ You began your study of macroeconomics with the core questions of the subject. What are the causes of

- Economic growth?
- Business cycles?
- Unemployment?
- Inflation?

In Chapter 19, you took your first look at each of these questions. You learned some facts about economic growth, business cycles, unemployment, and inflation. In Chapter 20, you learned how we measure the economy's output and the price level. These measures are used to calculate the rate of economic growth, business cycle fluctuations, and inflation. You discovered that making these measurements is not straightforward and that small measurement errors can have a big effect on our perceptions about how we are doing. ◆ In Chapter 21, you learned how we measure the state of the labour market—the levels of employment and unemployment and wages. And in Chapter 22, you studied the macroeconomic version of supply and demand—*aggregate supply* and *aggregate demand.* You saw that the aggregate supply–aggregate demand model is the big picture model. It explains both the long-term trends in economic growth and inflation and the short-term business cycle fluctuations in production, jobs, and inflation. ◆ The chapters that lie ahead of you look behind aggregate supply and aggregate demand, beginning on the demand side. In Chapters 23 through 28, you will study aggregate demand, inflation, and deflation and learn about the macroeconomics that Keynes developed as a response to the Great Depression. And you will learn about the effects of monetary and fiscal policies on aggregate demand. ◆ Then, in Chapters 29 through 32, you will study aggregate supply, economic growth and fluctuations, and policy challenges that we face in stabilizing our economy and speeding its growth. Here, you learn today's answer to the question posed by Adam Smith—what are the causes of differences in the wealth of nations? In Chapter 29, you study the economy at full employment and the forces that change potential GDP. In Chapter 30, you study the process of economic growth. In Chapter 31, you study the business cycle and in Chapter 32, the policy challenges. ◆ Before continuing your study of macroeconomics, spend a few minutes with John Maynard Keynes and Jean-Baptiste Say, the leading scholars who developed this subject. And spend a few minutes with one of today's leading macroeconomists, Robert Barro of Harvard University.

PROBING THE IDEAS

Macroeconomic Revolutions

The Economist

"The ideas of economists and political philosophers, both when they are right and when they are wrong, are more powerful than is commonly understood. Indeed the world is ruled by little else."

John Maynard Keynes
The General Theory of Employment, Interest, and Money

JOHN MAYNARD KEYNES, *born in England in 1883, was one of the outstanding minds of the twentieth century. He wrote on probability as well as economics, represented Britain at the Versailles peace conference at the end of World War I, was a master speculator on international financial markets (an activity he conducted from bed every morning and which made and lost him several fortunes), and played a prominent role in creating the International Monetary Fund. He was a member of the Bloomsbury Group, a circle of outstanding artists and writers that included E. M. Forster, Bertrand Russell, and Virginia Woolf. Keynes was a controversial and quick-witted figure. A critic once complained that Keynes had changed his opinion on some matters, to which Keynes retorted: "When I discover I am wrong, I change my mind. What do you do?"*

The Issues

During the Industrial Revolution, as technological change created new jobs and destroyed old ones, people began to wonder whether the economy could create enough jobs and sufficient demand to buy all the things that the new industrial economy could produce.

Jean-Baptiste Say argues that production creates incomes that are sufficient to buy everything that is produced—supply creates its own demand—an idea that came to be called Say's Law.

Say and Keynes would have had a lot to disagree about. Jean-Baptiste Say, born in Lyon, France, in 1767 (he was 9 years old when Adam Smith's *Wealth of Nations* was published), suffered the wrath of Napoleon for his views on government and the economy. In today's world, Say would be leading a radical conservative charge for a smaller and leaner government. Say was the most famous economist of his era on both sides of the Atlantic. His book, *Traité d'économie politique* (*A Treatise in Political Economy*), published in 1803, became a best-selling university economics textbook in both Europe and North America.

As the Great Depression of the 1930s became more severe and more prolonged, Say's Law looked less and less relevant. John Maynard Keynes revolutionized macroeconomics thinking by turning Say's Law on its head, arguing that production does not depend on supply. Instead, it depends on what people are willing to buy—on demand. Or as Keynes put it, production depends on effective demand. It is possible, argued Keynes, for people to refuse to spend all of their incomes. If businesses fail to spend on new capital the amount that people plan to save, demand might be less than supply. In this situation, resources might go unemployed and remain unemployed indefinitely.

The influence of Keynes persists even today, more than 60 years after the publication of his main work. But during the past 20 years, Nobel Laureate Robert E. Lucas, Jr., with significant contributions from a list of outstanding macroeconomists too long to name, has further revolutionized macroeconomics. Today, we know a lot about economic growth, unemployment, inflation, and business cycles. And we know how to use fiscal policy and monetary policy to improve macroeconomic performance. But we don't yet have all the answers. Macroeconomics remains a field of lively controversy and exciting research.

Then

In 1776, James Hargreaves, an English weaver and carpenter, developed a simple hand-operated machine called a spinning jenny (pictured here). Using this machine, a person could spin 80 threads at once. Thousands of hand-wheel spinners, operators of machines that could spin only one thread, lost their jobs. They protested by wrecking spinning jennies. In the long run, the displaced hand-wheel spinners found work, often in factories that manufactured the machines that had destroyed their previous jobs. From the earliest days of the Industrial Revolution to the present day, people have lost their jobs as new technologies have automated what human effort had previously been needed to accomplish.

Now

Advances in computer technology have made it possible for us to dial our own telephone calls to any part of the world and get connected in a flash. A task that was once performed by telephone operators, who made connections along copper wires, is now performed faster and more reliably by computers along fibre-optic cables. Just as the Industrial Revolution transformed the textile industry, so today's Information Revolution is transforming the telecommunications industry. In the process, the mix of jobs is changing. There are fewer jobs for telephone operators but more jobs for telephone systems designers, builders, managers, and marketers. In the long run, as people spend the income they earn in their changing jobs, supply creates its own demand, just as Say predicted. But does supply create its own demand in the short run, when displaced workers are unemployed?

Robert Barro, whom you can meet on the following pages, is one of the most distinguished macroeconomists. He has contributed to our understanding of economic growth, inflation, and the business cycle and played a significant role in the contemporary macroeconomic revolution.

TALKING WITH

ROBERT J. BARRO *is Robert C. Waggoner Professor of Economics at Harvard University and a senior fellow at the Hoover Institution of Stanford University. Born in 1944 in New York City, he was a physics undergraduate at the California Institute of Technology and an economics graduate student at Harvard. Professor Barro is one of the world's leading economists and has done research on every aspect of macroeconomics, with a focus in recent years on economic growth. In addition to his many scholarly books and articles, he writes extensively for a wider audience. His book,* Getting it Right: Markets and Choices in a Free Society *(MIT Press, 1996) explains, in non-technical language, the importance of property rights and free markets for achieving economic growth and a high standard of living. A new book,* Nothing Is Sacred: Economic Ideas for the New Millennium *(MIT Press, 2002), expands on these ideas. And his regular articles in* Business Week *and the* Wall Street Journal *provide an accessible analysis of an incredible range of current economic issues.*

Michael Parkin and Robin Bade talked with Robert Barro about his work and the progress that economists have made in understanding macroeconomic performance since the pioneering work of Keynes.

Robert J. Barro

Professor Barro, your first degree was in physics. Why did you switch to economics when you went to graduate school?

For me, economics provided an ideal combination of technical analysis with applications to social problems and policies. Physics—or really mathematics—provided a strong background for economic theory and econometrics, but it was not until later in graduate school that I thought I acquired good economic insights. Overall, the transition from physics to economics was a relatively easy one for me, and I have never regretted the choice to switch fields. (Perhaps it also helped that, after taking courses from the great Richard Feynman at Caltech, I recognized that I would never be an outstanding theoretical physicist.)

Your recent research has focused on the determinants of economic growth. What do we know about the determinants of growth? And what do we still need to discover?

A lot of progress has been made over the last decade in attaining an empirical understanding of the determinants of economic growth. There are no "silver bullets" for growth, but there are a number of favourable policies, institutions, and national characteristics that have been identified.

For example, growth is stimulated by a strong rule of law, high levels of human capital in the forms of education and health, low levels of non-productive government spending (and associated taxes), international openness, low fertility rates, and macroeconomic stability (including low and stable inflation). Given these and other factors, growth tends to be higher if a country starts off poorer. That is, convergence—in the sense of the poor tending to grow faster than the rich—holds in a conditional sense, when one holds constant an array of policies and national characteristics. However, convergence does not apply in an absolute sense because the poorest countries tend to have the worst policies and characteristics (which explains why they are observed to be poor).

> ***There are no "silver bullets" for growth, but there are a number of favourable policies, institutions, and national characteristics that have been identified.***

Is there anything that rich countries can do to help poor countries grow faster? Or does successful economic growth come only from self-help?

Mostly economic growth has to come from internal improvements in institutions and policies and from domestic accumulations of human and physical capital. There is no evidence that the rich countries can help through welfare programs, such as foreign aid and debt relief. On the contrary, there is some evidence that, because of the low quality of governance in most developing countries, foreign aid goes mainly to increased government spending and corruption. In the bad old days, the rich countries also provided governance (though not aimed especially at the interests of the governed). However, no one wants to return to the era of colonialism.

You've identified international openness as a characteristic that encourages growth. Is this an area in which the rich countries might do more by opening themselves to free trade with poor countries? Or is it enough for poor countries to just get on with opening their doors?

The rich countries could help to spur economic development by opening themselves more to trade in goods and services, technology, and financial transactions. Protectionist policies, notably in agriculture and textiles, are harmful to developing countries as well as to consumers in rich countries. President Bush's policies have been disgraceful in this area, notably in his protectionism during 2002 for steel and agriculture.

Inflation has been subdued in the United States for most of the 1990s and 2000s. Is this now a problem of the past that we can stop worrying about?

I am optimistic that the monetary authorities of the United States and many other countries have become committed to price stability and have learned that high inflation does not stimulate growth. Central banks seem also to have learned a lot about the mechanics of achieving price stability. One worry, however, is that U.S. monetary authorities—including the Federal Reserve—will become overconfident and will come to believe that they can fine-tune the real economy without losing price stability. For example, the Federal Reserve's interest rates reductions during the 2001 recession may have stimulated too much and could lead eventually to higher inflation.

> ***I am optimistic that the monetary authorities of the United States and many other countries have become committed to price stability and have learned that high inflation does not stimulate growth.***

How do economic growth and inflation interact? Why can't a country grow faster by keeping demand growth strong and inflating?

Inflation is inversely related to economic growth over the medium term—for example, periods of five years or more. This relationship is particularly evident at high inflation rates—say, above 10–15% per year—but probably also applies for more moderate inflation. The likely reason for the inverse relation is that high and volatile inflation makes it difficult for the price system to operate efficiently. It is possible that unanticipated monetary stimulus expands the real economy in the short run. However, this short-term benefit is not worth the cost over the medium and long term. Moreover, the stimulus works mainly when it comes as a surprise, and it is hard to be surprising in a systematic way.

Some years ago, you worked on the business cycle. What is your current view on the nature and causes of aggregate fluctuations? Are they primarily an efficient response to the uneven pace of technical change, or are they primarily the consequence of market failure and demand fluctuations?

Many factors are sources of business cycles, and economists have not been very successful at isolating the precise causes. Influences that seem to matter include variations in the rate of technological progress, shifts in the terms of trade, fiscal effects (particularly important during wartime), and monetary fluctuations. In some countries, shifts in labour relations and in regulatory policies are important. Other countries are influenced by major changes in the quality of governance, such as the recent deterioration of public institutions in Argentina.

I do not think that we know what portion of fluctuations represents efficient responses to shocks as opposed to excess volatility associated with market failure. We do know that many observed fluctuations stem from failures of government policy and institutions, so it is inappropriate to think of governments as typically smoothing out the excesses of the private sector.

What remains in today's macroeconomics of the contribution of Keynes?

Probably Keynesian economics is most influential today in analyses that stress the real effects of monetary policy—either as sources of business fluctuations or as ways to smooth out the cycle. This situation is ironic because Keynes himself deemphasized monetary shocks as a source of fluctuations. He stressed the excesses of the private economy—including the amplifying effects of multipliers and the sensitivity of investment to shifting expectations—and the potentially beneficial role of offsetting fiscal policies. Empirically, the multiplier seems to have existed only in the mind of Keynes.

What advice do you have for a student who is just starting to study economics? Is it a good subject in which to major? If so, what other subjects would you urge students to study alongside economics? Or is the path that you followed, starting with physics (or perhaps math) and then moving to economics for graduate school more effective?

Economics is an excellent field for an undergraduate to study whether one chooses to become an economist or—more likely—if one goes into other fields, such as business or law. Economists have found the framework or methodology that makes economics the core social science, and its impact has been felt greatly by other fields, such as political science, law, and history. These days, economic reasoning is being applied to the study of an array of social topics, including marriage and fertility, crime, democracy, and legal structure. As another example, I am currently participating in a project that involves the interactions between economics and religion. Partly this work is about how economic development and government policies affect religiosity and partly about how religious beliefs and participation influence economic and political outcomes. So perhaps in the future, economics will also be important for studies in theology. No doubt, many economists (including me) have imperialistic tendencies, but this is because they have a great product to sell. As to other complementary subjects to study, the most valuable one is probably mathematics, which provides many of the useful tools to carry out theoretical and empirical inquiries.

Economists have found the framework or methodology that makes economics the core social science …

EXPENDITURE MULTIPLIERS

CHAPTER 23

Economic Amplifier or Shock Absorber?

Céline Dion sings into a microphone in a barely audible whisper. Increasing in volume, through the magic of electronic amplification, her voice fills Toronto's Molson Amphitheatre. ◆ Ralph Klein, the premier of Alberta, and his secretary are being driven to a business meeting along one of Edmonton's less well-repaired streets. The car's wheels bounce and vibrate over some of the worst potholes in the nation, but its passengers are completely undisturbed and the secretary's notes are written without a ripple, thanks to the car's efficient shock absorbers. ◆ Investment and exports fluctuate like the volume of Céline Dion's voice and the uneven surface of an Edmonton street. How does the economy react to those fluctuations? Does it react like a limousine, absorbing the shocks and providing a smooth ride for the economy's passengers? Or does it behave like an amplifier, blowing up the fluctuations and spreading them out to affect the many millions of participants in an economic rock concert?

◆ You will explore these questions in this chapter. You will learn how a recession or an expansion begins when a change in investment or exports induces an amplified change in aggregate expenditure and real GDP. And you'll learn the crucial role played by business inventories in the transition from expansion to recession and back to expansion. *Reading Between the Lines* at the end of the chapter looks at the multiplier at work during the first quarter of 2002, when real GDP grew by a near record 1.5 percent in three months.

After studying this chapter, you will be able to

- **Explain how expenditure plans and real GDP are determined when the price level is fixed**
- **Explain the expenditure multiplier**
- **Explain how recessions and expansions begin**
- **Explain the relationship between aggregate expenditure and aggregate demand**
- **Explain how the multiplier gets smaller as the price level changes**

Expenditure Plans and GDP

THE COMPONENTS OF AGGREGATE EXPENDITURE are consumption expenditure (C), investment (I), government expenditures on goods and services (G), and net exports—exports (X) minus imports (M). The sum of these components is real GDP (Y). (See Chapter 20, p. 460). That is,

$$Y = C + I + G + X - M.$$

Two of these components—consumption expenditure and imports—depend on the level of real GDP. Because real GDP influences consumption expenditure and imports, and because consumption expenditure and imports are components of aggregate expenditure, there is a feedback loop between aggregate expenditure and GDP. You are going to learn how this feedback loop determines real GDP at a given price level.

The starting point is to consider the first piece of the feedback loop: the influence of real GDP on planned consumption expenditure and saving.

Consumption and Saving Plans

Several factors influence consumption expenditure and saving. The most direct influence, especially in the short term, is disposable income. **Disposable income** is real GDP or aggregate income (Y) minus net taxes (NT)—taxes minus transfer payments. And aggregate income equals real GDP. The equation for disposable income (YD) is

$$YD = Y - NT.$$

Disposable income is either spent on consumption goods and services—consumption expenditure (C)— or saved (S). So planned consumption expenditure plus planned saving equals disposable income. That is,

$$YD = C + S.$$

The table in Fig. 23.1 shows some examples of planned consumption expenditure and planned saving at different levels of disposable income. The greater the disposable income, the greater is consumption expenditure and the greater is saving. Also, at each level of disposable income, consumption expenditure plus saving equals disposable income.

The relationship between consumption expenditure and disposable income, with other things remaining the same, is called the **consumption function.** The relationship between saving and disposable income, with other things remaining the same, is called the **saving function.** Let's look at the consumption function and saving function in Fig. 23.1.

Consumption Function Figure 23.1(a) shows a consumption function. The y-axis measures consumption expenditure and the x-axis measures disposable income. Along the consumption function, the points labelled A through F correspond to the rows of the table. For example, point E shows that when disposable income is $800 billion, consumption expenditure is $750 billion. Along the consumption function, as disposable income increases, consumption expenditure also increases.

At point A on the consumption function, consumption expenditure is $150 billion even though disposable income is zero. This consumption expenditure is called *autonomous consumption,* and it is the amount of consumption expenditure that would take place in the short run even if people had no current income. You can think of this amount as the expenditure on the vital necessities of life.

When consumption expenditure exceeds disposable income, past savings are used to pay for current consumption. Such a situation cannot last forever, but it can occur temporarily.

Consumption expenditure in excess of autonomous consumption is called *induced consumption*—expenditure that is induced by an increase in disposable income.

45° Line Figure 23.1(a) also contains a 45° line, the height of which measures disposable income. At each point on this line, consumption expenditure equals disposable income. In the range over which the consumption function lies above the 45° line—between A and D—consumption expenditure exceeds disposable income. In the range over which the consumption function lies below the 45° line—between D and F—consumption expenditure is less than disposable income. And at the point at which the consumption function intersects the 45° line—at point D—consumption expenditure equals disposable income.

Saving Function Figure 23.1(b) shows a saving function. The x-axis is exactly the same as that in part (a). The y-axis measures saving. Again, the points marked A through F correspond to the rows of the table. For example, point *E* shows that when disposable income is $800 billion, saving is $50 billion. Along the saving function, as disposable income increases, saving also increases. At disposable incomes less than $600 billion (point *D*), saving is negative. Negative saving is called *dissaving*. At disposable incomes greater than $600 billion, saving is positive, and at $600 billion, saving is zero.

Notice the connection between the two parts of Fig. 23.1. When consumption expenditure exceeds disposable income in part (a), saving is negative in part (b). When consumption expenditure is less than disposable income in part (a), saving is positive in part (b). And when consumption expenditure equals disposable income in part (a), saving is zero in part (b).

When saving is negative (when consumption expenditure exceeds disposable income), past savings are used to pay for current consumption. Such a situation cannot last forever, but it can occur if disposable income falls temporarily.

FIGURE 23.1 Consumption Function and Saving Function

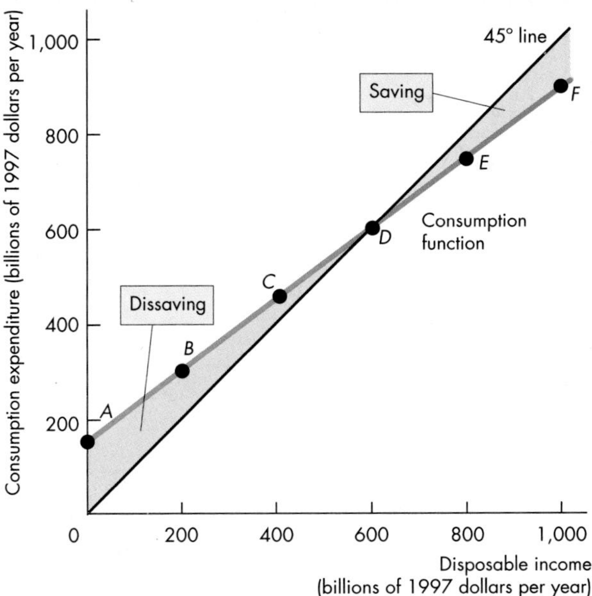

(a) Consumption function

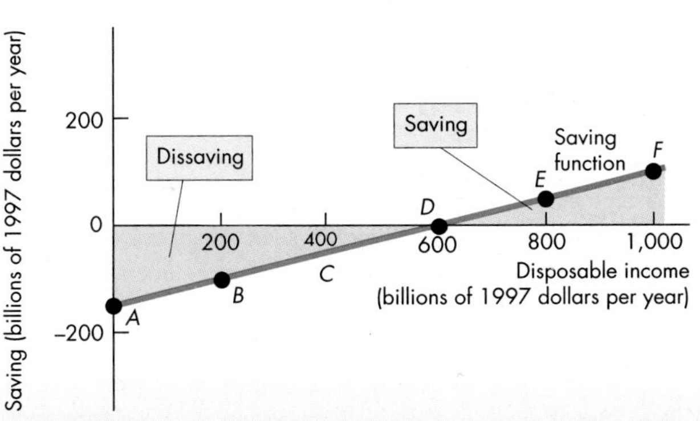

(b) Saving function

	Disposable income	Planned consumption expenditure	Planned saving
	(billions of 1997 dollars per year)		
A	0	150	–150
B	200	300	–100
C	400	450	–50
D	600	600	0
E	800	750	50
F	1,000	900	100

The table shows consumption expenditure and saving plans at various levels of disposable income. Part (a) of the figure shows the relationship between consumption expenditure and disposable income (the consumption function). The height of the consumption function measures consumption expenditure at each level of disposable income. Part (b) shows the relationship between saving and disposable income (the saving function). The height of the saving function measures saving at each level of disposable income. Points *A* through *F* on the consumption and saving functions correspond to the rows in the table. The height of the 45° line in part (a) measures disposable income. So along the 45° line, consumption expenditure equals disposable income. Consumption expenditure plus saving equals disposable income. When the consumption function is above the 45° line, saving is negative (dissaving occurs). When the consumption function is below the 45° line, saving is positive. At the point where the consumption function intersects the 45° line, all disposable income is consumed and saving is zero.

Marginal Propensity to Consume

The amount by which consumption expenditure changes when disposable income changes depends on the marginal propensity to consume. The **marginal propensity to consume** (*MPC*) is the fraction of a *change* in disposable income that is consumed. It is calculated as the *change* in consumption expenditure (ΔC) divided by the *change* in disposable income (ΔYD) that brought it about. That is,

$$MPC = \frac{\Delta C}{\Delta YD}.$$

In the table in Fig. 23.1, when disposable income increases from \$600 billion to \$800 billion, consumption expenditure increases from \$600 billion to \$750 billion. The \$200 billion increase in disposable income increases consumption expenditure by \$150 billion. The *MPC* is \$150 billion divided by \$200 billion, which equals 0.75.

The marginal propensity to consume is the slope of the consumption function. You can check this fact out in Fig. 23.2(a). Here, a \$200 billion increase in disposable income from \$600 billion to \$800 billion is the base of the red triangle. The increase in consumption expenditure that results from this increase in disposable income is \$150 billion and is the height of the triangle. The slope of the consumption function is given by the formula "slope equals rise over run" and is \$150 billion divided by \$200 billion, which equals 0.75—the *MPC.*

Marginal Propensity to Save

The amount by which saving changes when disposable income changes depends on the marginal propensity to save. The **marginal propensity to save** (*MPS*) is the fraction of a *change* in disposable income that is saved. It is calculated as the *change* in saving (ΔS) divided by the *change* in disposable income (ΔYD) that brought it about. That is,

$$MPS = \frac{\Delta S}{\Delta YD}.$$

In the table in Fig. 23.1, an increase in disposable income from \$600 billion to \$800 billion increases saving from zero to \$50 billion. The \$200 billion increase in disposable income increases saving by \$50 billion. The *MPS* is \$50 billion divided by \$200 billion, which equals 0.25.

FIGURE 23.2 Marginal Propensities to Consume and Save

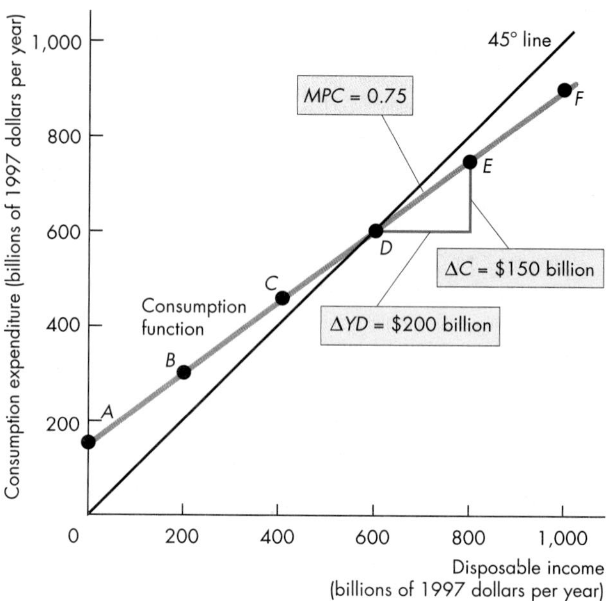

(a) Consumption function

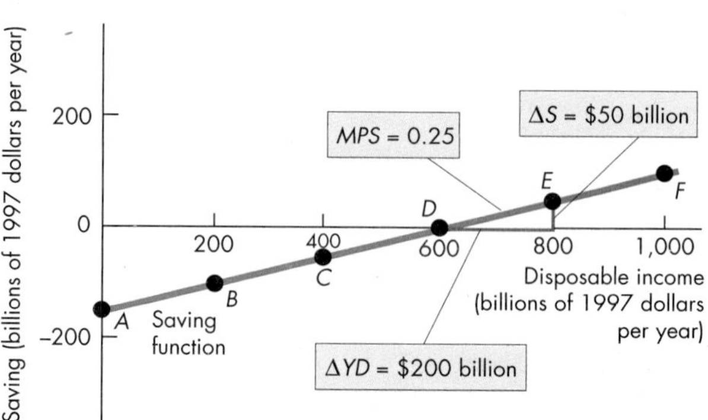

(b) Saving function

The marginal propensity to consume, *MPC*, is equal to the change in consumption expenditure divided by the change in disposable income, other things remaining the same. It is measured by the slope of the consumption function. In part (a), the *MPC* is 0.75.

The marginal propensity to save, *MPS*, is equal to the change in saving divided by the change in disposable income, other things remaining the same. It is measured by the slope of the saving function. In part (b), the *MPS* is 0.25.

The marginal propensity to save is the slope of the saving function. You can check this fact out in Fig. 23.2(b). Here, a \$200 billion increase in disposable income from \$600 billion to \$800 billion (the base of the red triangle) increases saving by \$50 billion (the height of the triangle). The slope of the saving function is \$50 billion divided by \$200 billion, which equals 0.25—the *MPS.*

The marginal propensity to consume plus the marginal propensity to save always equals 1. They sum to 1 because consumption expenditure and saving exhaust disposable income. Part of each dollar increase in disposable income is consumed, and the remaining part is saved. You can see that these two marginal propensities sum to 1 by using the equation:

$$\Delta C + \Delta S = \Delta YD.$$

Divide both sides of the equation by the change in disposable income to obtain

$$\frac{\Delta C}{\Delta YD} + \frac{\Delta S}{\Delta YD} = 1.$$

$\Delta C/\Delta YD$ is the *marginal propensity to consume* (*MPC*), and $\Delta S/\Delta YD$ is the *marginal propensity to save* (*MPS*), so

$$MPC + MPS = 1.$$

Other Influences on Consumption Expenditure and Saving

You've seen that a change in disposable income leads to changes in consumption expenditure and saving. A change in disposable income brings movements along the consumption function and saving function. A change in any other influence on consumption expenditure and saving shifts the consumption function and the saving function as shown in Fig. 23.3.

The main other influences are

1. Expected future disposable income
2. The real interest rate
3. Wealth

An increase in expected future disposable income makes people feel better off and leads to an increase in current consumption expenditure and a decrease in current saving. A fall in the real interest rate, other things remaining the same, encourages an increase in

FIGURE 23.3 Shifts in the Consumption and Saving Functions

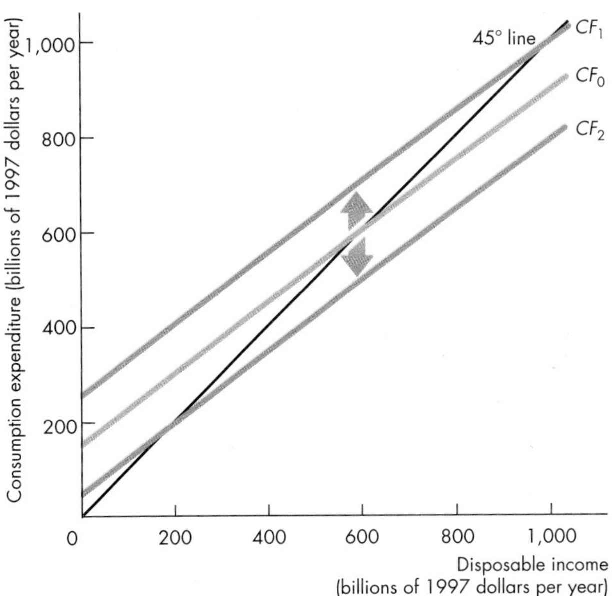

(a) Consumption function

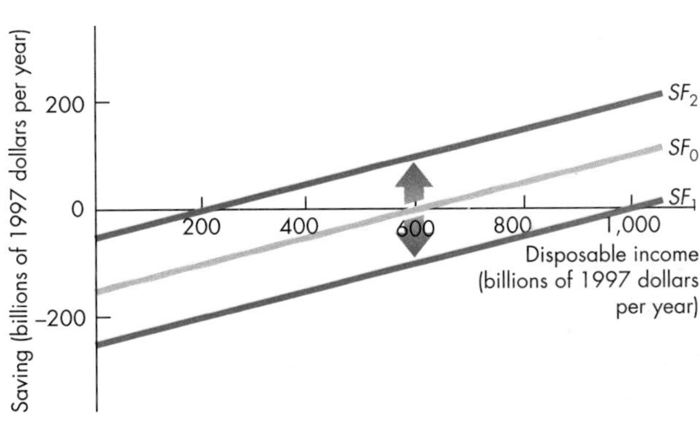

(b) Saving function

A fall in the real interest rate, an increase in wealth, or an increase in expected future disposable income shifts the consumption function upward from CF_0 *to* CF_1 and the saving function downward from SF_0 *to* SF_1.

A rise in the real interest rate, a decrease in wealth, or a decrease in expected future disposable income shifts the consumption function downward from CF_0 *to* CF_2 and shifts the saving function upward from SF_0 *to* SF_2.

borrowing and consumption expenditure and a decrease in saving. And an increase in wealth, other things remaining the same, stimulates consumption expenditure and decreases saving.

When expected future disposable income increases, the real interest rate falls, or when wealth increases, consumption expenditure increases and saving decreases. In Fig. 23.3 the consumption function shifts upward from CF_0 to CF_1, and the saving function shifts downward from SF_0 to SF_1.

When expected future disposable income decreases, the real interest rate rises, or when wealth decreases, consumption expenditure decreases and saving increases. The consumption function shifts downward from CF_0 to CF_2, and the saving function shifts upward from SF_0 to SF_2. Such shifts often occur when a recession begins because at such a time, expected future disposable income decreases.

We've studied the theory of the consumption function. Let's now see how that theory applies to the Canadian economy.

The Canadian Consumption Function

Figure 23.4 shows the Canadian consumption function. Each point identified by a blue dot represents consumption expenditure and disposable income for a particular year. (The dots are for the years 1961–2001. Five of the years are identified in the figure.) The line labelled CF_{61} is an estimate of the Canadian consumption function in 1961, and the line labelled CF_{01} is an estimate of the Canadian consumption function in 2001.

The slope of the consumption function in Fig. 23.4 is 0.7, which means that a $100 billion increase in disposable income brings a $70 billion increase in consumption expenditure. This slope, which is an estimate of the marginal propensity to consume, is an assumption that is at the middle of the range of values that economists have estimated for the marginal propensity to consume.

The consumption function shifts upward over time as other influences on consumption expenditure change. Of these other influences, expected future disposable income, the real interest rate, and wealth fluctuate and so bring upward *and* downward shifts in the consumption function. But rising wealth and rising expected future disposable income brings a steady upward shift in the consumption function. As the consumption function shifts upward, autonomous consumption expenditure increases.

FIGURE 23.4 The Canadian Consumption Function

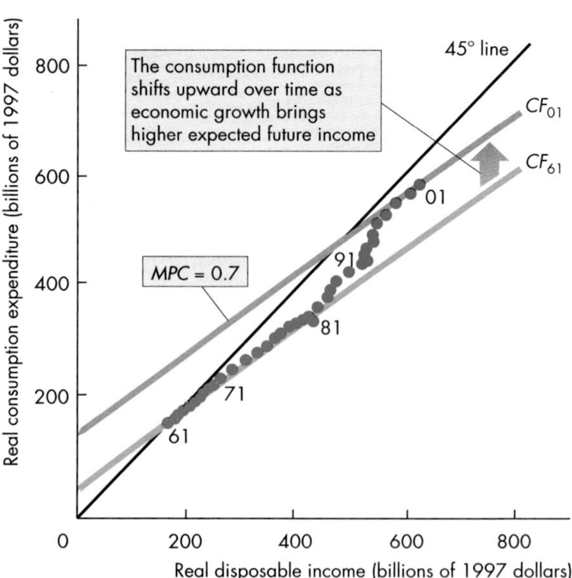

Each blue dot shows consumption expenditure and disposable income for a particular year. The lines CF_{61} and CF_{01} are estimates of the Canadian consumption function in 1961 and 2001, respectively. Here, the (assumed) marginal propensity to consume is 0.7.

Source: Statistics Canada, CANSIM tables 380-0002, 384-0013, 384-0035, and the authors' calculations.

Consumption as a Function of Real GDP

You've seen that consumption expenditure changes when disposable income changes. Disposable income changes when either real GDP changes or net taxes change. But net taxes—taxes minus transfer payments—are themselves related to real GDP. When real GDP increases, taxes increase and transfer payments decrease. Because net taxes depend on real GDP, disposable income depends on real GDP and so consumption expenditure depends not only on disposable income but also on real GDP. We use this link between consumption expenditure and real GDP to determine equilibrium expenditure. But before we do so, we need to look at one further component of aggregate expenditure: imports. Like consumption expenditure, imports also are influenced by real GDP.

Import Function

Canadian imports are determined by many factors, but in the short run, one factor dominates: Canadian real GDP. Other things remaining the same, the greater the Canadian real GDP, the larger is the quantity of Canadian imports.

The relationship between imports and real GDP is determined by the marginal propensity to import. The **marginal propensity to import** is the fraction of an increase in real GDP that is spent on imports. It is calculated as the change in imports divided by the change in real GDP that brought it about, other things remaining the same. For example, if a $100 billion increase in real GDP increases imports by $25 billion, the marginal propensity to import is 0.25.

In recent years, since the North American Free Trade Agreement (NAFTA) was implemented, Canadian imports have surged. For example, between 1991 and 2001, real GDP increased by $278 billion and imports increased by $167 billion. If no factors other than real GDP influenced imports during this period, these numbers would imply a marginal propensity to import of 0.6 ($167 billion divided by $278 billion). But other factors (such as NAFTA) increased imports, so the marginal propensity to import is smaller than 0.6. The marginal propensity to import might be as large as 0.3, and it has been increasing as the global economy has become more integrated.

REVIEW QUIZ

1. Which components of aggregate expenditure are influenced by real GDP?
2. Define the marginal propensity to consume. What is your estimate of your own marginal propensity to consume? After you graduate, will it change? Why or why not?
3. How do we calculate the effects of real GDP on consumption expenditure and imports?

Real GDP influences consumption and imports. But consumption and imports—along with investment, government expenditures, and exports—influence real GDP. Your next task is to study this second piece of the two-way link between aggregate expenditure and real GDP and see how all the components of aggregate planned expenditure interact to determine real GDP.

Equilibrium Expenditure at a Fixed Price Level

MOST FIRMS ARE LIKE YOUR LOCAL SUPERMARKET. They set their prices, advertise their products and services, and sell the quantities their customers are willing to buy. If they persistently sell a greater quantity than they plan to and are constantly running out of inventory, they eventually raise their prices. And if they persistently sell a smaller quantity than they plan to and have inventories piling up, they eventually cut their prices. But in the very short term, their prices are fixed. They hold the prices they have set, and the quantities they sell depend on demand, not supply.

The Aggregate Implications of Fixed Prices

Fixed prices have two immediate implications for the economy as a whole:

1. Because each firm's price is fixed, the *price level* is fixed.
2. Because demand determines the quantities that each firm sells, *aggregate demand* determines the aggregate quantity of goods and services sold, which equals real GDP.

So to understand how real GDP is determined when the price level is fixed, we must understand how aggregate demand is determined. Aggregate demand is determined by aggregate expenditure plans. We define **aggregate planned expenditure** as *planned* consumption expenditure plus *planned* investment plus *planned* government expenditures plus *planned* exports minus *planned* imports.

You've just studied planned consumption expenditure and planned imports and seen that these two components of aggregate planned expenditure are influenced by real GDP. The other components of aggregate expenditure—investment, government expenditures, and exports—are not influenced by real GDP. They fluctuate for many reasons but not because real GDP fluctuates.

You are now going to study a model called the *aggregate expenditure model*, which explains how consumption expenditure, imports, and real GDP are *simultaneously* determined by a feedback loop between expenditure plans and real GDP.

The Aggregate Expenditure Model

You are now going to discover how aggregate expenditure plans interact to determine real GDP when the price level is fixed. First, we will study the relationship between aggregate planned expenditure and real GDP. Second, we'll learn about the key distinction between *planned* expenditure and *actual* expenditure. And third, we'll study equilibrium expenditure, a situation in which aggregate planned expenditure and actual expenditure are equal.

The relationship between aggregate planned expenditure and real GDP can be described by either an aggregate expenditure schedule or an aggregate expenditure curve. The *aggregate expenditure schedule* lists aggregate planned expenditure generated at each level of real GDP. The *aggregate expenditure curve* is a graph of the aggregate expenditure schedule.

FIGURE 23.5 Aggregate Expenditure

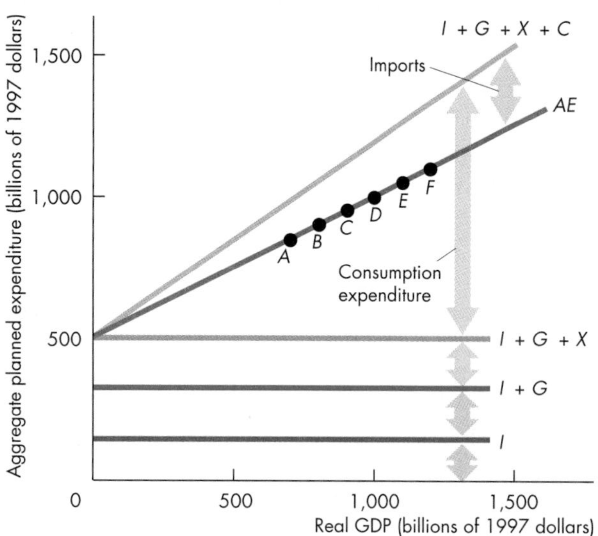

The aggregate expenditure schedule shows the relationship between aggregate planned expenditure and real GDP. Aggregate planned expenditure is the sum of planned consumption expenditure, investment, government expenditures, and exports minus imports. For example, in row *B* of the table, when real GDP is \$800 billion, planned consumption expenditure is \$560 billion, planned investment is \$150 billion, planned government expenditures on goods and services are \$180 billion, planned exports are \$170 billion, and planned imports are \$160 billion. So when real GDP is \$800 billion, aggregate planned expenditure is \$900 billion (\$560 + \$150 + \$180 + \$170 – \$160). The schedule shows that aggregate planned expenditure increases as real GDP increases.

This relationship is graphed as the aggregate expenditure curve *AE*. The components of aggregate expenditure that increase with real GDP are consumption expenditure and imports. The other components—investment, government expenditures, and exports—do not vary with real GDP.

	Real GDP (*Y*)	Consumption expenditure (*C*)	Investment (*I*)	Government expenditures (*G*)	Exports (*X*)	Imports (*M*)	Aggregate planned expenditure (*AE* = *C* + *I* + *G* + *X* – *M*)
		Planned expenditure (billions of 1997 dollars)					
	0	0	150	180	170	0	500
A	700	490	150	180	170	140	850
B	800	560	150	180	170	160	900
C	900	630	150	180	170	180	950
D	1,000	700	150	180	170	200	1,000
E	1,100	770	150	180	170	220	1,050
F	1,200	840	150	180	170	240	1,100

Aggregate Planned Expenditure and Real GDP

The table in Fig. 23.5 sets out an aggregate expenditure schedule together with the components of aggregate planned expenditure. To calculate aggregate planned expenditure at a given real GDP, we add the various components together. The first column of the table shows real GDP, and the second column shows the consumption expenditure generated by each level of real GDP. A \$700 billion increase in real GDP generates a \$490 billion increase in consumption expenditure—the *MPC* is 0.7.

The next two columns show investment and government expenditures on goods and services. Investment depends on such factors as the real interest rate and the expected future profit. But at a given point in time, these factors generate a particular level of investment. Suppose this level of investment is \$150 billion. Also, suppose that government expenditures on goods and services is \$180 billion.

The next two columns show exports and imports. Exports are influenced by income in the rest of the world, prices of foreign-made goods and services relative to the prices of similar Canadian-made goods and services, and foreign exchange rates. But exports are not directly affected by real GDP in Canada. Exports are a constant \$170 billion no matter what real GDP in Canada is. Imports increase as real GDP increases. A \$100 billion increase in real GDP generates a \$20 billion increase in imports—the marginal propensity to import is 0.2.

The final column shows aggregate planned expenditure—the sum of planned consumption expenditure, investment, government expenditures on goods and services, and exports minus imports.

Figure 23.5 plots an aggregate expenditure curve. Real GDP is shown on the *x*-axis, and aggregate planned expenditure is shown on the *y*-axis. The aggregate expenditure curve is the red line *AE*. Points *A* through *F* on that curve correspond to the rows of the table. The *AE* curve is a graph of aggregate planned expenditure (the last column) plotted against real GDP (the first column).

Figure 23.5 also shows the components of aggregate expenditure. The constant components—investment (I), government expenditures on goods and services (G), and exports (X)—are shown by the horizontal lines in the figure. Consumption expenditure (C) is the vertical gap between the lines labelled $I + G + X$ and $I + G + X + C$.

To construct the *AE* curve, subtract imports (M) from the line labelled $I + G + X + C$. Aggregate expenditure is expenditure on Canadian-made goods and services. But the components of aggregate expenditure—C, I, and G—include expenditure on imported goods and services. For example, if you buy a new cell phone, your expenditure is part of consumption expenditure. But if the cell phone is a Nokia made in Finland, your expenditure on it must be subtracted from consumption expenditure to find out how much is spent on goods and services produced in Canada—on Canadian real GDP. Money paid to Nokia for cell phone imports from Finland does not add to aggregate expenditure in Canada.

Because imports are only a part of aggregate expenditure, when we subtract imports from the other components of aggregate expenditure, aggregate planned expenditure still increases as real GDP increases, as you can see in Fig. 23.5.

Consumption expenditure minus imports, which varies with real GDP, is called **induced expenditure.** The sum of investment, government expenditures, and exports, which does not vary with real GDP, is called **autonomous expenditure.** Consumption expenditure and imports can also have an autonomous component—a component that does not vary with real GDP. Another way of thinking about autonomous expenditure is that it would be the level of aggregate planned expenditure if real GDP were zero.

In Fig. 23.5, autonomous expenditure is \$500 billion—aggregate planned expenditure when real GDP is zero. For each \$100 billion increase in real GDP, induced expenditure increases by \$50 billion.

The aggregate expenditure curve summarizes the relationship between aggregate *planned* expenditure and real GDP. But what determines the point on the aggregate expenditure curve at which the economy operates? What determines *actual* aggregate expenditure?

Actual Expenditure, Planned Expenditure, and Real GDP

Actual aggregate expenditure is always equal to real GDP, as we saw in Chapter 20 (p. 460). But aggregate *planned* expenditure is not necessarily equal to actual aggregate expenditure and therefore is not necessarily equal to real GDP. How can actual expenditure and planned expenditure differ from each other? Why don't expenditure plans get implemented? The main reason is that firms might end up with greater inventories than planned or with smaller inventories than planned. People carry out their consumption expenditure plans, the government implements its planned purchases of goods and services, and net exports are as planned. Firms carry out their plans to purchase new buildings, plant, and equipment. But one component of investment is the change in firms' inventories. If aggregate planned expenditure is less than real GDP, firms don't sell all the goods they produce and they end up with inventories they hadn't planned. If aggregate planned expenditure exceeds real GDP, firms sell more than they produce and inventories decrease below the level that firms had planned.

Equilibrium Expenditure

Equilibrium expenditure is the level of aggregate expenditure that occurs when aggregate *planned* expenditure equals real GDP. It is the level of aggregate

FIGURE 23.6 Equilibrium Expenditure

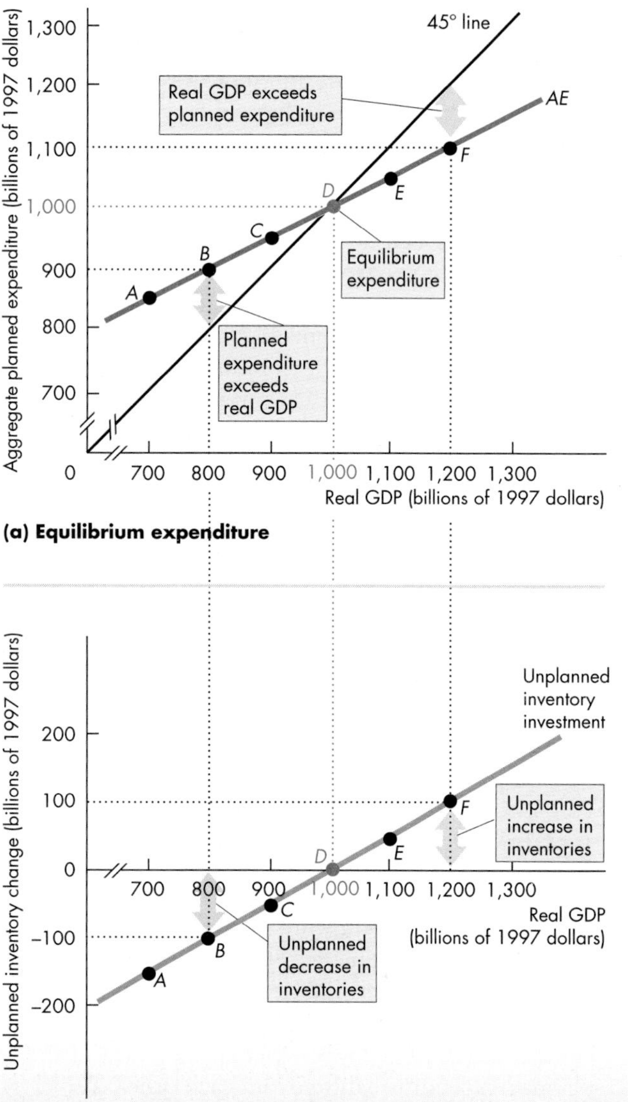

	Real GDP (*Y*)	Aggregate planned expenditure (*AE*)	Unplanned inventory change (*Y* – *AE*)
		(billions of 1997 dollars)	
A	700	850	–150
B	800	900	–100
C	900	950	–50
D	**1,000**	**1,000**	**0**
E	1,100	1,050	50
F	1,200	1,100	100

The table shows expenditure plans at different levels of real GDP. When real GDP is $1,000 billion, aggregate planned expenditure equals real GDP.

Part (a) of the figure illustrates equilibrium expenditure, which occurs when aggregate planned expenditure equals real GDP at the intersection of the 45° line and the *AE* curve. Part (b) of the figure shows the forces that bring about equilibrium expenditure. When aggregate planned expenditure exceeds real GDP, inventories decrease—for example, at point *B* in both parts of the figure. Firms increase production, and real GDP increases.

When aggregate planned expenditure is less than real GDP, inventories increase—for example, at point *F* in both parts of the figure. Firms decrease production, and real GDP decreases. When aggregate planned expenditure equals real GDP, there are no unplanned inventory changes and real GDP remains constant at equilibrium expenditure.

expenditure and real GDP at which everyone's spending plans are fulfilled. When the price level is fixed, equilibrium expenditure determines real GDP. When aggregate planned expenditure and actual aggregate expenditure are unequal, a process of convergence towards equilibrium expenditure occurs. And throughout this convergence process, real GDP adjusts. Let's examine equilibrium expenditure and the process that brings it about.

Figure 23.6(a) illustrates equilibrium expenditure. The table sets out aggregate planned expenditure at various levels of real GDP. These values are plotted as points *A* through *F* along the *AE* curve. The 45° line shows all the points at which aggregate planned expenditure equals real GDP. Thus where the *AE* curve lies above the 45° line, aggregate planned expenditure exceeds real GDP; where the *AE* curve lies below the 45° line, aggregate planned expenditure is less than real GDP; and where the *AE* curve intersects the 45° line, aggregate planned expenditure equals real GDP. Point *D* illustrates equilibrium expenditure. At this point, real GDP is $1,000 billion.

Convergence to Equilibrium

What are the forces that move aggregate expenditure towards its equilibrium level? To answer this question, we must look at a situation in which aggregate expenditure is away from its equilibrium level. Suppose that in Fig. 23.6, real GDP is $800 billion. With real GDP at $800 billion, actual aggregate expenditure is also $800 billion. But aggregate *planned* expenditure is $900 billion (point *B* in Fig. 23.6a). Aggregate planned expenditure exceeds *actual* expenditure. When people spend $900 billion and firms produce goods and services worth $800 billion, firms' inventories fall by $100 billion (point *B* in Fig. 23.6b). Recall that *investment* is the purchase of new plant, equipment and buildings and *additions to inventories.* Because the change in inventories is part of investment, *actual* investment is $100 billion less than *planned* investment.

Real GDP doesn't remain at $800 billion for very long. Firms have inventory targets based on their sales. When inventories fall below target, firms increase production to restore inventories to the target level. To increase inventories, firms hire additional labour and increase production. Suppose that they increase production in the next period by $100 billion. Real GDP increases by $100 billion to $900 billion. But again, aggregate planned expenditure exceeds real GDP. When real GDP is $900 billion, aggregate planned expenditure is $950 billion (point *C* in Fig. 23.6a). Again, inventories decrease, but this time by less than before. With real GDP of $900 billion and aggregate planned expenditure of $950 billion, inventories decrease by $50 billion (point *C* in Fig. 23.6b). Again, firms hire additional labour, and production increases; real GDP increases yet further.

The process that we've just described—planned expenditure exceeds real GDP, inventories decrease, and production increases—ends when real GDP has reached $1,000 billion. At this real GDP, there is equilibrium. Unplanned inventory changes are zero. Firms do not change their production.

You can do an experiment similar to the one we've just done but starting with a level of real GDP greater than equilibrium expenditure. In this case, planned expenditure is less than actual expenditure, inventories pile up, and firms cut production. As before, real GDP keeps on changing (decreasing this time) until it reaches its equilibrium level of $1,000 billion.

REVIEW QUIZ

1. What is the relationship between aggregate planned expenditure and real GDP in expenditure equilibrium?
2. How does equilibrium expenditure come about? What adjusts to achieve equilibrium?
3. If real GDP and aggregate expenditure are less than their equilibrium levels, what happens to firms' inventories? How do firms change their production? And what happens to real GDP?
4. If real GDP and aggregate expenditure are greater than their equilibrium levels, what happens to firms' inventories? How do firms change their production? And what happens to real GDP?

We've learned that when the price level is fixed, real GDP is determined by equilibrium expenditure. And you have seen how unplanned changes in inventories and the production response that they generate brings a convergence towards equilibrium expenditure. We're now going to study *changes* in equilibrium expenditure and discover an economic amplifier called the *multiplier.*

The Multiplier

INVESTMENT AND EXPORTS CAN CHANGE FOR many reasons. A fall in the real interest rate might induce firms to increase their planned investment. A wave of innovation, such as occurred with the spread of multimedia computers in the 1990s, might increase expected future profits and lead firms to increase their planned investment. An economic boom in the United States and Western Europe might lead to a large increase in their expenditure on Canadian-produced goods and services—on Canadian exports. These are all examples of increases in autonomous expenditure.

When autonomous expenditure increases, aggregate expenditure increases, and so do equilibrium expenditure and real GDP. But the increase in real GDP is *larger* than the change in autonomous expenditure. The **multiplier** is the amount by which a change in autonomous expenditure is magnified or multiplied to determine the change in equilibrium expenditure and real GDP.

It is easiest to get the basic idea of the multiplier if we work with an example economy in which there are no income taxes and no imports. So we'll first assume that these factors are absent. Then, when you understand the basic idea, we'll bring these factors back into play and see what difference they make to the multiplier.

The Basic Idea of the Multiplier

Suppose that investment increases. The additional expenditure by businesses means that aggregate expenditure and real GDP increase. The increase in real GDP increases disposable income, and with no income taxes, real GDP and disposable income increase by the same amount. The increase in disposable income brings an increase in consumption expenditure. And the increased consumption expenditure adds even more to aggregate expenditure. Real GDP and disposable income increase further, and so does consumption expenditure. The initial increase in investment brings an even bigger increase in aggregate expenditure because it induces an increase in consumption expenditure. The magnitude of the increase in aggregate expenditure that results from an increase in autonomous expenditure is determined by the *multiplier*.

The table in Fig. 23.7 sets out aggregate planned expenditure. When real GDP is $900 billion, aggregate planned expenditure is $925 billion. For each $100 billion increase in real GDP, aggregate planned expenditure increases by $75 billion. This aggregate expenditure schedule is shown in the figure as the aggregate expenditure curve AE_0. Initially, equilibrium expenditure is $1,000 billion. You can see this equilibrium in row *B* of the table and in the figure where the curve AE_0 intersects the 45° line at the point marked *B*.

Now suppose that autonomous expenditure increases by $50 billion. What happens to equilibrium expenditure? You can see the answer in Fig. 23.7. When this increase in autonomous expenditure is added to the original aggregate planned expenditure, aggregate planned expenditure increases by $50 billion at each level of real GDP. The new aggregate expenditure curve is AE_1. The new equilibrium expenditure, highlighted in the table (row *D'*), occurs where AE_1 intersects the 45° line and is $1,200 billion (point *D'*). At this real GDP, aggregate planned expenditure equals real GDP.

The Multiplier Effect

In Fig. 23.7, the increase in autonomous expenditure of $50 billion increases equilibrium expenditure by $200 billion. That is, the change in autonomous expenditure leads, like Céline Dion's electronic equipment, to an amplified change in equilibrium expenditure. This amplified change is the *multiplier effect*—equilibrium expenditure increases by *more than* the increase in autonomous expenditure. The multiplier is greater than 1.

Initially, when autonomous expenditure increases, aggregate planned expenditure exceeds real GDP. As a result, inventories decrease. Firms respond by increasing production so as to restore their inventories to the target level. As production increases, so does real GDP. With a higher level of real GDP, *induced expenditure* increases. Thus equilibrium expenditure increases by the sum of the initial increase in autonomous expenditure and the increase in induced expenditure. In this example, induced expenditure increases by $150 billion, so equilibrium expenditure increases by $200 billion.

Although we have just analyzed the effects of an *increase* in autonomous expenditure, the same analysis applies to a decrease in autonomous expenditure. If initially the aggregate expenditure curve is AE_1, equilibrium expenditure and real GDP are $1,200 billion. A decrease in autonomous expenditure of $50 billion shifts the aggregate expenditure

FIGURE 23.7 The Multiplier

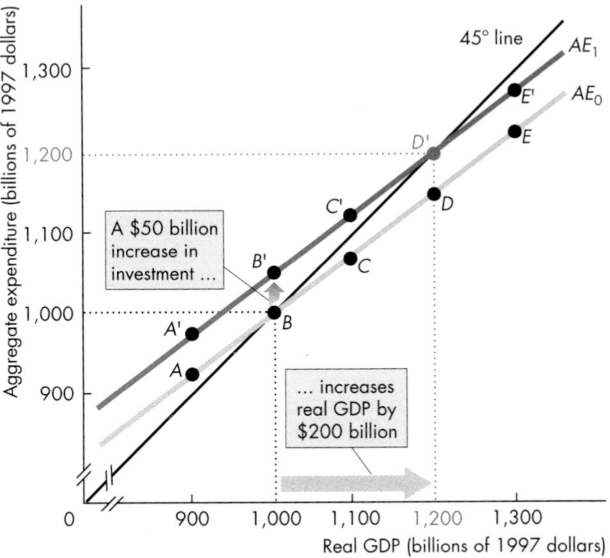

Real GDP (Y)	Aggregate planned expenditure Original (AE_0)		New (AE_1)	
	(billions of 1997 dollars)			
900	A	925	A'	975
1,000	**B**	**1,000**	B'	1,050
1,100	C	1,075	C'	1,125
1,200	D	1,150	**D'**	**1,200**
1,300	E	1,225	E'	1,275

A $50 billion increase in autonomous expenditure shifts the *AE* curve upward by $50 billion from AE_0 to AE_1. Equilibrium expenditure increases by $200 billion from $1,000 billion to $1,200 billion. The increase in equilibrium expenditure is 4 times the increase in autonomous expenditure, so the multiplier is 4.

curve downward by $50 billion to AE_0. Equilibrium expenditure decreases from $1,200 billion to $1,000 billion. The decrease in equilibrium expenditure ($200 billion) is larger than the decrease in autonomous expenditure that brought it about ($50 billion).

Why Is the Multiplier Greater Than 1?

We've seen that equilibrium expenditure increases by more than the increase in autonomous expenditure. This makes the multiplier greater than 1. How come? Why does equilibrium expenditure increase by more than the increase in autonomous expenditure?

The multiplier is greater than 1 because of induced expenditure—an increase in autonomous expenditure *induces* further increases in expenditure. If Rogers Cablesystems spends $10 million on a new pay-per-view system, aggregate expenditure and real GDP immediately increase by $10 million. But that is not the end of the story. Video system designers and computer producers now have more income, and they spend part of the extra income on cars, microwave ovens, vacations, and a host of other goods and services. Real GDP now increases by the initial $10 million plus the extra consumption expenditure induced by the $10 million increase in income. The producers of cars, microwave ovens, vacations, and other goods and services now have increased incomes, and they, in turn, spend part of the increase in their incomes on consumption goods and services. Additional income induces additional expenditure, which creates additional income.

We have seen that a change in autonomous expenditure has a multiplier effect on real GDP. But how big is the multiplier effect?

The Size of the Multiplier

The *multiplier* is the amount by which a change in autonomous expenditure is multiplied to determine the change in equilibrium expenditure that it generates. To calculate the multiplier, we divide the change in equilibrium expenditure by the change in autonomous expenditure. Let's calculate the multiplier for the example in Fig. 23.7. Initially, equilibrium expenditure is $1,000 billion. Then autonomous expenditure increases by $50 billion, and equilibrium expenditure increases by $200 billion, to $1,200 billion. So

$$\text{Multiplier} = \frac{\text{Change in equilibrium expenditure}}{\text{Change in autonomous expenditure}}$$

$$= \frac{\$200 \text{ billion}}{\$50 \text{ billion}} = 4.$$

The Multiplier and the Slope of the *AE* Curve

What determines the magnitude of the multiplier? The answer is the slope of the *AE* curve. The steeper the slope of the *AE* curve, the larger is the multiplier. To see why, think about what the slope of the *AE* curve tells you. It tells you by how much induced expenditure increases when real GDP increases. The steeper the *AE* curve, the greater is the increase in induced expenditure that results from a given increase in real GDP. Let's do a calculation to show the relationship between the slope of the *AE* curve and the multiplier.

The change in real GDP (ΔY) equals the change in induced expenditure (ΔN) plus the change in autonomous expenditure (ΔA). That is,

$$\Delta Y = \Delta N + \Delta A.$$

The slope of the *AE* curve equals the "rise," ΔN, divided by the "run," ΔY. That is,

$$\text{Slope of } AE \text{ curve} = \Delta N \div \Delta Y.$$

So

$$\Delta N = \text{Slope of } AE \text{ curve} \times \Delta Y.$$

Now use this equation to replace ΔN in the first equation above to give

$$\Delta Y = (\text{Slope of } AE \text{ curve} \times \Delta Y) + \Delta A.$$

Now, solve for ΔY as

$$(1 - \text{Slope of } AE \text{ curve}) \times \Delta Y = \Delta A$$

and rearrange to give

$$\Delta Y = \frac{\Delta A}{1 - \text{Slope of the } AE \text{ curve}}.$$

Finally, divide both sides of the previous equation by ΔA to give

$$\text{Multiplier} = \frac{\Delta Y}{\Delta A} = \frac{1}{1 - \text{Slope of } AE \text{ curve}}.$$

Using the numbers for Fig. 23.7, the slope of the *AE* curve 0.75, so the multiplier is

$$\text{Multiplier} = \frac{1}{1 - 0.75} = \frac{1}{0.25} = 4.$$

When there are no income taxes and no imports, the slope of the *AE* curve equals the marginal propensity to consume (*MPC*). So the multiplier is

$$\text{Multiplier} = \frac{1}{1 - MPC}.$$

There is another formula for the multiplier in this special case. Because the marginal propensity to consume (*MPC*) plus the marginal propensity to save (*MPS*) sum to 1, the term ($1 - MPC$) equals *MPS*. Therefore, another formula for the multiplier is

$$\text{Multiplier} = \frac{1}{MPS}.$$

Because the marginal propensity to save (*MPS*) is a number between 0 and 1, the multiplier is greater than 1.

Figure 23.8 illustrates the multiplier process. In round 1, autonomous expenditure increases by $50 billion (shown by the green bar). At this time, induced expenditure does not change, so aggregate expenditure and real GDP increase by $50 billion. In round 2, the larger real GDP induces more consumption expenditure. Induced expenditure increases by 0.75 times the increase in real GDP, so the increase in real GDP of $50 billion induces a further increase in expenditure of $37.5 billion. This change in induced expenditure (the green bar in round 2), when added to the previous increase in expenditure (the blue bar in round 2), increases aggregate expenditure and real GDP by $87.5 billion. The round 2 increase in real GDP induces a round 3 increase in expenditure. The process repeats through successive rounds. Each increase in real GDP is 0.75 times the previous increase. The cumulative increase in real GDP gradually approaches $200 billion.

So far, we've ignored imports and income taxes. Let's now see how these two factors influence the multiplier.

Imports and Income Taxes

The multiplier is determined, in general, not only by the marginal propensity to consume but also by the marginal propensity to import and by the marginal tax rate.

Imports make the multiplier smaller than it otherwise would be. To see why, think about what happens following an increase in investment. An increase in investment increases real GDP, which in

FIGURE 23.8 The Multiplier Process

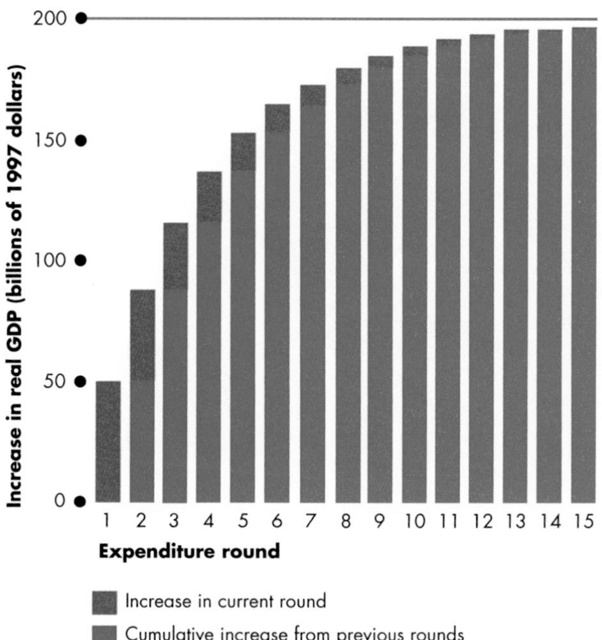

Autonomous expenditure increases in round 1 by $50 billion. As a result, real GDP increases by the same amount. With a marginal propensity to consume of 0.75, each additional dollar of real GDP induces an additional 0.75 of a dollar of aggregate expenditure. The round 1 increase in real GDP induces an increase in consumption expenditure of $37.5 billion in round 2. At the end of round 2, real GDP has increased by $87.5 billion. The extra $37.5 billion of real GDP in round 2 induces a further increase in consumption expenditure of $28.1 billion in round 3. Real GDP increases yet further to $115.6 billion. This process continues with real GDP increasing by ever-smaller amounts. When the process comes to an end, real GDP has increased by a total of $200 billion.

turn increases consumption expenditure. But part of the increase in consumption expenditure is expenditure on imported goods and services, not Canadian-produced goods and services. Only expenditure on Canadian-produced goods and services increases Canadian real GDP. The larger is the marginal propensity to import, the smaller is the change in Canadian real GDP.

Income taxes also make the multiplier smaller than it otherwise would be. Again, think about what happens following an increase in investment. An increase in investment increases real GDP. But because income taxes increase, disposable income increases by less than the increase in real GDP. Consequently, consumption expenditure increases by less than it would if taxes had not changed. The larger is the marginal tax rate, the smaller is the change in disposable income and real GDP.

The marginal propensity to import and the marginal tax rate together with the marginal propensity to consume determine the multiplier. And their combined influence determines the slope of the *AE* curve. The multiplier is equal to 1 divided by (1 minus the slope of the *AE* curve).

Figure 23.9 compares two situations. In Fig. 23.9(a), there are no imports and no taxes. The slope of the *AE* curve equals the marginal propensity to consume, which is 0.75, and the multiplier is 4. In Fig. 23.9(b), imports and income taxes decrease the slope of the *AE* curve to 0.5. In this case, the multiplier is 2.

Over time, the value of the multiplier changes as tax rates change and as the marginal propensity to consume and the marginal propensity to import change. These ongoing changes make the multiplier hard to predict. But they do not change the fundamental fact that an initial change in autonomous expenditure leads to a magnified change in aggregate expenditure and real GDP.

The math note on pp. 550–551 shows the effects of taxes, imports, and the *MPC* on the multiplier.

Now that we've studied the multiplier and the factors that influence its magnitude, let's use what we've learned to gain some insights into business cycle turning points.

Business Cycle Turning Points

At business cycle turning points, the economy moves from expansion to recession or from recession to expansion. Economists understand these turning points as seismologists understand earthquakes. They know quite a lot about the forces and mechanisms that produce them, but they can't predict them. The forces that bring business cycle turning points are the swings in autonomous expenditure such as investment and exports. The mechanism that gives momentum to the economy's new direction is the multiplier. Let's use what we've now learned to examine these turning points.

FIGURE 23.9 The Multiplier and the Slope of the *AE* Curve

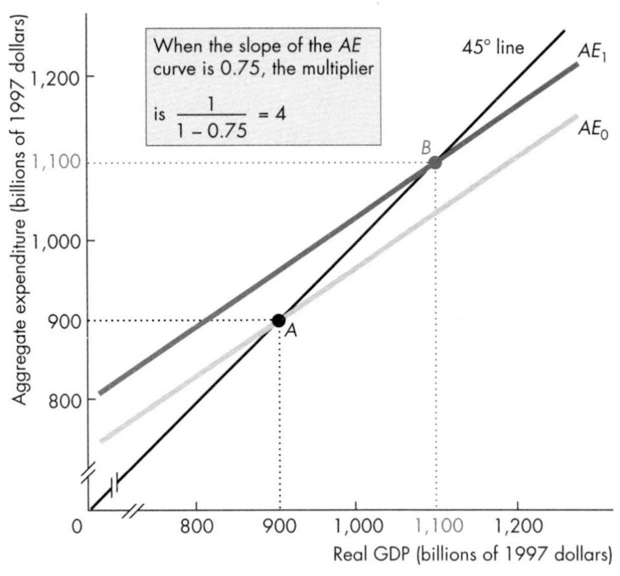

(a) Multiplier is 4

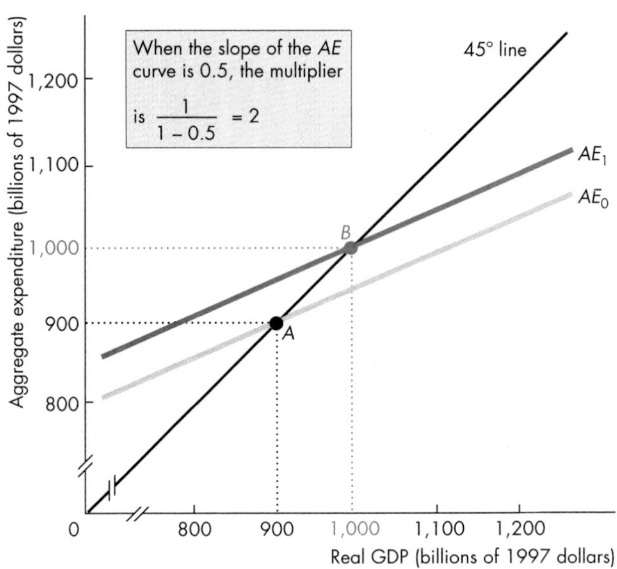

(b) Multiplier is 2

Imports and income taxes make the *AE* curve less steep and reduce the value of the multiplier. In part (a), with no imports and income taxes, the slope of the *AE* curve is 0.75 (the marginal propensity to consume) and the multiplier is 4. But with imports and income taxes, the slope of the *AE* curve is less than the marginal propensity to consume. In part (b), the slope of the *AE* curve is 0.5. In this case, the multiplier is 2.

An Expansion Begins An expansion is triggered by an increase in autonomous expenditure that increases aggregate planned expenditure. At the moment the economy turns the corner into expansion, aggregate planned expenditure exceeds real GDP. In this situation, firms see their inventories taking an unplanned dive. The expansion now begins. To meet their inventory targets, firms increase production, and real GDP begins to increase. This initial increase in real GDP brings higher incomes that stimulate consumption expenditure. The multiplier process kicks in, and the expansion picks up speed.

A Recession Begins The process we've just described works in reverse at a business cycle peak. A recession is triggered by a decrease in autonomous expenditure that decreases aggregate planned expenditure. At the moment the economy turns the corner into recession, real GDP exceeds aggregate planned expenditure. In this situation, firms see unplanned inventories piling up. The recession now begins. To lower their inventories, firms cut production, and real GDP begins to decrease. This initial decrease in real GDP brings lower incomes that cut consumption expenditure. The multiplier process reinforces the initial cut in autonomous expenditure, and the recession takes hold.

The Next Canadian Recession? Since 1991, the Canadian economy has been in a business cycle expansion. The last real GDP trough was in the first quarter of 1991. The science of macroeconomics cannot predict when the next recession will begin. A recession seemed possible in 1998 following a rapid buildup of inventories during 1997. But firms planned this inventory buildup. At the end of 2002, there was still no immediate prospect of the next recession. But it will surely come. And when it does, the mechanism you've just studied will operate.

REVIEW QUIZ

1. What is the multiplier? What does it determine? Why does it matter?
2. How do the marginal propensity to consume, the marginal propensity to import, and the marginal tax rate influence the multiplier?
3. If autonomous expenditure decreases, which phase of the business cycle does the economy enter?

The economy's potholes are changes in investment and exports. The economy does not operate like the shock absorbers on Ralph Klein's car. While the price level is fixed, the effects of the economic potholes are not smoothed out. Instead, they are amplified like Céline Dion's voice. But we've considered only the adjustments in spending that occur when the price level is fixed. What happens after a time lapse long enough for the price level to change? Let's answer this question.

The Multiplier and the Price Level

WHEN FIRMS CAN'T KEEP UP WITH SALES AND their inventories fall below target, they increase production, but at some point, they raise their prices. Similarly, when firms find unwanted inventories piling up, they decrease production, but eventually they cut their prices. So far, we've studied the macroeconomic consequences of firms changing their production levels when their sales change, but we haven't looked at the effects of price changes. When individual firms change their prices, the economy's price level changes.

To study the simultaneous determination of real GDP and the price level, we use the *aggregate supply–aggregate demand model*, which is explained in Chapter 22. But to understand how aggregate demand adjusts, we need to work out the connection between the aggregate supply–aggregate demand model and the equilibrium expenditure model that we've used in this chapter. The key to understanding the relationship between these two models is the distinction between the aggregate *expenditure* and aggregate *demand* and the related distinction between the aggregate *expenditure curve* and the aggregate *demand curve.*

Aggregate Expenditure and Aggregate Demand

The aggregate expenditure curve is the relationship between the aggregate planned expenditure and real GDP when all other influences on aggregate planned expenditure remain the same. The aggregate demand curve is the relationship between the aggregate quantity of goods and services demanded and the price level when all other influences on aggregate demand remain the same. Let's explore the links between these two relationships.

Aggregate Expenditure and the Price Level

When the price level changes, aggregate planned expenditure changes and the quantity of real GDP demanded changes. The aggregate demand curve slopes downward. Why? There are two main reasons:

- Wealth effect
- Substitution effects

Wealth Effect Other things remaining the same, the higher the price level, the smaller is the purchasing power of people's real wealth. For example suppose you have \$100 in the bank and the price level is 110. If the price level rises to 130, your \$100 buys fewer goods and services. You are less wealthy. With less wealth, you will probably want to try to spend a bit less and save a bit more. The higher the price level, other things remaining the same, the lower is aggregate planned expenditure.

Substitution Effects A rise in the price level today, other things remaining the same, makes current goods and services more costly relative to future goods and services and results in a delay in purchases—an *intertemporal substitution.* A rise in the price level, other things remaining the same, makes Canadian-produced goods more expensive relative to foreign-produced goods and services and increases imports and decreases exports—an *international substitution.*

When the price level rises, each of these effects reduces aggregate planned expenditure at each level of real GDP. As a result, when the price level *rises,* the *AE* curve shifts *downward.* A fall in the price level has the opposite effect. When the price level *falls,* the *AE* curve shifts *upward.*

Figure 23.10(a) shows the shifts of the *AE* curve.

When the price level is 110, the aggregate expenditure curve is AE_0, which intersects the 45° line at point *B*. Equilibrium expenditure is $1,000 billion. If the price level increases to 130, the aggregate expenditure curve shifts downward to AE_1, which intersects the 45° line at point *A*. Equilibrium expenditure is $900 billion. If the price level decreases to 90, the aggregate expenditure curve shifts upward to AE_2, which intersects the 45° line at point *C*. Equilibrium expenditure is $1,100 billion.

We've just seen that when the price level changes, other things remaining the same, the *AE* curve shifts and the equilibrium expenditure changes. And when the price level changes, other things remaining the same, there is a movement along the *AD* curve. Figure 23.10(b) shows these movements along the *AD* curve. At a price level of 110, the aggregate quantity of goods and services demanded is $1,000 billion—point *B* on the *AD* curve. If the price level rises to 130, the aggregate quantity of goods and services demanded decreases to $900 billion. There is a movement along the *AD* curve to point *A*. If the price level falls to 90, the aggregate quantity of goods and services demanded increases to $1,100 billion. There is a movement along the *AD* curve to point *C*.

Each point on the *AD* curve corresponds to a point of equilibrium expenditure. The equilibrium expenditure points *A*, *B*, and *C* in Fig. 23.10(a) correspond to the points *A*, *B*, and *C* on the *AD* curve in Fig. 23.10(b).

A change in the price level, other things remaining the same, shifts the *AE* curve and brings a movement along the *AD* curve. A change in any other influence on aggregate planned expenditure shifts *both* the *AE* curve and the *AD* curve. For example, an increase in investment or in exports increases both aggregate planned expenditure and aggregate demand and shifts both the *AE* curve and the *AD* curve. Figure 23.11 illustrates the effect of such an increase.

Initially, the aggregate expenditure curve is AE_0 in part (a) and the aggregate demand curve is AD_0 in part (b). The price level is 110, real GDP is $1,000 billion, and the economy is at point *A* in both parts of the figure. Now suppose that investment increases by $100 billion. At a constant price level of 110, the aggregate expenditure curve shifts upward to AE_1. This curve intersects the 45° line at an equilibrium expenditure of $1,200 billion (point *B*).

FIGURE 23.10 Aggregate Demand

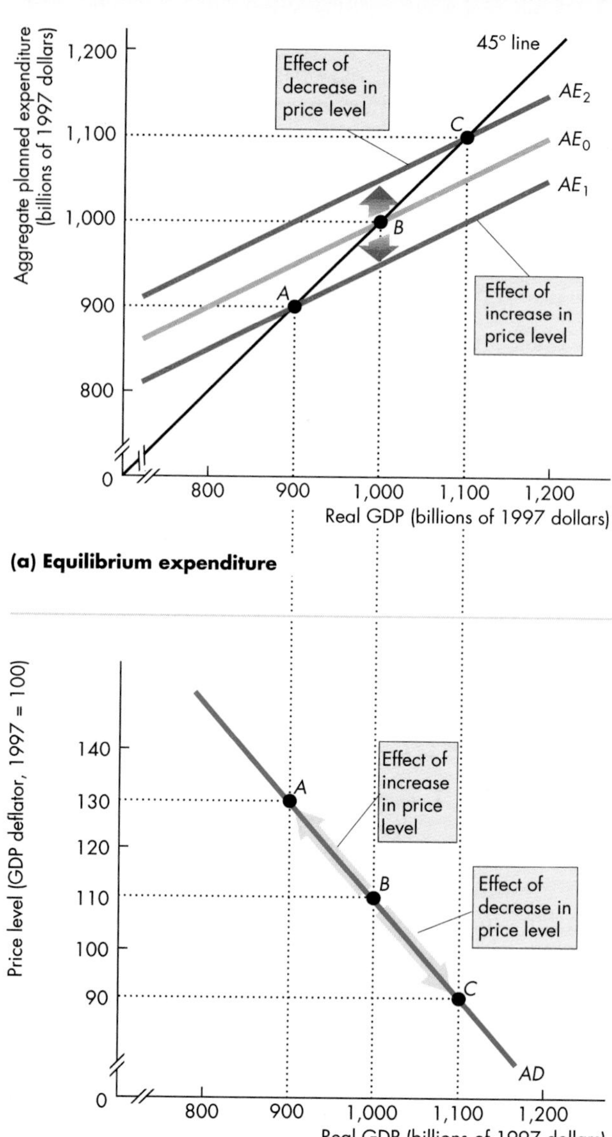

A change in the price level *shifts* the *AE* curve and results in a *movement along* the *AD* curve. When the price level is 110, the *AE* curve is AE_0 and equilibrium expenditure is $1,000 billion at point *B*. When the price level rises to 130, the *AE* curve is AE_1 and equilibrium expenditure is $900 billion at point *A*. When the price level falls to 90, the *AE* curve is AE_2 and equilibrium expenditure is $1,100 billion at point *C*. Points *A*, *B*, and *C* on the *AD* curve in part (b) correspond to the equilibrium expenditure points *A*, *B*, and *C* in part (a).

FIGURE 23.11 A Change in Aggregate Demand

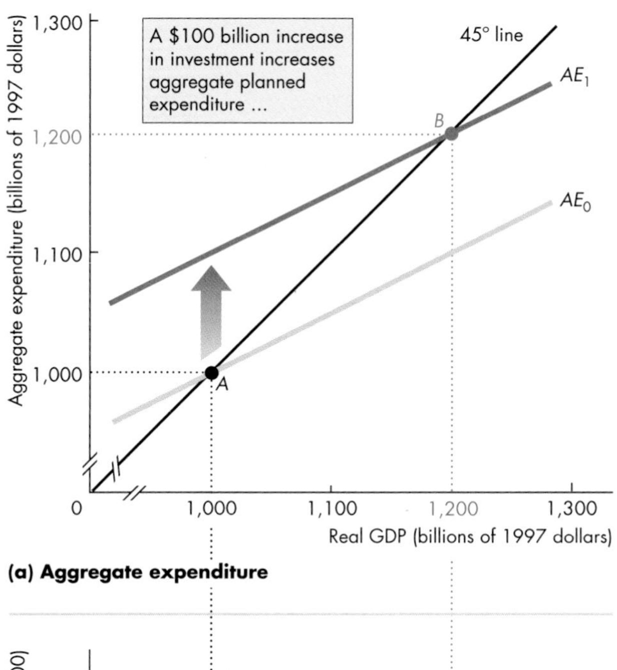

(a) Aggregate expenditure

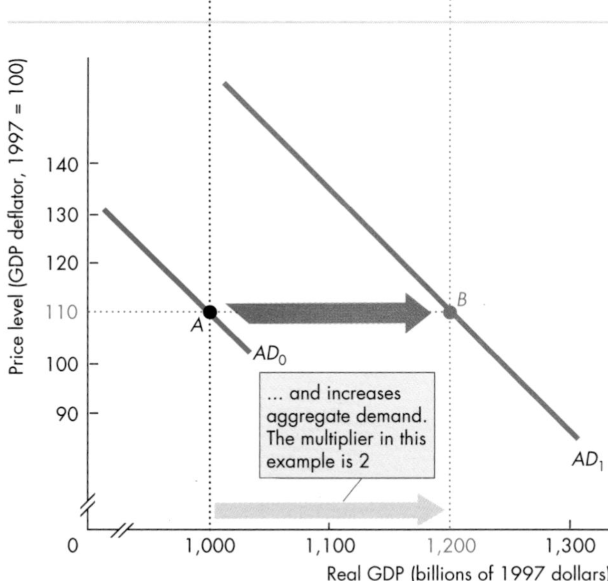

(b) Aggregate demand

The price level is 110. When the aggregate expenditure curve is AE_0 (part a), the aggregate demand curve is AD_0 (part b). An increase in autonomous expenditure shifts the *AE* curve upward to AE_1. In the new equilibrium, real GDP is $1,200 billion (at point *B*). Because the quantity of real GDP demanded at a price level of 110 increases to $1,200 billion, the *AD* curve shifts rightward to AD_1.

This equilibrium expenditure of $1,200 billion is the aggregate quantity of goods and services demanded at a price level of 110, as shown by point *B* in part (b). Point *B* lies on a new aggregate demand curve. The aggregate demand curve has shifted rightward to AD_1.

But how do we know by how much the *AD* curve shifts? The multiplier determines the answer. The larger the multiplier, the larger is the shift in the *AD* curve that results from a given change in autonomous expenditure. In this example, the multiplier is 2. A $100 billion increase in investment produces a $200 billion increase in the aggregate quantity of goods and services demanded at each price level. That is, a $100 billion increase in autonomous expenditure shifts the *AD* curve rightward by $200 billion.

A decrease in autonomous expenditure shifts the *AE* curve downward and shifts the *AD* curve leftward. You can see these effects by reversing the change that we've just described. If the economy is initially at point *B* on the aggregate expenditure curve AE_1, the aggregate demand curve is AD_1. A decrease in autonomous expenditure shifts the aggregate planned expenditure curve downward to AE_0. The aggregate quantity of goods and services demanded decreases from $1,200 billion to $1,000 billion, and the aggregate demand curve shifts leftward to AD_0.

Let's summarize what we have just discovered:

If some factor other than a change in the price level increases autonomous expenditure, the *AE* curve shifts upward and the *AD* curve shifts rightward.

The size of the *AD* curve shift depends on the change in autonomous expenditure and the multiplier.

Equilibrium GDP and the Price Level

In Chapter 22, we learned that aggregate demand and short-run aggregate supply determine equilibrium real GDP and the price level. We've now put aggregate demand under a more powerful microscope and have discovered that a change in investment (or in any component of autonomous expenditure) changes aggregate demand and shifts the aggregate demand curve. The magnitude of the shift depends on the multiplier. But whether a change in autonomous expenditure results ultimately in a change in real GDP, a change in the price level, or a combination of the two depends on aggregate supply. There are two time frames to consider: the short run and the long run. First we'll see what happens in the short run.

An Increase in Aggregate Demand in the Short Run Figure 23.12 describes the economy. In part (a), the aggregate expenditure curve is AE_0 and equilibrium expenditure is $1,000 billion—point *A*. In part (b), aggregate demand is AD_0 and the short-run aggregate supply curve is *SAS*. (Chapter 22, pp. 501–502 explains the *SAS* curve.) Equilibrium is at point *A*, where the aggregate demand and short-run aggregate supply curves intersect. The price level is 110, and real GDP is $1,000 billion.

Now suppose that investment increases by $100 billion. With the price level fixed at 110, the aggregate expenditure curve shifts upward to AE_1. Equilibrium expenditure increases to $1,200 billion—point *B* in part (a). In part (b), the aggregate demand curve shifts rightward by $200 billion, from AD_0 to AD_1. How far the aggregate demand curve shifts is determined by the multiplier when the price level is fixed. But with this new aggregate demand curve, the price level does not remain fixed. The price level rises, and as it does so, the aggregate expenditure curve shifts downward. The short-run equilibrium occurs when the aggregate expenditure curve has shifted downward to AE_2 and the new aggregate demand curve, AD_1, intersects the short-run aggregate supply curve. Real GDP is $1,130 billion, and the price level is 123 (at point *C*).

When price level effects are taken into account, the increase in investment still has a multiplier effect on real GDP, but the multiplier effect is smaller than it would be if the price level were fixed. The steeper the slope of the short-run aggregate supply curve, the larger is the increase in the price level and the smaller is the multiplier effect on real GDP.

An Increase in Aggregate Demand in the Long Run Figure 23.13 illustrates the long-run effect of an increase in aggregate demand. In the long run, real GDP equals potential GDP and there is full employment. Potential GDP is $1,000 billion, and the long-run aggregate supply curve is *LAS*. Initially, the economy is at point *A* (parts a and b).

Investment increases by $100 billion. The aggregate expenditure curve shifts to AE_1, and the aggregate demand curve shifts to AD_1. With no change in the price level, the economy would move to point *B* and real GDP would increase to $1,200 billion. But in the short run, the price level rises to 123 and real GDP increases to only $1,130 billion. With the higher price level, the *AE* curve shifts from AE_1 to AE_2. The economy is now in a short-run equilibrium at point *C*.

FIGURE 23.12 The Multiplier in the Short Run

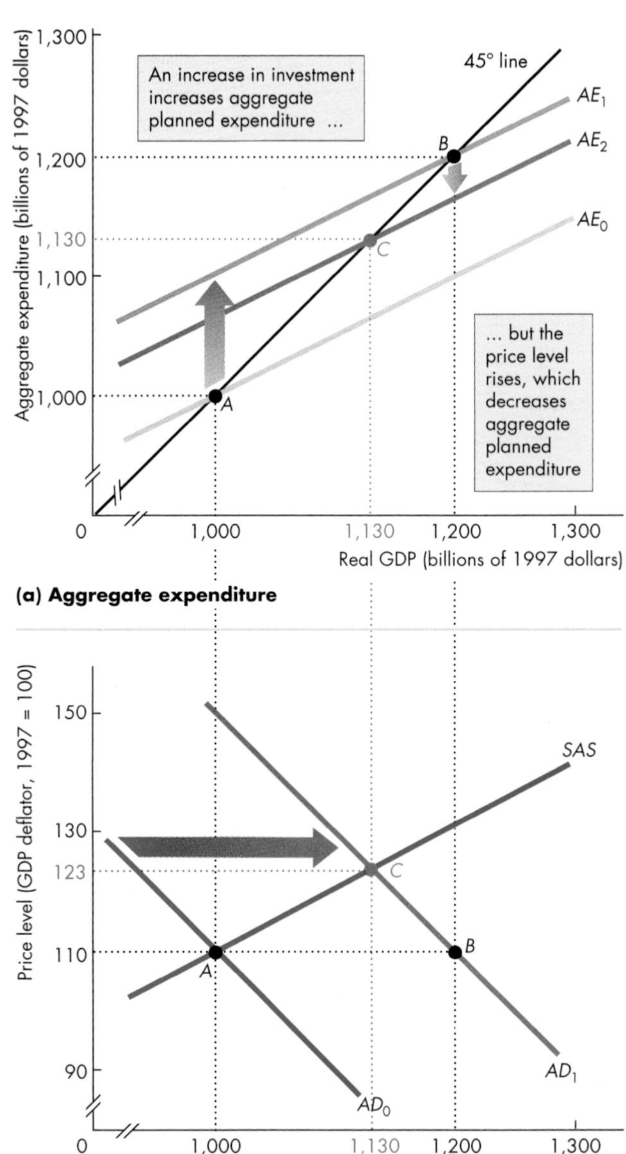

An increase in investment shifts the *AE* curve from AE_0 to AE_1 (part a) and shifts the *AD* curve from AD_0 to AD_1 (part b). The price level does not remain at 110 but rises, and the higher price level shifts the *AE* curve downward from AE_1 to AE_2. The economy moves to point *C* in both parts. In the short run, when prices are flexible, the multiplier effect is smaller than when the price level is fixed.

FIGURE 23.13 The Multiplier in the Long Run

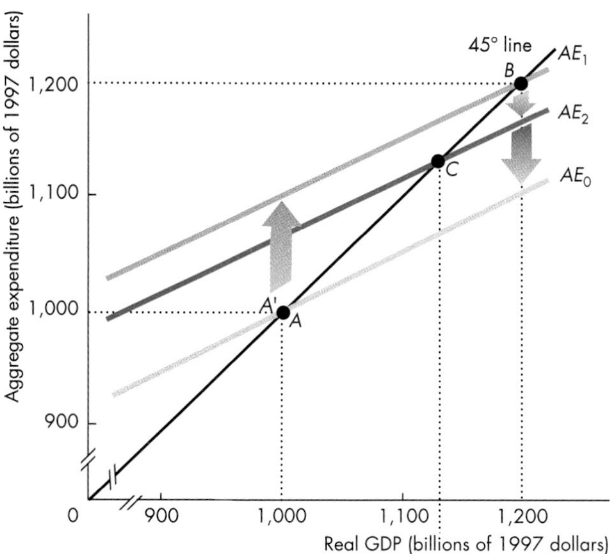

(a) Aggregate expenditure

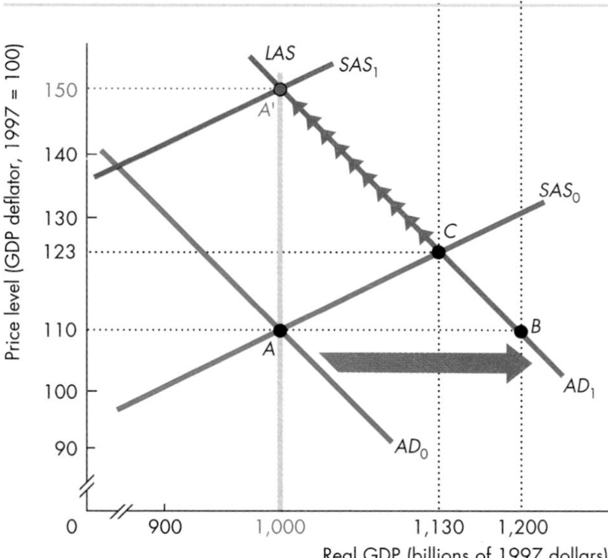

(b) Aggregate demand

Starting from point *A*, an increase in investment shifts the *AE* curve to AE_1 and shifts the *AD* curve to AD_1. In the short run, the economy moves to point *C*. In the long run, the money wage rate rises, the *SAS* curve shifts to SAS_1, the price level rises, the *AE* curve shifts back to AE_0, and real GDP decreases. The economy moves to point *A'*, and in the long run, the multiplier is zero.

Real GDP is now above potential GDP. The labour force is more than fully employed, and shortages of labour increase the money wage rate. The higher money wage rate increases costs, which decreases short-run aggregate supply and shifts the *SAS* curve leftward to SAS_1. The price level rises further, and real GDP decreases. There is a movement along AD_1, and the *AE* curve shifts downward from AE_2 towards AE_0. When the money wage rate and the price level have increased by the same percentage, real GDP is again equal to potential GDP and the economy is at point *A'*. In the long run, the multiplier is zero.

REVIEW QUIZ

1. How does a change in the price level influence the *AE* curve and the *AD* curve?
2. If autonomous expenditure increases with no change in the price level, what happens to the *AE* curve and the *AD* curve? Which curve shifts by an amount that is determined by the multiplier and why?
3. How does real GDP change in the short run when there is an increase in autonomous expenditure? Does real GDP change by the same amount as the change in aggregate demand? Why or why not?
4. How does real GDP change in the long run when there is an increase in autonomous expenditure? Does real GDP change by the same amount as the change in aggregate demand? Why or why not?

You are now ready to build on what you've learned about aggregate expenditure fluctuations and study the roles of fiscal policy and monetary policy in smoothing the business cycle. In Chapter 24, we study fiscal policy—government expenditures, taxes, and the deficit. In Chapters 25 and 26, we study monetary policy—interest rates and the quantity of money. But before you leave the current topic, look at *Reading Between the Lines* on pp. 548–549, which looks at the rapid expansion of real GDP that occurred in Canada during the first quarter of 2002.

READING BETWEEN THE LINES

The Aggregate Expenditure Multiplier in Action

THE VANCOUVER SUN, JUNE 1, 2002

Canadian economy on fire in early 2002: hot housing market helped

Canada's economy had its best quarter of the new millennium in the first months of 2002 as a hot housing market and a rebound in manufacturing and exports buoyed the country's gross domestic product by 1.5 per cent, Statistics Canada said Friday.

Canada emerged from the post-Sept. 11 economic shock, which caused a short-term economic contraction in the third quarter of 2001 and a lacklustre fourth quarter, to post its best performance since the fourth quarter of 1999. ...

Virtually all of the economic growth came in the first two months of the year and was a result of inventory stocks having become depleted and manufacturing orders picking up. Statistics Canada said "economic activity paused late in the quarter as GDP leveled off in March ... ."

Record low interest rates led to a record high in new housing construction, which surged 10.5 per cent, smashing levels set in the late 1980s. Urban housing starts were up dramatically across the country, except in Atlantic Canada. At the same time, the cost of existing homes jumped 9.9 per cent, its largest single-quarter jump since 1996.

Statistics Canada said household furnishings, appliances and recreational equipment were the manufacturing sector's greatest strengths, while new automobiles continued to fly off the lots as consumers took advantage of sales and low loan rates. ...

"But this party won't last, or at least it won't be nearly as raucous in the quarters ahead," said economist Avery Shenfeld of CIBC World Markets.

Essence of the Story

- During the first quarter of 2002, Canada's real GDP increased by 1.5 percent, the fastest quarterly expansion since the fourth quarter of 1999.
- Virtually all of the economic growth was a result of inventories that became depleted and manufacturing orders that picked up in January and February.
- Low interest rates stimulated housing construction, which increased by a record 10.5 percent.
- Production of household furnishings, appliances, and recreational equipment increased most, while new automobile sales were strong.
- Economist Avery Shenfeld of CIBC World Markets said "… this party won't last …"

Economic Analysis

■ During the first quarter of 2002, real GDP increased by \$16 billion, or 1.5 percent.

■ The table shows the amounts by which the components of aggregate expenditure increased.

■ On the average, an additional dollar of real GDP brings about 57 cents of additional consumption expenditure and about 32 cents of additional imports.

■ Using these two values, the slope of the *AE* curve is 0.25 and the multiplier, which equals $1/(1 - \text{Slope of } AE \text{ curve})$ equals $1/(1 - 0.25) = 1/0.75 = 1.33$.

■ The increase in consumption expenditure was \$6 billion less than the amount that is normally induced by a \$16 billion increase in real GDP. The consumption function shifted downward during the first quarter of 2002 by \$6 billion.

■ The decrease in autonomous consumption decreased autonomous expenditure by \$6 billion.

■ The increase in imports was \$1 billion less than the amount that is normally induced by a \$16 billion increase in real GDP. The import function shifted downward during the first quarter of 2002 by \$1 billion.

■ The decrease in autonomous imports increased autonomous expenditure by \$1 billion.

■ The increases in fixed investment (investment excluding the change in inventories), government expenditures, exports, and investment in inventories sum to \$17 billion.

■ Subtracting the changes in autonomous consumption and imports from \$17 billion gives an increase in autonomous expenditure of \$12 billion.

■ Based on the assumptions just described, Fig. 1 shows the *AE* curve in the fourth quarter of 2001, AE_0, and in the first quarter of 2002, AE_1.

■ The *AE* curve shifted upward by \$12 billion (the assumed increase in autonomous expenditure), and real GDP increased from \$1,032 billion to \$1,048 billion, an increase of \$16 billion.

■ Check that the increase in real GDP equals the increase in autonomous expenditure, \$12 billion, multiplied by 1.33, the multiplier.

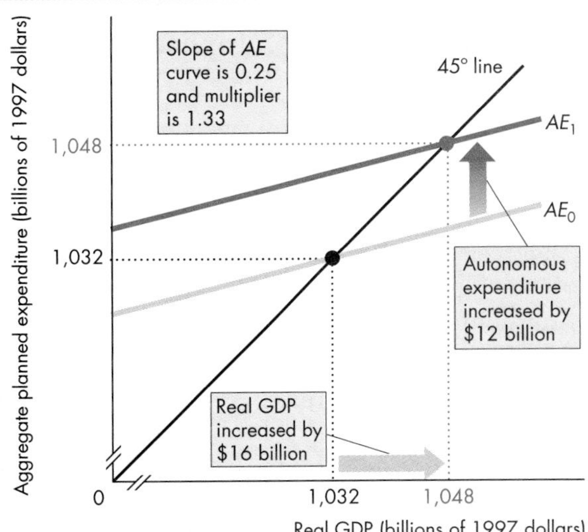

Figure 1 Increase in autonomous expenditure and multiplier

Item	Increase (billions of 1997 dollars)
Consumption expenditure	3
Fixed investment	4
Government expenditure	1
Exports	6
minus Imports	4
Investment in inventories	6
Real GDP	16

Mathematical Note
The Algebra of the Multiplier

THIS NOTE EXPLAINS THE MULTIPLIER IN GREATER detail than that presented on p. 540. We begin by defining the symbols we need:

- Aggregate planned expenditure, AE
- Real GDP, Y
- Consumption expenditure, C
- Investment, I
- Government expenditures, G
- Exports, X
- Imports, M
- Net taxes, NT
- Disposable income, YD
- Autonomous consumption expenditure, a
- Marginal propensity to consume, b
- Marginal propensity to import, m
- Marginal tax rate, t
- Autonomous expenditure, A

Aggregate Expenditure

Aggregate planned expenditure (AE) is the sum of the planned amounts of consumption expenditure (C), investment (I), government expenditures (G), and exports (X) minus the planned amount of imports (M). That is,

$$AE = C + I + G + X - M.$$

Consumption Function Consumption expenditure (C) depends on disposable income (YD), and we write the consumption function as

$$C = a + bYD.$$

Disposable income (YD) equals real GDP minus net taxes ($Y - NT$). So if we replace YD with ($Y - NT$), the consumption function becomes

$$C = a + b(Y - NT).$$

Net taxes equal real GDP (Y) multiplied by the marginal tax rate (t). That is,

$$NT = tY.$$

Use this equation in the previous one to obtain

$$C = a + b(1 - t)Y.$$

This equation describes consumption expenditure as a function of real GDP.

Import Function Imports depend on real GDP, and the import function is

$$M = mY.$$

Aggregate Expenditure Curve Use the consumption function and the import function to replace C and M in the aggregate planned expenditure equation. That is,

$$AE = a + b(1 - t)Y + I + G + X - mY.$$

Collect the terms on the right side of the equation that involve Y to obtain

$$AE = (a + I + G + X) + [b(1 - t) - m]Y.$$

Autonomous expenditure (A) is $(a + I + G + X)$, and the slope of the AE curve is $[b(1 - t) - m]$. So the equation for the AE curve, which is shown in Fig. 1, is

$$AE = A + [b(1 - t) - m]Y.$$

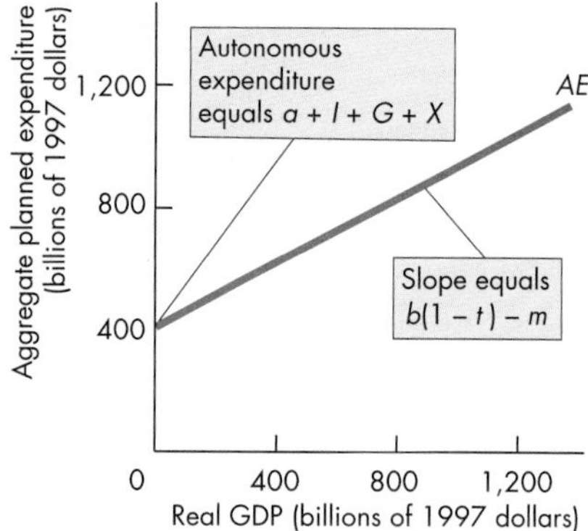

Figure 1 The *AE* curve

Equilibrium Expenditure

Equilibrium expenditure occurs when aggregate planned expenditure (AE) equals real GDP (Y). That is,

$$AE = Y.$$

In Fig. 2, the scales of the x-axis (real GDP) and the y-axis (aggregate planned expenditure) are identical, so the 45° line shows the points at which aggregate planned expenditure equals real GDP.

Figure 2 shows the point of equilibrium expenditure at the intersection of the AE curve and the 45° line.

To calculate equilibrium expenditure and real GDP, we solve the equations for the AE curve and the 45° line for the two unknown quantities AE and Y. So starting with

$$AE = A + [b(1 - t) - m]Y$$

$$AE = Y,$$

replace AE with Y in the AE equation to obtain

$$Y = A + [b(1 - t) - m]Y.$$

The solution for Y is

$$Y = \frac{1}{1 - [b(1 - t) - m]} A.$$

The Multiplier

The multiplier equals the change in equilibrium expenditure and real GDP (Y) that results from a change in autonomous expenditure (A) divided by the change in autonomous expenditure.

A change in autonomous expenditure (ΔA) changes equilibrium expenditure and real GDP (ΔY) by

$$\Delta Y = \frac{1}{1 - [b(1 - t) - m]} \Delta A.$$

So

$$\text{Multiplier} = \frac{1}{1 - [b(1 - t) - m]}.$$

The size of the multiplier depends on the slope of the AE curve, $b(1 - t) - m$. The larger the slope, the larger is the multiplier. So the multiplier is larger,

- The greater the marginal propensity to consume (b)
- The smaller the marginal tax rate (t)
- The smaller the marginal propensity to import (m)

An economy with no imports and no marginal taxes has $m = 0$ and $t = 0$. In this special case, the multiplier equals $1/(1 - b)$. If b is 0.75, then the multiplier is 4, as shown in Fig. 3.

In an economy with $b = 0.75$, $t = 0.2$, and $m = 0.1$, the multiplier is $1 \div [1 - 0.75(1 - 0.2) - 0.1]$, which equals 2. Make up some more examples to show the effects of b, t, and m on the multiplier.

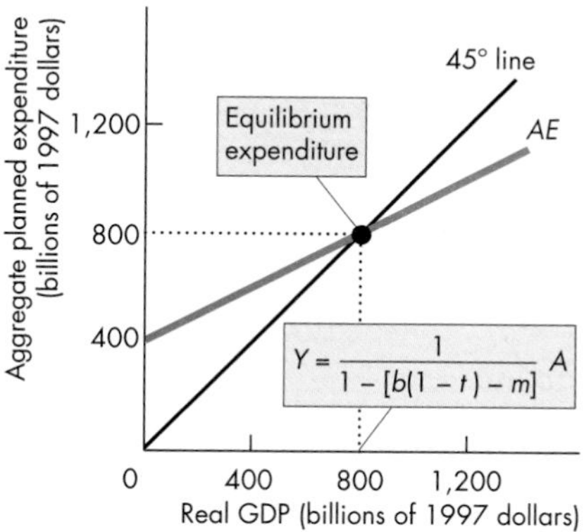

Figure 2 Equilibrium expenditure

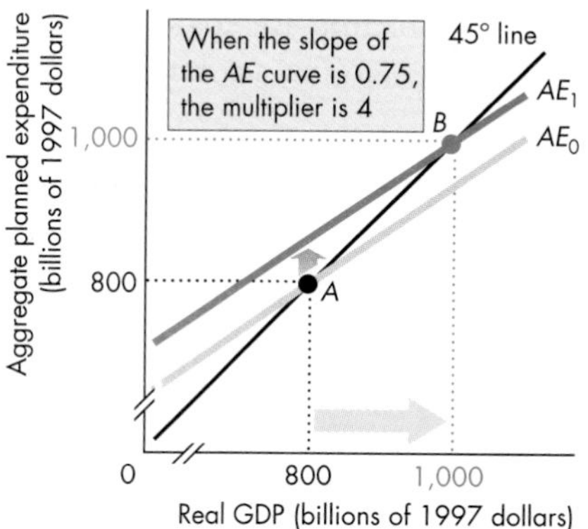

Figure 3 The multiplier

SUMMARY

KEY POINTS

Expenditure Plans and GDP (pp. 528–533)

- When the price level is fixed, expenditure plans determine real GDP.
- Consumption expenditure is determined by disposable income, and the marginal propensity to consume (*MPC*) determines the change in consumption expenditure brought about by a change in disposable income. Real GDP is the main influence on disposable income.
- Imports are determined by real GDP, and the marginal propensity to import determines the change in imports brought about by a change in real GDP.

Equilibrium Expenditure at a Fixed Price Level (pp. 533–537)

- Aggregate *planned* expenditure depends on real GDP.
- Equilibrium expenditure occurs when aggregate planned expenditure equals actual expenditure and real GDP.

The Multiplier (pp. 538–543)

- The multiplier is the magnified effect of a change in autonomous expenditure on real GDP.
- The multiplier equals 1 divided by (1 minus the slope of the *AE* curve).
- The multiplier is influenced by the marginal propensity to consume, the marginal propensity to import, and the marginal tax rate.

The Multiplier and the Price Level (pp. 543–547)

- The aggregate demand curve is the relationship between the quantity of real GDP demanded and the price level, other things remaining the same.
- The aggregate expenditure curve is the relationship between aggregate planned expenditure and real GDP, other things remaining the same.
- At a given price level, there is a given aggregate expenditure curve. A change in the price level changes aggregate planned expenditure and shifts the aggregate expenditure curve. A change in the price level also creates a movement along the aggregate demand curve.
- A change in autonomous expenditure that is not caused by a change in the price level shifts the aggregate expenditure curve and shifts the aggregate demand curve. The magnitude of the shift of the aggregate demand curve depends on the multiplier and on the change in autonomous expenditure.
- The multiplier decreases as the price level changes and the multiplier in the long run is zero.

KEY FIGURES

Figure 23.1	Consumption Function and Saving Function, 529
Figure 23.2	Marginal Propensities to Consume and Save, 530
Figure 23.5	Aggregate Expenditure, 534
Figure 23.6	Equilibrium Expenditure, 536
Figure 23.7	The Multiplier, 539
Figure 23.8	The Multiplier Process, 541
Figure 23.9	The Multiplier and the Slope of the *AE* Curve, 542
Figure 23.10	Aggregate Demand, 544
Figure 23.11	A Change in Aggregate Demand, 545
Figure 23.12	The Multiplier in the Short Run, 546
Figure 23.13	The Multiplier in the Long Run, 547

KEY TERMS

Aggregate planned expenditure, 533
Autonomous expenditure, 535
Consumption function, 528
Disposable income, 528
Equilibrium expenditure, 536
Induced expenditure, 535
Marginal propensity to consume, 530
Marginal propensity to import, 533
Marginal propensity to save, 530
Multiplier, 538
Saving function, 528

PROBLEMS

*1. You are given the following information about the economy of Heron Island:

Disposable income (millions of dollars per year)	Consumption expenditure (millions of dollars per year)
0	5
10	10
20	15
30	20
40	25

Calculate Heron Island's
a. Marginal propensity to consume.
b. Saving at each level of disposable income.
c. Marginal propensity to save.

2. You are given the following information about the economy of Spendthrift Island:

Disposable income (millions of dollars per year)	Saving (millions of dollars per year)
0	−10
50	−5
100	0
150	5
200	10
250	15
300	20

a. Calculate the marginal propensity to save.
b. Calculate consumption at each level of disposable income.
c. Calculate the marginal propensity to consume.
d. Why is the island called "spendthrift"?

*3. Turtle Island has no imports or exports, there are no income taxes, and the price level is fixed. The figure illustrates the components of aggregate planned expenditure.
a. What is autonomous expenditure?
b. What is the marginal propensity to consume?
c. What is aggregate planned expenditure when real GDP is \$6 billion?
d. If real GDP is \$4 billion, what is happening to inventories?
e. If real GDP is \$6 billion, what is happening to inventories?
f. What is the multiplier?

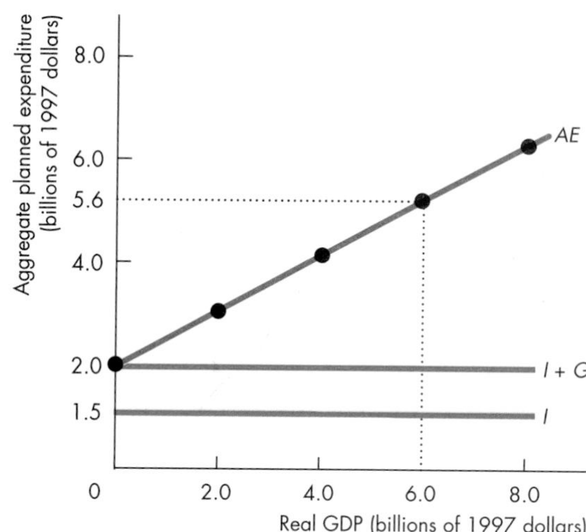

4. The spreadsheet lists the components of aggregate planned expenditure in Spice Bay. The numbers are in billions of cloves, the currency of Spice Bay.

	A	B	C	D	E	F	G
1		Y	C	I	G	X	M
2	A	100	110	50	60	60	15
3	B	200	170	50	60	60	30
4	C	300	230	50	60	60	45
5	D	400	290	50	60	60	60
6	E	500	350	50	60	60	75
7	F	600	410	50	60	60	90

In Spice Bay,
a. What is autonomous expenditure?
b. What is the marginal propensity to consume?
c. What is aggregate planned expenditure when real GDP is 200 billion cloves?
d. If real GDP is 200 billion cloves, what is happening to inventories?
e. If real GDP is 500 billion cloves, what is happening to inventories?
f. What is the multiplier in Spice Bay?

*5. You are given the following information about the economy of Zeeland: Autonomous consumption expenditure is \$100 billion, and the marginal propensity to consume is 0.9. Investment is \$460 billion, government expenditures on goods and services are \$400 billion, and net taxes are a constant \$400 billion—they do not vary with income.

a. What is the consumption function?
b. What is the equation that describes the aggregate expenditure curve?
c. Calculate equilibrium expenditure.
d. If investment falls to $360 billion, what is the change in equilibrium expenditure and what is the size of the multiplier?

6. You are given the following information about the economy of Antarctica: Autonomous consumption expenditure is $1 billion, and the marginal propensity to consume is 0.8. Investment is $5 billion, government expenditures on goods and services are $4 billion, and net taxes are a constant $4 billion—they do not vary with income.
   a. What is the consumption function?
   b. What is the equation that describes the aggregate expenditure curve?
   c. Calculate equilibrium expenditure.
   d. If investment falls to $3 billion, what is the change in equilibrium expenditure and what is the size of the multiplier?

*7. Suppose that in problem 5, the price level is 100 and real GDP equals potential GDP.
   a. If investment increases by $100 billion, what happens to the quantity of real GDP demanded?
   b. In the short run, does equilibrium real GDP increase by more than, less than, or the same amount as the increase in the quantity of real GDP demanded?
   c. In the long run, does equilibrium real GDP increase by more than, less than, or the same amount as the increase in the quantity of real GDP demanded?
   d. In the short run, does the price level in Zeeland rise, fall, or remain unchanged?
   e. In the long run, does the price level in Zeeland rise, fall, or remain unchanged?

8. Suppose that in problem 6, the price level is 100 and real GDP equals potential GDP.
   a. If investment increases by $1 billion, what happens to the quantity of real GDP demanded?
   b. In the long run, does equilibrium real GDP increase by more than, less than, or the same amount as the increase in the quantity of real GDP demanded?
   c. In the short run, does the price level in Antarctica rise, fall, or remain unchanged?

CRITICAL THINKING

1. Study *Reading Between the Lines* on pp. 548–549 and then:
   a. Describe the changes in the components of aggregate expenditure during the first quarter of 2002.
   b. Suppose that the assumptions about the extent to which a change in real GDP induces a change in consumption expenditure and imports on p. 549 are incorrect and that the slope of the *AE* curve is 0.3, not 0.25. What does this imply about the change in autonomous expenditure during the first quarter of 2002? What does it imply about the magnitude of the multiplier?
   c. Draw the *AE* curves for the fourth quarter of 2001 and first quarter of 2002 on the assumption that the slope of the *AE* curve is 0.3.

WEB EXERCISES

1. Use the link on the Parkin–Bade Web site to visit the Penn World Table Web site and obtain data on real GDP per person and consumption as a percentage of real GDP for Canada, China, South Africa, and Mexico since 1960.
   a. In a spreadsheet, multiply your real GDP data by the consumption percentage and divide by 100 to obtain data on real consumption expenditure per person.
   b. Make graphs like Fig. 23.4 that show the relationship between consumption and real GDP for these four countries.
   c. On the basis of the numbers you've obtained, in which country do you expect the multiplier to be largest (other things being equal)?
   d. What other data would you need to be able to calculate the multipliers for these countries?

2. You are a research assistant in the office of the Prime Minister. Draft a note for the Prime Minister that explains the power and limitations of the multiplier. The Prime Minister wants only 250 words of crisp, clear, jargon-free explanation together with a lively example.

FISCAL POLICY

CHAPTER 24

Balancing Acts on Parliament Hill

In 2001, the federal government spent about 15 cents of every dollar that Canadians earned and collected almost 17 cents of every dollar earned in taxes. What are the effects of government spending and taxes on the economy? Does a dollar spent by the government have the same effect as a dollar spent by someone else? Does it create jobs, or does it destroy them? ◆ Do taxes harm employment and economic growth? ◆ For many years during the 1980s and 1990s, the government had a large budget deficit and ran up a debt. During the late 1990s, spending cuts brought the deficit under control and created a surplus. But in 2001, your share of government debt stood at $18,000. Does it matter if the government doesn't balance its books? What are the effects of an ongoing government deficit and accumulating debt? Do they slow economic growth? Do they impose a burden on future generations—on you and your children? Was the deficit-cutting exercise of the late 1990s beneficial to our economy?

These are the fiscal policy issues that you will study in this chapter. We'll begin by describing the federal budget and the process of creating it. We'll also look at the recent history of the budget. We'll then use the multiplier analysis of Chapter 23 and the aggregate supply–aggregate demand model of Chapter 22 to study the effects of the budget on the economy. At the end of the chapter, in *Reading Between the Lines,* we'll look at the federal government's budget projections through 2008.

After studying this chapter, you will be able to

- **Describe how federal and provincial budgets are created**
- **Describe the recent history of federal and provincial revenues, outlays, and budget deficits**
- **Distinguish between automatic and discretionary fiscal policy**
- **Define and explain the fiscal policy multipliers**
- **Explain the effects of fiscal policy in both the short run and the long run**
- **Distinguish between and explain the demand-side and supply-side effects of fiscal policy**

Government Budgets

THE ANNUAL STATEMENT OF THE OUTLAYS AND revenues of the government of Canada, together with the laws and regulations that approve and support those outlays and revenues, make up the **federal budget**. Similarly, a **provincial budget** is an annual statement of the revenues and outlays of a provincial government, together with the laws and regulations that approve or support those revenues and outlays.

Before World War II, the federal budget had no purpose other than to finance the business of government. But since the late 1940s, the federal budget has assumed a second purpose, which is to pursue the government's fiscal policy. **Fiscal policy** is the use of the federal budget to achieve macroeconomic objectives such as full employment, sustained long-term economic growth, and price level stability. Our focus is this second purpose.

Budget Making

The federal government and Parliament make fiscal policy. The process begins with long drawn-out consultations between the Minister of Finance and Department of Finance officials and their counterparts in the provincial governments. These discussions deal with programs that are funded and operated jointly by the two levels of government. The Minister also consults with business and consumer groups on a wide range of issues.

After all these consultations, and using economic projections made by Department of Finance economists, the Minister develops a set of proposals, which are discussed in Cabinet and which become government policy. The Minister finally presents a budget plan to Parliament, which debates the plan and enacts the laws necessary to implement it.

Highlights of the 2002 Budget

Table 24.1 shows the main items in the federal budget. The numbers are projected amounts for the fiscal year beginning on April 1, 2002. The three main items shown are

- Revenues
- Outlays
- Budget balance

TABLE 24.1 The Federal Budget in 2002–03

Item	Projections (billions of dollars)	
Revenues	**174**	
Personal income taxes		82
Corporate income taxes		23
Indirect taxes		61
Investment income		8
Outlays	**171**	
Transfer payments		93
Expenditures on goods and services		42
Debt interest		36
Budget balance	**+3**	

Source: Department of Finance *Budget Plan* 2002.

Revenues Revenues are the federal government's receipts, which in the 2002–03 budget were projected at $174 billion. These revenues come from four sources:

1. Personal income taxes
2. Corporate income taxes
3. Indirect taxes
4. Investment income

The largest revenue source is *personal income taxes*, which in 2002–03 were projected to be $82 billion. These are the taxes paid by individuals on their incomes. The second largest source of revenue is *indirect taxes*, which in 2002–03 were projected to be $61 billion. These taxes include the Goods and Services Tax or GST and taxes on the sale of gasoline, alcoholic drinks, and a few other items. The smallest revenue sources are *corporate income taxes*, which are the taxes paid by companies on their profits, and *investment income*, which is the income from government enterprises and investments.

In 2002–03, corporate income taxes were projected to raise $23 billion and investment income was projected at $8 billion. Total federal government revenue in 2002–03 was projected at $174 billion.

Outlays Outlays are classified in three categories:

1. Transfer payments
2. Expenditures on goods and services
3. Debt interest

The largest outlay, and by a big margin, is *transfer payments.* Transfer payments are payments to individuals, businesses, other levels of government, and the rest of the world. In 2002–03, this item was $93 billion. It includes unemployment cheques and welfare payments to individuals, farm subsidies, grants to provincial and local governments, aid to developing countries, and dues to international organizations such as the United Nations.

Expenditures on goods and services are expenditures on final goods and services, and in 2002–03 this item totalled $42 billion. These expenditures include those on national defence, computers for Canada Customs and Revenue Agency, government cars, and highways. This component of the federal budget is *government expenditures on goods and services* that appears in the circular flow of expenditure and income and in the national income and product accounts (see Chapter 20, pp. 459–460).

Debt interest is the interest on the government debt. In 2002–03, this item was $36 billion—almost as much as government expenditures on goods and services. This interest payment is large because the government has a large debt—$538 billion. This large debt has arisen because, until recently, the federal government has had a large and persistent budget deficit.

Budget Balance The government's budget balance is equal to its revenues minus its outlays. That is,

Budget balance = Revenues – Outlays.

If revenues exceed outlays, the government has a **budget surplus.** If outlays exceed revenues, the government has a **budget deficit.** If revenues equal outlays, the government has a **balanced budget.** In 2002–03, with projected outlays of $171 billion and revenues of $174 billion, the government projected a budget surplus of $3 billion.

How typical is the federal budget of 2002–03? Let's look at its recent history.

The Budget in Historical Perspective

Figure 24.1 shows the government's revenues, outlays, and budget balance since 1971. To get a better sense of the magnitudes of these items, they are shown as percentages of GDP. Expressing them in this way lets us see how large the government is rela-

FIGURE 24.1 Revenues, Outlays, and the Budget Balance

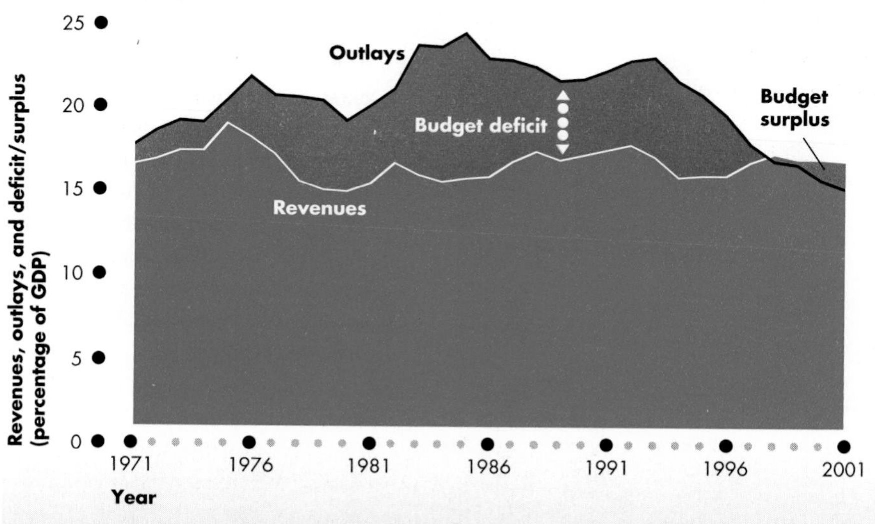

The figure records the federal government's revenues, outlays, and budget balance as percentages of GDP from 1971 to 2001. During the late 1970s, the budget deficit was small and decreasing, but during the 1980s, it became large and persisted. The budget deficit arose because revenues decreased and outlays increased as percentages of GDP. Spending cuts eliminated the deficit by 1997.

Source: Statistics Canada, CANSIM tables 380-0002 and 380-0007.

tive to the size of the economy, and also helps us to study *changes* in the scale of government over time. You can think of the percentages of GDP as telling you how many cents of each dollar that Canadians earn get paid to and spent by the government.

From 1971 through 1996, the federal budget was in deficit, and the average deficit over these years was 4.5 percent of GDP. The deficit climbed to a peak of 8.6 percent of GDP in 1985. It then decreased through the rest of the 1980s. During the recession of 1990–1991, the deficit increased again. The deficit remained above 4 percent of GDP for most of the 1980s and early 1990s.

Only in 1997 did the federal government finally eradicate its deficit. And it did so by cutting outlays, especially transfer payments to provincial governments.

Why did the government deficit grow during the early 1980s and remain high through the early 1990s? The immediate answer is that outlays increased while revenues remained relatively constant. But which components of outlays increased? And did all the sources of revenues remain constant?

To answer these questions, we need to examine each of the sources of revenues and outlays in detail. We'll begin by looking at the sources of revenues.

Revenues Figure 24.2 shows the components of government revenues (as percentages of GDP) since 1971. Total revenues have no strong trends. Throughout the 1980s, federal government revenues as a percentage of GDP increased slightly. The main source of this increase was an increase in personal income taxes. Corporate income taxes and indirect taxes decreased as a percentage of GDP.

The increase in personal income taxes resulted from increases in tax rates in successive budgets throughout the 1980s. The decrease in indirect taxes is mainly the result of replacing an old Federal Sales Tax with the current GST. This switch was intended to maintain revenues at a constant level, but this outcome was not realized.

Outlays Figure 24.3 shows the components of government outlays (as percentages of GDP) since 1971. Total outlays increased steadily from 1971 through 1985, were relatively flat through 1993, and then decreased sharply after 1993. The main source of the changing trends in outlays is transfer payments to provincial governments. These payments swelled during the 1980s and were cut drastically during the late 1990s.

FIGURE 24.2 Federal Government Revenues

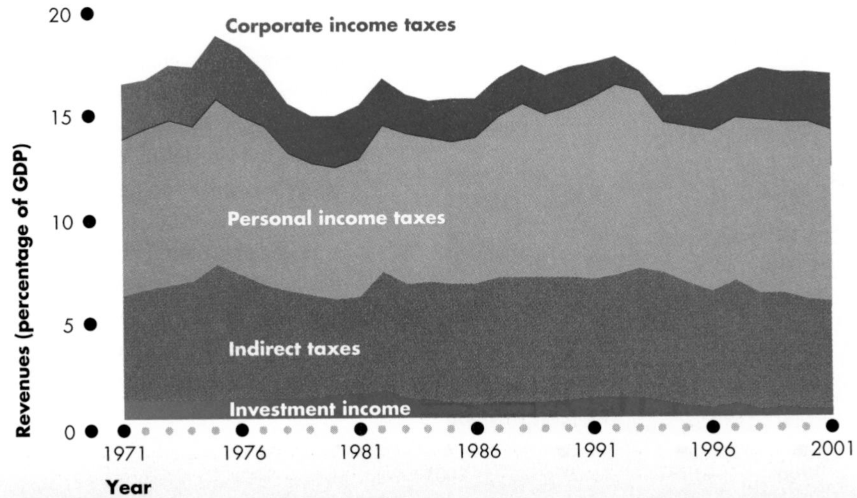

The figure shows four components of government revenues (as percentages of GDP): personal income taxes, corporate income taxes, indirect taxes, and investment income. Revenues from personal income taxes decreased during the late 1970s but trended upward during the 1980s and 1990s. Corporate income taxes decreased slightly. The other two components of revenues remained steady.

Source: Statistics Canada, CANSIM tables 380-0002 and 380-0007.

FIGURE 24.3 Federal Government Outlays

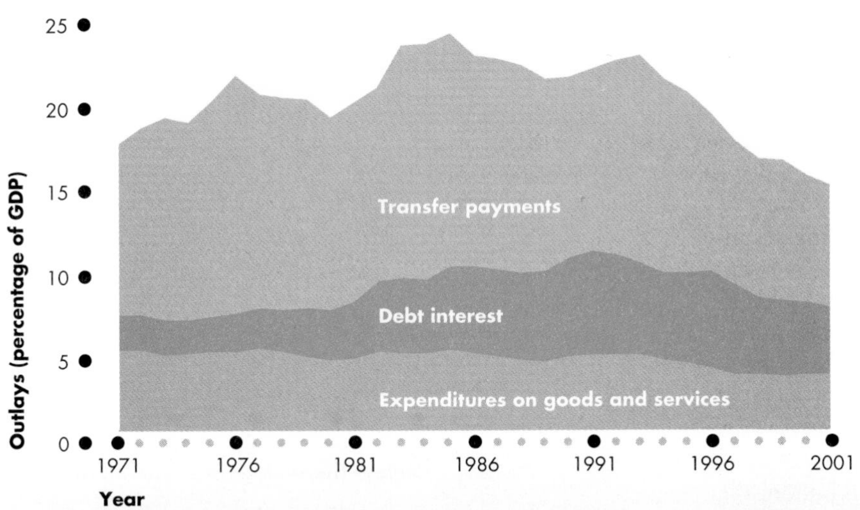

The figure shows three components of government outlays (as percentages of GDP): expenditures on goods and services, debt interest, and transfer payments. Expenditures on goods and services have been stable. Transfer payments increased during the 1970s and early 1980s, remained high through the early 1990s, and then decreased sharply during the 1990s. Debt interest increased steadily during the 1980s as the budget deficit fed on itself, but decreased during the late 1990s as surpluses began to lower the government's debt.

Source: Statistics Canada, CANSIM tables 380-0002 and 380-0007.

To understand the changes in debt interest, we need to see the connection between the budget deficit and government debt.

Deficit and Debt The government borrows to finance its deficit. And **government debt** is the total amount of government borrowing. It is the sum of past deficits minus the sum of past surpluses. When the government has a deficit, its debt increases. Once a persistent deficit emerged during the 1980s, the deficit began to feed on itself. The deficit led to increased borrowing; increased borrowing led to larger debt and larger interest payments; and larger interest payments led to a larger deficit and yet larger debt. That is the story of the increasing deficit of the 1980s.

Figure 24.4 shows the history of government debt since 1946. At the end of World War II, debt (as a percentage of GDP) was at an all-time high of 113 percent. Huge wartime deficits had increased debt to the point that it exceeded GDP. Postwar budget surpluses lowered the debt to GDP ratio through 1974, by which time it stood at 18 percent, its lowest point since World War II. Small deficits increased the debt to GDP ratio slightly through the 1970s, and large deficits increased it dramatically between 1981 and 1986. During the late 1980s, the ratio continued to

FIGURE 24.4 Federal Government Debt

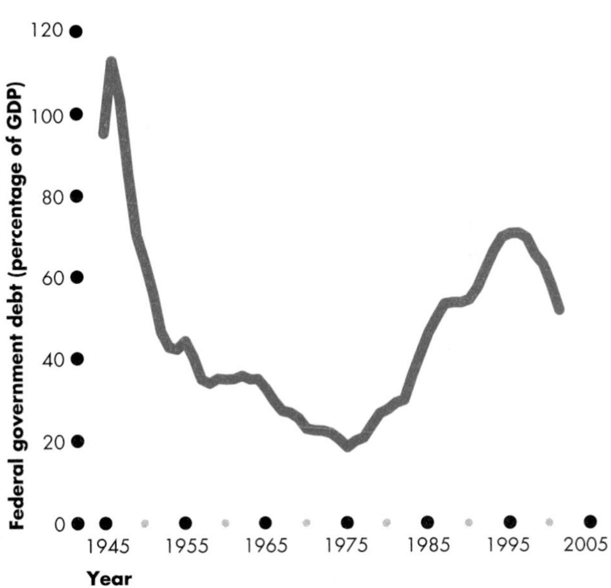

Federal government debt as a percentage of GDP decreased from 1946 through 1974, increased through 1997, and then began to decrease again.

Source: Statistics Canada, CANSIM tables 380-0002 and 385-0010.

increase but at a more moderate rate. It grew quickly again during the 1990–1991 recession, but its growth rate slowed after 1995 and debt interest decreased as a percentage of GDP.

Debt and Capital When individuals and businesses incur debts, they usually do so to buy capital—assets that yield a return. In fact, the main point of debt is to enable people to buy assets that will earn a return that exceeds the interest paid on the debt. The government is similar to individuals and businesses in this regard. Some government expenditure is investment—the purchase of public capital that yields a return. Highways, major irrigation schemes, public schools and universities, public libraries, and the stock of national defence capital all yield a social rate of return that probably far exceeds the interest rate the government pays on its debt.

But government debt, which is $538 billion, is much larger than the value of the public capital stock. This fact means that some government debt has been incurred to finance public consumption expenditure.

Provincial and Local Government Budgets

The *total government* sector of Canada includes provincial and local governments as well as the federal government. In 2001, when federal government outlays were $167 billion, provincial and local government outlays were $280 billion and total government outlays were $447 billion. Most provincial and local government outlays are on public hospitals and public schools, colleges, and universities.

Provincial government outlays and revenue sources vary a great deal across the provinces. Figure 24.5 shows the range of variation. Part (a) shows outlays as a percentage of provincial GDP. You can see that the outlays of Northern and Atlantic governments are the greatest, and those of the governments of Ontario, Alberta, and Saskatchewan are the least. Part (b) shows the sources of provincial revenues as a percentage of total outlays. The Northern and Atlantic provinces receive the largest transfers from the federal government, while Alberta, Ontario, and British Columbia receive the least.

Figure 24.6 shows the revenues, outlays, and deficits of the federal government and of total government between 1971 and 2001.

You can see that federal government outlays and revenues and total government outlays and revenues

FIGURE 24.5 Provincial Government Budgets

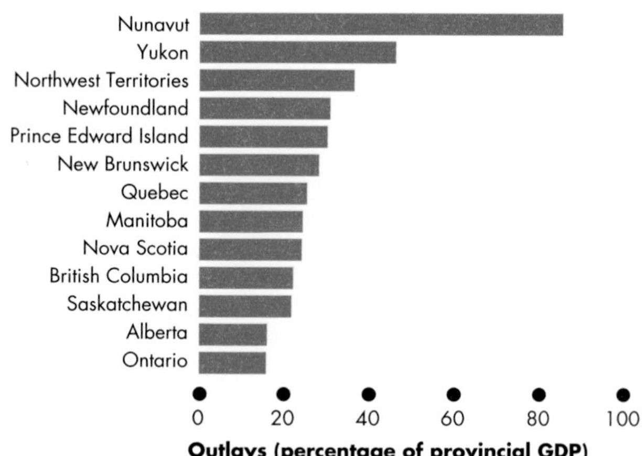

(a) Outlays

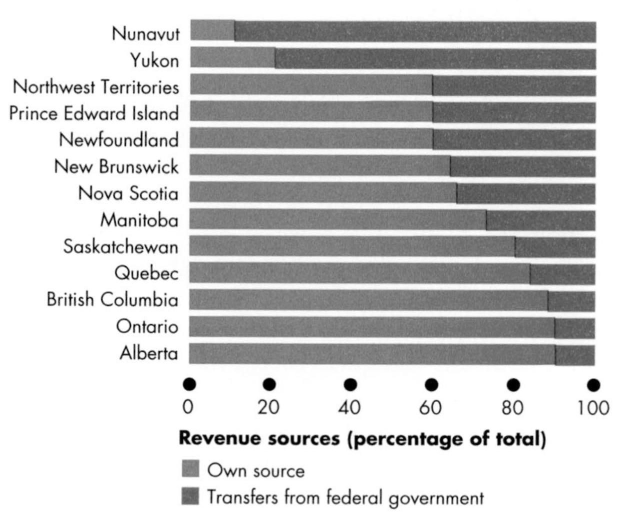

(b) Revenues

Provincial government budgets vary a lot across the provinces. As a percentage of provincial GDP, outlays (part a) are highest in Northern and Atlantic Canada and lowest in Ontario, Alberta, and Saskatchewan. The Northern and Atlantic regions receive the largest share of revenues from the federal government (part b) while Alberta, Ontario, and British Columbia receive the least.

Source: Statistics Canada, CANSIM tables 384-0002 and 385-0002.

FIGURE 24.6 Total Government Budgets

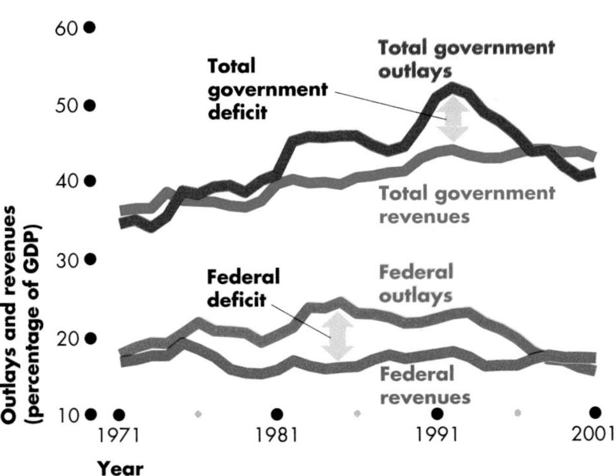

Total government is the sum of the federal, provincial, and local governments. Both the federal government deficit and the provincial government deficits increased from the early 1980s to the mid-1990s, so the total government deficit also increased. Both the federal government deficit and the provincial government deficits decreased after 1995 and turned to surpluses in the late 1990s, so the total government deficit also decreased and became a surplus.

Source: Statistics Canada, CANSIM tables 380-0002 and 380-0007.

FIGURE 24.7 Government Deficits Around the World in 2001

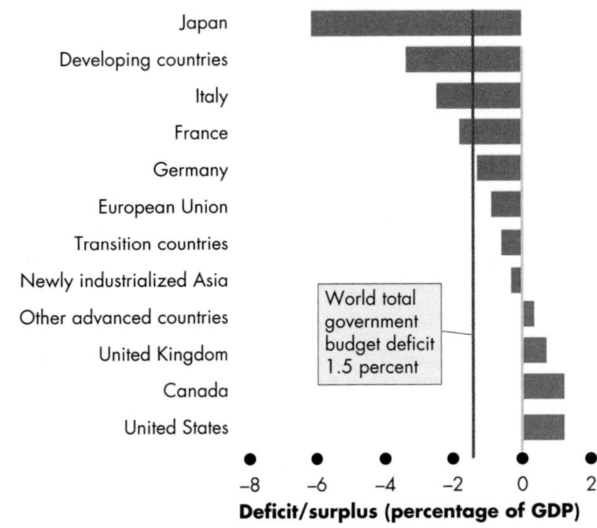

Governments in most countries had budget deficits in 2001. The largest ones were in Japan, the developing countries, Italy, and France. Canada, the United States, and a few other economies had surpluses.

Source: World Economic Outlook, October 2001 (Washington D.C.: International Monetary Fund), tables A15 and A20.

fluctuate in similar ways, but the total government is much larger than the federal government. In other words, the provincial and local governments are a large component of total government. You can also see that total government outlays fluctuate more than federal government outlays.

How does the Canadian government budget balance compare with budgets in other countries?

The Canadian Government Budget in Global Perspective

Is Canada unusual in having eliminated its budget deficit and now to be running a budget surplus? Do other countries have budget surpluses, or do they have budget deficits? Figure 24.7 answers these questions. In today's world, almost all countries have budget deficits. To compare countries, we measure the budget surplus or deficit as a percentage of GDP. The biggest deficit relative to GDP is found in Japan, where the deficit exceeds 6 percent of GDP. The developing countries, along with Italy and France, have deficits greater than the world average. Canada, the United States, and a small group of other countries are relatively unusual in having budget surpluses.

REVIEW QUIZ

1. What are the main items of government revenues and outlays?
2. Under what circumstances does the government have a budget surplus?
3. Explain the connection between a government deficit and a government debt.

Your next task is to study the effects of the government's budget on the economy and learn about fiscal policy multipliers.

Fiscal Policy Multipliers

FISCAL POLICY ACTIONS CAN BE EITHER AUTOmatic or discretionary. **Automatic fiscal policy** is a change in fiscal policy that is triggered by the state of the economy. For example, an increase in unemployment triggers an automatic increase in payments to the unemployed. A fall in incomes triggers an automatic decrease in tax revenues. That is, this type of fiscal policy adjusts automatically. **Discretionary fiscal policy** is a policy action that is initiated by an act of Parliament. It requires a change in tax laws or in some spending program. For example, a cut in income tax rates and an increase in defence spending are discretionary fiscal policy actions. That is, discretionary fiscal policy is a deliberate policy action.

We begin by studying the effects of *discretionary* changes in government spending and taxes. To focus on the essentials, we'll initially study a model economy that is simpler than the one in which we live. In our model economy, there is no international trade and the taxes are autonomous. **Autonomous taxes** are taxes that do not vary with real GDP. The government fixes them, and they change when the government changes them. But they do not vary automatically with the state of the economy.

The main example of an autonomous tax is the *property tax*. This tax varies across individuals and depends on the value of the property a person occupies. But unlike the income tax, it does not change simply because a person's income changes.

We use autonomous taxes in our model economy because they make the principles we are studying easier to understand. Once we've grasped the principles, we'll explore our real economy with its international trade and income taxes—taxes that *do* vary with real GDP.

Like our real economy, the model economy we study is bombarded by spending fluctuations. Business investment in new buildings, plant and equipment, and inventories fluctuates because of swings in profit expectations and interest rates. These fluctuations set up multiplier effects that begin a recession or an expansion. If a recession takes hold, unemployment increases and incomes fall. If an expansion becomes too strong, inflationary pressures build up. To minimize the effects of these swings in spending, the government might change either its expenditures on goods and services or taxes. By changing either of these items, the government can influence aggregate expenditure and real GDP, but the government's budget deficit or surplus also changes. An alternative fiscal policy action is to change both expenditures and taxes together so that the budget balance does not change. We are going to study the initial effects of these discretionary fiscal policy actions in the very short run when the price level is fixed. Each of these actions creates a multiplier effect on real GDP. These multipliers are the

- Government expenditures multiplier
- Autonomous tax multiplier

Government Expenditures Multiplier

The **government expenditures multiplier** is the magnification effect of a change in government expenditures on goods and services on equilibrium aggregate expenditure and real GDP.

Government expenditures are a component of aggregate expenditure. So when government expenditures on goods and services change, aggregate expenditure and real GDP change. The change in real GDP induces a change in consumption expenditure, which brings a further change in aggregate expenditure. A multiplier process ensues. This multiplier process is like the one described in Chapter 23 (pp. 538–543). Let's look at an example.

A Mackenzie Valley Pipeline Multiplier Canada's Arctic region is rich in natural gas. But to get that gas to Canadian and U.S. markets, a huge $6 billion pipeline would have to be built. Although it is a controversial project because of its potential impact on the environment, building a pipeline in this region would have a large multiplier effect. Construction workers would be hired who would spend much of their income in the Arctic region. Retail stores, schools, health care centres, hotels and motels, and recreational facilities would open and hire yet more people. Some of the income earned by this second wave of workers would also be spent in the region. The Arctic economy would expand until aggregate planned expenditure again equalled aggregate income.

The Size of the Multiplier Table 24.2 illustrates the government expenditures multiplier with a numerical example. The first data column lists various possible levels of real GDP. Our task is to find equilibrium expenditure and the change in real GDP when government expenditures change. The second column shows taxes. They are fixed at $200 billion,

TABLE 24.2 The Government Expenditures Multiplier

	Real GDP (*Y*)	Taxes (*T*)	Disposable income (*Y* – *NT*)	Consumption expenditure (*C*)	Investment (*I*)	Initial government expenditures (*G*)	Initial aggregate planned expenditure (*AE* = *C* + *I* + *G*)	New government expenditures (*G'*)	New aggregate planned expenditure (*AE'* = *C* + *I* + *G'*)
					(billions of dollars)				
A	900	200	700	525	200	200	925	250	975
B	**1,000**	**200**	**800**	**600**	**200**	**200**	**1,000**	250	1,050
C	1,100	200	900	675	200	200	1,075	250	1,125
D	**1,200**	**200**	**1,000**	**750**	**200**	200	1,150	**250**	**1,200**
E	1,300	200	1,100	825	200	200	1,225	250	1,275

regardless of the level of real GDP. (This is an assumption that keeps your attention on the key idea and makes the calculations easier to do.) The third column calculates disposable income. Because taxes are autonomous, disposable income equals real GDP minus the $200 billion of taxes. For example, in row *B*, real GDP is $1,000 billion and disposable income is $800 billion. The next column shows consumption expenditure. In this example, the *marginal propensity to consume* is 0.75. That is, a $1 increase in disposable income brings a 75-cent increase in consumption expenditure. Check this fact by calculating the increase in consumption expenditure when disposable income increases by $100 billion from row *B* to row *C*. Consumption expenditure increases by $75 billion. The next column shows investment, which is a constant of $200 billion. The next column shows the initial level of government expenditures, which is $200 billion. Aggregate planned expenditure is the sum of consumption expenditure, investment, and government expenditures.

Equilibrium expenditure and real GDP occur when aggregate planned expenditure equals actual expenditure. In this example, equilibrium expenditure is $1,000 billion (highlighted in row *B* of the table.)

The final two columns of the table show what happens when government expenditures increase by $50 billion, to $250 billion. Aggregate planned expenditure increases by $50 billion at each level of real GDP. At the initial real GDP of $1,000 billion (row *B*), aggregate planned expenditure increases to $1,050 billion.

Because aggregate planned expenditure now exceeds real GDP, inventories decrease. So firms increase production. Output, incomes, and expenditure increase. Increased incomes induce a further increase in consumption expenditure, which is less than the increase in income. Aggregate planned expenditure increases and eventually, a new equilibrium is reached. The new equilibrium is at a real GDP of $1,200 billion (highlighted in row *D*).

A $50 billion increase in government expenditures has increased equilibrium expenditure and real GDP by $200 billion. So the government expenditures multiplier is 4. The size of the multiplier depends on the marginal propensity to consume, which in this example is 0.75. The following formula shows the connection between the government expenditures multiplier and the marginal propensity to consume (*MPC*):

$$\text{Government expenditures multiplier} = \frac{1}{1 - MPC}.$$

Let's check this formula by using the numbers in the above example. The marginal propensity to consume is 0.75, so the government expenditures multiplier is 4.

Figure 24.8 illustrates the government expenditures multiplier. Initially, aggregate planned expenditure is shown by the curve labelled AE_0. The points on this curve, labelled *A* through *E*, correspond with

FIGURE 24.8 Government Expenditures Multiplier

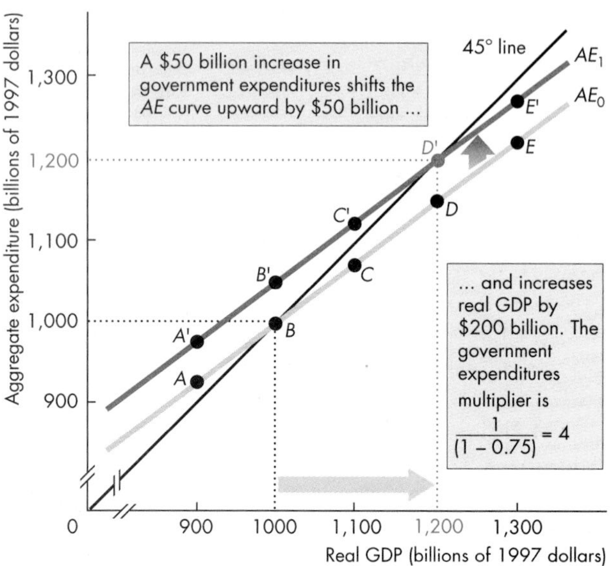

Initially, the aggregate expenditure curve is AE_0, and real GDP is $1,000 billion (at point *B*). An increase in government expenditures of $50 billion increases aggregate planned expenditure at each level of real GDP by $50 billion. The aggregate expenditure curve shifts upward from AE_0 to AE_1—a parallel shift.

At the initial real GDP of $1,000 billion, aggregate planned expenditure is now $1,050 billion. Because aggregate planned expenditure is greater than real GDP, real GDP increases. The new equilibrium is reached when real GDP is $1,200 billion—the point at which the AE_1 curve intersects the 45° line (at point *D'*). In this example, the government expenditures multiplier is 4.

the rows of Table 24.2. This aggregate expenditure curve intersects the 45° line at the equilibrium level of real GDP, which is $1,000 billion.

When government expenditures increase by $50 billion, the aggregate expenditure curve shifts upward by that amount to AE_1. With this new aggregate expenditure curve, equilibrium real GDP increases by $200 billion to $1,200 billion. The increase in real GDP is 4 times the increase in government expenditures. The government expenditures multiplier is 4.

You've seen that in the very short term, when the price level is fixed, an increase in government expenditures increases real GDP. But to produce more output, more people must be employed, so in the short term, an increase in government expenditures can create jobs.

Increasing its expenditures on goods and services is one way in which the government can try to stimulate the economy. A second way in which the government might act to increase real GDP in the very short run is by decreasing autonomous taxes. Let's see how this action works.

Autonomous Tax Multiplier

The **autonomous tax multiplier** is the magnification effect of a change in autonomous taxes on equilibrium aggregate expenditure and real GDP. An *increase* in taxes *decreases* disposable income, which *decreases* consumption expenditure. The amount by which consumption expenditure initially changes is determined by the marginal propensity to consume. In our example, the marginal propensity to consume is 0.75, so a $1 tax cut increases disposable income by $1 and increases aggregate expenditure initially by 75 cents.

This initial change in aggregate expenditure has a multiplier just like the government expenditures multiplier. We've seen that the government expenditures multiplier is $1/(1 - MPC)$. Because a tax *increase* leads to a *decrease* in expenditure, the autonomous tax multiplier is *negative*. And because a change in autonomous taxes changes aggregate expenditure initially by only *MPC* multiplied by the tax change, the

$$\text{Autonomous tax multiplier} = \frac{-MPC}{1 - MPC}.$$

In our example, the marginal propensity to consume is 0.75, so

$$\text{Autonomous tax multiplier} = \frac{-0.75}{1 - 0.75} = -3.$$

Figure 24.9 illustrates the autonomous tax multiplier. Initially, the aggregate expenditure curve is AE_0 and equilibrium expenditure is $1,000 billion. Taxes increase by $100 billion, and disposable income falls by that amount. With a marginal propensity to consume of 0.75, aggregate expenditure decreases initially by $75 billion and the aggregate expenditure curve shifts downward by that amount to AE_1. Equilibrium expenditure and real GDP decrease by $300 billion, to $700 billion. The autonomous tax multiplier is –3.

FIGURE 24.9 Autonomous Tax Multiplier

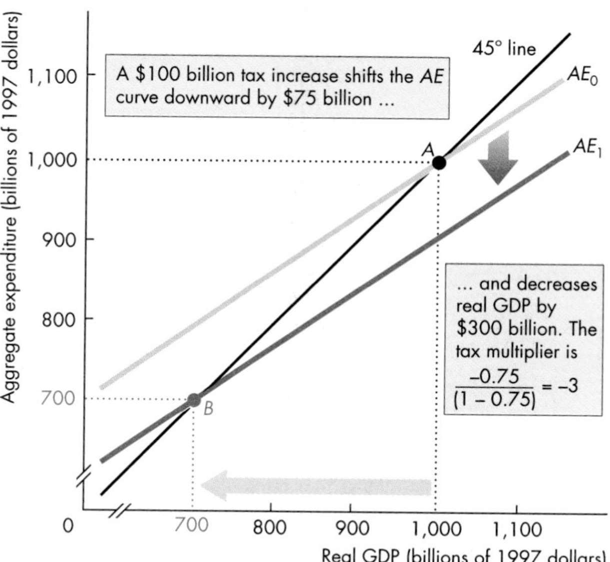

Initially, the aggregate expenditure curve is AE_0 and equilibrium expenditure is $1,000 billion. The marginal propensity to consume is 0.75. Autonomous taxes increase by $100 billion, so disposable income falls by $100 billion. The decrease in aggregate expenditure is found by multiplying this change in disposable income by the marginal propensity to consume and is $100 billion × 0.75 = $75 billion. The aggregate expenditure curve shifts *downward* by this amount to AE_1. Equilibrium expenditure decreases by $300 billion, from $1,000 billion to $700 billion. The autonomous tax multiplier is –3.

Autonomous Transfer Payments The autonomous tax multiplier also tells us the effects of a change in autonomous transfer payments. Transfer payments are like negative taxes, so an increase in transfer payments works like a decrease in taxes. Because the tax multiplier is negative, a decrease in taxes increases expenditure. An increase in transfer payments also increases expenditure. So the autonomous transfer payments multiplier is positive. It is

$$\text{Autonomous transfer payments multiplier} = \frac{MPC}{1 - MPC}.$$

Induced Taxes and Transfer Payments

In the examples we've studied so far, taxes are autonomous. But in reality, net taxes (taxes minus transfer payments) vary with the state of the economy.

On the revenue side of the budget, tax laws define tax *rates* to be paid, not tax *dollars* to be paid. Tax *dollars* paid depend on tax *rates* and incomes. But incomes vary with real GDP, so tax *revenues* depend on real GDP. Taxes that vary with real GDP are called **induced taxes**. When the economy expands, induced taxes increase because real GDP increases. When the economy is in a recession, induced taxes decrease because real GDP decreases.

On the outlay side of the budget, the government creates programs that entitle suitably qualified people and businesses to receive benefits. The spending on such programs is not fixed in dollars and it results in transfer payments that depend on the economic state of individual citizens and businesses. When the economy is in a recession, unemployment is high, the number of people experiencing economic hardship increases, and a larger number of firms and farms experience hard times. Transfer payments increase. When the economy expands, transfer payments decrease.

Induced taxes and transfer payments decrease the multiplier effects of changes in government expenditures and autonomous taxes. The reason is that they weaken the link between real GDP and disposable income and so dampen the effect of a change in real GDP on consumption expenditure. When real GDP increases, induced taxes increase and transfer payments decrease, so disposable income does not increase by as much as the increase in real GDP. As a result, consumption expenditure does not increase by as much as it otherwise would have done and the multiplier effect is reduced.

The extent to which induced taxes and transfer payments decrease the multiplier depends on the *marginal tax rate*. The marginal tax rate is the proportion of an additional dollar of real GDP that flows to the government in net taxes (taxes minus transfer payments). The higher the marginal tax rate, the larger is the proportion of an additional dollar of real GDP that is paid to the government and the smaller is the induced change in consumption expenditure. The smaller the change in consumption expenditure induced by a change in real GDP, the smaller is the multiplier effect of a change in government expenditures or autonomous taxes.

International Trade and Fiscal Policy Multipliers

Not all expenditure in Canada is on Canadian-produced goods and services. Some of it is on imports—on foreign-produced goods and services. Imports affect the fiscal policy multipliers in the same way that they influence the investment multiplier, as explained in Chapter 23 (see pp. 540–541). The extent to which an additional dollar of real GDP is spent on imports is determined by the *marginal propensity to import.* Expenditure on imports does not generate Canadian real GDP and does not lead to an increase in Canadian consumption expenditure. The larger the marginal propensity to import, the smaller are the government expenditures and autonomous tax multipliers.

The math note on pp. 576–577 explains the details of the effects of induced taxes and transfer payments and imports on the fiscal policy multipliers.

So far, we've studied *discretionary* fiscal policy. Let's now look at *automatic* stabilizers.

Automatic Stabilizers

Automatic stabilizers are mechanisms that stabilize real GDP without explicit action by the government. Their name is borrowed from engineering and conjures up images of shock absorbers, thermostats, and sophisticated devices that keep airplanes and ships steady in turbulent air and seas. But automatic fiscal stabilizers do not actually stabilize. They just make the fluctuations less severe. These stabilizers operate because income taxes and transfer payments fluctuate with real GDP. If real GDP begins to decrease, tax revenues also fall and transfer payments rise and the government's budget deficit changes. Let's look at the budget deficit over the business cycle.

Budget Deficit Over the Business Cycle Figure 24.10 shows the business cycle and fluctuations in the budget deficit between 1981 and 2001. Part (a) shows the fluctuations of real GDP around potential GDP. Part (b) shows the federal budget deficit. Both parts highlight recessions by shading those periods. By comparing the two parts of the figure, you can see the relationship between the business cycle and the budget deficit. As a rule, when the economy is in the expansion phase of a business cycle, the budget deficit declines. (In the figure, a declining deficit means a deficit that is getting closer to zero.) As the expansion slows before the recession begins, the

FIGURE 24.10 The Business Cycle and the Budget Deficit

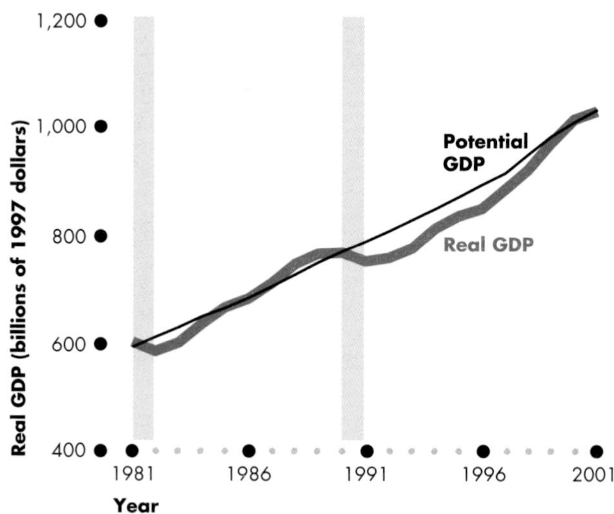

(a) Growth and recessions

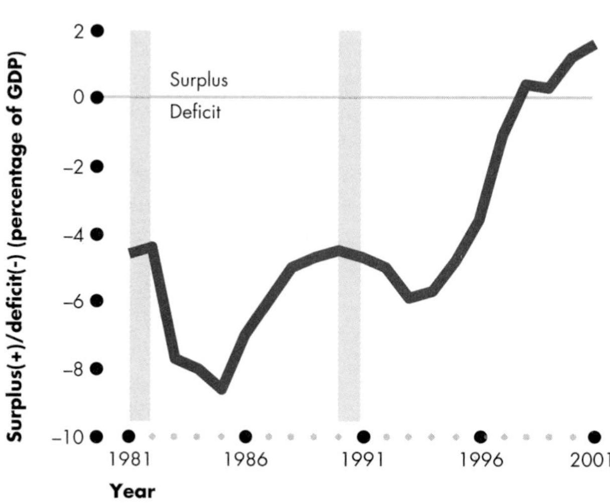

(b) Federal budget balance

As real GDP fluctuates around potential GDP (part a), the budget deficit fluctuates (part b). During a recession (shaded years), tax revenues decrease, transfer payments increase, and the budget deficit increases. The deficit also increases *before* a recession as real GDP growth slows and *after* a recession before real GDP growth speeds up.

Source: Statistics Canada, CANSIM tables 380-0002 and 380-0007.

budget deficit increases. It continues to increase during the recession and for a further period after the recession is over. Then, when the expansion is well underway, the budget deficit declines again.

The budget deficit fluctuates with the business cycle because both tax revenues and transfer payments fluctuate with real GDP. As real GDP increases during an expansion, tax revenues increase and transfer payments decrease, so the budget deficit automatically decreases. As real GDP decreases during a recession, tax revenues decrease and transfer payments increase, so the budget deficit automatically increases.

Fluctuations in investment and exports have a multiplier effect on real GDP. But fluctuations in tax revenues (and the budget deficit) act as an automatic stabilizer. They decrease the swings in disposable income and make the multiplier effect smaller. They dampen both expansions and recessions.

Cyclical and Structural Balances Because the government budget balance fluctuates with the business cycle, we need a method of measuring the balance that tells us whether it is a temporary cyclical phenomenon or a persistent phenomenon. A temporary and cyclical surplus or deficit vanishes when full employment returns. A persistent surplus or deficit requires government action to remove it.

To determine whether the budget balance is persistent or temporary and cyclical, economists have developed the concepts of the structural budget balance and the cyclical budget balance. The **structural surplus or deficit** is the budget balance that would occur if the economy were at full employment and real GDP were equal to potential GDP. The **cyclical surplus or deficit** is the actual surplus or deficit minus the structural surplus or deficit. That is, the cyclical surplus or deficit is the part of the budget balance that arises purely because real GDP does not equal potential GDP.

For example, suppose that the budget deficit is $10 billion. And suppose that economists have determined that there is a structural deficit of $2.5 billion. Then there is a cyclical deficit of $7.5 billion.

Figure 24.11 illustrates the concepts of the cyclical surplus or deficit and the structural surplus or deficit. The blue curve shows government outlays. The outlays curve slopes downward because transfer payments, a component of government outlays, decrease as real GDP increases. The green curve shows revenues. The revenues curve slopes upward

FIGURE 24.11 Cyclical and Structural Deficits and Surpluses

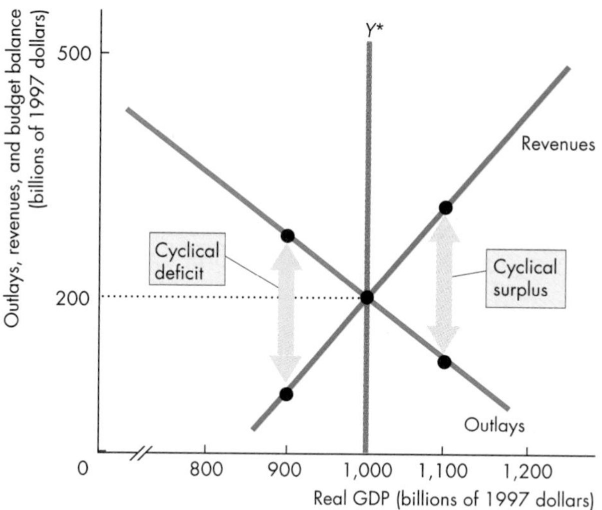

(a) Cyclical deficit and cyclical surplus

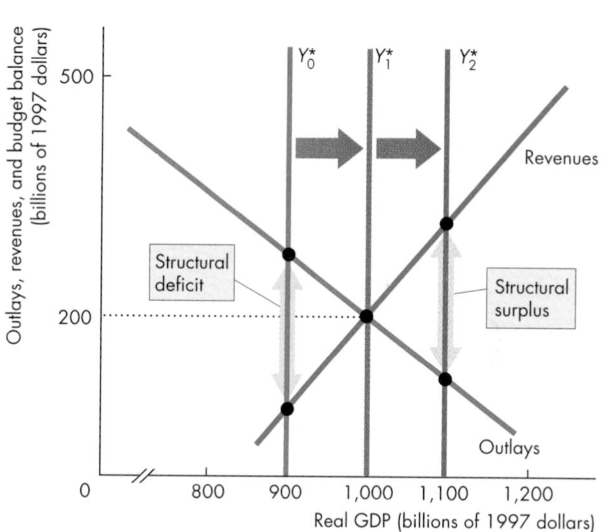

(b) Structural deficit and structural surplus

In part (a), potential GDP is $1,000 billion. When real GDP is less than potential GDP, the budget is in a *cyclical deficit.* When real GDP exceeds potential GDP, the budget is in a *cyclical surplus.* The government has a *balanced budget* when real GDP equals potential GDP. In part (b), when potential GDP is $900 billion, there is a *structural deficit.* But when potential GDP is $1,100 billion, there is a *structural surplus.*

because most components of tax revenues increase as incomes and real GDP increase.

In Fig. 24.11(a), potential GDP is $1,000 billion. If real GDP equals potential GDP, the government has a *balanced budget.* Outlays and revenues each equal $200 billion. If real GDP is less than potential GDP, outlays exceed revenues and there is a *cyclical deficit.* If real GDP is greater than potential GDP, outlays are less than revenues and there is a *cyclical surplus.*

In Fig. 24.11(b), potential GDP grows but the revenues curve and the outlays curve do not change. When potential GDP is $900 billion ($Y_0^*$), there is a *structural deficit.* When potential GDP grows to $1,000 billion ($Y_1^*$), there is a *structural balance* of zero. And when potential GDP grows to $1,100 billion ($Y_2^*$), there is a *structural surplus.*

The Canadian federal budget was in a structural deficit starting in the mid-1970s and continuing through the mid-1990s. That is, even if the economy had been at full employment, the budget would have been in deficit. Worse, the structural deficit was so large that even at the peak of a business cycle, the budget was in deficit. At the end of the 1990s, a budget surplus emerged. It is probable that this surplus was structural because the economy was close to full employment.

REVIEW QUIZ

1. What are the government expenditures multiplier and the autonomous tax multiplier? How do these multiplier effects work?
2. Which multiplier effect is larger: the multiplier effect of a change in government expenditures, or the multiplier effect of a change in autonomous taxes? Why is one larger than the other?
3. How do income taxes and imports influence the size of the fiscal policy multipliers?
4. How do income taxes and transfer payments work as automatic stabilizers to dampen the business cycle?
5. How do we tell whether a budget deficit needs government action to remove it?

Your next task is to see how, with the passage of more time and with some price level adjustments, these multiplier effects change.

Fiscal Policy Multipliers and the Price Level

WE'VE SEEN HOW REAL GDP RESPONDS TO changes in fiscal policy when the price level is fixed and all the adjustments that take place are in spending, income, and production. The period over which this response occurs is very short. Once production starts to change, regardless of whether it increases or decreases, prices also start to change. The price level and real GDP change together, and the economy moves to a new short-run equilibrium.

To study the simultaneous changes in real GDP and the price level, we use the *AS–AD* model of Chapter 22. In the long run, both the price level and the money wage rate respond to fiscal policy. As these further changes take place, the economy gradually moves towards a new long-run equilibrium. We also use the *AS–AD* model to study these adjustments.

We begin by looking at the effects of fiscal policy on aggregate demand and the aggregate demand curve.

Fiscal Policy and Aggregate Demand

You learned about the relationship between aggregate demand, aggregate expenditure, and equilibrium expenditure in Chapter 23 (pp. 543–545). You are now going to use what you learned there to work out what happens to aggregate demand, the price level, and real GDP when fiscal policy changes. We'll start by looking at the effects of a change in fiscal policy on aggregate demand.

Figure 24.12 shows the effects of an increase in government expenditures on aggregate demand. Initially, the aggregate expenditure curve is AE_0 in part (a), and the aggregate demand curve is AD_0 in part (b). The price level is 110, real GDP is $1,000 billion, and the economy is at point *A* in both parts of the figure. Now suppose that the government increases its expenditures by $50 billion. At a constant price level of 110, the aggregate expenditure curve shifts upward to AE_1. This curve intersects the 45° line at an equilibrium expenditure of $1,200 billion at point *B*. This amount is the aggregate quantity of goods and services demanded at a price level of 110, as shown by point *B* in part (b). Point *B* lies on a new aggregate demand curve. The aggregate demand curve has shifted rightward to AD_1.

The government expenditures multiplier determines the distance by which the aggregate demand

FIGURE 24.12 Government Expenditures and Aggregate Demand

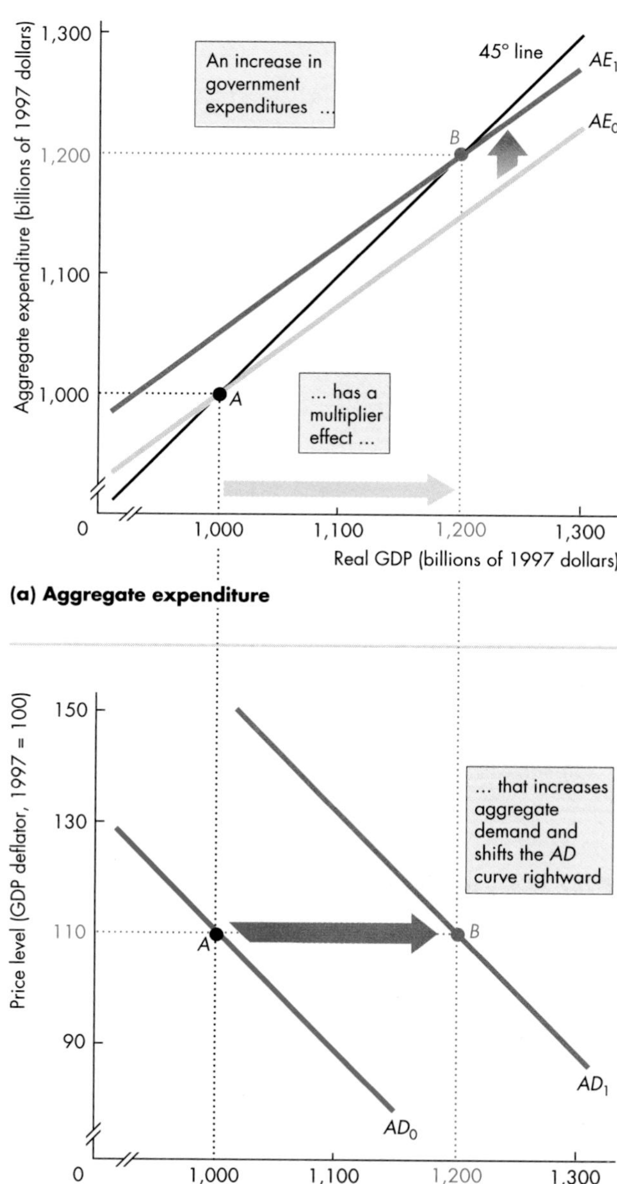

The price level is 110, aggregate planned expenditure is AE_0 (part a), and aggregate demand is AD_0 (part b). An increase in government expenditures shifts the *AE* curve to AE_1 and increases equilibrium real GDP to $1,200 billion. The aggregate demand curve shifts rightward to AD_1.

curve shifts rightward. The larger the multiplier, the larger is the shift in the aggregate demand curve resulting from a given change in government expenditures. In this example, a $50 billion increase in government expenditures produces a $200 billion increase in the aggregate quantity of goods and services demanded at each price level. The multiplier is 4. So the $50 billion increase in government expenditures shifts the aggregate demand curve rightward by $200 billion.

Figure 24.12 shows the effects of an increase in government expenditures. But a similar effect occurs for *any* expansionary fiscal policy. An **expansionary fiscal policy** is an increase in government expenditures or a decrease in taxes. But the distance that the aggregate demand curve shifts is smaller for a decrease in taxes than for an increase in government expenditures of the same size.

Figure 24.12 can also be used to illustrate the effects of a **contractionary fiscal policy**—a decrease in government expenditures or an increase in taxes. In this case, start at point *B* in each part of the figure and decrease government expenditures or increase taxes. Aggregate demand decreases and the aggregate demand curve shifts leftward from AD_1 to AD_0.

Equilibrium GDP and the Price Level in the Short Run We've seen how an increase in government expenditures increases aggregate demand. Let's now see how it changes real GDP and the price level. Figure 24.13(a) describes the economy. Aggregate demand is AD_0, and the short-run aggregate supply curve is *SAS*. (Check back to Chapter 22, pp. 501–502, to refresh your understanding of the *SAS* curve.) Equilibrium is at point *A*, where the aggregate demand and short-run aggregate supply curves intersect. The price level is 110, and real GDP is $1,000 billion.

An increase in government expenditures of $50 billion shifts the aggregate demand curve rightward from AD_0 to AD_1. While the price level is fixed at 110, the economy moves towards point *B* and real GDP increases towards $1,200 billion. But during the adjustment process, the price level does not remain constant. It gradually rises, and the economy moves along the short-run aggregate supply curve to the point of intersection of the short-run aggregate supply curve and the new aggregate demand curve—point *C*. The price level rises to 123, and real GDP increases to only $1,130 billion.

FIGURE 24.13 Fiscal Policy, Real GDP, and the Price Level

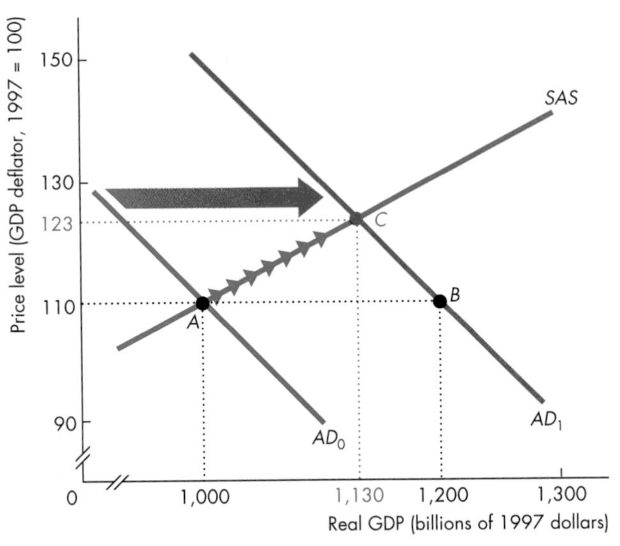

(a) Fiscal policy with unemployment

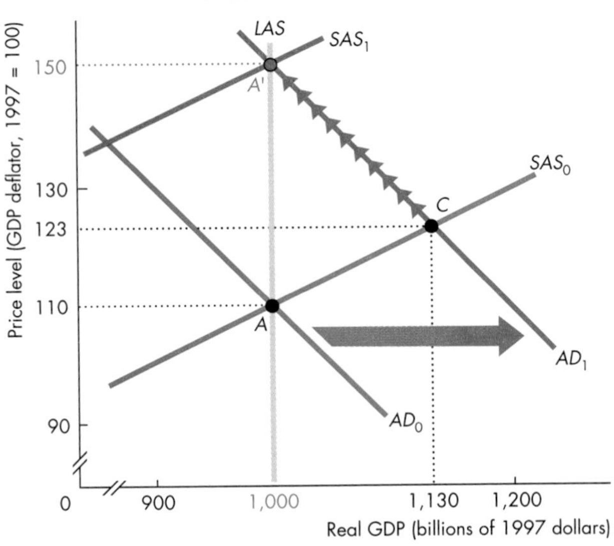

(b) Fiscal policy at full employment

An increase in government expenditures shifts the *AD* curve from AD_0 to AD_1 (part a). With a fixed price level, the economy would have moved to point *B*. But the price level rises, and in the short run, the economy moves to point *C*. The price level increases to 123, and real GDP increases to $1,130 billion.

At point *C*, real GDP exceeds potential GDP and unemployment is below the natural rate (part b). The money wage rate rises, and short-run aggregate supply decreases. The *SAS* curve shifts leftward to SAS_1, and in the long run, the economy moves to point *A'*. The price level rises to 150, and real GDP returns to $1,000 billion.

When we take the price level effect into account, the increase in government expenditures still has a multiplier effect on real GDP, but the effect is smaller than it would be if the price level remained constant. Also, the steeper the slope of the *SAS* curve, the larger is the increase in the price level, the smaller is the increase in real GDP, and the smaller is the government expenditures multiplier. But the multiplier is not zero.

In the long run, real GDP equals potential GDP—the economy is at full-employment equilibrium. When real GDP equals potential GDP, an increase in aggregate demand has the same short-run effect as we've just worked out, but its long-run effect is different. The increase in aggregate demand raises the price level but leaves real GDP unchanged at potential GDP.

To study this case, let's see what happens if the government embarks on an expansionary fiscal policy when real GDP equals potential GDP.

Fiscal Expansion at Potential GDP

Suppose that real GDP is equal to potential GDP, which means that unemployment is equal to the natural rate of unemployment. But suppose also that the unemployment rate and the natural rate are high and that most people, including the government, mistakenly think that unemployment is above the natural rate. In this situation, the government tries to lower the unemployment rate by using an expansionary fiscal policy.

Figure 24.13(b) shows the effect of an expansionary fiscal policy when real GDP equals potential GDP. In this example, potential GDP is $1,000 billion. Aggregate demand increases, and the aggregate demand curve shifts rightward from AD_0 to AD_1. The short-run equilibrium, point *C*, is an above full-employment equilibrium. Now the money wage rate begins to increase and short-run aggregate supply decreases. The *SAS* curve shifts leftward from SAS_0 to

SAS_1. The economy moves up the aggregate demand curve AD_1 towards point *A'*.

When all the wage and price adjustments have occurred, the price level is 150 and real GDP is again at potential GDP of $1,000 billion. The multiplier is zero. There has been only a temporary increase in real GDP but a permanent rise in the price level.

Limitations of Fiscal Policy

Because the short-run fiscal policy multipliers are not zero, expansionary fiscal policy can be used to increase real GDP and decrease the unemployment rate in a recession. Contractionary fiscal policy can also be used, if the economy is overheating, to decrease real GDP and help to keep inflation in check. But two factors limit the use of fiscal policy.

First, the legislative process is slow, which means that it is difficult to take fiscal policy actions in a timely way. The economy might be able to benefit from fiscal stimulation right now, but it will take Parliament many months, perhaps more than a year, to act. By the time the action is taken, the economy might need an entirely different fiscal medicine.

Second, it is not always easy to tell whether real GDP is below (or above) potential GDP. A change in aggregate demand can move real GDP away from potential GDP, or a change in aggregate supply can change real GDP and change potential GDP. This difficulty is a serious one because, as you've seen, fiscal stimulation might occur too close to full employment, in which case it will increase the price level and have no long-run effect on real GDP.

REVIEW QUIZ

1 How do changes in the price level influence the multiplier effects of fiscal policy on real GDP?
2 What are the long-run effects of fiscal policy on real GDP and the price level when real GDP equals potential GDP?

So far, we've ignored any potential effects of fiscal policy on aggregate supply. Yet many economists believe that the supply-side effects of fiscal policy are the biggest. Let's now look at these effects.

Supply-Side Effects of Fiscal Policy

TAX CUTS INCREASE DISPOSABLE INCOME AND increase aggregate demand. But tax cuts also strengthen incentives and increase aggregate supply. The strength of the supply-side effects of tax cuts is not known with certainty. Some economists believe that the supply-side effects are large and exceed the demand-side effects. Other economists, while agreeing that supply-side effects are present, believe that they are relatively small.

The controversy over the magnitude of the effects of taxes on aggregate supply is a political controversy. Generally speaking, people on the conservative or right wing of the political spectrum believe that supply-side effects are powerful, and people on the liberal or left wing of the political spectrum view supply-side effects as being small.

Regardless of which view is correct, we can study the supply-side effects of tax cuts by using the *AS–AD* model. Let's study the effects of taxes on potential GDP and then see how the supply-side effects and demand-side effects together influence real GDP and the price level.

Fiscal Policy and Potential GDP

Potential GDP depends on the full-employment quantity of labour, the quantity of capital, and the state of technology. Taxes can influence all three of these factors. The main tax to consider is the income tax. By taxing the incomes people earn when they work or save, the government weakens the incentives to work and save. The result is a smaller quantity of labour and capital and a smaller potential GDP. Also, the income tax weakens the incentive to develop new technologies that increase income. So the pace of technological change might be slowed, which slows the growth rate of potential GDP. Let's look at the effect of the income tax on both the quantity of labour and the quantity of capital.

Labour Market Taxes The quantity of labour is determined by demand and supply in the labour market. Figure 24.14(a) shows a labour market. The demand for labour is *LD* and the supply is *LS*. The equilibrium real wage rate is $15 an hour and 30 billion hours of labour per year are employed.

FIGURE 24.14 Supply-Side Effects of Taxes

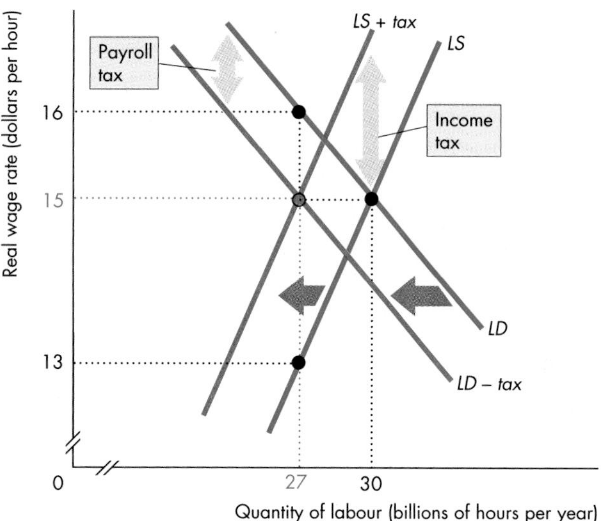

(a) The labour market

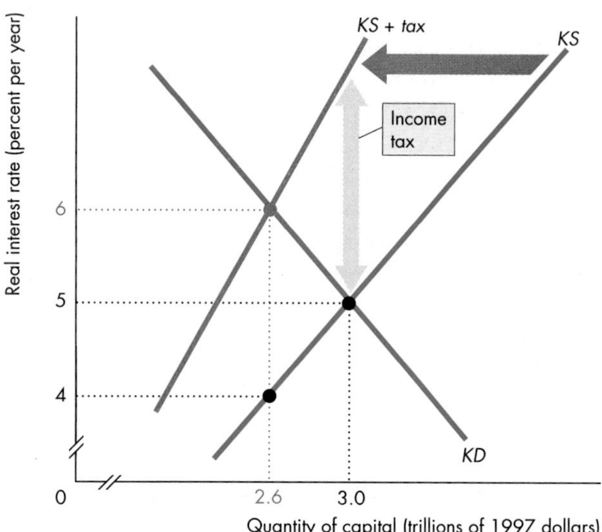

(b) The capital market

In part (a), an income tax decreases the supply of labour from *LS* to *LS* + *tax* and a payroll tax decreases the demand for labour from *LD* to *LD* – *tax*. The quantity of labour decreases. In part (b), the income tax decreases the supply of capital from *KS* to *KS* – *tax*. The quantity of capital decreases. With less labour and less capital, potential GDP decreases.

Now suppose that two taxes are introduced. An income tax weakens the incentive to work and decreases the supply of labour. The supply curve shifts leftward to *LS* + *tax*. A payroll tax makes it more costly to employ labour and decreases the demand for labour. The demand curve shifts leftward to *LD* – *tax*. With the new decreased supply and demand, the quantity of labour employed decreases to 27 billion hours a year. The *before-tax* real wage rate remains at \$15 an hour (but it might rise or fall depending on whether demand or supply decreases more). The *after-tax* real wage rate falls to \$13 an hour, and the cost of hiring labour rises to \$16 an hour.

Capital and the Income Tax The quantity of capital is determined by demand and supply in the capital market. Figure 24.14(b) shows the capital market. The demand for capital is *KD* and the supply is *KS*. The equilibrium real interest rate is 5 percent a year and the quantity of capital is \$3 trillion.

A tax on the income from capital weakens the incentive to save and decreases the supply of capital. The supply curve shifts leftward to *KS* + *tax*. With the new decreased supply, the quantity of capital decreases to \$2.6 trillion. The *before-tax* interest rate rises to 6 percent a year, and the *after-tax* interest rate falls to 4 percent a year.

Potential GDP and *LAS* Because the income tax decreases the equilibrium quantities of labour and capital, it also decreases potential GDP. But potential GDP determines long-run aggregate supply. So the income tax decreases long-run aggregate supply and shifts the *LAS* curve leftward.

Supply Effects and Demand Effects

Let's now bring the supply-side effects and demand-side effects of fiscal policy together. Figure 24.15(a) shows the most likely effects of a tax cut. The tax cut increases aggregate demand and shifts the *AD* curve rightward, just as before. But a tax cut that increases the incentive to work and save also increases aggregate supply. It shifts the long-run and short-run aggregate supply curves rightward. Here we focus on the short run and show the effect on the *SAS* curve, which shifts rightward to SAS_1. In this example, the tax cut has a large effect on aggregate demand and a small effect on aggregate supply. The aggregate demand curve shifts rightward by a larger amount

FIGURE 24.15 Two Views of the Supply-Side Effects of Fiscal Policy

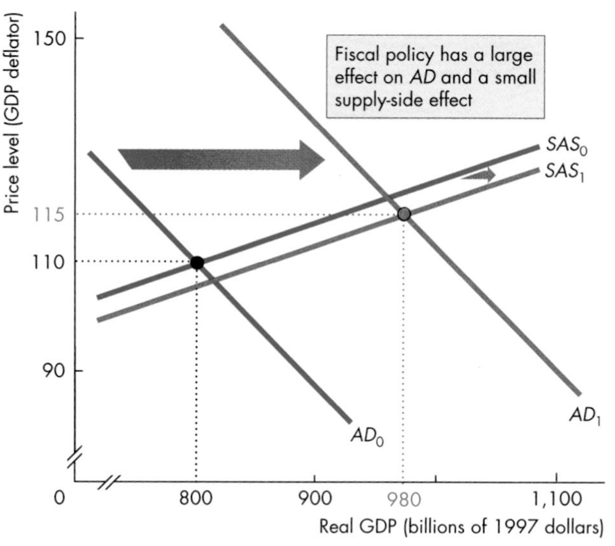

(a) The traditional view

A tax cut increases aggregate demand and shifts the *AD* curve rightward from AD_0 to AD_1 (both parts). Such a policy change also has a supply-side effect. If the supply-side effect is small, the *SAS* curve shifts rightward from SAS_0 to SAS_1 in part (a). The demand-side effect dominates the supply-side effect, real GDP increases, and the price level rises.

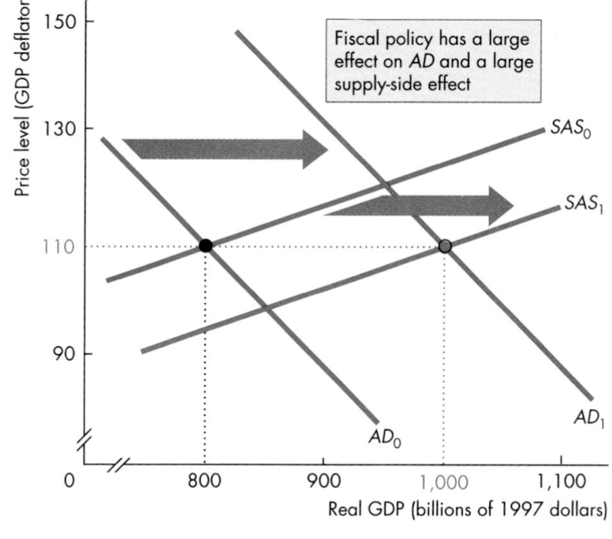

(b) The supply-side view

If the supply-side effect of a tax cut is large, the *SAS* curve shifts to SAS_1 in part (b). In this case, the supply-side effect is as large as the demand-side effect. Real GDP increases, and the price level remains constant. But if the supply-side effect were larger than the demand-side effect, the price level would actually fall.

than the rightward shift in the short-run aggregate supply curve. The outcome is a rise in the price level and an increase in real GDP. But notice that the price level rises by *less* and real GDP increases by *more* than would occur if there were no supply-side effects.

Figure 24.15(b) shows the effects that supply-siders believe occur. A tax cut still has a large effect on aggregate demand, but it has a similarly large effect on aggregate supply. The aggregate demand curve and the short-run aggregate supply curve shift rightward by similar amounts. In this particular case, the price level remains constant and real GDP increases. A slightly larger increase in aggregate supply would have brought a fall in the price level, a possibility that some supply-siders believe could occur.

The general point with which everyone agrees is that a tax cut that strengthens incentives increases real GDP by more and is less inflationary than an equal-size expansionary fiscal policy that does not change incentives or that weakens them.

REVIEW QUIZ

1 How do income taxes and payroll taxes influence the labour market, and how would a cut in these taxes influence real GDP?
2 How would an income tax cut influence aggregate supply and aggregate demand?
3 How would an income tax cut influence real GDP and the price level?

You've seen how fiscal policy influences the way real GDP fluctuates around its trend and how it influences potential GDP. *Reading Between the Lines* on pp. 574–575 looks further at Finance Minister John Manley's fiscal policy projections through 2008.

Your next task is to study the other main arm of macroeconomic policy: monetary policy.

Fiscal Policy Projections

OTTAWA CITIZEN, OCTOBER 31, 2002

Manley predicts $70B surplus by 2007

Finance Minister John Manley is projecting the government will have accumulated surpluses of more than $70 billion over this and the coming five years, money that will be used to continue transforming Canada into a "Northern tiger."

Even after setting aside about $30 billion over that time for unexpected emergencies or economic downturns, that if not needed will go to debt reduction, the federal government will still have more than $40 billion to fund promised improvements in health care, the child benefit, environmental cleanup and upgrades to city infrastructure, according to Mr. Manley's fiscal and economic update presented to the Commons finance committee yesterday.

The minister also hinted there will be more money for the military in his February budget to allow Canada to meet its defence and diplomatic responsibilities. ...

However, the update forecasts that this year there would be only $1 billion in surplus funds after setting aside $3 billion for unexpected emergencies.

And that's despite expected economic growth of 3.4 per cent this year, more than double the 1.5 per cent forecast in last year's budget, 3.4 per cent next year and an average of three per cent in each of the following five years....

TD Bank economist Don Drummond, a former associate deputy finance minister, said that while Mr. Manley "looks like he's awash in funds," he faces enormous spending pressures, noting that each of the major throne speech promises alone will cost billions.

He also noted that the big surpluses are well down the road.

The update projects annual surpluses of $1 billion this year, followed by $3.1 billion the year after, then $3.5 billion, $6.8 billion, $10.5 billion and $14.6 billion in 2007-08, not including about $30 billion that will be set aside for contingencies and prudence, including $7 billion in the last fiscal year of the forecast. ...

Essence of the Story

- Finance Minister John Manley projects budget surpluses that will accumulate to more than $70 billion by 2007.
- Of this amount, $30 billion will be spent on unexpected emergencies, be lost in economic downturns, or be used to pay down the national debt.
- The projected annual surpluses, excluding $30 billion on contingencies, are

$1 billion in 2002–03,
$3.1 billion in 2003–04,
$3.5 billion in 2004–05,
$6.8 billion in 2005–06,
$10.5 billion in 2006–07, and $14.6 billion in 2007–08.

- These surpluses will be spent on improvements in health care, the child benefit, environmental cleanup, upgrades to city infrastructure, and national defence.
- The 2002–03 surplus is small despite the fact that economic growth in that year was strong.

Economic Analysis

■ The table shows the federal government's budget projections through 2008.

■ The "Planning surplus" numbers, which are the "surpluses" referred to in the news article, are actually amounts that the government intends to spend on improvements in health care, the child benefit, environmental cleanup, upgrades to city infrastructure, and national defence.

■ The "Economic prudence" numbers are part of the $30 billion of "surplus" referred to in the news article. These amounts are expected to be spent or lost because of recession.

■ The "Contingency reserve" numbers are also part of the $30 billion of "surplus" referred to in the news article. And these amounts are the actual surplus that will be used to pay down the federal government's debt.

■ Figure 1 shows the rise and fall of government debt and the projected debt through 2008.

■ Even if the government ran surpluses that totalled $70 billion by 2008, the debt would still be more than 30 percent of GDP in 2008 and would follow the lower path in the figure.

■ The government says that its "Economic prudence" provision is to ensure that it never again has a deficit.

■ Figure 2 shows that a deficit will most likely arise in a recession.

■ In 2005, with real GDP at $1,250 billion and a structural surplus of $5 billion (the contingency reserve plus the economic prudence item for 2005), a recession that takes real GDP to 4 percent below potential GDP would create a deficit of around $3.5 billion.

You're The Voter

■ Do you think the federal government's projected surplus is too big, too small, or about right? Provide your reasons.

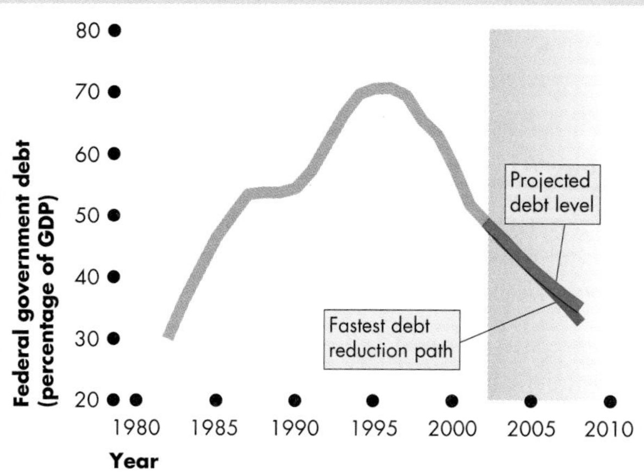

Figure 1 Paying off the federal government's debt

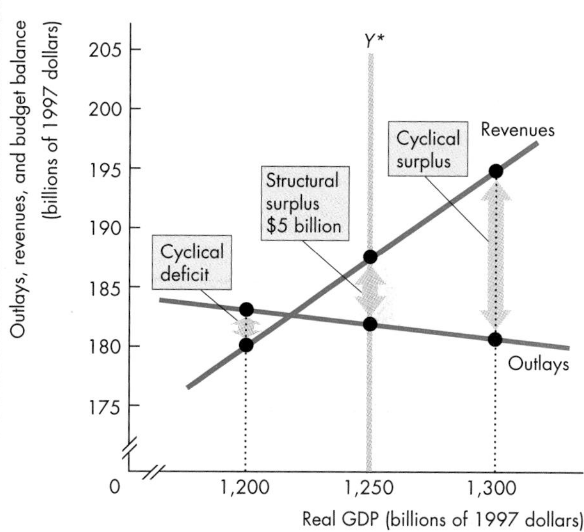

Figure 2 Cyclical and structural surpluses and deficits

Summary of Fiscal Projections: 2002–2008

Financial year	2002–03	2003–04	2004–05	2005–06	2006–07	2007–08
Item	Billions of dollars					
Revenues	173.9	184.1	191.9	201.5	211.2	221.0
Program spending	134.3	140.7	146.6	152.4	158.0	163.6
Debt interest	35.6	36.3	36.8	36.3	36.2	35.8
Planning surplus (planned increase in spending)	1.0	3.1	3.5	6.8	10.5	14.6
Economic prudence (unplanned increase in spending or decrease in revenue)	0.0	1.0	2.0	3.0	3.5	4.0
Total planned spending	170.9	181.1	188.9	198.5	208.2	218.0
Contingency reserve (planned surplus for reducing debt)	3.0	3.0	3.0	3.0	3.0	3.0

Mathematical Note
The Algebra of the Fiscal Policy Multipliers

THIS MATHEMATICAL NOTE DERIVES FORMULAS FOR the fiscal policy multipliers. We begin by defining the symbols we need:

- Aggregate planned expenditure, AE
- Real GDP, Y
- Consumption expenditure, C
- Investment, I
- Government expenditures, G
- Exports, X
- Imports, M
- Net taxes, NT
- Autonomous consumption expenditure, a
- Autonomous taxes, T_a
- Autonomous transfer payments, T_r
- Marginal propensity to consume, b
- Marginal propensity to import, m
- Marginal tax rate, t
- Autonomous expenditure, A

Equilibrium Expenditure

Aggregate planned expenditure is

$$AE = C + I + G + X - M.$$

The consumption function is

$$C = a + b(Y - NT).$$

Net taxes equals autonomous taxes minus autonomous transfer payments plus induced taxes, which is

$$NT = T_a - T_r + tY.$$

Use the last equation in the consumption function to give consumption expenditure as a function of GDP:

$$C = a - bT_a + bT_r + b(1 - t)Y.$$

The import function is

$$M = mY.$$

Use the consumption function and the import function to replace C and M in the aggregate planned expenditure equation to obtain

$$AE = a - bT_a + bT_r + b(1 - t)Y + I + G + X - mY.$$

Collect the terms that involve Y on the right-side of the equation to obtain

$$AE = (a - bT_a + bT_r + I + G + X) + [b(1 - t) - m]Y.$$

Autonomous expenditure (A) is given by

$$A = a - bT_a + bT_r + I + G + X$$

and the slope of the AE curve is $[b(1 - t) - m]$, so

$$AE = A + [b(1 - t) - m]Y.$$

Equilibrium expenditure occurs when aggregate planned expenditure (AE) equals real GDP (Y). That is,

$$AE = Y.$$

To calculate equilibrium expenditure, we solve the equation:

$$Y = A + [b(1 - t) - m]Y$$

to obtain

$$Y = \frac{1}{1 - [b(1 - t) - m]}A.$$

Government Expenditures Multiplier

The government expenditures multiplier equals the change in equilibrium expenditure (Y) that results from a change in government expenditures (G) divided by the change in government expenditures. Because autonomous expenditure is equal to

$$A = a - bT_a + bT_r + I + G + X,$$

the change in autonomous expenditure equals the change in government expenditures. That is,

$$\Delta A = \Delta G.$$

The government expenditures multiplier is found by working out the change in Y that results from the change in A. You can see from the solution for Y that

$$\Delta Y = \frac{1}{1 - [b(1 - t) - m]}\Delta G.$$

The government expenditures multiplier equals

$$\frac{1}{1 - [b(1 - t) - m]}.$$

In an economy in which $t = 0$ and $m = 0$, the government expenditures multiplier is $1/(1 - b)$. With $b = 0.75$, the government expenditures multiplier equals 4, as part (a) of the figure shows. Make up some examples and use the above formula to show how b, m, and t influence the government expenditures multiplier.

Autonomous Tax Multiplier

The autonomous tax multiplier equals the change in equilibrium expenditure (Y) that results from a change in autonomous taxes (T_a) divided by the change in autonomous taxes. Because autonomous expenditure is equal to

$$A = a - bT_a + bT_r + I + G + X,$$

the change in autonomous expenditure equals *minus* b multiplied by the change in autonomous taxes. That is,

$$\Delta A = -b\Delta T_a.$$

You can see from the solution for equilibrium expenditure Y that

$$\Delta Y = \frac{-b}{1 - [b(1 - t) - m]}\Delta T_a.$$

The autonomous tax multiplier equals

$$\frac{-b}{1 - [b(1 - t) - m]}.$$

In an economy in which $t = 0$ and $m = 0$, the autonomous tax multiplier is $-b/(1 - b)$. With $b = 0.75$, the autonomous tax multiplier equals -3, as part (b) of the figure shows. Make up some examples and use the above formula to show how b, m, and t influence the autonomous tax multiplier.

Autonomous Transfer Payments Multiplier

The autonomous transfer payments multiplier equals the change in equilibrium expenditure (Y) that results from a change in autonomous transfer payments (T_r) divided by the change in autonomous transfer payments. Because autonomous expenditure is equal to

$$A = a - bT_a + bT_r + I + G + X,$$

the change in autonomous transfer payments changes autonomous expenditure such that

$$\Delta A = b\Delta T_r.$$

Because transfer payments are like negative taxes, the autonomous transfer payments multiplier equals minus the autonomous tax multiplier. The autonomous transfer payments multiplier equals

$$\frac{b}{1 - [b(1 - t) - m]}.$$

In an economy in which $t = 0$ and $m = 0$, the autonomous transfer payments multiplier is $b/(1 - b)$. With $b = 0.75$, the autonomous transfer payments multiplier equals 3, as part (c) of the figure shows. Make up some examples and use the above formula to show how b, m, and t influence the autonomous transfer payments multiplier.

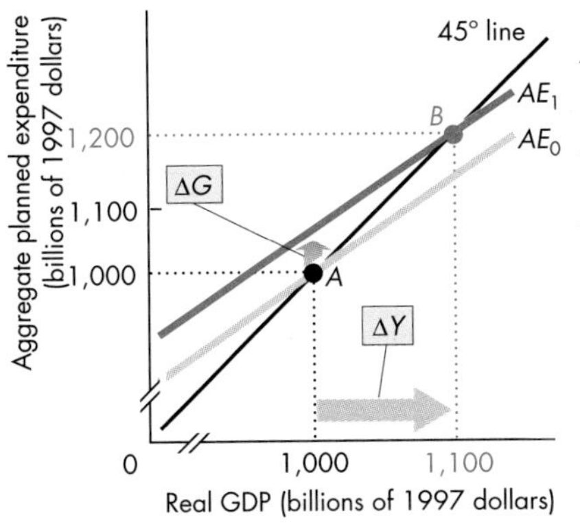

(a) Government expenditures multiplier

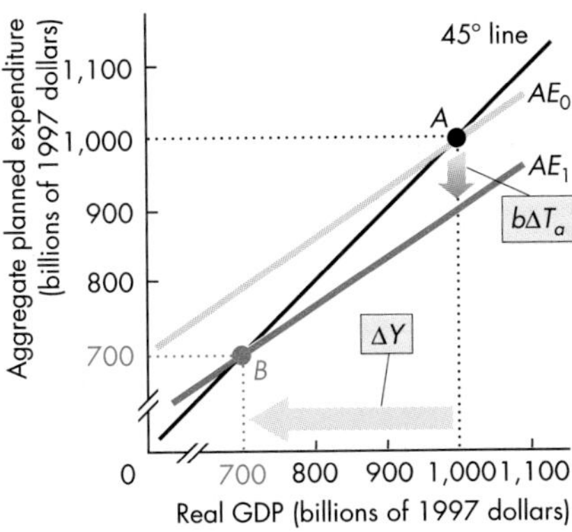

(b) Autonomous tax multiplier

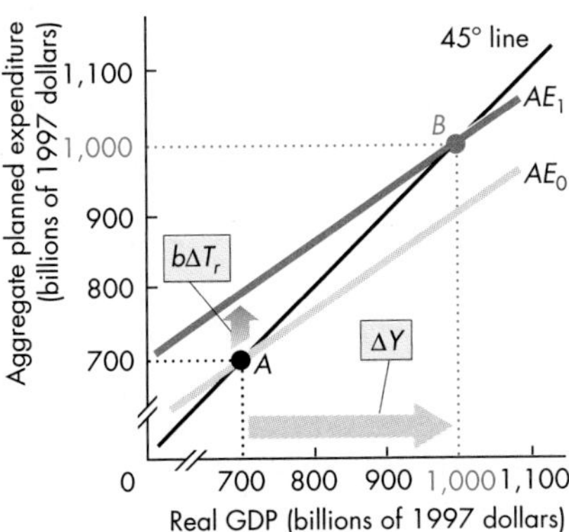

(c) Autonomous transfer payments multiplier

SUMMARY

KEY POINTS

Government Budgets (pp. 556–561)

- The federal budget finances the activities of the government and is used to stabilize real GDP.
- Federal revenues come from personal income taxes, corporate income taxes, indirect taxes, and investment income. Federal outlays include transfer payments, expenditures on goods and services, and debt interest.
- When government revenues exceed outlays, the government has a budget surplus.

Fiscal Policy Multipliers (pp. 562–568)

- Fiscal policy actions are discretionary or automatic.
- Government expenditures, taxes, and transfer payments have multiplier effects on real GDP.
- The government expenditures multiplier equals $1/(1 - MPC)$. The autonomous tax multiplier equals $-MPC/(1 - MPC)$.
- The transfer payments multiplier is equal to the magnitude of autonomous tax multiplier but is positive.
- Induced taxes and transfer payments and imports make the fiscal policy multipliers smaller.
- Income taxes and transfer payments act as automatic stabilizers.

Fiscal Policy Multipliers and the Price Level (pp. 568–571)

- An expansionary fiscal policy increases aggregate demand and shifts the aggregate demand curve rightward. It increases real GDP and raises the price level. (A contractionary fiscal policy has the opposite effects.)
- Price level changes dampen fiscal policy multiplier effects.
- At potential GDP, an expansionary fiscal policy raises the price level but leaves real GDP unchanged. The fiscal policy multipliers are zero.

Supply-Side Effects of Fiscal Policy (pp. 571–573)

- Fiscal policy has supply-side effects because increases in taxes weaken the incentives to work and save.
- A tax cut increases both aggregate demand and aggregate supply and increases real GDP, but the tax cut has an ambiguous effect on the price level.

KEY FIGURES

Figure 24.8 Government Expenditures Multiplier, 564
Figure 24.9 Autonomous Tax Multiplier, 565
Figure 24.10 The Business Cycle and the Budget Deficit, 566
Figure 24.11 Cyclical and Structural Deficits and Surpluses, 567
Figure 24.12 Government Expenditures and Aggregate Demand, 569
Figure 24.13 Fiscal Policy, Real GDP, and the Price Level, 570
Figure 24.15 Two Views of the Supply-Side Effects of Fiscal Policy, 573

KEY TERMS

Automatic fiscal policy, 562
Automatic stabilizers, 566
Autonomous tax multiplier, 564
Autonomous taxes, 562
Balanced budget, 557
Budget deficit, 557
Budget surplus, 557
Contractionary fiscal policy, 569
Cyclical surplus or deficit, 567
Discretionary fiscal policy, 562
Expansionary fiscal policy, 569
Federal budget, 556
Fiscal policy, 556
Government debt, 559
Government expenditures multiplier, 562
Induced taxes, 565
Provincial budget, 556
Structural surplus or deficit, 567

PROBLEMS

*1. In the economy of Zap, the marginal propensity to consume is 0.9. Investment is $50 billion, government expenditures on goods and services are $40 billion, and autonomous taxes are $40 billion. Zap has no exports and no imports.
   a. The government cuts its expenditures on goods and services to $30 billion. What is the change in equilibrium expenditure?
   b. What is the value of the government expenditures multiplier?
   c. The government continues to buy $40 billion worth of goods and services and cuts autonomous taxes to $30 billion. What is the change in equilibrium expenditure?
   d. What is the value of the autonomous tax multiplier?
   e. The government simultaneously cuts both its expenditures on goods and services and taxes to $30 billion. What is the change in equilibrium expenditure? Why does equilibrium expenditure decrease?

2. In the economy of Zip, the marginal propensity to consume is 0.8. Investment is $60 billion, government expenditures on goods and services are $50 billion, and autonomous taxes are $60 billion. Zip has no exports and no imports.
   a. The government increases its expenditures on goods and services to $60 billion. What is the change in equilibrium expenditure?
   b. What is the value of the government expenditures multiplier?
   c. The government continues to buy $60 billion worth of goods and services and increases autonomous taxes to $70 billion. What is the change in equilibrium expenditure?
   d. What is the value of the autonomous tax multiplier?
   e. The government simultaneously increases both its expenditures on goods and services and taxes by $10 billion. What is the change in equilibrium expenditure? Why does equilibrium expenditure increase?

*3. Suppose that the price level in the economy of Zap as described in problem 1 is 100. The economy is also at full employment.
   a. If the government of Zap increases its expenditures on goods and services by $10 billion, what happens to the quantity of real GDP demanded?
   b. How does Zap's aggregate demand curve change? Draw a two-part figure that is similar to Fig. 24.12 to illustrate the change in both the *AE* curve and the *AD* curve.
   c. In the short run, does equilibrium real GDP increase by more than, less than, or the same amount as the increase in the quantity of real GDP demanded?
   d. In the long run, does equilibrium real GDP increase by more than, less than, or the same amount as the increase in the quantity of real GDP demanded?
   e. In the short run, does the price level in Zap rise, fall, or remain unchanged?
   f. In the long run, does the price level in Zap rise, fall, or remain unchanged?

4. Suppose that the price level in the economy of Zip as described in problem 2 is 100. The economy is also at full employment.
   a. If the government of Zip decreases its expenditures on goods and services by $5 billion, what happens to the quantity of real GDP demanded?
   b. How does Zip's aggregate demand curve change? Draw a two-part figure that is similar to Fig. 24.12 to illustrate the change in both the *AE* curve and the *AD* curve.
   c. In the short run, does equilibrium real GDP decrease by more than, less than, or the same amount as the increase in the quantity of real GDP demanded?
   d. In the short run, does the price level in Zip rise, fall, or remain unchanged?
   e. Why does real GDP decrease by a smaller amount than the decrease in aggregate demand?

*5. The figure shows outlays and revenues of the government of Dreamland. Potential GDP is $40 million.

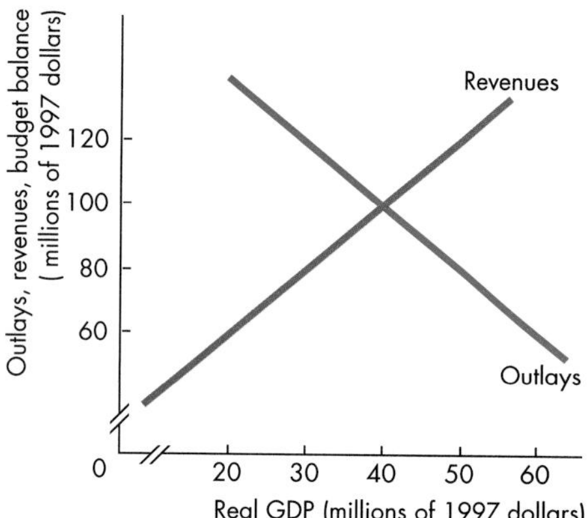

a. What is the government's budget balance if real GDP equals potential GDP?
b. Does Dreamland have a structural surplus or deficit if its real GDP is $40 million? What is the size of the structural surplus or deficit? Explain why.
c. What is the government's budget balance if real GDP is $30 million?
d. If Dreamland's real GDP is $30 million, does Dreamland have a structural surplus or deficit? What is its size? Explain why.
e. If Dreamland's real GDP is $50 million, does Dreamland have a structural surplus or deficit? What is its size? Explain why.

6. In problem 5, if Dreamland's real GDP is $50 million,
a. What is the government's budget balance?
b. Does Dreamland have a structural surplus? What is its size? Explain why.
c. What is the government's budget balance if potential GDP is $30 million?
d. If Dreamland's potential GDP is $30 million, does Dreamland have a structural surplus or deficit? What is its size? Explain why.
e. What would Dreamland's real GDP have to be for it to have neither a structural deficit or surplus nor a cyclical deficit or surplus if its potential GDP is $40 million?

CRITICAL THINKING

1. Study *Reading Between the Lines* on pp. 574–575 and then
a. Describe the overall plan for revenues and expenditures through 2008. Are government revenues and spending projected to increase as a percentage of GDP?
b. Do you think the government is planning a large enough budget surplus?
c. What do you predict would happen to aggregate demand if instead of spending, the government cut taxes to eliminate the "planning surplus"?
d. Suppose the government were to increase spending and turn its surplus into a deficit. What do you predict would be the short-run and long-run effects of such an action?

2. Thinking about the supply-side effects of the 2003 budget,
a. What would be the main effects of lower income tax rates on the level of potential GDP?
b. How would lower income taxes influence the real wage rate and the real interest rate?
c. What are the main costs of lower income taxes?

WEB EXERCISES

1. Use the link on the Parkin–Bade Web site to visit the Department of Finance and obtain data on the current federal budget. Use the information that you find, together with the fiscal policy multiplier analysis that you've learned about in this chapter, to predict the effects of the Canadian budget on real GDP and the price level. Explain reasons for your predictions.

2. Use the link on the Parkin–Bade Web site to visit Statistics Canada and obtain the most recent data you can find on the revenues, outlays, and budget surplus or deficit for Canada and for the province in which you live.
a. What are the main features of the two sets of budget data?
b. What are the main trends in the budget data?
c. Predict the effects of your province's budget on provincial GDP.

MONEY, BANKING, AND INTEREST RATES

Money Makes the World Go Around

Money, like fire and the wheel, has been around for a long time. Wampum (beads made from shells) was used as money by the First Nations of North America, and tobacco was used by early American colonists. Today, we use coins, bills, cheques, and debit and credit cards. Tomorrow, we'll use "smart cards" that keep track of spending. Are all these things money? ◆ When we deposit some coins or notes into a bank, is that still money? ◆ There are enough coins and Bank of Canada notes circulating today for every Canadian to have a wallet stuffed with more than $1,000. In addition, there is enough money deposited in banks and other financial institutions for every Canadian to have a deposit of more than $20,000. Why do we hold all this money? During 2001 and 2002, interest rates fell. What determines interest rates and what makes them fall or rise?

In this chapter, you'll study the functions of money, how banks and other financial institutions create money, and how interest rates are determined. At the end of the chapter, in *Reading Between the Lines*, we'll see how the growth in the use of debit cards and credit cards and the surprisingly small effect these electronic payment methods are having on the amount of currency we use.

After studying this chapter, you will be able to

- **Define money and describe its functions**
- **Explain the economic functions of banks and other depository institutions**
- **Describe some financial innovations that have changed the way we use money**
- **Explain how banks create money**
- **Explain what determines the demand for money**
- **Explain how interest rates are determined**
- **Explain how interest rates influence expenditure plans**

What Is Money?

WHAT DO WAMPUM, TOBACCO, AND NICKELS AND dimes have in common? Why are they all examples of money? To answer these questions, we need a definition of money. **Money** is any commodity or token that is generally acceptable as the means of payment. A **means of payment** is a method of settling a debt. When a payment has been made, there is no remaining obligation between the parties to a transaction. So what wampum, tobacco, and nickels and dimes have in common is that they have served (or still do serve) as the means of payment. But money has three other functions:

- Medium of exchange
- Unit of account
- Store of value

Medium of Exchange

A *medium of exchange* is an object that is generally accepted in exchange for goods and services. Money acts as such a medium. Without money, it would be necessary to exchange goods and services directly for other goods and services—an exchange called **barter.** For example, if you want to buy a hamburger, you offer the paperback novel you've just finished reading in exchange for it. Barter requires a *double coincidence of wants,* a situation that occurs when Erika wants to buy what Kazia wants to sell and Kazia wants to buy what Erika wants to sell. To get your hamburger, you must find someone who's selling hamburgers and who wants your paperback novel. Money guarantees that there is a double coincidence of wants because people with something to sell will always accept money in exchange for it. Money acts as a lubricant that smoothes the mechanism of exchange.

Unit of Account

A *unit of account* is an agreed measure for stating the prices of goods and services. To get the most out of your budget, you have to figure out whether seeing one more movie is worth its opportunity cost. But that cost is not dollars and cents. It is the number of ice-cream cones, cans of pop, or phone calls that you must give up. It's easy to do such calculations when all these goods have prices in terms of dollars and cents (see Table 25.1). If a movie costs $6 and a six-pack of pop costs $3, you know right away that seeing one more movie costs you 2 six-packs of pop. If jelly beans are 50¢ a pack, one more movie costs 12 packs of jelly beans. You need only one calculation to figure out the opportunity cost of any pair of goods and services.

TABLE 25.1 The Unit of Account Function of Money Simplifies Price Comparisons

Good	Price in money units	Price in units of another good
Movie	$6.00 each	2 six-packs of pop
Pop	$3.00 per six-pack	2 ice-cream cones
Ice cream	$1.50 per cone	3 packs of jelly beans
Jelly beans	50¢ per pack	2 local phone calls
Phone call	25¢ per call	1/2 pack of jelly beans

Money as a unit of account: The price of a movie is $6 and the price of a local phone call is 25¢, so the opportunity cost of a movie is 24 local phone calls ($6.00 ÷ 25¢ = 24).

No unit of account: You go to a movie theatre and learn that the price of a movie is 2 six-packs of pop. You go to a candy store and learn that a pack of jelly beans costs 2 local phone calls. But how many phone calls does seeing a movie cost you? To answer that question, you go to the convenience store and find that a six-pack of pop costs 2 ice-cream cones. Now you head for the ice-cream shop, where an ice-cream cone costs 3 packs of jelly beans. Now you get out your pocket calculator: 1 movie costs 2 six-packs of pop, or 4 ice-cream cones, or 12 packs of jelly beans, or 24 phone calls!

But imagine how troublesome it would be if your local movie theatre posted its price as 2 six-packs of pop, and if the convenience store posted the price of a six-pack of pop as 2 ice-cream cones, and if the ice-cream shop posted the price of a cone as 3 packs of jelly beans, and if the candy store priced a pack of jelly beans as 2 local phone calls! Now how much running around and calculating would you have to do to figure out how much that movie is going to cost you in terms of the pop, ice cream, jelly beans, or phone calls that you must give up to see it? You get the answer for pop right away from the sign posted at the movie theatre. But for all the other goods you'd have to visit many different stores to establish the price of each commodity in terms of another and then calculate prices in units that are relevant for your own decision. Cover up the column labelled "price in money units" in Table 25.1 and see how hard it is to figure out the number of local phone calls it costs to see one movie. It's enough to make a person swear off movies! How much simpler it is if all the prices are expressed in dollars and cents.

Store of Value

Any commodity or token that can be held and exchanged later for goods and services is called a *store of value.* Money acts as a store of value. If it did not, it would not be acceptable in exchange for goods and services. The more stable the value of a commodity or token, the better it can act as a store of value and the more useful it is as money. No store of value is completely safe. The value of a physical object—such as a house, a car, or a work of art—fluctuates over time. The values of commodities and tokens used as money also fluctuate, and when there is inflation, they persistently fall in value.

Money in Canada Today

In Canada today, money consists of

- Currency
- Deposits at banks and other financial institutions

Currency The coins and Bank of Canada notes that we use today are known as **currency.** Currency is money because the government declares it to be so. Look at a Bank of Canada note and notice the words

> "CE BILLET A COURS LÉGAL—THIS NOTE IS LEGAL TENDER."

Currency is the most convenient type of money for settling small debts and buying low-priced items.

Deposits Deposits at banks and other financial institutions are also money. Deposits are money because they can be converted into currency and because they are used to settle debts. When you write a cheque or use a debit card, you are telling your bank to transfer money from your account to the account of the person from whom you are buying. Bank deposits are the most convenient type of money for settling large debts and buying big-ticket items.

Official Measures of Money There is no unique measure of money. The two main measures used in Canada today are M1 and M2+. Figure 25.1 shows the items that make up these two measures. **M1** consists of currency held outside the banks plus demand deposits at chartered banks that are owned by individuals and businesses. M1 does *not* include currency held by banks, and it does not include currency and bank deposits owned by the government of Canada. **M2+** consists of M1 plus personal savings deposits and nonpersonal notice deposits at chartered banks plus all types of deposits at trust and mortgage loan companies, credit unions, caisses populaires, and other financial institutions.

FIGURE 25.1 Two Measures of Money

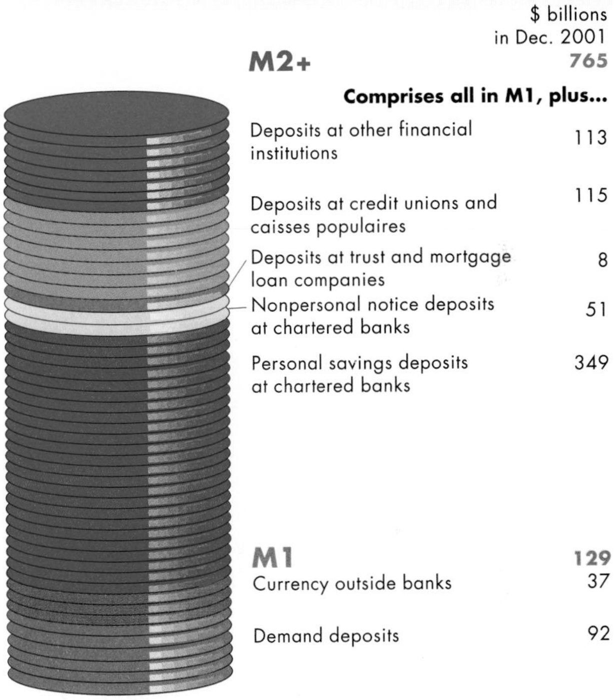

	$ billions in Dec. 2001
M2+	**765**
Comprises all in M1, plus...	
Deposits at other financial institutions	113
Deposits at credit unions and caisses populaires	115
Deposits at trust and mortgage loan companies	8
Nonpersonal notice deposits at chartered banks	51
Personal savings deposits at chartered banks	349
M1	**129**
Currency outside banks	37
Demand deposits	92

M1
- Currency held outside banks
- Demand deposits at chartered banks that are owned by individuals and businesses

M2+
- M1
- Personal savings deposits at chartered banks
- Nonpersonal notice deposits at chartered banks
- Deposits at trust and mortgage loan companies
- Deposits at credit unions and caisses populaires
- Deposits at other financial institutions

Source: Bank of Canada, *Banking and Financial Statistics,* table E1.

Are M1 and M2+ Really Money? Money is the means of payment. So the test of whether an item is money is whether it serves as a means of payment. Currency passes the test. But what about deposits? Deposit accounts on which cheques can be written are money because they can be transferred from one person to another by writing a cheque. Transferring a deposit is equivalent to handing over currency. Because M1 consists of currency plus demand deposits and each of these is a means of payment, M1 *is money.*

But what about M2+? Some of the savings deposits in M2+ are just as much a means of payment as the demand deposits in M1. You can use the automated teller machine (ATM) at the grocery store checkout or gas station and transfer funds directly from your savings account to pay for your purchase. But other savings deposits are not means of payment. They are known as *liquid assets.* **Liquidity** is the property of being instantly convertible into a means of payment with little loss in value. Because most of the deposits in M2+ are quickly and easily converted into currency or demand deposits, they are operationally similar to M1, but they are not means of payment.

Deposits Are Money but Cheques Are Not In defining money, we include, along with currency, deposits at banks and other financial institutions. But we do not count the cheques that people write as money. Why are deposits money and cheques not?

To see why deposits are money but cheques are not, think about what happens when Colleen buys some roller blades for $200 from Rocky's Rollers. When Colleen goes to Rocky's shop, she has $500 in her deposit account at the Laser Bank. Rocky has $1,000 in his deposit account—at the same bank, as it happens. The total deposits of these two people are $1,500. Colleen writes a cheque for $200. Rocky takes the cheque to the bank and deposits it. Rocky's bank balance rises from $1,000 to $1,200 and Colleen's balance falls from $500 to $300. The total deposits of Colleen and Rocky are still the same as before: $1,500. Rocky now has $200 more and Colleen has $200 less.

This transaction has transferred money from Colleen to Rocky. The cheque itself was never money. There wasn't an extra $200 worth of money while the cheque was in circulation. The cheque instructs the bank to transfer money from Colleen to Rocky.

If Colleen and Rocky use different banks, there is an extra step. Rocky's bank credits the cheque to Rocky's account and then takes the cheque to a cheque-clearing centre. The cheque is then sent to Colleen's bank, which pays Rocky's bank $200 and debits Colleen's account $200. This process can take a few days, but the principles are the same as when two people use the same bank.

Debit Cards Are Not Money So cheques are not money. But what about debit cards? Isn't presenting a debit card to pay for your roller blades the same thing as using money? Why aren't debit cards counted as part of the quantity of money?

A debit card works just like a cheque, which, as you've seen, is not money. A debit card is like an electronic cheque. When you use a debit card, money leaves your bank account and is deposited into the account of the person from whom you are buying at the instant of the transaction.

Credit Cards Are Not Money Sometimes you need ID and you pull out your driver's licence. Your credit card is another type of ID card—a special ID card that enables you to take a loan at the instant you buy something. When you sign a credit card sales slip, you are saying: "I agree to pay for these goods when the credit card company bills me." Once you get your statement from the credit card company, you must make the minimum payment due (or clear your balance). To make that payment you need money—you need to have currency or a bank deposit to pay the credit card company. So although you use a credit card when you buy something, the credit card is not the *means of payment* and it is not money.

REVIEW QUIZ

1 What makes something money? What functions does money perform? Why do you think packs of chewing gum don't serve as money?
2 What problems arise when a commodity is used as money?
3 What are the main components of money in Canada today?
4 What are two official measures of money in Canada? Are all the measures really money?
5 Why are cheques, debit cards, and credit cards not money?

We've seen that the main component of money in Canada is deposits at banks and other depository institutions. Let's take a closer look at these institutions.

Depository Institutions

A firm that takes deposits from households and firms and makes loans to other households and firms is called a **depository institution**. The deposits of three types of depository institution make up the nation's money:

- Chartered banks
- Credit unions and caisses populaires
- Trust and mortgage loan companies

Chartered Banks

A **chartered bank** is a private firm, chartered under the Bank Act of 1992 to receive deposits and make loans. In 2001, there were 11 Canadian-owned banks and 43 foreign-owned banks chartered by Parliament. In 2001, total deposits at chartered banks were $617 billion. A chartered bank's business is summarized in its balance sheet.

A bank's *balance sheet* lists its assets, liabilities, and net worth. *Assets* are what the bank *owns*, *liabilities* are what the bank *owes*, and *net worth*, which is equal to assets minus liabilities, is the value of the bank to its stockholders—its owners. A bank's balance sheet is described by the equation

$$\text{Liabilities} + \text{Net worth} = \text{Assets.}$$

Among a bank's liabilities are the deposits that are part of the nation's money. Your deposit at the bank is a liability to your bank (and an asset to you) because the bank must repay your deposit (and sometimes interest on it too) whenever you decide to take your money out of the bank.

Profit and Prudence: A Balancing Act The aim of a bank is to maximize the net worth of its stockholders. To achieve this objective, the interest rate at which a bank lends exceeds the interest rate at which it borrows. But a bank must perform a delicate balancing act. Lending is risky, and the more a bank ties up its deposits in high-risk, high-interest rate loans, the bigger is its chance of not being able to repay its depositors. And if depositors perceive a high risk of not being repaid, they withdraw their funds and create a crisis for the bank. So a bank must be prudent in the way it uses its deposits, balancing security for the depositors against profit for its stockholders.

Reserves and Loans To achieve security for its depositors, a bank divides its funds into two parts: reserves and loans. **Reserves** are cash in a bank's vault plus its deposits at the Bank of Canada. (We'll study the Bank of Canada in Chapter 26.) The cash in a bank's vaults is a reserve to meet depositors' demand for currency. The bank replenishes the ATM every time you and your friends raid it for cash for a midnight pizza. The account of a bank at the Bank of Canada is similar to your own bank account. Chartered banks use these accounts to receive and make payments. A chartered bank deposits cash into or draws cash out of its account at the Bank of Canada and writes cheques on that account to settle debts with other banks.

If a bank kept all its deposits as reserves, it wouldn't make any profit. In fact, it keeps only a small fraction of its funds in reserves and lends the rest. A bank has three types of assets:

1. *Liquid assets* are Canadian government Treasury bills and commercial bills. These assets are the banks' first line of defence if they need cash. They can be sold and instantly converted into cash with virtually no risk of loss. Because liquid assets are virtually risk-free, they have a low interest rate.
2. *Investment securities* are longer-term Canadian government bonds and other bonds. These assets can be sold quickly and converted into cash but at prices that fluctuate. Because their prices fluctuate, these assets are riskier than liquid assets but they have a higher interest rate.
3. *Loans* are commitments of fixed amounts of money for agreed-upon periods of time. Most banks' loans are made to corporations to finance the purchase of capital equipment and inventories and to households—personal loans—to finance purchases of consumer durable goods, such as cars or boats. The outstanding balances on credit card accounts are also bank loans. Loans are the riskiest assets of a bank because they cannot be converted into cash until they are due to be repaid. And some borrowers default and never repay. Because they are the riskiest of a bank's assets, loans also carry the highest interest rate.

Chartered bank deposits are one component of the nation's money. But other depository institutions also take deposits that form part—an increasing part—of the nation's money. The largest of these other depository institutions are the credit unions and caisses populaires.

Credit Unions and Caisses Populaires

A **credit union** is a cooperative organization that operates under the Co-operative Credit Association Act of 1992 and that receives deposits from and makes loans to its members. A caisse populaire is a similar type of institution that operates in Quebec. In 2001, the deposits in these institutions were $115 billion.

Trust and Mortgage Loan Companies

A **trust and mortgage loan company** is a privately owned depository institution that operates under the Trust and Loan Companies Act of 1992. It receives deposits and makes loans and in addition acts as a trustee for pension funds and for estates. In 2001, deposits in trust and mortgage loan companies that are included in M2+ were $8 billion.

Financial Legislation

Canada has historically made a sharp legal distinction between banks and other depository institutions. But the economic functions of all depository institutions have grown increasingly similar. This fact is recognized in laws governing these institutions that became effective in 1992. Today, the deposits in other depository institutions approach the same magnitude as those of the chartered banks. For example, the deposits in depository institutions such as trust and mortgage loan companies, credit unions, and caisses populaires were 31 percent of the M2+ definition of money in 1970 but 37 percent in 2001.

Paul Martin's Reform Proposal Former Finance Minister Paul Martin has proposed a more competitive framework for Canada's depository institutions, foreign banks, and insurance companies. His proposal, outlined in *Reforming Canada's Financial Services Sector: A Framework for the Future,* seeks to promote a more competitive and less regulated Canadian banking and financial system.

If the proposal (or something like it) made headway, chartered banks would be able to form joint ventures and strategic alliances, broaden their investments, and face more streamlined regulation. And the process for reviewing bank mergers would become more open. But chartered banks would face tougher competition from trust companies, credit unions, and foreign banks.

The Economic Functions of Depository Institutions

All depository institutions make a profit from the spread between the interest rate they pay on deposits and the interest rate at which they lend. Why can depository institutions get deposits at a low interest rate and lend at a higher one? What services do they perform that makes their depositors willing to put up with a low interest rate and their borrowers willing to pay a higher one?

Depository institutions provide four main services for which people are willing to pay:

- Creating liquidity
- Minimizing the cost of borrowing
- Minimizing the cost of monitoring borrowers
- Pooling risk

Creating Liquidity Depository institutions create liquidity. *Liquid* assets are those that are easily and with certainty convertible into money. Some of the liabilities of depository institutions are themselves money; others are highly liquid assets.

Depository institutions create liquidity by borrowing short and lending long. Borrowing short means taking deposits but standing ready to repay them on short notice (and even on no notice in the case of demand deposits). Lending long means making loan commitments for a prearranged, and often quite long, period of time. For example, when a person makes a deposit with a trust company, that deposit can be withdrawn at any time. But the trust company makes a lending commitment for perhaps more than 20 years to a homebuyer.

Minimizing the Cost of Borrowing Finding someone from whom to borrow can be a costly business. Imagine how troublesome it would be if there were no depository institutions. A firm that was looking for $1 million to buy a new production plant would probably have to hunt around for several dozen people from whom to borrow in order to acquire enough funds for its capital project. Depository institutions lower those costs. The firm that needs $1 million can go to a single depository institution to obtain those funds. The depository institution has to borrow from a large number of people, but it's not doing that just for this one firm and the $1 million that it wants to borrow. The depository institution can establish an organization that is capable of raising funds from a large number of depositors and can spread the cost of this activity over a large number of borrowers.

Minimizing the Cost of Monitoring Borrowers Lending money is a risky business. There is always a danger that the borrower may not repay. Firms are the biggest borrowers. They borrow to invest in projects that they hope will return a profit but sometimes those hopes are not fulfilled. Monitoring the activities of a borrower and ensuring that the best possible decisions are being taken to make a profit and to avoid a loss are costly and specialized activities. Imagine how costly it would be if each household that lent money to a firm had to incur the costs of monitoring that firm directly. By depositing funds with a depository institution, households avoid those costs. The depository institution performs the monitoring activity by using specialized resources that have a much lower cost than what each household would incur if it had to undertake the activity individually.

Pooling Risk As we noted above, lending money is risky. There is always a chance of not being repaid—of default. Lending to a large number of different individuals can reduce the risk of default. In such a situation, if one person defaults on a loan, it is a nuisance but not a disaster. In contrast, if only one person borrows and that person defaults on the loan, the entire loan is a write-off. Depository institutions enable people to pool risk in an efficient way. Thousands of people lend money to any one depository institution, and, in turn, the depository institution re-lends the money to hundreds, perhaps thousands, of individuals and firms. If any one firm defaults on its loan, that default is spread across all the depositors and no individual depositor is left exposed to a high degree of risk.

REVIEW QUIZ

1. What are Canada's main depository institutions?
2. Why don't banks keep all the money that people place on deposit in their vaults?
3. What are the main economic functions of depository institutions?
4. How do depository institutions create liquidity?
5. How do depository institutions pool risk?

How Banks Create Money

BANKS CREATE MONEY.[1] BUT THIS DOESN'T MEAN that they have smoke-filled back rooms in which counterfeiters are busily working. Remember, most money is deposits, not currency. What banks create is deposits, and they do so by making loans. But the amount of deposits they can create is limited by their reserves.

Reserves: Actual and Desired

We've seen that banks don't have \$100 in bills for every \$100 that people have deposited with them. In fact, a typical bank today has reserves of \$1.90 for every \$100 of deposits. No need for panic. These reserve levels are adequate for ordinary business needs.

The fraction of a bank's total deposits that are held in reserves is called the **reserve ratio.** The reserve ratio changes when a bank's customers make a deposit or withdrawal. Making a deposit increases the reserve ratio, and making a withdrawal decreases the reserve ratio.

The **desired reserve ratio** is the ratio of reserves to deposits that banks wish to hold. A bank's *desired reserves* are equal to its deposits multiplied by the desired reserve ratio. Actual reserves minus desired reserves are **excess reserves.** Whenever banks have excess reserves, they are able to create money.

To see how banks create money, we'll look at two model banking systems. In the first, there is only one bank; in the second, there are many banks.

Creating Deposits by Making Loans in a One-Bank Economy

In the model banking system that we'll study first, there is only one bank, and its desired reserve ratio is 25 percent. That is, for each dollar deposited, the bank keeps 25¢ in reserves and lends the rest. The balance sheet of the One-and-Only Bank is shown in Fig. 25.2(a). On January 1, its deposits are \$400 million and its reserves are 25 percent of this amount—\$100 million. Its loans are equal to deposits minus reserves and are \$300 million.

[1] In this section, we'll use the term *bank* to refer to any type of depository institution whose deposits are money—chartered banks, credit unions, caisses populaires, and trust and mortgage loan companies.

The story begins when Darth Vader retires and begins his quiet life in Winnipeg. He has been holding all his money in currency and has $1 million in Canadian money. On January 2, Darth puts his $1 million on deposit at the One-and-Only Bank. On the day that Darth makes his deposit, the One-and-Only Bank's balance sheet changes. The new situation is shown in Fig. 25.2(b). The bank now has $101 million in reserves and $401 million in deposits. It still has loans of $300 million.

FIGURE 25.2 Creating Money at the One-and-Only Bank

(a) Balance sheet on January 1

Assets (millions of dollars)		Liabilities (millions of dollars)	
Reserves	$100	Deposits	$400
Loans	$300		
Total	$400	Total	$400

(b) Balance sheet on January 2

Assets (millions of dollars)		Liabilities (millions of dollars)	
Reserves	$101	Deposits	$401
Loans	$300		
Total	$401	Total	$401

(c) Balance sheet on January 3

Assets (millions of dollars)		Liabilities (millions of dollars)	
Reserves	$101	Deposits	$404
Loans	$303		
Total	$404	Total	$404

In part (a) the One-and-Only Bank has deposits of $400 million, loans of $300 million, and reserves of $100 million. The bank's desired reserve ratio is 25 percent. When the bank receives a deposit of $1 million (part b), it has excess reserves. It lends $3 million and creates a further $3 million of deposits. Deposits increase by $3 million, and loans increase by $3 million (in part c). The bank has no excess reserves.

The bank now has *excess reserves.* With reserves of $101 million and a desired reserve ratio of 25 percent, the bank would like to have deposits of $404 million. Because the One-and-Only Bank is the only bank, the manager knows that the reserves will remain at $101 million. That is, she knows that when she makes a loan and creates a deposit, the amount lent remains on deposit at the One-and-Only Bank. She knows, for example, that all the suppliers of Sky's-the-Limit Construction are also depositors of One-and-Only. So she knows that if she makes the loan that Sky's-the-Limit has just requested, the deposit she creates will never leave One-and-Only. When Sky's-the-Limit uses part of its new loan to pay $100,000 to I-Dig-It Excavating Company for some excavations, the One-and-Only Bank simply moves the funds from Sky's-the-Limit's account to I-Dig-It's account.

So on January 3, the manager of One-and-Only calls Sky's-the-Limit's accountant and offers to lend the maximum that she can. How much does she lend? She lends $3 million. By lending $3 million, One-and-Only's balance sheet changes to the one shown in Fig. 25.2(c). Loans increase by $3 million to $303 million. The loan shows up in Sky's-the-Limit's deposit initially, and total deposits increase to $404 million—$400 million plus Darth Vader's deposit of $1 million plus the newly created deposit of $3 million. The bank now has no excess reserves and has reached the limit of its ability to create money.

The Deposit Multiplier

The **deposit multiplier** is the amount by which an increase in bank reserves is multiplied to calculate the increase in bank deposits. That is,

$$\text{Deposit multiplier} = \frac{\text{Change in deposits}}{\text{Change in reserves}}.$$

In the example we've just worked through, the deposit multiplier is 4. The $1 million increase in reserves created a $4 million increase in deposits.

The deposit multiplier is linked to the desired reserve ratio by the following equation:

$$\text{Deposit multiplier} = \frac{1}{\text{Desired reserve ratio}}.$$

In the example, the desired reserve ratio is 25 percent, or 0.25. That is,

$$\text{Deposit multiplier} = \frac{1}{0.25}$$
$$= 4.$$

Creating Deposits by Making Loans with Many Banks

If you told the loans officer at your own bank that she creates money, she wouldn't believe you. Bankers see themselves as lending the money they receive from others, not creating money. But in fact, even though each bank lends only what it receives, the banking *system* creates money. To see how, let's look at another example.

Figure 25.3 is going to keep track of what is happening in the process of money creation by a banking system in which each bank has a desired reserve ratio of 25 percent. The process begins when Art decides to decrease his currency holding and put $100,000 on deposit. Now Art's bank has $100,000 of new deposits and $100,000 of additional reserves. With a desired reserve ratio of 25 percent, the bank keeps $25,000 in reserves and lends $75,000 to Amy. Amy writes a cheque for $75,000 to buy a copy-shop franchise from Barb. At this point, Art's bank has a new deposit of $100,000, new loans of $75,000, and new reserves of $25,000. You can see this situation in Fig. 25.3 as the first row of the "running tally."

For Art's bank, that is the end of the story. But it's not the end of the story for the entire banking system. Barb deposits her cheque for $75,000 in another bank and its deposits and reserves increase by $75,000. This bank keeps 25 percent of its increase in deposits ($18,750) in reserves and lends $56,250 to Bob. And Bob writes a cheque to Carl to pay off a business loan. The current state of play is seen in the second row of the running tally in Fig. 25.3. Now total bank reserves have increased by $43,750 ($25,000 plus $18,750), total loans have increased by $131,250 ($75,000 plus $56,250), and total deposits have increased by $175,000 ($100,000 plus $75,000).

When Carl takes his cheque to his bank, its deposits and reserves increase by $56,250, $14,063 of which it keeps in reserve and $42,187 of which it lends. This process continues until there are no excess reserves in the banking system. But the process takes a lot of further steps. One additional step is shown in Fig. 25.3. The figure also shows the final tallies—reserves increase by $100,000, loans increase by $300,000, and deposits increase by $400,000.

The sequence in Fig. 25.3 is the first four stages of the process. To figure out the entire process, look closely at the numbers in the figure. At each stage, the loan is 75 percent (0.75) of the previous loan and the deposit is 0.75 of the previous deposit. Call that proportion L ($L = 0.75$). The complete sequence is

$$1 + L + L^2 + L^3 + \ldots .$$

Remember, L is a fraction, so at each stage in this sequence the amount of new loans gets smaller. The total number of loans made at the end of the process is the above sum, which is[2]

$$\frac{1}{(1 - L)}.$$

If we use the numbers from the example, the total increase in deposits is

$$\$100{,}000 + 75{,}000 + 56{,}250 + 42{,}187 + \ldots$$
$$= \$100{,}000\ (1 + 0.75 + 0.5625 + 0.42187 + \ldots)$$
$$= \$100{,}000\ (1 + 0.75 + 0.75^2 + 0.75^3 + \ldots)$$
$$= \$100{,}000 \times \frac{1}{(1 - 0.75)}$$
$$= \$100{,}000 \times \frac{1}{(0.25)}$$
$$= \$100{,}000 \times 4$$
$$= \$400{,}000$$

By using the same method, you can check that the totals for reserves and loans are the ones shown in Fig. 25.3.

[2] Both here and in the expenditure multiplier process in Chapter 23, the sequence of values is called a convergent geometric series. To find the sum of a series such as this, begin by calling the sum S. Then write the sum as

$$S = 1 + L + L^2 + L^3 + \ldots .$$

Multiply by L to get,

$$LS = L + L^2 + L^3 + \ldots$$

and then subtract the second equation from the first to get

$$S(1 - L) = 1$$

or

$$S = \frac{1}{(1 - L)}.$$

FIGURE 25.3 The Multiple Creation of Bank Deposits

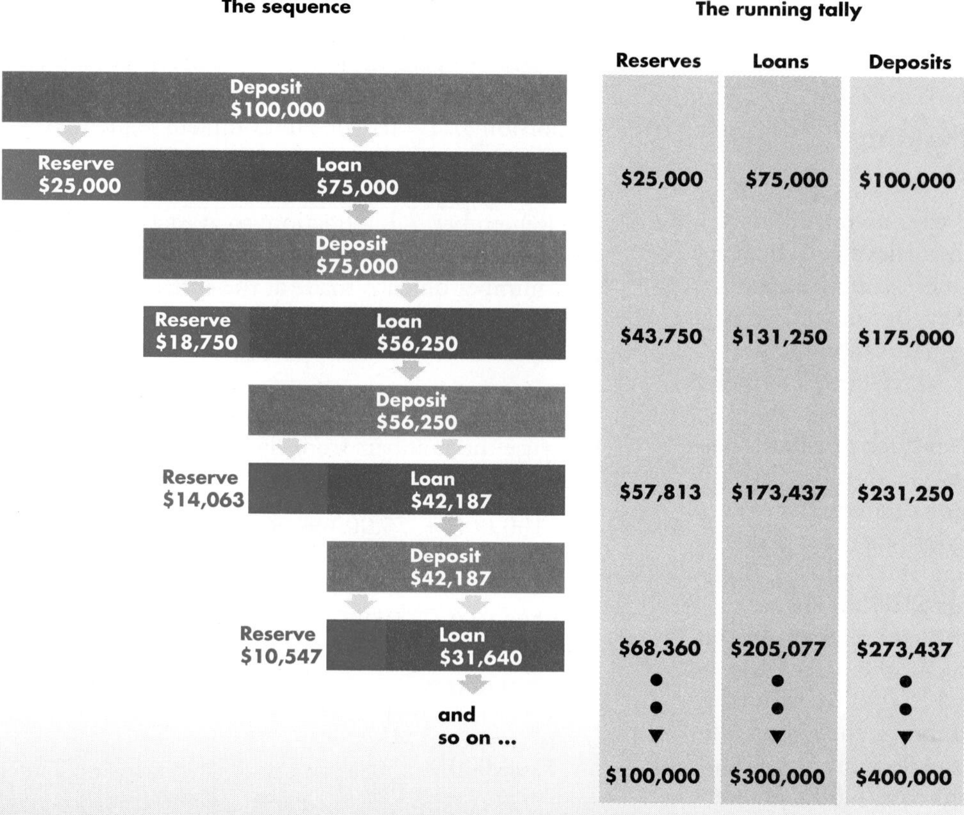

When a bank receives a deposit, it keeps 25 percent of it in reserves and lends the other 75 percent. The amount lent becomes a new deposit at another bank. The next bank in the sequence keeps 25 percent and lends 75 percent, and the process continues until the banking system has created enough deposits to eliminate its excess reserves. The running tally tells us the total amounts of deposits and loans created at each stage. At the end of the process, an additional $100,000 of reserves creates an additional $400,000 of deposits.

So even though each bank lends only part of the money it receives, the banking system as a whole creates money by making loans. The amount created is exactly the same in a multibank system as in a one-bank system.

The Deposit Multiplier in Canada The deposit multiplier in Canada works like the deposit multiplier we've just worked out for a model economy. But the deposit multiplier in Canada differs from the one we've just calculated for two reasons. First, the desired reserve ratio of Canadian banks is smaller than the 25 percent we used here. Second, not all the loans made by banks return to them in the form of reserves. Some of the loans remain outside the banks and are held as currency. The smaller desired reserve ratio makes the Canadian multiplier larger than the multiplier in the above example. But the other factor makes the Canadian multiplier smaller.

REVIEW QUIZ

1. How do banks create deposits by making loans, and what are the factors that limit the amount of deposits and loans that banks can create?
2. A bank manager tells you that he doesn't create money. He just lends the money that people deposit in the bank. How do you explain to him that he's wrong and that he does create money?
3. If banks receive new deposits of $100 million, what determines the total change in deposits that the banking system can create?

We've now seen how banks create money. Money has a powerful influence on the economy and this influence begins with interest rates. To understand how money influences interest rates, we must study the demand for money.

The Demand for Money

THE AMOUNT OF MONEY WE RECEIVE EACH WEEK in payment for our labour is income—a flow. The amount of money that we hold in our wallet or in a deposit account at the bank is an inventory—a stock. There is no limit to how much income we would like to receive each week. But there is a limit to how big an inventory of money each of us would like to hold on to and not spend.

The Influences on Money Holding

The quantity of money that people choose to hold depends on four main factors:

- The price level
- The interest rate
- Real GDP
- Financial innovation

The Price Level The quantity of money measured in dollars is *nominal money*. The quantity of nominal money demanded is proportional to the price level, other things remaining the same. That is, if the price level rises by 10 percent, people hold 10 percent more nominal money than before, other things remaining the same. If you hold $20 to buy your weekly movies and pop, you will increase your money holding to $22 if the prices of movies and pop—and your wage rate—increase by 10 percent.

The quantity of money measured in constant dollars (for example, in 1997 dollars) is called *real money*. Real money is equal to nominal money divided by the price level. It is the quantity of money measured in terms of what it will buy. In the above example, when the price level rises by 10 percent and you increase the amount of money that you hold by 10 percent, you keep your *real* money constant. Your $22 at the new price level buys the same quantity of goods and is the same quantity of *real money* as your $20 at the original price level. The quantity of real money held does not depend on the price level.

The Interest Rate A fundamental principle of economics is that as the opportunity cost of something increases, people try to find substitutes for it. Money is no exception. The higher the opportunity cost of holding money, other things remaining the same, the smaller is the quantity of real money demanded. But what is the opportunity cost of holding money? It is the interest rate that you must forgo on other assets that you could hold instead of money minus the interest rate that you can earn by holding money.

The interest rate that you earn on currency and demand deposits is zero. So the opportunity cost of holding these items is the interest rate on other assets such as a savings bond or Treasury bill. By holding money instead, you forgo the interest that you otherwise would have received. This forgone interest is the opportunity cost of holding money.

Money loses value because of inflation. So why isn't the inflation rate part of the cost of holding money? It is: Other things remaining the same, the higher the expected inflation rate, the higher are all interest rates and the higher, therefore, is the opportunity cost of holding money. The forces that make the interest rate change to reflect changes in the expected inflation rate are described in Chapter 28, pp. 666–667.)

Real GDP The quantity of money that households and firms plan to hold depends on the amount they are spending, and the quantity of money demanded in the economy as a whole depends on aggregate expenditure—real GDP.

Again, suppose that you hold an average of $20 to finance your weekly purchases of movies and pop. Now imagine that the prices of these goods and of all other goods remain constant but that your income increases. As a consequence you now spend more, and you keep a larger amount of money on hand to finance your higher volume of expenditure.

Financial Innovation Technological change and the arrival of new financial products—called **financial innovation**—change the quantity of money held. The major financial innovations are the widespread use of

1. Daily interest deposits
2. Automatic transfers between demand deposits and savings deposits
3. Automatic teller machines
4. Credit cards and debit cards

These innovations have occurred because the development of computing power has lowered the cost of calculations and record keeping.

We summarize the effects of the influences on money holding by using a demand for money curve.

The Demand for Money Curve

The **demand for money curve** is the relationship between the quantity of real money demanded and the interest rate when all other influences on the amount of money that people wish to hold remain the same.

Figure 25.4 shows a demand for money curve, *MD*. When the interest rate rises, everything else remaining the same, the opportunity cost of holding money rises and the quantity of real money demanded decreases—there is a movement along the demand for money curve. Similarly, when the interest rate falls, the opportunity cost of holding money falls, and the quantity of real money demanded increases—there is a movement down along the demand for money curve.

When any influence on the amount of money that people plan to hold changes, there is a change in the demand for money and the demand for money curve shifts. Let's study these shifts.

FIGURE 25.4 The Demand for Money

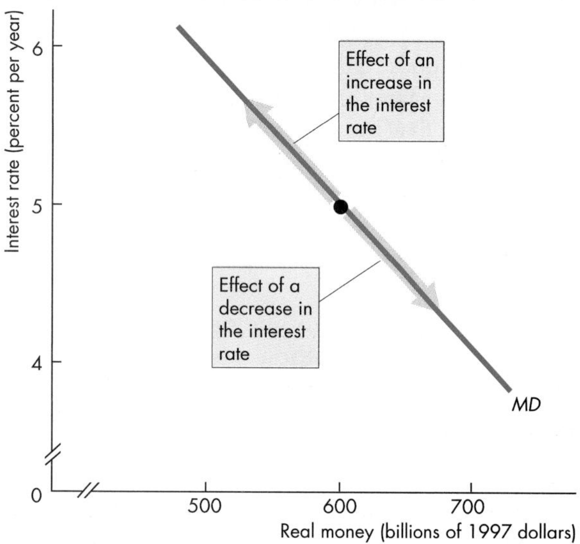

The demand for money curve, *MD*, shows the relationship between the quantity of real money that people plan to hold and the interest rate, other things remaining the same. The interest rate is the opportunity cost of holding money. A change in the interest rate brings a movement along the demand curve.

Shifts in the Demand for Money Curve

A change in real GDP or financial innovation changes the demand for money and shifts the demand for money curve. Figure 25.5 illustrates the change in the demand for money. A decrease in real GDP decreases the demand for money and shifts the demand curve leftward from MD_0 to MD_1. An increase in real GDP has the opposite effect. It increases the demand for money and shifts the demand curve rightward from MD_0 to MD_2.

The influence of financial innovation on the demand for money curve is more complicated. It might increase the demand for some types of deposits, decrease the demand for others, and decrease the demand for currency.

We'll look at the effects of changes in real GDP and financial innovation by studying the demand for money in Canada.

FIGURE 25.5 Changes in the Demand for Money

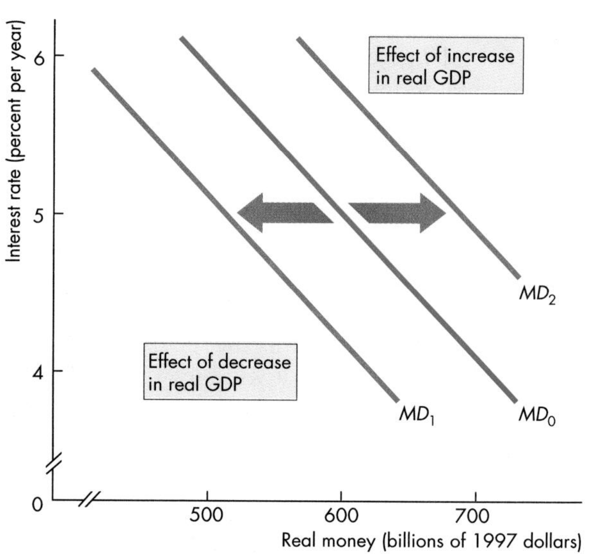

A decrease in real GDP decreases the demand for money. The demand curve shifts leftward from MD_0 to MD_1. An increase in real GDP increases the demand for money. The demand curve shifts rightward from MD_0 to MD_2. Financial innovation decreases the demand for some forms of money and increases the demand for other forms of money.

The Demand for Money in Canada

Figure 25.6 shows the relationship between the interest rate and the quantity of real money demanded in Canada between 1971 and 2001. Each dot shows the interest rate and the amount of real money held in a given year. In part (a), the measure of money is M1 and in part (b), it is M2+. In 1971, the demand for M1 (in part a) was MD_{71}. During the 1970s, real GDP increased by $200 billion, and this increase in real GDP increased the demand for M1 and shifted the demand for M1 curve rightward to MD_{81}. During the 1980s, real GDP increased by $150 billion, but the demand for M1 did not change. The reason is that during the 1980s the increased use of credit cards decreased the demand for M1. The increase in real GDP increased the demand for M1 and financial innovation decreased the demand for M1, so during the 1980s, the demand for M1 did not change. During the 1990s, real GDP increased by $280 billion and the demand for M1 increased again. The demand for M1 curve shifted rightward to MD_{01}.

In 1971, the demand for M2+ (in part b) was MD_{71}. The $200 billion increase in real GDP that occurred during the 1970s increased the demand for M2+ and the demand curve shifted rightward to MD_{81}. The $150 billion increase in real GDP that occurred during the 1980s increased the demand for M2+ and the demand curve shifted rightward. The further $280 billion increase in real GDP that occurred during the 1990s increased the demand for

FIGURE 25.6 The Demand for Money in Canada

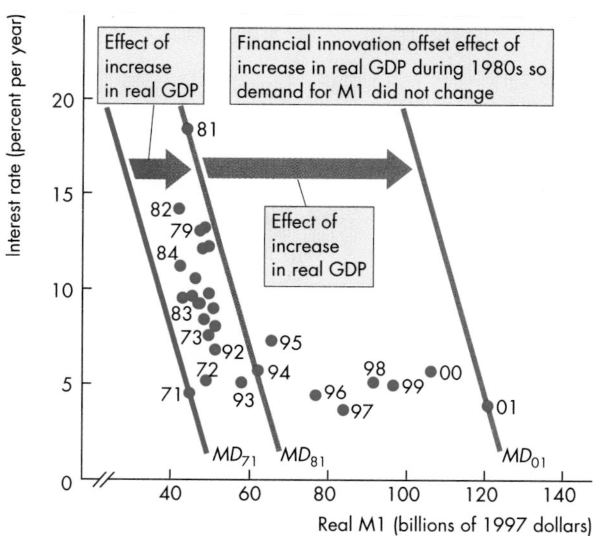

(a) Demand for M1

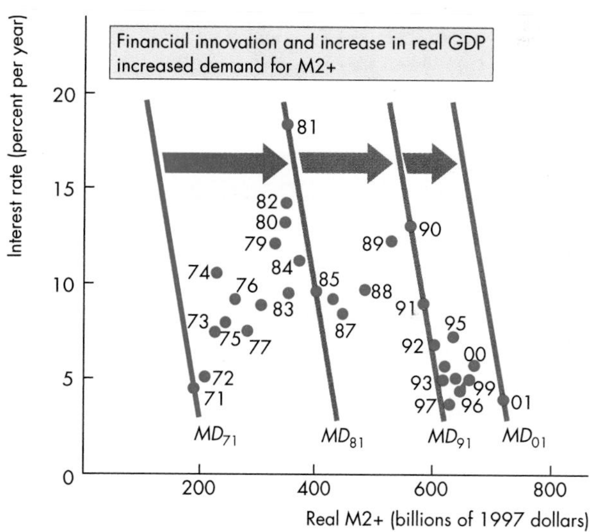

(b) Demand for M2+

The dots show the quantity of real money and the interest rate in each year between 1971 and 2001. In 1971, the demand for M1 was MD_{71} in part (a). The demand for M1 increased during the 1970s because real GDP grew and the demand curve shifted rightward to MD_{81}. The demand for M1 did not increase during the 1980s because financial innovation (mainly the spread of the use of credit cards) offset the effects of real GDP growth. The demand for M1 increased again during the 1990s.

In 1971, the demand for M2+ curve was MD_{71} in part (b). The growth of real GDP increased the demand for M2+ and by 1981 the demand curve had shifted rightward to MD_{81}. Real GDP growth and the development of interest-bearing accounts with cheque facilities further increased the demand for M2+ during the 1990s and the demand for M2+ curve shifted rightward to MD_{01}.

Source: Bank of Canada, *Banking and Financial Statistics*, tables E1 and F1, and authors' calculations and assumptions.

M2+ yet again. By 2001, the demand curve for M2+ had shifted rightward to MD_{01}.

You can see by comparing the two parts of Fig. 25.6 that the financial innovation that decreased the demand for M1 during the 1980s did not slow the growth of M2+. Because M1 is a component of M2+, the increased use of credit cards had the same effect on M2+ as it did on M1. But the development of new types of savings deposits with cheque facilities and the payment of more competitive interest rates on savings accounts increased the demand for M2+.

The opportunity cost of holding money is the interest forgone by not holding some other type of asset. But what is forgone depends partly on the interest that is paid on money itself. The interest rate on currency and demand deposits is zero. So for these components of money, the opportunity cost of holding money is the interest rate on non-money assets. But savings deposits and other types of deposits that are included in M2+ earn interest. So the opportunity cost of holding these forms of money is the interest rate on non-money assets minus the interest rate on these deposits.

REVIEW QUIZ

1. What are the main influences on the quantity of real money that people and businesses plan to hold?
2. What does the demand for money curve show?
3. How does an increase in the interest rate change the quantity of money demanded, and how would you use the demand for money curve to show the effects?
4. How does an increase in real GDP change the demand for money, and how would you use the demand for money curve to show the effects?
5. How have financial innovations changed the demand for M1 and the demand for M2+?

We now know what determines the demand for money. And we've seen that a key factor is the interest rate—the opportunity cost of holding money. But what determines the interest rate? Let's find out.

Interest Rate Determination

AN INTEREST RATE IS THE PERCENTAGE YIELD ON a financial security such as a *bond* or a *stock*. The **interest rate** is the amount received by a lender and paid by a borrower expressed as a percentage of the amount of the loan.

A bond is a promise to make a sequence of future payments. There are many different possible sequences but the simplest one is the case of a bond called a perpetuity. A *perpetuity* is a bond that promises to pay a specified fixed amount of money each year forever. The issuer of such a bond will never buy the bond back (redeem it); the bond will remain outstanding forever and will earn a fixed dollar payment each year. Because the payment each year is a fixed dollar amount, the interest rate on a bond varies as the price of the bond varies. In the case of a perpetuity, the formula that links the interest rate to the price of the bond is a particularly simple one. That formula is

$$\text{Interest rate} = \frac{\text{Dollar payment per year}}{\text{Price of bond}} \times 100.$$

This formula states that the higher the price of a bond, other things remaining the same, the lower is the interest rate. An example will make this relationship clear. Suppose the government of Canada sells a bond that promises to pay $10 a year. If the price of the bond is $100, the interest rate is 10 percent a year—$10 is 10 percent of $100. If the price of the bond is $50, the interest rate is 20 percent a year—$10 is 20 percent of $50. If the price of the bond is $200, the interest rate is 5 percent a year—$10 is 5 percent of $200.

You've just seen the link between the price of a bond and the interest rate. Because of this link, fluctuations in the interest rate bring fluctuations in the price of a bond. People try to anticipate these fluctuations and avoid holding bonds when they expect the price of a bond to fall. But they spread their risks. To do so, they divide their wealth between bonds (and other interest-bearing financial assets) and money, and the amount they hold as money depends on the interest rate. We can study the forces that determine the interest rate either in the market for bonds or the market for money. Because the Bank of Canada can influence the quantity of *money* (which we study in Chapter 26), we focus on the market for money.

Money Market Equilibrium

The supply of and the demand for money determine the interest rate. The actions of the Bank of Canada and the banking system determine the quantity of money supplied. On any given day, the quantity of money supplied is fixed. The quantity of *real* money supplied is equal to the nominal quantity supplied divided by the price level. At a given moment in time, there is a particular price level, and so the quantity of real money supplied is also a fixed amount. In Fig. 25.7, the quantity of real money supplied is $600 billion and the vertical line labelled *MS* is the supply of money curve.

On any given day, all the influences on the demand for money except for the interest rate are constant. But the lower the interest rate, the greater is the quantity of money demanded. Figure 25.7 shows a demand for money curve, *MD*.

FIGURE 25.7 Money Market Equilibrium

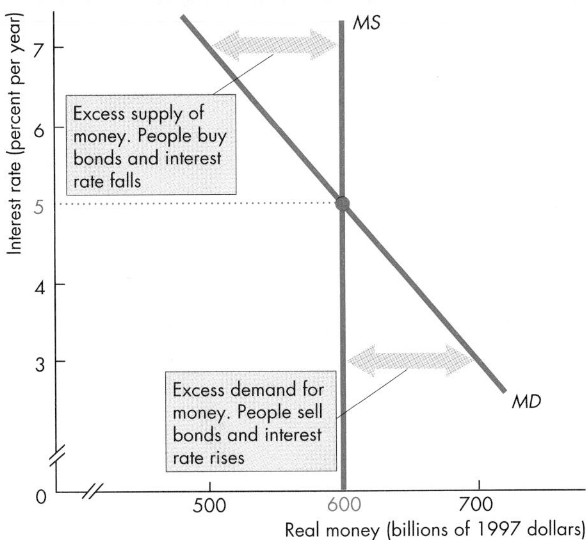

Money market equilibrium occurs when the interest rate has adjusted to make the quantity of money demanded equal to the quantity supplied. Here, equilibrium occurs at an interest rate of 5 percent a year. At interest rates above 5 percent a year, the quantity of money demanded is less than the quantity supplied, so people buy bonds, and the interest rate falls. At interest rates below 5 percent a year, the quantity of real money demanded exceeds the quantity supplied, so people sell bonds and the interest rate rises. Only at 5 percent a year is the quantity of real money in existence willingly held.

Equilibrium When the quantity of money supplied equals the quantity of money demanded, the money market is in equilibrium. Figure 25.7 illustrates equilibrium in the money market. Equilibrium is achieved by changes in the interest rate. If the interest rate is too high, people demand a smaller quantity of money than the quantity supplied. They are holding too much money. In this situation, they try to get rid of money by buying bonds. As they do so, the price of a bond rises and the interest rate falls to the equilibrium rate. Conversely, if the interest rate is too low, people demand a larger quantity of money than the quantity supplied. They are holding too little money. In this situation, they try to get more money by selling bonds. As they do so, the price of a bond falls and the interest rate rises to the equilibrium rate. Only when the interest rate is at the level at which people are holding the quantity of money supplied do they willingly hold the money and take no actions that change the interest rate.

Influencing the Interest Rate

Imagine that the economy is slowing down and the Bank of Canada wants to increase aggregate demand. To do so, it wants to lower the interest rate and encourage more borrowing and more expenditure on goods and services. What does the Bank of Canada do? How does it fiddle with the knobs to achieve a lower interest rate?

The answer is that the Bank of Canada changes the quantity of money in the economy. Chapter 26 (pp. 610–615) explains *how* the Bank of Canada changes the quantity of money. Here, we study the *effects* of a change in the quantity of money.

Suppose that initially, the quantity of real money is $600 billion. In Fig. 25.8, the supply of money curve is MS_0. With the demand for money given by the curve *MD*, the equilibrium interest rate is 5 percent a year.

Now suppose that the quantity of real money increases to $700 billion. The supply of money curve shifts rightward from MS_0 to MS_1. At an interest rate of 5 percent a year, people are now holding more money than they would like to hold. They attempt to decrease their money holding by buying bonds. As they do so, the price of a bond rises and the interest rate falls. When the interest rate has fallen to 3 percent a year, people are willing to hold the greater $700 billion quantity of real money.

Conversely, suppose that the economy is overheating and the Bank of Canada fears inflation. The Bank decides to take action to decrease aggregate demand. In this case, the Bank decreases the quantity of real money. Suppose that the Bank decreases the quantity of real money from the initial quantity of $600 billion to $500 billion. Now, in Fig. 25.8, the supply of money curve shifts leftward from MS_0 to MS_2. At an interest rate of 5 percent a year, people are now holding less money than they would like to hold. They attempt to increase their money holding by selling bonds. As they do so, the price of a bond falls and the interest rate rises. When the interest rate has risen to 7 percent, people are willing to hold the smaller $500 billion quantity of real money.

FIGURE 25.8 Interest Rate Changes

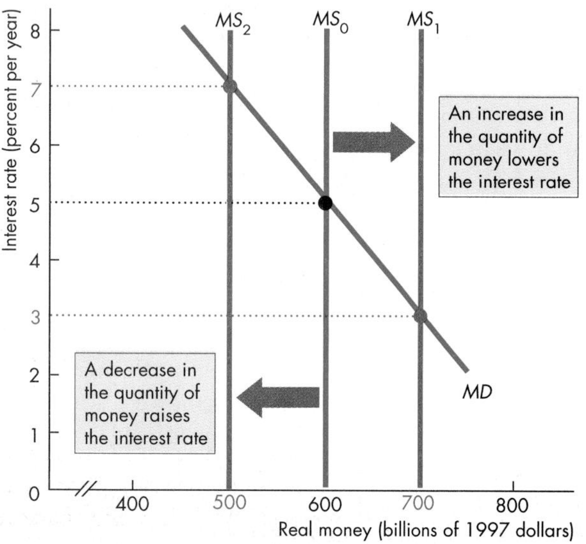

Initially, the quantity of real money is $600 billion and the interest rate is 5 percent a year. When the Bank of Canada increases the quantity of real money to $700 billion, the supply of money curve shifts rightward to MS_1 and the interest rate falls to 3 percent a year. When the Bank of Canada decreases the quantity of real money to $500 billion, the supply of money curve shifts leftward to MS_2 and the interest rate rises to 7 percent a year.

Influencing the Exchange Rate

The **exchange rate** is the price at which the Canadian dollar exchanges for another currency. For example, in October 2002, a Canadian dollar cost 63 U.S. cents. So the exchange rate at that time was 63 U.S. cents per Canadian dollar. The exchange rate is the price of the Canadian dollar determined by demand and supply in the global foreign exchange market. This market is described and studied in detail in Chapter 34 on pp. 815–823. Here, we'll look only at the influence of the interest rate on the exchange rate.

The interest rate that can be earned by moving funds into Canada is a key influence on the demand for Canadian dollars. People are constantly seeking the highest interest rate available, and when the interest rate that can be earned in one country rises with all other interest rates remaining the same, people move funds into that country. But to move funds into Canada, people must buy Canadian dollars in the foreign exchange market. And if more funds are moving into Canada, the demand for Canadian dollars increases.

An increase in the demand for Canadian dollars in the foreign exchange market raises the exchange rate. That is, the price of a Canadian dollar rises. So monetary policy actions that change the interest rate also change the exchange rate and in the same direction. Other things remaining the same, a rise in interest rates brings a rise in the exchange rate, and a fall in interest rates brings a fall in the exchange rate.

REVIEW QUIZ

1. What is a bond and what is the relationship between the price of a bond and the interest rate?
2. How is the interest rate determined?
3. What do people do if they are holding *less* money than they plan to hold and what happens to the interest rate?
4. What do people do if they are holding *more* money than they plan to hold and what happens to the interest rate?
5. What happens to the interest rate and the exchange rate if the quantity of money increases or decreases?

Your final task in this chapter is to study the influence of the interest rate on expenditure plans.

The Interest Rate and Expenditure Plans

YOU'VE SEEN THAT THE INTEREST RATE AFFECTS the quantity of money that people plan to hold. The interest rate also influences people's spending decisions. The reason is the same in both cases. The interest rate is an opportunity cost. But the interest rate that is relevant for the money holding decision is not quite the same as the interest rate that is relevant for a spending decision. Let's find out why.

Nominal Interest and Real Interest

We distinguish between two interest rates: the nominal interest rate and the real interest rate. The **nominal interest rate** is the percentage return on an asset such as a bond expressed in terms of money. It is the interest rate that is quoted in everyday transactions and news reports. The **real interest rate** is the percentage return on an asset expressed in terms of what money will buy. It is the nominal interest rate adjusted for inflation and is approximately equal to the nominal interest rate minus the inflation rate.

Suppose that the nominal interest rate is 10 percent a year and the inflation rate is 4 percent a year. The real interest rate is 6 percent a year—10 percent minus 4 percent.[3]

To see why the real interest rate is 6 percent, think about the following example. Jackie lends Joe $1,000 for one year. At the end of the year, Joe repays Jackie the $1,000 plus interest. At 10 percent a year, the interest is $100, so Jackie receives $1,100 from Joe.

Because of inflation, the money that Joe uses to repay Jackie is worth less than the money that Jackie originally lent to Joe. At an inflation rate of 4 percent a year, Jackie needs an extra $40 a year to compensate her for the fall in the value of money. So when Joe repays the loan, Jackie needs $1,040 to buy the same items that she could have bought for $1,000 when she made the loan. Because Joe pays Jackie $1,100, the interest that she *really* earns is $60, which is 6 percent of the $1,000 that she lent to Joe.

[3] The exact calculation allows for the change in the purchasing power of the interest as well as the amount of the loan. To calculate the *exact* real interest rate, use the formula: *real interest rate* = (*nominal interest rate* – *inflation rate*) divided by (1 + *inflation rate*/100). If the nominal interest rate is 10 percent and the inflation rate is 4 percent, the real interest rate is (10 – 4)÷(1 + 0.04) = 5.77 percent.

Interest Rate and Opportunity Cost

Now that you understand the distinction between the nominal interest rate and the real interest rate, let's think about the effects of interest rates on decisions.

The interest rate influences decisions because it is an opportunity cost. *The nominal interest rate is the opportunity cost of holding money.* And it is the nominal interest rate that is determined by the demand for real money and the supply of real money in the money market. To see why the nominal interest rate is the opportunity cost of holding money, think about the *real* interest rate on money compared with the real interest rate on other financial assets. Money loses value at the inflation rate. So the real interest rate on money equals *minus* the inflation rate. The real interest rate on other financial assets equals the nominal interest rate minus the inflation rate. So the difference between the real interest rate on money and the real interest rate on other financial assets is the nominal interest rate. By holding money rather than some other financial asset, we incur a *real* opportunity cost equal to the nominal interest rate.

The real interest rate is the opportunity cost of spending. Spending more today means spending less in the future. But spending one additional dollar today means cutting future spending by more than a dollar. And the real amount by which future spending must be cut is determined by the *real* interest rate.

A change in the real interest rate changes the opportunity cost of two components of aggregate expenditure:

- Consumption expenditure
- Investment

Consumption Expenditure

Other things remaining the same, the lower the real interest rate, the greater is the amount of consumption expenditure and the smaller is the amount of saving.

You can see why the real interest rate influences consumption expenditure and saving by thinking about the effect of the interest rate on a student loan. If the real interest rate on a student loan fell to 1 percent a year, students would be happy to take larger loans and spend more. But if the real interest rate on a student loan jumped to 20 percent a year, students would cut their expenditure, buying cheaper food and finding lower-rent accommodation for example, to pay off their loans as quickly as possible.

The effect of the real interest rate on consumption expenditure is probably not large. It is certainly not as powerful as the effect of disposable income that we studied in Chapter 23 (pp. 528–529). You can think of the real interest rate as influencing *autonomous consumption expenditure* (p. 532). The lower the real interest rate, the greater is autonomous consumption expenditure.

Investment

Other things remaining the same, the lower the real interest rate, the greater is the amount of investment.

The funds used to finance investment might be borrowed, or they might be the financial resources of the firm's owners (the firm's retained earnings). But regardless of the source of the funds, the opportunity cost of the funds is the real interest rate. The real interest paid on borrowed funds is an obvious cost. The real interest rate is also the cost of using retained earnings because these funds could be lent to another firm. The real interest rate forgone is the opportunity cost of using retained earnings to finance an investment project.

To decide whether to invest in new capital, firms compare the real interest rate with the expected profit rate from the investment. For example, suppose that Ford expects to earn 20 percent a year from a new car assembly plant. It is profitable for Ford to invest in this new plant as long as the real interest rate is less than 20 percent a year. That is, at a real interest rate below 20 percent a year, Ford will build this assembly plant; at a real interest rate in excess of 20 percent a year, Ford will not. Some projects are profitable at a high real interest rate, but other projects are profitable only at a low real interest rate. So the higher the real interest rate, the smaller is the number of projects that are worth undertaking and the smaller is the amount of investment.

The interest rate has another effect on expenditure plans—it changes net exports. Let's find out why.

Net Exports and the Interest Rate

Net exports change when the interest rate changes because, other things remaining the same, a change in the interest rate changes the exchange rate.

Net Exports and the Exchange Rate Let's first see why the exchange rate influences exports and imports. When a Canadian buys a Dell PC that is shipped from Texas, the price of the PC equals the U.S. dollar price converted into Canadian dollars. If the PC price is U.S.$2,000, and if the exchange rate is 66.67 U.S. cents per Canadian dollar, the PC price in Canada is $3,000. If the Canadian dollar rises to 75 U.S. cents per Canadian dollar, the PC price in Canada falls to $2,666.67. When the price of a U.S. PC falls, Canadians import more PCs.

Similarly, when a U.S. company buys a Nortel telephone system that is shipped from Ontario, the price of the system equals the Canadian dollar price converted into U.S. dollars. If the price of the telephone system is $6,000, and if the exchange rate is 66.67 U.S. cents per Canadian dollar, the price in the United States is U.S.$4,000. If the Canadian dollar rises to 75 U.S. cents per Canadian dollar, the price of the telephone system in the United States *rises* to $4,500. When the price of a Canadian telephone system rises, Americans buy fewer of them and Canada's exports decrease.

So when the Canadian dollar rises, imports increase, exports decrease, and net exports decrease. Similarly, when the Canadian dollar falls, imports decrease, exports increase, and net exports increase.

The Interest Rate and the Exchange Rate When the interest rate in Canada rises, and other things remain the same, the Canadian dollar exchange rate rises. The reason is that more people move funds into Canada to take advantage of the higher interest rate. But when money flows into Canada, the demand for Canadian dollars increases, so the Canadian dollar exchange rate (the price) rises. And when the interest rate in Canada falls, and other things remain the same, the Canadian dollar exchange rate falls.

Because the interest rate influences the exchange rate, it also influences net exports. A rise in the interest rate decreases net exports and a fall in the interest rate increases net exports, other things remaining the same.

Interest-Sensitive Expenditure Curve

Figure 25.9 illustrates the effects of the real interest rate on expenditure plans and summarizes those effects in the interest-sensitive expenditure curve. The **interest-sensitive expenditure curve** (the *IE* curve) shows the relationship between aggregate expenditure plans and the real interest rate when all other influences on expenditure plans remain the same.

FIGURE 25.9 The Interest Rate and Expenditure Plans

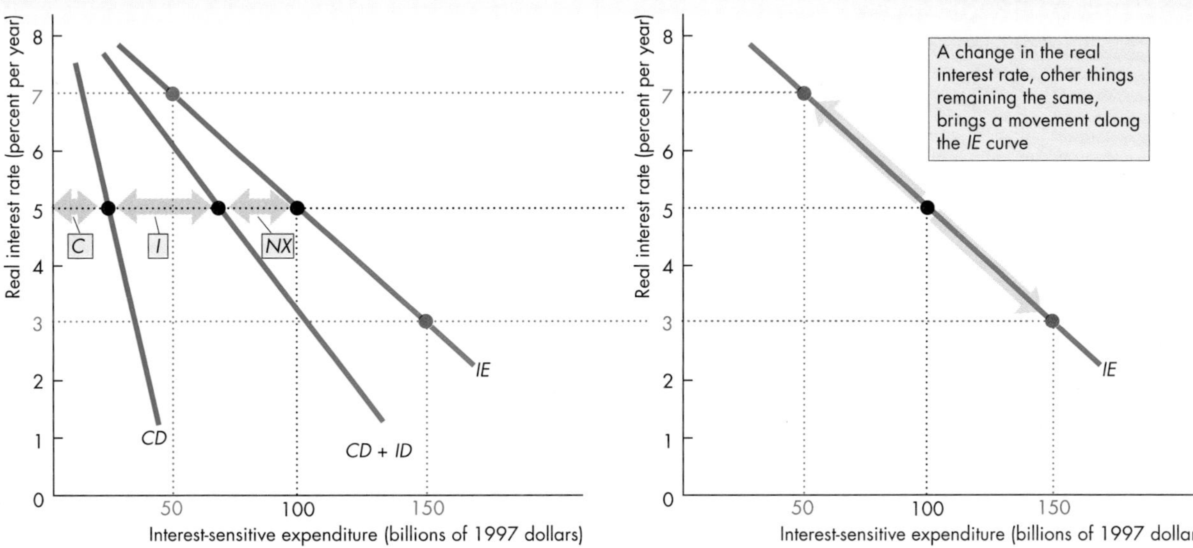

(a) The components of expenditure

(b) Aggregate expenditure plans

In part (a), when the interest rate is 5 percent a year, autonomous consumption expenditure is $20 billion, investment is $50 billion, net exports are $30 billion, and interest-sensitive expenditure is $100 billion. In part (b), when the real interest rate is 5 percent a year, interest-sensitive expenditure is $100 billion a year on the *IE* curve. Other things remaining the same, when the interest rate falls to 3 percent a year, interest-sensitive expenditure increases to $150 billion a year and when the interest rate rises to 7 percent a year, interest-sensitive expenditure decreases to $50 billion a year.

Figure 25.9(a) shows the components of interest-sensitive expenditure, autonomous consumption expenditure, investment, and net exports (*NX*). When the real interest rate is 5 percent a year, autonomous consumption expenditure is $20 billion on the curve *CD*. Investment is $50 billion, so when we add investment and autonomous consumption expenditure together, we get $70 billion on the curve *CD* + *ID*. Net exports are $30 billion, so when we add this amount to $70 billion, we obtain the sum of all the interest-sensitive components of aggregate expenditure, which is $100 billion on the *IE* curve.

In Fig. 25.9(b), as the real interest rate changes, interest-sensitive expenditure changes along the *IE* curve. Other things remaining the same, when the real interest rate falls to 3 percent a year, interest-sensitive expenditure increases to $150 billion. And when the real interest rate rises to 7 percent a year, interest-sensitive expenditure decreases to $50 billion.

REVIEW QUIZ

1. What is the real interest rate and how does it differ from the nominal interest rate?
2. Which interest rate influences the quantity of money that people plan to hold and why?
3. Which interest rate influences expenditure decisions and why?
4. How does the interest rate influence net exports?

Take a look at some recent trends in the way we use currency in Canada in *Reading Between the Lines* on pp. 600–601. You've now seen how the quantity of money influences the interest rate and how the interest rate influences expenditure plans. In the next chapter, we're going to discover how the Bank of Canada can change the quantity of money and interest rates. Then, in Chapter 27, we see how fiscal policy and monetary policy interact to influence the course of the economy.

Canada's Changing Demand for Money

FINANCIAL POST, DECEMBER 3, 2002

Odds stacked against cash

From consumer demands for speed and convenience to banks' hunger for fatter returns, a collusion of forces is ensuring that the use of paper money is sliding into decline.

"Cash is a very inefficient system, physical bills don't last very long before they need replacing, if you lose it there is no recourse and it costs a lot to count and process," says Joseph D'Cruz a professor of strategy at the Rotman School of Management at the University of Toronto. "Couple that with the very high level of trust Canadians place in their national banks and the rise of electronic banking is sure to drive down the use of cash."

If Canadians have trust in their banks, they seem to have less trust in their national currency. Retailers from Dominion to Tim Hortons and Shoppers Drug Mart have refused to accept bills in $50 or $100 denominations out of counterfeiting fears. Some stores, including Loblaws, have even started to put lowly $5 bills through a security scan. It's just one more reason that cash and other paper transactions, including cheques, are giving way to debit and credit charges. ...

... Interac Direct Payment—which polls Canadians annually to establish their preferred mode of payment for goods and services—says the use of electronic payment outstripped cash transactions in 1999. ... In 1995 well over half of all transactions were made in cash, by last year cash accounted for roughly 30% of transactions, according to Interac. ...

One of the last industries to resist accepting credit and debit has been fast food—because consumers spend roughly $5 each and the merchant pays a fee for customers to pay electronically. In Canada, however, fast food joints including McDonald's, Burger King, and Wendy's introduced debit payment several years ago.

Essence of the Story

- The use of paper money is decreasing, and the use of electronic credit and debit charges is increasing.
- Joseph D'Cruz, a professor of strategy at the Rotman School of Management at the University of Toronto, says that cash is an inefficient system and because Canadians trust their banks, electronic systems will continue to decrease the use of cash.
- Some retailers refuse to accept $50 bills or $100 bills because they fear counterfeiting, and some even put $5 bills through a security scan.
- A survey shows that cash payments decreased from more than 50 percent of transactions in 1995 to 30 percent in 2001.
- Because each transaction is small, the fast-food sector has been the most resistant to electronic transactions—but even in this sector, the use of cash is decreasing.

Economic Analysis

■ Figure 1 shows the amount of currency in Canada as a percentage of GDP since 1970. This percentage decreased during the 1970s and 1980s but increased during the early 1990s and was steady after 1994.

■ The news article emphasizes reasons why the amount of currency might have *decreased*. But why did currency increase during the 1990s?

■ Currency is one component of money, and the demand for money increases when real GDP increases.

■ In Figure 1, we graph currency *as a percentage of GDP* to remove the influence of GDP on the amount of currency held.

■ So Fig. 1 tells us that even holding real GDP constant, currency increased during the early 1990s and has not decreased during the 2000s.

■ The reason for the increase in currency is that the interest rate, which is the opportunity cost of holding currency, decreased during the 1990s.

■ Figure 2 shows the relationship between the amount of currency as a percentage of GDP against the interest rate on savings accounts at chartered banks.

■ You can see that, just as predicted by the theory of the demand for money, the lower the interest rate, the greater is the quantity of currency held.

■ As the opportunity cost of holding currency increased during the 1970s, the amount of currency held (as a percentage of GDP) decreased.

■ And as the opportunity cost of holding currency decreased during the 1990s, the amount of currency held (as a percentage of GDP) increased.

■ A change in the interest rate changes the quantity of currency demanded, but it does not change the demand for currency.

■ The demand for currency changes when some other influence on payment methods changes.

■ So what is left of the message in the news article? Are we using less currency as we switch increasingly to the use of debit cards?

■ Figure 2 provides part of the answer. The demand for currency has decreased. The demand curve of the 1990s is to the left of the demand curve of the 1970s.

■ But the demand for currency decreased during the early 1980s, not during the late 1990s when electronic payments technologies spread.

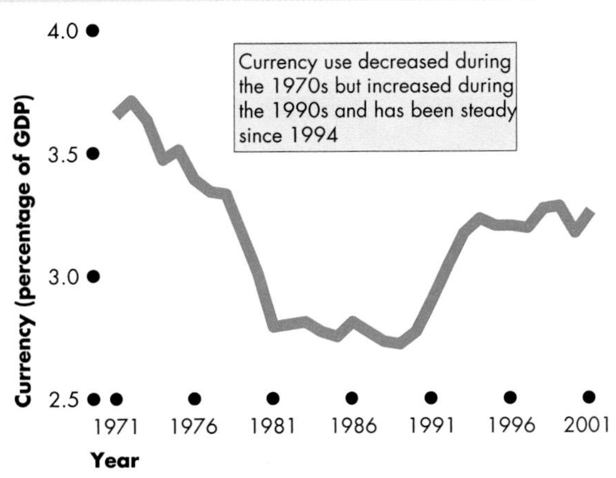

Figure 1 Trends in currency holding

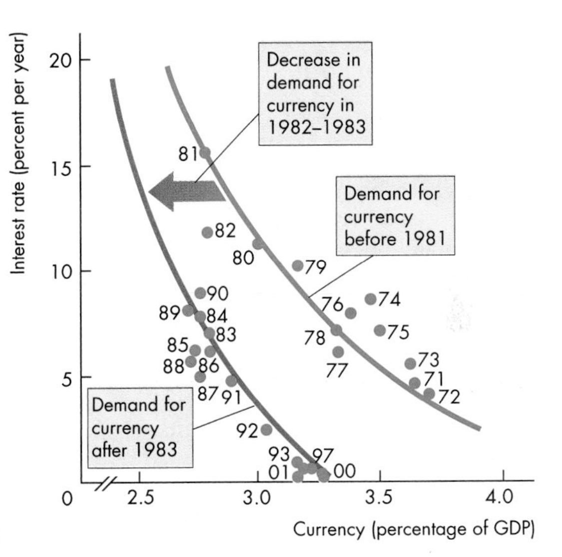

Figure 2 Currency holding and the interest rate

■ Most likely, the very high interest rate of 1981 made people think harder about how to be more economical in their use of currency, and the lesson was a permanent one.

■ Debit cards, which enable us to pay for purchases directly from our bank accounts, and credit cards, which enable us to buy on credit through the month and pay when we receive our own pay cheques, decrease our demand for currency.

■ As more and more businesses accept debit cards and credit cards and as more and more transactions are done by debit cards and credit cards, people will hold less cash.

■ But these changes are not visible in the aggregate data. Some other changes are working in the opposite direction to maintain the overall popularity of currency.

SUMMARY

KEY POINTS

What Is Money? (pp. 582–584)

- Money is the means of payment, a medium of exchange, a unit of account, and a store of value.
- M1 consists of currency and households' and businesses' demand deposits at chartered banks; M2+ consists of M1 plus savings deposits and other deposits at all types of depository institutions.

Depository Institutions (pp. 585–587)

- The depository institutions are the chartered banks, credit unions and caisses populaires, and trust and mortgage loan companies.
- Depository institutions provide four main economic services: They create liquidity, minimize the cost of obtaining funds, minimize the cost of monitoring borrowers, and pool risks.

How Banks Create Money (pp. 587–590)

- Banks create money by making loans.
- The total quantity of deposits that can be supported by a given amount of reserves (the deposit multiplier) is determined by the desired reserve ratio.

The Demand for Money (pp. 591–594)

- The quantity of money demanded is the amount of money that people plan to hold.
- The quantity of real money equals the quantity of nominal money divided by the price level.
- The quantity of real money demanded depends on the interest rate and real GDP. As the interest rate rises, the quantity of real money demanded decreases.

Interest Rate Determination (pp. 594–596)

- The interest rate adjusts to achieve equilibrium in the markets for money and financial assets.
- Money market equilibrium achieves an interest rate (and an asset price) that makes the quantity of real money available willingly held.
- If the quantity of real money increases, the interest rate falls and the prices of financial assets rise.

The Interest Rate and Expenditure Plans (pp. 597–599)

- The real interest rate (approximately) equals the nominal interest rate minus the inflation rate.
- The nominal interest rate is the opportunity cost of holding money. The real interest rate is the opportunity cost of consumption expenditure and investment.
- A fall in the interest rate increases interest-sensitive expenditure.

KEY FIGURES

Figure 25.1	Two Measures of Money, 583
Figure 25.2	Creating Money at the One-and-Only Bank, 588
Figure 25.3	The Multiple Creation of Bank Deposits, 590
Figure 25.4	The Demand for Money, 592
Figure 25.5	Changes in the Demand for Money, 592
Figure 25.7	Money Market Equilibrium, 595
Figure 25.8	Interest Rate Changes, 596
Figure 25.9	The Interest Rate and Expenditure Plans, 599

KEY TERMS

Barter, 582
Chartered bank, 585
Credit union, 586
Currency, 583
Demand for money curve, 592
Deposit multiplier, 588
Depository institution, 585
Desired reserve ratio, 587
Excess reserves, 587
Exchange rate, 596
Financial innovation, 591
Interest rate, 594
Interest-sensitive expenditure curve, 598
Liquidity, 584
M1, 583
M2+, 583
Means of payment, 582
Money, 582
Nominal interest rate, 597
Real interest rate, 597
Reserve ratio, 587
Reserves, 585
Trust and mortgage loan company, 586

PROBLEMS

*1. In Canada today, money includes which of the following items?
   a. Bank of Canada notes in the Bank of Montreal's cash machines
   b. Your Visa card
   c. The quarters inside public phones
   d. Canadian dollar coins in your pocket
   e. The cheque you have just written to pay for your rent
   f. The loan you took out last August to pay for your school fees

2. Which of the following items are money? Which are deposit money?
   a. Demand deposits at the CIBC
   b. Bell Canada stock held by individuals
   c. A "loonie"
   d. Canadian government securities

*3. Sara withdraws $1,000 from her savings account at the Lucky Trust and Mortgage Company, keeps $50 in cash, and deposits the balance in her demand deposit account at the Bank of Montreal. What is the immediate change in M1 and M2+?

4. Monica takes $10,000 from her savings account at Happy Credit Union and puts the funds into her demand deposit account at the Royal Bank. What is the immediate change in M1 and M2+?

*5. The banks in Zap have:

Reserves	$250 million
Loans	$1,000 million
Deposits	$2,000 million
Total assets	$2,500 million

   a. Construct the banks' balance sheet. If you are missing any assets, call them "other assets"; if you are missing any liabilities, call them "other liabilities."
   b. Calculate the banks' reserve ratio.
   c. If banks hold no excess reserves, calculate the deposit multiplier.

6. The banks in Zip have:

Reserves	$205 million
Loans	$3,750 million
Deposits	$4,000 million
Total assets	$4,200 million

   a. Construct the banks' balance sheet. If you are missing any assets, call them "other assets"; if you are missing any liabilities, call them "other liabilities."
   b. Calculate the banks' reserve ratio.
   c. If banks hold no excess reserves, calculate the deposit multiplier.

*7. The spreadsheet provides information about the demand for money in Minland. Column A is the interest rate, *R*. Columns B, C, and D show the quantity of money demanded at three different levels of real GDP: Y_0 is $10 billion, Y_1 is $20 billion, and Y_2 is $30 billion. The quantity of money supplied by the Minland central bank is $3.0 billion. Initially, real GDP is $20 billion.

	A	B	C	D
1	*R*	Y_0	Y_1	Y_2
2	7	1.0	1.5	2.0
3	6	1.5	2.0	2.5
4	5	2.0	2.5	3.0
5	4	2.5	3.0	3.5
6	3	3.0	3.5	4.0
7	2	3.5	4.0	4.5
8	1	4.0	4.5	5.0

What happens in Minland if
   a. The interest rate exceeds 4 percent a year?
   b. The interest rate is less than 4 percent a year?
   c. The interest rate equals 4 percent a year?

8. The Minland economy in problem 7 experiences a severe recession. Real GDP falls to $10 billion. The Minland central bank takes no action to change the quantity of money.
   a. What happens in Minland if the interest rate is 4 percent a year?
   b. What is the equilibrium interest rate?
   c. Compared with the situation in problem 7, does the interest rate in Minland rise or fall? Why?

*9. The Minland economy in problem 7 experiences a severe business cycle. Real GDP rises to $30 billion and then falls to $10 billion. The Minland central bank takes no action to change the quantity of money. What happens to the interest rate in Minland
   a. During the expansion phase of the cycle?
   b. During the recession phase of the cycle?

10. Financial innovation in Minland changes the demand for money. People plan to hold $0.5 billion less than the numbers in the spreadsheet.
   a. What happens to the interest rate if the Minland central bank takes no actions?

b. What happens to the interest rate if the Minland central bank decreases the quantity of money by $0.5 billion? Explain

*11. The figure shows the demand for real money curve in Upland.

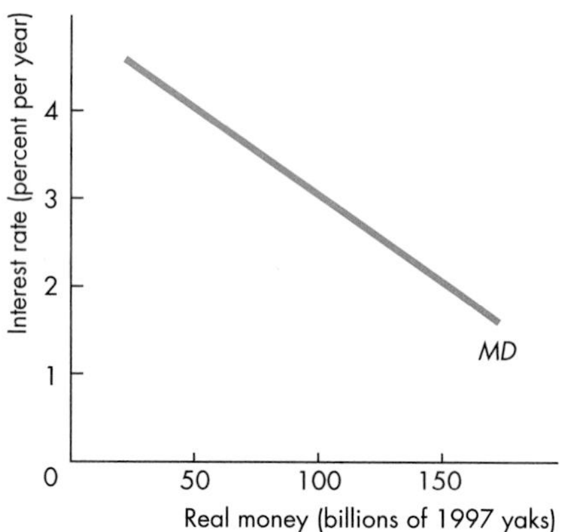

a. In the figure, draw the supply of money curve if the interest rate is 3 percent a year.
b. If the Upland central bank wants to lower the interest rate by 1 percentage point, by how much must it change the quantity of real money?

12. In problem 11, a new smart card replaces currency and the demand for money changes. Also, the new smart card causes business to boom and real GDP increases.
   a. Use the figure for problem 11 and draw a new demand for real money curve.
   b. If the Upland central bank wants to prevent the interest rate from changing, what must it do to the quantity of money?

*13. In problem 9, when Minland experiences a severe business cycle, what happens to autonomous consumption expenditure, investment, the exchange rate, and net exports
   a. During the expansion phase of the cycle?
   b. During the recession phase of the cycle?

14. In problem 10, what happens to autonomous consumption expenditure, investment, the exchange rate, and net exports in Minland if
   a. The central bank takes no action?
   b. The central bank decreases the quantity of money by $0.5 billion? Explain.

CRITICAL THINKING

1. Study *Reading Between the Lines* on pp. 600–601 and then answer the following questions:
   a. What changes in the payments technology are described in the news article?
   b. What does the news article imply has happened to the amount of currency held?
   c. What are the trends in currency use?
   d. Why did the use of currency increase during the 1990s?
   e. Does the increased use of currency during the 1990s contradict the news article?
   f. What do you expect the future trends in currency use to be and why?
2. Rapid inflation in Brazil caused the cruzeiro, the currency of Brazil, to lose its ability to function as money. People were unwilling to accept it because it lost value too fast. Which of the following commodities do you think would be most likely to take the place of the cruzeiro and act as money in the Brazilian economy?
   a. Tractor parts
   b. Packs of cigarettes
   c. Loaves of bread
   d. Impressionist paintings
   e. Baseball trading cards

WEB EXERCISES

1. Use the link on the Parkin–Bade Web site to visit Mark Bernkopf's Central Banking Resource Centre and read the article on Electronic Cash. Also read "The End of Cash" by James Gleick (first published in the *New York Times Magazine* on June 16, 1996). Then answer the following questions:
   a. What is e-cash?
   b. Mark Bernkopf asks: "Will 'e-cash' enable private currencies to overturn the ability of governments to make monetary policy?" Will it?
   c. When you buy an item on the Internet and pay by using a form of e-cash, are you using money? Explain why or why not.
   d. In your opinion, is the concern about e-cash a real concern or hype?

MONETARY POLICY

CHAPTER 26

Fiddling with the Knobs

Almost every month, the financial news reports on the Bank of Canada's view about whether the time is near for a further fall or rise in interest rates. What *is* the Bank of Canada? Why would the Bank of Canada want to change interest rates—especially upward? And how can the Bank of Canada influence interest rates? ◆ For most of the 1990s and 2000s the Consumer Price Index has risen slowly—inflation has been low—because the quantity of money in our economy has grown slowly. But during the 1970s, inflation rocketed as the pace of money creation exploded. What makes the quantity of money increase quickly at some times and more slowly at others? What role does the Bank of Canada play in changing the quantity of money? How does the quantity of money in existence influence interest rates? ◆ And how do interest rates influence the economy? Can the Bank of Canada speed up economic growth and lower unemployment by lowering interest rates? And can the Bank of Canada keep inflation in check by raising interest rates?

In this chapter, you will learn about the Bank of Canada and monetary policy. You will learn how the Bank of Canada influences interest rates and how interest rates influence the economy. You'll discover that interest rates depend, in part, on the amount of money in existence. You will also discover how the Bank of Canada changes the quantity of money to influence interest rates as it attempts to smooth the business cycle and keep inflation in check. In *Reading Between the Lines* at the end of the chapter, you will see the uncertainty that the Bank of Canada constantly faces as it tries to steer a steady course between inflation and recession.

After studying this chapter, you will be able to

- **Describe the structure of the Bank of Canada**
- **Describe the tools used by the Bank of Canada to conduct monetary policy**
- **Explain what an open market operation is and how it works**
- **Explain how the Bank of Canada changes the quantity of money**
- **Explain how the Bank of Canada influences interest rates**
- **Explain how the Bank of Canada influences the economy**

The Bank of Canada

THE BANK OF CANADA IS CANADA'S CENTRAL bank. A **central bank** is a public authority that supervises financial institutions and markets and conducts monetary policy. **Monetary policy** is the attempt to control inflation and moderate the business cycle by changing the quantity of money and adjusting interest rates and the exchange rate.

The **Bank of Canada** was established in 1935 and is directed by a governor who is appointed by the government of Canada. The seven people who have served as governor of the Bank of Canada are

- 1935–1954, Graham Towers
- 1955–1961, James Coyne
- 1961–1973, Louis Rasminsky
- 1973–1987, Gerald Bouey
- 1987–1994, John Crow
- 1994–2001, Gordon Thiessen
- 2001– , David Dodge

Both the Bank of Canada and the government of Canada play a role in determining Canada's monetary policy. And the Bank of Canada Act regulates the balance between these two power centres. The Act embodies the practices that have evolved over 60 years of experience. There are two possible models for the relationship between a country's central bank and its central government, and Canada has evolved from one model to the other. The two models are

- Independent central bank
- Subordinate central bank

Independent Central Bank An independent central bank is one that determines the nation's monetary policy without interference from the government. Public servants and politicians might comment on monetary policy but the Bank has no obligation to pay attention to these opinions.

The argument for an independent central bank is that it can pursue the long-term goal of price stability and can prevent monetary policy from being used for short-term, political advantage. This argument becomes more powerful when the government is running a budget deficit. One way of covering a deficit is for the central bank to buy government securities. But this action increases the quantity of money and creates inflation (see Chapter 27, p. 643 and Chapter 28, pp. 656–657). Another way of financing a government budget deficit is by selling securities to the general public. By taking a firm stand and being unwilling to print new money to pay for the government budget deficit, the central bank can force the government to face the higher interest rates that it brings upon itself by running a deficit.

Countries that have independent central banks today are Germany, the United States, and Switzerland. When the Bank of Canada was founded in 1935, it too was established as an independent central bank. Governors Towers and Coyne enjoyed substantial autonomy from the government of Canada. But in 1961, Governor James Coyne and Prime Minister John Diefenbaker clashed over who was in charge of monetary policy. Coyne resigned and for some time it was not clear whether the Bank of Canada was indeed independent (as the Act that established it proclaimed) or subordinate to the government (as the outcome of the Coyne–Diefenbaker clash seemed to imply).

The issue was resolved in 1967 when an amendment to the Bank of Canada Act redefined the relationship between the Bank and the government and made the Bank subordinate to the government.

Subordinate Central Bank Many central banks are subordinate to their governments. In the event of a difference of opinion between the central bank and government, the government carries the day and, if necessary, the central bank governor resigns if he or she is unwilling to implement the policies directed by the government. The argument for a subordinate central bank is that monetary policy affects the lives of everyone and so must be subject to democratic control.

Although the government (through the minister of finance) has final responsibility for Canada's monetary policy, this fact does not mean that the Bank of Canada is impotent. Because of its expertise and authority in the field and because of the quality of the analysis done by the Bank's staff of senior economists and advisors, the Bank (through the governor) has considerable power. Only a sharp, deep, and wide-ranging disagreement would bring a government to the point of forcing a governor's resignation. Also, there are times when a government wants to pursue unpopular monetary policies and, at such times, it is convenient for the government to hide behind the authority of the Bank of Canada.

We are now going to study the policy actions that the Bank of Canada takes. To understand these actions, we first must describe the Bank's balance sheet.

The Bank of Canada's Balance Sheet

Table 26.1 shows the balance sheet of the Bank of Canada. The numbers are for December 31, 2001. The assets on the left side are what the Bank of Canada owns and the liabilities on the right side are what it owes. Most of the Bank of Canada's assets are government of Canada securities. A small asset item is loans to chartered banks.

The most significant aspect of the Bank of Canada's balance sheet is on the liabilities side. The largest liability is Bank of Canada notes outside the Bank. These are the bank notes that we use in our daily transactions. Some of these bank notes are held by households and firms and others are in the tills and vaults of banks and other financial institutions.

The other economically significant but numerically small liability of the Bank of Canada is the deposits by chartered banks. These deposits are reserves of the chartered banks. The liabilities of the Bank of Canada are the largest component of the monetary base. The **monetary base** is the sum of Bank of Canada notes outside the Bank, chartered banks' deposits at the Bank of Canada, and coins held by households, firms, and banks. The government of Canada issues coins, so they do not appear as a liability of the Bank of Canada. The government of Canada also has deposits with the Bank of Canada.

You now know what the Bank of Canada is and you can describe the Bank's assets and liabilities. Your next task is to learn how the Bank goes about its work of making monetary policy.

TABLE 26.1 The Bank of Canada's Balance Sheet, December 31, 2001

Assets (billions of dollars)		Liabilities (billions of dollars)	
Government securities	39	Bank of Canada notes	39
Loans to banks	1	Banks' deposits	2
		Government deposits	1
Other assets	2		
Total assets	42	Total liabilities	42

[all the items are shown rounded to the nearest $1 billion].

Source: Bank of Canada, *Banking and Financial Statistics*, table B1.

Making Monetary Policy

Making monetary policy is like driving a very strange car. The car has an accelerator (lower interest rates) and a brake (higher interest rates). The accelerator and the brake work, but not very predictably. The driver (the Bank of Canada) cannot be sure how strong or how delayed the response to its actions will be. Also, to make the ride more interesting, the driver has only a rear view. The road just travelled can be seen, but the road ahead is invisible.

The objective is to drive the car at a constant speed over a terrain that alternates between uphill (tough economic times with a falling real GDP growth rate and rising unemployment) and downhill (easy economic times with a rising real GDP growth rate and falling unemployment). So sometimes the accelerator must be applied, sometimes the brake, and sometimes neither. You can see that to have a smooth ride, the driver must read the current situation and try to predict what lies ahead.

So to make monetary policy, the Bank of Canada must anticipate the future course of the economy and it must try to read that course from current economic conditions. To study the Bank's challenging task, economists break the monetary policy process into three pieces:

- Monetary policy objectives
- Monetary policy indicators
- Monetary policy tools

Monetary Policy Objectives

The objectives of monetary policy are ultimately political, and they stem from the mandate of the Bank that is set out in the Bank of Canada Act. These objectives are to

> regulate credit and currency in the best interests of the economic life of the nation... and to mitigate by its influence fluctuations in the general level of production, trade, prices and employment, so far as may be possible within the scope of monetary action...[1]

In simple language, these words have come to mean that the Bank's job is to control the quantity of money and interest rates in order to avoid inflation and, when possible, prevent excessive swings in real GDP growth and unemployment. In terms of the car

[1] This quotation is from the preamble of the Bank of Canada Act, 1935.

analogy, the Bank sees its job as being cautious in applying the accelerator and more aggressive in applying the brake.

This modern interpretation of the Bank's objectives is controversial. Some people believe that the emphasis is wrong and that the Bank should pay less attention to inflation and use its influence to avoid low real GDP growth and high unemployment. Or, the Bank should put more pressure on the gas pedal and less on the brake.

Monetary Policy Indicators

If inflation is raging too rapidly or unemployment is too high, there is nothing the Bank of Canada can do that will bring immediate relief. Furthermore, if the Bank is doing a good job, it will already have taken the actions it believes are the best available for dealing with *today's* situation. The actions the Bank takes today are designed to influence the economy many months into the future. **Monetary policy indicators** are the *current* features of the economy that the Bank looks at to determine whether it needs to apply the brake or the accelerator to the economy to influence its *future* real GDP growth, unemployment, and inflation.

The best monetary policy indicators are variables that the Bank of Canada can observe accurately and frequently, that are good predictors of the future course of real GDP growth, unemployment, and inflation (the objectives of policy), and that the Bank can control quickly.

The Bank of Canada's monetary policy indicators change as more research is done and the Bank learns more about which indicators work well and which are faulty. Today, the main monetary policy indicator is an interest rate called the overnight loans rate. The **overnight loans rate** is the interest rate on large-scale loans that chartered banks make to each other and to dealers in financial markets. The Bank of Canada sets a range for the overnight loans rate of half a percentage point and takes actions to keep the rate inside its desired range.[2] The overnight loans rate is like the cruise control on the Bank's strange car.

Figure 26.1 shows the overnight loans rate. This interest rate climbed steeply after 1975 and reached a peak of 18 percent in 1981. At this time, Governor Gerald Bouey was wrestling with double-digit inflation. Since 1981, the overnight loans rate has fluctuated, but it has generally followed a downward trend. This downward trend was interrupted during the late 1980s when Governor John Crow put the Bank on its current course of aiming for low inflation. The overnight loans rate has remained low through the low-inflation era of the 1990s and 2000s.

Monetary Policy Tools

The Bank of Canada controls the overnight loans rate by adjusting the reserves of the banks. These adjustments then spread through the banks to change the quantity of money, other interest rates, and the

FIGURE 26.1 The Main Monetary Policy Indicator: The Overnight Loans Rate

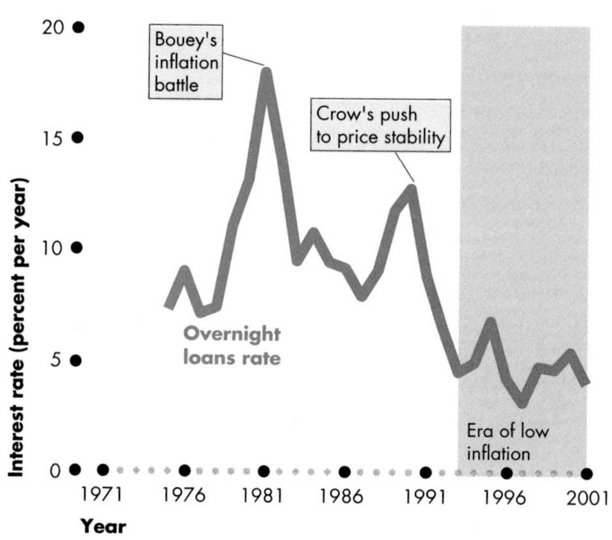

The Bank of Canada sets a target range for the overnight loans rate and then takes actions to keep this monetary policy indicator inside its target range. When the Bank wants to slow inflation, it takes actions that raise the overnight loans rate. When the Bank wants to increase real GDP, it takes actions that lower the overnight loans rate.

Source: Bank of Canada, *Banking and Financial Statistics*, table F1.

[2] Half a percentage point is sometimes called 50 *basis points*. A basis point is one-hundredth of one percentage point. For example, the Bank might set the range at 3.5 to 4.0 percent or from 7.1 to 7.6 percent. In each case, the range is half a percentage point or 50 basis points.

exchange rate. Four policy tools impact on bank reserves and the quantity of money:

- Required reserve ratio
- Bank rate and bankers' deposit rate
- Open market operations
- Government deposit shifting

Required Reserve Ratio Banks hold reserves in the form of currency and deposits at the Bank of Canada so that they can meet the demands of their customers. If the Bank of Canada chooses to do so, it can require the chartered banks to hold larger reserves than the banks themselves desire. Since 1992, banks in Canada have not been required to hold reserves. The *required reserve ratio is zero.* Before 1992, the Bank of Canada imposed reserve requirements on the banks. Required reserves were 8 percent of deposits before 1967. They then decreased steadily through the 1970s and 1980s and were finally abolished in 1992.

By changing the required reserve ratio, the Bank of Canada changes the amount of lending the banks can do and therefore changes the quantity of money. It also changes the magnitude of the deposit multiplier. The higher the reserve ratio, the smaller is the deposit multiplier (see Chapter 25, p. 588).

Required reserves act like a tax on the banks. When banks are required to hold either currency or deposits at the Bank of Canada, the banks earn no interest on either of these assets. So the banks are taxed by the Bank of Canada by an amount equal to the interest that they could have earned by lending these funds rather than by holding them as reserves. The *opportunity cost* of reserves is the loan interest forgone. By abolishing required reserves, the Bank of Canada has made the banks more profitable.

Bank Rate and Bankers' Deposit Rate The chartered banks hold tiny reserves relative to their deposits. The key reason the banks can manage with such small reserves is that the Bank of Canada stands ready to lend reserves to them to ensure that they can always meet their depositors' demands for currency. **Bank rate** is the interest rate that the Bank of Canada charges the chartered banks on the reserves it lends them.

The Bank of Canada can set bank rate at any level it chooses. At one time, the Bank linked bank rate to the interest rate on 3-month government of Canada Treasury bills. But today, bank rate is set as the upper end of the range of the Bank's target for the overnight loans rate. Because the Bank is willing to lend funds to the chartered banks at this interest rate, bank rate acts as a cap on the overnight loans rate. If the chartered banks can borrow from the Bank of Canada at bank rate, they will not borrow from another bank unless the rate is lower than or equal to bank rate.

The Bank of Canada pays the chartered banks interest at the *bankers' deposit rate* on their deposits at the Bank. The Bank of Canada sets this interest rate at bank rate minus half a percentage point, which also equals the low end of the Bank's target range for the overnight loans rate. If chartered banks can earn bank rate minus half a percentage point from the Bank of Canada, they will not make overnight loans to other banks unless they earn a higher interest rate than what the Bank of Canada is paying.

You can see now that the Bank of Canada can always make the overnight loans rate hit its target range by its setting of bank rate and bankers' deposit rate. But the Bank usually wants to keep the overnight loans rate inside its target range, not at one end of it. The other two policy tools are used to move the overnight loans rate around inside its target range.

Open Market Operations An **open market operation** is the purchase or sale of government of Canada securities—Treasury bills and government bonds—by the Bank of Canada from or to a chartered bank or the public. When the Bank of Canada buys securities, it pays for them with newly created monetary base. Its payment for the securities increases the chartered banks' deposits at the Bank of Canada. With extra reserves, the banks make new loans, the quantity of money increases, and interest rates fall. When the Bank of Canada sells securities, it receives payments that decrease the monetary base. Banks' reserves decrease, the banks cut lending, the quantity of money decreases, and interest rates rise.

Open market operations are the main method of controlling bank reserves and the quantity of money, and they are undertaken on a huge scale. In a typical week, the Bank of Canada might buy or sell government securities valued at several hundred million dollars. In some weeks, the Bank buys or sells more than a billion dollars worth of government securities. Some of these transactions occur to cope with seasonal fluctuations in the demand for money that arise from factors such as the timing of tax payments and Christmas shopping. Others occur because the Bank of Canada wants to raise or lower the overnight loans rate. Because open market operations are the main tool for controlling the quantity of money and influencing other interest rates, we study them in more detail later in this chapter (on pp. 611–615).

Government Deposit Shifting The government of Canada has deposits in accounts at chartered banks and the Bank of Canada. On a typical day, the government has about $2.5 billion in the bank and most of this money is on deposit at chartered banks. The government's deposit at the Bank of Canada is usually much smaller than the amount on deposit at the chartered banks.

Government deposit shifting is the transfer of government funds by the Bank of Canada from the government's account at the Bank of Canada to its accounts at the chartered banks, or from the government's accounts at the chartered banks to its account at the Bank of Canada. When the Bank of Canada shifts government funds from itself to the chartered banks, it increases chartered bank deposits and reserves. When the Bank shifts government funds from the chartered banks to itself, it decreases chartered bank deposits and reserves.

Table 26.2 shows the effects of government deposit shifting. Suppose the Bank of Canada writes cheques totalling $10 million on a government of Canada account and deposits those cheques into government of Canada accounts at the chartered banks. (To avoid benefiting or hurting an individual bank, these operations are spread across the banks according to an agreed-upon formula.)

Two sets of transactions now occur. First, government deposits decrease at the Bank of Canada and increase at the chartered banks. This transaction appears as –$10 million in government deposits in Bank of Canada liabilities and +$10 million in government deposits in chartered banks' liabilities. Second, chartered banks' reserves increase. This transaction appears as +$10 million in Bank of Canada liabilities and +$10 million in chartered banks' assets. The Bank of Canada has no net additional liabilities and the chartered banks have $10 million more assets and $10 million more liabilities.

The quantity of money has not changed because government deposits are not counted as money. But bank reserves have increased, so the banks can now increase their loans. And, when banks make loans they create money. The quantity of money increases.

By doing the transactions you've just seen in reverse, the Bank of Canada can decrease bank reserves and cause a contraction of loans, and the quantity of money decreases.

Government deposit shifting is done on a very small scale and is a way of fine-tuning the quantity of bank reserves from one day to another.

TABLE 26.2 The Effects of Government Deposit Shifting

(a) Bank of Canada's Balance Sheet

Change in assets		Change in liabilities	
		Government deposits	–$10 million
		Chartered bank deposits	+$10 million
Total assets	$0	Total liabilities	$0 million

(b) Chartered Banks' Balance Sheet

Change in assets		Change in liabilities	
Reserves (deposits at the Bank of Canada)	+$10 million	Government deposits	+$10 million
Total assets	+$10 million	Total liabilities	+$10 million

REVIEW QUIZ

1. What is the central bank of Canada?
2. What functions does a central bank perform?
3. What are the Bank of Canada's monetary policy objectives?
4. Why does the Bank of Canada need a monetary policy indicator and what is its main indicator?
5. What are the four policy tools that the Bank of Canada can use to attempt to achieve its monetary policy objectives?

We're now going to look in greater detail at the way the Bank of Canada influences the quantity of money and interest rates by using its main tool, the open market operation. We'll see first how the Bank changes the monetary base and second how the monetary base influences the quantity of money. We'll then see how the quantity of money influences interest rates and the exchange rate.

Controlling the Quantity of Money

The Bank of Canada constantly monitors and adjusts the quantity of money in the economy. When the Bank of Canada *buys* securities in an open market operation, the monetary base *increases*, banks increase their lending, and the quantity of money *increases*. When the Bank of Canada *sells* securities in an open market operation, the monetary base *decreases*, banks decrease their lending, and the quantity of money *decreases*.

Let's study these changes in the quantity of money, beginning with the effects of open market operations on the monetary base.

How an Open Market Operation Works

When the Bank of Canada conducts an open market operation, the reserves of the banking system—a part of the monetary base—change. To see why this outcome occurs, we'll trace the effects of an open market operation when the Bank of Canada buys securities.

Suppose the Bank of Canada buys $100 million of government securities in the open market. There are two cases to consider: when the Bank of Canada buys from a chartered bank, and when it buys from the public (a person or business that is not a chartered bank). The outcome is essentially the same in either case, but you need to be convinced of this fact. We'll start with the simpler case: the Bank of Canada buys securities from a chartered bank.

Buy from a Chartered Bank When the Bank of Canada buys $100 million of securities from the Royal Bank, two things happen:

1. The Royal Bank has $100 million less securities, and the Bank of Canada has $100 million more securities.
2. The Bank of Canada pays for the securities by crediting the Royal Bank's deposit account at the Bank of Canada with $100 million.

Figure 26.2(a) shows the effects of these actions on the balance sheets of the Bank of Canada and the Royal Bank. Ownership of the securities passes from the chartered bank to the Bank of Canada, so the Royal Bank's assets decrease by $100 million and the Bank of Canada's assets increase by $100 million, as shown by the blue arrow running from the Royal to

FIGURE 26.2 Bank of Canada Buys Securities in the Open Market

(a) The Bank of Canada buys securities from a chartered bank

The Bank of Canada

Assets	Liabilities
Securities +$100	Reserves of the Royal Bank +$100

The Bank of Canada buys securities from a bank ...

... and pays for the securities by increasing the reserves of the bank

Royal Bank

Assets	Liabilities
Securities –$100	
Reserves +$100	

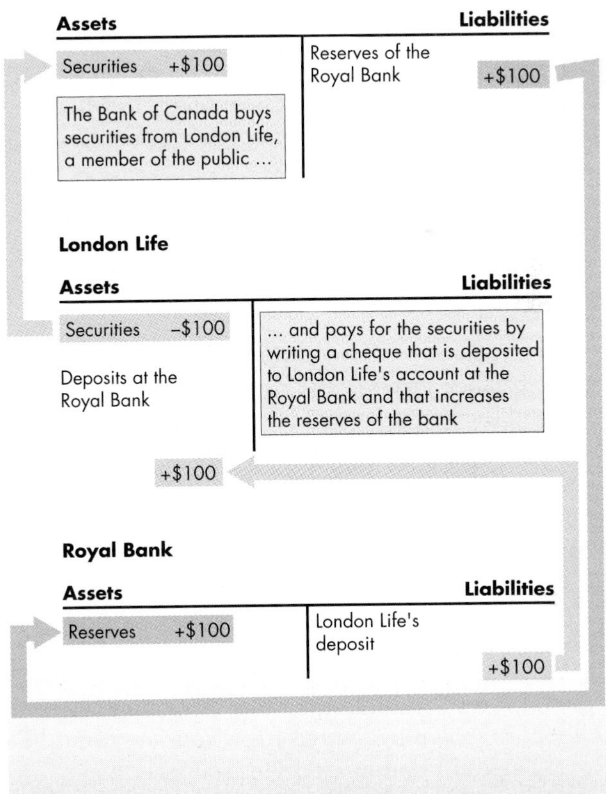

the Bank of Canada. The Bank of Canada pays for the securities by crediting the Royal Bank's deposit account at the Bank of Canada—its reserves—with $100 million, as shown by the green arrow running from the Bank of Canada to the Royal Bank. This action increases the monetary base and increases the reserves of the banking system.

The Bank of Canada's assets increase by $100 million, and its liabilities increase by $100 million. The chartered bank's total assets remain constant but their composition changes. Its deposit at the Bank of Canada increases by $100 million, and its holding of government securities decreases by $100 million. So the Royal Bank has additional reserves, which it can use to make loans.

We've just seen that when the Bank of Canada buys government securities from a bank, the bank's reserves increase. But what happens if the Bank of Canada buys government securities from the public—say from London Life, an insurance company?

Buy from the Public When the Bank of Canada buys $100 million of securities from London Life, three things happen:

1. London Life has $100 million less securities, and the Bank of Canada has $100 million more securities.
2. The Bank of Canada pays for the securities with a cheque for $100 million drawn on itself, which London Life deposits in its account at the Royal Bank.
3. The Royal Bank collects payment of this cheque from the Bank of Canada, and $100 million is deposited in the Royal Bank's deposit account at the Bank of Canada.

Figure 26.2(b) shows the effects of these actions on the balance sheets of the Bank of Canada, London Life, and the Royal Bank. Ownership of the securities passes from London Life to the Bank of Canada, so London Life's assets decrease by $100 million and the Bank of Canada's assets increase by $100 million, as shown by the blue arrow running from London Life to the Bank of Canada.

The Bank of Canada pays for the securities with a cheque payable to London Life, which London Life deposits in the Royal Bank. This transaction increases London Life's deposit at the Royal Bank by $100 million, as shown by the red arrow running from the Royal Bank to London Life. This transaction also increases the Royal Bank's reserves by $100 million, as shown by the green arrow running from the Bank of Canada to the Royal Bank. Just as when the Bank of Canada buys securities from a bank, this action increases the monetary base and increases the reserves of the banking system.

Again, the Bank of Canada's assets increase by $100 million, and its liabilities also increase by $100 million. London Life has the same total assets as before, but their composition has changed. It now has more money and less securities. The Royal Bank's total assets increase, and so do its liabilities. Its deposit at the Bank of Canada—its reserves—increases by $100 million, and its deposit liability to London Life increases by $100 million. Because its reserves have increased by the same amount as its deposits, the bank has excess reserves, which it can use to make loans.

We've now studied what happens when the Bank of Canada buys government securities from either a bank or from the public. If the Bank of Canada sells securities, all the events that you've just studied occur in reverse. Reserves decrease, and the banks are short of reserves.

The effects of an open market operation on the balance sheets of the Bank of Canada and the banks that we've just described are not the end of the story—they are just the beginning. With an increase in their reserves, the banks are able to make more loans, which increases the quantity of money. With a decrease in reserves, the banks must cut back on their loans, which decreases the quantity of money.

You learned how loans create deposits in Chapter 25. Here, we build on that basic idea but instead of studying the link between *bank reserves* and *bank deposits*, we examine the related broader link between the *monetary base* and the *quantity of money*.

Monetary Base and Bank Reserves

We've defined the monetary base as the sum of Bank of Canada notes outside the Bank, chartered banks' deposits at the Bank of Canada, and coins held by households, firms, and banks. The monetary base is held either by banks as reserves or by households and firms as currency.

When the monetary base increases, both bank reserves and currency held by households and firms increase. Banks can use the increase in bank reserves to make loans and create additional money. The increase in currency held by households and firms cannot be used to create additional money. An increase in currency held by households and firms is called a **currency drain**. A currency drain reduces the amount of additional money that can be created from a given increase in the monetary base.

The **money multiplier** is the amount by which a change in the monetary base is multiplied to determine the resulting change in the quantity of money. That is, the money multiplier is equal to the change in the quantity of money (M) divided by the change in the monetary base (MB):

$$\text{Money multiplier} = \frac{\Delta M}{\Delta MB}.$$

The money multiplier is related to but differs from the *deposit multiplier* that we studied in Chapter 25. The deposit multiplier is the amount by which a change in bank reserves is multiplied to determine the change in the bank deposits.

Let's now look at the money multiplier.

The Money Multiplier

Let's work out the money multiplier by studying the case in which the Bank of Canada *buys securities from the banks.* Figure 26.3 shows the events that follow this open market purchase by the Bank of Canada. These events are

1. Banks have excess reserves.
2. Banks lend excess reserves.
3. Bank deposits increase.
4. The quantity of money increases.
5. New money is used to make payments.
6. Some of the new money remains on deposit.
7. Some of the new money is a *currency drain.*
8. Desired reserves increase because deposits have increased.
9. Excess reserves decrease, but remain positive.

FIGURE 26.3 A Round in the Multiplier Process Following an Open Market Operation

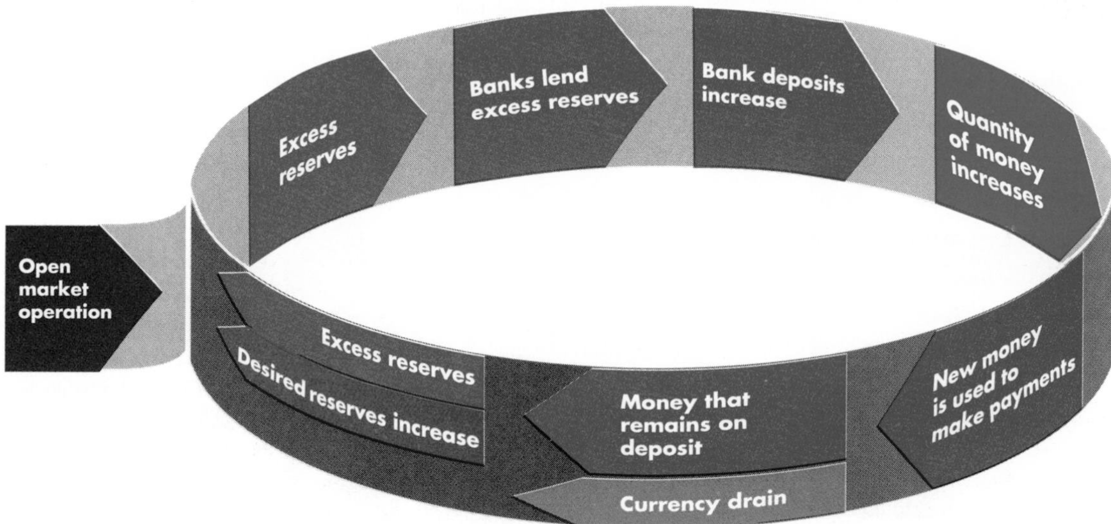

An open market operation increases bank reserves and creates excess reserves. Banks lend the excess reserves, new bank deposits are created, and the quantity of money increases. New money is used to make payments. Households and firms receiving payments keep some of the receipts as currency—a currency drain—and place the rest on deposit in banks. The increase in bank deposits increases banks' reserves but also increases banks' desired reserves. Desired reserves increase by less than the increase in actual reserves, so the banks still have some excess reserves, though less than before. The process repeats until excess reserves have been eliminated.

The sequence repeats in a series of rounds, but each round begins with a smaller quantity of excess reserves than did the previous one. The process continues until excess reserves have finally been eliminated.

You've seen that an open market operation creates excess reserves for the banks and that the reaction of the banks to this situation increases the quantity of money. But you've not yet seen the magnitude of the increase in the quantity of money.

Figure 26.4 illustrates the series of rounds and keeps track of the magnitudes of the increases in reserves, loans, deposits, currency, and money that result from an open market purchase of $100,000. In this figure, the *currency drain* is 33.33 percent of money and the *desired reserve ratio* is 10 percent of deposits.

The Bank of Canada buys $100,000 of securities from the banks. The banks' reserves increase by this amount, but deposits do not change. The banks have excess reserves of $100,000, and they lend those reserves. When the banks lend $100,000 of excess reserves, $66,667 remains in the banks as deposits and $33,333 drains off and is held outside the banks as currency. The quantity of money has now increased by $100,000—the increase in deposits plus the increase in currency holdings.

The increased bank deposits of $66,667 generate an increase in desired reserves of 10 percent of that amount, which is $6,667. Actual reserves have increased by the same amount as the increase in deposits—$66,667. So the banks now have excess reserves of $60,000. At this stage, we have gone around the circle shown in Fig. 26.3 once. The process we've just described repeats but begins with excess reserves of $60,000. Figure 26.4 shows the next two rounds. When the process comes to an end, the quantity of money has increased by $250,000.

FIGURE 26.4 The Multiplier Effect of an Open Market Operation

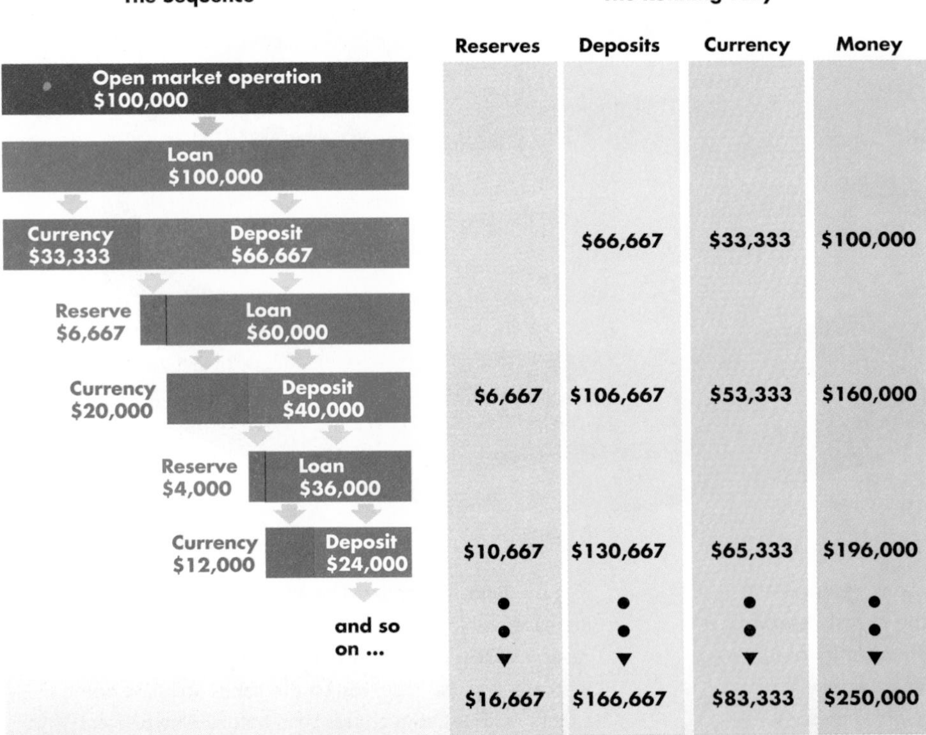

When a Bank of Canada open market operation gives the banks an additional $100,000 of reserves, the banks lend those reserves. Of the amount lent, $33,333 (33.33 percent) leaves the banks in a currency drain and $66,667 remains on deposit. With additional deposits, desired reserves increase by $6,667 (10 percent desired reserve ratio) and the banks lend $60,000. Of this amount, $20,000 leaves the banks in a currency drain and $40,000 remains on deposit. The process repeats until the banks have created enough deposits to eliminate their excess reserves. An additional $100,000 of reserves creates $250,000 of money.

The Canadian Money Multiplier

In the example you've just worked through, a \$100,000 open market purchase increases the quantity of money by \$250,000. The money multiplier is 2.5. What is the magnitude of the Canadian money multiplier? Let's look at some numbers.

The Canadian money multiplier is the change in the quantity of money divided by the change in the monetary base. Because there are two main definitions of money, there are two money multipliers: one for M1 and one for M2+. The M1 multiplier is about 2.2, and the M2+ multiplier is about 10. That is, a \$1 million increase in the monetary base brings (approximately) a \$2.2 million increase in M1 and a \$10 million increase in M2+. These multipliers are based on a desired reserve ratio for M1 of 0.12 (12 percent) and for M2+ of 0.01 (1 percent). That is, a \$100 increase in M1 increases desired reserves by \$12, while a \$100 increase in M2+ brings an increase in desired reserves of only \$1. These multipliers are also based on a currency drain of 0.36 (or 36 percent) for M1 and 0.08 (or 8 percent) for M2+. That is, a \$100 increase in M1 increases currency held by households and firms by \$36, while a \$100 increase in M2+ increases currency held by households and firms by \$8.

REVIEW QUIZ

1. What happens when the Bank of Canada buys securities in the open market?
2. What happens when the Bank of Canada sells securities in the open market?
3. What do the banks do when they have excess reserves, and how do their actions influence the quantity of money?
4. What do the banks do when they are short of reserves, and how do their actions influence the quantity of money?

The Bank of Canada's objective in changing the quantity of money is to influence the course of the economy—especially unemployment, real GDP growth, and inflation. The immediate effects of a change in the quantity of money are changes in the interest rate and the exchange rate. These changes create ripple effects that ultimately change the course of the economy. Let's now study these ripple effects.

Ripple Effects of Monetary Policy

YOU'VE SEEN HOW THE BANK OF CANADA CAN use its power in financial markets to change the quantity of money. And you learned in Chapter 25 that a change in the quantity of money changes the interest rate and the exchange rate.

We're now going to study the consequences of these changes in the interest rate and the exchange rate as they ripple through the economy.

When the Bank of Canada sells securities on the open market and decreases the monetary base, the quantity of money decreases, and the interest rate and the exchange rate rise. The higher interest rate decreases consumption expenditure and investment. And the higher exchange rate makes Canadian exports more expensive and imports cheaper. So net exports decrease. Tighter bank credit brings fewer loans, which reinforces the effects of higher interest rates on consumption expenditure and investment.

Similarly, when the Bank of Canada buys securities on the open market and increases the monetary base, the quantity of money increases, and the interest rate and the exchange rate fall. The lower interest rate increases consumption expenditure and investment. And the lower exchange rate makes Canadian exports cheaper and imports more costly. So net exports increase. Easier bank credit brings an expansion of loans, which reinforces the effects of lower interest rates on consumption expenditure and investment.

Figure 26.5 provides a schematic summary of these ripple effects. We're going to look at each stage in the transmission process. But before we do so, and so that we keep our eye on the ultimate objectives of monetary policy, we'll first use the *AS–AD* model and refresh our understanding of how a change in the quantity of money influences real GDP and the price level.

Monetary Policy to Lower Unemployment

Figure 26.6 shows an economy that is experiencing unemployment. Potential GDP is \$1,000 billion, but actual real GDP is only \$950 billion, at the intersection of the aggregate demand curve AD_0 and the short-run aggregate supply curve *SAS*. The price level is 105. With a large amount of unemployment,

FIGURE 26.5 The Channels for the Ripple Effects of Monetary Policy

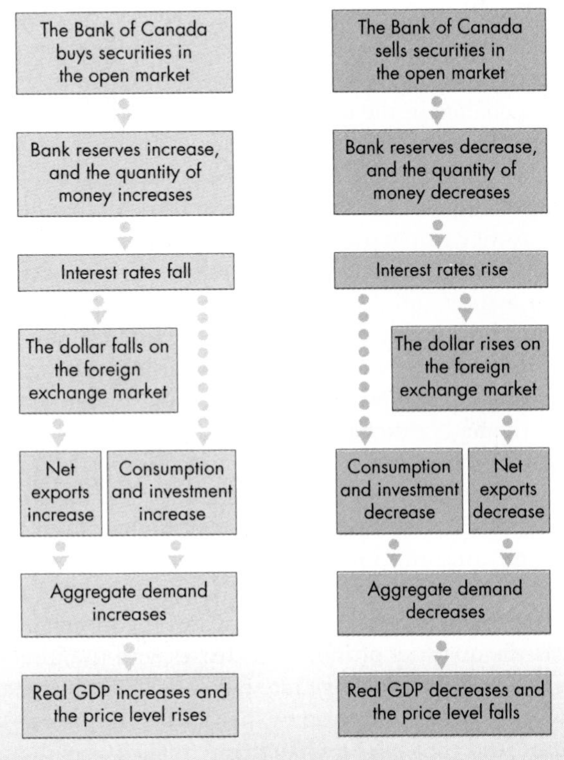

FIGURE 26.6 Monetary Policy to Lower Unemployment

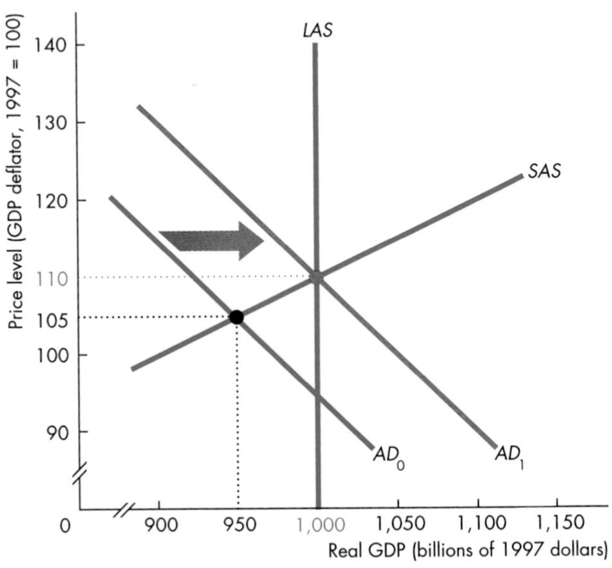

The aggregate demand curve is AD_0 and the short-run aggregate supply curve is *SAS*. The price level is 105, and real GDP is $950 billion. Long-run aggregate supply is *LAS*, and the economy is at a below full-employment equilibrium. An increase in the quantity of money shifts the aggregate demand curve rightward from AD_0 to AD_1. The price level rises to 110, and real GDP increases to $1,000 billion. Full employment is restored.

the money wage rate will eventually fall. As a result, the *SAS* curve will shift rightward, the price level will fall, and real GDP will increase, restoring full employment. But this automatic adjustment process is extremely slow.

To bring the economy to full employment more quickly, the Bank of Canada increases the quantity of money by conducting an open market operation in which it purchases government securities. Flush with excess reserves, banks make loans and the loans create money. With more money in their bank accounts, people increase their expenditure and aggregate demand increases.

In Fig. 26.6, the aggregate demand curve shifts rightward from AD_0 to AD_1. The new equilibrium is at the intersection point of AD_1 and *SAS*. The price level rises to 110, and real GDP increases to $1,000 billion. The economy is now at full employment.

Monetary Policy to Lower Inflation

Figure 26.7 shows an economy in which real GDP exceeds potential GDP and in which inflation is about to break out. Potential GDP is $1,000 billion and the long-run aggregate supply curve is *LAS*. Initially, the short-run aggregate supply curve is SAS_0, and the aggregate demand curve is AD_0. The price level is 115 and real GDP is $1,050 billion.

If the Bank of Canada does not take action, the money wage rate will begin to rise and the *SAS* curve will shift leftward to SAS_1. The price will rise to 125, and inflation will occur.

The Bank of Canada can prevent inflation by decreasing the quantity of money. By conducting an open market operation in which it sells securities, the Bank of Canada can decrease the quantity of money and shift the aggregate demand curve leftward to

FIGURE 26.7 Monetary Policy to Lower Inflation

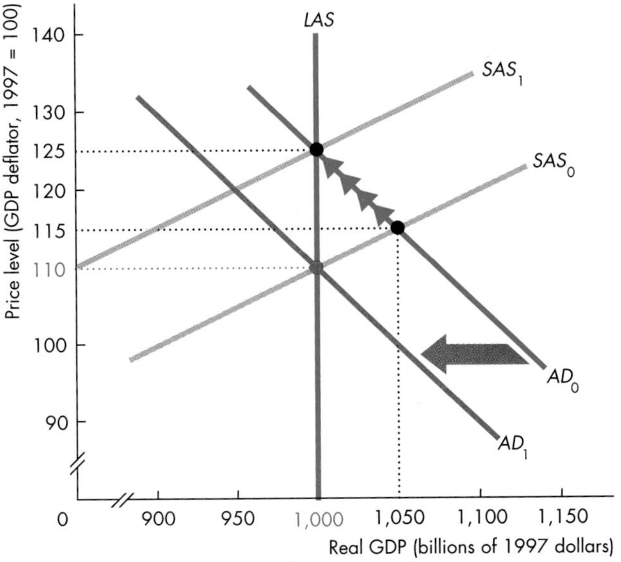

The economy is at an above full-employment equilibrium. The price level is 115, and real GDP is $1,050 billion. With no change in aggregate demand, the money wage rate rises and the short-run aggregate supply curve shifts to SAS_1. The price level rises to 125, and inflation occurs. If before the money wage rate rises, the Bank of Canada decreases the quantity of money so that the aggregate demand curve shifts to AD_1, the price level falls to 110 and the economy returns to full employment.

AD_1. If the Bank takes this action before the money wage rate has increased, the new equilibrium is at the intersection point of AD_1 and SAS_0. The price level falls to 110 and real GDP decreases to $1,000 billion. Inflation is avoided.

Time Lags in the Adjustment Process

To achieve its goal of full employment and the absence of inflation, the Bank of Canada needs a combination of good judgment and good luck. Too large an injection of money into an underemployed economy can bring inflation, as it did during the 1970s. And too large a decrease in the quantity of money in an inflationary economy can create unemployment, as it did in 1991.

The Bank is especially handicapped by the fact that the ripple effects of its policy actions are long and drawn out. Also, the economy does not always respond in exactly the same way to policy. Further, many factors other than policy are constantly changing and bringing a new situation for policy to respond to.

We'll look at each stage in the transmission process of monetary policy and see some of the problems that confront the Bank.

Interest Rate Fluctuations

The first effect of monetary policy is a change in the interest rate. This effect occurs quickly and relatively predictably. Figure 26.8 shows the fluctuations in three interest rates: the overnight loans rate, the 3-month Treasury bill rate, and the 10-year government bond rate (which is similar to the rate paid by big

FIGURE 26.8 Interest Rates

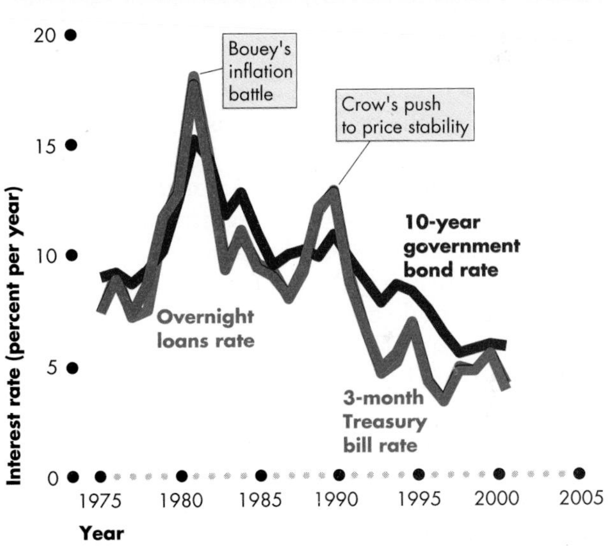

The short-term interest rates—the overnight loans rate and the 3-month Treasury bill rate—move closely together. The 10-year government bond rate moves in the same direction as the short-term rates but fluctuates less. The overnight loans rate climbed during the 1970s and peaked at 18 percent a year in 1981. The rate fell during the 1980s, but it increased again to peak at 13 percent a year in 1990. It fell again through the 1990s and remained low in the early 2000s.

Source: Bank of Canada, *Banking and Financial Statistics*, table F1.

corporations). The overnight loans rate is the one that the Bank of Canada targets directly and influences most closely. But notice how closely the 3-month Treasury bill rate follows the overnight loans rate. The 3-month Treasury bill rate is similar to the interest rate paid by Canadian businesses on short-term funds. These are short-term interest rates.

Notice also how the 10-year government bond rate moves with the short-term rates. It does not fluctuate as much as the short-term rates but its direction of change is the same.

Do the Bank of Canada's own actions make interest rates fluctuate? The answer is "yes." Figure 26.9 shows the relationship between the 3-month Treasury bill rate and the monetary base. Over time, the monetary base increases because the economy grows. So what matters for interest rates is not the absolute amount of monetary base, but the amount relative to GDP. The *x*-axis measures the monetary base as a percentage of GDP. During the 1970s and early 1980s, the Bank decreased the monetary base relative to GDP and interest rates rose. You can see the Bank at work as the movement up the line labelled MB_0. During the late 1990s and 2000s, the Bank increased the monetary base relative to GDP and interest rates fell. You can see the Bank at work as the movement down the line labelled MB_1.

But the relationship between monetary base and interest rates is not completely predictable. During the 1980s and early 1990s, the monetary base decreased relative to GDP and interest rates fell. The normal relationship broke down mainly because of ongoing decreases in the required reserve ratio.

FIGURE 26.9 Monetary Base and the Interest Rate

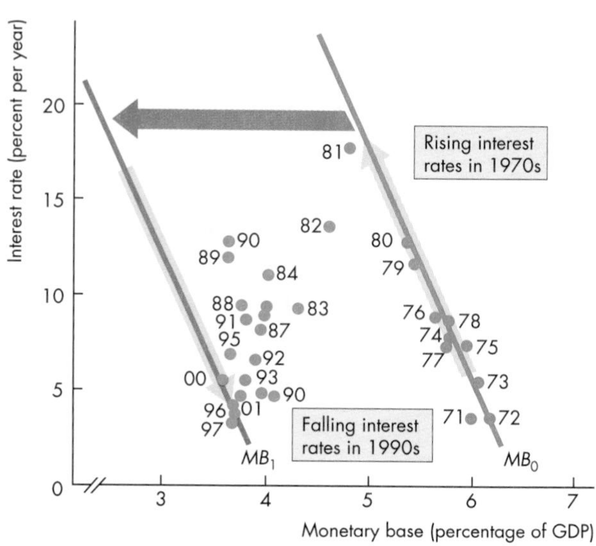

To increase interest rates during the 1970s and early 1980s, the Bank of Canada decreased the monetary base relative to GDP. To decrease interest rates during the late 1990s and 2000s, the Bank of Canada increased the monetary base relative to GDP. During the 1980s and early 1990s, the relationship between the monetary base and the interest rate changed as reserve requirements and other factors changed.

Sources: Bank of Canada and *Monetary Base and the Interest Rate*; data calculated in part from the Statistics Canada CANSIM II database, table 380–0002.

Money Target Versus Interest Rate Target

Because the demand for money fluctuates, the Bank of Canada prefers to target the interest rate rather than the quantity of money. To target the interest rate, the Bank changes the quantity of money supplied in response to changes in the demand for money.

Figure 26.10 illustrates the difference between money targeting and interest rate targeting. In part (a), the Bank keeps the quantity of money at $600 billion. The money supply curve is *MS*. The demand for money fluctuates between a high of MD_H and a low of *MD* and averages MD_A. The interest rate averages 5 percent a year. But as the demand for money fluctuates, the interest rate fluctuates between 4 percent when the demand for money is MD_L and 6 percent when the demand for money is MD_H.

In Fig. 26.10(b), the Bank keeps the interest rate at 5 percent a year. To achieve its target the quantity of money is $600 billion on the average and the supply of money curve is MS_A. But when the demand for money changes, so does the quantity of money. When the demand for money increases to MD_H, the Bank increases the quantity of money to $610 billion and the supply of money curve becomes MS_H. When the demand for money decreases to MD_L, the Bank decreases the quantity of money to $590 billion and the supply of money curve becomes MS_L.

The decision by the Bank of Canada to target the interest rate does not mean that the Bank has abandoned control of the quantity of money. The Bank achieves its interest rate target by controlling the quantity of money. If the Bank wants to stop the

FIGURE 26.10 Money Target Versus Interest Rate Target

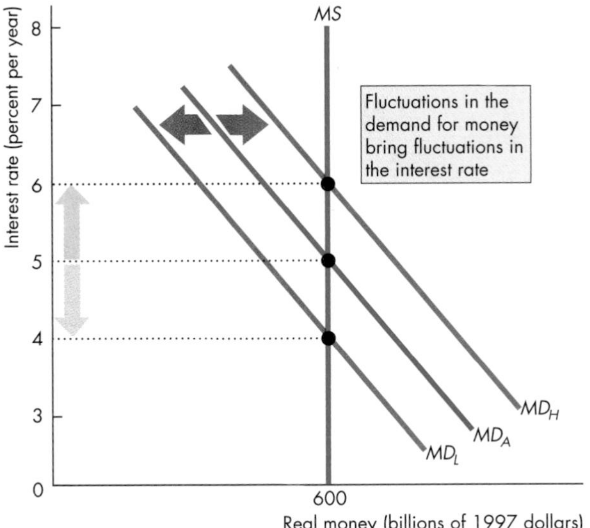

(a) Money target

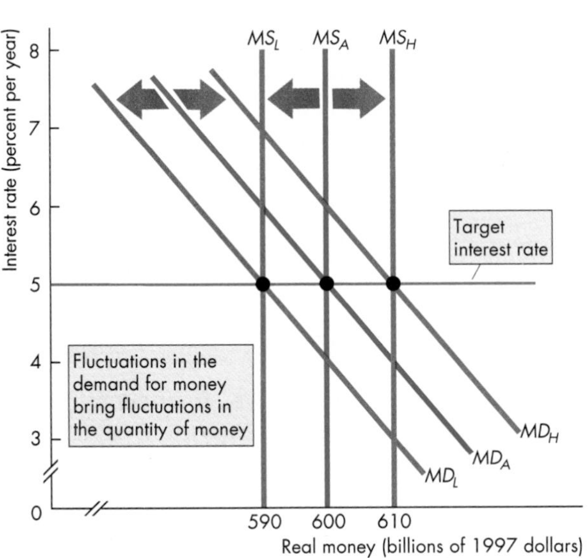

(b) Interest rate target

The demand for money fluctuates between MD_L and MD_H and on the average is MD_A. In part (a), the Bank of Canada keeps the quantity of money at $600 billion and the interest rate fluctuates between 4 percent and 6 percent a year and averages 5 percent a year. In part (b), the Bank of Canada keeps the interest rate at 5 percent a year and the quantity of money fluctuates between $590 billion ($MS_L$) and $610 billion ($MS_H$) and on the average is $600 billion ($MS_A$).

interest rate rising, it increases the quantity of money by increasing bank reserves. Flush with excess reserves, the banks increase the quantity of loans and bank deposits. And if the bank wants to stop the interest rate falling, it decreases the quantity of money by decreasing bank reserves. Short of reserves, banks decrease the quantity of loans and bank deposits.

The Exchange Rate

The exchange rate responds to changes in the interest rate in Canada relative to the interest rates in other countries. But other factors are also at work, which make the exchange rate hard to control and even harder to predict. The red line in Fig. 26.11 shows the gap between the Canadian and U.S. short-term interest

FIGURE 26.11 The Interest Rate and the Dollar

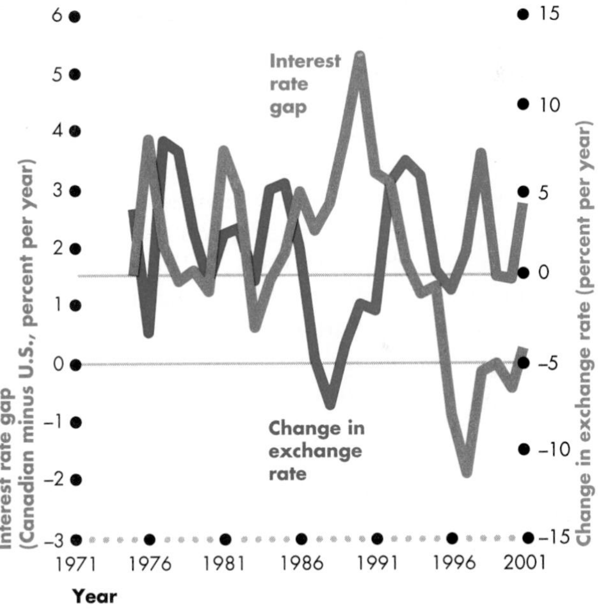

Other things remaining the same, when the gap between Canadian and U.S. short-term interest rates widens, the Canadian dollar rises in value or its value falls less quickly, and when the gap between Canadian and U.S. short-term interest rates narrows, the Canadian dollar falls in value or its value rises less quickly. Most of the time, other things do not remain the same, so the relationship between the interest rate gap and the exchange rate is weak.

Sources: Bank of Canada, *Banking and Financial Statistics*, tables F1 and I1, and authors' calculations.

rates. And the blue line shows the change in the Canadian dollar exchange rate against the U.S. dollar. You can see that sometimes when the interest rate gap widens (when the Canadian interest rate rises relative to the U.S. rate), the Canadian dollar rises or falls less quickly. Also, sometimes, when the interest rate gap narrows (when the Canadian interest rate falls relative to the U.S. rate), the Canadian dollar falls or rises less quickly. But the relationship between the interest rate gap and the exchange rate is weak. The exchange rate often changes independently of the interest rate gap.

Interest Rates, Aggregate Demand, and Real GDP Fluctuations

You've seen that the Bank of Canada's actions influence interest rates and the exchange rate. And you know that according to the *AS–AD* model, changes in the quantity of money, interest rates, and the exchange rate change aggregate demand and lead to changes in real GDP and the price level. But how powerful are the influences of money on real GDP? And how long does it take for these influences to occur?

Figure 26.12 answers these questions. The blue line shows the short-term interest rate minus the long-term interest rate. The Bank of Canada influences the short-term interest rate in the way that you studied earlier in this chapter. Changes in the short-term interest rate have some effect on the long-term interest rate, but this effect is small. The long-term interest rate is also influenced by saving and investment plans and by inflation expectations.

The red line in Fig. 26.12 is the real GDP growth rate *one year later.* You can see that when the short-term interest rate rises or the long-term interest rate falls, the real GDP growth rate slows down in the following year. The long-term interest rate fluctuates less than the short-term rate, so when the short-term rate rises above the long-term rate, it is because the Bank of Canada has pushed the short-term rate up. And when the short-term rate falls below the long-term rate, it is because the Bank of Canada has pushed the short-term rate down. So when the Bank of Canada stimulates aggregate demand (pushes the short-term rate down), the real GDP growth rate speeds up, and when the Bank of Canada lowers aggregate demand (pushes the short-term rate up), the real GDP growth rate slows. The inflation rate also increases and decreases in sympathy with these fluctuations in the real GDP growth rate. But the effects on the inflation rate take even longer.

FIGURE 26.12 Interest Rates and Real GDP Growth

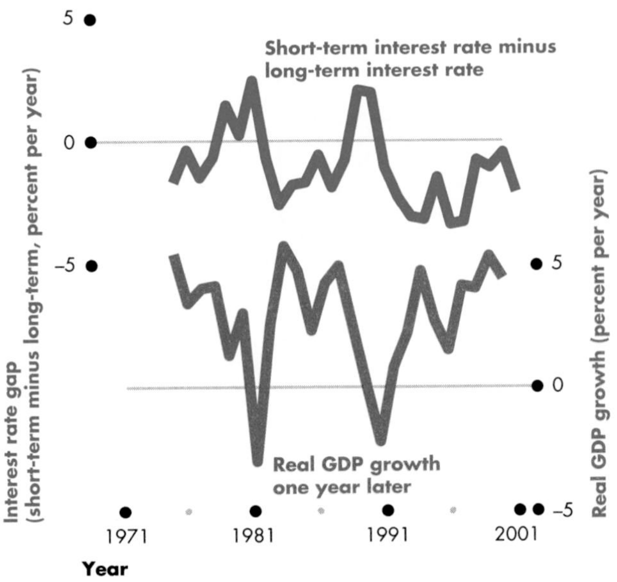

When the short-term interest rate rises relative to the long-term interest rate, the real GDP growth rate usually slows about one year later. Similarly, when the short-term interest rate falls relative to the long-term interest rate, the real GDP growth rate speeds up about one year later.

Sources: Bank of Canada and *Interest Rates and Real GDP Growth;* data calculated in part from the Statistics Canada CANSIM II database, table 380–0002.

REVIEW QUIZ

1. Describe the channels by which monetary policy ripples through the economy and explain why each channel operates.
2. Do interest rates fluctuate in response to the Bank of Canada's actions?
3. What change has occurred in the relationship between the monetary base and the interest rate?
4. How do the Bank of Canada's actions influence the exchange rate?
5. How do the Bank of Canada's actions influence real GDP and how long does it take for real GDP to respond to the Bank's policy actions?

We now look at the Bank of Canada in action.

The Bank of Canada in Action

YOU HAVE NOW LEARNED A GREAT DEAL ABOUT the Bank of Canada, the monetary policy actions it can take, and the effects of those actions on short-term interest rates. But you are possibly thinking: All this sounds nice in theory, but does it really happen? Does the Bank of Canada actually do the things we've learned about in this chapter? Indeed, it does happen, sometimes with dramatic effect, as two episodes in the life of the Bank of Canada show.

Gerald Bouey's Fight Against Inflation

Bank of Canada Governor Gerald Bouey eradicated a near double-digit inflation during the early 1980s. He did so by forcing interest rates sharply upward.

You know that to increase interest rates, the Bank must decrease the quantity of real money. In practice, because the economy is growing and because prices are rising, a slowdown in the growth rate of nominal money is enough to decrease the quantity of real money and increase interest rates.

In 1982, the quantity of money was held in check relative to the demand for money and interest rates increased sharply. The Treasury bill rate increased from 13 percent a year in 1980 to 18 percent a year in 1981. Mortgage rates—the rate at which house buyers borrow—increased to more than 20 percent a year. The economy went into severe recession. Real GDP shrank and the inflation rate slowed.

John Crow's Push for Price Stability

John Crow became governor of the Bank of Canada on February 1, 1987. Like his predecessor, Crow was a fierce inflation fighter and intent on holding the growth rate of money steady. But in October 1987, he was faced with one of the most severe crises that any central banker can face—a stock market crash. The Bank of Canada, in the company of other central banks around the world, feared the recession potential that might be signalled by the stock market crash. So to avoid any hint of financial tightness that might exacerbate a recessionary situation, the Bank of Canada permitted the quantity of money to grow quickly and short-term interest rates fell.

As the months passed, fears of recession were replaced by fears of a re-emergence of inflation. The Bank of Canada again slowed money growth and forced interest rates upward in a concerted attack on inflation. The Bank persisted in its focus on price stability despite a severe recession in 1990–1991.

Gordon Thiessen's and David Dodge's Balancing Acts

Gordon Thiessen succeeded John Crow in 1994 at a time of high unemployment. Many economists blamed the Bank for creating the 1990–1991 recession and for the absence of a strong recovery. Thiessen began the Bank's modern era of balancing the overriding goal of price stability with a strong secondary goal of trying to moderate the business cycle. Through 1995 and 1996, persistently high unemployment and slow economic growth combined with low inflation encouraged the Bank to lower interest rates and the economy embarked on what became a long and strong business cycle expansion. But inflation remained low.

This expansion was still underway but with increasing concern of a new recession when David Dodge succeeded Thiessen at the beginning of 2001. Soon thereafter, the United States went into recession and the U.S. slowdown, combined with the shock of September 11, brought ever lower interest rates both in the United States and Canada as the Bank sought to fight recession. As 2003 began, the Bank continued to walk a tightrope and began to consider raising interest rates again to hold back a possible upturn in the inflation rate.

REVIEW QUIZ

1. What were the policy challenges that Gerald Bouey and John Crow faced, and how did they respond to them?
2. What were the challenges that faced Gordon Thiessen during the 1990s and David Dodge during the 2000s, and how did they respond to them?

In the next chapter, we're going to learn how monetary policy and fiscal policy interact. But first, take a look at *Reading Between the Lines* on pages 622–623 and see the Bank of Canada's challenge in 2002.

READING BETWEEN THE LINES

Monetary Policy in Action

FINANCIAL POST, OCTOBER 17, 2002

Strong growth, inflation spike not enough to send rates up: Bank of Canada stands pat

Bank of Canada said yesterday global economic, financial and political uncertainties persuaded it to keep interest rates steady for the second month in a row, despite a strong domestic expansion and a spike in inflation.

While the central bank left little doubt it would eventually drive rates higher, analysts detected a more dovish outlook in its statement that decreased the chances of a rise before the end of the year.

The bank kept its target for overnight lending rates between banks at 2.75% while the bank rate—the interest rate at which the central bank lends money to major financial institutions—was maintained at 3%.

"It remains the bank's view, going forward, that timely removal of monetary stimulus will be required to achieve the inflation target over the medium term," the bank said in a statement.

"The pace of monetary tightening will depend on unfolding economic, financial, and geopolitical developments and their implications for pressures on capacity and inflation in Canada."

David Dodge, the Bank of Canada governor, has now held interest rates steady since July after pushing them up from 40-year lows of 2% in three rate rises this spring.

While the bank's decision to keep interest rates on hold at its announcement in September caught many economists by surprise, yesterday's statement was widely anticipated as external conditions have become even more precarious since then.

The equity rally of the past few days has given investors heart, but the bear still has the market firmly in its claws, the U.S. recovery remains stubbornly weak, risk tolerance is wilting and the possibility of a U.S. attack on Iraq has cast a pall of uncertainty over everything.

"These uncertainties and the weaker global outlook may dampen growth in aggregate demand for Canadian output in the near term," the bank said. ...

Essence of the Story

- The Bank of Canada decided to leave its target for the overnight lending rate at 2.75 percent and the bank rate at 3 percent in October 2002.
- Strong domestic expansion and a spike in inflation pointed to the need for an increase in the interest rate, but global economic, financial, and political uncertainties pointed in the opposite direction.
- The Bank said that it would eventually raise interest rates to avoid inflation moving above its target range.

Economic Analysis

- In the fall of 2002, Canada's inflation rate was rising and approaching 3 percent a year, the upper end of the Bank of Canada's target range.

- In the absence of other considerations, the inflation situation would call for monetary policy to decrease aggregate demand and remove an inflationary gap.

- But there were other considerations—global economic, financial, and political uncertainties—that pointed in the opposite direction.

- Figures 1 and 2 illustrate that possible range of uncertainty about real GDP and the inflation rate through 2003.

- If real GDP keeps growing rapidly, the small inflationary gap in late 2002 might become a large one in 2003. Or if real GDP growth slows, a recessionary gap might emerge.

- Similarly, the inflation rate might keep rising and burst through the upper end of the target range, or the rise in the inflation rate might slow.

- Figure 3 illustrates the possible developments during 2003 using the *AS–AD* model.

- Potential GDP in 2003 is projected to be $1,084 billion and the short-run aggregate supply curve is *SAS*.

- The Bank of Canada would like the aggregate demand curve to be AD_0 so that the economy attains full employment with real GDP at $1,084. The Bank would like the price level to rise by 2 percent to 115.

- If aggregate demand continues to grow quickly, the aggregate demand curve would shift to AD_1. In this case, with no actions by the Bank of Canada, real GDP would be $1,095 and the price level would rise to 119. To prevent this outcome, the Bank would need to increase the interest rate.

- Alternatively, if aggregate demand grows slowly, the aggregate demand curve would shift to AD_2. In this case, with no actions by the Bank of Canada, real GDP would be $1,073—below full employment—and the price level would rise to 111. To prevent this outcome, the Bank would need to *decrease* the interest rate.

- The Bank of Canada must operate in a permanent state of uncertainty about the future course of the economy.

You're The Voter

- Do you think the Bank of Canada should always err on the side of avoiding recession, even if that means risking rising inflation?

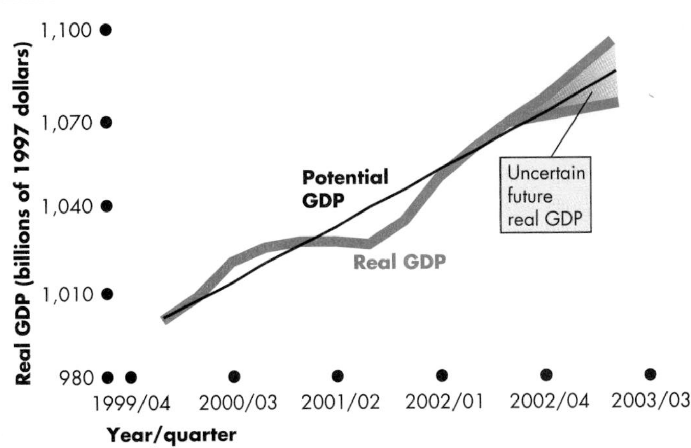

Figure 1 Real GDP and potential GDP

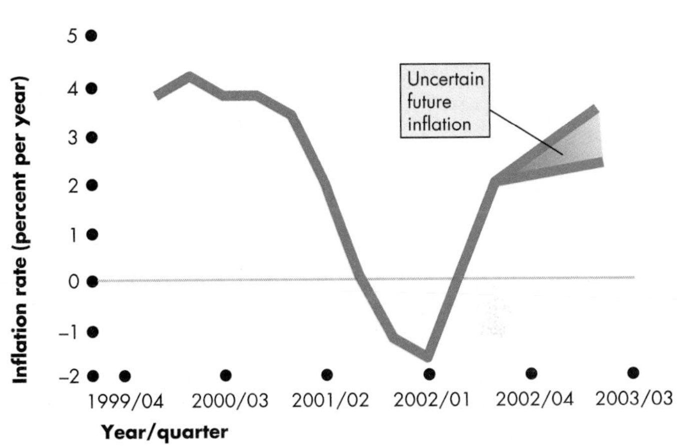

Figure 2 Inflation rate

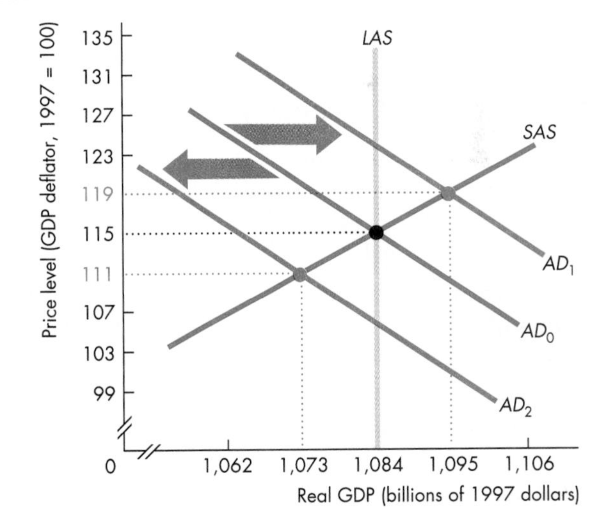

Figure 3 Aggregate supply and aggregate demand

- Do you think the Bank of Canada should always err on the side of avoiding inflation, even if that means risking recession?

SUMMARY

KEY POINTS

The Bank of Canada (pp. 606–610)

- The Bank of Canada is the central bank of Canada.
- The Bank of Canada's goals are to achieve low inflation, and as far as possible, to moderate the business cycle.
- The Bank of Canada can influence the economy by setting the required reserve ratio for banks, by setting bank rate and bankers' deposit rate, by open market operations, and by government deposit shifting.

Controlling the Quantity of Money (pp. 611–615)

- By buying government securities in the open market (an open market purchase), the Bank of Canada is able to increase the monetary base and the reserves available to banks.
- There follows an expansion of bank lending and the quantity of money increases.
- By selling government securities in the open market, the Bank of Canada is able to decrease the monetary base and bank reserves and decrease the quantity of money.

Ripple Effects of Monetary Policy (pp. 615–620)

- An increase in the quantity of money lowers the interest rate and the exchange rate, increases aggregate demand, and eventually increases real GDP and the price level.
- An increase in the quantity of money can fight unemployment, and a decrease in the quantity of money can fight inflation.
- The Bank of Canada targets the short-term interest rate, but to change the interest rate, the Bank must change the quantity of money.
- Changes in the short-term interest rate change real GDP about one year later and change the inflation rate with an even longer time lag.

The Bank of Canada in Action (p. 621)

- Since the early 1980s the Bank of Canada has been fighting inflation.
- Under Governor Gerald Bouey, the Bank increased the interest rate to a record level in 1981 and lowered the inflation rate, but at the cost of a severe recession.
- Under Governor John Crow, the Bank increased the interest rate during the late 1980s and almost eliminated inflation, but again at the cost of a severe recession.
- During the 1990s and 2000s, the Bank of Canada adjusted the interest rate to balance the primary goal of price stability with concerns for the business cycle.

KEY FIGURES

Figure 26.3 A Round in the Multiplier Process Following an Open Market Operation, 613
Figure 26.4 The Multiplier Effect of an Open Market Operation, 614
Figure 26.5 The Channels for the Ripple Effects of Monetary Policy, 616
Figure 26.6 Monetary Policy to Lower Unemployment, 616
Figure 26.7 Monetary Policy to Lower Inflation, 617
Figure 26.10 Money Target Versus Interest Rate Target, 619
Figure 26.12 Interest Rates and Real GDP Growth, 620

KEY TERMS

Bank of Canada, 606
Bank rate, 609
Central bank, 606
Currency drain, 613
Government deposit shifting, 610
Monetary base, 607
Monetary policy, 606
Monetary policy indicators, 608
Money multiplier, 613
Open market operation, 609
Overnight loans rate, 608

PROBLEMS

*1. You are given the following information about the economy of Nocoin: The banks have deposits of $300 billion. Their reserves are $15 billion, two-thirds of which is in deposits with the central bank. There is $30 billion in notes outside the banks. There are no coins!
   a. Calculate the monetary base.
   b. Calculate the quantity of money.
   c. Calculate the banks' reserve ratio.
   d. Calculate the currency drain as a percentage of the quantity of money.

2. You are given the following information about the economy of Freezone: The people and businesses in Freezone have bank deposits of $500 billion and hold $100 billion in notes and coins. The banks hold deposits at the Freezone central bank of $5 billion and they keep $5 billion in notes and coins in their vaults and ATMs. Calculate
   a. The monetary base.
   b. The quantity of money.
   c. The banks' reserve ratio.
   d. The currency drain as a percentage of the quantity of money.

*3. Suppose that in problem 1, the Bank of Nocoin, the central bank, undertakes an open market purchase of securities of $1 billion.
   a. What happens to the quantity of money?
   b. Explain why the change in the quantity of money is not equal to the change in the monetary base.
   c. Calculate the money multiplier.

4. Suppose that in problem 2, the Freezone central bank undertakes an open market sale of securities of $1 billion.
   a. What happens to the quantity of money?
   b. Explain why the change in the quantity of money is not equal to the change in the monetary base.
   c. Calculate the money multiplier.

*5. The figure shows the economy of Freezone. The aggregate demand curve is *AD* and the short-run aggregate supply curve is SAS_A. Potential GDP is $300 billion.
   a. What is the price level and real GDP?
   b. Does Freezone have an unemployment problem or an inflation problem? Why?
   c. What do you predict will happen in Freezone if the central bank takes no monetary policy actions?
   d. What monetary policy action would you advise the central bank to take, and what do you predict will be the effect of that action?

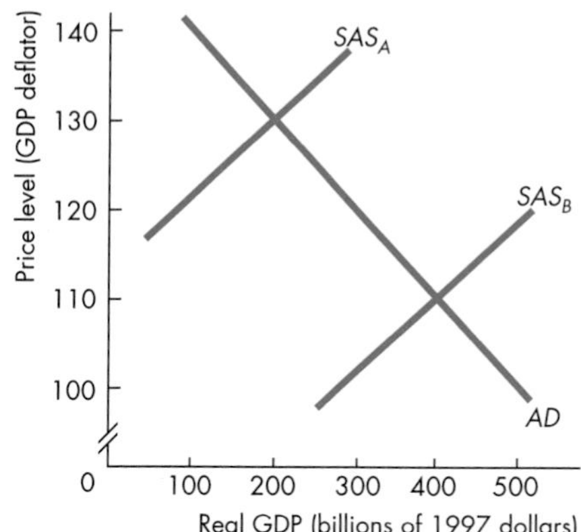

6. Suppose that in Freezone, shown in problem 5, the aggregate demand curve is *AD* and potential GDP is $300 billion, but the short-run aggregate supply curve is SAS_B.
   a. What is the price level and real GDP?
   b. Does Freezone have an unemployment problem or an inflation problem? Why?
   c. What do you predict will happen in Freezone if the central bank takes no monetary policy actions?
   d. What monetary policy action would you advise the central bank to take and what do you predict the effect of that action will be?

*7. Suppose that in Freezone, shown in problem 5, the short-run aggregate supply curve is SAS_B and potential GDP increases to $350 billion.
   a. What happens in Freezone if the central bank buys securities on the open market?
   b. What happens in Freezone if the central bank sells securities on the open market?
   c. Do you recommend that the central bank buy securities or sell securities? Why?

8. Suppose that in Freezone, shown in problem 5, the short-run aggregate supply curve is SAS_A and a drought decreases potential GDP to $250 billion.
   a. What happens in Freezone if the central bank buys securities on the open market?
   b. What happens in Freezone if the central bank sells securities on the open market?
   c. Do you recommend that the central bank buy securities or sell securities? Why?

*9. The figure shows that for a given real GDP, the demand for money in Minland fluctuates between MD_B and MD_C and on the average is MD_A.

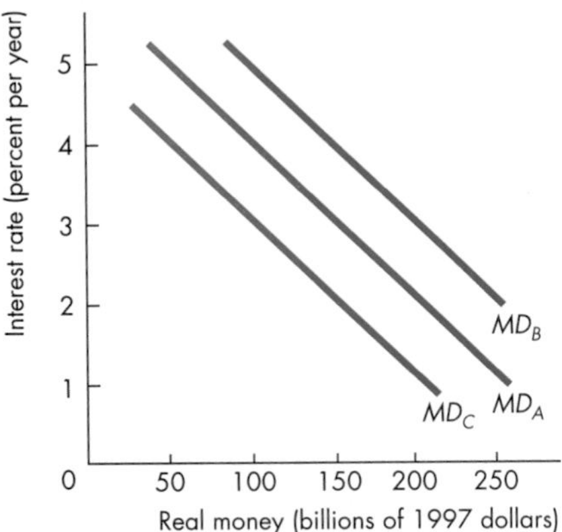

If the Minland central bank sets a target for the quantity of money at $150 billion,

a. What is the interest rate in Minland on the average?
b. What is the range of interest rates in Minland?
c. What do you expect to happen to aggregate demand, real GDP, and the price level when the demand for money changes but the quantity of money remains fixed?

10. Suppose that in Minland in problem 9, the central bank sets the interest rate target at 3 percent a year.

a. How does the Minland central bank prevent the interest rate from rising when the demand for money increases to MD_B?
b. How does the Minland central bank prevent the interest rate from falling when the demand for money decreases to MD_C?
c. Suppose that potential GDP decreases in Minland. Do you think that the Bank of Minland will maintain the 3 percent a year interest rate target? If not, do you think the Bank will try to raise the interest rate or lower it? What actions would the central bank have to take to change the interest rate?
d. If inflation breaks out in Minland, do you think that the Minland central bank will maintain its interest rate target? Why or why not?

CRITICAL THINKING

1. Study *Reading Between the Lines* on pp. 622–623 and then answer the following questions:
   a. Why did the Bank of Canada leave the interest rate unchanged in October 2002?
   b. What were the major uncertainties facing the Canadian economy during 2002?
   c. Was the Bank of Canada more concerned about inflation or recession during 2002?
   d. Do you think the Bank of Canada got its monetary policy right during 2002, or do you think it should have either raised or lowered the interest rate? Provide reasons.
2. Could the Bank of Canada have brought inflation under control during the early 1990s without creating a recession? If you think the answer is "no," do you think it was wise to lower inflation? If you think the answer is "yes," what would the Bank of Canada have had to do differently?

WEB EXERCISES

1. Use the link on the Parkin–Bade Web site to visit the Web site of the Bank of Canada and obtain the latest data on M1, M2+, and some short-term interest rates. Then answer the following questions.
   a. Is the Bank of Canada trying to slow the economy or speed it up? How can you tell?
   b. What open market operations do you think the Bank of Canada has undertaken during the past month?
   c. In the light of the Bank of Canada's recent actions, what ripple effects do you expect over the coming months?
   d. What do you think the effects of the Bank of Canada's recent actions will be on bond prices and stock prices?
2. Use the link on the Parkin–Bade Web site to visit the Web site of Statistics Canada and look at the current economic conditions. On the basis of the current state of the Canadian economy, do you predict that the Bank of Canada will raise interest rates, lower interest rates, or hold interest rates steady? Write a brief summary of your predictions and reasons.

Chapter

FISCAL AND MONETARY INTERACTIONS

CHAPTER 27

Sparks Fly in Ottawa

In 2002, the Parliament of Canada approved a federal government budget that showed a large surplus. Not far from Parliament Hill, on Sparks Street, the Bank of Canada pulls the nation's monetary policy levers that influence interest rates and the exchange rate. How does the government's fiscal policy interact with the Bank of Canada's monetary policy to influence interest rates, the exchange rate, and real GDP? ◆ Does it matter if fiscal and monetary policy come into conflict—creating sparks on Sparks Street? ◆ If a recession is looming on the horizon, is an interest rate cut by the Bank of Canada just as good as a tax cut by Parliament? If the economy is overheating, is an interest rate hike by the Bank of Canada just as good as a tax increase by Parliament?

We are going to answer these questions in this chapter. You already know a lot about the effects of fiscal policy and monetary policy. And you know that their ultimate effects work through their influences on both aggregate demand and aggregate supply. This chapter gives you a deeper understanding of the aggregate demand side of the economy and how the combined actions of the federal government and the Bank of Canada affect aggregate demand. In *Reading Between the Lines* at the end of the chapter, we look at what David Dodge, governor of the Bank of Canada, thinks about the appropriate roles for monetary and fiscal policy today.

After studying this chapter, you will be able to

- **Explain how fiscal policy and monetary policy interact to influence interest rates and aggregate demand**
- **Explain the relative effectiveness of fiscal policy and monetary policy**
- **Describe the Keynesian–monetarist controversy about policy and explain how the controversy was settled**
- **Explain how the mix of fiscal and monetary policies influences the composition of aggregate expenditure**
- **Explain how fiscal and monetary policy influence real GDP and the price level**

Macroeconomic Equilibrium

OUR GOAL IN THIS CHAPTER IS TO LEARN HOW changes in government expenditure and changes in the quantity of money interact to change real GDP, the price level, and the interest rate. But before we study the effects of *changes* in these policy variables, we must describe the state of the economy in which government expenditure and the quantity of money are given.

The Basic Idea

Aggregate demand and short-run aggregate supply determine real GDP and the price level. And the demand for and supply of real money determine the interest rate. But aggregate demand and the money market are linked together.

Other things remaining the same, the greater the level of aggregate demand, the higher are real GDP and the price level. A higher real GDP means a greater demand for money; a higher price level means a smaller supply of real money; so a greater level of aggregate demand means a higher interest rate.

Aggregate demand depends on the interest rate because consumption expenditure, investment, and net exports are influenced by the interest rate (see Chapter 25, pp. 597–599). So, other things remaining the same, the lower the interest rate, the greater is aggregate demand.

Only one level of aggregate demand and one interest rate are consistent with each other in macroeconomic equilibrium. Figure 27.1 describes this unique equilibrium.

AS–AD Equilibrium

In Fig. 27.1(a) the intersection of the aggregate demand curve, *AD*, and the short-run aggregate supply curve, *SAS*, determines real GDP at $1,000 billion and the price level at 110.

The equilibrium amounts of consumption expenditure, investment, government expenditures, and net exports lie behind the *AD* curve. But some components of these expenditures are influenced by the interest rate. And the interest rate, in turn, is determined by equilibrium in the money market. Assume that interest-sensitive expenditures total $100 billion, government expenditure is $100 billion, and the rest of real GDP totals $800 billion.

Money Market Equilibrium and Interest-Sensitive Expenditure

In Fig. 27.1(b) the intersection of the demand for money curve, *MD*, and the supply of money curve, *MS*, determines the interest rate at 5 percent a year.

The position of the *MD* curve depends on the level of real GDP. Suppose that the demand for money curve shown in the figure describes the demand for money when real GDP is $1,000 billion, which is equilibrium real GDP in Fig. 27.1(a).

The position of the *MS* curve depends on the quantity of nominal money and the price level. Suppose that the supply of money curve shown in the figure describes the quantity of real money when the price level is 110, which is the equilibrium price level in Fig. 27.1(a).

In Fig. 27.1(c), the *IE* curve determines the level of interest-sensitive expenditure at the equilibrium interest rate of 5 percent a year. Interest-sensitive expenditure is $100 billion, which is the level of this expenditure that lies behind the aggregate demand curve *AD* in Fig. 27.1(a).

Check the Equilibrium

The *AS–AD* equilibrium in Fig. 27.1(a), the money market equilibrium in Fig. 27.1(b), and interest-sensitive expenditure in Fig. 27.1(c) are consistent with each other. And there is no other equilibrium.

To check this claim, assume that aggregate demand is less than *AD* in Fig. 27.1(a) so that real GDP is less than $1,000 billion. If this assumption is correct, the demand for money curve lies to the left of *MD* in Fig. 27.1(b) and the equilibrium interest rate is less than 5 percent a year. With an interest rate less than 5 percent a year, interest-sensitive expenditure exceeds the $100 billion in Fig. 27.1(c). If interest-sensitive expenditure exceeds $100 billion, the *AD* curve lies to the right of the one we assumed and equilibrium real GDP exceeds $1,000 billion. So if we assume a real GDP of less than $1,000 billion, equilibrium real GDP is greater than $1,000 billion. There is an inconsistency. The assumed equilibrium real GDP is too small.

Now assume that aggregate demand is greater than *AD* in Fig. 27.1(a) so that real GDP exceeds $1,000 billion. If this assumption is correct, the demand for money curve lies to the right of *MD* in Fig. 27.1(b) and the equilibrium interest rate exceeds 5 percent a year. With an interest rate above 5 percent a year, interest-sensitive expenditure is less than the $100 billion in Fig. 27.1(c), in which case the

FIGURE 27.1 Equilibrium Real GDP, Price Level, Interest Rate, and Expenditure

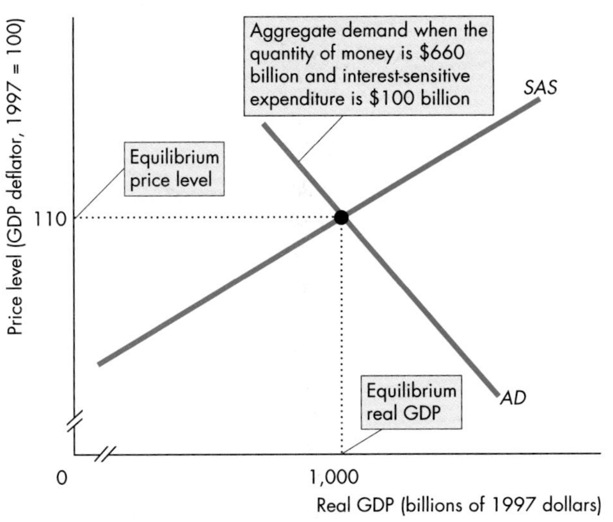

(a) Aggregate supply and aggregate demand

In part (a), the intersection of the aggregate demand curve, *AD*, and the short-run aggregate supply curve, *SAS*, determines real GDP at $1,000 billion and the price level at 110. Behind the *AD* curve, interest-sensitive expenditure is $100 billion, government expenditure is $100 billion, and the rest of real GDP is $800 billion. In part (b), when real GDP is $1,000 billion, the demand for money curve is *MD* and when the price level is 110, the supply of real money curve is *MS*. The intersection of the demand for money curve, *MD*, and the supply of money curve, *MS*, determines the interest rate at 5 percent a year. In part (c), on the *IE* curve, interest-sensitive expenditure is $100 billion at the equilibrium interest rate of 5 percent a year.

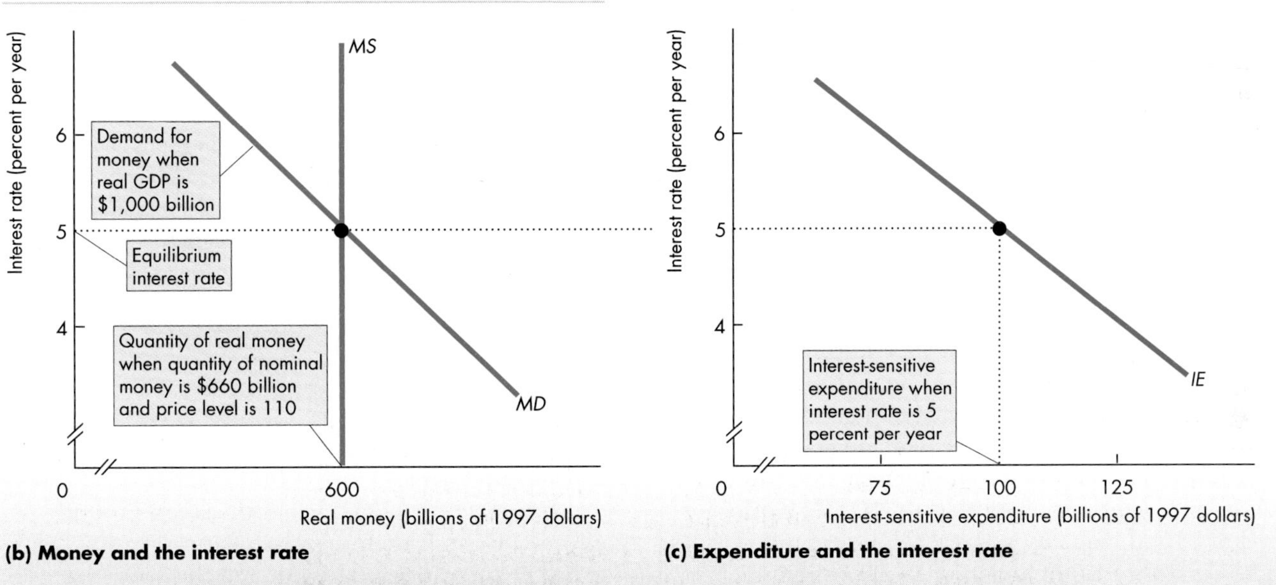

(b) Money and the interest rate

(c) Expenditure and the interest rate

AD curve must lie to the left of the one we assumed and equilibrium real GDP must be smaller than $1,000 billion. So if we assume that real GDP exceeds $1,000 billion, equilibrium real GDP is less than $1,000 billion. There is another inconsistency. The assumed equilibrium real GDP is too large.

Only one level of aggregate demand delivers the same money market equilibrium and *AS–AD* equilibrium. In this example, it is the aggregate demand curve *AD* in Fig. 27.1(a). Assuming this level of aggregate demand implies this level of aggregate demand. Assuming a lower level of aggregate demand implies a higher level. And assuming a higher level of aggregate demand implies a lower level.

Now that you understand how aggregate demand and the interest rate are simultaneously determined, let's study the effects of a change in government expenditures.

Fiscal Policy in the Short Run

REAL GDP GROWTH IS SLOWING, AND THE Finance Minister is concerned that a recession is likely. So the government decides to try to head off the recession by using fiscal policy to stimulate aggregate demand. A fiscal policy that increases aggregate demand is called an *expansionary fiscal policy.*

The effects of an expansionary fiscal policy are similar to those of throwing a pebble into a pond. There's an initial splash followed by a series of ripples that become ever smaller. The initial splash is the "first round effect" of the fiscal policy action. The ripples are the "second round effects." You've already met the first round effects in Chapter 24, so here is a refresher.

First Round Effects of Fiscal Policy

The economy starts out in the position shown in Fig. 27.1. Real GDP is $1,000 billion, the price level is 110, the interest rate is 5 percent a year, and interest-sensitive expenditure is $100 billion. The government now increases its expenditures on goods and services by $100 billion.

Figure 27.2 shows the first round effects of this action. The increase in government expenditures has a multiplier effect because it induces an increase in consumption expenditure. (You can refresh your memory about the government expenditures multiplier on pp. 562–564.) Let's assume that the multiplier is 2, so a $100 billion increase in government expenditure increases aggregate demand at a given price level by $200 billion. The aggregate demand curve shifts rightward from AD_0 to AD_1. At a price level of 110, the quantity of real GDP demanded increases from $1,000 billion to $1,200 billion.

Real GDP now starts to increase and the price level starts to rise. These are the first round effects of expansionary fiscal policy.

Second Round Effects of Fiscal Policy

Through the second round, real GDP increases and the price level rises until a new macroeconomic equilibrium is reached. But to find that equilibrium and to describe the changes that result from the initial increase in government expenditures, we must keep track of further changes in the money market and in expenditure plans.

FIGURE 27.2 First Round Effects of an Expansionary Fiscal Policy

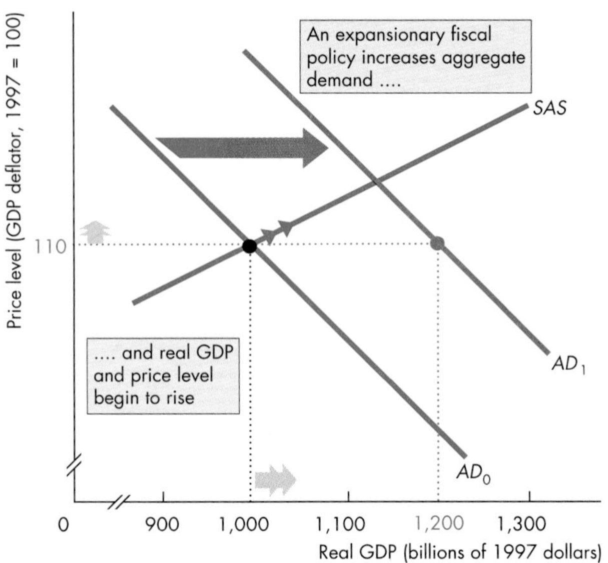

Initially, the aggregate demand curve is AD_0, real GDP is $1,000 billion, and the price level is 110. A $100 billion increase in government expenditures on goods and services has a multiplier effect and increases aggregate demand by $200 billion. The aggregate demand curve shifts rightward to AD_1. Real GDP begins to increase and the price level begins to rise. These are the first round effects of an expansionary fiscal policy.

It is easier to keep track of the second round effects if we split them into two parts: one that results from the increasing real GDP, and the other that results from the rising price level. We follow these effects in Fig. 27.3.

First, the increasing real GDP increases the demand for money. In Fig. 27.3(b), the demand for money curve shifts rightward. Eventually, it shifts to MD_1 and the interest rate rises to 6 percent a year. At this interest rate, interest-sensitive expenditure decreases to $75 billion in Fig. 27.3(c). The decrease in planned expenditure decreases aggregate demand and the aggregate demand curve shifts leftward to AD_2 in Fig. 27.3(a).

FIGURE 27.3 Second Round Effects of an Expansionary Fiscal Policy

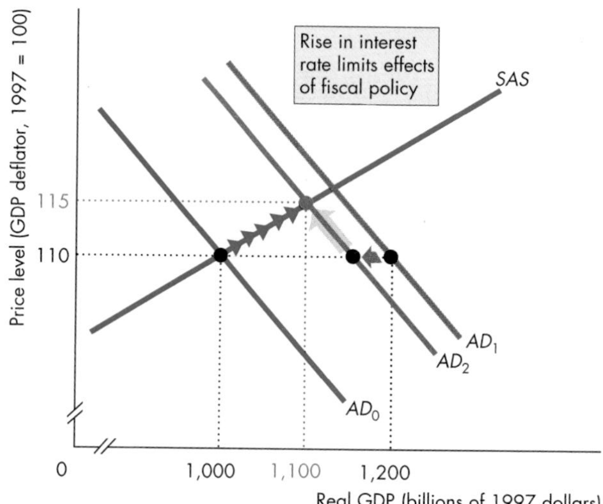

(a) Aggregate supply and aggregate demand

Initially, (part b), the money demand curve is MD_0, the real money supply curve is MS_0, and the interest rate is 5 percent a year. With an interest rate of 5 percent a year, interest-sensitive expenditure is $100 billion on the curve *IE* (part c). With increased government expenditures, the aggregate demand curve is AD_1 (part a). Real GDP is increasing, and the price level is rising. The increasing real GDP increases the demand for money and the money demand curve shifts rightward to MD_1. The higher interest rate decreases interest-sensitive expenditure, which decreases aggregate demand to AD_2. The rising price level brings a movement along the new *AD* curve. It does so because it decreases the quantity of real money. The money supply curve shifts leftward to MS_1, which in turn raises the interest rate further and decreases expenditure. The new equilibrium occurs when real GDP has increased to $1,100 billion and the price level has risen to 115.

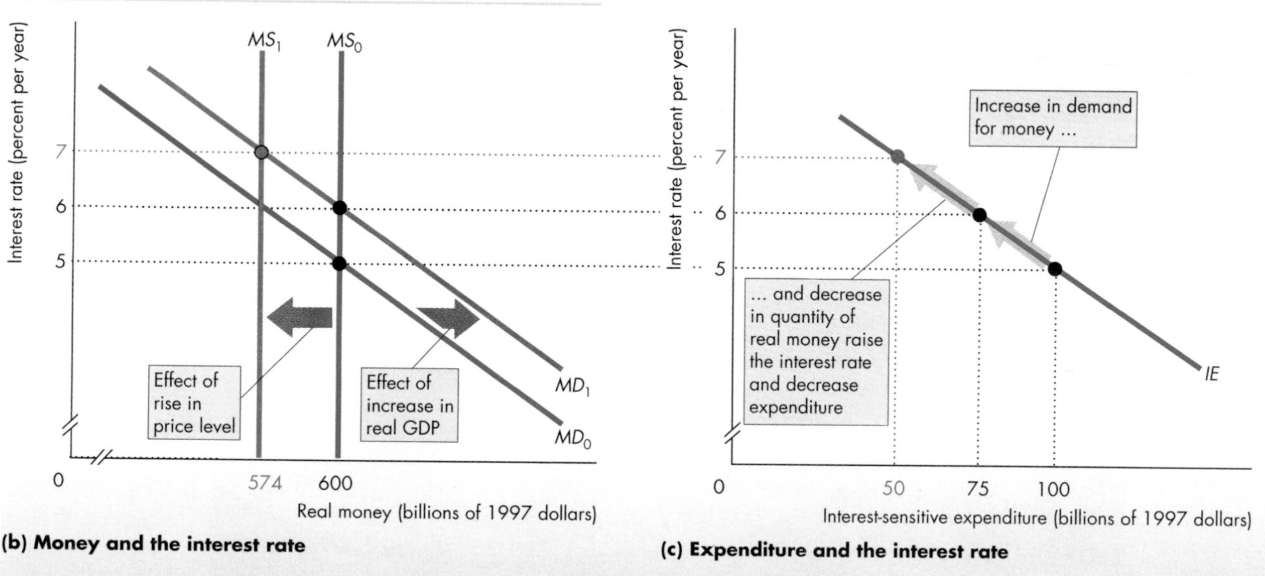

(b) Money and the interest rate

(c) Expenditure and the interest rate

Second, with a given quantity of nominal money, the rising price level decreases the quantity of real money. In Fig. 27.3(b), the money supply curve shifts leftward to MS_1. The decrease in the quantity of real money raises the interest rate further to 7 percent a year. In Fig. 27.3(c), the higher interest rate decreases interest-sensitive expenditure to $50 billion. Because this decrease in spending plans is induced by a rise in the price level, it decreases the quantity of real GDP demanded and is shown as a movement up along the aggregate demand curve AD_2 in Fig. 27.3(a).

During this second round process, real GDP is increasing and the price level is rising in a gradual movement up along the short-run aggregate supply curve as indicated by the arrows. In the new equilibrium, real GDP is $1,100 billion, the price level is 115, the interest rate is 7 percent a year, and interest-sensitive expenditure is $50 billion.

FIGURE 27.4 How the Economy Adjusts to an Expansionary Fiscal Policy

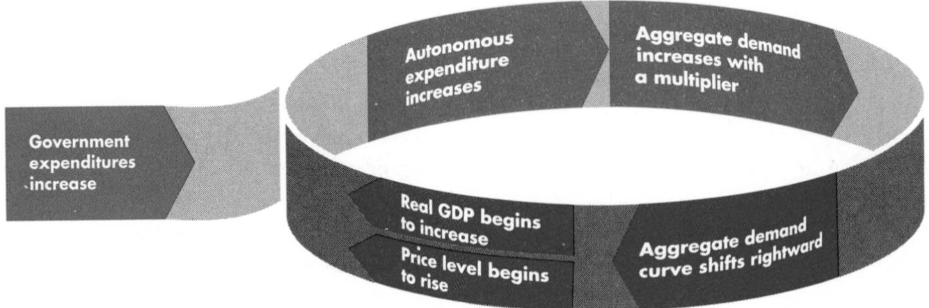

(a) First round effect of expansionary fiscal policy

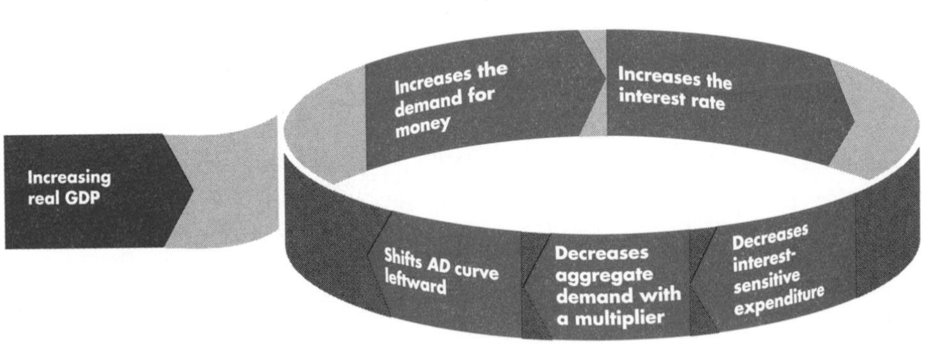

(b) Second round real GDP effect

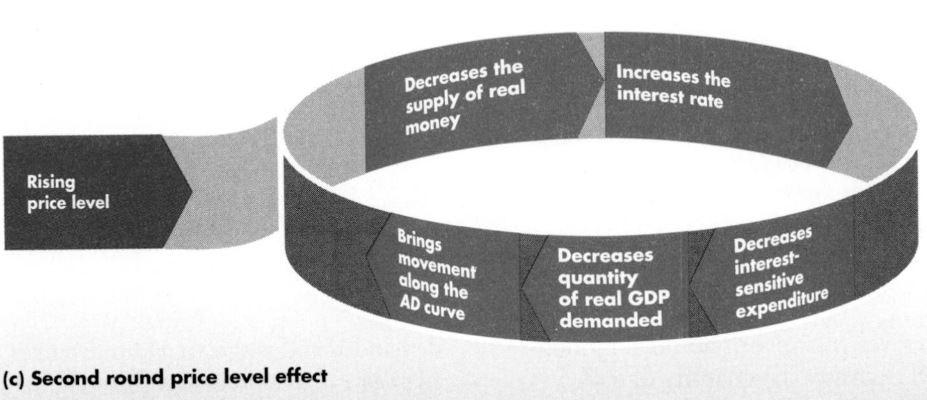

(c) Second round price level effect

Just as the initial equilibrium in Fig. 27.1 was consistent, so the new equilibrium is consistent. The *AS–AD* equilibrium in Fig. 27.3(a), the money market equilibrium in Fig. 27.3(b), and interest-sensitive expenditure in Fig. 27.3(c) are all consistent with each other. And there is no other equilibrium.

Figure 27.4(a) summarizes the first round effect of an expansionary fiscal policy action. Figure 27.4(b) summarizes the two parts of the second round adjustments as the economy responds.

Other Fiscal Policies

A change in government expenditures is only one possible fiscal policy action. Others are a change in transfer payments, such as an increase in unemployment compensation or an increase in social benefits and a change in taxes. All fiscal policy actions work by changing expenditure. But the magnitude of the initial change in expenditure differs for different fiscal actions. For example, changes in taxes and transfer payments change expenditure by smaller amounts than does a change in government expenditures on goods and services. But fiscal policies that change autonomous expenditure by a given amount and in a given direction have similar effects on equilibrium real GDP, the price level, and the interest rate regardless of the initial fiscal action. Let's take a closer look at the effect of the rise in the interest rate.

Crowding Out and Crowding In

Because an expansionary fiscal policy increases the interest rate, it decreases all the interest-sensitive components of aggregate expenditure. One of these components is investment, and the decrease in investment that results from an expansionary fiscal action is called **crowding out.**

Crowding out may be partial or complete. Partial crowding out occurs when the decrease in investment is less than the increase in government expenditures. This is the normal case—and the case we've just seen.

Complete crowding out occurs if the decrease in investment equals the initial increase in government expenditures. For complete crowding out to occur, a small change in the demand for real money must lead to a large change in the interest rate, and the change in the interest rate must lead to a large change in investment.

But another potential influence of government expenditures on investment works in the opposite direction to the crowding-out effect and is called "crowding in." **Crowding in** is the tendency for expansionary fiscal policy to *increase* investment. This effect works in three ways.

First, in a recession, an expansionary fiscal policy might create expectations of a more speedy recovery and bring an increase in expected profits. Higher expected profits might increase investment despite a higher interest rate.

Second, government expenditures might be productive and lead to more profitable business opportunities. For example, a new government-built highway might cut the cost of transporting a farmer's produce to a market and induce the farmer to invest in a new fleet of refrigerated trucks.

Third, if an expansionary fiscal policy takes the form of a cut in taxes on business profits, firms' after-tax profits increase and investment might increase.

The Exchange Rate and International Crowding Out

We've seen that an expansionary fiscal policy leads to higher interest rates. But a change in interest rates also affects the exchange rate. Higher interest rates make the dollar rise in value against other currencies. With interest rates higher in Canada than in the rest of the world, funds flow into Canada and people around the world demand more Canadian dollars. As the dollar rises in value, foreigners find Canadian-produced goods and services more expensive and Canadians find imports less expensive. Exports decrease and imports increase—net exports decrease. The tendency for an expansionary fiscal policy to decrease net exports is called **international crowding out.** The decrease in net exports offsets, to some degree, the initial increase in aggregate expenditure brought about by an expansionary fiscal policy.

REVIEW QUIZ

1 Describe macroeconomic equilibrium. What conditions are met in such an equilibrium? What are the links between aggregate demand, the money market, and investment?
2 What is an expansionary fiscal policy and what are its first round effects? What is happening at the end of the first round?
3 What are the second round effects of an expansionary fiscal policy action? Describe the forces at work and the changes that occur in the interest rate, investment, real GDP, and the price level.
4 What is crowding out? What is crowding in? How do they influence the outcome of a fiscal policy action?
5 How does an expansionary fiscal policy affect the exchange rate? What happens to imports and exports?

Monetary Policy in the Short Run

To study the effects of an expansionary monetary policy, we look at the first round effects and the second round effects, just as we did for fiscal policy. Figure 27.5 describes the economy, which is initially in the situation that we studied in Fig. 27.1. The quantity of money is $660 billion, the interest rate is 5 percent a year, interest-sensitive expenditure is $100 billion, real GDP is $1,000 billion, and the price level is 110.

The Bank of Canada now increases the quantity of money to $1,155 billion. With a price level of 110, the quantity of real money increases to $1,050 billion. Figure 27.5(a) shows the immediate effect. The real money supply curve shifts rightward from MS_0 to MS_1, and the interest rate falls from 5 percent to 1 percent a year. The lower interest rate increases interest-sensitive expenditure to $200 billion (part b). The increase in interest-sensitive expenditure

FIGURE 27.5 First Round Effects of an Expansionary Monetary Policy

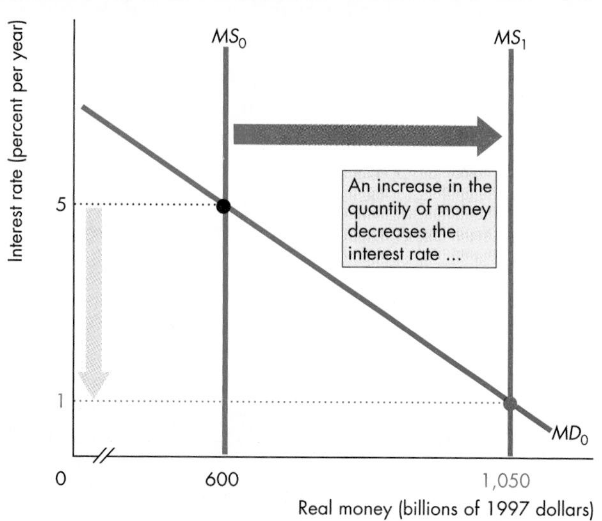

(a) Change in quantity of money

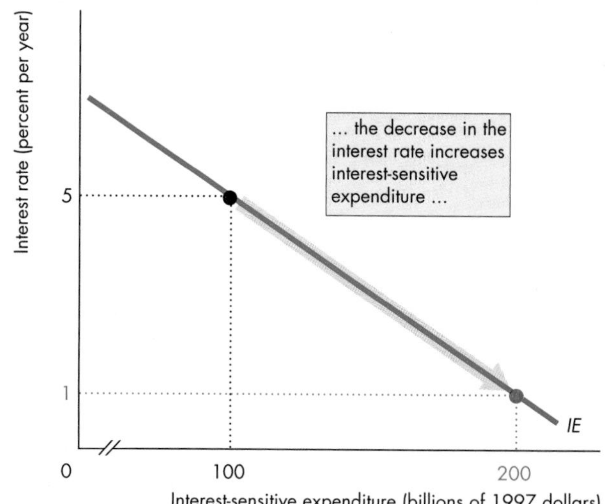

(b) Change in expenditure

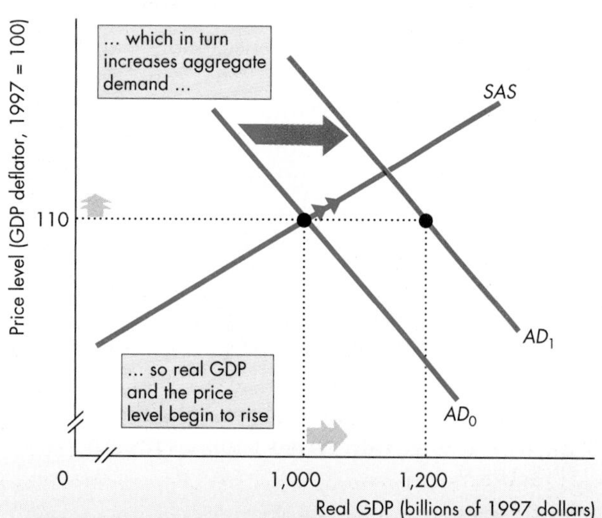

(c) Change in aggregate demand

Initially, the real money demand curve is MD_0, the real money supply curve is MS_0, and the interest rate is 5 percent a year (part a). With an interest rate of 5 percent a year, interest-sensitive expenditure is $100 billion on the *IE* curve (part b). The aggregate demand curve is AD_0. Equilibrium real GDP is $1,000 billion, and the price level is 110 (part c).

An increase in the quantity of money shifts the money supply curve rightward to MS_1 (part a). The interest rate falls to 1 percent a year and interest-sensitive expenditure increases to $200 billion (part b). The increase in expenditure increases aggregate demand and shifts the aggregate demand curve to AD_1 (in part c). Real GDP begins to increase and the price level begins to rise.

increases aggregate demand and shifts the *AD* curve rightward from AD_0 to AD_1 (part c). The increase in aggregate demand sets off a multiplier process in which real GDP and the price level begin to increase towards their equilibrium levels.

These are the first round effects of an expansionary monetary policy. An increase in the quantity of money lowers the interest rate and increases aggregate demand. Real GDP and the price level begin to increase.

Let's now look at the second round effects.

Second Round Effects

The increasing real GDP and rising price level set off the second round, which Fig. 27.6 illustrates. And as in the case of fiscal policy, it is best to break the second round into two parts: the consequence of increasing real GDP, and the consequence of the rising price level.

The increasing real GDP increases the demand for money from MD_0 to MD_1 in Fig. 27.6(a). The increased demand for money raises the interest rate to

FIGURE 27.6 Second Round Effects of an Expansionary Monetary Policy

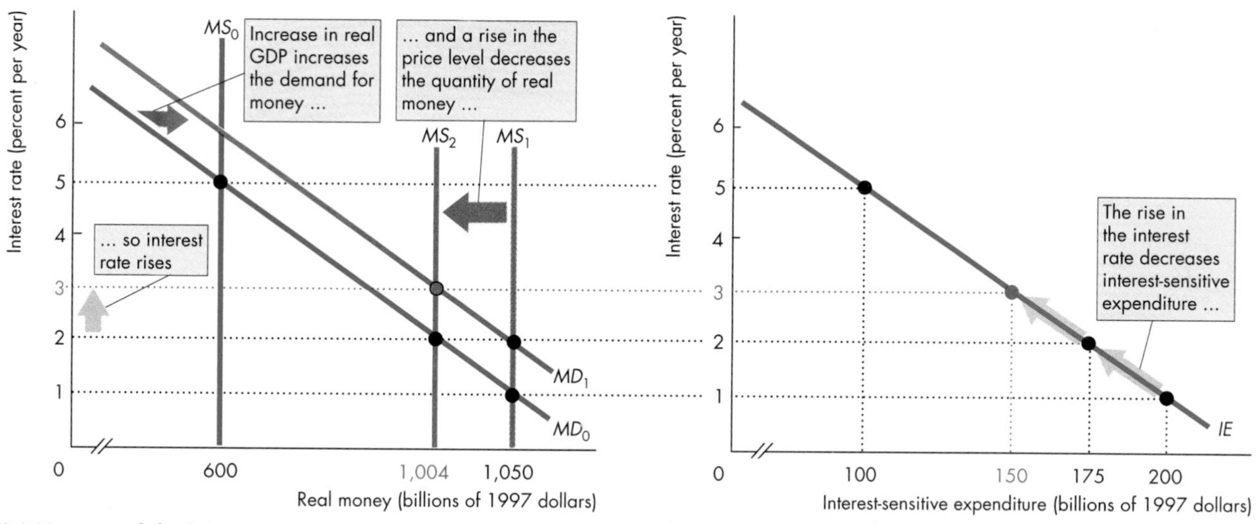

(a) Money and the interest rate

(b) Decrease in expenditure

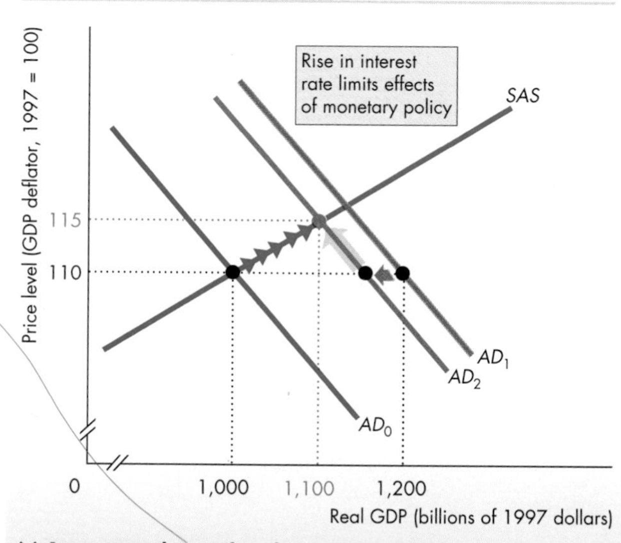

(c) Aggregate demand and aggregate supply

At the start of the second round, the money demand curve is still MD_0 (part a), the real money supply curve is MS_1, and the interest rate is 1 percent a year. With an interest rate of 1 percent a year, interest-sensitive expenditure is \$200 billion on the curve *IE* (part b). With the increased quantity of money and expenditure level, the aggregate demand curve is AD_1 (part c). Real GDP is increasing, and the price level is rising. The increasing real GDP increases the demand for money and the money demand curve shifts rightward to MD_1. The higher interest rate decreases interest-sensitive expenditure, which decreases aggregate demand to AD_2. The rising price level brings a movement along the new *AD* curve. It does so because the rising price level decreases the quantity of real money and the money supply curve shifts to MS_2. The interest rate raises further and expenditure decreases. The new equilibrium occurs when real GDP has increased to \$1,100 billion and the price level has risen to 115.

2 percent a year. The higher interest rate brings a decrease in interest-sensitive expenditure from $200 billion to $175 billion in Fig. 27.6(b). And the lower level of expenditure decreases aggregate demand and shifts the aggregate demand curve leftward from AD_1 to AD_2 in Fig. 27.6(c).

The rising price level brings a movement along the new aggregate demand curve in Fig. 27.6(c). This movement occurs because the rising price level decreases the quantity of real money. As the price level rises, the quantity of real money decreases to $1,004 billion and the money supply curve shifts leftward from MS_1 to MS_2 (part a). The interest rate rises further to 3 percent a year. And interest-sensitive expenditure decreases to $150 billion (part b).

In the new short-run equilibrium, real GDP has increased to $1,100 billion, and the price level has risen to 115, where aggregate demand curve AD_2 intersects the short-run aggregate supply curve *SAS*.

FIGURE 27.7 How the Economy Adjusts to an Expansionary Monetary Policy

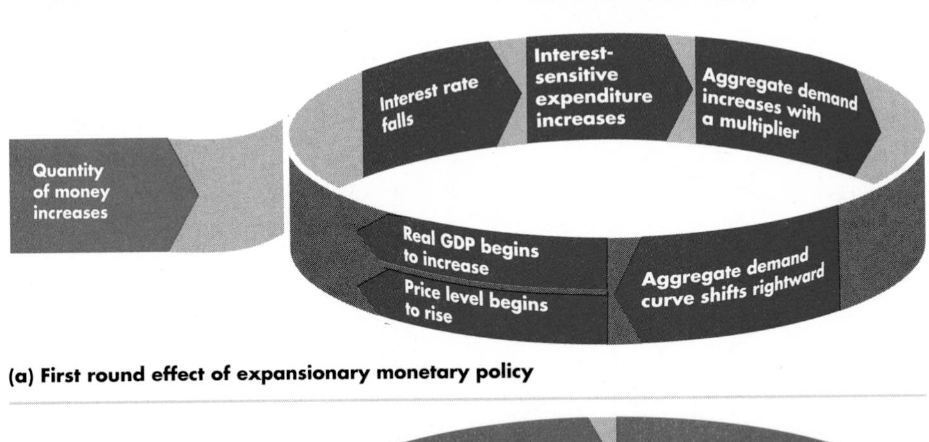

(a) First round effect of expansionary monetary policy

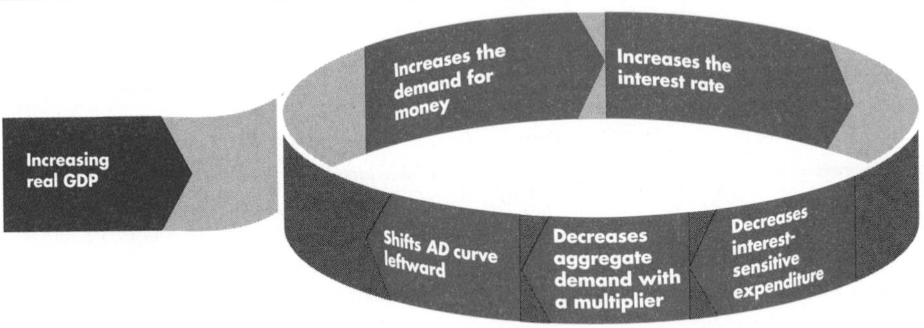

(b) Second round real GDP effect

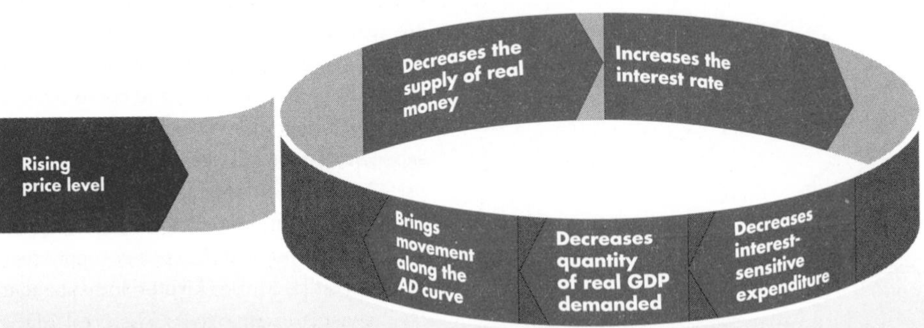

(c) Second round price level effect

The money demand curve is MD_1, the money supply curve is MS_2, and the interest rate is 3 percent a year in part (a). With an interest rate of 3 percent a year, interest-sensitive expenditure is \$150 billion (part b).

The new equilibrium is the only consistent one and is like that of Fig. 27.1. Figure 27.7 summarizes the adjustments that occur to bring the economy to this new equilibrium.

Money and the Exchange Rate

An increase in the money supply lowers the interest rate. If the interest rate falls in Canada but does not fall in the United States, Japan, and Western Europe, international investors buy the now higher-yielding foreign assets and sell the relatively lower-yielding Canadian assets. As they make these transactions, they sell Canadian dollars. So the dollar depreciates against other currencies. (This mechanism is explained in greater detail in Chapter 26, pp. 619–620.)

With a cheaper Canadian dollar, foreigners face lower prices for Canadian-produced goods and services and Canadians face higher prices for foreign-produced goods and services. Foreigners increase their imports from Canada, and Canadians decrease their imports from the rest of the world. Canadian net exports increase, and real GDP and the price level increase further.

REVIEW QUIZ

1. What are the first round effects of an expansionary monetary policy? What happens to the interest rate, investment and other components of interest-sensitive expenditure, aggregate demand, the demand for money, real GDP, and the price level in the first round?
2. What are the second round effects of an expansionary monetary policy? What happens to the interest rate, investment and other components of interest-sensitive expenditure, aggregate demand, the demand for money, real GDP, and the price level in the second round?
3. How does an expansionary monetary policy influence the exchange rate, imports, and exports?

Relative Effectiveness of Policies

WE'VE SEEN THAT AGGREGATE DEMAND AND REAL GDP are influenced by both fiscal and monetary policy. But which policy is the more potent? This question was once at the centre of a controversy among macroeconomists. Later in this section we'll look at that controversy and see how it was settled. But we begin by discovering what determines the effectiveness of fiscal policy.

Effectiveness of Fiscal Policy

The effectiveness of fiscal policy is measured by the magnitude of the increase in aggregate demand that results from a given increase in government expenditures (or decrease in taxes). The effectiveness of fiscal policy depends on the strength of the crowding-out effect. Fiscal policy is most powerful if no crowding out occurs. Fiscal policy is impotent if there is complete crowding out. And the strength of the crowding-out effect depends on two things:

1. The responsiveness of expenditure to the interest rate
2. The responsiveness of the quantity of money demanded to the interest rate

If expenditure is not very responsive to a change in the interest rate, the crowding-out effect is small. But if expenditure is highly responsive to a change in the interest rate, the crowding-out effect is large. Other things remaining the same, the smaller the responsiveness of expenditure to the interest rate, the smaller is the crowding-out effect and the more effective is fiscal policy.

The responsiveness of the quantity of money demanded to the interest rate also affects the size of the crowding-out effect. An increase in real GDP increases the demand for money and with no change in the quantity of money, the interest rate rises. But the extent to which the interest rate rises depends on the responsiveness of the quantity of money demanded to the interest rate. Other things remaining the same, the greater the responsiveness of the quantity of money demanded to the interest rate, the smaller is the rise in the interest rate, the smaller is the crowding-out effect, and the more effective is fiscal policy.

Effectiveness of Monetary Policy

The effectiveness of monetary policy is measured by the magnitude of the increase in aggregate demand that results from a given increase in the quantity of money. The effectiveness of monetary policy depends on the same two factors that influence the effectiveness of fiscal policy:

1. The responsiveness of the quantity of money demanded to the interest rate
2. The responsiveness of expenditure to the interest rate

The starting point for monetary policy is a change in the quantity of money that changes the interest rate. A given change in the quantity of money might bring a small change or a large change in the interest rate. The less responsive the quantity of money demanded to the interest rate, the greater is the change in the interest rate. So other things remaining the same, the larger the initial change in the interest rate, the more effective is monetary policy.

But effectiveness of monetary policy also depends on how much expenditure changes. If expenditure is not very responsive to a change in the interest rate, monetary actions do not have much effect on expenditure. But if expenditure is highly responsive to a change in the interest rate, monetary actions have a large effect on aggregate expenditure. The greater the responsiveness of expenditure to the interest rate, the more effective is monetary policy.

The effectiveness of fiscal policy and monetary policy that you've just studied was once controversial. During the 1950s and 1960s, this issue lay at the heart of what was called the Keynesian–monetarist controversy. Let's look at the dispute and see how it was resolved.

Keynesian–Monetarist Controversy

The Keynesian–monetarist controversy was an ongoing dispute in macroeconomics between two broad groups of economists. A **Keynesian** is a macroeconomist who regards the economy as being inherently unstable and as requiring active government intervention to achieve stability. Keynesian views about the functioning of the economy are based on the theories of John Maynard Keynes, published in Keynes' *General Theory* (see pp. 522–523). Traditionally Keynesians assigned a low degree of importance to monetary policy and a high degree of importance to fiscal policy. Modern Keynesians assign a high degree of importance to both types of policy. A **monetarist** is a macroeconomist who believes that most macroeconomic fluctuations are caused by fluctuations in the quantity of money and that the economy is inherently stable and requires no active government intervention. Monetarist views about the functioning of the economy are based on theories most forcefully set forth by Milton Friedman (see pp. 674–675). Traditionally monetarists assigned a low degree of importance to fiscal policy. But modern monetarists, like modern Keynesians, assign a high degree of importance to both types of policy.

The nature of the Keynesian–monetarist debate has changed over the years. During the 1950s and 1960s, it was a debate about the relative effectiveness of fiscal policy and monetary policy in changing aggregate demand. We can see the essence of that debate by distinguishing three views:

- Extreme Keynesianism
- Extreme monetarism
- Intermediate position

Extreme Keynesianism The extreme Keynesian hypothesis is that a change in the quantity of money has no effect on aggregate demand and a change in government expenditures on goods and services or in taxes has a large effect on aggregate demand. The two circumstances in which a change in the quantity of money has no effect on aggregate demand are

1. Expenditure is completely insensitive to the interest rate
2. The quantity of money demanded is highly sensitive to the interest rate

If expenditure is completely insensitive to the interest rate (if the *IE* curve is vertical), a change in the quantity of money changes the interest rate, but the change does not affect aggregate planned expenditure. Monetary policy is impotent.

If the quantity of money demanded is highly sensitive to the interest rate (if the *MD* curve is horizontal), people are willing to hold any amount of money at a given interest rate—a situation called a *liquidity trap*. With a liquidity trap, a change in the quantity of money affects only the amount of money held. It does not affect the interest rate. With an unchanged interest rate, expenditure remains constant. Monetary policy is impotent. Some people believe that Japan was in a liquidity trap during the late 1990s.

Extreme Monetarism The extreme monetarist hypothesis is that a change in government expenditures on goods and services or in taxes has no effect on aggregate demand and that a change in the quantity of money has a large effect on aggregate demand. Two circumstances give rise to these predictions:

1. Expenditure is highly sensitive to the interest rate
2. The quantity of money demanded is completely insensitive to the interest rate

If an increase in government expenditures on goods and services induces an increase in the interest rate that is sufficiently large to reduce expenditure by the same amount as the initial increase in government expenditures, then fiscal policy has no effect on aggregate demand. This outcome is complete crowding out. For this result to occur, either the quantity of money demanded must be insensitive to the interest rate—a fixed amount of money is held regardless of the interest rate—or expenditure must be highly sensitive to the interest rate—any amount of expenditure will be undertaken at a given interest rate.

The Intermediate Position The intermediate position is that both fiscal and monetary policy affect aggregate demand. Crowding out is not complete, so fiscal policy does have an effect. There is no liquidity trap and expenditure responds to the interest rate, so monetary policy does indeed affect aggregate demand. This position is the one that now appears to be correct and is the one that we've spent most of this chapter exploring. Let's see how economists came to this conclusion.

Sorting Out the Competing Claims

The dispute between monetarists, Keynesians, and those taking an intermediate position was essentially a disagreement about the magnitudes of two economic parameters:

1. The responsiveness of expenditure to the interest rate
2. The responsiveness of the demand for real money to the interest rate

If expenditure is highly sensitive to the interest rate or the demand for real money is barely sensitive to the interest rate, then monetary policy is powerful and fiscal policy relatively ineffective. In this case, the world looks similar to the claims of extreme monetarists. If expenditure is very insensitive to the interest rate, or the demand for real money is highly sensitive, then fiscal policy is powerful and monetary policy is relatively ineffective. In this case, the world looks similar to the claims of the extreme Keynesians.

By using statistical methods to study the demand for real money and expenditure and by using data from a wide variety of historical and national experiences, economists were able to settle this dispute. Neither extreme position turned out to be supported by the evidence and the intermediate position won. The demand curve for real money slopes downward. And expenditure *is* interest sensitive. Neither the money demand curve nor the interest-sensitive expenditure curve is vertical or horizontal, so the extreme Keynesian and extreme monetarist hypotheses are rejected.

Interest Rate and Exchange Rate Effectiveness

Although fiscal policy and monetary policy are alternative ways of changing aggregate demand, they have opposing effects on the interest rate and the exchange rate. A fiscal policy action that increases aggregate demand raises the interest rate and increases the exchange rate. A monetary policy action that increases aggregate demand lowers the interest rate and decreases the exchange rate. Because of these opposing effects on interest rates and the exchange rate, if the two policies are combined to increase aggregate demand, their separate effects on the interest rate and the exchange rate can be minimized.

REVIEW QUIZ

1. What two macroeconomic parameters influence the relative effectiveness of fiscal policy and monetary policy?
2. Under what circumstances is the Keynesian view correct and under what circumstances is the monetarist view correct?
3. How can fiscal policy and monetary policy be combined to increase aggregate demand yet at the same time keep the interest rate constant?

We're now going to look at expansionary fiscal and monetary policy at full employment.

Policy Actions at Full Employment

AN EXPANSIONARY FISCAL POLICY OR MONETARY policy can bring the economy to full employment. But it is often difficult to determine whether the economy is below full employment. So an expansionary fiscal policy or monetary policy might be undertaken when the economy is at full employment. What happens then? Let's answer this question starting with an expansionary fiscal policy.

Expansionary Fiscal Policy at Full Employment

Suppose the economy is at full employment and the government increases expenditure. All the effects that we worked out earlier in this chapter occur. Except that these effects determine only a *short-run equilibrium.* That is, the first round and second round effects of policy both occur in the short run. There is a third round, which is the long-run adjustment.

Starting out at full employment, an expansionary fiscal policy will create an above full-employment equilibrium in which there is an *inflationary gap.* The money wage rate begins to rise, short-run aggregate supply decreases, and a long-run adjustment occurs in which real GDP decreases to potential GDP and the price level rises.

Figure 27.8 illustrates the combined first and second round short-run effects and the third round long-run adjustment.

In Fig. 27.8, potential GDP is $1,000 billion. Real GDP equals potential GDP on aggregate demand curve AD_0 and short-run aggregate supply curve SAS_0. An expansionary fiscal action increases aggregate demand. The combined first round and second round effect increases aggregate demand to AD_1. Real GDP increases to $1,100 billion and the price level rises to 115. There is an inflationary gap of $100 billion.

With the economy above full employment, a shortage of labour puts upward pressure on the money wage rate, which now begins to rise. And a third round of adjustment begins. The rising money wage rate decreases short-run aggregate supply and the *SAS* curve starts moving leftward towards SAS_1.

As short-run aggregate supply decreases, real GDP decreases and the price level rises. This process

FIGURE 27.8 Fiscal Policy at Full Employment

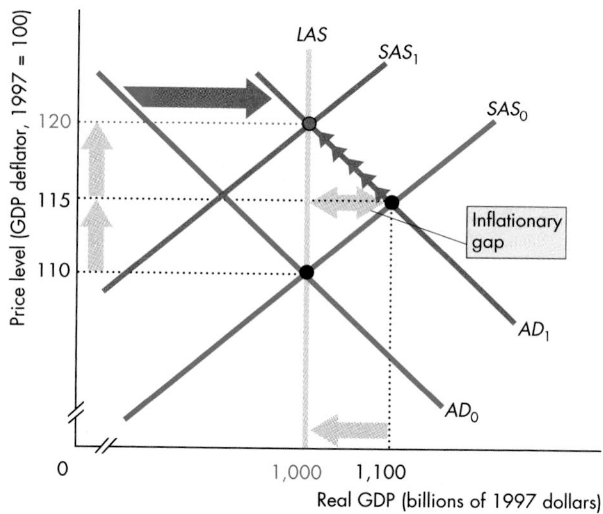

The long-run aggregate supply curve is *LAS* and initially the aggregate demand curve is AD_0 and the short-run aggregate supply curve is SAS_0. Real GDP is $1,000 billion and the GDP deflator is 110. Fiscal and monetary policy changes shift the aggregate demand curve to AD_1. At the new short-run equilibrium, real GDP is $1,100 billion and the GDP deflator is 115. Because real GDP exceeds potential GDP, the money wage rate begins to rise and the short-run aggregate supply curve begins to shift leftward to SAS_1. At the new long-run equilibrium, the GDP deflator is 120 and real GDP is back at its original level.

continues until the inflationary gap has been eliminated at full employment. At long-run equilibrium, real GDP is $1,000, which is potential GDP, and the price level is 120.

Crowding Out at Full Employment

You've just seen that when government expenditures increase at full employment, the long-run change in real GDP is zero. The entire effect of the increase in aggregate demand is to increase the price level. This outcome implies that at full employment, an increase in government expenditures *completely crowds out private expenditure* or *creates an international (net exports) deficit,* or results in a combination of the two.

The easiest way to see why is to recall that aggregate expenditure, which equals consumption expenditure, *C*, plus investment, *I*, plus government expenditures, *G*, plus net exports, *NX*, equals real GDP. That is,

$$Y = C + I + G + NX.$$

Comparing the initial situation with the outcome, real GDP has not changed. So aggregate expenditure, $C + I + G + NX$, is constant between the two situations.

But government expenditures have increased, so the sum of consumption, investment, and net exports must have decreased. If net exports don't change, consumption plus investment decreases by the full amount of the increase in government expenditures. If consumption and investment don't change, net exports decrease by an amount equal to the increase in government expenditures. A decrease in net exports is an increase in our international deficit.

You've now seen that the effects of expansionary fiscal policy are extremely sensitive to the state of the economy when the policy action is taken. At less than full employment, an expansionary fiscal policy can move the economy towards full employment. At full employment, an expansionary fiscal policy raises the price level, crowds out private expenditure, and creates an international deficit.

Expansionary Monetary Policy at Full Employment

Now suppose the economy is at full employment and the Bank of Canada increases the quantity of money. Again, all the effects that we worked out earlier in this chapter occur. But again, these effects determine only a *short-run equilibrium*. That is, the first round and second round effects of monetary policy both occur in the short run. And again, there is a third round, which is the long-run adjustment.

Starting out at full employment, an expansionary monetary policy will create an above full-employment equilibrium in which there is an *inflationary gap*. The money wage rate begins to rise, short-run aggregate supply decreases, and a long-run adjustment occurs in which real GDP decreases to potential GDP and the price level rises.

Figure 27.8, which illustrates the effects of an expansionary fiscal policy at full employment, also illustrates the effects of an expansionary monetary policy at full employment.

In the short run, an expansionary monetary policy increases real GDP and the price level. But in the long run, it increases only the price level and leaves real GDP unchanged at potential GDP.

Long-Run Neutrality

In the long run, a change in the quantity of money changes only the price level and leaves real GDP unchanged. The independence of real GDP from the quantity of money is an example of the long-run neutrality of money.

But long-run neutrality applies not only to real GDP but also to all real variables. The so-called **long-run neutrality** proposition is that in the long run, a change in the quantity of money changes the price level and leaves all real variables unchanged.

You can see this outcome in the case of real GDP in Fig. 27.8. With no change in real GDP, the demand for money does not change. The price level rises by the same percentage as the increase in the quantity of money, so the quantity of real money does not change. With no change in the demand for money and no change in the quantity of real money, the interest rate does not change. And with no change in the interest rate, expenditure remains the same. Finally, with no change in real GDP or the real interest rate, consumption expenditure, investment, government expenditures, and net exports are unchanged.

REVIEW QUIZ

1 Contrast the short-run effects of an expansionary fiscal policy on real GDP and the price level with its long-run effects when the policy action occurs at full employment.
2 Contrast the short-run effects of an expansionary monetary policy on real GDP and the price level with its long-run effects when the policy action occurs at full employment.
3 Explain crowding out at full employment.
4 Explain the long-run neutrality of money.

Policy Coordination and Conflict

SO FAR, WE'VE STUDIED FISCAL POLICY AND monetary policy in isolation from each other. We are now going to consider what happens if the two branches of policy are coordinated and if they come into conflict.

Policy coordination occurs when the government and the Bank of Canada work together to achieve a common set of goals. **Policy conflict** occurs when the government and the Bank of Canada pursue different goals and the actions of one make it harder (perhaps impossible) for the other to achieve its goals.

Policy Coordination

The basis for policy coordination is the fact that either fiscal policy or monetary policy can be used to increase aggregate demand. Starting from a *below full-employment equilibrium*, an increase in aggregate demand increases real GDP and decreases unemployment. If the size of the policy action is well judged, it can restore full employment. Similarly, starting from an *above full-employment equilibrium*, a decrease in aggregate demand decreases real GDP and can, if the size of the policy action is well judged, eliminate an *inflationary gap*. Because either a fiscal policy or a monetary policy action can achieve these objectives, the two policies can (in principle) be combined to also achieve the same outcome.

If either or both policies can restore full employment and eliminate inflation, why does it matter which policy is used? It matters because the two policies have different side effects—different effects on other variables about which people care. These side effects work through the influence of policy on two key variables:

- The interest rate
- The exchange rate

Interest Rate Effects An expansionary fiscal policy *raises* the interest rate, while an expansionary monetary policy *lowers* the interest rate. When the interest rate changes, investment changes, so an expansionary fiscal policy lowers investment (crowding out) while an expansionary monetary policy increases investment. So if an expansionary fiscal policy increases aggregate demand, consumption expenditure increases and investment decreases. But if an expansionary monetary policy increases aggregate demand, consumption expenditure and investment increase.

By coordinating fiscal policy and monetary policy and increasing aggregate demand with an appropriate combination of the two, it is possible to increase real GDP and lower unemployment with either no change in the interest rate or any desired change in the interest rate. A big dose of fiscal expansion and a small dose of monetary expansion raises the interest rate and decreases investment, while a small dose of fiscal expansion and a big dose of monetary expansion lowers the interest rate and increases investment.

The interest rate affects our long-term growth prospects because the growth rate of potential GDP depends on the level of investment. The connection between investment, capital, and growth is explained in Chapters 29 and 30.

Exchange Rate Effects An expansionary fiscal policy raises not only the interest rate but also the exchange rate. In contrast, an expansionary monetary policy *lowers* the exchange rate. When the exchange rate changes, net exports change. An expansionary fiscal policy lowers net exports (international crowding out) while an expansionary monetary policy increases net exports. So if full employment is restored by expansionary policy, net exports decrease with fiscal expansion and increase with monetary expansion.

Policy Conflict

Policy conflicts are not planned. But they sometimes happen. When they arise, it is usually because of a divergence of the political priorities of the government and the objectives of the Bank of Canada.

Governments (both federal and provincial) pay a lot of attention to employment and production over a short time horizon. They look for policies that make their re-election chances high. The Bank of Canada pays a lot of attention to price level stability and has a long time horizon. It doesn't have an election to worry about.

So a situation might arise in which the government wants the Bank to pursue an expansionary monetary policy but the Bank wants to keep its foot on the monetary brake. The government says that an increase in the quantity of money is essential to lower interest rates and the exchange rate and to boost investment and exports. The Bank says that the problem is with fiscal policy. Spending is too high and revenues too low. With fiscal policy too expansionary, interest rates and the exchange rate are high and they cannot be lowered permanently by monetary policy. To lower interest rates and give investment and exports a boost, fiscal policy must become contractionary. Only then can an expansionary monetary policy be pursued.

A further potential conflict between the government and the Bank of Canada concerns the financing of the government deficit. A government deficit can be financed either by borrowing from the general public or by borrowing from the Bank. If the government borrows from the general public, it must pay interest on its debt. If it borrows from the Bank, it pays interest to the Bank. But the government owns the Bank, so the interest comes back to the government. Financing a deficit by selling debt to the central bank costs the government no interest. So the temptation to sell debt to the central bank is strong.

But when the Bank of Canada buys government debt, it pays for the debt with newly created monetary base. The quantity of money increases. And such finance leads to inflation. In many countries—for example in Eastern Europe, Latin America, and Africa—government deficits are financed by the central bank. In Canada, they are not. Despite huge government deficits in the 1980s and early 1990s, the Bank of Canada has stood firm in its purchase of government debt. Only tiny amounts have been bought by the Bank to keep the monetary base growing at a rate that keeps up with real GDP growth and sustains a modest inflation rate. Figure 27.9 shows the Bank's contribution to financing the government of Canada's deficits since those deficits emerged in 1975. You can see that the Bank has been able to pursue its primary objective of price level stability despite the huge debts incurred by the government.

FIGURE 27.9 Debt Financing

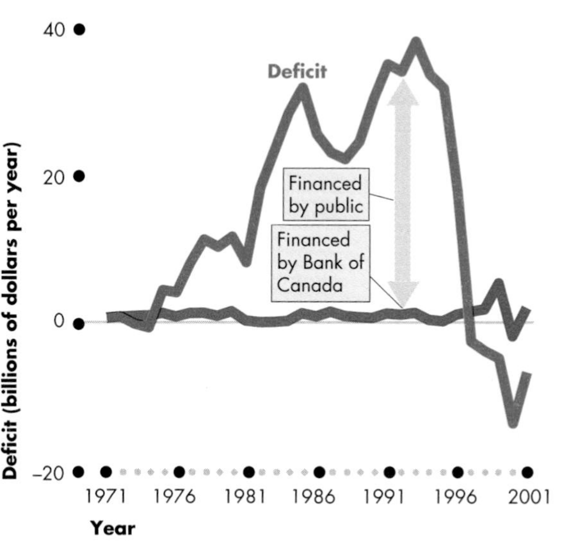

The federal government's budget deficit mushroomed after 1975. The deficit was financed mostly by selling bonds to the public. The Bank of Canada's monetary policy has created little new money to finance the deficit.

Source: Bank of Canada, *Banking and Financial Statistics*, table G4.

REVIEW QUIZ

1. What are the main things that can be achieved by coordinating fiscal policy and monetary policy?
2. What are the main sources of conflict in policy between the Bank of Canada and the government of Canada?
3. What are the main consequences of the government and the Bank of Canada pursuing conflicting policies? Are all the consequences bad?

You have now studied the interaction of fiscal policy and monetary policy. *Reading Between the Lines* on pp. 644–645 examines the views of David Dodge, governor of the Bank of Canada, on the appropriate roles for monetary and fiscal policy today.

You've seen that monetary and fiscal policy policies are alternative ways of changing aggregate demand and real GDP. But they have different effects on the interest rate and the exchange rate. You've seen what determines the relative effectiveness of fiscal and monetary policies and how the mix of these policies can influence the composition of aggregate expenditure. But you've also seen that the ultimate effects of these policies on real GDP and the price level depend not only on the behaviour of aggregate demand but also on aggregate supply and the state of the labour market. You will turn to the aggregate supply side of the economy in the next part. But first, in Chapter 28, we complete our study of aggregate demand by learning about inflation.

READING BETWEEN THE LINES

Monetary and Fiscal Tensions

CALGARY HERALD, SEPTEMBER 4, 2002

Central bank boss warns against big spending

The head of the Bank of Canada has warned the Chrétien government against eroding the country's hard-earned anti-inflation credibility.

The not-so-veiled warning by governor David Dodge came amid rising speculation that the prime minister is about to go on a social policy spending spree in advance of his retirement in 18 months.

It also came on the eve of what many analysts expect will be another interest rate increase aimed at reducing the stimulus that is already in the economy. Earlier this year, the bank rate was the lowest in more than four decades.

In a speech to other central bankers in Jackson Hole, Wyo., last weekend Dodge stressed the importance of the credibility that the bank and government have earned with "joint agreements on inflation-control targets" and "a framework that greatly reduces the probability of running a fiscal deficit and thus puts the debt-to-GDP ratio on a clear downward track."

"Fiscal and monetary credibility is high," Dodge said, noting that markets, businesses and individuals "trust" that the central bank will meet its inflation target and that the government will not start spending more than it takes in.

"Initially, the credibility of these policies was not high," Dodge noted. "So it was essential to demonstrate clearly our resolve to achieve greater fiscal prudence and lower inflation until credibility was gained."

To do that, he said, it meant that the bank at times had to keep interest rates higher, and that the government had to keep a tighter rein on spending than otherwise necessary.

Dodge also said it was fortunate the government in its last budget did not inject a lot of new spending into the economy.

"I say fortunately because... there was more underlying strength in the economy than we expected," Dodge explained.

He went on to note that the bank had already injected a lot of stimulus into the economy by cutting interest rates.

"Therefore, added fiscal stimulus was not necessary to get the economy going and the monetary stimulus provided is proving much easier to turn around."

Essence of the Story

- In a speech at a conference of central bankers, Bank of Canada governor David Dodge said that the joint agreements on inflation-control targets between the Bank and government have created a high degree of trust that inflation targets will be met.
- He warned against increasing government spending and said it was fortunate that in its last budget, the government did not inject a lot of new spending into the economy because the economy was already expanding strongly.
- He noted that the Bank of Canada had injected a lot of stimulus into the economy by cutting interest rates and that added fiscal stimulus was neither necessary nor as easy to reverse as monetary policy actions.

Economic Analysis

- David Dodge wants to maintain the credibility that the Bank of Canada has established and keep the inflation rate below 3 percent a year.

- He thinks that macroeconomic stability—low inflation *and* full employment—can best be achieved by using monetary policy alone.

- He fears that if fiscal policy were to become too expansionary, inflation could take off.

- Figure 1 illustrates David Dodge's concern.

- In Fig. 1, potential GDP is $1,084, but aggregate demand, AD_0, and short-run aggregate supply, SAS_0, intersect at a below-full employment equilibrium so there is a recessionary gap.

- If the Bank of Canada cuts the interest rate to stimulate demand, and if the government increases its expenditure, which also stimulates demand, the *AD* curve shifts rightward to AD_1.

- This expansionary fiscal and monetary policy brings an inflationary gap.

- With an inflationary gap, the money wage rate begins to rise and the *SAS* curve starts to shift leftward towards SAS_1.

- Real GDP falls back towards potential GDP, but inflation takes off as the price level rises to 127.

- Figure 2 shows what David Dodge would like to achieve.

- With the same initial recessionary gap, the Bank of Canada takes action to stimulate demand by cutting the interest rate.

- The government holds expenditure steady so that fiscal policy does not increase aggregate demand.

- The *AD* curve shifts rightward to AD_2 and full employment is achieved while the inflation rate remains low.

- If the Bank of Canada sees an inflationary gap, it can take quick action in the opposite direction—raise the interest rate—to decrease aggregate demand.

- In contrast, if increased government spending brings an inflationary gap, it is difficult to cut spending.

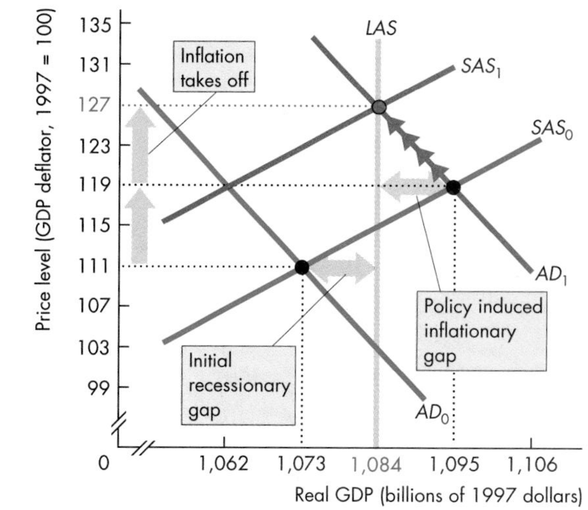

Figure 1 Fiscal and monetary stimulus

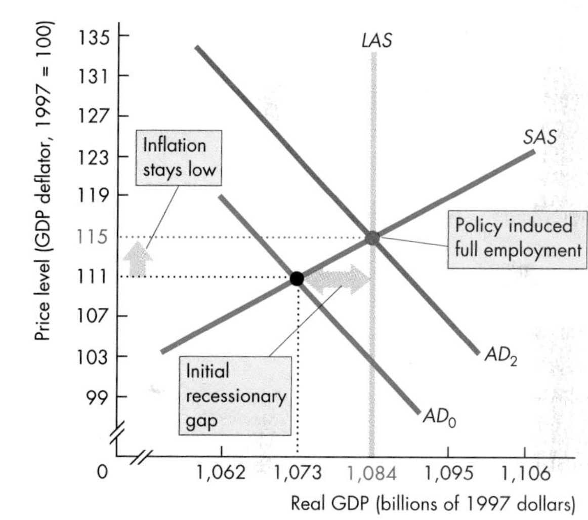

Figure 2 Monetary stimulus alone

You're The Voter

- Do you agree with David Dodge that monetary policy alone is the appropriate tool for achieving low inflation and full employment?

- Do you think there is ever a role for fiscal policy?

SUMMARY

KEY POINTS

Macroeconomic Equilibrium (pp. 628–629)

- Equilibrium real GDP, the price level, and the interest rate are determined simultaneously by equilibrium in the money market and equality of aggregate demand and aggregate supply.

Fiscal Policy in the Short Run (pp. 630–633)

- The first round effects of an expansionary fiscal policy are an increase in aggregate demand, increasing real GDP, and a rising price level.
- The second round effects are an increasing demand for money and a decreasing quantity of real money that increase the interest rate and limit the increase in real GDP and the rise in the price level.
- Interest-sensitive expenditure, which includes investment and net exports, decreases.

Monetary Policy in the Short Run (pp. 634–637)

- The first round effects of an expansionary monetary policy are a fall in the interest rate, an increase in aggregate demand, an increasing real GDP, and a rising price level.
- The second round effects are an increasing demand for money and a decreasing quantity of real money that increase the interest rate and limit the increase in real GDP and the rise in the price level.
- Interest-sensitive expenditure, which includes investment and net exports, increases.

Relative Effectiveness of Policies (pp. 637–639)

- The relative effectiveness of fiscal and monetary policy depends on the interest-sensitivity of both expenditure and the quantity of money demanded.
- The extreme Keynesian position is that only fiscal policy affects aggregate demand. The extreme monetarist position is that only monetary policy affects aggregate demand. Neither extreme is correct.
- The mix of fiscal and monetary policy influences the composition of aggregate demand.

Policy Actions at Full Employment (pp. 640–641)

- An expansionary fiscal policy at full employment increases real GDP and the price level in the short run but increases only the price level in the long run. Complete crowding out of investment occurs or the international deficit increases.
- An expansionary monetary policy at full employment increases real GDP and the price level in the short run but increases only the price level in the long run. Money is neutral—has no real effects—in the long run.

Policy Coordination and Conflict (pp. 642–643)

- Policy coordination can make changes in the interest rate and the exchange rate small.
- Policy conflict can avoid inflation in the face of a government deficit.

KEY FIGURES

Figure 27.1 Equilibrium Real GDP, Price Level, Interest Rate, and Expenditure, 629
Figure 27.2 First Round Effects of an Expansionary Fiscal Policy, 630
Figure 27.3 Second Round Effects of an Expansionary Fiscal Policy, 631
Figure 27.5 First Round Effects of an Expansionary Monetary Policy, 634
Figure 27.6 Second Round Effects of an Expansionary Monetary Policy, 635
Figure 27.8 Fiscal Policy at Full Employment, 640

KEY TERMS

Crowding in, 633
Crowding out, 633
International crowding out, 633
Keynesian, 638
Long-run neutrality, 641
Monetarist, 638
Policy conflict, 642
Policy coordination, 642

PROBLEMS

*1. In the economy described in Fig. 27.1, suppose the government decreases its expenditures on goods and services.
   a. Work out the first round effects.
   b. Explain how real GDP and the interest rate change.
   c. Explain the second round effects that take the economy to a new equilibrium.

2. In the economy described in Fig. 27.1, suppose the government increases its expenditures on goods and services by $25 billion.
   a. Work out the first round effects.
   b. Explain how real GDP and the interest rate change.
   c. Explain the second round effects that take the economy to a new equilibrium.
   d. Compare the equilibrium in this case with the one described in the chapter on pp. 630–632. In which case does real GDP change most? In which case does the interest rate change most? Why?

*3. In the economy described in Fig. 27.1, suppose the Bank of Canada decreases the quantity of money.
   a. Work out the first round effects.
   b. Explain how real GDP and the interest rate change.
   c. Explain the second round effects that take the economy to a new equilibrium.

4. In the economy described in Fig. 27.1, suppose the Bank of Canada increases the quantity of money by $250 billion.
   a. Work out the first round effects.
   b. Explain how real GDP and the interest rate change.
   c. Explain the second round effects that take the economy to a new equilibrium.
   d. Compare the equilibrium in this case with the one described in the chapter on pp. 634–636. In which case does real GDP change most? In which case does the interest rate change most? Why?

*5. The economies of two countries, Alpha and Beta, are identical in every way except the following: in Alpha, a change in the interest rate of 1 percentage point (for example, from 5 percent to 6 percent) results in a $1 billion change in the quantity of real money demanded. In Beta, a change in the interest rate of 1 percentage point results in a $0.1 billion change in the quantity of real money demanded.
   a. In which economy does an increase in government expenditures on goods and services have a larger effect on real GDP?
   b. In which economy is the crowding-out effect weaker?
   c. In which economy does a change in the quantity of money have a larger effect on equilibrium real GDP?
   d. Which economy, if either, is closer to the Keynesian extreme and which is closer to the monetarist extreme?

6. The economies of two countries, Gamma and Delta, are identical in every way except the following: in Gamma, a change in the interest rate of 1 percentage point (for example, from 5 percent to 6 percent) results in a $0.1 billion change in interest-sensitive expenditure. In Delta, a change in the interest rate of 1 percentage point results in a $10 billion change in interest-sensitive expenditure.
   a. In which economy does an increase in government expenditures on goods and services have a larger effect on real GDP?
   b. In which economy is the crowding-out effect weaker?
   c. In which economy does a change in the quantity of money have a larger effect on equilibrium real GDP?
   d. Which economy, if either, is closer to the Keynesian extreme and which is closer to the monetarist extreme?

*7. The economy is in a recession and the government wants to increase aggregate demand, stimulate exports, and increase investment. It has three policy options: increase government expenditures on goods and services, decrease taxes, and increase the quantity of money.
   a. Explain the mechanisms at work under each alternative policy.
   b. What is the effect of each policy on the composition of aggregate demand?
   c. What are the short-run effects of each policy on real GDP and the price level?
   d. Which policy would you recommend that the government adopt? Why?

8. The economy has an inflationary gap and the government wants to decrease aggregate demand, cut exports, and decrease investment.

It has three policy options: decrease government expenditures on goods and services, increase taxes, and decrease the quantity of money.

a. Explain the mechanisms at work under each alternative policy.
b. What is the effect of each policy on the composition of aggregate demand?
c. What are the short-run effects of each policy on real GDP and the price level?
d. Which policy would you recommend that the government adopt? Why?

*9. The economy is at full employment, but the government is disappointed with the growth rate of real GDP. It wants to increase real GDP growth by stimulating investment. At the same time, it wants to avoid an increase in the price level.

a. Suggest a combination of fiscal and monetary policies that will achieve the government's objective.
b. Which policy would you recommend that the government adopt?
c. Explain the mechanisms at work under your recommended policy.
d. What is the effect of your recommended policy on the composition of aggregate demand?
e. What are the short-run and long-run effects of your recommended policy on real GDP and the price level?

10. The economy is at full employment, and the government is worried that the growth rate of real GDP is too high because it is depleting the country's natural resources. The government wants to lower real GDP growth by lowering investment. At the same time it wants to avoid a fall in the price level.

a. Suggest a combination of fiscal and monetary policies that will achieve the government's objective.
b. Which policy would you recommend that the government adopt?
c. Explain the mechanisms at work under your recommended policy.
d. What is the effect of your recommended policy on the composition of aggregate demand?
e. What are the short-run and long-run effects of your recommended policy on real GDP and the price level?

CRITICAL THINKING

1. Study *Reading Between the Lines* on pp. 644–645 and then answer the following questions:

a. What does David Dodge think the government's fiscal policy should do?
b. What are your predictions about the effects of a large increase in government expenditure on real GDP, the price level, interest rates, investment, the exchange rate, and net exports?
c. What actions do you think that the Bank of Canada would need to take to ensure that an increase in government expenditure doesn't bring an increase in the inflation rate?
d. What would happen if the Bank of Canada decided to raise interest rates at the same time that the government increased its expenditure? Explain the likely effects on real GDP, the price level, investment, the exchange rate, and net exports.

WEB EXERCISES

1. Use the link on the Parkin–Bade Web site to visit Statistics Canada and look at the current economic conditions. On the basis of the current state of the Canadian economy, and in light of what you now know about fiscal and monetary policy interaction, what do you predict would happen to real GDP and the price level

a. If the Bank of Canada conducted an expansionary monetary policy?
b. If the Bank of Canada conducted a contractionary monetary policy?
c. If the government of Canada conducted an expansionary fiscal policy?
d. If the government of Canada conducted a contractionary fiscal policy?
e. If the Bank of Canada conducted an expansionary monetary policy and the government of Canada conducted a contractionary fiscal policy?
f. If the Bank of Canada conducted a contractionary monetary policy and the government of Canada conducted an expansionary fiscal policy?

2. What do you think the government of Canada should do with its fiscal surplus? Should it cut taxes, increase spending, or do some of both? How would your recommended actions influence real GDP, the price level, the interest rate, the exchange rate, and net exports?

INFLATION — CHAPTER 28

From Rome to Rio de Janeiro

At the end of the third century A.D., Roman Emperor Diocletian struggled to contain an inflation that raised prices by more than 300 percent a year. At the end of the twentieth century, Brazil's president, Fernando Henrique Cardoso, struggled to contain an inflation that hit a rate of 40 percent *per month*—or 5,600 percent a year. ◆ Today, Canada has remarkable price stability, but during the 1970s, the Canadian price level more than doubled—an inflation of more than 100 percent over the decade. Why do inflation rates vary? And why do serious inflations break out from time to time? ◆ Will inflation increase so our savings buy less? Or will inflation decrease so our debts are harder to repay? To make good decisions, we need good forecasts of inflation, and not for just next year but for many years into the future. How do people try to forecast inflation? And how do expectations of inflation influence the economy? ◆ Does the Bank of Canada face a tradeoff between inflation and unemployment? And does a low unemployment rate signal a rising inflation rate? How does inflation affect the interest rate?

We'll answer these questions in this chapter. We'll begin by reviewing what inflation is and how it is measured. And we'll end, in *Reading Between the Lines*, by looking at the views of Nobel Laureate George Akerlof on the links between inflation and unemployment in Canada.

After studying this chapter, you will be able to

- **Distinguish between inflation and a one-time rise in the price level**
- **Explain how demand-pull inflation is generated**
- **Explain how cost-push inflation is generated**
- **Describe the effects of inflation**
- **Explain the quantity theory of money**
- **Explain the short-run and long-run relationships between inflation and unemployment**
- **Explain the short-run and long-run relationships between inflation and interest rates**

Inflation and the Price Level

WE DON'T HAVE MUCH INFLATION TODAY, BUT during the 1970s, inflation was a major problem. **Inflation** is a process in which the *price level is rising* and *money is losing value.*

If the price level rises persistently, then people need more and more money to make transactions. Incomes rise, so firms must pay out more in wages and other payments to owners of factors of production. And prices rise, so consumers must take more money with them when they go shopping. But the value of money gets smaller and smaller.

A change in one price is not inflation. For example, if the price of a hot dog jumps to $25 and all other money prices fall slightly so that the price level remains constant, there is no inflation. Instead, the relative price of a hot dog has increased. If the price of a hot dog and all other prices rise by a similar percentage, there is inflation.

But a one-time jump in the price level is not inflation. Instead, inflation is an ongoing *process.* Figure 28.1 illustrates this distinction. The red line shows the price level rising continuously. That is inflation. The blue line shows a one-time jump in the price level. This economy is not experiencing inflation. Its price level is constant most of the time.

Inflation is a serious problem, and preventing inflation is the main task of monetary policy and the actions of the Bank of Canada. We are going to learn how inflation arises and see how we can avoid the situation shown in the cartoon. But first, let's see how we calculate the inflation rate.

"I told you the Fed should have tightened."

FIGURE 28.1 Inflation Versus a One-Time Rise in the Price Level

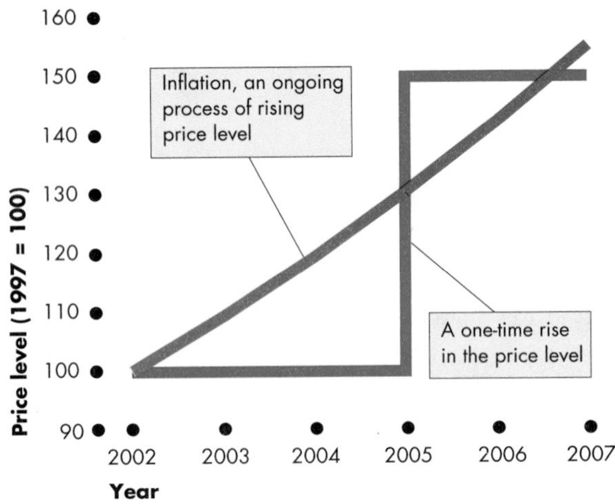

Along the red line, an economy experiences inflation because the price level is rising persistently. Along the blue line, an economy experiences a one-time rise in the price level.

To measure the inflation *rate,* we calculate the annual percentage change in the price level. For example, if this year's price level is 126 and last year's price level was 120, the inflation rate is 5 percent per year. That is,

$$\text{Inflation rate} = \frac{126 - 120}{120} \times 100$$
$$= 5 \text{ percent per year.}$$

This equation shows the connection between the *inflation rate* and the *price level.* For a given price level last year, the higher the price level in the current year, the higher is the inflation rate. If the price level is *rising,* the inflation rate is *positive.* If the price level rises at a *faster* rate, the inflation rate *increases.* Also, the higher the new price level, the lower is the value of money and the higher is the inflation rate.

Inflation can result from either an increase in aggregate demand or a decrease in aggregate supply. These two sources of impulses are called

1. Demand-pull inflation
2. Cost-push inflation

We'll first study a demand-pull inflation.

Demand-Pull Inflation

AN INFLATION THAT RESULTS FROM AN INITIAL increase in aggregate demand is called **demand-pull inflation.** Demand-pull inflation can arise from *any* factor that increases aggregate demand, such as an

1. Increase in the quantity of money
2. Increase in government expenditures
3. Increase in exports

Initial Effect of an Increase in Aggregate Demand

Suppose that last year the price level was 110 and real GDP was $1,000 billion. Potential GDP was also $1,000 billion. Figure 28.2(a) illustrates this situation. The aggregate demand curve is AD_0, the short-run aggregate supply curve is SAS_0, and the long-run aggregate supply curve is *LAS*.

In the current year, aggregate demand increases to AD_1. Such a situation arises if, for example, the Bank of Canada loosens its grip on the quantity of money, or the government increases its expenditures on goods and services, or exports increase.

With no change in potential GDP, and with no change in the money wage rate, the long-run aggregate supply curve and the short-run aggregate supply curve remain at *LAS* and SAS_0, respectively.

The price level and real GDP are determined at the point where the aggregate demand curve AD_1 intersects the short-run aggregate supply curve. The price level rises to 113, and real GDP increases above potential GDP to $1,050 billion. The economy experiences a 2.7 percent rise in the price level (a price level of 113 compared with 110 in the previous year) and a rapid expansion of real GDP. Unemployment falls below its natural rate. The next step in the unfolding story is a rise in the money wage rate.

Money Wage Rate Response

Real GDP cannot remain above potential GDP forever. With unemployment below its natural rate, there is a shortage of labour. In this situation, the

FIGURE 28.2 A Demand-Pull Rise in the Price Level

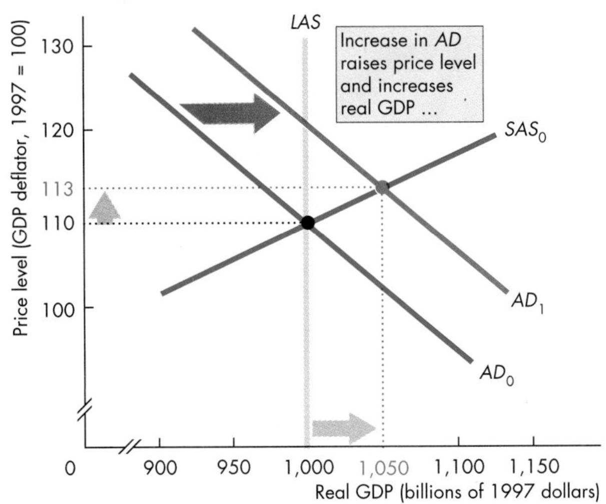

(a) Initial effect

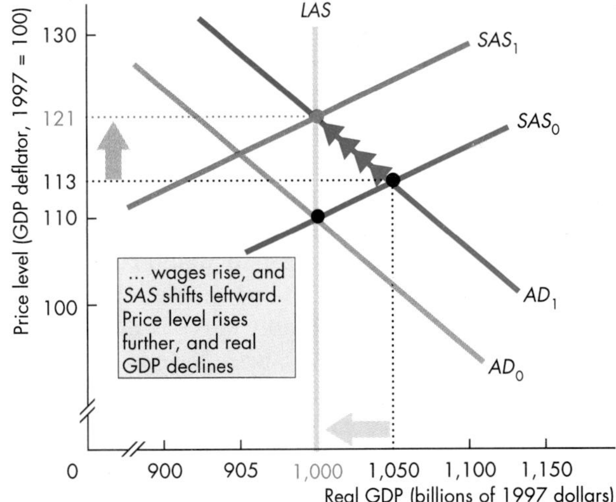

(b) Wages adjust

In part (a), the aggregate demand curve is AD_0, the short-run aggregate supply curve is SAS_0, and the long-run aggregate supply curve is *LAS*. The price level is 110, and real GDP is $1,000 billion, which equals potential GDP. Aggregate demand increases to AD_1. The price level rises to 113, and real GDP increases to $1,050 billion. In part (b), starting from above full employment, the money wage rate begins to rise and the short-run aggregate supply curve shifts leftward towards SAS_1. The price level rises further, and real GDP returns to potential GDP.

money wage rate begins to rise. As it does so, short-run aggregate supply decreases and the *SAS* curve starts to shift leftward. The price level rises further, and real GDP begins to decrease.

With no further change in aggregate demand—that is, the aggregate demand curve remains at AD_1—this process ends when the short-run aggregate supply curve has shifted to SAS_1 in Fig. 28.2(b). At this time, the price level has increased to 121 and real GDP has returned to potential GDP of $1,000 billion, the level from which it started.

A Demand-Pull Inflation Process

The process we've just studied eventually ends when, for a given increase in aggregate demand, the money wage rate has adjusted enough to restore the real wage rate to its full-employment level. We've studied a one-time rise in the price level like that described in Fig. 28.1. For inflation to proceed, aggregate demand must persistently increase.

The only way in which aggregate demand can persistently increase is if the quantity of money persistently increases. Suppose the government has a budget deficit that it finances by selling bonds. Also suppose that the Bank of Canada buys some of these bonds. When the Bank of Canada buys bonds, it creates more money. In this situation, aggregate demand increases year after year. The aggregate demand curve keeps shifting rightward. This persistent increase in aggregate demand puts continual upward pressure on the price level. The economy now experiences demand-pull inflation.

Figure 28.3 illustrates the process of demand-pull inflation. The starting point is the same as that shown in Fig. 28.2. The aggregate demand curve is AD_0, the short-run aggregate supply curve is SAS_0, and the long-run aggregate supply curve is *LAS*. Real GDP is $1,000 billion, and the price level is 110. Aggregate demand increases, shifting the aggregate demand curve to AD_1. Real GDP increases to $1,050 billion, and the price level rises to 113. The economy is at an above full-employment equilibrium. There is a shortage of labour, and the money wage rate rises. The short-run aggregate supply curve shifts to SAS_1. The price level rises to 121, and real GDP returns to potential GDP.

But the Bank of Canada increases the quantity of money again, and aggregate demand continues to increase. The aggregate demand curve shifts rightward to AD_2. The price level rises further to 125, and

FIGURE 28.3 A Demand-Pull Inflation Spiral

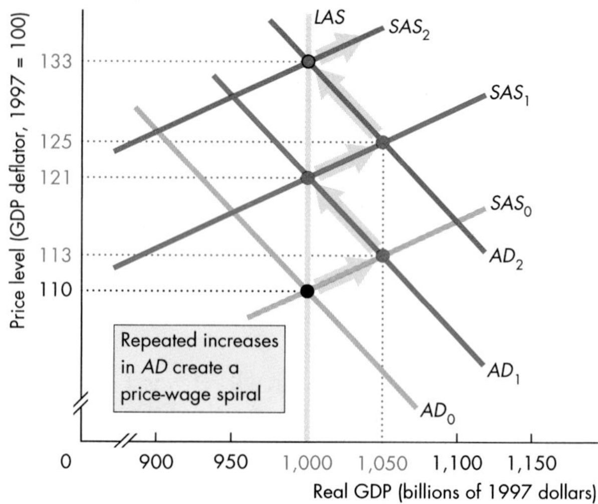

Each time the quantity of money increases, aggregate demand increases, and the aggregate demand curve shifts rightward from AD_0 to AD_1 to AD_2, and so on. Each time real GDP goes above potential GDP, the money wage rate rises and the short-run aggregate supply curve shifts leftward from SAS_0 to SAS_1 to SAS_2, and so on. The price level rises from 110 to 113, 121, 125, 133, and so on. There is a perpetual demand-pull inflation. Real GDP fluctuates between $1,000 billion and $1,050 billion.

real GDP again exceeds potential GDP at $1,050 billion. Yet again, the money wage rate rises and decreases short-run aggregate supply. The *SAS* curve shifts to SAS_2, and the price level rises further, to 133. As the quantity of money continues to grow, aggregate demand increases and the price level rises in an ongoing demand-pull inflation process.

The process you have just studied generates inflation—an ongoing process of a rising price level.

Demand-Pull Inflation in Chatham You may better understand the inflation process that we've just described by considering what is going on in an individual part of the economy, such as a Chatham ketchup-bottling plant. Initially, when aggregate demand increases, the demand for ketchup increases and the price of ketchup rises. Faced with a higher price, the ketchup plant works overtime and increases production. Conditions are good for workers in Chatham, and the ketchup factory finds it hard to hang onto its best people. To do so, it has to offer a higher money wage rate. As the wage rate rises, so do the ketchup factory's costs.

What happens next depends on what happens to aggregate demand. If aggregate demand remains constant (as in Fig. 28.2b), the firm's costs are increasing, but the price of ketchup is not increasing as quickly as its costs. Production is scaled back. Eventually, the money wage rate and costs increase by the same percentage as the rise in the price of ketchup. In real terms, the ketchup factory is in the same situation as it was initially—before the increase in aggregate demand. The plant produces the same amount of ketchup and employs the same amount of labour as before the increase in demand.

But if aggregate demand continues to increase, so does the demand for ketchup and the price of ketchup rises at the same rate as wages. The ketchup factory continues to operate above full employment, and there is a persistent shortage of labour. Prices and wages chase each other upward in an unending spiral.

Demand-Pull Inflation in Canada A demand-pull inflation like the one you've just studied occurred in Canada during the late 1960s and early 1970s. In 1960, inflation was a moderate 2 percent a year, but its rate increased slowly through the mid-1960s. Then, between 1966 and 1969, the inflation rate surged upward. Inflation then decreased slightly during 1970 and 1971, but it took off again in 1972. By 1973, the inflation rate was approaching 10 percent a year.

These increases in inflation resulted from increases in aggregate demand that had two main sources. The first was from the United States, where large increases in government expenditures and in the quantity of money increased aggregate demand in the entire world economy. The second source was an increase in Canadian government expenditures and the quantity of money.

With the economy above full employment, the money wage rate started to rise more quickly and the *SAS* curve shifted leftward. The Bank of Canada responded with a further increase in the money growth rate, and a demand-pull inflation spiral unfolded. By 1974, the inflation rate had reached double digits.

REVIEW QUIZ

1. How does demand-pull inflation begin? What are the initial effects of demand-pull inflation on real GDP?
2. When real GDP moves above potential GDP, what happens to the money wage rate and short-run aggregate supply? How do real GDP and the price level respond?
3. What must happen to create a demand-pull inflation spiral?

Next, let's see how shocks to aggregate supply can create cost-push inflation.

Cost-Push Inflation

AN INFLATION THAT RESULTS FROM AN INITIAL increase in costs is called **cost-push inflation.** The two main sources of increases in costs are

1. An increase in money wage rates
2. An increase in the money prices of raw materials

At a given price level, the higher the cost of production, the smaller is the amount that firms are willing to produce. So if money wage rates rise or if the prices of raw materials (for example, oil) rise, firms decrease their supply of goods and services. Aggregate supply decreases, and the short-run aggregate supply curve shifts leftward.[1] Let's trace the effects of such a decrease in short-run aggregate supply on the price level and real GDP.

Initial Effect of a Decrease in Aggregate Supply

Suppose that last year the price level was 110 and real GDP was $1,000 billion. Potential real GDP was also $1,000 billion. Figure 28.4 illustrates this situation. The aggregate demand curve was AD_0, the short-run aggregate supply curve was SAS_0, and the long-run aggregate supply curve was *LAS*. In the current year,

[1] Some cost-push forces, such as an increase in the price of oil accompanied by a decrease in the availability of oil, can also decrease long-run aggregate supply. We'll ignore such effects here and examine cost-push factors that change only short-run aggregate supply.

FIGURE 28.4 A Cost-Push Rise in the Price Level

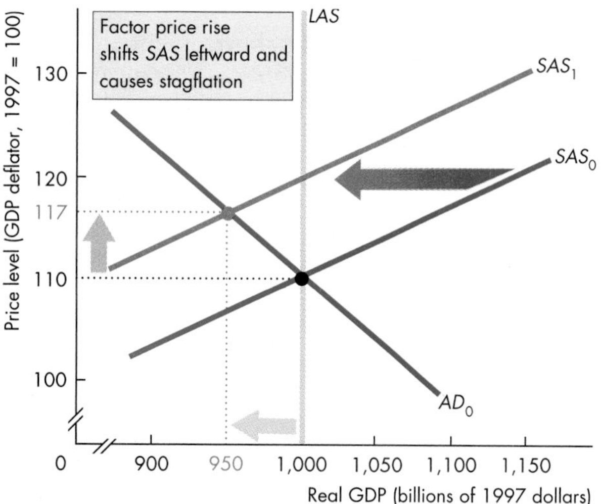

Initially, the aggregate demand curve is AD_0, the short-run aggregate supply curve is SAS_0, and the long-run aggregate supply curve is *LAS*. A decrease in aggregate supply (for example, resulting from a rise in the world price of oil) shifts the short-run aggregate supply curve to SAS_1. The economy moves to the point where the short-run aggregate supply curve SAS_1 intersects the aggregate demand curve AD_0. The price level rises to 117, and real GDP decreases to $950 billion.

the world's oil producers form a price-fixing organization that strengthens their market power and increases the relative price of oil. They raise the price of oil, and this action decreases short-run aggregate supply. The short-run aggregate supply curve shifts leftward to SAS_1. The price level rises to 117, and real GDP decreases to $950 billion. The combination of a rise in the price level and a fall in real GDP is called *stagflation.*

This event is a one-time rise in the price level, like that in Fig. 28.1. It is not inflation. In fact, a supply shock on its own cannot cause inflation. Something more must happen to enable a one-time supply shock, which causes a one-time rise in the price level, to be converted into a process of money growth and ongoing inflation. The quantity of money must persistently increase. And it often does increase, as you will now see.

Aggregate Demand Response

When real GDP falls, the unemployment rate rises above its natural rate. In such a situation, there is usually an outcry of concern and a call for action to restore full employment. Suppose that the Bank of Canada increases the quantity of money. Aggregate demand increases. In Fig. 28.5, the aggregate demand curve shifts rightward to AD_1. The increase in aggregate demand has restored full employment. But the price level rises to 121, a 10 percent increase over the initial price level.

A Cost-Push Inflation Process

The oil producers now see the prices of everything that they buy increase by 10 percent. So they increase the price of oil again to restore its new high relative price. Figure 28.6 continues the story.

The short-run aggregate supply curve now shifts to SAS_2, and another bout of stagflation ensues. The

FIGURE 28.5 Aggregate Demand Response to Cost Push

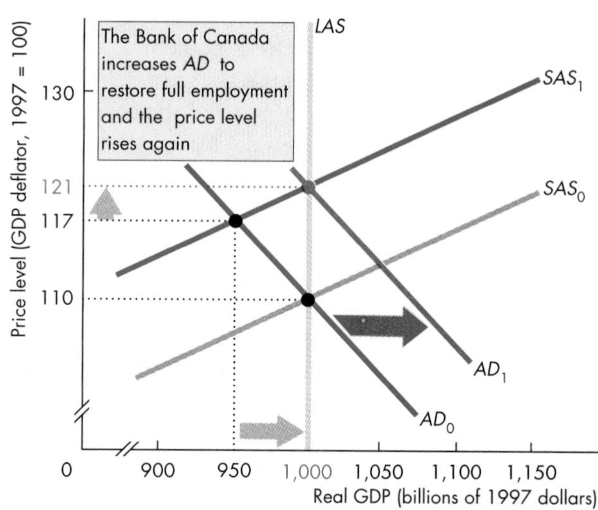

Following a cost-push increase in the price level, real GDP is below potential GDP and unemployment is above its natural rate. If the Bank of Canada responds by increasing aggregate demand to restore full employment, the aggregate demand curve shifts rightward to AD_1. The economy returns to full employment but the price level rises to 121.

price level rises further, to 129, and real GDP falls to \$950 billion. Unemployment increases above its natural rate. If the Bank of Canada responds yet again with an increase in the quantity of money, aggregate demand increases and the aggregate demand curve shifts to AD_2. The price level rises even higher—to 133—and full employment is again restored. A cost-push inflation spiral results. But if the Bank of Canada does not respond, the economy remains below full employment until the price of oil falls.

You can see that the Bank of Canada has a dilemma. If it increases the quantity of money to restore full employment, the Bank invites another oil price hike that will call forth yet a further increase in the quantity of money. Inflation will rage along at a rate decided by the oil-exporting nations. If the Bank of Canada keeps the lid on money growth, the economy operates with a high level of unemployment.

FIGURE 28.6 A Cost-Push Inflation Spiral

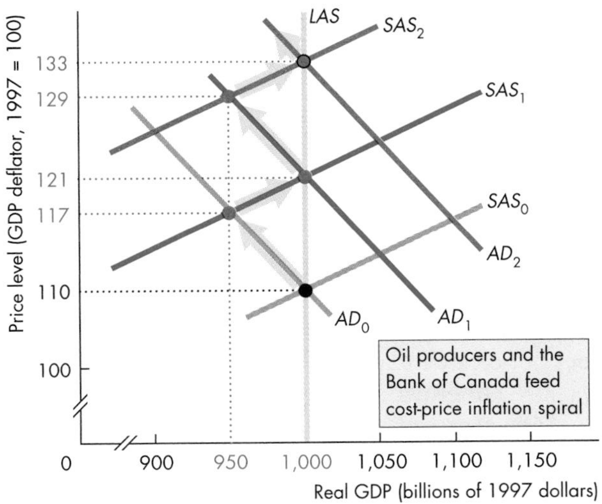

When a cost increase decreases short-run aggregate supply from SAS_0 to SAS_1, the price level rises to 117 and real GDP decreases to \$950 billion. The Bank of Canada responds with an increase in the quantity of money. The aggregate demand curve shifts from AD_0 to AD_1, the price level rises to 121, and real GDP returns to \$1,000 billion. A further cost increase occurs, which shifts the short-run aggregate supply curve again, this time to SAS_2. Stagflation is repeated, and the price level rises to 129. The Bank of Canada responds again, and the cost-price inflation spiral continues.

Cost-Push Inflation in Chatham What is going on in the Chatham ketchup-bottling plant when the economy is experiencing cost-push inflation? When the oil price increases, so do the costs of bottling ketchup. These higher costs decrease the supply of ketchup, increasing its price and decreasing the quantity produced. The ketchup plant lays off some workers. This situation will persist until either the Bank of Canada increases aggregate demand or the price of oil falls. If the Bank of Canada increases aggregate demand, as it did in the mid-1970s, the demand for ketchup increases and so does its price. The higher price of ketchup brings higher profits, and the bottling plant increases its production. The ketchup factory rehires the laid-off workers.

Cost-Push Inflation in Canada A cost-push inflation like the one you've just studied occurred in Canada during the 1970s. It began in 1974 when the Organization of the Petroleum Exporting Countries (OPEC) raised the price of oil fourfold. The higher oil price decreased aggregate supply, which caused the price level to rise more quickly and real GDP to shrink. The Bank of Canada then faced a dilemma: Would it increase the quantity of money and accommodate the cost-push forces, or would it keep aggregate demand growth in check by limiting money growth? In 1975, 1976, and 1977, the Bank of Canada repeatedly allowed the quantity of money to grow quickly and inflation proceeded at a rapid rate. In 1979 and 1980, OPEC was again able to push oil prices higher. On that occasion, the Bank of Canada decided not to respond to the oil price hike with an increase in the quantity of money. The result was a recession but also, eventually, a fall in inflation.

REVIEW QUIZ

1. How does cost-push inflation begin? What are the initial effects of a cost-push rise in the price level?
2. What is *stagflation* and why does cost-push inflation cause stagflation?
3. What must the Bank of Canada do to convert a one-time rise in the price level into a freewheeling cost-push inflation?

The Quantity Theory of Money

YOU'VE SEEN THAT REGARDLESS OF WHETHER IT originates in a demand-pull or a cost-push, to convert a one-time rise in the price level into an ongoing inflation, aggregate demand must increase. And although many factors can and do influence aggregate demand, only one factor can persistently increase in the long run: the quantity of money. This special place of money gives rise to a special long-run theory of inflation, called the quantity theory of money.

The **quantity theory of money** is the proposition that in the long run, an increase in the quantity of money brings an equal percentage increase in the price level. The basis of the quantity theory of money is a concept known as *the velocity of circulation* and an equation called *the equation of exchange.*

The **velocity of circulation** is the average number of times a dollar of money is used annually to buy the goods and services that make up GDP. GDP equals the price level (P) multiplied by real GDP (Y). That is,

$$GDP = PY.$$

Call the quantity of money M. The velocity of circulation, V, is determined by the equation

$$V = PY/M.$$

For example, if GDP is $1,000 billion ($PY =$ $1,000 billion) and the quantity of money is $250 billion, the velocity of circulation is 4. ($1,000 billion divided by $250 billion equals 4.)

The **equation of exchange** states that the quantity of money (M) multiplied by the velocity of circulation (V) equals GDP, or

$$MV = PY.$$

Given the definition of the velocity of circulation, this equation is always true—it is true by definition. With M equal to $250 billion and V equal to 4, MV is equal to $1,000 billion, the value of GDP.

The equation of exchange becomes the quantity theory of money by making two assumptions:

1. The velocity of circulation is not influenced by the quantity of money.
2. Potential GDP is not influenced by the quantity of money.

If these two assumptions are true, then the equation of exchange tells us that a change in the quantity of money brings about an equal proportional change in the price level. You can see why by solving the equation of exchange for the price level. Dividing both sides of the equation by real GDP (Y) gives

$$P = (V/Y) \times M.$$

In the long run, real GDP equals potential GDP, so if potential GDP and velocity are not influenced by the quantity of money, then the relationship between the change in the price level (ΔP) and the change in the quantity of money (ΔM) is

$$(\Delta P = (V/Y) \times \Delta M.$$

Divide this equation by $P = (V/Y) \times M$, and multiply by 100 to get

$$(\Delta P/P) \times 100 = (\Delta M/M) \times 100.$$

$(\Delta P/P) \times 100$ is the inflation rate and $(\Delta M/M) \times 100$ is the growth rate of the quantity of money. So this equation is the quantity theory of money: The percentage increase in the price level and the percentage increase in the quantity of money are equal.

Evidence on the Quantity Theory

Figure 28.7 summarizes some Canadian evidence on the quantity theory of money. The figure reveals that

1. On the average, the money growth rate exceeds the inflation rate.
2. The money growth rate is correlated with the inflation rate.

Money growth exceeds inflation because real GDP grows. Money growth that matches real GDP growth does not create inflation. But money growth in excess of real GDP growth does create inflation.

Money growth and inflation are correlated—move up and down together. For example, the rise in the inflation rate during the 1970s and the slight rebound in inflation during the late 1980s were accompanied by a rise in the money growth rate. The decreases in the inflation rate during the 1980s and 1990s were accompanied by decreases in the money growth rate. But the correlation is not perfect. Nor does it tell us that money growth *causes* inflation. Money growth might cause inflation; inflation might cause money growth; or some third variable might simultaneously cause inflation and money growth.

Figure 28.8 summarizes some international evidence on the quantity theory of money. It shows the inflation rate and the money growth rate for 60 countries. There is a clear tendency for high money

FIGURE 28.7 Money Growth and Inflation in Canada

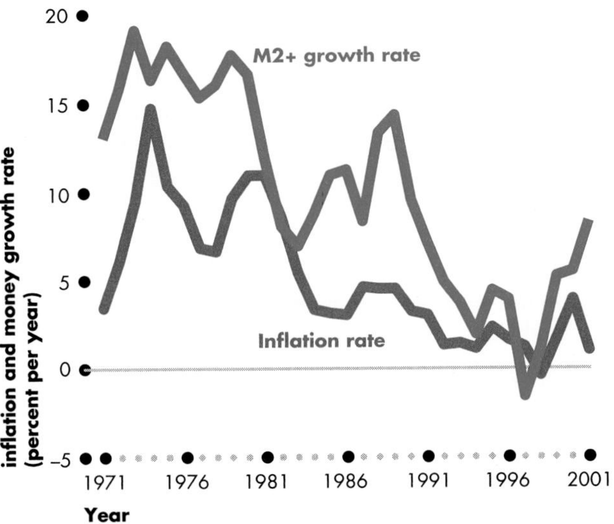

On the average, the money growth rate exceeds the inflation rate because real GDP grows. Money growth and inflation are correlated—they rise and fall together.

Source: Statistics Canada, CANSIM tables 176-0020, 380-0056, and authors' calculations.

growth to be associated with high inflation. The evidence is strongest for the high-inflation countries shown in Fig. 28.8(a), but it is also present for low-inflation countries, which are shown in Fig. 28.8(b).

REVIEW QUIZ

1. What is the quantity theory of money?
2. What is the velocity of circulation of money and how is it calculated?
3. What is the equation of exchange? Can the equation of exchange be wrong?
4. What does the long-run historical evidence and international evidence on the relationship between money growth and inflation tell us about the quantity theory of money?

We next turn to an examination of the effects of inflation.

FIGURE 28.8 Money Growth and Inflation in the World Economy

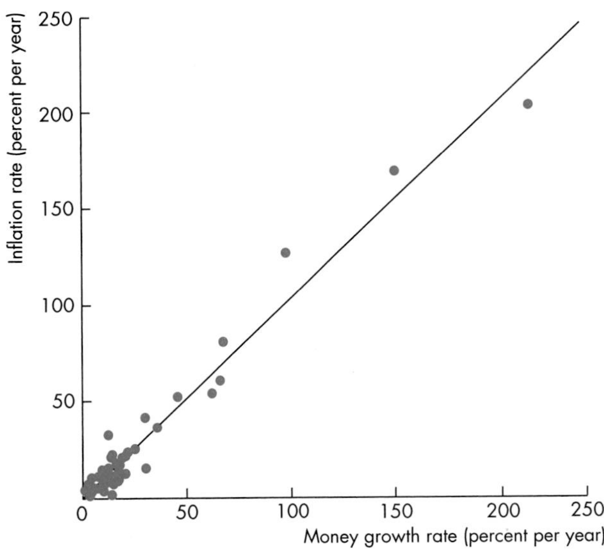

(a) 60 countries during the 1980s

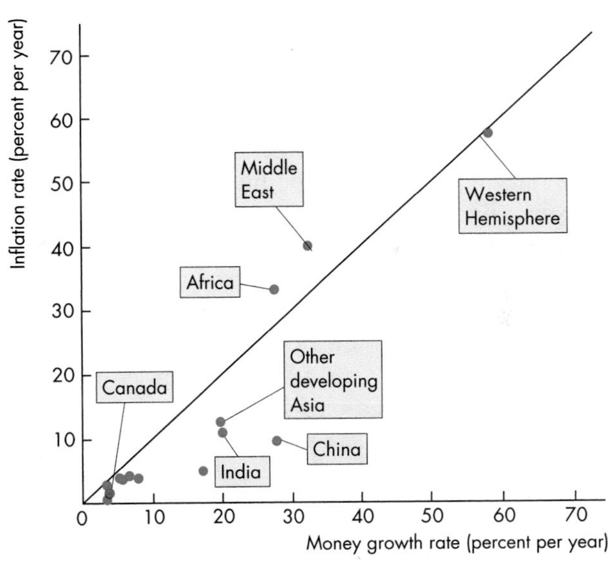

(b) 13 regions and countries during the 1990s

Inflation and money growth in 60 countries (in part a) and low-inflation countries (in part b) show a clear positive relationship between money growth and inflation.

Source: Federal Reserve Bank of St. Louis, *Review*, May/June 1988, p. 15.

Effects of Inflation

REGARDLESS OF WHETHER INFLATION IS DEMAND pull or cost push, the failure to correctly *anticipate* it results in unintended consequences. These unintended consequences impose costs in both labour markets and capital markets. Let's examine these costs.

Unanticipated Inflation in the Labour Market

Unanticipated inflation has two main consequences for the operation of the labour market:

- Redistribution of income
- Departure from full employment

Redistribution of Income Unanticipated inflation redistributes income between employers and workers. Sometimes employers gain at the expense of workers, and sometimes they lose. If an unexpected increase in aggregate demand increases the inflation rate, then the money wage rate will not have been set high enough. Profits will be higher than expected, and real wages will buy fewer goods than expected. In this case, employers gain at the expense of workers. But if aggregate demand is expected to increase at a rapid rate and it fails to do so, workers gain at the expense of employers. With a high inflation rate anticipated, the money wage rate is set too high and profits are squeezed. Redistribution between employers and workers creates an incentive for both firms and workers to try to forecast inflation correctly.

Departures from Full Employment Redistribution brings gains to some and losses to others. But departures from full employment impose costs on everyone. To see why, let's return to the ketchup-bottling plant in Chatham.

If the bottling plant and its workers do not anticipate inflation but inflation occurs, the money wage rate does not rise to keep up with inflation. The real wage rate falls, and the firm tries to hire more labour and increase production. But because the real wage rate has fallen, the firm has a hard time attracting the labour it wants to employ. It pays overtime rates to its existing work force, and because it runs its plant at a faster pace, it incurs higher plant maintenance and parts replacement costs. But also, because the real wage rate has fallen, workers begin to quit the bottling plant to find jobs that pay a real wage rate that is closer to one that prevailed before the outbreak of inflation. This labour turnover imposes additional costs on the firm. So even though its production increases, the firm incurs additional costs and its profits do not increase as much as they otherwise would. The workers incur additional costs of job search, and those who remain at the bottling plant wind up feeling cheated. They've worked overtime to produce the extra output, and when they come to spend their wages, they discover that prices have increased so their wages buy a smaller quantity of goods and services than expected.

If the bottling plant and its workers anticipate a high inflation rate that does not occur, they increase the money wage rate by too much and the real wage rate rises. At the higher real wage rate, the firm lays off some workers and the unemployment rate increases. The workers who keep their jobs gain, but those who become unemployed lose. Also, the bottling plant loses because its output and profits fall.

Unanticipated Inflation in the Market for Financial Capital

Unanticipated inflation has two consequences for the operation of the market for financial capital:

- Redistribution of income
- Too much or too little lending and borrowing

Redistribution of Income Unanticipated inflation redistributes income between borrowers and lenders. Sometimes borrowers gain at the expense of lenders, and sometimes they lose. When inflation is unexpected, interest rates are not set high enough to compensate lenders for the falling value of money. In this case, borrowers gain at the expense of lenders. But if inflation is expected and then fails to occur, interest rates are set too high. In this case, lenders gain at the expense of borrowers. Redistributions of income between borrowers and lenders create an incentive for both groups to try to forecast inflation correctly.

Too Much or Too Little Lending and Borrowing If the inflation rate turns out to be either higher or lower than expected, the interest rate does not incorporate a correct allowance for the falling value of money and the real interest rate is either lower or higher than it otherwise would be. When the real interest rate turns out to be too low, which occurs when inflation is *higher* than expected, borrowers wish they had borrowed more and lenders wish they had lent less. Both groups would have made different lending and borrowing decisions with greater foresight about the inflation rate. When the real interest rate turns out to be too high, which occurs when inflation is lower than expected, borrowers wish they had borrowed less and lenders wish they had lent more. Again, both groups would have made different lending and borrowing decisions with greater foresight about the inflation rate.

So unanticipated inflation imposes costs regardless of whether the inflation turns out to be higher or lower than anticipated. The presence of these costs gives everyone an incentive to forecast inflation correctly. Let's see how people go about this task.

Forecasting Inflation

Inflation is difficult to forecast for two reasons. First, there are several sources of inflation—the demand-pull and cost-push sources you've just studied. Second, the speed with which a change in either aggregate demand or aggregate supply translates into a change in the price level varies. This speed of response also depends, as you will see below, on the extent to which the inflation is anticipated.

Because inflation is costly and difficult to forecast, people devote considerable resources to improving inflation forecasts. Some people specialize in forecasting, and others buy forecasts from specialists. The specialist forecasters are economists who work for public and private macroeconomic forecasting agencies and for banks, insurance companies, labour unions, and large corporations. The returns these specialists make depend on the quality of their forecasts, so they have a strong incentive to forecast as accurately as possible. The most accurate forecast possible is the one that is based on all the relevant information available and is called a **rational expectation.**

A rational expectation is not necessarily a correct forecast. It is simply the best forecast available. It will often turn out to be wrong, but no other forecast that could have been made with the information available could be predicted to be better.

You've seen the effects of inflation when people fail to anticipate it. And you've seen why it pays to try to anticipate inflation. Let's now see what happens if inflation is correctly anticipated.

Anticipated Inflation

In the demand-pull and cost-push inflations that we studied in this chapter, the money wage rate is sticky. When aggregate demand increases, either to set off a demand-pull inflation or to accommodate a cost-push inflation, the money wage rate does not change immediately. But if people correctly anticipate increases in aggregate demand, they will adjust the money wage rate so as to keep up with anticipated inflation.

In this case, inflation proceeds with real GDP equal to potential GDP and unemployment equal to its natural rate. Figure 28.9 explains why. Suppose that last year the price level was 110 and real GDP was $1,000 billion, which is also potential GDP. The aggregate demand curve was AD_0, the aggregate supply curve was SAS_0, and the long-run aggregate supply curve was LAS.

Suppose that potential GDP does not change, so the LAS curve does not shift. Also suppose that aggregate demand is expected to increase and that the expected aggregate demand curve for this year is AD_1. In anticipation of this increase in aggregate demand, the money wage rate rises and the short-run aggregate supply curve shifts leftward. If the money wage rate rises by the same percentage as the price level rises, the short-run aggregate supply curve for next year is SAS_1.

If aggregate demand turns out to be the same as expected, the aggregate demand curve is AD_1. The short-run aggregate supply curve SAS_1 and AD_1 determine the actual price level at 121. Between last year and this year, the price level increased from 110 to 121 and the economy experienced an inflation rate of 10 percent, the same as the inflation rate that was anticipated. If this anticipated inflation is ongoing, in the following year aggregate demand increases (as anticipated) and the aggregate demand curve shifts to AD_2. The money wage rate rises to reflect the anticipated inflation, and the short-run aggregate supply curve shifts to SAS_2. The price level rises by a further 10 percent to 133.

What has caused this inflation? The immediate answer is that because people expected inflation, the money wage rate increased and the price level increased. But the expectation was correct. Aggregate demand was expected to increase, and it did increase. Because aggregate demand was *expected* to increase from AD_0 to AD_1, the short-run aggregate supply curve shifted from SAS_0 to SAS_1. Because aggregate demand actually did increase by the amount that was expected, the actual aggregate demand curve shifted from AD_0 to AD_1. The combination of the anticipated and actual shifts of the aggregate demand curve rightward produced an increase in the price level that was anticipated.

Only if aggregate demand growth is correctly forecasted does the economy follow the course described in Fig. 28.9. If the expected growth rate of aggregate demand is different from its actual growth rate, the expected aggregate demand curve shifts by an amount that is different from the actual aggregate demand curve. The inflation rate departs from its expected level, and to some extent, there is unanticipated inflation.

FIGURE 28.9 Anticipated Inflation

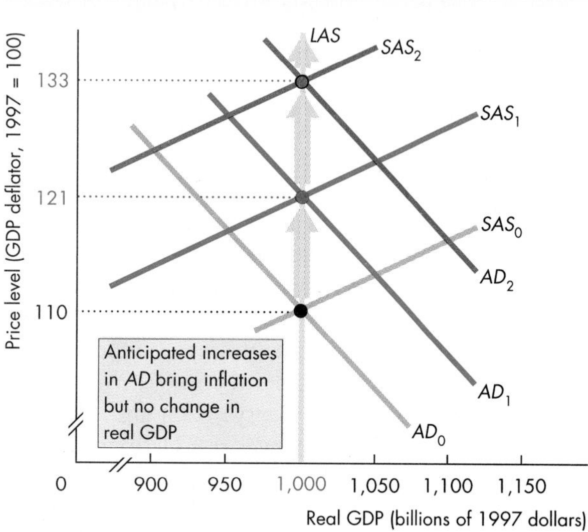

Potential real GDP is $1,000 billion. Last year, the aggregate demand curve was AD_0, and the short-run aggregate supply curve was SAS_0. The actual price level was the same as the expected price level—110. This year, aggregate demand is expected to increase to AD_1. The rational expectation of the price level changes from 110 to 121. As a result, the money wage rate rises and the short-run aggregate supply curve shifts to SAS_1. If aggregate demand actually increases as expected, the actual aggregate demand curve AD_1 is the same as the expected aggregate demand curve. Real GDP is $1,000 billion and the actual price level is 121. The inflation is correctly anticipated. Next year, the process continues with aggregate demand increasing as expected to AD_2 and the money wage rate rising to shift the short-run aggregate supply curve to SAS_2. Again, real GDP remains at $1,000 billion, and the price level rises, as anticipated, to 133.

Unanticipated Inflation

When aggregate demand increases by *more* than expected, there is some unanticipated inflation that looks just like the demand-pull inflation that you studied earlier. Some inflation is expected, and the money wage rate is set to reflect that expectation. The *SAS* curve intersects the *LAS* curve at the expected price level. Aggregate demand then increases but by more than expected. So the *AD* curve intersects the *SAS* curve at a level of real GDP that exceeds potential GDP. With real GDP above potential GDP and unemployment below its natural rate, the money wage rate rises. So the price level rises further. If aggregate demand increases again, a demand-pull inflation spiral unwinds.

When aggregate demand increases by *less* than expected, there is some unanticipated inflation that looks like the cost-push inflation that you studied earlier. Again, some inflation is expected, and the money wage rate is set to reflect that expectation. The *SAS* curve intersects the *LAS* curve at the expected price level. Aggregate demand then increases but by less than expected. So the *AD* curve intersects the *SAS* curve at a level of real GDP below potential GDP. Aggregate demand increases to restore full employment. But if aggregate demand is expected to increase by more than it actually does, the money wage rate again rises, short-run aggregate supply again decreases, and a cost-push spiral unwinds.

We've seen that only when inflation is unanticipated does real GDP depart from potential GDP. When inflation is anticipated, real GDP remains at potential GDP. Does this mean that an anticipated inflation has no costs?

The Costs of Anticipated Inflation

The costs of an anticipated inflation depend on its rate. At a moderate rate of 2 or 3 percent a year, the cost is probably small. But as the anticipated inflation rate rises, so does its cost, and an anticipated inflation at a rapid rate can be extremely costly.

Anticipated inflation decreases potential GDP and slows economic growth. These adverse consequences arise for three major reasons:

- Transactions costs
- Tax effects
- Increased uncertainty

Transactions Costs The first transactions costs are known as the "boot leather costs." These are costs that arise from an increase in the velocity of circulation of money and an increase in the amount of running around that people do to try to avoid incurring losses from the falling value of money.

When money loses value at a rapid anticipated rate, it does not function well as a store of value and people try to avoid holding money. They spend their incomes as soon as they receive them, and firms pay out incomes—wages and dividends—as soon as they receive revenue from their sales. The velocity of circulation increases. During the 1920s in Germany, when inflation reached *hyperinflation* levels (rates more than 50 percent a month), wages were paid and spent twice in a single day!

The range of estimates of the boot leather costs is large. Some economists put them at close to zero. Others estimate them to be as much as 2 percent of GDP for a 10 percent inflation. For a rapid inflation, these costs are much more.

The boot leather costs of inflation are just one of several transactions costs that are influenced by the inflation rate. At high anticipated inflation rates, people seek alternatives to money as means of payment and use tokens and commodities or even barter, all of which are less efficient than money as a means of payment. For example, in Russia during the 1990s, when inflation reached 1,000 percent a year, the U.S. dollar started to replace the increasingly worthless Russian ruble. Consequently, people had to keep track of the exchange rate between the ruble and the dollar hour by hour and had to engage in many additional and costly transactions in the foreign exchange market.

Because anticipated inflation increases transactions costs, it diverts resources from producing goods and services and it decreases potential GDP. The faster the anticipated inflation rate, the greater is the decrease in potential GDP and the farther leftward does the *LAS* curve shift.

Tax Effects Anticipated inflation interacts with the tax system and creates serious distortions in incentives. Its major effect is on real interest rates.

Anticipated inflation swells the dollar returns on investments. But dollar returns are taxed, so the effective tax rate rises. This effect becomes serious at even modest inflation rates. Let's consider an example.

Suppose the real interest rate is 4 percent a year and the tax rate is 50 percent. With no inflation, the nominal interest rate is also 4 percent a year and 50 percent of this rate is taxable. The real *after-tax* interest rate is 2 percent a year (50 percent of 4 percent). Now suppose the inflation rate is 4 percent a year, and the nominal interest rate is 8 percent a year. The *after-tax* nominal rate is 4 percent a year (50 percent of 8 percent). Now subtract the 4 percent inflation rate from this amount, and you see that the *after-tax real interest rate* is zero! The true tax rate on interest income is 100 percent.

The higher the inflation rate, the higher is the effective tax rate on income from capital. And the higher the tax rate, the higher is the interest rate paid by borrowers and the lower is the after-tax interest rate received by lenders.

With a low after-tax real interest rate, the incentive to save is weakened and the saving rate falls. With a high cost of borrowing, the amount of investment decreases. And with a fall in saving and investment, the pace of capital accumulation slows and so does the long-term growth rate of real GDP.

Increased Uncertainty When the inflation rate is high, there is increased uncertainty about the long-term inflation rate. Will inflation remain high for a long time, or will price stability be restored? This increased uncertainty makes long-term planning difficult and gives people a shorter-term focus. Investment falls, and so the growth rate slows.

But this increased uncertainty also misallocates resources. Instead of concentrating on the activities at which they have a comparative advantage, people find it more profitable to search for ways of avoiding the losses that inflation inflicts. As a result, inventive talent that might otherwise work on productive innovations works on finding ways of profiting from the inflation instead.

The implications of inflation for economic growth have been estimated to be enormous. Peter Howitt of Brown University, building on work by Robert Barro of Harvard University, has estimated that if inflation is lowered from 3 percent a year to zero, the growth rate of real GDP will rise by between 0.06 and 0.09 percentage points a year. These numbers might seem small, but they are growth rates. After 30 years, real GDP would be 2.3 percent higher and the present value of all the future output would be 85 percent of current GDP—$850 billion! In the rapid anticipated inflations of Brazil and Russia, the costs are much greater than the numbers given here.

REVIEW QUIZ

1. What is a rational expectation? Are people who form rational expectations ever wrong?
2. Why do people forecast inflation and what information do they use to do so?
3. How does anticipated inflation occur?
4. What are the effects of a rapid anticipated inflation? Does anticipated inflation bring an increase in real GDP?

You've seen that an increase in aggregate demand that is not fully anticipated increases both the price level and real GDP. It also decreases unemployment. Similarly, a decrease in aggregate demand that is not fully anticipated decreases the price level and real GDP. It also increases unemployment. Do these relationships mean that there is a tradeoff between inflation and unemployment? Does low unemployment always bring inflation and does low inflation bring high unemployment? We explore these questions.

Inflation and Unemployment: The Phillips Curve

THE AGGREGATE SUPPLY–AGGREGATE DEMAND model focuses on the price level and real GDP. Knowing how these two variables change, we can work out what happens to the inflation rate and the unemployment rate. But the model does not place inflation and unemployment at the centre of the stage.

A more direct way of studying inflation and unemployment uses a relationship called the Phillips curve. The Phillips curve approach uses the same basic ideas as the *AS–AD* model, but it focuses directly on inflation and unemployment. The Phillips curve is so named because New Zealand economist A.W. Phillips popularized it. A **Phillips curve** is a curve that shows a relationship between inflation and unemployment. There are two time frames for Phillips curves:

- The short-run Phillips curve
- The long-run Phillips curve

The Short-Run Phillips Curve

The **short-run Phillips curve** is a curve that shows the tradeoff between inflation and unemployment, holding constant

1. The expected inflation rate
2. The natural rate of unemployment

You've just seen what determines the expected inflation rate. The natural rate of unemployment and the factors that influence it are explained in Chapter 21, pp. 488–489 and Chapter 29, pp. 693–695.

Figure 28.10 shows a short-run Phillips curve, *SRPC*. Suppose that the expected inflation rate is 10 percent a year and the natural rate of unemployment is 6 percent, point *A* in the figure. A short-run Phillips curve passes through this point. If inflation

FIGURE 28.10 A Short-Run Phillips Curve

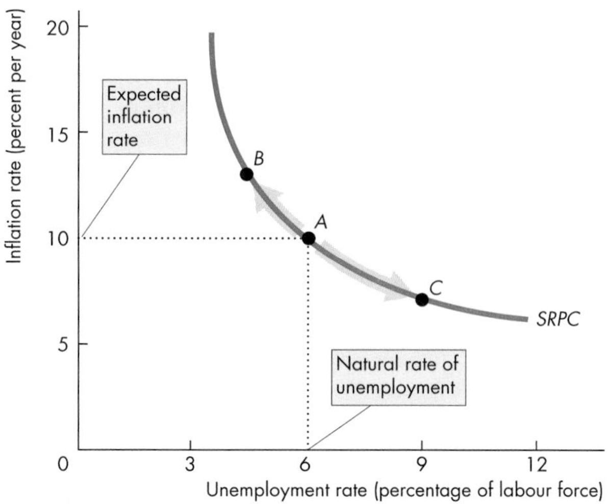

The short-run Phillips curve (*SRPC*) shows the relationship between inflation and unemployment at a given expected inflation rate and a given natural rate of unemployment. With an expected inflation rate of 10 percent a year and a natural rate of unemployment of 6 percent, the short-run Phillips curve passes through point *A*. An unanticipated increase in aggregate demand lowers unemployment and increases inflation—a movement up along the short-run Phillips curve. An unanticipated decrease in aggregate demand increases unemployment and lowers inflation—a movement down along the short-run Phillips curve.

rises above its expected rate, unemployment falls below its natural rate. This joint movement in the inflation rate and the unemployment rate is illustrated as a movement up along the short-run Phillips curve from point *A* to point *B* in the figure. Similarly, if inflation falls below its expected rate, unemployment rises above its natural rate. In this case, there is movement down along the short-run Phillips curve from point *A* to point *C*.

This negative relationship between inflation and unemployment along the short-run Phillips curve is explained by the aggregate supply–aggregate demand model. Figure 28.11 shows the connection between the two approaches. Initially, the aggregate demand curve is AD_0, the short-run aggregate supply curve is SAS_0, and the long-run aggregate supply curve is *LAS*. Real GDP is $1,000 billion, and the price level is 100. Aggregate demand is expected to increase, and the aggregate demand curve is expected to shift rightward to AD_1. Anticipating this increase in aggregate demand, the money wage rate rises, which shifts the short-run aggregate supply curve to SAS_1. What happens to actual inflation and real GDP depends on the *actual* change in aggregate demand.

First, suppose that aggregate demand actually increases by the amount expected, so the aggregate demand curve shifts to AD_1. The price level rises from 100 to 110, and the inflation rate is an anticipated 10 percent a year. Real GDP remains at potential GDP, and unemployment remains at its natural rate—6 percent. The economy moves to point *A* in Fig. 28.11, and it can equivalently be described as being at point *A* on the short-run Phillips curve in Fig. 28.10.

Alternatively, suppose that aggregate demand is expected to increase to AD_1 but actually increases by more than expected, to AD_2. The price level now rises to 113, a 13 percent inflation rate. Real GDP increases above potential GDP, and unemployment falls below its natural rate. We can now describe the economy as moving to point *B* in Fig. 28.11 or as being at point *B* on the short-run Phillips curve in Fig. 28.10.

Finally, suppose that aggregate demand is expected to increase to AD_1 but actually remains at AD_0. The price level now rises to 107, a 7 percent inflation rate. Real GDP falls below potential GDP, and unemployment rises above its natural rate. We can now describe the economy as moving to point *C* in Fig. 28.11 or as being at point *C* on the short-run Phillips curve in Fig. 28.10.

FIGURE 28.11 *AS–AD* **and the Short-Run Phillips Curve**

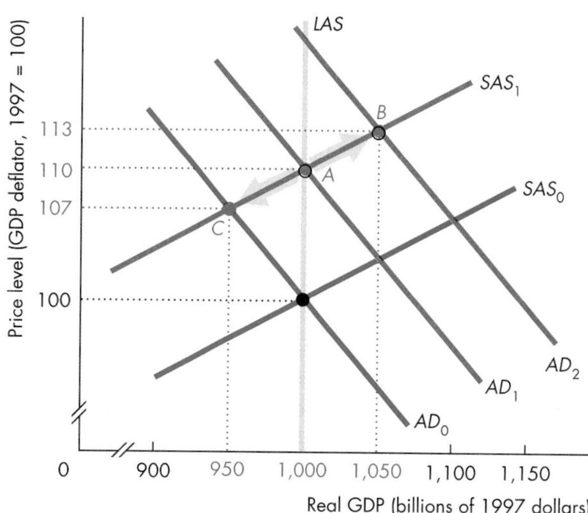

If aggregate demand is expected to increase and shift the aggregate demand curve from AD_0 to AD_1, then the money wage rate rises by an amount that shifts the short-run aggregate supply curve from SAS_0 to SAS_1. If aggregate demand increases as expected, the price level rises to 110, a 10 percent rise, and the economy is at point *A* in this figure and at point *A* on the short-run Phillips curve in Fig. 28.10. If, with the same expectations, aggregate demand increases and shifts the aggregate demand curve from AD_0 to AD_2, the price level rises to 113, a 13 percent rise, and the economy is at point *B* in this figure and at point *B* on the short-run Phillips curve in Fig. 28.10. If, with the same expectations, aggregate demand does not change, the price level rises to 107, a 7 percent rise, and the economy is at point *C* in this figure and at point *C* on the short-run Phillips curve in Fig. 28.10.

The short-run Phillips curve is like the short-run aggregate supply curve. A movement along the *SAS* curve that brings a higher price level and an increase in real GDP is equivalent to a movement along the short-run Phillips curve that brings an increase in the inflation rate and a decrease in the unemployment rate. (Similarly, a movement along the *SAS* curve that brings a lower price level and a decrease in real GDP is equivalent to a movement along the short-run Phillips curve that brings a decrease in the inflation rate and an increase in the unemployment rate.)

The Long-Run Phillips Curve

The **long-run Phillips curve** shows the relationship between inflation and unemployment when the actual inflation rate equals the expected inflation rate. The long-run Phillips curve is vertical at the natural rate of unemployment. In Fig. 28.12, it is the vertical line *LRPC.* The long-run Phillips curve tells us that any anticipated inflation rate is possible at the natural rate of unemployment. This proposition is consistent with the *AS–AD* model, which predicts that when inflation is anticipated, real GDP equals potential GDP and unemployment is at its natural rate.

When the expected inflation rate changes, the short-run Phillips curve shifts but the long-run Phillips curve does not shift. If the expected inflation rate is 10 percent a year, the short-run Phillips curve is $SRPC_0$. If the expected inflation rate falls to 7 percent a year, the short-run Phillips curve shifts downward to $SRPC_1$. The distance by which the short-run Phillips curve shifts downward when the expected inflation rate falls is equal to the change in the expected inflation rate.

FIGURE 28.12 Short-Run and Long-Run Phillips Curves

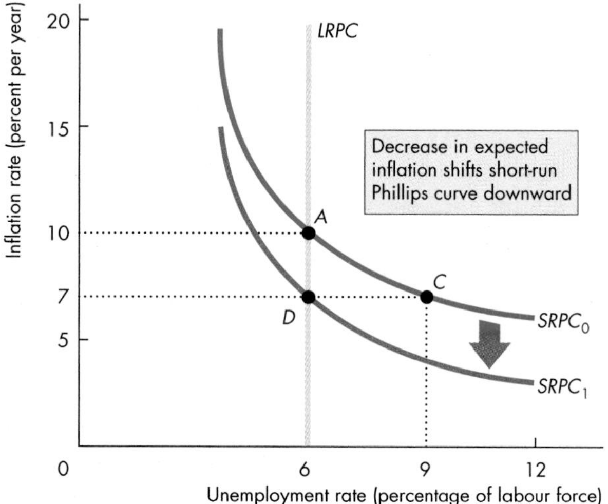

The long-run Phillips curve is *LRPC.* A fall in the expected inflation rate from 10 percent a year to 7 percent a year shifts the short-run Phillips curve downward from $SRPC_0$ and $SRPC_1$. The new short-run Phillips curve intersects the long-run Phillips curve at the new expected inflation rate—point *D.* With the original expected inflation rate (of 10 percent), a fall in the actual inflation rate to 7 percent a year increases the unemployment rate from 6 percent to 9 percent, at point *C.*

To see why the short-run Phillips curve shifts when the expected inflation rate changes, let's do a thought experiment. There is full employment, and a 10 percent a year anticipated inflation is raging. The Bank of Canada now begins an attack on inflation by slowing money growth. Aggregate demand growth slows, and the inflation rate falls to 7 percent a year. At first, this decrease in inflation is *un*anticipated, so the money wage rate continues to rise at its original rate. The short-run aggregate supply curve shifts leftward at the same pace as before. Real GDP decreases, and unemployment increases. In Fig. 28.12, the economy moves from point *A* to point *C* on $SRPC_0$.

If the actual inflation rate remains steady at 7 percent a year, this rate eventually comes to be expected. As this happens, wage growth slows and the short-run aggregate supply curve shifts leftward less quickly. Eventually, it shifts leftward at the same pace at which the aggregate demand curve is shifting rightward. The actual inflation rate equals the expected inflation rate, and full employment is restored. Unemployment is back at its natural rate. In Fig. 28.12, the short-run Phillips curve has shifted from $SRPC_0$ to $SRPC_1$ and the economy is at point *D.*

An increase in the expected inflation rate has the opposite effect to that shown in Fig. 28.12. Another important source of shifts in the Phillips curve is a change in the natural rate of unemployment.

Changes in the Natural Rate of Unemployment

The natural rate of unemployment changes for many reasons (see Chapter 29, pp. 693–695). A change in the natural rate of unemployment shifts both the short-run and long-run Phillips curves. Figure 28.13 illustrates such shifts. If the natural rate of unemployment increases from 6 percent to 9 percent, the long-run Phillips curve shifts from $LRPC_0$ to $LRPC_1$, and if expected inflation is constant at 10 percent a year, the short-run Phillips curve shifts from $SRPC_0$ to $SRPC_1$. Because the expected inflation rate is constant, the short-run Phillips curve $SRPC_1$ intersects the long-run curve $LRPC_1$ (point *E*) at the same inflation rate at which the short-run Phillips curve $SRPC_0$ intersects the long-run curve $LRPC_0$ (point *A*).

FIGURE 28.13 A Change in the Natural Rate of Unemployment

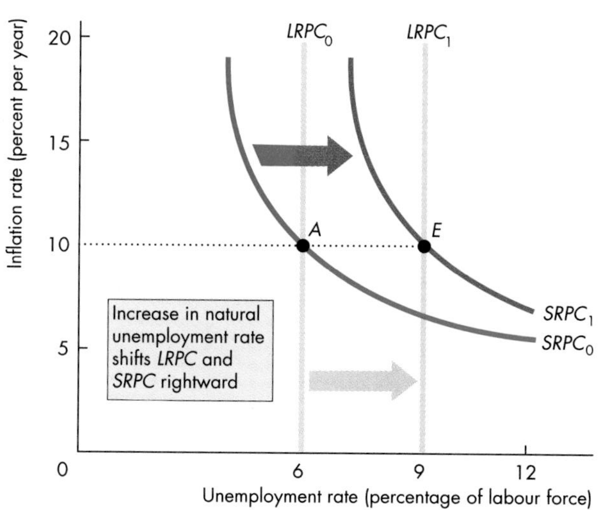

A change in the natural rate of unemployment shifts both the short-run and long-run Phillips curves. Here, the natural rate of unemployment increases from 6 percent to 9 percent, and the two Phillips curves shift right to $SRPC_1$ and $LRPC_1$. The new long-run Phillips curve intersects the new short-run Phillips curve at the expected inflation rate—point *E*.

The Canadian Phillips Curve

Figure 28.14(a) is a scatter diagram of inflation and unemployment since 1960. The data follow a course like a Formula 1 race track with 2001 almost at the same spot as 1961. Figure 28.14(b) interprets the data in terms of the Phillips curve. In 1960, the natural rate of unemployment was 5 percent so the long-run Phillips curve was $LRPC_1$. The expected inflation rate was 3 percent a year so the short-run Phillips curve, $SRPC_1$, intersects $LRPC_1$ at point *A*. During the 1970s and through 1982, the expected inflation rate and the natural rate of unemployment increased. The long-run curve shifted to $LRPC_2$ and the short-run curve shifted to $SRPC_2$. During the 1980s and 1990s, the expected inflation rate and the natural rate of unemployment decreased. The long-run curve shifted to $LRPC_3$ and the short-run curve shifted back to $SRPC_1$. The *SRPC* of 2001 is the same as that of 1960, but in 2001, the natural rate of unemployment is higher and the expected inflation rate is lower than in 1960.

FIGURE 28.14 Phillips Curves in Canada

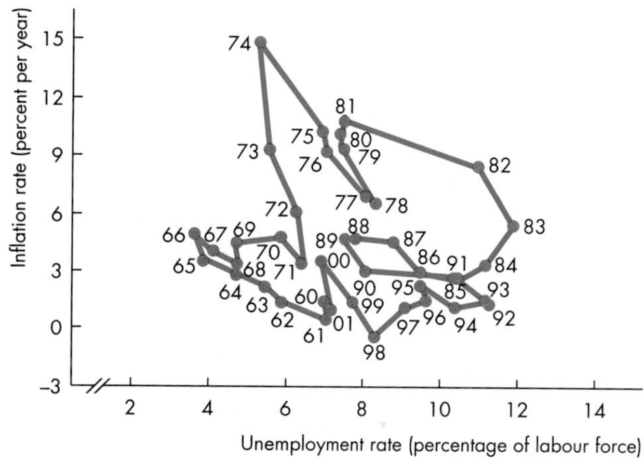

(a) The time sequence

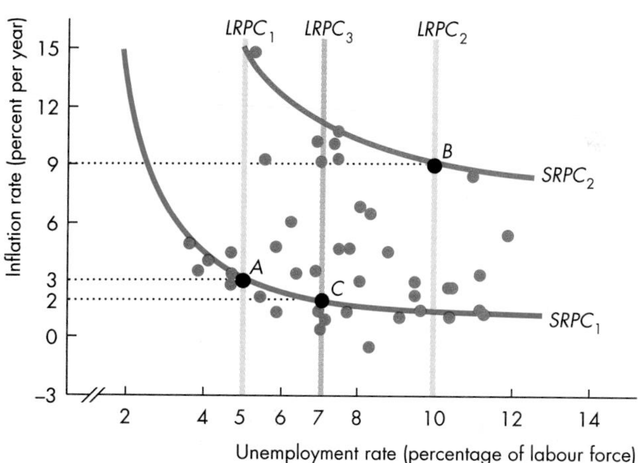

(b) Shifting Phillips curves

In part (a), each dot represents the combination of inflation and unemployment for a particular year in Canada.

Part (b) interprets the data with a shifting short-run Phillips curve. The black dots *A*, *B*, and *C* show the combination of the natural rate of unemployment and the expected inflation rate in different periods. The short-run Phillips curve was $SRPC_1$ during the 1960s and the late 1990s and early 2000s. It was $SRPC_2$ during the early 1970s and early 1980s. The long-run Phillips curve was $LRPC_1$ during the 1960s, $LRPC_2$ during the 1970s and early 1980s, and $LRPC_3$ during the 1990s.

Sources: Statistics Canada, CANSIM tables 380-0002 and 380-0056, and authors' calculations and assumptions.

REVIEW QUIZ

1. How would you use the Phillips curve to illustrate an unanticipated change in the inflation rate?
2. What are the effects of an unanticipated increase in the inflation rate on the unemployment rate?
3. If the expected inflation rate increases by 10 percentage points, how do the short-run Phillips curve and the long-run Phillips curve change?
4. If the natural rate of unemployment increases, what happens to the short-run Phillips curve and the long-run Phillips?
5. Does Canada have a stable short-run Phillips curve? Explain why or why not.
6. Does Canada have a stable long-run Phillips curve?

So far, we've studied the effects of inflation on real GDP, real wages, employment, and unemployment. But inflation lowers the value of money and changes the real value of the amounts borrowed and repaid. As a result, interest rates are influenced by inflation. Let's see how.

Interest Rates and Inflation

TODAY, BUSINESSES IN CANADA CAN BORROW AT interest rates of around 6 percent a year. Businesses in Russia pay interest rates of 60 percent a year, and those in Turkey pay 80 percent a year. Although Canadian interest rates have never been as high as these two cases, Canadian businesses faced interest rates of 20 percent or higher during the early 1980s. Why do interest rates vary so much both across countries and over time? Part of the answer is because risk differences make *real interest rates* vary across countries. Borrowers in high-risk countries pay higher interest rates than do those in low-risk countries. But another part of the answer is that the inflation rate varies.

Figure 28.15 shows that the higher the inflation rate, the higher is the nominal interest rate. This proposition is true for Canada over time in part (a) and the world in 2000 in part (b).

FIGURE 28.15 Inflation and the Interest Rate

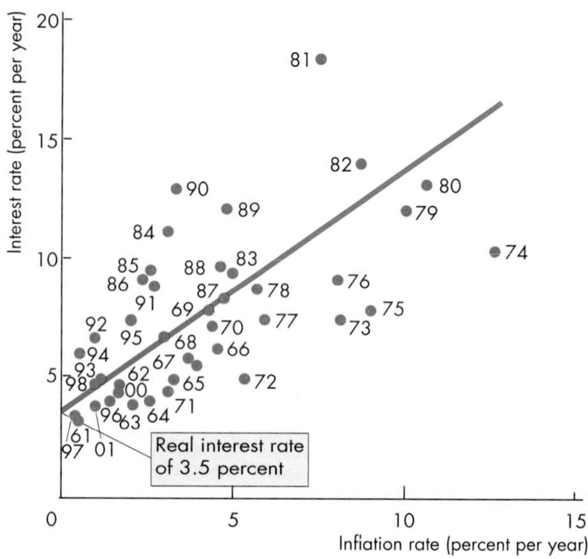

(a) Canada

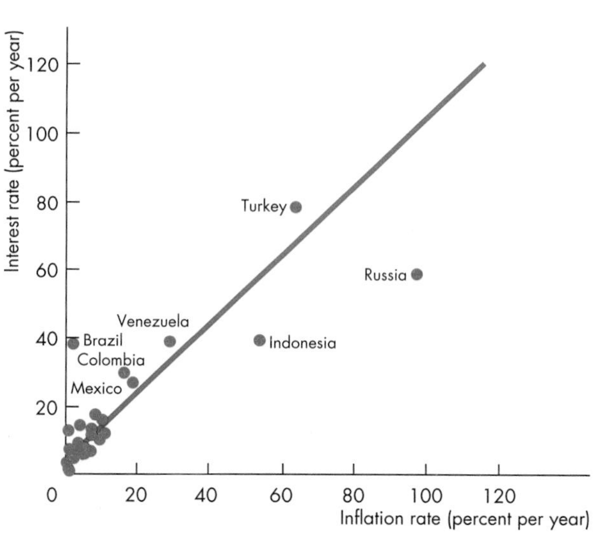

(b) Around the world

Other things remaining the same, the higher the inflation rate, the higher is the nominal interest rate. Part (a) shows this relationship between nominal interest rates and the inflation rate in Canada, and part (b) shows the relationship across a number of countries in 2000.

Sources: Statistics Canada, CANSIM tables 176-0043 and 380-0056 and International Monetary Fund, *International Financial Statistics Yearbook 2001*.

How Interest Rates Are Determined

The *real* interest rate is determined by investment demand and saving supply in the global market for financial capital. Investment demand and saving supply depend on the real interest rate. And the real interest rate adjusts to make investment plans and saving plans equal. You can think of the forces that determine the equilibrium real interest rate by using the standard demand and supply model. National real interest rates vary around the world-average real interest rate because of national differences in risk.

A *nominal* interest rate is determined by the demand for money and the quantity of money in each nation's money market. The demand for money depends on the nominal interest rate, and the quantity of money is determined by the central bank's monetary policy—the Bank of Canada's monetary policy in Canada. The nominal interest rate adjusts to make the quantity of money demanded equal to the quantity supplied. (Chapter 25, p. 595–596, explains the forces that determine the equilibrium nominal interest rate.)

Why Inflation Influences the Nominal Interest Rate

Because the real interest rate is determined in the global capital market and nominal interest rates are determined in each nation's money market, there is no tight and mechanical link between the two interest rates. But on the average, and other things remaining the same, a 1 percentage point rise in the inflation rate leads to a 1 percentage point rise in the nominal interest rate. Why? The answer is that the capital market and the money market are closely interconnected. The investment, saving, and demand for money decisions that people make are connected and the result is that the equilibrium nominal interest rate approximately equals the real interest rate plus the expected inflation rate.

To see why this relationship between the real interest rate and the nominal interest rate arises, think about the investment, saving, and demand for money decisions that people make. Imagine first that there is no inflation. Investment equals saving at a real interest rate of 6 percent a year. The demand for money equals the supply of money at a nominal interest rate of 6 percent a year. Teleglobe Canada is willing to pay an interest rate of 6 percent a year to get the funds it needs to pay for its global investment in new satellites. Sue and thousands of people like her are willing to save and lend Teleglobe Canada the amount it needs for its satellites if they can get a *real* return of 6 percent a year. (Sue is saving to buy a new car.) And Teleglobe Canada, Sue, and everyone else are willingly holding the quantity of (real) money supplied by the Bank of Canada.

Now imagine that the inflation rate is a steady and expected 4 percent a year. All dollar amounts, including satellite service profits and car prices, are rising by 4 percent a year. If Teleglobe Canada was willing to pay a 6 percent interest rate when there was no inflation, it is now willing to pay 10 percent interest. Its profits are rising by 4 percent a year, so it is *really* paying only 6 percent. Similarly, if Sue was willing to lend at a 6 percent interest rate when there was no inflation, she is now willing to lend only if she gets 10 percent interest. The price of the car Sue is planning to buy is rising by 4 percent a year, so she is *really* getting only a 6 percent interest rate.

Because borrowers are willing to pay the higher rate and lenders are willing to lend only if they get the higher rate when inflation is anticipated, the *nominal interest rate* increases by an amount equal to the expected inflation rate. The *real interest rate* remains constant.

At a nominal interest rate of 10 percent a year, people are willingly holding the quantity of (real) money supplied by the Bank of Canada. This quantity is less than that with zero inflation. The price level rises by more than the quantity of money, and the real quantity of money decreases because of the increase in inflation.

REVIEW QUIZ

1. What is the relationship between the real interest rate, the nominal interest rate, and the inflation rate?
2. Why does inflation change the nominal interest rate?

Reading Between the Lines on pp. 668–669 looks at the views of an economist who believes there is a long-run tradeoff between inflation and unemployment.

You have now completed your study of the aggregate demand side of the economy. Your task in the following chapters is to probe the supply side more deeply. We study the forces that determine aggregate supply in the short run and the long run and that bring economic growth and cycles.

READING BETWEEN THE LINES

Inflation–Unemployment Tradeoff

THE VANCOUVER SUN, JUNE 18, 2002

High jobless rate avoidable

Canada could have done more to stimulate employment through the 1990s without risking inflation, the winner of the 2001 Nobel Prize in Economics said Monday.

Dr. George Akerlof said during a meeting of the Canadian Institute for Advanced Research that the chairman of the U.S. Federal Reserve Board, Edward Greenspan, went against the advice of his staff and traditional economic theory and kept stimulating the economy with low interest rates as unemployment hit historic lows.

Canada took a more conservative and ideological approach.

The result was Canada had an unemployment rate much higher than that in the United States, where inflation stayed low even when unemployment fell below five per cent as a result of the investment generated by the economic stimulus program.

"The Canadian economy serves up a sober lesson," said Akerlof, who is a professor of economics at the University of California at Berkeley.

As the economy stalled in the past couple of years, the Bank of Canada lowered interest rates, but unemployment rates have been held high by the global recession, Akerlof said.

"You can't expect that Canada wouldn't have the same repercussions that are happening in the rest of the world," he said.

Akerlof recommended that in future, Canada adopt a policy similar to that employed in the U.S.

"I sincerely hope the Canadian unemployment of the 1990s is not going to repeat itself," he said.

...

Akerlof won the Nobel prize for work he did more than 30 years ago, describing how markets break down when buyers and sellers have conflicting needs and expectations.

Essence of the Story

- George Akerlof, a professor of economics at the University of California at Berkeley and a Nobel Laureate, says that Canada could have had higher employment (lower unemployment) with no higher inflation rate during the 1990s.

- He contrasted Canada with the United States and said that as the unemployment rate hit historic lows, the U.S. kept stimulating the economy with low interest rates.

- U.S. inflation stayed low even when unemployment fell below five percent because of the investment generated by the economic stimulus program.

- Canada took a more conservative and ideological approach and had an unemployment rate much higher than that in the United States.

Economic Analysis

- It is difficult to recognize the Canada portrayed by George Akerlof.
- Canada's unemployment rate was indeed higher than the U.S. unemployment rate.
- But the gap between the Canadian and U.S. unemployment rates, which opened up during the early 1980s (not the 1990s), was persistent and not cyclical.
- Figure 1 shows the unemployment rates in the two countries.
- Because the unemployment gap was persistent, it is likely that it represents an increase in the natural rate of unemployment in Canada.
- If Canada's natural rate of unemployment is higher than the U.S. rate, lowering interest rates to stimulate aggregate demand will bring no improvement in the unemployment situation, but will bring greater inflation.
- Canada had a more severe inflation problem than the United States during the early 1980s.
- But Canada brought its inflation under control and had lower inflation than the United States during the 1990s and 2000s.
- Figure 2 shows the inflation records in the two countries.
- George Akerlof says that U.S. unemployment fell because low interest rates brought a high investment rate.
- He implies that Canada's investment rate was too low and could have been boosted by lower interest rates.
- Figure 3 shows that generally Canada has invested a larger percentage of its GDP than the United States has invested.
- It is true that U.S. investment increased during the 1990s. But it increased from a very low level and began to catch up to Canada's higher investment rate.
- Canada chose to fight inflation and accept a temporarily higher unemployment rate. But the persistently higher unemployment rate in Canada is a natural phenomenon that cannot be changed with demand stimulation.

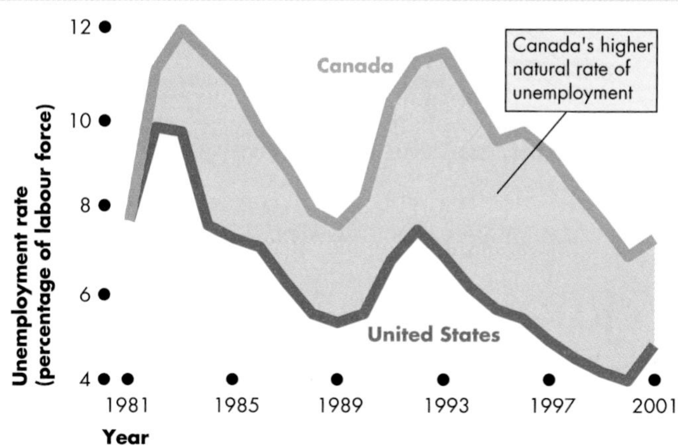

Figure 1 Unemployment in Canada and the United States

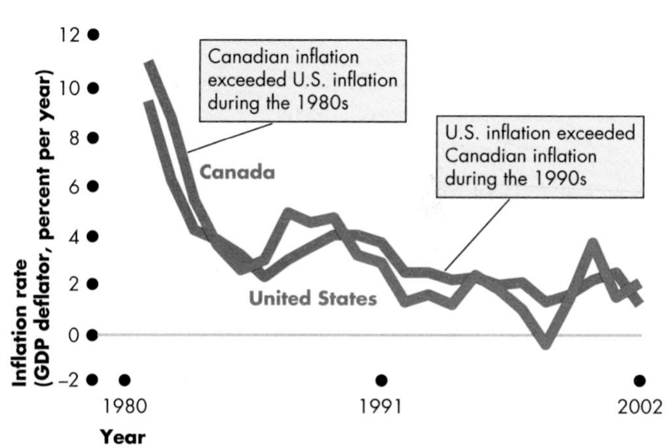

Figure 2 Inflation in Canada and the United States

Figure 3 Investment in Canada and the United States

SUMMARY

KEY POINTS

Inflation and the Price Level (p. 650)

- Inflation is a process of persistently rising prices and falling value of money.

Demand-Pull Inflation (pp. 651–653)

- Demand-pull inflation arises from increasing aggregate demand.
- Its main sources are increases in the quantity of money, government expenditures, or exports.

Cost-Push Inflation (pp. 653–655)

- Cost-push inflation can result from any factor that decreases aggregate supply.
- Its main sources are increasing money wage rates and increasing prices of key raw materials.

Quantity Theory of Money (pp. 656–657)

- The quantity theory of money is the proposition that money growth and inflation move up and down together in the long run.
- The Canadian and international evidence is consistent with the quantity theory on the average.

Effects of Inflation (pp. 658–662)

- Inflation is costly when it is unanticipated because it creates inefficiencies and redistributes income and wealth.
- People try to anticipate inflation to avoid its costs.
- Forecasts of inflation based on all the available relevant information are called rational expectations.
- A moderate anticipated inflation has a small cost. A rapid anticipated inflation is costly because it decreases potential GDP and slows economic growth.

Inflation and Unemployment: The Phillips Curve (pp. 662–666)

- The short-run Phillips curve shows the tradeoff between inflation and unemployment when the expected inflation rate and the natural rate of unemployment are constant.
- The long-run Phillips curve, which is vertical, shows that when the actual inflation rate equals the expected inflation rate, the unemployment rate equals the natural rate of unemployment.
- Unexpected changes in the inflation rate bring movements along the short-run Phillips curve.
- Changes in expected inflation shift the short-run Phillips curve.
- Changes in the natural rate of unemployment shift both the short-run and long-run Phillips curves.

Interest Rates and Inflation (pp. 666–667)

- The higher the expected inflation rate, the higher is the nominal interest rate.
- As the expected inflation rate rises, borrowers willingly pay a higher interest rate and lenders successfully demand a higher interest rate.
- The nominal interest rate adjusts to equal the real interest rate plus the expected inflation rate.

KEY FIGURES

Figure 28.2 A Demand-Pull Rise in the Price Level, 651
Figure 28.3 A Demand-Pull Inflation Spiral, 652
Figure 28.4 A Cost-Push Rise in the Price Level, 654
Figure 28.6 A Cost-Push Inflation Spiral, 655
Figure 28.9 Anticipated Inflation, 660
Figure 28.10 A Short-Run Phillips Curve, 662
Figure 28.12 Short-Run and Long-Run Phillips Curves, 664

KEY TERMS

Cost-push inflation, 653
Demand-pull inflation, 651
Equation of exchange, 656
Inflation, 650
Long-run Phillips curve, 664
Phillips curve, 662
Quantity theory of money, 656
Rational expectation, 659
Short-run Phillips curve, 662
Velocity of circulation, 656

PROBLEMS

*1. The figure shows an economy's long-run aggregate supply curve *LAS*; three aggregate demand curves AD_0, AD_1, and AD_2; and three short-run aggregate supply curves SAS_0, SAS_1, and SAS_2. The economy starts out on the curves AD_0 and SAS_0.

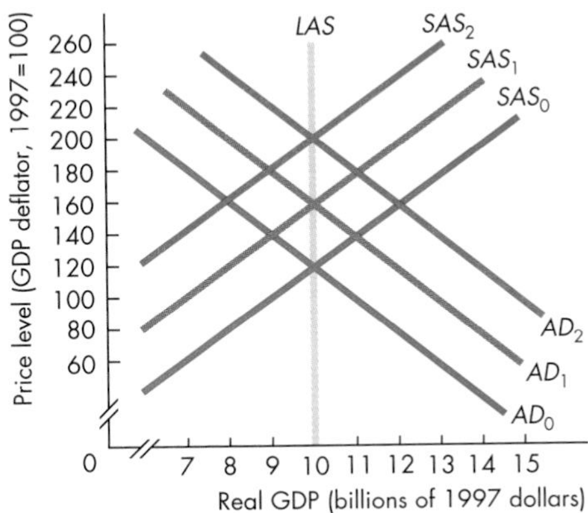

Some events occur that generate a demand-pull inflation.

a. List the events that might cause a demand-pull inflation.
b. Using the figure, describe the initial effects of a demand-pull inflation.
c. Using the figure, describe what happens as a demand-pull inflation spiral unwinds.

2. In the economy described in problem 1, some events then occur that generate a cost-push inflation.
   a. List the events that might cause a cost-push inflation.
   b. Using the figure, describe the initial effects of a cost-push inflation.
   c. Using the figure, describe what happens as a cost-push inflation spiral unwinds.

*3. Quantecon is a country in which the quantity theory of money operates. The country has a constant population, capital stock, and technology. In year 1, real GDP was $400 million, the price level was 200, and the velocity of circulation of money was 20. In year 2, the quantity of money was 20 percent higher than in year 1.
   a. What was the quantity of money in year 1?
   b. What was the quantity of money in year 2?
   c. What was the price level in year 2?
   d. What was the level of real GDP in year 2?
   e. What was the velocity of circulation in year 2?

4. In Quantecon described in problem 3, in year 3, the quantity of money falls to one-fifth of its year 2 level.
   a. What is the quantity of money in year 3?
   b. What is the price level in year 3?
   c. What is the level of real GDP in year 3?
   d. What is the velocity of circulation in year 3?
   e. If it takes more than one year for the full quantity theory effect to occur, what do you predict happens to real GDP in Quantecon in year 3? Why?

*5. The economy described in problem 1 starts out on the curves AD_0 and SAS_0. Some events now occur that generate a perfectly anticipated inflation.
   a. List the events that might cause a perfectly anticipated inflation.
   b. Using the figure, describe the initial effects of an anticipated inflation.
   c. Using the figure, describe what happens as an anticipated inflation proceeds.

6. In the economy described in problem 1, suppose that people anticipate deflation (a falling price level) but aggregate demand turns out not to change.
   a. What happens to the short-run and long-run aggregate supply curves? (Draw some new curves if you need to.)
   b. Using the figure, describe the initial effects of an anticipated deflation.
   c. Using the figure, describe what happens as it becomes obvious to everyone that the anticipated deflation is not going to occur.

*7. An economy has an unemployment rate of 4 percent and an inflation rate of 5 percent at point *A* in the figure. Some events then occur that move the economy to point *D*.
   a. Describe the events that could move the economy from point *A* to point *D*.
   b. Draw in the figure the economy's short-run and long-run Phillips curves when the economy is at point *A*.
   c. Draw in the figure the economy's short-run and long-run Phillips curves when the economy is at point *D*.

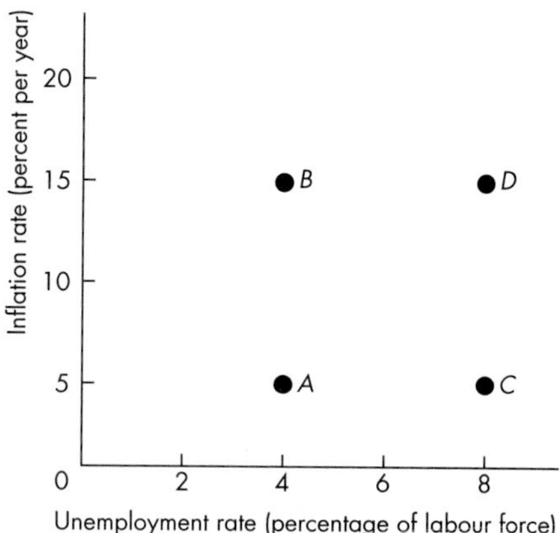

8. In the economy described in problem 7, some events occur that move the economy from point *B* to point *C*.
   a. Describe the events that could move the economy from point *B* to point *C*.
   b. Draw in the diagram the economy's short-run and long-run Phillips curves when the economy is at point *B*.
   c. Draw in the diagram the economy's short-run and long-run Phillips curves when the economy is at point *C*.

*9. An economy with a natural rate of unemployment of 4 percent and an expected inflation rate of 6 percent a year has the following inflation and unemployment history:

Year	Inflation rate (percent per year)	Unemployment rate (percentage of labour force)
1999	10	2
2000	8	3
2001	6	4
2002	4	5
2003	2	6

   a. Draw a graph of the economy's short-run and long-run Phillips curves.
   b. If the actual inflation rate rises from 6 percent a year to 8 percent a year, what is the change in the unemployment rate? Explain why it occurs.

10. For the economy described in problem 9, the natural rate of unemployment increases to 5 percent and the expected inflation rate falls to 5 percent a year. Draw the new short-run and long-run Phillips curves in the graph.

CRITICAL THINKING

1. Study *Reading Between the Lines* on pp. 668–669 and then answer the following questions:
   a. What does George Akerlof believe about the tradeoff between inflation and unemployment?
   b. Why, according to Akerlof, did the United States have a better unemployment performance than Canada?
   c. Do you think the data on inflation and unemployment are consistent with the view that the natural rate of unemployment is 7 percent? Explain why or why not.

WEB EXERCISES

1. Use the links on the Parkin–Bade Web site to obtain data on the growth rate of the quantity of money and the inflation rate in Canada since 2000.
   a. Calculate the average growth rate of the quantity of money since 2000.
   b. Calculate the average inflation rate since 2000.
   c. Make a graph of the growth rate of the quantity of money and the inflation rate since 2000.
   d. Interpret your graph and explain what it tells you about the forces that generate inflation and the relationship between money growth and inflation.
2. Use the links on the Parkin–Bade Web site to obtain data on the inflation rate and the unemployment rate in the United States during the 1990s and 2000s.
   a. Make a graph using the data you've obtained that is similar to Fig. 28.14.
   b. Describe the similarities and the differences in relationship between inflation and unemployment found in the United States and in Canada.

UNDERSTANDING AGGREGATE DEMAND AND INFLATION

Money Chasing Goods

Aggregate demand fluctuations bring recessions and expansions. If aggregate demand expands more rapidly than long-run aggregate supply, we get inflation. So understanding the forces that determine aggregate demand helps us to understand both the business cycle and inflation. ◆ It took economists a long time to achieve this knowledge, and we still don't know enough about aggregate demand to be able to forecast it more than a few months ahead. But we do know the basic factors that influence aggregate demand. And we know a lot about how those factors interact to send shock waves rippling through the economy. ◆ Fundamentally, aggregate demand is a monetary phenomenon. The quantity of money is the single most significant influence on aggregate demand. This insight was first outlined more than 200 years ago by David Hume, a Scottish philosopher and close friend of Adam Smith. Said Hume, "In every Kingdom into which money begins to flow in greater abundance than formerly, everything takes a new face: labour and industry gain life; the merchant becomes more enterprising, the manufacturer more diligent and skilful, and even the farmer follows his plough with greater alacrity and attention." Milton Friedman and other economists known as monetarists also emphasize the central role of money. Money lies at the centre of Keynes' theory of aggregate demand as well. But Keynes also called attention to the power of independent changes in government expenditures, taxes, and business investment to influence aggregate demand. In the modern world, we also recognize the effect of changes in exports on aggregate demand. ◆ The chapters in this part explain the factors that influence aggregate demand and help you to understand how they interact to bring multiplier effects on aggregate expenditure. Chapter 23 explained the effects of changes in business investment and the multiplier effect they have on consumption expenditure and aggregate expenditure. This chapter also explained how changes in business inventories trigger changes in production and incomes. Chapter 24 looked at fiscal policy and applied the model of Chapter 23 to study the effects of changes in government expenditures and taxes. Chapter 25 brought money into the picture and explained what money is, how banks create it, and what determines the interest rate. Chapter 26 showed how the Bank of Canada controls the quantity of money and influences interest rates and expenditure. Chapter 27 returned to the aggregate supply–aggregate demand framework and explained how fiscal policy and monetary policy interact. Chapter 28 explained inflation and showed how the trend in money growth determines the trend in inflation and how fluctuations in aggregate demand bring fluctuations in inflation, employment, and unemployment. ◆ Many economists have developed the insights you've learned in these chapters. One of the truly outstanding ones is Milton Friedman, whom you can meet on the next page. You can also meet one of today's leading macroeconomists, Michael Woodford of Princeton University.

PROBING THE IDEAS

Understanding Inflation

The Economist

"Inflation is always and everywhere a monetary phenomenon."

Milton Friedman
The Counter-Revolution in Monetary Theory

MILTON FRIEDMAN *was born into a poor immigrant family in New York City in 1912. He was an undergraduate at Rutgers and graduate student at Columbia University during the Great Depression. Today, Professor Friedman is a Senior Fellow at the Hoover Institution at Stanford University. But his reputation was built between 1946 and 1983, when he was a leading member of the "Chicago School," an approach to economics developed at the University of Chicago and based on the views that free markets allocate resources efficiently and that stable and low money supply growth delivers macroeconomic stability.*

Friedman has advanced our understanding of the forces that determine aggregate demand and clarified the effects of the quantity of money and for this work, he was awarded the (much overdue, in the opinion of his many admirers) 1977 Nobel Prize for Economic Science.

By reasoning from basic economic principles, Friedman predicted that persistent demand stimulation would not increase output but would cause inflation. When output growth slowed and inflation broke out in the 1970s, Friedman seemed like a prophet, and for a time, his policy prescription, known as monetarism, was embraced around the world.

The Issues

The combination of history and economics has taught us a lot about the causes of inflation. Severe inflation—hyperinflation—arises from a breakdown of the normal fiscal policy processes at times of war or political upheaval. Tax revenues fall short of government spending, and newly printed money fills the gap between them. As inflation increases, the quantity of money that is needed to make payments increases, and a shortage of money can even result. So the rate of money growth increases yet further, and prices rise yet faster. Eventually, the monetary system collapses. Such was the experience of Germany during the 1920s and Brazil during the 1990s.

In earlier times, when commodities were used as money, inflation resulted from the discovery of new sources of money. The most recent occurrence of this type of inflation was at the end of the nineteenth century when gold, then used as money, was discovered in Australia, the Klondike, and South Africa.

In modern times, inflation has resulted from increases in the quantity of money that has accommodated increases in costs. The most dramatic such inflations occurred during the 1970s when the Bank of Canada, the Federal Reserve, and other central banks around the world accommodated oil price increases.

To avoid inflation, money growth must be held in check. But at times of severe cost pressure, central banks feel a strong tug in the direction of avoiding recession and accommodating the cost pressure.

Yet some countries have avoided inflation more effectively than others have. One source of success is central bank independence. In low-inflation countries, such as Germany and Japan, the central bank decides how much money to create and at what level to set interest rates, and does not take instructions from the government. In high-inflation countries, such as Angola and Zimbabwe, the central bank takes direct orders from the government about interest rates and money growth. The architects of the new monetary system for the European Community based on the euro noticed this connection between central bank independence and inflation and modelled the constitution for the European Central Bank on the independent German central bank.

Then

When inflation is especially rapid, as it was in Germany in 1923, money becomes almost worthless. In Germany at that time, bank notes were more valuable as fire kindling than as money, and the sight of people burning Reichmarks was a common one. To avoid having to hold money for too long, wages were paid and spent twice a day. Banks took deposits and made loans, but at interest rates that compensated both depositors and the bank for the falling value of money—interest rates that could exceed 100 percent a month. The price of a dinner would increase during the course of an evening, making lingering over coffee a very expensive pastime.

Now

In 1994, Brazil had a computer-age hyperinflation, an inflation rate that was close to 50 percent a month. Banks installed ATMs on almost every street corner and refilled them several times an hour. Brazilians tried to avoid holding currency. As soon as they were paid, they went shopping and bought enough food to get them through to the next payday. Some shoppers filled as many as six carts on a single monthly trip to the supermarket. Also, instead of using currency, Brazilians used credit cards whenever possible. But they paid their card balances off quickly because the interest rate on unpaid balances was 50 percent a month. Only at such a high interest rate did it pay banks to lend to cardholders, because banks themselves were paying interest rates of 40 percent a month to induce depositors to keep their money in the bank.

Many economists today are working on aggregate demand and inflation. One distinguished contributor, whom you can meet on the following pages, is Michael Woodford of Princeton University.

TALKING WITH

MICHAEL WOODFORD *is Harold H. Helm '20 Professor of Economics and Banking at Princeton University. Born in 1955 in Chicopee, Massachusetts, he was an undergraduate at the University of Chicago and a doctoral student at the Yale Law School before pursuing his doctorate in economics at the Massachusetts Institute of Technology. Professor Woodford's research on money and monetary policy has challenged much traditional thinking, and his ideas about a (future) world without money are attracting a great deal of interest. His advanced text,* Interest and Prices: Foundations of a Theory of Monetary Policy, *is being published by Princeton University Press.*

Michael Parkin and Robin Bade talked with Michael Woodford about his work and the progress that economists have made in designing effective monetary policy rules.

Michael Woodford

Why, after completing law school, did you decide to become an economist?

Almost every class in law school was full of economic reasoning. I became fascinated by economic analysis, and thought that I would have to get a better foundation in economics in order to think clearly about legal issues. In the end I found that I liked economics enough to become an economist.

I am able to address questions of public policy, which is what had originally drawn me to law, but in a way that also allows me to indulge a taste for thinking about what the world might be like or should be like, and not simply the way that it already is.

In a world as rapidly changing as ours is, I think that the perspective provided by economics is essential for understanding which kinds of laws and rules make sense.

You are a supporter of rules for monetary policy. Why are rules so important?

In my view, rules are important not because central bankers can't be relied upon to take the public interest to heart, or because they don't know what they're doing, but because the effects of monetary policy depend critically upon what the private sector expects about future policy, and hence about the future course of the economy. Thus effective monetary policy depends more on the successful *management of expectations* than on any direct consequences of the current level of interest rates.

In order to steer people's expectations about future monetary policy in the way that it would like, a central bank needs to communicate details about how policy will be conducted in the future. The best way to do this is by being explicit about the rule that guides its decision making. The central bank also needs to establish a reputation for actually following the rule.

Following the rule means not always doing what might seem best in given current conditions. What is best for the economy now will be independent of what people may have expected in the past. But if the central bank doesn't feel bound to follow through on its prior commitments, people will learn that they don't mean anything. Then those commitments will not shape people's expectations in the desired way.

There is actually a strong parallel between monetary policy rules and the law, and the desirability of rules is an example of the perspective that I gained from the study of law. A judge doesn't simply seek to determine, in each individual case, what outcomes would do the most good, given the individual circumstances. Instead, the judge makes a decision based on rules established either by precedent or by statute. Because the law is rule-based, people are able to forecast more accurately the consequences of their contemplated actions.

A central banker is often portrayed as the captain of the economic ship, steering it skillfully between the rocks of inflation and unemployment in a choppy sea. But a ship's captain doesn't need to care about how the ocean will interpret his actions. So the parallel isn't a good one. In my view, the role of a central banker is more similar to that of a judge than to that of a ship's captain. Both central bankers and judges care enormously about the effects of their decisions on the expectations of people whose behaviour depends on expected future decisions.

> *"Following the rule means* **not** *always doing what might seem best in given current conditions."*

The rule that you favour is different from that suggested by Milton Friedman. What is wrong with the Friedman rule?

Friedman's rule involves a target for the growth rate of some definition of the quantity of money. I don't think that the best monetary rule involves a target of any kind for the growth rate of a monetary aggregate. Friedman's rule is not the worst sort of rule, as simple rules go, but we can do better.

Just a century ago, no one had any idea how to establish a reasonably predictable monetary standard except by guaranteeing the convertibility of money into a precious metal such as gold. We didn't have the surprisingly modern concept of index numbers and today's routinely calculated price indexes like the CPI that enable us to measure, to a decent approximation, the purchasing power of the dollar.

We now understand that pegging the value of money to something like gold is a cruder solution to the problem than is necessary. We don't need to leave the value of money hostage to the vagaries of the gold market simply in order to maintain confidence that a dollar means *something*.

Friedman recognizes the value of a well-managed fiat currency, but supposes that there is unlikely to be much predictability to the value of money unless the central bank is committed to a fixed target growth path for the quantity of money. But that again is a more indirect solution to the problem of maintaining a stable and predictable value for money than is necessary.

And there is a potentially large cost of such a crude approach when the relation between one's favourite monetary aggregate and the value of money shifts over time. A focus on stabilizing a monetary aggregate means less stability than would otherwise have been possible in the purchasing power of money.

So what would be a good monetary rule?

First, there should be a clearly defined target in terms of variables that policymakers actually care about, such as the inflation rate, rather than an "intermediate target" such as a monetary aggregate. Second, the central bank should be as clear as possible about the decision making process through which it determines the level of interest rates that is believed to be consistent with achieving the target.

"Inflation targeting," as currently practised in the United Kingdom, Canada, and New Zealand, is an example of the general approach that I would advocate. But I think that central banks of the inflation-targeting countries could do a better job of explaining the procedures used to determine the interest rate that is judged to be consistent with the inflation target—they could be more transparent.

And all of these countries could better explain to the public the ways in which variables other than inflation are also taken into consideration. I'm not sure that inflation targeting needs to be *stricter*, in the sense that considerations other than inflation should be more scrupulously ruled out. But I think that it is desirable to make it more of a *rule*.

One of the most intriguing issues that you've worked on is the question of what determines the price level in a "cashless economy." How would we control inflation in such a world?

One advantage of the approach the monetary policy that I've just mentioned is that the form of policy rule that is appropriate need not change much at all if we were to progress to a "cashless economy." As long as the central bank can still control the overnight interest rate—the overnight loans rate in Canada—the *rule* for adjusting the interest rate need not change. Yet there might no longer be any meaning to a target path for a monetary aggregate in such a world.

The critical question is whether a central bank would still be able to control the overnight interest rate in such a world. Some argue that central banks only control interest rates in the interbank market for reserves because the private sector cannot supply a good substitute for reserves and the central bank is therefore a monopoly supplier. They then worry that if private substitutes for reserves were available, central banks would lose control of the interest rate.

But this line of reasoning assumes, as do most textbooks (even the good ones!), that central banks can change the interest rate *only* by changing the *opportunity cost* of holding reserves, which should only be possible in the presence of market power. But central banks can change the overnight interest rate *without* changing the opportunity cost of holding reserves. Indeed, the Bank of Canada already does so. It pays interest on reserves and maintains a fixed difference between the interest rate on reserves and the discount rate—the rate at which it stands willing to lend reserves to the banks. The overnight rate fluctuates inside the range of these two rates, so by changing the interest rate on reserves, the Bank of Canada controls the overnight rate but doesn't change the opportunity cost of holding reserves.

Every central bank, including the Federal Reserve, would have to adjust the interest rate in a way similar to this in a "cashless economy."

Where do you stand on the sources of aggregate fluctuations? Are they primarily an efficient response to the uneven pace of technical change, or are they primarily the consequence of market failure and demand fluctuations?

I don't think that they are primarily an *efficient* response to variations in technical progress or to other real disturbances of that kind. I think that there are important distortions that often result in *inefficient* responses of the economy to real disturbances, and this is why monetary policy matters. But I do think that real disturbances are important—for example, I don't think that exogenous variations in monetary policy have been responsible for too much of the economic instability in the U.S. economy in recent decades—and I think that their supply-side effects are important, too.

The important issue, to my mind, is not whether the disturbances are thought to have more to do with supply or demand factors; it is whether the economy can be relied upon to respond efficiently to them, regardless of the nature of monetary policy. I don't think that that occurs automatically. The goal of good monetary policy is to bring about such a world: one in which monetary policy is not itself a source of disturbances, and in which the responses to real disturbances are efficient ones. The first part simply requires that monetary policy be systematic, but the second part depends upon the choice of a monetary policy rule of the right sort.

What advice do you have for a student who is just starting to study economics? Is it a good subject in which to major? What other subjects would you urge students to study alongside economics?

I think economics is an excellent major for students with many different interests. Most people who study economics are probably looking for an edge in the business world, and economics is valuable for that. But it's also all extremely valuable background for people interested in careers in law, government, or public policy. And of course, to some of us, the subject is interesting in its own right. I find that the challenges just get deeper the farther I get into the subject.

Probably the most important other subject for someone thinking of actually becoming an economist is mathematics. This is often the determining factor as to how well a student will do in graduate study, because the research literature is a good deal more mathematical than many people suspect from their undergraduate economics courses. But economics is not a branch of mathematics. It's a subject that seeks to understand people and social institutions, and so all sorts of other subjects—history, politics, sociology, psychology, moral and political philosophy—are useful background for an economist, too. I don't at all regret the amount of time I spent in liberal arts courses as an undergraduate.

PART 9 AGGREGATE SUPPLY AND ECONOMIC GROWTH

THE ECONOMY AT FULL EMPLOYMENT

CHAPTER 29

Production and Jobs

Over time, we become more productive and our incomes grow. For each hour we worked in 2001, we earned twice what we earned in 1961. What makes production and incomes grow? Why did productivity grow during a recession? ◆ Our population also grows every year. How does population size influence employment, wage rates, and potential GDP? ◆ We hear a lot about the need to increase our national saving to invest in new capital, the importance of education, and the need to support science and technology. How do capital accumulation, education, and advances in technology influence employment, wage rates, and potential GDP? ◆ You know that when we talk about full employment, we don't mean there is *no* unemployment. But what determines the amount of unemployment when the economy is at full employment?

◆ We'll answer these questions in this chapter. We'll discover how changes in population, capital, and technology influence production, jobs, and incomes over long periods of time. We'll learn about the forces that create unemployment when the economy is at full employment. And in *Reading Between the Lines* at the end of this chapter, we'll compare productivity in Canada with that in the United States.

After studying this chapter, you will be able to

- **Describe the relationship between the quantity of labour employed and real GDP**
- **Explain what determines the demand for labour and the supply of labour and how labour market equilibrium determines employment, the real wage rate, and potential GDP**
- **Explain how an increase in the population, an increase in capital, and an advance in technology change employment, the real wage rate, and potential GDP**
- **Explain what determines unemployment when the economy is at full employment**

Real GDP and Employment

TO PRODUCE MORE OUTPUT, WE MUST USE MORE inputs. We can increase real GDP by employing more labour, increasing the quantity of capital, or developing technologies that are more productive. In the short term, the quantity of capital and the state of technology are fixed. So to increase real GDP in the short term, we must increase the quantity of labour employed. Let's look at the relationship between real GDP and the quantity of labour employed.

Production Possibilities

When you studied the limits to production in Chapter 2 (see p. 34), you learned about the *production possibilities frontier*, which is the boundary between those combinations of goods and services that can be produced and those that cannot. We can think about the production possibilities frontier for any pair of goods or services when we hold the quantities of all other goods and services constant. Let's think about the production possibilities frontier for two special items: real GDP and the quantity of leisure time.

Real GDP is a measure of the final goods and services produced in the economy in a given time period (see Chapter 20, p. 458). We measure real GDP as a number of 1997 dollars, but the measure is a *real* one. Real GDP is not a pile of dollars. It is a pile of goods and services. Think of it as a number of big shopping carts filled with goods and services. Each cart contains some of each kind of different goods and services produced, and one cartload of items costs $100 billion. To say that real GDP is $1,000 billion means that real GDP is 10 very big shopping carts of goods and services.

The quantity of leisure time is the number of hours we spend not working. It is the time we spend playing or watching sports, seeing movies, and hanging out with friends. Leisure time is a special type of good or service.

Each hour that we spent pursuing fun could have been an hour that we spent working. So when the quantity of leisure time increases by one hour, the quantity of labour employed decreases by one hour. If we spent all our time having fun rather than working, we would not produce anything. Real GDP would be zero. The more leisure time we forgo to work, the greater is the quantity of labour employed and the greater is real GDP.

The relationship between leisure time and real GDP is a *production possibilities frontier* (*PPF*). Figure 29.1(a) shows an example of this frontier. The economy has 45 billion hours of leisure time available. If people use all these hours to pursue leisure, no labour is employed and real GDP is zero. As people forgo leisure and work more, real GDP increases. If people spent 20 billion hours working and took 25 billion hours in leisure, real GDP would be $1,000 billion at point *A*. If people spent all the available hours working, real GDP would be $1,500 billion.

The bowed-out *PPF* displays increasing opportunity cost. In this case, the opportunity cost of a given amount of real GDP is the amount of leisure time forgone to produce it. As real GDP increases, each additional unit of real GDP costs an increasing amount of forgone leisure. The reason is that we use the most productive labour first, and as we use more labour, we use increasingly less productive labour.

The Production Function

The **production function** is the relationship between real GDP and the quantity of labour employed when all other influences on production remain the same. The production function shows how real GDP varies as the quantity of labour employed varies, other things remaining the same.

Because one more hour of labour employed means one less hour of leisure, the production function is like a mirror image of the leisure time–real GDP *PPF*. Figure 29.1(b) shows the production function for the economy whose *PPF* is shown in Fig. 29.1(a). You can see that when the quantity of labour employed is zero, real GDP is also zero. And as the quantity of labour employed increases, so does real GDP. When 20 billion labour hours are employed, real GDP is $1,000 billion (at point *A*).

A decrease in leisure hours and the corresponding increases in the quantity of labour employed and real GDP bring a movement along the production possibilities frontier and along the production function (*PF*). The arrows along the *PPF* and the *PF* in Fig. 29.1 show these movements. Such movements occurred when employment and real GDP surged during World War II.

But the increase in real GDP during World War II changed for an additional reason. Labour became more productive. Let's study the influences on the productivity of labour.

FIGURE 29.1 Production Possibilities and the Production Function

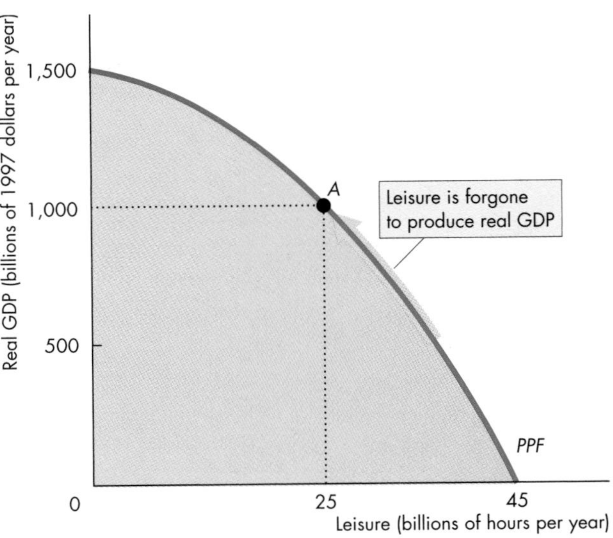

(a) Production possibility frontier

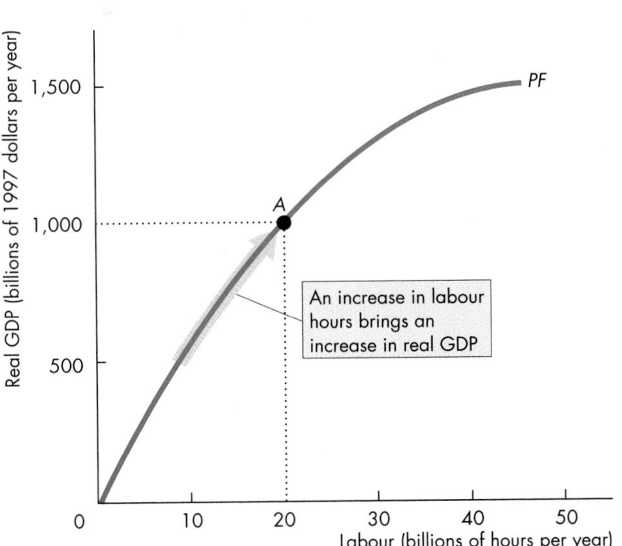

(b) Production function

On the production possibilities frontier in part (a), if we enjoy 45 billion hours of leisure, we produce no real GDP. If we forgo 20 billion hours of leisure time to work and spend 25 billion hours of leisure time, we produce a real GDP of $1,000 billion, at point *A*. At point *A* on the production function in part (b), we use 20 billion hours of labour to produce $1,000 billion of real GDP.

Changes in Productivity

When we talk about *productivity*, we usually mean labour productivity. **Labour productivity** is real GDP per hour of labour. Three factors influence labour productivity:

- Physical capital
- Human capital
- Technology

Physical Capital A farm worker equipped with only a stick and primitive tools can cultivate almost no land and grow barely enough food to feed a single family. A farmer equipped with a steel plow pulled by an animal can cultivate more land and produce enough food to feed a small village. A farmer equipped with a modern tractor, plow, and harvester can cultivate thousands of hectares and produce enough food to feed hundreds of people.

By using physical capital on our farms and in our factories, shops, and offices, we enormously increase labour productivity. And the more physical capital we use, the greater is our labour productivity, other things remaining the same.

Human Capital An economy's **human capital** is the knowledge and skill that people have obtained from education and on-the-job training.

The average university graduate has a greater amount of human capital than the average high school graduate possesses. Consequently, the university graduate is able to perform some tasks that are beyond the ability of the high school graduate. The university graduate is more productive. For the nation as a whole, the greater the amount of schooling its citizens complete, the greater is its real GDP, other things remaining the same.

Regardless of how much schooling a person has completed, not much production is accomplished on the first day at work. Learning about the new work environment consumes the newly hired worker. But as time passes and experience accumulates, the worker becomes more productive. We call this on-the-job education activity **learning-by-doing**.

Learning-by-doing can bring incredible increases in labour productivity. The more experienced the labour force, the greater is its labour productivity, and other things remaining the same, the greater is real GDP.

World War II provides a carefully documented example of the importance of this source of increase in labour productivity. In the shipyards that produced the transport vessels called Liberty ships, labour productivity increased by an astonishing 30 percent purely as a result of learning-by-doing.

Technology A student equipped with a pen can complete a readable page of writing in perhaps 10 minutes. This same task takes 5 minutes with a typewriter and 2 minutes with a computer. Travelling on foot from Toronto to Vancouver takes a person (a fit person!) more than 100 days. In a car, the trip takes a comfortable 5 days. And in an airplane, the trip takes 5 hours. These are examples of the enormous impact of technology on productivity. Imagine the profound effect of these advances in technology on the productivity of a movie director who works in both Toronto and Vancouver!

Shifts in the Production Function

Any influence on production that increases labour productivity shifts the production function upward. Real GDP increases at each level of labour hours. In Fig. 29.2(a), the production function is initially PF_0. Then an increase in physical capital and human capital or an advance in technology occurs. The production function shifts upward to PF_1.

At each quantity of labour employed, real GDP is greater on the new production function than it was on the original one. For example, at 20 billion hours, real GDP increases from $1,000 billion (point *A*) to $1,100 billion (point *B*).

Figure 29.2(b) shows how the production function in Canada shifted upward between 1981 and 2001. Along the production function PF_{01}, labour productivity is 42 percent greater than that on PF_{81}. Labour productivity in Canada increased by 1.8 percent a year.

REVIEW QUIZ

1. What is the relationship between the leisure hours–real GDP *PPF* and the production function?
2. What does the outward-bowed shape of the leisure hours–real GDP *PPF* imply about the opportunity cost of real GDP and why is the *PPF* bowed outward?
3. Why does the production function shift upward when capital increases and/or technology advances?

FIGURE 29.2 An Increase in Labour Productivity

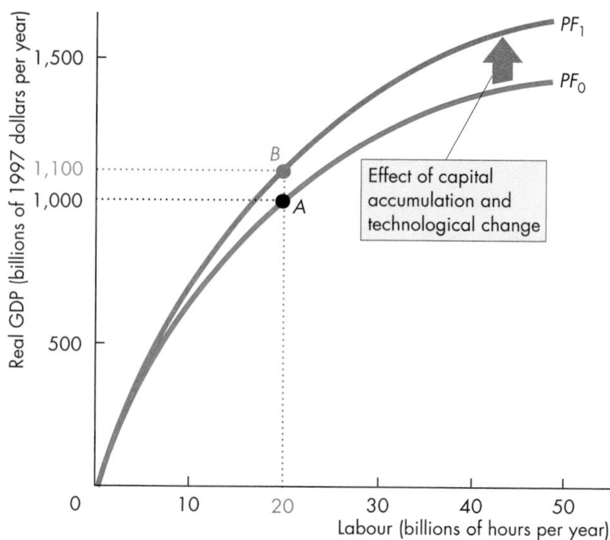

(a) An increase in labour productivity

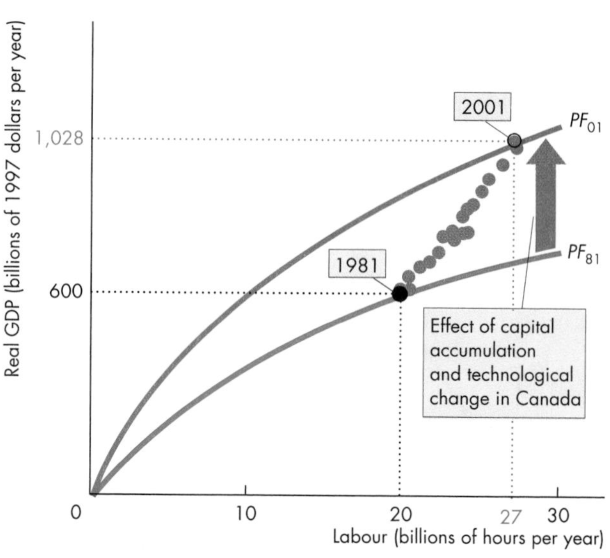

(b) The Canadian production function

On PF_0 in part (a), 20 billion labour hours produce a real GDP of $1,000 billion (point *A*). An increase in capital or an advance in technology increases labour productivity and shifts the production function upward to PF_1. Now, 20 billion labour hours produce a real GDP of $1,100 billion (point *B*). Canadian real GDP has increased (part b) because labour has become more productive and the quantity of labour has increased.

The Labour Market and Aggregate Supply

YOU'VE SEEN THAT IN A GIVEN YEAR, WITH A given amount of physical and human capital and given technology, real GDP depends on the quantity of labour hours employed. To produce more real GDP, we must employ more labour hours. The labour market determines the quantity of labour hours employed and the quantity of real GDP supplied. We'll learn how by studying

- The demand for labour
- The supply of labour
- Labour market equilibrium and potential GDP
- Aggregate supply

The Demand for Labour

The **quantity of labour demanded** is the number of labour hours hired by all the firms in the economy. The **demand for labour** is the relationship between the quantity of labour demanded and the real wage rate when all other influences on firms' hiring plans remain the same. The **real wage rate** is the quantity of goods and services that an hour of labour earns. In contrast, the **money wage rate** is the number of dollars that an hour of labour earns. A real wage rate is equal to a money wage rate divided by the price of a good. For the economy as a whole, the average real wage rate equals the average money wage rate divided by the price level multiplied by 100. So we express the real wage rate in constant dollars. (Today, we express this real wage rate in 1997 dollars.)

The *real* wage rate influences the quantity of labour demanded because what matters to firms is how much output they must sell to earn the number of dollars they pay (the money wage rate).

We can represent the demand for labour as either a demand schedule or a demand curve. The table in Fig. 29.3 shows part of a demand for labour schedule. It tells us the quantity of labour demanded at three different real wage rates. For example, if the real wage rate falls from $40 an hour to $35 an hour, the quantity of labour demanded increases from 15 billion hours a year to 20 billion hours a year. (You can find these numbers in rows *A* and *B* of the table.) The demand for labour curve is *LD*. Points *A*, *B*, and *C* on the curve correspond to rows *A*, *B*, and *C* of the demand schedule.

FIGURE 29.3 The Demand for Labour

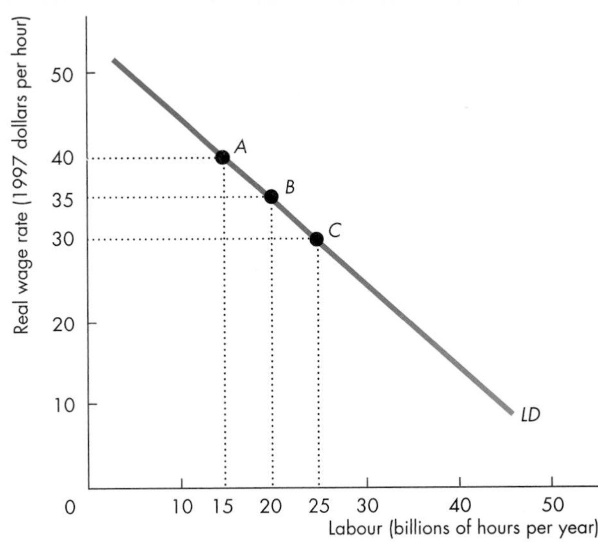

	Real wage rate (1997 dollars per hour)	Quantity of labour demanded (billions of hours per year)
A	40	15
B	35	20
C	30	25

The table shows part of a demand for labour schedule. Points *A*, *B*, and *C* on the demand for labour curve correspond to the rows of the table. The lower the real wage rate, the greater is the quantity of labour demanded.

Why does the quantity of labour demanded *increase* as the real wage rate *decreases*? That is, why does the demand for labour curve slope downward? To answer these questions, we must learn about the marginal product of labour.

The Marginal Product of Labour The **marginal product of labour** is the additional real GDP produced by an additional hour of labour when all other influences on production remain the same. The marginal product of labour is governed by the **law of diminishing returns,** which states that as the quantity of labour increases, other things remaining the same, the marginal product of labour decreases.

The Law of Diminishing Returns Diminishing returns arise because the amount of capital is fixed. Two people operating one machine are not twice as productive as one person operating one machine. Eventually, as more labour hours are hired, workers get in each other's way and output barely increases.

Marginal Product Calculation We calculate the marginal product of labour as the change in real GDP divided by the change in the quantity of labour employed. Figure 29.4(a) shows some calculations, and Fig. 29.4(b) shows the marginal product curve.

In Fig. 29.4(a), when the quantity of labour employed increases from 10 billion hours to 20 billion hours, an increase of 10 billion hours, real GDP increases from $600 billion to $1,000 billion, an increase of $400 billion. The marginal product of labour equals the increase in real GDP ($400 billion) divided by the increase in the quantity of labour employed (10 billion hours), which is $40 an hour.

When the quantity of labour employed increases from 20 billion hours to 30 billion hours, an increase of 10 billion hours, real GDP increases from $1,000 billion to $1,300 billion, an increase of $300 billion. The marginal product of labour equals $300 billion divided by 10 billion hours, which is $30 an hour.

In Fig. 29.4(b), as the quantity of labour employed increases, the marginal product of labour diminishes. Between 10 billion and 20 billion hours (at 15 billion hours), marginal product is $40 an hour. And between 20 billion and 30 billion hours (at 25 billion hours), marginal product is $30 an hour.

The diminishing marginal product of labour limits the demand for labour.

Diminishing Marginal Product and the Demand for Labour Firms are in business to maximize profits. Each hour of labour that a firm hires increases output and adds to costs. Initially, an extra hour of labour produces more output than the real wage that the labour costs. Marginal product exceeds the real wage rate. But each additional hour of labour produces less additional output than the previous hour—the marginal product of labour diminishes.

As a firm hires more labour, eventually the extra output from an extra hour of labour is exactly what that hour of labour costs. At this point, marginal product equals the real wage rate. Hire one less hour and marginal product exceeds the real wage rate. Hire one more hour and the real wage rate exceeds marginal product. In either case, profit is less.

FIGURE 29.4 Marginal Product and the Demand for Labour

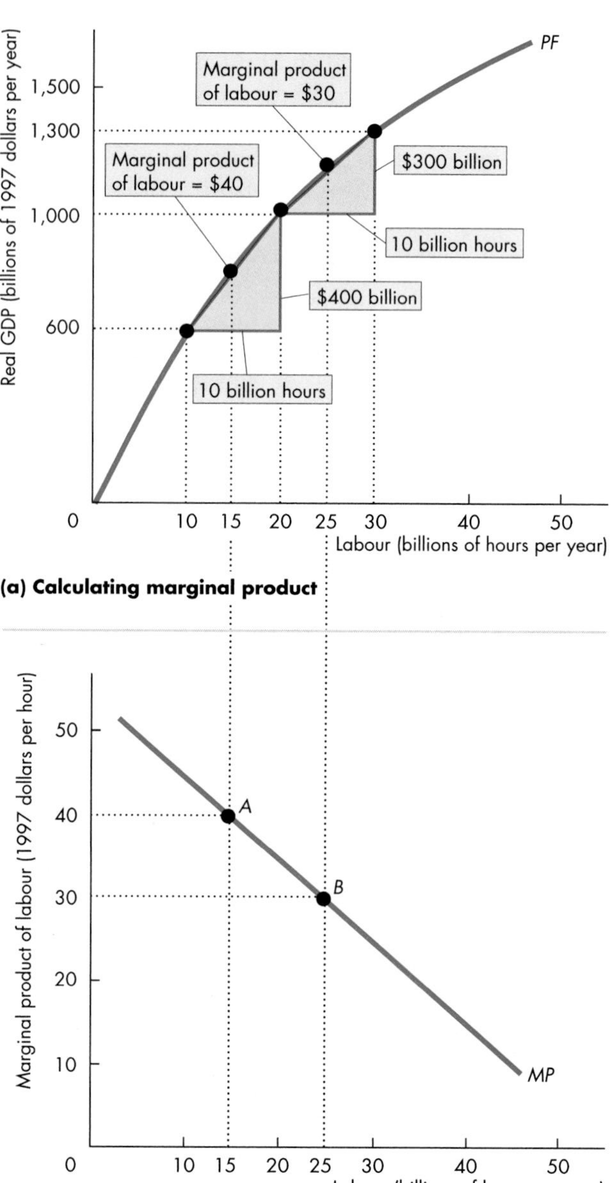

Between 10 billion and 20 billion hours, the marginal product of labour is $40 an hour. Between 20 billion and 30 billion hours, the marginal product of labour is $30 an hour. At 15 billion hours (midway between 10 billion and 20 billion), the marginal product of labour is $40 an hour at point *A* on the *MP* curve. The *MP* curve is the demand for labour curve.

Because marginal product diminishes as the quantity of labour employed increases, the lower the real wage rate, the greater is the quantity of labour that a firm can profitably hire. The marginal product curve is the same as the demand for labour curve.

You might gain a clearer understanding of the demand for labour by looking at an example.

Demand for Labour in a Ketchup Factory

Suppose that when a ketchup factory employs one additional hour of labour, output increases by 11 bottles. Marginal product is 11 bottles an hour. If the money wage rate is $5.50 an hour and ketchup sells for 50¢ a bottle, the real wage rate is 11 bottles an hour. (We calculate the factory's real wage rate as the money wage rate of $5.50 an hour divided by a price of 50¢ a bottle, which equals a real wage rate of 11 bottles an hour.) Because marginal product diminishes, we know that if the firm did not hire this hour of labour, marginal product would exceed 11 bottles. Because the firm can hire the hour of labour for a real wage rate of 11 bottles, it just pays it to do so.

If the price of ketchup remains at 50¢ a bottle and the money wage rate falls to $5.00 an hour, the real wage rate falls to 10 bottles an hour and the firm increases the quantity of labour demanded.

Similarly, if the money wage rate remains at $5.50 an hour and the price of ketchup rises to 55¢ a bottle, the real wage rate falls to 10 bottles an hour and the firm increases the quantity of labour demanded.

When the firm pays a real wage rate equal to the marginal product of labour, it is maximizing profit.

Changes in the Demand for Labour When the marginal product of labour changes, the demand for labour changes and the demand for labour curve shifts. You've seen that an increase in capital (both physical and human) and an advance in technology that increases productivity shift the production function upward. These same forces increase the demand for labour and shift the demand for labour curve rightward.

The Supply of Labour

The **quantity of labour supplied** is the number of labour hours that all the households in the economy plan to work. The **supply of labour** is the relationship between the quantity of labour supplied and the real wage rate when all other influences on work plans remain the same.

We can represent the supply of labour as either a supply schedule or a supply curve. The table in Fig. 29.5 shows a supply of labour schedule. It tells us the quantity of labour supplied at three different real wage rates. For example, if the real wage rate rises from $15 an hour (row *A*) to $35 an hour (row *B*), the quantity of labour supplied increases from 15 billion hours a year to 20 billion hours a year. The curve *LS* is a supply of labour curve. Points *A*, *B*, and *C* on the curve correspond to rows *A*, *B*, and *C* of the supply schedule.

The *real* wage rate influences the quantity of labour supplied because what matters to people is not the number of dollars they earn (the money wage rate) but what those dollars will buy.

FIGURE 29.5 The Supply of Labour

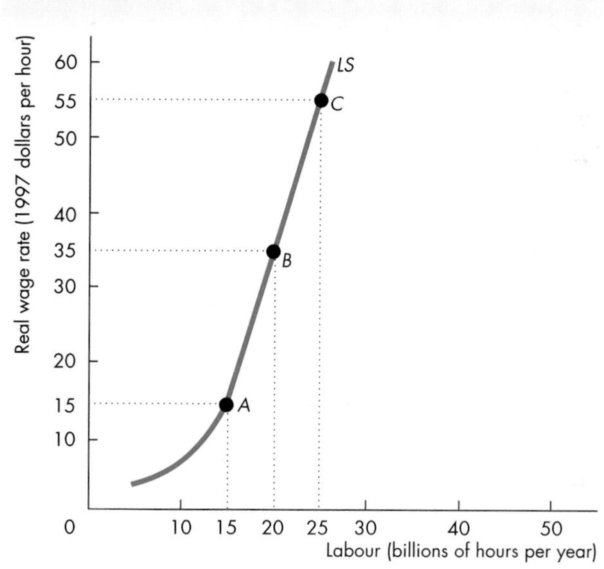

	Real wage rate (1997 dollars per hour)	Quantity of labour supplied (billions of hours per year)
A	15	15
B	35	20
C	55	25

The table shows part of a supply of labour schedule. Points *A*, *B*, and *C* on the supply of labour curve correspond to the rows of the table. The higher the real wage rate, the greater is the quantity of labour supplied.

The quantity of labour supplied increases as the real wage rate increases for two reasons:

- Hours per person increase
- Labour force participation increases

Hours per Person In choosing how many hours to work, a household considers the opportunity cost of not working. This opportunity cost is the real wage rate. The higher the real wage rate, the greater is the opportunity cost of taking leisure and not working. And as the opportunity cost of taking leisure rises, so the more the household chooses to work, other things remaining the same.

But other things don't remain the same. The higher the real wage rate, the greater is the household's income. And the higher the household's income, the more it wants to consume. One item that it wants to consume more of is leisure.

So a rise in the real wage rate has two opposing effects. By increasing the opportunity cost of leisure, it makes the household want to consume less leisure and to work more. And by increasing the household's income, it makes the household want to consume more leisure and to work fewer hours. For most households, the opportunity cost effect is stronger than the income effect. So the higher the real wage rate, the greater is the amount of work that the household chooses to do.

Labour Force Participation Some people have productive opportunities outside the labour force. These people choose to work only if the real wage rate exceeds the value of these other productive activities. For example, a parent might spend time caring for her or his child. The alternative is day care. The parent will choose to work only if he or she can earn enough per hour to pay the cost of child care and have enough left to make the work effort worthwhile. The higher the real wage rate, the more likely it is that a parent will choose to work and so the greater is the labour force participation rate.

Labour Supply Response The quantity of labour supplied increases as the real wage rate rises. But the quantity of labour supplied is not highly responsive to the real wage rate. A large percentage change in the real wage rate brings a small percentage change in the quantity of labour supplied.

Let's now see how the labour market determines employment, the real wage rate, and potential GDP.

Labour Market Equilibrium and Potential GDP

The forces of supply and demand operate in labour markets just as they do in the markets for goods and services. The price of labour is the real wage rate. A rise in the real wage rate eliminates a shortage of labour by decreasing the quantity demanded and increasing the quantity supplied. A fall in the real wage rate eliminates a surplus of labour by increasing the quantity demanded and decreasing the quantity supplied. If there is neither a shortage nor a surplus, the labour market is in equilibrium.

In macroeconomics, we study the economy-wide labour market to determine the total quantity of labour employed and the average real wage rate.

Labour Market Equilibrium Figure 29.6(a) shows a labour market in equilibrium. The demand curve *LD* and the supply curve *LS* are the same as those in Fig. 29.3 and Fig. 29.5, respectively.

If the real wage rate exceeds $35 an hour, the quantity of labour supplied exceeds the quantity demanded and there is a surplus of labour. In this situation, the real wage rate falls.

If the real wage rate is less than $35 an hour, the quantity of labour demanded exceeds the quantity supplied and there is a shortage of labour. In this situation, the real wage rate rises.

If the real wage rate is $35 an hour, the quantity of labour demanded equals the quantity supplied and there is neither a shortage nor a surplus of labour. In this situation, the labour market is in equilibrium and the real wage rate remains constant. The equilibrium level of employment is 20 billion hours a year. This equilibrium is a *full-employment equilibrium.*

Potential GDP You've seen that the quantity of real GDP depends on the quantity of labour employed. The production function tells us how much real GDP a given amount of employment can produce. At the equilibrium level of employment, there is full employment. And the level of real GDP at full employment is *potential GDP*. So the equilibrium level of employment produces potential GDP.

Figure 29.6(b) shows potential GDP. The equilibrium level of employment in Fig. 29.6(a) is 20 billion hours. The production function in Fig. 29.6(b) tells us that 20 billion hours of labour can produce a real GDP of $1,000 billion. This amount is potential GDP.

FIGURE 29.6 The Labour Market and Potential GDP

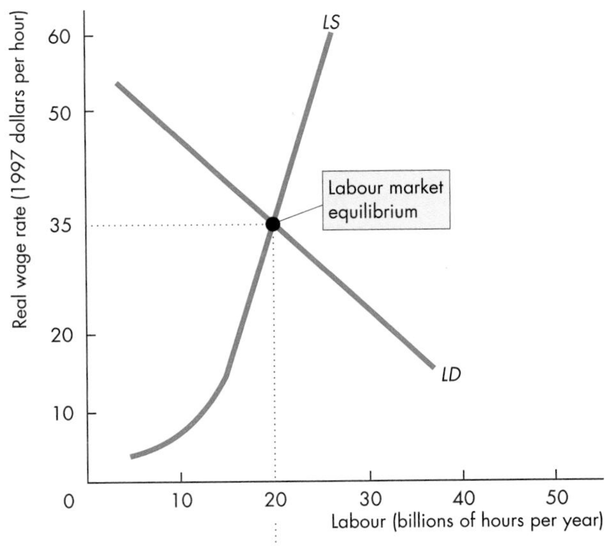

(a) The labour market

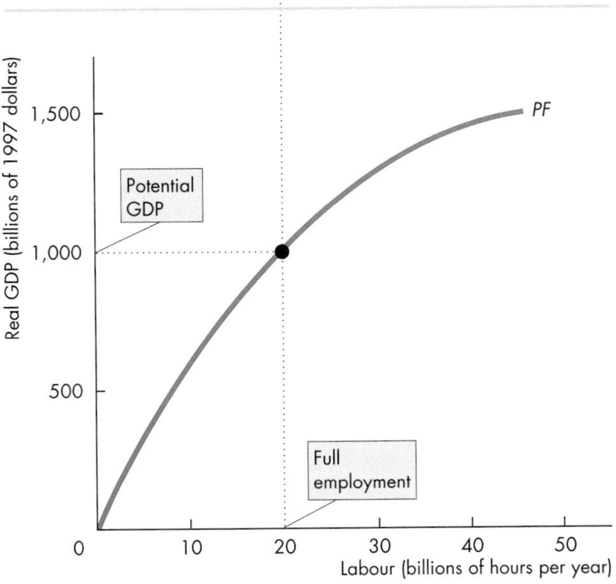

(b) Potential GDP

Full employment occurs (part a) when the quantity of labour demanded equals the quantity of labour supplied. The real wage rate is $35 an hour, and employment is 20 billion hours a year. Part (b) shows how potential GDP is determined. It is the quantity of real GDP determined by the production function and the full-employment quantity of labour.

Aggregate Supply

The **long-run aggregate supply curve** is the relationship between the quantity of real GDP supplied and the price level when real GDP equals potential GDP. Figure 29.7 shows this relationship as the vertical *LAS* curve. Along the long-run aggregate supply curve, as the price level changes, the money wage rate also changes to keep the real wage rate at the full-employment equilibrium level in Fig. 29.6(a). With no change in the real wage rate and no change in employment, real GDP remains at potential GDP.

The **short-run aggregate supply curve** is the relationship between the quantity of real GDP supplied and the price level when the money wage rate and potential GDP remain constant. Figure 29.7 shows a short-run aggregate supply curve as the upward-sloping *SAS* curve. Along the short-run aggregate supply curve, as the price level rises, the money wage rate remains fixed, so the real wage rate *falls*. In Fig. 29.6,

FIGURE 29.7 The Aggregate Supply Curves

A rise in the price level accompanied by a rise in the money wage rate that keeps the real wage rate at its full-employment equilibrium level keeps the quantity of real GDP supplied constant at potential GDP. There is a movement along the *LAS* curve. A rise in the price level with no change in the money wage rate lowers the real wage rate and brings an increase in employment and in the quantity of real GDP supplied. There is a movement up along the *SAS* curve.

when the real wage rate falls, the quantity of labour demanded increases and real GDP increases.

When the economy is at a point on its short-run aggregate supply curve above potential GDP, the real wage rate is below the full-employment equilibrium level. And when the economy is at a point on the short-run aggregate supply curve below potential GDP, the real wage rate is above the full-employment equilibrium level. In both cases, the quantity of labour that firms employ departs from the quantity that households would like to supply.

Production is efficient in the sense that the economy operates on its production possibilities frontier. But production is inefficient in the sense that the economy operates at the wrong point on the frontier. When the real wage rate is below the full-employment equilibrium, people do too much work and produce too much real GDP. When the real wage rate is above the full-employment equilibrium, people do too little work and produce too little real GDP.

When the real wage rate departs from its full-employment equilibrium level, the resulting shortage or surplus of labour brings market forces into play that move the real wage rate and quantity of labour employed back towards their full-employment levels.

The appendix on pp. 698–703 explains in detail how to derive the *LAS* and *SAS* curves.

REVIEW QUIZ

1. Why does a rise in the real wage rate bring a decrease in the quantity of labour demanded, other things remaining the same?
2. Why does a rise in the real wage rate bring an increase in the quantity of labour supplied, other things remaining the same?
3. What happens in the labour market if the real wage rate is above or below the full-employment level?
4. How is potential GDP determined?
5. What is the relationship between full-employment equilibrium in the labour market and long-run aggregate supply?
6. What is the relationship between the labour market and short-run aggregate supply?

You have studied the forces that determine full-employment real wages, employment, and potential GDP. Let's now look at *changes* in full-employment equilibrium.

Changes in Potential GDP

REAL GDP WILL INCREASE IF

1. The economy recovers from recession.
2. Potential GDP increases.

Recovery from recession means that the economy moves along the real GDP–leisure *PPF* from a point at which real GDP and employment are too low relative to the full-employment equilibrium point. Equivalently, the economy moves along the short-run aggregate supply curve. Economists have a lot to say about such a move. Chapters 23–28 explain this type of short-term change in real GDP.

Increasing potential GDP means expanding production possibilities. We're going to study such an expansion in the rest of this chapter and in Chapter 30. We begin this process here by examining two influences on potential GDP:

- An increase in population
- An increase in labour productivity

An Increase in Population

As the population increases and the additional people reach working age, the supply of labour increases. With more labour available, the economy's production possibilities expand. But does the expansion of production possibilities mean that potential GDP increases? And does it mean that potential GDP *per person* increases?

The answers to these questions have intrigued economists for many years. And they cause heated political debate today. In China, for example, families are under enormous pressure to limit the number of children they have. In some other countries, such as France, the government encourages large families. We can study the effects of an increase in population by using the model of the full-employment economy in Fig. 29.8.

In Fig. 29.8(a), the demand for labour is *LD* and initially the supply of labour is LS_0. At full employment, the real wage rate is $35 an hour and the level of employment is 20 billion hours a year. In Fig. 29.8(b), the production function (*PF*) shows that with 20 billion hours of labour employed, potential GDP is $1,000 billion. We're now going to work out what happens when the population increases.

FIGURE 29.8 The Effects of an Increase in Population

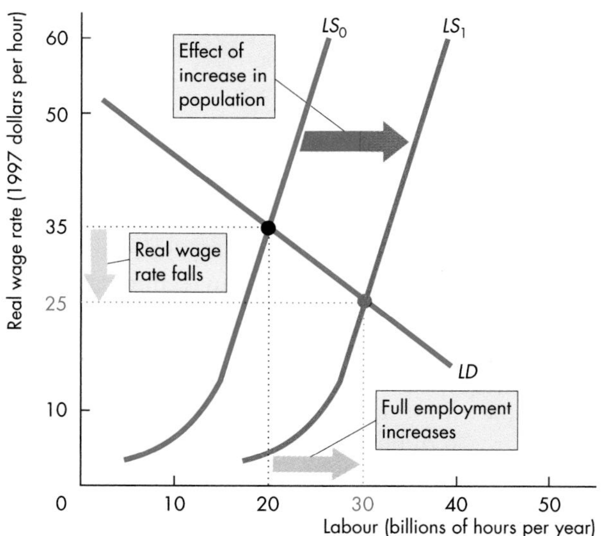

(a) The labour market

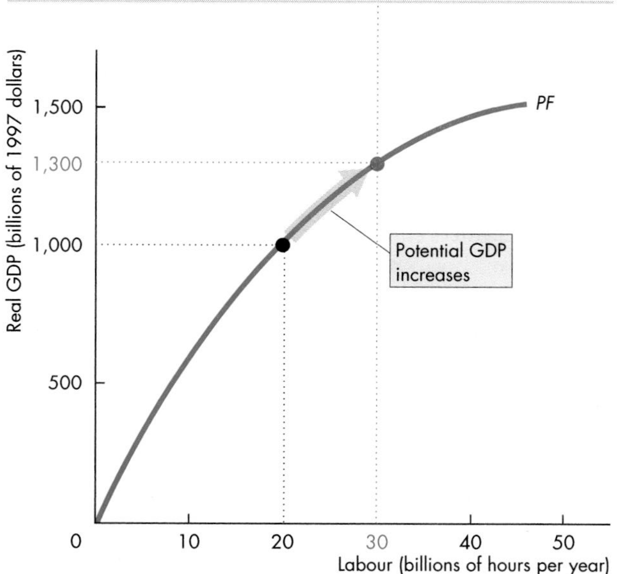

(b) Potential GDP

An increase in population increases the supply of labour. In part (a), the real wage rate falls, and the full-employment quantity of labour increases. In part (b), the increase in full employment increases potential GDP. Because the marginal product of labour diminishes, the increased population increases potential GDP but potential GDP per hour of work decreases.

An increase in the population increases the number of people of working age, and the supply of labour increases. The labour supply curve shifts rightward to LS_1. At a real wage rate of \$35 an hour, there is now a surplus of labour. So the real wage rate falls. In this example, it falls until it reaches \$25 an hour. At \$25 an hour, the quantity of labour demanded equals the quantity of labour supplied. Equilibrium employment increases to 30 billion hours a year.

Figure 29.8(b) shows the effect of the increase in equilibrium employment on real GDP. As the full-employment quantity of labour increases from 20 billion hours to 30 billion hours, potential GDP increases from \$1,000 billion to \$1,300 billion.

So at full employment, an increase in population increases full employment, increases potential GDP, and lowers the real wage rate.

An increase in population also decreases potential GDP per hour of work. You can see this decrease by dividing potential GDP by total labour hours. Initially, with potential GDP at \$1,000 billion and labour hours at 20 billion, potential GDP per hour of work was \$50. With the increase in population, potential GDP is \$1,300 billion and labour hours are 30 billion. Potential GDP per hour of work is \$43.33. Diminishing returns are the source of the decrease in potential GDP per hour of work.

You've seen that an increase in population increases potential GDP and decreases potential GDP per work hour. Some people challenge this conclusion and argue that people are the ultimate economic resource. They claim that a larger population brings forth a greater amount of scientific discovery and technological advance. Consequently, they argue that an increase in population never takes place in isolation. It is always accompanied by an increase in labour productivity. Let's now look at the effects of this influence on potential GDP.

An Increase in Labour Productivity

We've seen that three factors increase labour productivity:

- An increase in physical capital
- An increase in human capital
- An advance in technology

Saving and investment increase the quantity of physical capital over time. Education and on-the-job training and experience increase human capital. Research and development efforts bring advances in technology. In Chapter 30, we study how all these forces interact to determine the growth rate of potential GDP.

Here, we study the *effects* of an increase in physical capital, an increase in human capital, or an advance in technology on the labour market and potential GDP. We'll see how potential GDP, employment, and the real wage rate change when any of these three influences on labour productivity changes.

An Increase in Physical Capital If the quantity of physical capital increases, labour productivity increases. With labour being more productive, the economy's production possibilities expand. How does such an expansion of production possibilities change the real wage rate, employment, and potential GDP?

The additional capital increases the real GDP that each quantity of labour can produce. It also increases the marginal product of labour and so increases the demand for labour. Some physical capital replaces some types of labour, so the demand for those types of labour decreases when capital increases. But an increase in physical capital creates a demand for the types of labour that build, sell, and maintain the additional capital. The increases in demand for labour are always larger than the decreases in demand, and the economy-wide demand for labour increases.

With an increase in the economy-wide demand for labour, the real wage rate rises and the quantity of labour supplied increases. Equilibrium employment increases.

Potential GDP now increases for two reasons. First, a given level of employment produces more real GDP. Second, full employment increases.

An Increase in Human Capital If the quantity of human capital increases, labour productivity increases. Again, with labour being more productive, the economy's production possibilities expand. And this expansion of production possibilities changes the equilibrium real wage rate, full employment, and potential GDP in a similar manner to the effects of a change in physical capital.

An Advance in Technology As technology advances, labour productivity increases. And exactly as in the case of an increase in capital, the economy's production possibilities expand. Again, just as in the case of an increase in capital, the new technology increases the real GDP that each quantity of labour can produce and increases the marginal product of labour and the demand for labour.

With an increase in the demand for labour, the real wage rate rises, the quantity of labour supplied increases, and equilibrium employment increases. And again, potential GDP increases because a given level of employment produces more real GDP and because full employment increases.

Illustrating the Effects of an Increase in Labour Productivity Figure 29.9 shows the effects of an increase in labour productivity that results from an increase in capital or an advance in technology. In part (a), the demand for labour initially is LD_0 and the supply of labour is *LS*. The real wage rate is \$35 an hour, and full employment is 20 billion hours a year.

In part (b), the production function initially is PF_0. With 20 billion hours of labour employed, potential GDP is \$1,000 billion.

Now an increase in capital or an advance in technology increases the productivity of labour. In Fig. 29.9(a), the demand for labour increases and the demand curve shifts rightward to LD_1. In Fig. 29.9(b), the productivity of labour increases and the production function shifts upward to PF_1.

In Fig. 29.9(a), at the original real wage rate of \$35 an hour, there is now a shortage of labour. So the real wage rate rises. In this example, it keeps rising until it reaches \$45 an hour. At \$45 an hour, the quantity of labour demanded equals the quantity of labour supplied and full employment increases to 22.5 billion hours a year.

Figure 29.9(b) shows the effects of the increase in full employment combined with the new production function on potential GDP. As full employment increases from 20 billion hours to 22.5 billion hours, potential GDP increases from \$1,000 billion to \$1,500 billion.

Potential GDP per hour of work also increases. You can see this increase by dividing potential GDP by total labour hours. Initially, with potential GDP at \$1,000 billion and labour hours at 20 billion, potential GDP per hour of work was \$50. With the increase in labour productivity, potential GDP is \$1,500 billion and labour hours are 22.5 billion, so potential GDP per hour of work is \$66.67.

We've just studied the effects of an increase in population and an increase in labour productivity separately. In reality, these changes occur together. We can see the combined effects by examining an episode in the life of the Canadian economy.

FIGURE 29.9 The Effects of an Increase in Labour Productivity

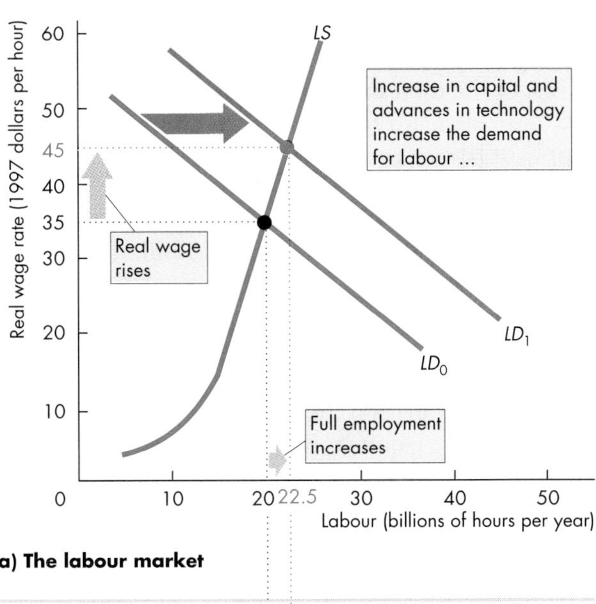

(a) The labour market

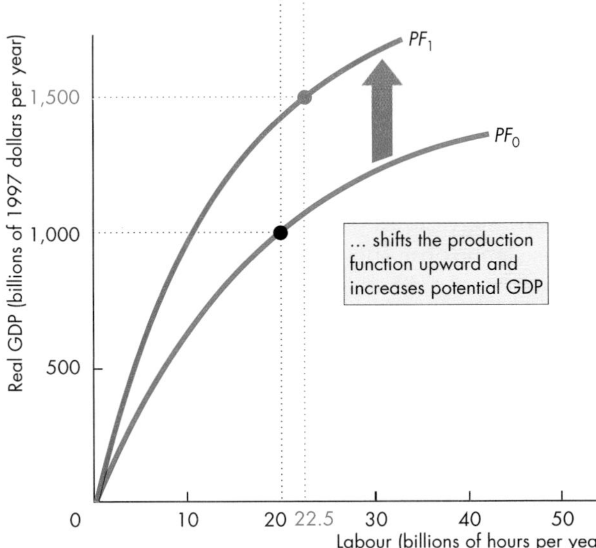

(b) Potential GDP

An increase in labour productivity shifts the demand for labour curve rightward from LD_0 to LD_1 (part a) and the production function upward from PF_0 to PF_1 (part b). The real wage rate rises from \$35 to \$45 an hour, and full employment increases from 20 billion to 22.5 billion hours. Potential GDP increases from \$1,000 billion to \$1,500 billion. Potential GDP increases because labour becomes more productive and full employment increases.

Population and Productivity in Canada

The Canadian economy was close to full employment in 1998. It was also close to full employment in 1980. We're going to compare these two years and look at the forces that moved the economy from one full-employment equilibrium to another.

In 1980, real GDP in Canada was \$582 billion, employment was 20 billion hours, and the real wage rate was \$15.77 an hour. (We are using 1997 dollars.)

By 1998, real GDP had increased to \$919 billion, labour hours had increased to 25 billion, and the real wage rate had risen to \$19.66 an hour. (Again, we are using 1997 dollars.)

The factors that you've just studied—an increase in population, increases in physical and human capital, and advances in technology—brought these changes.

Population Increase In 1980, the working-age population of Canada was 18.7 million. By 1998, this number had increased to 23.2 million. The 1998 working-age population was 24 percent larger than the 1980 working-age population. Recall that labour hours were 20 billion in 1980. A 24 percent increase would take labour hours in 1998 to 24.8 billion. But labour hours actually increased to 25 billion. Why? The increased labour productivity increased the real wage rate, which increased the quantity of labour supplied by increasing the labour force participation rate.

Capital Increase In 1980, the capital stock in Canada was estimated to be \$1.4 trillion (in 1997 dollars). By 1998, the capital stock had increased to \$2.4 trillion. This increase in capital increased labour productivity. But the increase in capital was not the only influence on labour productivity. Technological advances also occurred.

Technological Advances In 1980, we were just getting into the information revolution. Personal computers had just arrived. They were slow, had little memory, and had no hard drive, much less the CD-ROM and DVD drives of today. The Internet existed as a tool used by academic researchers for e-mail and file transfers, but no one had imagined the World Wide Web. Telephones couldn't remember numbers or record messages. Communication was slower and more costly than it was to become by 1998.

Production processes were beginning to be computerized but on a limited scale. Banks equipped with ATMs were in the future. Supermarkets with laser scanners were only a dream. Robots in car facto-

FIGURE 29.10 Full Employment in Canada: 1980 and 1998

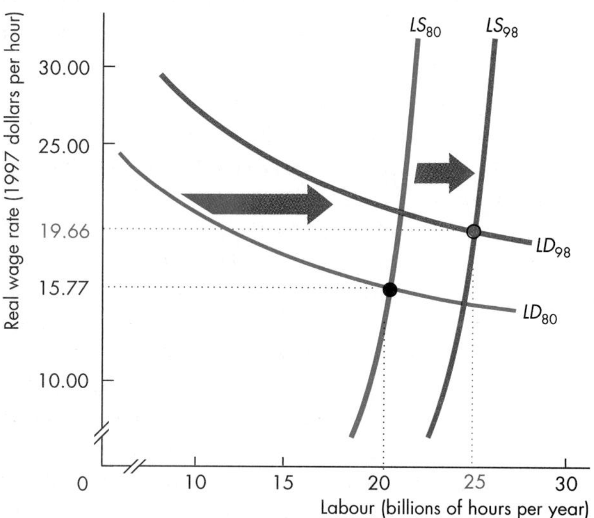

(a) The Canadian labour market in 1980 and 1998

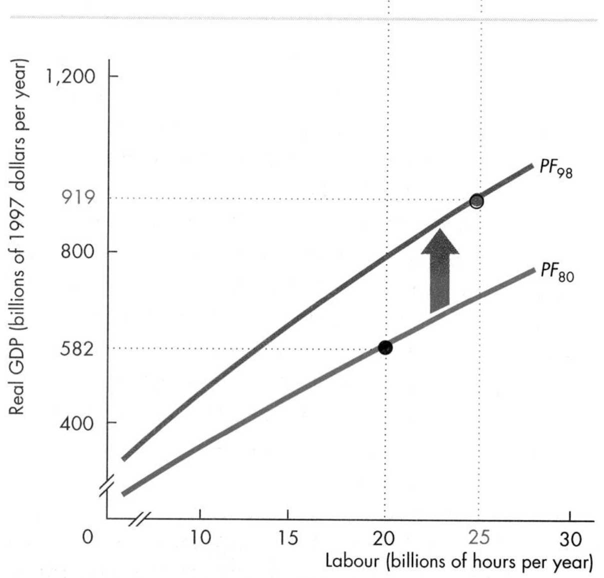

(b) The Canadian production function in 1980 and 1998

In 1980, the real wage rate was $15.77 an hour and the quantity of labour employed was 20 billion hours at the intersection of LD_{80} and LS_{80} (part a). Potential GDP was $582 billion on PF_{80} (part b). By 1998, the real wage rate had increased to $19.66 an hour and the quantity of labour employed had increased to 25 billion hours at the intersection of LD_{98} and LS_{98} (part a). Potential GDP had increased to $919 billion on PF_{98} (part b).

ries and coal mines were still unknown. The biotechnology sector had yet to be developed. The combined effects of capital accumulation and technological advance have made our farms and factories, shops and offices more productive.

Figure 29.10 shows these effects along with the effects of the increase in population that occurred. In 1980, the demand for labour curve was LD_{80}, the supply of labour curve was LS_{80}, the full-employment real wage rate was $15.77 an hour, and 20 billion hours of labour were employed. The production function in 1980 was PF_{80}. With 20 billion hours of labour employed, real GDP (and potential GDP) was $582 billion.

By 1998, the increase in population had increased the working-age population by 24 percent. This increase in population increased the supply of labour and shifted the labour supply curve rightward to LS_{98}.

The accumulation of capital and advances in technology increased labour productivity. The demand for labour increased, and the demand for labour curve shifted rightward to LD_{98}. And the production function shifted upward to PF_{98}.

The real wage rate increased to $19.66 an hour, and employment increased to 25 billion hours. At this quantity of labour, real GDP (and potential GDP) increased to $919 billion.

So in Canada, the effects of an increase in capital and advances in technology have been larger than the effects of increases in population. The forces that increase labour productivity have been strong enough to overcome the effects of an increase in population.

REVIEW QUIZ

1. When the population increases but nothing else changes, why does real GDP per hour of work decrease?
2. How does an increase in capital change the real wage rate, full employment, and potential GDP?
3. How do advances in technology change the real wage rate, full employment, and potential GDP?
4. If, as some people suggest, capital accumulation and technological change always accompany an increase in population, is it possible for potential GDP per hour of work to decrease?

Unemployment at Full Employment

SO FAR, WE'VE FOCUSED ON THE FORCES THAT determine the real wage rate, the quantity of labour employed, and potential GDP. And we've studied the effects of changes in population, capital, and technology on these variables. We're now going to bring unemployment into the picture.

In Chapter 21 (p. 480), we learned how unemployment is measured. We described how people become unemployed—they lose jobs, leave jobs, and enter or re-enter the labour force—and we classified unemployment—it can be frictional, structural, seasonal, and cyclical. We also learned that we call the unemployment rate at full employment the *natural rate of unemployment.*

But measuring, describing, and classifying unemployment do not *explain* it. Why is there always some unemployment? Why does its rate fluctuate? Why was the unemployment rate lower during the 1960s and the late 1990s than during the 1980s and early 1990s?

The forces that make the unemployment rate fluctuate around the natural rate take some time to explain, and we study these forces in Chapters 27–32. Here, we look at the churning economy and the reasons why we have unemployment at full employment.

Unemployment is ever present for two broad reasons:

- Job search
- Job rationing

Job Search

Job search is the activity of looking for an acceptable vacant job. There are always some people who have not yet found a suitable job and who are actively searching for one. The reason is that the labour market is in a constant state of change. The failure of existing businesses destroys jobs. The expansion of existing businesses and the startup of new businesses that use new technologies and develop new markets create jobs. As people pass through different stages of life, some enter or re-enter the labour market. Others leave their jobs to look for better ones, and still others retire. This constant churning in the labour market means that there are always some people looking for jobs, and these people are the unemployed.

The amount of job search depends on a number of factors, one of which is the real wage rate. In Figure 29.11, when the real wage rate is $35 an hour, the economy is at a full-employment equilibrium. The amount of job search that takes place at this wage rate generates unemployment at the natural rate. If the real wage rate is above the full-employment equilibrium—for example, at $45 an hour—there is a surplus of labour. At this higher real wage rate, more job search takes place and the unemployment rate rises above the natural rate. If the real wage rate is below the full-employment equilibrium—for example, at $25 an hour—there is a shortage of labour. At this real wage rate, less job search takes place and the unemployment rate falls below the natural rate.

The market forces of supply and demand move

FIGURE 29.11 Job Search Unemployment

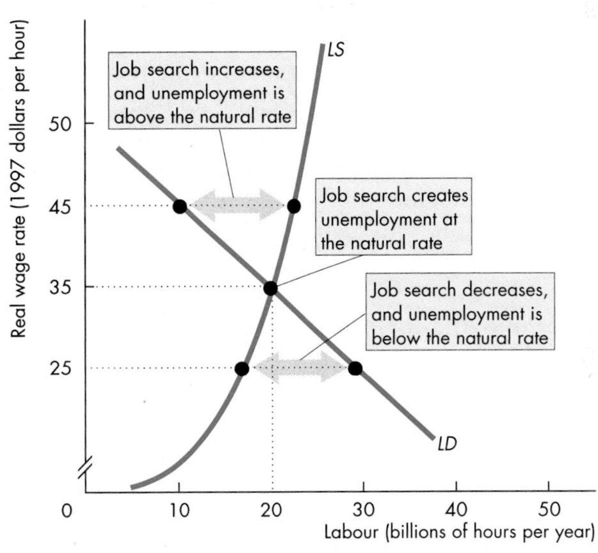

When the real wage rate is at its full-employment level—$35 an hour in this example—job search puts unemployment at the natural rate. If the real wage rate is above the full-employment level, there is a surplus of labour. Job search increases, and unemployment rises above the natural rate. If the real wage rate is below the full-employment level, there is a shortage of labour. Job search decreases, and unemployment falls below the natural rate.

the real wage rate towards the full-employment equilibrium. And these same forces move the amount of job search towards the level that creates unemployment at the natural rate.

But other influences on the amount of job search bring changes, over time, in the natural rate of unemployment. The main sources of these changes are

- Demographic change
- Unemployment compensation
- Structural change

Demographic Change An increase in the proportion of the population that is of working age brings an increase in the entry rate into the labour force and an increase in the unemployment rate. This factor has been important in the Canadian labour market in recent years. The bulge in the birth rate that occurred from the late 1940s through the late 1950s increased the proportion of new entrants into the labour force during the 1970s and brought an increase in the natural rate of unemployment.

As the birth rate declined, the bulge moved into higher age groups, and the proportion of new entrants declined during the 1980s. During this period, the natural rate of unemployment decreased.

Another demographic trend is an increase in the number of households with two paid workers. When one of these workers becomes unemployed, it is possible, with income still flowing in, to take longer to find a new job. This factor might have increased frictional unemployment.

Unemployment Compensation The length of time that an unemployed person spends searching for a job depends, in part, on the opportunity cost of job search. An unemployed person who receives no unemployment compensation faces a high opportunity cost of job search. In this situation, search is likely to be short and the person is likely to accept a less attractive job rather than continue a costly search process. An unemployed person who receives generous unemployment compensation faces a low opportunity cost of job search. In this situation, search is likely to be prolonged. The unemployed worker will continue to search for an ideal job.

The extension of unemployment compensation to larger groups of workers during the late 1960s and 1970s lowered the opportunity cost of job search. Consequently, the amount of job search and the natural rate of unemployment increased during those years.

Structural Change Labour market flows and unemployment are influenced by the pace and direction of technological change. Sometimes, technological change brings a *structural slump*, a condition in which some industries die and some regions suffer while other industries are born and other regions flourish. When these events occur, labour turnover is high—the flows between employment and unemployment increase and the number of unemployed people increases. The decline of industries in the Maritimes and the rapid expansion of industries in the Ottawa Valley illustrate the effects of technological change and were a source of the increase in unemployment during the 1970s and early 1980s. While these changes were taking place, the natural rate of unemployment increased.

Job Rationing

You've learned that markets *allocate* scarce resources by adjusting the market price to make buying plans and selling plans agree. Another word that has a meaning similar to "allocate" is "ration." Markets *ration* scarce resources by adjusting prices. In the labour market, the real wage rate rations employment and therefore rations jobs. Changes in the real wage rate keep the number of people seeking work and the number of jobs available in balance.

But the real wage rate is not the only possible instrument for rationing jobs. And in some industries, the real wage rate is set above the market equilibrium level. **Job rationing** is the practice of paying a real wage rate above the equilibrium level and then rationing jobs by some method.

Two reasons why the real wage rate might be set above the equilibrium level are

- Efficiency wage
- Minimum wage

Efficiency Wage It is costly for a firm to pay its workers more than the market wage rate. But doing so also brings benefits. An **efficiency wage** is a real wage rate that is set above the full-employment equilibrium wage rate that balances the costs and benefits of this higher wage rate to maximize the firm's profit.

The cost of paying a higher wage is direct. It is the addition to the firm's wage bill. The benefits of paying a higher wage rate are indirect.

First, a firm that pays a high wage rate can attract the most productive workers. Second, the firm can get greater productivity from its work force if it threatens to fire those who do not perform at the desired standard. The threat of losing a well-paid job stimulates greater work effort. Third, workers are less likely to quit their jobs, so the firm faces a lower rate of labour turnover and lower training costs. Fourth, the firm's recruiting costs are lower. The firm always faces a steady stream of available new workers.

Faced with benefits and costs, a firm offers a wage rate that balances productivity gains from the higher wage rate against its additional cost. This wage rate maximizes the firm's profit and is the efficiency wage.

Minimum Wage A **minimum wage** law determines the lowest wage rate at which a firm may legally hire labour. If the minimum wage is set *below* the equilibrium wage, the minimum wage has no effect. The minimum wage law and market forces are not in conflict. But if a minimum wage is set *above* the equilibrium wage, the minimum wage is in conflict with the market forces and does have some effects on the labour market.

In Canada, provincial governments set the minimum wages. In 2003, the minimum wage ranged from lows of $5.90 an hour in Alberta and $6.00 an hour in Newfoundland and Nova Scotia to highs of $7.30 an hour in Quebec and the Yukon and $8.00 an hour in British Columbia. The minimum wage increases from time to time and has fluctuated relative to the average wage of all workers.

Job Rationing and Unemployment Regardless of the reason, if the real wage rate is set above the equilibrium level, the natural rate of unemployment increases. The above-equilibrium real wage rate decreases the quantity of labour demanded and increases the quantity of labour supplied. So even at full employment, the quantity of labour supplied exceeds the quantity of labour demanded.

The surplus of labour is an addition to the amount of unemployment. The unemployment that results from a non-market wage rate and job rationing increases the natural rate of unemployment because it is added to the job search that takes place at full-employment equilibrium.

Economists broadly agree that efficiency wages can create persistent unemployment. And most economists believe that the minimum wage contributes to unemployment, especially among low-skilled young workers. But David Card of the University of California at Berkeley and Alan Krueger of Princeton University have challenged this view. And the challenge has been rebutted.

Card and Krueger say that an increase in the minimum wage works like an efficiency wage. It makes workers more productive and less likely to quit. Most economists remain skeptical about this suggestion. If higher wages make workers more productive and reduce labour turnover, why don't firms freely pay the wage rates that encourage the correct work habits? Daniel Hamermesh of the University of Texas at Austin says that firms anticipate increases in the minimum wage and cut employment *before* they occur. Looking for the effects of an increase in the minimum wage *after* it has occurred misses its effects. Finis Welch of Texas A&M University and Kevin Murphy of the University of Chicago say that regional differences in economic growth and not changes in the minimum wage explain the facts that Card and Krueger found.

REVIEW QUIZ

1. Why does the economy experience unemployment at full employment?
2. Why does the natural rate of unemployment fluctuate?
3. What is job rationing and why does it occur?
4. How does an efficiency wage influence the real wage rate, employment, and unemployment?
5. How does the minimum wage create unemployment?

In this chapter, you've seen how the economy operates at full employment. *Reading Between the Lines* on pp. 696–697 compares productivity in Canada with that in the United States.

In the next chapter, we study the rate of growth of the full-employment economy. We study the interactions of capital accumulation, technological change, and population growth in the process of economic growth.

Canada–U.S. Productivity Gap

NATIONAL POST, OCTOBER 8, 2002

Bank CEOs fear Canada falling further behind U.S.

Productivity gap grows

The leaders of two major banks warned yesterday about the widening gap in productivity between Canada and the United States, with one saying it could be this country's main economic threat.

Gordon Nixon, chief executive of the Royal Bank of Canada, said Canada's future prosperity is "far from guaranteed" because our productivity, regulatory efficiency and innovation lag those of many other countries.

"Our failure to achieve better productivity growth, and the widening gap with the United States, may well be the single biggest threat to our long-term prosperity," he said in a speech at Queen's University in Kingston.

"Our competitive performance is Canada's only lasting source of economic vitality and the wealth creation that we need to sustain our way of life."

Though Canada's economy is growing at an envious rate compared to other G7 countries, our standard of living has fallen 20% relative to the U.S., he said. "Clearly, we need a strategy that will help Canadians catch up to Americans in terms of per capita income. And in time, even surpass them."

Charles Baillie, chairman of TD Financial Group, warned Canada will find it harder to maintain top jobs and keep creative young people without a sustained effort to reach a standard of living similar to that in the United States.

Mr. Baillie and TD Group are sponsoring a forum today in Ottawa on how to restore the country's competitive edge with the United States.

While closing the gap on individual incomes is the goal, the larger objective is to improve the quality of life for Canadians, Mr. Baillie said in an interview. ...

Essence of the Story

- Gordon Nixon, chief executive of the Royal Bank of Canada, believes that the widening gap between Canadian and U.S. productivity is a serious problem.

- He noted that although Canada's real GDP growth was rapid during 2002, our standard of living has fallen 20 percent relative to that in the United States and we need a strategy for catching up to or even surpassing U.S. per capita income.

- Charles Baillie, chairman of TD Financial Group, said that if we don't achieve the same standard of living as that in the United States, we will find it hard to keep creative young people in Canada.

Economic Analysis

■ Comparisons of Canada and the United States reveal a widening gap in production per person and incomes.

■ Different methods of making the comparison lead to slightly different numbers, but the picture that Fig. 1 presents is reasonably accurate.

■ Figure 1 shows the ratio of real GDP per person in Canada to real GDP per person in the United States, with the values converted to a common currency using the OECD's estimates of the purchasing power parity exchange rate between the Canadian and U.S. dollars in 1997, the base year for the comparison.

■ The figure illustrates Gordon Nixon's and Charles Baillie's concerns.

■ The productivity gap widened from 10 percent in the late 1970s to almost 20 percent in the late 1990s.

■ Because income per person equals the value of production per person, the income gap between Canada and the United States has widened in the same way as the productivity gap.

■ Figure 2 illustrates the production functions in Canada and the United States. With more productive capital and technologies, the U.S. production function, PF_{US}, is above the Canadian production function, PF_C.

■ Figure 3 illustrates the implications of the greater productivity for the labour market.

■ The U.S. demand for labour curve, LD_{US}, is above the Canadian demand for labour curve, LD_C.

■ The supply of labour (per person) is assumed to be the same in both countries—a reasonable assumption—and the labour supply curve in both countries is *LS*.

■ The equilibrium real wage rate and employment level are higher in the United States than in Canada.

■ But the gap in real wage rates is smaller than the gap in production per employed person because the higher real wage rate in the United States induces a greater number of hours per person.

■ Figure 3 implies that Canadians enjoy more leisure time than Americans, so the productivity gap overstates the difference in overall economic well-being.

You're The Voter

■ Do you agree with Gordon Nixon and Charles Baillie that Canada's low productivity is a major problem?

■ Can you suggest some actions that the government of Canada might take to close the productivity gap?

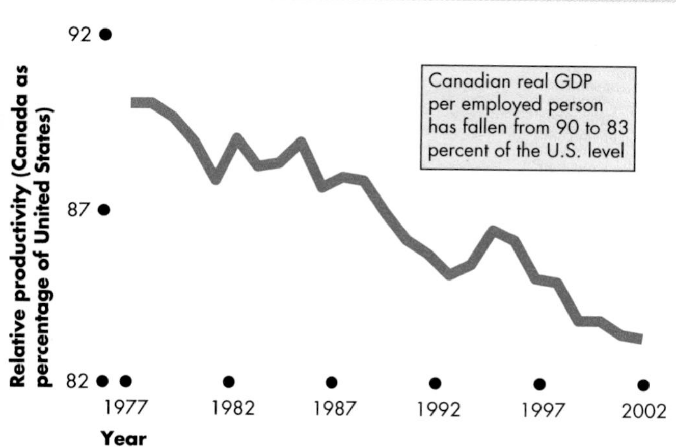

Figure 1 Canadian versus U.S. productivity

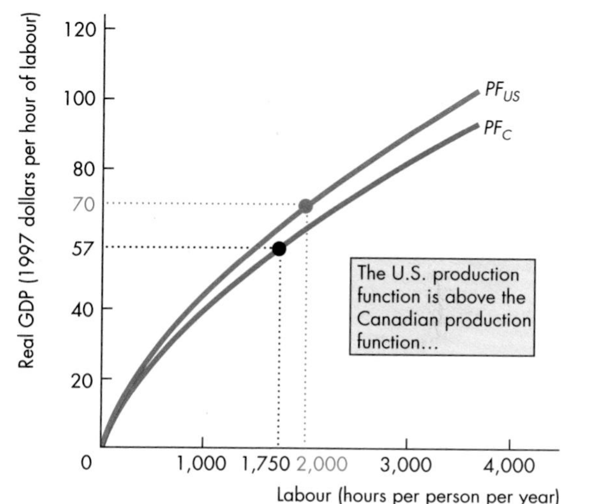

Figure 2 Canadian and U.S. production functions

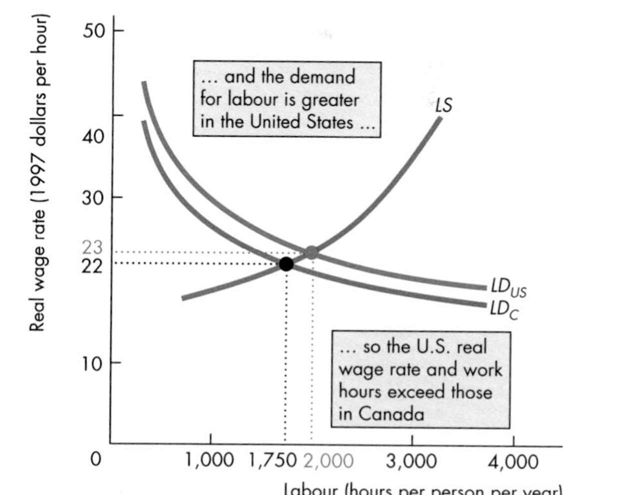

Figure 3 Canadian and U.S. labour markets

Deriving the Aggregate Supply Curves

THIS APPENDIX EXPLAINS HOW TO DERIVE THE long-run aggregate supply curve and the short-run aggregate supply curve. It shows the links between the labour market, the production function, and the aggregate supply curves and fills in the steps from Figure 29.6 to Figure 29.7 on p. 687 in this chapter.

Deriving the Long-Run Aggregate Supply Curve

FIGURE A29.1 SHOWS HOW TO DERIVE THE LONG-run aggregate supply curve. Part (a) shows the labour market. The demand and supply curves shown are similar to those in Fig. 29.6(a) on p. 687. The equilibrium, a real wage of $35 an hour and employment of 20 billion hours, is exactly the same equilibrium that was determined in that figure.

Figure A29.1(b) shows the production function. This production function is similar to that in Fig. 29.1(b) on p. 687. We know from the labour market (part a) that 20 billion hours of labour are employed. Part (b) tells us that when 20 million hours of labour are employed, real GDP is $1,000 billion.

Figure A29.1(c) shows the long-run aggregate supply curve. That curve tells us that real GDP is $1,000 billion regardless of the price level. To see why, look at what happens when the price level changes.

Start with a GDP deflator of 100. The economy is at point *J* in part (c) of the figure. That is, the GDP deflator is 100 and real GDP is $1,000 billion. We've determined, in part (a), that the real wage rate is $35 an hour. With a GDP deflator of 100, the money wage rate (the wage rate in current dollars) is also $35 an hour.

What happens to real GDP if the GDP deflator falls from 100 to 80 (a 20 percent decrease in the price level)? If the money wage rate remains at $35 an hour, the real wage rate rises and the quantity of labour supplied exceeds the quantity demanded. In the long run, the money wage rate will fall. It falls to $28 an hour. With a money wage rate of $28 an hour and a GDP deflator of 80, the real wage rate is still $35 an hour ($28 divided by 80 and multiplied by 100 equals $35). With the lower money wage rate but a constant real wage rate, employment remains at 20 billion hours and real GDP remains at $1,000 billion. The economy is at point *K* in Fig. A29.1(c).

What happens to real GDP if the GDP deflator rises from 100 to 120 (a 20 percent increase in the price level)? If the money wage rate stays at $35 an hour, the real wage rate falls and the quantity of labour demanded exceeds the quantity supplied. In the long run, the money wage rate rises. It keeps rising until it reaches $42 an hour. At that money wage rate, the real wage rate is $35 an hour ($42 divided by 120 and multiplied by 100 equals $35) and the quantity of labour demanded equals the quantity supplied. Employment remains at 20 billion hours and real GDP remains at $1,000 billion. The economy is at point *I* in Fig. A29.1(c).

Points *J*, *K*, and *I* in part (c) all lie on the long-run aggregate supply curve. We have considered only three price levels. We can consider any price level and we will reach the same conclusion: a change in the price level generates a proportionate change in the money wage rate and leaves the real wage rate unchanged. Employment and real GDP are also unchanged.

Because in the long run the price level *and the money wage rate* adjust to achieve full employment, the real wage rate, employment, and real GDP remain constant as the price level changes. In the long run, one level of real GDP—potential GDP—occurs at any price level and the *LAS* curve is vertical.

FIGURE A29.1 The Labour Market and Long-Run Aggregate Supply

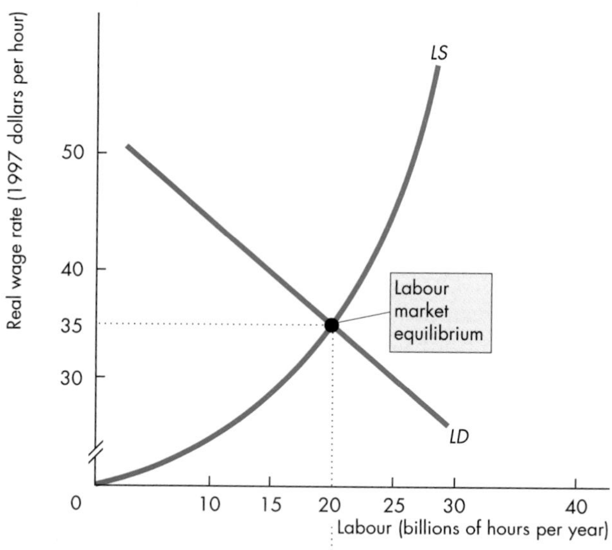

(a) The labour market

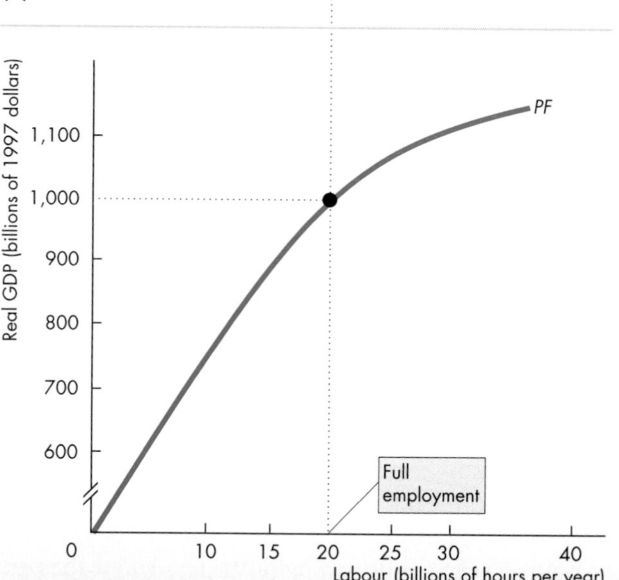

(b) Potential GDP

(c) Long-run aggregate supply curve

Equilibrium in the labour market determines the real wage rate and employment. The demand for labour curve (*LD*) intersects the supply of labour curve (*LS*) at a real wage rate of $35 an hour and 20 billion hours of employment (part a). The production function (*PF*) and employment of 20 billion hours determine real GDP at $1,000 billion (part b). Potential GDP is $1,000 billion and in the long run, real GDP supplied is $1,000 billion regardless of the price level. The long-run aggregate supply curve (*LAS*) is the vertical line in part (c). If the GDP deflator is 100, the economy is at point *J*. If the GDP deflator is 120, the money wage rate rises to keep the real wage rate constant at $35 an hour, employment remains at 20 billion hours, and real GDP is $1,000 billion. The economy is at point *I*. If the GDP deflator is 80, the money wage rate falls to keep the real wage rate constant at $35 an hour, employment remains at 20 billion hours, and real GDP is $1,000 billion. The economy is at point *K*.

Changes in Long-Run Aggregate Supply

Long-run aggregate supply can change for two reasons:

- Change in labour supply
- Change in labour productivity

Change in Labour Supply The supply of labour can change for many reasons, but the biggest one is a change in the population. Over time, the population grows and the supply of labour increases.

We study and illustrate the effects of these labour market changes and their effects on potential GDP on pp. 688–689. An increase in the supply of labour means the supply of labour curve shifts rightward. The real wage rate falls and full employment increases. Potential GDP increases.

Now that we've derived the long-run aggregate supply curve, you can see when potential GDP changes, long-run aggregate supply also changes and the long-run aggregate supply curve shifts. Because an increase in the supply of labour increases potential GDP, it also increases long-run aggregate supply and shifts the long-run aggregate supply curve rightward. The new (vertical) long-run aggregate supply curve is located at the increased level of potential GDP.

Change in Labour Productivity An increase in labour productivity means that a given amount of labour can produce a larger quantity of real GDP. The production function shifts upward and the demand for labour curve shifts rightward. The real wage rate rises, full employment increases. Potential GDP increases.

We study and illustrate the effects of an increase in productivity on the quantity of labour, the real wage rate, and potential GDP on pp. 689–691.

Again, because an increase in labour productivity increases potential GDP, it also increases long-run aggregate supply and shifts the long-run aggregate supply curve rightward. The new (vertical) long-run aggregate supply curve is located at the increased level of potential GDP.

Whether the real wage rate increases when long-run aggregate supply increases depends on the source of the increase in potential GDP. If the source is an increase in the supply of labour, the real wage rate falls. If the source is an increase in labour productivity, the real wage rate rises.

Short-Run Aggregate Supply

SHORT-RUN AGGREGATE SUPPLY IS THE RELATIONship between the quantity of real GDP supplied and the price level when the money wage rate and all other influences on production plans remain the same. We are now going to learn about the connection between short-run aggregate supply and the labour market. Before we can derive the short-run aggregate supply curve, we must understand how the labour market works when the money wage rate is fixed.

Short-Run Equilibrium in the Labour Market

When the money wage rate is fixed, a change in the price level changes the real wage rate. Suppose the money wage rate is $35 an hour and the GDP deflator is 100. Then the real wage rate is also $35 an hour.

Now suppose that the money wage rate remains at $35 an hour but the GDP deflator rises to 116.7. In this case, the real wage rate falls to $30 an hour. A money wage rate of $35 an hour and a GDP deflator of 116.3 enables people to buy the same goods and services that a money wage rate of $30 an hour buys when the GDP deflator is 100.

Alternatively, suppose that the GDP deflator falls to 87.5. In this case, the real wage rate rises to $40 an hour. A money wage rate of $35 an hour with a GDP deflator of 87.5 buys the same quantity of goods and services that a money wage rate of $40 an hour buys when the GDP deflator is 100.

Figure A29.2 shows the labour market in the short run at the three different price levels we've just considered. As before, the demand for labour is *LD* and the supply of labour is *LS*. The money wage rate is constant at $35 an hour and the higher the price level, the lower is the real wage rate. The three points *B*, *C*, and *D* in Fig. A29.2 tell us the quantities of labour demanded at the three different real wage rates. If the price level is 87.5, the real wage rate is $40 an hour and the quantity of labour demanded is 15 billion hours a year, (indicated by point *B*). If the price level is 100, the real wage rate is $35 an hour and the quantity of labour demanded is 20 billion hours a year, (indicated by point *C*). And if the price level is 116.7, the real wage rate is $30 an hour and

FIGURE A29.2 The Labour Market in the Short Run

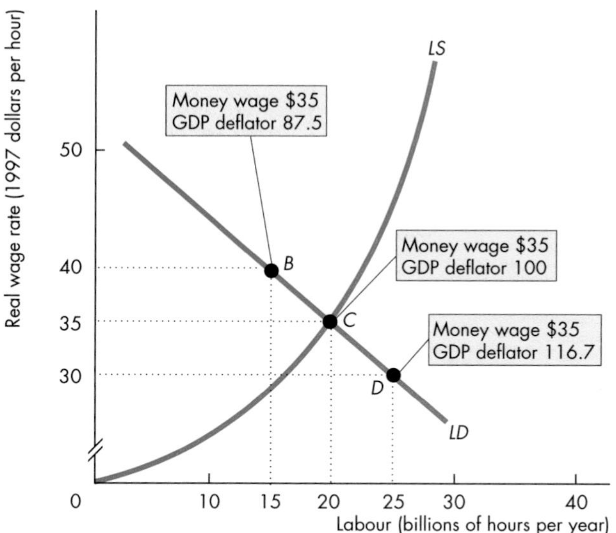

The labour demand curve is *LD* and the labour supply curve is *LS*. The money wage rate is fixed at $35 an hour. If the GDP deflator is 100, the *real* wage rate is $35 an hour and 20 billion hours of labour are employed. The economy operates at point *C*. If the GDP deflator is 87.5, the real wage rate is $40 an hour and 15 billion hours of labour are employed. The economy operates at point *B*. If the GDP deflator is 116.7, the real wage rate is $30 an hour and 25 billion hours of labour are employed. The economy operates at point *D*.

the quantity of labour demanded is 25 billion hours a year (indicated by point *D*).

You can see that when the money wage rate is fixed and the price level rises, the real wage rate falls, and the quantity of labour *demanded* increases. But what determines the quantity of labour *employed*?

Employment with Sticky Wages When the real wage rate is not at its long-run equilibrium level, there are many possible ways in which the level of employment could be determined. It is assumed that when the labour market is not at full employment, firms decide the level of employment and households supply whatever quantity firms demand. Provided that firms pay the agreed money wage rate, households supply whatever quantity of labour firms demand. In the short run, households are willing to be "off" their labour supply curves.

In Fig. A29.2, with a money wage rate of $35 an hour and a price level of 87.5 (point *B* in the figure) the actual level of employment is 15 billion hours. In this situation, people supply less labour than they would like to. If the GDP deflator is 116.7, the real wage rate is $30 an hour and employment is 25 billion hours (point *D* in the figure). In this case, people supply more labour than they would like to.

It is easy to understand why people might supply less labour than they would like to. But why would people supply *more* labour than they would like to? In the long run, they would not. But in the short run, during the life of an existing wage contract, it is quite likely that people will agree to supply whatever quantity of labour their employer demands. The employer gives the employee an "all-or-nothing" choice. The employee must either work the hours requested or find another job.

Deriving the Short-Run Aggregate Supply Curve

The short-run aggregate supply curve is the relationship between the quantity of real GDP supplied and the price level when the money wage rate and all other influences on production plans remain the same. Along the short-run aggregate supply curve, when the price level changes, the *real wage rate also changes*, which means that employment and real GDP also change. The short-run aggregate supply curve is upward sloping.

Figure A29.3 shows the derivation of the short-run aggregate supply curve. Part (a) shows the aggregate labour market. The demand and supply curves are the same as those in Fig. A29.2. The long-run equilibrium, a real wage of $35 an hour and employment of 20 billion hours, is exactly the same equilibrium that was determined in that figure.

Focus first on part (a). It shows the three short-run equilibrium levels of the real wage rate and employment that we discovered in Fig. A29.2. The money wage rate is fixed at $35 an hour. If the price level is 100, the real wage rate is also $35 an hour and 20 billion hours of labour are employed—point *C*. If the price level is 87.5, the real wage rate is $40 an hour and employment is 15 billion hours—point *B*. If the price level is 116.7, the real wage rate is $30 an hour and employment is 25 billion hours—point *D*.

FIGURE A29.3 The Labour Market and Short-Run Aggregate Supply

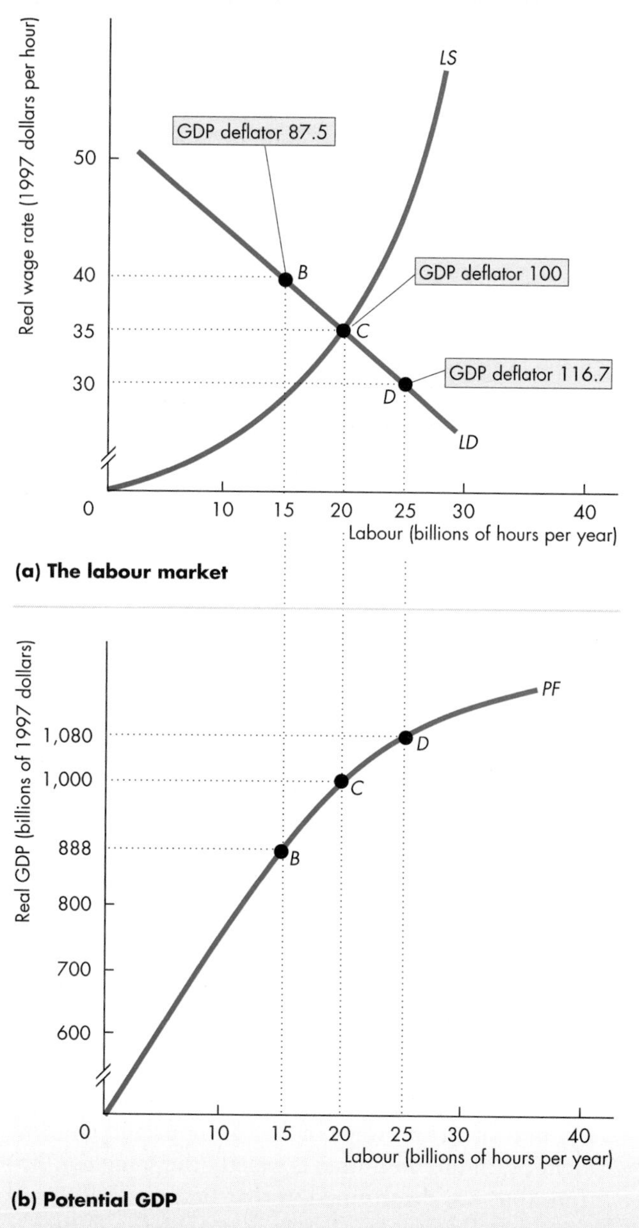

(a) The labour market

(b) Potential GDP

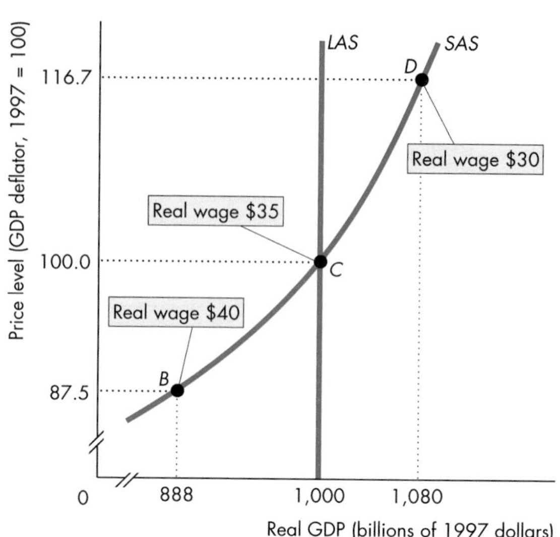

(c) Aggregate supply curves

The money wage rate is fixed at $35 an hour. In part (a), the demand for labour curve (*LD*) intersects the supply of labour curve (*LS*) at a real wage rate of $35 an hour and 20 billion hours of employment. If the GDP deflator is 100, the economy operates at point *C*. In part (b), the production function (*PF*) determines real GDP at $1,000 billion. The economy is at point *C* on its long-run aggregate supply curve (*LAS*), in part (c). If the GDP deflator is 87.5, the real wage rate is $40 an hour and the economy is at point *B*. Employment is 15 billion hours (part a) and real GDP is $888 billion (part b). The economy is at point *B* on its short-run aggregate supply curve (*SAS*) in part (c). If the GDP deflator is 116.7, the real wage rate is $30 an hour and the economy is at point *D*. Employment is 25 billion hours (part a) and real GDP is $1,080 billion (part b). The economy is at point *D* on its short-run aggregate supply curve in part (c).

Figure A29.3(b) shows the production function. We know from the labour market (part a) that at different price levels, different quantities of labour are employed. Part (b) shows the real GDP produced by these employment levels. For example, when employment is 15 billion hours, real GDP is $888 billion—point *B*. When employment is 20 billion hours, real GDP is $1,000 billion—point *C*. And when employment is 25 billion hours, real GDP is $1,080 billion—point *D*.

Figure A29.3(c) shows the short-run aggregate supply curve. It also shows the long-run aggregate supply curve, *LAS*, that we derived in Fig. A29.1. The short-run aggregate supply curve, *SAS*, is derived from the labour market and production function. To see how, first focus on point *B* in all three parts of the figure. At point *B*, the price level is 87.5. From the labour market (part a) we know that when the price level is 87.5, the real wage is $40 an hour, and 15 billion hours of labour are employed. At this employment level, we know from the production function (part b) that real GDP is $888 billion. That's what point *B* on the *SAS* curve in part (c) tells us—when the price level is 87.5, the quantity of real GDP supplied is $888 billion. The other two points on the *SAS* curve, *C* and *D*, are derived in the same way. At point *D*, the price level is 116.7 so the real wage rate is $30 an hour and 25 billion hours of labour are employed (part a). This employment level produces a real GDP of $1,080 billion (part b).

The short-run aggregate supply curve intersects the long-run aggregate supply curve at the price level that delivers the equilibrium real wage rate in the labour market. In this example, that price level is 100. At labour market equilibrium, the economy is at full employment and real GDP equals potential GDP. At price levels above 100, the quantity of real GDP supplied in the short run exceeds potential GDP; at price levels below 100, the quantity of real GDP supplied in the short run falls short of potential GDP.

Changes in Short-Run Aggregate Supply

Short-run aggregate supply can change for two reasons:

- Change in long-run aggregate supply
- Change in money wage rate

Change in Long-Run Aggregate Supply Anything that changes long-run aggregate supply also changes short-run aggregate supply. That is, anything that increases potential GDP increases the quantity of real GDP supplied at each and every price level. Both long-run aggregate supply and short-run aggregate supply increase and both curves shift rightward.

A key feature of the *SAS* curve is that it intersects the *LAS* curve at the price level that puts the real wage rate at its full-employment level. That is, the real wage rate at which the labour market is in equilibrium. So if long-run aggregate supply changes and the *LAS* curve shifts, the short-run aggregate supply curve also shifts. And the new *SAS* curve intersects the new *LAS* curve at the price level that makes the real wage rate equal to its *new* full-employment level.

Change in Money Wage Rate Short-run aggregate supply changes and long-run aggregate supply remains unchanged if the money wage rate changes and all other influences on production plans remain the same. A rise in the money wage rate with a given price level means that the real wage rate has increased. Faced with a higher real wage rate, firms decrease the quantity of labour demanded. Employment decreases and firms produce less output, so the quantity of real GDP supplied decreases.

But the changes that we've just described would occur at any given price level. So short-run aggregate supply decreases. The *SAS* curve shifts leftward.

Short-Run Changes in the Quantity of Real GDP Supplied

Even if short-run aggregate supply does not change, real GDP can change in the short run. The reason is that there can be a *change in the quantity of real GDP supplied*, which appears as a *movement along the SAS curve*. These changes in real GDP are brought about by changes in aggregate demand. All the factors that can change aggregate demand result in a shift of the aggregate demand curve and movement along the *SAS* curve. Real GDP changes and so does the price level. They both change in the same direction. An increase in aggregate demand brings an increase in real GDP and a rise in the price level; a decrease in aggregate demand brings a decrease in real GDP and a fall in the price level.

The Shape of the Short-Run Aggregate Supply Curve

The short-run aggregate supply curve that we've derived in Fig. A29.3(c) is *curved*. Along this *SAS* curve, as the price level rises, real GDP increases. But for given increments in the price level, the increments in real GDP become successively smaller. In contrast, the *SAS* curve in Fig. 29.7 on p. 687, like that in Chapter 22, is linear—a curve that graphs as a straight line. Along a linear *SAS* curve, as the price level rises, real GDP increases. You can regard the linear *SAS* curve as an approximation over a small range of real GDP in the neighbourhood of potential GDP. The farther the economy moves away from potential GDP, the less close is the approximation.

SUMMARY

KEY POINTS

Real GDP and Employment (pp. 680–682)

- To produce real GDP, we must forgo leisure time.
- As the quantity of labour increases, real GDP increases.
- Labour productivity increases if the amount of physical capital or human capital increases or if technology advances.

The Labour Market and Aggregate Supply (pp. 683–688)

- The quantity of labour demanded increases as the real wage rate falls, other things remaining the same.
- The diminishing marginal product of labour is the reason the quantity of labour demanded increases as the real wage rate falls.
- The quantity of labour supplied increases as the real wage rate rises, other things remaining the same.
- At full-employment equilibrium, the quantity of labour demanded equals the quantity of labour supplied.
- Potential GDP is real GDP produced by the full-employment quantity of labour.
- Along the long-run aggregate supply curve, the real wage rate is constant at its full-employment level. Along the short-run aggregate supply curve, the real wage rate, employment, and real GDP change.

Changes in Potential GDP (pp. 688–692)

- An increase in population increases the supply of labour, lowers the real wage rate, increases the quantity of labour employed, and increases potential GDP. It decreases potential GDP per hour of work.
- An increase in capital or an advance in technology increases labour productivity. It shifts the production function upward and the demand for labour curve rightward. The real wage rate rises, full employment increases, and potential GDP increases.

Unemployment at Full Employment (pp. 693–695)

- The unemployment rate at full employment is the natural rate of unemployment.
- Unemployment is ever present because of job search and job rationing.
- Job-search unemployment is influenced by demographic change, unemployment compensation, and structural change.
- Job-rationing unemployment arises from efficiency wages and the minimum wage.

KEY FIGURES

Figure 29.1 Production Possibilities and the Production Function, 681
Figure 29.3 The Demand for Labour, 683
Figure 29.4 Marginal Product and the Demand for Labour, 684
Figure 29.5 The Supply of Labour, 685
Figure 29.6 The Labour Market and Potential GDP, 687
Figure 29.7 The Aggregate Supply Curves, 687
Figure 29.8 The Effects of an Increase in Population, 689
Figure 29.9 The Effects of an Increase in Labour Productivity, 691
Figure 29.11 Job Search Unemployment, 693

KEY TERMS

Demand for labour, 683
Efficiency wage, 694
Human capital, 681
Job rationing, 694
Job search, 693
Labour productivity, 681
Law of diminishing returns, 683
Learning-by-doing, 681
Long-run aggregate supply curve, 687
Marginal product of labour, 683
Minimum wage, 695
Money wage rate, 683
Production function, 680
Quantity of labour demanded, 683
Quantity of labour supplied, 685
Real wage rate, 683
Short-run aggregate supply curve, 687
Supply of labour, 685

PROBLEMS

*1. Robinson Crusoe lives on a desert island on the equator. He has 12 hours of daylight every day to allocate between leisure and work. The table shows seven alternative combinations of leisure and real GDP in Crusoe's economy:

Possibility	Leisure (hours per day)	Real GDP (dollars per day)
A	12	0
B	10	10
C	8	18
D	6	24
E	4	28
F	2	30
G	0	30

a. Make a graph of Crusoe's *PPF* for leisure and real GDP.
b. Make a table and a graph of Crusoe's production function.
c. Find the marginal product of labour for Crusoe at different quantities of labour.

2. The people of Nautica have a total of 100 hours every day to allocate between leisure and work. The table shows the opportunity cost of real GDP in terms of leisure time forgone in the economy of Nautica:

Possibility	Leisure (hours per day)	Opportunity cost of leisure (dollars of real GDP per hour)
A	0	0
B	20	5
C	40	10
D	60	15
E	80	20
F	100	25

a. Make a table and a graph of Nautica's *PPF* for leisure and real GDP.
b. Make a table and a graph of Nautica's production function.
c. Find the marginal product of labour for Nautica at different quantities of labour.

*3. Use the information provided in problem 1 about Robinson Crusoe's economy. Also, use the information that Crusoe must earn $4.50 an hour. If he earns less than this amount, he does not have enough food on which to live. He has no interest in earning more than $4.50 an hour. At a real wage rate of $4.50 an hour, he is willing to work any number of hours between zero and the total available to him.

a. Make a table that shows Crusoe's demand for labour schedule and draw Crusoe's demand for labour curve.
b. Make a table that shows Crusoe's supply of labour schedule and draw Crusoe's supply of labour curve.
c. What are the full-employment equilibrium real wage rate and quantity of labour in Crusoe's economy?
d. Find Crusoe's potential GDP.

4. Use the information provided in problem 2 about the economy of Nautica. Also, use the information that the people of Nautica are willing to work 20 hours a day for a real wage rate of $10 an hour. And for each 50¢ an hour *increase* in the real wage, they are willing to work an *additional* hour a day.

a. Make a table that shows Nautica's demand for labour schedule and draw Nautica's demand for labour curve.
b. Make a table that shows Nautica's supply of labour schedule and draw Nautica's supply of labour curve.
c. Find the full-employment equilibrium real wage rate and quantity of labour in Nautica's economy.
d. Find Nautica's potential GDP.

*5. Robinson Crusoe, whose economy is described in problems 1 and 3, gets a bright idea. He diverts a stream and increases his food production by 50 percent. That is, each hour that he works produces 50 percent more real GDP than before.

a. Make a table that shows Crusoe's new production function and new demand for labour schedule.
b. Find the new full-employment equilibrium real wage rate and quantity of labour in Crusoe's economy.
c. Find Crusoe's new potential GDP.
d. Explain and interpret the results you obtained in parts (a), (b), and (c).

6. Nautica's economy, described in problems 2 and 4, experiences a surge in its population. The supply of labour increases, and 50 percent more hours are supplied at each real wage rate.
   a. Make a table that shows Nautica's new supply of labour schedule.
   b. Find the new full-employment equilibrium real wage rate and quantity of labour in Nautica's economy.
   c. Find Nautica's new potential GDP.
   d. Explain and interpret the results you obtained parts in (a), (b), and (c).

*7. The figure describes the labour market on Cocoa Island. In addition (not shown in the figure), a survey tells us that when Cocoa Island is at full employment, people spend 1,000 hours a day in job search.

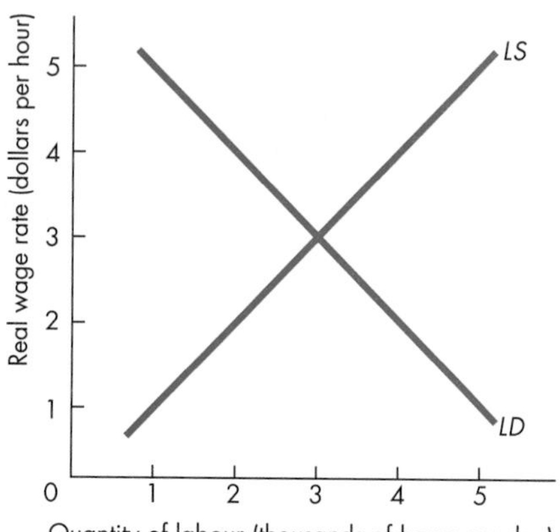

   a. Find the full-employment equilibrium real wage rate and quantity of labour employed.
   b. Find potential GDP on Cocoa Island. (*Hint*: The demand for labour curve tells you the *marginal* product of labour. How do we calculate the marginal product of labour?)
   c. Calculate the natural rate of unemployment on Cocoa Island.

8. On Cocoa Island described in the figure and in problem 7, the government introduces a minimum wage of $4 an hour.
   a. Find the new equilibrium real wage rate and quantity of labour employed.
   b. What now is potential GDP on Cocoa Island?
   c. Calculate the new natural rate of unemployment on Cocoa Island.
   d. How much of the unemployment results from the minimum wage?

CRITICAL THINKING

1. Study the news article about the productivity gap between Canada and the United States in *Reading Between the Lines* on pp. 696–697 and then
   a. Describe the productivity difference between Canada and the United States.
   b. List the factors that influence a nation's production function that might explain why there is a gap between U.S. and Canadian productivity.
   c. List the factors that influence a nation's production function that might explain why the gap between U.S. and Canadian productivity has widened.
   d. List the factors that influence a nation's production function that might be manipulated by Canadian economic policy to narrow the gap between U.S. and Canadian productivity.
2. You are working for the Finance Minister and must write a memo for the minister that provides a checklist of policy initiatives that will increase potential GDP. Be as imaginative as possible, but justify each of your suggestions with reference to the concepts and tools that you have learned about in this chapter.

WEB EXERCISES

1. Use the links on the Parkin–Bade Web site to obtain information about the economy of Russia during the 1990s. Try to figure out what happened to the production possibilities frontier and production function and to the demand for labour and supply of labour in Russia during the 1990s. Tell a story about the Russian economy during those years using only the concepts and tools that you have learned about in this chapter.
2. Use the links on the Parkin–Bade Web site to obtain information about the economy of China during the 1990s. Try to figure out what happened to the production possibilities frontier and production function and to the demand for labour and supply of labour in China during the 1990s. Tell a story about the Chinese economy during those years using only the concepts and tools that you have learned about in this chapter.

ECONOMIC GROWTH

CHAPTER 30

Transforming People's Lives

Real GDP *per person* in Canada more than doubled between 1961 and 2001. If you live in a dorm, chances are it was built during the 1960s and equipped with two electrical outlets: one for a desk lamp and one for a bedside lamp. Today, with the help of a power bar (or two), your room bulges with a personal computer, television and VCR or DVD player, stereo system, microwave, refrigerator, coffee maker, and toaster—the list goes on. What has brought about this growth in production, incomes, and living standards? ◆ We see even greater economic growth if we look at modern Asia. On the banks of the Li River in Southern China, Songman Yang breeds cormorants, amazing birds that he trains to fish and to deliver their catch to a basket on his simple bamboo raft. Songman's work, the capital equipment and technology he uses, and the income he earns are similar to those of his ancestors going back some 2,000 years. Yet all around Songman, in China's bustling cities, people are participating in an economic miracle. They are creating businesses, investing in new technologies, developing local and global markets, and transforming their lives. Why are incomes in China growing so rapidly?

◆ In this chapter, we study the forces that make real GDP grow, that make some countries grow faster than others, and that make our own growth rate sometimes slow down and sometimes speed up. And at the end of the chapter, in *Reading Between the Lines*, we examine Canada's recent growth performance and compare it with that of other major industrial countries.

After studying this chapter, you will be able to

- **Describe the long-term growth trends in Canada and other countries and regions**
- **Identify the main sources of long-term real GDP growth**
- **Explain the productivity growth slowdown in Canada during the 1970s and the speedup during the 1990s**
- **Explain the rapid economic growth rates being achieved in Asia**
- **Explain the theories of economic growth**

Long-Term Growth Trends

THE LONG-TERM GROWTH TRENDS THAT WE study in this chapter are the trends in *potential GDP.* We are interested in long-term growth primarily because it brings rising incomes *per person.* So we begin by looking at some facts about the level and the growth rate of real GDP per person in Canada and around the world. Let's look first at real GDP per person in Canada over the past 75 years.

Growth in the Canadian Economy

Figure 30.1 shows real GDP *per person* in Canada for the 75 years from 1926 to 2001. The average growth rate over this period is 2.2 percent a year.

The earliest years in the graph are dominated by two extraordinary events: the Great Depression of the 1930s and World War II of the 1940s. The fall in real GDP during the depression and the bulge during the war obscure the changes in the long-term growth trend that occurred within these years. Averaging out the depression and the war, the long-term growth rate was close to its 75-year average of 2.2 percent a year.

The 1950s had slow growth but then, during the 1960s, the growth rate speeded and averaged 3.6 percent a year. The 1970s growth slowed to 2.8 percent a year and in the 1980s the growth rate slowed to a crawl of 1.0 percent a year. After 1996, the growth rate increased again and for the five years between 1996 and 2001, the growth rate was back at its 75-year average.

A major goal of this chapter is to explain why our economy grows and why the long-term growth rate varies. Why did growth speed up during the 1960s, slow through the 1970s and 1980s, and then speed up again during the late 1990s and 2000s? Another goal is to explain variations in the growth rate across countries. Let's look at some facts about the growth rates of other nations and compare them with Canada's growth rate.

FIGURE 30.1 Economic Growth in Canada: 1926–2001

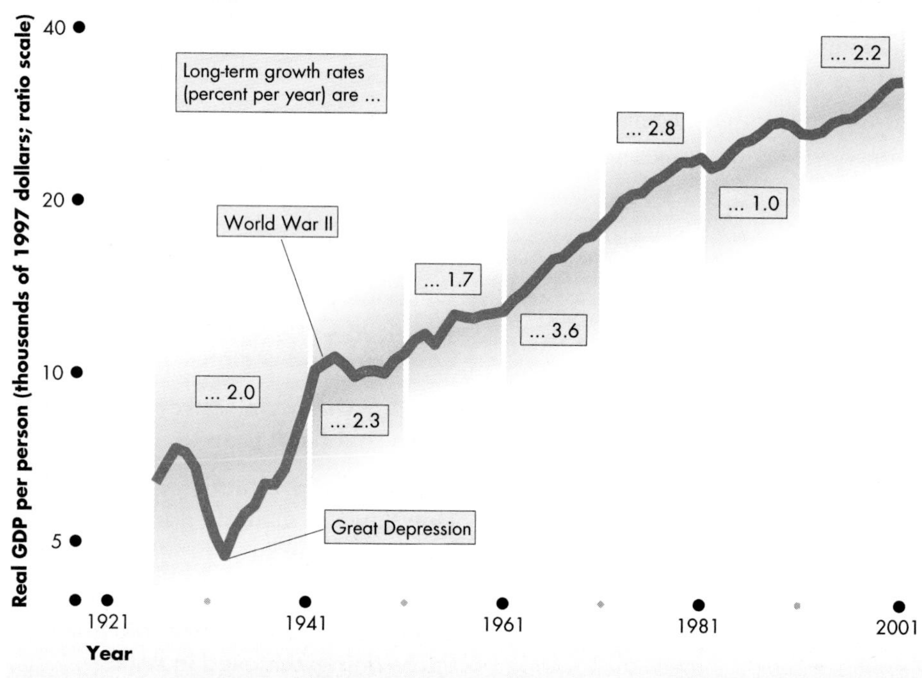

During the 75 years from 1926 to 2001, real GDP per person in Canada grew by 2.2 percent a year, on the average. Growth was the most rapid during the 1960s and slowest during the 1980s.

Sources: F.H. Leacy (ed.), *Historical Statistics of Canada*, 2nd ed., catalogue 11-516, series A1, F32, F55, Statistics Canada, Ottawa, 1983; Statistics Canada, CANSIM tables 380-0002 and 051-0005, and authors' calculations.

Real GDP Growth in the World Economy

Figure 30.2 shows real GDP per person in Canada and in other countries between 1961 and 2001. (The data shown in this figure are in 1985 U.S. dollars.) Part (a) looks at the seven richest countries—known as the G7 nations. Among these nations, the United States has the highest real GDP per person.

In 2001, Canada had the second-highest real GDP per person and Japan the third. Before the 1990s, Canada and Japan grew faster than the United States and were catching up. Japan also grew faster than the Europe Big 4 (France, Germany, Italy, and the United Kingdom) and overtook Europe in the mid-1980s. But during the 1990s, the Japanese economy stagnated while Europe's continued to expand, so by 2001, these nations had similar levels of real GDP per person.

Not all countries are growing faster than, and catching up with, Canada. Figure 30.2(b) looks at some of these. Western Europe (other than the Big 4) grew faster than Canada before 1975, slowed to the Canadian growth rate during the 1980s, and fell farther behind during the 1990s. After a brief period of catch-up, the former Communist countries of Central Europe have fallen increasingly behind Canada, and by 2001, they were as far behind as they had been 30 years earlier.

Africa and Central and South America have grown more slowly than Canada. Real GDP per person in Central and South America slipped from a comparative high of 35 percent of the Canadian level of real GDP per person in 1980 to 25 percent in 2001. Africa

FIGURE 30.2 Economic Growth Around the World: Catch-Up or Not?

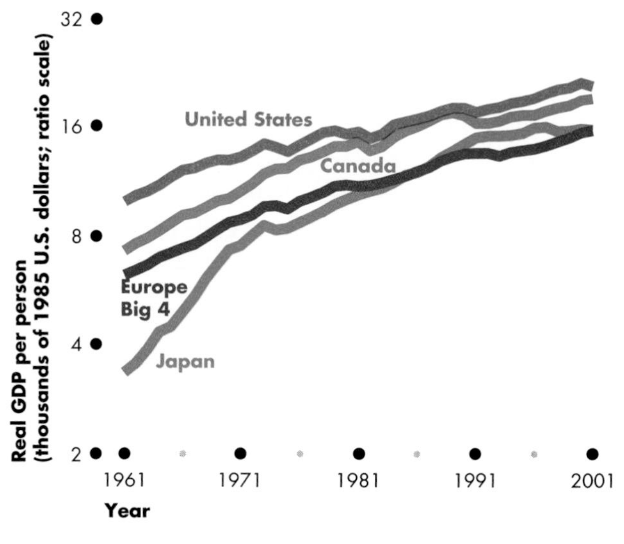

(a) Catch-up?

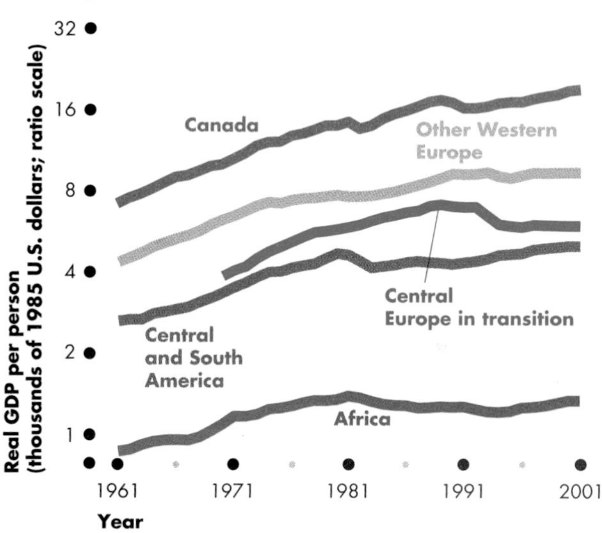

(b) No catch-up?

Real GDP per person has grown throughout the world economy. Among the rich industrial countries (part a), real GDP growth has been faster in Canada, the Europe Big 4 (France, Germany, Italy, and the United Kingdom), and Japan than in the United States, and these countries have narrowed the gap. The most spectacular growth was in Japan during the 1960s. Real GDP per person in Canada became close to the U.S. level during the 1980s but slipped back during the 1990s. Among a wider range of countries (part b), there is little sign of catch-up. The gap between real GDP per person in Canada and other Western European countries has remained constant. The gaps between Canada and Central Europe, Central and South America, and Africa have widened.

Sources: 1960–1992: Robert Summers and Alan Heston, New Computer Diskette, January 15, 1995, distributed by the National Bureau of Economic Research to update "The Penn World Table: An Expanded Set of International Comparisons, 1950–1988," *Quarterly Journal of Economics*, May 1991, 327–368. 1993–2001: *World Economic Outlook* (Washington, DC: International Monetary Fund, October 2001).

slipped from 11 percent of the Canadian level of real GDP per person in 1960 to 7 percent in 2001.

Taking both parts of Fig. 30.2 together, we can see that the catch-up in real GDP per person that is visible in part (a) is not a global phenomenon.

Hong Kong, Korea, Singapore, and Taiwan have experienced spectacular growth, which you can see in Fig. 30.3. During the 1960s, real GDP per person in these economies ranged from 10 to 25 percent of that in Canada. But by 2001, two of them, Hong Kong and Singapore, had caught up with Canada and the other two were close behind.

Figure 30.3 shows that China is also catching up, but more slowly and from a very long way behind.

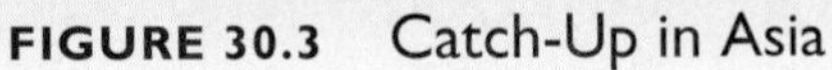

FIGURE 30.3 Catch-Up in Asia

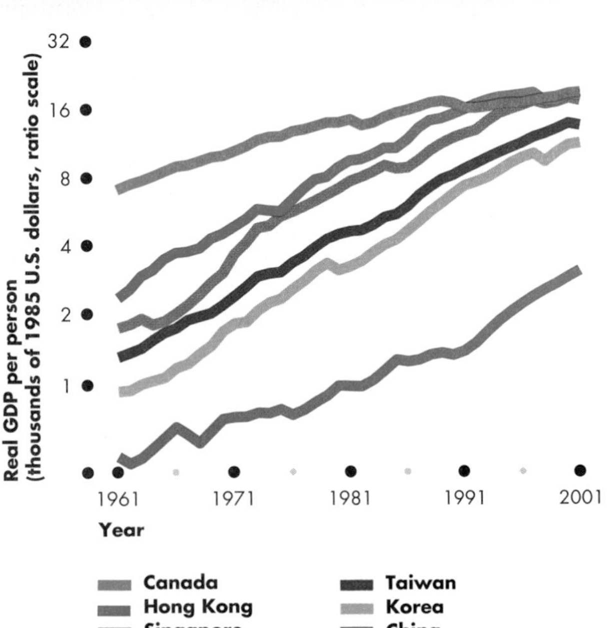

Catch-up has occurred in five economies in Asia. After starting out in 1960 with real GDP per person as low as 10 percent of that in Canada, Hong Kong, Korea, Singapore, and Taiwan have substantially narrowed the gap between them and Canada. And from being a very poor developing country in 1960, China now has a real GDP per person that equals that of Hong Kong in 1960. China is growing at a rate that is enabling it to continue to catch up with Canada.

Sources: See Fig. 30.2.

China's real GDP per person increased from 5 percent of Canada's level in 1961 to 15 percent in 2001.

The four small Asian economies shown in Fig. 30.3 are like fast trains running on the same track at similar speeds and with a roughly constant gap between them. Hong Kong is the lead train and runs about 15 years in front of Korea, which is the last train. Real GDP per person in Korea in 2001 was similar to that in Hong Kong in 1986, 15 years earlier. Between 1961 and 2001, Hong Kong transformed itself from a poor developing economy into one of the world's richest economies.

China is now doing what Hong Kong has done. If China continues its rapid growth, the world economy will become a dramatically different place, because China is equivalent to more than 200 countries of the size of Hong Kong. Whether China will continue on its current path of rapid growth is impossible to predict.

REVIEW QUIZ

1. What has been the average economic growth rate in Canada over the past 75 years? In which periods was growth the most rapid and in which periods was it the slowest?
2. Describe the gaps between the levels of real GDP per person in Canada and other countries. For which countries are the gaps narrowing? For which countries are the gaps widening? And for which countries are the gaps remaining unchanged?
3. Compare the growth rates and levels of real GDP per person in Hong Kong, Korea, Singapore, Taiwan, China, and Canada. How far is China behind the other Asian economies?

The facts about economic growth in Canada and around the world raise some big questions that we're now going to answer. We'll study the causes of economic growth in three stages. First, we'll look at the preconditions for growth and the activities that sustain it. Second, we'll learn how economists measure the relative contributions of the sources of growth—an activity called *growth accounting.* And third, we'll study three theories of economic growth that seek to explain how the influences on growth interact to determine the growth rate. Let's take our first look at the causes of economic growth.

The Causes of Economic Growth: A First Look

MOST HUMAN SOCIETIES HAVE LIVED FOR centuries and even thousands of years, like Songman Yang and his ancestors, with no economic growth. The key reason is that they have lacked some fundamental social institutions and arrangements that are essential preconditions for economic growth. Let's see what these preconditions are.

Preconditions for Economic Growth

The most basic precondition for economic growth is an appropriate *incentive* system. Three institutions are crucial to the creation of incentives:

1. Markets
2. Property rights
3. Monetary exchange

Markets enable buyers and sellers to get information and to do business with each other, and market prices send signals to buyers and sellers that create incentives to increase or decrease the quantities demanded and supplied. Markets enable people to specialize and trade and to save and invest. But markets need property rights and monetary exchange.

Property rights are the social arrangements that govern the ownership, use, and disposal of factors of production and goods and services. They include the rights to physical property (land, buildings, and capital equipment), to financial property (claims by one person against another), and to intellectual property (such as inventions). Clearly established and enforced property rights give people an assurance that a capricious government will not confiscate their income or savings.

Monetary exchange facilitates transactions of all kinds, including the orderly transfer of private property from one person to another. Property rights and monetary exchange create incentives for people to specialize and trade, to save and invest, and to discover new technologies.

No unique political system is necessary to deliver the preconditions for economic growth. Liberal democracy, founded on the fundamental principle of the rule of law, is the system that does the best job. It provides a solid base on which property rights can be established and enforced. But authoritarian political systems have sometimes provided an environment in which economic growth has occurred.

Early human societies, based on hunting and gathering, did not experience economic growth because they lacked these preconditions. Economic growth began when societies evolved the three key institutions that create incentives. But the presence of an incentive system and the institutions that create it does not guarantee that economic growth will occur. It permits economic growth but does not make that growth inevitable.

The simplest way in which growth happens when the appropriate incentive system exists is that people begin to specialize in the activities at which they have a comparative advantage and trade with each other. You saw in Chapter 2 how everyone can gain from such activity. By specializing and trading, everyone can acquire goods and services at the lowest possible cost. Equivalently, people can obtain a greater volume of goods and services from their labour.

As an economy moves from one with little specialization to one that reaps the gains from specialization and exchange, its production and consumption grow. Real GDP per person increases, and the standard of living rises.

But for growth to be persistent, people must face incentives that encourage them to pursue three activities that generate ongoing economic growth:

- Saving and investment in new capital
- Investment in human capital
- Discovery of new technologies

These three sources of growth, which interact with each other, are the primary sources of the extraordinary growth in productivity during the past 200 years. Let's look at each in turn.

Saving and Investment in New Capital

Saving and investment in new capital increase the amount of capital per worker and increase real GDP per hour of labour—labour productivity. Labour productivity took the most dramatic upturn when the amount of capital per worker increased during the Industrial Revolution. Production processes that use hand tools can create beautiful objects, but production methods that use large amounts of capital per worker, such as auto plant assembly lines, are much more productive. The accumulation of capital on farms, in textile factories, in iron foundries and steel mills, in coal mines, on building sites, in chemical plants, in auto plants, in banks and insurance companies, and in shopping malls has added incredibly to the productivity of our economy. The next time you see a movie set in the Old West or colonial times, look carefully at the small amount of capital around. Try to imagine how productive you would be in such circumstances compared with your productivity today.

Investment in Human Capital

Human capital—the accumulated skill and knowledge of human beings—is the most fundamental source of economic growth. It is a source of both increased productivity and technological advance.

The development of one of the most basic human skills—writing—was the source of some of the earliest major gains in productivity. The ability to keep written records made it possible to reap ever-larger gains from specialization and exchange. Imagine how hard it would be to do any kind of business if all the accounts, invoices, and agreements existed only in people's memories.

Later, the development of mathematics laid the foundation for the eventual extension of knowledge about physical forces and chemical and biological processes. This base of scientific knowledge was the foundation for the technological advances of the Industrial Revolution 200 years ago and of today's information revolution.

But much human capital that is extremely productive is much more humble. It takes the form of millions of individuals learning and repetitively doing simple production tasks and becoming remarkably more productive in the tasks.

One carefully studied example illustrates the importance of this kind of human capital. Between 1941 and 1944 (during World War II), U.S. shipyards produced some 2,500 units of a cargo ship, called the Liberty Ship, to a standardized design. In 1941, it took 1.2 million person-hours to build one ship. By 1942, it took 600,000 person-hours, and by 1943, it took only 500,000. Not much change occurred in the capital employed during these years. But an enormous amount of human capital was accumulated. Thousands of workers and managers learned from experience and accumulated human capital that more than doubled their productivity in two years.

Discovery of New Technologies

Saving and investment in new capital and the accumulation of human capital have made a large contribution to economic growth. But technological change—the discovery and the application of new technologies and new goods—has made an even greater contribution.

People are many times more productive today than they were a hundred years ago. We are not more productive because we have more steam engines per person and more horse-drawn carriages per person. Rather, it is because we have engines and transportation equipment that use technologies that were unknown a hundred years ago and that are more productive than the old technologies were. Technological change makes an enormous contribution to our increased productivity. It arises from formal research and development programs and from informal trial and error, and it involves discovering new ways of getting more out of our resources.

To reap the benefits of technological change, capital must increase. Some of the most powerful and far-reaching fundamental technologies are embodied in human capital—for example, language, writing, and mathematics. But most technologies are embodied in physical capital. For example, to reap the benefits of the internal combustion engine, millions of horse-drawn carriages and horses had to be replaced by automobiles; more recently, to reap the benefits of computerized word processing, millions of typewriters had to be replaced by PCs and printers.

REVIEW QUIZ

1. What economic activities that lead to economic growth do markets, property rights, and monetary exchange facilitate?
2. What are the roles of saving and investment in new capital, the growth of human capital, and the discovery of new technologies in economic growth?
3. Provide some examples of how human capital has created new technologies that are embodied in both human and physical capital.

What is the quantitative contribution of the sources of economic growth? To answer this question, economists use growth accounting.

Growth Accounting

THE QUANTITY OF REAL GDP SUPPLIED (Y) depends on three factors:

1. The quantity of labour (L)
2. The quantity of capital (K)
3. The state of technology (T)

The purpose of **growth accounting** is to calculate how much real GDP growth results from growth of labour and capital and how much is attributable to technological change.

The key tool of growth accounting is the **aggregate production function,** which we write as

$$Y = F(L, K, T).$$

In words, the quantity of real GDP supplied is determined by (is a function F of) the quantities of labour and capital and of the state of technology. The larger L, K, or T, the greater is Y. And the faster L and K grow and T advances, the faster Y grows.

So understanding what makes labour and capital grow and technology advance is the key to understanding economic growth. Labour growth depends primarily on population growth. And the growth rate of capital and the pace of technological advance determine the growth rate of labour productivity.

FIGURE 30.4 Real GDP per Hour of Labour

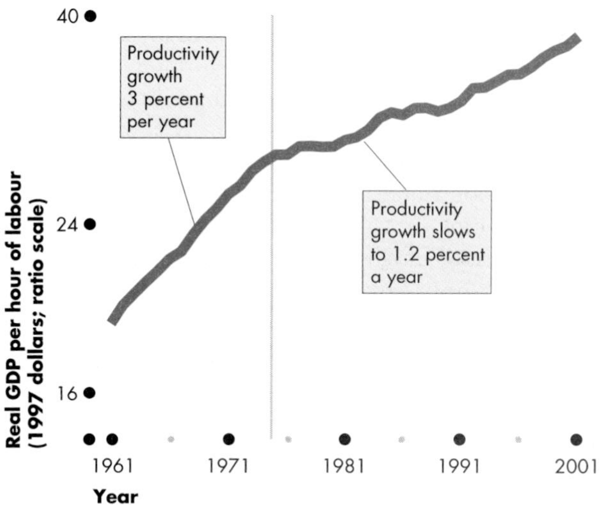

Real GDP divided by aggregate hours equals real GDP per hour of labour, which is a broad measure of productivity. During the 1960s and late 1990s, the productivity growth rate was high. It slowed between 1973 and 1983.

Sources: Statistics Canada, CANSIM tables 282-0022 and 380-0002, and authors' calculations.

Labour Productivity

Labour productivity is real GDP per hour of labour. Labour productivity is calculated by dividing real GDP Y by aggregate labour hours L.

Labour productivity determines how much income an hour of labour generates. Figure 30.4 shows labour productivity for the period 1961–2001. Productivity growth was most rapid during the 1960s. It slowed down in 1973 and remained low for about 10 years. Productivity growth then speeded up again in what has been called the new economy of the 1990s.

Why did productivity grow fastest during the 1960s and late 1990s? Why did it slow down in 1973 and then speed up again during the 1990s?

Growth accounting answers these questions by dividing the growth in labour productivity into two components and then measuring the contribution of each. The components are

- Growth in capital per hour of labour
- Technological change

Capital is physical capital. Technological change includes everything that contributes to labour productivity growth that is not included in the growth in capital per hour. In particular, it includes human capital growth. Human capital growth and technological change are intimately related. Technology advances because knowledge advances. And knowledge is part of human capital. So "technological change" is a broad catchall concept.

The analytical engine of growth accounting is a relationship called the productivity curve. Let's learn about this relationship and see how it is used.

The Productivity Curve

The **productivity curve** is a relationship that shows how real GDP per hour of labour changes as the amount of capital per hour of labour changes with a given state of technology. Figure 30.5 illustrates the productivity curve. Capital per hour of labour is measured on the *x*-axis, and real GDP per hour of labour is measured on the *y*-axis. The figure shows *two* productivity curves. One is the curve labelled PC_0, and the other is the curve labelled PC_1.

An increase in the quantity of capital per hour of labour increases real GDP per hour of labour, which is shown by a movement along a productivity curve. For example, on PC_0, when capital per hour of labour is $30, real GDP per hour of labour is $20. If capital per hour of labour increases to $60, real GDP per hour of labour increases to $25.

Technological change increases the amount of GDP per hour of labour that can be produced by a given amount of capital per hour of labour. Technological change shifts the productivity curve upward. For example, if capital per hour of labour is $30 and a technological change increases real GDP per hour of labour from $20 to $25, the productivity curve shifts upward from PC_0 to PC_1 in Fig. 30.5. Similarly, if capital per hour of labour is $60, the same technological change increases real GDP per hour of labour from $25 to $32 and shifts the productivity curve upward from PC_0 to PC_1.

To calculate the contributions of capital growth and technological change to productivity growth, we need to know the shape of the productivity curve. The shape of the productivity curve reflects a fundamental economic law—the law of diminishing returns. The **law of diminishing returns** states that as the quantity of one input increases with the quantities of all other inputs remaining the same, output increases but by ever smaller increments. For example, in a factory that has a given amount of capital, as more labour is hired, production increases. But each *additional* hour of labour produces less *additional* output than the previous hour produced. Two typists working with one computer type fewer than twice as many pages per day as one typist working with one computer.

Applied to capital, the law of diminishing returns states that if a given number of hours of labour use more capital (with the same technology), the *additional* output that results from the *additional* capital gets smaller as the amount of capital increases. One typist working with two computers types fewer than twice as many pages per day as one typist working with one computer. More generally, one hour of labour working with $40 of capital produces less than twice the output of one hour of labour working with $20 of capital. But how much less? The answer is given by the *one-third rule.*

FIGURE 30.5 How Productivity Grows

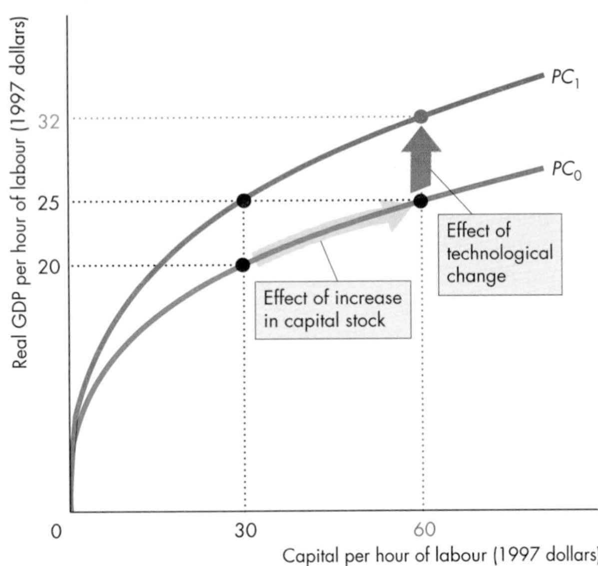

Productivity is measured by real GDP per hour of labour, and it can grow for two reasons: (1) Capital per hour of labour increases, and (2) technological advances occur. The productivity curve, PC_0, shows the effects of an increase in capital per hour of labour on productivity. Here, when capital per hour of labour increases from $30 to $60, real GDP per hour of labour increases from $20 to $25 along the productivity curve PC_0. Technological advance shifts the productivity curve upward. Here, an advance in technology shifts the productivity curve from PC_0 to PC_1. When capital per hour of labour is $60, real GDP per hour of labour increases from $25 to $32.

The One-Third Rule Robert Solow of MIT estimated a U.S. productivity curve and discovered the **one-third rule** that, on the average, with no change in technology, a 1 percent increase in capital per hour of labour brings a *one-third of 1 percent* increase in real GDP per hour of labour. This one-third rule is used to calculate the contributions of an increase in capital per hour of labour and technological change to the growth of real GDP. Let's do such a calculation.

Suppose that capital per hour of labour grows by 3 percent a year and real GDP per hour of labour grows by 2.5 percent a year. The one-third rule tells us that capital growth has contributed one-third of

3 percent, which is 1 percent, to the growth of real GDP per hour of labour. The rest of the 2.5 percent growth of real GDP per hour of labour comes from technological change. That is, technological change has contributed 1.5 percent, which is the 2.5 percent growth of real GDP per hour of labour minus the estimated 1 percent contribution of capital growth.

Accounting for the Productivity Growth Slowdown and Speedup

We can use the one-third rule to study Canadian productivity growth and the productivity growth slowdown. Figure 30.6 tells the story, starting in 1961.

Booming Sixties and Early Seventies In 1961, capital per hour of labour was $48 and real GDP per hour of labour was $19 at the point marked 61 on PC_{61} in Fig. 30.6. By 1973, real GDP per hour of labour had expanded by 47 percent, to $28, and capital per hour of labour had increased by 36 percent, to $65. With no change in technology, the economy would have moved to point *A* on PC_{61}, where real GDP per hour of labour has increased by 12 percent (1/3 of 36 percent). But rapid technological change shifted the productivity curve upward to PC_{73}, and the economy moved to the point marked 73 on that curve.

Slowdown During the 23 years from 1973 to 1996, real GDP per hour of labour expanded by only 25 percent, to $35. At the same time, capital per hour of labour increased by 43 percent, to $93. With no change in technology, the economy would have moved to point *B* on PC_{73} in Fig. 30.6, where real GDP per hour of labour has increased by 14 percent (1/3 of 43 percent). But a small amount of technological change shifted the productivity curve upward to PC_{96}, and the economy moved to the point marked 96 on that curve. So the productivity growth slowdown occurred because the contribution of technological change to real GDP growth slowed.

Growth Again During the 5 years from 1996 to 2001, real GDP per hour of labour expanded by 8.5 percent, to $38. At the same time, capital per hour of labour increased by 4.5 percent, to $97. With no change in technology, the economy would have moved to point *C* on PC_{96} in Fig. 30.6, where real GDP per hour of labour has increased by 1.5 percent (1/3 of 4.5 percent). But a speedup in the pace of technological change shifted the productivity curve upward to PC_{01}, and the economy moved to the point marked 01 on that curve. Although technological change speeded, its pace was slower than that during the 1960s.

The growth accounting exercise that we've just worked through suggests that the so-called new economy of the late 1990s was not such a spectacular or unusual growth phenomenon.

FIGURE 30.6 Growth Accounting and the Productivity Growth Slowdown

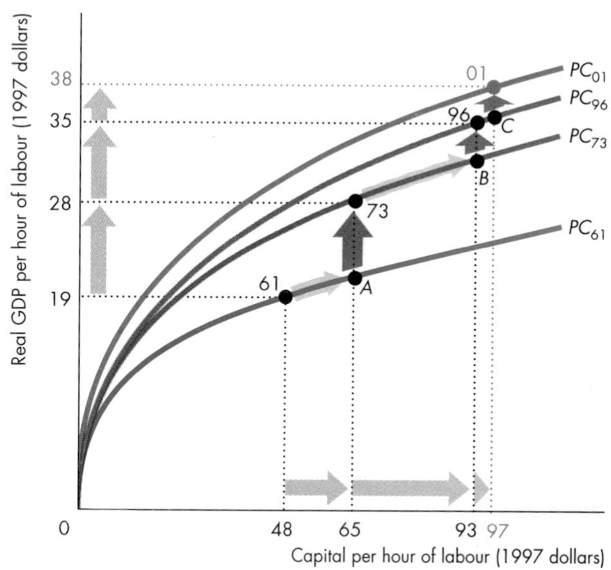

Between 1961 and 1973, a period in which productivity growth was rapid, capital per hour of labour increased from $48 to $65 and technological progress shifted the productivity curve upward from PC_{61} to PC_{73}. Between 1973 and 1996, a period in which productivity growth was slow, capital per hour of labour increased from $65 to $93 and technological progress shifted the productivity curve upward from PC_{73} to PC_{96}. Between 1996 and 2001, a period in which productivity growth speeded, capital per hour of labour increased from $93 to $97 and technological progress shifted the productivity curve upward from PC_{96} to PC_{01}. Although productivity growth increased after 1996, its pace was slower than that of the 1960s and early 1970s.

Sources: Statistics Canada, CANSIM tables 282-0022, 378-0004, and 380-0002, and authors' calculations.

Technological Change During the Productivity Growth Slowdown

Technological change did not stop during the productivity growth slowdown. But its focus changed from increasing productivity to coping with

- Energy price shocks
- The environment

Energy Price Shocks Energy price increases that occurred in 1973–1974 and in 1979–1980 diverted research efforts towards saving energy rather than increasing productivity. Airplanes became more fuel efficient, but they didn't operate with smaller crews. Real GDP per litre of fuel increased faster, but real GDP per hour of labour increased more slowly.

The Environment The 1970s saw an expansion of laws and resources devoted to protecting the environment and improving the quality of the workplace. The benefits of these actions—cleaner air and water and safer factories—are not counted as part of real GDP. So the growth of these benefits is not measured as part of productivity growth.

Achieving Faster Growth

Growth accounting tells us that to achieve faster economic growth, we must either increase the growth rate of capital per hour of labour or increase the pace of technological advance (which includes improving human capital). The main suggestions for achieving these objectives are

- Stimulate saving
- Stimulate research and development
- Target high-technology industries
- Encourage international trade
- Improve the quality of education

Stimulate Saving Saving finances investment, which brings capital accumulation. So stimulating saving can stimulate economic growth. The East Asian economies have the highest growth rates and the highest saving rates. Some African economies have the lowest growth rates and the lowest saving rates.

Tax incentives can increase saving. Registered Retirement Savings Plans (RRSPs) are a tax incentive to save. Economists claim that a tax on consumption rather than income provides the best saving incentive.

Stimulate Research and Development Everyone can use the fruits of *basic* research and development efforts. For example, all biotechnology firms can use advances in gene-splicing technology. Because basic inventions can be copied, the inventor's profit is limited, and the market allocates too few resources to this activity.

Governments can use public funds to finance basic research, but this solution is not foolproof. It requires a mechanism for allocating the public funds to their highest-valued use. The National Science and Engineering Research Council of Canada is one possibly efficient channel for allocating public funds to universities to finance and stimulate basic research.

Target High-Technology Industries Some people say that by providing public funds to high-technology firms and industries, a country can become the first to exploit a new technology and can earn above-average profits for a period while others are busy catching up. This strategy is risky and just as likely to use resources inefficiently as to speed growth.

Encourage International Trade Free international trade stimulates growth by extracting all the available gains from specialization and exchange. The fastest-growing nations today are those with the fastest-growing exports and imports.

Improve the Quality of Education The free market produces too little education because it brings benefits beyond those valued by the people who receive the education. By funding basic education and by ensuring high standards in basic skills such as language, mathematics, and science, governments can contribute to a nation's growth potential. Education can also be stimulated and improved by using tax incentives to encourage improved private provision.

REVIEW QUIZ

1. Explain how the one-third rule isolates the contributions of capital growth and technological change to productivity growth.
2. Explain how growth accounting gives us information about the factors that contributed to the productivity growth slowdown of the 1970s. Why did the slowdown occur?

Growth Theories

WE'VE SEEN THAT REAL GDP GROWS WHEN THE quantities of labour and capital (which includes human capital) grow and when technology advances. Does this mean that the growth of labour and capital and technological advances *cause* economic growth? It might mean that. But there are other possibilities. *One* of these factors might be the cause of real GDP growth, and the others might be the *effect.* We must try to discover how the influences on economic growth interact with each other to make some economies grow quickly and others grow slowly. And we must probe the reasons why a country's long-term growth rate sometimes speeds up and sometimes slows down.

Growth theories are designed to study the interactions among the several factors that contribute to growth and to disentangle cause and effect. They are also designed to enable us to study the way the different factors influence each other.

Growth theories are also designed to be universal. They are not theories about the growth of poor countries only or rich countries only. They are theories about why and how poor countries become rich and rich countries continue to get richer.

We're going to study three theories of economic growth, each one of which gives some insights into the process of economic growth. But none provides a definite answer to the basic questions: What causes economic growth and why do growth rates vary? Economics has some way to go before it can provide a definite answer to these most important of questions. The three growth theories we study are

- Classical growth theory
- Neoclassical growth theory
- New growth theory

Classical Growth Theory

Classical growth theory is the view that real GDP growth is temporary and that when real GDP per person rises above the subsistence level, a population explosion eventually brings real GDP per person back to the subsistence level. Adam Smith, Thomas Robert Malthus, and David Ricardo, the leading economists of the late eighteenth century and early nineteenth century, proposed this theory, but the view is most closely associated with the name of Malthus and is sometimes called the *Malthusian theory.*

Many people today are Malthusians! They say that if today's global population of 6.2 billion explodes to 11 billion by 2200, we will run out of resources and return to a primitive standard of living. We must act, say the Malthusians, to contain the population growth.

The Basic Classical Idea To understand classical growth theory, let's transport ourselves back to the world of 1776, when Adam Smith is first explaining the idea. Most of the 2.5 million people who live in the newly emerging nations of North America work on farms or on their own land and perform their tasks using simple tools and animal power. They earn an average of 2 shillings (a bit less than $12 in today's money) for working a 10-hour day.

Then advances in farming technology bring new types of plows and seeds that increase farm productivity. As farm productivity increases, farm production increases and some farm workers move from the land to the cities, where they get work producing and selling the expanding range of farm equipment. Incomes rise, and the people seem to be prospering. But will the prosperity last? Classical growth theory says it will not.

Advances in technology—in both agriculture and industry—lead to an investment in new capital, which makes labour more productive. More and more businesses start up and hire the now more productive labour. The greater demand for labour raises the real wage rate and increases employment.

At this stage, economic growth has occurred and everyone has benefited from it. Real GDP has increased, and the real wage rate has increased. But the classical economists believe that this new situation can't last because it will induce a population explosion.

Classical Theory of Population Growth When the classical economists were developing their ideas about population growth, an unprecedented population explosion was underway. In Britain and other Western European countries, improvements in diet and hygiene had lowered the death rate while the birth rate remained high. For several decades, population growth was extremely rapid. For example, after being relatively stable for several centuries, the population of Britain increased by 40 percent between 1750 and 1800 and by a further 50 percent between 1800 and 1830. Meanwhile, an estimated 1 million people (about 20 percent of the 1750 population) left Britain for North

America and Australia before 1800, and outward migration continued on a similar scale through the nineteenth century. These facts are the empirical basis for the classical theory of population growth.

To explain the high rate of population growth, the classical economists used the idea of a **subsistence real wage rate,** which is the minimum real wage rate needed to maintain life. If the actual real wage rate is less than the subsistence real wage rate, some people cannot survive and the population decreases. In classical theory, when the real wage rate exceeds the subsistence real wage rate, the population grows. But a rising population brings diminishing returns to labour. So labour productivity eventually decreases. This implication led to economics being called the *dismal science.* The dismal implication is that no matter how much technological change occurs, real wage rates are always pushed back towards the subsistence level.

FIGURE 30.7 Classical Growth Theory

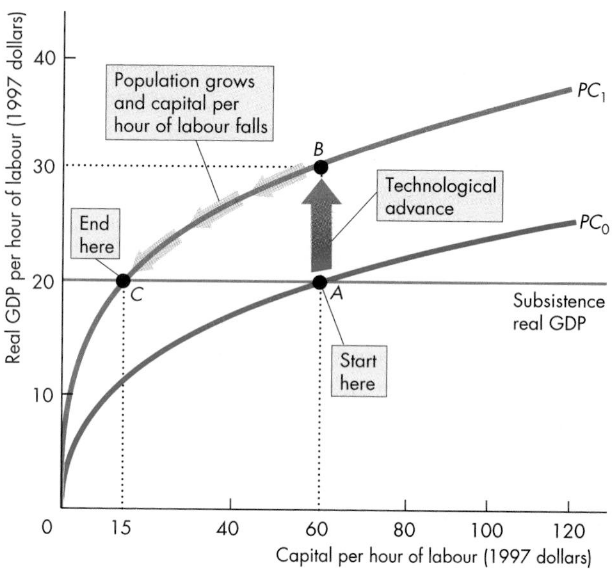

The economy starts out at point *A* with capital per hour of labour of \$60 and real GDP per hour of labour of \$20—the subsistence level—on productivity curve PC_0. A technological advance shifts the productivity curve upward to PC_1 and the economy moves to point *B*. The population grows, and both capital and real GDP per hour of labour decrease. The process ends at point *C* when real GDP per hour of labour is back at its subsistence level.

Classical Theory and the Productivity Curve Figure 30.7 illustrates the classical growth theory using the productivity curve. Initially, the productivity curve is PC_0. Subsistence real GDP is \$20 an hour, shown by the horizontal line in the graph. The economy starts out at point *A*, with \$60 of capital per hour of labour and \$20 of real GDP per hour of labour, the subsistence level. Because real GDP is at the subsistence level, the population is constant.

Then a technological advance occurs, which shifts the productivity curve upward to PC_1. The economy now moves to point *B* on PC_1, and real GDP per hour of labour rises to \$30. Now earning more than the subsistence wage, people have more children and live longer. The population grows.

A growing population means that labour hours grow, so capital per hour of labour falls. As capital per hour of labour falls, there is a movement down along the productivity curve PC_1. Real GDP per hour of labour falls and keeps falling as long as the population grows and capital per hour of labour falls.

This process ends when real GDP per hour of labour is back at the subsistence level at point *C* on productivity curve PC_1. The population stops growing and capital per hour of labour stops falling.

Repeated advances in technology play out in the same way as the advance that we've just studied. No matter how productive our economy becomes, population growth lowers capital per hour of labour and drives real GDP per hour of labour towards the subsistence level. Living standards temporarily improve while the population is expanding, but when the population expansion ends, the standard of living is back at the subsistence level.

Classical Theory and Capital Accumulation In the story you've just worked through, the total quantity of capital didn't change. Suppose that people save and invest, so capital grows. Doesn't a growing quantity of capital prevent the dismal conclusion of classical theory? It does not. *Anything* that raises real GDP per hour of labour above the subsistence level triggers a population explosion that eventually wipes out the gains from greater productivity.

The dismal conclusion of classical growth theory is a direct consequence of the assumption that the population explodes if real GDP per hour of labour exceeds the subsistence level. To avoid this conclusion, we need a different view of population growth.

The neoclassical growth theory that we'll now study provides a different view.

Neoclassical Growth Theory

Neoclassical growth theory is the proposition that real GDP per person grows because technological change induces a level of saving and investment that makes capital per hour of labour grow. Growth ends only if technological change stops.

Robert Solow of MIT suggested the most popular version of neoclassical growth theory in the 1950s. But Frank Ramsey of Cambridge University in England first developed this theory in the 1920s.

Neoclassical theory's big break with its classical predecessor is its view about population growth. So we'll begin our account of neoclassical theory by examining its views about population growth.

The Neoclassical Economics of Population Growth The population explosion of eighteenth-century Europe that created the classical theory of population eventually ended. The birth rate fell, and while the population continued to increase, its rate of increase became moderate. This slowdown in population growth seemed to make the classical theory less relevant. It also eventually led to the development of a modern economic theory of population growth.

The modern view is that although the population growth rate is influenced by economic factors, the influence is not a simple and mechanical one like that proposed by the classical economists. Key among the economic influences on population growth is the opportunity cost of a woman's time. As women's wage rates increase and their job opportunities expand, the opportunity cost of having children increases. Faced with a higher opportunity cost, families choose to have fewer children and the birth rate falls.

A second economic influence works on the death rate. The technological advance that brings increased productivity and increased incomes brings advances in health care that extend lives.

These two opposing economic forces influence the population growth rate. As incomes increase, both the birth rate and the death rate decrease. It turns out that these opposing forces almost offset each other, so the rate of population growth is independent of the rate of economic growth.

This modern view of population growth and the historical trends that support it contradict the views of the classical economists and call into question the modern doomsday conclusion that the planet will one day be swamped with too many people to feed.

Neoclassical growth theory adopts this modern view of population growth. Forces other than real GDP and its growth rate determine population growth.

Technological Change In the neoclassical theory, the rate of technological change influences the rate of economic growth but economic growth does not influence the pace of technological change. It is assumed that technological change results from chance. When we get lucky, we have rapid technological change, and when bad luck strikes, the pace of technological advance slows.

Target Rate of Return and Saving The key assumption in the neoclassical growth theory concerns saving. Other things remaining the same, the higher the real interest rate, the greater is the amount that people save. To decide how much to save, people compare the rate of return with a *target rate of return.* If the rate of return exceeds the target rate of return, saving is sufficient to make capital per hour of labour grow. If the target rate of return exceeds the rate of return, saving is not sufficient to maintain the current level of capital per hour of labour, so capital per hour of labour shrinks. And if the rate of return equals a target rate of return, saving is just sufficient to maintain the quantity of capital per hour of labour at its current level.

The Basic Neoclassical Idea To understand neoclassical growth theory, imagine the world of the mid-1950s, when Robert Solow is explaining his idea. Canadians are enjoying post–World War II prosperity. Income per person is around $12,000 a year in today's money. The population is growing at about 1 percent a year. People are saving and investing about 20 percent of their incomes, enough to keep the quantity of capital per hour of labour constant. Income per person is growing, but not by much.

Then technology begins to advance at a more rapid pace across a range of activities. The transistor revolutionizes an emerging electronics industry. New plastics revolutionize the manufacture of household appliances. The national highway system revolutionizes road transportation. Jet airliners start to replace piston-engine airplanes and speed air transportation.

These technological advances bring new profit opportunities. Businesses expand, and new businesses are created to exploit the newly available profitable technologies. Investment and saving increase. The economy enjoys new levels of prosperity and growth. But will the prosperity last? And will the growth last? Neoclassical growth theory says that the *prosperity* will last but the *growth* will not last unless technology keeps advancing.

According to the neoclassical growth theory, the prosperity will persist because there is no classical population growth to induce lower wages.

But growth will stop if technology stops advancing, for two related reasons. First, high profit rates that result from technological change bring increased saving and capital accumulation. But second, capital accumulation eventually results in diminishing returns that lower the rate of return, and that eventually decrease saving and slow the rate of capital accumulation.

Neoclassical Theory and the Productivity Curve Figure 30.8 illustrates the neoclassical growth theory using the productivity curve. Initially, the productivity curve is PC_0 and the economy is at point *A*, with $60 of capital per hour of labour and real GDP of $20 an hour.

The slope of the productivity curve measures the additional output that results from an additional unit of capital—the marginal product of capital or rate of return on capital. People have a target rate of return that can be illustrated by a straight line with a slope equal to the target rate of return.

At point *A* on productivity curve PC_0, the slope of the *PC* curve equals the slope of the target rate of return line. If the quantity of capital per hour of labour were less than $60, the real interest rate would exceed the target rate of return and capital per hour of labour would grow. If the quantity of capital per hour of labour were greater than $60, the rate of return would be less than the target rate of return and capital per hour of labour would shrink. But when the quantity of capital per hour of labour is $60, the rate of return equals the target rate of return and capital per hour of labour is constant.

Now a technological advance occurs that shifts the productivity curve upward to PC_1. The economy now moves to point *B* on PC_1, and real GDP per hour of labour rises to $30. It is at this point in the classical theory that forces kick in to drive real GDP per hour of labour back to the subsistence level. But in the neoclassical theory, no such forces operate. Instead, at point *B*, the rate of return exceeds the target rate of return. (You can see why by comparing the slopes of PC_1 at point *B* and the target rate of return line.)

With a high rate of return available, saving and investment increase and the quantity of capital per hour of labour increases. There is a movement up along the productivity curve PC_1, and real GDP per hour of labour increases.

This growth process eventually ends because, as the quantity of capital per hour of labour increases, the rate of return falls. At point *C*, where the process ends, the real interest rate again equals the target rate of return.

Throughout the process you've just studied, real GDP per hour of labour grows but the growth rate gradually decreases and eventually growth ends.

FIGURE 30.8 Neoclassical Growth Theory

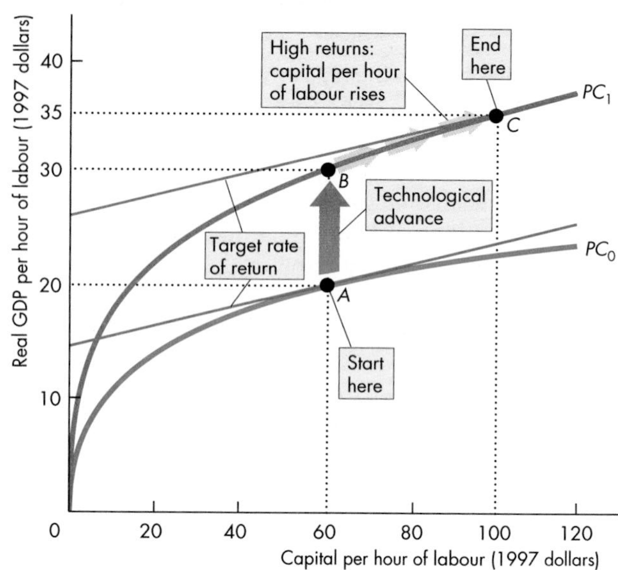

The economy starts on productivity curve PC_0 at point *A*. The slope of the productivity curve measures the rate of return, so at point *A* the rate of return equals the target rate of return. A technological advance shifts the productivity curve upward to PC_1 and the economy moves to point *B*. The rate of return exceeds the target rate of return, and the quantity of capital per hour of labour increases—a movement up along the productivity curve PC_1. Growth ends when the rate of return again equals the target rate of return at point *C*.

But if another advance in technology occurs, the process you've just seen repeats. Ongoing advances in technology constantly increase the rate of return, inducing the saving that increases capital per hour of labour. The growth process persists as long as technology advances. And the growth rate fluctuates because technological progress occurs at a variable rate.

A Problem with Neoclassical Growth Theory All economies have access to the same technologies, and capital is free to roam the globe seeking the highest available rate of return. Given these facts, neoclassical growth theory implies that growth rates and income levels per person around the globe will converge. While there is some sign of convergence among the rich countries, as Fig. 30.2(a) shows, convergence is slow, and it does not appear to be imminent for all countries, as Fig. 30.2(b) shows.

New growth theory attempts to overcome this shortcoming of neoclassical growth theory. It also attempts to explain how the rate of technological change is determined.

New Growth Theory

New growth theory holds that real GDP per person grows because of the choices people make in the pursuit of profit and that growth can persist indefinitely. Paul Romer of Stanford University developed this theory during the 1980s, but the ideas go back to work by Joseph Schumpeter during the 1930s and 1940s.

The theory begins with two facts about market economies:

- Discoveries result from choices.
- Discoveries bring profit and competition destroys profit.

Discoveries and Choices When people discover a new product or technique, they think of themselves as being lucky. They are right. But the pace at which new discoveries are made—and at which technology advances—is not determined by chance. It depends on how many people are looking for a new technology and how intensively they are looking.

Discoveries and Profits Profit is the spur to technological change. The forces of competition squeeze profits, so to increase profit, people constantly seek either lower-cost methods of production or new and better products for which people are willing to pay a higher price. Inventors can maintain a profit for several years by taking out a patent or copyright. But eventually, a new discovery is copied, and profits disappear.

Two further facts play a key role in the new growth theory:

- Discoveries are a public capital good.
- Knowledge is capital that is not subject to the law of diminishing returns.

Discoveries Are a Public Capital Good Economists call a good a *public good* when no one can be excluded from using it and when one person's use does not prevent others from using it. National defence is one example of a public good. Knowledge is another.

When in 1992, Marc Andreesen and his friend Eric Bina developed a browser they called Mosaic, they laid the foundation for Netscape Navigator and Internet Explorer, two pieces of capital that have increased productivity unimaginably.

While patents and copyrights protect the inventors or creators of new products and production processes and enable them to reap the returns from their innovative ideas, once a new discovery has been made, everyone can benefit from its use. And one person's use of a new discovery does not prevent others from using it. Your use of a Web browser doesn't prevent someone else from using that same browser simultaneously.

Because knowledge is a public good, as the benefits of a new discovery spread, free resources become available. These resources are free because nothing is given up when they are used. They have a zero opportunity cost. Knowledge is even more special because it is not subject to diminishing returns.

Knowledge Capital Not Subject to Diminishing Returns Production is subject to diminishing returns when one resource is fixed and the quantity of another resource changes. Adding labour to a fixed amount of equipment or adding equipment to a fixed amount of labour both bring diminishing marginal product—diminishing returns.

But increasing the stock of knowledge makes labour and machines more productive. Knowledge capital does not bring diminishing returns.

The fact that knowledge capital does *not* experience diminishing returns is the central novel proposition of the new growth theory. And the implication of this simple and appealing idea is astonishing. The new growth theory has no growth-stopping mechanism like those of the other two theories. As physical capital accumulates, the rate of return falls. But the incentive to innovate and earn a higher profit becomes stronger. So innovation occurs, which increases the rate of return. Real GDP per hour of labour grows indefinitely as people find new technologies that yield a higher real interest rate.

The growth rate depends on people's ability to innovate and the rate of return. Over the years, the ability to innovate has changed. The invention of language and writing (the two most basic human capital tools) and later the development of the scientific method and the establishment of universities and research institutions brought huge increases in the rate of return. Today, a deeper understanding of genes is bringing profit in a growing biotechnology industry. And astonishing advances in computer technology are creating an explosion of profit opportunities in a wide range of information-age industries.

New Growth Theory and the Productivity Curve Figure 30.9 illustrates new growth theory. Like Fig. 30.8, which illustrates neoclassical growth theory, Fig. 30.9 contains a productivity curve and a target rate of return curve.

But unlike in neoclassical theory, the productivity curve in the new growth theory never stands still. The pursuit of profit means that technology is always advancing and human capital is always growing. The result is an ever upward-shifting *PC* curve. As physical capital is accumulated, diminishing returns lower its rate of return. But ever-advancing productivity counteracts this tendency and keeps the rate of return above the target rate of return curve.

Advancing technology and human capital growth keep the *PC* curve shifting upward in Fig. 30.9 from PC_0 to PC_1 to PC_2 and beyond. As the productivity curve shifts upward, capital per hour of labour and real GDP per hour of labour increase together along the line labelled "*Ak* line."

The new growth theory implies that although the productivity curve shows diminishing returns, if capital is interpreted more broadly as physical capital, human capital, and the technologies they embody, then real GDP per hour of labour grows at the same rate as the growth in capital per hour of labour. Real GDP per hour of labour is proportional to capital per hour of labour.

FIGURE 30.9 New Growth Theory

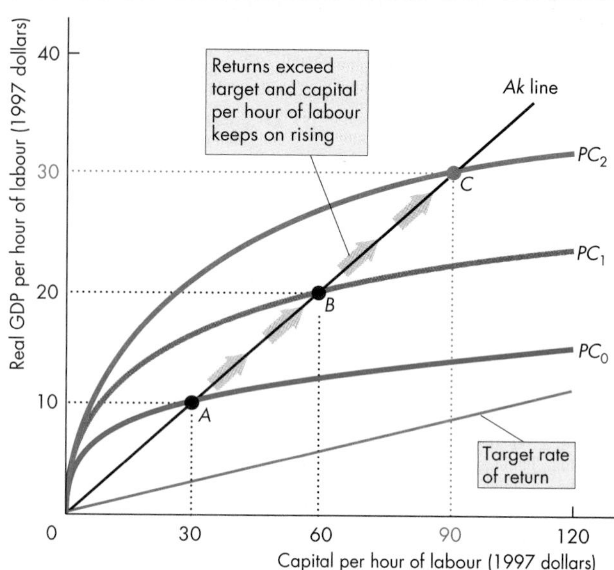

In new growth theory, economic growth results from incentives to innovate and from capital that does not experience diminishing returns. The productivity curve, *PC*, keeps shifting upward, and real GDP per hour of labour and capital per hour of labour grow along the *Ak* line.

Real GDP per hour of labour y is related to capital per hour of labour k by the equation:

$$y = Ak.$$

In Fig 30.9, $A = (1/3)$. When capital per hour of labour is \$30, real GDP per hour of labour is \$10 at point *A*. People look for yet more profit and accumulate yet more capital. The economy expands to point *B*, with capital per hour of labour of \$60 and real GDP per hour of labour of \$20. In pursuit of further profit, technology keeps advancing and capital per hour of labour rises to \$90 with real GDP per hour of labour of \$30, at point *C*. Real GDP per hour of labour and capital per hour of labour increase without limit.

A Perpetual Motion Economy The new growth theory sees the economy as a perpetual motion machine, which Fig. 30.10 illustrates. Insatiable wants lead us to pursue profit, innovate, and create new and better products. New firms start up and old firms go out of business. As firms start up and die, jobs are created and destroyed. New and better jobs

FIGURE 30.10 A Perpetual Motion Machine

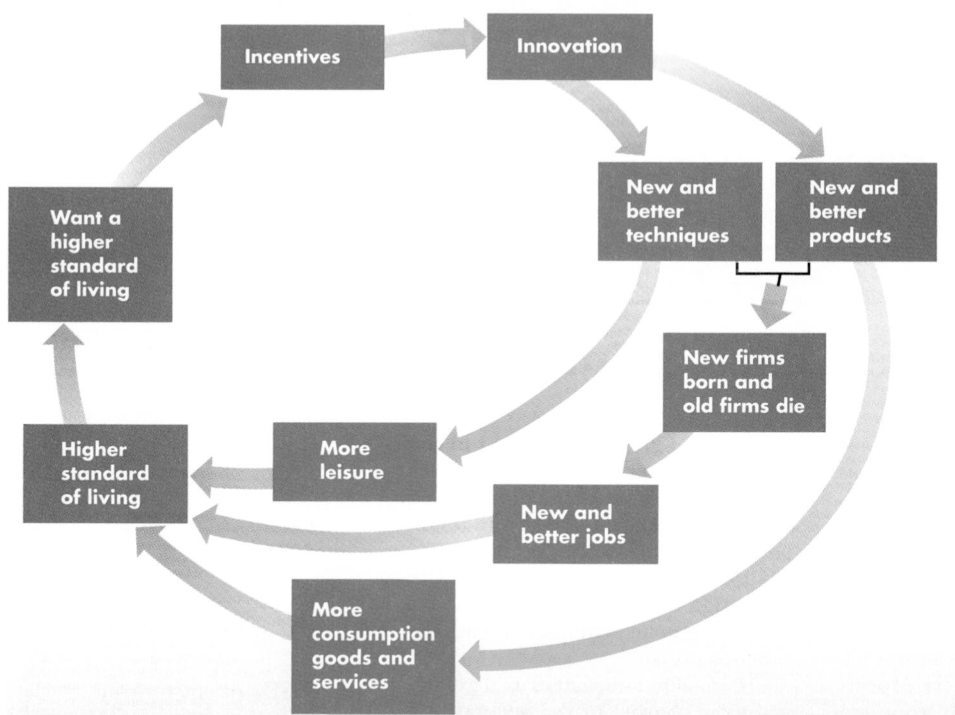

People want a higher standard of living and are spurred by profit incentives to make the innovations that lead to new and better techniques and new and better products, which in turn lead to the birth of new firms and the death of some old firms, new and better jobs, and more leisure and more consumption goods and services. The result is a higher standard of living. But people want a still higher standard of living, and the growth process continues.

Source: Based on a similar figure in *These Are the Good Old Days: A Report on U.S. Living Standards*, Federal Reserve Bank of Dallas 1993 Annual Report.

lead to more leisure and more consumption. But our insatiable wants are still there, so the process continues, going around and around a circle of wants, profits, innovation, and new products.

Sorting Out the Theories

Which theory is correct? Probably none, but they all teach us something of value. The classical theory reminds us that our physical resources are limited and that with no advances in technology, we must eventually hit diminishing returns. Neoclassical theory reaches essentially the same conclusion, but not because of a population explosion. Instead, it emphasizes diminishing returns to capital and reminds us that we cannot keep growth going just by accumulating physical capital. We must also advance technology and accumulate human capital. We must become more creative in our use of scarce resources. New growth theory emphasizes the possible capacity of human resources to innovate at a pace that offsets diminishing returns.

REVIEW QUIZ

1. What is the key idea of classical growth theory that leads to the dismal outcome?
2. What, according to the neoclassical growth theory, is the fundamental cause of economic growth?
3. What is the key proposition of the new growth theory that makes growth persist?

Economic growth is the single most decisive factor influencing a country's living standard. But another is the extent to which the country fully employs its scarce resources. In the next part, we study economic fluctuations and recessions. But before embarking on this new topic, take a look at *Reading Between the Lines* on pp. 724–725 and compare Canada's recent economic growth with that of other major industrial countries.

Forecasting Economic Growth

THE GLOBE AND MAIL, SEPTEMBER 21, 2002

Economists cut back estimates

Forecasters are growing pessimistic about the outlook for growth in the major industrial countries, according to a survey.

In its latest poll, Consensus Economics Inc. found that economists have marked down their growth forecasts for most European countries for this year and 2003. Canadian forecasters trimmed their estimates slightly from what they were expecting in August while their counterparts in the United States raised their hopes a bit.

Each month, London-based Consensus Economics surveys about 240 forecasts in more than 20 countries on where their own economies are heading. The latest survey was conducted Sept. 9.

The consensus among the 13 Canadians in the poll was that Canada's economy will grow 3.4 per cent this year and 3.5 per cent in 2003. That compares with the August predictions of 3.5 per cent for this year and 3.7 per cent for 2003.

Canada grew much faster in the second quarter than all the other Group of Seven leading industrialized countries, the company said in its report, but "questions remain over whether the second-quarter results are a sign of Canadian economic resilience or of an economy lagging the U.S. downturn."

Canadian forecasters said growth will slow sharply in the second half from its robust 5-per-cent annual rate expansion in the first half.

U.S. forecasters lifted their expectations for 2002 growth to 2.4 per cent this month from the 2.3-per-cent expansion they anticipated in August, but left their 2003 prediction of 3.1-per-cent growth unchanged. The outlook for German growth this year has slipped to 0.5 per cent from 1 per cent in the June survey, while forecasters in Britain are now expecting only 1.6-per-cent growth, compared with 1.8 per cent in June.

Essence of the Story

- Each month, Consensus Economics Inc. surveys about 240 economists in more than 20 countries on where their own economies are heading.
- In September 2002, economists lowered their growth forecasts for most European countries for 2002 and 2003.
- Canadian forecasters lowered their estimates slightly while U.S. forecasters increased their estimates.
- Canada grew much faster in the second quarter of 2002 than all the other G7 countries.

Economic Analysis

- The G7 is the seven industrial countries: Canada, France, Germany, Italy, Japan, the United Kingdom, and the United States.

- Consensus Economics Inc. says that Canada was the fastest growing G7 economy in 2002.

- Most reports on economic growth (including this one) do not distinguish between short-term growth of real GDP at different phases of the business cycle and the growth rate of *potential* GDP, which excludes the effects of the business cycle.

- The fact that Canada was the fastest-growing G7 economy in 2002 was a consequence of Canada's current business cycle expansion, which remained strong while other economies slowed.

- The ranking of countries in the growth league table depends on the time period over which we measure growth.

- Figure 1 shows the growth rate of real GDP in the G7 countries between 1972 and 2002. (The data for 2002 are forecasts by the International Monetary Fund made in October 2002.)

- Over this thirty-year period, Japan has grown much more than Canada, the European members of the G7 (Europe Big 4), and the United States, all of which have grown by similar amounts.

- Figure 2 shows growth during the decade 1992–2002. Over this period, Canada tops the table and the United States places second. But the United States was top until 2000. Over this time frame, Japan comes in last.

- Figure 3 looks at the International Monetary Fund (IMF) growth forecast for 2002. Over this very short period, Canada is first and the United States is second, followed by the United Kingdom, France, and Italy, with Germany and Japan coming last.

- Growth rates differ across countries because of differences in saving rates and differences in the pace of technological change.

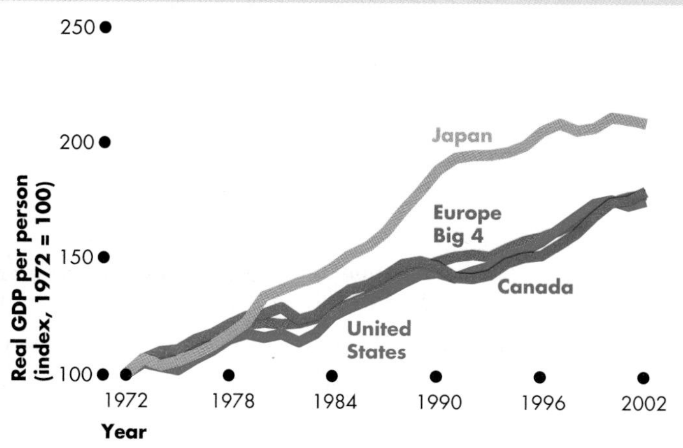

Figure 1 Growth since 1972

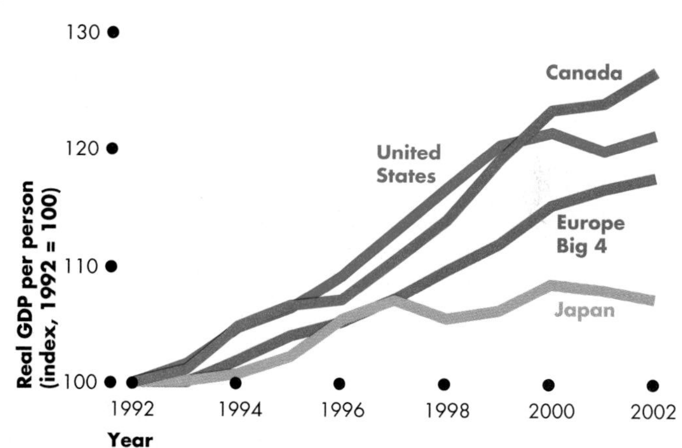

Figure 2 Growth since 1992

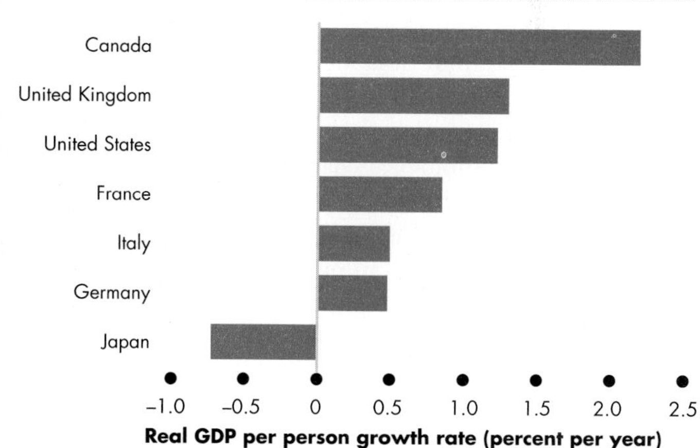

Figure 3 Growth in 2002

SUMMARY

KEY POINTS

Long-Term Growth Trends (pp. 708–710)

- Between 1926 and 2001, real GDP per person in Canada grew at an average rate of 2.2 percent a year. Growth was most rapid during the 1960s and slowest during the 1980s.
- The real GDP per person gaps between Canada and Hong Kong, Korea, Taiwan, and China have narrowed. The gaps between Canada and Central and South America, Africa, and Central Europe have widened.

The Causes of Economic Growth: A First Look (pp. 711–712)

- Economic growth requires an *incentive* system created by markets, property rights, and monetary exchange.
- Economic growth occurs when people save, invest in physical and human capital, and discover new technologies.

Growth Accounting (pp. 713–716)

- Growth accounting measures the contributions of capital accumulation and technological change to productivity growth.
- Growth accounting uses the productivity curve and the one-third rule: A 1 percent increase in capital per hour of labour brings a one-third of 1 percent increase in real GDP per hour of labour.
- During the productivity growth slowdown of the 1970s, technological change made no contribution to real GDP growth.
- It might be possible to achieve faster growth by stimulating saving, stimulating research and development, targeting high-technology industries, encouraging more international trade, and improving the quality of education.

Growth Theories (pp. 717–723)

- In classical theory, when technological advances increase real GDP per person above the *subsistence* level, a population explosion brings diminishing returns to labour and real GDP per person returns to the subsistence level.
- In neoclassical growth theory, when technological advances increase saving and investment, an increase in the capital stock brings diminishing returns to capital and eventually, without further technological change, the capital stock and real GDP per person stop growing.
- In new growth theory, when technological advances increase saving and investment, an increase in the capital stock *does not* bring diminishing returns to capital and growth persists indefinitely.

KEY FIGURES

Figure 30.1 Economic Growth in Canada: 1926–2001, 708
Figure 30.5 How Productivity Grows, 714
Figure 30.6 Growth Accounting and the Productivity Growth Slowdown, 715
Figure 30.7 Classical Growth Theory, 718
Figure 30.8 Neoclassical Growth Theory, 720
Figure 30.9 New Growth Theory, 722

KEY TERMS

Aggregate production function, 713
Classical growth theory, 717
Growth accounting, 713
Labour productivity, 713
Law of diminishing returns, 714
Neoclassical growth theory, 719
New growth theory, 721
One-third rule, 714
Productivity curve, 713
Subsistence real wage rate, 718

PROBLEMS

*1. The following information has been discovered about the economy of Longland. The economy's productivity curve is

Capital per hour of labour (1997 dollars per hour)	Real GDP per hour of labour (1997 dollars per hour)
10	3.80
20	5.70
30	7.13
40	8.31
50	9.35
60	10.29
70	11.14
80	11.94

Does this economy conform to the one-third rule? If so, explain why. If not, explain why not and explain what rule, if any, it does conform to. Explain how you would do the growth accounting for this economy.

2. The following information has been discovered about the economy of Flatland. The economy's productivity curve is

Capital per hour of labour (1997 dollars per hour)	Real GDP per hour of labour (1997 dollars per hour)
20	6.00
40	7.50
60	8.44
80	9.14
100	9.72
120	10.20
140	10.62
160	11.00

Does this economy conform to the one-third rule? If so, explain why. If not, explain why not and explain what rule, if any, it does conform to. Explain how you would do the growth accounting for this economy.

*3. In Longland, described in problem 1, capital per hour of labour in 1999 was $40 and real GDP per hour of labour was $8.31. In 2001, capital per hour of labour was $50 and real GDP per hour of labour was $10.29 an hour.
   a. Does Longland experience diminishing returns? Explain why or why not.
   b. Use growth accounting to find the contribution of the change in capital between 1999 and 2001 to the growth of productivity in Longland.
   c. Use growth accounting to find the contribution of technological change between 1999 and 2001 to the growth of productivity in Longland.

4. In Flatland, described in problem 2, capital per hour of labour in 1999 was $60 and real GDP per hour of labour was $8.44. In 2001, capital per hour of labour was $120 and real GDP per hour of labour was $12.74 an hour.
   a. Does Flatland experience diminishing returns? Explain why or why not.
   b. Use growth accounting to find the contribution of the change in capital between 1999 and 2001 to the growth of productivity in Flatland.
   c. Use growth accounting to find the contribution of technological change between 1999 and 2001 to the growth of productivity in Flatland.

*5. The following information has been discovered about the economy of Cape Despair. Subsistence real GDP is $15 an hour. Whenever real GDP per hour rises above this level, the population grows, and when real GDP per hour of labour falls below this level, the population falls. The productivity curve in Cape Despair is as follows:

Capital per hour of labour (1997 dollars per hour)	Real GDP per hour of labour (1997 dollars per hour)
20	8
40	15
60	21
80	26
100	30
120	33
140	35
160	36

Initially, the population of Cape Despair is constant, and real GDP is at its subsistence level. Then a technological advance shifts the productivity curve upward by $7 at each level of capital per hour of labour.
   a. What are the initial capital per hour of labour and real GDP per hour of labour?

b. What happens to real GDP per hour of labour immediately following the technological advance?
c. What happens to the population growth rate following the technological advance?
d. What is the eventual quantity of capital per hour of labour in Cape Despair?

6. Martha's Island is an economy that behaves according to the neoclassical growth model. The economy has no growth, a target rate of return of 10 percent a year, and the following productivity curve:

Capital per hour of labour (1997 dollars per hour)	Real GDP per hour of labour (1997 dollars per hour)
40	16
80	30
120	42
160	52
200	60
240	66
280	70
320	72

A technological advance shifts the productivity curve upward.
a. What is the initial capital per hour of labour on Martha's Island?
b. What is the initial real GDP per hour of labour?
c. What happens to the return from capital immediately following the technological advance?
d. What happens to the return on capital and the quantity of capital per hour of labour?

*7. Romeria is a country that behaves according to the predictions of new growth theory. The target rate is 3 percent a year. A technological advance increases the demand for capital and raises the rate of return to 5 percent a year. Describe the events that happen in Romeria and contrast them with the events in Martha's Island in problem 6.

8. Suppose that in Romeria, described in problem 7, technological advance slows and the rate of return falls to 3 percent a year. Describe what happens in Romeria.

CRITICAL THINKING

1. After studying *Reading Between the Lines* on pp. 724–725, answer the following questions:
   a. How does the growth rate of real GDP in Canada compare with that of the other G7 nations over the past 30 years, 10 years, and 1 year?
   b. Do you think Canada's real GDP growth is faster than other countries because Canada's potential GDP growth is faster or because Canada has moved from below full employment to above full employment in the comparisons?
   c. Explain why faster real GDP growth does not necessarily mean faster improvements in the standard of living.
2. Is faster economic growth always a good thing? Argue the case for faster growth and the case for slower growth and then reach a conclusion on whether growth should be increased or decreased.

WEB EXERCISES

1. Use the links on the Parkin–Bade Web site to obtain data on real GDP per person for Canada, China, South Africa, and Mexico since 1960.
   a. Draw a graph of the data.
   b. Which country has the lowest real GDP per person and which has the highest?
   c. Which country has experienced the fastest growth rate since 1960 and which the slowest?
   d. Explain why the growth rates in these four countries are ranked in the order you have discovered.
   e. Return to the Penn World Table Web site and obtain data for any four other countries that interest you. Describe and explain the patterns that you find for these countries.
2. Write a memo to your member of Parliament in which you set out the policies you believe the Canadian government must follow to speed up the growth rate of real GDP in Canada.

THE BUSINESS CYCLE

CHAPTER 31

Must What Goes Up Always Come Down?

The 1920s were years of unprecedented prosperity for Canadians. After the horrors of World War I (1914–1918), the economic machine was back at work, producing such technological marvels as cars and airplanes, telephones and vacuum cleaners. Houses and apartments were being built at a frantic pace. Then, almost without warning, in October 1929 came a devastating stock market crash. Overnight, the values of stocks trading on Wall Street and Bay Street fell by 30 percent. During the four succeeding years, there followed the most severe economic contraction in recorded history. By 1933, real GDP had fallen by 30 percent and unemployment had increased to 20 percent of the labour force. What caused the Great Depression? ◆ By the standard of the Great Depression, recent recessions have been mild. But recessions have not gone away. Our economy has experienced 15 recessions since 1920, 10 of which have occurred since the end of World War II in 1945. In 1981, real GDP fell by 3.2 percent. It fell again in 1990 and 1991 by more than 2 percent. It was not until mid-1992 that real GDP returned to its 1989 level. Since the 1990–1991 recession, real GDP has soared. By the end of 2002, it was some 42 percent higher than it had been in the 1990–1991 recession and 39 percent higher than its peak before the 1990–1991 recession. What causes a repeating sequence of recessions and expansions in our economy? Must what goes up always come down? Will we have another recession? When? *Reading Between the Lines* at the end of the chapter explores this question in the context of the state of the Canadian economy at the end of 2002.

◆ We are going to explore the business cycle in this chapter. You will see how all the strands of macroeconomics that you've been following come together and weave a complete picture of the forces and mechanisms that generate economic growth and fluctuations in production, employment and unemployment, and inflation.

After studying this chapter, you will be able to

- **Distinguish among the different theories of the business cycle**
- **Explain the Keynesian and monetarist theories of the business cycle**
- **Explain the new classical and new Keynesian theories of the business cycle**
- **Explain real business cycle theory**
- **Describe the origins of and the mechanisms at work during recessions in the 1990s**
- **Describe the origins of and the mechanisms at work during the Great Depression**

Cycle Patterns, Impulses, and Mechanisms

CYCLES ARE A WIDESPREAD PHYSICAL PHENOMENON. In a tennis match, the ball cycles from one side of the court to the other and back again. Every day, the earth cycles from day to night and back to day. A child on a rocking horse creates a cycle as the horse swings back and forth.

The tennis ball cycle is the simplest. It is caused by the actions of the players. Each time the ball changes direction (at each turning point), the racquet (an outside force) is applied. The day-night-day cycle is the most subtle. The rotation of the earth causes this cycle. No new force is applied each day to make the sun rise and set. It happens because of the design of the objects that interact to create the cycle. Nothing happens at a turning point (sunrise and sunset) that is any different from what is happening at other points except that the sun comes into or goes out of view. The child's rocking horse cycle is a combination of these two cases. To start the horse rocking, some outside force must be exerted (as in the tennis ball cycle). But once the horse is rocking, the to-and-fro cycle continues for some time with no further force being applied (as in the day-night-day cycle). The rocking horse cycle eventually dies out unless the horse is pushed again, and each time the horse is pushed, the cycle temporarily becomes more severe.

The economy is a bit like all three of these examples. It can be hit by shocks (like a tennis ball) that send it in one direction or another, it can cycle indefinitely (like the turning of day into night), and it can cycle in swings that get milder until another shock sets off a new burst of bigger swings (like a rocking horse). While none of these analogies is perfect, they all contain some insights into the business cycle. Different theories of the cycle emphasize different impulses (different tennis racquets) and different cycle mechanisms (different solar system and rocking horse designs).

Although there are several different theories of the business cycle, they all agree about one aspect of the cycle: the central role played by investment and the accumulation of capital.

The Role of Investment and Capital

Whatever the shocks are that hit the economy, they hit one crucial variable: investment. Recessions begin when investment in new capital slows down, and they turn into expansions when investment speeds up. Investment and capital interact like the spinning earth and the sun to create an ongoing cycle.

In an expansion, investment proceeds at a rapid rate and the capital stock grows quickly. But rapid capital growth means that the amount of capital per hour of labour is growing. Equipped with more capital, labour becomes more productive. But the *law of diminishing returns* begins to operate. The law of diminishing returns states that as the quantity of capital increases, with the quantity of labour remaining the same, the gain in productivity from an additional unit of capital eventually diminishes. Diminishing returns to capital bring a fall in the profit rate and with a lower profit rate, the incentive to invest weakens. As a result, investment eventually falls. When it falls by a large amount, recession begins.

In a recession, investment is low and the capital stock grows slowly. In a deep recession, the capital stock might actually decrease. Slow capital growth (or even a decreasing capital stock) means that the amount of capital per hour of labour is decreasing. With a low amount of capital per hour of labour, businesses begin to see opportunities for profitable investment and the pace of investment eventually picks up. As it does so, recession turns into expansion.

The *AS–AD* Model

Investment and capital are a crucial part of the business cycle mechanism, but they are just one part. To study the broader business cycle mechanism, we need a broader framework—the *AS–AD* model. We can use the *AS–AD* model to describe all theories of the business cycle. The theories differ in what they identify as the impulse and in the cycle mechanism. But all theories can be thought of as making assumptions about the factors that make either aggregate supply or aggregate demand fluctuate and about how those assumptions interact to create a business cycle. Business cycle impulses can affect either the supply side or the demand side of the economy or both. There are no pure supply-side theories, so we classify the theories as either

1. Aggregate demand theories
2. Real business cycle theory

We'll study the aggregate demand theories first. Then we'll study real business cycle theory, which is a more recent approach that isolates a shock that has both aggregate supply and aggregate demand effects.

Aggregate Demand Theories of the Business Cycle

Three types of aggregate demand theory of the business cycle have been proposed. They are

- Keynesian theory
- Monetarist theory
- Rational expectations theories

Keynesian Theory

The **Keynesian theory of the business cycle** regards volatile expectations as the main source of economic fluctuations. This theory is distilled from Keynes' *General Theory of Employment, Interest, and Money.* We'll explore the Keynesian theory by looking at its main impulse and the mechanism that converts that impulse into a real GDP cycle.

Keynesian Impulse The impulse in the Keynesian theory of the business cycle is *expected future sales and profits.* A change in expected future sales and profits changes the demand for new capital and changes the level of investment.

Keynes reasoned that profit expectations would be volatile because most of the events that shape the future are unknown and impossible to forecast. So, he reasoned, news or even rumours about future influences on profit (such as tax rate changes, interest rate changes, advances in technology, global economic and political events, or any of the thousands of other relevant factors) have large effects on the expected profit rate.

To emphasize the volatility and diversity of sources of changes in expected sales and profits, Keynes described these expectations as *animal spirits.*

Keynesian Cycle Mechanism In the Keynesian theory, once a change in animal spirits has changed investment, a cycle mechanism begins to operate that has two key elements. First, the initial change in investment has a multiplier effect. The change in investment changes *aggregate* expenditure, real GDP, and disposable income. The change in disposable income changes consumption expenditure, and aggregate demand changes by a multiple of the initial change in investment. (This mechanism is described in detail in Chapter 23, p. 538 and pp. 544–545.) The aggregate demand curve shifts leftward in a recession and rightward in an expansion.

The second element of the Keynesian cycle mechanism is a sticky money wage rate together with a horizontal *SAS* curve. With a horizontal *SAS* curve, swings in aggregate demand translate into swings in real GDP with no changes in the price level.

Figure 31.1 illustrates the Keynesian cycle. The long-run aggregate supply curve is *LAS,* the short-run aggregate supply curve is *SAS,* and the aggregate demand curve is AD_0. Initially, the economy is at full employment (point *A*) with real GDP at $1,000 billion and the price level at 110.

A fall in animal spirits decreases investment and a multiplier process decreases aggregate demand. The aggregate demand curve shifts leftward to AD_1. With

FIGURE 31.1 The Keynesian Cycle

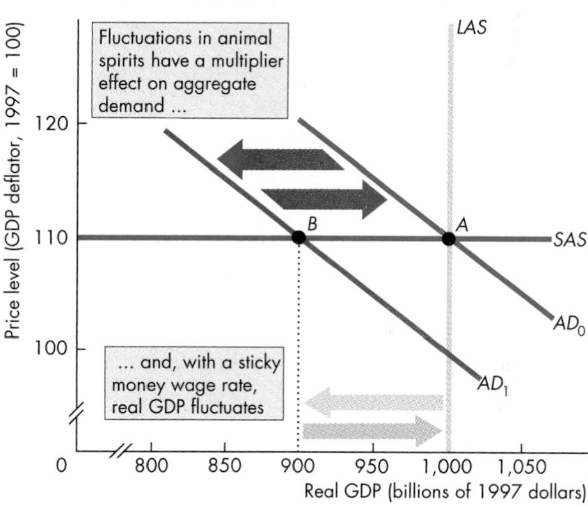

The economy is operating at point *A* at the intersection of the long-run aggregate supply curve (*LAS*), the short-run aggregate supply curve (*SAS*), and the aggregate demand curve (AD_0). A Keynesian recession begins when a fall in animal spirits decreases investment. Aggregate demand decreases and the *AD* curve shifts leftward to AD_1. With a sticky money wage rate, real GDP decreases to $900 billion and the price level does not change. The economy moves to point *B*. An increase in animal spirits has the opposite effect and takes the economy back to point *A*. The economy cycles by bouncing between point *A* and point *B*.

a fixed money wage rate, real GDP decreases to $900 billion and the economy moves to point *B*.

Unemployment has increased and there is a surplus of labour, but the money wage rate does not fall and the economy remains at point *B* until some force moves it away.

That force is a rise in animal spirits, which increases investment. The multiplier process kicks in again and aggregate demand increases. The *AD* curve shifts back to AD_0 and real GDP increases in an expansion to $1,000 billion again.

As long as real GDP remains below potential GDP ($1,000 billion in this example), the money wage rate and the price level remain constant. And real GDP cycles between points *A* and *B*.

Keynes at Above-Full Employment If animal spirits increase investment at full employment, an inflationary gap arises. Real GDP increases temporarily, but soon returns to potential GDP at a higher price level. Figure 31.2 shows this case.

Starting from full employment, at point *A*, an increase in aggregate demand shifts the aggregate demand curve rightward from AD_0 to AD_1. Real GDP increases to $1,100 billion at point *C*. There is now an inflationary gap. Once real GDP exceeds potential GDP and unemployment falls below the natural rate, the money wage rate begins to rise. As it does so, the short-run aggregate supply curve begins to shift from SAS_0 towards SAS_1. Real GDP now begins to decrease and the price level rises. The economy follows the arrows from point *C* to point *D*, the eventual long-run equilibrium.

The Keynesian business cycle is like a tennis match. It is caused by outside forces—animal spirits—that change direction and set off a process that ends at an equilibrium that must be hit again by the outside forces to disturb it.

On the downside, when aggregate demand decreases and unemployment rises, the money wage rate does not change. It is completely rigid in the downward direction. With a decrease in aggregate demand and no change in the money wage rate, the economy gets stuck in a below full-employment equilibrium. There are no natural forces operating to restore full employment. The economy remains in that situation until animal spirits are lifted and investment increases again.

On the upside, if an increase in aggregate demand creates an inflationary gap, the money wage rate rises and the price level also rises. Real GDP returns to potential GDP.

FIGURE 31.2 A Keynesian Inflationary Gap

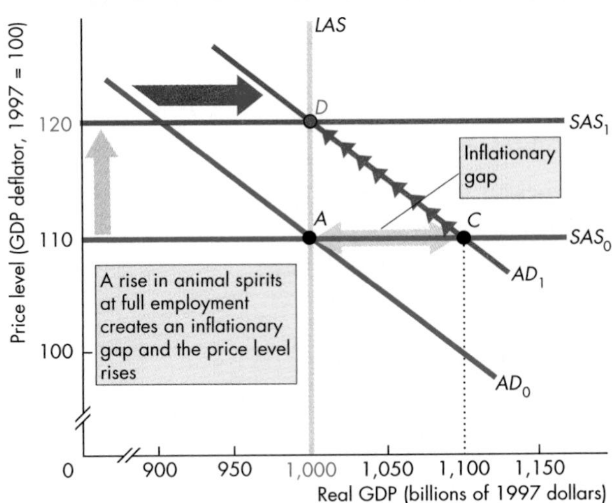

The economy is initially at full employment at point *A*. A Keynesian expansion begins when a rise in animal spirits increases investment. Aggregate demand increases and the *AD* curve shifts rightward from AD_0 to AD_1. With a sticky money wage rate, real GDP increases to $1,100 billion at point *C*. There is now an inflationary gap. The money wage rate rises and the *SAS* curve shifts from SAS_0 towards SAS_1. Real GDP decreases and the price level rises as the economy heads towards point *D*.

Monetarist Theory

The **monetarist theory of the business cycle** regards fluctuations in the quantity of money as the main source of economic fluctuations. This theory is distilled from the writings of Milton Friedman and several other economists. We'll explore the monetarist theory as we did the Keynesian theory, by looking first at its main impulse and second at the mechanism that creates a cycle in real GDP.

Monetarist Impulse The impulse in the monetarist theory of the business cycle is the *growth rate of the quantity of money*. A speedup in money growth brings expansion, and a slowdown in money growth brings recession. The source of the change in the growth rate of the quantity of money is the monetary policy actions of the Bank of Canada.

Monetarist Cycle Mechanism In the monetarist theory, once the Bank of Canada has changed the money growth rate, a cycle mechanism begins to operate that, like the Keynesian mechanism, first affects aggregate demand. When the money growth rate increases, the quantity of real money in the economy increases. Interest rates fall. The foreign exchange rate also falls—the dollar loses value on the foreign exchange market. These initial financial market effects begin to spill over into other markets. Investment and exports increase, and consumers spend more on durable goods. These initial changes in expenditure have a multiplier effect, just as investment has in the Keynesian theory. Through these mechanisms a speedup in money growth shifts the aggregate demand curve rightward and brings an expansion. Similarly, a slowdown in money growth shifts the aggregate demand curve leftward and brings a recession.

The second element of the monetarist cycle mechanism is the response of aggregate supply to a change in aggregate demand. The short-run aggregate supply curve is upward sloping. With an upward-sloping *SAS* curve, swings in aggregate demand translate into swings in both real GDP and the price level. But monetarists believe that real GDP deviations from full employment are temporary.

In monetarist theory, the money wage rate is only *temporarily sticky*. When aggregate demand decreases and unemployment rises above the natural rate, the money wage rate eventually begins to fall. As the money wage rate falls, so does the price level. And through a period of adjustment, real GDP returns to potential GDP and the unemployment rate returns to the natural rate. When aggregate demand increases and unemployment falls below the natural rate, the money wage rate begins to rise. As the money wage rate rises, so does the price level. And through a period of adjustment, real GDP returns to potential GDP and the unemployment rate returns to the natural rate.

Figure 31.3 illustrates a monetarist recession and recovery. The economy is initially at full employment (point *A*) on the long-run aggregate supply curve (*LAS*), the aggregate demand curve (AD_0), and the short-run aggregate supply curve (SAS_0). A slowdown in the money growth rate decreases aggregate demand, and the aggregate demand curve shifts leftward to AD_1. Real GDP decreases to $950 billion, and the economy goes into recession (point *B*).

Unemployment increases and there is a surplus of labour. The money wage rate begins to fall. As the money wage rate falls, the short-run aggregate supply curve starts to shift rightward towards SAS_1. The price level falls, and real GDP begins to expand as the economy moves to point *C*, its new full-employment equilibrium.

The monetarist business cycle is like a rocking horse. It needs an outside force to get it going, but once going, it rocks back and forth (but just once). Starting from full employment, when the quantity of money decreases (or its growth rate slows), the economy cycles with a recession followed by expansion. And if the quantity of money increases (or its growth rate speeds) the economy also cycles but with an expansion followed by recession.

FIGURE 31.3 A Monetarist Recession

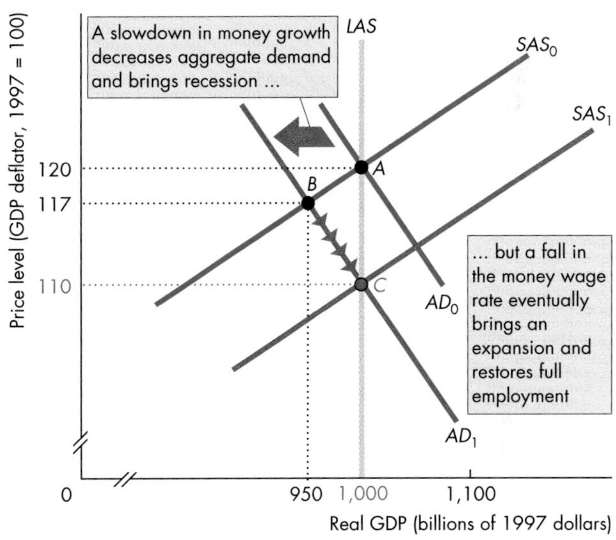

The economy is initially at full employment at point *A*. Real GDP is $1,000 billion and the price level is 120. A monetarist recession begins when a slowdown in money growth decreases aggregate demand. The *AD* curve shifts leftward from AD_0 to AD_1. With a sticky money wage rate, real GDP decreases to $950 billion and the price level falls to 117 as the economy moves from point *A* to point *B*. With a surplus of labour, the money wage rate falls and the *SAS* curve shifts rightward to SAS_1. The price level falls further, and real GDP returns to potential GDP at point *C*.

Figure 31.4 shows the effects of this opposite case in which the quantity of money increases. Here, starting out at point *C*, an increase in the quantity of money increases aggregate demand and shifts the *AD* curve to AD_2. Both real GDP and the price level increase as the economy moves to point *D*, where SAS_1 and AD_2 intersect. With real GDP above potential GDP and unemployment below the natural rate, the money wage rate begins to rise and the *SAS* curve starts to shift leftward towards SAS_2. As the money wage rate rises, the price level also rises and real GDP decreases. The economy moves from point *D* to point *E*, its new full-employment equilibrium.

Although monetarists think that the money wage rate will fall when real GDP is less than potential GDP—when there is a recessionary gap—they do not see this process as being a rapid one.

FIGURE 31.4 A Monetarist Expansion

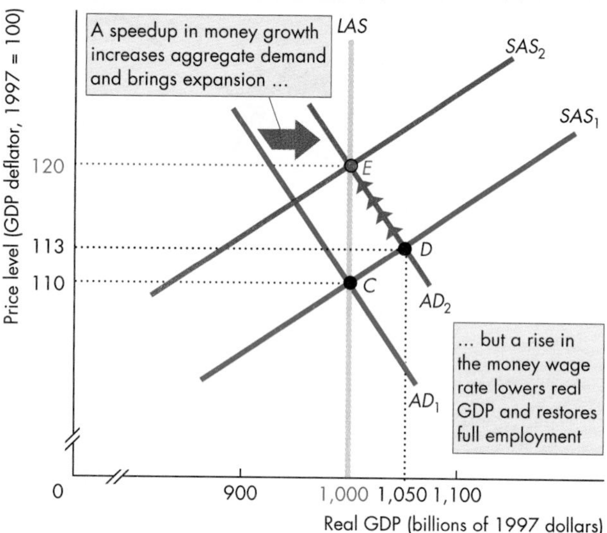

Starting at point *C*, a monetarist expansion begins when an increase in money growth increases aggregate demand and shifts the *AD* curve rightward to AD_2. With a sticky money wage rate, real GDP rises to $1,050 billion, the price level rises to 113, and the economy moves to point *D*. With a shortage of labour, the money wage rate rises and the *SAS* curve shifts towards SAS_2. The price level rises and real GDP decreases to potential GDP as the economy heads towards point *E*.

Rational Expectations Theories

A **rational expectation** is a forecast that is based on all the available relevant information. Rational expectations theories of the business cycle are theories based on the view that the money wage rate is determined by a rational expectation of the price level. Two distinctly different rational expectations theories of the cycle have been proposed. A **new classical theory of the business cycle** regards *unanticipated* fluctuations in aggregate demand as the main source of economic fluctuations. This theory is based on the work of Robert E. Lucas, Jr. and several other economists, including Thomas J. Sargent and Robert J. Barro (see pp. 524–526). A different **new Keynesian theory of the business cycle** also regards *unanticipated* fluctuations in aggregate demand as the main source of economic fluctuations but also leaves room for *anticipated* demand fluctuations to play a role. We'll explore these theories as we did the Keynesian and monetarist theories, by looking first at the main impulse and second at the cycle mechanism.

Rational Expectations Impulse The impulse that distinguishes the rational expectations theories from the other aggregate demand theories of the business cycle is the *unanticipated change in aggregate demand.* A larger than anticipated increase in aggregate demand brings an expansion, and a smaller than anticipated increase in aggregate demand brings a recession. Any factor that influences aggregate demand—for example, fiscal policy, monetary policy, or developments in the world economy that influence exports—whose change is not anticipated, can bring a change in real GDP.

Rational Expectations Cycle Mechanisms To describe the rational expectations cycle mechanisms, we'll deal first with the new classical version. When aggregate demand decreases, if the money wage rate doesn't change, short-run aggregate supply remains unchanged, so real GDP and the price level both decrease. The fall in the price level increases the *real* wage rate, and employment decreases and unemployment rises. In the new classical theory, these events occur only if the decrease in aggregate demand is not anticipated. If the decrease in aggregate demand *is* anticipated, the price level is expected to fall and both firms and workers will agree to a lower money wage rate. By doing so, they can prevent the real wage from rising and avoid a rise in the unemployment rate.

Similarly, if firms and workers anticipate an increase in aggregate demand, they expect the price level to rise and will agree to a higher money wage rate. By doing so, they can prevent the real wage rate from falling and avoid a fall in the unemployment rate below the natural rate.

Only fluctuations in aggregate demand that are unanticipated and not taken into account in wage agreements bring changes in real GDP. *Anticipated* changes in aggregate demand change the price level but they leave real GDP and unemployment unchanged and do not create a business cycle.

New Keynesian economists, like new classical economists, believe that the money wage rate is influenced by rational expectations of the price level. But new Keynesians emphasize the long-term nature of most wage contracts. They say that *today's* money wage rate is influenced by *yesterday's* rational expectations. These expectations, which were formed in the past, are based on old information that might now be known to be incorrect. After they have made a long-term wage agreement, both firms and workers might anticipate a change in aggregate demand, which they expect will change the price level. But because they are locked into their agreement, they are unable to change the money wage rate. So the money wage rate is sticky in the new Keynesian theory and with a sticky money wage rate, even an *anticipated* change in aggregate demand changes real GDP.

New classical economists believe that long-term contracts are renegotiated when conditions change to make them outdated. So they do not regard long-term contracts as an obstacle to money wage flexibility, provided both parties to an agreement recognize the changed conditions. If both firms and workers expect the price level to change, they will change the agreed money wage rate to reflect that shared expectation. In this situation, anticipated changes in aggregate demand change the money wage rate and the price level and leave real GDP unchanged.

The distinctive feature of both versions of the rational expectations theory of the business cycle is the role of *unanticipated* changes in aggregate demand. Figure 31.5 illustrates their effect on real GDP and the price level.

Potential GDP is $1,000 billion and the long-run aggregate supply curve is *LAS*. Aggregate demand is expected to be *EAD*. Given potential GDP and *EAD*, the money wage rate is set at the level that is expected to bring full employment. At this money wage rate, the short-run aggregate supply curve is *SAS*.

Imagine that initially aggregate demand equals expected aggregate demand, so there is full employment. Real GDP is $1,000 billion and the price level is 110, at point *A*. Then, unexpectedly, aggregate demand turns out to be less than expected and the aggregate demand curve shift leftward to AD_0. Many different aggregate demand shocks, such as a slowdown in the money growth rate or a collapse of exports, could have caused this shift. A recession begins. But aggregate demand is expected to be at *EAD*, so the money wage rate doesn't change and the short-run aggregate supply curve remains at *SAS*. Real GDP decreases to $950 billion and the price level falls to 107. The economy moves to point *B*. Unemployment increases and there is a surplus of labour.

FIGURE 31.5 A Rational Expectations Business Cycle

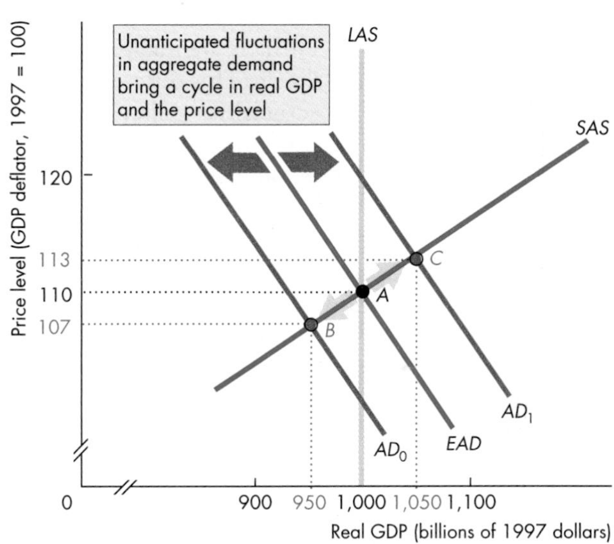

The economy is expected to be at point *A*. As long as aggregate demand is *expected* to be *EAD*, there is no change in the money wage rate and the *SAS* curve does not shift. A rational expectations recession begins when an unanticipated decrease in aggregate demand shifts the *AD* curve leftward to AD_0. Real GDP decreases to $950 billion and the price level falls to 107, at point *B*. A rational expectations expansion begins when an unanticipated increase in aggregate demand shifts the *AD* curve rightward to AD_1. Real GDP increases to $1,050 billion and the price level rises to 113, at point *C*.

A shock that takes aggregate demand to a level that exceeds *EAD* brings an expansion. The aggregate demand curve shifts rightward to AD_1. A speedup in the money growth rate or an export boom might have increased aggregate demand. But aggregate demand is expected to be at *EAD*, so the money wage rate doesn't change and the short-run aggregate supply curve remains at *SAS*. Real GDP increases to $1,050 billion and the price level rises to 113. The economy moves to point *C*. Unemployment is below the natural rate.

Fluctuations in aggregate demand between AD_0 and AD_1 around expected aggregate demand *EAD* bring fluctuations in real GDP and the price level between points *B* and *C*.

The two versions of the rational expectations theory differ in their predictions about the effects of a change in expected aggregate demand. The new classical theory predicts that as soon as expected aggregate demand changes, the money wage rate also changes so the *SAS* curve shifts. The new Keynesian theory predicts that the money wage rate changes only gradually when new contracts are made so that the *SAS* curve moves only slowly. This difference between the two theories is crucial for policy. According to the new classical theory, anticipated policy actions change the price level only and have no effect on real GDP and unemployment. The reason is that when policy is expected to change, the money wage rate changes so the *SAS* curve shifts and offsets the effects of the policy action on real GDP. In contrast, in the new Keynesian theory, because the money wage rate changes only when new contracts are made, even anticipated policy actions change real GDP and can be used in an attempt to stabilize the cycle.

Like the monetarist business cycle, these rational expectations cycles are similar to rocking horses. They need an outside force to get going, but once going the economy rocks around its full employment point. The new classical horse rocks faster and comes to rest more quickly than does the new Keynesian horse.

AS–AD General Theory

All the theories of the business cycle that we've considered can be viewed as particular cases of the more general *AS–AD* theory. In this more general theory, the impulses of both the Keynesian and monetarist theories can change aggregate demand. A multiplier effect makes aggregate demand change by more than any initial change in one of its components. The money wage rate can be viewed as responding to changes in the expected price level. Even if the money wage is flexible, it will change only to the extent that price level expectations change. As a result, the money wage rate will adjust gradually.

Although in all three business cycle theories that we've considered, the cycle is caused by fluctuations in aggregate demand, the possibility that an occasional aggregate supply shock might occur is not ruled out by the aggregate demand theories.

A recession could occur because aggregate supply decreases. For example, a widespread drought that cuts agricultural production could create a recession in an economy that has a large agricultural sector. But these aggregate demand theories of the business cycle regard aggregate supply shocks as rare rather than normal events. Aggregate demand fluctuations are the normal ongoing sources of fluctuations.

REVIEW QUIZ

1. What, according to Keynesian theory, is the main business cycle impulse?
2. What, according to Keynesian theory, are the main business cycle mechanisms? Describe the roles of *animal spirits*, the multiplier, and a sticky money wage rate in this theory.
3. What, according to monetarist theory, is the main business cycle impulse?
4. What, according to monetarist theory, are the business cycle mechanisms? Describe the roles of the Bank of Canada and the quantity of money in this theory.
5. What, according to new classical theory and new Keynesian theory, causes the business cycle? What are the roles of rational expectations and unanticipated fluctuations in aggregate demand in these theories?
6. What are the differences between the new classical theory and the new Keynesian theory concerning the money wage rate over the business cycle?

A new theory of the business cycle challenges the mainstream and traditional aggregate demand theories that you've just studied. It is called the real business cycle theory. Let's look at this new theory of the business cycle.

Real Business Cycle Theory

THE NEWEST THEORY OF THE BUSINESS CYCLE, known as **real business cycle theory** (or RBC theory), regards random fluctuations in productivity as the main source of economic fluctuations. These productivity fluctuations are assumed to result mainly from fluctuations in the pace of technological change, but they might also have other sources such as international disturbances, climate fluctuations, or natural disasters. The origins of real business cycle theory can be traced to the rational expectations revolution set off by Robert E. Lucas, Jr., but the first demonstration of the power of this theory was given by Edward Prescott and Finn Kydland and by John Long and Charles Plosser. Today, real business cycle theory is part of a broad research agenda called *dynamic general equilibrium analysis*, and hundreds of young macroeconomists do research on this topic.

We'll explore RBC theory by looking first at its impulse and second at the mechanism that converts that impulse into a cycle in real GDP.

The RBC Impulse

The impulse in RBC theory is the *growth rate of productivity that results from technological change.* Real business cycle theorists believe this impulse to be generated mainly by the process of research and development that leads to the creation and use of new technologies.

Most of the time, technological change is steady and productivity grows at a moderate pace. But sometimes productivity growth speeds up and occasionally productivity *decreases*—labour becomes less productive, on the average.

A period of rapid productivity growth brings a strong business cycle expansion, and a *decrease* in productivity triggers a recession.

It is easy to understand why technological change brings productivity growth. But how does it *decrease* productivity? All technological change eventually increases productivity. But if, initially, technological change makes a sufficient amount of existing capital (especially human capital) obsolete, productivity temporarily decreases. At such a time, more jobs are destroyed than created and more businesses fail than start up.

FIGURE 31.6 The Real Business Cycle Impulse

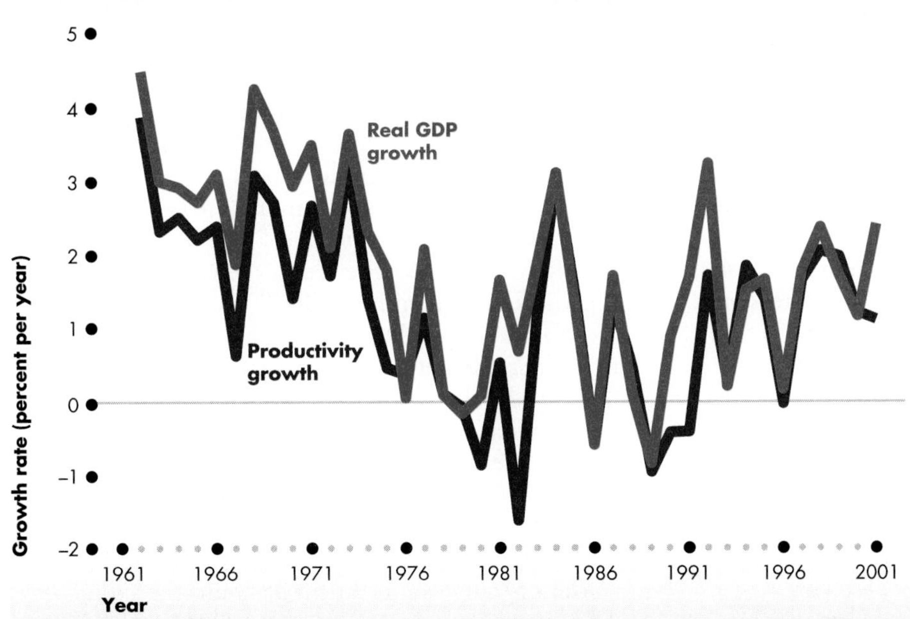

The real business cycle impulse is fluctuations in the growth rate of productivity that are caused by changes in technology. The fluctuations in productivity growth shown here are calculated by using growth accounting (the one-third rule) to remove the contribution of capital accumulation to productivity growth. Productivity fluctuations are correlated with real GDP fluctuations. Economists are not sure what the productivity variable actually measures or what causes it to fluctuate.

Sources: Statistics Canada, CANSIM tables 282-0002, 378–0004, and 380-0002, and authors' calculations.

To isolate the RBC theory impulse, economists use growth accounting, which is explained in Chapter 30, pp. 713–716. Figure 31.6 shows the RBC impulse for Canada from 1961 to 2001. You can see that fluctuations in productivity growth are correlated with real GDP fluctuations. But this RBC impulse is a catchall variable and no one knows what it actually measures or what causes it to fluctuate.

The RBC Mechanism

According to RBC theory, two immediate effects follow from a change in productivity that get an expansion or a contraction going. They are

1. Investment demand changes.
2. The demand for labour changes.

We'll study these effects and their consequences during a recession. In an expansion, they work in the direction opposite to what is described here.

Technological change makes some existing capital obsolete and temporarily decreases productivity. Firms expect the future profits to fall and see their labour productivity falling. With lower profit expectations, they cut back their purchases of new capital, and with lower labour productivity, they plan to lay off some workers. So the initial effect of a temporary fall in productivity is a decrease in investment demand and a decrease in the demand for labour.

Figure 31.7 illustrates these two initial effects of a decrease in productivity. Part (a) shows investment demand, *ID*, and saving supply, *SS*. (In real business cycle theory, saving depends on the real interest rate.) Initially, investment demand is ID_0, and the equilibrium investment and saving are $100 billion at a real interest rate of 6 percent a year. A decrease in productivity decreases investment demand and the *ID* curve shifts leftward to ID_1. The real interest rate falls to 4 percent a year, and investment and saving decrease to $70 billion.

Part (b) shows the demand for labour, *LD*, and the supply of labour, *LS* (which are explained in Chapter 29, pp. 683–686). Initially, the demand for labour is LD_0, and equilibrium employment is 20 billion hours a year at a real wage rate of $15 an hour. The decrease in productivity decreases the demand for labour, and the *LD* curve shifts leftward to LD_1.

Before we can determine the new level of employment and real wage rate, we need to take a ripple effect into account—the key ripple effect in RBC theory.

The Key Decision: When to Work? According to RBC theory, people decide when to work by doing a cost–benefit calculation. They compare the return from working in the current period with the *expected* return from working in a later period. You make such a comparison every day in school. Suppose your goal in this course is to get an A. To achieve this goal, you work pretty hard most of the time. But during the few days before the midterm and final exams, you work especially hard. Why? Because you believe that the return from studying just prior to the exam is greater than the return from studying when the exam is a long time away. So during the term, you take time off for the movies and other leisure pursuits, but at exam time, you work every evening and weekend.

Real business cycle theory says that workers behave like you. They work fewer hours, sometimes zero hours, when the real wage rate is temporarily low, and they work more hours when the real wage rate is temporarily high. But to properly compare the current wage rate with the expected future wage rate, workers must use the real interest rate. If the real interest rate is 6 percent a year, a real wage of $1 an hour earned this week will become $1.06 a year from now. If the real wage rate is expected to be $1.05 an hour next year, today's real wage of $1 looks good. By working longer hours now and shorter hours a year from now, a person can get a 1 percent higher real wage. But suppose the real interest rate is 4 percent a year. In this case, $1 earned now is worth $1.04 next year. Working fewer hours now and more next year is the way to get a 1 percent higher real wage.

So the when-to-work decision depends on the real interest rate. The lower the real interest rate, other things remaining the same, the smaller is the supply of labour. Many economists believe this *intertemporal substitution* effect to be of negligible size. RBC theorists believe that the effect is large, and it is the key element in the RBC mechanism.

You've seen in Fig. 31.7(a) that the decrease in investment demand lowers the real interest rate. This fall in the real interest rate lowers the return to current work and decreases the supply of labour. In Fig. 31.7(b) the labour supply curve shifts leftward to LS_1. The effect of a productivity shock on the demand for labour is larger than the effect of the fall in the real interest rate on the supply of labour. That is, the *LD* curve shifts farther leftward than does the *LS* curve. The real wage rate falls to $14.50 an hour and employment decreases to 19.5 billion hours. A recession has begun, and it is intensifying.

FIGURE 31.7 Capital and Labour Markets in a Real Business Cycle

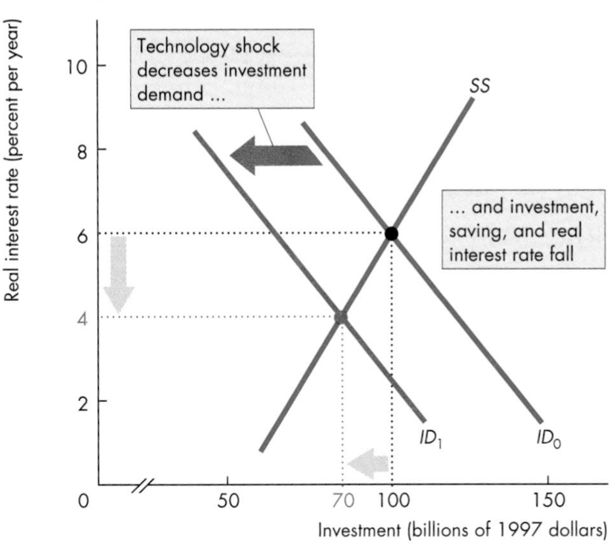

(a) Investment, saving, and interest rate

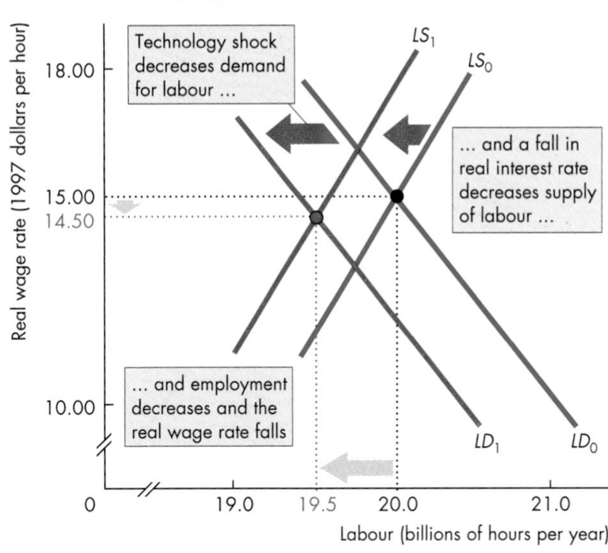

(b) Labour and wage rate

Saving supply is SS and, initially, investment demand is ID_0 (part a). The real interest rate is 6 percent a year, and saving and investment are \$100 billion. In the labour market (part b) the demand for labour is LD_0 and the supply of labour is LS_0. The real wage rate is \$15 an hour, and employment is 20 billion hours.

A technological change temporarily decreases productivity, and both investment demand and the demand for labour decrease. The two demand curves shift leftward to ID_1 and LD_1. In part (a), the real interest rate falls to 4 percent a year and investment and saving decrease. In part (b) the fall in the real interest rate decreases the supply of labour (the when-to-work decision) and the supply curve shifts leftward to LS_1. Employment decreases to 19.5 billion hours, and the real wage rate falls to \$14.50 an hour. A recession is underway.

Real GDP and the Price Level The next part of the RBC story traces the consequences of the changes you've just seen for real GDP and the price level. With a decrease in employment, aggregate supply decreases, and with a decrease in investment demand, aggregate demand decreases. Figure 31.8 illustrates these effects, using the *AS–AD* framework. Initially, the long-run aggregate supply curve is LAS_0, and the aggregate demand curve is AD_0. The price level is 110, and real GDP is \$1,000 billion. There is no short-run aggregate supply curve in this figure because the *SAS* curve has no meaning in RBC theory. The labour market moves relentlessly towards its equilibrium, and the money wage rate adjusts freely (either increases or decreases) to ensure that the real wage rate keeps the quantity of labour demanded equal to the quantity supplied. In RBC theory, unemployment is always at the natural rate, and the natural rate fluctuates over the business cycle because the amount of job search fluctuates.

The decrease in employment decreases total production, and aggregate supply decreases. The *LAS* curve shifts leftward to LAS_1. The decrease in investment demand decreases aggregate demand, and the *AD* curve shifts leftward to AD_1. The price level falls to 107, and real GDP decreases to \$950 billion. The economy is in a recession.

What Happened to Money? The name *real* business cycle theory is no accident. It reflects the central prediction of the theory. Real things, not nominal or monetary things, cause the business cycle. If the quantity of money changes, aggregate demand changes. But if there is no real change—with

FIGURE 31.8 *AS–AD* in a Real Business Cycle

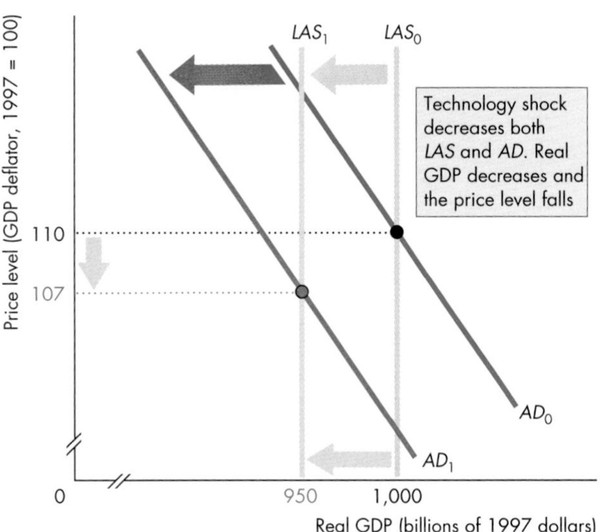

Initially, the long-run aggregate supply curve is LAS_0 and the aggregate demand curve is AD_0. Real GDP is $1,000 billion (which equals potential GDP), and the price level is 110. There is no *SAS* curve in the real business cycle theory because the money wage rate is flexible. The technological change described in Fig. 31.7 temporarily decreases potential GDP, and the *LAS* curve shifts leftward to LAS_1. The fall in investment decreases aggregate demand, and the *AD* curve shifts leftward to AD_1. Real GDP decreases to $950 billion, and the price level falls to 107. The economy has gone into recession.

no change in the use of resources and no change in potential GDP—the change in the quantity of money changes only the price level. In real business cycle theory, this outcome occurs because the aggregate supply curve is the *LAS* curve, which pins real GDP down at potential GDP. So a change in aggregate demand changes only the price level.

Cycles and Growth The shock that drives the business cycle of RBC theory is the same as the force that generates economic growth: technological change. On the average, as technology advances, productivity grows. But it grows at an uneven pace. You saw this fact when you studied growth accounting in Chapter 30. There, we focused on slow-changing trends in productivity growth. Real business cycle theory uses the same idea but says that there are frequent shocks to productivity that are mostly positive but that are occasionally negative.

Criticisms of Real Business Cycle Theory

RBC theory is controversial, and when economists discuss it, they often generate more heat than light. Its detractors claim that its basic assumptions are just too incredible. The money wage rate *is* sticky, they claim, so to assume otherwise is at odds with a clear fact. Intertemporal substitution is too weak, they say, to account for large fluctuations in labour supply and employment with small changes in the real wage rate.

But what really kills the RBC story, say most economists, is an implausible impulse. Technology shocks are not capable of creating the swings in productivity that growth accounting reveals. These swings in productivity are caused by something, they concede, but they are as likely to be caused by *changes in aggregate demand* as by technology. If the fluctuations in productivity are caused by aggregate demand fluctuations, then the traditional demand theories are needed to explain them. Fluctuations in productivity do not cause the cycle but are caused by it!

Building on this theme, the critics point out that the so-called productivity fluctuations that growth accounting measures are correlated with changes in the growth rate of money and other indicators of changes in aggregate demand.

Defence of Real Business Cycle Theory

The defenders of RBC theory claim that the theory works. It explains the macroeconomic facts about the business cycle and is consistent with the facts about economic growth. In effect, a single theory explains *both economic growth and business cycles.* The growth accounting exercise that explains slowly changing trends also explains the more frequent business cycle swings. Its defenders also claim that RBC theory is consistent with a wide range of *micro*economic evidence about labour supply decisions, labour demand and investment demand decisions, and information on the distribution of income between labour and capital.

RBC theorists acknowledge that money growth and the business cycle are correlated. That is, rapid money growth and expansion go together, and slow money growth and recession go together. But, they argue, causation does not run from money to real GDP as the traditional aggregate demand theories state. Instead, RBC theorists view causation as running from real GDP to money—so-called reverse causation. In a recession, the initial fall in investment demand that lowers the real interest rate decreases the demand for bank loans and lowers the profitability of banking. So banks increase their reserves and decrease their loans. The quantity of bank deposits and hence the quantity of money decreases. This reverse causation is responsible for the correlation between money growth and real GDP according to real business cycle theory.

Its defenders also argue that the RBC view is significant because it at least raises the possibility that the business cycle is efficient. The business cycle does not signal an economy that is misbehaving; it is business as usual. If this view is correct, it means that policy designed to smooth the business cycle is misguided. Only by taking out the peaks can the troughs be smoothed out. But peaks are bursts of investment to take advantage of new technologies in a timely way. So smoothing the business cycle means delaying the benefits of new technologies.

REVIEW QUIZ

1. What, according to real business cycle theory, causes the business cycle? What is the role of fluctuations in the rate of technological change?
2. How, according to real business cycle theory, does a fall in productivity growth influence investment demand, the real interest rate, the demand for labour, the supply of labour, employment, and the real wage rate?
3. How, according to real business cycle theory, does a fall in productivity growth influence long-run aggregate supply, aggregate demand, real GDP, and the price level?

You've now reviewed the main theories of the business cycle. Your next task is to examine some actual business cycles. In pursuing this task, we'll focus on two episodes of recession during the 1990s and on the Great Depression of the 1930s.

Recessions During the 1990s

THE 1990S HAVE BROUGHT SOME INTERESTING business cycle experience. In Canada, we had a recession during 1990–1991 followed by a period of sustained expansion. In contrast, Japan experienced a decade of slow growth and ended the decade in serious recession. In 1999, while the three-fifths of the global economy that includes Canada, the United States, and Western Europe continued to expand vigorously, the other two-fifths that includes Japan, some other East Asian countries, and Central Europe were in recession.

In the theories of the business cycle that you've studied, recessions and expansions can be triggered by a variety of forces, some on the aggregate demand side and some on the aggregate supply side. We'll study the shocks that triggered some of these 1990s episodes and the processes at work during them. We'll focus on two cases:

- The recession of 1990–1991
- Japanese stagnation

The Recession of 1990–1991

Three forces were at work in Canada during 1990 that appear to have contributed to the recession and subsequent sluggish growth. They were

- The Bank of Canada's anti-inflation policy
- A slowdown in economic expansion in the United States
- The Canada–United States Free Trade Agreement

The Bank of Canada's Anti-Inflation Policy The Bank of Canada began to pursue low inflation targets in 1988. But because of the time lags involved in the operation of monetary policy, the policy began to bite in 1989 and to bite hard in 1990. The best evidence available suggests that the long-term effects of price stability will be extremely beneficial to Canadians. But its short-term effects are costly.

To achieve price stability, the Bank of Canada must slow the growth rate of money. The extent to which the Bank did slow money growth can be seen in Fig. 31.9. The growth rate of the narrow definition of money, M1, slowed in 1989 to almost zero during 1990. The growth rate of the M2+ definition of money also slowed, but more gently.

FIGURE 31.9 Money Growth: 1989–1995

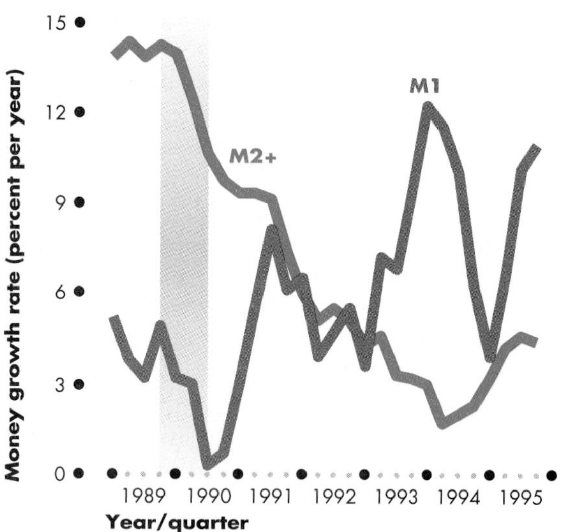

The Bank of Canada began to pursue the goal of low inflation in 1988 and the growth rate of the M2+ money began to slow during 1989. It slowed even further during 1990. The narrow definition of money, M1, barely grew during 1990.

Source: Bank of Canada, *Banking and Financial Statistics*, table E1.

FIGURE 31.10 U.S. and Canadian Real GDP Growth: 1989–1995

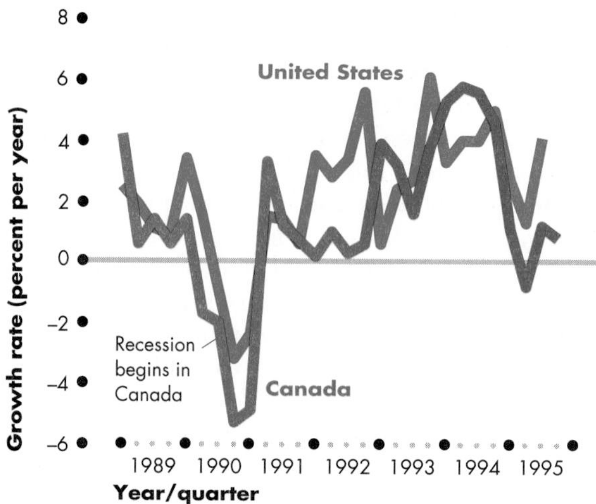

The United States had a recession in 1990, but Canada's recession preceded that in the United States by one quarter. The Canadian recession was deeper than the U.S. recession and with the exception of the first quarter of 1991, Canadian real GDP growth rate was below that of the United States throughout the recession.

Sources: Statistics Canada, CANSIM table 380-0002 and Bureau of Economic Analysis.

A Slowdown in Economic Expansion in the United States After its longest ever period of peacetime expansion, U.S. real GDP growth began to slow in 1989 and 1990 and the United States went into recession in mid-1990, a quarter of a year behind Canada. You can see the performance of real GDP growth in the United States (and Canada) by looking at Fig. 31.10. You can see that the U.S. recession not only lagged behind Canada's recession but was also less severe than Canada's. Also, the U.S. recovery during 1991 and 1992 was more rapid than Canada's.

The slowdown of the U.S. economy brought slower growth in the demand for Canada's exports, which resulted in lower export prices and smaller export volumes.

The Canada–United States Free Trade Agreement The first tariff cuts under the Free Trade Agreement with the United States occurred on January 1, 1989, and the second phase of cuts came a year later. The gradual elimination of tariffs on most of Canada's trade with the United States will result in a rationalization of production activities on both sides of the border. The long-term effects of this rationalization are expected to be beneficial to Canada (and the United States). But like the Bank of Canada's price stability policy, tariff cuts impose costs in the short term. These costs arise because initially, tariff cuts destroy more jobs than they create. Production cutbacks in sectors that must contract precede production increases in sectors that must expand. The result is a temporary decrease in both short-run and long-run aggregate supply as structural unemployment increases.

The elimination of tariffs changes the profitability of businesses, bringing gains to some industries and firms and losses to others. It is easy to see who the immediate winners and losers are. But it is difficult to predict where the gains and losses will ultimately be when the new tariff structure has been in place for some time. As a result, tariff cuts bring an increase in uncertainty that decreases investment in new buildings, plant, and equipment. This decrease in investment decreases aggregate demand.

Let's see how the events we've just described influenced the Canadian economy in 1990–1991.

Aggregate Demand and Aggregate Supply in the 1990–1991 Recession The Canadian economy in the first quarter of 1990, on the eve of the 1990–1991 recession, is shown in Fig. 31.11. The aggregate demand curve was AD_0, the short-run aggregate supply curve was SAS_0, real GDP was $767 billion, and the price level was 89.

The 1990–1991 recession was caused by a decrease in both aggregate demand and aggregate supply. Aggregate demand decreased, initially, because of the slowdown in the growth rate of the quantity of money. This initial source was soon reinforced by the slowdown in the U.S. economy that brought a decline in the growth of exports. These two factors, together with increased uncertainty arising from tariff cuts, triggered a massive decline in investment. The resulting decrease in aggregate demand is shown in Fig. 31.11 by the shift of the aggregate demand curve leftward to AD_1. Aggregate supply decreased partly because of the effects of the Free Trade Agreement and partly because the money wage rate continued to increase throughout 1990 at a rate similar to that in 1989. This decrease in aggregate supply is shown as the shift in the short-run aggregate supply curve leftward to SAS_1. (The figure does not show the long-run aggregate supply curve.)

The combined effect of the decreases in aggregate supply and aggregate demand was a decrease in real GDP to $741 billion—a 3.4 percent decrease—and a rise in the price level to 92—a 3.4 percent rise.

What happened in the labour market during this recession?

FIGURE 31.11 The 1990–1991 Recession

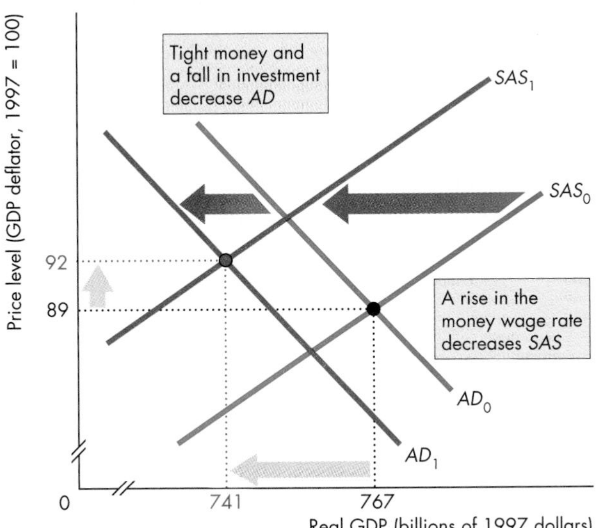

At the beginning of 1990, real GDP was $767 billion and the GDP deflator was 89. Sectoral reallocations resulting from the Canada–U.S. Free Trade Agreement together with increases in the money wage rate decreased aggregate supply, and the short-run aggregate supply curve shifted leftward to SAS_1. Tight monetary policy, a slowdown in the U.S. economy, and increased uncertainty shifted the aggregate demand curve leftward to AD_1. Real GDP decreased to $741 billion, and the economy went into recession.

The Labour Market in the 1990s The unemployment rate increased persistently from the beginning of 1990 to the end of 1992. Figure 31.12 shows two

FIGURE 31.12 Employment and Real Wages

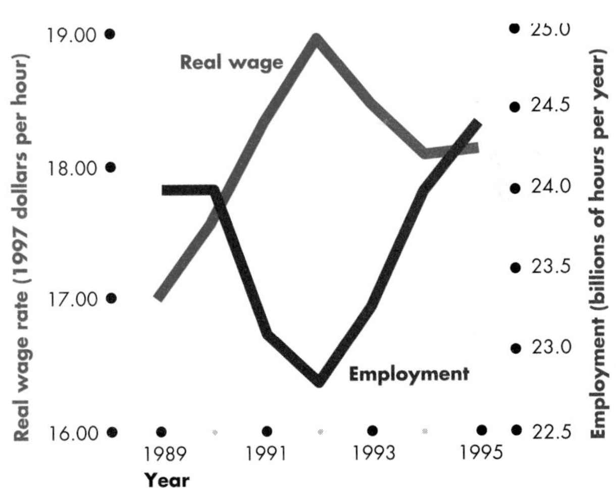

During 1990–1991, the economy was in a recession. Employment decreased, and the real wage rate increased. During the expansion that followed, employment increased and the real wage rate decreased.

Sources: Statistics Canada, CANSIM tables 282-0002, 282-0022, and 380-0001 and authors' calculations.

other facts about the labour market during this period—facts about employment and the real wage rate. As employment decreased through 1990 and 1991, the real wage rate increased. During the recovery, employment increased and the real wage rate decreased. These movements in employment and the real wage rate suggest that the forces of supply and demand do not operate smoothly in the labour market. The money wage rate rose because people didn't anticipate the slowdown in inflation. When inflation did slow down, the real wage increased and the quantity of labour demanded decreased.

Japanese Stagnation

Between 1992 and 2002, when real GDP in Canada expanded by more than 40 percent, Japan's real GDP expanded by a mere 10 percent—a growth rate of less than 1 percent per year. Between 1997 and 2002, Japan's real GDP barely changed.

Why has Japan experienced such a low rate of economic growth during the 1990s and stagnation since 1997? Several factors seem to have combined to produce Japan's problems. And these factors together with the fiscal policies and monetary policies that Japan has pursued provide valuable information about the validity of the alternative theories of the business cycle that you studied earlier in this chapter.

The main factors that have contributed to Japan's weak economy and ultimate recession are

- Collapse of asset prices
- Fiscal policy
- Monetary policy
- Structural rigidities

Collapse of Asset Prices During the second half of the 1980s, land prices and stock prices in Japan increased *threefold.* This increase was much larger than that in Canada, the United States, and Europe. Asset prices increased for three main reasons.

First, investors believed Japan's medium-term and long-term prospects were bright. Second, financial deregulation brought an increase of foreign investment into Japan. Japan's banks expanded loans to finance the purchase of assets whose prices were rising. Third, the Bank of Japan (the nation's central bank) lowered interest rates between 1985 and 1987 and permitted a rapid growth rate of money. The motivation for rapid monetary expansion was to prevent the yen from rising and the U.S. dollar from falling in the foreign exchange market. (See Chapter 34, pp. 822–823 for an explanation of how monetary policy influences the foreign exchange rate.)

Asset prices collapsed in 1990. And the collapse created a wealth effect. Saving and consumption were not much affected by the decrease in wealth. But investment expenditure decreased sharply and so did aggregate demand. And with a lower investment rate, the capital stock and potential GDP grew more slowly.

Fiscal Policy From 1991 through 1996, Japan pursued ambitious and substantial fiscal policies to stimulate the economy. In 1991, the government of Japan had a budget surplus equal to 3 percent of GDP. By 1996, this surplus had been transformed into a deficit equal to more than 7 percent of GDP. Six major *discretionary* actions occurred, which are detailed in Table 31.1, that added 12.9 percent to aggregate expenditure. With its associated multiplier effects, this represents an enormous increase in aggregate demand relative to what it would have been in the absence of stimulation. But the stimulation was not persistent during the 1990s.

The removal of temporary tax cuts and cuts in government investment expenditures *lowered* aggregate expenditure by 3 percent of real GDP in 1996–1997. This fiscal policy tightening decreased aggregate demand and contributed to the recession of 1998.

Monetary Policy The Bank of Japan lowered its official interest rate (called the official discount rate or ODR) from 6 percent in 1991 to 1.75 percent by the end of 1993 and to 0.5 percent by 1995. The ODR

TABLE 31.1 Fiscal Stimulation in Japan

Date proposed	Total stimulation (percent of GDP)
August 1992	2.3
April 1993	2.8
September 1993	1.3
February 1994	3.2
September 1995	3.0
Mid-1996–mid-1997	−3.0
April 1998	3.3
Total	**12.9**

Source: Bank of Japan.

FIGURE 31.13 Japan's Sliding Growth Rate

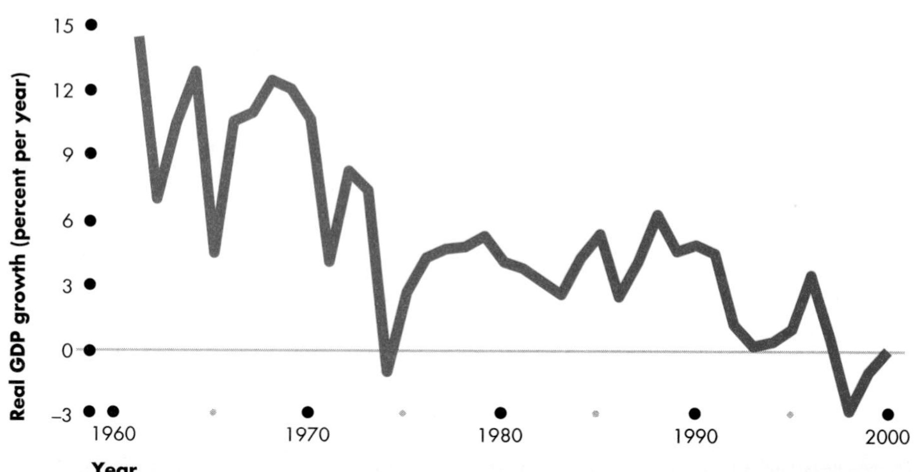

Japan's economic growth rate has been on a slide for many years. Growth of 10 percent a year on the average during the 1960s was followed by growth of 4 percent a year on the average during the 1970s and 1980s and by less than 1 percent a year on the average during the 1990s.

Sources: The Penn World Table: An Expanded Set of International Comparisons, 1950–1988, *Quarterly Journal of Economics*, May 1991, 327–368. 1993–2001, *World Economic Outlook*, International Monetary Fund, Washington D.C., October 2002.

has remained at this level since 1995. Despite these large cuts in the interest rate, a lower inflation rate meant that the real interest rate did not fall as much and so did not act as a stimulus to investment. Also, a strong yen limited the growth of export demand.

Since 1996, a weaker yen and lower real short-term interest rates have had a small but positive effect on aggregate demand in Japan.

Structural Problems Market distortions in agriculture, transportation, retail and wholesale trades, and construction that protect inefficient farms and firms create a lack of competition and low productivity growth. Rich countries such as the United States, Canada, and those in Western Europe have experienced a process of de-industrialization as manufacturing processes have migrated to poorer countries and have been replaced by rapid expansion in the service sector. Japan has not shared this experience.

Japan's structural problems are real, supply-side problems. These problems have brought a gradually falling growth rate of real GDP over many years. Figure 31.13 shows this steadily falling growth rate.

This aspect of Japan's business cycle is an example of a real business cycle. It is a slowdown in productivity growth that slows the rate of increase in long-run aggregate supply. Slower productivity growth works through the real business cycle mechanism described earlier in this chapter. It reduces the demand for capital and labour and decreases potential GDP.

If this explanation for Japan's problems is the correct one, no amount of fiscal and monetary stimulation will end the recession.

REVIEW QUIZ

1. What events triggered Canada's 1990–1991 recession?
2. What role was played by external shocks and by policy?
3. What mechanisms translated the shocks into a recession?
4. What factors contributed to the slow growth and eventual stagnation in Japan?

You've now seen how business cycle theory can be used to interpret Canada's recession of 1990–1991 and Japan's stagnation of the 1990s. We're now going to use business cycle theory to explain the greatest of recessions—the Great Depression that engulfed the global economy during the 1930s.

The Great Depression

THE LATE 1920S WERE YEARS OF ECONOMIC boom. New houses and apartments were built on an unprecedented scale, new firms were created, and the capital stock of the nation expanded. At the beginning of 1929, Canadian real GDP equalled potential GDP and the unemployment rate was only 2.9 percent.

But as that eventful year unfolded, increasing signs of economic weakness began to appear. The most dramatic events occurred in October when the stock market collapsed. Stocks lost more than one-third of their value in two weeks. The four years that followed were a period of monstrous economic depression.

We'll describe the recession by using the *AS–AD* model and identify the forces that made aggregate demand and aggregate supply change.

Figure 31.14 shows the dimensions of the Great Depression and the changes in aggregate demand and aggregate supply that occurred. On the eve of the Great Depression in 1929, the economy was on aggregate demand curve AD_{29} and short-run aggregate supply curve SAS_{29}. Real GDP was $87 billion (1997 dollars) and the GDP deflator was 7.1.

In 1930, there was a widespread expectation that the price level would fall, and the money wage rate fell. With a lower money wage rate, short-run aggregate supply increased. But increased pessimism and uncertainty decreased investment and the demand for consumer durables. Aggregate demand decreased. In 1930, the economy went into recession as real GDP decreased by about 7 percent. The price level also fell by a similar amount.

In a normal recession, the economy might have remained below full employment for a year or so and then started an expansion. But the recession of 1930 was not a normal one. In 1930 and for the next two years, the economy was further bombarded with huge negative aggregate demand shocks (the sources of which we'll look at in a moment). The aggregate demand curve shifted leftward all the way to AD_{33}. With a depressed economy, the price level was expected to fall and the money wage rate fell in line with those expectations. As a result, the aggregate supply curve shifted rightward to SAS_{33}. But the size of the shift of the short-run aggregate supply curve was much less than the decrease in aggregate demand. As a result, the aggregate demand curve and the short-run aggregate supply curve intersected in 1933 at a real GDP of $60 billion (a decrease of 31 percent from 1929) and a GDP deflator of 5.8 (a fall of 18 percent from 1929).

FIGURE 31.14 The Great Depression

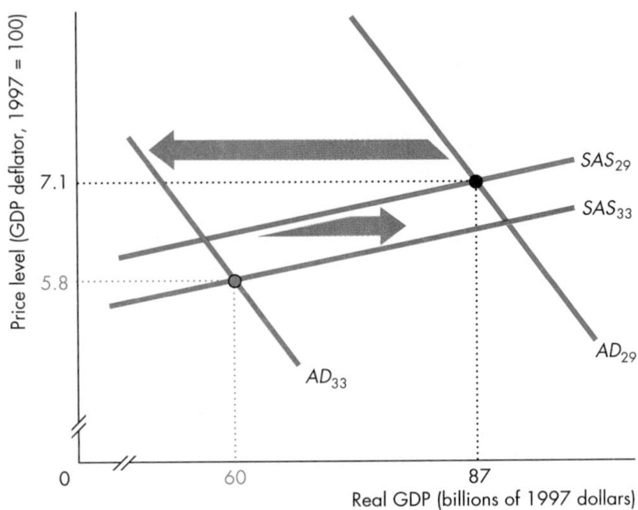

In 1929, real GDP was $87 billion and the GDP deflator was 7.1—at the intersection of AD_{29} and SAS_{29}. In 1930, increased pessimism and uncertainty decreased aggregate demand. Real GDP and the price level fell, and the economy went into recession. In the next three years, decreases in money growth and investment decreased aggregate demand and shifted the aggregate demand curve to AD_{33}. With the price level expected to fall, the money wage rate fell and the short-run aggregate supply curve shifted to SAS_{33}. By 1933, real GDP had decreased to $60 billion (69 percent of its 1929 level) and the price level had fallen to 5.8 (82 percent of its 1929 level).

Although the Great Depression brought enormous hardship, the distribution of that hardship was uneven. Twenty percent of the work force had no jobs at all. Also at that time, there were virtually no organized social assistance and unemployment programs in place. So many families had virtually no income. But the pocketbooks of those who kept their jobs barely noticed the Great Depression. It is true that the money wage rate fell. But at the same time, the price level fell by almost exactly the same percentage, so the real wage rate remained constant. So those who had jobs continued to be paid a wage rate that had roughly the same buying power at the depth of the Great Depression as in 1929.

You can begin to appreciate the magnitude of the Great Depression if you compare it with the 1990–1991 recession. In 1990, real GDP fell by 3.4 percent. In comparison, from 1929 to 1933, it fell by 31 percent. A 1999 Great Depression of the same magnitude would lower income per person to its level of more than 20 years earlier.

Why the Great Depression Happened

The late 1920s were years of economic boom, but they were also years of increasing uncertainty. The main source of increased uncertainty was international. The world economy was going through tumultuous times. The patterns of world trade were changing as Britain, the traditional economic powerhouse of the world, began its period of relative economic decline and new economic powers such as Japan began to emerge. International currency fluctuations and the introduction of restrictive trade policies by many countries (see Chapter 33) further increased the uncertainty faced by firms. There was also domestic uncertainty arising from the fact that there had been such a strong boom in recent years, especially in the capital goods sector and housing. No one believed that this boom could continue, but there was great uncertainty as to when it would end and how the pattern of demand would change.

This environment of uncertainty led to a slowdown in consumer spending, especially on new homes and household appliances. By the fall of 1929, the uncertainty had reached a critical level and contributed to the stock market crash. The stock market crash, in turn, heightened people's fears about economic prospects in the foreseeable future. Fear fed fear. Investment collapsed. The building industry almost disappeared. An industry that had been operating flat out just two years earlier was now building virtually no new houses and apartments. It was this drop in investment and a drop in consumer spending on durables that led to the initial decrease in aggregate demand.

At this stage, what became the Great Depression was no worse than many previous recessions had been. What distinguishes the Great Depression from previous recessions are the events that followed between 1930 and 1933. But economists, even to this day, have not come to agreement on how to interpret those events. One view, argued by Peter Temin, is that spending continued to fall for a wide variety of reasons—including a continuation of increasing pessimism and uncertainty.[1] According to Temin's view, the continued contraction resulted from a collapse of expenditure that was independent of the decrease in the quantity of money. The investment demand curve shifted leftward. Milton Friedman and Anna J. Schwartz have argued that the continuation of the contraction was almost exclusively the result of the subsequent worsening of financial and monetary conditions in the United States.[2] According to Friedman and Schwartz, it was a severe cut in the quantity of U.S. money that lowered U.S. aggregate demand and that prolonged the contraction and deepened the depression. Recently, Ben Bernanke, Barry Eichengreen, and James Hamilton have added further to our understanding of the Great Depression by explaining how it was transmitted among countries by the attempts of central banks to increase their gold reserves.[3]

As a result of these recent efforts to probe more deeply into the causes of the Great Depression, the range of disagreement has narrowed. Everyone now agrees that increased pessimism and uncertainty lowered investment demand, and that there was a massive contraction of the quantity of real money. Temin and his supporters assign primary importance to the fall in autonomous expenditure and secondary importance to the fall in the quantity of money. Friedman and Schwartz and their supporters assign primary responsibility to the quantity of money and regard the other factors as being of limited importance.

Let's look at the contraction of U.S. money a bit more closely. Between 1929 and 1933, the nominal quantity of money in the United States decreased by 20 percent. This decrease in money was not directly induced by the Federal Reserve's actions. The *monetary base* (currency in circulation and bank reserves) hardly fell at all. But the bank deposits component of money suffered an enormous collapse. It did so primarily because a large number of banks failed. Before

[1]Peter Temin, *Did Monetary Forces Cause the Great Depression?* (New York: W. W. Norton, 1976).

[2]This explanation was developed by Milton Friedman and Anna J. Schwartz in *A Monetary History of the United States 1867–1960* (Princeton: Princeton University Press, 1963), Chapter 7.

[3]Ben Bernanke, "The Macroeconomics of the Great Depression: A Comparative Approach," *Journal of Money, Credit, and Banking,* 28 (1995), pp. 1–28; Barry Eichengreen, *Golden Fetters: The Gold Standard and the Great Depression, 1919–1939* (New York: Oxford University Press, 1992); and James Hamilton, "The Role of the International Gold Standard in Propagating the Great Depression," *Contemporary Policy Issues,* 6 (1988), pp. 67–89.

the Great Depression, fuelled by increasing stock prices and booming business conditions, bank loans expanded. But after the stock market crash and the downturn, many borrowers found themselves in hard economic times. They could not pay the interest on their loans, and they could not meet the agreed repayment schedules. Banks had deposits that exceeded the realistic value of the loans that they had made. When depositors withdrew funds from the banks, the banks lost reserves and many of them simply couldn't meet their depositors' demands to be repaid.

Bank failures feed on themselves and create additional failures. Seeing banks fail, people become anxious to protect themselves and so take their money out of the banks. Such were the events in the United States in 1930. The quantity of notes and coins in circulation increased and the volume of bank deposits declined. But the very action of taking money out of the bank to protect one's wealth accelerated the process of banking failure. Banks were increasingly short of cash and unable to meet their obligations.

Monetary contraction also occurred in Canada, although on a less serious scale than in the United States. In Canada, the quantity of money declined during 1929 to 1933 but at a steady 5 percent a year in contrast to the whopping 20 percent in the United States. Also, we had much less severe problems with bank failures than Americans did.

What role did the stock market crash of 1929 play in producing the Great Depression? It certainly created an atmosphere of fear and panic, and probably also contributed to the overall air of uncertainty that dampened investment spending. It also reduced the wealth of stockholders, encouraging them to cut back on their consumption spending. But the direct effect of the stock market crash on consumption, although a contributory factor to the Great Depression, was not the major source of the drop in aggregate demand. It was the collapse in investment arising from increased uncertainty that brought the 1930 decline in aggregate demand.

But the stock market crash was a predictor of severe recession. It reflected the expectations of stockholders concerning future profit prospects. As those expectations became pessimistic, people sold their stocks. There were more sellers than buyers and the prices of stocks were bid lower and lower. That is, the behaviour of the stock market was a consequence of expectations about future profitability and those expectations were lowered as a result of increased uncertainty.

Can It Happen Again?

Since, even today, we have an incomplete understanding of the causes of the Great Depression, we are not able to predict such an event or to be sure that it cannot occur again. But there are some significant differences between the economy of the 2000s and that of the 1930s that make a severe depression much less likely today than it was 60 years ago. The most significant features of the economy that make severe depression less likely today are

- Bank deposit insurance
- Bank of Canada's role as lender of last resort
- Taxes and government spending
- Multi-income families

Let's examine these in turn.

Bank Deposit Insurance In 1967, the government of Canada established the Canada Deposit Insurance Corporation (CDIC). The CDIC insures bank deposits for up to $60,000 per deposit so that most depositors need no longer fear bank failure. If a bank fails, the CDIC pays the deposit holders.

Similar arrangements have been introduced in the United States, where deposits up to $100,000 are insured by the Federal Deposit Insurance Corporation. With government-insured bank deposits, the key event that turned a fairly ordinary recession into the Great Depression is most unlikely to occur. It was the fear of bank failure that caused people to withdraw their deposits from banks. The aggregate consequence of these individually rational acts was to cause the very bank failures that were feared. With deposit insurance, most depositors have nothing to lose if a bank fails and so have no incentive to take actions that are likely to give rise to that failure.

Although bank failure was not a severe problem in Canada during the Great Depression, it clearly was an important factor in intensifying the depression in the United States. And the severity of the U.S. depression had an impact on Canada and the rest of the world.

Bank of Canada's Role as Lender of Last Resort The Bank of Canada is the lender of last resort in the Canadian economy. If a single bank is short of reserves, it can borrow reserves from other banks. If the entire banking system is short of reserves, banks can borrow from the Bank of Canada. By making reserves available (at a suitable interest rate), the Bank of Canada is able to make the quantity of reserves in the banking system respond flexibly to the demand for those reserves. Bank failure can be prevented, or at least contained, to cases where bad management practices are the source of the problem. Widespread failures of the type that occurred in the Great Depression can be prevented.

It is interesting to note, in this regard, that during the weeks following the October 1987 stock market crash, Bank of Canada Governor John Crow and Federal Reserve Chairman Alan Greenspan used every opportunity available to remind the world banking and financial community of their ability and readiness to maintain calm financial conditions and to supply sufficient reserves to ensure that the banking system did not begin to contract.

Taxes and Government Spending The government sector was a much smaller part of the economy in 1929 than it has become today. On the eve of that earlier recession, government expenditures on goods and services were less than 11 percent of GDP. Today, government expenditures exceed 20 percent of GDP. Government transfer payments were about 5 percent of GDP in 1929. Today, they are 20 percent of GDP.

A larger level of government expenditures on goods and services means that when recession hits, a large component of aggregate demand does not decline. But it is government transfer payments that are the most sensitive economic stabilizer. When the economy goes into recession and depression, more people qualify for unemployment benefits and social assistance. As a consequence, although disposable income decreases, the extent of the decrease is moderated by the existence of such programs. Consumption expenditure, in turn, does not decline by as much as it would in the absence of such government programs. The limited decline in consumption spending further limits the overall decrease in aggregate expenditure, thereby limiting the magnitude of an economic downturn.

Multi-Income Families At the time of the Great Depression, families with more than one wage earner were much less common than they are today. The labour force participation rate in 1929 was 58 percent. Today, it is 66 percent. Thus even if the unemployment rate increased to around 20 percent today, close to 53 percent of the adult population would actually have jobs. During the Great Depression, only 46 percent of the adult population had work. Multi-income families have greater security than single-income families. The chance of both (or all) income earners in a family losing their jobs simultaneously is much lower than the chance of a single earner losing work. With greater family income security, family consumption is likely to be less sensitive to fluctuations in family income that are seen as temporary. Thus when aggregate income falls, it does not induce a cut in consumption. For example, during the 1982 and 1990–1991 recessions, as real GDP fell personal consumption expenditure actually increased.

For the four reasons we have just reviewed, it appears the economy has better shock-absorbing characteristics today than it had in the 1920s and 1930s. Even if there is a collapse of confidence leading to a decrease in investment, the recession mechanism that is now in place will not translate that initial shock into the large and prolonged decrease in real GDP and increase in unemployment that occurred more than 60 years ago.

Because the economy is now more immune to severe recession than it was in the 1930s, even a stock market crash of the magnitude that occurred in 1987 had barely noticeable effects on spending. A crash of a similar magnitude in 1929 resulted in the near collapse of housing investment and consumer durable purchases. In the period following the 1987 stock market crash, investment and spending on durable goods hardly changed.

None of this is to say that there might not be a deep recession or even a Great Depression in the future. But it would take a very severe shock to trigger one.

◆ We have now completed our study of the business cycle. You can put what you've learned to work examining the prospects for expansion and recession in the United States and Canada in *Reading Between the Lines* on pp. 750–751.

We have also completed our study of the science of macroeconomics and learned about the influences on long-term economic growth and inflation as well as the business cycle. We have discovered that these issues pose huge policy challenges. How can we speed up the rate of economic growth while at the same time keeping inflation low and avoiding big swings of the business cycle? Our task in the next chapter is to study these macroeconomic policy challenges.

READING BETWEEN THE LINES

Fighting a North American Recession

OTTAWA CITIZEN, NOVEMBER 7, 2002

U.S. Fed battles prospect of double-dip

Increasingly worried that U.S. economic growth is close to stalling, Federal Reserve officials cut a key short-term interest rate yesterday to its lowest level in more than four decades to help lift the economy over what they called "this current soft spot."

The Fed's top policy-making group, the Federal Open Market Committee, cut its target for overnight interest rates by a half-percentage point to 1.25 per cent. Separately, the Fed reduced a companion rate governing what banks pay when they borrow from a regional Federal Reserve bank to only 0.75 per cent, the lowest in the Fed's 89-year history.

Those extraordinarily low rates are a sign of how seriously Fed Chairman Alan Greenspan and other Fed officials regard the failure of the U.S. economy to sustain a stronger recovery this year.

In Ottawa last night, Finance Minister John Manley said the lack of confidence in the U.S. economy shown in yesterday's steeper-than-expected interest-rate cut makes the Canadian government more cautious about risks in its fiscal forecasts. "If the U.S. economy goes back into recession, it will definitely affect us," he told business executives and financial workers at a budget-consultation meeting. ...

The half-point rate cut is seen as good news for the Canadian economy, which itself emitted further symptoms of weakness yesterday with news that builders have cut construction plans and that bankruptcies have edged up.

"With this kind of a shot in the arm, maybe the U.S. economy will improve in '03 and that will help Canada," said Patti Croft, economist at Sceptre Investment Counsel Ltd.

Statistics Canada said the value of building permits fell in September for the second straight month in both residential and the non-residential sectors, and Industry Canada said there were 7,347 business and consumer bankruptcies in September, up six per cent from 6,920 a year earlier. ...

Essence of the Story

- The U.S. economy was in a weak expansion from recession in November 2002 and the Federal Reserve (the Fed) wanted to avoid a slip into a second recession.
- To prevent recession, the Fed cut overnight interest rates by a half-percentage point to 1.25 percent and cut the discount rate (like Canada's bank rate) to 0.75 percent, the lowest in the Fed's 89-year history.
- The Canadian economy also showed symptoms of slower growth with the value of building permits falling for a second straight month and bankruptcies increasing.
- The cut in the U.S. interest rate was seen as good news for Canada.
- Finance Minister John Manley said that a U.S. recession would place a strain on the Canadian government's budget.

Economic Analysis

- The United States went into recession in March 2001 and a new expansion probably began before the end of 2001.

- But the expansion was slow and real GDP remained below potential GDP through 2002.

- Figure 1 shows the path of potential GDP and real GDP in the United States from the first quarter of 2000 to the third quarter of 2002.

- In mid-2001, the U.S. economy moved from above-full employment equilibrium with an inflationary gap to below-full employment equilibrium with a recessionary gap.

- Figure 2 illustrates the situation in the United States at the end of 2002 using the *AS–AD* model.

- Potential GDP was $9,600 billion on long-run aggregate supply curve *LAS*. Short-run aggregate supply was *SAS* and aggregate demand was AD_0.

- Equilibrium real GDP was $9,550 billion, the price level was 111, and there was a recessionary gap of $50 billion.

- The Federal Reserve feared that aggregate demand might decrease towards AD_1, which would bring recession.

- To try to avoid recession, the Federal Reserve cut the interest rate. The hope was that the lower interest rate would increase aggregate demand towards AD_2 and restore full employment.

- Figure 3 illustrates the situation in Canada at the end of 2002 using the *AS–AD* model.

- Potential GDP was $1,065 billion on long-run aggregate supply curve *LAS*. Short-run aggregate supply was *SAS* and aggregate demand was AD_0.

- Equilibrium real GDP was $1,065 billion, the price level was 108, and there was full employment.

- A recession in the United States would decrease Canadian aggregate demand towards AD_1, and bring recession in Canada.

- Signs of a decrease in Canadian aggregate demand—falling building permits and increasing bankruptcies—were already present in the fourth quarter of 2002.

- The forces leading to a decrease in Canadian aggregate demand might be countered by a higher real GDP in the United States.

- If U.S. aggregate demand increased to AD_2 (in Fig. 2), U.S. demand for Canadian-produced goods and services would increase, so Canadian aggregate demand might remain close to AD_0 (in Fig. 3) with the economy at full employment.

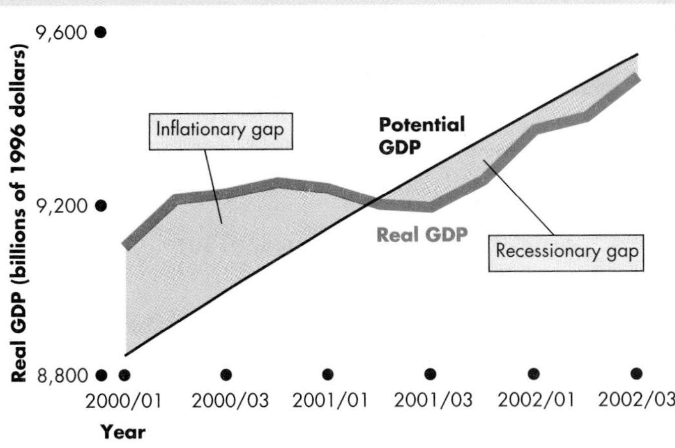

Figure 1 U.S. real GDP and potential GDP: 2000–2002

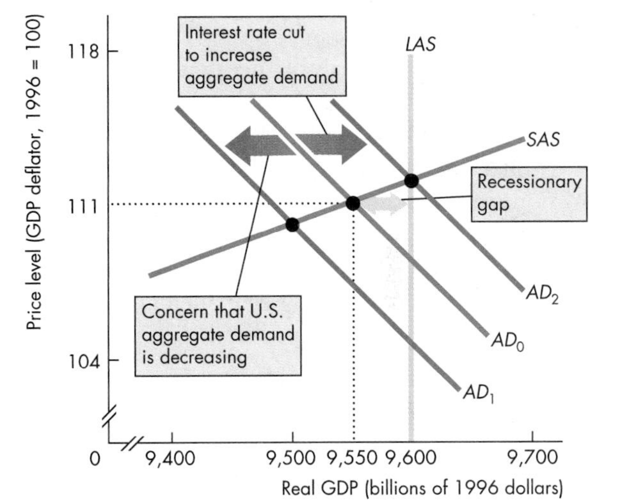

Figure 2 *AS* and *AD* in the U.S. economy in 2002

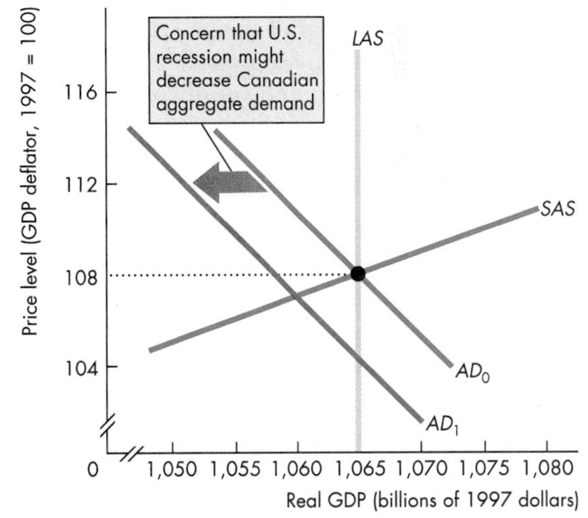

Figure 3 *AS* and *AD* in the Canadian economy in 2002

SUMMARY

KEY POINTS

Cycle Patterns, Impulses, and Mechanisms (pp. 730)

- The economy can be hit (like a tennis ball), cycle indefinitely (like the turning of day into night), and cycle in swings that get milder until another shock hits (like a rocking horse).

Aggregate Demand Theories of the Business Cycle (pp. 731–736)

- Keynesian business cycle theory identifies volatile expectations about future sales and profits as the main source of economic fluctuations.
- Monetarist business cycle theory identifies fluctuations in the quantity of money as the main source of economic fluctuations.
- Rational expectations theory identifies unanticipated fluctuations in aggregate demand as the main source of economic fluctuations.

Real Business Cycle Theory (pp. 737–741)

- In real business cycle (RBC) theory, economic fluctuations are caused by fluctuations in the influence of technological change on productivity growth.
- A temporary slowdown in the pace of technological change decreases investment demand and both the demand for labour and supply of labour.

Recessions During the 1990s (pp. 741–745)

- The 1990–1991 recession resulted from tight monetary policy, a slowdown in the United States, and adjustments to the Canada–United States Free Trade Agreement.
- The Japanese slowdown and recession of the 1990s was triggered by an asset price collapse combined with structural problems. Policy stimulation occurred but it was not sufficient to prevent recession, and a tightening of fiscal policy in 1996 and 1997 contributed to the 1998 recession.

The Great Depression (pp. 746–749)

- The Great Depression started with increased uncertainty, which brought a decrease in investment (especially in housing) and spending on consumer durables.
- There then followed a near total collapse of the financial system. Banks failed and the quantity of money decreased, resulting in a continued decrease in aggregate demand.
- The Great Depression itself produced a series of reforms that make a repeat of such a depression much less likely.

KEY FIGURES

Figure 31.1 The Keynesian Cycle, 731
Figure 31.2 A Keynesian Inflationary Gap, 732
Figure 31.3 A Monetarist Recession, 733
Figure 31.5 A Rational Expectations Business Cycle, 735
Figure 31.7 Capital and Labour Markets in a Real Business Cycle, 739
Figure 31.8 *AS–AD* in a Real Business Cycle, 740
Figure 31.11 The 1990–1991 Recession, 743

KEY TERMS

Keynesian theory of the business cycle, 731
Monetarist theory of the business cycle, 732
New classical theory of the business cycle, 734
New Keynesian theory of the business cycle, 734
Rational expectation, 734
Real business cycle theory, 737

PROBLEMS

*1. The figure shows the economy of Virtual Reality. When the economy is in a long-run equilibrium, it is at points *B*, *F*, and *J*. When a recession occurs in Virtual Reality, the economy moves away from these points to one of the three other points identified in each part of the figure.

   a. If the Keynesian theory is the correct explanation for the recession, to which points does the economy move?
   b. If the monetarist theory is the correct explanation for the recession, to which points does the economy move?
   c. If the new classical rational expectations theory is the correct explanation for the recession, to which points does the economy move?
   d. If the new Keynesian rational expectations theory is the correct explanation for the recession, to which points does the economy move?
   e. If real business cycle theory is the correct explanation for the recession, to which points does the economy move?

2. The figure shows the economy of Vital Signs. When the economy is in a long-run equilibrium, it is at points *A*, *E*, and *I*. When an expansion occurs in Vital Signs, the economy moves away from these points to one of the three other points identified in each part of the figure.

   a. If the Keynesian theory is the correct explanation for the expansion, to which points does the economy move?
   b. If the monetarist theory is the correct explanation for the expansion, to which points does the economy move?
   c. If the new classical rational expectations theory is the correct explanation for the expansion, to which points does the economy move?
   d. If the new Keynesian rational expectations theory is the correct explanation for the expansion, to which points does the economy move?
   e. If real business cycle theory is the correct explanation for the expansion, to which points does the economy move?

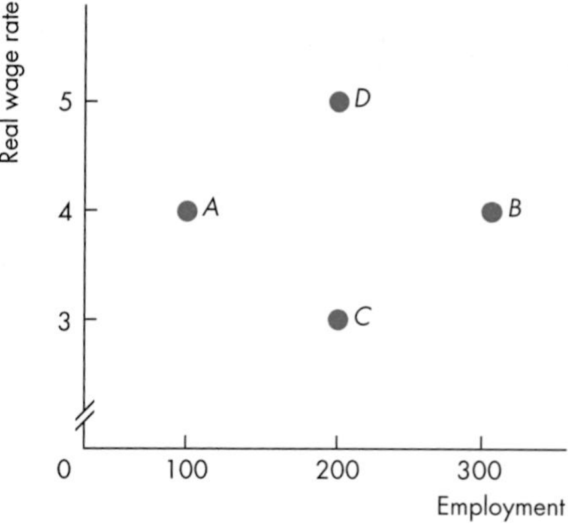

(a) Labour market

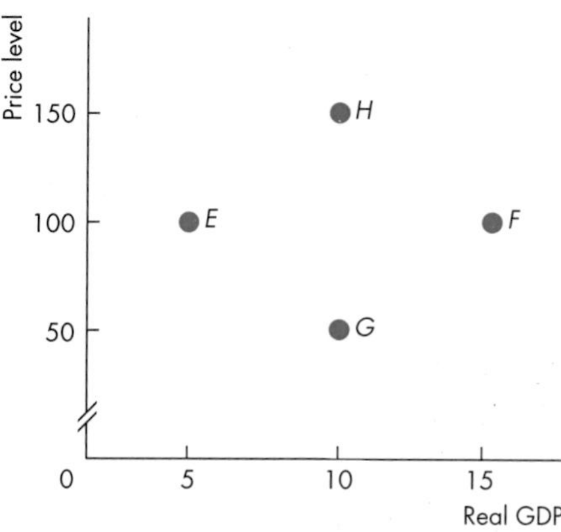

(b) *AS–AD*

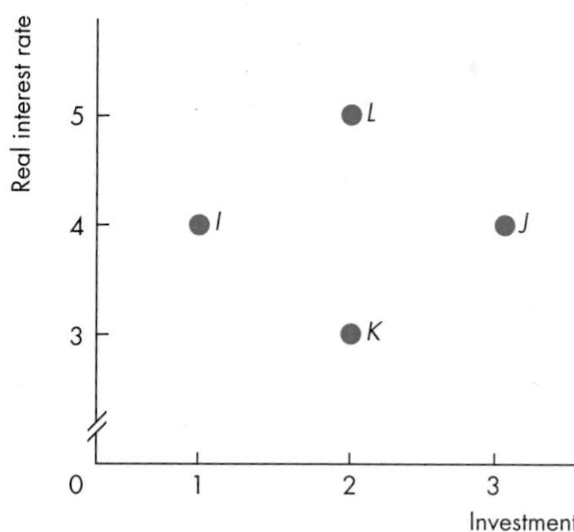

(c) Investment

*3. Suppose that when the recession occurs in Virtual Reality, the economy moves to *D*, *G*, and *K*. Which theory of the business cycle, if any, explains this outcome?

4. Suppose that when the expansion occurs in Vital Signs, the economy moves to *D*, *H*, and *L*. Which theory of the business cycle, if any, explains this outcome?

*5. Suppose that when the recession occurs in Virtual Reality, the economy moves to *C*, *G*, and *K*. Which theory of the business cycle, if any, explains this outcome?

6. Suppose that when the expansion occurs in Vital Signs, the economy moves to *C*, *H*, and *L*. Which theory of the business cycle, if any, explains this outcome?

*7. Suppose that when the recession occurs in Virtual Reality, the economy moves to *D*, *H*, and *K*. Which theory of the business cycle, if any, explains this outcome?

8. Suppose that when the expansion occurs in Vital Signs, the economy moves to *D*, *G*, and *L*. Which theory of the business cycle, if any, explains this outcome?

*9. Suppose that when the recession occurs in Virtual Reality, the economy moves to *C*, *H*, and *K*. Which theory of the business cycle, if any, explains this outcome?

10. Suppose that when the expansion occurs in Vital Signs, the economy moves to *C*, *G*, and *L*. Which theory of the business cycle, if any, explains this outcome?

*11. Suppose that when the recession occurs in Virtual Reality, the economy moves to *D*, *G*, and *L*. Which theory of the business cycle, if any, explains this outcome?

12. Suppose that when the expansion occurs in Vital Signs, the economy moves to *C*, *H*, and *K*. Which theory of the business cycle, if any, explains this outcome?

*13. Suppose that when the recession occurs in Virtual Reality, the economy moves to *C*, *G*, and *L*. Which theory of the business cycle, if any, explains this outcome?

14. Suppose that when the expansion occurs in Vital Signs, the economy moves to *D*, *H*, and *K*. Which theory of the business cycle, if any, explains this outcome?

CRITICAL THINKING

1. Study *Reading Between the Lines* on pp. 750–751 and then answer the following questions:
   a. What does this news article see as the uncertainties for the Canadian economy in 2003?
   b. What does the article regard as symptoms that slower growth might be ahead?
   c. How would a U.S. recession affect John Manley's budget problems?
   d. What policy actions, if any, do you think the Bank of Canada or Parliament of Canada needs to take in 2003 and 2004 to keep the economy growing and to prevent a new recession?
   e. Do you think any policy actions the Bank of Canada or Parliament of Canada might take can work if the U.S. economy goes into recession?
   f. What is the main danger facing Canada in 2003, inflation or recession?
2. Describe the changes in real GDP, employment and unemployment, and the price level that occurred during the Great Depression years of 1929–1933.

WEB EXERCISES

1. Use the links on the Parkin–Bade Web site to obtain information on the current state of the Canadian economy. Then
   a. List all of the features of the economy during the current year that you can think of that are consistent with a pessimistic outlook for the next two years.
   b. List all of the features of the economy during the current year that you can think of that are consistent with an optimistic outlook for the next two years.
   c. Drawing on the pessimistic and optimistic factors that you have listed in parts (a) and (b) and on your knowledge of macroeconomic theory, explain how you think the Canadian economy is going to evolve over the next year or two.

MACROECONOMIC POLICY CHALLENGES

What Can Policy Do?

From 1995 through 2000, the Canadian economy performed well. Real GDP expanded, unemployment fell, the inflation rate was steady, and a federal government budget deficit was turned into a surplus. ◆ But by 2001, growth was slowing, and in 2002 unemployment turned upward. ◆ Canada was not alone in facing a growth slowdown. Every other major country in the so-called Group of Seven saw its economy slow. ◆ Prime ministers and finance ministers began to talk of stimulus packages. And some people talked about a concerted global stimulus package. But not everyone agreed that the economy needed government stimulation. ◆ What can and should policymakers do to achieve a desirable macroeconomic performance?

In this chapter, we're going to study the challenges of achieving sustainable long-term growth and low unemployment, and of avoiding inflation. We're also going to review the alternative views on these issues. At the end of the chapter, in *Reading Between the Lines*, you can examine the macroeconomic policy problems facing the Canadian economy and the global economy today.

After studying this chapter, you will be able to

- **Describe the goals of macroeconomic policy**
- **Describe the main features of fiscal policy and monetary policy since 1971**
- **Explain how fiscal policy and monetary policy influence long-term economic growth**
- **Distinguish between and evaluate fixed-rule and feedback-rule policies to stabilize the business cycle**
- **Evaluate fixed-rule and feedback-rule policies to contain inflation and explain why lowering inflation usually brings recession**

Policy Goals

MACROECONOMIC POLICY GOALS FALL INTO TWO big categories: domestic and international. We will study international macroeconomic policy issues in Chapters 33 and 34. Here, we focus on domestic policy. The four main domestic macroeconomic policy goals are to

- Achieve the highest sustainable rate of potential GDP growth
- Smooth out avoidable business cycle fluctuations
- Maintain low unemployment
- Maintain low inflation

Potential GDP Growth

Rapid sustained real GDP growth can make a profound contribution to economic well-being. With a growth rate of 2 percent a year, it takes more than 30 years for production to double. With a growth rate of 5 percent a year, production more than doubles in just 15 years. And with a growth rate of 10 percent a year, as some Asian countries are achieving, production doubles in just 7 years. The limits to *sustainable* growth are determined by the availability of natural resources, by environmental considerations, and by the willingness of people to save and invest in new capital and new technologies rather than consume everything they produce.

How fast can the economy grow over the long term? Between 1988 and 2001, through a complete business cycle, potential GDP grew at a rate of 2.7 percent a year in Canada. But the Canadian population grew at a rate of 1.1 percent a year, so the growth rate of real GDP per person was about 1.6 percent a year. A growth rate of real GDP per person of 1.6 percent a year means that output per person would double every 45 years. Most economists believe that the Canadian economy can maintain a long-term growth rate of potential GDP of more than 2.7 percent a year. A few economists believe that with the right policies, sustainable growth of 5 percent a year is possible. This growth rate would double output per person every 18 years, increase it more than sixfold over 48 years, and increase it more than twelvefold in 65 years. So increasing the long-term growth rate is of critical importance.

The Business Cycle

Potential GDP probably does not grow at a constant rate. Fluctuations in the pace of technological advance and in the pace of investment in new capital bring fluctuations in potential GDP. So some fluctuations in real GDP represent fluctuations in potential GDP. But when real GDP grows less quickly than potential GDP, output is lost, and when real GDP grows more quickly than potential GDP, bottlenecks arise. Keeping real GDP growth steady and equal to potential GDP growth avoids these problems.

It is not known how smooth real GDP growth can be made. Real business cycle theory regards all the fluctuations in real GDP as fluctuations in potential GDP. The aggregate demand theories regard most of the fluctuations in real GDP as being avoidable deviations from potential GDP.

Unemployment

When real GDP grows more slowly than potential GDP, unemployment rises above the natural rate of unemployment. The higher the unemployment rate, the longer is the time taken by unemployed people to find jobs. Productive labour is wasted, and there is a slowdown in the accumulation of human capital. If high unemployment persists, serious psychological and social problems arise for the unemployed workers and their families.

When real GDP grows more quickly than potential GDP, unemployment decreases and falls below the natural rate of unemployment. The lower the unemployment rate, the harder it becomes for expanding industries to get the labour they need to keep growing. If extremely low unemployment persists, serious bottlenecks and production dislocations occur.

Keeping unemployment at the natural rate avoids both of these problems. But just what is the natural rate of unemployment? Assessments vary. The actual average unemployment rate over the most recent business cycle—1988 to 2001—was 8.9 percent. Few economists would think the natural rate to be as high as this number. And most believe that the natural rate has fallen in recent years. Real business cycle theorists believe that the natural rate fluctuates and always equals the actual unemployment rate.

If the natural rate of unemployment becomes high, then a goal of policy becomes lowering the natural rate itself. This goal is independent of smoothing the business cycle.

Inflation

When inflation fluctuates unpredictably, money becomes less useful as a measuring rod for conducting transactions. In extreme cases, it becomes useless and is abandoned as the means of payment. Borrowers and lenders and employers and workers must take on extra risks. Keeping the inflation rate steady and predictable avoids these problems.

What is the most desirable inflation rate? Some economists say that the *rate* of inflation doesn't matter much as long as the rate is *predictable.* But most economists believe that price stability, which they translate as an inflation rate of between 0 and 3 percent a year, is desirable. The reason why zero is not the target is that some price increases are due to quality improvements—a measurement bias in the price index—so a *measured* inflation rate of between 0 and 3 percent a year is equivalent to price stability.

FIGURE 32.1 Macroeconomic Performance: Real GDP and Inflation

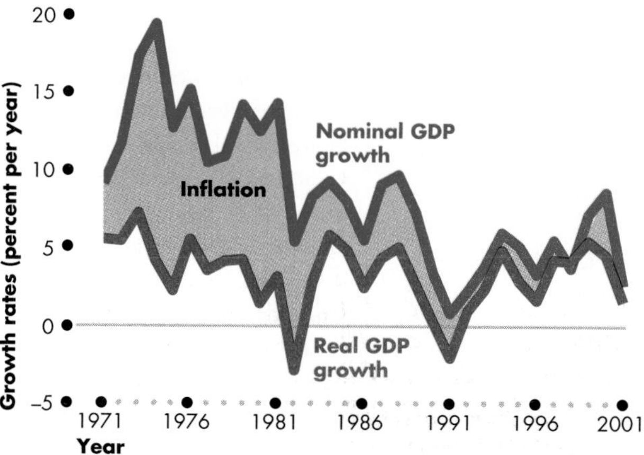

Real GDP growth and inflation fluctuate a great deal, and during the 1970s, inflation (the height of the green shaded area) mushroomed and real GDP growth slowed. This macroeconomic performance falls far short of the goals of a high and stable real GDP growth rate and low and predictable inflation.

Sources: Statistics Canada, CANSIM table 380-0002 and authors' calculations.

The Two Core Policy Indicators: Real GDP Growth and Inflation

Although macroeconomic policy pursues the four goals we've just considered, the goals are not independent ones. Three of these goals—increasing the real GDP growth rate, smoothing the business cycle, and maintaining low unemployment—are linked together. Real GDP growth tells us directly about the long-term goal of high sustainable growth and the business cycle. It also has a strong link to unemployment. If growth becomes too rapid, unemployment falls below the natural rate, and if growth becomes too slow, unemployment rises above the natural rate. So keeping real GDP growing steadily at its maximum sustainable rate is equivalent to avoiding business fluctuations and keeping unemployment at the natural rate.

There are some connections between real GDP growth and inflation, but over the long run, these two variables are largely independent. So two variables, real GDP growth and inflation, are the core policy targets.

Policy performance, judged by the two core policy targets—real GDP growth and inflation—is shown in Fig. 32.1. Here the red line shows real GDP growth. As we've noted, real GDP growth has averaged 3.3 percent a year. But the growth rate has fluctuated between a high of 7.2 percent in 1973 and a low of –2.9 percent in 1982. The height of the green shaded area shows inflation. The inflation rate exploded during the 1970s, and then fell through the 1980s. During the 1990s, inflation has been low.

REVIEW QUIZ

1. Why does macroeconomic stabilization policy try to achieve the highest sustainable rate of potential GDP growth, small business cycle fluctuations, low unemployment, and low inflation?
2. Can stabilization policy keep the unemployment rate below the natural rate?
3. Why are real GDP growth and inflation the two core policy indicators?

We've examined the policy goals. Let's now look at the policy tools and the way they have been used.

Policy Tools and Performance

THE TOOLS THAT ARE USED TO TRY TO ACHIEVE macroeconomic performance objectives are fiscal policy and monetary policy.

Fiscal policy, which is described in Chapter 24, is the use of the federal budget to achieve macroeconomic objectives. The detailed fiscal policy tools are tax rates, benefit rates, and government expenditures on goods and services. These tools work by influencing aggregate supply and aggregate demand in the ways explained in Chapter 22.

Monetary policy, which is described in Chapter 26, is the adjustment of the quantity of money and interest rates by the Bank of Canada to achieve macroeconomic objectives. These tools work by changing aggregate demand.

How have these policy tools been used in Canada? Let's answer this question by summarizing the main directions of fiscal and monetary policy in recent years.

Fiscal Policy Since 1971

Figure 32.2 gives a broad summary of fiscal policy from 1971 to 2001. It shows the levels of government revenues and outlays and the budget balance (each as a percentage of GDP). So that you can see the political context of fiscal policy, the figure also shows the election years and the names of the incumbent prime ministers.

Fiscal policy was neutral during the early 1970s, when Pierre Trudeau was prime minister. It then became expansionary before the 1976 election. Trudeau won that election, and during his next term as prime minister, spending exploded and so did the deficit. At this time, fiscal policy was strongly expansionary.

The Progressive Conservatives replaced the Liberals, and Brian Mulroney became prime minister in 1984. The Mulroney years were a period of spending cuts and modest tax increases and overall fiscal policy was contractionary during these years.

The Liberals returned to power in the election of 1993, and during 1994 through 1998, Prime Minister Jean Chrétien and Finance Minister Paul

FIGURE 32.2 The Fiscal Policy Record: A Summary

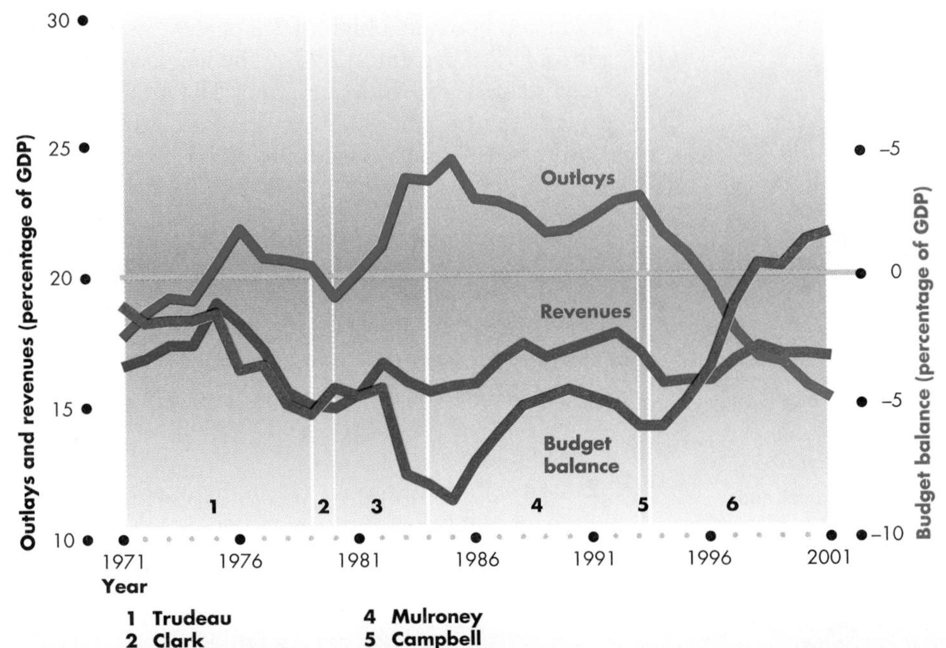

Source: Statistics Canada, CANSIM tables 380-0002 and 380-0007.

When Pierre Trudeau was prime minister, fiscal policy was expansionary—outlays and the deficit increased. When Brian Mulroney was prime minister, fiscal policy was contractionary—outlays were cut, revenues increased, and deficit decreased. When Jean Chrétien was prime minister, fiscal policy continued to be contractionary—outlays were cut further and the deficit was eventually eliminated. Cyclical fluctuations in outlays, revenues, and the deficit followed the business cycle.

Martin cut outlays and reduced the deficit. By 1998, aided by strong real GDP growth, the deficit was finally eliminated and a surplus was achieved for the first time since 1970.

Recall that the Canadian economy experienced a recession during 1982 and again during 1990–1991. You can see, in Fig. 32.2, that in these two recessions, outlays increased, revenues decreased, and the deficit increased. But when the economy expanded after the recessions, outlays decreased, revenues increased, and the deficit decreased.

Let's now look at monetary policy.

Monetary Policy Since 1971

Figure 32.3 shows three broad measures of monetary policy. They are the growth rate of M2+, the overnight loans rate, and the real overnight loans rate.

The M2+ growth rate provides a broad indication of the influence of monetary policy on aggregate demand.

The overnight loans rate is the interest rate on large-scale loans that chartered banks make to each other and to dealers in financial markets. The Bank of Canada sets a target range for the overnight loans rate and takes actions to keep the rate inside its target range (see Chapter 26, p. 608). Movements in the overnight loans rate tell us how the Bank is acting to change money growth. When the overnight loans rate rises, the Bank is tightening; and when it falls, the Bank is loosening its grip on money growth.

The real overnight rate tells us how the Bank of Canada's actions eventually ripple through the economy to influence spending plans. It is the real interest rate, not the nominal rate, to which expenditure plans respond.

Figure 32.3 also identifies the election years, the prime ministers, and the Bank of Canada governors. The Bank has had four governors during this period. Notice that the term of a governor does not coincide with the term of a government, and the governor's term extends across the terms of several governments.

There are four distinct phases of monetary policy. In the first phase, between 1971 and 1980, inflation was rapid and so was money growth. During this

FIGURE 32.3 The Monetary Policy Record: A Summary

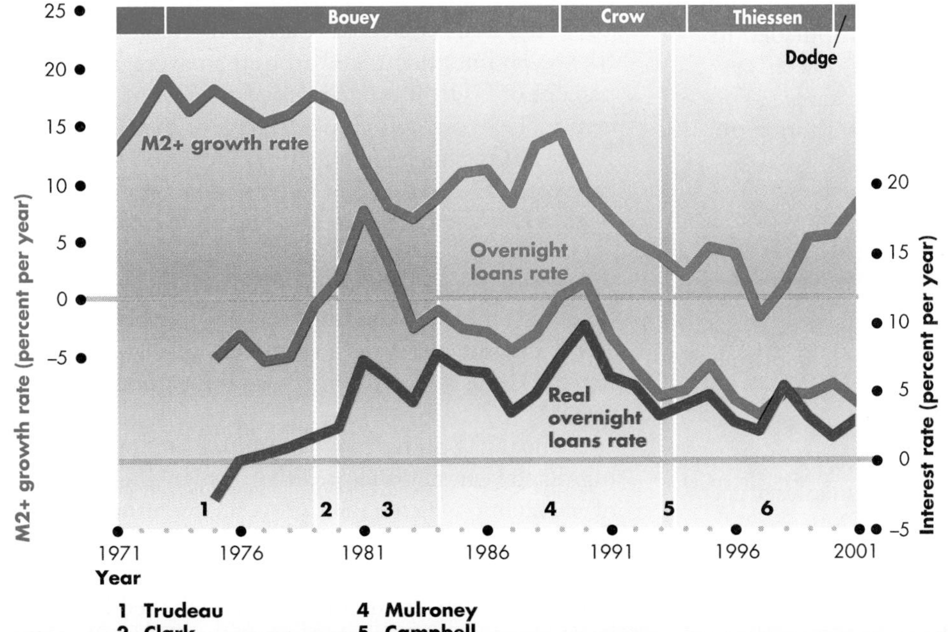

Monetary policy is summarized here by the growth rate of M2+ and by the overnight loans rate. The M2+ growth rate was extremely high during the first Trudeau term but slowed during Trudeau's second term. It increased and then decreased again during Mulroney's term. M2+ growth remained low during most of Chrétien's term but began to increase in the late 1990s and 2000s.

Sources: Bank of Canada and *The Monetary Summary Record: A Summary;* data calculated in part from the Statistics Canada CANSIM II database, table 380-0031.

period, the nominal interest rate was not much higher than the inflation rate, so the real interest rate was close to zero.

In the second phase, during the early 1980s, Bank of Canada governor Gerald Bouey embarked on a concerted anti-inflation policy. The money growth rate fell, and interest rates increased. As a result of these actions, the inflation rate fell from around 10 percent a year to less than 5 percent a year.

In the third phase, which began in 1989 when John Crow was governor of the Bank of Canada, a further attack on inflation was launched to achieve price stability. The money growth rate fell again, and interest rates increased.

In the fourth phase, which began in 1994 when Gordon Thiessen became governor of the Bank of Canada and which has continued into David Dodge's term as governor, the challenge has been to keep inflation at its new low level but to pursue a monetary policy that permits the economy to expand and to bring lower unemployment. The M2+ growth trend has been downward, and falling inflation has lowered the nominal interest rate and achieved a remarkably steady real interest rate.

You can see that monetary policy has had a long-term anti-inflation focus rather than a short-term business cycle focus. You can also see that there is no tendency for monetary policy to be linked to the timing of elections. The Bank of Canada has pursued its monetary policy to achieve its economic objectives and has been immune from political pressures to change the course of monetary policy for short-term political gains.

REVIEW QUIZ

1. What were the main features and effects of fiscal policy during the terms of the various prime ministers during the 1980s and 1990s?
2. What were the main features and effects of monetary policy during the 1980s and 1990s? In which periods was monetary policy inflationary? In which periods was it used to fight inflation?

Now that we've examined the goals of policy and the policy actions of the past, we're going to look at ways in which policy might be used better to achieve its goals.

Long-Term Growth Policy

THE SOURCES OF THE LONG-TERM GROWTH OF potential GDP, which are explained in Chapter 30 (pp. 711–712), are the accumulation of physical and human capital and the advance of technology. Chapter 30 briefly examines the range of policies that might achieve faster growth. Here, we probe more deeply into the problem of boosting the long-term growth rate.

Monetary policy can contribute to long-term growth by keeping the inflation rate low. (Chapter 28, pp. 660–661, explains some connections between inflation and growth.) Fiscal policy and other policies can also contribute to growth by influencing the private decisions on which long-term growth depends in three areas. All growth policies increase

- National saving
- Investment in human capital
- Investment in new technologies

National Saving

National saving equals private saving plus government saving. Figure 32.4 shows the private and government components of national saving between 1971 and 2001. Over this period, national saving (the green line) fluctuated around an average of 20 percent of GDP. It ranged between a low of 17 percent in 1993 and a high of 27 percent in 1974.

Private saving (the blue line) increased to 25 percent of GDP in 1975 and remained fairly steady until 1993 when it began to decrease. By 2001, private saving had decreased to 15 percent of GDP. Government saving (the vertical gap between the blue line and the green line) was positive before 1976, became negative (government dissaving) during the 1980s and early 1990s, and returned to positive in 1997.

The data you have just examined are for *gross* saving. Each year, national wealth grows by the amount of *net* saving, which equals gross saving minus the value of capital that is scrapped during the year. Figure 32.4 shows net saving as a percentage of GDP. You can see that net national saving (the red line) has had a downward trend through the period 1971 to 2001. Gross national saving minus net national saving is the average depreciation of capital. In 1971, depreciation was about 11 percent of GDP. Over the period from 1971 to 2001, depreciation gradually increased to 13 percent of GDP. Because depreciation has gradually increased, the fluctuations in net national saving are similar to those in gross national saving.

Canadian investment, which is one of the engines of real GDP growth, is not limited by Canadian saving. The reason is that Canadians can borrow abroad to finance domestic investment. And foreigners can invest some of their saving directly in Canadian businesses. Either way, the foreign saving boosts Canadian real GDP growth. Also, because all investment, regardless of how it is financed, creates jobs, the boost in Canadian incomes leads to an increase in national saving. Further, by using foreign saving along with domestic saving, Canadians can invest in a wider range of potentially profitable business enterprises and can better spread their risks across traditional and high-return new technologies.

FIGURE 32.4 Saving Rates in Canada: 1971–2001

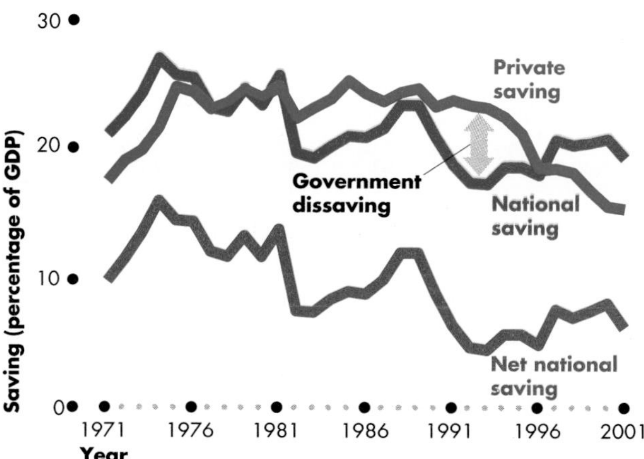

Gross national saving (green line) ranged between 17 percent in 1993 and 27 percent in 1974. Private saving (blue line) increased to 25 percent of GDP in 1975, remained steady until 1993, then decreased. Government saving (the vertical gap between the blue line and the green line) was positive before 1975, became negative during the 1980s and early 1990s, and positive again in the late 1990s. Net national saving (red line) has fluctuated, but it has had a downward trend.

Source: Statistics Canada, CANSIM table 380–0031.

How can national saving be increased? The two points of attack are

- Increasing government saving
- Increasing private saving

Increasing Government Saving Government saving was negative between 1976 and 1997, and its average during the 1990s was –0.7 percent of GDP. But government saving increased after 1993 as the federal budget deficit was gradually eliminated and replaced by a surplus. Maintaining a federal budget surplus will be hard work and will be achieved only by resisting increases in social programs and educational and health-care expenditures.

Increasing Private Saving Private saving has fallen from its average of 24 percent of GDP in the period 1975 to 1993. Private saving in 2001 was the lowest it has been since 1971. The main way in which government actions can boost private saving is by increasing the after-tax rate of return on saving. This is what government policy has sought to do, but on only one type of asset: Registered Retirement Savings Plans (RRSPs) and pension funds. By putting their savings into RRSPs and pension funds, people can avoid income tax on their interest income. But they cannot use their RRSPs (without a tax penalty) until they retire. Also, there are limits to the amount that can be accumulated tax-free in an RRSP and a pension fund each year.

Private saving probably could be stimulated more effectively by cutting taxes on interest income and capital gains and by replacing the lost government revenue from such a tax cut with an increase in the Goods and Services Tax (GST) or an increase in the tax on labour income. But such a move would be regarded as inequitable and probably not politically feasible. So governments are limited to making minor changes to the taxation of interest income, and these changes will have negligible effects on the saving rate.

Private Saving and Inflation Inflation erodes the value of money and other financial assets such as bonds, and uncertainty about future inflation discourages saving. So a monetary policy that preserves stable prices and minimizes uncertainty about the future value of money stimulates saving. Chapter 28 (pp. 660–661) spells out the broader connection between inflation and real GDP and explains why low inflation brings greater output and faster growth.

Investment in Human Capital

The accumulation of human capital plays a crucial role in economic growth, and three areas are relevant: education, on-the-job experience, and health care. Economic research shows that education, on-the-job training, and good health yield high rates of return.

On the average, the greater the number of years a person remains in school, the higher are that person's earnings. A university graduate earns more, on the average, than does a college graduate, who in turn earns more than does a high school graduate. Again on the average, a person with ten years of work experience earns more than an otherwise identical person who has no work experience. Similarly, and again on the average, the better a person's health, the more productive is that person.

So, by providing subsidized education, governments can increase the rate of investment in human capital and boost the rate of real GDP growth. By keeping unemployment low, the government can increase the number of people who have work experience and again increase the rate of investment in human capital. And by providing comprehensive high-quality health-care services, the government can help to build a more productive labour force.

But if education, on-the-job experience, and good health yield higher earnings, why, you might be wondering, does the government need a policy that increases the rate of investment in human capital? Why can't people simply be left to get on with making their own decisions about how much human capital to acquire?

The answer is that the *social* returns to human capital probably exceed the *private* returns. Some of the productivity of human capital comes from the *interactions* of people who are well endowed with human capital. The greater the number of well-educated, experienced, and healthy people, the greater is the productivity of each person. The design and production of just about every good and service benefits from team efforts.

When each person makes a decision about how much education or on-the-job training to get, the benefits that will accrue to others are ignored. So, left to ourselves, we would probably accumulate too little human capital. For this reason, free schooling and heavily subsidized college and university education is efficient. Tax deductibility of interest on student loans is also efficient. Countries that provide a good basic education and health care for everyone have a better economic growth performance, on the average, than countries that do not.

Investment in New Technologies

Investment in new technologies is the third area in which policy can influence economic growth. As Chapter 30 explains, investment in new technologies is special for two reasons. First, it appears not to run into the problem of diminishing returns that plague the other types of capital and the other factors of production. Second, the benefits of new technologies spill over to influence all parts of the economy, not just the firms undertaking the investment. For these reasons, increasing the rate of investment in new technologies is a promising way of boosting long-term growth. But how can government policy influence the pace of technological change?

The government can fund and provide tax incentives for research and development activities. Through the Natural Sciences Research Council, the universities, and various research establishments, the government funds a large amount of basic research.

Considering the payoff from faster growth and the payoff, therefore, from improved knowledge about the forces that create growth, it is surprising that more is not spent, both on research and development and on economic research on the causes of growth.

REVIEW QUIZ

1. Why do long-term growth policies focus on increasing saving and increasing investment in human capital and new technologies?
2. What has been the trend in the net national saving rate in Canada since 1971?
3. What actions can the government take that might increase the saving rate?
4. What actions can the government take that might increase the rate of investment in human capital?
5. What actions can the government take that might increase investment in new technologies?

We've seen how government might use its fiscal and monetary policies to influence long-term growth. How can it influence the business cycle and unemployment? Let's now address this question.

Business Cycle and Unemployment Policy

MANY DIFFERENT FISCAL AND MONETARY POLICIES can be pursued to stabilize the business cycle and cyclical unemployment. But all these policies fall into three broad categories:

- Fixed-rule policies
- Feedback-rule policies
- Discretionary policies

Fixed-Rule Policies

A **fixed-rule policy** specifies an action to be pursued independently of the state of the economy. An everyday life example of a fixed rule is a stop sign. It says, "Stop regardless of the state of the road ahead—even if no other vehicle is trying to use the road." One fixed-rule policy, proposed by Milton Friedman, is to keep the quantity of money growing at a constant rate year in and year out, regardless of the state of the economy, to make the *average* inflation rate zero. Another fixed-rule policy is to balance the federal budget. Fixed rules are rarely followed in practice, but they have some merits in principle. Later in this chapter, we will study how they would work if they were pursued.

Feedback-Rule Policies

A **feedback-rule policy** specifies how policy actions respond to changes in the state of the economy. A yield sign is an everyday feedback rule. It says, "Stop if another vehicle is attempting to use the road ahead, but otherwise, proceed." A macroeconomic feedback-rule policy is one that changes the quantity of money, interest rates, or even tax rates in response to the state of the economy. Some feedback rules guide the actions of policymakers. For example, the Bank of Canada used a feedback rule when it kept pushing interest rates ever higher through 1994 in response to persistently falling unemployment and strong real GDP growth. Other feedback-rule policies are automatic. Examples are the automatic increase in tax revenues and decrease in transfer payments during an expansion and the automatic decrease in tax revenues and increase in transfer payments during a recession.

Discretionary Policies

A **discretionary policy** responds to the state of the economy in a possibly unique way that uses all the information available, including perceived lessons from past "mistakes." An everyday discretionary policy occurs at an unmarked intersection. Each driver uses discretion in deciding whether to stop and how slowly to approach the intersection. Most macroeconomic policy actions have an element of discretion because every situation is to some degree unique. For example, through 1994, the Bank of Canada raised interest rates several times but by small increments. The Bank might have delayed cutting rates until it was sure that lower rates were needed and then cut them in larger increments. The Bank used discretion based on lessons it had learned from earlier expansions. But despite the fact that all policy actions have an element of discretion, they can be regarded as modifications of a basic feedback-rule policy.

We'll study the effects of business cycle policy by comparing the performance of real GDP and the price level under a fixed rule and a feedback rule. Because the business cycle can result from demand shocks or supply shocks, we need to consider these two cases. We'll begin by studying demand shocks.

Stabilizing Aggregate Demand Shocks

We'll study an economy that starts out at full employment and has no inflation. Figure 32.5 illustrates this situation. The economy is on aggregate demand curve AD_0 and short-run aggregate supply curve *SAS*. These curves intersect at point *A* on the long-run aggregate supply curve, *LAS*. The GDP deflator is 110, and real GDP is $1,000 billion. Now suppose that there is an unexpected and temporary decrease in aggregate demand. Let's see what happens.

Perhaps investment decreases because of a wave of pessimism about the future, or perhaps exports decrease because of a recession in the rest of the world. Regardless of the origin of the decrease in aggregate demand, the aggregate demand curve shifts leftward, to AD_1 in Fig. 32.5. Aggregate demand curve AD_1 intersects the short-run aggregate supply curve, *SAS*, at point *B* where the GDP deflator is 105 and real GDP is $950 billion. The economy is in a recession. Real GDP is less than potential GDP, and unemployment is above its natural rate.

FIGURE 32.5 A Decrease in Aggregate Demand

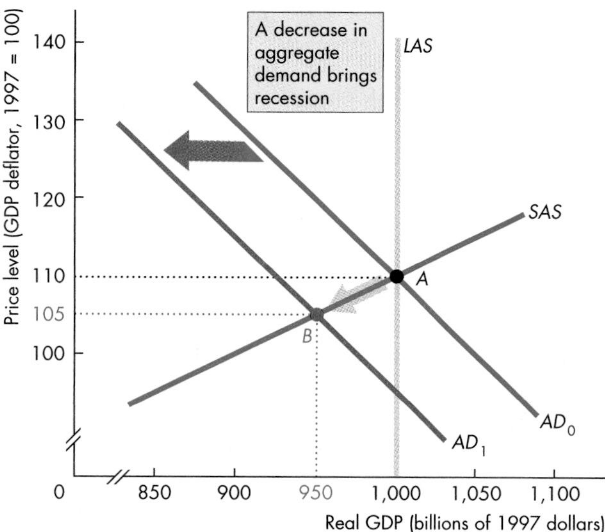

The economy starts out at full employment on aggregate demand curve AD_0 and short-run aggregate supply curve *SAS*, the two curves intersecting on the long-run aggregate supply curve, *LAS*, at point *A*. Real GDP is $1,000 billion, and the GDP deflator is 110. A fall in aggregate demand (due to pessimism about future profits, for example) unexpectedly shifts the aggregate demand curve to AD_1. Real GDP falls to $950 billion, and the GDP deflator falls to 105. The economy is in a recession at point *B*.

Suppose that the decrease in aggregate demand from AD_0 to AD_1 is temporary. As confidence in the future improves, firms' investment picks up, or as economic expansion proceeds in the rest of the world, exports gradually increase. As a result, the aggregate demand curve gradually returns to AD_0, but it takes some time to do so.

We are going to work out how the economy responds under two alternative policies during the period in which aggregate demand gradually increases to its original level: a fixed rule and a feedback rule.

Fixed Rule: Monetarism The fixed rule that we'll study here is one in which government expenditures on goods and services, taxes, and the quantity of money remain constant. Neither fiscal policy nor monetary policy responds to the depressed economy. This rule is advocated by monetarists. A **monetarist** is an economist who believes that fluctuations in the quantity of money are the main source of economic fluctuations—the monetarist theory of the business cycle (see Chapter 31, pp. 732–734).

Figure 32.6(a) illustrates the response of the economy under a fixed rule when the decrease in aggregate demand to AD_1 is *temporary.* Starting from the recession at point *B*, aggregate demand gradually returns to its original level and the aggregate demand curve shifts rightward to AD_0. Real GDP and the GDP deflator gradually increase as the economy returns to point *A* in Fig. 32.6(a). Throughout this process, real GDP growth is more rapid than usual but beginning from below potential GDP. Throughout the adjustment, unemployment remains above the natural rate.

Figure 32.6(b) illustrates the response of the economy under a fixed rule when the decrease in aggregate demand to AD_1 is *permanent.* Again starting from the recession at point *B* and with unemployment above the natural rate, the money wage rate falls. Short-run aggregate supply increases and the *SAS* curve shifts rightward to SAS_1. Real GDP gradually increases towards $1,000 billion and the GDP deflator falls towards 95, at point *C*. Throughout the adjustment, real GDP is less than potential GDP and unemployment exceeds the natural rate.

Let's contrast the adjustment under a fixed-rule policy with that under a feedback-rule policy.

Feedback Rule: Keynesian Activism The feedback rule that we'll study is one in which government expenditures on goods and services increase, tax rates decrease, and the quantity of money increases when real GDP falls below potential GDP. In other words, both fiscal policy and monetary policy become expansionary when real GDP is less than potential GDP. When real GDP exceeds potential GDP, both policies operate in reverse, becoming contractionary. This rule is advocated by Keynesian activists. A **Keynesian activist** is an economist who believes that fluctuations in aggregate demand combined with sticky wages (and/or sticky prices) are the main source of economic fluctuations—the Keynesian and new Keynesian theories of the business cycle (see Chapter 31, pp. 731–732 and pp. 734–735).

Figure 32.6(c) illustrates the response of the economy under this feedback-rule policy. Starting from the recession at point *B*, the expansionary fiscal and monetary policies shift the aggregate

FIGURE 32.6 Two Stabilization Policies: Aggregate Demand Shock

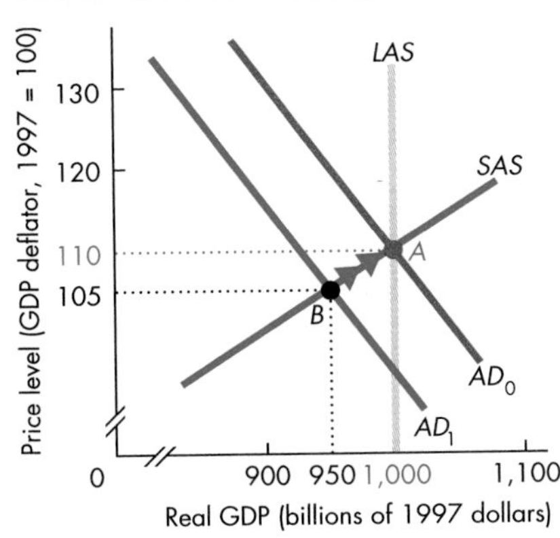

(a) Fixed rule: temporary demand shock

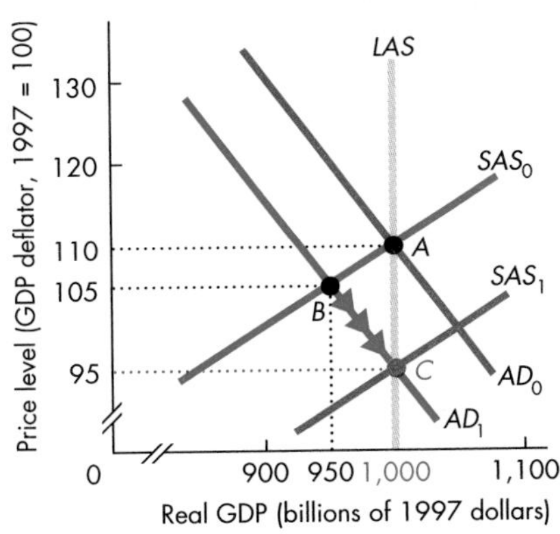

(b) Fixed rule: permanent demand shock

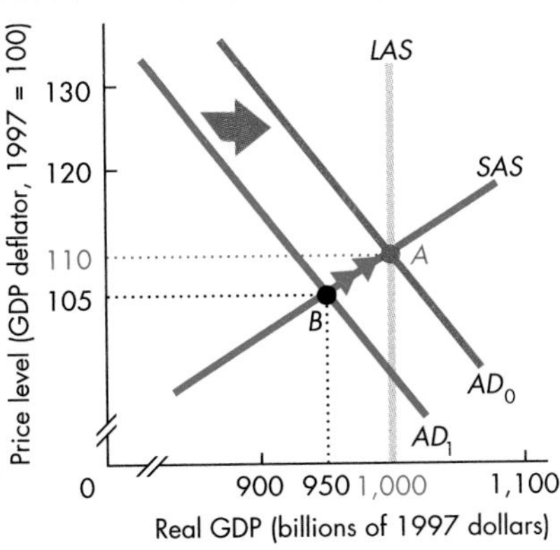

(c) Feedback rule

Aggregate demand is AD_1 and the economy is in a recession at point *B*. Real GDP is $950 billion, and the GDP deflator is 105. In part (a) the aggregate demand shock is temporary and a fixed-rule policy is pursued. Aggregate demand gradually increases to AD_0. Real GDP increases to $1,000 billion, and the GDP deflator increases to 110 at point *A*. In part (b), the demand shock is permanent and a fixed-rule policy is pursued. Aggregate demand remains at AD_1. Eventually the money wage rate falls and the *SAS* curve shifts to SAS_1. The price level falls to 95, and real GDP increases to $1,000 billion at point *C*. In part (c), a feedback rule is pursued. With the economy in recession, expansionary fiscal and monetary policies increase aggregate demand and shift the aggregate demand curve from AD_1 to AD_0. Real GDP increases to $1,000 billion, and the GDP deflator increases to 110 at point *A*.

demand curve immediately to AD_0 and the economy moves back to point *A*. As other influences increase aggregate demand, fiscal and monetary policies become contractionary to hold the aggregate demand curve steady at AD_0. Real GDP is held steady at $1,000 billion, and the GDP deflator remains at 110.

The Two Rules Compared Under a fixed-rule policy, the economy goes into a recession and stays there for as long as it takes for aggregate demand to increase again under its own steam. Only gradually does the aggregate demand curve return to its original position and the recession come to an end.

Under a feedback-rule policy, the policy action pulls the economy out of its recession. Once back at potential GDP, real GDP is held there by a gradual, policy-induced decrease in aggregate demand that exactly offsets the increase in aggregate demand coming from private spending decisions.

The price level and real GDP decrease and increase by exactly the same amounts under the two policies, but real GDP stays below potential GDP for longer with a fixed rule than it does with a feedback rule.

So Feedback Rules Are Better? Isn't it obvious that a feedback rule is better than a fixed rule? Can't the government and the Bank of Canada use feedback rules to keep the economy close to full employment with a stable price level? Of course, unforecasted events—such as a collapse in business confidence—will hit the economy from time to time. But by responding with a change in tax rates, spending, interest rates, and the quantity of money, can't the government and the Bank minimize the damage from such a shock? It appears to be so from our analysis, and the Bank did a pretty good job through the late 1990s and into the 2000s.

Despite the apparent superiority of a feedback rule, many economists remain convinced that a fixed rule stabilizes aggregate demand more effectively than a feedback rule does. These economists assert that fixed rules are better than feedback rules because

- Potential GDP is not known.
- Policy lags are longer than the forecast horizon.
- Feedback-rule policies are less predictable than fixed-rule policies.

Let's look at these assertions.

Knowledge of Potential GDP To decide whether a feedback policy needs to stimulate or retard aggregate demand, it is necessary to determine whether real GDP is currently above or below potential GDP. But potential GDP is not known with certainty. It depends on a large number of factors, one of which is the level of employment when unemployment is at its natural rate. But uncertainty and disagreement exist about how the labour market works, so we can only estimate the natural rate of unemployment. As a result, there is uncertainty about the *direction* in which a feedback policy should be pushing the level of aggregate demand.

Policy Lags and the Forecast Horizon The effects of policy actions taken today are spread out over the next two years or even more. But no one is able to forecast accurately that far ahead. The forecast horizon of the policymakers is less than one year. Further, it is not possible to predict the precise timing and magnitude of the effects of policy actions. So a feedback policy that reacts to today's economy may be inappropriate for the state of the economy at that uncertain future date when the policy's effects are felt.

For example, suppose that today the economy is in recession. The Bank of Canada reacts with an increase in the money growth rate. When the Bank steps on the monetary accelerator, the first reaction is a fall in interest rates. Some time later, lower interest rates produce an increase in investment and the purchases of consumer durable goods. Some time still later, this increase in expenditure increases income; higher income in turn induces higher consumption expenditure. Later yet, the higher expenditure increases the demand for labour, and eventually, money wage rates and prices rise. The industries and regions in which spending increases occur vary, and so does the impact on employment. It can take from nine months to two years for an initial action by the Bank to cause a change in real GDP, employment, and the inflation rate.

By the time the Bank's actions are having their maximum effect, the economy has moved on to a new situation. Perhaps a world economic slowdown has added a new negative effect on aggregate demand that is offsetting the Bank's expansionary actions. Or perhaps a boost in business confidence has increased aggregate demand yet further, adding to the Bank's own expansionary policy. Whatever the situation, the Bank can take the appropriate actions today only if it can forecast those future shocks to aggregate demand.

To smooth the fluctuations in aggregate demand, the Bank of Canada needs to take actions today that are based on a forecast of what will be happening over a period stretching two or more years into the future. It is no use taking actions a year from today to influence the situation that then prevails. By then it will be too late.

If the Bank is good at economic forecasting and bases its policy actions on its forecasts, then the Bank can deliver the type of aggregate demand-smoothing performance that we assumed in the model economy that we studied earlier in this chapter. But if the Bank takes policy actions that are based on today's economy rather than on the forecasted economy a year into the future, then those actions will often be inappropriate ones.

When unemployment is high and the Bank puts its foot on the accelerator, it speeds the economy back to full employment. But the Bank might not be able to see far enough ahead to know when to ease off the accelerator and gently tap the brake, holding the economy at its full-employment point. Usually, the Bank keeps its foot on the accelerator for too long, and after the Bank has taken its foot off the accelerator pedal, the economy races through the full-employment point and starts to experience shortages and inflationary pressures. Eventually, when inflation increases and unemployment falls below its natural rate, the Bank steps on the brake and pushes the economy back below full employment.

According to advocates of fixed rules, the Bank's own reactions to the current state of the economy are one of the major sources of fluctuations in aggregate demand and the major factor that people have to forecast to make their own economic choices.

During 1994, the Bank of Canada tried hard to avoid the problems just described. It increased interest rates early in the expansion and by small increments. In 1995, after real GDP growth slowed but before any serious signs of recession were on the horizon, it began to cut interest rates. And in 1997, before inflation turned seriously upward, the Bank squeezed the monetary brake. Whether the Bank now knows enough to avoid some of the mistakes of the past is too early to tell. But its actions during the period 1992 to 2001 were gentler and better timed than those in previous cycles.

The problems with feedback rules for fiscal policy are more severe than those for monetary policy because of the lags in the implementation of fiscal policy. The Bank of Canada can take actions relatively quickly, but before a fiscal policy action can be taken, the entire legislative process must be completed. So even before a fiscal policy action is implemented, the economy may have moved on to a new situation that calls for a different feedback policy from the one that is in the legislative pipeline.

Predictability of Policies To make decisions about long-term contracts for employment (wage contracts) and for borrowing and lending, people have to anticipate the future course of prices—the future inflation rate. To forecast the inflation rate, it is necessary to forecast aggregate demand. And to forecast aggregate demand, it is necessary to forecast the policy actions of the government and the Bank of Canada.

If the government and the Bank of Canada stick to rock-steady, fixed rules for tax rates, spending programs, and money growth, then policy itself cannot be a contributor to unexpected fluctuations in aggregate demand.

In contrast, when a feedback rule is being pursued, there is more scope for the policy actions to be unpredictable. The main reason is that feedback rules are not written down for all to see. Rather, they have to be inferred from the behaviour of the government and the Bank of Canada.

So with a feedback policy, it is necessary to predict the variables to which the government and Bank of Canada react and the extent to which they react. Consequently, a feedback rule for fiscal and monetary policies can create more unpredictable fluctuations in aggregate demand than a fixed rule can.

Economists disagree about whether those bigger fluctuations offset the potential stabilizing influence of the predictable changes the Bank of Canada makes. No agreed measurements have been made to settle this dispute. Nevertheless, the unpredictability of the Bank in its pursuit of feedback policies is an important fact of economic life. And the Bank does not always go out of its way to make its reactions clear. Even in parliamentary testimony, Bank of Canada governors are reluctant to make the Bank's actions and intentions entirely plain. Rather they like to create a degree of mystery about what they are doing and place a smokescreen between themselves and the rest of the government economic policy-making machine.

It is not surprising that the Bank of Canada seeks to keep *some* of its actions behind a smokescreen. First, the Bank wants to maintain as much freedom of action as possible and so does not want to state with too great a precision the feedback rules that it will follow in any given circumstances. Second, the Bank is part of a political process and, although legally independent of the federal government, is not immune to subtle influence. For at least these two reasons, the Bank does not specify feedback rules as precisely as the one we've analyzed in this chapter. As a result, the Bank cannot deliver an economic performance that has the stability that we generated in the model economy.

To the extent to which the Bank's actions are discretionary and unpredictable, they lead to unpredictable fluctuations in aggregate demand. These fluctuations, in turn, produce fluctuations in real GDP, employment, and unemployment.

If it is difficult for the Bank to pursue a predictable feedback stabilization policy, it is probably impossible for Parliament to do so. The stabilization policy of Parliament is formulated in terms of spending programs and tax laws. Because these programs and laws are the outcome of a political process that is constrained only by the Constitution, there can be no effective way in which a predictable feedback fiscal policy can be adhered to.

We reviewed three reasons why feedback-rule policies might not be more effective than fixed-rule policies in controlling aggregate demand. But there is a fourth reason why some economists prefer fixed rules: Not all shocks to the economy are on the demand side. Let's now see how aggregate supply fluctuations affect the economy under a fixed rule and a feedback rule. We will also see why the economists who believe that aggregate supply fluctuations are the dominant ones also favour a fixed rule rather than a feedback rule.

Stabilizing Aggregate Supply Shocks

Real business cycle theorists believe that fluctuations in real GDP (and in employment and unemployment) are caused not by fluctuations in aggregate demand but by fluctuations in productivity growth. According to real business cycle theory, there is no useful distinction between long-run aggregate supply and short-run aggregate supply. Because money wage rates are flexible, the labour market is always in equilibrium and unemployment is always at its natural rate. The vertical long-run aggregate supply curve is also the short-run aggregate supply curve. Fluctuations occur because of shifts in the long-run aggregate supply curve. Normally, the long-run aggregate supply curve shifts to the right—the economy expands. But the pace at which the long-run aggregate supply curve shifts to the right varies. Also, on occasion, the long-run aggregate supply curve shifts leftward, bringing a decrease in aggregate supply and a decrease in real GDP.

If real business cycle theory is correct, economic policy that influences the aggregate demand curve has no effect on real GDP. But it does affect the price level. If a feedback-rule policy is used to increase aggregate demand every time real GDP decreases, and if real business cycle theory is correct, the feedback-rule policy will make price level fluctuations more severe than they otherwise would be.

Figure 32.7 illustrates these alternative policy responses to a decrease in aggregate supply. The economy starts out at point *A* on aggregate demand curve AD_0 and long-run aggregate supply curve LAS_0 at a GDP deflator of 110 and with real GDP equal to $1,000 billion. Now suppose that the long-run aggregate supply curve shifts to LAS_1. A decrease in long-run aggregate supply can occur as a result of a severe drought or other natural catastrophe or perhaps as the result of a disruption of international trade such as the OPEC embargo of the 1970s.

Fixed Rule With a fixed rule, the fall in the long-run aggregate supply has no effect on the policies of the Bank of Canada or the government and no effect on aggregate demand. The aggregate demand curve remains AD_0. Real GDP decreases to $950 billion, and the price level increases to 120 at point *B*.

Feedback Rule Now suppose that the Bank of Canada and the government use feedback rules. In particular, suppose that when real GDP decreases, the Bank increases the quantity of money and Parliament enacts a tax cut to increase aggregate demand. In this example, aggregate demand increases and the aggregate demand curve shifts to AD_1. The policy goal is to bring real GDP back to $1,000 billion. But the long-run aggregate supply curve has shifted, and so potential GDP has decreased to $950 billion. The increase in aggregate demand cannot bring forth an increase in output if the economy does not have the capacity to produce that output. So real GDP stays at $950 billion, but the price level rises further—to 130 at point *C*. You can see that in this case the attempt to stabilize real GDP using a feedback-rule policy has no effect on real GDP but generates a substantial price level increase.

FIGURE 32.7 Responding to a Productivity Growth Slowdown

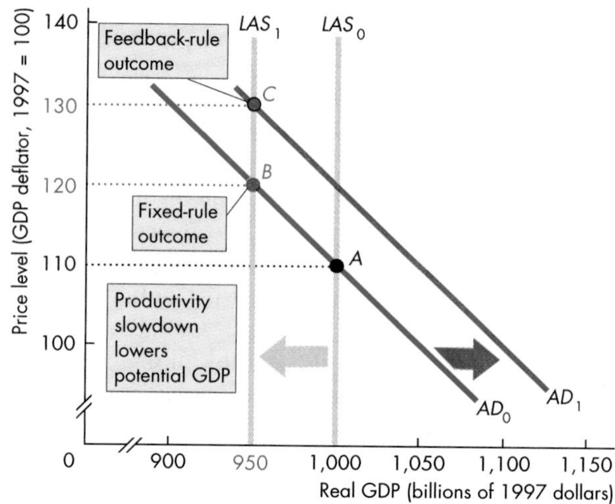

Initially the economy is at point *A*. A productivity growth slowdown shifts the long-run aggregate supply curve from LAS_0 to LAS_1. Real GDP decreases to $950 billion, and the price level rises to 120 at point *B*. With a fixed rule, there is no change in the quantity of money, taxes, or government expenditures; aggregate demand stays at AD_0 and that is the end of the matter. With a feedback rule, the Bank increases the quantity of money and Parliament cuts taxes or increases expenditures, intending to increase real GDP. Aggregate demand shifts to AD_1, but the result is an increase in the price level—to 130—with no change in real GDP, at point *C*.

We've now seen some of the shortcomings of using feedback rules for stabilization policy. Some economists believe that these shortcomings are serious and want to constrain Parliament and the Bank of Canada so that they use fixed rules. Others, regarding the potential advantages of feedback rules as greater than their costs, advocate the continued use of such policies but with an important modification that we'll now look at.

Natural Rate Policies

The business cycle and unemployment policies we've considered have been directed at smoothing the business cycle and minimizing *cyclical unemployment.* It is also possible to pursue policies aimed at lowering the natural rate of unemployment. But there are no costless ways of lowering the natural rate of unemployment. Let's look at two possible ways.

One policy tool is unemployment compensation. To lower the natural rate of unemployment, the government might lower the unemployment compensation rate, or shorten the period for which compensation is paid, or restrict compensation to people who undertake training programs that increase the likelihood of their finding jobs. With lower compensation, an unemployed person would spend less time looking for a job and would accept a job even it was not a good match for the person's skills. But such a policy might create hardship and have a cost that exceeds the cost of a high natural rate of unemployment.

The government might lower the minimum real wage rate. It could achieve a cut in the minimum wage either by holding the minimum money wage rate constant and letting inflation cut the minimum real wage rate or by cutting the minimum money wage rate. A lower minimum wage increases the quantity of labour demanded and lowers unemployment. Again, the government faces the trade-off.

REVIEW QUIZ

1 What is a fixed-rule fiscal policy and what is a fixed-rule monetary policy? Can you provide two examples of fixed rules in everyday life (other than those in the text)?
2 What is a feedback fiscal policy and what is a feedback monetary policy? When might a feedback policy be used? Can you provide two examples of feedback rules in everyday life (other than those in the text)?
3 Why do some economists say that feedback rules do not necessarily deliver a better macroeconomic performance than fixed rules? Do you agree or disagree with them? Why?

We've studied growth policy and business cycle and unemployment policy. Let's now study anti-inflation policy.

Anti-Inflation Policy

THERE ARE TWO INFLATION POLICY PROBLEMS. In times of price level stability, the problem is to prevent inflation from breaking out. In times of inflation, the problem is to reduce its rate and restore price stability. Preventing inflation from breaking out means avoiding both demand-pull and cost-push forces. Avoiding demand-pull inflation is the flip side of avoiding demand-driven recession and is achieved by stabilizing aggregate demand. So the business cycle and unemployment policy we've just studied is also an anti-inflation policy. But avoiding cost-push inflation raises some special issues that we need to consider. So we will look at two issues for inflation policy:

- Avoiding cost-push inflation
- Slowing inflation

Avoiding Cost-Push Inflation

Cost-push inflation is inflation that has its origins in cost increases (see Chapter 28, pp. 653–655). In 1973–1974 and again in 1979, the world oil price exploded. Cost shocks such as these become inflationary if they are accommodated by an increase in the quantity of money. Such an increase in the quantity of money can occur if a monetary policy feedback rule is used. A fixed-rule policy for the quantity of money makes cost-push inflation impossible. Let's see why.

Figure 32.8 shows the economy at full employment. Aggregate demand is AD_0, short-run aggregate supply is SAS_0, and long-run aggregate supply is LAS. Real GDP is $1,000 billion, and the price level is 110 at point *A*. Now suppose that OPEC tries to gain a temporary advantage by increasing the price of oil. The short-run aggregate supply curve shifts leftward from SAS_0 to SAS_1.

Monetarist Fixed Rule Figure 32.8(a) shows what happens if the Bank of Canada follows a fixed rule for monetary policy and the government follows a fixed rule for fiscal policy. Suppose that the fixed rule is for zero money growth and no change in taxes or government expenditures on goods and services. With these fixed rules, the Bank and the government pay no attention to the fact that there has been an increase in the price of oil. No policy actions are taken. The short-run aggregate supply curve has shifted to SAS_1, but the aggregate demand curve remains at AD_0. The price level rises to 120, and real

FIGURE 32.8 Responding to an OPEC Oil Price Increase

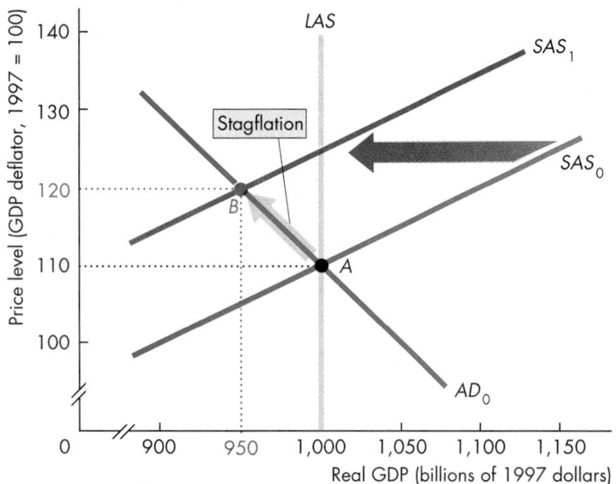

(a) Fixed rule

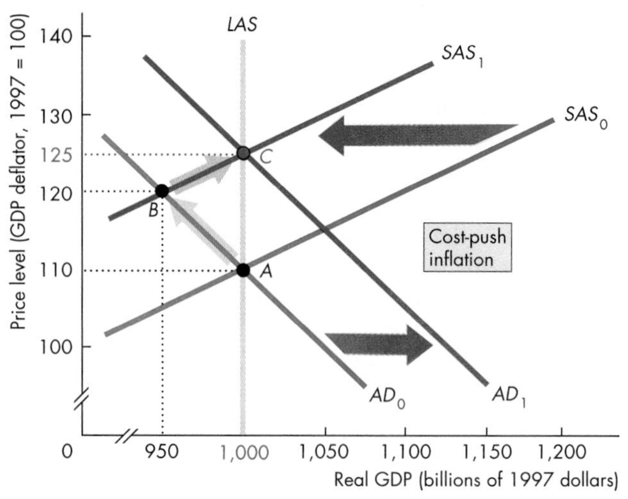

(b) Feedback rule

The economy starts out at point *A* on AD_0 and SAS_0, with a price level of 110 and real GDP of $1,000 billion. OPEC forces up the price of oil, and the short-run aggregate supply curve shifts to SAS_1. Real GDP decreases to $950 billion, and the price level increases to 120 at point *B*. With a fixed-rule policy (part a), aggregate demand remains at AD_0. The economy stays in a recession at point *B* until the price of oil falls and the economy returns to its original position. With a feedback-rule policy (part b), the Bank injects additional money and the government increases spending. The aggregate demand curve shifts to AD_1. Real GDP returns to $1,000 billion (potential GDP), but the price level increases to 125 at point *C*. The economy is set for another round of cost-push inflation.

GDP falls to $950 billion at point *B*. The economy has experienced *stagflation*. With unemployment above the natural rate, the money wage rate will eventually fall. The low level of real GDP and low sales will probably also bring a fall in the price of oil. These events shift the short-run aggregate supply curve back to SAS_0. The price level will fall to 110, and real GDP will increase to $1,000 billion. But this adjustment might take a long time.

Keynesian Feedback Rule Figure 32.8(b) shows what happens if the Bank and government operate a feedback rule. The starting point *A* is the same as before—the economy is on SAS_0 and AD_0 with a price level of 110 and real GDP of $1,000 billion. OPEC raises the price of oil, and the short-run aggregate supply curve shifts to SAS_1. Real GDP decreases to $950 billion, and the price level rises to 120 at point *B*.

A feedback rule is followed. With potential GDP perceived to be $1,000 billion and with actual real GDP at $950 billion, the Bank pumps money into the economy and the government increases its spending and lowers taxes. Aggregate demand increases, and the aggregate demand curve shifts rightward to AD_1. The price level rises to 125, and real GDP returns to $1,000 billion at point *C*. The economy moves back to full employment but at a higher price level. The economy has experienced *cost-push inflation*.

The Bank of Canada responded in the way we've just described to the first wave of OPEC price rises in the mid-1970s. OPEC saw the same advantage in forcing up the price of oil again. A new rise in the price of oil decreased aggregate supply, and the short-run aggregate supply curve shifted leftward once more. If the Bank had chased it with an increase in aggregate demand, the economy would have been in a freewheeling inflation. Realizing this danger, the Bank did *not* respond to the second wave of OPEC price increases in the early 1980s as it had done before. Instead, the Bank held firm and even slowed the growth of aggregate demand to further dampen the inflation consequences of OPEC's actions.

Incentives to Push Up Costs You can see that there are no checks on the incentives to push up *nominal* costs if the Bank accommodates price hikes. If some group sees a temporary gain from pushing up the price at which it is selling its resources and if the Bank always accommodates the increase to prevent unemployment and slack business conditions from emerging, then cost-push elements will have a free rein. But when the Bank pursues a fixed-rule policy, the incentive to attempt to steal a temporary advantage from a price increase is severely weakened. The cost of higher unemployment and lower output is a consequence that each group will have to face and recognize.

So a fixed rule can deliver steady inflation, while a feedback rule, in the face of cost-push pressures, leaves inflation free to rise at the whim of whichever group believes a temporary advantage to be available from pushing up its price.

Slowing Inflation

So far, we've concentrated on *avoiding* inflation. But often the problem is not to avoid inflation but to tame it. Canada was in such a situation during the late 1970s and early 1980s. How can inflation, once it has set in, be cured? We'll look at two cases:

- A surprise inflation reduction
- A credible announced inflation reduction

A Surprise Inflation Reduction We'll use two equivalent approaches to study the problem of lowering inflation: the aggregate supply–aggregate demand model and the Phillips curve. The *AS–AD* model tells us about real GDP and the price level, while the Phillips curve, which is explained in Chapter 28 (pp. 662–664), lets us keep track of inflation and unemployment.

Figure 32.9 illustrates the economy at full employment with inflation raging at 10 percent a year. In part (a), the economy is on aggregate demand curve AD_0 and short-run aggregate supply curve SAS_0. Real GDP is $1,000 billion, and the price level is 110. With real GDP equal to potential GDP on the *LAS* curve, the economy is at full employment. Equivalently, in part (b), the economy is on its long-run Phillips curve, *LRPC*, and short-run Phillips curve, $SRPC_0$. The inflation rate of 10 percent a year is anticipated, so unemployment is at its natural rate, 6 percent of the labour force.

Next year, aggregate demand is *expected* to increase and the aggregate demand curve in Fig. 32.9(a) is expected to shift rightward from AD_0 to AD_1. In expectation of this increase in aggregate demand, the money wage rate increases and shifts the short-run aggregate supply curve from SAS_0 to SAS_1. If expectations are fulfilled, the price level rises to 121—a 10 percent inflation—and real GDP remains at potential GDP. In part (b), the economy remains at its original position—unemployment is at the natural rate, and the inflation rate is 10 percent a year.

Now suppose that people expect the Bank not to change its policy, but the Bank actually tries to slow inflation. It raises interest rates and slows money growth. Aggregate demand growth slows, and the aggregate demand curve (in part a) shifts rightward from AD_0 not to AD_1 as people expect but only to AD_2.

With no change in the expected inflation rate, the money wage rate rises by the same amount as before and the short-run aggregate supply curve shifts leftward from SAS_0 to SAS_1. Real GDP decreases to $950 billion, and the price level rises to 118.8—an inflation rate of 8 percent a year. In Fig. 32.9(b), the economy moves along the short-run Phillips curve $SRPC_0$ as unemployment rises to 9 percent and inflation falls to 8 percent a year. The Bank's policy has succeeded in slowing inflation, but at the cost of recession. Real GDP is below potential GDP, and unemployment is above its natural rate.

A Credible Announced Inflation Reduction Suppose that instead of simply slowing down the growth of aggregate demand, the Bank announces its intention ahead of its action and in a credible and convincing way so that its announcement is believed. That is, the Bank's policy is anticipated. Because the lower level of aggregate demand is expected, the money wage rate increases at a pace that is consistent with the lower level of aggregate demand. The short-run aggregate supply curve (in Fig. 32.9a) shifts leftward from SAS_0 but only to SAS_2. Aggregate demand increases by the amount expected, and the aggregate demand curve shifts from AD_0 to AD_2. The price level rises to 115.5—an inflation rate of 5 percent a year—and real GDP remains at potential GDP.

In Fig. 32.9(b), the lower expected inflation rate shifts the short-run Phillips curve downward to $SRPC_1$, and inflation falls to 5 percent a year, while unemployment remains at its natural rate of 6 percent.

FIGURE 32.9 Lowering Inflation

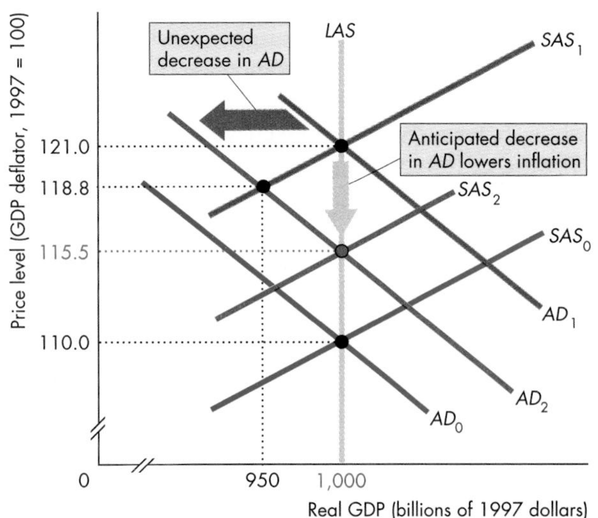

(a) Aggregate demand and aggregate supply

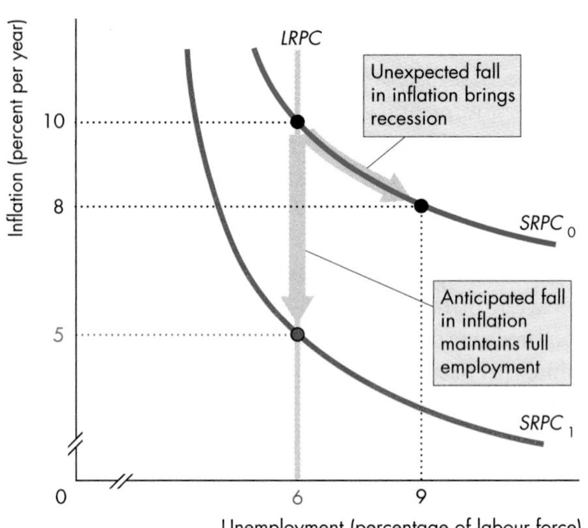

(b) Phillips curves

In part (a), aggregate demand is AD_0, short-run aggregate supply is SAS_0, and real GDP and potential GDP are $1,000 billion on the long-run aggregate supply curve *LAS*. The aggregate demand curve is expected to shift and actually shifts to AD_1. The short-run aggregate supply curve shifts to SAS_1. The price level rises to 121, but real GDP remains at $1,000 billion. Inflation is proceeding at 10 percent a year, and this inflation rate is anticipated. In part (b), which shows this same situation, the economy is on the short-run Phillips curve $SRPC_0$ and on the long-run Phillips curve *LRPC*. Unemployment is at the natural rate of 6 percent, and inflation is 10 percent a year.

An unexpected slowdown in aggregate demand growth means that the aggregate demand curve shifts from AD_0 to AD_2, real GDP decreases to $950 billion, and inflation slows to 8 percent (price level is 118.8). Unemployment rises to 9 percent as the economy slides down $SRPC_0$. An anticipated, credible, announced slowdown in aggregate demand growth means that when the aggregate demand curve shifts from AD_0 to AD_2, the short-run aggregate supply curve shifts from SAS_0 to SAS_2. The short-run Phillips curve shifts to $SRPC_1$. Inflation slows to 5 percent, real GDP remains at $1,000 billion, and unemployment remains at its natural rate of 6 percent.

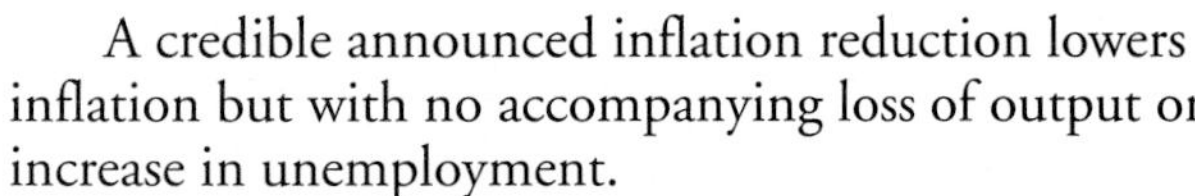

A credible announced inflation reduction lowers inflation but with no accompanying loss of output or increase in unemployment.

Inflation Reduction in Practice

When the Bank of Canada slowed inflation in 1981, we paid a high price. The Bank's policy action was unpredicted. It occurred in the face of wages that had been set at too high a level to be consistent with the growth of aggregate demand that the Bank subsequently allowed. The consequence was recession—a decrease in real GDP and a rise in unemployment. Could the Bank have lowered inflation without causing recession by telling people far enough ahead of time that it did indeed plan to lower inflation?

The answer appears to be no. The main reason is that people expect the Bank to behave in line with its record, not with its stated intentions. How many times have you told yourself that it is your firm intention to take off 5 unwanted kilograms or to keep within your budget and put a few dollars away for a rainy day, only to discover that, despite your very best intentions, your old habits win out in the end?

To form expectations of the Bank's actions, people look at the Bank's past *actions*, not its stated intentions. On the basis of such observations—called Bank-watching—they try to work out what the Bank's policy is, to forecast its future actions, and to forecast the effects of those actions on aggregate demand and inflation. The Bank of Canada has built a reputation for being anti-inflationary. That reputation is valuable because it helps the Bank to contain inflation and lowers the cost of eliminating inflation if it temporarily returns. The reason is that with a low expected inflation rate, the short-run Phillips curve is in a favourable position (like $SRPC_1$ in Fig. 32.9b). The Bank's actions during the 1990s were designed to keep inflation expectations low and prevent the gains made during the 1980s recession from being eroded.

Balancing the Inflation and Real GDP Objective: The Taylor Rule

John Taylor, formerly an economics professor at Stanford University and now Undersecretary of the Treasury for International Affairs in the Bush administration, has suggested a policy feedback rule that he says would deliver a better performance than what central banks have achieved.

The idea is to target inflation but also to be explicit about the extent to which the interest rate will be changed in response to both inflation and deviations of real GDP from potential GDP. By being explicit and always following the same rule, central bank watching becomes a simpler task and smaller forecasting errors might be made, which translates into smaller deviations of real GDP from potential GDP and smaller deviations of the unemployment rate from the natural rate.

If the Bank of Canada followed the Taylor rule with a target inflation rate of 2 percent a year and an average real overnight loans rate of 3 percent a year, it would set a target for the overnight loans rate equal to 5 percent plus one-half of the amount by which the inflation rate exceeds 2 percent a year, plus one-half of the percentage gap between real GDP and potential GDP. And the Bank would move the actual overnight loans rate gradually towards the target rate.

Figure 32.10 shows the overnight loans rate and the target rate if the Taylor rule were followed. You can see that the Bank of Canada's actual policy is similar to the Taylor rule. So if the Bank announced that it were using the Taylor rule, it would not be changing the way it acts, but by being explicit about the formula that determines the overnight loans rate, it would take the mystery and unpredictability out of its policy actions.

But you can also see that the Bank of Canada's actions have not exactly followed the Taylor rule. During the recessions of the early 1980s and early 1990s, the Bank set the overnight loans rate higher than the Taylor rule. The reason could be that the Bank has a lower target inflation rate or places less weight on real GDP fluctuations than does the Taylor rule.

FIGURE 32.10 The Overnight Loans Rate and the Taylor Rule

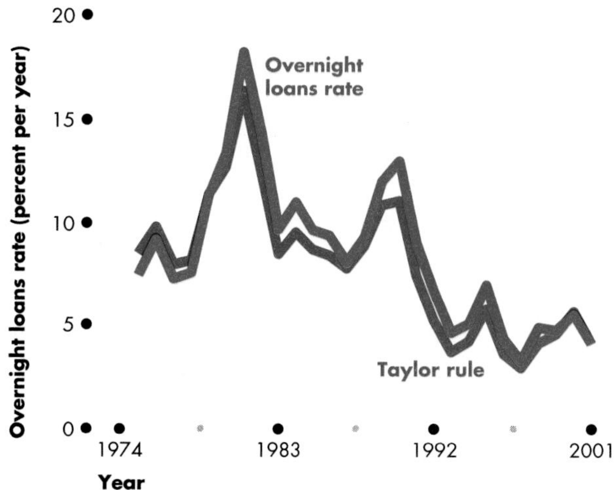

The green line shows the overnight loans interest rate between 1975 and 2001. The orange line shows what the overnight rate would have been if the Bank of Canada had followed the Taylor rule and adjusted the overnight loans rate to place equal emphasis on achieving low inflation and full employment.

Sources: Bank of Canada, *Banking and Financial Statistics*, table F1, and authors' calculations.

REVIEW QUIZ

1. Why does a fixed rule provide more effective protection against cost-push inflation than does a feedback rule?
2. Why does a recession usually result as inflation is being tamed?
3. How does establishing a reputation of being an inflation fighter improve the Bank of Canada's ability to maintain low inflation and to lower the cost of fighting inflation?

Reading Between the Lines on pp. 774–775 looks Canada's stabilization challenge at the end of 2002 as the world economy appeared to be slowing.

You've now completed your study of macroeconomics. In the remaining chapters, we shift our focus to the international economy.

The Stabilization Policy Balancing Act

NATIONAL POST, OCTOBER 12, 2002

Canadian job growth surges ahead:

Best 9-months in 15 years: 'emerging cracks' enough to prevent near-term rate hike

The Canadian economy blasted through forecasts to pump out another 40,700 jobs in September, but analysts said the labour market showed signs of tiring and that, combined with a minefield of global uncertainties, should keep the Bank of Canada from raising interest rates next week. ...

The economy has created almost as many jobs so far this year as in all of 1999, when the world economy was roaring. That year, 433,000 jobs were generated.

Despite September's employment gain, the unemployment rate jumped to 7.7%, from 7.5%, because more people felt confident enough to start looking for work—another sign of a strength—analysts said. The participation rate rose to a 12-year high of 67.2%. But analysts spotted weaknesses concealed in the strong headline numbers. ...

Among the cracks:

- All the gains were part-time. Full-time jobs fell by 5,000 in the month, the first drop in a year.
- the manufacturing sector lost 16,900 jobs.
- almost half the gains were in self-employment;
- the private sector generated gains of only 8,600;
- for the third quarter as a whole, total hours worked fell 0.9% at annual rates.
- the rise in the unemployment rate could be psychologically damaging ...

Many analysts said that, if anything, the world has become a more uncertain place ... with banking concerns brewing in Japan and Germany and corporate credit concerns adding to an ugly outlook for the world economy. ...

Essence of the Story

- The Canadian economy created 40,700 jobs in September 2002.
- Despite September's increase in employment, the unemployment rate increased because the labour force participation rate increased.
- Most of the jobs created were part-time and aggregate hours decreased. Only one job in five was in the private sector (four in five were in the public sector).
- The global economic outlook appeared uncertain.

Economic Analysis

■ Figure 1 illustrates the Canadian economy at the start of 2002. Potential GDP was $1,045 billion, long-run aggregate supply was LAS_0, short-run aggregate supply was SAS_0, and aggregate demand was AD_0. Equilibrium real GDP was $1,030 billion, so there was a recessionary gap of $15 billion.

■ Potential GDP increased to $1,065 billion by the third quarter of 2002, and the long-run aggregate supply curve shifted rightward to LAS_1.

■ During 2002, short-run aggregate supply increased slightly to SAS_1 and aggregate demand increased strongly to AD_1.

■ Equilibrium real GDP increased to $1,065 billion, and the economy was at a full-employment equilibrium.

■ Figure 2 illustrates the uncertain outlook for 2003 that confronts the Bank of Canada as it makes decisions about monetary policy.

■ By the third quarter of 2003, potential GDP will be around $1,095 billion so the long-run aggregate supply curve will be *LAS* in Fig. 2.

■ The *SAS* curve in 2003 will depend on the change in *LAS* and the change in the money wage rate. The *SAS* curve for 2003 in Fig. 2 assumes that these two influences exactly offset each other.

■ If aggregate demand increases to AD_0 in Fig. 2, real GDP will increase to $1,095—potential GDP—and the price level will rise to 110—an inflation rate of less than 2 percent a year. The Bank of Canada would like to deliver this outcome.

■ But if aggregate demand continues to increase as strongly as it did in 2002, by the third quarter of 2003, the *AD* curve will be at AD_1 in Fig. 2. Real GDP will exceed potential GDP and the inflation rate will be increasing.

■ To try to avoid such an inflation, the Bank of Canada would increase the interest rate, hoping to keep aggregate demand at AD_0 and achieve full employment.

■ A global recession will decrease Canadian aggregate demand towards AD_2, and bring recession in Canada.

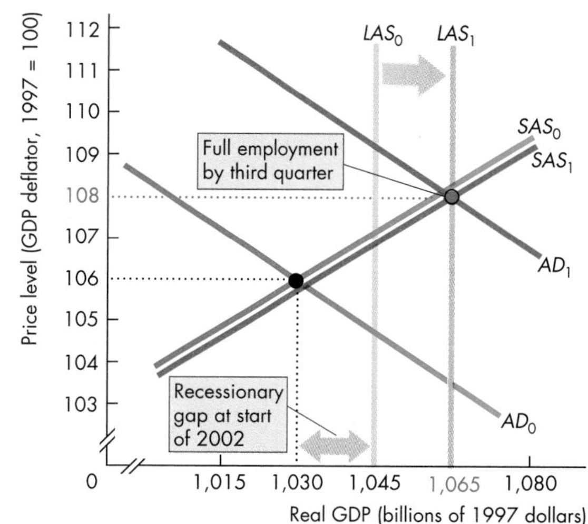

Figure 1 The Canadian economy in 2002

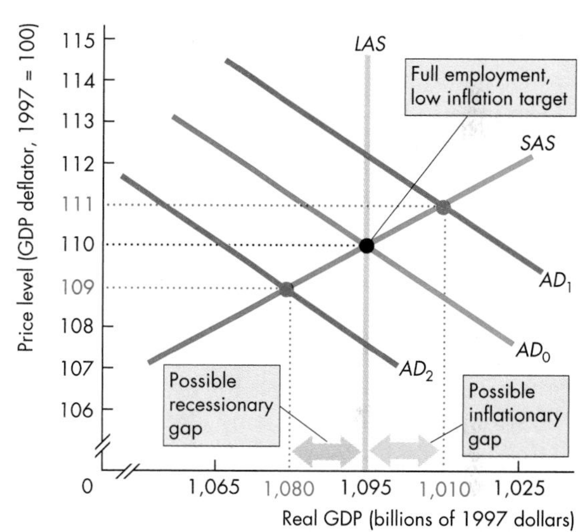

Figure 2 The uncertain outlook for 2003

SUMMARY

KEY POINTS

Policy Goals (pp. 756–757)

- The goals of macroeconomic policy are to achieve the highest sustainable rate of potential GDP growth, smooth the business cycle, maintain low unemployment, and avoid inflation.
- The two core policy indicators are real GDP growth and inflation.

Policy Tools and Performance (pp. 758–760)

- Fiscal policy was expansionary during the Trudeau years and contractionary during the Mulroney and Chrétien years.
- There have been four phases of monetary policy since 1971: (1) permit inflation to rise, (2) bring inflation down, (3) eliminate inflation, and (4) keep inflation low and encourage expansion.

Long-Term Growth Policy (pp. 760–762)

- Policies to increase the long-term growth rate focus on increasing saving and investment in human capital and new technologies.
- To increase the saving rate, government saving must increase or incentives for private saving must be strengthened by increasing after-tax returns.
- Human capital investment might be increased with improved education and by improving on-the-job training programs and health care.
- Investment in new technologies can be encouraged by tax incentives.

Business Cycle and Unemployment Policy (pp. 763–769)

- In the face of an aggregate demand shock, a fixed-rule policy takes no action. Real GDP and the price level fluctuate.
- In the face of an aggregate demand shock, a feedback-rule policy takes offsetting fiscal and monetary action. An ideal feedback rule keeps the economy at full employment, with stable prices.
- Some economists say that a feedback rule creates fluctuations because it requires greater knowledge of the economy than we have, operates with time lags that extend beyond the forecast horizon, and introduces unpredictability about policy reactions.
- In the face of a productivity growth slowdown, both rules have the same effect on output. A feedback rule brings a higher inflation rate than does a fixed rule.

Anti-Inflation Policy (pp. 769–773)

- A fixed rule minimizes the threat of cost-push inflation. A feedback rule validates cost-push inflation and leaves the price level and inflation rate free to move to wherever they are pushed.
- Inflation can be tamed, at little or no cost in terms of lost output or excessive unemployment, by slowing the growth of aggregate demand in a credible and predictable way. But usually, when inflation is slowed down, a recession occurs.

KEY FIGURES

Figure 32.1 Macroeconomic Performance: Real GDP and Inflation, 757
Figure 32.2 The Fiscal Policy Record: A Summary, 758
Figure 32.3 The Monetary Policy Record: A Summary, 759
Figure 32.6 Two Stabilization Policies: Aggregate Demand Shock, 765
Figure 32.7 Responding to a Productivity Growth Slowdown, 768
Figure 32.8 Responding to an OPEC Oil Price Increase, 770
Figure 32.9 Lowering Inflation, 772

KEY TERMS

Discretionary policy, 763
Feedback-rule policy, 763
Fixed-rule policy, 763
Keynesian activist, 764
Monetarist, 764

PROBLEMS

*1. A productivity growth slowdown has occurred. Explain its possible origins and describe a policy package that is designed to speed up growth again.

2. A nation is experiencing a falling saving rate. Explain its possible origins and describe a policy package that is designed to increase the saving rate.

*3. The economy shown in the figure is initially on aggregate demand curve AD_0 and short-run aggregate supply curve *SAS*. Then aggregate demand decreases, and the aggregate demand curve shifts leftward to AD_1.

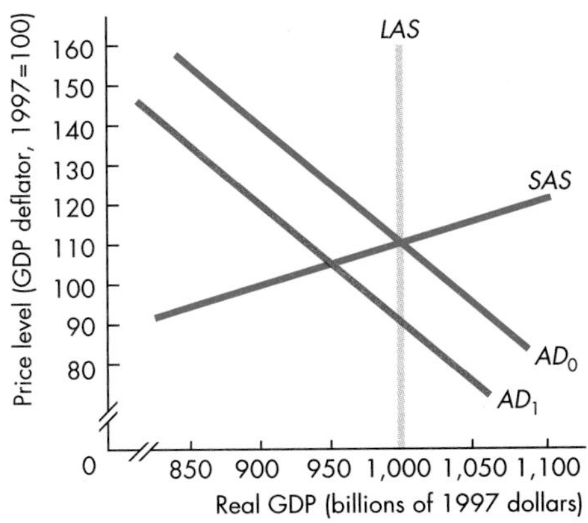

a. What is the initial equilibrium real GDP and price level?
b. If the decrease in aggregate demand is temporary and the government follows a fixed-rule fiscal policy, what happens to real GDP and the price level? Trace the immediate effects and the adjustment as aggregate demand returns to its original level.
c. If the decrease in aggregate demand is temporary and the government follows a feedback-rule fiscal policy, what happens to real GDP and the price level? Trace the immediate effects and the adjustment as aggregate demand returns to its original level.
d. If the decrease in aggregate demand is permanent and the government follows a fixed-rule fiscal policy, what happens to real GDP and the price level?
e. If the decrease in aggregate demand is permanent and the government follows a feedback-rule fiscal policy, what happens to real GDP and the price level?

4. The economy shown in the figure is initially on aggregate demand curve *AD* and short-run aggregate supply curve SAS_0. Then short-run aggregate supply decreases, and the short-run aggregate supply curve shifts leftward to SAS_1.

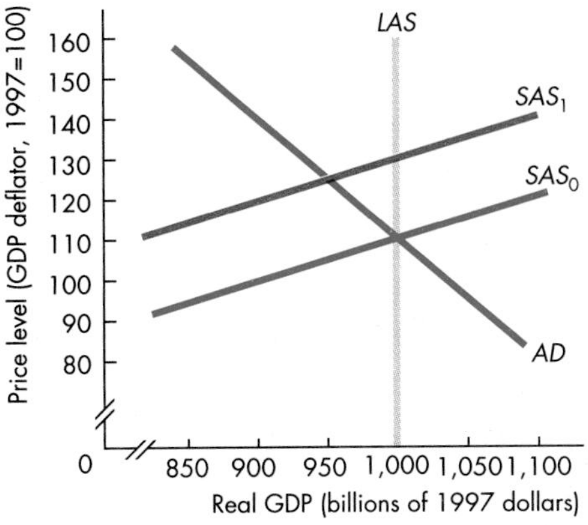

a. What is the initial equilibrium real GDP and price level?
b. What type of event could have caused the decrease in short-run aggregate supply?
c. If the Bank of Canada follows a fixed-rule monetary policy, what happens to real GDP and the price level? Trace the immediate effects and the adjustment as aggregate demand and short-run aggregate supply return to their original level.
d. If the Bank of Canada follows a feedback-rule monetary policy, what happens to real GDP and the price level? Trace the immediate effects and the adjustment as aggregate demand and short-run aggregate supply respond to the policy action.

*5. The economy is experiencing 10 percent inflation and 7 percent unemployment. Real GDP growth has sagged to 1 percent a year. The stock market has crashed.
a. Explain how the economy might have got into its current state.
b. Set out policies for the Bank of Canada and Parliament to pursue that will lower inflation, lower unemployment, and speed real GDP growth.
c. Explain how and why your proposed policies will work.

6. The inflation rate has fallen to less than 1 percent a year, and the unemployment rate has fallen to less than 4 percent. Real GDP is growing at almost 5 percent a year. The stock market is at a record high.
   a. Explain how the economy might have got into its current state.
   b. Set out policies for the Bank of Canada and Parliament to pursue that will maintain low inflation, low unemployment, and rapid real GDP growth.
   c. Explain how and why your proposed policies will work.
*7. When the economies of Indonesia, Korea, Thailand, Malaysia, and the Philippines entered into recession in 1997, the International Monetary Fund (IMF) made loans but only on the condition that the recipients of the loans increase interest rates, raise taxes, and cut government expenditures.
   a. Would you describe the IMF prescription as a feedback-rule policy or a fixed-rule policy?
   b. What do you predict the effects of the IMF policies would be?
   c. Do you have any criticisms of the IMF policies? What would you have required these countries to do? Why?
8. As the Canadian economy continued to expand and its stock market soared to new record levels during 1998, the Bank of Canada cut interest rates.
   a. Would you describe the Bank's actions as a feedback-rule policy or a fixed-rule policy?
   b. What do you predict the effects of the Bank's policies would be?
   c. Do you have any criticisms of the Bank's policies? What monetary policy would you have pursued? Why?

CRITICAL THINKING

1. Study *Reading Between the Lines* on pp. 774–775 and then
   a. Do you think the labour market indicators reported in the news article indicate expansion or recession? Explain your answer.
   b. Describe the cracks that were appearing in the Canadian economy that suggested a slower growth rate in 2003.
   c. What are David Dodge's views on the appropriate fiscal policy reported in the news article? Do you agree with those views? Why or why not?
   d. What was the likely influence of the United States, Japan, and Germany on the Canadian economy during 2003?
2. Suppose the economy is booming and inflation is beginning to rise, but it is widely agreed that a massive recession is just around the corner. Weigh the advantages and disadvantages of the government pursuing a fixed rule and a feedback rule for *fiscal* policy.
3. Suppose the economy is in a recession and inflation is falling. It is widely agreed that a strong recovery is just around the corner. Weigh the advantages and disadvantages of the Bank of Canada pursuing a fixed-rule policy and a feedback-rule policy.

WEB EXERCISES

1. Use the links on the Parkin–Bade Web site to review the Bank of Canada's latest *Monetary Policy Report* and the latest *Annual Financial Report of the Government of Canada*. Write a summary and critique of these reports.
2. Use the link on the Parkin–Bade Web site to review the latest *World Economic Outlook*.
   a. What are the major macroeconomic stabilization policy problems in the world today?
   b. What is the general direction in which policy actions are pushing the global economy?

UNDERSTANDING AGGREGATE SUPPLY AND ECONOMIC GROWTH

Expanding the Frontier

Economics is about how we cope with scarcity. We cope by making choices that balance marginal benefits and marginal costs so that we use our scarce resources efficiently. ◆ These choices determine how much work we do; how hard we work at school to learn the mental skills that form our human capital and that determine the kinds of jobs we get and the incomes we earn; and how much we save for future big-ticket expenditures. These choices also determine how much businesses and governments spend on new capital—on auto assembly lines, computers and fibre cables for improved Internet services, shopping malls, highways, bridges, and tunnels; and how intensively existing capital and natural resources are used and therefore how quickly they wear out or are used up. Most significant of all, these choices determine the problems that scientists, engineers, and other inventors work on to develop new technologies. ◆ All the choices we've just described determine two vital measures of economic performance:

- Real GDP
- Economic growth

Real GDP is determined by the quantity of labour, the quantity of capital, and the state of technological knowledge. And economic growth—the growth rate of real GDP—is determined by growth in the quantity of labour, capital accumulation, and technological advances. ◆ Economic growth, maintained at a steady rate over a number of decades, is the single most powerful influence on any society. It brings a transformation that continues to amaze thoughtful people. Economic growth that is maintained at a rapid rate can transform a society in years, not decades. Such transformations are taking place right now in many Asian countries. These transformations are economic miracles. ◆ The four chapters in this part studied the miracle of rapid economic growth, the forces that shape our capacity to produce goods and services, and the forces that from time to time interrupt the growth process. ◆ Chapter 29 explains how labour market equilibrium determines potential GDP. Chapter 30 studies the process of economic growth in the fast-growing economies of Asia and Canada. It explains how growth is influenced by technological change and the incentives that stimulate it. Chapter 31 studies the business cycle that interrupts growth, and Chapter 32 reviews the policy debate and looks at alternative approaches to speeding growth, smoothing the business cycle, and containing inflation. ◆ Modern ideas about economic growth owe much to two economists, Joseph Schumpeter and Paul Romer, whom you can meet on the following pages.

PROBING THE IDEAS

Incentives to Innovate

The Economist

"Economic progress, in capitalist society, means turmoil."

JOSEPH SCHUMPETER
Capitalism, Socialism, and Democracy

JOSEPH SCHUMPETER, *the son of a textile factory owner, was born in Austria in 1883. He moved from Austria to Germany during the tumultuous 1920s when those two countries experienced hyperinflation. In 1932, in the depths of the Great Depression, he came to the United States and became a professor of economics at Harvard University.*

This creative economic thinker wrote about economic growth and development, business cycles, political systems, and economic biography. He was a person of strong opinions who expressed them strongly and delighted in verbal battles.

Schumpeter has become the unwitting founder of modern growth theory. He saw the development and diffusion of new technologies by profit-seeking entrepreneurs as the source of economic progress. But he saw economic progress as a process of creative destruction—the creation of new profit opportunities and the destruction of currently profitable businesses. For Schumpeter, economic growth and the business cycle were a single phenomenon.

When Schumpeter died, in 1950, he had achieved his self-expressed life ambition: He was regarded as the world's greatest economist.

The Issues

Technological change, capital accumulation, and population growth all interact to produce economic growth. But what is cause and what is effect? And can we expect productivity and income per person to keep growing?

Thc classical economists of the eighteenth and nineteenth centuries believed that technological advances and capital accumulation were the engines of growth. But they also believed that no matter how successful people were at inventing more productive technologies and investing in new capital, they were destined to live at the subsistence level. These economists based their conclusion on the belief that productivity growth causes population growth, which in turn causes productivity to decline. These classical economists believed that whenever economic growth raises incomes above the subsistence level, the population will increase. They went on to reason that the increase in population brings diminishing returns that lower productivity. As a result, incomes must always return to the subsistence level. Only when incomes are at the subsistence level is population growth held in check.

A new approach, called neoclassical growth theory, was developed by Robert Solow of MIT, during the 1950s. Solow, who was one of Schumpeter's students, received the Nobel Prize for Economic Science for this work.

Solow challenged the conclusions of the classical economists. But the new theories of economic growth developed during the 1980s and 1990s went further. They stand the classical belief on its head. Today's theory of population growth is that rising income slows the population growth rate because it increases the opportunity cost of having children and lowers the opportunity cost of investing in children and equipping them with more human capital, which makes them more productive. Productivity and income grow because technology advances, and the scope for further productivity growth, which is stimulated by the search for profit, is practically unlimited.

Then

In 1830, a strong and experienced farm worker could harvest three acres of wheat in a day. The only capital employed was a scythe to cut the wheat, which had been used since Roman times, and a cradle on which the stalks were laid, which had been invented by Flemish farmers in the fifteenth century. With newly developed horse-drawn plows, harrows, and planters, farmers could plant more wheat than they could harvest. But despite big efforts, no one had been able to make a machine that could replicate the swing of a scythe. Then in 1831, 22-year-old Cyrus McCormick built a machine that worked. It scared the horse that pulled it, but it did in a matter of hours what three men could accomplish in a day. Technological change has increased productivity on farms and brought economic growth. Do the facts about productivity growth mean that the classical economists, who believed that diminishing returns would push us relentlessly back to a subsistence living standard, were wrong?

&

Now

Today's technologies are expanding our horizons beyond the confines of our planet and are expanding our minds. Geosynchronous satellites bring us global television, voice and data communication, and more accurate weather forecasts, which, incidentally, increase agricultural productivity. In the foreseeable future, we might have superconductors that revolutionize the use of electric power, virtual reality theme parks and training facilities, pollution-free hydrogen cars, wristwatch telephones, and optical computers that we can talk to. Equipped with these new technologies, our ability to create yet more dazzling technologies increases. Technological change begets technological change in an (apparently) unending process and makes us ever more productive and brings ever higher incomes.

Today's revolution in the way economists think about economic growth has been led by Paul Romer, a professor of economics at Stanford University, whom you can meet on the following pages.

TALKING WITH

PAUL ROMER *is Professor of Economics at the Graduate School of Business at Stanford University and the Royal Bank Fellow of the Canadian Institute for Advanced Research. Born in 1955 in Denver, Colorado, he earned his B.S. in Mathematics (1977) and his Ph.D. in Economics (1983) from the University of Chicago.*

Paul Romer

Professor Romer has transformed the way economists think about economic growth. He believes that sustained economic growth arises from competition among firms. Firms try to increase their profits by devoting resources to creating new products and developing new ways of making existing products.

Michael Parkin and Robin Bade talked with Professor Romer about his work, how he was influenced by Joseph Schumpeter and Robert Solow, and the insights economic growth offers us.

Professor Romer, why did you decide to become an economist?

As an undergraduate, I studied math and physics and was interested in becoming a cosmologist. During my senior year, I concluded that job prospects in physics were not very promising, so I decided to go to law school. I was an undergraduate at the University of Chicago, where the law and economics movement first emerged. In the fall of my senior year, I took my first economics course to prepare for law school. My economics professor, Sam Peltzman presented a simple piece of economic analysis that changed my life. He argued that the demand for economists was likely to grow for decades. The government, which employs economists, would grow in size. Businesses that deal with the government would want their own economists. The legal profession that serves businesses would also need more economists. Because of all these demands, many students would want to take economics courses. This meant that there would be many job openings for economists at universities. Moreover, he claimed, being a professor of economics was a lot like being a cosmologist and far more fun than being a lawyer. I could take fragmentary bits of evidence and try to make sense of them using mathematical equations. So I tore up my law school applications, applied to graduate school in economics, and never looked back.

What are the truly important lessons about the causes economic growth?

As a physics major, I felt that the description economists used for growth violated a basic law of physics: the conservation of mass. Economists seemed to be saying that GDP, the output of a nation, was a bunch of stuff that was "produced" and that the quantity of stuff produced has grown steadily over time and will continue to do so. But this can't be right. We have the same amount of stuff, or elements from the periodic table, that we had 100,000 years ago. Because there are many more people now, in terms of kilograms of matter per person, we know that we are vastly poorer than our ancestors were 100,000 years ago. Yet we clearly have a higher standard of living. How could this be? This basic question indicates that thinking about growth as a production process that generates stuff is a dead-end. Instead, economic growth has to be about rearranging the fixed amount of matter that we have to work with and making new combinations that seem a lot more valuable. The key insight is that economic growth comes from increases in value, not increases in the amount of matter.

Can you give us an example of an increase in value?

For tens of thousands of years, we treated iron oxide, ordinary rust, like dirt. When we lived in caves, we learned how to use it as a pigment for decorating cave walls. We took the low-value dirt and put it to the higher-valued use of making cave paintings. Later, we learned how to extract the iron from iron ore to make bridges and rails. Later still, we learned how to arrange the iron atoms together with carbon atoms and make steel. Recently, we learned how to take iron oxide and put it on magnetic tape and use it to store sound and pictures. The iron, oxygen, and carbon atoms have always been here. We have a higher standard of living because we have learned how to arrange these atoms in ways that we find more valuable.

What kind of policy implications does this kind of thinking lead to?

Policy makers must encourage institutions to become more efficient at discovering new recipes to rearrange matter. Consider the transistor as an example. We take silicon and mix it with a few impurities and some metal in just the right way, and we get a computer chip worth thousands of times what the raw ingredients were worth. Research grants, subsidies for education, and institutions like the nonprofit private university encourage the production of new recipes or ideas. But so do venture capitalists who help new-technology startups, competitive markets that allow the firms with better instructions or ideas to quickly displace existing firms, and labour laws that let inefficient firms lay off workers when more efficient new firms come on the scene. We must let firms like Digital Electronics or Wang Computers shrink, maybe even fail, if we want to make room for new firms like Intel to enter the scene and thrive.

> ***We take silicon and mix it with a few impurities and some metal in just the right way, and we get a computer chip worth thousands of times what the raw ingredients were worth.***

Were the classical economists wrong in their view that population growth and diminishing returns are the dominant long-term influences on production and incomes? Or is the current global population explosion part of a process that will ultimately prove them correct?

Classical economists like Malthus and Ricardo were right when they argued that we have a fixed amount of natural resources to work with. Malthus pointed out that resource scarcity will lead to falling standards of living if we continue to work with the same set of recipes or instructions for using our resources. Where he went wrong was in assuming that there was little scope for us to find new recipes for taking resources such as land, water, carbon dioxide, nitrogen, and sunshine and converting them into carbohydrates and proteins that we can eat.

The classical economists got half of the story right. We do live in a world with scarce resources. They missed the other half. There is an incomprehensibly large number of different formulas we can use to recombine these scarce resources into things we value, such as protein or entertainment.

Scarcity is a very important part of economics and our lives. For example, we know that there is an absolute limit on the number of people who can live on the earth. One way or another, we know that the rate of population growth will slow down. It's only a question of how and when. But will this ultimately lead to a period when standards of living fall as Malthus predicted? I doubt it. As countries get rich, population growth slows. As a larger fraction of the worldwide population becomes educated, these people will help us to discover new things, like plants that are more efficient at taking carbon dioxide out of the atmosphere, and more efficient distribution systems. Thus standards of living for all humans will continue to improve.

During the past decade, China and several other economies in East Asia have experienced rapid, unheralded growth rates. Why?

These countries took some of the recipes, formulas, and instructions for generating value that already existed in the advanced countries of the world and put them to use within their borders. It's the same process that the Japanese followed after the Meiji restoration at the end of the last century. These countries noticed that other people in the world knew a lot about how to create value and realized that by trading with these people, they could share in the gains.

What lessons from East Asia can, in principle, be applied in Africa and Central Europe?

The basic insight is that there are huge potential gains from trade. Poor countries can supply their natural and human resources. Rich countries can supply their know-how. When these are combined, everyone can be better off. The challenge is for a country to arrange its laws and institutions so that both sides can profitably engage in trade. If there are barriers to trade or if the government cannot protect basic property rights and prevent crime, trade can't take place. For example, the Japanese have been able to borrow many ideas about manufacturing and design and even to improve on some of these ideas. But because they have barriers that limit entry of foreign firms into the retail sector, they still waste vast quantities of resources on a very inefficient distribution system.

What does today's thinking about economic growth owe to Joseph Schumpeter and Robert Solow?

Schumpeter worked at a time before most economists had learned to work with equations. He coined the phrase "creative destruction," which describes the process by which companies like Wang shrink or go out of business when new firms come in. He also described in words how important monopoly profits are in the process of innovation. There were many other economists, including Alfred Marshall, who described these same issues in verbal terms and also struggled to express these ideas in terms of equations.

Robert Solow was part of the post-World War II generation of economists who truly mastered the use of equations and wrote eloquently using both words and equations. As a result, his ideas have been far more influential than Schumpeter's. Many economists in the 1950s were trying to get a grasp on the economic effects of knowledge, formulas, recipes, and instructions. Solow called these things "technology" and gave us a wonderfully concise and workable way to think about how technology interacts with other economic inputs such as capital and labour. He also linked the methods that he and several economists were using to measure technology with this framework for thinking about the behaviour of the economy as a whole. His work on growth was a masterful piece of invention, synthesis, and exposition.

Recent economists have taken Solow's mathematical framework and extended it to bring in some of the elements that Schumpeter described in words, like creative destruction and monopoly power. One of the great things about ideas is that they build on each other. In Isaac Newton's famous phrase, those of us working on growth today are "able to see farther because we stand on the shoulders of giants." Newton was another person who was pretty good with equations and could turn a good phrase.

Is economics a worthwhile subject to major in? What can one do with an economics degree?

Economics is an excellent training ground for developing mathematical and verbal skills. But students should supplement the courses in economics with courses in mathematics and science that force them to practise working with equations, graphs, and numbers. There is no substitute for such practice. Innate ability is far less important than most students think.

If you can learn how to write readable prose and use the basic tools of mathematics, you can do almost anything.

They should also take courses that force them to write, revise, and edit. I took an English course in college that taught me the basics of how to edit, and it is one of the best investments I made. You can't tell what you will end up doing or what skills you will need later in life. But if you can learn how to write readable prose and use the basic tools of mathematics, you can do almost anything.

PART 10 THE GLOBAL ECONOMY

CHAPTER 33 TRADING WITH THE WORLD

Silk Routes and Sucking Sounds

Since ancient times, people have expanded their trading as far as technology allowed. Marco Polo opened up the silk route between Europe and China in the thirteenth century. Today, container ships laden with cars and electronics and Boeing 747s stuffed with farm-fresh foods ply sea and air routes, carrying billions of dollars' worth of goods. Why do people go to such great lengths to trade with those in other nations? ◆ In 1994, Canada entered into a free trade agreement with the United States and Mexico—the North American Free Trade Agreement, or NAFTA. Some people predicted a "giant sucking sound" as jobs were transferred from high-wage Michigan and Ontario to low-wage Mexico. Can we compete with a country that pays its workers a fraction of Canadian wages? Are there any industries, besides perhaps the software and movie industries, in which we have an advantage? ◆ Canada exports lumber to the United States for homebuilding. But U.S. lumber producers say that Canadian producers receive an unfair subsidy from their government, so the United States has imposed a tariff on Canadian lumber imports. Do tariffs benefit the importing country? We examine this question in *Reading Between the Lines.*

◇ In this chapter, we're going to learn about international trade and discover how *all* nations can gain from trading with other nations. We'll discover that all nations can compete, no matter how high their wages. We'll also explain why, despite the fact that international trade brings benefits to all, governments restrict trade.

After studying this chapter, you will be able to

- **Describe the trends and patterns in international trade**
- **Explain comparative advantage and explain why all countries can gain from international trade**
- **Explain why international trade restrictions reduce the volume of imports and exports and reduce our consumption possibilities**
- **Explain the arguments that are used to justify international trade restrictions and show how they are flawed**
- **Explain why we have international trade restrictions**

Patterns and Trends in International Trade

THE GOODS AND SERVICES THAT WE BUY FROM people in other countries are called **imports.** The goods and services that we sell to people in other countries are called **exports.** What are the most important things that we import and export? Most people would probably guess that a rich nation such as Canada imports raw materials and exports manufactured goods. Although that is one feature of Canadian international trade, it is not its most important feature. The vast bulk of our exports *and* imports is manufactured goods. We sell foreigners earth-moving equipment, airplanes, telecommunications equipment, and scientific equipment. We buy televisions, VCRs, blue jeans, and T-shirts from foreigners. Also, we are a major exporter of agricultural products and raw materials. We also import and export a huge volume of services.

Trade in Goods

Of the goods that we trade, manufactured goods account for 50 percent of our exports and 70 percent of our imports. Industrial materials (raw materials and semimanufactured items) account for 40 percent of our exports and 15 percent of our imports, and agricultural products account for only 5 percent of our exports and 2 percent of our imports. Our largest individual export and import items are capital goods and automobiles.

But goods account for only 80 percent of our exports and imports. The rest of our international trade is in services.

Trade in Services

You may be wondering how a country can "export" and "import" services. Here are some examples.

If you take a vacation in France and travel there on an Air France flight from Montreal, you import transportation services from France. The money you spend in France on hotel bills and restaurant meals is also classified as the import of services. Similarly, the money spent by a French student on vacation in Canada is a Canadian export of services to France.

When we import TV sets from South Korea, the owner of the ship that transports them might be Greek and the company that insures them might be British. The payments that we make for the transportation and insurance are Canadian imports of services. Similarly, when a Canadian shipping company transports timber from British Columbia to Tokyo, the transportation cost is a Canadian export of a service to Japan. Our international trade in these types of services is large and growing.

Geographical Patterns of International Trade

Canada has trading links with every part of the world, but the United States is our biggest trading partner. In 2001, 82 percent of our exports went to the United States and 71 percent of our imports came from the United States. Our trade with the European Union is also large—7 percent of our exports and 11 percent of our imports in 2001. Other major trading partners include the countries of Latin America and Japan. But our trade with Japan is only 2 percent of exports and 3 percent of imports.

Trends in the Volume of Trade

In 1978, we exported 25 percent of total output and imported 25 percent of the goods and services that we bought. In 2001, we exported 43 percent of total output and imported 38 percent of the goods and services that we bought.

On the export side, capital goods, automobiles, food, and raw materials have remained large items and held a roughly constant share of total exports. But the composition of imports has changed. Food and raw material imports have fallen steadily. Imports of fuel increased during the 1970s but decreased during the 1980s. Imports of machinery have grown and today approach 30 percent of total imports.

Net Exports and International Borrowing

The value of exports minus the value of imports is called **net exports.** In 2001, Canadian net exports were $57 billion. Our exports were $57 billion more than our imports. When we export more than we import, as we did in 2001, we lend to foreigners or buy some of their assets. When we import more than we export, we borrow from foreigners or sell some of our assets to them.

The Gains from International Trade

THE FUNDAMENTAL FORCE THAT GENERATES international trade is *comparative advantage.* And the basis of comparative advantage is divergent *opportunity costs.* You met these ideas in Chapter 2, when we learned about the gains from specialization and exchange between Tom and Nancy.

Tom and Nancy each specialize in producing just one good and then trade with each other. Most nations do not go to the extreme of specializing in a single good and importing everything else. But nations can increase the consumption of all goods if they redirect their scarce resources towards the production of those goods and services in which they have a comparative advantage.

To see how this outcome occurs, we'll apply the same basic ideas that we learned in the case of Tom and Nancy to trade among nations. We'll begin by recalling how we can use the production possibilities frontier to measure opportunity cost. Then we'll see how divergent opportunity costs bring comparative advantage and gains from trade for countries as well as for individuals even though no country completely specializes in the production of just one good.

Opportunity Cost in Farmland

Farmland (a fictitious country) can produce grain and cars at any point inside or along its production possibilities frontier, *PPF*, shown in Fig. 33.1. (We're holding constant the output of all the other goods that Farmland produces.) The Farmers (the people of Farmland) are consuming all the grain and cars that they produce, and they are operating at point *A* in the figure. That is, Farmland is producing and consuming 15 million tonnes of grain and 8 million cars each year. What is the opportunity cost of a car in Farmland?

We can answer that question by calculating the slope of the production possibilities frontier at point *A*. The magnitude of the slope of the frontier measures the opportunity cost of one good in terms of the other. To measure the slope of the frontier at point *A*, place a straight line tangential to the frontier at point *A* and calculate the slope of that straight line. Recall that the formula for the slope of a line is the change in the value of the variable measured on the *y*-axis divided by the change in the value of the variable measured on the *x*-axis as we move along the line. Here, the variable measured on the *y*-axis is millions of tonnes of grain, and the variable measured on the *x*-axis is millions of cars. So the slope is the change in the number of tonnes of grain divided by the change in the number of cars.

As you can see from the red triangle at point *A* in the figure, if the number of cars produced increases by 2 million, grain production decreases by 18 million tonnes. Therefore the magnitude of the slope is 18 million divided by 2 million, which equals 9. To get one more car, the people of Farmland must give up 9 tonnes of grain. So the opportunity cost of 1 car is 9 tonnes of grain. Equivalently, 9 tonnes of grain cost 1 car. For the people of Farmland, these opportunity costs are the prices they face. The price of a car is 9 tonnes of grain, and the price of 9 tonnes of grain is 1 car.

FIGURE 33.1 Opportunity Cost in Farmland

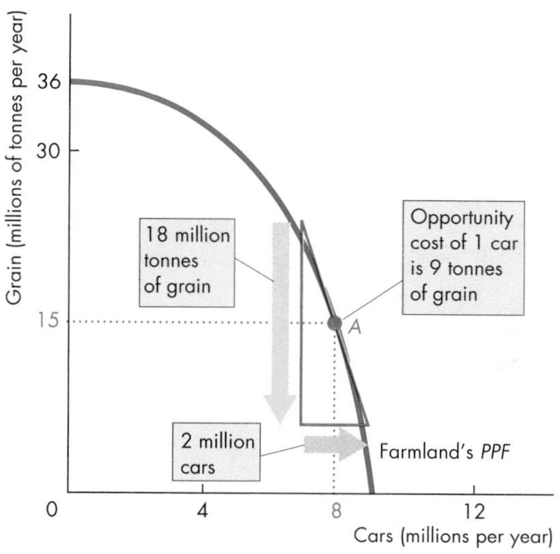

Farmland produces and consumes 15 million tonnes of grain and 8 million cars a year. That is, it produces and consumes at point *A* on its production possibilities frontier. Opportunity cost is equal to the magnitude of the slope of the production possibilities frontier. The red triangle tells us that at point *A*, 18 million tonnes of grain must be forgone to get 2 million cars. That is, at point *A*, 2 million cars cost 18 million tonnes of grain. Equivalently, 1 car costs 9 tonnes of grain or 9 tonnes of grain cost 1 car.

Opportunity Cost in Mobilia

Figure 33.2 shows the production possibilities frontier of Mobilia (another fictitious country). Like the Farmers, the Mobilians consume all the grain and cars that they produce. Mobilia consumes 18 million tonnes of grain a year and 4 million cars, at point *A*'.

Let's calculate the opportunity costs in Mobilia. At point *A*', the opportunity cost of a car is equal to the magnitude of the slope of the red line tangential to the production possibilities frontier, *PPF*. You can see from the red triangle that the magnitude of the slope of Mobilia's production possibilities frontier is 6 million tonnes of grain divided by 6 million cars, which equals 1 tonne of grain per car. To get one more car, the Mobilians must give up 1 tonne of grain. So the opportunity cost of 1 car is 1 tonne of grain, or equivalently, the opportunity cost of 1 tonne of grain is 1 car. These are the prices faced in Mobilia.

Comparative Advantage

Cars are cheaper in Mobilia than in Farmland. One car costs 9 tonnes of grain in Farmland but only 1 tonne of grain in Mobilia. But grain is cheaper in Farmland than in Mobilia—9 tonnes of grain cost only 1 car in Farmland, while that same amount of grain costs 9 cars in Mobilia.

Mobilia has a comparative advantage in car production. Farmland has a comparative advantage in grain production. A country has a comparative advantage in producing a good if it can produce that good at a lower opportunity cost than any other country. Let's see how opportunity cost differences and comparative advantage generate gains from international trade.

FIGURE 33.2 Opportunity Cost in Mobilia

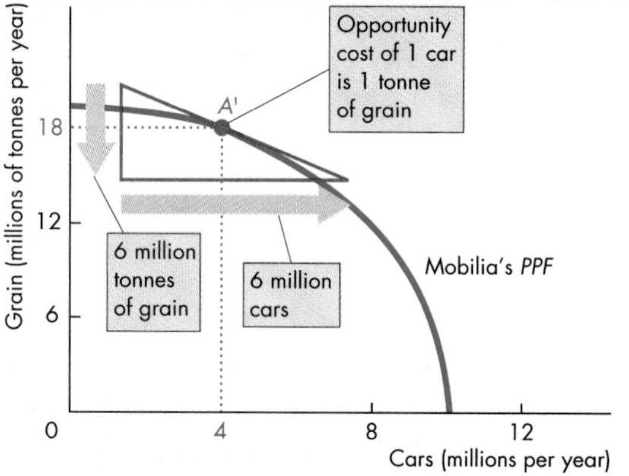

Mobilia produces and consumes 18 million tonnes of grain and 4 million cars a year. That is, it produces and consumes at point *A*' on its production possibilities frontier. Opportunity cost is equal to the magnitude of the slope of the production possibilities frontier. The red triangle tells us that at point *A*', 6 million tonnes of grain must be forgone to get 6 million cars. That is, at point *A*', 6 million cars cost 6 million tonnes of grain. Equivalently, 1 car costs 1 tonne of grain or 1 tonne of grain costs 1 car.

The Gains from Trade: Cheaper to Buy Than to Produce

If Mobilia bought grain for what it costs Farmland to produce it, then Mobilia could buy 9 tonnes of grain for 1 car. That is much lower than the cost of growing grain in Mobilia, for there it costs 9 cars to produce 9 tonnes of grain. If the Mobilians can buy grain at the low Farmland price, they will reap some gains.

If the Farmers can buy cars for what it costs Mobilia to produce them, they will be able to obtain a car for 1 tonne of grain. Because it costs 9 tonnes of grain to produce a car in Farmland, the Farmers would gain from such an opportunity.

In this situation, it makes sense for Mobilians to buy their grain from Farmers and for Farmers to buy their cars from Mobilians. But at what price will Farmland and Mobilia engage in mutually beneficial international trade?

The Terms of Trade

The quantity of grain that Farmland must pay Mobilia for a car is Farmland's **terms of trade** with Mobilia. Because Canada exports and imports many different goods and services, we measure the terms of trade in the real world as an index number that averages the terms of trade over all the items we trade.

The forces of international supply and demand determine the terms of trade. Figure 33.3 illustrates these forces in the Farmland-Mobilia international car market. The quantity of cars *traded internationally* is measured on the *x*-axis. On the *y*-axis, we measure the price of a car. This price is expressed as the *terms of trade*: tonnes of grain per car. If no international trade takes place, the price of a car in Farmland is 9 tonnes of grain, its opportunity cost, indicated by point *A* in

FIGURE 33.3 International Trade in Cars

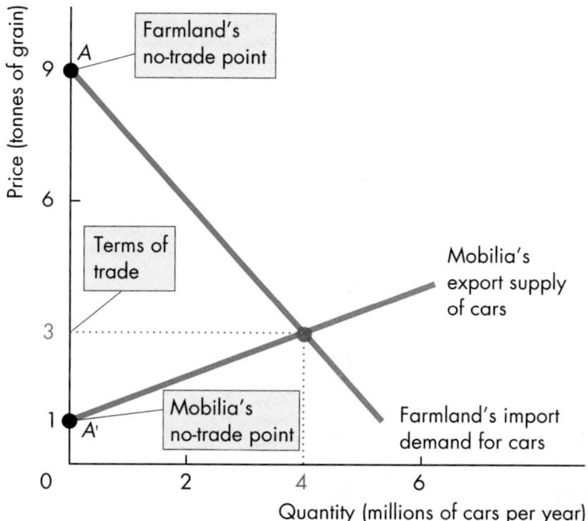

Farmland's import demand curve for cars is downward sloping, and Mobilia's export supply curve of cars is upward sloping. Without international trade, the price of a car is 9 tonnes of grain in Farmland (point *A*) and 1 tonne of grain in Mobilia (point *A'*).

With free international trade, the price (terms of trade) is determined where the export supply curve intersects the import demand curve: 3 tonnes of grain per car. At that price, 4 million cars a year are imported by Farmland and exported by Mobilia. The value of grain exported by Farmland and imported by Mobilia is 12 million tonnes a year, the quantity required to pay for the cars imported.

the figure. Again, if no trade takes place, the price of a car in Mobilia is 1 tonne of grain, its opportunity cost, indicated by point *A'* in the figure. The no-trade points *A* and *A'* in Fig. 33.3 correspond to the points identified by those same letters in Figs. 33.1 and 33.2. The lower the price of a car (terms of trade), the greater is the quantity of cars that the Farmers are willing to import from the Mobilians. This fact is illustrated by the downward-sloping curve, which shows Farmland's import demand for cars.

The Mobilians respond in the opposite direction. The higher the price of a car (terms of trade), the greater is the quantity of cars that Mobilians are willing to export to Farmers. This fact is reflected in Mobilia's export supply of cars—the upward-sloping line in Fig. 33.3.

The international market in cars determines the equilibrium terms of trade (price) and quantity traded. This equilibrium occurs where the import demand curve intersects the export supply curve. In this case, the equilibrium terms of trade are 3 tonnes of grain per car. Mobilia exports and Farmland imports 4 million cars a year. Notice that the terms of trade are lower than the initial price in Farmland but higher than the initial price in Mobilia.

Balanced Trade

The number of cars exported by Mobilia—4 million a year—is exactly equal to the number of cars imported by Farmland. How does Farmland pay for its cars? The answer is by exporting grain. How much grain does Farmland export? You can find the answer by noticing that for 1 car, Farmland must pay 3 tonnes of grain. So for 4 million cars, Farmland pays 12 million tonnes of grain. Farmland's exports of grain are 12 million tonnes a year, and Mobilia imports this same quantity of grain.

Mobilia is exchanging 4 million cars for 12 million tonnes of grain each year, and Farmland is doing the opposite: exchanging 12 million tonnes of grain for 4 million cars. Trade is balanced between these two countries. The value received from exports equals the value paid out for imports.

Changes in Production and Consumption

We've seen that international trade makes it possible for Farmers to buy cars at a lower price than they can produce them and sell their grain for a higher price. International trade also enables Mobilians to sell their cars for a higher price and buy grain for a lower price. Everyone gains. How is it possible for *everyone* to gain? What are the changes in production and consumption that accompany these gains?

An economy that does not trade with other economies has identical production and consumption possibilities. Without trade, the economy can consume only what it produces. But with international trade, an economy can consume different quantities of goods from those that it produces. The production possibilities frontier describes the limit of what a country can produce, but it does not describe the limits to what it can consume. Figure 33.4 will help you to see the distinction between production possibilities and consumption possibilities when a country trades with other countries.

FIGURE 33.4 Expanding Consumption Possibilities

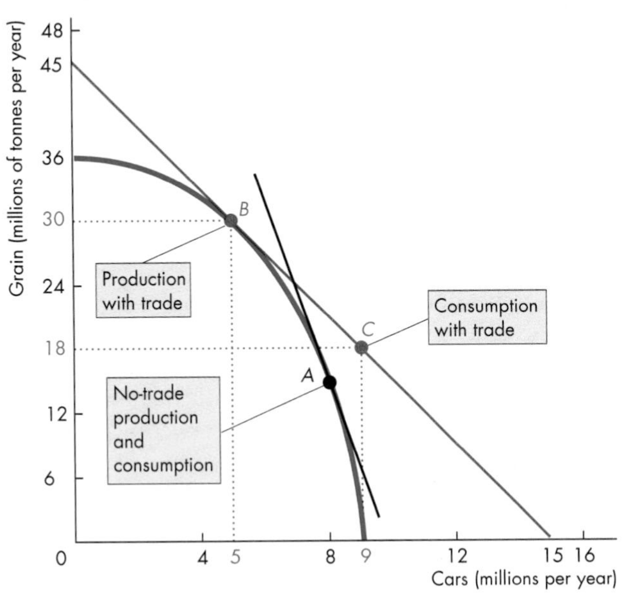

(a) Farmland

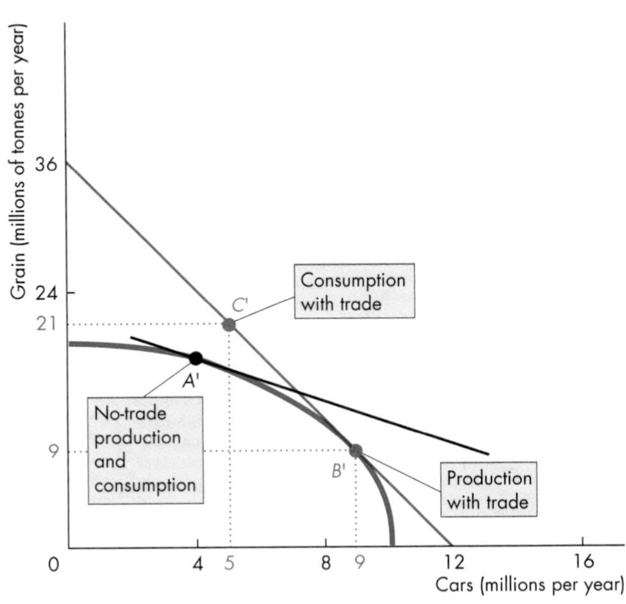

(b) Mobilia

With no international trade, the Farmers produce and consume at point *A* and the opportunity cost of a car is 9 tonnes of grain (the slope of the black line in part a). Also, with no international trade, the Mobilians produce and consume at point *A'* and the opportunity cost of 1 tonne of grain is 1 car (the slope of the black line in part b). Goods can be exchanged internationally at a price of 3 tonnes of grain for 1 car along the red line in each part of the figure. In part (a), Farmland decreases its production of cars and increases its production of grain, moving from *A* to *B*. It exports grain and imports cars, and it consumes at point *C*. The Farmers have more of both cars and grain than they would if they produced all their own consumption goods—at point *A*. In part (b), Mobilia increases car production and decreases grain production, moving from *A'* to *B'*. Mobilia exports cars and imports grain, and it consumes at point *C'*. The Mobilians have more of both cars and grain than they would if they produced all their own consumption goods—at point *A'*.

First of all, notice that the figure has two parts: part (a) for Farmland and part (b) for Mobilia. The production possibilities frontiers that you saw in Figs. 33.1 and 33.2 are reproduced here. The slopes of the two black lines in the figure represent the opportunity costs in the two countries when there is no international trade. Farmland produces and consumes at point *A*, and Mobilia produces and consumes at *A'*. Cars cost 9 tonnes of grain in Farmland and 1 tonne of grain in Mobilia.

Consumption Possibilities The red line in each part of Fig. 33.4 shows the country's consumption possibilities with international trade. These two red lines have the same slope, and the magnitude of that slope is the opportunity cost of a car in terms of grain on the world market: 3 tonnes per car. The *slope* of the consumption possibilities line is common to both countries because its magnitude equals the *world* price. But the position of a country's consumption possibilities line depends on the country's production possibilities. A country cannot produce outside its production possibilities curve, so its consumption possibilities curve touches its production possibilities curve. So Farmland could choose to consume at point *B* with no international trade or, with international trade, at any point on its red consumption possibilities line.

Free Trade Equilibrium With international trade, the producers of cars in Mobilia can get a higher price for their output. As a result, they increase the quantity of car production. At the same time, grain producers in Mobilia get a lower price for their grain, and so they reduce production. Producers in Mobilia adjust their output by moving along their production possibilities frontier until the opportunity cost in Mobilia equals the world price (the opportunity cost in the world market). This situation arises when Mobilia is producing at point *B'* in Fig. 33.4(b).

But the Mobilians do not consume at point *B'*. That is, they do not increase their consumption of cars and decrease their consumption of grain. Instead, they sell some of their car production to Farmland in exchange for some of Farmland's grain. They trade internationally. But to see how that works out, we first need to check in with Farmland to see what's happening there.

In Farmland, producers of cars now get a lower price and producers of grain get a higher price. As a consequence, producers in Farmland decrease car production and increase grain production. They adjust their outputs by moving along the production possibilities frontier until the opportunity cost of a car in terms of grain equals the world price (the opportunity cost on the world market). They move to point *B* in part (a). But the Farmers do not consume at point *B*. Instead, they trade some of their additional grain production for the now cheaper cars from Mobilia.

The figure shows us the quantities consumed in the two countries. We saw in Fig. 33.3 that Mobilia exports 4 million cars a year and Farmland imports those cars. We also saw that Farmland exports 12 million tonnes of grain a year and Mobilia imports that grain. So Farmland's consumption of grain is 12 million tonnes a year less than it produces, and its consumption of cars is 4 million a year more than it produces. Farmland consumes at point *C* in Fig. 33.4(a).

Similarly, we know that Mobilia consumes 12 million tonnes of grain more than it produces and 4 million cars fewer than it produces. Mobilia consumes at point *C'* in Fig. 33.4(b).

Calculating the Gains from Trade

You can now literally see the gains from trade in Fig. 33.4. Without trade, Farmers produce and consume at *A* (part a)—a point on Farmland's production possibilities frontier. With international trade, Farmers consume at point *C* in part (a)—a point *outside* the production possibilities frontier. At point *C*, Farmers are consuming 3 million tonnes of grain a year and 1 million cars a year more than before. These increases in consumption of both cars and grain, beyond the limits of the production possibilities frontier, are the Farmers' gains from international trade.

Mobilians also gain. Without trade, they consume at point *A'* in part (b)—a point on Mobilia's production possibilities frontier. With international trade, they consume at point *C'*—a point outside their production possibilities frontier. With international trade, Mobilia consumes 3 million tonnes of grain a year and 1 million cars a year more than it would without trade. These are the gains from international trade for Mobilia.

Gains for All

Trade between the Farmers and the Mobilians does not create winners and losers. It creates only winners. Farmers selling grain and Mobilians selling cars face an increased demand for their products because the net demand by foreigners is added to domestic demand. With an increase in demand, the price rises.

Farmers buying cars and Mobilians buying grain face an increased supply of these products because the net foreign supply is added to domestic supply. With an increase in supply, the price falls.

Gains from Trade in Reality

The gains from trade that we have just studied between Farmland and Mobilia in grain and cars occur in a model economy—in a world economy that we have imagined. But these same phenomena occur every day in the real global economy.

Comparative Advantage in the Global Economy We buy TVs and VCRs from Korea, machinery from Europe, and fashion goods from Hong Kong. In exchange, we sell machinery, grain and lumber, airplanes, computers, and financial services. All this international trade is generated by comparative advantage, just like the international trade between Farmland and Mobilia in our model economy. All international trade arises from comparative advantage, even when trade is in similar goods such as tools and machines. At first thought, it seems puzzling that countries exchange manufactured goods. Why doesn't each developed country produce all the manufactured goods its citizens want to buy?

Trade in Similar Goods Why does Canada produce automobiles for export and at the same time import large quantities of automobiles from the United States, Japan, Korea, and Western Europe? Wouldn't it make more sense to produce all the cars that we buy here in Canada? After all, we have access to the best technology available for producing cars. Auto workers in Canada are surely as productive as their fellow workers in the United States, Western Europe, and Asian countries. So why does Canada have a comparative advantage in some types of cars and Japan and Europe in others?

Diversity of Taste and Economies of Scale The first part of the answer is that people have a tremendous diversity of taste. Let's stick with the example of cars. Some people prefer a sports car, some prefer a limousine, some prefer a regular, full-size car, some prefer a sport utility vehicle, and some prefer a minivan. In addition to size and type of car, there are many other dimensions in which cars vary. Some have low fuel consumption, some have high performance, some are spacious and comfortable, some have a large trunk, some have four-wheel drive, some have front-wheel drive, some have a radiator grille that looks like a Greek temple, others resemble a wedge. People's preferences across these many dimensions vary. The tremendous diversity in tastes for cars means that people value variety and are willing to pay for it in the marketplace.

The second part of the answer to the puzzle is *economies of scale*—the tendency for the average cost to be lower, the larger the scale of production. In such situations, larger and larger production runs lead to ever lower average costs. Production of many goods, including cars, involves economies of scale. For example, if a car producer makes only a few hundred (or perhaps a few thousand) cars of a particular type and design, the producer must use production techniques that are much more labour-intensive and much less automated than those employed to make hundreds of thousands of cars in a particular model. With short production runs and labour-intensive production techniques, costs are high. With very large production runs and automated assembly lines, production costs are much lower. But to obtain lower costs, the automated assembly lines have to produce a large number of cars.

It is the combination of diversity of taste and economies of scale that determines opportunity cost, produces comparative advantages, and generates such a large amount of international trade in similar commodities. With international trade, each car manufacturer has the whole world market to serve. Each producer can specialize in a limited range of products and then sell its output to the entire world market. This arrangement enables large production runs on the most popular cars and feasible production runs even on the most customized cars demanded by only a handful of people in each country.

The situation in the market for cars is also present in many other industries, especially those producing specialized equipment and parts. For example, Canada exports illustration software but imports database software, exports telecommunications systems but imports PCs, exports specialized video equipment but imports VCRs. International trade in similar but slightly different manufactured products is profitable.

REVIEW QUIZ

1. What is the fundamental source of the gains from international trade?
2. In what circumstances can countries gain from international trade?
3. What determines the goods and services that a country will export?
4. What determines the goods and services that a country will import?
5. What is comparative advantage and what role does it play in determining the amount and type of international trade that occurs?
6. How can it be that all countries gain from international trade and that there are no losers?
7. Provide some examples of comparative advantage in today's world.
8. Why does Canada both export and import automobiles?

You've now seen how free international trade brings gains for all. But trade is not free in our world. We'll now take a brief look at the history of international trade restrictions and also work out the effects of international trade restrictions. We'll see that free trade brings the greatest possible benefits and that international trade restrictions are costly.

International Trade Restrictions

GOVERNMENTS RESTRICT INTERNATIONAL TRADE to protect domestic industries from foreign competition by using two main tools:

1. Tariffs
2. Nontariff barriers

A **tariff** is a tax that is imposed by the importing country when an imported good crosses its international boundary. A **nontariff barrier** is any action other than a tariff that restricts international trade. Examples of nontariff barriers are quantitative restrictions and licensing regulations limiting imports. First, let's look at tariffs.

The History of Tariffs

The Canadian economy has always been protected by a tariff. Figure 33.5 shows the history of that tariff, from Confederation through 2001. The figure shows tariffs as a percentage of total imports—the average tariff rate. As you can see, the average tariff rate climbed from the early 1870s to exceed 20 percent by the late 1880s. The rate fluctuated but gradually decreased through the early 1920s. It increased again during the Great Depression years of the early 1930s. During these years, most countries increased their tariff rates in what became a "beggar-my-neighbour" policy. The average tariff then decreased through the late 1930s and continued its decrease throughout the years after World War II. Today, the average tariff rate is less than 1 percent.

The reduction in tariffs after World War II followed the signing in 1947 of the **General Agreement on Tariffs and Trade** (GATT). From its formation, GATT organized a series of "rounds" of negotiations that resulted in a steady process of tariff reduction. One of these, the Kennedy Round that began in the early 1960s, resulted in large tariff cuts starting in 1967. Another, the Tokyo Round, resulted in further tariff cuts in 1979. The final round, the Uruguay Round, started in 1986 and was completed in 1994.

The Uruguay Round was the most ambitious and comprehensive of the rounds and led to the creation of the **World Trade Organization** (WTO). Membership of the WTO brings greater obligations for countries to observe the GATT rules. Canada signed the Uruguay Round agreements, and Parliament ratified them in 1994.

In addition to the agreements under the GATT

FIGURE 33.5 Canadian Tariffs: 1867–2001

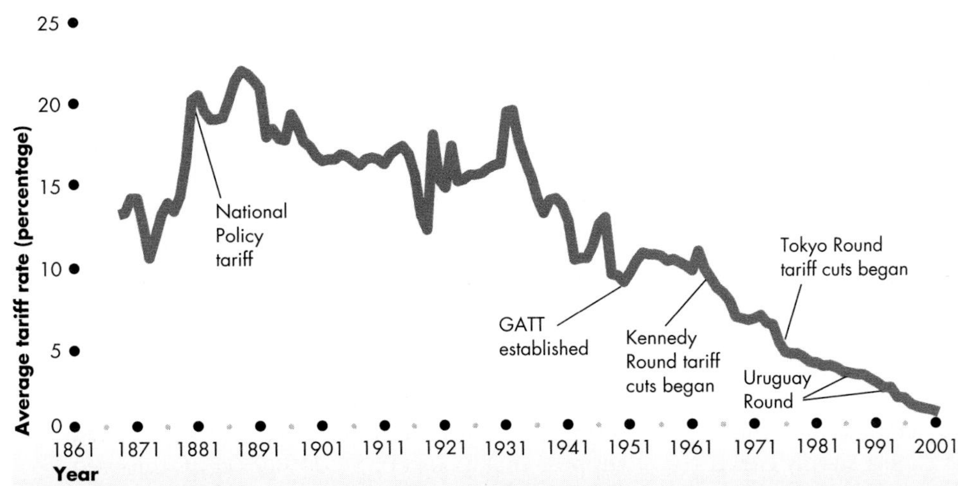

Canadian tariffs were in place before Confederation. Tariffs increased sharply in the 1870s and remained high until the 1930s. Since the establishment of the GATT in 1947, tariffs have steadily declined in a series of negotiating rounds, the most significant of which are identified in the figure. Tariffs are now as low as they have ever been.

Sources: Statistics Canada, *Historial Statistics of Canada*, Series G485, CANSIM tables 380-0002 and 380-0007, and authors' calculations.

and the WTO, Canada is a party to the **North American Free Trade Agreement** (NAFTA), which became effective on January 1, 1994, and under which barriers to international trade between the United States, Canada, and Mexico will be virtually eliminated after a 15-year phasing-in period.

In other parts of the world, trade barriers have virtually been eliminated among the member countries of the European Union, which has created the largest unified tariff-free market in the world. In 1994, discussions among the Asia-Pacific Economic Cooperation (APEC) led to an agreement in principle to work towards a free-trade area that embraces China, all the economies of East Asia and the South Pacific, and the United States and Canada. These countries include the fastest-growing economies and hold the promise of heralding a global free-trade area.

The effort to achieve freer trade underlines the fact that trade in some goods is still subject to a high tariff. Textiles and footwear are among the goods that face the highest tariffs, and rates on these items average more than 10 percent. Some individual items face a tariff much higher than the average. For example, when you buy a pair of blue jeans for $20, you pay about $5 more than you would if there were no tariffs on textiles. Other goods that are protected by tariffs are agricultural products, energy and chemicals, minerals, and metals. The meat, cheese, and sugar that you consume cost significantly more because of protection than they would with free international trade.

The temptation for governments to impose tariffs is a strong one. First, tariffs provide revenue to the government. Second, they enable the government to satisfy special interest groups in import-competing industries. But, as we'll see, free international trade brings enormous benefits that are reduced when tariffs are imposed. Let's see how.

How Tariffs Work

To see how tariffs work, let's return to the example of trade between Farmland and Mobilia. Figure 33.6 shows the international market for cars in which these two countries are the only traders. The volume of trade and the price of a car are determined at the point of intersection of Mobilia's export supply curve of cars and Farmland's import demand curve for cars.

In Fig. 33.6, these two countries trade cars and grain in exactly the same way that we saw in Fig. 33.3.

FIGURE 33.6 The Effects of a Tariff

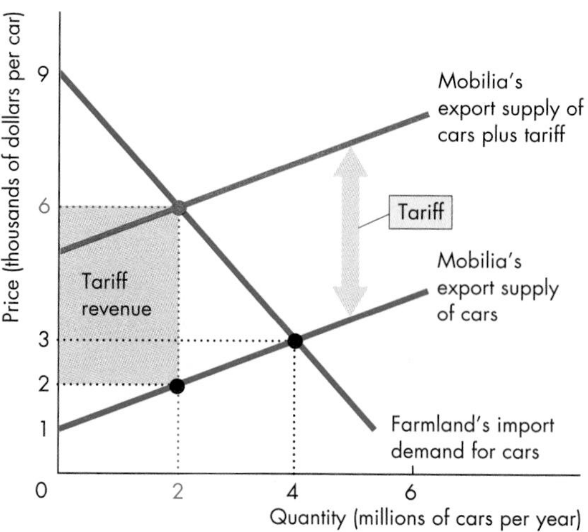

Farmland imposes a tariff on car imports from Mobilia. The tariff increases the price that Farmers have to pay for cars. It shifts the supply curve of cars in Farmland leftward. The vertical distance between the original supply curve and the new one is the amount of the tariff, $4,000 per car. The price of cars in Farmland increases, and the quantity of cars imported decreases. The government of Farmland collects a tariff revenue of $4,000 per car—a total of $8 billion on the 2 million cars imported. Farmland's exports of grain decrease because Mobilia now has a lower income from its exports of cars.

Mobilia exports cars, and Farmland exports grain. The volume of car imports into Farmland is 4 million a year, and the world market price of a car is 3 tonnes of grain. Figure 33.6 expresses prices in dollars rather than in units of grain and is based on a money price of grain of $1 a tonne. With grain costing $1,000 a tonne, the money price of a car is $3,000.

Now suppose that the government of Farmland, perhaps under pressure from car producers, decides to impose a tariff on imported cars. In particular, suppose that a tariff of $4,000 per car is imposed. (This is a huge tariff, but the car producers of Farmland are pretty fed up with competition from Mobilia.) What happens?

- The supply of cars in Farmland decreases.
- The price of cars in Farmland rises.
- The quantity of cars imported by Farmland decreases.
- The government of Farmland collects the tariff revenue.
- Resource use is inefficient.
- The *value* of exports changes by the same amount as the *value* of imports, and trade remains balanced.

Change in the Supply of Cars Farmland cannot buy cars at Mobilia's export supply price. It must pay that price plus the $4,000 tariff. So the supply curve in Farmland shifts leftward. The new supply curve is that labelled "Mobilia's export supply of cars plus tariff." The vertical distance between Mobilia's original export supply curve and the new supply curve is the tariff of $4,000 a car.

Rise in Price of Cars A new equilibrium occurs where the new supply curve intersects Farmland's import demand curve for cars. That equilibrium is at a price of $6,000 a car, up from $3,000 with free trade.

Fall in Imports Car imports fall from 4 million to 2 million cars a year. At the higher price of $6,000 a car, domestic car producers increase their production. Domestic grain production decreases as resources are moved into the expanding car industry.

Tariff Revenue Total expenditure on imported cars by the Farmers is $6,000 a car multiplied by the 2 million cars imported ($12 billion). But not all of that money goes to the Mobilians. They receive $2,000 a car, or $4 billion for the 2 million cars. The difference—$4,000 a car, or a total of $8 billion for the 2 million cars—is collected by the government of Farmland as tariff revenue.

Inefficiency The people of Farmland are willing to pay $6,000 for the marginal car imported. But the opportunity cost of that car is $2,000. So there is a gain from trading an extra car. In fact, there are gains—willingness to pay exceeds opportunity cost—all the way up to 4 million cars a year. Only when 4 million cars are being traded is the maximum price that a Farmer is willing to pay equal to the minimum price that is acceptable to a Mobilian. Restricting trade reduces the gains from trade.

Trade Remains Balanced With free trade, Farmland was paying $3,000 a car and buying 4 million cars a year from Mobilia. The total amount paid to Mobilia for imports was $12 billion a year. With a tariff, Farmland's imports have been cut to 2 million cars a year and the price paid to Mobilia has also been cut to only $2,000 a car. The total amount paid to Mobilia for imports has been cut to $4 billion a year. Doesn't this fact mean that Farmland now has a balance of trade surplus? It does not.

The price of cars in Mobilia has fallen. But the price of grain remains at $1 a tonne. So the relative price of cars has fallen, and the relative price of grain has increased. With free trade, the Mobilians could buy 3,000 tonnes of grain for the price of one car. Now they can buy only 2,000 tonnes for the price of a car. With a higher relative price of grain, the quantity demanded by the Mobilians decreases and Mobilia imports less grain. But because Mobilia imports less grain, Farmland exports less grain. In fact, Farmland's grain industry suffers from two sources. First, there is a decrease in the quantity of grain sold to Mobilia. Second, there is increased competition for inputs from the now-expanded car industry. The tariff leads to a contraction in the scale of the grain industry in Farmland.

It seems paradoxical at first that a country imposing a tariff on cars hurts its own export industry, lowering its exports of grain. It may help to think of it this way: Mobilians buy grain with the money they make from exporting cars to Farmland. If they export fewer cars, they cannot afford to buy as much grain. In fact, in the absence of any international borrowing and lending, Mobilia must cut its imports of grain by exactly the same amount as the loss in revenue from its export of cars. Grain imports into Mobilia are cut back to a value of $4 billion, the amount that can be paid for by the new lower revenue from Mobilia's car exports. Trade is still balanced. The tariff cuts imports and exports by the same amount. The tariff has no effect on the *balance* of trade, but it reduces the *volume* of trade.

The result that we have just derived is perhaps one of the most misunderstood aspects of international economics. On countless occasions, politicians and others call for tariffs to remove a balance of trade deficit or argue that lowering tariffs would produce a balance of trade deficit. They reach this conclusion by failing to work out all the implications of a tariff.

Let's now look at nontariff barriers.

Nontariff Barriers

The two main forms of nontariff barriers are

1. Quotas
2. Voluntary export restraints

A **quota** is a quantitative restriction on the import of a particular good, which specifies the maximum amount of the good that may be imported in a given period of time. A **voluntary export restraint** (VER) is an agreement between two governments in which the government of the exporting country agrees to restrain the volume of its own exports.

Quotas are especially prominent in textiles and agriculture. Voluntary export restraints are used to regulate trade between Japan and Canada.

How Quotas and VERs Work

To see how a quota works, suppose that Farmland imposes a quota that restricts its car imports to 2 million cars a year. Figure 33.7 shows the effects of this action. The quota is shown by the vertical red line at 2 million cars a year. Because it is illegal to exceed the quota, car importers buy only that quantity from Mobilia, for which they pay $2,000 a car. But because the import supply of cars is restricted to 2 million cars a year, people are willing to pay $6,000 per car. This is the price of a car in Farmland.

The value of imports falls to $4 billion, exactly the same as in the case of the tariff in Fig. 33.6. So with lower incomes from car exports and with a higher relative price of grain, Mobilians cut back on their imports of grain in exactly the same way that they did under a tariff.

The key difference between a quota and a tariff lies in who collects the gap between the import supply price and the domestic price. In the case of a tariff, it is the government of the importing country. In the case of a quota, it goes to the person who has the right to import under the import quota regulations.

A VER is like a quota arrangement in which quotas are allocated to each exporting country. The effects of VERs are similar to those of quotas but differ from them in that the gap between the domestic price and the export price is captured not by domestic importers but by the foreign exporter. The government of the exporting country has to establish procedures for allocating the restricted volume of exports among its producers.

FIGURE 33.7 The Effects of a Quota

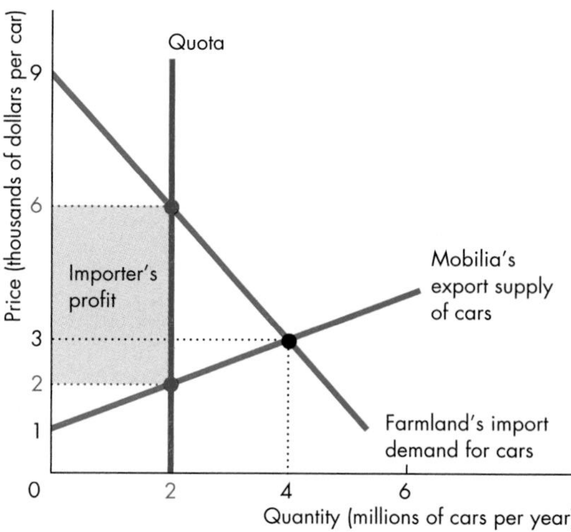

Farmland imposes a quota of 2 million cars a year on car imports from Mobilia. That quantity appears as the vertical line labelled "Quota." Because the quantity of cars supplied by Mobilia is restricted to 2 million, the price at which those cars will be traded increases to $6,000. Importing cars is profitable because Mobilia is willing to supply cars at $2,000 each. There is competition for import quotas.

REVIEW QUIZ

1. What are the tools that a country can use to restrict international trade?
2. What do international trade restrictions do to the gains from international trade?
3. Which is best for a country: restricted trade, no trade, or free trade? Why?
4. What does a tariff on imports do to the volume of imports and the volume of exports?
5. In the absence of international borrowing and lending, how do tariffs and other international trade restrictions influence the total value of imports and exports and the balance of trade—the value of exports minus the value of imports?

We're now going to look at some commonly heard arguments for restricting international trade and see why they are almost never correct.

The Case Against Protection

FOR AS LONG AS NATIONS AND INTERNATIONAL trade have existed, people have debated whether a country is better off with free international trade or with protection from foreign competition. The debate continues, but for most economists, a verdict has been delivered and is the one you have just seen. Free trade promotes prosperity for all; protection is inefficient. We've seen the most powerful case for free trade in the example of how Farmland and Mobilia both benefit from their comparative advantage. But there is a broader range of issues in the free trade versus protection debate. Let's review these issues.

Three arguments for restricting international trade are

- The employment argument
- The infant-industry argument
- The dumping argument

Let's look at each in turn.

The Employment Argument

The argument that protection saves jobs goes as follows: When we buy shoes from Brazil or shirts from Taiwan, Canadian workers in these industries lose their jobs. With no earnings and poor prospects, these workers become a drain on welfare and spend less, causing a ripple effect of further job losses. The proposed solution to this problem is to ban imports of cheap foreign goods and protect Canadian jobs. This argument for protection does not withstand scrutiny for three reasons.

First, free trade does cost some jobs, but it also creates other jobs. It brings about a global rationalization of labour and allocates labour resources to their highest-valued activities. Because of international trade in textiles, tens of thousands of workers in Canada have lost their jobs because textile mills and other factories have closed. But tens of thousands of workers in other countries have gotten jobs because textile mills have opened there. And tens of thousands of Canadian workers have gotten better-paying jobs than those of textile workers because other export industries have expanded and created more jobs than have been destroyed.

Second, imports create jobs. They create jobs for retailers that sell imported goods and firms that service those goods. They also create jobs by creating incomes in the rest of the world, some of which are spent on imports of Canadian-made goods and services.

Although protection does save particular jobs, it does so at inordinate cost. A striking example of the cost of quotas is that of the quotas on the import of textiles. Quotas imposed under an international agreement called the Multifiber Arrangement (that is being phased out) have protected textile jobs, especially in the United States. The U.S. International Trade Commission (ITC) has estimated that because of quotas, 72,000 jobs exist in textiles that would otherwise disappear and annual clothing expenditure in the United States is $U.S. 15.9 billion or $U.S. 160 per family higher than it would be with free trade. Equivalently, the ITC estimates that each textile job saved costs $U.S. 221,000 a year.

The Infant-Industry Argument

The so-called **infant-industry argument** for protection is that it is necessary to protect a new industry to enable it to grow into a mature industry that can compete in world markets. The argument is based on the idea of *dynamic comparative advantage*, which can arise from *learning-by-doing* (see Chapter 2).

Learning-by-doing is a powerful engine of productivity growth, and comparative advantage does evolve and change because of on-the-job experience. But these facts do not justify protection.

First, the infant-industry argument is valid only if the benefits of learning-by-doing *not only* accrue to the owners and workers of the firms in the infant industry but also *spill over* to other industries and parts of the economy. For example, there are huge productivity gains from learning-by-doing in the manufacture of aircraft. But almost all of these gains benefit the stockholders and workers of Boeing and other aircraft producers. Because the people making the decisions, bearing the risk, and doing the work are the ones who benefit, they take the dynamic gains into account when they decide on the scale of their activities. In this case, almost no benefits spill over to other parts of the economy, so there is no need for government assistance to achieve an efficient outcome.

Second, even if the case is made for protecting an infant industry, it is more efficient to do so by a subsidy to the firms in the industry, with the subsidy out of taxes.

The Dumping Argument

Dumping occurs when a foreign firm sells its exports at a price below its cost of production. Dumping might be used by a firm that wants to gain a global monopoly. In this case, the foreign firm sells its output at a price below its cost to drive domestic firms out of business. When the domestic firms have gone, the foreign firm takes advantage of its monopoly position and charges a higher price for its product. Dumping is usually regarded as a justification for temporary countervailing tariffs.

But there are powerful reasons to resist the dumping argument for protection. First, it is virtually impossible to detect dumping because it is hard to determine a firm's costs. As a result, the test for dumping is whether a firm's export price is below its domestic price. But this test is a weak one because it can be rational for a firm to charge a low price in markets in which the quantity demanded is highly sensitive to price and a higher price in a market in which demand is less price-sensitive.

Second, it is hard to think of a good that is produced by a natural *global* monopoly. So even if all the domestic firms were driven out of business in some industry, it would always be possible to find several and usually many alternative foreign sources of supply and to buy at prices determined in competitive markets.

Third, if a good or service were a truly global natural monopoly, the best way of dealing with it would be by regulation—just as in the case of domestic monopolies. Such regulation would require international cooperation.

The three arguments for protection that we've just examined have an element of credibility. The counterarguments are in general stronger, however, so these arguments do not make the case for protection. But they are not the only arguments that you might encounter. The many other arguments that are commonly heard are quite simply wrong. They are fatally flawed. The most common of them are that protection

- Maintains national security
- Allows us to compete with cheap foreign labour
- Brings diversity and stability
- Penalizes lax environmental standards
- Protects national culture
- Prevents rich countries from exploiting developing countries

Maintains National Security

The national security argument for protection is that a country must protect industries that produce defence equipment and armaments and industries on which the defence industries rely for their raw materials and other intermediate inputs. This argument for protection does not withstand close scrutiny.

First, it is an argument for international isolation, for in a time of war, there is no industry that does not contribute to national defence. Second, if the case is made for boosting the output of a strategic industry, it is more efficient to achieve this outcome with a subsidy to the firms in the industry that is financed out of taxes. Such a subsidy would keep the industry operating at the scale judged appropriate, and free international trade would keep the prices faced by consumers at their world market levels.

Allows Us to Compete with Cheap Foreign Labour

With the removal of tariffs in Canadian trade with Mexico, people said we would hear a "giant sucking sound" as jobs rushed to Mexico (shown in the cartoon). Let's see what's wrong with this view.

The labour cost of a unit of output equals the wage rate divided by labour productivity. For example, if a Canadian auto worker earns $30 an hour and produces 15 units of output an hour, the average labour cost of a unit of output is $2. If a Mexican auto assembly worker earns $3 an hour and produces 1 unit of output an hour, the average labour cost of a unit of output is $3. Other things remaining the same, the higher a worker's productivity, the higher is the worker's wage rate. High-wage workers have high productivity. Low-wage workers have low productivity.

Although high-wage Canadian workers are more productive, on the average, than low-wage Mexican workers, there are differences across industries. Canadian labour is relatively more productive in some activities than in others. For example, the productivity of Canadian workers in producing financial services and telephone systems is relatively higher than their productivity in the production of metals and some standardized machine parts. The activities in which Canadian workers are relatively more productive than their Mexican counterparts are those in which Canada has a *comparative advantage*. By engaging in free trade, increasing our production and exports of the goods and services in which we have a comparative advantage and decreasing our produc-

"I don't know what the hell happened—one minute I'm at work in Flint, Michigan, then there's a giant sucking sound and suddenly here I am in Mexico."

tion and increasing our imports of the goods and services in which our trading partners have a comparative advantage, we can make ourselves and the citizens of other countries better off.

Brings Diversity and Stability

A diversified investment portfolio is less risky than one that has all the eggs in one basket. The same is true for an economy's production. A diversified economy fluctuates less than an economy that produces only one or two goods.

But big, rich, diversified economies such as those of Canada, the United States, Japan, and Europe do not have this type of stability problem. Even a country such as Saudi Arabia that produces only one good (in this case, oil) can benefit from specializing in the activity at which it has a comparative advantage and then investing in a wide range of other countries to bring greater stability to its income and consumption.

Penalizes Lax Environmental Standards

Another argument for protection is that many poorer countries, such as Mexico, do not have the same environmental policies that we have and, because they are willing to pollute and we are not, we cannot compete with them without tariffs. So if they want free trade with the richer and "greener" countries, they must clean up their environments to our standards.

This argument for international trade restrictions is weak. First, not all poorer countries have significantly lower environmental standards than Canada has. Many poor countries and the former communist countries of Eastern Europe do have bad environment records. But some countries enforce strict laws. Second, a poor country cannot afford to be as concerned about its environment as a rich country can. The best hope for a better environment in Mexico and in other developing countries is rapid income growth through free trade. As their incomes grow, developing countries will have the *means* to match their desires to improve their environment. Third, poor countries have a comparative advantage at doing "dirty" work, which helps rich countries achieve higher environmental standards than they otherwise could.

Protects National Culture

The national culture argument for protection is one of the most commonly heard argument in Canada and Europe.

The expressed fear is that free trade in books, magazines, movies, and television programs means U.S. domination and the end of local culture. So, the reasoning continues, it is necessary to protect domestic "culture" industries from free international trade to ensure the survival of a national cultural identity.

Protection of these industries is common and takes the form of nontariff barriers. For example, local content regulations on radio and television broadcasting and in magazines is often required.

The cultural identity argument for protection has no merit. Writers, publishers, and broadcasters want to limit foreign competition so that they can earn larger economic profits. There is no actual danger to national culture. In fact, many of the creators of so-called American cultural products are not Americans but the talented citizens of other countries, ensuring the survival of their national cultural identities in Hollywood! Also, if national culture is in danger, there is no surer way of helping it on its way out than by impoverishing the nation whose culture it is. And protection is an effective way of doing just that.

Prevents Rich Countries from Exploiting Developing Countries

Another argument for protection is that international trade must be restricted to prevent the people of the rich industrial world from exploiting the poorer people of the developing countries, forcing them to work for slave wages.

Wage rates in some developing countries are indeed very low. But by trading with developing countries, we increase the demand for the goods that these countries produce and, more significantly, we increase the demand for their labour. When the demand for labour in developing countries increases, the wage rate also increases. So, far from exploiting people in developing countries, trade improves their opportunities and increases their incomes.

We have reviewed the arguments that are commonly heard in favour of protection and the counter-arguments against them. There is one counter-argument to protection that is general and quite overwhelming: Protection invites retaliation and can trigger a trade war. The best example of a trade war occurred during the Great Depression of the 1930s when the United States introduced the Smoot-Hawley tariff. Country after country retaliated with its own tariff, and in a short period, world trade had almost disappeared. The costs to all countries were large and led to a renewed international resolve to avoid such self-defeating moves in the future. They also led to the creation of GATT and are the impetus behind NAFTA, APEC, and the European Union.

REVIEW QUIZ

1. Can we save jobs, stimulate the growth of new industries, or to restrain foreign monopoly by restricting international trade?
2. Can we achieve national security goals, compensate for low foreign wages, make the economy more diversified, compensate for costly environmental policies, protect national culture, or to protect developing countries from being exploited by restricting international trade?
3. Is there any merit to the view that we should restrict international trade for any reason? What is the main argument against international trade restrictions?

Why Is International Trade Restricted?

WHY, DESPITE ALL THE ARGUMENTS AGAINST PROtection, is trade restricted? There are two key reasons:

- Tariff revenue
- Rent seeking

Tariff Revenue

Government revenue is costly to collect. In the developed countries such as Canada, a well-organized tax collection system is in place that can generate billions of dollars of income tax and sales tax revenues. This tax collection system is made possible by the fact that most economic transactions are done by firms that must keep properly audited financial records. Without such records, the revenue collection agencies (for example, Canada Customs and Revenue Agency) would be severely hampered in the work. Even with audited financial accounts, some proportion of potential tax revenue is lost. Nonetheless, for the industrialized countries, income taxes and sales taxes are the major sources of revenue and the tariff plays a very small role.

But governments in developing countries have a difficult time collecting taxes from their citizens. Much economic activity takes place in an informal economy with few financial records. So only a small amount of revenue is collected from income taxes and sales taxes in these countries. The one area in which economic transactions are well recorded and audited is in international trade. So this activity is an attractive base for tax collection in these countries and is used much more extensively than in the developed countries.

Rent Seeking

Rent seeking is the major reason why international trade is restricted. Rent seeking is lobbying and other political activity that seeks to capture the gains from trade. Free trade increases consumption possibilities *on the average*, but not everyone shares in the gain and some people even lose. Free trade brings benefits to some and imposes costs on others, with total benefits exceeding total costs. It is the uneven distribution of costs and benefits that is the principal source of impediment to achieving more liberal international trade.

Let's return to our example of trade in cars and grain between Farmland and Mobilia. In Farmland, the benefits from free trade accrue to all the producers of grain and to those producers of cars who would not have to bear the costs of adjusting to a smaller car industry. Those costs are transition costs, not permanent costs. The costs of moving to free trade are borne by those car producers and their employees who have to become grain producers.

The number of people who gain will, in general, be enormous in comparison with the number who lose. The gain per person will therefore be rather small. The loss per person to those who bear the loss will be large. Because the loss that falls on those who bear it is large, it will pay those people to incur considerable expense to lobby against free trade. On the other hand, it will not pay those who gain to organize to achieve free trade. The gain from trade for any one individual is too small for that individual to spend much time or money on a political organization to achieve free trade. The loss from free trade will be seen as being so great by those bearing that loss that they *will* find it profitable to join a political organization to prevent free trade. Each group is optimizing—weighing benefits against costs and choosing the best action for itself. The anti-free trade group will, however, undertake a larger quantity of political lobbying than the pro-free trade group.

Compensating Losers

If, in total, the gains from free international trade exceed the losses, why don't those who stand to gain from free trade offer to compensate those who stand to lose so that everyone votes for free trade?

The main answer is that there are serious obstacles to providing direct and correctly calculated compensation. First, the cost of identifying the losers from free trade and of estimating the value of their losses would be enormous.

Second, it would never be clear whether a person who has fallen on hard times is suffering because of free trade or for other reasons, perhaps reasons that are largely under the control of the individual.

Third, some people who look like losers at one point in time may, in fact, end up gaining. The young auto worker that loses her job in Windsor and becomes a computer assembly worker in Ottawa resents the loss of work and the need to move. But a year or two later, looking back on events, she counts herself fortunate. She has made a move that has increased her income and given her greater job security.

Despite the absence of explicit compensation, those who lose from a change in protection do receive some compensation. But compensation is not restricted to the losers from changes in trade policy. In Canada (and in all the other rich industrial countries) elaborate schemes are in place to ensure that people who suffer from economic change receive help during their transition to new activities.

Two major forms of compensation in Canada arise from interprovincial fiscal transfers and employment insurance. Interprovincial fiscal transfers result in tax dollars collected in the rich and expanding regions of the country being spent in the poorer regions. Employment insurance provides substantial compensation for workers who lose their jobs regardless of the reason for the job loss. Jobs lost because of changes in international protection are included among those for which benefits are paid.

But because we do not explicitly compensate the losers from free international trade, protectionism remains a popular and permanent feature of our national economic and political life.

Compensating Losers from Protection

There is no general presumption that it is the ones who lose from a tariff cut that should be compensated. Protection brings losses to the consumer and the view might be taken that the winners from protection should compensate the losers from protection. When this perspective is taken, the removal of protection would mean the removal of the compensation of the losers by the winners and no further adjustments would be needed. What is fair is a tricky matter (see Chapter 5, pp. 114–117).

REVIEW QUIZ

1. What are the two main reasons for imposing tariffs on imports?
2. What type of country most benefits from the revenue from tariffs? Provide some examples of such countries.
3. If international trade restrictions are costly, why do we use them? Why don't the people who gain from trade organize a political force that is strong enough to ensure that their interests are protected?

The North American Free Trade Agreement

THE NORTH AMERICAN FREE TRADE AGREEment came into effect on January 1, 1994. It was the outgrowth of an earlier Canada–United States Free Trade Agreement, which was signed in October 1987. Both agreements were struck only after several years of intense negotiations and, on the Canadian side of the border, an intense political debate. First, let's look at the terms of the Canada–United States agreement of 1987 and at the progress made in achieving freer trade between two of the world's largest trading partners.

The Terms of the Canada–United States Agreement

The main terms of the Canada–United States Free Trade Agreement are:

- Tariffs to be phased out through 1999
- Nontariff barriers to be reduced
- Free trade in energy products, with energy resource sharing in times of national shortage
- More freedom of trade in services
- Future negotiations to eliminate subsidies
- Creation of dispute-settling mechanisms

Removal of Tariffs Scheduled tariff cuts began on January 1, 1989 and were completed on January 1, 1998. But tariff protection remains in place and an atmosphere of tension prevails in many areas. Agriculture remains effectively protected with new tariffs that have replaced old quotas. And a series of so-called *countervailing duties* has been introduced to offset the effects of domestic subsidies. Further, several so-called *antidumping duties* have also been introduced in cases in which it is alleged that products are being exported at a price below the cost of production.

Nontariff Barriers Nontariff barriers such as government procurement policies of buying local products are removed by the agreement. Subsequent to entering into the free trade agreement, Canada and the United States took on additional obligations as members of the WTO that require the removal of agricultural quotas. Many agricultural quotas have been removed but they have been replaced with tariffs. So despite the free trade agreement, we remain a long way from achieving free trade in agricultural products.

Energy Products Free trade in energy products existed before the free trade agreement but the agreement ratified the intent to maintain that arrangement. The agreement that scarce energy resources will be shared in times of national shortage became a controversial one. In effect, what the energy sharing clause amounts to is an agreement that governments will not intervene in energy markets to prevent firms from selling their energy to the other country.

Trade in Services International trade in services has been expanding more quickly than trade in manufactured goods in recent years. The free trade agreement, recognizing this factor and seeking to facilitate further expansion of trade in services between the United States and Canada, incorporates two principles: the *right of establishment* and *national treatment.* The right of establishment means that American firms have the right to set up branches in Canada and Canadian firms have the right to set up operations in the United States. National treatment means that each country will treat the goods and firms and investors of the other country as if they were operating within its own borders.

Future Negotiations on Subsidies In both the United States and Canada, there are many subsidies, especially on agricultural products. The presence of subsidies causes problems and makes it legitimate under the agreement for the country importing subsidized goods to impose countervailing duties. As we have just noted, several such duties have been imposed.

Dispute-Settling Mechanisms The Free Trade Agreement included two dispute-settling mechanisms: one to settle disputes relating to all aspects of the agreement, and the other to deal with applications of countervailing duties and antidumping laws in either country. For example, the United States has applied for and received permission to impose countervailing duties on Canadian exports of durum wheat, lumber products, poultry, and live hogs. In each case, the United States accuses Canada of subsidizing these industries unfairly so that Canadian exports are cheaper than U.S. producers can supply these goods.

The Extension of the Agreement: NAFTA

The North American Free Trade Agreement (NAFTA) is an agreement between Canada, the United States, and Mexico that has six objectives. They are to

1. Eliminate trade barriers
2. Promote conditions of fair competition
3. Increase investment opportunities
4. Protect intellectual property rights
5. Create an effective dispute resolution mechanism
6. Establish a framework for the expansion of the agreement to include other nations in the hemisphere

Effects of the Free Trade Agreement

Working out the effects of an agreement as complex as NAFTA is difficult, and there is no general consensus on what the effects have been. The theory that you have studied in this chapter predicts that the removal of tariffs will produce an increase in the *volume* of international trade. That is, the theory predicts that Canadians will increasingly specialize in those activities at which they have a comparative advantage and Mexicans and Americans will specialize in a different range of activities and that the three countries will exchange a larger volume of goods and services.

As predicted, trade among the three countries has increased. During the first five years of NAFTA, Canada's trade with the United States increased by 80 percent and Canada's trade with Mexico doubled.

The trade expansion that followed the entry of Mexico in 1995 was especially dramatic. Mexico's exports increased by 31 percent (in U.S. dollar value) in 1995 and by 21 percent in 1996, compared with increases that averaged less than 15 percent a year during the two years before the agreement. But trade expansion with Mexico has not been in one direction. Mexico's imports also increased following the agreement by 23 percent in both 1996 and 1997.

During the 1990s, Canada's exports expanded from less than 30 percent of total production to 36 percent, and Canada's imports have increased from 27 percent to 34 percent of total expenditure.

Canada greatly increased its exports of advertising services, office and telecommunications equipment, paper, and transportation services. And its imports of meat and dairy products, communications services, clothing, furniture, and processed foods and beverages also increased by a large percentage.

These huge changes in exports and imports brought gains from increased specialization and exchange. But they also brought a heavy toll of adjustment. Thousands of jobs were lost in the declining sectors and new jobs were created in the expanding sectors. The amount of job destruction in the years following the free trade agreement was historically high and the unemployment rate rose for three successive years. Only during the Great Depression did the rate of job destruction exceed that in the late 1980s and early 1990s. To what extent a high rate of labour market turnover was caused by the free trade agreement is unclear and controversial. But the net outcome of NAFTA appears to be strongly positive. More than a million new Canadian jobs were created between 1994 and 1999.

REVIEW QUIZ

1. By when, under the Canada–United States Free Trade Agreement, were all tariffs on trade between Canada and the United States intended to be phased out? What progress and setbacks have we experienced?
2. What effect has NAFTA had on nontariff barriers?
3. What effect has NAFTA had on trade in services?
4. How has the volume of trade among Canada, the United States, and Mexico changed during the period since NAFTA was established?

You've now seen how free international trade enables all nations to gain from specialization and trade. By producing goods in which we have a comparative advantage and trading some of our production for that of others, we expand our consumption possibilities. Placing impediments on that trade decreases the gains from specialization and trade. By opening our country up to free international trade, the market for the things that we sell expands and the relative price rises. The market for the things that we buy also expands, and the relative price falls.

Reading Between the Lines on pp. 804–805 looks at a recent example of an international trade dispute between the United States and Canada—the lumber dispute. This dispute provides a clear example of the economic cost of restricting international trade.

READING BETWEEN THE LINES

Tariffs in Action: Lumber

THE GLOBE AND MAIL, JULY 27, 2002

Officials applaud softwood victory

Canadian forestry officials applauded a first-round victory in the bitter softwood dispute, but warned there is no quick relief for an industry still facing crippling duties.

The punitive duties, which have shut dozens of sawmills across Canada and cost thousands of forestry workers their jobs, were imposed to support allegations by the U.S. industry that Canadian lumber is unfairly subsidized.

The World Trade Organization said yesterday the United States was not justified in using cross-border pricing comparisons for calculating duties on lumber imports.

While the WTO accepted the U.S. argument that Canada's stumpage system does violate WTO subsidy rules, Frank Dottori, president of Montreal-based lumber producer Tembec Inc., said he was "ecstatic" with the ruling. "We hope the Americans respect this third-party ruling and see it as an opportunity to stop persecuting us and move forward," he said. ...

Mr. De Jong said the decision will not bestow immediate benefits on the lumber industry, which is currently paying a 27-per-cent duty on about $10-billion worth of lumber shipments into the key U.S. market. ...

"The American lumber lobby will probably try to minimize the importance of the decision and stick to their guns," said Carl Grenier, president of the Free Trade Lumber Council, whose members account for about 40 per cent of Canadian lumber exports to the United States.

Mr. Grenier said the U.S. trade position is driven by a powerful industry lobby, not by government, and that he expects that lobby to continue to forcefully argue its case. ...

Essence of the Story

- A 27-percent duty on Canadian lumber exports to the United States has shut dozens of sawmills across Canada and cost thousands of forestry workers their jobs.
- The U.S. lumber industry claims that Canadian lumber is unfairly subsidized.
- The World Trade Organization agrees that Canadian lumber is subsidized but says that the United States is not justified in calculating duties on lumber imports by comparing the Canadian and U.S. prices.
- While Canadian lumber producers hope that this ruling paves the way for tariff cuts, U.S. lumber producers are a powerful lobby and one that will be hard to overcome.

Economic Analysis

■ The U.S. tariff on Canadian lumber damages Canada, but it also damages the United States.

■ Figure 1 shows the U.S. market for lumber.

■ The demand curve of U.S. buyers of lumber is *D*.

■ There are two supply curves: the supply curve of the Canadian producers, S_C, and the supply curve of U.S. producers, S_{US}. We'll assume that Canada can supply any quantity at a price of $100 per load.

■ With no tariff, the quantity of lumber bought in the United States is QC_0. Of this amount, QP_0 is produced in the United States and the rest is imported from Canada, as shown by the arrow in Fig. 1.

■ Now the United States puts a 27-percent tariff on the import of lumber. Canadian lumber is now supplied to the U.S. market at the original supply price, $100, plus the tariff, $27, so the supply curve of lumber from Canada shifts to become S_C + *tariff*.

■ With the tariff, the quantity of lumber bought in the United States is QC_1. Of this amount, QP_1 is produced in the United States and the rest is imported from Canada, as shown by the arrow in Fig. 1.

■ The tariff decreases U.S. consumption and imports and increases U.S. production.

■ Figure 2 shows the winners and the losers in the United States.

■ The winners include U.S lumber producers, who gain additional producer surplus, which is shown by the blue area in Fig. 2.

■ Another winner is the U.S. government, which collects additional revenue, shown by the purple area in Fig. 2.

■ The sum of the blue, red, purple, and gray areas is the loss of consumer surplus that results from the tariff.

■ The Canadian subsidy has no influence on the effects of the tariff. A deadweight loss arises—the decrease in consumer surplus exceeds the increase in producer surplus—regardless of whether Canadian lumber producers receive a subsidy.

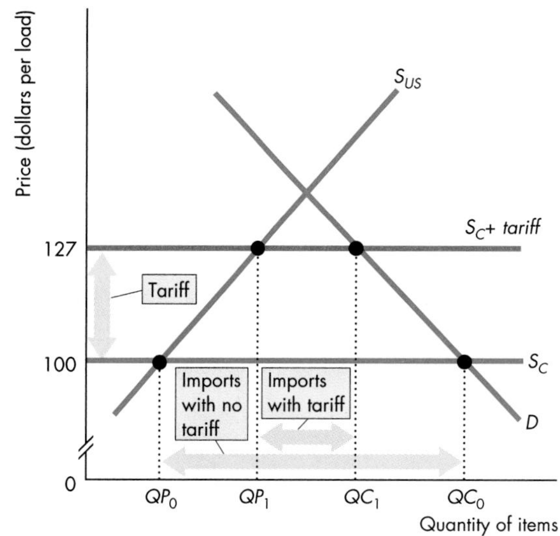

Figure 1 Tariffs and imports

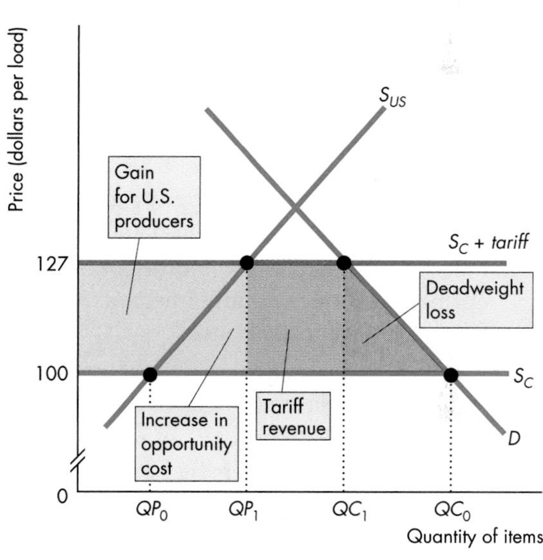

Figure 2 Winners and losers

SUMMARY

KEY POINTS

Patterns and Trends in International Trade (p. 786)

- Large flows of trade take place between countries, most of which is in manufactured goods exchanged among rich industrialized countries.
- Since 1978, the volume of Canadian international trade has increased to more than one-third of total production.

The Gains from International Trade (pp. 787–792)

- Comparative advantage is the fundamental source of the gains from trade.
- Comparative advantage exists when opportunity costs between countries diverge.
- By increasing its production of goods in which it has a comparative advantage and then trading some of the increased output, a country can consume at points outside its production possibilities frontier.
- In the absence of international borrowing and lending, trade is balanced as prices adjust to reflect the international supply of and demand for goods.
- The world price balances the production and consumption plans of the trading parties. At the equilibrium price, trade is balanced.
- Comparative advantage explains the international trade that takes place in the world.
- But trade in similar goods arises from economies of scale in the face of diversified tastes.

International Trade Restrictions (pp. 793–796)

- Countries restrict international trade by imposing tariffs and nontariffs, such as quotas and VERS.
- International trade restrictions raise the domestic price of imported goods, lower the volume of imports, and reduce the total value of imports.
- They also reduce the total value of exports by the same amount as the reduction in the value of imports.

The Case Against Protection (pp. 797–800)

- Arguments that protection is necessary to save jobs, to protect infant industries, and to prevent dumping are weak.
- Arguments that protection is necessary for national security, allows us to compete with cheap foreign labour, makes the economy diversified and stable, penalizes lax environmental standards, protects national culture, and prevents exploitation of developing countries are fatally flawed.

Why Is International Trade Restricted? (pp. 800–801)

- Trade is restricted because tariffs raise government revenue and because protection brings a small loss to a large number of people and a large gain per person to a small number of people.

The North American Free Trade Agreement (pp. 802–803)

- NAFTA is an agreement between Canada, the United States, and Mexico, which began in 1995 and grew from a previous Canada–U.S. agreement.
- Under NAFTA, trade has expanded more rapidly than before the agreement.

KEY FIGURES

Figure 33.1 Opportunity Cost in Farmland, 787
Figure 33.2 Opportunity Cost in Mobilia, 788
Figure 33.3 International Trade in Cars, 789
Figure 33.4 Expanding Consumption Possibilities, 790
Figure 33.6 The Effects of a Tariff, 794
Figure 33.7 The Effects of a Quota, 796

KEY TERMS

Dumping, 798
Exports, 786
General Agreement on Tariffs and Trade, 793
Imports, 786
Infant-industry argument, 797
Net exports, 786
Nontariff barrier, 793
North American Free Trade Agreement, 794
Quota, 796
Tariff, 793
Terms of trade, 788
Voluntary export restraint, 796
World Trade Organization, 793

PROBLEMS

*1. The table provides information about Virtual Reality's production possibilities.

TV sets (per day)		Computers (per day)
0	and	36
10	and	35
20	and	33
30	and	30
40	and	26
50	and	21
60	and	15
70	and	8
80	and	0

a. Calculate Virtual Reality's opportunity cost of a TV set when it produces 10 sets a day.
b. Calculate Virtual Reality's opportunity cost of a TV set when it produces 40 sets a day.
c. Calculate Virtual Reality's opportunity cost of a TV set when it produces 70 sets a day.
d. Using the answers to parts (a), (b), and (c), sketch the relationship between the opportunity cost of a TV set and the quantity of TV sets produced in Virtual Reality.

2. The table provides information about Vital Sign's production possibilities.

TV sets (per day)		Computers (per day)
0	and	18.0
10	and	17.5
20	and	16.5
30	and	15.0
40	and	13.0
50	and	10.5
60	and	7.5
70	and	4.0
80	and	0

a. Calculate Vital Sign's opportunity cost of a TV set when it produces 10 sets a day.
b. Calculate Vital Sign's opportunity cost of a TV set when it produces 40 sets a day.
c. Calculate Vital Sign's opportunity cost of a TV set when it produces 70 sets a day.
d. Using the answers to parts (a), (b), and (c), sketch the relationship between the opportunity cost of a TV set and the quantity of TV sets produced in Vital Sign.

*3. Suppose that with no international trade, Virtual Reality in problem 1 produces and consumes 10 TV sets a day and Vital Sign produces and consumes 60 TV sets a day. Now suppose that the two countries begin to trade with each other.
a. Which country exports TV sets?
b. What adjustments are made to the amount of each good produced by each country?
c. What adjustments are made to the amount of each good consumed by each country?
d. What can you say about the terms of trade (the price of a TV set expressed as computers per TV set) under free trade?

4. Suppose that with no international trade, Virtual Reality in problem 1 produces and consumes 50 TV sets a day and Vital Sign produces and consumes 20 TV sets a day. Now suppose that the two countries begin to trade with each other.
a. Which country exports TV sets?
b. What adjustments are made to the amount of each good produced by each country?
c. What adjustments are made to the amount of each good consumed by each country?
d. What can you say about the terms of trade (the price of a TV set expressed as computers per TV set) under free trade?

*5. Compare the total quantities of each good produced in problems 1 and 2 with the total quantities of each good produced in problems 3 and 4.
a. Does free trade increase or decrease the total quantities of TV sets and computers produced in both cases? Why?
b. What happens to the price of a TV set in Virtual Reality in the two cases? Why does it rise in one case and fall in the other?
c. What happens to the price of a computer in Vital Sign in the two cases? Why does it rise in one case and fall in the other?

6. Compare the international trade in problem 3 with that in problem 4.
a. Why does Virtual Reality export TV sets in one of the cases and import them in the other case?
b. Do the TV producers or the computer producers gain in each case?
c. Do consumers gain in each case?

*7. The figure depicts the international market for soybeans.

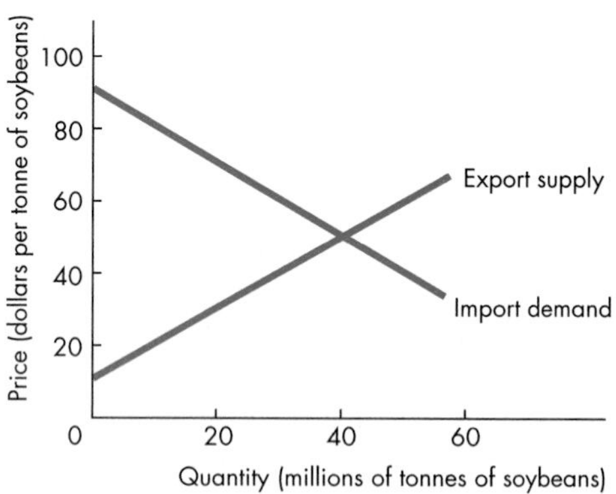

a. If the two countries did not engage in international trade, what would be the prices of soybeans in the two countries? Show the prices on the graph.
b. What is the world price of soybeans if there is free trade between these countries?
c. What quantities of soybeans are exported and imported?
d. What is the balance of trade?

8. If the country in problem 7 that imports soybeans imposes a tariff of $20 per tonne, what is the world price of soybeans and what quantity of soybeans gets traded internationally? What is the price of soybeans in the importing country? Calculate the tariff revenue.

*9. The importing country in problem 7 imposes a quota of 30 million tonnes on imports of soybeans.
a. What is the price of soybeans in the importing country?
b. What is the revenue from the quota?
c. Who gets this revenue?

10. The exporting country in problem 7 imposes a VER of 30 million tonnes on its exports of soybeans.
a. What is the world price of soybeans now?
b. What is the revenue of soybean growers in the exporting country?
c. Which country gains from the VER?

CRITICAL THINKING

1. Study *Reading Between the Lines* on pp. 804–805 and then answer the following questions:
a. Why did the United States impose a tariff on lumber imports from Canada?
b. What are the effects of the tariff on lumber?
c. Who are the winners and who are the losers from the tariff on lumber?
d. Modify the figures on page 805 to show the effects of a Canadian subsidy to lumber producers on the consumer surplus, producer surplus, and deadweight loss in the United States.

WEB EXERCISES

1. Visit the Parkin–Bade Web site and study the Web *Reading Between the Lines* on steel dumping, and then answer the following questions:
a. What is the argument in the news article for limiting steel imports?
b. Evaluate the argument. Is it correct or incorrect in your opinion? Why?
c. Would you vote to eliminate steel imports? Why or why not?
d. Would you vote differently if you lived in another steel-producing country? Why or why not?

2. Use the links on the Parkin–Bade Web site to view a NAFTA report card on agriculture. Then answer the following questions:
a. What does NAFTA seek to achieve in agriculture trade?
b. What has NAFTA achieved to date?
c. What are the obstacles to greater gains for North American trade in agricultural products?
d. Would you vote to maintain NAFTA? Why or why not?
e. Would you vote to expand NAFTA to include other countries? Why or why not?

INTERNATIONAL FINANCE

CHAPTER 34

¥€$!

Yes! The yen (¥), the euro (€), and the U.S. dollar ($) are the world's three big currencies. The yen (the currency of Japan) and the dollar (the currency of the United States) have been around for a long time. The euro is new. It was launched on January 1, 1999, as the fledgling currency of 11 members of the European Union. But it is already an international currency. Most of the world's international trade and finance is conducted using these three currencies. ◆ In 1976, an American needed 1.01 U.S. dollars to buy a Canadian dollar. But in 2002, 63 U.S. cents was sufficient to buy a Canadian dollar. Many currencies have fallen by much more than the Canadian dollar. In 1997 and 1998, during the Asian financial crisis, the currency of Indonesia fell against our dollar to less than one-third of its pre-crisis value. ◆ Why do currency values fluctuate? Is there anything we can do or should do to stabilize the value of the dollar? ◆ In 2001, Canadian receipts from the rest of the world for exports and debt interest exceeded the amount paid by Canadians for imports by $30 billion. But during most of the 1990s, imports and debt interest exceeded exports. Through those years, foreigners bought Canadian assets on a grand scale. Cadbury Schweppes (a British firm) bought George Weston's chocolate company and foreign companies now own Canada's four biggest makers of chocolate bars. Why have foreigners bought so many Canadian businesses?

In this chapter, we're going to discover what determines the amount of international borrowing and lending, and why the dollar fluctuates against other currencies. At the end of the chapter, in *Reading Between the Lines*, we'll look at a projection of the Canadian dollar exchange rate through 2026.

After studying this chapter, you will be able to:

- **Explain how international trade is financed**
- **Describe a country's balance of payments accounts**
- **Explain what determines the amount of international borrowing and lending**
- **Explain why Canada is an international borrower**
- **Explain how the foreign exchange value of the dollar is determined**
- **Explain why the foreign exchange value of the dollar fluctuates**

Financing International Trade

WHEN A SONY STORE IN CANADA IMPORTS CD players from Japan, it does not pay for them with Canadian dollars—it uses Japanese yen. And when an Irish railroad company buys a locomotive from GM in London, Ontario, it pays in Canadian dollars. Whenever we buy things from another country, we use the currency of that country to make the transaction. It doesn't make any difference what the item being traded is; it might be a consumption good or a capital good, a building, or even a firm.

We're going to study the markets in which money—different types of currency—is bought and sold. But first we're going to look at the scale of international trading and borrowing and lending and at the way in which we keep our records of these transactions. Such records are called the balance of payments accounts.

Balance of Payments Accounts

A country's **balance of payments accounts** record its international trading, borrowing, and lending. There are in fact three balance of payments accounts:

1. Current account
2. Capital account
3. Official settlements account

The **current account** records payments for imports of goods and services from abroad, receipts from exports of goods and services sold abroad, net interest paid abroad, and net transfers (such as foreign aid payments). The *current account balance* equals exports minus imports, net interest payments, and net transfers. The **capital account** records foreign investment in Canada minus Canadian investment abroad. The **official settlements account** records the change in official Canadian reserves. **Official Canadian reserves** are the government's holdings of foreign currency. If Canadian official reserves increase, the *official settlements account balance* is negative. The reason is that holding foreign money is like investing abroad. Canadian investment abroad is a minus item in the capital account and in the official settlements account. (By the same reasoning, if official Canadian reserves decrease, the *official settlements account balance* is positive.)

The sum of the balances on the three accounts always equals zero. That is, to pay for a current account deficit, we must either borrow more from abroad than we lend abroad or use our official reserves to cover the shortfall.

Table 34.1 shows the Canadian balance of payments accounts in 2001. Items in the current account and capital account that provide foreign currency to Canada have a plus sign; items that cost Canada foreign currency have a minus sign. The table shows that in 2001, exports plus net transfers exceeded imports plus net interest payments and the current account had a surplus of $30 billion.

What do we do with our current account surplus? We lend it to the rest of the world. The capital account tells us by how much. We borrowed $90 billion (foreign investment in Canada) but made loans of $108 billion (Canadian investment abroad). Thus our net foreign lending was $18 billion. A statistical discrepancy arises because of illegal and hidden transactions, which in 2001 was $9 billion.

Our current account surplus minus our net foreign lending and the statistical discrepancy is the

TABLE 34.1 Canadian Balance of Payments Accounts in 2001

Current account	**Billions of dollars**
Imports of goods and services	–416
Exports of goods and services	+471
Net interest payments	–27
Net transfers	+2
Current account balance	+30
Capital account	
Foreign investment in Canada	+90
Canadian investment abroad	–108
Capital account balance	–18
Statistical discrepancy	–9
Official settlements account	
Increase in official Canadian reserves	–3

Source: Statistics Canada, CANSIM tables 376-0001 and 376-0002.

change in official Canadian reserves. In 2001, reserves increased because our current account surplus of $30 billion exceeded our net foreign lending of $18 billion plus the statistical discrepancy of $9 billion by $3 billion. When our reserves change, we record an *increase* in reserves as a negative number in our international accounts. Why? Because an increase in our reserves is like making a loan to the rest of the world.

The numbers in Table 34.1 give a snapshot of the balance of payments accounts in 2001. Figure 34.1 puts that snapshot into perspective by showing the balance of payments between 1981 and 2001. Because the economy grows and the price level rises, changes in the dollar value of the balance of payments do not convey much information. To remove the influences of growth and inflation, Fig. 34.1 shows the balance of payments as a percentage of nominal GDP.

As you can see, the capital account balance is almost a mirror image of the current account balance. The official settlements balance is very small in comparison with the balances of these other two accounts. A large current account deficit (and capital account surplus) emerged during the 1980s but declined after 1993. By 1996 we had a small surplus and after two more years of deficit, the early 2000s saw an increasing surplus.

You can understand the balance of payments and the way the accounts are linked together if you think about the income and expenditure, borrowing and lending, and bank account of an individual.

Individual Analogy An individual's current account records the income from supplying the services of productive resources and the expenditure on goods and services. Consider, for example, Joanne. She worked in 2002 and earned an income of $25,000. Joanne has $10,000 worth of investments that earned her an interest income of $1,000. Joanne's current account shows an income of $26,000. Joanne spent $18,000 buying goods and services for consumption. She also bought a new house, which cost her $60,000. So Joanne's total expenditure was $78,000. The difference between her expenditure and income is $52,000 ($78,000 minus $26,000). This amount is Joanne's current account deficit.

To pay for expenditure of $52,000 in excess of her income, Joanne has to use the money that she has in the bank or has to take out a loan. In fact, Joanne took a mortgage of $50,000 to help buy her house. This mortgage was the only borrowing that Joanne did, so her capital account surplus was $50,000. With a current account deficit of $52,000 and a capi-

FIGURE 34.1 The Balance of Payments: 1981–2001

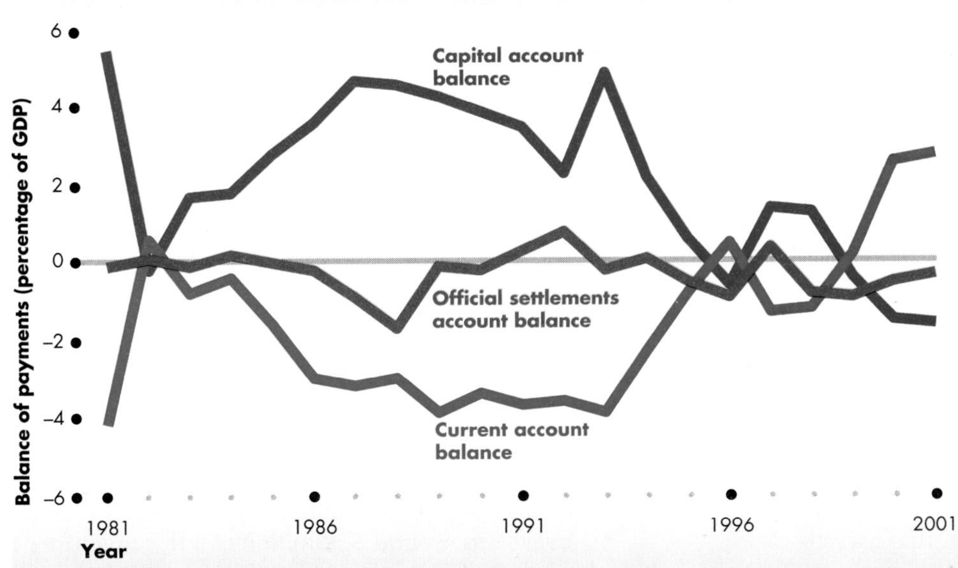

Source: Statistics Canada, CANSIM tables 376-0001 and 376-0002.

During the 1980s, a large current account deficit arose. That deficit decreased after 1993 and by the early 2000s an increasing surplus arose. The capital account balance mirrors the current account balance. When the current account balance is negative, the capital account balance is positive—we borrow from the rest of the world. Fluctuations in the official settlements account balance are small in comparison with fluctuations in the current account balance and the capital account balance.

tal account surplus of $50,000, Joanne is still $2,000 short. She got that $2,000 from her own bank account. Her cash holdings decreased by $2,000.

Joanne's income from her work is analogous to a country's income from its exports. Her income from her investments is analogous to a country's interest income from foreigners. Her purchases of goods and services, including her purchase of a house, are analogous to a country's imports. Joanne's mortgage—borrowing from someone else—is analogous to a country's borrowing from the rest of the world. The change in her own bank account is analogous to the change in the country's official reserves.

Borrowers and Lenders, Debtors and Creditors

A country that has a current account deficit and that borrows more from the rest of the world than it lends to it is called a **net borrower**. Similarly, a **net lender** is a country that lends more to the rest of the world than it borrows from it.

From 1999 through 2001, Canada was a net lender. But most years, Canada has been a net borrower. During the 57 years between the end of World War II and 2001, Canada was a net lender in only 15 years, and most of those were in the 1940s. During the 1990s alone, Canada borrowed $140 billion (net) from the rest of the world. Canada's cumulative borrowing since the end of World War II is $265 billion. Only in the past few years has Canada been a net lender in recent memory. The year of greatest foreign borrowing was 1993, when Canada borrowed (net) almost $30 billion from the rest of the world.

Most countries are net borrowers. But like Canada today, a small number of countries, including Japan and oil-rich Saudi Arabia, are net lenders. For the world as a whole, net foreign borrowing equals net foreign lending.

A net borrower might be going deeper into debt or might simply be reducing its net assets held in the rest of the world. The total stock of foreign investment determines whether a country is a debtor or creditor. A **debtor nation** is a country that during its entire history has borrowed more from the rest of the world than it has lent to it. It has a stock of outstanding debt to the rest of the world that exceeds the stock of its own claims on the rest of the world. A **creditor nation** is a country that has invested more in the rest of the world than other countries have invested in it.

At the heart of the distinction between a net borrower/net lender and a debtor/creditor nation is the distinction between flows and stocks, which you have encountered many times in your study of macroeconomics. Borrowing and lending are flows—amounts borrowed or lent per unit of time. Debts are stocks—amounts owed at a point in time. The flow of borrowing and lending changes the stock of debt. But the outstanding stock of debt depends mainly on past flows of borrowing and lending, not on the current period's flows. The current period's flows determine the *change* in the stock of debt outstanding.

Canada is a debtor nation. In 2001, the net international debt of Canadians was $203 billion. To put this number in perspective, it is $6,500 per person, or 20 percent of total income. Other debtor nations are a diverse group. They include the United States as well as the poor capital-hungry nations of the developing regions of Central and South America, Asia, and Africa. The international debt of the developing countries grew from less than one-third to more than half of their gross domestic product during the 1980s and 1990s and created what was called the "Third World debt crisis."

Should we be concerned that Canada is a net borrower and debtor nation? The answer to this question depends on what we do with the funds that we borrow. If borrowing finances investment that in turn generates economic growth and higher income, borrowing is not a problem. If borrowing finances consumption, then higher interest payments are being incurred, and as a consequence, consumption will eventually have to be reduced. In this case, the more the borrowing and the longer it goes on, the greater is the reduction in consumption that will eventually be necessary.

Has Canada Borrowed for Consumption or Investment?

In 1998, the last time we had a current account deficit, we borrowed $12 billion from abroad. Did we borrow for consumption or investment? In 1998, private investment in buildings, plant, and equipment was $176 billion. Government investment in a wide range of public buildings and structures such as highways was around $20 billion. All this investment added to the nation's capital and much of it increased productivity. Government also spends on education and health-care services, which increase *human capital.* Our international borrowing has financed private and public investment, not consumption.

Current Account Balance

What determines a country's current account balance and net foreign borrowing? You've seen that net exports (*NX*) is the main item in the current account. We can define the current account balance (*CAB*) as

$$CAB = NX + \text{Net interest income} + \text{Net transfers.}$$

Fluctuations in net exports are the main source of fluctuations in the current account balance. The other two items have trends but they do not fluctuate much. So we can study the current account balance by looking at what determines net exports.

Net Exports

Net exports are determined by the government budget and private saving and investment. To see how net exports are determined, we need to recall some of the things that we learned about the National Income Accounts in Chapter 20. Table 34.2 will refresh your memory and summarize some calculations.

Part (a) lists the national income variables that are needed, with their symbols. Part (b) defines three balances. **Net exports** is the value of exports of goods and services minus the value of imports of goods and services.

The **government sector balance** is equal to net taxes minus government expenditures on goods and services. If that number is positive, the government sector has a surplus and it is lent to other sectors; if that number is negative, the government sector has a deficit that must be financed by borrowing from other sectors. The government sector balance is the sum of the balances of the federal, provincial, and municipal governments.

The **private sector balance** is equal to saving minus investment. If saving exceeds investment, a private sector has a surplus and it is lent to other sectors. If investment exceeds saving, borrowing from other sectors finances a private sector deficit.

Part (b) also shows the values of these balances for Canada in 2001. As you can see, net exports were

TABLE 34.2 Net Exports, the Government Budget, Saving, and Investment

	Symbols and equations	Canada in 2001 (billions of dollars)
(a) Variables		
Exports*	X	473
Imports*	M	416
Government expenditures	G	231
Net taxes	NT	280
Investment	I	184
Saving	S	192
(b) Balances		
Net exports	$X - M$	473 – 416 = 57
Government sector	$NT - G$	280 – 231 = 49
Private sector	$S - I$	192 – 184 = 8
(c) Relationship among balances		
National accounts	$Y = C + I + G + X - M$	
	$= C + S + NT$	
Rearranging:	$X - M = S - I + NT - G$	
Net exports	$X - M$	57
Equals:		
Government sector	$NT - G$	49
Plus		
Private sector	$S - I$	8

Source: Statistics Canada, CANSIM tables 380-0002 and 380-0034.

* The national income accounts' measures of exports and imports are different from the balance of payments' accounts measures by small amounts.

$57 billion, a surplus of $57 billion. The government sector's revenue from net taxes was $280 billion and it purchased $231 billion worth of goods and services. The government sector surplus was $49 billion. The private sector saved $192 billion and invested $184 billion, so it had a surplus of $8 billion.

Part (c) shows the relationship among the three balances. From the national income accounts, we know that real GDP (*Y*) is the sum of consumption expenditure (*C*), investment (*I*), government expenditures (*G*), and net exports ($X - M$). It also equals the sum of consumption expenditure (*C*), saving (*S*), and net taxes (*NT*). Rearranging these equations tells us that net exports ($X - M$) is the sum of the government sector surplus ($NT - G$) and the private sector surplus ($S - I$). In Canada in 2001, the government sector had a surplus of $49 billion and the private sector had a surplus of $8 billion. The government sector surplus plus the private sector surplus equals net exports of $57 billion.

FIGURE 34.2 The Twin Deficits

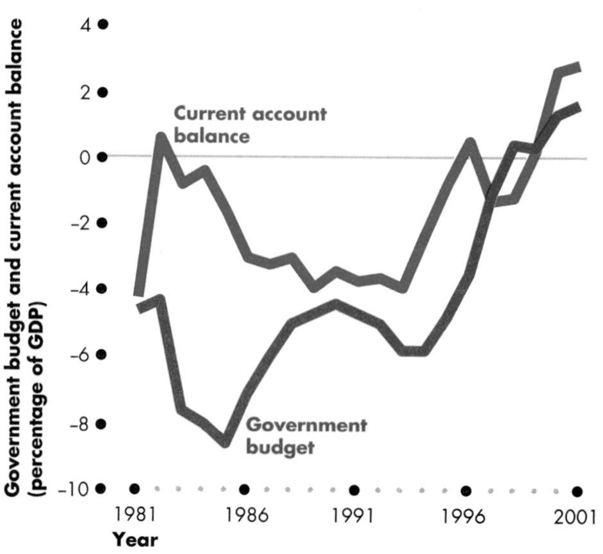

The current account balance and the government budget balance move in similar ways and look like twin deficits. But this relationship broke down during the early 1980s when the private sector surplus swelled.

Source: Statistics Canada, CANSIM tables 376-0001 and 380-0007.

The Twin Deficits

You've seen that net exports equals the sum of the government surplus and the private surplus. And net exports plus debt interest (and other small transfers) equals the current account balance. What is the relationship over time between the current account balance and the government budget balance? How do these balances fluctuate over time? Figure 34.2 answers this question. It shows the government budget (the red line) and the current account balance (the blue line).

You can see that, with an important exception during the early 1980s, there is a tendency for the current account to go into a deeper deficit when the government budget goes into a deeper deficit. Because of the tendency for the government budget deficit and the current account deficit to move in the same direction they have been called the **twin deficits.**

Why are the two deficits linked? They are linked because capital is highly mobile in today's world. If the Canadian government increases expenditure or lowers taxes, total spending in Canada rises. But with the economy at or near full employment, the extra goods and services demanded are sucked in from the rest of the world. Imports increase. Capital flows in to pay for those imports. Saving and investment don't change. This relationship broke down during the early 1980s because we were in recession and investment decreased relative to saving.

REVIEW QUIZ

1. When a Canadian art dealer buys a painting from a French gallery, which currency gets used to make the transaction?
2. When a German car maker buys parts from a Windsor car maker, which currency gets used to make the transaction?
3. What types of transactions do we record in the balance of payments accounts?
4. What transactions does the current account record? What transactions does the capital account record? What transactions does the official settlements account record?
5. How are the current account balance, the government sector balance, and the private sector balance related?

The Exchange Rate

WHEN WE BUY FOREIGN GOODS OR INVEST IN another country, we have to obtain some of that country's currency to make the transaction. When foreigners buy Canadian-produced goods or invest in Canada, they have to obtain some Canadian dollars. We get foreign currency, and foreigners get Canadian dollars in the foreign exchange market. The **foreign exchange market** is the market in which the currency of one country is exchanged for the currency of another. The foreign exchange market is not a place like a downtown flea market or produce market. The market is made up of thousands of people—importers and exporters, banks, and specialists in the buying and selling of foreign exchange—called foreign exchange brokers. The foreign exchange market opens on Monday morning in Hong Kong, which is still Sunday evening in Montreal and Toronto. As the day advances, markets open in Singapore, Tokyo, Bahrain, Frankfurt, London, New York, Montreal, Toronto, and Vancouver. As the West Coast markets close, Hong Kong is only an hour away from opening for the next day of business. The sun barely sets on the foreign exchange market. Dealers around the world are in continual contact by telephone and on a typical day in 2001, $1.5 trillion changed hands.

The price at which one currency exchanges for another is called a **foreign exchange rate.** For example, in October 2002, one Canadian dollar bought 63 U.S. cents. The exchange rate was 63 U.S. cents per dollar.

Figure 34.3 shows the exchange rate of the Canadian dollar in terms of the U.S. dollar between 1971 and 2001. On the average over this period, the Canadian dollar has depreciated against the U.S. dollar.

Currency depreciation is a fall in the value of one currency in terms of another currency. For example when the Canadian dollar fell from 101 U.S. cents in 1976 to 94 U.S. cents in 1977, the Canadian dollar depreciated by 7 percent.

Currency appreciation is the rise in the value of one currency in terms of another currency. From 1986 to 1991, the value of the Canadian dollar increased against the U.S. dollar—the Canadian dollar appreciated.

We've just expressed the value of the Canadian dollar in terms of the U.S. dollar. But we can express the value of the dollar in terms of any currency. Also, we can express the exchange rate of the U.S. dollar in terms of the Canadian dollar as a number of Canadian dollars per U.S. dollar.

When the Canadian dollar depreciates against the U.S. dollar, the U.S. dollar appreciates against the Canadian dollar.

Why does the Canadian dollar fluctuate in value? Why does it sometimes depreciate and sometimes appreciate? What happened between 1976 and 1986 and again between 1992 and 2001 to make the Canadian dollar depreciate? And what happened between 1986 and 1991 to make the Canadian dollar appreciate against the U.S. dollar? To answer these questions, we need to understand the forces that determine the exchange rate.

The exchange rate is the price of one country's money in terms of another country's money. And like all prices, the exchange rate is determined by demand and supply.

FIGURE 34.3 The Exchange Rate

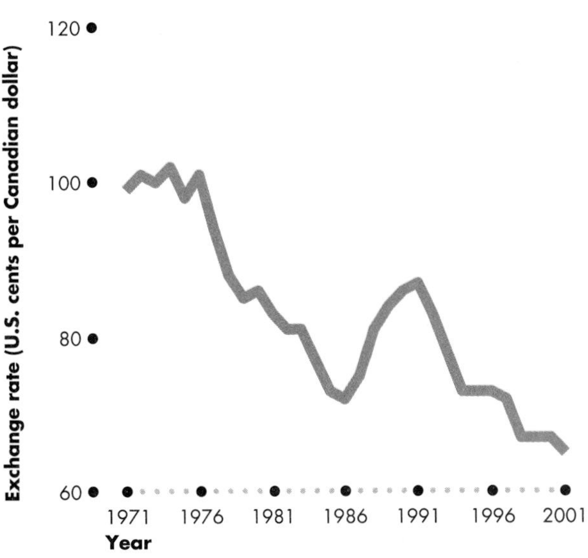

The Canadian dollar exchange rate, expressed as U.S. cents per Canadian dollar, shows that the Canadian dollar fell in value—depreciated—against the U.S. dollar from 1976 through 1986. The Canadian dollar rose in value against the U.S. dollar—appreciated—from 1986 through 1991 and then depreciated again.

Source: Bank of Canada, *Banking and Financial Statistics*, table J1.

Demand in the Foreign Exchange Market

The quantity of Canadian dollars demanded in the foreign exchange market is the amount that traders plan to buy during a given time period at a given exchange rate. This quantity depends on many factors but the main ones are

- The exchange rate
- Interest rates in Canada and other countries
- The expected future exchange rate

Let's look first at the relationship between the quantity of Canadian dollars demanded in the foreign exchange market and the exchange rate.

The Law of Demand for Foreign Exchange

People do not buy dollars because they enjoy them. The demand for dollars is a *derived demand.* People demand Canadian dollars so that they can buy Canadian-made goods and services (Canadian exports). They also demand dollars so they can buy Canadian assets such as bank accounts, bonds, stocks, businesses, and real estate. Nevertheless, the law of demand applies to dollars just as it does to anything else that people value.

Other things remaining the same, the higher the exchange rate, the smaller is the quantity of Canadian dollars demanded in the foreign exchange market. For example, if the price of the Canadian dollar rose from 68 U.S. cents to 75 U.S. cents but nothing else changed, the quantity of Canadian dollars that people plan to buy in the foreign exchange market would decrease. The exchange rate influences the quantity of dollars demanded for two reasons:

- Exports effect
- Expected profit effect

Exports Effect The larger the value of Canadian exports, the larger is the quantity of Canadian dollars demanded on the foreign exchange market. But the value of Canadian exports depends on the exchange rate. The lower the exchange rate, with other things remaining the same, the cheaper are Canadian-produced goods and services and the more Canada exports. So the quantity of Canadian dollars demanded on the foreign exchange market increases.

Expected Profit Effect The larger the expected profit from holding Canadian dollars, the greater is the quantity of Canadian dollars demanded. But expected profit depends on the exchange rate. The lower the exchange rate, other things remaining the same, the larger is the expected profit from buying Canadian dollars and the greater is the quantity of Canadian dollars demanded.

To understand this effect, suppose that today, a Canadian dollar costs 68 U.S. cents. Tina thinks the dollar will be worth 70 U.S. cents by the end of the month and Jack thinks it will be worth 67 U.S. cents. In this situation, Tina buys Canadian dollars but Jack does not. Now suppose that expectations remain the same, but that today a Canadian dollar costs 65 U.S. cents. Now both Tina and Jack buy Canadian dollars. So the quantity of dollars demanded increases.

For the two reasons we've just reviewed, other things remaining the same, when the foreign exchange rate rises, the quantity of Canadian dollars demanded decreases and when the foreign exchange rate falls, the quantity of Canadian dollars demanded increases.

Figure 34.4 shows the demand curve for Canadian dollars in the foreign exchange market. When the foreign exchange rate rises, other things remaining the same, there is a decrease in the quantity of Canadian dollars demanded and a movement up along the demand curve as shown by the arrow. When the exchange rate falls, other things remaining the same, there is an increase in the quantity of Canadian dollars demanded and a movement down along the demand curve as shown by the arrow.

Changes in the Demand for Dollars

A change in any other influence on the quantity of Canadian dollars that people plan to buy brings a change in the demand for dollars and a shift in the demand curve for dollars. Demand either increases or decreases. These other influences are

- Interest rates in Canada and other countries
- The expected future exchange rate

Interest Rates in Canada and Other Countries People and businesses buy financial assets to make a return. The higher the interest rate that people can make on Canadian assets compared with foreign assets, the more Canadian assets they buy. What matters is not the level of Canadian interest rates, but the

FIGURE 34.4 The Demand for Dollars

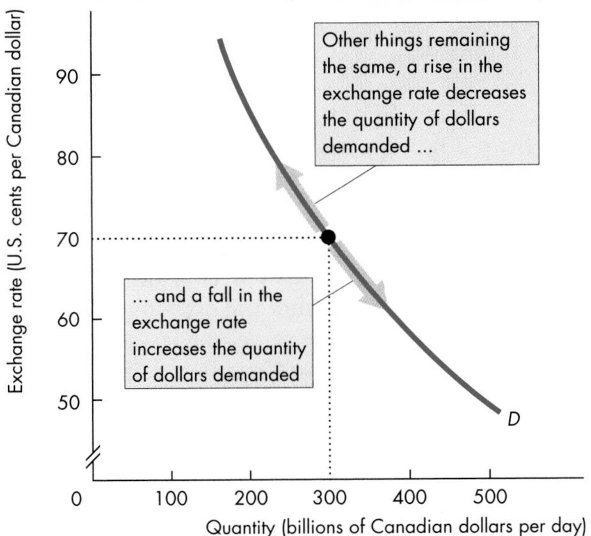

The quantity of Canadian dollars that people plan to buy depends on the exchange rate. Other things remaining the same, if the exchange rate rises, the quantity of dollars demanded decreases and there is a movement up along the demand curve for dollars. If the exchange rate falls, the quantity of dollars demanded increases and there is a movement down along the demand curve for dollars.

Canadian interest rate minus the foreign interest rate, a gap that is called the **Canadian interest rate differential.** If the Canadian interest rate rises and the foreign interest rate remains constant, the Canadian interest rate differential increases. The larger the Canadian interest rate differential, the greater is the demand for Canadian assets and the greater is the demand for Canadian dollars on the foreign exchange market.

The Expected Future Exchange Rate Other things remaining the same, the higher the expected future exchange rate, the greater is the demand for Canadian dollars. To see why, suppose you are American Express's finance manager. The exchange rate is 70 U.S cents per dollar and you think that by the end of the month, it will be 75 U.S. cents per dollar. You spend $U.S.700,000 today and buy $C1,000,000. At the end of the month, the Canadian dollar is 75 U.S. cents, as you predicted it would be, and you sell the $C1,000,000. You get $U.S.750,000. You've made a profit of $U.S.50,000. The higher the expected future exchange rate, other things remaining the same, the greater is the expected profit and the greater is the demand for Canadian dollars.

Figure 34.5 summarizes the influences on the demand for dollars. A rise in the Canadian interest rate differential or a rise in the expected future exchange rate increases the demand for Canadian dollars and shifts the demand curve rightward from D_0 to D_1. A fall in the Canadian interest rate differential or a fall in the expected future exchange rate decreases the demand for Canadian dollars and shifts the demand curve leftward from D_0 to D_2.

FIGURE 34.5 Changes in the Demand for Dollars

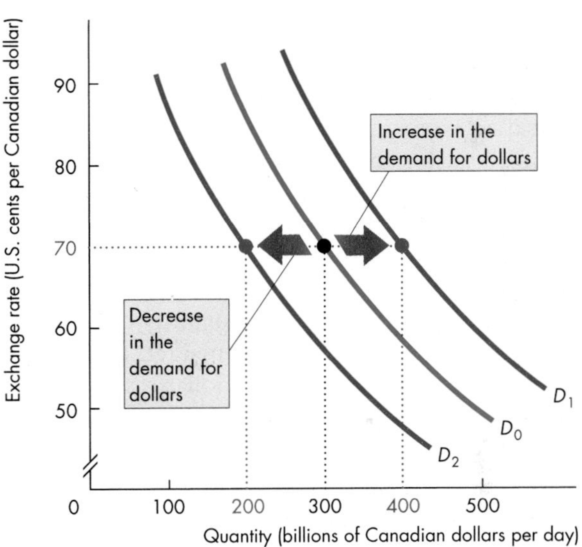

A change in any influence on the quantity of Canadian dollars that people plan to buy, other than today's exchange rate, brings a change in the demand for Canadian dollars.

The demand for Canadian dollars

Increases if:	*Decreases if:*
■ The Canadian interest rate differential increases	■ The Canadian interest rate differential decreases
■ The expected future exchange rate rises	■ The expected future exchange rate falls

Supply in the Foreign Exchange Market

The quantity of Canadian dollars supplied in the foreign exchange market is the amount that traders plan to sell during a given time period at a given exchange rate. This quantity depends on many factors but the main ones are

- The exchange rate
- Interest rates in Canada and other countries
- The expected future exchange rate

Let's look first at the relationship between the quantity of Canadian dollars supplied in the foreign exchange market and the exchange rate.

The Law of Supply of Foreign Exchange

People supply dollars in the foreign exchange market when they buy other currencies. And they buy other currencies so they can buy foreign-made goods and services (Canadian imports). People also supply dollars and buy foreign currencies so they can buy foreign assets such as bank accounts, bonds, stocks, businesses, and real estate. The law of supply applies to dollars just as it does to anything else that people plan to sell.

Other things remaining the same, the higher the exchange rate, the greater is the quantity of dollars supplied in the foreign exchange market. For example, if the price of the Canadian dollar rose from 68 U.S. cents to 75 U.S. cents but nothing else changed, the quantity of Canadian dollars that people plan to sell in the foreign exchange market would increase. Why does the exchange rate influence the quantity of dollars supplied?

The exchange rate influences the quantity of dollars supplied for two reasons:

- Imports effect
- Expected profit effect

Imports Effect The larger the value of Canadian imports, the larger is the quantity of foreign currency demanded to pay for these imports. And when people buy foreign currency, they supply Canadian dollars. So the larger the value of Canadian imports, the greater is the quantity of Canadian dollars supplied on the foreign exchange market. But the value of Canadian imports depends on the exchange rate. The higher the exchange rate, with other things remaining the same, the cheaper are foreign-produced goods and services to Canadians, and the more Canada imports. So the greater is the quantity of Canadian dollars supplied.

Expected Profit Effect The larger the expected profit from holding a foreign currency, the greater is the quantity of that currency demanded and the greater is the quantity of Canadian dollars supplied in the foreign exchange market. But the expected profit from holding a foreign currency depends on the exchange rate. The higher the exchange rate, other things remaining the same, the larger is the expected profit from selling Canadian dollars and the greater is the quantity of Canadian dollars supplied.

For the two reasons we've just reviewed, other things remaining the same, when the foreign

FIGURE 34.6 The Supply of Dollars

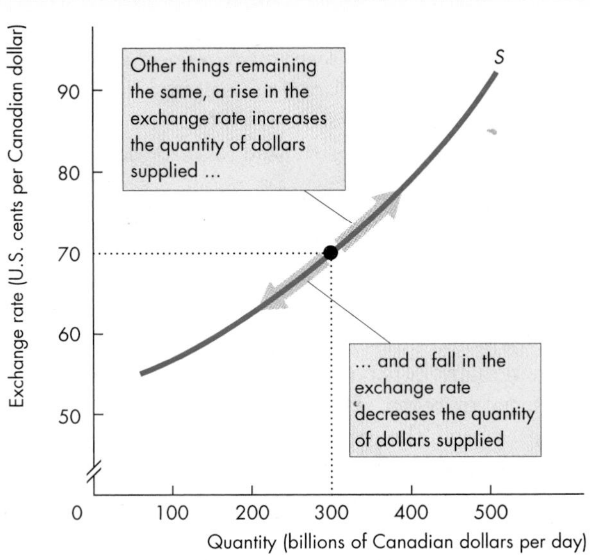

The quantity of Canadian dollars that people plan to sell depends on the exchange rate. Other things remaining the same, if the exchange rate rises, the quantity of Canadian dollars supplied increases and there is a movement up along the supply curve of dollars. If the exchange rate falls, the quantity of Canadian dollars supplied decreases and there is a movement down along the supply curve of dollars.

exchange rate rises, the quantity of dollars supplied increases and when the foreign exchange rate falls, the quantity of Canadian dollars supplied decreases. Figure 34.6 shows the supply curve for Canadian dollars in the foreign exchange market. In this figure, when the foreign exchange rate rises, other things remaining the same, there is an increase in the quantity of Canadian dollars supplied and a movement up along the supply curve as shown by the arrow. When the exchange rate falls, other things remaining the same, there is a decrease in the quantity of Canadian dollars supplied and a movement down along the supply curve as shown by the arrow.

Changes in the Supply of Dollars

A change in any other influence on the quantity of Canadian dollars that people plan to sell in the foreign exchange market brings a change in the supply of dollars and a shift in the supply curve of dollars. Supply either increases or decreases. These other influences parallel the other influences on demand but have exactly the opposite effects. These influences are

- Interest rates in Canada and other countries
- The expected future exchange rate

Interest Rates in Canada and Other Countries The larger the Canadian interest rate differential, the smaller is the demand for foreign assets, and the smaller is the supply of Canadian dollars on the foreign exchange market.

The Expected Future Exchange Rate Other things remaining the same, the higher the expected future exchange rate, the smaller is the supply of dollars. To see why, suppose the Canadian dollar is trading at 70 U.S. cents per dollar today and you think that by the end of the month, the dollar will be worth 75 U.S. cents per dollar. You were planning on selling Canadian dollars today, but you decide to hold off and wait until the end of the month. If you supply dollars today, you get only 70 U.S. cents. But at the end of the month, if the dollar is worth 75 U.S. cents as you predict, you'll get 75 U.S. cents for each dollar you supply. You'll make a profit of 5 U.S. cents per dollar. So the higher the expected future exchange rate, other things remaining the same, the smaller is the expected profit from selling Canadian dollars today and the smaller is the supply of Canadian dollars today.

Figure 34.7 summarizes the influences on the supply of Canadian dollars. A rise in the Canadian interest rate differential or a rise in the expected future exchange rate decreases the supply of Canadian dollars and shifts the demand curve leftward from S_0 to S_1. A fall in the Canadian interest rate differential or a fall in the expected future exchange rate increases the supply of Canadian dollars and shifts the supply curve rightward from S_0 to S_2.

FIGURE 34.7 Changes in the Supply of Dollars

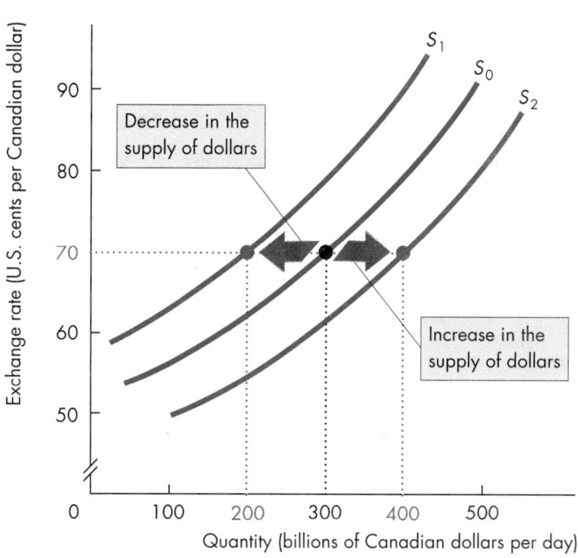

A change in any influence on the quantity of Canadian dollars that people plan to sell, other than today's exchange rate, brings a change in the supply of Canadian dollars.

The supply of Canadian dollars

Increases if:	*Decreases if:*
■ The Canadian interest rate differential decreases	■ The Canadian interest rate differential increases
■ The expected future exchange rate falls	■ The expected future exchange rate rises

Market Equilibrium

Figure 34.8 shows how demand and supply in the foreign exchange market determine the exchange rate. The demand curve is *D* and the supply curve is *S*. As in other markets you've studied, price (the exchange rate) acts as a regulator. If the exchange rate is too high, there is a surplus—the quantity supplied exceeds the quantity demanded. For example, in Fig. 34.8, if the exchange rate is 80 U.S. cents per Canadian dollar, there is a surplus of Canadian dollars.

If the exchange rate is too low, there is a shortage—the quantity supplied is less than the quantity demanded. For example, in Fig. 34.8, if the exchange rate is 60 U.S. cents per Canadian dollar, there is a shortage of Canadian dollars.

At the equilibrium exchange rate, there is neither a shortage nor a surplus. The quantity supplied equals the quantity demanded. In Fig. 34.8, the equilibrium exchange rate is 70 U.S. cents per Canadian dollar. At this exchange rate, the quantity demanded and the quantity supplied are each $300 billion a day.

The foreign exchange market is constantly pulled to its equilibrium by the forces of supply and demand. Foreign exchange dealers are constantly looking for the best price they can get. If they are selling, they want the highest price available. If they are buying, they want the lowest price available. Information flows from dealer to dealer through the worldwide computer network and the price adjusts second by second to keep buying plans and selling plans in balance. That is, price adjusts minute by minute to keep the market at its equilibrium.

FIGURE 34.8 Equilibrium Exchange Rate

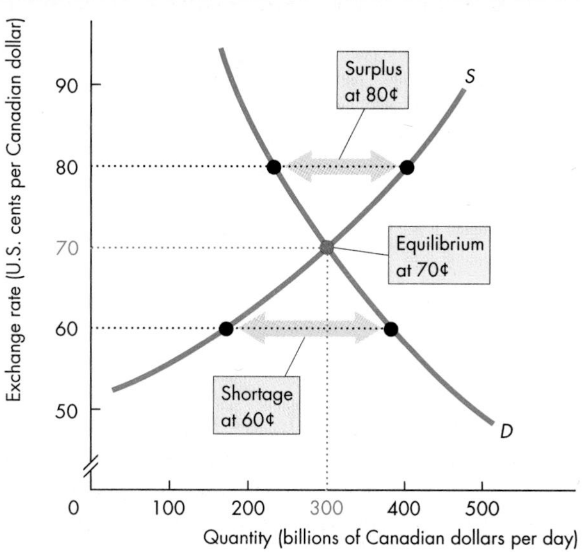

The demand curve for dollars is *D* and the supply curve is *S*. If the exchange rate is 80 U.S. cents per dollar, there is a surplus of dollars and the exchange rate falls. If the exchange rate is 60 U.S. cents per dollar, there is a shortage of dollars and the exchange rate rises. If the exchange rate is 70 U.S. cents per dollar, there is neither a shortage nor a surplus of dollars and the exchange rate remains constant. The market is in equilibrium.

Changes in the Exchange Rate

If the demand for dollars increases and the supply of dollars does not change, the exchange rate rises. If the demand for dollars decreases and the supply of dollars does not change, the exchange rate falls. Similarly, if the supply of dollars decreases and the demand for dollars does not change, the exchange rate rises. If the supply of dollars increases and the demand for dollars does not change, the exchange rate falls.

These predictions about the effects of changes in demand and supply are exactly the same as for any other market.

Why the Exchange Rate Is Volatile Sometimes the dollar depreciates and at other times it appreciates but the quantity of dollars traded each day barely changes. Why? The main reason is that supply and demand are not independent of each other in the foreign exchange market.

When we studied the demand for dollars and the supply of dollars, we saw that the demand side and the supply side of the market have some common influences. A change in the expected future exchange rate or a change in the Canadian interest rate differential changes both demand and supply and in opposite directions. These common influences explain why the exchange rate can be volatile at times even though the quantity of dollars traded does not change.

Everyone in the market is potentially either a demander or a supplier. Each has a price above which he or she will sell and below which he or she will buy. Let's see how these common supply and demand effects work by looking at two episodes: one in which the dollar appreciated and one in which it depreciated.

An Appreciating Dollar: 1986–1991 Between 1986 and 1991 the Canadian dollar appreciated. It rose from 72 U.S. cents in 1986 to 87 U.S. cents in 1991. Figure 34.9(a) explains why this happened. In 1986, the demand and supply curves were those labelled D_{86} and S_{86}. The exchange rate was 72 U.S. cents per dollar—where the supply and demand curves intersect. During the next five years, people expected the Canadian dollar to appreciate. They expected a higher future exchange rate. As a result, the demand for dollars increased and the supply of dollars decreased. The demand curve shifted from D_{86} to D_{91} and the supply curve shifted from S_{86} to S_{91}. These two shifts reinforced each other and the exchange rate increased to 87 U.S. cents per dollar.

A Depreciating Dollar: 1991–2001 Between 1991 and 2001, the dollar fell from 87 U.S. cents to 65 U.S. cents per dollar. Figure 34.9(b) explains this fall. In 1991, the demand and supply curves were those labelled D_{91} and S_{91}. The exchange rate was 87 U.S. cents per dollar. During the 1990s, traders expected the Canadian dollar to depreciate. They expected a lower exchange rate. As a result, the demand for dollars decreased and the supply of dollars increased. The demand curve shifted leftward to D_{01} and the supply curve shifted rightward to S_{01}. The exchange rate fell to 65 U.S. cents per dollar.

Exchange Rate Expectations

The changes in the exchange rate that we've just examined occurred mainly because the exchange rate was *expected to change.* This explanation sounds a bit like a self-fulfilling forecast. But what makes expectations change? The answer is new information about the deeper forces that influence the value of money. Two such forces are

- Purchasing power parity
- Interest rate parity

FIGURE 34.9 Exchange Rate Fluctuations

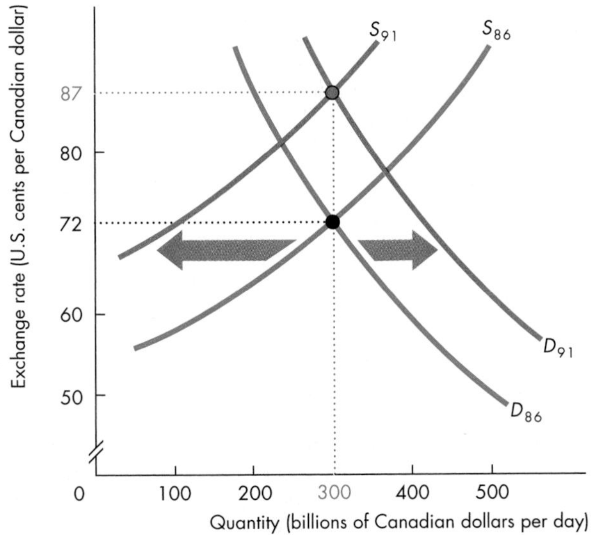

(a) 1986 to 1991

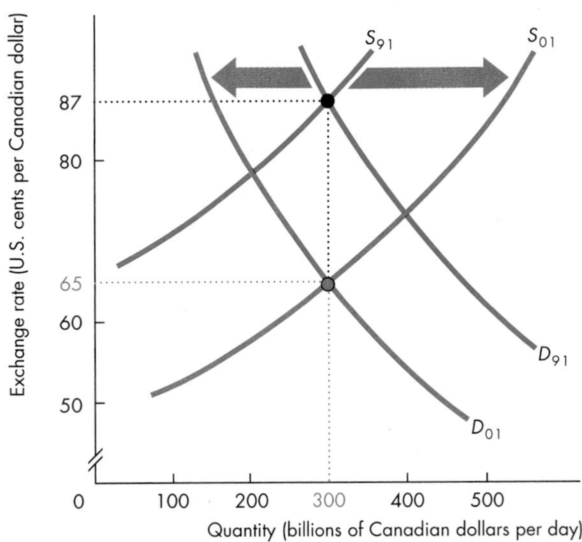

(b) 1991 to 2001

The exchange rate fluctuates because changes in demand and supply are not independent of each other. Between 1986 and 1991 (part a), the Canadian dollar appreciated from 72 U.S. cents to 87 U.S. cents per dollar. This appreciation occurred because an increase in the expected future exchange rate increased the demand for dollars and decreased the supply. Between 1991 and 2001 (in part b), the exchange rate fell from 87 U.S. cents to 65 U.S. cents per dollar. This depreciation occurred because a decrease in the expected future exchange rate decreased the demand for dollars and increased the supply.

Purchasing Power Parity Money is worth what it will buy. But two kinds of money, Canadian dollars and U.S. dollars for example, might buy different amounts of goods and services. Suppose a Big Mac costs $4 (Canadian) in Toronto and $3 (U.S.) in New York. If the Canadian dollar exchange rate is 75 U.S. cents per Canadian dollar, the two monies have the same value. You can buy a Big Mac in either Toronto or New York for either $4 Canadian or $3 U.S.

The situation we've just described is called **purchasing power parity,** which means *equal value of money.* If purchasing power parity does not prevail, some powerful forces go to work. To understand these forces, let's suppose that the price of a Big Mac in New York rises to $4 U.S. but in Toronto it remains at $4 Canadian. Suppose the exchange rate remains at 75 U.S. cents per Canadian dollar. In this case, a Big Mac in Toronto still costs $4 Canadian or $3 U.S. But in New York, it costs $4 U.S. or $5.33 Canadian. Money buys more in Canada than in the United States. Money is not of equal value in both countries.

If all (or most) prices have increased in the United States and have not increased in Canada, then people will generally expect that the value of the Canadian dollar on the foreign exchange market must rise. In this situation, the exchange rate is expected to rise. The demand for Canadian dollars increases and the supply of Canadian dollars decreases. The exchange rate rises, as expected. If the exchange rate rises to $1.00 U.S. per Canadian dollar and there are no further price changes, purchasing power parity is restored. A Big Mac now costs $4 in either Canadian or U.S. dollars in both New York and Toronto.

If prices increase in Canada but remain constant in other countries, then people will generally expect that the value of the Canadian dollar on the foreign exchange market is too high and that it is going to fall. In this situation, the exchange rate is expected to fall. The demand for Canadian dollars decreases and the supply of Canadian dollars increases. The exchange rate falls, as expected.

Ultimately, the value of money is determined by the price level, which in turn is determined by aggregate supply and aggregate demand (see Chapter 22) So the deeper forces that influence the exchange rate have tentacles that spread throughout the economy. If the price level rises more quickly in Canada than in other countries, the exchange rate falls. And if the price level rises more slowly in Canada than in other countries, the exchange rate rises.

Interest Rate Parity Money is worth what it can earn. Again two kinds of money, Canadian dollars and U.S. dollars for example, might earn different amounts. For example, suppose a Canadian dollar bank deposit in Toronto earns 4 percent a year and a U.S. dollar bank deposit in New York earns 5 percent a year. In this situation, why does anyone deposit money in Toronto? Why doesn't all the money flow to New York? The answer is: because of exchange rate expectations. Suppose people expect the Canadian dollar to appreciate by 1 percent a year. This 1 percent appreciation must be added to the 4 percent interest to obtain a return of 5 percent a year that an American can earn by depositing funds in a Toronto bank. The two returns are equal. This situation is one of **interest rate parity,** which means *equal interest rates.*

Adjusted for risk, interest rate parity always prevails. Funds move to get the highest return available. If for a few seconds a higher return is available in Toronto than in New York, the demand for Canadian dollars rises and the exchange rate rises until the expected interest rates are equal.

The Bank of Canada in the Foreign Exchange Market

The Bank of Canada influences the quantity of money and the Canadian interest rate (see Chapter 25, pp. 594–595). So the Bank of Canada influences the exchange rate through its monetary policy. When interest rates in Canada rise relative to those in other countries, the demand for Canadian dollars increases, the supply decreases, and the exchange rate rises. (Similarly, when interest rates in Canada fall relative to those in other countries, the demand for Canadian dollars decreases, the supply increases, and the exchange rate falls.)

But the Bank of Canada can intervene directly in the foreign exchange market. It can buy or sell dollars and try to smooth out fluctuations in the exchange rate. Let's look at the foreign exchange interventions that the Bank can make.

Suppose the Bank of Canada wants the exchange rate to be steady at 70 U.S. cents per dollar. If the exchange rate rises above 70 U.S. cents, the Bank sells dollars. If the exchange rate falls below 70 U.S. cents, the Bank buys dollars. By these actions, it changes the supply of dollars and keeps the exchange rate close to its target rate of 70 U.S. cents per Canadian dollar.

Figure 34.10 shows the Bank of Canada's intervention in the foreign exchange market. The supply

FIGURE 34.10 Foreign Exchange Market Intervention

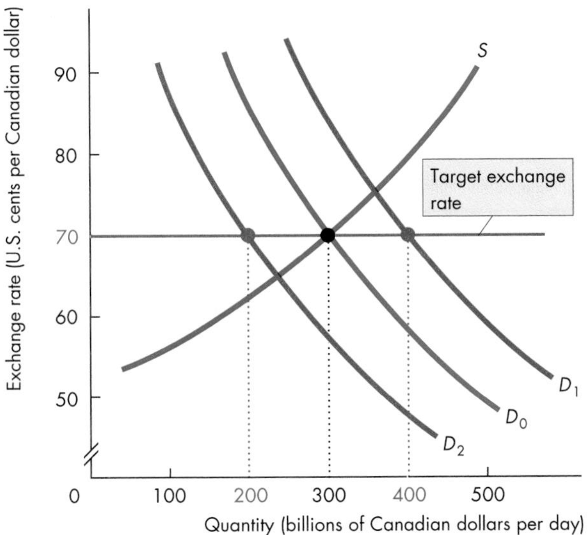

Initially, the demand for dollars is D_0, the supply of dollars is S, and the exchange rate is 70 U.S. cents per dollar. The Bank of Canada can intervene in the foreign exchange market to keep the exchange rate close to its target rate (70 U.S. cents in this example). If demand increases from D_0 to D_1, the Bank sells dollars to increase supply. If demand decreases from D_0 to D_2, the Bank buys dollars to decrease supply. Persistent intervention on one side of the market cannot be sustained.

of dollars is S and initially the demand for dollars is D_0. The equilibrium exchange rate is 70 U.S. cents per dollar. This exchange rate is the Bank's target rate, shown by the horizontal red line.

When the demand for dollars increases and the demand curve shifts rightward to D_1, the Bank of Canada sells $100 billion. This action increases the supply of dollars by $100 billion and prevents the exchange rate from rising. When the demand for dollars decreases and the demand curve shifts leftward to D_2, the Bank buys $100 billion. This action decreases the supply of dollars by $100 billion and prevents the exchange rate from falling.

If the demand for dollars fluctuates between D_1 and D_2 and on the average is D_0, the Bank of Canada can repeatedly intervene in the way we've just seen. Sometimes the Bank buys and sometimes it sells but, on the average, it neither buys nor sells.

But suppose the demand for dollars increases permanently from D_0 to D_1. The Bank cannot now maintain the exchange rate at 70 U.S. cents indefinitely. For to do so, the Bank would have to sell dollars every day. When the Bank sells dollars in the foreign exchange market, it buys foreign currency. So the Bank would be piling up foreign currency.

Now suppose the demand for dollars decreases permanently from D_0 to D_2. Again the Bank cannot maintain the exchange rate at 70 U.S. cents indefinitely. In this situation, to hold the exchange rate at 70 U.S. cents per dollar the Bank would have to buy dollars every day. When the Bank buys dollars in the foreign exchange market, it uses its holdings of foreign currency. So the Bank would be losing foreign currency. Eventually, it would run out of foreign currency and would then have to abandon its attempt to fix the exchange rate.

REVIEW QUIZ

1. What is the exchange rate and how is it determined?
2. What are the influences of interest rates and the expected future exchange rate on the demand for and supply of dollars in the foreign exchange market?
3. How do changes in the expected future exchange rate influence the actual exchange rate?
4. How do purchasing power parity and interest rate parity affect exchange rate expectations?
5. How can the Bank of Canada influence the foreign exchange market?

Reading Between the Lines on pages 824–825 looks at a projection of the Canadian dollar through 2026.

In the final chapter, we expand our view of the global economy and study global stock markets. These are the markets in which firms borrow the funds that finance their investment in new capital. Those funds often cross national borders, and when they do so, they move through the foreign exchange markets and show up in the balance of payments capital accounts that you've studied in this chapter. Keep what you've learned about the balance of payments and the foreign exchange market in mind as you work through the stock markets chapter.

Exchange Rate Projections

FINANCIAL POST, NOVEMBER 5, 2002

Loonie to rise above US80 cents: climb to take 15 years

The Canadian dollar, now worth just over US64 cents, is heading back up to more than US80 cents, a level not seen since the early 1990s and then only briefly, a major economic think-tank is forecasting.

But that increase in the exchange rate will take more than 15 years, according to the new DRI-WEFA forecast.

Still, the loonie's worst days are now behind it, thanks to higher interest rates here than in the U.S., relatively low and stable inflation, and healthy trade and budget surpluses, it says.

"These factors combined are expected to impart modest upward pressure on the Canadian dollar, moving it... through the US70 cents barrier in 2004 and to the US80 cents level by 2018," says the Canadian arm of the international economic research firm.

And that's not the peak.

The loonie will continue to rise steadily after 2018, reaching a peak of US84.5 cents sometime between 2021 and 2026, which is the outer limit of the near quarter-century forecast.

"DRI-WEFA has been forecasting slight upward pressures on the Canadian dollar for several years now," it notes. "This is the obvious forecast given the strong fundamentals, in spite of the fact that history has not been kind."

The think-tank assumes "a reasonably healthy spread will be maintained over U.S. interest rates."

And that's despite what it says will be lower inflation here, averaging close to two per cent compared with 2.4% in the U.S. ...

Essence of the Story

- DRI-WEFA, an international economy forecasting firm, says that the Canadian dollar will rise from US64 cents in 2002 to more than US70 cents during 2004, to US80 cents by 2018, and to US84.5 cents sometime between 2021 and 2026.
- Higher interest rates and a lower inflation rate in Canada than in the U.S. and healthy trade and budget surpluses will be the sources of the strength of the Canadian dollar.
- The Canadian inflation rate will average 2 percent a year compared with 2.4 percent a year in the United States.

Economic Analysis

- Exchange rate forecasting over a 25-year horizon is impossible, and the DRI-WEFA projections are not worth much.

- Despite the fact that we can't forecast the exchange rate, we can predict that it is unlikely that a currency will remain either undervalued or overvalued relative to purchasing power parity (PPP) for two decades.

- The DRI-WEFA projection implies that the Canadian dollar will remain undervalued for the next 25 years and is almost certainly going to be incorrect.

- Figure 1 shows the history of the Canadian dollar since 1970 with the DRI-WEFA projection through 2026.

- Figure 2 shows the path that the Canadian dollar would have followed since 1970 and would follow through 2026 based on the DRI-WEFA projection of the inflation differential between Canada and the United States—Canadian inflation rate minus U.S. inflation rate.

- Figure 3 shows the fluctuations of the Canadian dollar around PPP. It shows an overvalued Canadian dollar during the 1970s, early 1980s, and around 1990 and an undervalued dollar in the mid 1980s, late 1990s, and 2000s.

- The DRI-WEFA projects another 25 years of undervaluation. More likely, the dollar will alternate between undervaluation and overvaluation, but at unpredictable times.

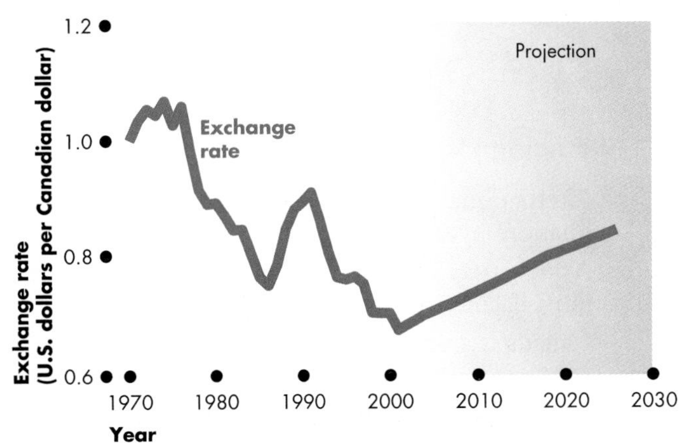

Figure 1 The Canadian dollar: 1970 to 2026

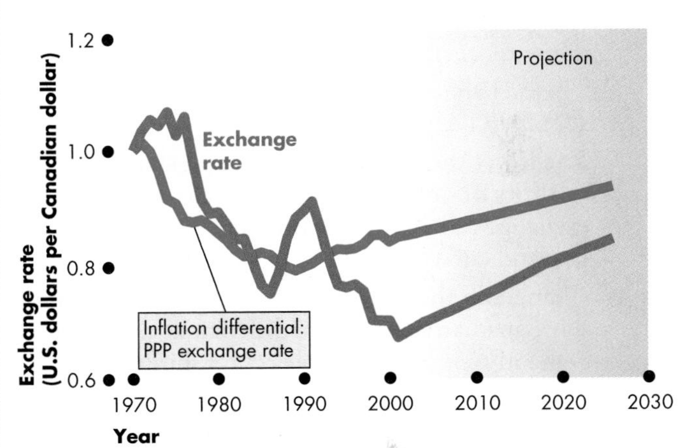

Figure 2 The effects of inflation differences: 1970 to 2026

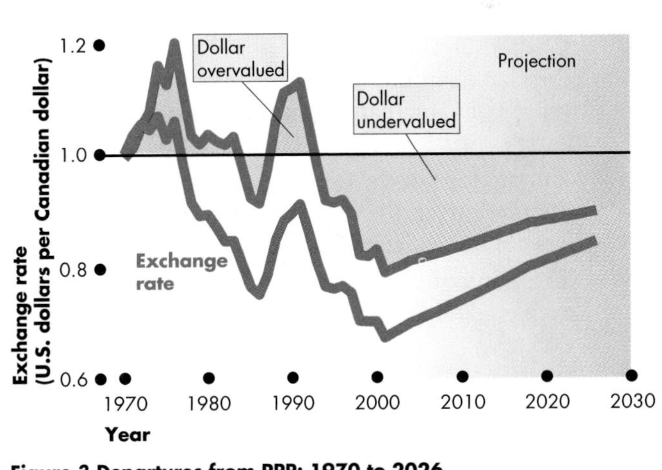

Figure 3 Departures from PPP: 1970 to 2026

SUMMARY

KEY POINTS

Financing International Trade (pp. 810–814)

- International trade, borrowing, and lending are financed by using foreign currency.
- A country's international transactions are recorded in its balance of payments accounts.
- Canada is a net borrower and a debtor nation.
- The net exports surplus is equal to the government sector surplus plus the private sector surplus.

The Exchange Rate (pp. 815–823)

- Foreign currency is obtained in exchange for domestic currency in the foreign exchange market.
- The exchange rate is determined by demand and supply in the foreign exchange market.
- The lower the exchange rate, the greater is the quantity of dollars demanded. A change in the exchange rate brings a movement along the demand curve for dollars.
- Changes in the expected future exchange rate and the Canadian interest rate differential change the demand for Canadian dollars and shift the demand curve.
- The lower the exchange rate, the smaller is the quantity of dollars supplied. A change in the exchange rate brings a movement along the supply curve of dollars.
- Changes in the expected future exchange rate and the Canadian interest rate differential change the supply of Canadian dollars and shift the supply curve.
- Fluctuations in the exchange rate occur because fluctuations in the demand for and supply of dollars are not independent.
- The Bank of Canada can intervene in the foreign exchange market to smooth fluctuations in the dollar.

KEY FIGURES AND TABLE

Figure 34.1 The Balance of Payments: 1981–2001, 811
Figure 34.3 The Exchange Rate, 815
Figure 34.8 Equilibrium Exchange Rate, 820
Figure 34.9 Exchange Rate Fluctuations, 821
Figure 34.10 Foreign Exchange Market Intervention, 823
Table 34.2 Net Exports, the Government Budget, Saving, and Investment, 813

KEY TERMS

Balance of payments accounts, 810
Canadian interest rate differential, 817
Capital account, 810
Creditor nation, 812
Currency appreciation, 815
Currency depreciation, 815
Current account, 810
Debtor nation, 812
Foreign exchange market, 815
Foreign exchange rate, 815
Government sector balance, 813
Interest rate parity, 822
Net borrower, 812
Net exports, 813
Net lender, 812
Official Canadian reserves, 810
Official settlements account, 810
Private sector balance, 813
Purchasing power parity, 822
Twin deficits, 814

PROBLEMS

*1. The citizens of Silecon, whose currency is the grain, conducted the following transactions in 2002:

Item	Billions of grains
Imports of goods and services	350
Exports of goods and services	500
Borrowing from the rest of the world	60
Lending to the rest of the world	200
Increase in official holdings of foreign currency	10

a. Set out the three balance of payments accounts for Silecon.
b. Does the Silecon central bank intervene in the foreign exchange market?

2. The citizens of Spin, whose currency is the wheel, conducted the following transactions in 2002:

Item	Billions of wheels
Imports of goods and services	100
Exports of goods and services	120
Borrowing from the rest of the world	4
Lending to the rest of the world	24
Increase in official holdings of foreign currency	0

a. Set out the three balance of payments accounts for Spin.
b. Does the central bank intervene in the foreign exchange market?

*3. The figure at the bottom of the page shows the flows of income and expenditure in Dream Land in 2000. The amounts are in millions of dollars. GDP in Dream Land is $120 million.
a. Calculate Dream Land's net exports.
b. Calculate saving in Dream Land.
c. How is Dream Land's investment financed?

4. The figure shows the flows of income and expenditure in Dream Land in 2001. The amounts are in millions of dollars. Dream Land's GDP has increased to $130 million but all the other items whose values are provided in the figure remain the same as they were in 2000.
a. Calculate Dream Land's net exports in 2001.
b. Calculate saving in Dream Land in 2001.
c. How is Dream Land's investment financed?

*5. The table on the next page tells you about Ecflex, a country whose currency is the band. The official settlements balance is zero. Net interest income and net transfers from abroad are zero.

Calculate for Ecflex its
a. Imports of goods and services
b. Current account balance
c. Capital account balance
d. Net taxes
e. Private sector balance

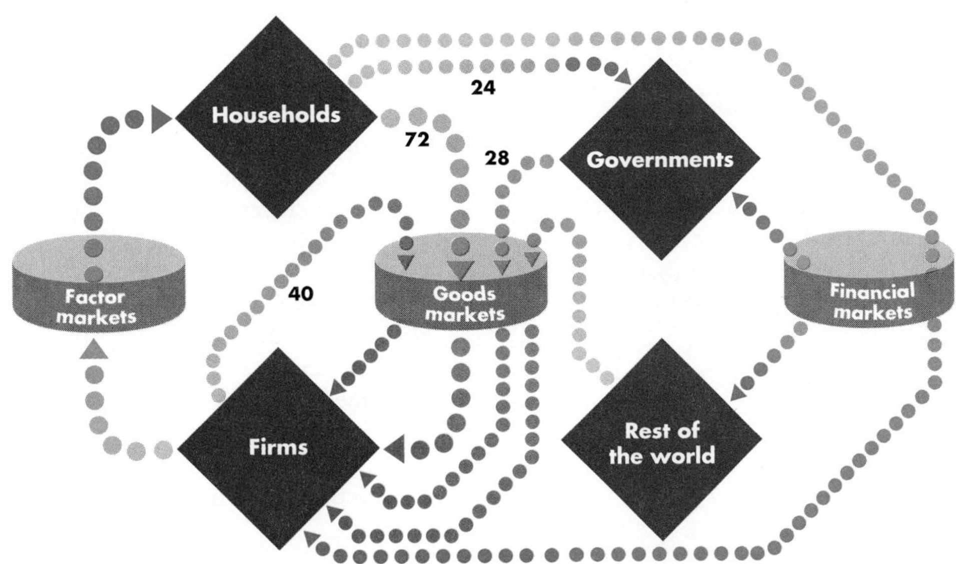

Item	Billions of bands
GDP	100
Consumption expenditure	60
Government expenditures on goods and services	24
Investment	22
Exports of goods and services	20
Government budget deficit	4

6. The following table tells you about Ecfix, a country whose currency is the rock:

Item	Billions of rocks
GDP	400
Consumption expenditure	240
Government expenditures on goods and services	100
Investment	100
Exports of goods and services	80
Saving	90

   Calculate for Ecfix its
   a. Imports of goods and services
   b. Current account balance
   c. Government sector balance
   d. Net taxes
   e. Private sector balance

*7. A country's currency appreciates, and its official reserves increase. What can you say about
   a. Intervention in the foreign exchange market by the country's central bank?
   b. The possible central bank sources of the currency appreciation?
   c. The possible private actions behind the appreciation?

8. A country has a lower inflation rate than all other countries. It has more rapid economic growth. The central bank does not intervene in the foreign exchange market. What can you say about each of the following (and why)?
   a. The exchange rate
   b. The current account balance
   c. The expected exchange rate
   d. The interest rate differential
   e. Interest rate parity
   f. Purchasing power parity

CRITICAL THINKING

1. Study *Reading Between the Lines* on pp. 824–825 and then answer the following questions:
   a. What does DRI-WEFA predict will happen to the Canadian dollar exchange rate during the next 25 years?
   b. Are the projections consistent with purchasing power parity?
   c. Are the projections consistent with interest rate parity?
   d. What could happen over the next 25 years to make the Canadian dollar either rise much faster than the DRI-WEFA projection, or fall rather than rise?

WEB EXERCISES

1. Use the link on the Parkin–Bade Web site to visit Statistics Canada and find data on the exchange rate and international trade.
   a. When did Canada last have a current account surplus?
   b. When did official Canadian reserves last increase?
   c. Does Canada have a surplus or a deficit in its trade in services?
   d. What has happened to foreign investment in Canada during the past ten years?
   e. Do you think that Canada's balance of payments record is a matter for concern? Why or why not?
2. Use the link on the Parkin–Bade Web site to visit PACIFIC (an exchange rate service) and read the page on purchasing power parity.
   a. What is purchasing power parity?
   b. Which currencies are the most overvalued relative to the U.S. dollar today?
   c. Which currencies are the most undervalued relative to the U.S. dollar today?
   d. Can you offer some suggestions as to why some currencies are overvalued and some are undervalued?
   e. Do you think that the information on overvaluation and undervaluation is useful to currency speculators? Why or why not?

CHAPTER 35

GLOBAL STOCK MARKETS

Irrational Exuberance?

On December 5, 1996, Alan Greenspan, chairman of the U.S. Federal Reserve, said that stock market investors were suffering from *irrational exuberance.* It appeared that some people agreed with Mr. Greenspan, for when the New York Stock Exchange opened the next morning, the Dow Jones Industrial Average immediately dropped by 2.3 percent. During the American night, stock prices in Japan, Hong Kong, Germany, and Britain had dropped an average of almost 4 percent. ◆ Alan Greenspan's remark was prompted by an extraordinary rise in stock prices in the United States and around the world that began in 1994 and was to continue through 1999. During these years, the Dow (as the Dow Jones Industrial Average is known) tripled! It then stopped climbing and eventually nose-dived following September 11, 2001, but only temporarily. By January 2002, prices were back at the pre-September 11 levels. ◆ How are stock prices determined? Do investors suffer from "irrational exuberance" or are their buying and selling decisions rational? Do Canadian stock prices behave like those in the United States? How does the economy influence the stock market? And how does the stock market influence the economy?

◆ You are going to probe some interesting questions in this chapter. But first, a warning: You will not learn in this chapter which stocks to buy and how to get rich. You will, though, learn some important lessons about traps to avoid that could easily make you poor. And you will see in *Reading Between the Lines* at the end of the chapter how it is impossible to predict when a falling stock market will turn the corner and start rising.

After studying this chapter, you will be able to

- **Explain what a firm's stock is and how its rate of return and price are related**
- **Describe the global markets in which stocks are traded and the stock price indexes**
- **Describe the long-term performance of stock prices and earnings**
- **Explain what determines the price of stock and why stock prices are volatile**
- **Explain why it is rational to diversify a stock portfolio rather than to hold the one stock that has the highest expected return**
- **Explain how the stock market influences the economy and how the economy influences the stock market**

Stock Market Basics

ALL FIRMS GET SOME OF THEIR FINANCIAL capital from the people who own the firm. A large firm has possibly millions of owners from whom it raises billions of dollars in financial capital. These owners are the firm's stockholders—the holders of stock issued by the firm.

What Is Stock?

Stock is a tradable security that a firm issues to certify that the stockholder owns a share of the firm. Figure 35.1 shows a famous stock certificate that has become a collector's item—a Walt Disney Company stock certificate. The value of a firm's stock is called the firm's **equity capital** (or just equity). The terms "stock" and "equity" are often used interchangeably.

A stockholder has *limited liability*, which means that if the firm can't pay all its debts, a stockholder's liability for the firm's debts is limited to the amount invested in the firm by that stockholder. For example, when Enron collapsed, its stockholders lost everything they had invested in the firm's stock, but they weren't forced to contribute anything to make up for Enron's remaining debts.

FIGURE 35.1 A Stock Certificate

The Walt Disney Company issues a colourful stock certificate to record the ownership of its common stock. Attractive share certificates, like postage stamps and coins, become collectors' items.

Source: © Disney Enterprises Inc.

Stockholders receive a **dividend,** which is a share of the firm's profit, in proportion to their stock holdings. For example, holders of stock in PepsiCo received a dividend of 58 cents per share during 2002.

Firms issue two types of stock:

- Preferred stock
- Common stock

Preferred stock entitles its owner to a pre-agreed dividend before common stock dividends are paid and to first claim on the firm's assets in the event that it is liquidated.

Common stock holders are entitled to a share of the firm's assets and earnings and to a vote (one vote per share held) in the selection of the firm's directors.

When a firm issues stock, the buyer of the stock invests directly in the firm. For example, in March 1986, Microsoft Corporation issued 161 million shares of common stock for $21 a share and raised a total of $3.4 billion. The buyers of those shares paid Microsoft Corporation.

Most stockholders buy stock not from the firm that issues it but from other holders who bought the stock from yet other holders. People buy and sell stock on a stock exchange. For example, on an average day during the past ten years, 14 million Microsoft shares have changed hands. Microsoft doesn't receive anything from these transactions and doesn't even keep track of who owns its stock. It hires another firm, Mellon Investor Services, to do that job and to issue stock certificates.

What Is a Stock Exchange?

A **stock exchange** is an organized market on which people can buy and sell stock. The stocks of major Canadian corporations are traded on the Toronto Stock Exchange, which is the centre of Canada's major stock market. Canadian stocks are also traded, along with the stocks of global and U.S. corporations, in the United States on the New York Stock Exchange (NYSE). High-tech stocks are traded on the National Association of Securities Dealers Automated Quotation (NASDAQ) system.

Some stock exchanges—the New York Stock Exchange is one of them—are physical trading arenas. Traders shout and signal their buy and sell orders on the trading floor of the exchange. In the case of the New York Stock Exchange, trades take place on the trading floor on Wall Street in New York City.

Other stock exchanges—the Toronto Stock Exchange is one of them—do not have a trading floor. These more recently upgraded stock exchanges trade through a computer and telecommunications network that links together buyers and sellers from all parts of the world. For example, the NASDAQ computer system enables more than 1.3 million traders in 83 countries to trade more than 4,000 (mainly high-tech) stocks.

NASDAQ is a global stock exchange with large operations in Canada, Japan, and Europe as well as the United States. The other major stock exchanges in the global economy are those in London, Frankfurt, Tokyo, and Hong Kong.

Stock Prices and Returns

You can find the price and other information about the stocks of most of the large firms in the daily newspaper. You can also find the same information (and much more) on a newspaper's Web site. The Web sites of the stock exchanges and of major stock dealers also provide a wealth of data on stocks. You can also install software such as MarketBrowser that provides an easy way of viewing stock prices and making graphs of the recent price history. (The Parkin–Bade Web site provides the links that will get you to these Web resources.)

To read the stock market reports, you need to know the meaning of a few technical terms that we'll now review.

The point of buying stock is to earn an income from it. A **stock price** is the price at which one share of a stock trades on a stock exchange. The price is expressed like any other price: in dollars and cents. For example, on October 11, 2002, the price of a share of Bombardier stock was $3.83. The price can change from minute to minute and almost certainly will change over the trading day, and it can be tracked on the Internet (with a short time delay). Because the price keeps changing, in addition to tracking the current price, people also pay attention to the high and low prices during the previous year and the change from day to day.

The annual **return** on a stock consists of the stock's dividend plus its capital gain (or minus its capital loss) during the year. A stock's **capital gain** is the increase in its price, and a stock's **capital loss** is the decrease in its price. For example, between October 2001 and October 2002, the price of Bombardier stock fell from $17.37 to $3.83, a capital loss of $13.54.

The absolute return—the number of dollars returned by the stock—is not very informative because the stock might be cheap or costly. More informative is the return per dollar invested. So we express the return, or its components, as a percentage of the stock price. The dividend expressed as a percentage of the stock price is called the stock's **dividend yield.** For example, during the year from October 2001 to October 2002, Bombardier paid dividends of 18¢. Expressed as a percentage of the price of the stock in October 2002, the dividend yield was 4.7 percent.

The return on a stock expressed as a percentage of the stock price is called the stock's **rate of return.** For example, the return of a Bombardier share in the year from October 2001 to October 2002 was a dividend of 18¢ minus a capital loss of $13.54, or a loss of $13.36. The rate of return was –$13.36 as a percentage of $17.37, the price of a share in October 2001, which is –76.9 percent—a loss of almost 77 percent.

Earnings and the Price-Earnings Ratio

A firm's accounting profit is called the firm's **earnings.** A firm's directors decide how much of the earnings to pay out as dividends and how much to retain—called *retained earnings*—to invest in new capital and expand the firm.

Because they are the ultimate source of income for stockholders, a lot of attention is paid to a firm's earnings. And those earnings must be calculated and reported to meet standards of accuracy determined by government regulations and accounting standards. Following the Enron debacle in the United States, these standards have been reviewed and will be the object of an ongoing review for some time.

Earnings are the source of stockholder returns, but it is the relationship between a stock's price and earnings that matters most to the stockholder. So another number that is routinely calculated for each stock is its **price-earnings ratio**—the stock price divided by the most recent year's earnings. For example during 2001, Bombardier reported earnings of 11¢ per share, so its price-earnings ratio was $3.83 divided by 11¢, which equals 34.8.

The price-earnings ratio is the inverse of earnings per dollar invested. For example, because in October 2002 the price of a share of Bombardier stock was

\$3.83 and the earnings per share during 2002 were 11¢, earnings per dollar invested were 11¢ ÷ \$3.83 = 0.0287, or 2.87 percent. Check that 0.0287, earnings per dollar invested, equals the inverse of the price-earnings ratio and equals 1/34.8.

Now that you've reviewed some of the key vocabulary of the stock market, let's look at the stock market report.

Reading the Stock Market Report

Figure 35.2 shows part of a *Financial Post* stock market page. (The format varies from one newspaper to another, but the content is similar in all of them.) You can see some numbers for Bombardier that might seem familiar. They are some of the numbers that we've just used to illustrate the technical terms used in the report. Figure 35.2 also provides the CHUM (radio and television company line of the report).

The first two columns show the range of prices for the stock (expressed in dollars) over the preceding year. This information is useful because it tells you about the volatility of the stock. Some stocks fluctuate a lot more than others. By glancing at the numbers in these two columns, you can get a quick sense of how volatile the price is. In this example, the price of CHUM stock ranged from a high of \$64.50 to a low of \$40.00 (its current price), a range of \$24.50 and more than 50 percent of its current price.

Following the firm's name is the ticker symbol, BBD for Bombardier and CHM for CHUM. This symbol appears on real-time reports of the stock price. You need to know the symbol for any stocks that you own so that you can easily check their prices during the trading day.

The dividend paid expressed in dollars comes next. In this example, Bombardier paid 0.18 or 18¢ a share and CHUM paid 0.08 or 8¢ a share. The dividend yield—the dividend as a percentage of the stock's closing price—comes next, followed by the price-earnings ratio. The next column records the volume of trades in hundreds during the day. This number is the actual number of shares bought and sold. In this example, 287,800 Bombardier shares and 252,200 CHUM shares changed hands during the day.

The next three columns show the range of prices over the day and the closing price, and the final column shows the change in price from the previous day.

Stock Price Indexes

Because thousands of different stocks are traded on the world's stock markets every business day, we need a handy way of summarizing the thousands of different stock prices. Investors want to know not only how their own stocks have performed, but also how they have performed relative to other stocks on the average.

To make these comparisons and to indicate the general movements in the market, index numbers of the average stock prices are calculated and published. You will encounter hundreds of different stock price indexes. The three main U.S. stock price indexes are

FIGURE 35.2 Reading the Stock Market Report

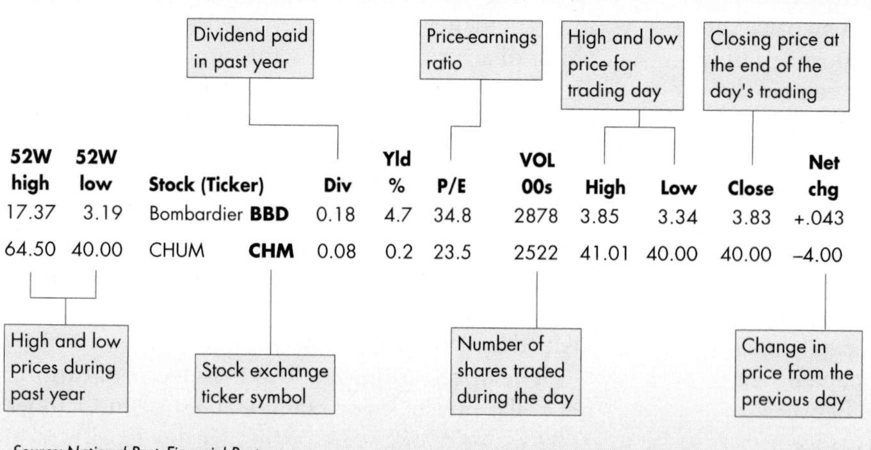

52W high	52W low	Stock (Ticker)	Div	Yld %	P/E	VOL 00s	High	Low	Close	Net chg
17.37	3.19	Bombardier **BBD**	0.18	4.7	34.8	2878	3.85	3.34	3.83	+.043
64.50	40.00	CHUM **CHM**	0.08	0.2	23.5	2522	41.01	40.00	40.00	–4.00

Source: National Post, Financial Post.

The stock market report provides information each day on the high and low prices over the previous year, dividend, price-earnings ratio, volume of shares traded, the price range over the day, the day's closing price, and price change from the previous day.

- S&P Composite Index
- Dow Jones Industrial Average (DJIA)
- NASDAQ Index

S&P Composite Index The S&P Composite Index is an average of the prices of 500 stocks traded on the New York Stock Exchange, the NASDAQ, and the American Stock Exchange. The index is calculated and published by Standard & Poor's (S&P), a New York financial information and services company. Figure 35.3 shows the breadth of coverage of this index, which provides one of the most comprehensive guides to the state of the stock market. Notice in Fig. 35.3 the importance of consumer products in the index.

DJIA The DJIA, or "the Dow," as it is often called, is perhaps the best-known stock price index. The Dow Jones Company is the owner of the *Wall Street Journal*, and because of this link, the Dow is the most widely and rapidly reported barometer of the state of the New York stock market.

FIGURE 35.3 The Scope of the S&P Composite

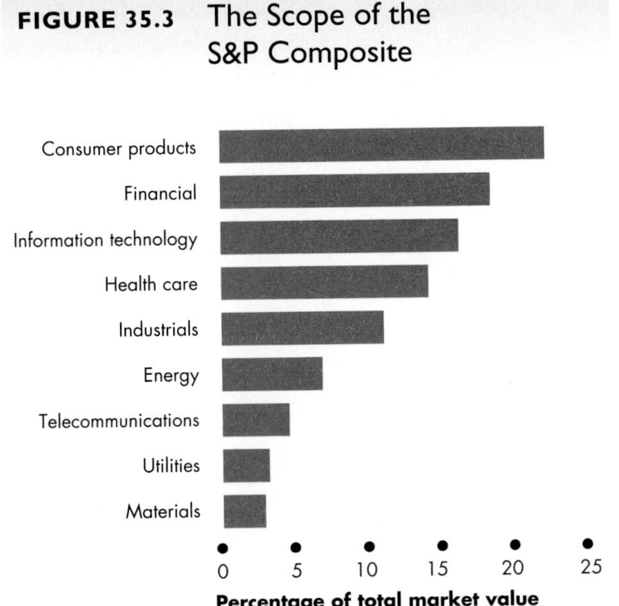

The 500 stocks in the S&P Composite Index cover all parts of the economy. Consumer products are the largest component of the index.

Source: www.spglobal.com.

Although the DJIA is widely quoted, it is not as broadly representative as the S&P Composite Index. It is an average of the prices of just 30 stocks of major U.S. corporations traded on the New York Stock Exchange. In 2002, these corporations are: Philip Morris Companies, Inc.; Eastman Kodak Co.; J.P. Morgan Chase & Co.; General Motors Corp.; E.I. DuPont de Nemours & Co.; SBC Communications, Inc.; Caterpillar, Inc.; Merck & Co., Inc.; International Paper Co.; Minnesota Mining & Manufacturing Co.; Exxon Mobil Corp.; Honeywell International, Inc.; General Electric Co.; Hewlett-Packard Co.; Procter & Gamble Co.; Alcoa, Inc.; Coca-Cola Co.; Boeing Co.; Citigroup, Inc.; United Technologies Corp.; Johnson & Johnson; AT&T Corp.; Walt Disney Co.; McDonald's Corp.; American Express Co.; International Business Machines Corp.; Wal-Mart Stores, Inc.; Home Depot, Inc.; Intel Corp.; and Microsoft Corp.

NASDAQ The NASDAQ Index is the average price of the stocks traded on this global electronic stock exchange. Like the Dow, this index looks at only part of the market—in this case, the high-tech part.

Four indexes track the state of the world's other major stock markets. They are the

- S&P/TSX
- FTSE 100
- DAX
- Nikkei

S&P/TSX The S&P/TSX is an index of the stock prices of the 300 largest Canadian corporations traded on the Toronto Stock Exchange. It is Canada's main stock price index and is comparable to the S&P 500 for the United States.

FTSE 100 The FTSE 100 (pronounced "footsie") is an index calculated by FTSE, a financial information services firm owned by the *Financial Times* (FT) and the London Stock Exchange (SE). (The *Financial Times* is Europe's leading business and financial daily newspaper and rivals the *Wall Street Journal* outside the United States.)

DAX The DAX index is an average of prices on the Frankfurt stock exchange in Germany.

Nikkei The Nikkei index is the average of prices on the Tokyo stock exchange.

Stock Price Performance

How has the stock market performed in recent years and over the longer term? Do stock prices generally rise? How much do they fluctuate? To answer these questions, we'll look at some actual stock price data, using the S&P/TSX and the S&P 500 (composite). But first, we need to make two technical points.

Inflation Adjustments Stock prices, like all prices, need to be corrected for inflation. So rather than looking at the actual index numbers, we deflate them to remove the effects of inflation and examine *real* stock price indexes.

Ratio Scale Graphs Stock prices rise and fall, but over the long term, they rise. The interesting question about stock price changes is not the absolute change but the percentage change. For example a ten-point change in the S&P was a 1 percent change in 2002, but it was a 10 percent change in 1982. To reveal percentage changes, we graph stock prices using a ratio scale (or logarithmic scale). On a ratio scale, the distance between 1 and 10 equals that between 10 and 100 and between 100 and 1000. Each distance represents a tenfold increase.

Stock Prices

Figure 35.4 shows the real S&P/TSX for the period since 1956 when the index begins, and the S&P 500 over the past 130 years, both placed on a base of 1975 = 1,000 and measured on a ratio scale.

Both indexes move together, but the S&P 500 climbs more than the S&P/TSX. Notice the general upward trend of the real stock price index. In 2001, the S&P was 33 times its 1871 value. This increase translates to a 2.7 percent per year increase on the average.

This average rate of increase masks some subperiods of spectacular increases and spectacular decreases in stock prices. The largest increases occurred during the "roaring twenties" and the "booming nineties." Between 1920 and 1929, on the eve of the Great Depression, stock prices increased by almost 19 percent a year. Between 1991 and 2000, they increased by 15 percent a year, and between 1995 and 2000, the rate of increase hit 24 percent a year.

FIGURE 35.4 Stock Prices

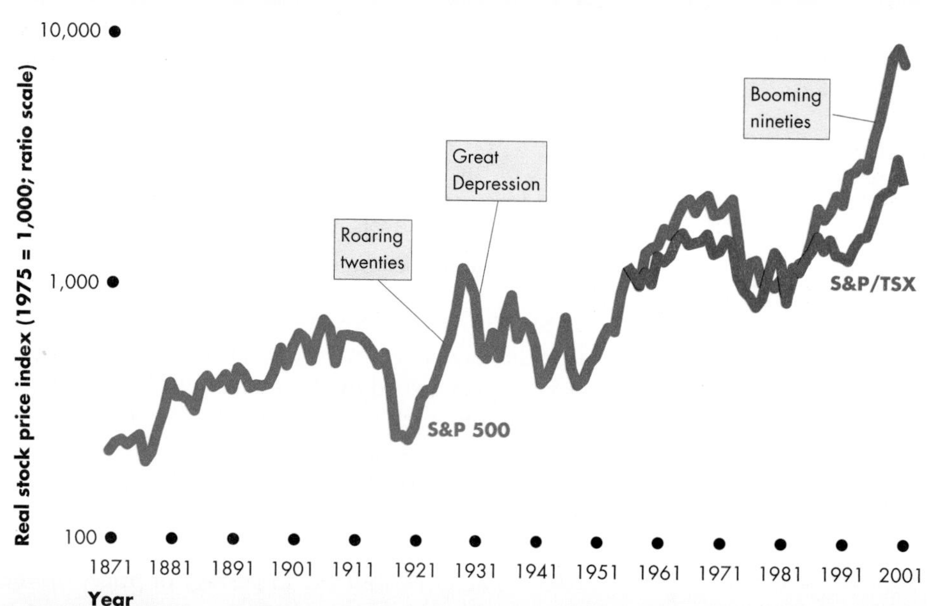

In 2001, average stock prices stood at 33 times their 1871 level (after adjusting for the effects of inflation). This increase translates to an average increase of 2.7 percent a year. Earnings per share stood at 14 times their 1871 level (after adjusting for the effects of inflation). This increase translates to an average increase of 2.7 percent a year. Stock prices increased fastest during the "roaring twenties" and the "booming nineties."

Sources: Reprinted by permission of Robert J. Shiller, Professor of Economics, Yale University (www.econ.yale.edu/~shiller) and adapted in part by the Statistics Canada CANSIM II database, table 176–0047.

The most spectacular period of falling stock prices occurred during World War I (1914–1918), the opening years of the Great Depression (the early 1930s), and the mid-1970s.

Earnings Per Share

Stocks are worth owning because of what they earn. Like stock prices, earnings per share have increased over the long term. But the rate of increase in earnings per share is less than the rate of increase in stock prices. Earnings per share in 2001 were 14 times their 1871 level, which translates to a growth rate of 2 percent per year on the average.

Figure 35.5 looks at the price-earnings ratio for the S&P/TSX over the years since 1956 and for the S&P 500 over the 130 years from 1871 to 2001. The average S&P price-earnings ratio has been 13.9. But there is a lot of variation around this average value. The low values of around 6 occurred in 1916, 1950, and 1979. The high values of around 27 occurred in 1894, 1921, 1931, and the period from 1998 into 2001.

Figure 35.5 is important for the perspective in which it places the stock market's recent performance. Stock prices were high and increased rapidly during the late 1990s and into 2001. And the price-earnings ratio increased to a level not seen since the opening years of the Great Depression.

Figure 35.5 also provides a reminder that in all previous periods when the price-earnings ratio was above average, it eventually fell below the average.

Being a ratio of stock prices and earnings, the price-earnings ratio can change either because stock prices change or because earnings change. The price-earnings ratio can fall sharply either because stock prices fall sharply or because earnings rise sharply. But all the cases in which the price-earnings ratio has fallen sharply are ones in which stock prices have fallen sharply. For this reason, some people are concerned that the stock market of the 1990s and 2000 increased by too much and that a sharp fall is coming some time in the future.

What does it mean to say that stock prices have increased by too much? To answer this question, we need to understand the forces that determine stock prices and the relationship between prices and earnings. That is the task of the next section.

FIGURE 35.5 The Price-Earnings Ratio

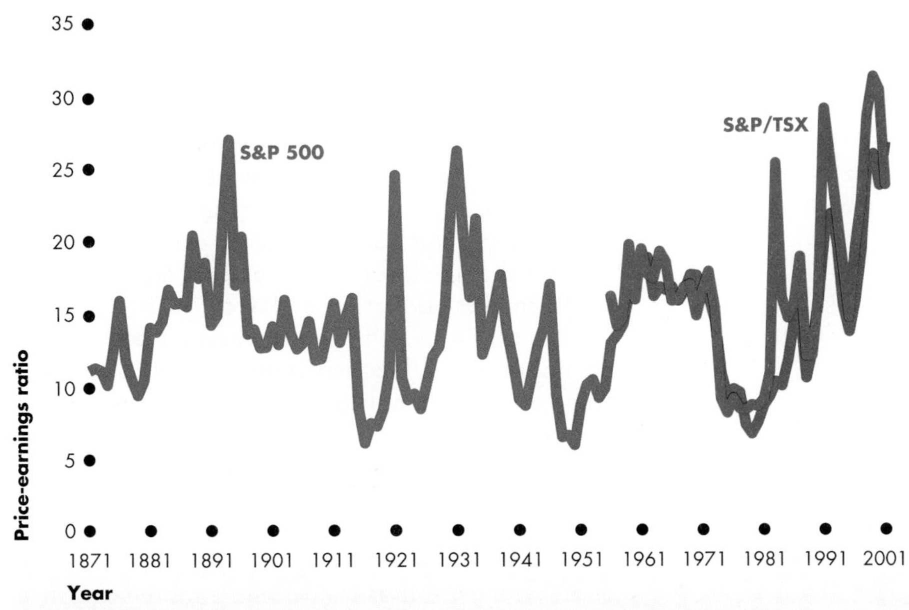

The S&P price-earnings ratio has swung between a low of around 6 in 1916, 1950, and 1979 and a high of around 27 in 1894, 1921, 1931, and 1998–2001. The S&P average price-earnings ratio is 13.9. When the price-earnings ratio exceeds the average, it eventually falls below the average. The S&P/TSX price-earnings ratio follows a similar path to that of the S&P.

Sources: Reprinted by permission of Robert J. Shiller, Professor of Economics, Yale University (www.econ.yale.edu/~shiller) and adapted in part by the Statistics Canada CANSIM II database, table 176–0047.

REVIEW QUIZ

1 What is a stock and what is the distinction between a preferred stock and a common stock?
2 What are the two sources of return from a stock?
3 What is a stock market and what are the leading stock exchanges in the United States, Canada, and around the world?
4 What is a price-earnings ratio and how is it calculated?
5 What is the most comprehensive stock price index for the United States? How does it differ from some other major indexes?
6 Describe the major trends and fluctuations in stock prices, earnings per share, and the price-earnings ratio.

How Are Stock Prices Determined?

YOU'VE SEEN THAT STOCK PRICES GENERALLY RISE over long periods but fluctuate a lot over shorter periods. What determines the price of a stock? Why is the long-term trend upward? Why do stock prices fluctuate so much?

There is no firm and universally agreed-upon answer to these questions. Instead, there are two possible types of answers. They are that prices are determined by

- Market fundamentals
- Speculative bubbles

Market Fundamentals

The price of a stock is the amount that people *on the average* are willing to pay for the opportunity that the stock provides to earn a dividend and a capital gain. If a stock price exceeds what people are willing to pay, they sell the stock and its price falls. If a stock price is less than what people are willing to pay, they buy and the stock price rises. The price always settles down at the amount that people are willing to pay.

The *market fundamentals* price that people are willing to pay is a price that is based on the deep sources of value that make a stock worth holding. These sources of value are

1. The activities of the firm that issued the stock
2. The stream of profits that these activities generate
3. The stream of dividend payments to stockholders
4. The degree of uncertainty surrounding profits and dividends
5. The attitudes of stockholders towards the timing and uncertainty of the stream of dividends

We're now going to discover how these deep sources of value of a firm's stock combine to determine the market fundamentals price of the stock. To do so, we're going to figure out how much you would be willing to pay for a stock or be willing to accept to sell it.

Price, Value, and Willingness to Pay The market fundamentals value of a stock is the price that people *on the average* are willing to pay for the opportunity that the stock provides to earn a dividend and a capital gain. To figure out how this price is determined, let's look at your decision to buy or sell a stock.

Suppose the price of a stock that you own is $1. You're trying to figure out whether to buy 50 more units of this stock or to sell the 50 units you own. If you sell, you have $50 more to spend, and if you buy, you have $50 less to spend—a $100 difference. You can spend $100 today on something that you will enjoy. In the language of the economist, you will get some utility from what you buy—the marginal utility of $100 worth of consumption. Alternatively, you can buy more stock and sell it later, say, after a year. If you buy the stock, you'll receive the dividend plus the stock's market price at the end of the year.

For it to be worth buying, you must believe that the utility you will receive from owning the stock is going to be worth at least the $1 a share you must pay for it.

But comparing what you must pay with what you'll gain is a difficult exercise for two main reasons. First, you must compare an amount paid in the present with an amount received in the future. And second, you must compare a definite price today with an uncertain dividend and future price.

Present Versus Future People are impatient. We prefer good things to happen sooner rather than later, other things remaining the same. Suppose that you're offered the chance to take an exotic trip that really excites you and are told that you can go right away or after a year. Which would you choose (other things remaining the same)? Most of us would take the trip right away. Because we prefer good things now more than later, we must be compensated for delaying consumption.

Certainty Versus Uncertainty People prefer certainty to uncertainty, other things remaining the same. Suppose you're offered the opportunity to pay $50 for a chance to win $100 on the flip of a coin. Would you accept the offer? Most people would not. Accepting the offer would give you a 50 percent chance of gaining $50 and a 50 percent chance of losing $50. On the average, you get nothing from this offer. Your *expected return* is zero. Most people need to be compensated for taking risks, and the bigger the risk, the bigger is the compensation that must be offered to make bearing the risk worthwhile.

In figuring out what you're willing to pay for a stock, you can see that, for two reasons, you will not be willing to pay as much as the amount that you expect to receive in dividends and from selling the stock. You're going to get the returns later and you're going to face uncertainty, and you must be compensated for both of these consequences of buying a stock.

Discounting Future Uncertain Returns Another way of expressing the relationship between the price you're willing to pay and what you expect to get back is to *discount* the uncertain future amount. You get a discount when a shop lowers the price of an item. And you will insist on a discount if you buy a stock.

To determine the discounted price, we multiply the original price by a **discount factor.** If you get a 20 percent discount on something, you pay 80 percent, or 0.8, of the original price. The discount factor is 0.8.

We can use the idea of a discount factor to link the highest price you're willing to pay for a stock to the amount you'll get back from the stock a year later. Let's call this price P. Suppose that your discount factor is 0.8, and suppose that you believe that the stock will pay a dividend of 5¢ and that its price next year will be $1.20. Then the highest price that you're willing to pay for a stock is

$$P = 0.8 \times (\$0.05 + \$1.20) = \$1.$$

In this example, you would be on the fence. If the price were a bit less than $1, you'd buy, and if the price were a bit more than $1, you'd sell the stock that you already own.

Because people buy if the price is less than the price they are willing to pay and sell if the price is greater than the price they are willing to pay, the market price moves towards the average of what people are willing to pay. If the price exceeded the average of what people are willing to pay, there would be more sellers than buyers and the price would fall. If the price was less than the average of what people are willing to pay, there would be more buyers than sellers and the price would rise. Only if the price equals the average of what people are willing to pay is there no tendency for it to rise or fall.

The Stock Price Equation Call the price of a stock P_1, the dividend D_1, the price at the end of a year P_2, and the discount factor b_1. Then the stock price is the expected value of the discounted uncertain future dividend and stock price. That is,

$$P_1 = \text{Expected value of } [b_1(D_1 + P_2)].$$

Expected Future Stock Price You've seen that the stock price depends on expectations about the future stock price. That is, to figure out what you're willing to pay for a stock today, you must forecast next period's stock price.

The market fundamentals method assumes that an investor's forecast of a future stock price is a rational expectation. A **rational expectation** is a forecast that uses all the available information, including knowledge of the relevant economic forces that influence the variable being forecasted.

But the stock price equation tells us how the price at one time depends on the expected price a year later. This same stock price equation relationship applies to the current period and all future periods. So if we call next period's discount factor b_2, next period's dividend D_2, and the price at the end of next period P_3, you can see that the stock price equation next year will be

$$P_2 = \text{Expected value of } [b_2(D_2 + P_3)].$$

That is, the price next period depends on the expected dividend next period and the price at the end of the next period.

This relationship repeats period after period into the future. And each period's expected future price depends on the dividend expected in that period along with the price at the end of the period.

Table 35.1 illustrates the link between the current price and the expected future price, dividend, and discount factor. In period 1, the price depends on expectations about the price in period 2. In period 2, the price depends on expectations about the price in period 3. And in period 3, the price depends on expectations about the price in period 4. This relationship repeats indefinitely to period *N*.

Because each period's price depends on the expected price in the following period, the dividend stream, $D_1, D_2, D_3, \ldots D_N$, is the only fundamental that determines the price of a stock.

Market Fundamental Price The market fundamental stock price depends only on the stream of expected future dividend payments. If the expected dividend rises, so does the stock price. And starting from a given dividend, if the dividend is expected to grow at a faster rate, the stock price rises.

But dividends depend on profit, or earnings, so if earnings are expected to increase, dividends will also be expected to increase—if not right away, then at some point in the future. So if earnings increase, the stock price increases. And starting from a given level of earnings, if earnings are expected to grow more quickly, the stock price rises.

TABLE 35.1 Rational Expectations

$$P_1 = \text{Expected value of } [b_1(D_1 + P_2)]$$

$$P_2 = \text{Expected value of } [b_2(D_2 + P_3)]$$

$$P_3 = \text{Expected value of } [b_3(D_3 + P_4)]$$

$$P_N = \text{Expected value of } [b_N(D_N + P_{N+1})]$$

The market fundamentals are the expected dividends that will be earned out into the indefinite future. Rational expectations of future prices and future discount factors are driven by this one fundamental.

Notice that it is changes in expected future earnings and dividends that drive changes in stock price, not changes in actual earnings or dividends. But expectations about the future don't change without reason. And when earnings change, investors project those changes into the future. So fluctuations in earnings might be expected to bring similar fluctuations in stock prices.

In reality, the link between earnings and stock prices is a loose one. You can see just how loose by glancing back at Fig. 35.5 and noting the large swings that range between 6 and 27 in the price-earnings ratio. The booming stock prices of the late 1990s, for example, outpaced the growth of earnings during that same period by a huge margin.

For this reason, some economists believe that stock prices can be understood only as speculative bubbles. Let's now look at this approach.

Speculative Bubbles

A **speculative bubble** is a price increase followed by a price plunge, both of which occur because people expect them to occur and act on that expectation.

Suppose that most people believe that stock prices are going to rise by 30 percent next year. With such a huge price rise, stocks provide the best available rate of return. The demand for stocks increases, and stock prices rise by the expected amount immediately.

Conversely, suppose that most people believe that stock prices are going to *fall* by 30 percent next year. With such a huge price fall, stockholders will earn less than people who simply sit on cash. In this situation, the demand for stocks collapses and a selling spree brings stock prices tumbling by the expected amount.

Why might either of these events occur? And why would a bubble burst? Why would a price collapse follow a price rise?

Guessing Other People's Guesses Part of the answer to the questions just posed arises from the fact that forecasting future stock prices means forecasting other people's forecasts—or, more accurately, guessing other people's guesses.

The most famous English economist of the twentieth century, John Maynard Keynes, described the challenge of the stock market investor as being like that of trying to win the prize in a "select the most beautiful person" contest. Each entrant must pick the most beautiful person from a group of ten photographs. The winner is selected at random from all those who chose the photograph that most other entrants chose. So the challenge is not to pick the most beautiful person, but to pick the one that most people will pick. Or is it to pick the one that most people think that most people will pick? Or is it to pick the one that most people think that most people think that most people will pick? And so on!

Because no one knows the correct choice and because everyone faces the same challenge and shares the same sources of information, people are likely to use similar rules of thumb and theories to guide them. So people might behave in a herdlike way and form and act upon similar expectations.

The booming stock market of the 1990s provides an example of the possibility of a speculative bubble.

The Booming Nineties: A Bubble?

Some economists believe that the booming stock market of the 1990s occurred because the market fundamentals changed. They see the stock price rise as the consequence of a "new economy" in which the rational expectation is that earnings will grow in the future at a more rapid rate than in the past.

Other economists believe that the market of the booming nineties was a speculative bubble. Prominent among those who take this view is Robert Shiller, a professor at Yale University, who explains his view in a popular and readable book, *Irrational Exuberance.*

According to Robert Shiller, the late 1990s stock price rise was a bubble encouraged by 12 "precipitating factors":

1. The arrival of the Internet at a time of solid earnings growth
2. A sense that the United States had triumphed over its former rivals
3. A cultural change that favours business and profit
4. A Republican Congress and cuts in capital gains taxes
5. The baby boom and its perceived effects on the stock market
6. An expansion of media reporting of business news
7. Increasingly optimistic forecasts by "experts"
8. The expansion of pension plans with fixed contributions
9. The growth of mutual funds
10. The fall in inflation
11. The expansion of stock trading opportunities
12. A rise of gambling opportunities

Many of these factors directly influence stockholder expectations, and all of them encouraged an optimistic outlook for stock prices during the late 1990s. Probably no one investor thought that all of these factors would bring rising stock prices, but almost every investor believed that more than one of the factors would bring rising prices.

According to the speculative bubble view, the factors that encourage rising stock prices eventually weaken, prices stop rising and possibly crash. Some people see the falling stock prices of 2001 and 2002 as the bursting of a bubble.

But through 2002, the Internet and the information age remained a strong force for rising prices. So did the expansion of trading opportunities, especially on-line opportunities. The major new factor was the long-term campaign against terrorism. But the effects of this campaign on average stock prices were not clear at the end of 2002. The global economy was still adjusting to a new situation by reallocating resources away from travel and tourism and towards security and defence goods and services. Some sectors were expanding, and some were shrinking. The impact on average stock prices might be positive or negative.

REVIEW QUIZ

1. What is the market fundamentals view of the forces that determine stock prices?
2. What is the speculative bubble view of the forces that determine stock prices?
3. List five factors that you think might have encouraged the booming stock market of the 1990s.

You've seen that there are two views about the forces that determine stock prices. No one knows which view is correct. And no one can predict stock prices. For these reasons, rational stockholders diversify their holdings across a number of stocks. Let's see how diversification spreads risks.

Risk and Return

STOCK PRICES FLUCTUATE IN UNPREDICTABLE ways, and stockholders might receive a large capital gain or incur a large capital loss. But stocks differ in both their expected return and risk, and generally, the greater the risk, the higher is the expected return from a stock. We call the additional return that is earned for bearing an additional risk a **risk premium.** Let's see why a risk premium arises.

Risk Premium

Recall the stock price equation:

$$P_1 = \text{Expected value of } [b_1(D_1 + P_2)].$$

Suppose that two stocks have the same expected dividend, D_1, and the same expected future price, P_2, but one is riskier than the other. Because people dislike risk and must be compensated for bearing it, a riskier return is discounted more than a safe return—the discount factor, b_1, is smaller for the riskier return. Because b_1 is smaller, the price of a stock, P_1, is lower for the riskier stock. But if the price of the riskier stock is lower, the expected return from holding it is greater than the expected return from the safer stock.

Because expected return increases with risk, a person earns the highest expected return by holding only the one stock that has the highest expected return.

But this investment strategy is not usually the best one. The reason is that by diversifying stock holdings across a number of different stocks, an investor can lower the risk. To do so, the investor must accept a lower expected return. There is a tradeoff between risk and expected return.

Let's see how and why diversification lowers risk. To do so, we'll look at some actual stock purchases that you could have made in January 2001 and see what your investments would have been worth in 2002 with different degrees of diversification.

Portfolio Diversification

Table 35.2 shows the prices of five stocks in January 2001 and January 2002. Suppose that in January 2001, you had $1,000 to invest and put it all into just one of these five stocks.

You might have been lucky and chosen Procter & Gamble (P&G), in which case your $1,000 grew to $1,139 over the year. But you might have been very unlucky and chosen Enron, in which case you lost your entire investment.

Now suppose that instead of investing in only one of these stocks, you had put $500 into each of Enron and Procter & Gamble. In this case, your investment would have been worth $569.50 at the end of the year—a loss, but not as big as if you'd gone for only Enron.

Now imagine that you diversified even more, putting $200 each into Enron, Microsoft, Procter & Gamble, McDonald's, and Wal-Mart. In this case, your investment would have been worth $834 at the beginning of 2002.

You could spread your risks even more by investing in a mutual fund—a fund that is managed by investment specialists and that is diversified across a large number of stocks.

You can see from this example that lowering risk means accepting a lower return. The highest return across the five stocks in Table 35.2 comes from buying only Procter & Gamble. But at the beginning of 2001, you might equally have thought that buying Enron would provide the highest return. Because you can't predict which individual stock is going to perform best, it pays to diversify and take a lower expected return in return for a lower risk.

TABLE 35.2 Five Stock Prices in January 2001 and January 2002

	Price in January 2001	Price in January 2002	Value in 2002 of $1,000 in 2001
Enron	60	0	0
McDonald's	29	27	931
Microsoft	61	64	1,049
P&G	72	82	1,139
Wal-Mart	57	60	1,053

REVIEW QUIZ

1 Why do stocks' returns include a risk premium?
2 How does diversification across a number of stocks lower the risk that a stockholder faces?

We next look at the links between the stock market and the rest of the economy.

The Stock Market and the Economy

THE LINKS BETWEEN THE STOCK MARKET AND THE rest of the economy that we're now going to look at run in two directions: effects from the rest of the economy *on* the stock market and effects on the rest of the economy *from* the stock market. We'll look first at influences *on* the stock market, which fall into three broad groups:

- Trends and cycles in earnings growth
- Central bank monetary policy
- Taxes

Trends and Cycles in Earnings Growth

You've seen that expected future earnings are the fundamental influence on stock prices. Current earnings are known, but future earnings can only be forecasted. And the central question on which investors must take a position is the *expected growth rate* of earnings.

If earnings are expected to grow more rapidly, the fundamental value of a stock rises relative to current earnings—its price-earnings ratio rises. Conversely, if earnings are expected to grow more slowly, the fundamental value of a stock falls relative to current earnings—its price-earnings ratio falls.

The nature and pace of technological change and the state of the business cycle are the main influences on earnings growth. And expectations about future earnings growth are based on the best information that people can obtain about future technological change and business cycle developments.

The long-term trend in earnings growth has been remarkably constant at about 2 percent a year (after the effects of inflation are removed). But earnings growth has fluctuated a great deal around its trend. Figure 35.6 shows these fluctuations. The figure highlights the interesting fact that there have been only three main periods during which earnings have grown rapidly to reach a new higher level: the 1890s, 1950s and 1960s, and 1990s. There was only one other period of rapid earnings growth, from 1921 to 1931, but this episode was a temporary burst of growth from an extremely low level that did not take earnings back to their previous peak of 1918.

Each period during which earnings grew rapidly to a new level was one in which far-reaching new technologies spread. During the 1890s, it was the

FIGURE 35.6 Three Bursts of Earnings Growth

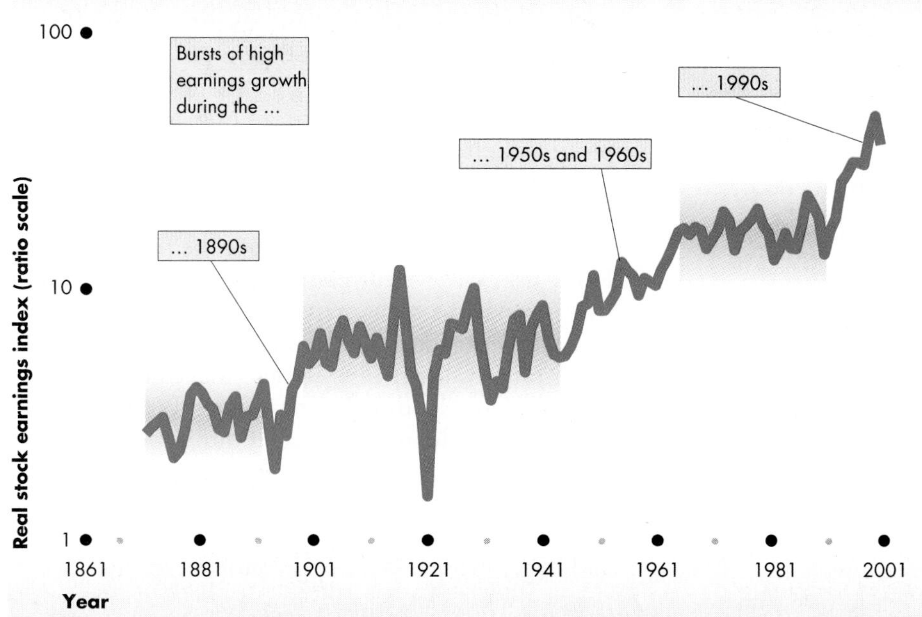

Earnings grew rapidly during three periods of rapid technological change: the 1890s (railroad, telegraph, electricity); 1950s and 1960s (highway system, plastics, transistor, and television); and 1990s (Internet and information technologies).

Source: Reprinted by permission of Robert J. Shiller, Professor of Economics, Yale University (www.econ.yale.edu/~schiller).

railroad, telegraph, and electricity. During the 1950s and 1960s, it was the highway system, plastics, the transistor, and television. And during the 1990s, it was the Internet and associated information technologies.

Although earnings are the fundamental source of value for stocks, the connection between earnings growth and stock prices cannot be used to make reliable predictions of stock prices. Stock prices did increase more rapidly than usual during the periods of rapid earnings growth. But they outpaced earnings growth—increased by more than was justified by the growth of earnings. And during the 1920s, stock prices grew beyond the levels that were supported by the underlying earnings fundamentals.

Some people have argued that the 1990s were special—unique—and marked a new era for permanently faster earnings growth arising from the information technologies that brought the exploding Internet. Does the earnings growth rate change permanently when a major new technology spreads? And are we living today in a "new economy"?

A New Economy? It is a well-documented fact that the spread of the Internet was unusually rapid. Not since the spread of television during the 1950s has there been such a rapid penetration of a new technology.

It is also a solid fact that the pace of earnings growth was unusually rapid during the 1990s—13 percent a year compared to the long-term average of 2 percent a year. But as you can see in Fig. 35.6, earnings growth was similarly rapid in earlier periods, only to return to its long-term average growth rate.

The only exception to this tendency to return to the preceding long-term average growth rate occurred more than 200 years ago, in an event called the Industrial Revolution. The Industrial Revolution was possibly unique, not because it saw the introduction of powerful new technologies but because it was a period in which for the first time in human history, research and the development of new technologies became commercially viable activities. People began to make a living by inventing new technologies rather than merely by producing goods and services. Before this period, invention and innovation had been a spasmodic and relatively rare event. The last really big invention had been the chronometer, a reliable method of keeping time on ships that improved the reliability of navigation.

It is still too soon to be sure, but more and more people are coming to the view that the "new economy" is just another stage in the evolution of the old economy. If this view is correct, the stock market of the early 2000s remains overvalued relative to its fundamentals. If the "new economy" view is correct, the stock market has correctly incorporated the future earnings growth that the new economy will bring.

Central Bank Monetary Policy

The U.S. Federal Reserve (Fed) and the European Central Bank (ECB) are the most powerful central banks in today's world. Their actions influence global stock markets. Whether you've studied monetary policy or not, you can understand how a central bank influences the stock market by seeing how interest rates affect stock prices.

If the Fed or ECB take actions that raise interest rates, stock prices usually fall. Conversely, if monetary policy lowers interest rates, stock prices usually rise. But policy influences on stock prices are short lived, and the timing of the influences depends on whether the policy actions are anticipated or they surprise the market.

Interest Rates and Stock Prices When the economy is expanding too rapidly and the policy goal is to slow down the growth of spending, interest rates are pushed upward. Higher interest rates make borrowing more costly and lending more rewarding. People who are borrowing to finance their expenditure face higher costs, and some of them cut back on spending.

Lower spending and higher saving translate into a smaller demand for the output of firms and smaller profits. With smaller profits expected, the prices of stocks fall.

Higher interest rates also encourage some stockholders to sell risky stocks and put their funds into lower-risk, lower-return bonds and other securities that now yield a higher return. This action increases the supply of stocks and lowers stock prices further.

Similarly, lower interest rates make borrowing less costly and lending less rewarding. People who are borrowing to finance their expenditure face lower costs, and some of them increase their spending.

Greater spending and lower saving translate into a greater demand for the output of the nation's firms, and larger profits. With larger profits expected, the prices of stocks rise.

Lower interest rates on bonds and other securities also encourage some bond holders to sell bonds and put their funds into higher-risk, higher-return stocks. This action increases the demand for stocks and raises stock prices still further.

Anticipating Policy Because monetary policy actions influence stock prices in the way we've just seen, it is profitable to anticipate future policy actions. If interest rates are expected to rise in the near future, then stock prices are expected to fall in the near future. Selling stocks before the price falls and buying them back after the price has fallen is profitable. So if a large number of people expect a rise in interest rates, they will sell stock. The selling action increases supply and lowers the stock price before the interest rate rises. Monetary policy has caused the stock price to fall, but the stock price falls *before* the policy action occurs. (This timing relationship is an example of the *post hoc* fallacy— see pp. 13–14.)

Taxes

Taxes can influence stock prices in a number of ways, some direct and some indirect. Three types of tax can affect stock markets:

- Capital gains tax
- Corporate profits tax
- Transactions (Tobin) tax

Capital Gains Tax The capital gains tax is a tax on the income that people earn when they *realize* a capital gain. A **realized capital gain** is a capital gain that is obtained when a stock is sold for a higher price than the price paid for it. People who hold onto stocks that have increased in value also enjoy a capital gain, but they do not pay a tax on that gain until they sell the stock and realize the gain.

When a capital gains tax is introduced or when the rate of capital gains tax is increased, stock prices fall, other things remaining the same. The reason is that the capital gains tax lowers the after-tax return on stocks and so lowers the price that people are willing to pay for stocks.

The lowering of the capital gains tax rate in the United States during the 1980s and 1990s probably contributed to the booming stock prices of the 1990s.

Corporate Profits Tax The corporate profits tax is an income tax on the profits of corporations. If this tax is increased, corporate after-tax profits fall. The firm has smaller earnings from which to pay dividends and invest in new capital. So the market fundamentals value of a firm falls, and so do stock prices.

Transactions (Tobin) Tax Transactions on the stock market are not taxed. But their value is enormous, and a tax set at a tiny rate would raise a huge amount of tax revenue for the government.

James Tobin, an economist at Yale University (who died in 2002), proposed that stock market transactions be taxed—hence the name "the Tobin tax." Tobin believed that such a tax would discourage speculative buying and selling of stocks and make the stock market more efficient. The evidence on transactions taxes in other markets, notably real estate markets, does not support the view that a transactions tax lowers speculation.

Let's now change directions and look at influences *from* the stock market to the rest of the economy. We'll look at the influences of stock prices on

- Wealth, consumption expenditure, and saving
- The distribution of wealth

Wealth, Consumption Expenditure, and Saving

Wealth is the market value of assets. The influence of wealth on consumption expenditure and saving is called the **wealth effect.** *Disposable income* equals income minus taxes. A household can do only two things with its disposable income: spend it on consumption goods and services or save it. The **saving rate** is saving as a percentage of disposable income. The greater is wealth, the smaller is the saving rate.

How do stock prices influence the saving rate? The answer depends on how we measure saving (and, related, how we measure disposable income).

There are two definitions of saving that are equivalent, provided that we measure everything in a consistent way. The first definition is

$$\text{Saving} = \begin{matrix}\text{Disposable}\\ \text{income}\end{matrix} - \begin{matrix}\text{Consumption}\\ \text{expenditure.}\end{matrix}$$

The second definition arises from the fact that saving adds to wealth. That is,

$$\begin{matrix}\text{Wealth at}\\ \text{end of year}\end{matrix} = \begin{matrix}\text{Wealth at}\\ \text{start of year}\end{matrix} + \begin{matrix}\text{Saving during}\\ \text{the year,}\end{matrix}$$

or

$$\text{Saving} = \text{Change in wealth.}$$

The first definition of saving focuses on the fact that saving is what is left over after buying consumer goods and services. The second definition focuses on the fact that saving adds to wealth.

Because the two definitions of saving are equivalent, it must be the case that

$$\begin{matrix}\text{Disposable} \\ \text{income}\end{matrix} = \begin{matrix}\text{Consumption} \\ \text{expenditure}\end{matrix} + \begin{matrix}\text{Change in} \\ \text{wealth.}\end{matrix}$$

In the data on income and wealth, disposable income does not include capital gains and losses. In the data on wealth, capital gains and losses *are* included. So there is a measurement discrepancy between saving measured using the first definition, which excludes capital gains, and saving measured using the second definition, which includes capital gains.

Figure 35.7 shows you what has happened to the saving rate based on the first measure and excluding capital gains. The saving rate was on an upward trend in Canada during the 1960s and 1970s. It was roughly constant in the United States. But during the 1990s, the saving rate collapsed in both countries. By 2000, the U.S. personal saving rate was less than 1 percent.

This collapse of the personal saving rate coincided with the explosion of stock prices through the 1990s.

You might expect that if people are enjoying capital gains on the stock market, they will think of these gains as being part of their saving. So they will not be concerned if their saving rate *excluding* capital gains falls. So what happened to the saving rate defined to include capital gains? Figure 35.8 answers this question for the period 1981–2001. While the saving rate excluding capital gains was collapsing, the saving rate including capital gains increased from about 7 percent in the early 1980s to around 20 percent in the late 1990s.

Which measure of saving is the correct one?

FIGURE 35.7 The Personal Saving Rate

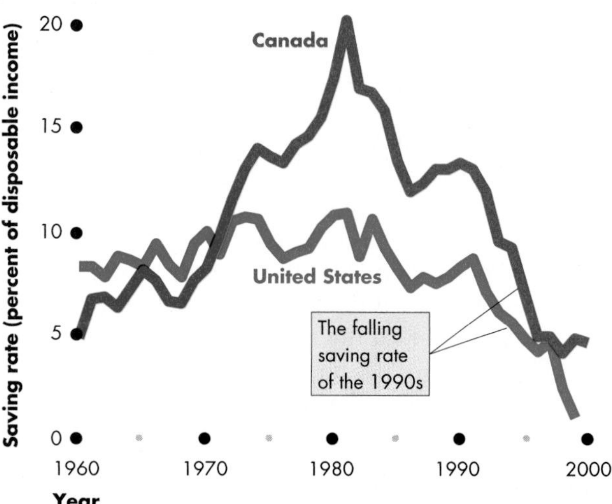

The personal saving rate increased in Canada and was flat in the United States before 1980. The saving rate fell in both countries during the 1980s and 1990s.

Sources: U.S. Bureau of Economic Analysis and adapted in part from the Statistics Canada CANSIM II database, table 380-0031.

FIGURE 35.8 Two Views of the Personal Saving Rate

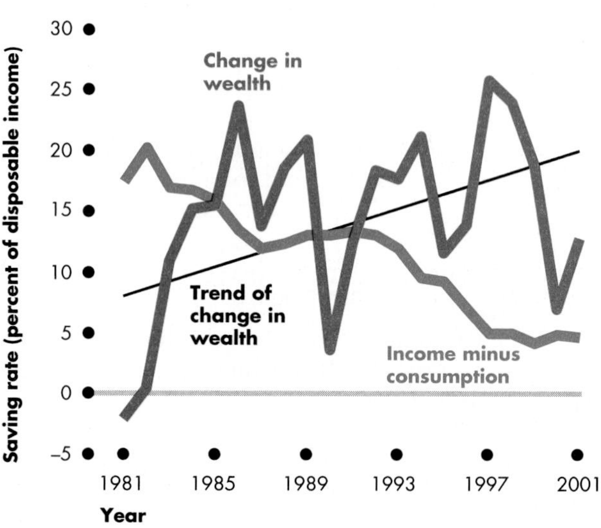

The personal saving rate including capital gains—the change in wealth—increased, while the saving rate excluding capital gains—disposable income minus consumption—collapsed.

Sources: Statistics Canada, CANSIM tables 378-0004 and 380-0031.

Neither! The rate that excludes capital gains is incorrect because it omits an important source of changes in wealth. But the rate that includes capital gains is incorrect because those gains are not realized. And if everyone attempted to realize their gains, the stock market would almost surely crash, thereby wiping out some unknown proportion of the gains. So the truth lies at some unknown place between the two available measures.

The Distribution of Wealth

When stock prices are rising as rapidly as they did from 1995 to 2000, stockholders enjoy spectacular increases in their wealth. Do all income groups share in these increases in wealth? Or are the increases concentrated among the already wealthy?

The answer to this question depends on the distribution of stockholdings. It turns out that the wealthier households are those that tend to hold stocks. So the wealthiest have gained the most.

The only wealth distribution data available is for the United States, and it ends in 1998. But these data tell an amazing story. You can see the data in Fig. 35.9. Here, we plot the mean wealth in 1992, 1995, and 1998 of households in five income groups ranging from those who earn less than $10,000 a year to those who earn more than $100,000 a year. The wealth data are in 1998 dollars, which means that they are adjusted to remove the effects of inflation.

Notice that the wealth of the four lowest-income groups barely changes. In contrast, the wealth of the highest-income group increases. In fact, the increase in wealth of the highest-income group exceeds the level of wealth of the next highest group. Between 1995 and 1998, households that have an income of $100,000 or more a year enjoyed an increase in average wealth of more than $300,000. The average wealth of households that earn between $50,000 and $99,999 was only $275,000 in 1998.

While we cannot be sure that all the wealth changes shown in Fig. 35.9 resulted from the rising stock prices, much of the change must have come from that source. Whether the changes in the distribution of wealth will be permanent depends on the future of stock prices. If stock prices collapse, much of the gain in wealth by the highest-income group will be reversed. And many families will wish that they had not lowered their saving rate.

FIGURE 35.9 Wealth Redistribution

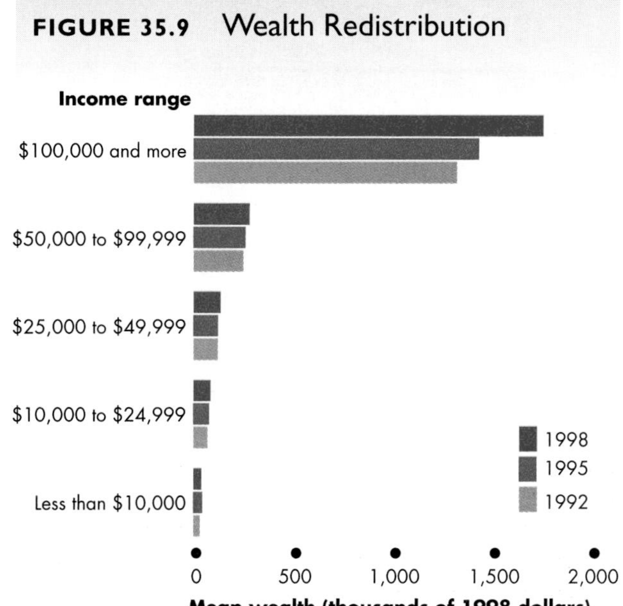

The wealth of the highest-income households increased between 1995 and 1998 by more than the level of wealth of other households.

Source: Board of Governors of the Federal Reserve System.

REVIEW QUIZ

1. What are the main trends in earnings growth?
2. What events are associated with the three periods of rapid earnings growth?
3. How does monetary policy influence the stock market?
4. How do taxes influence the stock market?
5. How does the stock market influence saving?
6. How does the stock market influence the distribution of wealth?

You've learned the two main approaches to understanding stock prices, seen why portfolio diversification is a good idea, and seen how the stock market and the economy interact. To reinforce your appreciation of the impossibility of predicting stock prices, we look at the stock market at the end of 2002 in *Reading Between the Lines* on pp. 846–847.

Stock Price Uncertainties

THE GLOBE AND MAIL, DECEMBER 3, 2002

Analysts just can't agree: recovery or bear respite?

The stock markets have been rallying for the better part of seven weeks, but analysts continue to disagree over whether this is a full-fledged recovery or just a bear market taking a breather.

"I think, so far, that is the $64-million question, or the $8-trillion question," said Ross Healy, president of Strategic Analysis Corp.

The S&P/TSX composite index rose 5.2 per cent last month, and is up 17 per cent from its Oct. 9 low. Over the same period, the S&P 500 in the United States is up 20.3 per cent. However, that hasn't convinced many experts that the 2½-year bear market is at an end.

"Unfortunately, I think no matter how adamant that the born-again bulls are, or I suppose, for that matter, how adamant the unrepentant bears are, things are murky ... they are not cut and dried," Mr. Healy said.

What is cut and dried is that as a bear market bottoms, valuations become so attractive that they tend to draw investors into the market, he said. He doesn't see that yet.

He said the U.S. market is trading at about three times or more book value, far above the 1.6 times of the 1990 bear market. The dividend yield was far higher in 1990 than in today's market. Moreover, he pointed out, the price/earnings multiple on the Standard & Poor's 500-stock index stands at a relatively high 30 times trailing earnings.

Many market watchers zero in on the multiple on next year's earnings, which is significantly lower than the trailing multiple, but that is based on expectations that earnings will grow sharply next year. "I don't see 20- or 25-per-cent increase in earnings year over year next year," he said.

...

Essence of the Story

- Stock prices fell for two and a half years to October 2002—a bear market.
- The S&P/TSX composite index increased by 5.2 percent in November 2002 and by 17 percent over its October 9 low.
- Over the same period, the S&P 500 in the United States increased by 20.3 percent.
- Uncertainty persisted over whether price increase would continue—whether the bear market was gone and a rising bull market had begun.
- Reasons to believe that the market was not ready to begin a new long period of rising prices were: a high ratio of stock prices to the book value of firms, a low dividend yield, and a high price-earnings ratio.
- Earnings would need to grow by an unlikely 20 percent to 25 percent to support a rising market.

Economic Analysis

■ This news article reports the rising stock prices of November 2002 and notes the uncertainty about the continuation of the increase.

■ Figure 1 shows the stock market of the 1990s and 2000s. The graph shows the S&P/TSX composite index.

■ The bull market—rising prices—began in the early 1990s and, with a brief pause in 1998, continued until August 2000.

■ A bear market—falling prices—began in September 2000.

■ The stock market never moves relentlessly in one direction. It is constantly fluctuating around its general trend and in November 2002, prices increased. They had also increased during November 2001.

■ Figure 2 expands our view of November and December 2002.

■ Stock prices increased for about a month and then fell before returning in mid-December to their previous peak of December 2, the date of the news article.

■ If stock prices are determined by market fundamentals, it is unlikely that a new bull market began at the end of 2002.

■ Uncertainty about continued economic growth in the United States, Japan, and Germany made Canada's continued strong expansion equally uncertain.

■ If in early 2003, real GDP growth slows and business profits are weak, stock prices will reflect these fundamentals and fall further.

■ If real GDP growth speeds up and business profits are strong, stock prices will reflect these more encouraging fundamentals and a bull market will begin.

■ At the end of 2002 (the date of the news article), slow growth and weak profits appeared more likely than fast growth and high profits.

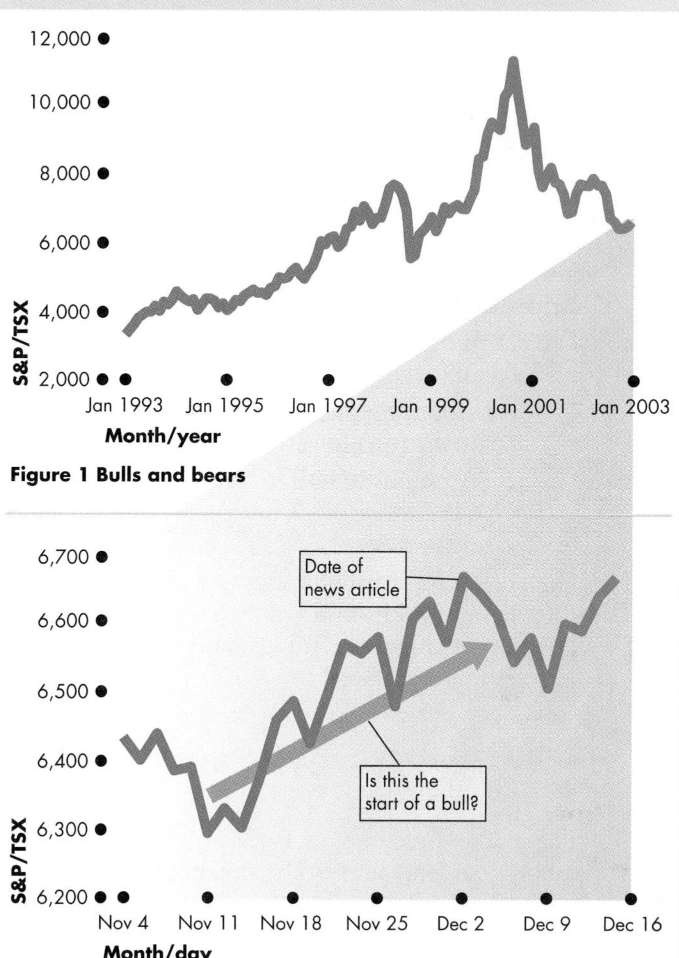

Figure 1 Bulls and bears

Figure 2 Bull or short-lived adjustment?

SUMMARY

KEY POINTS

Stock Market Basics (pp. 830–836)

- A stock is a tradable security issued by a firm to certify that its holder owns a share of the firm, is entitled to receive a share of the firm's profit (a dividend), and vote at stockholder meetings.
- The return on a stock consists of a dividend plus a capital gain (or minus a capital loss).
- A firm's accounting profit (called earnings) is used to calculate the price-earnings ratio.
- The S&P Composite, DJIA, NASDAQ, and S&P/TSX indexes provide information about average stock prices.
- The S&P price-earnings ratio between 1871 and 2001 has ranged from 6 to 27 and averaged 13.9. The S&P/TSX price-earnings ratio follows a similar path to that of S&P.

How Are Stock Prices Determined? (pp. 836–839)

- The market fundamental stock price is the discounted present value of the stream of expected future dividend payments, which in turn depend on expected future earnings.
- Some economists believe that stock prices can be understood only as speculative bubbles—periods of rising prices followed by price plunges, both of which occur because people expect them to occur and act on that expectation.

Risk and Return (p. 840)

- Stocks differ in their expected return and risk, and the greater the risk, the higher is the stock's risk premium.
- An investor can lower the risk faced by diversifying across a number of stocks because the returns on different stocks are not perfectly correlated.

The Stock Market and the Economy (pp. 841–845)

- Technological change and the state of the business cycle influence earnings growth and stock prices.
- Earnings growth has come in three main bursts: the 1890s, 1950s and 1960s, and 1990s.
- Each period of rapid earnings growth was also a time of the spread of major new technologies.
- When interest rates rise, stock prices fall, and when interest rates fall, stock prices rise. The change in stock prices precedes anticipated monetary policy actions.
- The capital gains tax and corporate profits tax affect stock prices. A transactions (Tobin) tax would probably not deter speculation.
- As stock prices increased during the 1990s, the saving rate excluding capital gains collapsed but the saving rate including capital gains increased.
- As stock prices increased during the 1990s, the distribution of wealth became more unequal.

KEY FIGURES AND TABLE

Figure 35.2	Reading the Stock Market Report, 832
Figure 35.5	The Price-Earnings Ratio, 835
Figure 35.6	Three Bursts of Earnings Growth, 841
Figure 35.7	The Personal Saving Rate, 844
Figure 35.8	Two Views of the Personal Saving Rate, 844
Figure 35.9	Wealth Redistribution, 845
Table 35.1	Rational Expectations, 838

KEY TERMS

Capital gain, 831
Capital loss, 831
Discount factor, 837
Dividend, 830
Dividend yield, 831
Earnings, 831
Equity capital, 830
Price-earnings ratio, 831
Rate of return, 831
Rational expectation, 837
Realized capital gain, 843
Return, 831
Risk premium, 840
Saving rate, 843
Speculative bubble, 838
Stock, 830
Stock exchange, 830
Stock price, 831
Wealth, 843
Wealth effect, 843

PROBLEMS

*1. On January 2, 2001, the price of a share of Coca-Cola stock was $60.81. On December 31, 2001, the price was $47.15. During 2001, Coca-Cola paid dividends that totaled 54¢ a share. Coca-Cola's reported accounting profit during 2001 was $1.58 per share.
   a. What was the dividend yield on Coca-Cola stock during 2001?
   b. What was the return on Coca-Cola stock during 2001?
   c. What was the capital gain or loss on Coca-Cola stock during 2001?
   d. What was the rate of return on Coca-Cola stock during 2001?
   e. What were Coca-Cola's earnings during 2001?
   f. What was Coca-Cola's price-earnings ratio on December 31, 2001?

2. On January 2, 2001, the price of a share of General Motors (GM) stock was $52.19. On December 31, 2001, the price was $48.60. During 2001, GM paid a dividend of $2 a share. GM's reported accounting profit during 2001 was $1.40 per share.
   a. What was the dividend yield on GM stock during 2001?
   b. What was the return on GM stock during 2001?
   c. What was the capital gain or loss on GM stock during 2001?
   d. What was the rate of return on GM stock during 2001?
   e. What were GM's earnings during 2001?
   f. What was GM's price-earnings ratio on December 31, 2001?

*3. The financial pages report that the Dow is up by 5 percent, the S&P is up by 8 percent, and the NASDAQ is up by 15 percent. Write a report that interprets these numbers. What can you infer from the data about the changes in stock prices in different sectors of the economy?

4. The financial pages report that the Dow is down by 15 percent, the S&P is down by 10 percent, and the NASDAQ is down by 25 percent. Write a short report that interprets these numbers. What can you infer from the data about the changes in stock prices in different sectors of the economy?

*5. You are trying to figure out whether to buy some stock. You are confident that the stock will pay a dividend of $3 a share next year, and you think that you'll be able to sell the stock at the end of the year for $30 a share. Your discount factor is 0.9. What is the most that you'd be willing to pay for this stock?

6. You are trying to figure out whether to buy some stock. You are confident that the stock will pay a dividend of $5 a share next year, and you think that you'll be able to sell the stock at the end of the year for $30 a share. Your discount factor is 0.8. What is the most that you'd be willing to pay for this stock?

*7. The price of a stock that you're thinking of buying is $20 a share. Your discount factor is 0.75. The firm has announced its dividend for next year of $1 per share. What is the lowest expected price next year that would make it rational for you to go ahead and buy the stock?

8. The price of a stock that you're thinking of buying is $100 a share. Your discount factor is 0.7. The firm has announced that it will pay no dividend next year. What is the lowest expected price next year that would make it rational for you to go ahead and buy the stock?

*9. Suppose there are two pharmaceutical stocks that you might buy: Merck and Pfizer. Merck will provide a return of 50 percent if the firm makes a major breakthrough on its new drug and a 10 percent return otherwise. There is only a 10 percent chance that the firm will make the breakthrough. Pfizer will provide a return of 20 percent if the firm achieves a cost saving and a 15 percent return otherwise. There is a 50 percent chance that the firm will achieve the cost saving.
   a. What is the expected return from investing in Merck?
   b. What is the expected return from investing in Pfizer?
   c. What is the chance of making a return of 50 percent by investing only in Merck?
   d. What is the chance of making a return of 10 percent by investing only in Merck?
   e. What is the chance of making a return of 20 percent by investing only in Pfizer?
   f. What is the chance of making a return of 15 percent by investing only in Pfizer?
   g. If you invest in both Merck and Pfizer in equal amounts, what is your expected return?

h. If you invest in both Merck and Pfizer in equal amounts, what is your chance of making a return of 50 percent?
i. If you invest in both Merck and Pfizer in equal amounts, what is your chance of making a return of 10 percent?
j. Explain why it might be rational to diversify across Merck and Pfizer.

10. Suppose there are two soft drink stocks that you might buy: Coke and Pepsi. Coke will provide a return of 20 percent if the firm's Harry Potter advertising campaign is successful and a 10 percent return otherwise. There is a 60 percent chance that the advertising campaign will be successful. Pepsi will provide a return of 16 percent if the firm achieves a cost saving and a 14 percent return otherwise. There is a 50 percent chance that the firm will achieve the cost saving.
    a. What is the expected return from investing in Coke?
    b. What is the expected return from investing in Pepsi?
    c. What is the chance of making a return of 20 percent by investing only in Coke?
    d. What is the chance of making a return of 10 percent by investing only in Coke?
    e. What is the chance of making a return of 16 percent by investing only in Pepsi?
    f. What is the chance of making a return of 14 percent by investing only in Pepsi?
    g. If you invest in both Coke and Pepsi in equal amounts, what is your expected return?
    h. If you invest in both Coke and Pepsi in equal amounts, what is your chance of making a return of 20 percent?
    i. If you invest in both Coke and Pepsi in equal amounts, what is your chance of making a return of 10 percent?
    j. Explain why it might be rational to diversify across Coke and Pepsi.

CRITICAL THINKING

1. Study *Reading Between the Lines* on pp. 846–847 and then answer the following questions:
    a. What happened to stock prices during 2002 on the average?
    b. Does the performance of stock prices during 2002 look like the result of rational expectations of the fundamentals or of the bursting of a speculative bubble?
    c. Assuming that the performance of stock prices during 2002 was the result of rational expectations, what does that performance imply about expectations for profits in 2003 and beyond?
    d. What economic development is needed before a new sustained increase in stock prices begins?

WEB EXERCISES

1. Use the link on the Parkin–Bade Web site to visit the New York, London, Frankfurt, Tokyo, and Toronto stock exchanges.
    a. Get the latest index numbers from these stock exchanges and get the indexes a year ago.
    b. On the basis of the data you have obtained, calculate the percentage changes in the indexes over the past year.
    c. Which of the stock markets has delivered the largest percentage gain? Can you think of reasons for the differences in performance of the five stock markets?
2. Use the link on the Parkin–Bade Web site to obtain data on the prices and dividend payments over the past year for five stocks that interest you. Also obtain the value of the S&P/TSX, the DJIA, S&P Composite, and NASDAQ indexes for the same period.
    a. For each stock, calculate the rate of return assuming that you bought the stock one year ago.
    b. For each index, calculate the percentage change over the past year and compare the performance of each stock with the indexes.

UNDERSTANDING THE GLOBAL ECONOMY

It's a Small World

The scale of international trade, borrowing, and lending, both in absolute dollar terms and as a percentage of total world production expands every year. One country, Singapore, imports and exports goods and services in a volume that exceeds its Gross Domestic Product. The world's largest nation, China, returned to the international economic stage during the 1980s and is now a major producer of manufactured goods. ◆ International economic activity is large because today's economic world is small and because communication is so incredibly fast. But today's world is not a new world. From the beginning of recorded history, people have traded over large and steadily increasing distances. The great Western civilizations of Greece and Rome traded not only around the Mediterranean but also into the Gulf of Arabia. The great Eastern civilizations traded around the Indian Ocean. By the Middle Ages, the East and the West were trading routinely overland on routes pioneered by Venetian traders and explorers such as Marco Polo. When, in 1497, Vasco da Gama opened a sea route between the Atlantic and Indian Oceans around Africa, a new trade between East and West began, which brought tumbling prices of Eastern goods in Western markets. ◆ The European discovery of America and the subsequent opening up of Atlantic trade continued the process of steady globalization. So the developments of the 1990s, amazing though many of them are, represent a continuation of an ongoing expansion of human horizons. These three chapters studied the interaction of nations in today's global economy. ◆ Chapter 33 described and explained international trade in goods and services. In this chapter, you came face to face with one of the biggest policy issues of all ages: free trade versus protection and the globalization debate. The chapter explained how all nations can benefit from free international trade. ◆ Chapter 34 explained some of the fundamentals of international borrowing and lending and the exchange rate. It explained the poorly understood fact that the size of a nation's international deficit depends not on how efficient it is, but on how much its citizens save relative to how much they invest. Nations with low saving rates, everything else being the same, have international deficits. ◆ Finally, Chapter 35 studied global stock markets. It described these markets and it explained how stock prices are determined and why they are volatile and impossible to predict. ◆ The global economy is big news these days. And it has always attracted attention. On the next page, you can meet the economist who first understood comparative advantage, David Ricardo. And you can meet one of today's leading international economists, Jagdish Bhagwati of Columbia University.

PROBING THE IDEAS

Gains from International Trade

THE ECONOMIST

Gains from International Trade
"Under a system of perfectly free commerce, each country naturally devotes its capital and labour to such employments as are most beneficial to each."

DAVID RICARDO
The Principles of Political Economy and Taxation, 1817

DAVID RICARDO *(1772–1832) was a highly successful 27-year-old stockbroker when he stumbled on a copy of Adam Smith's* Wealth of Nations *(see p. 54) on a weekend visit to the country. He was immediately hooked and went on to become the most celebrated economist of his age and one of the all-time great economists. One of his many contributions was to develop the principle of comparative advantage, the foundation on which the modern theory of international trade is built. The example he used to illustrate this principle was the trade between England and Portugal in cloth and wine.*

The General Agreement on Tariff and Trade was established as a reaction against the devastation wrought by beggar-my-neighbour tariffs imposed during the 1930s. But it is also a triumph for the logic first worked out by Smith and Ricardo.

THE ISSUES

Until the mid-eighteenth century, it was generally believed that the purpose of international trade was to keep exports greater than imports and pile up gold. If gold was accumulated, it was believed, the nation would prosper; if gold was lost through an international deficit, the nation would be drained of money and impoverished. These beliefs are called *mercantilism*, and the *mercantilists* were pamphleteers who advocated with missionary fervor the pursuit of an international surplus. If exports did not exceed imports, the mercantilists wanted imports restricted.

In the 1740s, David Hume explained that as the quantity of money (gold) changes, so also does the price level, and the nation's *real* wealth is unaffected. In the 1770s, Adam Smith argued that import restrictions would lower the gains from specialization and make a nation poorer. Thirty years later, David Ricardo proved the law of comparative advantage and demonstrated the superiority of free trade. Mercantilism was intellectually bankrupt but remained politically powerful.

Gradually, through the nineteenth century, the mercantilist influence waned and North American and Western Europe prospered in an environment of increasingly free international trade. But despite remarkable advances in economic understanding, mercantilism never quite died. It had a brief and devastating revival in the 1920s and 1930s when tariff hikes brought about the collapse of international trade and accentuated the Great Depression. It subsided again after World War II with the establishment of the General Agreement on Tariffs and Trade (GATT).

But mercantilism lingers on. The often expressed view that the United States should restrict Japanese imports and reduce its deficit with Japan and fears that NAFTA will bring economic ruin to Canada are modern manifestations of mercantilism. It would be interesting to have David Hume, Adam Smith, and David Ricardo commenting on these views. But we know what they would say—the same things that they said to the eighteenth-century mercantilists. And they would still be right today.

Then

In the eighteenth century, when mercantilists and economists were debating the pros and cons of free international exchange, the transportation technology that was available limited the gains from international trade. Sailing ships with tiny cargo holds took close to a month to cross the Atlantic Ocean. But the potential gains were large, and so was the incentive to cut shipping costs. By the 1850s, the clipper ship had been developed, cutting the journey from Boston to Liverpool to only 12¼ days. Half a century later, 10,000-ton steamships were sailing between North America and England in just 4 days. As sailing times and costs declined, the gains from international trade increased and the volume of trade expanded.

Now

The container ship has revolutionized international trade and contributed to its continued expansion. Today, most goods cross the oceans in containers—metal boxes—packed into and piled on top of ships like this one. Container technology has cut the cost of ocean shipping by economizing on handling and by making cargoes harder to steal, lowering insurance costs. It is unlikely that there would be much international trade in goods such as television sets and VCRs without this technology. High-value and perishable cargoes such as flowers and fresh foods, as well as urgent courier packages, travel by air. Every day, dozens of cargo-laden 747s fly between every major North American city and to destinations across the Atlantic and Pacific oceans.

Jagdish Bhagwati, whom you can meet on the following pages, is one of the most distinguished international economists. He has contributed to our understanding of the effects of international trade and trade policy on economic growth and development and has played a significant role in helping to shape today's global trading arrangements.

TALKING WITH

JAGDISH BHAGWATI *is*

University Professor at Columbia University. Born in India in 1934, he studied at Cambridge University in England, MIT, and Oxford University before returning to India. He returned to teach at MIT in 1968 and moved to Columbia in 1980. A prolific scholar: Professor Bhagwati also writes in leading newspapers and magazines throughout the world. He has been much honoured for both his scientific work and his impact on public policy. His greatest contributions are in international trade but extend also to developmental problems and the study of political economy.

Michael Parkin and Robin Bade talked with Jagdish Bhagwati about his work and the progress that economists have made in understanding the benefits of international economic integration since the pioneering work of Ricardo.

Jagdish Bhagwati

Professor Bhagwati, what attracted you to economics?

When you come from India where poverty hits the eye, it is easy to be attracted to economics, which can be used to bring prosperity and create jobs to pull up the poor into gainful employment.

I learned later that there are two broad types of economist: those who treat the subject as an arid mathematical toy, and those who see it as a serious social science.

If Cambridge, where I went as an undergraduate, had been interested in esoteric mathematical economics, I would have opted for something else. But the Cambridge economists from whom I learned—many among the greatest figures in the discipline—saw economics as a social science. I therefore saw the power of economics as a tool to address India's poverty and was immediately hooked.

Who had the greatest impact on you at Cambridge?

Most of all, it was Harry Johnson, a young Canadian of immense energy and profound analytical gifts. Quite unlike the shy and reserved British dons, Johnson was friendly, effusive, and supportive of students who flocked around him. He would later move to Chicago where he became one of the most influential members of the market-oriented Chicago school. Another was Joan Robinson, arguably the world's most impressive female economist.

When I left Cambridge for MIT, going from one Cambridge to the other, I was lucky to transition from one phenomenal set of economists to another. At MIT, I learned much from future Nobel laureates Paul Samuelson and Robert Solow—both would later become great friends and colleagues when I joined the MIT faculty in 1968.

After Cambridge and MIT, you went to Oxford and then back to India. What did you do in India?

I joined the Planning Commission in New Delhi, where my first big job was to find ways of raising the bottom 30 percent of India's population out of poverty to a "minimum income" level.

And what did you prescribe?

My main prescription was to "grow the pie." My research suggested that the share of the bottom 30 percent of the pie did not seem to vary dramatically with differences in economic and political systems. So, growth in the pie seemed to be the principal (but not the only) component of an antipoverty strategy. To supplement growth's good effects on the poor, the Indian planners were also dedicated to education, health, social reforms, and land reforms. Also, the access of the lowest-income and socially disadvantaged groups to the growth process and its benefits was to be improved in many ways, such as extension of credit without collateral.

Today, this strategy has no rivals. Much empirical work shows that where growth has occurred, poverty has lessened. It is nice to know that one's basic take on an issue of such central importance to humanity's well-being has been borne out by experience!

My main prescription was to "grow the pie"... Today, this strategy has no rivals. Much empirical work shows that where growth has occurred, poverty has lessened.

You left India in 1968 to come to America and an academic job at MIT. Why?

While the decision to emigrate often reflects personal factors—and they were present in my case—the offer of a Professorship from MIT certainly helped me make up my mind. At the time, it was easily the world's most celebrated Department: Serendipitously, the highest-ranked Departments at MIT were not in engineering and the sciences but in linguistics (which had Noam Chomsky) and economics (which had Paul Samuelson). Joining the MIT faculty was a dramatic breakthrough: I felt stimulated each year by several fantastic students and by several of the world's most creative economists.

We hear a lot in the popular press about fair trade and level playing fields. What's the distinction between free trade and fair trade? How can the playing field be unlevel?

Free trade simply means allowing no trade barriers such as tariffs, subsidies, and quotas. Trade barriers make domestic prices different from world prices for traded goods. When this happens, resources are not being used efficiently. Basic economics from the time of Ricardo tells us why free trade is good for us and why barriers to trade harm us, though our understanding of this doctrine today is far more nuanced and profound than it was at its creation.

Fair trade, on the other hand, is almost always a sneaky way of objecting to free trade. If your rivals are hard to compete with, you are not likely to get protection simply by saying that you cannot hack it. But if you say that your rival is an "unfair" trader, that is an easier sell! As international competition has grown fiercer, cries of "unfair trade" have therefore multiplied. The lesser rogues among the protectionists ask for "free and fair trade," whereas the worst ones ask for "fair, not free, trade."

Fair trade ... is almost always a sneaky way of objecting to free trade.

At the end of World War II, the General Agreement on Tariffs and Trade (GATT) was established and there followed several rounds of multilateral trade negotiations and reductions in barriers to trade. How do you assess the contribution of GATT and its successor, the World Trade Organization (WTO)?

The GATT has made a huge contribution by overseeing massive trade liberalization in industrial goods among the developed countries. GATT rules, which "bind" tariffs to negotiated ceilings, prevent the raising of tariffs and have prevented tariff wars like those of the 1930s in which mutual and retaliatory tariff barriers were raised to the detriment of everyone.

The GATT was folded into the WTO at the end of the Uruguay Round of trade negotiations and is institutionally stronger. For instance, it has a binding Dispute Settlement Mechanism, whereas the GATT had no such teeth. It is also more ambitious in its scope, extending to new areas such as environment, intellectual property protection, and investment rules.

Running alongside the pursuit of multilateral free trade has been the emergence of bilateral trade agreements such as NAFTA and the EU. How do you view the bilateral free trade areas in today's world?

Unfortunately, there has been an explosion of bilateral free trade areas today. By some estimates, the ones in place and others being plotted approach 400! Each bilateral agreement gives preferential treatment to its trading partner over others. Because there are now so many bilateral agreements, such as between United States and Israel and between United States and Jordan, the result is a chaotic pattern of different tariffs depending on where a product comes from. Also, "rules of origin" must be agreed upon to determine whether a product is, say, Jordanian or Taiwanese if Jordan qualifies for a preferential tariff but Taiwan does not, and Taiwanese inputs enter the Jordanian manufacture of the product.

I have called the resulting criss-crossing of preferences and rules of origin the "spaghetti bowl" problem. The world trading system is choking under these proliferating bilateral deals. Contrast this complexity against the simplicity of a multilateral system with common tariffs for all WTO members.

We now have a world of uncoordinated and inefficient trade policies. The EU makes bilateral free trade agreements with different non-EU countries, so the United States follows with its own bilateral agreements; and with Europe and the United States doing it, the Asian countries, long wedded to multilateralism, have now succumbed to the mania.

Instead, if the United States had provided leadership by rewriting rules to make the signing of such bilateral agreements extremely difficult, this plague on the trading system today might well have been averted.

> ***We now have a world of uncoordinated and inefficient trade policies.***

Despite the benefits that economics points to from multilateral free trade, the main organization that pursues this goal, the WTO, is having a very hard time with the anti-globalization movement. What can we say about globalization that puts the WTO and its work in proper perspective?

The anti-globalization movement contains a diverse set of activists. Essentially, they all claim to be stakeholders in the globalization phenomenon. But there are those who want to drive a stake through the system, as in Dracula films, and there are those who want to exercise their stake in the system. The former want to be heard; the latter, to be listened to. For a while, the two disparate sets of critics were milling around together, seeking targets of opportunity at international conferences such as WTO's November 2000 meeting in Seattle where the riots broke out. Now things have settled down; and the groups that want to work systematically and seriously at improving the global economy's functioning are much more in play.

But the WTO is also seen, inaccurately for the most part, as imposing trade sanctions that override concerns such as environmental protection. For example, U.S. legislation bans the importing of shrimp that is harvested without the use of turtle-excluding devices. India and others complained, but the WTO upheld the U.S. legislation. Ignorant of the facts, demonstrators took to the streets dressed as turtles protesting the WTO decision!

What advice do you have for a student who is just starting to study economics? Is economics a good subject in which to major?

I would say: enormously so. In particular, we economists bring three unique insights to good policymaking.

First, economists look for second and subsequent-round effects of actions.

Second, we correctly emphasize that a policy cannot be judged without using a counterfactual. It is a witticism that an economist, when asked how her husband was, said: compared to what?

Third, we uniquely and systematically bring the principle of social cost and benefit to our policy analysis.

CANADIAN
ECONOMY
DATABASE

CANADIAN ECONOMY DATABASE

THE FOLLOWING DATA TABLES PROVIDE A DESCRIPTION of some of the main features of the Canadian economy from 1926 to 2001.

You can make graphs of these data by using *Economics in Action* on the Parkin–Bade Web site. To do so, open the table of contents page for *any* chapter, click on Data Graphing and then click on Canada Historical.

These data are updated annually on the Parkin–Bade Web site.

Sources

CANSIM series: Statistics Canada, Ottawa

HSC series: Statistics Canada, *Historical Statistics of Canada*, Second Edition, F. H. Leacy (ed.), Ottawa, 1983.

HSC(1) series: The MacMillan Company of Canada Limited, *Historical Statistics of Canada*, M.C. Urquhart (ed.), Toronto, 1965.

A break in a series is indicated by ^{b}.

Variables

1. Real GDP
HSC series F55 and CANSIM series v1992292. The data for 1926–1960 are F55 multiplied by the 1961 ratio of v1992292 to F55.

2. Real consumption expenditure
HSC series F33 and CANSIM series v1992262. The data for 1926–1960 are F33 multiplied by the 1961 ratio of v1992262 to F33.

3. Real investment
HSC is F55 minus the sum of F33, F34, and F51 plus F52; CANSIM series is v1992292 minus the sum of v1992262, v1992268, 1992282 plus v1992286. The data for 1926–1960 are *HSC* multiplied by the 1961 ratio of CANSIM to *HSC*.

4. Real government expenditure
HSC series F34 and CANSIM series v1992268. The data for 1926–1960 are F34 multiplied by the 1961 ratio of v1992268 to F34.

5. Real exports
HSC series F51 and CANSIM series v1992282. The data for 1926–1960 are F51 multiplied by the 1961 ratio of v1992282 to F51.

6. Real imports
HSC series F52 and CANSIM series v1992286. The data for 1926–1960 are F51 multiplied by the 1961 ratio of v1992286 to F52.

7. Real net exports
Real exports *minus* real imports.

8. Potential GDP
Real GDP trends and authors' assumptions and calculations.

9. Fluctuations around potential GDP
Percentage deviation of real GDP from potential GDP.

10. Real GDP growth rate
Annual percentage change in real GDP.

11. GDP deflator
HSC series K172 and CANSIM series v647710 and v3860248. The data for 1961–1980 are v647710 multiplied by the 1981 ratio of v3860248 to v647710. The data for 1926–1960 are K172 multiplied by the 1961 ratio of the above calculation to K172.

12. CPI
Statistics Canada, CANSIM series v737344.

13. Inflation rate
Annual percentage change in the GDP deflator.

14. Inflation rate
Annual percentage change in the CPI.

15. Labour force
CANSIM series v21051 and v2461098.

16. Labour force participation rate
CANSIM series v21051, v21056, and v2461245.

17. Average weekly hours
HSC series E128, E129, E130, E131, E132, E133, E134, E135; Statistics Canada, CANSIM series v2461119 and v2641490, and authors' calculations.

18. Unemployment rate
HSC series D127, D132, and D491 and CANSIM series v2461224.

19. Long-term interest rate
HSC(1) series H605, *HSC* series J475, and Bank of Canada series B14013.

20. Short-term interest rate
HSC series J471 and Bank of Canada series B14060.

21. Federal government revenues
HSC series H18 and CANSIM series v499985.

22. Federal government outlays
HSC series H34 and CANSIM series v500016.

23. Federal government surplus(+)/deficit(-)
HSC series H18 and H34 and CANSIM series v499985 and v500016.

24. Gross federal debt
CANSIM series v151537.

25. M1
Bank of Canada series B2033.

26. M2+
Bank of Canada series B2037.

27. M1 velocity
Series 1 multiplied by series 11 divided by series 25.

28. M2+ velocity
Series 1 multiplied by series 11 divided by series 26.

29. Exchange rate
HSC series J562 and CANSIM series v37426.

30. Current account
HSC series G83 and CANSIM series v114421.

Year		1926	1927	1928	1929	1930	1931	1932	1933	1934	1935
Real GDP (billions of 1997 dollars)	1	61.2	67.0	73.1	73.4	70.3	61.4	55.0	51.3	57.6	62.1
Real consumption expenditure (billions of 1997 dollars)	2	35.6	39.8	43.6	46.3	44.3	42.2	38.9	37.9	39.9	41.6
Real investment (billions of 1997 dollars)	3	12.4	14.5	16.3	14.4	12.7	4.2	1.0	0.0	2.8	4.5
Real government expenditures (billions of 1997 dollars)	4	10.0	10.5	10.6	11.9	13.0	13.8	13.3	11.2	11.9	12.4
Real exports (billions of 1997 dollars)	5	12.1	12.2	13.8	13.0	11.3	10.1	9.4	9.5	10.7	11.8
Real imports (billions of 1997 dollars)	6	8.9	9.9	11.1	12.1	11.0	8.8	7.6	7.2	7.7	8.2
Real net exports (billions of 1997 dollars)	7	3.2	2.3	2.7	0.9	0.3	1.3	1.8	2.2	3.0	3.5
Potential GDP (billions of 1997 dollars)	8	62.0	63.8	65.7	67.7	69.7	71.8	73.9	76.1	78.4	80.8
Fluctuations around potential GDP (percentage)	9	–1.2	5.0	11.3	8.5	0.8	–14.5	–25.6	–32.6	–26.6	–23.2
Real GDP growth rate (percent per year)	10	—	9.5	9.1	0.4	–4.3	–12.7	–10.4	–6.7	12.1	7.8
GDP deflator (1997 = 100)	11	8.7	8.6	8.5	8.6	8.4	7.9	7.1	7.0	7.1	7.1
CPI (1992 = 100)	12	10.9	10.8	10.8	11.0	10.9	9.8	8.9	8.5	8.6	8.7
Inflation rate (GDP deflator percent per year)	13	—	–1.1	–0.6	1.1	–2.5	–6.2	–9.3	–1.7	1.4	0.3
Inflation rate (CPI percent per year)	14	0	–0.9	0	1.9	–0.9	–10.1	–9.2	–4.5	1.2	1.2
Labour force (millions)	15	3.7	3.8	3.9	4.0	4.1	4.2	4.2	4.3	4.3	4.4
Labour force participation rate (percentage)	16	57.8	57.9	58.0	58.1	58.2	58.3	58.2	58.0	57.9	57.8
Average weekly hours (hours per week)	17	—	—	—	—	—	—	—	—	—	—
Unemployment rate (percentage)	18	2.9	1.8	1.7	2.9	9.1	11.6	17.6	19.3	14.5	14.2
Long-term interest rate (percent per year)	19	4.9	4.6	4.5	4.9	4.7	4.6	5.1	4.6	4.0	3.6
Short-term interest rate (percent per year)	20	—	—	—	—	—	—	—	—	2.5	1.5
Federal government revenues (billions of dollars)	21	0.4	0.4	0.5	0.5	0.4	0.3	0.3	0.3	0.4	0.4
Federal government outlays (billions of dollars)	22	0.4	0.4	0.4	0.4	0.4	0.4	0.5	0.5	0.5	0.5
Federal government surplus (+)/deficit(–) (billions of dollars)	23	0	0.1	0.1	0	–0.1	–0.1	–0.2	–0.1	–0.1	–0.2
Gross federal debt (billions of dollars)	24	2.8	2.8	2.7	2.7	2.6	2.7	2.9	3.1	3.2	3.5
M1 (billions of dollars)	25	—	—	—	—	—	—	—	—	—	—
M2+ (billions of dollars)	26	—	—	—	—	—	—	—	—	—	—
M1 velocity (GDP/M1)	27	—	—	—	—	—	—	—	—	—	—
M2+ velocity (GDP/M2+)	28	—	—	—	—	—	—	—	—	—	—
Exchange rate (U.S. dollars per Canadian dollar)	29	1.00	1.00	1.00	1.00	1.00	0.96	0.88	0.92	1.01	0.99
Current account balance (billions of dollars)	30	0.1	0	0	–0.3	–0.3	–0.2	–0.1	0	0.1	0.1

1936	1937	1938	1939	1940	1941	1942	1943	1944	1945	1946	1947	1948	1949	
64.8	71.3	71.9	77.2	88.1	100.8	119.5	124.3	129.2	126.3	123.0	128.2	131.4	136.4	1
43.5	46.2	45.6	46.9	50.3	53.7	55.1	56.7	60.8	66.9	74.4	79.6	77.7	82.1	2
4.0	8.3	8.8	11.3	6.4	0.5	−20.7	−29.9	−38.0	−19.0	9.5	19.5	23.6	23.4	3
12.5	12.6	14.1	15.0	26.5	38.3	80.2	87.7	100.7	69.3	32.8	24.7	23.4	25.9	4
14.2	14.5	13.1	14.4	16.4	21.6	19.3	26.8	25.9	25.2	21.2	21.0	21.7	20.4	5
9.3	10.3	9.6	10.3	11.5	13.3	14.3	17.0	20.2	16.0	14.8	16.7	15.0	15.4	6
4.8	4.2	3.4	4.1	4.9	8.3	5.0	9.8	5.7	9.2	6.3	4.4	6.7	5.0	7
83.2	85.7	88.2	90.9	93.6	97.3	101.1	105.1	109.3	113.7	118.3	123.2	128.2	133.6	8
−22.1	−16.7	−18.5	−15.0	−5.8	3.6	18.2	18.2	18.2	11.1	3.9	4.1	2.4	2.1	9
4.4	10.0	0.8	7.4	14.1	14.4	18.6	4.0	4.0	−2.2	−2.7	4.3	2.5	3.8	10
7.4	7.6	7.6	7.5	7.9	8.5	8.9	9.2	9.4	9.7	10.0	10.8	12.2	12.7	11
8.8	9.1	9.2	9.2	9.5	10.1	10.5	10.7	10.8	10.9	11.2	12.3	14.0	14.5	12
3.3	2.6	0	−0.9	4.7	7.9	4.5	3.5	3.1	2.5	2.9	8.8	12.3	4.3	13
1.1	3.4	1.1	0	3.3	6.3	4.0	1.9	0.9	0.9	2.8	9.8	13.8	3.6	14
4.5	4.5	4.6	4.6	4.6	4.5	4.6	4.6	4.5	4.5	4.8	4.9	5.0	5.2	15
57.6	57.5	57.4	57.2	56.6	55.4	56.5	58.0	57.4	56.2	55.0	54.9	54.6	54.4	16
—	—	—	—	—	—	—	—	—	44.1	42.7	42.5	42.3	42.2	17
12.8	9.1	11.4	11.4	9.0	4.1	2.7	1.4	1.2	1.4	[b]3.4	2.2	2.3	2.8	18
[b]3.0	3.2	3.1	3.2	3.3	3.1	3.1	3.0	3.0	2.9	2.6	2.6	2.9	2.8	19
0.9	0.7	0.6	0.7	0.7	0.6	0.5	0.5	0.4	0.4	0.4	0.4	0.4	0.5	20
0.5	0.5	0.5	0.6	0.9	1.5	2.3	2.8	2.7	3.0	3.0	2.9	2.8	2.6	21
0.5	0.5	0.6	0.7	1.3	1.9	4.4	5.3	5.2	5.1	2.6	2.2	2.2	2.4	22
−0.1	0	−0.1	−0.1	−0.4	−0.4	−2.1	−2.6	−2.6	−2.1	0.4	0.7	0.6	0.1	23
3.5	3.6	3.6	3.7	4.0	5.0	6.6	8.8	11.8	14.9	17.9	17.7	17.2	16.9	24
—	—	—	—	—	—	—	—	—	—	—	—	—	—	25
—	—	—	—	—	—	—	—	—	—	—	—	—	—	26
—	—	—	—	—	—	—	—	—	—	—	—	—	—	27
—	—	—	—	—	—	—	—	—	—	—	—	—	—	28
1.00	1.00	0.99	0.96	0.90	0.90	0.90	0.90	0.90	0.91	1.00	1.00	1.00	0.97	29
0.2	0.2	0.1	0.1	0.2	0.5	0.1	0.7	0.1	0.7	[b]0.08	0	0.1	0	30

Year		1950	1951	1952	1953	1954	1955	1956	1957	1958	1959
Real GDP (billions of 1997 dollars)	1	146.7	154.1	167.8	176.5	174.3	190.7	206.9	211.7	216.6	224.8
Real consumption expenditure (billions of 1997 dollars)	2	87.5	88.2	94.4	100.9	104.6	113.6	122.1	126.6	131.2	138.5
Real investment (billions of 1997 dollars)	3	27.8	26.2	23.4	26.0	21.8	29.3	37.5	38.0	35.2	38.0
Real government expenditures (billions of 1997 dollars)	4	27.9	36.4	44.8	46.2	44.4	45.4	46.6	45.8	47.2	46.8
Real exports (billions of 1997 dollars)	5	20.3	22.2	24.7	24.5	23.6	25.4	27.3	27.5	27.4	28.5
Real imports (billions of 1997 dollars)	6	16.8	18.9	19.5	21.2	20.2	22.9	26.5	26.2	24.4	26.9
Real net exports (billions of 1997 dollars)	7	3.5	3.3	5.2	3.3	3.4	2.5	0.7	1.3	3.0	1.6
Potential GDP (billions of 1997 dollars)	8	139.1	145.0	151.1	157.6	164.4	171.5	179.0	186.9	195.3	204.1
Fluctuations around potential GDP (percentage)	9	5.5	6.3	11.0	12.0	6.0	11.2	15.5	13.3	10.9	10.2
Real GDP growth rate (percent per year)	10	7.6	5.0	8.9	5.1	–1.2	9.4	8.4	2.4	2.3	3.8
GDP deflator (1997 = 100)	11	13.0	14.5	15.1	15.1	15.3	15.4	16.0	16.3	16.6	16.9
CPI (1992 = 100)	12	14.9	16.4	16.9	16.7	16.8	16.8	17.1	17.6	18.0	18.3
Inflation rate (GDP deflator percent per year)	13	2.4	11.3	4.4	–0.2	1.6	0.6	3.7	2.1	1.5	2.0
Inflation rate (CPI percent per year)	14	2.8	10.1	3.0	–1.2	0.6	0	1.8	2.9	2.3	1.7
Labour force (millions)	15	5.2	5.2	5.3	5.4	5.5	5.6	5.8	6.0	6.1	6.2
Labour force participation rate (percentage)	16	53.7	53.7	53.5	53.1	52.9	52.9	53.5	54.0	53.9	53.8
Average weekly hours (hours per week)	17	42.3	41.7	41.5	41.3	40.7	41.0	41.0	40.4	40.2	40.7
Unemployment rate (percentage)	18	3.6	2.4	2.9	3.0	4.6	4.4	3.4	4.6	7.0	6.0
Long-term interest rate (percent per year)	19	2.8	3.2	3.6	3.7	3.1	3.1	3.6	4.2	4.5	5.0
Short-term interest rate (percent per year)	20	0.6	0.8	1.1	1.7	1.4	1.6	2.9	3.8	2.3	4.8
Federal government revenues (billions of dollars)	21	3.1	4.0	4.6	4.7	4.4	4.7	5.5	5.4	5.1	5.8
Federal government outlays (billions of dollars)	22	2.9	3.8	4.6	4.7	4.7	4.8	5.2	5.5	6.0	6.3
Federal government surplus (+)/deficit(–) (billions of dollars)	23	0.2	0.2	–0.1	0	–0.2	–0.1	0.3	–0.1	–0.8	–0.4
Gross federal debt (billions of dollars)	24	16.7	16.7	16.8	17.4	17.6	17.6	18.7	18.0	18.0	19.7
M1 (billions of dollars)	25	—	—	—	4.2	4.4	4.8	4.8	4.8	5.4	5.2
M2+ (billions of dollars)	26	—	—	—	—	—	—	—	—	—	—
M1 velocity (GDP/M1)	27	—	—	—	6.3	6.1	6.1	6.9	7.2	6.6	7.3
M2+ velocity (GDP/M2+)	28	—	—	—	—	—	—	—	—	—	—
Exchange rate (U.S. dollars per Canadian dollar)	29	[b]0.95	0.95	1.02	1.02	1.03	1.01	1.02	1.04	1.03	1.04
Current account balance (billions of dollars)	30	–0.1	–0.1	0	–0.1	–0.1	–0.2	–0.3	–0.4	–0.3	–0.4

1960	1961	1962	1963	1964	1965	1966	1967	1968	1969	1970	1971	1972	1973	
231.3	237.9	254.2	267.1	284.6	303.0	322.9	332.5	350.3	369.0	378.6	399.6	420.9	451.2	1
143.3	144.9	152.3	158.7	167.1	176.9	185.6	192.5	201.1	210.9	214.5	227.4	243.1	260.0	2
37.3	33.9	39.4	41.6	46.2	54.5	58.8	52.5	54.3	60.9	52.3	56.8	61.1	70.6	3
47.9	54.5	57.0	59.0	62.1	64.9	70.7	76.9	81.9	85.4	92.9	96.8	99.8	104.5	4
29.7	31.9	33.4	36.4	41.4	43.2	49.1	54.3	61.2	66.1	72.3	75.8	82.3	91.1	5
26.9	27.4	28.0	28.5	32.1	36.5	41.4	43.6	48.1	54.4	53.4	57.3	65.5	75.1	6
2.8	4.5	5.4	7.9	9.2	6.8	7.7	10.6	13.0	11.7	18.9	18.6	16.9	16.0	7
212.0	225.8	240.1	254.9	270.2	285.9	302.1	318.7	335.7	353.1	370.8	388.3	406.3	423.7	8
9.1	5.3	5.8	4.8	5.3	6.0	6.9	4.3	4.3	4.5	2.1	2.9	3.6	6.5	9
2.9	2.8	6.8	5.1	6.5	6.5	6.6	3.0	5.3	5.3	2.6	5.5	5.4	7.2	10
17.1	17.2	17.5	17.8	18.3	18.9	19.9	20.8	21.6	22.5	23.6	24.4	25.9	28.3	11
18.5	18.7	18.9	19.2	19.6	20.0	20.8	21.5	22.4	23.4	24.2	24.9	26.1	28.1	12
1.3	0.4	1.6	2.1	2.6	3.5	5.3	4.1	4.0	4.3	4.9	3.5	6.0	9.2	13
1.1	1.1	1.1	1.6	2.1	2.0	4.0	3.4	4.2	4.5	3.4	2.9	4.8	7.7	14
6.4	6.5	6.6	6.7	6.9	7.1	7.4	7.7	7.9	8.2	8.4	8.6	8.9	9.3	15
54.2	54.1	53.9	53.8	54.1	54.4	55.1	55.5	55.5	55.8	57.8	58.1	58.6	59.7	16
40.7	40.5	40.3	40.2	40.2	40.1	39.8	39.1	38.7	38.1	37.5	37.4	37.4	36.8	17
7.0	7.1	5.9	5.5	4.7	3.9	[b]3.3	3.8	4.5	4.4	5.7	6.2	6.2	5.6	18
5.1	5.0	5.1	5.1	5.1	5.3	5.7	6.0	6.7	7.6	7.9	7.0	7.2	7.6	19
3.2	2.8	4.1	3.6	3.8	4.0	5.0	4.6	6.3	7.2	6.0	3.5	3.6	5.5	20
6.2	6.6	6.7	7.0	8.0	8.8	9.6	10.5	11.7	13.9	14.9	16.5	18.8	21.9	21
6.6	7.1	7.6	7.7	8.1	8.6	9.8	11.0	12.2	13.2	15.1	17.2	19.6	21.8	22
−0.3	−0.5	−0.9	−0.7	−0.1	0.2	−0.2	−0.5	−0.5	0.7	−0.2	−0.7	−0.9	0.1	23
20.4	20.9	22.8	24.5	26.2	26.8	27.7	29.8	32.0	34.4	35.8	39.9	43.8	46.2	24
5.5	5.9	6.1	6.3	6.7	7.1	7.7	8.4	8.9	9.2	9.8	11.5	13.2	14.6	25
—	—	—	—	—	—	—	—	34.0	37.1	40.9	46.2	53.3	63.5	26
7.2	6.9	7.3	7.6	7.8	8.1	8.4	8.2	8.5	9.0	9.1	8.5	8.3	8.7	27
—	—	—	—	—	—	—	—	2.2	2.2	2.2	2.1	2.0	2.0	28
1.03	0.99	0.94	0.93	0.93	0.93	0.93	0.93	0.93	0.93	0.96	0.99	1.01	1.00	29
−0.3	−0.3	−0.3	−0.2	−0.1	−0.4	−0.4	−0.3	−0.3	−0.5	0.1	−0.3	−0.6	−0.5	30

Year		1974	1975	1976	1977	1978	1979	1980	1981	1982	1983
Real GDP (billions of 1997 dollars)	1	469.9	480.3	506.7	524.2	545.6	568.5	576.4	594.1	576.7	592.7
Real consumption expenditure (billions of 1997 dollars)	2	273.5	284.8	300.2	309.2	319.7	328.6	335.2	338.9	330.5	339.9
Real investment (billions of 1997 dollars)	3	79.9	75.5	81.8	78.4	81.4	97.8	97.7	117.0	88.1	95.5
Real government expenditures (billions of 1997 dollars)	4	111.1	118.6	120.9	126.5	128.8	130.1	134.5	136.2	139.0	141.3
Real exports (billions of 1997 dollars)	5	88.7	83.0	91.9	99.0	109.8	113.8	115.9	120.2	118.7	126.3
Real imports (billions of 1997 dollars)	6	83.3	81.6	88.0	88.9	94.0	101.7	106.9	118.2	99.6	110.3
Real net exports (billions of 1997 dollars)	7	5.4	1.4	3.8	10.1	15.8	12.1	9.0	1.9	19.1	15.9
Potential GDP (billions of 1997 dollars)	8	440.4	463.2	484.4	504.0	524.1	547.7	565.7	581.3	598.3	616.7
Fluctuations around potential GDP (percentage)	9	6.7	3.7	4.6	4.0	4.1	3.8	1.9	2.2	–3.6	–3.9
Real GDP growth rate (percent per year)	10	4.1	2.2	5.5	3.5	4.1	4.2	1.4	3.0	–2.9	2.8
GDP deflator (1997 = 100)	11	32.5	35.8	39.1	41.8	44.6	48.8	54.1	60.1	65.1	68.7
CPI (1992 = 100)	12	31.1	34.5	37.1	40.0	43.6	47.6	52.4	58.9	65.3	69.1
Inflation rate (GDP deflator percent per year)	13	14.9	10.2	9.2	6.8	6.6	9.5	10.9	11.0	8.3	5.5
Inflation rate (CPI percent per year)	14	10.7	10.9	7.5	7.8	9.0	9.2	10.1	12.4	10.9	5.8
Labour force (millions)	15	9.6	10.0	10.5	10.8	11.1	11.5	11.9	12.2	12.3	12.5
Labour force participation rate (percentage)	16	60.5	61.1	61.5	61.8	62.6	63.6	64.2	65.0	64.4	64.7
Average weekly hours (hours per week)	17	36.0	35.5	35.4	35.4	35.7	35.8	35.2	34.7	34.5	34.5
Unemployment rate (percentage)	18	5.3	6.9	[b]7.0	8.0	8.3	7.5	7.5	7.6	11.0	11.9
Long-term interest rate (percent per year)	19	8.9	9.0	9.2	8.7	9.3	10.2	12.5	15.2	14.3	11.8
Short-term interest rate (percent per year)	20	7.8	7.4	8.9	7.3	8.7	11.7	12.7	17.8	13.7	9.3
Federal government revenues (billions of dollars)	21	29.0	30.9	34.5	35.3	36.7	42.0	49.1	63.4	65.1	67.4
Federal government outlays (billions of dollars)	22	28.4	35.4	38.7	43.5	48.2	52.5	60.8	71.7	83.6	91.0
Federal government surplus (+)/deficit(–) (billions of dollars)	23	0.6	–4.5	–4.2	–8.2	–11.4	–10.4	–11.8	–8.3	–18.5	–23.6
Gross federal debt (billions of dollars)	24	49.1	55.1	61.9	69.7	82.4	100.5	110.6	127.7	144.5	173.1
M1 (billions of dollars)	25	15.5	19.0	19.4	21.7	23.6	24.6	27.3	27.4	28.5	30.8
M2+ (billions of dollars)	26	73.7	87.3	102.0	117.8	136.7	160.9	187.5	209.6	226.3	241.6
M1 velocity (GDP/M1)	27	9.9	9.1	10.2	10.1	10.3	11.3	11.4	13.0	13.2	13.2
M2+ velocity (GDP/M2+)	28	2.1	2.0	1.9	1.9	1.8	1.7	1.7	1.7	1.7	1.7
Exchange rate (U.S. dollars per Canadian dollar)	29	1.02	0.98	1.01	0.94	0.88	0.85	0.86	0.83	0.81	0.81
Current account balance (billions of dollars)	30	–1.1	–2.1	–1.9	–1.9	–2.3	–2.5	–1.8	–3.7	0.6	–0.8

1984	1985	1986	1987	1988	1989	1990	1991	1992	1993	1994	1995	1996	1997	
626.4	660.3	677.8	705.7	740.6	759.8	762.4	747.9	754.8	772.5	810.0	832.1	845.2	882.7	1
355.1	373.6	388.5	404.7	422.4	437.4	443.1	437.2	444.8	452.7	467.0	476.9	488.9	510.7	2
108.8	121.3	125.0	137.9	153.9	163.0	149.2	137.5	131.8	133.6	146.6	150.7	151.8	183.0	3
143.0	149.2	151.9	153.9	161.0	165.5	171.6	176.6	178.6	178.7	176.5	175.6	173.5	171.8	4
149.8	158.0	166.3	171.8	188.1	190.5	199.5	204.1	220.2	244.3	276.3	301.3	319.1	348.6	5
130.3	141.8	154.0	162.6	184.9	196.6	201.1	207.6	220.5	236.7	256.4	272.3	288.2	331.3	6
19.4	16.2	12.4	9.2	3.2	–6.1	–1.6	–3.5	–0.3	7.5	19.9	29.0	30.9	17.3	7
634.6	657.7	679.2	699.4	721.8	740.6	751.1	760.0	770.2	784.3	805.2	829.6	857.2	890.8	8
–1.3	0.4	–0.2	0.9	2.6	2.6	1.5	–1.6	–2.0	–1.5	0.6	0.3	–1.4	–0.9	9
5.7	5.4	2.6	4.1	4.9	2.5	0.3	–1.9	0.9	2.3	4.9	2.7	1.6	4.4	10
70.9	73.2	75.4	78.8	82.4	86.1	88.9	91.5	92.7	94.0	95.1	97.2	98.8	100.0	11
72.1	75.0	78.1	81.5	84.8	89.0	93.3	98.5	100.0	101.8	102.0	104.2	105.9	107.6	12
3.2	3.2	3.0	4.5	4.6	4.5	3.3	2.9	1.3	1.4	1.2	2.2	1.6	1.2	13
4.3	4.0	4.1	4.4	4.0	5.0	4.8	5.6	1.5	1.8	0.2	2.2	1.6	1.6	14
12.7	13.0	13.3	13.5	13.8	14.0	14.2	14.3	14.4	14.5	14.6	14.8	14.9	15.2	15
65.0	65.5	66.0	66.4	66.8	67.2	67.1	66.5	65.7	65.4	65.2	64.9	64.7	64.9	16
34.6	34.8	34.8	34.7	35.3	35.7	35.2	34.5	34.0	34.5	34.9	34.6	34.4	34.2	17
11.3	10.7	9.6	8.8	7.8	7.5	8.1	10.3	11.2	11.4	10.4	9.4	9.6	9.1	18
12.8	11.0	9.5	10.0	10.2	9.9	10.9	9.8	8.8	7.8	8.6	8.3	7.5	6.4	19
11.1	9.4	9.0	8.2	9.5	12.1	12.8	8.8	6.6	4.8	5.5	7.1	4.2	3.2	20
73.5	80.2	88.6	97.3	106.6	113.7	120.9	125.8	130.1	128.7	131.9	140.3	148.0	162.6	21
102.2	112.3	114.4	120.6	128.9	138.5	151.5	161.2	164.4	167.2	165.9	172.4	166.1	160.1	22
–28.7	–32.2	–25.8	–23.3	–22.4	–24.8	–30.6	–35.4	–34.4	–38.5	–34.0	–32.1	–18.1	2.5	23
209.3	250.5	284.0	318.3	349.9	380.0	406.6	444.6	476.1	514.4	557.6	595.9	634.9	651.1	24
31.1	34.4	36.7	39.8	42.6	44.1	43.7	46.2	49.2	56.5	61.0	65.5	77.9	86.5	25
262.6	291.2	324.6	351.9	398.8	456.0	499.7	534.8	562.1	582.5	593.1	619.3	643.5	633.7	26
14.3	14.1	13.9	14.0	14.3	14.8	15.5	14.8	14.2	12.8	12.6	12.3	10.7	10.2	27
1.7	1.7	1.6	1.6	1.5	1.4	1.4	1.3	1.2	1.2	1.3	1.3	1.3	1.4	28
0.77	0.73	0.72	0.75	0.81	0.84	0.86	0.87	0.83	0.78	0.73	0.73	0.73	0.72	29
–0.4	–2.0	–3.9	–4.5	–4.6	–6.5	–5.8	–6.4	–6.3	–7.0	–4.4	–1.5	1.2	–2.8	30

Year		1998	1999	2000	2001
Real GDP (billions of 1997 dollars)	1	919.0	967.6	1013.1	1026.9
Real consumption expenditure (billions of 1997 dollars)	2	524.9	545.6	566.3	581.4
Real investment (billions of 1997 dollars)	3	184.9	200.9	219.3	206.4
Real government expenditures (billions of 1997 dollars)	4	177.3	180.7	185.0	191.2
Real exports (billions of 1997 dollars)	5	380.3	416.8	451.7	433.8
Real imports (billions of 1997 dollars)	6	348.4	376.5	409.3	385.9
Real net exports (billions of 1997 dollars)	7	31.9	40.4	42.4	47.8
Potential GDP (billions of 1997 dollars)	8	926.4	962.8	1001.1	1035.1
Fluctuations around potential GDP (percentage)	9	–0.8	0.5	1.2	–0.8
Real GDP growth rate (percent per year)	10	4.1	5.3	4.7	1.4
GDP deflator (1997 = 100)	11	99.6	101.3	105.2	106.3
CPI (1992 = 100)	12	108.6	110.5	113.5	116.4
Inflation rate (GDP deflator percent per year)	13	–0.4	1.7	3.8	1.0
Inflation rate (CPI percent per year)	14	0.9	1.7	2.7	2.6
Labour force (millions)	15	15.4	15.7	16.0	16.2
Labour force participation rate (percentage)	16	65.1	65.6	65.9	66.0
Average weekly hours (hours per week)	17	33.9	34.2	34.5	33.8
Unemployment rate (percentage)	18	8.3	7.6	6.8	7.2
Long-term interest rate (percent per year)	19	5.5	5.7	5.9	5.8
Short-term interest rate (percent per year)	20	4.7	4.7	5.5	3.7
Federal government revenues (billions of dollars)	21	167.5	177.1	193.2	191.4
Federal government outlays (billions of dollars)	22	163.7	172.3	179.5	184.7
Federal government surplus (+)/deficit(–) (billions of dollars)	23	3.8	4.8	13.7	6.7
Gross federal debt (billions of dollars)	24	645.7	648.4	648.2	644.9
M1 (billions of dollars)	25	93.6	101.2	116.1	133.8
M2+ (billions of dollars)	26	641.4	675.0	712.4	771.8
M1 velocity (GDP/M1)	27	9.8	9.7	9.2	8.2
M2+ velocity (GDP/M2+)	28	1.4	1.5	1.5	1.4
Exchange rate (U.S. dollars per Canadian dollar)	29	0.67	0.67	0.67	0.65
Current account balance (billions of dollars)	30	–2.8	0.5	6.9	7.5

GLOSSARY

Above full-employment equilibrium A macroeconomic equilibrium in which real GDP exceeds potential GDP. (p. 510)

Absolute advantage A person has an absolute advantage if that person can produce more goods with a given amount of resources than another person can; a country has an absolute advantage if its output per unit of inputs of all goods is larger than that of another country. (p. 45)

After-tax income Total income minus tax payments by households to governments. (p. 348)

Aggregate demand The relationship between the quantity of real GDP demanded and the price level. (p. 505)

Aggregate hours The total number of hours worked by all the people employed, both full time and part time, during a year. (p. 483)

Aggregate planned expenditure The expenditure that households, firms, governments, and foreigners plan to undertake in given circumstances. It is the sum of planned consumption expenditure, planned investment, planned government expenditures on goods and services, and planned exports minus planned imports. (p. 533)

Aggregate production function The relationship between the quantity of real GDP supplied and the quantities of labour and capital and the state of technology. (pp. 500, 713)

Allocative efficiency A situation in which we cannot produce more of any good without giving up some of another good that we value more highly. (p. 39)

Anti-combine law A law that regulates and prohibits certain kinds of market behaviour, such as monopoly and monopolistic practices. (p. 394)

Automatic fiscal policy A change in fiscal policy that is triggered by the state of the economy. (p. 562)

Automatic stabilizers Mechanisms that stabilize real GDP without explicit action by the government. (p. 566)

Autonomous expenditure The sum of those components of aggregate planned expenditure that are not influenced by real GDP. Autonomous expenditure equals the sum of investment, government expenditures, exports, and the autonomous parts of consumption expenditure and imports. (p. 535)

Autonomous tax multiplier The magnification effect of a change in autonomous taxes on equilibrium expenditure and real GDP. (p. 564)

Autonomous taxes Taxes that do not vary with real GDP. (p. 562)

Average cost pricing rule A rule that sets price to cover cost including normal profit, which means setting the price equal to average total cost. (pp. 277, 398)

Average fixed cost Total fixed cost per unit of output. (p. 224)

Average product The average product of a factor of production. It equals total product divided by the quantity of the factor employed. (p. 219)

Average tax rate The percentage of income that is paid in tax. (pp. 359, 382)

Average total cost Total cost per unit of output. (p. 224)

Average variable cost Total variable cost per unit of output. (p. 224)

Balance of payments accounts A country's record of international trading, borrowing, and lending. (p. 810)

Balanced budget A government budget in which revenues and outlays are equal. (p. 557)

Bank of Canada The central bank of Canada. (p. 606)

Bank rate The interest rate that the Bank of Canada charges the chartered banks on the reserves it lends them. (p. 609)

Barriers to entry Legal or natural constraints that protect a firm from potential competitors. (p. 262)

Barter The direct exchange of one good or service for other goods and services. (p. 582)

Base period The period in which the CPI is defined to be 100. (p. 490)

Below full-employment equilibrium A macroeconomic equilibrium in which potential GDP exceeds real GDP. (p. 510)

Big tradeoff The conflict between equity and efficiency. (pp. 10, 115, 361)

Bilateral monopoly A situation in which a single seller (a monopoly) faces a single buyer (a monopsony). (p. 345)

Black market An illegal trading arrangement in which the price exceeds the legally imposed price ceiling. (p. 126)

Budget deficit A government's budget balance that is negative—outlays exceed revenues. (p. 557)

Budget line The limits to a household's consumption choices. (p. 172)

Budget surplus A government's budget balance that is positive—revenues exceed outlays. (p. 557)

Business cycle The periodic but irregular up-and-down movement in production and jobs. (p. 8)

Canadian interest rate differential A gap equal to the Canadian interest rate minus the foreign interest rate. (p. 817)

Capacity output The output at which average total cost is a minimum—the output at the bottom of the U-shaped *ATC* curve. (p. 287)

Capital The tools, equipment, buildings, and other constructions that businesses now use to produce goods and services. (p. 4)

Capital account A record of foreign investment in a country minus its investment abroad. (p. 810)

Capital accumulation The growth of capital resources. (p. 40)

Capital consumption The decrease in the capital stock that results from wear and tear and obsolescence. (p. 461)

Capital gain The increase in the price of a stock. (p. 831)

Capital loss The decrease in the price of a stock. (p. 831)

Capture theory A theory of regulation that states that the regulations are supplied to satisfy the demand of producers to maximize producer surplus—to maximize economic profit. (p. 395)

Cartel A group of firms that has entered into a collusive agreement to restrict output and increase prices and profits. (p. 295)

Central bank A public authority that supervises financial institutions and markets and conducts monetary policy. (p. 606)

Ceteris paribus Other things being equal—all other relevant things remaining the same. (p. 13)

Chain-weighted output index An index that uses the prices of two adjacent years to calculate the real GDP growth rate. (p. 466)

Change in demand A change in buyers' plans that occurs when some influence on those plans other than the price of the good changes. It is illustrated by a shift of the demand curve. (p. 63)

Change in supply A change in sellers' plans that occurs when some influence on those plans other than the price of the good changes. It is illustrated by a shift of the supply curve. (p. 67)

Change in the quantity demanded A change in buyers' plans that occurs when the price of a good changes but all other influences on buyers' plans remain unchanged. It is illustrated by a movement along the demand curve. (p. 65)

Change in the quantity supplied A change in sellers' plans that occurs when the price of a good changes but all other influences on sellers' plans remain unchanged. It is illustrated by a movement along the supply curve. (p. 68)

Chartered bank A private firm, chartered under the Bank Act of 1992 to receive deposits and make loans. (p. 585)

Classical growth theory A theory of economic growth based on the view that real GDP growth is temporary and that when real GDP per person increases above subsistence level, a population explosion brings real GDP back to subsistence level. (p. 717)

Coase theorem The proposition that if property rights exist, if only a small number of parties are involved, and transactions costs are low, then private transactions are efficient. (p. 419)

Collusive agreement An agreement between two (or more) producers to restrict output, raise the price, and increase profits. (p. 295)

Command system A method of organizing production that uses a managerial hierarchy. (p. 201)

Comparative advantage A person or country has a comparative advantage in an activity if that person or country can perform the activity at a lower opportunity cost than anyone else or any other country. (p. 42)

Competitive market A market that has many buyers and many sellers, so no single buyer or seller can influence the price. (p. 60)

Complement A good that is used in conjunction with another good. (p. 63)

Constant returns to scale Features of a firm's technology that lead to constant long-run average cost as output increases. When constant returns to scale are present, the *LRAC* curve is horizontal. (p. 231)

Consumer equilibrium A situation in which a consumer has allocated all his or her available income in the way that, given the prices of goods and services, maximizes his or her total utility. (p. 157)

Consumer Price Index (CPI) An index that measures the average of the prices paid by urban consumers for a fixed "basket" of the consumer goods and services. (p. 490)

Consumer surplus The value of a good minus the price paid for it, summed over the quantity bought. (p. 107)

Consumption expenditure The total payment for consumer goods and services. (p. 459)

Consumption function The relationship between consumption expenditure and disposable income, other things remaining the same. (p. 528)

Contestable market A market in which firms can enter and leave so easily that firms in the market face competition from potential entrants. (p. 302)

Contractionary fiscal policy A decrease in government expenditures or an increase in taxes. (p. 569)

Cooperative equilibrium The outcome of a game in which the players make and share the monopoly profit. (p. 301)

Copyright A government-sanctioned exclusive right granted to the inventor of a good, service, or productive process to produce, use, and sell the invention for a given number of years. (p. 425)

Cost of living The amount of money it takes to buy the goods and services that the average family consumes. (p. 7)

Cost-push inflation An inflation that results from an initial increase in costs. (p. 653)

Credit union A cooperative organization that operates under the Co-operative Credit Association Act of 1992 and that receives deposits and makes loans to its members. (p. 586)

Creditor nation A country that during its entire history has invested more in the rest of the world than other countries have invested in it. (p. 812)

Cross elasticity of demand The responsiveness of the demand for a good to a change in the price of a substitute or complement, other things remaining the same. It is calculated as the percentage change in the quantity demanded of the good divided by the percentage change in the price of the substitute or complement. (p. 91)

Cross-section graph A graph that shows the values of an economic variable for different groups in a population at a point in time. (p. 18)

Crowding in The tendency for expansionary fiscal policy to increase investment. (p. 633)

Crowding out The tendency for an expansionary fiscal policy action to decrease investment. (p. 633)

Crown Corporation A publicly owned firm in Canada. (p. 394)

Currency The coins and Bank of Canada notes that we use today. (p. 583)

Currency appreciation The rise in the value of one currency in terms of another currency. (p. 815)

Currency depreciation The fall in the value of one currency in terms of another currency. (p. 815)

Currency drain An increase in currency held outside the banks. (p. 613)

Current account A record of the payments for imports of goods and services, receipts from exports of goods and services, net interest paid abroad, and net transfers. (pp. 449, 810)

Cyclical surplus or deficit The actual surplus or deficit minus the structural surplus or deficit. (p. 567)

Cyclical unemployment The fluctuations in unemployment over the business cycle. (p. 488)

Deadweight loss A measure of inefficiency. It is equal to the decrease in consumer surplus and producer surplus that results from an inefficient level of production. (p. 112)

Debtor nation A country that during its entire history has borrowed more from the rest of the world than it has lent to it. (p. 812)

Deflation A falling cost of living—a process in which the price level is falling. (pp. 7, 447)

Demand The relationship between the quantity of a good that consumers plan to buy and the price of the good when all other influences on buyers' plans remain the same. It is described by a demand schedule and illustrated by a demand curve. (p. 62)

Demand curve A curve that shows the relationship between the quantity demanded of a good and its price when all other influences on consumers' planned purchases remain the same. (p. 62)

Demand for labour The relationship between the quantity of labour demanded and the real wage rate when all other influences on firms' hiring plans remain the same. (p. 683)

Demand for money curve The relationship between the quantity of money demanded and the interest rate when all other influences on the amount of money that people wish to hold remain the same. (p. 592)

Demand-pull inflation An inflation that results from an initial increase in aggregate demand. (p. 651)

Deposit multiplier The amount by which an increase in bank reserves is multiplied to calculate the increase in bank deposits. (p. 588)

Depository institution A firm that takes deposits from households and firms and makes loans to other households and firms. (p. 585)

Depreciation The decrease in the capital stock that results from wear and tear and obsolescence. (p. 461)

Derived demand Demand for a factor of production, which is derived from the demand for the goods and services produced by that factor. (p. 317)

Desired reserve ratio The ratio of reserves to deposits that banks wish to hold. (p. 587)

Diminishing marginal rate of substitution The general tendency for a person to be willing to give up less of good *y* to get one more unit of good *x*, and at the same time remain indifferent, as the quantity of good *x* increases. (p. 176)

Diminishing marginal returns The tendency for the marginal product of an additional unit of a factor of production to be less than the marginal product of the previous unit of the factor. (p. 221)

Diminishing marginal utility The decrease in marginal utility as the quantity consumed increases. (p. 155)

Direct relationship A relationship between two variables that move in the same direction. (p. 20)

Discount factor The discounted price is the original price multiplied by the discount factor. (p. 837)

Discounting The conversion of a future amount of money to its present value. (p. 326)

Discouraged workers People who are available and willing to work but have not made specific efforts to find a job within the previous four weeks. (pp. 445, 482)

Discretionary fiscal policy A policy action that is initiated by an act of Parliament. (p. 562)

Discretionary policy A policy that responds to the state of the economy in a possibly unique way that uses all the information available, including perceived lessons from past "mistakes." (p. 763)

Diseconomies of scale Features of a firm's technology that lead to rising long-run average cost as output increases. (p. 230)

Disposable income Aggregate income minus taxes plus transfer payments. (pp. 507, 528)

Dividend The share of a firm's profit paid to stockholders. (p. 830)

Dividend yield The dividend paid on a stock expressed as a percentage of the stock price. (p. 831)

Dumping The sale by a foreign firm of exports at a lower price than the cost of production. (p. 798)

Duopoly A market structure in which two producers of a good or service compete. (p. 295)

Dynamic comparative advantage A comparative advantage that a person or country possesses as a result of having specialized in a particular activity and then, as a result of learning-by-doing, having become the producer with the lowest opportunity cost. (p. 45)

Earnings A firm's accounting profit. (p. 831)

Economic depreciation The change in the market value of capital over a given period. (p. 196)

Economic efficiency A situation that occurs when the firm produces a given output at the least cost. (p. 199)

Economic growth The expansion of production possibilities that results from capital accumulation and technological change. (pp. 40, 439)

Economic growth rate The percentage change in the quantity of goods and services produced from one year to the next. (p. 468)

Economic model A description of some aspect of the economic world that includes only those features of the world that are needed for the purpose at hand. (p. 12)

Economic profit A firm's total revenue minus its opportunity cost. (p. 197)

Economic rent The income received by the owner of a factor of production over and above the amount required to induce that owner to offer the factor for use. (p. 334)

Economic theory A generalization that summarizes what we think we understand about the economic choices that people make and the performance of industries and entire economies. (p. 12)

Economic welfare A comprehensive measure of the general state of economic well-being. (p. 468)

Economics The social science that studies the choices that we make as we cope with scarcity and the institutions that have evolved to influence and reconcile our choices. (p. 2)

Economies of scale Features of a firm's technology that lead to a falling long-run average cost as output increases. (pp. 211, 230)

Economies of scope Decreases in average total cost that occur when a firm uses specialized resources to produce a range of goods and services. (p. 211)

Efficiency wage A real wage rate that is set above the full-employment equilibrium wage rate and that balances the costs and benefits of this higher wage rate to maximize the firm's profit. (p. 694)

Efficient allocation Resource use is efficient when we produce the goods and services that we value most highly. (p. 104)

Elastic demand Demand with a price elasticity greater than 1; other things remaining the same, the percentage change in the quantity demanded exceeds the percentage change in price. (p. 87)

Elasticity of demand The responsiveness of the quantity demanded of a good to a change in its price, other things remaining the same. (p. 84)

Elasticity of supply The responsiveness of the quantity supplied of a good to a change in its price, other things remaining the same. (p. 94)

Employment-to-population ratio The percentage of people of working age who have jobs. (p. 482)

Entrants People who enter the labour force. (p. 485)

Entrepreneurship The human resource that organizes the other three factors of production: labour, land, and capital. Entrepreneurs come up with new ideas about what and how to produce, make business decisions, and bear the risks that arise from their decisions. (p. 4)

Equation of exchange An equation that states that the quantity of money multiplied by the velocity of circulation equals GDP. (p. 656)

Equilibrium expenditure The level of aggregate expenditure that occurs when aggregate planned expenditure equals real GDP. (p. 536)

Equilibrium price The price at which the quantity demanded equals the quantity supplied. (p. 70)

Equilibrium quantity The quantity bought and sold at the equilibrium price. (p. 70)

Equity capital The value of a firm's stock—also called the firm's equity. (p. 830)

Excess reserves A bank's actual reserves minus its desired reserves. (p. 587)

Exchange rate The price at which the Canadian dollar exchanges for another currency. (p. 596)

Excise tax A tax on the sale of a particular commodity. (p. 386)

Expansion A business cycle phase between a trough and a peak—a phase in which real GDP increases. (p. 440)

Expansionary fiscal policy An increase in government expenditures or a decrease in taxes. (p. 569)

Exports The goods and services that we sell to people in other countries. (pp. 460, 786)

External benefits Benefits that accrue to people other than the buyer of the good. (p. 254)

External costs Costs that are not borne by the producer of the good but borne by someone else. (p. 254)

External diseconomies Factors outside the control of a firm that raise the firm's costs as the industry produces a larger output. (p. 251)

External economies Factors beyond the control of a firm that lower the firm's costs as the industry produces a larger output. (p. 251)

Externality A cost or a benefit that arises from production and falls on someone other than the producer, or a cost or a benefit that arises from consumption and falls on someone other than the consumer. (p. 414)

Factors of production The resources that businesses use to produce goods and services. (p. 4)

Farm Marketing Board A regulatory agency that intervenes in an agricultural market to stabilize the price of an agricultural product. (p. 139)

Federal budget The annual statement of the outlays and revenues of the government of Canada, together with the laws and regulations that approve and support those outlays and revenues. (p. 556)

Feedback-rule policy A rule that specifies how policy actions respond to changes in the state of the economy. (p. 763)

Final good An item that is bought by its final user during the specified time period. (p. 458)

Financial innovation The development of new financial products—new ways of borrowing and lending. (p. 591)

Firm An institution that hires factors of production and organizes those factors to produce and sell goods and services. (p. 196)

Fiscal policy The government's attempt to achieve macroeconomic objectives such as full employment, sustained economic growth, and price level stability by setting and changing taxes, making transfer payments, and purchasing goods and services. (pp. 451, 507, 556)

Fixed-rule policy A rule that specifies an action to be pursued independently of the state of the economy. (p. 763)

Flow A quantity per unit of time. (p. 461)

Foreign exchange market The market in which the currency of one country is exchanged for the currency of another. (p. 815)

Foreign exchange rate The price at which one currency exchanges for another. (p. 815)

Four-firm concentration ratio A measure of market power that is calculated as the percentage of the value of sales accounted for by the four largest firms in an industry. (p. 206)

Free rider A person who consumes a good without paying for it. (p. 376)

Frictional unemployment The unemployment that arises from normal labour turnover—from people entering and leaving the labour force and from the ongoing creation and destruction of jobs. (p. 487)

Full employment A situation in which the quantity of labour demanded equals the quantity supplied. At full employment, there is no cyclical unemployment—all unemployment is frictional, structural, and seasonal. (p. 488)

Game theory A tool that economists use to analyze strategic behaviour—behaviour that takes into account the expected behaviour of others and the recognition of mutual interdependence. (p. 293)

GDP deflator One measure of the price level, which is the average of current-year prices as a percentage of base-year prices. (p. 466)

General Agreement on Tariffs and Trade An international agreement signed in 1947 to reduce tariffs on international trade. (p. 793)

Goods and services All the objects that people value and produce to satisfy their wants. (p. 3)

Government budget deficit The deficit that arises when the government spends more than it collects in taxes. (p. 449)

Government budget surplus The surplus that arises when the government collects more in taxes than it spends. (p. 449)

Government debt The total amount of borrowing that the government has undertaken. It equals the sum of past budget deficits minus the sum of past budget surpluses. (p. 559)

Government deposit shifting The transfer of government funds by the Bank of Canada from the government's account at the Bank of Canada to its accounts at the chartered banks or from the government's accounts at the chartered banks to its account at the Bank of Canada. (p. 610)

Government expenditures Goods and services bought by the government. (p. 460)

Government expenditures multiplier The magnification effect of a change in government expenditures on goods and services on equilibrium expenditure and real GDP (p. 562)

Government sector balance An amount equal to net taxes minus government expenditures on goods and services. (p. 813)

Great Depression A decade (1929–1939) of high unemployment and stagnant production throughout the world economy. (p. 438)

Gross domestic product (GDP) The market value of all final goods and services produced within a country during a given time period. (p. 458)

Gross investment The total amount spent on purchases of new capital and on replacing depreciated capital. (p. 461)

Growth accounting A method of calculating how much real GDP growth results from growth of labour and capital and how much is attributable to technological change. (p. 713)

Growth rate cycle downturn A pronounced, pervasive, and persistent decline in the growth rate of aggregate economic activity. (p. 478)

Growth recession A slowdown in the growth rate of real GDP but with the growth rate not becoming negative. (p. 440)

Herfindahl–Hirschman Index A measure of market power that is calculated as the square of the market share of each firm (as a percentage) summed over the largest 50 firms (or over all firms if there are fewer than 50) in a market. (p. 206)

Human capital The knowledge and skill that people obtain from education, on-the-job training, and work experience. (pp. 4, 681)

Implicit rental rate The firm's opportunity cost of using its own capital. (p. 196)

Imports The goods and services that we buy from people in other countries. (pp. 460, 786)

Incentive An inducement to take a particular action. (p. 11)

Incentive system A method of organizing production that uses a market-like mechanism inside the firm. (p. 201)

Income effect The effect of a change in income on consumption, other things remaining the same. (p. 180)

Income elasticity of demand The responsiveness of demand to a change in income, other things remaining the same. It is calculated as the percentage change in the quantity demanded divided by the percentage change in income. (p. 92)

Indifference curve A line that shows combinations of goods among which a consumer is indifferent. (p. 175)

Induced expenditure The sum of the components of aggregate planned expenditure that vary with real GDP. Induced expenditure equals consumption expenditure minus imports. (p. 535)

Induced taxes Taxes that vary with real GDP. (p. 565)

Inelastic demand A demand with a price elasticity between 0 and 1; the percentage change in the quantity demanded is less than the percentage change in price. (p. 87)

Infant-industry argument The argument that it is necessary to protect a new industry to enable it to grow into a mature industry that can compete in world markets. (p. 797)

Inferior good A good for which demand decreases as income increases. (p. 64)

Inflation A rising cost of living—a process in which the price level is rising and money is losing value. (pp. 7, 447, 650)

Inflation rate The percentage change in the price level from one year to the next. (p. 492)

Inflationary gap The amount by which real GDP exceeds potential GDP. (p. 511)

Intellectual property rights Property rights for discoveries owned by the creators of knowledge. (p. 425)

Interest The income that capital earns. (p. 5)

Interest rate The amount received by a lender and paid by a borrower expressed as a percentage of the amount of the loan. (p. 594)

Interest rate parity A situation in which the rates of return on assets in different currencies are equal. (p. 822)

Interest-sensitive expenditure curve The relationship between aggregate expenditure plans and the real interest rate when all other influences on expenditure plans remain the same. (p. 598)

Intermediate good An item that is produced by one firm, bought by another firm, and used as a component of a final good or service. (p. 458)

International crowding out The tendency for an expansionary fiscal policy to decrease net exports. (p. 633)

Inverse relationship A relationship between variables that move in opposite directions. (p. 21)

Investment The purchase of new plant, equipment, and buildings and additions to inventories. (p. 460)

Job leavers People who voluntarily quit their jobs. (p. 485)

Job losers People who are laid off, either permanently or temporarily, from their jobs. (p. 485)

Job rationing The practice of paying a real wage rate above the equilibrium level and then rationing jobs by some method. (p. 694)

Job search The activity of looking for an acceptable vacant job. (p. 693)

Keynesian A macroeconomist who regards the economy as being inherently unstable and requiring active government intervention to achieve stability. (p. 638)

Keynesian activist An economist who believes that fluctuations in aggregate demand combined with sticky wages (and/or sticky prices) are the main source of economic fluctuations. (p. 764)

Keynesian theory of the business cycle A theory that regards volatile expectations as the main source of economic fluctuations. (p. 731)

Labour The work time and work effort that people devote to producing goods and services. (p. 4)

Labour force The sum of the people who are employed and who are unemployed. (pp. 444, 480)

Labour force participation rate The percentage of the working-age population who are members of the labour force. (p. 482)

Labour productivity Real GDP per hour of labour. (pp. 681, 713)

Labour union An organized group of workers whose purpose is to increase wages and to influence other job conditions. (p. 341)

Land All the gifts of nature that we use to produce goods and services. (p. 4)

Law of demand Other things remaining the same, the higher the price of a good, the smaller is the quantity demanded of it. (p. 61)

Law of diminishing returns As a firm uses more of a variable input, with a given quantity of other inputs (fixed inputs), the marginal product of the variable input eventually diminishes. (pp. 221, 683, 714)

Law of supply Other things remaining the same, the higher the price of a good, the greater is the quantity supplied of it. (p. 66)

Learning-by-doing People become more productive in an activity (learn) just by repeatedly producing a particular good or service (doing). (pp. 45, 681)

Legal monopoly A market structure in which there is one firm and entry is restricted by the granting of a public franchise, government licence, patent, or copyright. (p. 262)

Limit pricing The practice of setting the price at the highest level that inflicts a loss on an entrant. (p. 303)

Linear relationship A relationship between two variables that is illustrated by a straight line. (p. 28)

Liquidity The property of being instantly convertible into a means of payment with little loss in value. (p. 584)

Local public good A public good that is consumed by all the people who live in a particular area. (p. 385)

Long run A period of time in which the quantities of all resources can be varied. (p. 218)

Long-run aggregate supply curve The relationship between the quantity of real GDP supplied and the price level in the long run when real GDP equals potential GDP. (pp. 500, 687)

Long-run average cost curve The relationship between the lowest attainable average total cost and output when both plant size and labour are varied. (p. 229)

Long-run industry supply curve A curve that shows how the quantity supplied by an industry varies as the market price varies after all the possible adjustments have been made, including changes in plant size and the number of firms in the industry. (p. 251)

Long-run macroeconomic equilibrium A situation that occurs when real GDP equals potential GDP—the economy is on its long-run aggregate supply curve. (p. 509)

Long-run neutrality The proposition that in the long run, a change in the quantity of money changes the price level and leaves all real variables unchanged. (p. 641)

Long-run Phillips curve A curve that shows the relationship between inflation and unemployment when the actual inflation rate equals the expected inflation rate. (p. 664)

Lorenz curve A curve that graphs the cumulative percentage of income or wealth against the cumulative percentage of households. (p. 349)

Low-income cutoff The income level, determined separately for different types of families (for example, single persons, couples, one parent) that is selected such that families with incomes below that limit normally spend 54.7 percent or more of their income on food, shelter, and clothing. (p. 352)

M1 A measure of money that consists of currency held outside the banks plus demand deposits at chartered banks that are owned by individuals and businesses. (p. 583)

M2+ A measure of money that consists of M1 plus personal savings deposits, and nonpersonal notice deposits at chartered banks plus all types of deposits at trust and mortgage loan companies, credit unions, caisses populaires, and other financial institutions. (p. 583)

Macroeconomic long run A time frame that is sufficiently long for real GDP to return to potential GDP so that full employment prevails. (p. 500)

Macroeconomic short run A period during which real GDP has fallen below or risen above potential GDP. (p. 501)

Macroeconomics The study of the effects on the national economy and the global economy of the choices that individuals, businesses, and governments make. (p. 2)

Margin When a choice is changed by a small amount or by a little at a time, the choice is made at the margin. (p. 11)

Marginal benefit The benefit that a person receives from consuming one more unit of a good or service. It is measured as the maximum amount that a person is willing to pay for one more unit of the good or service. (pp. 11, 38, 104)

Marginal benefit curve A curve that shows the relationship between the marginal benefit of a good and the quantity of that good consumed. (p. 38)

Marginal cost The opportunity cost of producing one more unit of a good or service. It is the best alternative forgone. It is calculated as the increase in total cost divided by the increase in output. (pp. 11, 37, 104, 224)

Marginal cost pricing rule A rule that sets the price of a good or service equal to the marginal cost of producing it. (pp. 276, 398)

Marginal external benefit The benefit from an additional unit of a good or service that people other than the consumer enjoy. (p. 421)

Marginal external cost The cost of producing an additional unit of a good or service that falls on people other than the producer. (p. 417)

Marginal private benefit The benefit from an additional unit of a good or service that the consumer of that good or service receives. (p. 421)

Marginal private cost The cost of producing an additional unit of a good or service that is borne by the producer of that good or service. (p. 417)

Marginal product The increase in total product that results from a one-unit increase in the variable input, with all other inputs remaining the same. It is calculated as the increase in total product divided by the increase in the variable input employed, when the quantities of all other inputs are constant. (p. 219)

Marginal product of labour The additional real GDP produced by an additional hour of labour when all other influences on production remain the same. (p. 683)

Marginal propensity to consume The fraction of a change in disposable income that is consumed. It is calculated as the change in consumption expenditure divided by the change in disposable income. (p. 530)

Marginal propensity to import The fraction of an increase in real GDP that is spent on imports. (p. 533)

Marginal propensity to save The fraction of an increase in disposable income that is saved. It is calculated as the change in saving divided by the change in disposable income. (p. 530)

Marginal rate of substitution The rate at which a person will give up good *y* (the good measured on the *y*-axis) to get an additional unit of good *x* (the good measured on the *x*-axis) and at the same time remain indifferent (remain on the same indifference curve). (p. 176)

Marginal revenue The change in total revenue that results from a one-unit increase in the quantity sold. It is calculated as the change in total revenue divided by the change in quantity sold. (p. 238)

Marginal revenue product The change in total revenue that results from employing one more unit of a factor of production (labour) while the quantity of all other factors remains the same. It is calculated as the increase in total revenue divided by the increase in the quantity of the factor (labour). (p. 318)

Marginal social benefit The marginal benefit enjoyed by society—by the consumer of a good or service (marginal private benefit) plus the marginal benefit enjoyed by others (marginal external benefit). (p. 421)

Marginal social cost The marginal cost incurred by the entire society—by the producer and by everyone else on whom the cost falls— and is the sum of marginal private cost and marginal external cost. (p. 417)

Marginal tax rate The percentage of an additional dollar of income that is paid in tax. (p. 382)

Marginal utility The change in total utility resulting from a one-unit increase in the quantity of a good consumed. (p. 155)

Marginal utility per dollar spent The marginal utility from a good divided by its price. (p. 157)

Market Any arrangement that enables buyers and sellers to get information and to do business with each other. (p. 46)

Market demand The relationship between the total quantity demanded of a good and its price. It is illustrated by the market demand curve. (p. 163)

Market failure A state in which the market does not allocate resources efficiently. (p. 374)

Market income The wages, interest,

rent, and profit earned in factor markets and before paying income taxes. (p. 348)

Market power The ability to influence the market, and in particular the market price, by influencing the total quantity offered for sale. (p. 262)

Means of payment A method of settling a debt. (p. 582)

Microeconomics The study of the choices that individuals and businesses make, the way those choices interact, and the influence governments exert on them. (p. 2)

Minimum efficient scale The smallest quantity of output at which the long-run average cost curve reaches its lowest level. (p. 231)

Minimum wage A regulation that makes the hiring of labour below a specified wage rate illegal. (pp. 129, 695)

Monetarist A macroeconomist who believes that fluctuations in the quantity of money are the main source of economic fluctuations. (pp. 638, 764)

Monetarist theory of the business cycle A theory that regards fluctuations in the quantity of money as the main source of economic fluctuations. (p. 732)

Monetary base The sum of the Bank of Canada notes outside the Bank of Canada, chartered banks' deposits at the Bank of Canada, and coins held by households and firms. (p. 607)

Monetary policy The attempt to control inflation and moderate the business cycle by changing the quantity of money and adjusting interest rates and the exchange rate. (pp. 451, 507, 606)

Monetary policy indicators The current features of the economy that the Bank of Canada looks at to determine whether it needs to apply the brake or the accelerator to the economy to influence its future real GDP growth, unemployment, and inflation. (p. 608)

Money Any commodity or token that is generally acceptable as the means of payment. (p. 582)

Money multiplier The amount by which a change in the monetary base is multiplied to determine the resulting change in the quantity of money. (p. 613)

Money wage rate The number of dollars that an hour of labour earns. (p. 683)

Monopolistic competition A market structure in which a large number of firms compete by making similar but slightly different products. (pp. 205, 284)

Monopoly A market structure in which there is one firm, which produces a good or service that has no close substitutes and in which the firm is protected from competition by a barrier preventing the entry of new firms. (pp. 205, 262)

Monopsony A market in which there is a single buyer. (p. 344)

Multiplier The amount by which a change in autonomous expenditure is magnified or multiplied to determine the change in equilibrium expenditure and real GDP. (p. 538)

Nash equilibrium The outcome of a game that occurs when player A takes the best possible action given the action of player B and player B takes the best possible action given the action of player A. (p. 294)

National saving The sum of private saving (saving by households and businesses) and government saving. (p. 461)

Natural monopoly A monopoly that occurs when one firm can supply the entire market at a lower price than two or more firms can. (pp. 262, 397)

Natural rate of unemployment The unemployment rate when the economy is at full employment. There is no cyclical unemployment; all unemployment is frictional, structural, and seasonal. (pp. 488, 500)

Negative externality An externality that arises from either production or consumption and that imposes an external cost. (p. 414)

Negative relationship A relationship between variables that move in opposite directions. (p. 21)

Neoclassical growth theory A theory of economic growth that proposes that real GDP per person grows because technological change induces a level of saving and investment that makes capital per hour of labour grow. (p. 719)

Net borrower A country that is borrowing more from the rest of the world than it is lending to it. (p. 812)

Net exports The value of exports minus the value of imports. (pp. 460, 786, 813)

Net investment Net increase in the capital stock—gross investment minus depreciation. (p. 461)

Net lender A country that is lending more to the rest of the world than it is borrowing from it. (p. 812)

Net present value The present value of the future flow of marginal revenue product generated by capital minus the cost of the capital. (p. 328)

Net taxes Taxes paid to governments minus transfer payments received from governments. (p. 460)

New classical theory of the business cycle A rational expectations theory of the business cycle that regards unanticipated fluctuations in aggregate demand as the main source of economic fluctuations. (p. 734)

New growth theory A theory of economic growth based on the idea that real GDP per person grows because of the choices that people make in the pursuit of profit and that growth can persist indefinitely. (p. 721)

New Keynesian theory of the business cycle A rational expectations theory of the business cycle that regards unanticipated fluctuations in aggregate demand as the main source of economic fluctuations but leaves room for anticipated demand fluctuations to play a role. (p. 734)

Nominal GDP The value of the final goods and services produced in a given year valued at the prices that prevailed in that same year. It is a more precise name for GDP. (p. 465)

Nominal interest rate The percentage return on an asset such as a bond expressed in terms of money. (p. 597)

Nonrenewable natural resources Natural resources that can be used only once and that cannot be replaced once they have been used. (p. 331)

Nontariff barrier Any action other

than a tariff that restricts international trade. (p. 793)

Normal good A good for which demand increases as income increases. (p. 64)

Normal profit The expected return for supplying entrepreneurial ability. (p. 197)

North American Free Trade Agreement An agreement, which became effective on January 1, 1994, to eliminate all barriers to international trade between the United States, Canada, and Mexico after a 15-year phasing-in period. (p. 794)

Official Canadian reserves The government's holdings of foreign currency. (p. 810)

Official settlements account A record of the change in a country's official reserves. (p. 810)

Oligopoly A market structure in which a small number of firms compete. (pp. 205, 291)

One-third rule The rule that, with no change in technology, a 1 percent increase in capital per hour of labour brings, on the average, a one-third of 1 percent increase in real GDP per hour of labour. (p. 714)

Open market operation The purchase or sale of government of Canada securities—Treasury bills and government bonds—by the Bank of Canada from or to a chartered bank or the public. (p. 609)

Opportunity cost The highest-valued alternative that we give up to get something. (p. 11)

Output-inflation tradeoff A tradeoff that arises because a policy action that lowers inflation also lowers output and a policy action that boosts output also increases inflation. (p. 10)

Overnight loans rate The interest rate on large-scale loans that chartered banks make to each other and to dealers in financial markets. (p. 608)

Patent A government-sanctioned exclusive right granted to the inventor of a good, service, or productive process to produce, use, and sell the invention for a given number of years. (p. 425)

Payoff matrix A table that shows the payoffs for every possible action by each player for every possible action by each other player. (p. 293)

Peak The point at which a business cycle turns from expansion into recession. (p. 440)

Perfect competition A market in which there are many firms each selling an identical product; there are many buyers; there are no restrictions on entry into the industry; firms in the industry have no advantage over potential new entrants; and firms and buyers are well informed about the price of each firm's product. (pp. 205, 238)

Perfect price discrimination Price discrimination that extracts the entire consumer surplus. (p. 273)

Perfectly elastic demand Demand with an infinite price elasticity; the quantity demanded changes by an infinitely large percentage in response to a tiny price change. (p. 87)

Perfectly inelastic demand Demand with a price elasticity of zero; the quantity demanded remains constant when the price changes. (p. 86)

Phillips curve A curve that shows a relationship between inflation and unemployment. (p. 662)

Pigovian taxes Taxes that are used as an incentive for producers to cut back on an activity that creates an external cost. (p. 420)

Policy conflict A situation in which the government and the Bank of Canada pursue different goals and the actions of one make it harder for the other to achieve its goals. (p. 642)

Policy coordination A situation in which the government and the Bank of Canada work together to achieve a common set of goals. (p. 642)

Political equilibrium The outcome that results from the choices of voters, politicians, and bureaucrats. (p. 375)

Positive externality An externality that arises from either production or consumption and that provides an external benefit. (p. 414)

Positive relationship A relationship between two variables that move in the same direction. (p. 20)

Potential GDP The quantity of real GDP at full employment. (pp. 439, 489)

Poverty A situation in which a household's income is too low to be able to buy the quantities of food, shelter, and clothing that are deemed necessary. (p. 352)

Preferences A description of a person's likes and dislikes. (p. 38)

Present value The amount of money that, if invested today, will grow to be as large as a given future amount when the interest that it will earn is taken into account. (p. 326)

Price ceiling A regulation that makes it illegal to charge a price higher than a specified level. (p. 125)

Price discrimination The practice of selling different units of a good or service for different prices or of charging one customer different prices for different quantities bought. (p. 263)

Price-earnings ratio The stock price divided by the most recent year's earnings. (p. 831)

Price effect The effect of a change in the price on the quantity of a good consumed, other things remaining the same. (p. 179)

Price elasticity of demand A units-free measure of the responsiveness of the quantity demanded of a good to a change in its price, when all other influences on buyers' plans remain the same. (p. 84)

Price floor A regulation that makes it illegal to charge a price lower than a specified level. (p. 129)

Price level The average level of prices as measured by a price index. (pp. 447, 466)

Price taker A firm that cannot influence the price of the good or service it produces. (p. 238)

Principal–agent problem The problem of devising compensation rules that induce an agent to act in the best interest of a principal. (p. 202)

Principle of minimum differentiation The tendency for competitors to make themselves identical as they try to appeal to the maximum number of clients or voters. (p. 379)

Private sector balance An amount equal to saving minus investment. (p. 813)

Privatization The process of selling publicly owned corporations to private shareholders. (p. 394)

Producer surplus The price of a good minus the opportunity cost of producing it, summed over the quantity sold. (p. 109)

Product differentiation Making a product slightly different from the product of a competing firm. (pp. 205, 284)

Production efficiency A situation in which the economy cannot produce more of one good without producing less of some other good. (p. 35)

Production function The relationship between real GDP and the quantity of labour employed when all other influences on production remain the same. (p. 680)

Production possibilities frontier The boundary between the combinations of goods and services that can be produced and the combinations that cannot. (p. 34)

Productivity curve A relationship that shows how real GDP per hour of labour changes as the amount of capital per hour of labour changes with a given state of technology. (p. 713)

Profit The income earned by entrepreneurship. (p. 5)

Progressive income tax A tax on income at an average rate that increases with the level of income. (p. 359)

Property rights Social arrangements that govern the ownership, use, and disposal of resources or factors of production, goods, and services that are enforceable in the courts. (pp. 46, 418)

Proportional income tax A tax on income at a constant average rate, regardless of the level of income. (p. 359)

Provincial budget The annual statement of the outlays and revenues of a provincial government, together with the laws and regulations that approve and support those outlays and revenues. (p. 556)

Public good A good or service that can be consumed simultaneously by everyone and from which no one can be excluded. (p. 376)

Public interest theory A theory of regulation that states that regulations are supplied to satisfy the demand of consumers and producers to maximize the sum of consumer surplus and producer surplus—that is, to attain efficiency. (p. 395)

Public provision The production of a good or service by a public authority that receives its revenue from the government. (p. 423)

Purchasing power parity The equal value of different monies. (p. 822)

Quantity demanded The amount of a good or service that consumers plan to buy during a given time period at a particular price. (p. 61)

Quantity of labour demanded The number of labour hours hired by all the firms in the economy. (p. 683)

Quantity of labour supplied The number of labour hours that all households in the economy plan to work. (p. 685)

Quantity supplied The amount of a good or service that producers plan to sell during a given time period at a particular price. (p. 66)

Quantity theory of money The proposition that in the long run, an increase in the quantity of money brings an equal percentage increase in the price level. (p. 656)

Quota A restriction on the quantity of a good that a farm is permitted to produce. (p. 140)

Quota A quantitative restriction on the import of a particular good, which specifies the maximum amount that can be imported in a given time period. (p. 796)

Rand Formula A requirement that all workers represented by a union must pay union dues, whether they join the union or not. (p. 341)

Rate of return The return on a stock expressed as a percentage of the stock price. (p. 831)

Rate of return regulation A regulation that requires the firm to justify its price by showing that the price enables it to earn a specified target percent return on its capital. (p. 399)

Rational expectation The most accurate forecast possible, a forecast that uses all the available information, including knowledge of the relevant economic forces that influence the variable being forecasted. (pp. 659, 734, 837)

Rational ignorance The decision not to acquire information because the cost of doing so exceeds the expected benefit. (p. 380)

Real business cycle theory A theory that regards random fluctuations in productivity as the main source of economic fluctuations. (p. 737)

Real GDP (Real gross domestic product) The value of final goods and services produced in a given year when valued at constant prices. (pp. 439, 465)

Real income A household's income expressed as a quantity of goods that the household can afford to buy. (p. 173)

Real interest rate The percentage return on an asset expressed in terms of what money will buy. It is the nominal interest rate adjusted for inflation and is approximately equal to the nominal interest rate minus the inflation rate. (p. 597)

Real wage rate The quantity of goods and services that an hour's work can buy. It is equal to the money wage rate divided by the price level and multiplied by 100. (pp. 484, 683)

Realized capital gain A capital gain that is obtained when a stock is sold for a higher price than the price paid for it. (p. 843)

Recession A significant decline in activity spread across the economy, lasting for more than a few months, visible in industrial production, employment, real income, and wholesale-retail trade. (p. 440)

Recessionary gap The amount by which potential GDP exceeds real GDP. (p. 510)

Re-entrants People who re-enter the labour force. (p. 485)

Regressive income tax A tax on

income at an average rate that decreases with the level of income. (p. 359)

Relative price The ratio of the price of one good or service to the price of another good or service. A relative price is an opportunity cost. (pp. 60, 173)

Renewable natural resources Natural resources that can be used repeatedly without depleting what is available for future use. (p. 331)

Rent The income that land earns. (p. 5)

Rent ceiling A regulation that makes it illegal to charge a rent higher than a specified level. (p. 125)

Rent seeking Any attempt to capture a consumer surplus, a producer surplus, or an economic profit. (p. 270)

Reserve ratio The fraction of a bank's total deposits that are held in reserves. (p. 587)

Reserves Cash in a bank's vault plus the bank's deposits at the Bank of Canada. (p. 585)

Return The return on a stock is the sum of the stock's dividend plus its capital gain (or minus its capital loss). (p. 831)

Risk premium The additional return that is earned for bearing an additional risk. (p. 840)

Saving The amount of income that households have left after they have paid their taxes and bought their consumption goods and services. (p. 460)

Saving function The relationship between saving and disposable income, other things remaining the same. (p. 528)

Saving rate Saving as a percentage of disposable income. (p. 843)

Scarcity The state in which the resources available are insufficient to satisfy people's wants. (p. 2)

Scatter diagram A diagram that plots the value of one variable against the value of another. (p. 19)

Search activity The time spent looking for someone with whom to do business. (p. 126)

Seasonal unemployment Unemployment that arises because the number of jobs available has decreased because of the season. (p. 488)

Short run The short run in microeconomics has two meanings. For the firm, it is the period of time in which the quantity of at least one input is fixed and the quantities of the other inputs can be varied. The fixed input is usually capital—that is, the firm has a given plant size. For the industry, the short run is the period of time in which each firm has a given plant size and the number of firms in the industry is fixed. (p. 218)

Short-run aggregate supply curve A curve that shows the relationship between the quantity of real GDP supplied and the price level in the short run when the money wage rate, other resource prices, and potential GDP remain constant. (pp. 501, 687)

Short-run industry supply curve A curve that shows the quantity supplied by the industry at each price when the plant size of each firm and the number of firms in the industry remain the same. (p. 245)

Short-run macroeconomic equilibrium A situation that occurs when the quantity of real GDP demanded equals the quantity of real GDP supplied—at the point of intersection of the *AD* curve and the *SAS* curve. (p. 508)

Short-run Phillips curve A curve that shows the tradeoff between inflation and unemployment, when the expected inflation rate and the natural rate of unemployment remain the same. (p. 662)

Shutdown point The output and price at which the firm just covers its total variable cost. In the short run, the firm is indifferent between producing the profit-maximizing output and shutting down temporarily. (p. 244)

Single-price monopoly A monopoly that must sell each unit of its output for the same price to all its customers. (p. 263)

Slope The change in the value of the variable measured on the *y*-axis divided by the change in the value of the variable measured on the *x*-axis. (p. 24)

Speculative bubble A price increase followed by a price plunge, both of which occur because people expect them to occur and act on that expectation. (p. 838)

Standard of living The level of consumption that people enjoy, on the average, and is measured by average income per person. (p. 6)

Stock A quantity that exists at a point in time. (p. 461)

Stock A tradable security that a firm issues to certify that the stockholder owns a share of the firm. (p. 830)

Stock exchange An organized market on which people can buy and sell stock. (p. 830)

Stock price The price at which one share of a firm's stock trades on a stock exchange. (p. 831)

Strategies All the possible actions of each player in a game. (p. 293)

Structural surplus or deficit The budget balance that would occur if the economy were at full employment and real GDP were equal to potential GDP. (p. 567)

Structural unemployment The unemployment that arises when changes in technology or international competition change the skills needed to perform jobs or change the locations of jobs. (p. 488)

Subsidy A payment that the government makes to private producers. (pp. 140, 424)

Subsistence real wage rate The minimum real wage rate needed to maintain life. (p. 718)

Substitute A good that can be used in place of another good. (p. 63)

Substitution effect The effect of a change in price of a good or service on the quantity bought when the consumer (hypothetically) remains indifferent between the original and the new consumption situations—that is, the consumer remains on the same indifference curve. (p. 181)

Sunk cost The past cost of buying a plant that has no resale value. (p. 218)

Supply The relationship between the quantity of a good that producers plan to sell and the price of the good when all other influences on producers' plans remain the same. It is described by a supply schedule and illustrated by a supply curve. (p. 66)

Supply curve A curve that shows the relationship between the quantity supplied and the price of a good when all other influences on producers' planned sales remain the same. (p. 66)

Supply of labour The relationship between the quantity of labour supplied and the real wage rate when all other influences on work plans remain the same. (p. 685)

Symmetry principle A requirement that people in similar situations be treated similarly. (p. 116)

Tariff A tax that is imposed by the importing country when an imported good crosses its international boundary. (p. 793)

Technological change The development of new goods and of better ways of producing goods and services. (p. 40)

Technological efficiency A situation that occurs when the firm produces a given output by using the least amount of inputs. (p. 199)

Technology Any method of producing a good or service. (p. 198)

Terms of trade The quantity of goods and services that a country exports to pay for its imports of goods and services. (p. 788)

Time-series graph A graph that measures time (for example, months or years) on the *x*-axis and the variable or variables in which we are interested on the *y*-axis. (p. 18)

Total cost The cost of all the productive resources that a firm uses. (p. 223)

Total fixed cost The cost of the firm's fixed inputs. (p. 223)

Total income Market income plus cash payments to households by governments. (p. 348)

Total product The total output produced by a firm in a given period of time. (p. 219)

Total revenue The value of a firm's sales. It is calculated as the price of the good multiplied by the quantity sold. (pp. 88, 238)

Total revenue test A method of estimating the price elasticity of demand by observing the change in total revenue that results from a change in the price, when all other influences on the quantity sold remain the same. (p. 88)

Total utility The total benefit that a person gets from the consumption of goods and services. (p. 154)

Total variable cost The cost of all the firm's variable inputs. (p. 223)

Tradeoff A constraint that involves giving up one thing to get something else. (p. 9)

Transactions costs The costs that arise from finding someone with whom to do business, of reaching an agreement about the price and other aspects of the exchange, and of ensuring that the terms of the agreement are fulfilled. The opportunity costs of conducting a transaction. (pp. 210, 419)

Trend The general tendency for a variable to move in one direction. (p. 18)

Trough The point at which a business cycle turns from recession into expansion. (p. 440)

Trust and mortgage loan company A privately owned depository institution that operates under the Trust and Loan Companies Act of 1992. (p. 586)

Twin deficits The tendency for the government budget deficit and the current account deficit to move in the same direction. (p. 814)

Unemployment A state in which a person does not have a job but is available for work, willing to work, and has made some effort to find work within the previous four weeks. (p. 444)

Unemployment rate The percentage of the people in the labour force who are unemployed. (pp. 444, 481)

Unit elastic demand Demand with a price elasticity of 1; the percentage change in the quantity demanded equals the percentage change in price. (p. 86)

Utilitarianism A principle that states that we should strive to achieve "the greatest happiness for the greatest number of people." (p. 114)

Utility The benefit or satisfaction that a person gets from the consumption of a good or service. (p. 154)

Value The maximum amount that a person is willing to pay for a good. The value of one more unit of the good or service is its marginal benefit. (p. 106)

Velocity of circulation The average number of times a dollar of money is used annually to buy the goods and services that make up GDP. (p. 656)

Voluntary export restraint An agreement between two governments in which the government of the exporting country agrees to restrain the volume of its own exports. (p. 796)

Voucher A token that the government provides to households, which they can use to buy specified goods and services. (p. 424)

Wages The income that labour earns. (p. 5)

Wealth The market value of all the things that people own—the market value of their assets. (pp 461, 843)

Wealth effect The influence of wealth on consumption expenditure and saving. (pp. 843)

Working-age population The total number of people aged 15 years and over. (p. 480)

World Trade Organization An international organization that places greater obligations on its member countries to observe the GATT rules. (p. 793)

INDEX

Key terms and pages on which they are defined appear in **boldface**.

Above full-employment equilibrium, 510–511
Absolute advantage, 45
After-tax income, 348
Aggregate demand
  aggregate demand curve, 505–506
  in Canada (1961-2001), 514
  changes in, 506–508
  defined, **505**
  expansionary fiscal policy and, 630
  expectations, 506–507
  and fiscal policy, 507, 568–570
  fluctuations in, 512–513
  increase in, effect of, 512, 651
  long run increase, 546–547
  and monetary policy, 507
  quantity of real GDP demanded, changes in, 506
  real GDP, effect on, 620, 628
  in recession of 1990-1991, 743
  response to increase in money, 654
  shifts in aggregate demand curve, 508
  shocks. *See* Aggregate demand shocks
  short run increase, 546
  substitution effects, 506
  theories of. *See* Aggregate demand theories
  wealth effect, 505–506
  world economy and, 507–508
Aggregate demand shocks
  feedback-rule policies, 764–765, 765
  fixed rule policy, 764
  forecast horizon, 766–767
  policy lags, 766–767
  potential GDP, 766
  predictability of policies, 767
  stabilization of, 764–767
Aggregate demand theories
  AS–AD general theory, 736
  Keynesian theory, 731–732
  monetarist theory, 732–734
  new classical theory of the business cycle, 734
  new Keynesian theory of the business cycle, 734
  rational expectations theories, 734–736
Aggregate expenditure
  aggregate planned expenditure, 533
  algebra of, 550
  components of, 528
  consumption expenditure, 528–531
  curve, 534, 550
  defined, 460
  equilibrium expenditure, 536–537
  fixed prices, aggregate implications of, 533
  import function, 533
  model, 534
  multiplier. *See* Multiplier
  and price level, 543–545
  and real GDP, 533, 535–536
  saving, 528–531
  schedule, 534
  slope of curve, and multiplier, 540, 542
Aggregate hours, 483–484
Aggregate income, 459, 460
Aggregate planned expenditure
  autonomous expenditure, 535
  defined, **533**
  and equilibrium expenditure, 536–537
  induced expenditure, 535
  and real GDP, 535
Aggregate production function, 500, 713
Aggregate supply
  aggregate production function, 500
  in Canada (1961–2001), 514
  changes in, 503–504
  decrease in, 513, 653–654
  fluctuations in, 513
  fundamentals, 500
  and labour market, 683–688
  long-run, 500–501, 700
  long-run, and labour market, 699
  long-run aggregate supply curve, 500–501, 502, 687, 698–700
  movements along supply curves, 502
  potential GDP, changes in, 503
  in recession of 1990–1991, 743
  shocks, stabilization of, 767–768
  short-run, 501–502, 700–703
  short-run aggregate supply curve, 501, 502, 687–688, 701–703
Aggregate supply–aggregate demand *(AS–AD)* model
  see also Aggregate demand; Aggregate supply
  and business cycle, 730
  equilibrium, 628–629
  general theory of the business cycle, 736
  and macroeconomic performance, 500
  short-run Phillips curve and, 663
Agricultural markets
  and bumper harvest, 138
  elasticity of demand, 138
  farm marketing boards. *See* Farm marketing board
  inventory holders, behaviour of, 138
  inventory speculation, 138
  and poor harvest, 137
  production, fluctuations in, 138
  stabilization of farm revenues, 137–141
  unregulated, 137–138
Air pollution, 415–416
Air pollution debate *(Reading between the lines),* 426–427
Airport security tax *(Reading between the lines),* 142–143
Alchian, Armen, 211
Allocative efficiency, 39
Anarchy, State, and Utopia (Nozick), 116
Anti-combine law, 394
  anti-competitive agreements, 406–407
  bank mergers, 407
  Bell Canada Enterprises case, 406
  in Canada, 406
  Canada Packers and Labatt case, 407
  Chrysler case, 406
  NutraSweet case, 406
  public *vs.* special interest, 407
Anti-inflation policy
  cost-push inflation, avoidance of, 769–771
  feedback-rule policies, 770–771
  fixed-rule policy, 769–770
  incentives to push up costs, 771
  inflation slowdown, 771–773
  Turner rule, 773
Anticipated inflation, 659–661
AS–AD model. *See* Aggregate supply–aggregate demand *(AS–AD)* model
Asia, and real GDP growth, 710
Automatic fiscal policy, 562
Automatic stabilizers, 566–568
Autonomous expenditure, 535
Autonomous tax multiplier, 564–565, 577
Autonomous taxes, 562
Autonomous transfer payments multiplier, 565, 577
Average cost pricing rule, 277, 398
Average fixed cost, 224
Average product, 219
Average product curves, 222
Average tax rate, 359, 382
Average total cost, 224
Average total cost curve, 224–225
Average variable cost, 224

Balance of payments accounts
capital account, 810
current account, 810
defined, **810**
official Canadian reserves, 810
official settlements account, 810
Balanced budget, 557, 567–568
Bank deposit insurance, 748
Bank of Canada
see also Monetary policy
balance sheet, 607
banks' accounts at, 585
Bouey's fight against inflation, 621
Crow and price stability, 621
Dodge's balancing act, 621
establishment of, **606**
and foreign exchange market, 822–823
interest rates and, 595–596
lender of last resort, role as, 748–749
monetary base, 607, 612–613
quantity of money, control over, 611–615
Thiessen's balancing act, 621
Bank of Canada Act, 606
Bank rate, 609
Banks
assets, types of, 585
balancing act, 585
bankers' deposit rate, 609
central bank. *See* Central bank
creation of money, 587–590
deposit creation through loans (multiple-bank economy), 589–590
deposit creation through loans (one-bank economy), 587–588
deposit multiplier, 588–589
investment securities, 585
liquid assets, 585
loans, 585
mergers, and anti-combine law, 407
reserves, 585, 587, 612–613
Bar chart, 18
Barriers to entry
and concentration measures, 208
defined, **262**
legal barriers to entry, 262
natural, 262–263
Barro, Robert, 661
Barter, 582
Base period, 490
Becker, Gary, 191, 192–194
Below full-employment equilibrium, 510
Bentham, Jeremy, 190–191
Best affordable point, 178
Bhagwati, Jagdish, 854–856
Biased CPI, 493
Big tradeoff, 10, **115, 361**
Bilateral monopoly, 345
Black markets, 126
Boat rides, marginal utility of *(Reading between the lines),* 166–167
Book sellers war *(Reading between the lines),* 304–305
Brazil, hyperinflation in, 449, 675
Break-even point, 240
Budget deficit
cyclical surplus or deficit, 567
defined, **449, 557**
over the business cycle, 566–567
structural surplus or deficit, 567
Budget equation, 173–174
Budget line, 154, **172,** 180
Budget surplus
cyclical surplus or deficit, 567
defined, **449, 557**
structural surplus or deficit, 567
Bureaucracy model of public enterprise, 404–405
Bureaucrats, 375, 380
Business cycle
aggregate demand theories, 731–736
AS–AD general theory, 736
and *AS–AD* model, 730
in Canada, 479, 515
capital, role of, 730
capital in, 739
dates, 478
defined, **8,** 478
discretionary policies, 763
expansion, 8
feedback-rule policies, 763
fixed-rule policies, 763
forecasts, 471
growth rate cycle downturn, 478
investment, role of, 730
Keynesian theory, 731–732
labour markets in, 739
and macroeconomic equilibrium, 510–511
macroeconomic policy goal, 756
monetarist theory, 732–734
most recent Canadian business cycle, 440
and multiplier, 541–542
new classical theory, 734
new Keynesian theory, 734
peak, 8
phases, 8, 478
rational expectations theories, 734–736
real business cycle theory, 737–741
recession, 8
trough, 8
turning points, 8, 541–542
Business organizations
corporation, 203
partnership, 202–203
pros and cons of different types, 203
relative importance of types of, 204
sole proprietorship, 202
types of, 202–203

Caisse populaire, 586
Canada
aggregate hours (1961–2001), 483
aggregate supply and aggregate demand (1961–2001), 514
anti-combine law in, 406
balance of payments (1981–2001), 811
balance of payments accounts (2001), 810
borrower and debtor status, 812
borrowing, reasons for, 812–813
budget, in global perspective, 561
budget highlights (2002), 556–557
business cycle, 515
business cycle, most recent, 440
business cycle and budget deficit, 566
business cycle patterns, 479
capital, increase of, 691
changing demand for money *(Reading between the lines),* 600–601
concentration measures, 207
consumption function, 532
cost-push inflation in, 655
CPI (1971–2001), 492
CPI basket, 490
current account balance, 449–450
demand for money in, 593–594
demand-pull inflation in, 653
deposit multiplier, 590
distribution of income, 5
drug dealing penalties, 136
economic growth, long-term, 441
economic growth in, 41, 439–441, 442, 514
employment in, 481
evolving economy (1961–2001), 515–516
exchange rate, 815
expansion, most recent, 8
farm marketing boards in, 139
federal government debt, 559
fiscal policy record (1971–2001), 759
full employment in, 692
gains from international trade, 44–45
GDP balloon, 467
government budget balance, 450
government tax revenues, 382
gross domestic product, measurement of, 463–464
growth rate cycles, 479
illegal drug market in, 135–136
imports since NAFTA, 533
income distribution in, 348
income distribution trends (1980–1998), 352
income Lorenz curve (1998), 349
income redistribution, 360
inflation and the interest rate, 666
inflation in, 447, 515
inflation rate (1971–2001), 492
interest rate and the dollar, 619
interest rates, 617
interest rates and real GDP growth, 620

international balance, 449–450
international deficit, 450
job creation in, 444
labour force participation rate, 481
labour market trends, 317
long-term growth, 708
low income incidence, by family characteristics, 353
macroeconomic performance: real GDP and inflation, 757
minimum wage in, 130
monetary base and the interest rate, 618
monetary policy record (1971–2001), 759
money growth (1989–1995), 742
money growth and inflation, 657
money in, 583
money multiplier, 615
next recession, 542
North American economy, market structure of, 209
official Canadian reserves, 810
overnight loans rate and Taylor rule, 773
personal saving rate, 844
Phillips curve in, 665
population increase in, 691
population labour force categories, 480
production function, 682, 692
production per person, in past 30 years, 40
productivity in, 691–692
provincial government budgets, 560
quintile shares (1998), 349
real GDP, level of, 709
real GDP, *vs.* China's real GDP, 470–471
real GDP growth (1989–1995), 742
real GDP per hour of labour, 713
real wage rate (1961–2001), 484
revenues, outlays and budget balance (1971–2001), 557
saving rates (1971–2001), 761
tariffs (1867–2001), 793
technological advances in, 691–692
total government budgets, 561
twin deficit, 814
unemployment, 445, 481
unemployment and real GDP, 489
unemployment by demographic group, 487
unemployment by duration, 486
unemployment by reason, 486
welfare challenge in, 361
Canada–United States Free Trade Agreement, 742–743, 802
Canada–U.S. productivity gap *(Reading between the lines),* 696–697
Canadian dollar
see also Exchange rate; Foreign exchange market
appreciation of (1986–1991), 821
demand for, 816–817
depreciation of (1991–2001), 821
and interest rates, 619
supply of, 818, 819
Canadian interest rate differential, 817
Capacity output, 287
Capital
business cycle, role in, 730
and debt, 560
defined, **4,** 461
demand curve, 329
demand for, 325–326
demand for, and income taxes, 572
depreciation, 461
economic depreciation, 196–197
equity, 830
human capital, 4, 40
implicit rental rate, 196
increase in Canada, 691
interest, 5
marginal product of capital, 228
physical, 681, 690
quantity changes, and potential GDP, 503
in real business cycle, 739
substitutability of, for labour, 322
supply curve, 330
supply of, 329–330
unequal ownership of, 358
Capital account, 810
Capital accumulation, 40, 718–719
Capital consumption, 461
Capital gain, 831
Capital gains tax, 843
Capital loss, 831
Capital markets
capital demand curve, 329
defined, 325
demand for capital, 325–326
discounting, 326
equilibrium, 330
and interest rate, 330–331
net present value, 328
present value, 326–328
supply curve of capital, 330
supply of capital, 329–330
unanticipated inflation and, 658–659
Capture theory, 395–396, 398, 400–401
Card, David, 130, 695
Cartel
defined, **295,** 401
regulation, 401–402
Causation, and graphs, 20
Cause and effect, identification of, 13
Central bank
defined, **606**
independent central bank, 606
subordinate central bank, 606
Ceteris paribus
defined, **13**
graphing relationships among more than two variables, 26–27
Chain-weighted output index, 466
Change in demand
vs. change in quantity demanded, 64–65
defined, **63**
expected future prices, 63–64
factors, 63–64
income, 64
in perfect competition, 246
permanent, 250–251
population, 64
and preferences, 64
price and quantity, effect on, 72–73, 74–75
prices of related goods, 63
Change in quantity demanded, 65
Change in supply
vs. change in quantity supplied, 68–69
defined, **67**
expected future prices, 68
factors, 67–68
price and quantity, effect on, 73, 74–75, 84
prices of productive resources, 67
prices of related goods, 67–68
suppliers, number of, 68
technology, 68
Change in the quantity supplied, 68–69
Chartered banks, 585
see also Banks
Cheques, *vs.* deposits, 584
China, real GDP in, 470–471, 710
Choices, as tradeoffs, 9–10
Circular flow model, 459–460
Classical growth theory, 717–719
Coase, Ronald, 210, 419, 432–433
Coase theorem, 419, 425
Collusion
cheating on agreement, 297–298
monopolistic competition, impossibility in, 284
payoff matrix, 298
profit maximization, 296
Collusive agreement, 295
Command systems, 201
Common stock, 830
Comparative advantage, 42–43, 787, **788,** 791
Competition
and choices, 254
and efficiency, 254–255
and equilibrium, 254
perfect competition. *See* Perfect competition
Competition Act, 406–407
Competition policy
anti-combine law, 406–407
economic theory of regulation, 394–396
market intervention, 394
public ownership, 403–405
regulation. *See* Regulation
Competitive equilibrium, efficiency of, 110

Competitive market
competitive equilibrium, efficiency of, 110
defined, **60**
efficiency of, 106, 110–113
fairness of, 114–117
"invisible hand," 111
obstacles to efficiency, 111–113
Complement
and cross elasticity of demand, 92
defined, **63,** 68
and indifference curves, 177–178
Concentration measures
and barriers to entry, 208
for Canadian economy, 207
firm turnover, 208
four-firm concentration ratio, 206
geographical scope of markets, 208
Herfindahl-Hirschman Index, 206–207
limitations of, 207–209
market and industry correspondence, 208–209
Constant returns to scale, 231
Consumer behaviour
best affordable point, 178
income effect, 180–182
predictions, 178–182
price effect, 179–180
Consumer equilibrium, 157
Consumer Price Index (CPI)
base period, 490
basket, 490–491
biased, 493
calculation of, 491–492
commodity substitution bias, 193
construction of, 490–492
defined, **490**
inflation measurement, 492
and inflation rate, 492
monthly CPI report *(Reading between the lines),* 494–495
monthly price survey, 491
new goods bias, 193
outlet substitution bias, 193
quality change bias, 193
reading CPI numbers, 490
Consumer surplus
and consumer efficiency, 164
defined, **107**
and paradox of value, 165
and price discrimination, 271–272
Consumption
household. *See* Household consumption choices
negative consumption externalities, 414
positive consumption externalities, 414
Consumption expenditure
consumption function, 528
defined, **459,** 461
and disposable income, 528
factors influencing, 528–531
interest rate, 597–598
marginal propensity to consume, 530
and real GDP, 532
and stock markets, 843–844
Consumption function
algebra of, 550
in Canada, 532
defined, **528**
Consumption possibilities
budget equation, 173–174
divisible and indivisible goods, 172
household consumption choices, 154
international trade and, 790–791
Contestable market, 302–303
Contractionary fiscal policy, 569
Cooperative equilibrium, 301
Copyright, 262, **425**
Corporation, 203
Correlation, and graphs, 20
Cost-benefit analysis, forerunner of, 149
Cost curves
long-run average cost curve, 229, 230
and prices of productive resources, 227
and product curves, 226–227
shifts in, 226–227
and technological change, 226–227
Cost of living
defined, **7**
deflation, 7
inflation, 7
prices in different currencies, 7
Cost-push inflation, 769–771
aggregate demand response, 654
aggregate supply, decrease in, 653–654
in Canada, 655
defined, **653**
example of, 655
process, 654–655
Costs
of anticipated inflation, 660–661
average costs, 224–225
average fixed cost, 224
average total cost, 224
average variable cost, 224
boot leather costs of inflation, 661
defined, 108
of economic growth, 40, 443–444
of education *(Reading between the lines),* 48–49
explicit, 196
external. *See* External costs
implicit, 196
long-run cost. *See* Long-run cost
main sources of increases in, 653
marginal cost, 11, 224
marginal external cost, 417
marginal private cost, 417
opportunity cost. *See* Opportunity cost
owner's resources, 197
vs. price, 108–109
private, 417
selling costs, 289–290
short-run. *See* Short-run cost
sunk cost, 218
total cost, 223, 241
total fixed cost, 223
total variable cost, 223
transactions, 210–211, 419
Cournot, Antoine-Augustin, 148
Credit cards, 584
Credit unions, 586
Creditor nation, 812
Cross elasticity of demand, 91–92
Cross-section graphs, 18
Crowding in, 633
Crowding out, 633, 640–641
Crown corporations
budget maximization at zero price, 405
budget maximization with marginal cost pricing, 404–405
bureaucracy model of public enterprise, 404–405
defined, **394,** 403
efficiency, 403–404
in reality, 405
Currency, 583
Currency appreciation, 815
Currency depreciation, 815
Currency drain, 613
Current account
balance, 813
defined, **449, 810**
Currie, Janet, 370–372
Curved line, slope of, 25–26
Cyclical surplus or deficit, 567
Cyclical unemployment, 488, 763–769

DAX index, 833
Deadweight loss, 112, 269, 398
Debit cards, 584
Debtor nation, 812
Decision time frame
long run, 218
short run, 218
Deficits
borrowing to finance, 559
government budget deficit, 449, 557
importance of, 450
international, 449–450
twin deficits, 814
worldwide, 461
Deflation, 7, 447
Degree of specialization differences, 358
Demand
aggregate demand. *See* Aggregate demand
buying plans, determination of, 61
for capital, 325–326
change in demand. *See* Change in demand
computer prices *(Reading between the lines),* 76–77
defined, **62**
derived demand, 317

for dollars, changes in, 816–817
elastic demand, 87
elasticities of. *See* Elasticities of demand
in foreign exchange market, 816
and higher price, 61
income elastic demand, 92
income inelastic demand, 92
increase in, 63
inelastic demand, 87
for labour. *See* Demand for labour
law of demand, 61
market demand, 163–164
market demand for labour, 322
for money. *See* Demand for money
in monopoly, 265
in perfect competition, 239
perfectly elastic demand, 87
perfectly inelastic demand, 86
price elasticity. *See* Price elasticity of demand
quantity demanded, 61, 64–65
for regulation, 394–395
schedule, 62
unit elastic demand, 86
and willingness to pay, 106

Demand curve
aggregate demand curve, 505–506
from budget line and indifference curve, 180
for capital, 329
defined, **62**
demand for money curve, 592
equation, 78
and income effect, 180
kinked demand curve model, 291
labour demand curve, 319
as marginal benefit curve (willingness-to-pay), 106, 164
movement along, 65
relative price *vs.* money price, 106
shift of, 65
straight-line, and elasticity, 87
willingness and ability to pay, 62

Demand for labour
changes in, 321, 685
defined, **683**
derived demand, 317
diminishing marginal product and, 684–685
elasticity of, 322
labour demand curve, 319
law of diminishing returns, 683, 684
long-run demand for labour, 321
marginal product calculation, 684
marginal product of labour, 683
market demand for labour, 322
quantity of labour demanded, 683
short-run demand for labour, 321
and unions, 343

Demand for money
in Canada, 593–594
curve, 592
financial innovation, 591
and interest rate, 591
interest rate target *vs.* money target, 618–619
and price level, 591
and real GDP, 591

Demand for money curve, 592

Demand-pull inflation
aggregate demand increase, initial effect of, 651
in Canada, 653
defined, **651**
example of, 652–653
money wage rate response, 651–652
process, 652

Demsetz, Harold, 211

Deposit multiplier, 588–589, 590

Depository institutions
borrowing costs, minimization of, 586–587
caisse populaire, 586
chartered banks, 585
credit unions, 586
defined, **585**
economic functions of, 586–587
financial legislation, 586
liquidity, creation of, 586
monitoring borrowers, 587
Paul Martin's reform proposal, 586
pooling risk, 587
trust and mortgage loan company, 586

Deposits
bank deposit insurance, 748
creation of, in multiple-bank economy, 589–590
creation of, in one-bank economy, 587–588
as money, 583, 584

Depreciation, 461

Deregulation, 402–403

Derived demand, 317

Desired reserve ratio, 587

Developing economies, inflation in, 7

Diminishing marginal rate of substitution, 176

Diminishing marginal returns, 221

Diminishing marginal utility, 155

Direct relationship, 20

Discount factor, 837

Discounting, 326

Discouraged worker, 445, 482

Discoveries, 721

Discretionary fiscal policy, 562

Discretionary policies, 763

Discrimination, and economic inequality, 357–358

Diseconomies of scale, 230–231

Disposable income, 507, 528

Dividend, 830

Dividend yield, 831

Divisible goods, 172

Division of labour, 55

DJIA, 833

Domestic airline monopoly *(Reading between the lines)*, 278–279

Dominant firm oligopoly, 292

Double counting, 458

The Dow, 833

Dumping, 798

Duopoly, 295–299, 301–302

Dupuit, Jules, 148, 149

Dynamic comparative advantage, 45

E-books *(Reading between the lines)*, 184–185

Earnings
defined, **831**
growth, trends and cycles in, 841–842
per share, 835

Econometrics, 13

Economic accounting
economic depreciation, 196–197
economic profit, 197
explicit costs, 196
implicit costs, 196
implicit rental rate, 196
normal profit, 197
opportunity costs, 196–197
owner's resources, cost of, 197
summary of, 197

Economic depreciation, 196–197

Economic efficiency, 199, 199–200, 254

Economic growth
during Asia Crisis, 41
benefits of, 443
in Canada, 41, 439–441, 442, 514
and capital accumulation, **40**
causes of, 711–712
costs of, 40, 443–444
defined, **40, 439**
forecasting economic growth *(Reading between the lines)*, 724–725
growth accounting. *See* Growth accounting
growth theories. *See* Growth theories
in Hong Kong, 41
human capital, investment in, 712, 762
incentive system, 711
long-term growth policy, 760–762
long-term growth trends, 708–710
and macroeconomic equilibrium, 510
measurement of, 439
see also Economic growth rate
preconditions for, 711
productivity growth slowdown, 439
saving and investment in new capital, 711–712, 760–761
and technological change, 40, 712, 762
worldwide, 441–443, 709–710

Economic growth rate
business cycle forecasts, 471
defined, **468**
economic welfare comparisons, 468–470

international comparisons, 470–471
Economic inequality
after-tax income, distribution of, 348
discrimination, 357–358
human capital, 354–356
and life cycle stages, 351
Lorenz curve, 349–350
measurement of, 348–353
poor, characteristics of, 352–353
poverty, 352
rich, characteristics of, 352–353
sources of, 354–358
trends in, 351–352
trends in *(Reading between the lines),* 362–363
unequal ownership of capital, 358
wealth, distribution of, 350
Economic model
defined, **12**
described, 20
graphs used in, 20–23
unrelated variables, 23
variables moving in opposite directions, 21–22
variables moving in same direction, 20–21
variables with a maximum or minimum, 22
Economic profit, 197, 238–239, 241
Economic questions
macroeconomic questions, 6–8
microeconomics questions, 3–5
Economic rent, 334–335
Economic rents and opportunity costs on the ice *(Reading between the lines),* 336–337
Economic theory, 12–13
Economic theory of government, 374–375
Economic theory of regulation, 394–396
Economic way of thinking
choices and tradeoffs, 9
incentives, 11
margins, 11
opportunity cost, 11
Economic welfare
defined, **468**
environmental quality, 469
health and life expectancy, 469
household production, 468
leisure, 469
overadjustment for inflation, 468
political freedom, 469–470
social justice, 469–470
underground economic activity, 468–469
Economics
agreement and disagreement, 14
cause and effect, identification of, 13
definition of, **2**
fallacy of composition, 13
human behaviour, analysis of, 190–191
Keynesian economics, 438
macroeconomics, 2
microeconomics, 2
model building, 12
observation and measurement, 12
obstacles and pitfalls, 13
post hoc fallacy, 13–14
scarcity and, 2
as social science, 12–14
task of economic science, 12
testing models, 12–13
The Economics of Discrimination (Becker), 192
Economies of scale
constant returns to scale, 231
defined, **211, 230**
diseconomies of scale, 230–231
international trade, 792
minimum efficient scale, 231
and monopoly, 275–276
Economies of scope
defined, **211**
and monopoly, 275–276
Economies of team production, 211
Education, costs and benefits of *(Reading between the lines),* 48–49
Education quality, 716
Efficiency
see also Inefficiency
allocative efficiency, 39
and competition, 254–255
of competitive market, 106, 110–113
consumer efficiency, and consumer surplus, 164
Crown corporations, 403–404
economic, 199–200, 254
economists' use of term, 104
efficient allocation, 104
and fairness, 116
and inefficiency, 105
and marginal benefit, 104
marginal benefit equals marginal cost, 105
marginal benefit exceeds marginal cost, 105
and marginal cost, 104–105
marginal cost exceeds marginal benefit, 105
and monopolistic competition, 287, 290
of monopoly, 255, 269
obstacles to, 111–113
of perfect competition, 255, 269
pharmaceutical drug market *(Reading between the lines),* 118–119
and price discrimination, 274
and product innovation, 288–289
production efficiency, 35, 39
public goods and, 255
and rent ceilings, 127
resources. *See* Resources
and taxes, 134
technological, 199, 254
Efficiency wage, 694–695
Efficient allocation, 255
Efficient allocation, 104
Ehrlich, Paul, 368
Elastic demand, 87
Elasticities of demand
cross elasticity of demand, 91–92
glossary of, 97
income elasticity of demand, 92
labour, 322
price elasticity of demand. *See* Price elasticity of demand
for product, 322
real-world income elasticities of demand, 93
Elasticity of supply
calculation of, 94–95
defined, **94**
factors influencing, 95–96
in global oil market *(Reading between the lines),* 98–99
glossary of, 97
resource substitution possibilities, 95–96
and tax division, 133
time frame for supply decision, 96
Emission charges, 420
Employment Insurance program, 359
Employment-to-population ratio, 482–483
Energy price shocks, 716
Entrants, 485
Entrepreneurship
defined, **4**
profit, 5
Entry, effects of, 247–248
Environment
pollution. *See* Pollution
quality of, 469
trade barriers and, 799
Equality of opportunity, 116
Equation of exchange, 656
Equilibrium
above full-employment equilibrium, 510–511
AS-AD, 628–629
below full-employment equilibrium, 510
capital markets, 330
competitive equilibrium, efficiency of, 110
consumer equilibrium, 157
cooperative equilibrium, 301
exchange rate, 820
expenditure. *See* Equilibrium expenditure
in foreign exchange market, 820
GDP, and price level, 545–547, 569–570
labour market, 324, 686
long-run, 249
macroeconomic. *See* Macroeconomic equilibrium
market equilibrium, 70–71, 79

money market equilibrium, 595, 628
Nash equilibrium, 294, 298–299
political, 381, 395
rent-seeking, 270–271
short-run, 246
Equilibrium expenditure
algebra of, 551, 576
convergence to, 537
defined, **536–537**
multiplier. *See* Multiplier
Equilibrium price, 70
Equilibrium quantity, 70
Equity. *See* Fairness
Equity capital, 830
Excess reserves, 587
Exchange rate
see also Foreign exchange market
changes in, 820–821
currency appreciation, 815
currency depreciation, 815
defined, 507, **596**
equilibrium, 820
and expansionary fiscal policy, 633
expectations, 821
expected future exchange rate, 817, 819
and interest rate, 598
monetary policy and, 619–620
and net exports, 598
policy effects, 642
projections *(Reading between the lines)*, 824–825
volatility of, 820
Excise tax, 386–387
Exit, effects of, 248
Expansion, 8, **440**, 478, 542, 734
Expansionary fiscal policy
adjustment to, 632
crowding in, 633
crowding out, 633
defined, **569,** 630
first round effects, 630
at full employment, 640–641
and interest-sensitive components of aggregate expenditure, 633
international crowding out, 633
second round effects, 630–632
Expansionary monetary policy
economic adjustment, 636
exchange rate, effect on, 637
first round effects, 634–635
at full employment, 641
money, effect on, 637
second round effects, 635–637
Expectations, 506–507
Expected future prices, 63–64, 68
Expected profit effect, 816, 818–819
Expenditure
aggregate. *See* Aggregate expenditure
approach, 463
autonomous, 535
consumption. *See* Consumption expenditure
equilibrium, 536–537
government expenditures, 460
induced, 535
and interest rate, 597–599
interest-sensitive expenditure curve, 598–599
marketing, 289
and price elasticity of demand, 89
Explicit costs, 196
Exports
defined, **460, 786**
effect, 816
net exports, 460, 786, 813–814
External benefits
defined, 112, **254**
and efficiency, 112
efficiency, obstacle to, 255
knowledge, and government actions, 423–425
marginal external benefit, 421
External costs
defined, 112, **254**
and efficiency, 112
efficiency, obstacle to, 255
government actions, 420–421
marginal external cost, 417
and output, 417
valuation of, 417
External diseconomies, 251–253
External economies, 251–253
Externalities
defined, **414**
knowledge, 421–425
negative, 414
negative consumption externalities, 414
negative production externalities, 414
pollution, 415–421
positive, 414
positive consumption externalities, 414
positive production externalities, 414
and property rights, 432–433
Extreme Keynesian hypothesis, 638
Extreme monetarist hypothesis, 639

Factor markets
capital markets, 325–331
defined, 46
demand and supply in, 316
economic rent, and opportunity cost, 334–335
income, 334
labour market, 317–324
natural resource markets, 331–333
prices and incomes in competitive factor markets, 316
Factors of production
capital, 4
defined, **4**
entrepreneurship, 4
labour, 4
land, 4
sale of services of, 5
"Fair results" ideas, 115
Fairness
big tradeoff, 115
of competitive market, 114–117
and efficiency, 116
"fair results" ideas, 115
farm marketing board, 141
pharmaceutical drug market *(Reading between the lines),* 118–119
price hike in natural disaster, 116–117
and rent ceilings, 127
symmetry principle, 116
unfair results, 114–115
unfair rules, 116
utilitarian, 114–115
Fallacy of composition, 13
Farm marketing board
defined, **139**
fairness of, 141
inefficiency of, 141
price floor, 139–140
quotas, 140
subsidy, 140–141
Federal budget, 556
Feedback-rule policies, 763, 764–765, 765, 768, 770–771
Final good, 458
Financial flows
household saving, 460
investment, financing of, 460–461
national saving, 461
Financial innovation, 591
Financial property, 46
Firm turnover, 208
Firms
command systems, 201
concentration measures, 206–209
constraints, 198
coordination of production, 210–211
decision time frames, 218
defined, **196**
earnings, 831–832
economic problem of, 196–198
and economies of scale, 211
economies of scope, 211
economies of team production, 211
goal of, 196
incentive systems, 201
information and organization, 201–204
information constraints, 198
long-run cost, 228–231
market constraints, 198
vs. markets, 210–211
and opportunity cost, 196–197
output. *See* Output
in perfect competition. *See* Perfect competition
perfect competition, decisions in, 240–245
principal-agent problem, 202
profit, measurement of, 196

relative importance of types of, 204
short-run cost, 223–227
technology constraints, 198, 219–222
transactions costs, 210–211
types of, 202–203
Fiscal policy
and aggregate demand, 507, 568–570
automatic fiscal policy, 562
autonomous expenditure, changes in, 633
contractionary fiscal policy, 569
defined, **451, 507, 556,** 758
demand-side effects, 572–573
discretionary fiscal policy, 562, 763
effectiveness of, 637
expansionary fiscal policy. *See* Expansionary fiscal policy
feedback-rule policies, 763
first round effects, 630
fiscal expansion at potential GDP, 570–571
fixed-rule policies, 763
income tax, and demand for capital, 572
interest rates and exchange rates, effects on, 639, 642
Japanese, in 1990s, 744
Keynesian-monetarist controversy, 638–639
labour market taxes, 571–572
limitations of, 571
monetary and fiscal tensions *(Reading between the lines),* 644–645
other fiscal policies, 633
policy conflict, 642–643
policy coordination, 642
and potential GDP, 571–572
projections *(Reading between the lines),* 574–575
second round effects, 630–632
in short run, 630–633
since 1971, 758–759
supply-side effects, 571–573
Fiscal policy multipliers
algebra of, 576–577
automatic stabilizers, 566–568
autonomous tax multiplier, 564–565, 577
autonomous transfer payments multiplier, 565, 577
equilibrium expenditure, 576
government expenditures multiplier, 562–564, 576–577
and international trade, 566
and price level, 568–571
Fixed prices, aggregate implications of, 533
Fixed-rule policies, 763, 764, 768, 769–770
Flat-rate income tax, 359
Flow, 461
Forecasting economic growth *(Reading between the lines),* 724–725
Foreign exchange market
see also Exchange rate
Bank of Canada and, 822–823
Canadian interest rate differential, 817
defined, **815**
demand for dollars, changes in, 816–817
demand in, 816
expected profit effect, 816, 818–819
exports effect, 816
imports effect, 818
interest rate parity, 822
and interest rates, 816–817, 819
law of demand for foreign exchange, 816
law of supply in foreign exchange, 818–819
market equilibrium, 820
purchasing power parity, 822
supply in, 818
supply of dollars, changes in, 819
Foreign exchange rate, 815
see also Exchange rate
Four-firm concentration ratio, 206
Free rider, 376
Free-rider problem
creation of, 376
defined, 112, 374
Free trade agreements, 742–743, 793–794, 802–803
Frictional unemployment, 487–488
Friedman, Milton, 674–675
FTSE 100, 833
Full employment
in Canada, 692
crowding out, 640–641
defined, **488**
and expansionary fiscal policy, 640–641
and expansionary monetary policy, 641
Keynes, at above-full employment, 732
and potential GDP, 489
unanticipated inflation and, 658
unemployment at, 693–695

Gains from trade, 43–45, 787–792, 852–853
Game theory
cooperative equilibrium, 301
defined, **293**
games, features of, 293
Nash equilibrium, 294, 298–299
payoff matrix, 293, 298
price-fixing game, 295–299
price wars, 302
prisoners' dilemma, 293–294
real-world games, 301–303
repeated duopoly game, 301–302
sequential entry game in contestable market, 302–303
strategies, 293
tit-for-tat strategy, 301
trigger strategy, 301
Game tree, 302
GDP. *See* Gross domestic product (GDP)
GDP deflator, 466–467
General Agreement on Tariffs and Trade (GATT), 793
The General Theory of Employment, Interest and Money (Keynes), 438
Geographical scope of markets, 208
Germany
economic growth in, 442–443
hyperinflation in, 66–75
Global economy. *See* World economy
Global oil market, elasticity of demand and supply in *(Reading between the lines),* 98–99
Goods
complement, 63, 68
divisible, 172
final good, 458
illegal goods, 135–136
indivisible, 172
inferior good, 64, 92
intermediate good, 458
international trade in, 786
luxuries, 89
markets, 46
necessities, 89
normal good, 64
public goods, 112
substitute, 63, 67
Goods and services
defined, **3**
factors of production, 4
how they are produced, 4
what are produced, 3
for whom they are produced, 5
Government
big tradeoff, 10, 361
bureaucrats, 375, 380
deficits. *See* Deficits
economic theory of, 374–375
expenditures, and possibility of severe depression, 749
income maintenance programs, 359
income redistribution, 359–361
knowledge, actions for dealing with, 423–425
licence, 262
and market failure, 374
market intervention, 394
pollution, actions for coping with, 420–421
public choice model, 375
public choice theory, 380, 381
public interest theory, 381
purpose of, 374
saving, increasing, 761
size and growth, 381
subsidized services, 359–360
taxes. *See* Taxes
and voters, 375, 381

Government budgets
balance, 557
balanced budget, 557, 567–568
budget deficit, 449, 557
budget making, 556
budget surplus, 449, 557
Canadian budget in global perspective, 561
cyclical surplus or deficit, 567
federal budget, 556
highlights of 2002 budget, 556–557
in historical perspective, 557–558
outlays, 557, 558–559
provincial budget, 556, 560–561
revenues, 558
structural surplus or deficit, 567
Government debt, 559–560
Government deposit shifting, 610
Government expenditures, 460
Government expenditures multiplier, 562–564, 576–577
Government sector balance, 813
Graphs
bar chart, 18
breaks in axes, 20
causation, 20
correlation, 20
cross-section graphs, 18
demand curves. *See* Demand curve
described, 17
direct relationship, 20
in economic models, 20–23
inverse relationship, 21
linear relationship, 20–21, 28
making a graph, 17
misleading, 20
negative relationship, 21
positive relationship, 20
product curves, 219–222
ratio scale graphs, 834
relationships among more than two variables, 26–27
scatter diagram, 19
slope of relationship, 24–26
supply curves. *See* Supply curve
time-series graphs, 18
unrelated variables, 23
variables moving in opposite directions, 21–22
variables moving in same direction, 20–21
variables with a maximum or minimum, 22
Great Depression
causes of, 747–748
changes during, 746
described, 8, **438,** 746
magnitude of, 747
real GDP, decrease in, 441, 478
reoccurrence, possibility of, 748–749
uneven distribution of hardship, 746–747
Gross domestic product (GDP)
and circular flow of expenditure and income, 459–460
defined, **458**
determination of, 460
equilibrium, and price level, 545–547, 569–570
expenditure approach, 463
and expenditure plans, 528–533
final goods and services, 458
in given time period, 458
growth and fluctuations, 462
income approach, 463–464
market value, 458
measurement of, 463–464
vs. net domestic product, 462
nominal GDP, 465
potential GDP. *See* Potential GDP
produced within country, 458
quarterly GDP report *(Reading between the lines),* 472–473
real GDP. *See* Real gross domestic product (real GDP)
Gross investment, 461
Growth accounting
aggregate production function, 713
defined, **713**
faster growth, achievement of, 716
growth in 1960s, 715
growth in 1970s, 715
growth slowdown, 715
growth speedup, 715
and labour productivity, 713
one-third rule, 714–715
productivity curve, 713–714
productivity growth slowdown and speedup, 713
purpose of, 713
technological change during slowdown, 716
Growth rate cycle downturn, 478
Growth recession, 440
Growth theories
classical growth theory, 717–719
defined, **721**
neoclassical growth theory, 719–721
new growth theory, 721–723
GST, 385

Hamermesh, Daniel, 130
Health and life expectancy, 469
Herfindahl–Hirschman Index, 206–207
Heston, Alan, 470
High-technology industries, 716
Hong Kong
dynamic comparative advantage, 45
economic growth in, 41
Hotelling, Harold, 332, 368
Hotelling principle, 332–333
Household choice model
budget equation, 173–174
budget line, 172
consumer behaviour, prediction of, 178–182
work-leisure choices, 182–183
Household consumption choices
budget line, 154
consumption possibilities, 154
diminishing marginal utility, 155
divisible and indivisible goods, 172
indifference curve. *See* Indifference curve
marginal utility, 155
prediction of consumer behaviour. *See* Consumer behaviour
preference map, 175
and preferences, 154
total utility, 154–155
utility, 154–156
Household production, 468
Household work-leisure choices
labour supply, 182
labour supply curve, 183
Housing markets
black markets, 126
inefficiency of rent ceilings, 127
long-run adjustments, 125
regulation of, 125–126
and rent ceilings, 124–128
response to decrease in supply, 124
search activity, 126
Howitt, Peter, 661
Human capital
accumulation of, 762
and capital accumulation, 40
defined, **4**
and economic growth, 712
and economic inequality, 354–356
and labour productivity, **681**–682
and potential GDP, 690
and unemployment, 446
Human Capital (Becker), 192
Hume, David, 852
Hyperinflation, 448–449, 661

Illegal goods
free market for drugs, 135
and heavy penalties, 136
legalization, effect of, 136
market for illegal drugs, 135–136
prohibition, 136
taxes on, 136
Implicit costs, 196
Implicit rental rate, 196
Imports
defined, **460, 786**
effect, 818
marginal propensity to import, 533
and multiplier, 540–541
since NAFTA, 533
Incentive, 11
Incentive pay, 202
Incentive systems, 201
Income
after-tax, 348
aggregate, 459, 460
approach, 463–464

change in, and budget equation, 174
and demand, 64
disposable, 507, 528
distribution. *See* Income distribution
earning an income, 5
economic rent, 334–335
effect. *See* Income effect
elastic demand, 92
expected future income, 330
in factor markets, 334
inelastic demand, 92
Lorenz curve, 349–350
market, 348
median, 348
mode, 348
proportion spent on good, and elasticity, 90
real income, 173
redistribution. *See* Income redistribution
rise in, and marginal utility theory, 162
and saving decisions, 329–330
total, 348
wage gap, 5
vs. wealth, 350–351

Income distribution
after-tax income, 348
bell-shaped, 348
in Canada, 5, 348
positively skewed, 348
trends in Canada (1980-1998), 352

Income effect
calculation of, 181
defined, **180**
demand, effect on, 61
and demand curve, 180
inferior good, price changes in, 182
labour supply, 323

Income elasticity of demand
defined, **92**
real-world, 93

Income maintenance programs, 359

Income redistribution
big tradeoff, 361
income maintenance programs, 359
income taxes, 359
scale of, 360
subsidized services, 359–360
and taxes, 374
unanticipated inflation, 658

Income taxes
average tax rate, **382**
corporate profits tax, 384, 843
and demand for capital, 572
effect of, 383–384
and income redistribution, 359
marginal tax rate, 382
median voter model, 384
and multiplier, 540–541
personal income tax, 382
progressive income taxes, 384

Income-time budget line, 182

Increasing marginal returns, 220–221

Indifference curve
and close substitutes, 177
and complements, 177–178
defined, **175**
degree of substitutability, 177–178
demand curve and, 180
diminishing marginal rate of substitution, 176
marginal rate of substitution (MRS), 176

Indivisible goods, 172

Induced expenditure, 535

Induced taxes, 565

Inefficiency
see also Efficiency
and efficiency, 105
farm marketing board, 141
housing markets, 127
minimum wage, 130
tariffs, 795

Inefficient overprovision, and governments, 381

Inelastic demand, 87

Infant-industry argument, 797

Inferior good
defined, **64**
and income elasticity of demand, 92
price change, effect of, 182

Inflation
anti-inflation policy. *See* Anti-inflation policy
anticipated, 659–660
boot leather costs, 661
in Canada, 447, 515
capital market, effect on, 658–659
causes of, 674–675
cost-push inflation, 653–655, 769–771
costs of anticipated inflation, 660–661
and CPI, 492
defined, **7, 447, 650**
deflation, 7, 447
demand-pull inflation, 651–653
in developing economies, 7
effects of, 658–661
forecasting, 659
hyperinflation, 448–449, 661
inflation-unemployment tradeoff *(Reading between the lines)*, 668–669
and interest rates, 666–667
Keynesian inflationary gap, 732
labour market, effect on, 658
and macroeconomic equilibrium, 510
macroeconomic policy goal, 757
macroeconomic policy indicator, 757
and monetary policy, 616–617
and money growth in Canada, 657
and money growth in world economy, 657
output-inflation tradeoff, 10
Phillips curve, 662–665
and price level, 650
and private saving, 761
problem of, 448–449
rational expectation, 659
reduction of, 771–773
stagflation, 654, 770
stock price, adjustments on, 834
Taylor rule, 773
transactions costs, 661
unanticipated, 658–659, 660
uncertainty, increase in, 661
and unemployment, 662–665
worldwide, 448

Inflation rate
calculation of, 492
defined, 447, **492**

Inflationary gap, 511

Innovation, 262, 275, 288–289, 780–781

Intellectual property, 46

Intellectual property rights, 425

Interest
defined, **5**
and savings decision, 330

Interest rate
in Canada, 617
Canadian interest rate differential, 817
and capital markets, 330–331
changes, 328
consumption expenditure, 597–598
defined, **594**
and demand for money, 591
determination, 594–595, 667
and the dollar, 619
and exchange rate, 598
and expenditure plans, 597–599
and foreign exchange market, 816–817, 819
and inflation, 666–667
influences on, 595–596
investment and, 598
and monetary base, 618
monetary policy and, 617–618
money market equilibrium, 595
and net exports, 598
nominal interest rate, 597, 667
and opportunity cost, 597
policy effects, 642
real GDP, effect on, 620
real interest rate, 597
and stock prices, 842–843

Interest rate parity, 822

Interest-sensitive expenditure curve, 598–599

Intermediate good, 458

International crowding out, 633

International finance
balance of payments accounts, 810–812
creditor nation, 812
current account balance, 813
debtor nation, 812
exchange rate. *See* Exchange rate
net borrower, 812

net exports, 813–814
twin deficits, 814
International trade
absolute advantage, 45
balanced trade, 789
comparative advantage, 42–43, 788, 791
consumption, changes in, 789–790
consumption possibilities, 790–791
dynamic comparative advantage, 45
economies of scale, 792
encouragement of, 716
financing. *See* International finance
and fiscal policy multipliers, 566
free trade agreements, 793–794
gains from trade, 43–45, 787–792, 852–853
geographical patterns, 786
in goods, 786
international borrowing, 786
net exports, 786
opportunity cost, 787–788
patterns and trends, 786
production, changes in, 789–790
restrictions. *See* Trade barriers
in services, 786
in similar goods, 792
taste, diversity of, 792
terms of trade, 788–789
volume of trade trends, 786
Internet, and stock market, 842
Invention, 262
Inventories
inventory holders, behaviour of, 138
speculative markets in, 138
Inverse relationship, 21
Investment
business cycle, role in, 730
defined, **460,** 461
and economic growth, 711–712
financing of, 460–461
gross investment, 461
and interest rate, 598
net investment, 461
"Invisible hand," 111
Involuntary part-time rate, 481

Japan
asset prices, collapse of, 744
economic growth in, 442–443
fiscal policy in 1990s, 744
monetary policy in 1990s, 744–745
real GDP, level of, 709
recession in, 8
sliding growth rate, 745
stagnation in, 744–745
structural problems, 745
Job leavers, 485
Job losers, 485
Job rationing
defined, **694**
efficiency wage, 694–695
and minimum wage, 695
and unemployment, 695
Job search, 693–694
Jobs, 444
see also Labour market
Joint unlimited liability, 203

Keynes, John Maynard, 438
Keynesian, 638
Keynesian activist, 764
Keynesian economics, 438
Keynesian inflationary gap, 732
Keynesian-monetarist controversy, 638–639
Keynesian theory of the business cycle, 731–732
Kinked demand curve model, 291
Knowledge
copyright, 425
and diminishing returns, 721–722
patent, 425
private benefits *vs.* social benefits, 421–423
public provision, 423–424
subsidy, 424
voucher, 424–425
Krueger, Alan, 130, 695
Kyoto Protocol in *AS-AD* model *(Reading between the lines),* 516–517

Labour
defined, **4**
demand for. *See* Demand for labour
full-employment quantity of, changes in, 503
high-skilled, 354–355
low-skilled, 354–355
substitutability of capital for, 322
supply of. *See* Supply of labour
wages, 5
Labour force
defined, **444, 480**
entrants, 485
re-entrants, 485
Labour force participation rate, 482
Labour Force Survey, 480
Labour market
aggregate hours, 483–484
and aggregate supply, 683–688
demand for labour. *See* Demand for labour
diminishing marginal revenue product, 318
discrimination in, 357–358
employment-to-population ratio, 482–483
equilibrium, 324, 686
human capital in, 354–356
indicators, 480–483
involuntary part-time rate, 481
labour force participation rate, 482
and long-run aggregate supply, 699
for low-skilled labour, and technological change, 129
marginal revenue product of labour, 318
market power in, 341–344
and minimum wage, 128–130
monopsony, 344
in 1990s, 743–744
and potential GDP, 686
profit maximization, 320
in real business cycle, 739
real wage rate, 484
and short-run aggregate supply, 702
short-run equilibrium, 700–701
structural change, 694
supply of labour. *See* Supply of labour
taxes, 571–572
and technological change, 128
tracking health of, 480–484
trends in Canada, 317
unanticipated inflation, effect of, 658
unemployment rate, 481
Labour productivity
defined, **681, 713**
growth accounting and, 713
growth slowdown and speedup, 715–716
and human capital, 681–682
increase in, 682
physical capital, 681
and potential GDP, 689–691
and technology, 682
Labour union
binding arbitration, 341
collective bargaining, 341
in competitive labour market, 342–343
constraints, 342
defined, **341**
demand for labour and, 343
lockout, 341
monopsony and, 345
objectives, 341–342
organization of, 341
Rand formula, 341
strike, 341
union-nonunion wage differentials, 343–344
Land
defined, **4**
rent, 5
Land pollution, 416
Lardner, Dionysius, 148
Law of demand, 61, 148–149
Law of diminishing returns
capital growth and, 730
defined, **221, 683, 714**
and marginal product of labour, 683, 684
and productivity curve, 714
Law of supply, 66, 148–149
Learning-by-doing, 45, 681
Legal monopoly, 262
Leisure, 182–183, 469
Limit pricing, 303

Limited liability, 203
Linear equation, 28
Linear relationship, 20–21, 28
Liquidity, 584
Living standards. *See* **Standard of living**
Local public good, 385–386
Long run
  defined, **218**
  macroeconomic long run, 500
Long-run adjustments, 247–248
Long-run aggregate supply, 500–501, 700
Long-run aggregate supply curve, 500–501, 502, **687,** 698–700
Long-run average cost curve, 229, 230
Long-run cost
  constant returns to scale, 231
  diminishing marginal product of capital, 228
  diminishing returns, 228
  diseconomies of scale, 230–231
  economies of scale, 230
  long-run average cost curve, 229, 230
  minimum efficient scale, 231
  production function, 228
  and short-run cost, 228–229
Long-run decisions in perfect competition, 240
Long-run equilibrium, 249
Long-run industry supply curve, 251–253
Long-run macroeconomic equilibrium, 509
Long-run neutrality, 641
Long-run Phillips curve, 664
Long-run supply curve, 96
Long-run supply of labour, 128
Long-term contracts, 202
Long-term growth trends, 708–710
Lorenz curve, 349–350
Low-income cutoff, 352
Luxuries, 89

M1, 583, 584
M2+, 583, 584
Macroeconomic equilibrium
  above full-employment equilibrium, 510–511
  AS-AD equilibrium, 628–629
  below full-employment equilibrium, 510
  and business cycle, 510–511
  and economic growth, 510
  and inflation, 510
  long-run macroeconomic equilibrium, 509
  money market equilibrium and interest-sensitive expenditure, 628
  short-run macroeconomic equilibrium, 508–509
Macroeconomic issues
  economic growth, 439–444
  inflation, 447–449
  surpluses and deficits, 449–450
  unemployment, 444–446
Macroeconomic long run, 500
Macroeconomic short run, 501
Macroeconomics
  business cycle goal, 756
  cost of living, 7
  defined, **2**
  fiscal policy, 451
  fluctuation of economy, 8
  inflation goal, 757
  issues, 438
  monetary policy, 451
  origins of, 438
  policy challenges and tools, 451
  policy goals, 756–757
  policy indicators, 757
  potential GDP growth as goal, 756
  short-term *vs.* long-term goals, 438
  stabilization policy balancing act *(Reading between the lines),* 774–775
  standard of living, 6
  three big questions, 6–8
  tradeoffs, 10
  unemployment goal, 756
Malthus, Thomas Robert, 368–369
Maple syrup, perfect competition in *(Reading between the lines),* 256–257
Margin, 11
Marginal analysis
  power of, 159
  profit-maximizing output, 242
Marginal benefit
  defined, **11, 38, 104**
  and efficiency, 104, 105
  equals marginal cost, effect of, 105
  exceeds marginal cost, effect of, 105
  marginal external benefit, 421
  marginal private benefits, 421
  marginal social benefit, 421
  and preferences, 38
  principle of decreasing marginal benefit, 38, 104
  and value, 106
  willingness-and-ability-to-pay, 62
Marginal benefit curve
  defined, **38**
  as demand curve, 106
Marginal cost
  and average costs, 225
  curve, as supply curve, 109
  defined, **11, 37, 104, 224**
  and efficiency, 104–105, 105
  equals marginal benefit, effect of, 105
  exceeds marginal benefit, effect of, 105
  marginal external cost, 417
  marginal private cost, 417
  marginal social cost, 417
  as minimum supply-price, 108
  and output, 224
  principle of increasing marginal cost, 104
  and production possibilities frontier, 37
Marginal cost pricing rule, 276–277, **398**
Marginal external benefit, 421
Marginal external cost, 417
Marginal private benefits, 421
Marginal private cost, 417
Marginal product, 219
Marginal product curve, 220–221
Marginal product of capital, 228
Marginal product of labour, 683, 684
Marginal propensity to consume, 530
Marginal propensity to import, 533
Marginal propensity to save, 530–531
Marginal rate of substitution (MRS), **176**
Marginal revenue
  defined, **238**
  and elasticity, 265
  and price, 264
Marginal revenue product, 318
Marginal social benefit, 421
Marginal social cost, 417
Marginal tax rate, 382, 565
Marginal utility, 155
  see also Marginal utility theory
Marginal utility per dollar spent, 157–159
Marginal utility theory
  assumptions, 162
  boat rides *(Reading between the lines),* 166–167
  and elasticity, 164
  implications, 162
  income, rise in, 162
  individual demand, 163
  market demand, 163
  movie prices, fall in, 159
  pop prices, rise in, 160–161
  predictions of, 159–164
  value, *vs.* price, 164–165
Market demand, 163–164
Market economy
  circular flows in, 46, 47
  coordinating decisions, 47
  market, 46
  property rights, 46
Market equilibrium
  best deal for buyers and sellers, 71
  defined, 70
  equation, 79
  labour market, 324
  price, 70
  price adjustments, 71
  price as regulator, 70–71
  quantity, 70
Market failure
  defined, **374**
  and government, 374
Market income, 348
Market intervention
  anti-combine law, 394

Crown corporations, 394
regulation, 394
Market power
defined, **262**
in labour market, 341–344
Market structure, 208, 209
Market types, 205
Marketing
expenditures, 289
in monopolistic competition, 289–290
and product differentiation, 284–285
selling costs, 289–290
total costs, 289–290
Markets
agricultural. *See* Agricultural markets
black markets, 126
and competitive environment, 205–209
competitive market. *See* Competitive market
concentration measures, 206–209
contestable market, 302–303
coordinating decisions, 47
coordination of production, 210
defined, **46**
domination by small number of firms, 206–207
factor markets. *See* Factor markets
vs. firms, 210–211
geographical scope of, 208
goods markets, 46
housing markets. *See* Housing markets
illegal goods, 135–136
labour market. *See* Labour market
and prices, 60
two sides of, 60
Marshall, Alfred, 148–149
McCallum, John, 434–436
McMillan, John, 150–152
Means of payment, 582
Median income, 348
Mercantilism, 852–853
Microeconomics
defined, **2**
"for whom" tradeoffs, 9–10
goods and services, production of, 3–5
"how" tradeoffs, 9
three big questions, 3–5
tradeoffs, 9–10
"what" tradeoffs, 9
Minimum efficient scale, 231
Minimum wage
defined, **129**
inefficiency of, 130
and job rationing, **695**
in monopsony, 345–346
in practice, 130
and unemployment, 129
Misallocation of resources, 35
Mode income, 348
Momentary supply curve, 96, 137
Monetarist, 638, 764
Monetarist theory of the business cycle, 732–734
Monetary base, 607, 612–613, 618
Monetary policy
in action *(Reading between the lines),* 622–623
and aggregate demand, 507
aggregate demand and, 620
bank rate, 609
bankers' deposit rate, 609
defined, **451, 507, 606,** 758
discretionary policies, 763
effectiveness of, 638
exchange rate, 619–620
expansionary monetary policy. *See* Expansionary monetary policy
feedback-rule policies, 763
fixed-rule policies, 763
government deposit shifting, 610
and inflation, 616–617
interest rate fluctuations, 617–618
interest rate target *vs.* money target, 618–619
interest rates and exchange rates, effects on, 639, 642
Japanese, in 1990s, 744–745
Keynesian-monetarist controversy, 638–639
monetary and fiscal tensions *(Reading between the lines),* 644–645
objectives, 607–608
open market operations, 609
overnight loans rate, 608
policy conflict, 642–643
policy coordination, 642
real GDP fluctuations, 620
required reserve ratio, 609
ripple effects of, 615–620
in short run, 634–637
since 1971, 759–760
and stock market, 842–843
task of making monetary policy, 607
time lags in adjustment process, 617
tools, 608–610
unemployment and, 615–617
Monetary policy indicators, 608
Money
in Canada today, 583
creation of, by banks, 587–590
currency, 583
defined, **582**
demand for, 591–594
demand for money curve, 592
deposits, 583
M1, 583, 584
M2+, 583, 584
as medium of exchange, 582
nominal money, 591
official measures of, 583–584
quantity of, control over, 611–615
quantity theory of money, 656–657
real business cycle theory and, 739–740
as store of value, 583
as unit of account, 582–583
Money market equilibrium, 595, 628
Money multiplier
in Canada, 615
chartered banks, purchase of securities from, 613–614
defined, **613**
Money wage rate
changes, 504, 651–652
defined, **683**
Monopolistic competition
collusion, impossibility of, 284
defined, **205, 284**
and efficiency, 287, 290
examples of, 285
excess capacity, 287–288
free entry and exit, 285
and innovation, 288–289
large number of firms, 284
long-run profit, 287
marketing and, 289–290
output and price, 286–288
product development, 288–289
product differentiation, 284–285
short-run profit, 286–287
small market share, 284
Monopoly
barriers to entry, 262–263
bilateral monopoly, 345
defined, 112, **205**
domestic airline monopoly *(Reading between the lines),* 278–279
efficiency, effect on, 112, 255
elastic demand, 265
examples of, 262
key features, 262–263
legal monopoly, 262
maximization of profit, 266–267
natural monopoly, 262–263, 276–277
no close substitutes, 262
policy issues. *See* Monopoly policy issues
price discrimination. *See* Price discrimination
price-setting strategies, 263
regulation of, 263
see also Monopoly policy issues
single-price monopoly. *See* Single-price monopoly
Monopoly policy issues
average cost pricing rule, 277
economies of scale, 275
and economies of scope, 275–276
gains from monopoly, 275–276
incentives to innovation, 275
marginal cost pricing rule, 276–277
natural monopoly, regulation of, 276–277
two-part tariff, 277
Monopsony
defined, **344**
labour market in, 344–345

and labour unions, 345
and minimum wage, 345–346
tendencies, 345
Multi-income families, 749
Multiplier
in action *(Reading between the lines),* 548–549
and aggregate expenditure curve, 540, 542
algebra of, 551
basic idea of, 538
and business cycle turning points, 541–542
defined, **538**
deposit multiplier, 588–589
expansion, 542
fiscal policy multipliers. *See* Fiscal policy multipliers
greater than 1, 539
imports and, 540–541
income taxes and, 540–541
in long run, 547
money multiplier, 613–614
multiplier effect, 538–539
and price level, 543–547
recession, 542
size of, 539
symbols, definition of, 550
Murphy, Kevin, 130

NASDAQ index, 833
Nash, John, 294
Nash equilibrium, 294, 298–299
National Income and Expenditure Accounts, 463, 813
National saving, 461, 760–761
National security argument, 798
Natural monopoly
average cost pricing rule, 277, 398
capture theory, 398, 400–401
defined, **262, 397**
inflating costs, 400
marginal cost pricing rule, 276–277, 398
profit maximization, 276
public interest theory, 398, 400–401
rate-of-return regulation, 399–400
regulation of, 276–277, 397–400
Natural rate of unemployment, 488, 500, 664, 768–769
Natural rate policies, 768–769
Natural resource markets, 331–333
Necessities, 89
Negative externalities
defined, **414**
negative consumption externalities, 414
negative production externalities, 414
pollution, 415–421
Negative relationship, 21, 29
Negative slope, 24
Neoclassical growth theory, 719–721, 780
Net borrower, 812
Net domestic product, 462
Net exports
defined, **460, 786, 813**
and exchange rate, 598
and interest rate, 598
Net investment, 461
Net present value, 328
Net taxes, 460
New classical theory of the business cycle, 734
New Keynesian theory of the business cycle, 734
Nikkei index, 833
Nominal GDP, 465
Nominal interest rate, 597, 667
Nonrenewable natural resources, 331, 332
Nontariff barrier
defined, **793**
quota, 796
voluntary export restraint (VER), 796
Normal good, 64
Normal profit, 197, 277
Normative statements, 12
Nortel Networks *(Reading between the lines),* 212–213
North American economy, market structure of, 209
North American Free Trade Agreement, 533, **794,** 803
North American recession *(Reading between the lines),* 750–751
Nozick, Robert, 116

Observation and measurement, 12
Obstacles to efficiency
deadweight loss, 112
external benefits, 112
external costs, 112
monopoly, 112
overproduction, 113
price ceilings, 112
price floor, 112
public goods, 112
quotas, 112
subsidies, 112
taxes, 112
underproduction, 112
Official Canadian reserves, 810
Official settlements account, 810
Oligopoly
book sellers war *(Reading between the lines),* 304–305
defined, **205, 291**
dominant firm, 292
duopoly, 295–299
games, 293–300
kinked demand curve model, 291
price-fixing game, 295–299
price wars, 302
prisoners' dilemma, 293–294
public interest theory, 401
R&D game, 299–300
real-world games, 301–303
regulation, 401–402
repeated duopoly game, 301–302
sequential entry game in contestable market, 302–303
One-third rule, 714–715
Open market operations
chartered banks, buying from, 611–612, 613–614
defined, **609**
how it works, 611–612
public, purchase from, 612
securities on open market, purchase of, 611–612
Opportunity cost
defined, **11,** 60
and economic rent, 334–335
and economic rent *(Reading between the lines),* 336–337
and firms, 196
implicit rental rate of capital, 196
increase in, 36
and interest rate, 597
in international trade, 787–788
of leisure, 182, 183
marginal cost. *see* Marginal cost
and production possibilities, 35–36
as ratio, 35–36
relative price, 60
of reserves, 609
and search activity, 126
Organization of Oil Exporting Countries (OPEC), 83, 401
Outlays, 557, 558–559
Outlet substitution, 193
Output
average product, 219
break-even point, 240
capacity output, 287
decision, and costs, 218
economies of scale. *See* Economies of scale
and external costs, 417
long-run cost, 228–231
and marginal cost, 224
marginal product, 219
in monopolistic competition, 286–288
in perfect competition, 246–249
product curves, 219–222
product schedules, 219
productivity growth slowdown, 439
profit-maximizing output, 240–241, 242
and quantity of labour, 219
short-run cost, 223–227
short-run technology constraint, 219–222
and single-price monopoly, 266–267
total product, 219
Output-inflation tradeoff, 10
Overnight loans rate, 608
Overproduction, 113
Ownership, as incentive, 202

Paradox of value, 164–165
Partnership, 202–203
Patent, 262, **425**
Payoff matrix, 293, 298
Peak, 8, **440**
Perfect competition
  change in demand, 246
  and changing tastes, 250–252
  defined, **205, 238**
  demand, price and revenue in, 239
  economic profit, 238–239
  efficiency of, 255, 269
  entry, effects of, 247–248
  exit, effects of, 248
  external economies and diseconomies, 251–253
  firm's decisions in, 240–245
  how it arises, 238
  long-run adjustments, 247–248
  long-run decisions, 240
  long-run equilibrium, 249
  in maple syrup *(Reading between the lines),* 256–257
  marginal revenue, 238–239
  and market power, 262
  output and price decision, 268
  output in, 246–249
  permanent change in demand, 250–251
  plant size, changes in, 248–249
  price in, 246–249
  price takers, 238
  profit in, 246–249
  profit-maximizing output, 240–241, 242
  revenue, 238–239
  short-run decisions, 240
  short-run equilibrium, 246
  short-run industry supply curve, 245
  short run profits and losses, 243
  short-run supply curve, 244
  vs. single-price monopoly, 268–271
  technological change, 253
  total revenue, 238
Perfect price discrimination, 273–274
Perfectly elastic demand, 87
Perfectly inelastic demand, 86
Perpetual motion economy, 722–723
Perpetuity, 594
Personal saving rate, 844
Pharmaceutical drugs, and efficiency and equity *(Reading between the lines),* 118–119
Phillips, A.W., 662
Phillips curve
  in Canada, 665
  defined, **662**
  long-run, 663
  natural rate of unemployment, changes in, 664
  short-run, 662–663
Physical capital, 681, 690
Pigovian taxes, 420
Policy conflict, 642–643
Policy coordination, 642
Political equilibrium, 375, 381, 395–396
Political freedom, 469–470
Political marketplace, 375
Politicians, 375
Pollution
  acid rain, 415
  air-borne substances, 415–416
  air pollution, 415–416
  air pollution debate *(Reading between the lines),* 426–427
  Coase theorem, 419
  demand for pollution-free environment, 415
  emission charges, 420
  global warming, 416
  government action, 420–421
  land pollution, 416
  marketable permits, 420–421
  ozone layer depletion, 416
  Pigovian taxes, 420
  private costs, 417
  and production, 418
  property rights and, 418
  social costs, 417
  sources of, 415–417
  water pollution, 416
Population
  in Canada, 691
  and change in demand, 64
  changes in, and job search, 694
  classical theory of population growth, 717–718
  increases in, 688–689
  neoclassical economics of population growth, 719
  and resource depletion, 368–369
Portfolio diversification, 840
Positive externalities
  defined, **414**
  knowledge, 421–425
  positive consumption externalities, 414
  positive production externalities, 414
Positive relationship, 20, 29
Positive slope, 24
Positive statements, 12
Post hoc fallacy, 13–14, 130
Potential entry, 208
Potential GDP
  and aggregate demand shocks, 766
  capital quantity, changes in, 503
  changes in, 503–504, 688–692
  defined, **439,** 440, **489**
  fiscal expansion at, 570–571
  and fiscal policy, 571–572
  fluctuations of real GDP around, 440
  and full employment, 489, 500
  full-employment quantity of labour, change in, 503
  growth, as macroeconomic policy goal, 756
  human capital, increase in, 690
  and labour market, 686, 687
  labour productivity, increases in, 689–691
  and *LAS* curve, 572
  long-term growth policy, 760–762
  money wage rate changes, 504
  physical capital, increase in, 690
  population, increases in, 688–689
  resource prices, changes in, 504
  technological advances, 504, 690
Poverty, 352
Preference map, 175
Preferences
  defined, **38**
  and demand, 64
  household consumption choices, 154
  and indifference curves, 175–178
  and marginal benefit curve, 38
  utility. *See* Utility
Preferred stock, 830
Present value, 326–328
Price
  adjustments, 71
  average, and price elasticity of demand, 85–86
  change in, and budget equation, 173–174
  vs. cost, 108–109
  defined, 108
  expected future prices, 63–64, 68
  fall in, and marginal utility theory, 159
  fixed, 533
  and Hotelling principle, 332–333
  increases, in natural disaster, 116–117
  index, 60
  long-run changes in, 252
  and marginal revenue, 264
  and markets, 60
  minimum supply price, 67
  in monopolistic competition, 286–288
  in perfect competition, 239, 246–249
  prediction of changes in, 72–75
  and product differentiation, 284
  of productive resources, 67, 227
  as regulator, 70–71
  of related goods, 63, 67–68
  relative price. *See* Relative price
  rise in, and marginal utility theory, 160–161
  and shortage, 71
  and single-price monopoly, 266–267
  and stock prices, 836
  and surplus, 71
  vs. value, 106–107, 164–165
  wars, 302
Price ceilings
  defined, **125**
  efficiency, effect on, 112
  in housing market, 125–126
Price discrimination
  and consumer surplus, 271–272
  defined, **263,** 271
  discrimination among groups of buyers, 272

discrimination among units of a good, 272
efficiency and, 274
and marginal cost pricing rule, 276
perfect price discrimination, 273–274
vs. price differences, 271
and profit, 271, 272–273
rent seeking, 274

Price-earnings ratio, 831–832, 835
Price effect, 179–180
Price elasticity of demand
agricultural market, 138
along straight-line demand curve, 87
average price and quantity, 85–86
calculation of, 85
defined, **84**
elastic demand, 87
and expenditure, 89
factors influencing, 89–90
in global oil market *(Reading between the lines),* 98–99
inelastic demand, 87
and marginal revenue, 265
and marginal utility, 164
minus sign and, 86
percentage change, 86
perfectly elastic demand, 87
perfectly inelastic demand, 86
proportion of income spent on good, 90
proportionate change, 86
substitutes, closeness of, 89
and tax division, 132
time elapsed since price change, 90
total revenue and, 88
unit elastic demand, 86
units-free measure, 86

Price-fixing *(Reading between the lines),* 408–409
Price floor
in agricultural market, 139–140
defined, **129**
efficiency, effect on, 112
minimum wage as, 129

Price level
and aggregate demand curve, 505–506
and aggregate expenditure, 543–545
calculation of, 466–467
defined, **447, 466**
and demand for money, 591
and equilibrium GDP, 545–547, 569–570
and fiscal policy multipliers, 568–571
GDP deflator, 466–467
and inflation, 650
and multiplier, 543–547
real business cycle theory and, 739
and real GDP, 466–467, 505–506
and substitution effect, 543–544
and wealth effect, 543

Price takers, 238
Principal–agent problem, 202
Principle of minimum differentiation, 379

Print-on-demand books *(Reading between the lines),* 184–185
Prisoners' dilemma, 293–294
Private costs, 417
Private saving, 761
Private sector balance, 813
Privatization, 394, 405
Producer surplus, 109
Product curves
average, 222
defined, 219
diminishing marginal returns, 221
increasing marginal returns, 220–221
marginal product curve, 220–221
total product curve, 220

Product development, in monopolistic competition, 288–289
Product differentiation
defined, **205, 284**
marketing and, 284–285
price and, 284
quality and, 284

Product schedules, 219
Production
economies of scale, 211
economies of scope, 211
economies of team production, 211
fluctuations in, 138
function, 228
household, 468
labour intensity of production process, 322
limits to, 39
negative production externalities, 414
organization of, 201–204
overproduction, 113
and pollution, 418
positive production externalities, 414
private cost of, 417
specialization, 42
underproduction, 112

Production efficiency, 35, 39
Production function, 680, 681, 682, 692
Production possibilities frontier
defined, **34**
guns *vs.* butter example, 34–35
and leisure time, 680
and marginal cost, 37
and opportunity cost, 35–36
production at point on, 35
and real GDP, 680
tradeoff along, 35

Productivity. *See* Labour productivity
Productivity curve
classical growth theory, 718
defined, **713**–714
neoclassical theory, 720
and new growth theory, 722

Productivity growth slowdown, 439
Professional association, 341
Profit
defined, **5**
economic, 197, 238–239, 241
of firm, 196
normal, 197, 277
and price discrimination, 271, 272–273
in short run, 243

Profit maximization
collusion, 296
labour market, 320
in monopoly, 266–267
natural monopoly, 276
in perfect competition, 246–249

Profit-maximizing output, 240–241, 242
Progressive income tax, 359
Property rights
Coase theorem, 419
defined, **46**
and externalities, 432–433
intellectual property rights, 425
pollution and, **418**

Property taxes, 385–386
Proportional income tax, 359
Protectionism. *See* Trade barriers
Provincial budget, 556
Public choice model, 375
Public choice theory, 380, 381, 394, 402
Public franchise, 262
Public goods
benefit of, 377
bureaucrats, role of, 380
defined, 112, **376**
discoveries, 721
efficiency, obstacle to, 255
efficient quantity of, 378
free-rider problem, 112, 374, 376
increase in demand for *(Reading between the lines),* 388–389
local public good, 385–386
nonexcludable, 376
nonrivalry, 376
political equilibrium, 381
principle of minimum differentiation, 379
private provision, 378
public provision, 378
rational ignorance, 380

Public interest theory, 381, **395,** 398, 400–401, 401
Public ownership, 394, 403–405
Public provision, 423–424
Purchasing power parity, 822

Quality, and product differentiation, 284
Quantity
average, and price elasticity of demand, 85–86
efficient quantity of public goods, 378
equilibrium quantity, 70
long-run changes in, 252
prediction of changes in, 72–75

Quantity demanded
change in, *vs.* change in demand, 64–65
defined, **61**

Quantity of labour demanded, 683
Quantity of labour supplied, 685

Quantity supplied
change in, *vs.* change in supply, 68–69
defined, **66**
Quantity theory of money, 656–657
Quarterly GDP report *(Reading between the lines),* 472–473
Quotas
in agricultural market, 140
defined, **140, 796**
efficiency, effect on, 112
how they work, 796

Rand formula, 341
Rate of return, 831
Rate-of-return regulation, 399–400
Ratio scale graphs, 834
Rational expectation, 659, 734, 837, 839
Rational expectations theories, 734–736
Rational ignorance, 380
Rawls, John, 115
Rawski, Thomas, 470–471
R&D game, in oligopoly, 299–300
Re-entrants, 485
Reading between the lines
aggregate expenditure multiplier in action, 548–549
air pollution debate, 426–427
airport security tax, 142–143
Canada–U.S. productivity gap, 696–697
Canada's changing demand for money, 600–601
cost and benefit of education, 48–49
demand and supply: computer prices, 76–77
domestic airline monopoly, 278–279
doughnut, cost of, 232–233
efficiency and equity in market for drugs, 118–119
elasticities of demand and supply in global oil market, 98–99
exchange rate projections, 824–825
fiscal policy projections, 574–575
forecasting economic growth, 724–725
inequality, trends in, 362–363
inflation-unemployment tradeoff, 668–669
Kyoto Protocol in *AS–AD* model, 516–517
marginal utility of boat ride, 166–167
monetary and fiscal tensions, 644–645
monetary policy in action, 622–623
monthly CPI report, 494–495
multiplier in action, 548–549
Nortel Networks, 212–213
North American recession, 750–751
oligopoly in action: book sellers war, 304–305
perfect competition in maple syrup, 256–257
public good, increase in demand for, 388–389
quarterly GDP report, 472–473
regular books *vs.* print-on-demand books, 184–185
rents and opportunity costs on the ice, 336–337
stabilization policy balancing act, 774–775
stock price uncertainties, 846–847
tariffs in action: lumber, 804–805
technology stocks, 452–453
vitamin price-fixing, 408–409
Real business cycle theory
criticisms of, 740
defence of, 740–741
defined, **737**
impulse, 737–738
mechanism, 738–740
shocks to productivity, 740
Real gross domestic product (real GDP)
aggregate demand, effect of, 620, 628
and aggregate expenditure, 533, 535–536
and aggregate planned expenditure, 535
aggregate production function, 500
base-year prices value of, 465–467
calculation of, 465–466
in Canada, 470–471
chain-weighted output index, 466
in China, 470–471
and consumption expenditure, 532
defined, **439, 465**
and demand for money, 591
and employment, 680–682
exclusions, 439
fluctuations around potential GDP, 440
growth of, in world economy, 709–710
long-run neutrality, 641
macroeconomic policy indicator, 757
monetary policy, effect of, 620
nominal GDP calculation, 465
per person, 441
potential GDP, changes in, 688
and price level, 465–467, 505–506
production function, 680, 681
and production possibilities frontier, 680
and productivity curve, 713–714
quantity of real GDP demanded. *See* Aggregate demand
quantity of real GDP supplied. *See* Aggregate supply
real business cycle theory and, 739
short-run changes in, 703
Taylor rule, 773
and unemployment, 489
Real income, 173
Real interest rate, 597
Real property, 46
Real wage rate
defined, **484, 683**
increases in, 686
job rationing and, 694
subsistence, 718
Real-world income elasticities of demand, 93
Realized capital gain, 843
Recession
anti-inflation policy, 741
defined, 8, **440**
Great Depression. *See* Great Depression
growth recession, 440
in Japan, 8
Japanese stagnation, 744–745
likelihood of severe depression, 748–749
monetarist, 733
most recent, in historical perspective, 441
multiplier and, 542
of 1990-1991, 741–744
North American recession *(Reading between the lines),* 750–751
in Russia, 8
working definition of, 478
Recessionary gap, 510
Regressive income tax, 359
Regulation
average cost pricing rule, 277, 398
capture theory, 395–396, 399, 400–401
cartel, 401–402
demand for, 394–395
and deregulation, 402–403
described, 394
economic theory of, 394–396
housing markets, 125–126
marginal cost pricing rule, 276–277, 398
monopoly, 263
natural monopoly, 276–277, 397–400
oligopoly, 401–402
political equilibrium, 395–396
public choice theory predictions, 402
public interest theory, 395, 398, 400–401, 401
rate-of-return, 399–400
regulatory process, 396–397
scope of, 396
supply of, 395
Reinventing the Bazaar: A Natural History of Markets (McMillan), 150
Relative price
and budget equation, 173
defined, **60, 173**
in demand curve, 106
in supply curve, 108
Renewable natural resources, 331–332
Rent, 5
Rent ceilings, 124–128, **125**
Rent seeking, 270, 274, 800–801
Research and development, 716
Reservation wage, 322
Reserve ratio, 587
Reserves
defined, **585**

desired reserve ratio, 587
excess reserves, 587
and monetary base, 612–613
official Canadian reserves, 810
opportunity cost of, 609
required reserve ratio, 609
reserve ratio, 587
Resources
allocative efficiency, 39
depletion of, 368–369
efficient allocation of, 104
efficient use of, 37–39, 254
factors of production. *See* Factors of production
misallocation of, 35
owner's, costs of, 197
production efficiency, 35, 39
substitution possibilities, and elasticity of supply, 95–96
unused, 35
Retained earnings, 831
Return, 831
Revenue
marginal revenue, 238–239
in perfect competition, 239
from tariffs, 800
total revenue, 238, 241
Ricardo, David, 852–853
Risk premium, 840
Romer, Paul, 782–784
Russia, recession in, 8

Sales tax, 131, 134, 385
Saving
decisions, 329–330
defined, **460,** 461
and disposable income, 528
and economic growth, 711–712
factors influencing, 528–531
government, 761
marginal propensity to save, 530–531
national saving, 760–761
private, 761
stimulation of, 716
target rate of, 719
Saving function, 528–529
Saving rate, 843
Scarcity
defined, **2**
wants, and, 61
Scatter diagram, 19
Schumpeter, Joseph, 780–781
Search activity, 126
Seasonal unemployment, 488
Selling costs, 289–290
Sequential entry game in contestable market, 302–303
Services, international trade in, 786
Shiller, Robert, 839
Short run
defined, **218**
macroeconomic short run, 501
profits and losses, 243
temporary plant shutdown, 244
Short-run aggregate supply, 501–502, 700–703
Short-run aggregate supply curve, 501, 502, **687**–688, 701–703
Short-run cost
average costs, 224–225
average total cost curve, 224–225
cost curves and product curves, 226–227
and long-run cost, 228–229
marginal cost, 224
total cost, 223
total cost curves, 223
total fixed cost, 223
total variable cost, 223
Short-run decisions in perfect competition, 240
Short-run equilibrium, 246
Short-run industry supply curve, 245
Short-run macroeconomic equilibrium, 508–509
Short-run Phillips curve, 662–663
Short-run supply curve, 96, 244
Short-run technology constraint
product curves, 219–222
product schedules, 219
Shortages
housing, 126
and price, 71
Shutdown point, 244
Simon, Julian, 369
Singapore, and dynamic comparative advantage, 45
Single-price monopoly
vs. competition, 268–271
creation of monopoly, 270
defined, **263**
efficiency of, 269
elasticity, and marginal revenue, 265
output and price decision, 266–267, 268
price, and marginal revenue, 264
purchasing a monopoly, 270
redistribution of surpluses, 270
rent seeking, 270
social cost of, 270
Slope
across arc, 25–26
curved line, 25–26
defined, **24**
negative slope, 24
of point on curve, 25
positive slope, 24
straight line, 24–25, 28–29
Smith, Adam, 13, 46, 54, 111, 852
Social insurance taxes, 384–385
Social justice, 469–470
Social security programs, 359
Sole proprietorship, 202
Solow, Robert, 714, 719, 780
S&P Composite Index, 833
S&P/TSX, 833
Speculative bubbles, 838–839
Stabilization policy balancing act *(Reading between the lines),* 774–775
Stagflation, 654, 770
Standard of living
defined, **6**
determination of, 6
tradeoffs, 10
worldwide, 6
Sticky wages, 701
Stock
capital gain, 831
capital loss, 831
common stock, 830
defined, **461**
dividend, 830
dividend yield, 831
earnings per share, 835
portfolio diversification, 840
preferred stock, 830
return on, 831
risk premium, 840
Stock exchange, 830–831
Stock markets
anticipating policy, 843
basics, 830–835
and consumption expenditure, 843–844
earnings growth trends and cycles, 841–842
and the economy, 841–845
and monetary policy, 842–843
in new economy, 842
reports, 832
return on a stock, 831
and saving rate, 843
stock, 830
stock exchange, 830–831
stock price, 831
and taxes, 843
and wealth, 843–845
Stock price
certainty *vs.* uncertainty, 837
defined, **831**
determination of, 836–839
discount factor, 837
equation, 837
expected future stock price, 837–838
history of, 834–835
indexes, 832–833
inflation adjustments, 834
and interest rates, 842–843
market fundamental price, 838
market fundamentals, 836–838
performance, 834
present *vs.* future, 837
price, value and willingness to pay, 836
ratio scale graphs, 834
realized capital gain, 843
speculative bubbles, 838–839
uncertainties *(Reading between the lines),* 846–847

Straight lines
demand curve, and elasticity, 87
equations, 28
linear equation, 28
linear relationship, 28
negative relationships, 29
position of, 29
positive relationship, 29
slope of, 24–25, 28–29
Strategies, 293
Structural surplus or deficit, 567
Structural unemployment, 488
Subsidies
in agricultural market, 140–141
defined, **140, 424**
efficiency, effect on, 112
and knowledge, 424
Subsidized services, 359–360
Subsistence real wage rate, 718
Substitute
close substitutes, 177
closeness of, and elasticity of demand, 89
and cross elasticity of demand, 91
defined, **63,** 67
degree of substitutability, 177–178
diminishing marginal rate of substitution, 176
and indifference curves, 177
lack of, in monopoly, 262
marginal rate of substitution (MRS), 176
Substitution effect
and aggregate demand, 506
defined, **181**
demand, effect on, 61
international substitution, 543
intertemporal substitution, 543
labour supply, 323
price level and, 543–544
Summers, Lawrence H., 56–58
Summers, Robert, 470
Sunk cost, 218
Supply
aggregate supply. *See* Aggregate supply
of capital, 329–330
change in. *See* Change in supply
computer prices *(Reading between the lines),* 76–77
defined, **66**
of dollars, 818
elasticity of. *See* Elasticity of supply
in foreign exchange market, 818
graph of, 67
of labour. *See* Supply of labour
law of supply, 66
minimum supply price, 67
of nonrenewable natural resource, 332
quantity supplied, 66, 68–69
of regulation, 395
of renewable natural resource, 331–332
schedule, 66
selling plans, determination of, 66
Supply curve
of capital, 330
defined, **66**
equation, 78
labour supply curve, 183, 323
long-run, 96
long-run aggregate supply curve, 500–501, 502
long-run industry supply curve, 251–253
as marginal cost curve, 109
momentary, 96, 137
relative price, 108
short-run, 96, 244
short-run aggregate supply curve, 501, 502
short-run industry supply curve, 245
Supply of labour
backward-bending labour supply curve, 323
changes in, 323–324
defined, **685**
hours per person, 686
income effect, 323
labour force participation, 686
labour supply curve, 183
long-run supply of labour, 128
market supply of labour, 323
quantity of labour supplied, 685
and real wage rate increases, 686
substitution effect, 323
work-leisure choice, 182–183, 322–324
Supply-side effects of fiscal policy, 571–573
Surplus
consumer surplus, 107, 164
deadweight loss, 112
government budget surplus, 449, 557
international, 449–450
and price, 71
producer surplus, 109
redistribution, in monopoly, 270
Symmetry principle, 116

Target rate of return, 719
Tariffs
defined, **793**
effects of, 794, 795
history of, 793–794
how they work, 794–795
inefficiency, 795
lumber *(Reading between the lines),* 804–805
revenue from, 800
Tastes, changes in, and perfect competition, 250–252
Taxes
airport security tax *(Reading between the lines),* 142–143
anticipated inflation, effect of, 661
autonomous taxes, 562
capital gains, 843
corporate profits tax, 384, 843
and efficiency, 134
efficiency, effect on, 112
and elasticity of demand, 132
and elasticity of supply, 133
excise tax, 386–387
government tax revenues, 382
GST, 385
illegal drugs, 136
and income redistribution, 374
income taxes, 359, 382–384
induced taxes, 565
labour market, 571–572
net taxes, 460
perfectly elastic demand and, 132
perfectly elastic supply and, 133
perfectly inelastic demand and, 132
perfectly inelastic supply and, 133
Pigovian taxes, 420
vs. prohibition, 136
property taxes, 385–386
sales tax, 131, 134, 385
social insurance taxes, 384–385
and stock market, 843
transactions (Tobin) tax, 843
Team production, economies of, 211
Technological change
in Canada, 691–692
and change in supply, 68
and cost curves, 226–227
defined, **40**
and economic growth, 40, 712, 762
and labour market, 128
neoclassical theory, 719
in perfect competition, 253
and potential GDP, 504, 690
during productivity growth slowdown, 716
Technological efficiency, 199, 254
Technology
constraints, 198, 219–222
defined, **198**
and labour productivity, 682
Technology stocks *(Reading between the lines),* 452–453
Terms of trade, 788–789
A Theory of Justice (Rawls), 115
Time-series graphs, 18
Tit-for-tat strategy, 301
Tobin, James, 843
Total cost, 223, 241
Total cost curves, 223
Total fixed cost, 223
Total income, 348
Total product, 219
Total product curve, 220
Total revenue, 88, 238, 241
Total revenue test, 88
Total utility, 154–155
Total variable cost, 223
Trade
international. *See* International trade

social institutions and, 46
Trade barriers
argument against, 797–800
cheap foreign labour argument, 798–799
compensation for losers, 801
developing countries, exploitation of, 800
diversity argument, 799
dumping argument, 798
employment argument, 797
environmental standards argument, 799
infant-industry argument, 797
national culture argument, 799
national security argument, 798
nontariff barriers, 796
protectionism, case against, 797–800
quotas, 796
reasons for, 800–801
rent seeking, 800–801
revenue from tariffs, 800
stability argument, 799
tariffs, 793–795
voluntary export restraint (VER), 796
Tradeoff
along production possibilities frontier, 35
big tradeoff, 10, 115, 361
defined, **9**
guns *vs.* butter, 9
inflation-unemployment tradeoff *(Reading between the lines),* 668–669
macroeconomic tradeoffs, 10
microeconomic tradeoffs, 9–10
output-inflation tradeoff, 10
standard of living, 10
Transactions costs, 210–211, **419,** 661
Transactions (Tobin) tax, 843
Transfer payments
autonomous, 565
and induced taxes, 565
Trend, 18
Trigger strategy, 301
Trough, 8, **440**
Trust and mortgage loan company, 586
Turner rule, 773
Twin deficits, 814
Two-part tariff, 277

Unanticipated inflation, 658–659, 660
Underground economy, 468–469
Underproduction, 112
Unemployment
anatomy of, 485–487
in Canada, 445
compensation, 694
cyclical, 488, 763–769
defined, **444**
demographics of, 486–487
discouraged worker, 445, 482
discretionary policies, 763
duration of, 486
feedback-rule policies, 763
fixed-rule policies, 763
frictional, 487–488
at full employment, 693–695
and inflation, 662–665
inflation-unemployment tradeoff *(Reading between the lines),* 668–669
job rationing, 694–695
job search, 693–694
lost human capital, 446
lost production and incomes, 446
macroeconomic policy goal, 756
and minimum wage, 129
monetary policy and, 615–617
natural rate of unemployment. *See* Natural rate of unemployment
Phillips curve, 662–665
problem of, 446
and real GDP, 489
reasons for, 693–695
seasonal, 488
sources of, 485–486
structural, 488
structural change of labour market, 694
types of, 487–488
worldwide, 446
Unemployment rate
defined, **444–445, 481**
labour market indicator, 481
Unions. *See* Labour union
Unit elastic demand, 86
United States
air pollution, trends in, 416
business organizations, types of, 204
economic expansion, slowdown of, 742
economic growth in, 442–443
market structure of U.S. economy, 209
real GDP growth (1989-1995), 742
Units-free measure, 86
Unlimited liability, 202
Unused resources, 35
Utilitarianism, 114–115
Utility
consumer equilibrium, 157
defined, **154**
diminishing marginal utility, 155
marginal analysis, power of, 159
marginal utility, 155
marginal utility per dollar spent, 157–159
marginal utility theory. *See* Marginal utility theory
maximization of, 157–159
temperature, analogy to, 155–156
total utility, 154–155
units of, 159
utility-maximization choice, 157
Value
and consumer surplus, 107
defined, **106**
paradox of, 164–165
vs. price, 106–107, 164–165
and stock prices, 836
Velocity of circulation, 656
Vitamin price-fixing *(Reading between the lines),* 408–409
Voluntary export restraint (VER), 796
Voter preferences, 381
Voters, 375, 381
Voucher, 424–425

Wages, 5
Wants, 61
Water pollution, 416
Wealth
and assortative mating, 358
defined, **461, 843**
distribution of, 350, 845
vs. income, 350–351
sources of economic wealth, 54–55
and stock market, 843–845
Wealth effect
and aggregate demand, 505–506
defined, **843**
price level and, 543
and stock market, 843
Wealth of Nations (Smith), 13, 46, 54–55, 111
Welch, Finis, 130
Welfare programs, 359
When-to-work decision, 738
Willingness to pay
and demand, 106
and stock prices, 837
Women
degree of specialization differences, 358
discrimination, and economic inequality, 357–358
wage differentials, 5, 357
Woodford, Michael, 676–678
Work-leisure choices. *See* Household work-leisure choices
Working-age population, 480
World economy
and aggregate demand, 507–508
comparative advantage, 791
deficits, 461
economic growth, 441–443
inflation, 448
inflation and money growth, 657
real GDP growth, 709–710
standard of living, 6
unemployment, 446
World Trade Organization (WTO), 793

Zaire, hyperinflation in, 449

CREDITS

Photo Credits

Part 1: p. 54, Corbis-Bettman; p. 55 (left), Culver Pictures, p. 55 (right), Bruce Ando/Tony Stone Images.

Part 2: p. 148, Stock Montage; p. 149 (left), National Archives; p. 149 (right), PhotoDisc, Inc.

Part 3: p. 190, Corbis-Bettman; p. 191 (left), Keystone-Mast Collection (V22542) UCR/California Museum of Photography, University of California, Riverside; p. 191 (right), China Tourism Press/Getty Images; p. 192, Loren Santow.

Part 4: p. 205 (left), PhotoDisc, Inc.; p. 205 (left, inset), Dick Morton; p. 205 (right), Dick Morton; p. 205 (right, inset), © Reuters NewMedia Inc./CORBIS/MAGMA; p. 213, Jonathan Hayward/CP Photo Archive; p. 310, Stock Montage; p. 311 (left), Culver Pictures; p. 311 (right), Don Wilson/West Stock.

Part 5: p. 368, Corbis-Bettman; p. 369 (left), courtesy of The Bostonian Society/Old State House; p. 369 (right), Mark E. Gibson.

Part 6: p. 432, David Joel/David Joel Photography, Inc.; p. 433 (left), Jim Baron/The Image Finders; p. 433 (right), Patrick Mullen.

Part 7: p. 522, Stock Montage; p. 523 (left), Corbis-Bettman; p. 523 (right), Mug Shots, First Light.

Part 8: p. 674, Marshall Henrichs/Addison-Wesley; p. 675 (left), UPI/Corbis-Bettman; p. 675 (right), © Carlos Humberto TDC/Contact Press Images.

Part 9: p. 780, Corbis-Bettman; p. 781 (left), North Wind Picture Archives; p. 781 (right), PhotoDisc, Inc.; p. 782, Christopher Irion.

Part 10: p. 852, Corbis-Bettman; p. 853 (left), North Wind Picture Archives; p. 853 (right), © M. Timothy O'Keefe/Weststock.

Figure and Table Credits

The sources below were extracted from the Statistics Canada CANSIM II database <http://cansim2.statcan.ca/cgi-win/CNSMCGI.EXE>.

Figure 1.4: "The Distribution of Income in Canada," adapted from the Statistics Canada publication National Income and Expenditure Accounts, quarterly estimates, third quarter 2002, catalogue 13-001.

Figure 13.1: "Examples of Monopolistic Competition," adapted from the Statistics Canada publication Industrial Organization and Concentration in Manufacturing Industries, catalogue 31C0024, 2002.

Figure 14.2: "Labour Market Trends in Canada," adapted from the Statistics Canada CANSIM II database, tables 282-0002, 282-0022, and 380-0001.

Figure 14.5: "Capital Market Trends in Canada," adapted from the Statistics Canada CANSIM II database, tables 378-0004 and 176-0043.

Figure 15.1: "The Distribution of Income in Canada in 1998," adapted from the Statistics Canada publication Income in Canada, 2000, catalogue 75-202, 2002.

Figure 15.2: "Canadian Quintile Shares in 1998," adapted from the Statistics Canada publication Income in Canada, 2000, catalogue 75-202, 2002.

Figure 15.3: "The Income Lorenz Curve in 1998," adapted from the Statistics Canada publication Income in Canada, 2000, catalogue 75-202, 2002.

Figure 15.4: "Lorenz Curves for Income and Wealth," adapted from the Statistics Canada publication Income in Canada, 2000, catalogue 75-202, 2002.

Figure 15.5: "Trends in the Distribution of Income: 1980–1998," adapted from the Statistics Canada publication Income Distribution by Size in Canada, catalogue 13-207, 1998.

Figure 15.10: "Income Redistribution," adapted from the Statistics Canada publication Income in Canada, 2000, catalogue 75-202, 2002.

Figure 19.1: "Economic Growth in Canada," adapted from the Statistics Canada CANSIM II database, v1992292.

Figure 19.2: "The Most Recent Canadian Business Cycle," adapted from the Statistics Canada CANSIM II database, v1992292.

Figure 19.3: "Long-Term Growth, Economic Growth in Canada," adapted from the Statistics Canada CANSIM II database, v1992292, and from the Statistics Canada publication *Historical Statistics of Canada*, catalogue 11-516, series F55, 1983.

Figure 19.6: "Unemployment in Canada," adapted from the Statistics Canada CANSIM II database, table 282-0002, and from the Statistics Canada publication *Historical Statistics of Canada*, catalogue 11-516, 1983.

Figure 20.1: "The Circular Flow of Expenditure and Income," adapted from the Statistics Canada CANSIM II database, table 380-0002.

Table 20.1: "The Expenditure Approach," adapted from the Statistics Canada CANSIM II database, table 380-0002.

Table 20.2: "GDP: The Income Approach," adapted from the Statistics Canada CANSIM II database, table 380-0001.

Figure 20.3: "GDP: The Income Approach," adapted from the Statistics Canada CANSIM II database, table 380-0003.

Figure 21.1: Business cycle dates and growth cycle dates: the Economic Cycle Research Institute; Real GDP, Statistics Canada, CANSIM II database, v1992292.

Figure 21.2: "Population Labour Force Categories," adapted from the Statistics Canada CANSIM II database, tables 282-0002 and 051-0001, and from the Statistics Canada publication *Labour Force Historical Review*, catalogue 71F0004, 2001.

Figure 21.3: "Employment, Unemployment and the Labour Force: 1961–2001," adapted from the Statistics Canada CANSIM II database, tables 282-0002, and from the Statistics Canada publication *Labour Force Historical Review*, catalogue 71F0004, 2001.

Figures 21.4, 21.5: "The Changing Face of the Labour Market," data calculated and adapted from the Statistics Canada CANSIM II database, table 282-0002.

Figure 21.6: "Real Wage Rates: 1961–2001," data calculated from the Statistics Canada CANSIM II database, tables 282-0002, 282-0022, and 380-0001.

Figure 21.8: "Unemployment by Reason," adapted from the Statistics Canada publication *Labour Force Historical Review*, catalogue 71F0004, 2001.

Figure 21.9: "Unemployment by Duration," adapted from the Statistics Canada publication *Labour Force Historical Review*, catalogue 71F0004, 2001.

Figure 21.10: "Unemployment by Demographic Group," adapted from the Statistics Canada CANSIM II database, table 282-0002.

Figure 21.11: "Unemployment and the Real GDP," adapted from the Statistics Canada CANSIM II database, tables 282-0002 and 380-0002.

Figure 21.12: "The CPI Basket," adapted from the Statistics Canada publication *Your Guide to the Consumer Price Index*, catalogue 62-557, 1996.

Figure 21.13: "The CPI and the Inflation Rate," adapted from the Statistics Canada CANSIM II database, table 326-0002.

Figure 22.14: "Aggregate Supply and Aggregate Demand 1961–2001," adapted from the Statistics Canada CANSIM II database, tables 326-0002 and 380-0003.

Figure 23.4: "The Canadian Consumption Function," data calculated from the Statistics Canada CANSIM II database, tables 380-0002, 384-0013, and 384-0035.

Figure 24.1: "Revenues, Outlays, and the Budget Balance," adapted from the Statistics Canada CANSIM II database, tables 380-0002 and 380-0007.

Figure 24.2: "Federal Government Revenues," adapted from the Statistics Canada CANSIM II database, tables 380-0002 and 380-0007.

Figure 24.3: "Federal Government Outlays," adapted from the Statistics Canada CANSIM II database, tables 380-0002 and 380-0007.

Figure 24.4: "Federal Government Debt," adapted from the Statistics Canada CANSIM II database, tables 380-0002 and 385-0010.

Figure 24.5: "Provincial Government Budgets," adapted from the Statistics Canada CANSIM II database, tables 384-0002 and 385-0002.

Figure 24.6: "Total Government Budgets," adapted from the Statistics Canada CANSIM II database, tables 380-0002 and 380-0007.

Figure 24.10: "The Business Cycle and the Budget Deficit," adapted from the Statistics Canada CANSIM II database, tables 380-0002 and 380-0007.

Figure 28.7: "Money Growth and Inflation in Canada," data calculated from the Statistics Canada CANSIM database, tables 176-0020 and 380-0056.

Figure 28.14: "Phillips Curves in Canada," data calculated from the Statistics Canada CANSIM II database, tables 380-0002 and 380-0056.

Figure 28.15: "Inflation and the Interest Rate," data calculated in part from the Statistics Canada CANSIM II database, tables 176-0043 and 380-0056.

Figure 30.6: "Growth Accounting and the Productivity Growth Slowdown," data calculated from the Statistics Canada CANSIM II database, tables 282-0002, 378-0004, and 380-0002.

Figure 31.6: "The Real Business Cycle Impulse," data calculated from the Statistics Canada CANSIM II database, tables 282-0002, 378-0004, and 380-0002.

Figure 31.10: "U.S. and Canadian Real GDP Growth: 1989–1995," data calculated in part from the Statistics Canada CANSIM II database, table 380-0002.

Figure 31.12: "Employment and Real Wages," data calculated from the Statistics Canada CANSIM II database, tables 282-0002, 282-0022, and 380-0001.

Figure 32.1: "Macroeconomic Performance: Read GDP and Inflation," data calculated from the Statistics Canada CANSIM II database, table 380-0002.

Figure 32.2: "The Fiscal Policy Record: A Summary," adapted from the Statistics Canada CANSIM II database, tables 380-0002 and 380-0007.

Figure 32.4: "Savings Rate in Canada: 1970–2001," adapted from the Statistics Canada CANSIM II database, table 380-0031.

Figure 33.5: "Canadian Tariffs: 1867–2001," adapted from the Statistics Canada CANSIM II database, tables 380-0002 and 380-0007, and from the Statistics Canada publication *Historical Statistics of Canada*, catalogue 11-516, series G485, 1983.

Table 34.1: "Canadian Balance of Payments Accounts in 2001," adapted from the Statistics Canada CANSIM II database, tables 376-0001 and 376-0002.

Figure 34.1: "The Balance of Payments: 1981–2001," adapted from the Statistics Canada CANSIM II database, tables 376-0001 and 376-0002.

Table 34.2: "Net Exports, the Government Budget, Saving and Investment," adapted from the Statistics Canada CANSIM database, tables 380-0002 and 380-0034.

Figure 34.2: "The Twin Deficits," adapted from the Statistics Canada CANSIM II database, tables 376-0001 and 376-0007.

Figure 35.8: "Two Views of the Personal Saving Rate," adapted from the Statistics Canada CANSIM II database, tables 378-0004 and 380-0031.